Barry S. Levine • Sarah Kerrigan
Editors

Principles of Forensic Toxicology

Fifth Edition

 Springer

Editors
Barry S. Levine
Chesapeake Toxicology Resources
8415 Progress Dr. Suite V
Frederick, MD, USA

Sarah Kerrigan
Department of Forensic Science
Sam Houston State University
Huntsville, TX, USA

ISBN 978-3-030-42919-5   ISBN 978-3-030-42917-1   (eBook)
https://doi.org/10.1007/978-3-030-42917-1

The editors will choose an exemption template and provide a figure

This Springer imprint is published by the registered company Springer Nature Switzerland AG
The registered company address is: Gewerbestrasse 11, 6330 Cham, Switzerland

Preface

First published in 1999, *Principles of Forensic Toxicology* is now in its twentieth year of production. The book has remained a trusted textbook for students, and a reference book for laboratorians for two decades.

Although the structure of the book remains unchanged, the fifth edition has been extensively revised to reflect new analytical methods, drugs, and special topics.

A total of seven new chapters are included, bringing the total number of chapters to 40.

In *Part I—Introduction*, a new chapter on drug-facilitated crimes was added. This complements the existing chapters on human performance and postmortem toxicology, in addition to performance-enhancing, pain management, and forensic drug testing.

Significant updates were made with regard to *Part II—Methodologies*. Specimen preparation, chromatography and mass spectrometry chapters were extensively updated to reflect contemporary and emerging analytical approaches. New chapters on quantitative analytical methods, derivatization, statistics for forensic toxicology, and metrological traceability and measurement uncertainty were also added. These new additions further complement the existing method validation chapter and should provide a valuable resource to personnel in accredited forensic laboratories, and students preparing for the workplace.

In *Part III—Analytes*, novel psychoactive substances (NPS), emerging drugs and new therapeutic agents were included throughout. Although the landscape of drug use is ever-changing, significant updates were made to include designer benzodiazepines, novel synthetic opioids, fentalogs, synthetic cannabinoids, cathinones, newer psychedelics, and other drugs.

Finally, in *Part IV—Special Topics*, two new chapters were added, including drugs in embalmed tissues and oral fluid testing, an area of growing importance in forensic toxicology.

It is hoped that this new fifth edition is as comprehensive as it is contemporary and remains a staple resource for students and laboratorians alike for many years to come.

Frederick, MD, USA
Huntsville, TX, USA

Barry S. Levine
Sarah Kerrigan

Contents

Part IV   Special Topics

Contributors

William H. Anderson, Ph.D. NMS Labs, Horsham, PA, USA

Fred S. Apple, Ph.D. Hennepin Co. Medical Center, University of Minnesota, Minneapolis, MN, USA

Larry Broussard, Ph.D. Louisiana State University Health Sciences Center, New Orleans, LA, USA

Patrick Buzzini Department of Forensic Science, Sam Houston State University, Huntsville, TX, USA

Yale H. Caplan, Ph.D. National Scientific Services, Inc., Baltimore, MD, USA

Kenneth Cole, Ph.D. Annapolis, MD, USA

Michele M. Crosby, Ph.D. University of Tampa, Tampa, FL, USA

Dennis J. Crouch, B.S., MBA Utah Toxicology-Expert Services, Sandy, UT, USA

Anne Z. DePriest, Pharm.D, BCPS Janssen Scientific Affairs, Nashville, TN, USA

Laurel Farrell ANSI National Accreditation Board, Cary, NC, USA

Kenneth E. Ferslew, Ph.D. East Tennessee State University, Johnson City, TN, USA

Madeleine J. Gates Department of Forensic Science, Sam Houston State University, Huntsville, TX, USA

Lindsay Glicksberg, Ph.D. Southwestern Institute of Forensic Sciences, Dallas, TX, USA

Bruce A. Goldberger, Ph.D. Department of Pathology, Immunology and Laboratory Medicine, Forensic Medicine Division, University of Florida College of Medicine, Gainesville, FL, USA

Megan Grabenauer, Ph.D. RTI International, Research Triangle Park, NC, USA

Teresa Gray, Ph.D. Harris County Institute of Forensic Sciences, Houston, TX, USA

Rebecca L. Hartman, Ph.D. Monroe County Office of the Medical Examiner, Rochester, NY, USA

Justin M. Holler Chesapeake Toxicology Resources, Frederick, MD, USA

Marilyn A. Huestis, Ph.D. Institute on Emerging Health Professions, Thomas Jefferson University, Philadelphia, PA, USA

Daniel S. Isenschmid, Ph.D. NMS Labs, Horsham, PA, USA

Amanda J. Jenkins, Ph.D. UMass Memorial Medical Center/UMASS Medical School, Worcester, MA, USA

Robert D. Johnson Tarrant County Medical Examiner's Office, Fort Worth, TX, USA

A. Wayne Jones, Ph.D. Magasinsgrand, Linköping, Sweden

Rebecca A. Jufer-Phipps, Ph.D. Office of the Chief Medical Examiner, Baltimore, MD, USA

Sarah Kerrigan, Ph.D. Department of Forensic Science, Sam Houston State University, Huntsville, TX, USA

Robert Kronstrand, Ph.D. National Board of Forensic Medicine, Dep. Forensic Genetics and Forensic Toxicology, Linköping, Sweden

Gary W. Kunsman, Ph.D. Broward County Medical Examiner and Trauma Services, Ft. Lauderdale, FL, USA

Thomas Kupiec, Ph.D. ARL Bio Pharma, Oklahoma City, OK, USA

Marc LeBeau, Ph.D. FBI Laboratory, Quantico, VA, USA

Dayong Lee, Ph.D. Houston Forensic Science Center, Inc., Houston, TX, USA

Barry S. Levine, Ph.D. Office of the Chief Medical Examiner, Baltimore, MD, USA

Jamie McAllister, Ph.D. FireTox, LLC, New Market, MD, USA

Madeline Montgomery, Ph.D. FBI Laboratory, Quantico, VA, USA

Karla A. Moore, Ph.D (Deceased)

James H. Nichols, Ph.D. Vanderbilt University School of Medicine, Nashville, TN, USA

Joseph J. Saady, Ph.D. Saady Consulting Inc., Richmond, VA, USA

Melinda K. Shelby, Ph.D. Aegis Sciences Corporation, Nashville, TN, USA

Michael L. Smith, Ph.D. Huestis and Smith Toxicology, LLC, Severna Park, MD, USA

Erin A. Spargo, Ph.D. Southwestern Institute of Forensic Sciences, Dallas, TX, USA

Vina Spiehler, Ph.D. Spiehler & Associates, Newport Beach, CA, USA

David T. Stafford, Ph.D. (Deceased)

Shawn P. Vorce Chesapeake Toxicology Resources, Frederick, MD, USA

Tate Yeatman Palm Beach County Sheriff's Office Crime Laboratory, West Palm Beach, FL, USA

Part I

Introduction

Postmortem Forensic Toxicology

1

Barry S. Levine

Abstract

Forensic toxicology is defined as the application of toxicology for the purposes of the law. Until the middle of the twentieth century, forensic toxicology was practiced almost exclusively as a result of investigating a fatality. Therefore, analyses were performed on specimens from deceased individuals. Today, forensic pathologists rely heavily upon forensic toxicology testing to determine how alcohol, drugs, or poisons may have caused or contributed to death.

Keywords

Postmortem · Toxicology · Specimens · Analysis · Interpretation

History

Although the study of the science of toxic substances and poisons began in the early 1800s, knowledge of poisons and poisonings has existed for thousands of years. Writings from ancient Egypt and Greece report poisonings due to herbs, plants, and food. For instance, the Greeks used hemlock as a means of state-sponsored execution, Socrates being the most famous case. Poisonings by opium, arsenic, and hydrocyanic acid were also reported throughout Europe during the Middle Ages. It was during this period that Philippus Aureolus Theophrastus Bombastus von Hohenheim—or Paracelsus—observed that any substance could be a poison, depending on its dose (Fig. 1.1).

In 1814, M.J.B. Orfila, the chairman of the Legal Medicine Department at the Sorbonne in France, made the first attempt to systematically study and categorize poisons. In his book *Traité des Poisons ou Toxicologie Generale*, he established six classes of poisons, basing the six classes mainly on their toxic effects. He also isolated arsenic from a variety of postmortem specimens, and he was the first to state that poisons must be absorbed, or enter the blood, to manifest their toxic effects.

In 1851, Jean Servais Stas developed the first effective method for extracting alkaloids from biological specimens. Specifically, his method detected nicotine in postmortem specimens obtained from Gustave Fougnies, who was allegedly poisoned by his brother-in-law. The extraction procedure used by Stas was modified several years later by F.J. Otto. This method, which enabled the isolation of purer alkaloid substances, became known as the Stas–Otto method and remains the basis for drug extraction to this day.

B. S. Levine (✉)
Office of the Chief Medical Examiner, Baltimore, MD, USA
e-mail: blevine@som.umaryland.edu

" What is there that is not poison?
All things are poison and nothing without poison.
Solely the dose determines that a thing is not a poison."

Fig. 1.1 Paracelsus's statement about dose in Paracelsus's *Third Defense*

Forensic toxicology did not develop in the United States until the beginning of the twentieth century. Under Charles Norris, New York City replaced its coroner system with a medical examiner system. The medical examiner's office included a toxicology laboratory directed by Alexander Gettler, the first forensic toxicologist in the United States. Gettler directed the laboratory for 41 years and trained the first generation of forensic toxicologists in the country.

The ubiquitous use of alcohol drove the development of analytical methods to study alcohol's pharmacokinetics. Maurice Nicloux and Erik Widmark performed detailed pharmacokinetic studies on alcohol, developing a formula relating body weight, amount consumed, and blood alcohol concentration. To address the problem of drinking and driving, Rolla Harger developed an instrument, the Drunkometer, which measured alcohol concentration in breath. Then Robert Borkenstein developed the Breathalyzer®, which became the standard for breath alcohol testing for many years.

Types of Postmortem Forensic Toxicology Cases

The most obvious use for postmortem forensic toxicologic analyses lies in suspected drug intoxication cases, which are not readily diagnosed at autopsy. In intravenous drug deaths, a recent injection site may be observable, and oral intoxications may be inferred from a large amount of unabsorbed tablet fragments in the stomach. However, the only other anatomic findings indicating drug intoxication are pulmonary congestion and edema. In some cases, investigation at the scene may indicate the causative agent or agents. Nevertheless, a toxicology laboratory analysis is needed to identify and quantify the substances present in the biological specimens in order to determine whether these drugs caused or contributed to death.

Toxicologic investigations are also important in deaths other than drug intoxications, such as homicides and accidental deaths. Many medical examiner or coroner's offices routinely perform drug screens on all homicides, for example, for the following reasons:

- Many homicides are drug related.
- The abuse of drugs may provide a motive for homicide.
- An individual under the pharmacologic effects of drugs has a greater chance of committing or falling victim to homicides.

A drug-of-abuse screen can provide information related to solving a particular homicide case. Often, postmortem carbon monoxide analysis can also be relevant, since arson deaths are considered homicides.

In certain accidental deaths, impairment issues may have significant forensic relevance. Comprehensive testing for both therapeutic drugs and drugs of abuse, such as alcohol, is routinely requested in driver motor vehicle fatalities to ascertain the potential role of drugs in the accident.

Toxicologic analyses may even be important in deaths due to natural causes. For instance, deaths from seizures occur with or without anatomic findings. Being able to quantify blood levels of anticonvulsant drugs, for example, would allow the medical examiner to identify whether the deceased had been undermedicated or noncompliant. Conversely, the presence of anticonvulsant drugs in an individual who had no prior seizure history may require investigation. Patient compliance may also be an issue in deaths of individuals being treated for depression or mental illness.

Investigations of natural deaths may require postmortem clinical chemistry assays, and in these assays, vitreous humor is the specimen of choice. Vitreous urea nitrogen values are useful evidence in determining death from dehydration or renal malfunction. Markedly elevated vitreous glucose concentrations would indicate antemortem hyperglycemia.

Death Investigation

There are two main systems of death investigation in the United States: the coroner system and the medical examiner system. Regardless of the type of investigation, the types of cases under their jurisdiction are similar.

In general, any unnatural or suspicious death is subject to investigation: deaths involving trauma or violence, deaths that are potential suicides, or deaths that potentially result from criminal activity. Even apparently natural deaths, if occurring suddenly or unexpectedly, fall under the jurisdiction of the medical examiner or coroner.

Specific governmental subdivisions may also define specific circumstances of death that require an investigation. Each coroner or medical examiner has the authority to conduct investigations, perform autopsies, request toxicologic analysis, or employ the services of any other forensic experts deemed necessary to arrive at the final determination of cause and manner of death.

Though both systems handle similar types of cases, there are some significant differences in how the director of each system is chosen and in which credentials are required in order to be a director. A coroner is elected by the people or appointed by a governmental authority. A medical examiner is appointed usually by the health department. A coroner is not required to have any particular training or experience in medicine, whereas a medical examiner must be a physician, usually a pathologist, with specific training in forensic medicine.

Specimen Acquisition

A critical and often overlooked component of the forensic autopsy is the collection of proper specimens for toxicologic analysis. Since it is difficult if not impossible to acquire quality specimens after an autopsy has been completed, the pathologist must ensure that all necessary specimens are made available to the toxicologist.

Blood

The single most important specimen to be collected is blood. Blood should be obtained during all inspections and limited or complete autopsies. Ideally, two blood specimens should be collected, one from the heart (50–100 mL) and the other from a peripheral site, such as the femoral or ileac veins. In certain situations, heart blood can be contaminated either by trauma or from the release of drugs from tissue sites; in these cases, the alternate blood specimen can be used for analysis. No more than 10–20 mL of the peripheral blood specimen should be collected; the collection of a greater volume indicates that you might not have a pure peripheral blood specimen. If subdural or epidural clots exist, blood from these sites should also be collected. These specimens could be useful when there is some period between an injury and death. Sodium fluoride (1% w/v) and potassium oxalate (0.2%, w/v) are often used as preservative and anticoagulant, respectively.

Vitreous Humor

In addition to blood, collect vitreous humor in all postmortem cases. Vitreous humor displays good stability and resides in an anatomically isolated area. Therefore, it is more resistant to putrefactive changes than are other specimens. As previously stated, postmortem clinical assays can be performed on vitreous humor. Ethanol analysis in vitreous humor can also help in the interpretation of postmortem blood ethanol concentrations. Although sodium fluoride may be used as a preservative, an unpreserved vitreous humor specimen is often retained for electrolyte determination.

Urine

All available urine should be collected in all autopsied cases. The utility of urine in postmortem cases is similar to its uses in other types of drug testing. Many drugs and metabolites are present in higher concentration in urine than in blood. Drugs also remain in the urine for days or longer after use. Some color and immunoassay tests can be performed rapidly without pretreating the specimens.

Bile

In the absence of urine, bile from the gallbladder can be used as an alternate waste fluid for screening. Because bile can concentrate certain drugs such as narcotics and benzodiazepines, all available bile should be collected.

Liver

Drug metabolism occurs in the liver, so parent drugs and their metabolites may be present in higher concentrations in the liver than in the blood, thus making detection easier. Many drugs like the tricyclic antidepressants are sequestered in the liver. One drawback to using the liver is that drug detection requires treating the specimen first. Liver is also a useful specimen for comprehensive drug testing when there are limited fluid volumes, as may be encountered in baby and infant deaths. The collection of 30 to 50 grams of liver is sufficient for all toxicological testing.

Antemortem Specimens

When an individual is treated in the hospital prior to death, the collection of these specimens by the postmortem toxicology laboratory may be vital in cause of death determination. In drug intoxication cases, metabolism and medical intervention may cause a significant decrease in drug concentration or even the removal of the drug from the blood. Moreover, administration of drugs in the hospital for palliative care, such as morphine, may be detected in the postmortem specimens, but may be unrelated to the cause of death. However, there are also limitations in the use of these specimens in death investigation cases. Specimen volume is often limited, preventing the performance of a comprehensive drug screen. For that reason, it is best to only test the antemortem specimens either after a screen on the postmortem specimens or after consultation with the pathologist so as to target the testing that is needed.

Other Specimens

Lung tissue is frequently collected in cases involving the inhalation of volatile substances. Spleen, being a source of red cells, can be used for carbon monoxide analysis when blood is unavailable or unsuitable for analysis. In overdoses, stomach contents can provide easy identification of the ingested substance or substances if tablets are still intact. A large amount of drug would also be present in the stomach contents, thus facilitating analytical identification. Hair can also be used to identify long-term drug use; moreover, metals such as arsenic can be detected in hair.

Specimen Receipt and Accessioning

Once the pathologist or investigator acquires the specimens, they are transported to the laboratory. Specimens should be enumerated. Each should be individually packaged and labeled with the decedent's name and autopsy or case number and accompanied by the following documentation:

- Relevant demographic information about the deceased (age, sex, and race).
- The name and address of the contributor.
- A brief history of the case:
  - If the cause of death is known, listing this is usually sufficient.
  - If the cause of death is pending, then a brief summary of the known history suffices.
  - List any suspected drug use or involvement; this directs the laboratory regarding any nonroutine testing that may be required.
  - Indicate the types of analyses requested by the contributor. Many coroner or medical examiner offices use a standard request form when submitting specimens for toxicologic analysis (Fig. 1.2). This form may also serve as the external chain-of-custody form.

OFFICE OF THE CHIEF MEDICAL EXAMINER
  REQUEST FOR TOXICOLOGIC ANALYSIS

LABORATORY # _____

NAME _____   DATE OF REQUEST _____

MEDICAL EXAMINER _____   DATE OF DEATH _____

PATHOLOGIST _____   AUTOPSY# _____

_____ CHECK HERE IF DECOMPOSED   CLASSIFICATION: Natural _____ Other _____

_____ CHECK HERE IF SUSPECTED BIOHAZARD   AGE _____ RACE _____ SEX _____

_____ CHECK HERE IF DRUG DEATH AND DEATH CERTIFICATE SIGNED (non-pending)

Cause of Death: _____

Brief History: _____

Note Any Drugs Suspected: _____

SAMPLES SUBMITTED:

____ BLOOD (HEART)	_____		____ SPLEEN	_____
____ BLOOD (FEMORAL)	_____		____ LUNG	_____
____ BLOOD (SUBCLAVIAN)	_____		____ BRAIN	_____
____ BLOOD (PERIPHERAL)	_____		____ SPINAL FLUID	
____ BLOOD _____	_____		____ SWABS	V_A_O_
____ URINE	_____		____ EVIDENCE	
____ BILE	_____		____ HOSP SPEC	A_B_C_
____ VITREOUS HUMOR	_____			D_E_F_
____ LIVER	_____			
____ KIDNEY	_____		____ ____	_____
____ STOMACH CONTENTS	_____		____ ____	_____

ANALYSES REQUESTED :
____ ALCOHOL
____ CARBON MONOXIDE   _____ DRUG TESTING
                                                  _____ ROUTINE
                                                  _____ RULE OUT TOXICOLOGY - PENDING
                                                  _____ DRUG DEATH LIKELY - PENDING

____ OTHER _____

FOR LABORATORY USE ONLY   ‖ Received:
                                                                          ‖ Date
SAMPLE	ALCOHOL, ETHYL	OTHER VOLATILE	‖ Time
_____	_____ %	_____ %	‖ Initials:
_____	_____ %	_____ %	
_____	_____ %	_____ %	‖ Blood Fluoride
_____	_____ %	_____ %	‖ Tube Prepared:
_____	CARBON MONOXIDE _____	% SATURATED	‖ Volume:
			‖ Initials:

Reviewed by: _____

Fig. 1.2 An example of a toxicology request form

Specimens received in the laboratory are then accessioned. All specimens should be checked against the request sheet and the contributor notified of any discrepancies. Each case is then assigned a laboratory number and each specimen is labeled with that number. Choice of specimens for analysis should be made on the basis of laboratory policy or case history. All remaining specimens should then be placed in the freezer for storage or future analysis.

Analytical Process

The analytical process begins after the accessioning process is complete. The process used on postmortem specimens is both similar to and different from the process used to analyze toxicology specimens from living individuals. For example, commercially available immunoassays can be used to screen postmortem urine specimens; occasionally, postmortem urine specimens require centrifugation prior to immunoassay. Tests designed to detect adulteration, such as pH and specific gravity, need not be performed because the specimen is collected directly from the bladder by the pathologist or autopsy assistant during the autopsy.

Section II of this book will deal with the analytical process in more detail, but the following is a brief overview of the process.

Separation

The initial step in the process for postmortem specimens is analyte separation. Except for some drug classes that can be analyzed directly in urine specimens, the analytes of interest usually require separation from the biological matrix. For example, volatile substances can be separated from an aqueous matrix by heating the specimen in a sealed container at 60–80 °C. The gaseous phase above the matrix layer will contain volatile substances that can be sampled and analyzed.

Protein precipitation is another relatively simple separation technique. Inorganic acids such as tungstic acid and trichloroacetic acid may be used to precipitate protein. Alternatively, organic solvents such as methanol or acetonitrile may be used. Color tests, solid-phase extraction, and immunoassays may benefit from this sample preparation step.

Liquid–liquid extraction (LLE) and solid-phase extraction (SPE) are commonly used to isolate compounds of interest from postmortem specimens. In LLE, a drug is partitioned between two immiscible liquid phases. Ionization and solubility characteristics can affect separation of basic, neutral, and acidic drugs. For instance, a basic drug will be nonionized in an alkaline medium; adjusting the matrix pH to alkaline allows basic drugs to leave the matrix and enter an immiscible organic solvent. Similarly, acidic drugs can be extracted after acidifying the biological matrix. This process allows for the removal of contaminating aqueous components and permits easy concentration of the extract by evaporation.

In SPE, the drug is partitioned between a liquid and a solid (stationary) phase. The general process of SPE involves column conditioning, sample application, column washing, and analyte elution. Postmortem specimens may require additional sample preparation steps prior to SPE because whole blood and tissues may contain clots or particulate matter that prevent the flow of specimens or solvents through the column. Specimen dilution, sonication, centrifugation, filtration, or protein precipitation may be necessary. A hybrid technique between LLE and SPE is supported liquid extraction (SLE) where the buffered specimen is applied to a column containing a diatomaceous earth material. An extraction solvent is then applied to the column, collecting the nonionized drug for concentration and detection.

Identification by Spectrophotometry, Chromatography, Mass Spectrometry, and Immunoassay

After separation, toxic substances are identified. Identification techniques in forensic toxicology can be grouped into spectrophotometry, chromatography, mass spectrometry, and immunoassay techniques.

The use of spectrophotometry in today's postmortem forensic toxicology laboratory is limited to some simple color tests and the detection system in some commercially available immunoassays. Color tests are easy to use and can be performed directly on the specimen or on a protein-free filtrate of the specimen. Color tests may be used to screen postmortem specimens for salicylate and acetaminophen.

Gas chromatography (GC)-based techniques are widely used in the postmortem toxicology laboratory for the identification and quantification of drugs. Various components of the chromatographic system can be modified to enhance resolution, sensitivity, and specificity. The stationary phase can be changed to improve resolution of a particular group of substances. Temperature programming of the stationary phase permits the identification of substances with differing volatilities within a single chromatographic run. Detector selection can assist various analyses. The flame ionization detector (FID), for example, is a general detector for all compounds containing carbon and hydrogen atoms. The addition of a rubidium bead increases sensitivity to nitrogen-containing compounds (nitrogen–phosphorus detector, NPD). Halogenated compounds such as benzodiazepines can be analyzed at very low detection limits with an electron capture detector. For polar and thermally labile compounds, liquid chromatography (LC) is a preferred chromatographic technique. A variety of stationary phases and detectors exist, and mobile phase composition can be varied, either between runs or within a run. Within-run mobile phase modification is known as gradient elution and is analogous to temperature programming in GC. Mass spectrometry (MS) ionizes the chemical species and separates the molecular fragments based upon their mass-to-charge (m/z) ratio.

Immunoassays are based on competitive binding between an antibody reagent with labeled drug (reagent) and drug in the specimen. A separation step may be required prior to measurement. These assays have several advantages over other techniques. They can be performed directly on urine specimens or on blood or tissue specimens after pretreatment, and they have good sensitivity to a particular drug or drug class. A number of commercially available immunoassays, differing primarily in the type of drug label used are in use today. Each has distinct advantages that dictate its particular application. Although immunoassay-based techniques are not specific for a particular drug, this feature may be exploited for the identification of drugs within a particular class of drug (e.g., benzodiazepines, barbiturates, opiates).

Confirmation

Each identification technique individually can indicate the presence or absence of a particular analyte. However, for a substance to be reported as positive, at least two different analytical techniques must be used. The use of a second or confirmatory technique is a fundamental principle in forensic toxicology. Two different immunoassays would not be acceptable because of antibody similarity among commercially available immunoassays.

More definitive confirmatory techniques provide structural information about the substance itself. Mass spectrometry, in combination with a separation technique such as GC or LC, is currently the benchmark confirmatory technique used in the field. For example, a gas chromatographic retention time plus a full-scan electron ionization mass spectrum can be compared to a standard to provide conclusive identification in most but not all circumstances. For drugs present in lower concentrations, selected ion monitoring of three major ions may be sufficient. LC-MS-based techniques also allow additional flexibility with respect to ionization techniques and mass spectral data acquisition.

Quantification

That a substance is present does not necessarily mean that it was a cause of death. For this determination, the substances in the relevant specimens must be quantified.

Quantification of drugs in blood is most commonly associated with toxicity or lethality. In chromatographic methods, the signal generated by the detector will be proportional to the amount of substance present. By preparing calibrators of known concentration, response factors can be calculated to quantify the analyte in the case specimens.

In certain circumstances, the quantification of drugs in tissue may have particular utility. When blood specimens are unavailable, the liver is usually used as a substitute specimen. Moreover, the amount of drug in the liver is often helpful in interpreting postmortem tricyclic antidepressant concentrations.

Analytes

Ethanol

Ethanol is the most frequently encountered drug in the postmortem forensic toxicology laboratory. Specimens should be analyzed for ethanol in all postmortem cases.

One approach is to initially analyze the heart blood for ethanol. If it is negative, no further analyses are required. If it is above a predetermined cutoff such as 0.01 or 0.02 g/dL, then peripheral blood, vitreous humor, and urine should also be quantified. There are numerous reasons for this approach. In some cases, such as chest trauma, the heart blood can be contaminated, causing a spuriously high concentration of ethanol. An interpretation based on this single analysis would lead to false conclusions, whereas a peripheral blood sample would give a better indication of antemortem ethanol concentration. In head trauma cases, the analysis of subdural blood can indicate blood ethanol concentration at the time of injury, especially if there is a significant period of time between injury and death.

Quantification of ethanol in urine or vitreous humor is useful for several reasons, such as ascertaining the absorptive status of the individual. Post-absorption, the average vitreous humor/blood ethanol concentration ratio is about 1.18. If an individual was still absorbing ethanol at the time of death, then this ratio would be decreased. This is significant if blood ethanol concentration at a prior event is estimated. The average urine/blood ratio in the post-absorptive state is 1.3, but there are wide variations in this ratio. Therefore, both specimens should be analyzed if information about absorptive status is required.

Urine and vitreous humor analysis can also help determine whether a measured blood ethanol concentration resulted from antemortem consumption or from postmortem ethanol formation. A variety of microorganisms can produce ethanol as well as acetaldehyde and n-propanol from various sugars or fatty acids, but urine and vitreous humor are resistant to this process. Therefore, a positive blood ethanol concentration in conjunction with a positive vitreous humor and urine ethanol concentration would suggest antemortem ethanol consumption. Conversely, a negative vitreous humor and urine ethanol concentration could indicate postmortem ethanol formation in the blood.

Methods of Ethanol Analysis

Ethanol analysis on postmortem specimens can be conducted by a variety of methods. Enzymatic methods use alcohol dehydrogenase, which converts ethanol to acetaldehyde and reduces nicotinamide adenine dinucleotide from its oxidized (NAD⁺) to reduced (NADH) form. Using spectrophotometric detection, the increase in absorbance at 340 nm is directly proportional to the amount of ethanol in the specimen. This reversible reaction is shifted toward the production of NADH by adding a trapping agent such as hydrazine or semicarbazide, which reacts with acetaldehyde to produce a stable derivative. These assays were developed for serum or plasma specimens and are widely utilized in clinical (hospital) settings.

GC is the preferred analytical technique. Specimens can be analyzed directly after dilution with an aqueous internal standard, or by heating the diluted specimen to 60 °C in a sealed container and sampling the vapor. Analysis of this headspace permits quantification without interference from the biological matrix. It has the sensitivity and precision to quantify ethanol concentrations as low as 0.01 g/dL. Multiple volatile compounds, including other alcohols, acetone, or hydrocarbons, can be separated, identified, and quantified by GC-based methods, often in combination with an FID.

There are a number of combinations that provide confirmation of the presence of ethanol. Retention time agreement between two GC columns with different polarities is commonly used. This can be achieved with a single injection using headspace dual-column GC-FID, although headspace GC-MS can also be used.

Interpretation

The interpretation of blood ethanol concentrations in postmortem specimens, provided that no postmortem ethanol formation occurred, is similar to the interpretation of blood specimens of living individuals. Alcohol is a dose-dependent central nervous system depressant that can impair mental and physical functions. This impairment can manifest itself in reductions in judgment, attention, perception, and multitasking abilities (divided attention tasks). As the blood ethanol concentration increases, more overt symptoms of alcohol impairment may be observable. A blood ethanol concentration at or above 0.40 g/dL can be consistent with causing death in the absence of other pathological findings due to ethanol intoxication.

More details on ethanol will be provided in Chap. 19.

Carbon Monoxide

Carbon monoxide (CO) is produced by the incomplete combustion of organic material. CO is the causative agent in many fire deaths. In general, fire deaths can be explained by thermal injuries, smoke, and soot inhalation, or a combination of the two. CO binds with great affinity to hemoglobin (Hb), forming carboxyhemoglobin (CO-Hb) and reducing the blood's oxygen-carrying capabilities. The unit of measurement of CO is "percent saturation" (% sat) and is defined as the percent of total Hb which is CO-Hb.

Methods
CO may be measured in several ways. For instance, CO may be measured directly through microdiffusion or GC. A microdiffusion screening test uses a Conway cell. The outer well contains the specimen and an agent that releases the CO from Hb. The released CO reduces the palladium chloride in the center well to metallic palladium, producing a black film. Chromatographic methods also require the release of CO from Hb, usually by the addition of potassium ferricyanide to the blood in a sealed container. The released CO can be passed through a molecular sieve gas chromatographic column and measured directly with a thermal conductivity detector or after catalytic reduction to methane using a flame ioniza-

tion detector. The % sat is obtained either by measuring Hb to correct for the Hb content of the specimen or by analyzing a second aliquot of specimen after saturating with CO. This latter method removes the need to measure Hb because % sat is calculated by dividing the area of the CO peak in the untreated sample by the area generated from the saturated sample and then multiplying by 100.

CO content in a blood specimen can also be measured directly as CO-Hb by spectrophotometry. These methods are based on the difference in absorption spectra between various forms of Hb, and a large number have been published. Certain automated systems can simultaneously measure these Hb species by measuring absorbances at wavelengths where these spectra intersect. In some spectrophotometric methods, methemoglobin (met-Hb), a form of Hb where the iron is in the +3 valence state, can adversely affect spectrophotometric methods. Treating the blood with sodium hydrosulfite reduces met-Hb to Hb but does not affect CO-Hb. Therefore, postmortem specimens should be treated when these spectrophotometric methods are used. If blood is unavailable for analysis, a tissue fluid may have sufficient Hb to permit CO quantification; otherwise, spleen is an acceptable specimen.

Interpretation
The interpretation of CO-Hb levels is relatively straightforward. In general, values less than 10% are considered normal and are not associated with significant smoke inhalation. Smokers generally have higher basal CO levels than do nonsmokers. This implies that any fire death with normal % sat occurred prior to or shortly after the start of the fire, assuming that no medical treatment had ensued. Saturation values greater than 50% are consistent with death resulting from smoke and soot inhalation. Lower lethal concentrations can be observed in individuals with anemia or with compromised respiratory systems. Unlike other deaths from gaseous substances, CO can be detected in decomposed bodies because it is bound to Hb.

More details on carbon monoxide will be provided in Chap. 30.

Drugs

The most involved aspect of postmortem forensic toxicology is the analysis of drugs. Postmortem laboratories must have methodologies for the identification, confirmation, and quantification of both therapeutic and abused drugs.

The most common approach is to develop a protocol or a battery of tests to comprehensively screen for drugs. The scope of testing will depend on the type of investigation and contextual information. A negative screening test may require no additional analytical work. However, a positive screening test (presumptive positive) may require more specialized testing in the form of confirmation and quantification. No single analytical method is appropriate for all drugs; rather, a combination of methods provides a wide range of testing.

Figure 1.3 illustrates one comprehensive approach. Color tests are simple assays that can be done quickly to screen for certain drugs; several color tests can be included in a comprehensive approach. An alkaline extraction followed by GC with nitrogen–phosphorus or MS detection and temperature programming can identify drugs within the following classes: antiarrhythmics, antidepressants, antihistamines, benzodiazepines, narcotics, neuroleptics, and sympathomimetic amines. Not all drugs within a class can be detected at appropriate concentrations, and the toxicologist must know which drugs will be identified and at which detection limits. A weak acid extraction followed by GC or LC can identify acid and neutral drugs such as barbiturates and anticonvulsants. A variety of commercially avail-

able immunoassays can identify amphetamines, barbiturates, benzodiazepines, buprenorphine, cannabinoids, cocaine, opiates, oxycodone phencyclidine, and other drugs. Due to the proliferation of new psychoactive substances (NPS), mass spectrometry–based screening is gaining popularity due to its increased scope of testing.

The interpretation of drug results can be easy or difficult. The presence of drugs or metabolites in the bile or urine will indicate exposure, but assessment of toxicity is usually impossible.

Quantification of drugs in the blood, on the other hand, is better correlated with toxicity or fatality and must be interpreted in light of available history. A high concentration of a drug or a group of drugs in the blood of an individual with suicidal ideation, a suicide note, and no anatomic cause of death at autopsy is consistent with a suicidal drug or multiple drug intoxication. The ratio of parent-to-metabolite concentrations may indicate an acute death. A therapeutic postmortem blood concentration in an individual treated in the hospital for several days may indicate much higher concentrations at an earlier time. Often, hospital laboratories perform drug testing on urine specimens without associated blood quantifications. The postmortem laboratory should obtain hospital blood specimens so that toxicity can be assessed. Of course, the clinical picture as documented by the hospital is extremely critical to this overall assessment. When dealing with clinical specimens, it should be noted that a variety of additives are used in commercial blood tubes. Many contain only an anticoagulant (e.g., heparin, EDTA, citrate) and no pre-

Fig. 1.3 One approach to comprehensive drug testing (DA = abused drugs, neg = negative, pos = positive, MS = mass spectrometry)

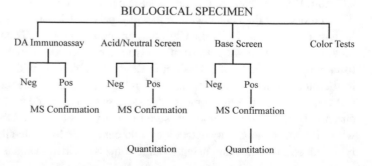

COMPREHENSIVE DRUG TESTING - ONE APPROACH

servative. This should be considered during sample selection, testing, and interpretation of results.

A series of drugs, each present in therapeutic concentrations, may have additive effects when present in combination. In some instances, effects may be synergistic (potentiating or supra-additive), whereby the overall effect is greater than the sum of the individual effects. A drug need not be present in toxic amounts to play a role in an individual's death. Therapeutic drug use may reduce judgment or performance, leading to an accident. Moreover, certain behavior may be altered by a drug, leading an individual to become a victim of violent activity.

One point that must be emphasized is that a laboratory's routine testing procedures are established to identify a large cross section of therapeutic and abused drugs. Each laboratory must determine the type of testing offered based on available resources. Not every drug available can be detected in a routine testing protocol; even within a drug class, some drugs may be identified and others not. It is crucial for the laboratory administration to understand the capabilities and limitations of the laboratory's routine testing procedures and communicate this to the client. These facts reinforce the need for drug history when a case is submitted. If the suspected agent is not identified routinely, then additional (targeted) testing can be done. Alternatively, a specimen can be sent to a reference laboratory for testing.

One complication in the interpretation of postmortem blood drug concentration is whether the measured drug concentration accurately reflects the concentration at death. Some drugs have been shown to redistribute after death, especially those with high volumes of distribution. For instance, tricyclic antidepressants may redistribute into the heart blood from the liver, producing an artificially high blood concentration. Measurement of these drugs in peripheral blood or tissues can minimize the possibility of misinterpreting results. The phenomenon of postmortem redistribution (PMR) is discussed in Chap. 34.

It is also possible that drug concentrations decrease during the postmortem interval. In vitro, cocaine degrades into benzoylecgonine (chemical hydrolysis) and ecgonine methyl ester (enzymatic hydrolysis) under alkaline conditions or in the absence of a chemical preservative. The presence of a cholinesterase inhibitor and storage of blood at reduced temperature can reduce this loss once the specimen is collected. Oxidation, light sensitivity, and other factors can also contribute to drug instability. These are discussed in more detail in Chap. 33.

Reporting

After the analytical work is completed, all data should be submitted for review by appropriately qualified personnel. These reviews should include all aspects of the technical and administrative processes. The results should also be reviewed in the context of the case. Consultation with the pathologist or medical examiner may clarify any unresolved issues. Once this review has been completed, a final report can be generated for final disposition.

Further Reading

Baselt RC (2020) Disposition of toxic drugs and chemicals in man, 12th edn. Biomedical Publications, Seal Beach, CA

Caplan YH, Goldberger BA (eds) (2015) Garriott's Medicolegal aspects of alcohol, 6th edn. Tuscon, Lawyers and Judges

Dinis-Oliveira RJ, Vieira D, Magalhaes T (2016) Guidelines for the collection of biological samples for clinical and forensic toxicological analysis. Forensic Sci Res 1:42–51

Dolinak D (2013) Forensic toxicology a physiologic perspective. Academic Forensic Pathology Inc, Calgary

Moffat AC, Osselton MD, Widdop B, Watts J (eds) (2011) Clarke's analysis of drugs and poisons, 4th edn. London, Pharmaceutical Press

Human Performance Toxicology

Gary W. Kunsman and Rebecca L. Hartman

Abstract

The evaluation of human performance, often termed psychomotor performance, is a daily occurrence for most people. Whether the ability to perform routine yet complex psychomotor tasks is determined on the highway or in the workplace, such monitoring occurs frequently. Inability to perform may affect the safety of other persons and have economic and legal implications. Many factors may affect an individual's ability to perform routine tasks such as operating machinery or driving a car, but psychoactive drugs, including alcohol (ethanol), are frequently implicated.

Keywords

Impaired driving · Drugs · Alcohol · DRE · Psychomotor impairment · Cognitive impairment

G. W. Kunsman
Broward County, District 17 Medical Examiner's Office, Fort Lauderdale, FL, USA

R. L. Hartman (✉)
Monroe County Office of the Medical Examiner, Rochester, NY, USA
e-mail: RebeccaHartman@monroecounty.gov

Definition

The field of human performance toxicology combines aspects of psychology, toxicology, and pharmacology. Modern psychology is not a study of the mind, as the term suggests (a combination of the Greek terms *psyche* for mind and *logos* for subject of discourse), but is more accurately defined as the study of behavior. Behavior encompasses the manner of one's conduct and one's response to environmental stimuli; the study of behavior is a science that deals with human action and seeks generalizations of human behavior in society. Performance is defined as the execution of an action, the manner of reacting to stimuli, and the carrying out of an action or behavior. It involves the effective use of higher brain centers in the coordination and control of motor functions resulting in movements appropriate to a given stimulus. Human performance toxicology or behavioral toxicology, then, is the study of the human response to environmental conditions and stimuli [and ability to function] under the influence of drugs.

This field of study was originally the realm of psychologists. They were interested in learning how people learn, and they applied both respondent conditioning (classical or Pavlovian) and operant conditioning (Skinner) in an effort to understand the learning process. An offshoot of this research attempted to elucidate the neurochemical basis for responding to external stimuli.

© Springer Nature Switzerland AG 2020
B. S. Levine, S. Kerrigan (eds.), *Principles of Forensic Toxicology*,
https://doi.org/10.1007/978-3-030-42917-1_2

Over time, this research led to establishing fields of study such as skills acquisition, human engineering, and motor performance testing, the area of psychology that has most significantly affected human performance toxicology.

Forensic toxicologists have become interested in human performance toxicology because it is a natural extension of their involvement in the medicolegal implications of drug use, misuse, and abuse. The effects of drugs on skills acquisition, learning, and performance have broad social and economic implications both on the road and in the workplace. The toxicologist uses "real-life" tests and laboratory-based psychomotor tests to monitor the behavioral effects of drugs.

It is important to note that drugs may alter normal behavior by either enhancing or impairing performance. In behavioral or human performance toxicology, the impairing effects of drugs are typically of more interest. In fact, those drugs, such as stimulants, that enhance performance in the short term often impair performance when they are used chronically over an extended period. In addition, the "crash" phase associated with abuse of such compounds can also be impairing. Therefore, toxicologists generally speak mainly of performance decrements when they refer to the behavioral effects of drugs.

Laboratory Psychomotor Performance Testing

To evaluate the effects of drugs and environmental conditions (e.g., illness, disease, exposure to toxicants in the workplace) on driving and workplace safety and efficiency, a large number of psychomotor tests have been developed. Since laboratory experiments provide a controlled environment, human performance testing most frequently occurs in this setting.

Although evaluation of performance on actual tasks (e.g., testing the effects of alcohol on automobile driving using closed-course or on-the-road studies) provides data more directly applicable to understanding and evaluating the behavioral effects of drugs on "real-life" tasks, such studies are not often practical. The high cost

and risk associated with such real-life studies is often prohibitive, and researchers turn to laboratory-based studies as an effective alternative. Laboratory studies also allow for subdividing a task into its component parts, which is often not feasible in non-laboratory studies.

The effects of a drug on performance are not typically predictable from a single test, in part because laboratory-based tests do not exactly simulate the performance of interest. Most tasks, such as driving, may be considered to be routine yet complex psychomotor tasks. This simply means that behaviors such as driving a car may be performed routinely and may seem uncomplicated, but are in fact a series of small tasks that must be performed simultaneously or in close association with each other to accomplish the larger task. Workplace and driving performance may be considered to be a series of vigilance and divided-attention tasks. Testing batteries, therefore, are believed to more adequately provide predictive value of the effects of drugs on human performance.

In a field study, it is generally difficult to subdivide tasks into their component parts and measure performance on each aspect of that task. The ability to subdivide tasks in this manner allows the investigator to determine exactly what part of a behavior is impaired and in what way. For example, it is important to be able to differentiate whether a task is impaired as a result of a loss of visual acuity or due to a reduction in cognitive ability. When assessing a large task as a whole unit, it is generally difficult to determine which portion of the behavior is impaired. In the laboratory study, the investigator is evaluating a number of small tasks which are either a portion of the larger task or which model the types of behaviors used in that larger task in an effort to assess each portion of the whole task.

Although there are many advantages to the laboratory study, some aspects of this type of experimentation are less desirable than the field study. Probably the most significant is directly related to the above discussion. When a task is subdivided into its component parts, it is no longer truly the whole task. It then becomes possible to assess impairment in the real-life task only by association instead of directly, as in the field study. This is frequently a question raised in reference to laboratory studies that attempt to relate impairment to driving. A serious question of validity is raised when a subject's performance is impaired on reaction time tasks or divided-attention tasks and the investigator extrapolates these results to suggest that driving, a task that involves reaction time and divided attention, will also be impaired under the same drug conditions. As well as validity (i.e., Does a task that measures driving ability look like the actual driving task?), there are also issues of learning, training, and practice effects that must be accounted for in the laboratory studies. These effects are minimized when a well-controlled study uses properly validated performance tests. Often, however, the time frame in which subjects learn new performance tests does not compare to the degree of practice and expertise they have developed in the performance of routine yet complex psychomotor tasks such as driving. Highly practiced tasks tend to be more resistant to drug effects than less well-learned tasks; therefore, impairment noted on such laboratory tasks may not reflect the same type or degree of impairment on the real-life task. One way in which laboratory testing is overcoming some of these disadvantages is through the application of increasingly sophisticated and more realistic simulators. For example, current technology has provided automobile and flight simulators that so accurately reflect the real task that they are used for training drivers and pilots. Such simulators overcome the problems of validity and are probably less susceptible to learning and practice effects. The simulator also allows for the measurement of the subtasks that constitute the larger task or behavior.

Various psychomotor tests are available for use in laboratory studies. Despite their differences, they may be grouped into three major categories: perceptual performance tasks, cognitive performance tasks, and motor performance tasks.

Perceptual performance tasks measure the acuity of the senses, especially vision and hearing. The most common task in this category is time estimation, in which the test subject is required to estimate the passage of a fixed time interval, typically 30 s. This task evaluates mental acuity. Many drugs alter the subject's ability to estimate the passage of time.

Cognitive performance tests measure intellectual function. Many different types of tasks fall into this category. Vigilance tasks measure the ability to recognize specific information and require the subject to discriminate a specific signal from among a group of choices, e.g., the subject monitors several dials and reports when one varies from the others. These types of tests model many modern workplace tasks as well as aspects of the driving task. Another form of cognitive test uses simple arithmetic problems to evaluate concentration and mental processing time. These tasks include a wide array of mathematical problems such as requiring the subject to perform a series of simple two- or three-digit addition or subtraction problems. One session of these tasks can include a series of 25–50 problems, and answers to each problem are typically required within 5–10 s.

Motor performance tests evaluate the integrity and function of motor pathways. This type of testing is also referred to as psychomotor or sensorimotor testing. The most basic of the motor performance tests is the tapping rate task. This is a test of pure motor speed in which the subject strikes a key or alternate keys on a keypad as rapidly as possible over a short time span. This task has no cognitive component and, therefore, allows for analyzing the motor component of other tasks in a performance test battery.

Among the most popular and frequently used motor tests are the reaction time tests, which evaluate motor response. Reaction time is a basic performance skill that is fundamental to all activity. Although many different variations of these tests are available, the essential element of the task is a button press in response to a critical stimulus. Reaction time tasks may be classified as either simple reaction time or choice reaction time. The simple reaction time tasks evaluate only motor response: how rapidly a response is made after the stimulus is presented. In the choice reaction time tasks, the subject must choose a single stimulus from among a number of alternatives. These tasks evaluate sensorimotor performance in that they have both a motor response component and a recognition time component.

Another popular type of motor performance test is the tracking task. These tests measure visual–motor coordination and contain elements of reaction time, fine and course motor control, and attention. The tracking task also has many variations. These tests are commonly used in behavioral studies because the elements of the tracking tasks are also present in automobile driving.

The motor performance test that provides the most sensitive measure of the impairing effects of drugs is the divided-attention task. This type of test involves the simultaneous performance of two or more subtasks. Many possible combinations of tasks are available, e.g., two tracking tasks or a tracking task and a choice reaction time task. The essential requirement for choosing the best combinations of tasks is that the subject's capacity to absorb and respond to all relevant information be taxed. The information processing demands of the combined tasks must be such that either one or both tasks are performed at a lower performance level than when either task is performed alone. The critical concern in task selection is that the combination of tasks must not overload the subject to such a degree that one of the tasks is neglected. The requirement to share attention is a common feature in everyday tasks such as automobile driving.

Another important aspect of the laboratory-based performance study is the subjective test, in which the subjects self-report their mood, feelings, and impressions using a quantifiable scale. Such self-reporting provides useful information about drug effects, duration, and the subject's perceptions regarding impairment.

Application

The question of behavioral toxicology or impairment is a separate issue from whether the drug in question is used appropriately or abused. Although it is common to think that forensic toxicology in general and human performance toxicology in particular are interested only in the use of illicit drugs (e.g., heroin, marijuana, cocaine, and others), numerous therapeutic drugs including antidepressants, benzodiazepines, muscle relaxants, opioids, antihistamines, and anticonvulsants also have significant behavioral effects. The toxicologist must focus on both licit and illicit drugs and must evaluate the effects of therapeutic drugs when administered in the prescribed manner for their normal medical applications, as well as when they are incorrectly administered or abused.

A classic example of this type of problem is the study of the benzodiazepines. When these drugs are used appropriately as anxiolytics, they may improve driving behavior. Individuals with prescriptions and other chronic users may also exhibit tolerance to some of the deleterious effects. However, they are often used in higher doses and for a longer period of time than prescribed or recommended, or recreationally, or in conjunction with popular drugs of abuse, or to supplement methadone maintenance by heroin addicts. In such cases these drugs may adversely affect driving behavior.

When evaluating the behavioral effects of a drug, it is also important to consider the metabolic profile of that drug. The presence of active metabolites is certainly important in evaluating the behavioral effects of drugs, because they contribute to the parent drug's effect. The presence of inactive metabolites, although exerting no behavioral effects themselves, may provide some information about the approximate time that a drug was used or frequency of intake.

The specimen of choice in human performance toxicology varies with the application. The specimen most commonly used for establishing dose and concentration/effect relationships is blood. Because blood is most intimately in contact with the central nervous system (CNS), it provides the best information concerning how a drug, its active metabolites, and their concentrations are related to performance impairment. This is why blood is usually the preferred specimen for driving under the influence (DUI) evaluation. Alternate specimens such as urine, oral fluid, sweat, and hair are becoming increasingly popular due to ease and noninvasiveness of collection, but it is unlikely that a direct behavioral/concentration relationship can be established using these specimens. Detection windows for the different

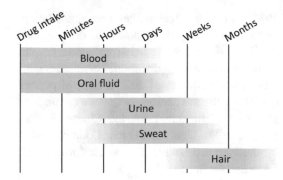

Fig. 2.1 Approximate drug detection windows for matrices utilized for human performance toxicological analysis

matrices inform specimen choice relative to the desired application. Drugs are concentrated in urine for excretion and thus may be detectable for days, whereas oral fluid typically indicates recent use (hours), and hair can establish use or exposure over months (Fig. 2.1).

Alcohol and Driving

The most commonly studied drug with performance-impairing effects is alcohol, and the most frequently studied task is driving. Even studies that examine the impairing effects of other drugs typically use alcohol as a standard of comparison. This is likely because drinking alcohol and driving is such a common occurrence and has such profound social and economic implications. Epidemiological studies have shown that 40–60% of all fatally injured drivers have a blood alcohol concentration (BAC) ≥0.10 g/dL, and 30–40% of those have a BAC >0.15 g/dL. The central issue in the history of the relationship between drinking and driving has been to establish a causal link between alcohol use and driving impairment and automobile accidents and to use this information to effect societal change.

History

The impairing effects of alcohol have been well known and well documented throughout recorded history. Although its impairing effects have

always had significant societal consequences, these consequences probably have even greater significance and cost in our industrial and mechanized society.

The invention of the steam locomotive and the advent of railway transportation in the mid-1800s brought to light the adverse consequences of combining high-speed travel with alcohol. By 1843, the New York Central Railroad prohibited employees from drinking while on duty. Along with the invention of the automobile and its rapid growth in popularity as a means of personal transportation came the problem of drinking and driving. An editorial as early as 1904 made the correlation between drinking before driving and automobile accidents. In 1910, the New York City traffic code noted that the misuse of alcohol was a factor in traffic safety. Even Henry Ford commented that the use of alcohol was incompatible with the speed at which Americans operated their automobiles, their machinery, and their lives in general.

The growth of industry in the United States in the early twentieth century was accompanied by an ever-increasing awareness of safety issues, not only in factories but also on the roads and in the home. The safety movement gained impetus in 1912 with the formation of the National Council for Industrial Safety, which became the National Safety Council (NSC) in 1914. By 1924, the National Safety Council had expanded its interests to include highway safety and therefore, by implication, the effects of alcohol on driving. The work of this organization has been continued and expanded by the National Highway Traffic Safety Administration (NHTSA), a division of the Department of Transportation.

Despite the awareness of the behavioral effects of alcohol throughout history, scientific documentation and evaluation of these effects did not begin until the early 1900s. Erik Widmark, from the University of Lund in Sweden, was among the first to quantify the amount of alcohol in various body fluids and correlate those concentrations to measures of impairment, subsequently applying that information to traffic safety issues. By the early 1920s, Widmark had developed a protocol for physicians to follow when evaluating drivers suspected of driving under the influence (DUI) of alcohol. This protocol consisted of behavioral and physiological measures including pupillary reaction to light, signs of ataxia (lack of voluntary muscle control/coordination), the Romberg test, finger-to-finger test, odor of alcohol on the breath, and general appearance. The evaluation concluded with drawing blood to analyze for the presence of alcohol.

In the United States, Herman Heise spurred the interest in alcohol and traffic safety in the early 1930s. From 1935 to 1938, the Evanston study reported on 270 drivers hospitalized after involvement in automobile accidents in Evanston, Illinois. During the same period, the police tested a sample of 1750 drivers for BAC. The Drunkometer, invented by Rolla Harger of Indiana University, was used to evaluate BAC in these drivers by measuring alcohol in the breath. The recent invention of this breath-testing device allowed researchers to overcome the legal and logistical problems associated with collecting blood or urine from these randomly stopped drivers. Richard Holcomb of the Northwestern University Traffic Institute reported the results of this study in 1938. Holcomb found that the chances of having an accident increased geometrically with the presence of any alcohol in the blood, to the extent that each 0.02 g/dL rise in BAC doubled the risk of accident.

The first legislation making DUI an offense in the United States was passed in Indiana in March 1939 and in Maine in April 1939. These statutes established a three-level offense based on BAC. A BAC of ≤ 0.05 g/dL was considered presumptive evidence of no guilt, >0.15 g/dL was considered presumptive evidence of guilt, and a BAC between these two concentrations was considered supportive evidence of DUI. This legislation was based on the joint statement issued in 1938 by the Committee to Study Problems of Motor Vehicle Accidents (a special committee of the American Medical Association) and the Committee on Alcohol and Other Drugs (a committee of the NSC). The Committee on Alcohol and Other Drugs (its name later changed to the Alcohol, Drugs and Impairment Division) has remained active in this area since its formation in

1936. The committee makes recommendations toward controlling the problem of drinking and driving, including legislative matters, law enforcement issues, education, chemical testing methods and equipment, and training of personnel. The recommendations of the two committees also formed the basis for the Chemical Tests Section of the Uniform Vehicle Code published by the National Committee on Uniform Traffic Laws and Ordinances in 1946.

In 1953, Implied Consent legislation was passed in New York State and was soon included in the Uniform Vehicle Code; implied consent laws have since been passed in all 50 states. The implied consent legislation provides that, as a condition precedent to being issued a driver's license, an applicant agrees, by implication, to submit to a chemical test in any case in which he is suspected of DUI. Refusal to submit to the test results in the loss of driving privileges.

In 1958, the Symposium on Alcohol and Road Traffic at Indiana University issued a statement that a BAC of 0.05 g/dL definitely impairs the driving ability of some individuals. It further posited that as the BAC increases, an increasing proportion of individuals experience impairment, until the BAC reaches 0.10 g/dL—at which point all individuals are definitely impaired. In 1960, the Committee on Alcohol and Drugs released a statement recommending that DUI laws be amended to reflect a 0.10 g/dL BAC as presumptive evidence of guilt. The Uniform Vehicle Code was amended to reflect this recommendation in 1962.

Another study conducted by Indiana University, the Grand Rapids Study, was published in 1964. This study essentially confirmed the results of the Evanston study and also stated that drivers with BAC >0.04 g/dL tend to have more single-vehicle accidents and also more severe accidents than do sober drivers. The study reviewed data collected from drivers stopped at four different locations as well as drivers involved in accidents at those sites. All individuals were interviewed and submitted breath specimens, which were later analyzed using the Breathalyzer®, a breath-testing device developed by Robert Borkenstein of Indiana University in 1954. It also found that accident-related factors other than alcohol decreased in significance when the driver's BAC was >0.08 g/dL (i.e., at a BAC >0.08 g/dL, alcohol was the most significant risk factor in having an accident) and that accident involvement increased rapidly when the driver's BAC was >0.05 g/dL. The researchers found no evidence that a BAC of 0.01–0.04 g/dL was associated with an elevated risk of accident. Drivers with BAC 0.04–0.08 g/dL had a greater risk of accident, but alcohol was not necessarily more significant than other risk factors. In terms of the relative probability of having an accident, the following statistics were generated:

- Drivers with a BAC of 0.04 g/dL were just as likely to have an accident as sober drivers.
- Drivers with a BAC of 0.06 g/dL were twice as likely as sober drivers to cause an accident.
- Drivers with a BAC of 0.10 g/dL were more than six times as likely as sober drivers to cause an accident.
- Drivers with a BAC of 0.15 g/dL were more than 25 times as likely as sober drivers to cause an accident.

Federal intervention in the drinking and driving problem began in earnest in 1966 with the passage of the National Highway Safety Act. This act required that a report be submitted to Congress detailing how the problem of the drunken driver was being addressed. This report was submitted in 1968 by the NHTSA. Since its inception, NHTSA has relied heavily on the recommendations of the National Safety Council and has enforced its recommendations, proposals, and legislative initiatives in individual states by withholding federal highway funds when states were not in compliance. In 1971, the committee released a resolution regarding alcohol impairment in which they stated that any individual, regardless of previous experience with alcohol, has impaired driving performance with a BAC $\geq$0.08 g/dL. During the past five decades, regulations and legislation concerning the drinking and driving problem have continued to proliferate. As of the early 2000s, all US jurisdictions

established a *per se* limit of 0.08 g/dL BAC for driving while impaired (with lower limits for individuals younger than the legal drinking age). In 2013, the National Transportation Safety Board (NTSB) recommended lowering the *per se* limit to 0.05 g/dL (consistent with several other countries) to help combat road fatalities. Similar positions were endorsed by the American Medical Association and the World Health Organization. Efforts to lower the legal alcohol limit for motor vehicle operators were also supported by the National Safety Council in 2016. Utah became the first state to decrease the *per se* limit to 0.05 g/dL in January 2019.

Specimens for Alcohol Testing

Breath and blood are the primary specimens for alcohol analysis in human performance toxicology. Several devices are available for measuring the amount of alcohol in breath, and they use a number of different analytical methodologies. Law enforcement personnel may prefer breath as a specimen because its collection is a noninvasive procedure and collection and analysis are typically performed together. Blood specimens, in contrast, must be drawn by a trained healthcare professional, and urine must be obtained under controlled conditions and under direct observation. These specimens must also be forwarded under chain of custody to a laboratory for analysis, whereas breath-testing devices provide instantaneous results. However, admissibility of breath tests depends on jurisdiction and associated regulations. Numerous studies have shown that a properly collected breath sample accurately reflects BAC at the time of its collection. Breath samples, therefore, can provide a measure of impairment because the alcohol measured in breath is directly proportional to BAC.

Several key factors in breath alcohol analysis must be considered. The most important is that end-expiratory breath is the only acceptable breath sample. Only the terminal portion of the expired breath is in equilibrium with the arterial blood (Henry's law) and therefore reflects BAC. The presence of residual alcohol in the mouth arising from recent ingestion of alcohol, regurgitation of gastric contents, or belching can cause an artificially high alcohol reading on breath-testing devices. Many breath-testing devices report an error when mouth alcohol is detected, thereby negating the breath test. In an effort to avoid contamination by mouth alcohol, a minimum 15-minute waiting period and rinsing the mouth with water before testing are recommended. When alcohol is present in the breath, it is generally the dominant exogenous species present and its concentration is greater than that of any other organic volatile that may be present. Therefore, no other species such as acetone or isopropanol will interfere with alcohol analysis.

Analysis of blood for BAC in a laboratory setting is also relatively easy to accomplish. Because alcohol is volatile and because relevant or active concentrations of alcohol in blood tend to be considerably higher than those of most drugs, BAC can be measured by headspace gas chromatography after simple dilution with an internal standard solution (typically N-propanol in water); no extraction is required. With proper calibration, results typically reflect high accuracy and precision. This is discussed in more detail in Chap. 19.

Epidemiology

Since the 1970s, NHTSA and/or the Insurance Institute for Highway Safety has conducted five National Roadside Surveys (NRS) of drinking and driving in the United States. The latest of these surveys was conducted in 2013–2014. Data was collected during a 2-hour daytime period on a Friday and four different 2-hour sessions at night, 10 PM to midnight and 1 AM to 3 AM on Friday and Saturday nights. In this study, 1.5% of the drivers on weekend nights had a BrAC (breath alcohol content, analogous to BAC) greater than or equal to 0.08 g/210 L breath. This represented a significant decline in the number of "legally impaired" drivers from the 1973 study where 7.5% of the drivers had a BrAC greater than or equal to 0.08 g/210 L. A similar decline was observed throughout the range of positive BACs. As expected, the percentage of daytime drivers

with a BrAC greater than or equal to 0.08 g/210 L was much lower than the nighttime drivers (0.4%). A similar project took place in Europe between January 2007 and July 2009. In the Driving Under the Influence of Drugs, Alcohol and Medicines (DRUID) study, over 42,000 random drivers from twelve European countries volunteered to provide blood samples for alcohol testing. Samples were taken at all times of the day and all days of the week. The prevalence of alcohol in European drivers (BAC ≥ 0.01 g/dL) was 3.48%. The common legal BAC limit was 0.05 g/dL at the time and 1.49% of drivers had a BAC above that limit. However, substantial variation was observed for the different countries. For example, in Italy, 5.23% of all drivers had a BAC above 0.05 g/dL, while in Norway, the corresponding number was 0.07%. In response to the alcohol-driving prevalence established by the DRUID project, European recommendations included establishing lower BAC limits (than their typical 0.05 g/dL) in target groups such as inexperienced drivers and those taking more than one substance. They also recommended mandating testing for drivers involved in crashes that resulted in injury, standardizing and regulating rehabilitation measures for impaired drivers, evaluation for addiction in repeat offenders with ≥ 0.16 g/dL, and license withdrawal in a standardized manner.

Behavioral and Physiological/ Psychomotor Effects of Alcohol

Alcohol exerts a wide variety of behavioral effects, as documented in numerous studies. It generally causes feelings of happiness and reduces the ability of aversive events to control behavior. Decreased inhibitions can lead to higher-risk behaviors. Higher doses cause loud, vigorous behavior, and even higher doses cause loss of consciousness and finally death.

Although individuals may respond differently to different doses of alcohol, behavioral effects tend to fall within BAC ranges. When the blood alcohol reaches 0.05 g/dL, individuals tend to exhibit an increased talkativeness, mild excitement, and a higher-pitched voice. As BAC reaches 0.10–0.15 g/dL, individuals become more talkative, cheerful, loud, boisterous, and then sleepy. When BAC exceeds 0.15 g/dL, the individual experiences nausea, and vomiting may occur, followed by lethargy and then stupor. Alcohol effects are generally more pronounced and pleasurable while BAC is rising than when it is falling. Many of the effects of alcohol show tolerance that is a result of both increased metabolism and increased experience. Subjective tests indicate that as BAC increases, individuals report elation, friendliness, and vigor. As BAC decreases, these same individuals report anger, depression, and fatigue.

Behavioral tolerance develops with repeated alcohol use. Those tasks learned under the influence of alcohol are often performed better when repeated at that blood concentration than when no alcohol is present. In general, the more complex the task, the more significant is the impairment at lower BACs. It is important to note, however, that between-study and between-subject variability is large, especially at concentrations below 0.08 g/dL. Often the results of studies refer only to some of the subjects tested, and the results generally indicate population tendencies and not absolute measures of behavioral effects.

Even at low concentrations, alcohol disrupts performance and can interfere with complex activities such as driving. Alcohol use decreases visual acuity and peripheral vision, and these effects increase significantly as the BAC rises above 0.07 g/dL. A decreased sensitivity to taste and smell at low alcohol doses has also been noted. Individuals under the influence of alcohol also exhibit an altered time sense, typically a slowed sense of the passage of time. With alcohol concentrations of 0.08 g/dL, sensitivity to pain decreases. Judgment may start to be impaired even at low BAC, and individuals under the influence of alcohol tend to underestimate their own impairment. Choice reaction time is impaired at 0.05 g/dL as measured by an increased latency to respond to the stimulus and a decrease in accuracy. Some studies have noted hand–eye coordination deficits at 0.05 g/dL and impairment in vigilance tasks at 0.06 g/dL, probably as a reflec-

tion of drowsiness. Body sway, as measured by the Romberg test and a device called the wobble board, was above normal at 0.05 g/dL; sway degrades to staggering and reeling with increasing BAC. Most tests of driving skill both on the road and in simulators show impairment at 0.05 g/dL. Numerous epidemiological studies also confirm the adverse effects of alcohol on driving performance.

Standardized Field Sobriety Tests

Law enforcement agencies attempt to reduce the number of impaired drivers through intervention and education. In the past few decades, laboratory researchers, law enforcement, governmental agencies, and the courts have combined their efforts to address this issue. It is through these efforts that the Standardized Field Sobriety Test and the Drug Evaluation and Classification program have arisen.

As police officers patrol traffic, they often encounter impaired drivers. This encounter initiates a three-phase process, culminating in the officer's decision to either arrest or release the driver. The officer proceeds through these three phases collecting information to determine whether the driver is truly impaired and the cause of that impairment:

1. Phase one is the initial observation of the vehicle in motion and how the driver stops the vehicle. The officer first notes poor driving performance such as weaving within a lane, unsignaled lane changes, rapid changes in speed, and other behaviors consistent with impaired driving. The officer gains additional information about the driver's level of impairment by observing how long it takes for the driver to respond to the officer's signal to stop and how the driver stops the vehicle.

2. Phase two of the arrest decision involves the officer's first direct contact with the driver. At this time the officer interviews the driver, who remains in the car, and evaluates the driver's physical appearance and condition. Officers are trained to notice breath odor, eye condi-

tion, demeanor, face color, dexterity, speech, and clothing appearance. If the officer's observations warrant it, the driver is asked to step from the car, providing another observation period. For example, if the driver needs help exiting the vehicle or staggers and stumbles when doing so, this further indicates the driver's level of impairment.

3. Phase three begins after the driver has exited the vehicle. At this time the officer administers several psychomotor tests and a preliminary breath test. By this point the officer should have enough information to make a decision about arresting or releasing the driver. If the driver is arrested, an evidential breath test is obtained or specimens (blood, urine, and/or oral fluid) are collected for laboratory analysis.

Standardized field sobriety tests were developed in the 1970s with funding by NHTSA. Several tests have been used over the years by officers in various jurisdictions, and three of these psychomotor tests were chosen for general use to provide an objective measure of impairment. Testing and scoring were standardized through laboratory studies and have been subsequently validated in field studies. The three tests that constitute the standardized field sobriety test are the one-leg stand (OLS), the walk and turn (WAT), and horizontal gaze nystagmus (HGN). Their predictive ability to measure impairment at 0.08 g/dL BAC or 0.08 g/210 L of breath is 82% for the WAT (i.e., 82% of those judged impaired as measured by the WAT have a ≥0.08 g/dL BAC), 85% for the OLS, and 87% for the HGN. When the three tests are used in combination, predictive ability increases to 89.7% and correlation with measured BAC increases.

The WAT test is a divided-attention task in two stages: instruction and walking. The officer gives instructions while requiring the suspect to place one foot in front of the other on a line and maintain balance throughout the instructions. The instructions explicitly include not beginning until told to do so. The suspect must then take nine heel-to-toe steps along a straight line, turn around by a series of small steps without lifting

the foot used in the ninth step [officer demonstrates], and then take nine more heel-to-toe steps along the same line. Impairment is measured (scored) by the number of observed clues, i.e., the failure to perform a certain aspect of the task. The WAT includes nine clues:

• Cannot balance during instructions
• Starts before instructions are completed
• Stops while walking
• Does not touch heel to toe
• Steps off the line
• Uses arms to balance
• Loses balance on turns or turns incorrectly (as demonstrated/explained by the officer)
• Takes incorrect number of steps
• Cannot do test (e.g., steps off the line three or more times)

If the suspect exhibits two or more clues on this test or is unable to complete the test, there is an 82% probability that the BAC is ≥0.08 g/dL (g/210 L).

The OLS is also a divided-attention task in two stages—instruction, and balancing and counting. The officer gives instructions while requiring the suspect to keep both heels together and arms down at his/her sides. After the instructions, the suspect is required to raise one leg approximately six inches off the ground and count rapidly from 1001 to 1030. The OLS has five clues that indicate impairment:

• Sways while balancing
• Uses arms to balance
• Hops (to maintain balance)
• Puts foot down
• Cannot do test (e.g., puts foot down three or more times)

If the subject exhibits two or more clues on this test or is unable to complete the test, there is an 85% predictability that the BAC is ≥0.08 g/dL (g/210 L). For both the WAT and the OLS, the instructional phase is a key component of the divided-attention task, testing the suspect's ability to listen to and comprehend the instructions without initiating the test prematurely. Due to physiological limitations, test results may not be valid for individuals over the age of 60 or who are more than 50 pounds overweight, nor may it be valid for individuals who wear high heels or have leg injuries or inner ear disorders.

The HGN test measures CNS motor pathways. Nystagmus is the involuntary jerking of the eyes, and horizontal nystagmus occurs as the eyes gaze toward the side. Nystagmus is a normal phenomenon that is not caused but is enhanced by alcohol. HGN is the most sensitive test in the battery. Because it is an involuntary reaction, it is less subject to decreased sensitivity in experienced drinkers than other psychomotor tests. In the HGN test, the subject is told to keep the head still and follow the stimulus that the officer presents. The stimulus is usually a pen or pencil that the officer holds in front of the subject and moves slowly from a position directly in front of the subject to either the left or right. The officer observes the suspect's eyes for smooth tracking and the onset of nystagmus. Studies have shown that the earlier that nystagmus occurs (the shorter the angle from directly in front of the subject), the greater the BAC. In fact, BAC and the angle of onset of nystagmus seem to have a dose–response relationship. The HGN test offers six clues (three per eye):

- Lack of smooth pursuit (eye cannot follow a slowly moving object smoothly)
- Pronounced nystagmus at maximum deviation
- Onset of nystagmus before 45° (from straight ahead)

If four or more clues are observed on this test, there is an 87% predictability that the suspect's BAC is ≥0.08 g/dL (g/210 L). The test results may not be valid for individuals with brain tumors, some types of brain disease, or inner ear disorders.

Drugs and Driving

The correlation between BAC and impairment has been extensively studied and is well understood. Characteristic effects have been described over a range of blood alcohol concentrations to the extent that certain behaviors or a range of behavior can be expected without directly observing supporting evidence of impairment in an individual. This has allowed statutory thresholds for alcohol impairment to be established and is the basis for *per se* laws. Unlike alcohol, this is not the case for other drugs.

Epidemiology

Although the prevalence of alcohol-positive drivers has decreased over the last several decades with study and legislation, awareness of drugged driving has increased. The first time the NRS evaluated drug prevalence in US drivers was in 2007. In the latest study, conducted 2013–2014, 7898 drivers provided samples of oral fluid and/or blood for drug testing. Of day- and nighttime drivers, 11.6% and 15.2%, respectively, tested positive for illegal drugs (including those in combination with medicinal drugs, 2.3% and 2.0%, respectively). Another 10.7% and 7.4% of day- and nighttime drivers, respectively, tested positive for prescription and/or over-the-counter drugs without illegal drugs. Those positive for both alcohol (BrAC ≥0.005 g/dL) and drug(s) represented approximately 0.56% and 2.09% of day- and nighttime drivers, respectively. Among nighttime drivers, delta-9-tetrahydrocannabinol (THC) was the most common drug found (12.7%), along with opioids (4.7%), stimulants (2.2%), benzodiazepines (1.9%), and antidepressants (1.6%). Compared to the 2007 survey, the prevalence of drug-positive (illicit and medication) nighttime drivers increased ($p < 0.05$). In particular, the prevalence of THC increased by 46% (to 12.7%, or 12.6% excluding cases that would not have been detected by the 2007 scope).

In the drug prevalence portion of the DRUID study, oral fluid and/or blood samples were collected from almost 50,000 drivers from 13 European countries. It was estimated that 1.90% of the drivers in Europe had used illicit drugs, 1.36% had used medicinal drugs, and 0.39% had used combinations of drugs. The prevalence of alcohol with drugs (licit or illicit) was 0.37%.

While this represents a substantial difference from the US numbers, it is worth considering that there were differences in the methodology and also large differences between the countries. For example, the prevalence of illicit drugs was highest in Spain (7.6%) and lowest in Sweden (0.1%). Similarly to the US data, THC was the most common substance (1.32%), followed by benzodiazepines (0.90%) and cocaine (0.42%). The opioids were divided into illicit opiates (0.07%) and medicinal opiates and opioids (0.35%). Recommendations of the DRUID project included training officers as drug recognition experts, treating drugged drivers separately from drinking drivers, basing legal regulations on science (including combining impairment with legal limits), and license withdrawal combined with rehabilitation programs for repeat offenders and/or addicts.

Drug Evaluation and Classification Program

The Drug Evaluation and Classification (DEC) program arose from the need to recognize drug impairment in the driving population. The Los Angeles Police Department pioneered the drug recognition procedure to provide a mechanism for obtaining compelling evidence that a driver was impaired at the time of apprehension. The DEC program was validated in 1984 at Johns Hopkins University in a controlled laboratory evaluation jointly sponsored by the NHTSA and the National Institute on Drug Abuse (NIDA) and in a 1985 NHTSA-sponsored field validation study. Using these studies, NHTSA developed a standardized curriculum for training police officers as drug recognition experts (DREs). In 1987, several pilot programs were initiated using this curriculum. Since that time, the number of DEC programs has continued to grow, and DRE training is available nationwide under the auspices of NHTSA. The program has also expanded elsewhere in the world, to places such as Canada, the UK, and Hong Kong.

The DEC program uses a standardized, systematic approach to determine if a subject is impaired, whether the impairment is due to drug

use, and identify a broad category of drugs that might cause the impairment. The DRE administers a series of physiological and psychomotor tests. The DRE's observations are the basis of an opinion concerning impairment resulting from the use of one or more drugs from within seven drug categories: CNS depressants, CNS stimulants, hallucinogens, dissociative anesthetics, narcotic analgesics, inhalants, and cannabis. Biological specimens are collected and toxicological analyses are performed. In combination, the DRE evaluation, toxicology, and observed driving behaviors can be used to evaluate drug-associated impairment.

Properly trained DREs can correctly predict the presence of certain drug categories in the majority of cases of impaired driving. However, the DEC process is not a field test; it is a postarrest investigative procedure that should be administered in a controlled environment, not at the roadside. Moreover, the DEC program does not determine exactly which drugs are present, but instead narrows the possibilities to broad categories (classes) of drugs. The DEC process is thus not a substitute for chemical tests; specimens must be collected for toxicological examination to provide objective support for the subjective opinion of the DRE.

Drug Recognition Evaluation

The DRE's evaluation has 12 components:

1. *Breath alcohol test.* The breath alcohol test is used to determine if the observed impairment is a result of alcohol consumption and if the degree of impairment is consistent with the concentration of alcohol. A low or negative breath alcohol result may be the DRE's first indication that other impairing drugs are present.
2. *Interview of the arresting officer.* The DRE interviews the arresting officer to develop a fuller understanding of the suspect and to gain important information the suspect may have revealed to the officer at the scene early in the arrest process.

3. *Preliminary examination of the suspect.* This examination is a structured series of questions, specific observations, and simple tests. This is the first opportunity for the DRE to directly examine the suspect and assess the possibility of injury, illness, or some non-drug-related condition as the cause of impairment. This examination is also the beginning of the systematic assessment of the suspect's appearance and behavior for any evidence of drug influence.

4. *Examination of the eyes.* Three tests are used in examining the eyes: HGN, vertical nystagmus, and lack of convergence. Presence or absence of these signs points to different drug categories.

5. *Divided-attention psychophysical tests.* Divided-attention tasks evaluate an individual's ability to perform multiple tasks simultaneously. These tasks, which are particularly sensitive to the impairing effects of drugs, are the WAT, the OLS, the modified Romberg balance test, and the finger-to-nose test.

6. *Vital signs examination.* Measurements are taken of the suspect's pulse, blood pressure, and body temperature. Certain drug categories will elevate these vital signs while other categories depress them.

7. *Dark room examination.* The size of the suspect's pupils is evaluated under three lighting conditions: near-total darkness, indirect light, and direct light. Some drug categories affect the pupil size by causing either dilation or constriction.

8. *Examination of muscle tone.* Certain categories of drugs cause muscle rigidity; others cause muscle flaccidity, while some have no effect on muscle tone.

9. *Examination for injection sites.* Some drugs are administered intravenously. Frequent use of such drugs may cause scarring, leaving track marks along the veins of the arms.

10. *Suspect's statements and other observations.* The DRE interviews the suspect concerning his or her drug use. The scope and direction of the interview is based on the DRE's opinion of the suspect's impairment and drug use drawn from the nine preceding steps.

11. *Opinion of the evaluator.* Based on all of the information gathered through the previous 10 steps, the DRE forms an opinion concerning whether the suspect is under the influence of drugs and what drug categories may be responsible for the suspect's impairment.

12. *Toxicological examination.* The evaluation culminates in the collection of blood and/or urine specimens for toxicological analysis to substantiate the DRE's opinion of impairment. Although specimen collection used to be the last ordinal step of the process, certain drugs (such as cannabinoids) can have rapidly changing concentrations throughout the course of the DRE evaluation. In 2018, in response to toxicologists' recommendations, the 12-step process was revised to allow for earlier ("out of order") specimen collection.

Toxicology

The opinion of the DRE concerning the suspect's state of impairment and the category of drug responsible for that impairment is a subjective evaluation. The determination of the presence of an impairing drug in the suspect's specimens by the toxicology laboratory provides objective scientific support for the DRE's opinion. The type of specimens submitted to the laboratory for analysis and the type of analyses performed often vary between jurisdictions.

Blood/Urine

In general, blood is considered a more suitable specimen than urine for analysis in DUI/DWI cases. It tends to have detection windows on the order of hours to a couple of days (depending on the substance, amount consumed, frequency of use, etc.). Although urine is an excellent specimen for toxicology screening, no direct relationship exists between impairment and the urine concentration of a drug. The identification of a drug in urine, therefore, only indicates that the suspect has been exposed to that drug. By contrast, this and urine's longer detection windows make it the preferred specimen for drug-facilitated crimes, including sexual assault. The detection of a drug in blood suggests that the drug is the cause of the suspect's observed impairment. It is important to note, however, that there is no well-established direct correlation between blood concentration and performance impairment for any drug other than alcohol. Thus, drug *per se* laws tend to be considerably more controversial (and not supported by science; e.g., cannabis) unless they are in the form of zero-tolerance legislation.

It is the observed impairment (as noted by a DRE), in combination with a confirmed blood concentration of a drug, that provides corroborating evidence that the impairment is related to the use and presence of that drug. The same type of DRE-observed impairment coupled with a confirmed urine concentration of a drug provide only a reasonable probability that the observed impairment is drug-related, because drugs can remain in the urine for several days after use. Merely confirming the presence of a drug or metabolite in blood or urine does not constitute proof of impairment. When formulating an opinion, a forensic toxicologist must consider the driving behavior, objective signs/symptoms, and the toxicology results.

Oral Fluid

Drugs detected in oral fluid are often indicative of recent use, and oral fluid could therefore serve as an alternative matrix for DUID testing in combination with observed impairment (by a DRE, for example). It has been increasingly studied for this purpose since the early 2000s. In fact, some places, such as Belgium, use oral fluid for both screening and confirmation in DUID cases.

From the standpoint of specimen collection, oral fluid is advantageous relative to blood because it can be easily and noninvasively sampled at almost any location by nonmedical personnel, such as law enforcement officers. Not only does this make sampling easier and cheaper, but it could also significantly reduce the time between the observed impairment and sampling—beneficial particularly for drugs (such as cannabis) that may be rapidly eliminated from blood. Capitalizing on the ease of sampling, roadside screening tests are available (and cur-

rently in use or under evaluation in many jurisdictions) for the most common drug classes. The devices can often test for more than one class of drugs at once, and a typical test battery could include amphetamine, methamphetamine/MDMA, cocaine, opiates, THC, benzodiazepines, and/or methadone. The devices use lateral flow immunoassays that are widely used in clinical point-of-care testing. The test kits are combined with readers that interpret the test and print results on a display. Given the technique used, the results carry all the limitations of a laboratory-based immunoassay. Therefore, confirmatory testing in a forensic toxicology laboratory (on a blood or oral fluid specimen) is still necessary. Scope, selectivity, and sensitivity must be carefully evaluated to show appropriateness for the needs of the jurisdiction. In recent years, a great deal of effort has been invested in developing and validating such tests. Roadside drug testing has been used in Australia since 2004 to test for THC, methamphetamine, and later MDMA. It has also been introduced in many other countries, including approximately half of the countries in Europe, Canada and some states in the United States.

Oral fluid concentrations appear to correlate to blood concentrations for some drugs, but not for others. Currently it is not recommended to use oral fluid concentrations to estimate blood concentrations or vice versa. Weakly basic drugs which are uncharged at blood pH 7.4 can cross the membrane into oral fluid and become ionized at the lower oral fluid pH of 4–6, thereby "trapping" them in the oral fluid because they cannot recross the membrane in their ionized state. This phenomenon is called "ion trapping" and can lead to elevated concentrations in oral fluid relative to blood—increasing detectability but potentially also concentration variability. A further complication is oral cavity contamination. For drugs that are smoked or inhaled, oral fluid concentrations immediately after intake are often extremely high. Although this makes them more easily detectable (even if a short sample was drawn due to dry mouth), concentrations do not necessarily reflect those in blood. As oral fluid testing indicates recent use and not impairment, testing cannot replace impairment testing by

DRE officers except in jurisdictions using *per se* limits in oral fluid for DUID.

Scope of Testing

Toxicology testing in DUID cases requires that the scope of testing as well as the limit of detection is properly selected to cover all relevant drugs. When making these decisions, it is important to consider the expected blood concentrations and detection times as well as the prevalence of different drugs in the sample population. In collaboration with the NSC's Alcohol, Drugs and Impairment Division, recommendations for scope and sensitivity of testing for impaired driving investigations have been published. The most recent guidelines recommend a tiered approach: They divide the drugs for DUID testing into a mandatory Tier I and recommended Tier II and provide recommended cutoffs for each drug in blood, urine, and oral fluid. Tier I drugs represent some of the most commonly encountered substances that can be identified using instrumental approaches that are widely available (i.e., immunoassay and gas chromatography–mass spectrometry). Tier II drugs include an expanded scope of drugs that may require more sophisticated approaches that may not be available in all laboratories (e.g., liquid chromatography–mass spectrometry). Some of the recommendations are listed below. In addition to these recommendations, the scope of testing might need to be expanded based on local drug trends in the population served by the laboratory. Standards for the scope and sensitivity of toxicology testing in impaired driving investigations are also anticipated (ANSI/ASB 120).

Drug Class Effects

The DEC program provides a standardized framework to observe behavior and collect physiologic data in an effort to determine if observed impairment is secondary to drug effects. Through the 12-step program, the DRE looks for a combination of behaviors and physiological indicators that may suggest that an individual is under the influence of a particular drug(s) or drug class(es).

Each of the seven categories of drugs is associated with a set of observable and measurable signs. The drug categories used in the DEC program do not directly correspond to traditional drug classes. The drugs are categorized on the basis of the signs they generate during the various examinations of the DEC process and not on their pharmacological properties (Table 2.1).

CNS Depressants

Alcohol is the most commonly used CNS depressant and is the prototypical drug in this category. In general, all members of this category produce behavioral and physiological effects similar to alcohol. Other drugs in this category include members of the barbiturate, benzodiazepine, antidepressant, and antipsychotic drug classes as well many others. Drugs in this category typically result in a dose-related slowing of reflexes, loss of social inhibitions, loss of coordination, impaired divided attention, impaired judgment, increased risk-taking behavior, and emotional instability. Tier I drugs include carisoprodol, meprobamate, and zolpidem as well as nine benzodiazepines and metabolites. Tier II drugs include atypical antipsychotics, barbiturates, carbamazepine, chlordiazepoxide, chlorpheniramine, cyclobenzaprine, diphenhydramine, doxylamine, gabapentin, GHB, hydroxyzine, lamotrigine, mirtazapine, novel benzodiazepines, phenytoin, pregabalin, topiramate, tricyclic antidepressants, valproic acid, and zopiclone.

CNS Stimulants

Cocaine and members of the amphetamine class of drugs, especially methamphetamine, are the most commonly used CNS stimulants. Psychomotor stimulants improve mood and cause intense feelings of pleasure ("high") after intravenous, intranasal, and smoked administration. Chronic use causes stereotypy (senseless repetition of a meaningless act to the exclusion of other behaviors) and often leads to paranoid behavior, psychosis (amphetamine psychosis and cocaine-induced psychosis), and violence. Low doses can overcome fatigue effects on cognitive, perceptual, and psychomotor tasks with improvement measured on some tasks. However, fatigue

Table 2.1 DRE drug influence symptomatology matrix[a]

Major indicators[b]	CNS depressants	CNS stimulants	Hallucinogens	Dissociative anesthetics	Narcotic analgesics	Inhalants	Cannabis
HGN	Present	None	None	Present	None	Present	None
Vertical gaze nystagmus	Present (high dose)	None	None	Present	None	Present (high dose)	None
Lack of convergence	Present	None	None	Present	None	Present	Present
Pupil size	Normal (1)	Dilated	Dilated	Normal	Constricted	Normal (4)	Dilated (6)
Reaction to light	Slow	Slow	Normal (3)	Normal	Little or none visible	Slow	Normal
Pulse rate	Down (2)	Up	Up	Up	Down	Up	Up
Blood pressure	Down	Up	Up	Up	Down	Up/down (5)	Up
Body temperature	Normal	Up	Up	Up	Down	Up/down/normal	Normal
Muscle tone	Flaccid	Rigid	Rigid	Rigid	Flaccid	Normal or flaccid	Normal
General indicators	Disorientation Droopy eyelids Drowsiness Drunk-like behavior Fumbling Slow, sluggish reactions Thick, slurred speech Uncoordinated Unsteady walk	Anxiety Body tremors Dry mouth Euphoria Exaggerated reflexes Excited Eyelid tremors Grinding teeth Increased alertness Insomnia Irritability Redness of the nasal area Restlessness Runny nose Talkative	Body tremors Dazed appearance Difficulty with speech Flashbacks Hallucinations Memory loss Nausea Paranoia Perspiring Poor perception of time and distance Synesthesia Uncoordinated Note: With LSD, Piloerection may be observed (goose bumps, hair standing on end)	Blank stare Confusion Chemical odor (PCP) Cyclic behavior Difficulty with speech Disoriented Early HGN onset Hallucinations Incomplete verbal responses Increased pain threshold "Moonwalking" Noncommunicative Perspiring (PCP) Possibly violent Sensory distortions Slow, slurred speech Slowed responses Warm to touch (PCP)	Constricted pupils Depressed reflexes Droopy eyelids Drowsiness Dry mouth Euphoria Facial itching Inability to concentrate Nausea "On the nod" Puncture marks Slow, low, raspy speech Slow breathing Slow deliberate movements Note: tolerant users exhibit relatively little psychomotor impairment	Bloodshot eyes Confusion Disoriented Flushed face Intense headaches Lack of muscle control Noncommunicative Odor of substance Possible nausea Residue of substance Slow, thick, slurred speech Watery eyes	Altered time/distance perception Alteration in thought formation Body tremors Bloodshot eyes Disoriented Drowsiness Eyelid tremors Euphoria Impaired memory Increased appetite Lack of concentration Mood changes Odor of marijuana Possible paranoia Rebound dilation Relaxed inhibitions Sedation

Duration of effects	Ultrashort: a few minutes Short up to 5 h Intermediate: 6–8 h Long: 8–14 h	Cocaine: 5–90 min Amphetamines: 4–8 h Meth: 12 plus h	Duration varies widely from one hallucinogen to another: LSD: 10–12 h Psilocybin: 2–3 h	PCP onset: 1–5 min Peak effects:15–30 min Exhibits effects up to 4–6 h DXM: onset 15–30 min Effects 3–6 h	Heroin: 4–6 h Methadone: up to 24 h Others: vary	6–8 h for most volatile solvents Anesthetic gases and aerosols—very short duration	2–3 h—exhibit and feel effects (impairment may last up to 24 h, without awareness of effects)
Usual methods of administration	Injected (occasionally) Insufflation Oral	Insufflation Injected Oral Smoked	Insufflation Oral Smoked Transdermal	Injected Insufflation Oral Smoked Transdermal	Injected Insufflation Oral Smoked	Insufflation	Oral Smoked Transdermal
Overdose signs	Clammy skin Coma Dilated pupils Rapid, weak pulse Shallow breathing	Agitation Hallucinations Increased body temperature	Intense bad "trip" Hyperthermia Convulsions	Long intense "trip"	Cold, clammy skin Coma Convulsions Slow, shallow breathing	Cardiac arrhythmia Possible psychosis Respiration ceases Severe nausea/vomiting Risk of death	Excessive vomiting Fatigue Panic reactions Paranoia Possible psychosis

(1) Soma, Quaaludes, and some antidepressants usually dilate pupils

(2) Quaaludes, ETOH, and some antidepressants may elevate

(3) Certain psychedelic amphetamines may cause slowing

(4) Normal, but may be dilated

(5) Down with anesthetic gases, up with volatile solvents and aerosols

(6) Pupil size possibly normal

a DRE drug influence symptomatology matrix was kindly provided by the International Association of Chiefs of Police Drug Evaluation and Classification (DEC) Program

b These indicators are the most consistent with the category; keep in mind that there may be variations due to individual reaction, dose taken, and drug interactions

is also associated with the "crash" phase and impairment may be observed as the drug wears off. Retrospective studies suggest that chronic use results in prolonged deficits in motor and cognitive performance. Tier I drugs include methamphetamine, amphetamine, MDMA (3,4-methylenedioxymethamphetamine), MDA (3,4-methylenedioxyamphetamine), cocaine, benzoylecgonine, and cocaethylene. Tier II drugs include cathinones, methylphenidate and mitragynine.

Hallucinogens

Members of this drug category cause an altered or distorted perception of reality in the user. The most commonly used hallucinogens are LSD, psilocybin (the naturally occurring hallucinogen found in some species of mushrooms), MDMA, and MDA (MDMA/MDA have some stimulant and some entactogenic and hallucinogenic properties). Phencyclidine (PCP) also produces a distorted view of the self and reality but is classified as a dissociative anesthetic in the DEC program. Marijuana, used at high doses, can also act as a hallucinogen, but cannabis constitutes a category unto itself in the DEC program.

The subjective effects of hallucinogens are difficult to study. In general, the hallucinatory experience starts out with colored visions of tunnel, spiral, and lattice shapes that move. Meaningful images start to become incorporated into these visions and finally there is a rapid succession of meaningful scenes. Apart from the hallucinations, the drug-induced hallucinatory experience often involves feelings of deep insight into oneself and the world, deep religious feelings, and an increase in the ability to enjoy and appreciate art and especially music. Performance is usually impaired by hallucinogens because the user has difficulty remaining motivated and attending to the task. No hallucinogens (apart from MDMA and MDA, listed under stimulants) are included in Tier I but testing is recommended in Tier II.

Dissociative Anesthetics

This category produces analgesia and amnesia without respiratory depression, resulting in a state in which the patient appears dissociated from his environment but not necessarily asleep. It includes PCP and its structural analogs, along with dextromethorphan and ketamine. In addition to having anesthetic properties and hallucinogenic effects, PCP also acts as an analgesic, a CNS depressant, and a stimulant. After high doses or chronic use of dissociatives, an acute psychosis that resembles schizophrenia may develop. Under the influence of a dissociative anesthetic, an individual may experience disorientation, slurred speech, agitation, excitement, hallucinations, and an altered perception of self and will typically be passive with a fixed, blank stare. This constellation of effects makes it difficult to predict or anticipate an individual user's response. Dissociative anesthetics are not included in Tier I but Tier II compounds include dextromethorphan, ketamine, and PCP.

Narcotic Analgesics

This category comprises the opiates (natural derivatives of opium such as heroin, morphine, and codeine) and the opioids (synthetic analogs of the opiates such as hydromorphone, hydrocodone, fentanyl, methadone, and others). The first use of opiates causes dysphoria, nausea, and vomiting, but tolerance to these effects develops. Opiates cause a sleepy, dreamy state and when taken intravenously cause "rushes" or feelings of intense pleasure. Chronic opiate use causes constipation and decreases sexual performance, but if doses are not too high, chronic use does not interfere with intellectual or physical abilities. The narcotic analgesic abuser experiences an increased awareness of sights and sounds, altered time sense (slowed for some, hastened for others), and a subjective belief in enhanced creativity. During the period of early analgesic use, the abuser experiences euphoria and relaxation. With continued use there is a shift toward unpleasant mood states and an increase in psychiatric symptoms, with decreased activity, social isolation, and aggression. Low and moderate doses have little performance effect apart from sedation. With higher doses there is a loss of motivation, and drug-seeking behavior will interfere with task performance. Tolerance develops rapidly to most effects of the narcotic analgesics. Tier I drugs include 13 opioids (including fentanyl, morphine, hydrocodone, oxycodone, buprenorphine, methadone, and tramadol). Tier II drugs include tapentadol as well as fentanyl analogs and novel opioids.

Inhalants

This category comprises the volatile organic solvents (e.g., toluene, gasoline, trichloroethylene), hydrocarbon gases (e.g., butane, freon, propane), anesthetic gases (e.g., halothane, nitrous oxide), nitrites (isobutyl nitrite, amyl nitrite, and butyl nitrite), and halogenated hydrocarbons (e.g., difluoroethane). Inhalation of the fumes of these substances results in euphoria and a CNS depression similar to that caused by alcohol. Abusers may also experience disorientation, confusion, and a sensation of floating. No inhalants are included in Tier I but testing is recommended in Tier II.

Cannabis

The cannabinoids are a family of compounds, some of which are psychoactive, found in the *Cannabis sativa* plant (phytocannabinoids) and synthetic compounds with cannabinoid receptor activity. Hundreds of cannabinoids have been identified, but delta-9-tetrahydrocannabinol (THC) is the primary psychoactive agent found in cannabis. THC is available as marijuana, hashish, hash oil, and Marinol (a synthetic form of THC used as an antiemetic). At high doses, cannabis acts like a hallucinogen, but at low doses, the drug is reported to cause a pleasurable high that may take several trials to experience and can usually be turned off at will. Systematic measures of mood have indicated that the mood of a user usually reflects the mood of the others who are present. Cannabis causes temporal disintegration, which means that the individual loses the ability to store information in the short term and is easily distracted. Time is usually overestimated. Performance on simple tasks may show little or no signs of impairment if the user applies adequate focus, but impairment manifests in divided-attention and complex tasks. Most performance deficits appear to be due to a lack of motivation and an inability to attend to a task, but impairing effects are measurable. Performance on the standardized field sobriety test is significantly impaired after commonly used doses of marijuana, and in driving tests subjects' ability to maintain lateral position within the lane is impaired. Tier I drugs include THC and its primary metabolites 11-OH-THC and THCCOOH (carboxy-THC); Tier II drugs include the synthetic cannabinoids.

Further Reading

ANSI/ASB 120: Standard for the analytical scope and sensitivity of forensic toxicology testing in impaired driving investigations

Berning A, Compton R, Wochinger K (2015) Results of the 2013–2014 National Roadside Survey of Alcohol and Drug Use by Drivers. NHTSA, Washington, DC

Bosker WM, Huestis MA (2009) Oral fluid testing for drugs of abuse. Clin Chem 55(11):1910–1931

Caplan YH, Goldberger BA (eds) (2015) Garriott's medicolegal aspects of alcohol, 6th edn. Lawyers and Judges Publishing Co, Tucson, AZ

Drug Evaluation and Classification Program: Drug Recognition Expert Course (participant manual). NHTSA and IACP, 2015

Drummer OH (2006) Drug testing in oral fluid. Clin Biochem Rev 27(3):147–159

Hancock SD, McKim WA (2018) Drugs and behavior: An introduction to behavioral pharmacology, 8th edn. Prentice Hall, Upper Saddle River, NY

Houwing S et al. (2011) Prevalence of alcohol and other psychoactive substances in drivers in general traffic, part I: General results. DRUID (Driving under the Influence of Drugs, Alcohol and Medicines)

Logan BK et al (2018) Recommendations for toxicological investigation of drug-impaired driving and motor vehicle fatalities-2017 update. J Anal Toxicol 42:63–68

O'Hanlon JF, de Gier JJ (eds) (1986) Drugs and driving. Taylor and Francis, Philadelphia, PA

Talpins S, Hayes C, Kimball T (2018) Drug Evaluation and Classification Program: Saving lives and preventing crashes. Arlington, VA, National Traffic Law Center

Society of Forensic Toxicologists maintains a list of recommended reading for the various drugs in Tiers I and II. This list can be found at: http://soft-tox.org/duid_literature

Drug-Facilitated Crimes

3

Marc LeBeau and Madeline Montgomery

Abstract

Drug-facilitated crimes have been occurring for well over a century. Toxicologists must appreciate the unique aspects of these cases in order to provide meaningful analyses of specimens that are collected from alleged victims of drug-facilitated crimes. The challenges include the drugs used, reporting of the crime, delays in evidence collection, and proper management of the cases. These challenges require laboratories to ensure that their analytical methods are sensitive enough to have a reasonable chance of detecting the presence of the strong, but often low-dose central nervous system (CNS) depressants used in drug-facilitated crimes.

Keywords

Drug-facilitated crimes · Drug-facilitated sexual assault · Challenges · CNS depressants Ethanol · Testing

This is publication 19–21 of the FBI Laboratory Division. Names of commercial manufacturers are provided for identification purposes only, and inclusion does not imply endorsement of the manufacturer, or its products or services by the FBI. The views expressed are those of the authors and do not necessarily reflect the official policy or position of the FBI or the US Government.

M. LeBeau (✉) · M. Montgomery
FBI Laboratory, Quantico, VA, USA
e-mail: malebeau@fbi.gov; mamontgomery@fbi.gov

Defining Drug-Facilitated Crimes

Any criminal action in which an incapacitating agent is used to assist the perpetrator in the commission of the crime may be classified as a "drug-facilitated crime." Typically, these include human trafficking, kidnapping, robberies, caregiver neglect, and sexual assaults. The incapacitating agent may be surreptitiously administered to the victim or the victim may voluntarily ingest it not realizing the consequences. Sometimes victims are misled as to the drug's true identity before they consume it—an aspirin is not always an aspirin. The media has portrayed so-called drink spiking as a popular means for a perpetrator to secretly drug their victims. While there have certainly been such cases, surreptitious administration is not always as simple as slipping a pill into a beverage. Pills contain insoluble components that may be noticeable if put into a drink. Further, the flavor is likely to be changed when a drink is spiked.

Victims of drug-facilitated crimes often describe some level of amnesia and many have reported becoming far more intoxicated than they believe they should from the amount of alcohol consumed. Some remember being a victim of a crime. Others have no direct memory of the crime but suspect that they may be a victim. Still others have neither memory nor suspicion of a crime and are only later uncovered as victims in investigations of other cases.

History of Drug-Facilitated Crimes

Despite the recent media attention to drug-facilitated crimes, the concept itself is not new. In the early twentieth century, the owner of Chicago's Lone Star Saloon—Mickey Finn—served a drink laced with chloral hydrate to the male patrons of his bar. When the men passed out from the drink, Finn would move them to an alley behind the bar and take their money. To this day, it is common to refer to drink spiking as "slipping someone a Mickey."

Around this same time, one of the first cases of drug-facilitated sexual assault was successfully prosecuted in Patterson, New Jersey. The case involved a young girl who was provided a spiked cocktail. When she lost consciousness, she was taken into a back room and sexually assaulted by four men, but died from an overdose of the drug. Her body was dumped into the local river and found the next morning. In a four-day trial in 1901, three of the men were convicted and sentenced to 30 years for second-degree murder in her death, but a fourth was convicted of sexually assaulting the girl while she was incapacitated. He received a 15-year sentence.

Over the last two decades, there has been a rise in the number of reported drug-facilitated crimes, particularly drug-facilitated sexual assaults. While it is unclear if there is an actual increase in the commission of these crimes or if greater awareness has prompted more reporting and improved investigations, the upsurge directly impacts toxicology laboratories responsible for assisting in these cases. But even with the trend of increased reporting, for many reasons these crimes remain underreported.

Challenges of Drug-Facilitated Crimes for Forensic Toxicologists

Drug-facilitated crimes present several challenges for forensic toxicologists who assist in these investigations. One of the challenges is the large number of drugs that can be used in these crimes. Despite the popular belief that only two or three drugs serve as the primary chemical sub-

mission agents, any substance that depresses the central nervous system (CNS) can be used. Drugs may also be co-ingested with one or more other CNS depressants, such as alcohol. The resulting depressant effect on the CNS can be severe, at times mimicking a general anesthetic agent and resulting in incapacitation, making the victim vulnerable and/or unable to consent to a sexual act.

The Society of Forensic Toxicologists (SOFT) lists over 100 drugs that should be considered in the toxicological testing of drug-facilitated crimes. Since CNS depression is the main pharmacological effect needed to commit drug-facilitated crimes and many drugs have this effect, symptomatology alone makes it nearly impossible to pinpoint the drug(s) involved. Therefore, the toxicological analysis may offer the best evidence for identifying the causative agent(s).

It is important to recognize that most drug-facilitated crimes are *not* reported to law enforcement. Victims of human trafficking, as well as children or the elderly drugged by their caregivers, are often incapable of reporting the crime. Men who are drugged by prostitutes and robbed may be reluctant to involve law enforcement. Sexual assault victims are also unlikely to report. Numerous studies have found that only a fraction of sexual assaults (including forcible sexual assaults) are reported to police. This has been tied to many different factors which include the relationship the victim has with the offender, fear of reprisal, belief that nothing would happen to the offender, desire to keep family members from learning of the incident, or fear of the justice system. When drugs are used to facilitate these crimes, it is not surprising that even fewer are reported due to the victim's uncertainty of many of the key aspects of the crime. And even when these crimes are reported, it is common that there is a delay in doing so, as the victims wait to try to fill in memory gaps from the time around the suspected crime. Delays impact the collection of useful biological evidence and the ability of the toxicological analysis to detect the presence of any drugs or metabolites that may have been used in the crime.

Because of the many challenges related to the toxicological analyses in these cases, negative findings alone should not be used to rule out the occurrence of a crime. Testing results may be affected by the variety of potential drugs used to facilitate a crime and the variability in the time that each is metabolized and eliminated. When a specific drug (or drugs) is not uncovered in the investigation, a negative toxicological finding must be cautiously interpreted. The negative finding must be equally appreciated as either due to no exposure to an incapacitating drug, that an incapacitating drug was not found because the sample was collected too late for the laboratory's methods to detect the drug, or that the laboratory did not specifically test for the drug that was used.

Most Common Drugs Detected in Alleged Drug-Facilitated Crimes

Ethanol

Ethanol is the drug most commonly detected in these crimes. This is in part due to its legal and social acceptance throughout much of the world; it is often voluntarily consumed by victims and can be given by perpetrators without suspicion. Ethanol, on its own or in combination with other CNS depressants, can cause all of the symptoms that a perpetrator of drug-facilitated crimes desires: decreased inhibitions, impaired perceptions, amnesia, and loss of consciousness. The reader is referred to Chap. 19 for information on the pharmacokinetics of ethanol.

Ethanol consumption factors such as the current state of gastric contents and motility, quantity ingested, and the person's tolerance impact the length of time that ethanol is detectable in a blood or urine specimen. When a reliable history is available concerning the amount of ethanol consumed in an alleged drug-facilitated crime, calculations may be performed to estimate a range of blood alcohol concentrations that the victim may have reached. This is done to understand the role that ethanol alone may have had in the case. In alleged alcohol-facilitated sexual assaults, such calculations can be used to form the basis of an opinion as to whether an average drinker at the estimated blood alcohol concentration range would likely exhibit signs of severe intoxication or have been in a state to reasonably consent to the sexual act.

Cannabinoids

The second most commonly detected drug class in many of the epidemiological studies of drug-facilitated crimes are cannabinoids. Marijuana users may experience CNS depressant effects that include impaired memory and altered time perceptions. Detection times in urine vary but may exceed 100 h after a single dose. Chapter 24 provides a more detailed review of cannabinoids.

Benzodiazepines and Z-Drugs

Benzodiazepines are one of the world's most widely prescribed classes of drugs, so it is not surprising that they are also common findings in drug-facilitated crimes. Additionally, the popularity of the z-drugs has led to their frequent finding in these cases. The reader is referred to Chap. 20 for details on the pharmacodynamic effects of benzodiazepines and Chap. 21 for the effects of the z-drugs. Benzodiazepines and z-drugs (alone or in combination with other CNS depressants) can cause anterograde amnesia, as well as complete unconsciousness.

The detection times for these drugs in urine samples vary from individual to individual, as well as from one drug to the next. Table 3.1 summarizes reported detection time ranges for select benzodiazepines and zolpidem in urine samples. Some studies have demonstrated the value of analytical methods that focus on glucuronide-conjugated benzodiazepine metabolites to extend detection times in urine samples.

It is important to recognize that while the media has labeled flunitrazepam as a substance "commonly used" in drug-facilitated crimes, there have been very few proven cases to support

Table 3.1 Urinary detection time ranges of select benzo-diazepines and zolpidem following single-dose administration

Drug (targeted metabolite)	Reported detection time ranges in urine
Alprazolam (alpha-hydroxyalprazolam)	26–61 h
Clonazepam (7-aminoclonazepam)	14–28 d
Diazepam (oxazepam glucuronide)	12–23 d
Flunitrazepam (7-aminoflunitrazepam)	5–28 d
Triazolam (alpha-hydroxytriazolam)	2–35 h
Zolpidem (zolpidem carboxylic acid)	Up to 72 h

this claim. While flunitrazepam is a powerful and relatively fast-acting benzodiazepine, there are many other benzodiazepines that work just as efficiently and are more readily available for use in these crimes.

GHB and Precursors

Gamma-hydroxybutyrate (GHB) and its precursors, gamma-butyrolactone and 1,4-butanediol, are some of the more challenging substances for toxicologists investigating drug-facilitated crimes. These compounds remain very easy to obtain, are fast-acting, have sedative properties, and can cause amnesia and complete unconsciousness. Further, they are rapidly metabolized and eliminated after ingestion. Chapter 21 provides complete information on the pharmacology of these drugs.

Another complicating factor for GHB is that it is a naturally occurring substance in all humans as a by-product of gamma-aminobutyric acid (GABA) metabolism. Additionally, studies have found that GHB concentrations may increase *in vitro* during storage. Therefore, care must be used in interpreting a finding of GHB in samples collected from alleged victims of drug-facilitated crimes. As a precaution, GHB concentrations of less than 2 mg/L in a blood sample or 10 mg/L in a urine sample should be considered as endogenous. This coupled with the rapid metabolism

and elimination means that blood concentrations resulting from a single oral dose of GHB (or one of its analogs) may only be discernable from endogenous GHB concentrations for only 4 to 6 h after ingestion. In urine samples, GHB may be distinguishable from endogenous GHB for as little as a few hours to as many as 12 h after it is consumed.

First-Generation Antihistamines

The first-generation antihistamines (e.g., brompheniramine, chlorpheniramine, diphenhydramine, doxylamine, hydroxyzine) have CNS depressant effects. In fact, some are specifically marketed as sleep aids. When combined with ethanol, an additive CNS depressant effect is to be expected. See Chap. 29 for more information about the pharmacology of these drugs. There have been few published studies that explore antihistamine detection times in urine samples following a single-dose administration with current instrumentation and methodologies. One limited study did find doxylamine in a urine sample collected up to 10 d following a single dose.

Opiates/Opioids

While the focus on the opioid crisis in the United States and other countries has been on deaths from these drugs, it must also be recognized that the CNS depressant effects of opiates and opioids, coupled with their oftentimes voluntary ingestion, make users vulnerable to drug-facilitated crimes. It should also be acknowledged that the number of cases of opioid-facilitated crimes is likely very underrepresented due to lack of reporting. Chapter 22 describes the pharmacokinetics and pharmacodynamics of opiates and opioids.

Ketamine

The media has portrayed ketamine as a common drug used in drug-facilitated crimes, but it has not been reported as a frequent finding in the scientific literature. There are some unique aspects of the drug that do make it particularly effective for perpetrators of these crimes. Chapter 26 describes the pharmacology of ketamine and other dissociatives. One group has reported detecting the presence of norketamine in urine for only two to five days following single-dose administration to monkeys.

Overcoming the Toxicological Challenges of Drug-Facilitated Crimes

While many of the challenges of drug-facilitated crimes are outside of the control of forensic toxicologists, consistent management of cases and abiding by testing recommendations will lead to better understanding of these crimes.

Testing Recommendations

A urine sample collected as soon as practical, but no later than 120 h (5 d) after an alleged drugging, is the preferred specimen in most drug-facilitated crimes. Therefore, several authoritative groups have published recommended testing limits for urine samples.

The Society of Forensic Toxicologists developed a comprehensive list of drugs believed to have played some role in drug-facilitated crimes in the United States. The drugs are listed by class under their generic names, but also include their common trade names and street names to help simplify communication between toxicologists and customers. Key metabolites of the listed drugs are also included. Each drug has a recommended minimum performance limit for toxicological testing for the drug in urine samples (Table 3.2). These limits were established based on capabilities reported from member laboratories using what is considered "standard laboratory instrumentation." The intention is to encourage laboratories to strive to develop and validate methods for specific use in toxicological investigations of drug-facilitated crimes. These recommended performance limits are considered the highest concentrations that laboratories should use to screen urine samples collected from alleged victims of drug-facilitated crimes. If the laboratory has the capability to test at concentrations even lower than those listed, they are encouraged to do so. Further, if a laboratory cannot achieve the recommended testing limits for any suspected analytes, they are encouraged to inform their customers, withhold testing for those analytes, and help identify a laboratory that can achieve the testing limits.

The United Nations Office on Drugs and Crime (UNODC) adopted the approach championed by SOFT. They did so by expanding SOFT's list to include drugs and metabolites that were more prevalent outside of the United States. Additionally, the UNODC encouraged capable laboratories to analyze victim hair samples in alleged drug-facilitated cases with delayed reporting as hair may provide even longer detection windows compared to blood or urine samples.

Finally, a standard has been proposed through the Academy Standards Board (ASB) that abbreviates the list of drugs or metabolites to those that the ASB's Toxicology Consensus Body believes *must* be tested for in urine samples collected from *all* alleged victims of drug-facilitated crimes. The list includes high-dose sedatives (ethanol and GHB), antidepressants (amitriptyline, nortriptyline, imipramine, desipramine, and trazodone), antihistamines (brompheniramine, chlorpheniramine, diphenhydramine, doxylamine, and norchlorcyclizine), barbiturates (butalbital and phenobarbital), benzodiazepines (alpha-hydroxyalprazolam, 7-aminoclonazepam, lorazepam, nordiazepam, oxazepam, and temazepam), cannabinoids (carboxy-tetrahydrocannabinol), select stimulants (methylenedioxyamphetamine, methylenedioxymethamphetamine, amphetamine, methamphetamine, benzoylecgonine), opioids (fentanyl, norfentanyl, codeine, morphine, hydrocodone, hydromorphone, oxycodone, oxymorphone, and tramadol), and some miscellaneous substances (cyclobenzaprine, dextromethorphan, norketamine, zolpidem carboxylic acid, zopiclone, carisoprodol, and meprobamate).

Table 3.2 Adapted from Society of Forensic Toxicologists (SOFT) drug-facilitated crimes committee recommended minimum performance limits for common DFC drugs and metabolites in urine samples

Target drug (Metabolite)	Recommended performance	Target drug (Metabolite)	Recommended performance	Target drug (Metabolite)	Recommended performance
Analgesics:		*Antidepressants:*		*Antihistamines and cough/cold treatments:*	
Buprenorphine (norbuprenorphine)	1 ng/mL	Amitriptyline (nortriptyline)	10 ng/mL	Brompheniramine	10 ng/mL
Fentanyl (norfentanyl)		Citalopram/Escitaopram		Carbinoxamine	
Dihydrocodeine	10 ng/mL	Desipramine		Cetirizine	
Heroin (6-monoacetyl morphine/morphine)		Doxepin (nordoxepin)		Chlorpheniramine	
Hydrocodone (dihydrocodeine/hydromorphone/norhydrocodone)		Fluoxetine (norfluoxetine)		Dextromethorphan (dextrorphan)	
Hydromorphone		Imipramine (desipramine)		Diphenhydramine	
Meperidine (normeperidine)		Nortriptyline		Doxylamine	
Methadone (EDDP)		Paroxetine		Hydroxyzine (cetirizine/norchlorcyclizine)	
Morphine		Sertraline (norsertraline)		Meclizine	
Oxycodone (noroxycodone/oxymorphone)		Trazodone (mCPP)		Promethazine	
Oxymorphone		Venlafaxine (norvenlafaxine)		Tetrahydrozoline	
Propoxyphene (norpropoxyphene)		*Barbiturates:*		*Stimulants:*	
Tapentadol (desmethyltapentadol)		Amobarbital	25 ng/mL	Amphetamine	50 ng/mL
Tramadol (n-desmethyltramadol/o-desmethyltramadol)		Butalbital		Cocaine (benzoylecgonine/cocaethylene/methylecgonine)	
Antipsychotics:		Pentobarbital		Methamphetamine	
Chlorpromazine	10 ng/mL	Phenobarbital		Methylphenidate (ritalinic acid)	
Clozapine (norclozapine)		Primidone		MDA	
Olanzapine		Secobarbital		MDMA	
Quetiapine (norquetiapine/7-hydroxyquetiapine)					
Thioridazine					
Ziprasidone					

Benzodiazepines:

Compound	Cutoff
Clonazepam (7-aminoclonazepam)	5 ng/mL
Flunitrazepam (7-aminoflunitrazepam)	
Triazolam (α-hydroxytriazolam)	
Alprazolam (α-hydroxyalprazolam)	10 ng/mL
Bromazepam (α-hydroxybromazepam)	
Chlordiazepoxide (nordiazepam)	
Clobazam	
Clorazepate (nordiazepam/oxazepam)	
Clotiazepam	
Diazepam (nordiazepam/oxazepam/temazepam)	
Estazolam	
Etizolam	
Flubromazepam	
Flurazepam (desalkylflurazepam)	
Loprazolam	
Lorazepam	
Lormetazepam	
Midazolam (α-hydroxymidazolam)	
Oxazepam	
Prazepam	
Temazepam (oxazepam)	
Tetrazepam	

High dose sedatives:

Compound	Cutoff
Ethanol	0.01 gram percent
Gamma-hydroxybutyrate (GHB)	10 mg/L
Gamma-butyrolactone (GHB)	
1,4-Butanediol (GHB)	

Miscellaneous:

Compound	Cutoff
Carisoprodol (meprobamate)	
Clonidine	
Cyclobenaprine (norcyclobenzaprine)	
Eszopiclone (zopiclone-n-oxide)	
Gabapentin	
Ketamine (norketamine)	
Meprobamate	
Phencyclidine	
Phenytoin	10 ng/mL
Pregabalin	
Suvoxerant	
Scopolamine	
Tetrahydrocannabinol (11-carboxy-THC)	
Topiramate	
Valproic acid	
Zaleplon	
Zopiclone (zopiclone-n-oxide)	
Zolpidem (zolpidem-phenyl-4-carboxylic acid)	

Management of Cases

The goal of determining if an individual was exposed to an incapacitating substance one or more days before biological specimens were collected is not typical for most forensic toxicology laboratories. Many forensic toxicology laboratories test specimens from persons suspected of impaired driving that were collected a short time after traffic stops. Postmortem toxicology involves testing of biological samples collected at autopsies with the goal of helping to establish if drugs or poisons may have been responsible for the individual's death. And while workplace testing can involve random collection of samples to identify recreational drug use by employees or applicants, testing limits are generally higher than those needed for drug-facilitated crimes. This means that laboratories that accept these cases for toxicological analyses will likely need to adapt their approach to managing them.

Investigative information is often critical for successful analyses in alleged drug-facilitated crimes, as it will guide the laboratory to the most likely drugs involved and thereby tested. The UNODC publication provided guidance on the types of information that may be useful for toxicologists in typical drug-facilitated crimes. Requested information includes the length of delay in specimen collection after the alleged drug exposure; an estimate of the number of times the victim urinated prior to providing evidentiary samples; any recreational, prescription, and over-the-counter drugs voluntarily ingested by the victim; all drugs known to be available to the alleged perpetrator; the amount of alcohol consumed by the victim; and specific symptoms reported by the victim. Further, the UNODC document provides guidelines on how laboratories may improve sensitivity of their analytical methods by hydrolyzing urine specimens prior to analysis in order to free conjugated metabolites, increasing the extracted specimen volume, or through the use of special derivatives and selective detectors.

Conclusions

It is telling that cases of drug-facilitated crimes are now recognized as a separate subdiscipline of forensic toxicology, in part for the unique challenges that accompany these cases. The challenges are centered on the vast number of drugs that may be used and how they impact victim reporting, delays in collection of specimens, and the laboratory's ability to provide meaningful analyses. The forensic toxicologist can overcome many of these challenges by ensuring good communication with its customers and properly planning for these cases.

Further Reading

ANSI/ASB STD 121. Standard for the analytical scope and sensitivity of forensic toxicology urine testing in drug-facilitated crime investigations

Forsman M, Nyström I, Roman M, Berglund L, Ahlner J, Kronstrand R (2009) Urinary detection times and excretion patterns of flunitrazepam and its metabolites after a single oral dose. J Anal Toxicol 33(8):491–501

Kilpatrick DG, Resnick HS, Ruggiero KJ, Conoscenti LM, McCauley J (2007) Drug-facilitated, incapacitated, and forcible rape: a national study. National Criminal Justice Reference Service, Charleston, SC

LeBeau M, Andollo W, Hearn WL, Baselt R, Cone E, Finkle B, Fraser D et al (1999) Recommendations for toxicological investigations of drug-facilitated sexual assaults. J Forensic Sci 44(1):227–230

LeBeau MA (2010) Laboratory management of drug-facilitated sexual assault cases. Forensic Sci Rev 22(1):113–119

Lin D-L, Huang T-Y, Liu H-C, Yin R-M (2005) Urinary excretion of α-hydroxytriazolam following a single dose of Halcion®. J Anal Toxicol 29(2):118–123

Negrusz A, Moore CM, Stockham TL, Poiser KR, Kern JL, Palaparthy R, Le NLT, Janicak PG, Levy NA (2000) Elimination of 7-aminoflunitrazepam and flunitrazepam in urine after a single dose of Rohypnol®. J Forensic Sci 45(5):1031–1040

Negrusz A, Bowen AM, Moore CM, Dowd SM, Strong MJ, Janicak PG (2003) Elimination of 7-aminoclonazepam in urine after a single dose of clonazepam. Anal Bioanal Chem 376(8):1198–1204

SOFT Drug-Facilitated Crimes Committee (2017) Recommended minimum performance limits for common DFC drugs and metabolites in urine samples. Society of Forensic Toxicologists. https://www.soft-tox.org/files/MinPerfLimits_DFC2017.pdf

Temte V, Kjeldstadli K, Bruun LD, Birdal M, Bachs L, Karinen R, Middelkoop G, Øiestad E, Høiseth G (2018) An experimental study of diazepam and alprazolam kinetics in urine and oral fluid following single oral doses. J Anal Toxicol 43(2):104–111

United Nations Office on Drugs and Crime (2011) Guidelines for the forensic analysis of drugs facilitating sexual assault and other criminal acts. United Nations, Vienna

Wang X, Wang R, Zhang Y, Liang C, Ye H, Cao F, Rao Y (2012) Extending the detection window of diazepam by directly analyzing its glucuronide metabolites in human urine using liquid chromatography–tandem mass spectrometry. J Chromatogr A 1268:29–34

Forensic Drug Testing

4

Amanda J. Jenkins

Abstract

The testing of biological specimens has become a major component in the identification and the treatment of drug misuse. Testing has been performed under the auspices of the military, the criminal justice system, the public sector, and the private sector. Urine remains the primary specimen for drug abuse testing, but other specimens such as oral fluid, sweat, and hair have also been used. Each testing program is different, but there are common components throughout the programs. Specimens are collected under a chain of custody that documents the location of the specimen from collection to disposal. No single test is used to identify a positive specimen; positive results are reported only after a positive initial test and a positive confirmation test. Concentration cutoffs are employed to distinguish negative from positive specimens. The analytical methods used must be validated prior to use on donor specimens. Moreover, a quality assurance program must be in place for all aspects of the process, from specimen collection to specimen testing to reporting of results. Some programs, such as the Department of Health and Human Services Program, require specimen validity tests to ensure the integrity of the specimen prior to receipt in the laboratory. To ensure continued acceptable laboratory performance, proficiency testing programs and laboratory accreditation are also components of the forensic drug-testing process.

Drug use has become a significant medical and social problem in the United States (US). Financial and human resources have been expended in attempts to combat this problem. Actions have included drug interdiction; criminal penalties for cultivation, distribution, possession, and use of illicit drugs; and medical treatment of offenders and those individuals with drug use disorders. Chemical testing of biological specimens is generally accepted to be the most objective method for determining drug use.

Keywords

Workplace drug testing · Urine · Hair · Sweat · Oral Fluid · Accreditation · Forensic Drug Testing in Society

The Military

In the US, the military establishment was the first to initiate testing of its employees. Testing was motivated by concern about how the use of illegal

A. J. Jenkins (✉)
UMass Memorial Medical Center/UMASS Medical School, Worcester, MA, USA
e-mail: amanda.jenkins@umassmemorial.org

© Springer Nature Switzerland AG 2020
B. S. Levine, S. Kerrigan (eds.), *Principles of Forensic Toxicology*,
https://doi.org/10.1007/978-3-030-42917-1_4

drugs affected the combat readiness of US Armed Forces. In 1971, Congress directed the Secretary of Defense to devise methods for the identification and treatment of military personnel who abused drugs. Under the 1990 General Military Law 10 U.S.C. 1090, the Secretary of Defense and the Secretary of Transportation (who had responsibility for the Coast Guard, currently it is the Department of Homeland Security) were required to write regulations, implement testing procedures, and provide facilities to identify and treat military personnel who were drug dependent. Such individuals are barred from military service and referred to civilian treatment programs. Furthermore, in 1990, the military instituted a "drug-free workplace" policy to preclude the hiring of drug-dependent individuals.

Potential military recruits must undergo drug testing as part of the application process. Drug-dependent individuals already serving in the armed forces that "cannot or will not be rehabilitated" face disciplinary action and/or discharge.

The Criminal Justice System

Drug testing is increasingly used within the criminal justice system to monitor drug use within prison populations. Urinalysis is the method of choice and, under President George H.W. Bush's 1991 National Drug Control Strategy, was considered a high priority for its ability to identify and monitor criminal offenders involved with drugs. In addition to a nationwide control strategy, some states mandate that drug-testing programs be initiated at the time of arrest and during pretrial release proceedings, probation, and parole. Several US cities have initiated drug-testing programs for arrestees. In some jurisdictions drug testing of drug offenders is not mandated.

The Public Sector

In 1983, as a result of a study conducted by the National Transportation Safety Board concerning the involvement of drugs (including alcohol) in train accidents, the Federal Railway Administration and the National Institute on Drug Abuse (NIDA) began to develop drug use regulations for the Department of Transportation. During this time, national concern about drug abuse was increasing, and many companies in the oil, chemical, transportation, and nuclear industries began implementing their own drug-testing programs. These programs varied in their procedures and standards, which resulted in much controversy and litigation.

In 1986, the executive branch of the federal government became actively involved in developing drug use regulations when President Reagan issued Executive Order No. 12564 (Federal Register 1986 51:32889, 32890). The order instructed the directors of each federal executive agency to develop testing programs for employees in sensitive positions. The objective of this order was to provide a "drug-free" federal workplace. The Office of Management and Budget estimated the cost of implementing these programs at $18 million per year (although the General Accounting Office was unable to verify this estimate).

A conference convened by NIDA in March 1986 produced a consensus document describing the conditions under which testing could be conducted:

- All individuals must be informed they are subject to testing.
- The confidentiality of the test results must be assured.
- All positive results on the initial screen must be confirmed with alternate methodology.
- Random screening for drug use under a well-defined program is appropriate and legally defensible in certain circumstances.

In 1988 NIDA of the Federal Department of Health and Human Services [DHHS] issued mandatory scientific and technical procedural guidelines (including standards for laboratory accreditation) for federal drug-testing programs (Federal Register 1988 53:11970). According to the guidelines, urine would be the testing specimen of choice. The guidelines included specimen collection, procedures for transmitting samples to testing laboratories, assay procedures, evaluation of test results, quality control measures, record-keeping and reporting requirements, and standards and procedures for DHHS accreditation of drug-testing laboratories. The intent of these guidelines was to ensure the accuracy and integrity of the test results and the privacy of the individuals tested. In July of 1988, DHHS/NIDA implemented the National Laboratory Certification Program (NLCP). The Division of Workplace Programs of the Substance Abuse and Mental Health Services Administration (SAMHSA) within DHHS administers and directs the NLCP. The Research Triangle Institute (RTI International) (Research Triangle Park, North Carolina) operates the program under contract.

In 1989, the Nuclear Regulatory Commission final rule (54FR24468) was published in the Federal Register. Implemented on January 3, 1990, the rule incorporated most of the DHHS mandatory guidelines, although the program did permit on-site testing under specific conditions.

The US Department of Transportation (DOT), having published an interim final rule on November 21, 1988, that established drug-testing procedures applicable to transportation employees, released its final rule in 1989 for implementation on January 2, 1990. These regulations covered employees in six transportation industries, namely, vehicle, aviation, railroad, mass transit, pipeline, and maritime. Implementation of the program in the Mass Transit Administration was delayed because a federal appellate court overturned the rule, stating that the agency did not have the statutory authority to issue standards requiring drug testing. To remedy this problem, Congress passed the Omnibus Transportation Employee Drug Testing Act of 1991. This act required the Department of Transportation to prepare regulations that would expand the existing program to include intrastate operations and the drug ethanol. The final DOT rules were applicable to large and small employers. The legislation was implemented on January 1, 1995, with respect to employers with more than 50 covered employees, and on January 1, 1996, with respect to employers with fewer than 50 employees. This legislation affects more than 7.4 million transportation workers in the United States.

These programs have been revised in the last 20 years to include revisions of the initial and confirmatory drugs; changes in cutoff concentrations for reporting; addition of specimen validity tests; qualifications, training, and certification of Medical Review Officers (MROs); and the introduction of the instrumented initial testing facility program [DHHS].

Since President Reagan's executive order, states and municipalities have increased employee drug testing. Programs throughout the US differ with regard to policy and testing procedures. While many states require drug-testing laboratories to be accredited, they may differ as to when an employee may be subject to testing and when and how samples are collected. Today many police, fire, and correctional department personnel across the United States are subject to testing.

The Private Sector

Since the mid-1980s, private sector employees have also been subject to drug testing. Surveys have estimated that in 1985, 25% of Fortune 500 companies were screening job applicants for drug use. In 1987, approximately 50% of Fortune 100 companies were conducting preemployment and for-cause testing. A large proportion of those companies were involved in the manufacturing and utility industries. According to the Institute for a Drug-Free Workplace 97% of Fortune 500 companies have drug-free workplace policies. Although the majority use accredited laboratories to conduct the testing, not all use a Medical Review Officer or require confirmatory testing of presumptive positive results. Urine is typically the specimen of choice, but blood, oral fluid, and hair are also used.

Other Segments of Society

Drug testing is not limited to the workplace or the criminal justice system. Professional and amateur athletes who compete at national and international levels may be subject to such testing. Testing of high school athletes is controversial, but today parents may privately test their children by collecting samples and sending them to laboratories for anonymous testing. In recent years, public secondary schools have been provided with federal money to test students. Random testing, usually for marijuana, stimulants, and opiates, typically involves high school age children. However, some school districts test middle school students. Athletes and those involved in school-related competitive extracurricular activities may be subject to testing. In addition, some districts test students who drive to school and in order to attend the school prom. National estimates indicate that during the school year 2004–2005, 14% of US public school districts conducted random drug testing in their high schools. Students subjected to testing were mainly athletes but approximately 65% randomly tested other students engaged in extracurricular activities.

Several politicians have endorsed the concept of drug testing for welfare recipients and possibly using testing results to limit eligibility for these benefits. Applicants to federal job training programs may also be subject to drug testing in the future. The insurance industry is also currently testing life insurance applicants for illicit drug use. In medicine, hospital emergency rooms, prenatal clinics, and delivery rooms test individuals for illicit drugs as part of diagnostic care. Depending on individual circumstances, these test specimens may or may not become forensic specimens.

Status of Forensic Drug Testing in the United States

The economic and social cost to the United States due to illicit drug use has been investigated. One study showed that approximately 35% of state prison inmates and 40% of juvenile offenders in long-term correctional facilities admitted to being under the influence of illicit drugs while committing the crime for which they were incarcerated. Drug defendants comprised 31% of defendants in criminal cases filed in federal district courts in the 12-month period ending March 31, 2018. This was an increase of 3% from the previous year. During the same period, defendants charged with crimes involving drugs other than marijuana increased by 8%, while marijuana-related offenses declined 17%. The majority of adult illicit drug users are employed full or part time and although the number of individuals testing positive has declined since the mid-1980s, the positive rate is approximately 5%. The economic impact of such use has been estimated to exceed $150 billion per year. This cost includes lost productivity due to increased sick time, lateness, increased number of workplace accidents, and worker's compensation claims.

An estimated 30 million working Americans are tested for illegal drugs each year. In the forensic arena, the generally accepted objective of drug testing is to detect and deter drug use among individuals subject to the testing. In addition, athletes are tested to determine whether they have used drugs that may improve performance and, therefore, result in an unfair competitive advantage. In the criminal justice system, prison inmates are tested so that individuals who may benefit from drug rehabilitation programs can be identified.

Employees may be tested in the workplace in several situations: during preemployment background checks, before promotion, return to duty, at random, for cause, follow-up, and postaccident. Employers may test job applicants to identify those individuals who may pose a safety risk to themselves or others. Random drug testing of employees may be conducted as a potential deterrent to illicit drug use and consequent safety risks. Companies may drug-screen for cause if a supervisor has reasonable suspicion (such as behavior or accident) that the employee is abusing drugs. Postaccident drug screening may be conducted in order to include or exclude drug use as a possible cause of the accident.

The Testing Process

Testing may be highly regulated with safeguards built into the system to protect the rights of the individual tested, such as the DHHS guidelines for federal employees. Alternatively, drug testing may be conducted informally, with no regulation and few safeguards, as in the case of a high school athlete whose parent collects a specimen. Workplace drug testing is unique in that single test results may be the only piece of evidence involved in the hiring and/or firing of an individual. Therefore, every test result may produce litigation.

The quality of the result is only as good as the quality of the entire process. This process begins at the collection site, continues with the transportation of the specimen to the testing laboratory; the accessioning, testing, data review, and report generation; and transmission of the results to a qualified individual for interpretation. In regulated workplace drug testing, this individual is known as a Medical Review Officer (MRO).

Collection and testing facilities must follow forensic toxicology standards. Instructions for collection facilities cover procedures for collecting the specimens, maintaining specimen integrity, and establishing a chain of custody. Currently in workplace drug testing, urine is the specimen of choice, and the collection may be witnessed. In federally regulated programs, this occurs, for example, if a donor's previous drug test was reported by an MRO as positive, adulterated, or substituted. Standards for testing laboratories cover facilities, standard operating procedures, security, chain of custody, testing methods and validation, quality assurance, reporting methods, confidentiality, personnel, and laboratory accreditation.

The testing facility must have the physical capacity to perform the work required. This means adequate space and adequate security that limits access not only to the physical premises but also to data in electronic and paper format. The facility must also have a sufficient number of qualified personnel and appropriate instrumentation to conduct the required tests, including those required for screening and for confirmatory assays.

Collecting the specimen initiates a chain of custody, i.e., procedures that account for the integrity, identification, and security of each specimen by tracking its handling and storage

from point of collection to final disposition. The chain of custody is documented on a custody and control form (CCF). The collection site must offer adequate facilities for specimen collection and sufficient numbers of trained personnel.

Documentation of the collection process appears on the CCF and on the specimen and container. Typically, the donor initials a label on the container, along with the date the specimen was collected. Trained collection personnel also sign the container, and "seals of integrity" are placed on the container to prevent tampering after collection. All federal agency collections utilize a single-use container and the collector, in the presence of the donor, then pours the urine into two specimen bottles, labeled A and B. The specimen is then packaged for transport to the testing facility by courier, express delivery, or US mail. Upon receipt at the laboratory, trained personnel accession the specimen into the laboratory's information management system. The specimen container is examined for evidence of tampering, e.g., breakage of seals and incomplete documentation (such as failure of one party to initial the container). It is also examined to ensure a match between the information on the specimen and that on the accompanying custody and control form. If there is a mismatch, the submitting agency must be contacted and discrepancies corrected. The laboratory then gives the specimen an accession number, and an internal chain of custody is initiated for specimen testing. The initial screen reflects testing for the classes of drugs identified by the submitting agency. All positive screening results are then confirmed using a second sample aliquot and an alternate technique. Laboratories under federal and military drug-testing programs screen using immunoassay with confirmation by gas/liquid chromatography/ [tandem] mass spectrometry.

The mandatory guidelines for federal workplace drug-testing programs, effective in 2010, introduced a new type of testing facility, the instrumented initial testing facility [IITF]. These facilities perform initial drug tests and specimen validity tests. An IITF must report a test result to an agency's MRO within an average of three working days after receiving the specimen. A negative result may be reported when each drug test is negative, and each validity test indicates that the specimen is a valid urine sample. A urine specimen is reported as dilute when the creatinine concentration is > 5 mg/dL but < 20 mg/dL and the specific gravity is ≥1.002 but <1.003. A DHHS accredited IITF must reject a urine specimen for testing when a fatal flaw occurs. Fatal flaws include the following: (a) the specimen identification number on the specimen does not match the ID number on federal CCF; (b) the specimen label/seal is missing, is broken, or shows evidence of tampering; and (c) the collector's printed name and signature are missing on the federal CCF [see Section 15.1. of the 2017 guidelines]. Specimens must be sent to a HHS-certified laboratory for additional testing if results may be positive, adulterated, substituted, or invalid. A list of HHS-accredited laboratories and IITFs is published monthly in the Federal Register and is also available at http://www.samhsa.gov/workplace.

The current mandatory DHHS guidelines, published in the Federal Register, effective October 1, 2017, apply to executive agencies [5 U.S.C.105]; the uniformed services [5 U.S.C.2101(3) except as defined in 5 U.S.C. 2101(2)]; any other employment unit of the federal government except the US Postal Service, Postal Rate Commission, and Judicial and Legislative Branches; the Intelligence Community [Executive Order 12333]; laboratories and IITFs that provide drug-testing services to federal agencies; collectors who provide such services to federal agencies; and MROs who provide review and interpretation of results to federal agencies. The guidelines *do not* apply to drug testing outside Executive Order 12564, such as individuals in the criminal justice system [arrestees, parolees].

Highlights of these guidelines include the following:

- A federal agency may collect urine and/or an alternate specimen.
- A donor is expected to provide a minimum volume of urine [45 mL].
- A federal agency must test each specimen for marijuana and cocaine.

- A federal agency may test each specimen for amphetamines, opioids, and phencyclidine.
- A federal agency must conduct specimen validity tests on each urine specimen to include:
  - Creatinine [Cr]
  - Specific gravity if Cr is less than 20 mg/dL
  - pH
  - Oxidizing adulterants
  - Additional testing if the specimen demonstrates unusual characteristics [odor, color]
- A federal agency may test for additional drugs if the collection was for reasonable suspicion or postaccident testing [limited to Schedule I and II drugs under the US Controlled Substances Act].
- A single-use collection container with a way to measure temperature must be used and two specimen bottles [A and B].
  - The collector must measure the temperature of the urine specimen within 4 min of receipt from the donor. Acceptable range is 32–38 °C or 90–100 °F.
- A DHHS-accredited laboratory must not discard specimens reported as positive, adulterated, substituted, or an invalid result for a minimum of 1 year. These specimens must be maintained in secure frozen storage at −20 °C or less.

Testing Methodologies

Initial Test/Screening

According to the 2017 updated DHHS guidelines, an initial test may be an immunoassay or an alternate technology such as spectrometry. The guidelines provide guidance on how these assays must be validated.

Screening by immunoassay typically involves no extraction, minimal specimen handling, and semiquantitative results. These tests have high sensitivity and moderate specificity. Many of the commercially available immunoassay tests cross-react with multiple drugs within a class, due to the choice of target analyte. (For detailed information about cross-reactivities of individual assays, see Ropero-Miller and Goldberger's

Handbook of Workplace Drug Testing in "Further Reading.") These assays may also be sensitive to interferences from additives that a donor may have used to adulterate the specimen. Such adulterants include bleach, glutaraldehyde, ammonia, soap, nitrite, and vinegar.

Commercial assays are based upon radioimmunoassay (RIA), enzyme-multiplied immunoassay technique (EMIT®), enzyme-linked immunosorbent assay (ELISA), cloned enzyme donor immunoassay (CEDIA), fluorescence polarization immunoassay (FPIA), and kinetic interaction of particles (KIMS). Tests typically screen for the original "HHS 5" drug classes that include amphetamines, cannabinoids, cocaine, phencyclidine, and opiates. Commercial assays developed to measure these drugs target certain analytes within each class. Therefore, for the amphetamine assay, methamphetamine and/or amphetamine may be the target analyte (meaning that during assay development, antibodies are produced to this specific analyte). In the cannabinoid assay, the inactive metabolite of delta-9-tetrahydrocannabinol (THC), delta-9-carboxy-THC (THCA), is the target analyte. For the cocaine assay, the target analyte is benzoylecgonine, and for the opiate assay, morphine. The tests are conducted using mandated cutoff concentrations. Refer to Table 4.1 for the current [effective October 1, 2017] analyte and cutoff concentrations for the NLCP. Samples that screen positive by immunoassay are known as presumptive positive specimens. The presence of the specific drug must be confirmed by an alternate analytical technique.

Specimen Validity Tests

In order to verify that the specimen collected is human urine, several validity tests may be performed. In regulated drug testing, specimen validity tests are conducted on each urine sample. These tests include creatinine, pH, and a minimum of one test for oxidizing adulterants. If the creatinine is less than 20 mg/dL, the specific gravity must also be measured. In addition, if the specimen exhibits unusual characteristics such as an abnormal odor or color, or produces reactions which interfere with testing, additional testing

may be performed. Oxidizing adulterants include tests for nitrite, chromium VI, halogens, glutaraldehyde, pyridine, and surfactants.

Validity tests utilize methodologies which include pH meter [pH], colorimetry [pH, nitrite, and halogen], multiwavelength spectrometry [nitrite, surfactant] ion chromatography [nitrite, chromium VI], capillary electrophoresis [nitrite, halogen], atomic absorption spectrometry [chromium VI], ICP-MS [chromium VI, halogen], aldehyde test [glutaraldehyde], and GC/MS [glutaraldehyde, pyridine]. The DHHS 2017 guidelines delineate the requirements for conducting these tests.

Urine specimens may be reported as adulterated, dilute, or substituted, following initial and confirmatory testing of 2 aliquots [2017 guidelines]:

- Adulterated. A specimen that has been altered by the addition of an exogenous substance or an abnormal concentration of an endogenous substance:
  - pH<4 or $\geq$ 11
  - Nitrite$\geq$ 500 mcg/mL
  - Chromium [VI]$\geq$ 50 mcg/mL
  - Halogen$\geq$ 200 mcg/mL nitrite equivalent or $\geq$ 50 mcg/mL chromium [VI] equivalent cutoff
  - Glutaraldehyde$\geq$ LOQ of the test
  - Pyridine$\geq$ 200 mcg/mL nitrite equivalent or $\geq$ 50 mcg/mL chromium [VI] equivalent cutoff
  - Surfactant$\geq$ 100 mcg/mL dodecylbenzene sulfonate equivalent
- Dilute. A specimen in which the creatinine and specific gravity are lower than normal but still physiologically possible for human urine:
  - Creatinine $\geq$ 2 but < 20 mg/dL *and* specific gravity > 1.0010 but <1.0030
  - Creatinine >5 but < 20 mg/dL *and* specific gravity $\geq$ 1.002 but <1.003 on a single aliquot
- Substituted. A specimen that is not the donor's urine. The specimen may produce validity results outside the physiologically possible range for human urine:
  - Creatinine < 2 mg/dL on both initial and confirmatory tests on 2 aliquots *and* spe-

Table 4.1 Urine cutoff concentrations and reporting requirements for DHHS-accredited laboratories (effective October 1, 2017)

Initial test target	Initial test cutoff (ng/mL)	Confirmation test target and cutoff (ng/mL)	
Amphetamine/methamphetamine	500	Amphetamine	250
		Methamphetamine	250
MDMA/MDA	500	MDMA	250
		MDA	250
Cocaine metabolite (benzoylecgonine)	150	Benzoylecgonine	100
Marijuana metabolite (THCA)	50	THCA	15
Phencyclidine	25	Phencyclidine	25
6-Acetylmorphine	10	6-Acetylmorphine	10
Codeine/morphine	2000	Codeine	2000
		Morphine	2000
Hydrocodone/hydromorphone	300	Hydrocodone	100
		Hydromorphone	100
Oxycodone/oxymorphone	100	Oxycodone	100
		Oxymorphone	100

cific gravity ≤ 1.0010 or ≥1.0200 on both initial and confirmatory tests on 2 aliquots

- A result may be reported as *invalid* under several circumstances including:
  - Inconsistent creatinine and specific gravity results
  - Possible presence of chromium [VI] or a halogen or an oxidizing adulterant or surfactant
  - Interference on initial or confirmatory tests on 2 separate aliquots

Confirmation: Chromatography/Mass Spectrometry

The initial document and four revisions of the Mandatory Guidelines for Federal Workplace Drug-Testing Programs required the use of gas chromatography/mass spectrometry (GC/MS) for confirmation of presumptive positive urine specimens. The 5th revision of the guidelines, effective May 1, 2010, allowed for the use of additional technologies which combine chromatographic separation with mass spectrometric identification. These include LC/MS, LC/MS/MS, and GC/MS/MS.

According to the 2017 updated DHHS guidelines, the confirmatory test must use mass spectrometric identification. The guidelines provide guidance on how these assays must be validated.

Each assay measures specific drugs and metabolites: amphetamine, methamphetamine, methylenedioxymethamphetamine (MDMA), methylenedioxyamphetamine (MDA), delta-9-carboxy-THC (THCA), morphine, codeine, 6-acetylmorphine, hydrocodone, hydromorphone, oxycodone, oxymorphone, benzoylecgonine, and phencyclidine. Assays generally use liquid–liquid or solid-phase extraction, with or without derivatization. Table 4.1 lists the current cutoff concentrations for the confirmation testing under the federal program, with reporting requirements.

For amphetamines, derivatives such as trifluoroacetyl, trichloroacetyl, and heptafluorobutyryl have been utilized after basic liquid–liquid extraction or solid-phase extraction using modified XAD-2 resin or hydrophobic cation exchange columns. The class of drugs to which the amphetamines belong, namely, sympathomimetic amines, have similar chemical structures. Therefore, when developing an assay for amphetamines, it is important to evaluate the assay for interference from similar drugs such as pseudoephedrine, ephedrine, phentermine, and phenylpropanolamine. Potential interference includes co-elution and similar mass ions and ion ratios. Procedures that do not use chiral columns or derivatives will not permit the differentiation between the licit l-isomer, the illicit d-isomer, and racemic mixtures of the parent compound. Chiral derivatizing reagents such as

N-trifluroacetyl-1-prolyl chloride and (-)-menthylchloroformate allow methamphetamine isomers to be distinguished using a non-chiral chromatographic column. False-positive results may occur if extracts are derivatized with 4-carbethoxyhexafluorobutyryl chloride, heptafluorobutyric anhydride, or N-trifluroacetyl-1-prolyl chloride. In this instance, methamphetamine is formed by thermoconversion of ephedrine or pseudoephedrine. This typically occurs at high GC injection port temperatures and when significant concentrations of pseudoephedrine/ephedrine are present in the specimen.

The major metabolite of delta-9-tetrahydrocannabinol is the carboxy acid that is present in urine in both free and conjugated forms. This metabolite is typically measured in urine specimens utilizing base hydrolysis followed by acidification and liquid–liquid extraction. Extracts may be derivatized with bis(trimethylsilyl)-trifluoroacetamide and 1% trimethylchlorosilane to form the trimethylsilyl derivative. C_{18} bonded phase adsorption columns or basic anion exchange resin may also be used after base hydrolysis. Trimethylanilinium hydroxide and iodopropane form propyl THC-carboxy acid derivatives.

Positive cocaine samples are confirmed by measuring the presence of the metabolite benzoylecgonine. Benzoylecgonine may be extracted from urine utilizing liquid–liquid, solid-phase, or "dilute and shoot" procedures. For solid phase, Amberlite XAD-2 extraction material has been used in addition to hydrophobic cation exchange columns.

Opiate-positive samples are confirmed by measuring morphine, codeine, 6-acetylmorphine, hydrocodone, hydromorphone, oxycodone, and oxymorphone. Morphine, a metabolite of heroin and codeine is present in the free form that is subsequently conjugated with glucuronic acid. Initial methods developed for opiate analysis utilized liquid–liquid extraction procedures. Samples may be hydrolyzed with acid or with glucuronidase, alkalinized, and extracted with an organic solvent solution such as methylene chloride isobutanol (9:1, v/v). After further acid–base extraction and re-extraction into organic solvent, acetyl derivatives are formed by reaction with acetic anhydride and pyridine. Other procedures have formed perfluoroester derivatives with a solution of pentafluoropropanol and pentafluoropropionic anhydride. More recent GC/MS methods for determination of opiates have utilized copolymeric bonded phase extraction cartridges such as hydrophobic cation exchange columns.

Opiate assays should be evaluated for potential interference from opiate metabolites and structurally similar compounds. In measuring 6-acetylmorphine, techniques should be developed to avoid chemical and enzymatic hydrolysis. The derivatizing reagent used for opiate analysis should be chosen with care since some opiates form similar derivatives. For example, formation of acetyl derivatives will convert both morphine and 6-acetylmorphine to heroin (diacetylmorphine), rendering them indistinguishable. Further, the mass spectrum of the trimethylsilyl derivative of hydromorphone resembles the trimethylsilyl derivative of morphine.

Confirmatory assays for the detection of phencyclidine have utilized liquid–liquid and solid-phase extraction techniques. Samples are alkalinized and extracted with organic solvents such as n-butyl chloride [1-chlorobutane]. Hydrophobic cation exchange solid-phase methods have also been described.

In many assays, deuterated internal standards are used. Additionally, assays that use phenylcyclohexylamine (amphetamines), meclofenamic acid (cannabinoids), ketamine (cocaine metabolite and phencyclidine), nalorphine (opiates), and difluorophencyclidine (phencyclidine) as internal standards have been described.

Benzodiazepines and barbiturates may also be measured in forensic drug testing. Screening assays are typically immunoassay based but confirmation may utilize GC, HPLC, LC/MS, and GC/MS technology. Refer to drug-/drug class–specific chapters for more information on analytical methods.

Oral Fluid

The secretary of HHS proposed the use of oral fluid [OF] as a specimen for federal workplace drug-testing programs [Federal Register Vol. 80 No.94, May 15, 2015 Notices]. Following a public comment period, the Mandatory Guidelines for Federal Workplace Drug Testing Programs Oral/Fluid were published in the Federal Register, Vol. 84, No. 207, October 25, 2019, effective January 1, 2020. There is no requirement for federal agencies to use OF; they may choose urine, OF, or both specimen types. The collection process will be under observation. In order to permit split specimen testing, two specimens are collected from the donor. All devices must have an indicator which shows that an adequate volume of OF has been collected [minimum of 1-mL undiluted OF]. IITF are not permitted to test OF specimens. If an individual is unable to provide an OF specimen, the collection of a urine specimen may be authorized.

The rules state that a federal agency must ensure a OF specimen is tested for marijuana and cocaine; is authorized to test the specimen for opioids amphetamines, and phencyclidine; and is authorized upon MRO request to determine specimen validity to include determination of the albumin concentration or IgG or a specific adulterant. If the specimen exhibits abnormal characteristics [unusual odor or color], additional testing may be performed. Table 4.2 illustrates the analytes and cutoff concentrations for drugs in OF.

An OF specimen may be reported as adulterated when the presence of an adulterant is verified by an initial and confirmatory test with separate aliquots. An invalid result is reported if interference occurs on the initial test on two separate aliquots; interference occurs with confirmation testing on two separate aliquots and the laboratory is unable to identify the interfering substance; the physical appearance of the specimen indicates that analyzing the sample may damage instruments; the specimen was tested and the appearance of the split samples are clearly different; or the concentration of a biomarker [e.g. IgG or albumin] is not consistent with that established for human OF on both the initial and second test on two separate aliquots.

Quality Control

The validity of testing results is assured through maintaining a laboratory-wide quality assurance program and, specifically, using good quality control. This includes the use of appropriate reference standard materials that are typically purchased from commercial vendors. These materials must be validated prior to use. In addition, appropriate control materials should be assayed concurrent with client specimens to serve as a check on the assay. Negative and positive control samples should be run with each batch of specimens; control samples may be blind or open but ideally examples of both should be run. Open control samples are those specimens that the analyst knows are controls; the analyst also knows the identity of the drugs present and the concentration. These serve to check that assay parameters are correct. Blind controls are those in which the identity of the control is blinded to the analyst in some way, i.e., the analyst may not know a sample is a control, or may not know the drug involved or its concentration. These samples are added to the run list by the quality assurance officer in the laboratory and are then evaluated by that individual.

Assays used for screening and confirmation must be validated. With commercial immunoassays, the laboratory should still generate validation data, especially if the laboratory does not follow the manufacturer's recommended procedure. Typical modifications include dilution of assay reagents or extension of reagent shelf-life in order to decrease costs. For GC/MS and LC/MS assays, sample preparation, extraction, and instrumental analysis must be validated. Therefore, specimen handling, matrix considerations, and optimal extraction conditions should be evaluated. Each assay must be quantitative due to mandated cutoff concentrations.

To validate the assay, four issues must be addressed: method validation, instrument performance, assay calibration, and quality control issues.

A laboratory must demonstrate that the analytical method is acceptable for the intended purpose and that the assay produces accurate and reliable data. Therefore, the laboratory must evaluate basic characteristics such as accuracy, precision, linearity, specificity, sensitivity, carryover potential, and "ruggedness" of the method. Additional parameters include stability of the analyte, recovery from the matrix, use of partial

Table 4.2 Oral fluid [undiluted] cutoff concentrations and reporting requirements for DHHS-accredited laboratories

Initial test target	Initial test cutoff (ng/mL)	Confirmation test target and cutoff (ng/mL)	
Amphetamine/methamphetamine	50	Amphetamine	25
		Methamphetamine	25
MDMA/MDA	50	MDMA	25
		MDA	25
Cocaine/benzoylecgonine	15	Cocaine	8
		Benzoylecgonine	8
Marijuana (THC)	4	THC	2
Phencyclidine	10	Phencyclidine	10
6-Acetylmorphine	4	6-Acetylmorphine	2
Codeine/morphine	30	Codeine	15
		Morphine	15
Hydrocodone/hydromorphone	30	Hydrocodone	15
		Hydromorphone	15
Oxycodone/oxymorphone	30	Oxycodone	15
		Oxymorphone	15

sample volumes, and identification and concentration of internal standard. For LC/MS assays, ion suppression and process efficiency should be assessed.

Accuracy and precision determine the error of the method. Accuracy is a measure of the degree to which the experimental mean agrees with the true or theoretical concentration or amount of substance and may be determined by analysis of standard reference materials or comparing laboratory prepared standards and controls with an established reference method. The generally accepted accuracy range is ±20% in forensic urine drug testing. Precision is a measure of reproducibility, or the variability of measurements within a batch or set of samples. Precision may be assessed by testing multiple samples during a single analytical run or batch (within-run precision) and a single measurement over several runs (between-run precision). The result of this testing is expressed as coefficient of variation (CV) and is calculated as follows:

$$\%CV = \frac{\text{Standard deviation}}{\text{Mean}} \times 100$$

CV values <15% are considered acceptable in forensic urine drug testing.

Linearity is determined by evaluating responses from a series of standards as a function of the concentration of the analyte. The result is evaluated by using a statistical method such as least squares regression analysis. The correlation coefficient (r) provides a measure of the degree of linearity. A method's linearity may be determined when the correlation coefficient (r) exceeds a defined value such as 0.99 and the quantitative concentration of each point is within ±20% of the target value. The limit of detection (LOD) of a method is the lowest concentration of drug that produces a detectable response. The limit of quantitation (LOQ) is the lowest concentration of analyte that can be accurately and precisely measured. The LOD may be determined by assaying negative or blank samples over time to determine the degree of noise or background in the system. The LOD is then calculated as mean of the signal intensity plus 3 standard deviations (SD). Similarly, the LOQ is the mean plus 10 SDs. Alternatively, blank specimens may be assayed with specimens of low analyte concentration, using a signal to noise ratio of 3:1 for LOD and 10:1 for LOQ.

Specificity refers to the ability of the method to measure an analyte in the presence of all potential analytes. Assays should be challenged with endogenous substances in addition to structurally related compounds. For example, an assay for methamphetamine and amphetamine should be challenged with sympathomimetic amines such as pseudoephedrine, phentermine, and phenylpropanolamine. Potential interfering compounds that are not structurally related may include over-the-counter medications.

Carryover refers to the contamination of a sample by the preceding sample. A laboratory should determine the concentration of drug that may result in carryover for each analyte. Drug standards of increasing concentration, over the range that the laboratory may reasonably expect to encounter, are injected with a solvent or reagent blank immediately following each standard.

Each method should be further evaluated to establish criteria to monitor instrument performance. For GC/MS techniques this should include tuning procedures, checking for water and air leaks, and evaluating chromatographic performance, which includes peak shape, resolution, and signal abundance. Calibration curves are typically multipoint or historical. Historical calibration refers to a historical multipoint calibration curve in which the calibration is determined and then the laboratory verifies that the calibration has not changed between batches by assaying positive and negative control samples and case specimens. One of the control samples must be at the cutoff concentration.

For the federal FUDT program, each batch of samples must contain positive and negative quality control specimens. The target concentration of one control must be 125% the cutoff concentration. Quality control results may be evaluated by utilizing a fixed criterion for the quantitative range, for example, ±20% of target concentration. Alternatively, Westgard quality control rules may be used. In this case, the laboratory establishes out-of-control limits for the assay based upon the validated mean and standard deviation for the control in question.

A laboratory must delineate criteria for designating positive results. For screening assays, this should include review of calibration and control data. For mass spectrometric assays, this should include chromatographic criteria [such as relative retention time], [transition] ion ratios, mass spectral matches, and determination of the quantitative results. In addition, the laboratory standard operating procedure manual should include details of dilution protocols, reinjection of extracts, evaluation of carryover, and data presentation.

Data Review

In the testing laboratory, data should be reviewed during each stage of the testing process. This includes review of specimen accessioning, aliquot chain of custody, quality control results, screening data, and confirmation data. Finally, before a report is generated, a senior scientist should review the complete case:

- At the bench, the analyst conducting the assay reviews the data.
- The supervisor of that section in the laboratory may then review the data.
- If the screening result is negative, a negative-certifying scientist will review the data before the results are recorded in a data management system.
- All positive results will also be reviewed and the specimen processed for confirmation. A positive-certifying scientist then reviews the screening and confirmation data.
- At this time the results for each specimen, including chain of custody documentation, are reviewed. If the data are valid, the result is reported.

Reporting

Reporting of results should be secure. Reports are typically sent electronically because telephone reporting is prohibited under the federal workplace drug-testing program. Reports utilize standardized forms and provide certified copies. In the federal program, the results are sent only to the Medical Review Officer.

MRO Review

The MRO is a licensed physician responsible for receiving laboratory results. This physician must have knowledge of substance abuse disorders and the appropriate training and experience to evaluate and interpret an individual's drug-testing results. In addition, they must pass an examination administered by a nationally recognized entity that has been approved by the Secretary of Health and Human Services. Every five years after initial certification, the MRO must complete requalification training and pass a requalification examination.

The donor provides his/her medical records to the MRO in addition to relevant medical history. The MRO must give the donor the opportunity to discuss the drug-testing results before making a final determination. If a drug test result is positive but there is an alternate medical explanation, the MRO will report the result as negative to the employer. If there is no explanation, the result is reported as positive. The MRO also reviews adulterated, substituted, rejected, and invalid test results. The MRO must also review negative results since many results for double-blind performance samples are sent to them. This review permits a continuous quality control program for specimen testing.

Proficiency Testing

As part of a comprehensive quality assurance program, laboratories must subject their work to independent evaluation. This is most commonly accomplished through enrolling in proficiency programs, which are typically established and administered by independent consultants or accrediting organizations.

On a regular basis, proficiency programs provide participating laboratories with samples that may be fortified with the drugs of interest. The laboratory is required to analyze these samples according to normal routine testing procedures, providing qualitative and quantitative data. The results of the testing must be reported to the accrediting agency by a specified date.

Proficiency checks test the ability of the laboratory not only to provide accurate results but also to provide accurate data review and reporting procedures and ensure that the laboratory completes work in a timely manner. The accrediting agency then compares a participant's results with those obtained by other laboratories and also with laboratories chosen to act as reference facilities.

Results of proficiency tests may be used to identify strengths and weaknesses in laboratory operations. Resources may then be more effectively utilized, whether in personnel, method development, instrumentation, etc. Acceptable proficiency testing results increase a laboratory's confidence in its analytical process.

The proficiency testing programs used by a laboratory must reflect the complexity of the work produced by that laboratory. For example, a laboratory that measures only ethanol in blood needs only subscribe to a blood alcohol proficiency program. However, laboratories providing comprehensive services in multiple biological matrices must participate in more rigorous programs and/or several programs, since one program is usually insufficient to test the qualitative and quantitative capabilities of a laboratory that assays multiple drugs in several biological specimens.

Accreditation/Certification

Government

As a result of President Reagan's Executive Order 12564, approximately 1.8 million federal employees, 600,000 Nuclear Regulatory Commission licensees, and 7 million Department of Transportation industry employees are tested for drugs. Laboratories conducting drug testing for these employees are subject to the "Mandatory

Guidelines for Federal Workplace Drug Testing Programs" published in the *Federal Register.* These guidelines cover requirements for personnel, quality assurance, analytical methodologies, and standard operating procedures for urine drug testing. The technical and scientific requirements detailed in section B of the guidelines form the basis of the National Laboratory Certification Program (NLCP). In December 1988, 10 laboratories were certified under this program; by July 1997, 69 laboratories had been certified. As of December 4, 2018, 26 laboratories and 1 IITF met the minimum standards to conduct urine drug testing for federal agencies.

Non-Government

The College of American Pathologists (CAP) Laboratory Accreditation Program began in the 1960s as an extension of the CAP proficiency program. In the 1980s, the CAP Toxicology Resource Committee, under the chairmanship of the Toxicology Commissioner, created the Forensic Urine Drug Testing Accreditation Program [currently known as the Forensic Drug Testing Accreditation Program]. Its mission was to oversee workplace drug testing performed by nonfederal employers. This program is intended to improve laboratory testing through peer review of testing practices by on-site inspections and the use of proficiency testing. In a manner similar to that of the NLCP, accreditation standards cover personnel, quality assurance, resources and facilities, analytical procedures, proficiency testing, and laboratory safety.

On-Site Testing

On-site drug testing is the testing of samples at the specimen collection site or site of current or future employment. Some regulated workplace programs prohibit this practice, but it is increasingly used in the criminal justice system and in the off-shore oil and shipping indus-

tries. The advantage of such testing is that results are available within a short period of time. This is important in certain industries when decisions regarding fitness for duty and access to safety-sensitive facilities must be made quickly.

Testing may take several forms. If the company has a large number of employees at one site, the drug testing of an employee's urine may be instrument based with immunoassay technology. In recent years, "quick" tests have been developed. These are usually based on immunoassay technology but are self-contained and require no instrumentation. If the specimen tests negative, no further action may be required. However, if the specimen is positive, the drug-testing program should require that a portion of the specimen be sent to a laboratory for confirmation. (Some programs send a percentage of specimens, regardless of testing status, to a laboratory for confirmation.)

On-site drug-testing programs may limit testing to one or two drugs/drug classes such as opiates and cannabinoids, or may perform more comprehensive screening to include ethanol, amphetamines, cocaine, methadone, barbiturates, and benzodiazepines. When on-site devices were initially marketed, they utilized urine as the testing specimen. However, several devices currently being marketed use OF to test for ethanol. More sophisticated devices that use a reader are now available to test OF for cannabinoids, amphetamines, opiates, benzodiazepines, and cocaine use.

The validity of specimen collection, handling, security, chain of custody, quality control, and reporting procedures must be assured when on-site testing is performed. A study of 11 on-site drug-testing facilities funded by NIDA made the following recommendations for ensuring testing quality:

- Establish criteria for training and demonstrating personnel competence.
- Use a standardized custody and control form.

- Establish guidelines that ensure the security of specimens and records.
- Establish minimum standards for quality assurance, quality control, and system supervision.

Specimens

Many biological specimens may be tested for drugs of abuse. Urine is the most common specimen type since high drug concentrations and metabolites are typically found.

Alternate specimens provide certain advantages over urine. Blood, breath, saliva [oral fluid], semen, nails, hair, meconium, sweat, breast milk, sebum, earwax, and nasal secretions may all have potential as drug-testing matrices. Blood is a useful matrix if the intent of the testing is to relate drug concentrations to pharmacological effects. Nails and hair can detect long-term or chronic use. In general, the potential advantages of using biological matrices as an alternative to urine include less invasive collection requirements, availability of multiple samples, ability to detect parent or the pharmacologically active moiety, greater analyte stability, a lower disease risk, and easier shipment and storage.

Urine

Regulated workplace drug testing utilizes urine as the specimen of choice for identifying cocaine metabolite, phencyclidine, opiates, marijuana metabolite, amphetamine/methamphetamine, and MDMA. In nonregulated workplace drug testing, urine is also used to test for additional drugs or drug classes such as methadone, benzodiazepines, buprenorphine, and ethanol.

The advantages of urine include ease of collection, ease of testing, the presence of high concentrations of the parent drug and/or metabolites, and the relative inexpensiveness of testing. The limitations of using urine as a testing matrix include the following: drug concentrations cannot be related to impairment; drugs and/or metabolites may remain in urine for one to seven days,

therefore reflecting only recent use; urine collection procedures may be embarrassing or uncomfortable to an individual if the testing procedures mandate witnessing the void; and specimens may be adulterated or tampered with. Such adulteration may include substitution of the specimen, dilution with water, or addition of substances to alter the testing results. Compounds that have been used to adulterate samples include alcohol, ammonia, ascorbic acid, Visine®, lemon juice, salt, peroxide, vinegar, detergent, golden seal root, and bleach. These adulterants may affect urine pH, specific gravity, and chloride levels.

Potentially adulterated specimens may be detected by measuring the above parameters. For instance, diluted samples may be identified by monitoring the specimen's creatinine and specific gravity. Potentially adulterated specimens may also be detected by observing sample smell and appearance. Some adulterants, such as salt, may not completely dissolve in the specimen, whereas an adulterant like Drano® produces a green precipitate. Foam may be visible in specimens adulterated with soap or detergent.

Screening procedures are typically more sensitive to the effects of adulterants than confirmation techniques. Since most screening procedures utilize immunoassay technology, a substance that interferes with the antibody will impact the results. Adulterants may also cause absorbance in enzyme and fluorescence immunoassays. The impact of adulterants is also dependent on the drug being assayed. For example, THCA assays are especially sensitive to the effects of adulterants. The effects may cause a positive or a negative result. Results may also be dependent on the particular immunoassay technology utilized. Detergent causes a false-negative EMIT THCA result but causes the RIA to measure THCA at elevated concentrations.

Hair

Hair, comprised of approximately 65– 95% protein (keratin, melanin), 1–9% lipid, and trace elements, polysaccharides, and water, is an epidermal outgrowth of the hair follicle. The base of the follicle is a bulb that contains matrix cells for producing the cell matrices present in the shaft, namely, the hair cuticle, cortex, and medulla. Drugs may enter the hair by several mechanisms such as diffusion from the blood supplying the hair follicle, absorption of sebaceous gland secretions, absorption of drugs from sweat deposited on the skin surface, and absorption through the hair shaft of drug particles deposited on the surface by the external environment.

Hair has been used as a testing matrix in forensic toxicology for many years, initially to identify exposure to metals such as arsenic, lead, and mercury. More recently, hair has been utilized to detect drugs of abuse. To date, heroin, 6-acetylmorphine, codeine, morphine, methamphetamine, amphetamine, caffeine, cocaine and metabolites, nicotine and cotinine, delta-9-tetrahydrocannabinol, barbiturates, benzodiazepines, phencyclidine, methadone, and several therapeutic drugs have been measured in hair. In such testing, head hair is typically utilized, although axillae, arm, and beard hair have been used.

Existing analytical methodologies may be used to assay hair for drugs. However, more attention must be given to sample collection, sample preparation, and the method's analytical sensitivity. Head hair samples are usually plucked using tweezers or cut as close to the scalp as possible. Samples may be collected from different scalp areas but the vertex or crown is the most common. Since head hair grows approximately 1 cm per month, segmental analysis may be possible to determine time of use. If this testing is to be done, the head hair should be aligned after collection, to identify the root and tip ends. Approximately 150–200 strands (or 50 mg) are needed. Sample preparation for analysis will include a washing step in which the hair is washed in a buffer, water, or methanol in order to remove potential external contaminants. (However, repeated washings may remove drug from the hair itself.) After washing, the hair may be incubated in buffer or organic solvent for a period of time prior to solid-phase extraction of the supernatant. Alternatively, the hair may be digested by enzyme or acid/base hydrolysis prior to extraction. Some investigators have pulverized the hair producing a powder for analysis. Most testing methods utilize solid-phase extraction followed by GC/MS or tandem mass spectrometry analysis for the identification and quantitation of drugs in hair.

Advantages of hair as a drug-testing matrix include the ease and noninvasiveness of collection and the ability of the specimen to measure long-term drug use. In addition, hair may be the only sample available for testing under certain circumstances, such as in death investigations of skeletal remains or traumatic injury. Another advantage is the stability of the specimen, permitting hazard-free storage and transportation. Limitations of hair as a drug-testing matrix include the cost, which is estimated to be at least twice the cost of testing urine. Drug concentrations in hair have not been correlated with dose or time of administration. In addition, most investigators consider issues of environmental contamination to be significant; active drug use may not be able to be differentiated from passive exposure. Recent research suggests that there may be a potential for bias regarding race and hair color in hair testing, because drugs may be preferentially bound to pigmented hair.

Sweat

Sweat, or perspiration, is produced as the body's response to exercise or thermal stress. Sweat is produced by eccrine glands located over most of the body surface. Apocrine sweat glands, located in the axillae, pubic, and mammary areas, also produce sweat. In addition, water is lost from the skin by a process known as insensible perspiration. This results from passive diffusion of substances through the dermal and epidermal layers of skin. Though the body excretes drugs in sweat, the mechanism by which drugs are deposited into sweat is ill defined. Transfer from the extensive blood supply throughout the skin is a possible mechanism.

Several devices have been invented to collect sweat to test for drugs of abuse. These collection devices typically consist of a tamper-proof adhesive membrane with an absorbent patch. The individual wears the patch for a period of time, commonly ranging from one day to one week. The patch is then removed and sent to a laboratory for testing. At the laboratory, the absorbent patch or collection pad is soaked and agitated in an aqueous buffer before subjecting the supernatant to testing. Testing procedures developed for the analysis of drugs of abuse in sweat have used solid-phase extraction followed by GC/MS. Other testing methodologies have utilized ELISA and RIA. The following drugs have been detected in sweat: ethanol, amphetamine, methamphetamine, barbiturates, benzodiazepines, buprenorphine, cocaine, codeine, heroin, methadone, 6-acetylmorphine, phencyclidine, and delta-9-tetrahydrocannabinol. Typically, the parent drug is the principal analyte detected in sweat. Therefore, assays targeted to drug metabolites would not be sufficiently sensitive for this type of testing. The range of drug concentrations found in sweat are as follows: from 2 to 4000 ng/mL for cocaine, negative to 0.6 g/L for ethanol, and 40 to 600 ng/patch for methadone.

Sweat collection devices have been approved by the US Food and Drug Administration for clinical and drugs of abuse testing. They are currently used to monitor drug abstinence in criminal justice and drug treatment programs. The advantages of testing for drugs in sweat is the noninvasive collection technique for providing a cumulative specimen. These semiocclusive sweat collection patches are impermeable to environmental contaminants and cannot be replaced after removal. However, adulterants may be injected into the patch and in this way adversely affect subsequent testing. Additional limitations of this matrix include the lack of information regarding drug incorporation into sweat and the paucity of pharmacokinetic data relating dose to drug concentrations. This renders interpretation of results problematic. The minimum dose to produce a positive result and the minimum length of time the patch should be worn

to optimize collection are unknown. Testing of the sweat patch costs approximately the same as testing urine. However, the entire patch is usually consumed in the analysis, preventing further testing. Currently, sweat testing is not utilized in the regulated workplace drug-testing industry.

Saliva (Oral Fluid)

Saliva is a colorless fluid secreted by the salivary glands. These are compound racemose glands with many lobes that may be subdivided into major and minor glands. The major glands (parotid, submandibular, and sublingual) are located outside the buccal cavity and contain a long duct system in order to deposit secretions into the mouth. The minor glands (labial, buccal, palatine, and lingual) have short ducts and are located in the walls of the mouth and under the tongue. Drugs may enter the saliva through the processes of passive diffusion, ultrafiltration, and active transport. The partition of drugs between plasma and saliva has been described utilizing the principles of drug transfer across biological membranes.

As a drug-testing matrix, saliva has been useful in therapeutic drug monitoring, the insurance industry (HIV, benzoylecgonine, cotinine), and the transportation industry (ethanol). Specimens may be collected by several techniques: secretions from individual glands may be collected by isolating the gland followed by cannulation, by tilting the head forward and allowing the saliva to drain freely from the mouth into a container, by expectorating into a container, or by placing a cotton swab or gauze in the mouth and allowing the saliva to be absorbed over a period of time or until saturated. In all cases except the first example, it is more accurate to state that oral fluid [OF] is being collected. This includes not only saliva but cellular material, food particulates, and bacteria. For multiple drug analysis, several milliliters of OF are necessary. Therefore, collection techniques may incorporate stimulation of saliva flow. This may be achieved by chewing a piece of Teflon® or Parafilm®, or placing citric acid crystals in the mouth. Changes in saliva flow result in alterations in pH that will affect the concentration of drugs in saliva.

Many drugs have been detected in OF including ethanol, amphetamines, barbiturates, benzodiazepines, caffeine, cocaine, THC, opiates, and phencyclidine. Parent drug is typically the principal analyte. In one study, peak OF concentrations of cocaine after intravenous administration of 40 mg to human subjects ranged from 428 to 1927 ng/mL. After smoked administration of a similar dose, peak saliva concentrations ranged from 15,000 to >500,000 ng/mL (high concentrations of drugs after smoking are due to drug contamination of the oral cavity). Drug detection times were slightly longer in OF than plasma after administration by both routes. However, in both matrices this time was short, approximately 10h. After smoking cocaine, anhydroecgonine methyl ester (AEME), the pyrolysis product of cocaine, may be detected in OF. Similarly, after heroin and marijuana smoking, high concentrations of the parent drug are detected in OF in the immediate period following drug administration. Since saliva may be considered a filtrate of blood, conventional screening and confirmation methodologies may be utilized to analyze drugs in this matrix. Sample preparation may include cell disruption, centrifugation, and filtration.

The advantages of OF as a drug-testing matrix include noninvasiveness and relative ease of collection; determination of pharmacokinetic parameters for drug appearance, metabolism, and excretion; possibility of relating drug concentrations to pharmacological effects; and adulteration or substitution that is less likely. The limitations include low specimen volume, the lack of data regarding drug deposition in this matrix, relatively short drug detection times, relatively low drug concentrations requiring sensitive analytical techniques, and appearance of the parent drug as a major analyte, thereby limiting the usefulness of assays targeted towards metabolites. Further, inhalation, sublingual, buccal, and smoked routes of drug administration will result in contamination of the oral cavity immediately following drug use, which complicates interpretation of drug concentrations in OF. Collection methods will alter the amount of parent drug and metabolites excreted in OF.

Further Reading

Armbruster DA, Tillman MD, Hubbs LM (1994) Limit of detection (LOD)/ limit of quantitation (LOQ): comparison of the empirical and the statistical methods exemplified with GC–MS assays of abused drugs. Clin Chem 40:1233–1238

Cone EJ, Welch MJ, Grigson Babecki MB (eds) (1995) Hair testing for drugs of abuse. Rockville, MD: International Research on Standards and Technology, National Institutes of Health, U.S. Department of Health and Human Services, National Institute on Drug Abuse. NIH Publication No. 95-3727

Department of Health and Human Services Substance Abuse and Mental Health Services Administration Drug Testing Advisory Board. Scientific meeting on drug testing of alternative specimens and technologies, April 28–30, 1997. Rockville, MD: SAMHSA, 1997

Department of Health and Human Services Substance Abuse and Mental Health Services Administration Revised Mandatory Guidelines for Federal Workplace Drug Testing Programs. Federal Register Volume 82, No.13 Monday, January 23, 2017/Notices p 7920–7970

Department of Health and Human Services Substance Abuse and Mental Health Services Administration Proposed Mandatory Guidelines for Federal Workplace Drug Testing Programs for the inclusion of oral fluid. Federal Register Volume 80, No.94 Friday, May 15, 2015/Notices p 28054–28101

Federal Judicial Caseload Statistics (2018) https://www.uscourts.gov/statistics-reports

Goldberger BA, Cone EJ (1994) Confirmatory tests for drugs in the workplace by gas chromatography-mass spectrometry. J Chromat A674:73–86

Goldberger BA, Huestis MA, Wilkins DG (1997) Commonly practiced quality control and quality assurance procedures for gas chromatography/mass spectrometry analysis in forensic urine drug-testing laboratories. Forensic Sci Rev 9:59–78

Goldberger BA, Jenkins AJ (1992) Testing of abused drugs in urine by immunological techniques. AACC Therapeut Drug Monitor Toxicol 13(8):7–25

Huestis MA, Mitchell JM, Cone EJ (1994) Lowering the federally mandated cannabinoid immunoassay cut-off increases true-positive results. Clin Chem 40(5):729–733

Institute for a drug-free workplace. http://www.drugfree-workplace.org

Jenkins AJ, Goldberger BA (eds) (2002) On-site drug testing. Humana Press Inc., Totowa, NJ

Jenkins AJ (1998) Detecting drugs of abuse in saliva. AACC Therapeut Drug Monitor Toxicol 19(3):65–74

Karch SB (ed) (2006) Drug abuse handbook, 2nd edn. CRC Press LLC, Boca Raton, FL

Kintz P (ed) (1996) Drug testing in hair. CRC Press LLC, Boca Raton, FL

Ropero-Miller JD, Goldberger BA (eds) (2009) Handbook of workplace drug testing, 2nd edn. AACC Press, Washington, DC

Shults TF (ed) (2009) Medical review officer handbook, 9th edn. Quadrangle Research, LLC, Research Triangle Park, NC

Sniegoski L, Welch M (1996) Interlaboratory studies on the analysis of hair for drugs of abuse: results from the fourth exercise. J Anal Toxicol 20:242

Spiehler V (1997) Detecting drugs of abuse in sweat. AACC Therapeut Drug Monitor Toxicol 18(2):37–45

Wong SH, Sunshine I (eds) (1997) Handbook of analytical therapeutic drug monitoring and toxicology. CRC Press LLC, Boca Raton, FL

Wu AHB, Ostheimer D, Cremese M, Forte E, Hill D (1994) Characterization of drug interferences caused by coelution of substances in gas chromatography/mass spectrometry confirmation of targeted drugs in full-scan and selected ion-monitoring modes. Clin Chem 40(2):216–220

Performance-Enhancing Drug Testing

5

Dennis J. Crouch and Melinda K. Shelby

Abstract

The use of performance-enhancing drugs by athletes has achieved greater public awareness over the past 30 to 40 years. Originally associated with the Olympic games, the use of these drugs has expanded to include not only professional athletes, but amateur athletes as well. The specific drug classes abused are a function of the sports themselves; athletes in endurance sports will use different drugs than competitors in sports that require a steady hand. As a result of this drug use, sponsoring organizations have instituted drug testing protocols in an attempt to prevent the use of these drugs. Among the classes of drugs included in these protocols are anabolic steroids, stimulants, diuretic/masking agents, narcotic analgesics, and peptide hormones. Urine is the primary specimen of choice for testing. The testing follows the same parameters as other forensic testing where a screening test is followed by confirmation testing. Each organization establishes its own testing regimen and its own procedures for sanctioning athletes that tests positive for a banned drug.

D. J. Crouch (✉)
Utah Toxicology-Expert Services, Sandy, UT, USA
e-mail: Denny.crouch@comcast.net

M. K. Shelby
Aegis Sciences Corporation, Nashville, TN, USA
e-mail: Melinda.shelby@aegislabs.com

Keywords

Steroids · Hormones · Stimulants · Diuretics · Adulteration · Urine · Sports-testing

Introduction

The use of performance-enhancing drugs has traditionally been associated with athletes competing or aspiring to compete in the Olympic Games. However, the use of these drugs has escalated dramatically such that today their use is a significant problem in middle and high schools, colleges and universities, organized amateur sports, and professional sports. The attributes of performance-enhancing (PE) drugs (actual or perceived) such as competitive advantage, muscle development, and improved self-image have contributed to the use of these drugs even by recreational athletes and in certain workplace settings. Testing for PE drugs is now common at all levels of sport and in safety-sensitive work environments such as the military, police, security officers, and firefighters. Some applications for testing have both sports and workplace implications such as the testing of professional athletes. Medical examiner investigations of the deaths of high school, amateur, collegiate, professional, and even aspiring athletes have exposed the potential toxicity and lethality of PE drugs.

© Springer Nature Switzerland AG 2020
B. S. Levine, S. Kerrigan (eds.), *Principles of Forensic Toxicology*,
https://doi.org/10.1007/978-3-030-42917-1_5

PE drug testing can, in part, be differentiated from the array of forensic drug testing applications by the scope of drugs tested. Testing programs often include tens if not a few hundred drugs and metabolites. Typically, programs include testing for marijuana, common stimulants and opioids, and anabolic androgenic steroids (AAS). However, as demonstrated in Table 5.1, programs may also include diuretics, "masking agents," glucocorticosteroids, beta-2-agonists, aromatase inhibitors, and other drugs affecting the production and actions of estrogen, peptide hormones, growth factors, alcohol, beta-blockers, and synthetic cannabinoids. Substances may be prohibited in certain sports, during competition or at all times. The international scope of athletic competitions, the breadth of testing applications, and the number of drugs require that PE drug testing laboratories have diverse analytical capabilities and a highly trained technical staff.

It is believed that the ancient Greeks used various herbs and mushrooms during competitions in attempts to improve their competiveness. In the late 1800s, French athletes reportedly used cocktails of coca leaves and wine to combat fatigue and prolong exercise routines. By the 1950s, stimulant use was reported in the Oslo Winter Olympics and allegations of AAS use by Russian and other eastern European athletes surfaced. The abuse of PE drugs reached a critical juncture when stimulant use was implicated in the deaths of several cyclists including a Danish rider in the 1960 Olympics in Rome. Because of the mounting evidence of PE use by competitive athletes, the International Olympic Committee (IOC) developed a drug-testing program that was implemented in the 1968 Games and further

Table 5.1 PE drug testing: Drug classes and sample drugs

Drug class	Example drugs
Steroids and anabolics	Endogenous Steroids and precursors: Androstenedione, Androstendiol, Dehydroepiandrosterone, Testosterone, Dihydrotestosterone
	Exogenous: Nandrolone, Stanazolol, Methyltestosterone, Oxandrolone, Tetrahydrogesterone, Trenbolone, Methandienone, Boldenone
	Others: Clenbuterol, Androgen Receptor Modulators, Testosterone/Epitestosterone ratio (T/E ratio)
Stimulants	Amphetamine, Methamphetamine, Methylphenidate, Phentermine, Methylenedioxyamphetamine, Methylenedioxymethamphetamine, Cocaine
	Others: Ephedrine, Pseudoephedrine, Methylhexaneamine, Modafinil, Selegiline
Diuretics and masking agents	Diuretics: Furosemide, Hydrochlorothiazide, Amiloride, Canrenone, Triamterine, Bumetanide
	Others: Epitestosterone, Probenecid
Opioids	Morphine, Codeine, Oxycodone, Hydrocodone, Hydromorphone, Fentanyl, Meperidine, Pentazocine, Propoxyphene
Peptide hormones	Human Growth Hormone (hGH), Insulin-like Growth Factor (IGF-1), Human Chorionic Gonadotropin (hCH), Luteninzing Hormone (LH), Insulin
	Erythropoetin (EPO)
Marijuana and synthetic cannabinoids	THC, THC metabolites, JWH-018, JWH-073, JWH-200, WIN 55211, HU-308, HU-331, CP-4797
Other drugs	Alcohol: Ethanol
	Beta Blockers: Alprenolol, Atenolol, Nadolol, Pindolol, Timolol, Propranolol, Metaprolol
	Beta-2-Agonists: Salbutamol, Salmeterol, Terbutaline, Formeterol
	Glucocorticosteroids: Budesonide, Betamethasone, Dexamethasone, Methylprednisolone, Prednisolone
	Aromatase Inhibitors: Anasterole, Formestane, Exemestane
	Selective Estrogen Receptor Modulators & Anti-Estrogens: Tamoxifen, Raloxifene, Clomiphene, Fluvestrant
	Misuse of Prescription Drugs
	"and Related Compounds"
	Gene doping

refined for the 1972 Games in Munich, Germany. Testing for AAS lagged behind stimulant testing until the mid-1970s when radioimmunoassay (RIA) tests for AAS were introduced. Subsequently, AAS testing using gas chromatograph (GC)-mass spectrometry (MS) was developed and the first widespread AAS testing occurred during the 1976 Olympics in Montreal.

The availability of robust and affordable mass spectrometers has been a significant factor in the development of effective testing methods for PE drugs and in the proliferation of testing programs. Because of diversity of tested drugs, consequences of the testing, and the sensitivity and specificity needed to detect and confirm the presence of these drugs and their characteristic metabolites, technologies such as gas chromatography-mass spectrometry (GC-MS), gas chromatography-tandem mass spectrometry (GC-MS/MS), high performance liquid chromatography-mass spectrometry (LC-MS or HPLC-MS), and high performance liquid chromatography-tandem mass spectrometry (LC-MS/MS or HPLC-MS/MS) are typically used.

Testing Approach

It is important to recognize that the details of many PE drug-testing programs are confidential and that programs are extremely variable in their application, drugs tested, and consequences. Consequences from a first positive test may be referral to qualified assessment and treatment specialists or suspension from competition. Penalties for subsequent positive tests vary from treatment to suspension or a permanent ban from competition. Because of program variability, it is difficult if not impossible, to discuss the nuances of each program. Therefore, presented are representative anti-doping approaches with some discussion of their variability.

PE testing under the World Anti-Doping Agency (WADA) regulation is among the most comprehensive (Table 5.1). The WADA list of banned substances and methods is divided into those that are banned at all times and those that

are banned within a competition. The groups of drug classes that are banned at all times include:

- Anabolic androgenic steroids, endogenous and exogenous
- Peptide hormones, growth factors, related substances, and mimetics
- Beta-2 agonists
- Hormone and metabolic modulators
- Diuretics and masking agents

Prohibited methods at all times include:

- Manipulation of blood and blood components
- Chemical and physical manipulation
- Gene doping

Groups of substances banned in competition include:

- Stimulants
- Narcotics
- Cannabinoids
- Glucocorticoids
- Beta-blockers (certain sports)
- Alcohol (certain sports)

Other programs focus on their testing efforts, in part because of financial considerations. Testing such as that required by the National Collegiate Athletic Association (NCAA), high schools, institutionally by colleges and universities, and professional sports is usually limited to a subset of the drugs and drug classes shown in Table 5.1. Because of its mission and international scope, WADA includes multiple drugs in most of the banned drug classes. Alternate programs are often modeled after WADA and its prohibited-substances list, but usually do not contain nearly as many drugs/class. The drugs tested may also vary by reason for testing. For example, under WADA's program, alcohol and beta-blockers are only banned in certain sports. Many programs limit out-of-competition testing to analyses for commonly abused drugs, AAS, masking agents, and perhaps an expanded list of stimulants. For cause testing, it may target a single drug such as alcohol or marijuana.

Blood specimens are collected in a limited number of testing programs and for only a very limited number of tests. For example, blood may be used for ethanol testing (blood or breath) and testing for indications of transfusions and other blood-doping activities. Tests for reticulocyte counts, hematocrit, and hemoglobin concentrations are often performed in cycling and Olympic endurance events such as cross-country skiing. Urine is by far the predominant specimen collected and analyzed in anti-doping programs. Although collection protocols vary, most collections are witnessed and specimen identification and handling and analysis procedures follow strict chain-of-custody protocols. Most programs specify "split specimen" collections and designate the specimen bottles as "A" and "B." Testing is performed on specimen A and specimen B is reserved for retests (see below). Specimen validity criteria are program dependent, but frequently include a minimum volume and specific gravity (SG), pH, and/or creatinine measurements. Minimum volumes of 30 mL and 15 mL, respectively, for the A and B bottles are typical. WADA's program has a unique requirement designed to ensure that specimens are not too dilute. The athlete must provide a specimen with a SG ≥ 1.005 as a collection requirement before the athlete is released from the collection site.

Specimen testing follows the typical forensic model of screening followed by confirmation of presumptive positive screen results. Screening and confirmation analyses are performed on urine from bottle A. Bottle B urine is only tested at the request of the athlete or his/her authorized representative. In contrast to workplace testing, often both bottle A and B samples are tested in the same laboratory. One or more approved observers can usually witness bottle B testing. Many anti-doping programs specify screen and confirmation cutoff concentrations and laboratories must demonstrate that the detected drugs or metabolites are present at concentrations $\geq$ cutoff before they can be reported. The WADA program has a decidedly different approach. WADA specifies Minimum Required Performance Levels (MRPL) for laboratories in their program. For example, the MRPL for most AAS is 10 ng/mL,

meaning that laboratories must be capable of detecting **at least** 10 ng/mL of a specified AAS or its metabolite(s). However, the laboratory **may** test to lower concentrations if they have sufficient analytical sensitivity. The WADA program has a limited number of substances termed "threshold substances." These substances fit the more traditional cutoff concentration model. For example, the laboratory must demonstrate that marijuana metabolite (THC-COOH), morphine, and ephedrine were confirmed at concentrations of ≥ 15 ng/mL, 1000 ng/mL, and 10,000 ng/mL, respectively, before these drugs can be reported.

Quality control and batch configuration varies. For those programs adhering to the cutoff model, screening and confirmation batches typically include the following: (1) a drug-free urine sample, (2) one or more calibrators, and (3) sufficient quality control samples to ensure discrimination between positive and negative samples when the drug concentration is near the cutoff. For programs not using specified cutoff concentrations, screening and confirmation batches typically include a drug-free urine sample and one or more quality control samples containing the drug.

Because urine is tested in the vast majority of PE programs, drug metabolites are frequently detected. The inclusion of metabolites greatly expands the number of compounds actually banned in most programs. Inclusion of metabolites also affects extraction protocols, analysis procedures, and data evaluation and interpretation. For example, metabolites of the many AAS, opioids, and marijuana must be hydrolyzed before they can be efficiently extracted. Urinary metabolites are often too polar to be analyzed by GC methods without derivatization. Metabolites detected in the urine may not be unique and may result from metabolic pathways shared with other drugs [e.g., morphine (may be detected as a metabolite of codeine) and amphetamine (may be detected as a metabolite of methamphetamine)].

Analyzing urine for PE drugs is also challenging because urine volume varies with the athlete's degree of hydration. Following competition or training, the athlete may be dehydrated and drugs and drug metabolites may be transiently concentrated in the urine. Concentration increases the likelihood of detection, but confounds interpretation. Conversely, overhydration dilutes the urine, decreases the concentration, reduces the likelihood of detection, and also affects interpretation. As a consequence, many programs attempt to "normalize" or "correct" the drug/metabolite (or cutoff) concentration to a predetermined standard such as a creatinine of 20 mg/dL or a SG of 1.020. Normalizing or correcting the SG is more widely accepted and is more easily defended than normalizing the creatinine.

The following formula may be used to correct a specimen concentration to a SG of 1.020:

$$\text{Corrected specimen concentration} = \left(\text{Measured drug concentration in specimen}\right) \times \left[\left(1.020 - 1\right) / \left(\text{specimen SG} - 1\right)\right].$$

If the measured SG and concentration of the drug in the specimen were 1.010 and 50 ng/mL, respectively, then:

$$\text{Corrected specimen concentration}$$
$$= \left(50 \text{ng} / \text{mL}\right) \times \left(1.020 - 1\right) / \left(1.010 - 1\right).$$

$$\text{Corrected specimen concentration} = 100 \text{ng} / \text{mL}$$

Correction of the urinary drug/metabolite concentration for SG provides a valuable interpretative tool, especially when monitoring an athlete for reuse or continued use of a PE drug.

Drugs and Drug Classes

Anabolic-Androgen Steroids and Anabolic Agents

Anabolic agents are among the most used and detected of all PE agents. AAS and other anabolic agents promote nitrogen retention, protein synthesis, and the development of lean muscle mass. Clinically, AAS may be used in the treatment of metastatic breast cancer, wasting diseases, types of anemia, male hypogonadism, and delayed male puberty. Anecdotally, AAS are claimed to increase strength, conditioning, and duration of workouts, improve recovery after workouts or injury, and promote aggressiveness. Theoretically, the physiological effects of steroids should benefit athletes. However, controlled clinical studies demonstrating the PE benefits of steroids are rare although there is a general acceptance scientifically that the use of AAS has a positive effect on muscle development, strength, and endurance.

For the purposes of this discussion, the AAS are divided into two broad classifications: synthetic and endogenous (Table 5.1). Synthetic steroids are manufactured, have effects similar to testosterone, and include drugs such as nandrolone, stanozolol, trenbolone, methyltestosterone, methandienone, oxandrolone, boldenone, and a continuing onslaught of designer steroids such as tetrahydrogestrinone (THG). Endogenous steroids include testosterone (T), epitestosterone (E), dehydroepiandrosterone (DHEA), dihydrotestosterone (DHT), androstenedione (A-dione) and androstenediol (A-diol) and are produced in the body primarily by the testis or adrenal glands (Fig. 5.1). As shown in Table 5.2, MS is used to both screen and confirm AAS in the urine. Most AAS substances are extensively metabolized and their Phase 1 metabolites are conjugated; therefore, hydrolysis of the urine is required for efficient extraction and detection. Sample preparation for screening usually involves isolation of the free and conjugated metabolites using solid-phase extraction (SPE), enzymatic hydrolysis, liquid-liquid extraction (LLE) of the hydrolysates, and formation of trimethylsilyl derivatives prior to GC-MS analysis. Although LC-MS, LC-MS/MS, and GC-MS/MS and full-scan MS acquisition are sometimes used, selected ion monitoring (SIM) using GC-MS remains the standard screening approach. Confirmation of synthetic AAS presumptively identified during screening may be by any of the

Fig. 5.1 Abbreviated steroid pathway

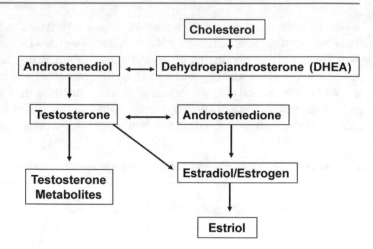

Table 5.2 PE drug testing: Methodologies used for different drug classes

Drug class	Screen techniques	Confirmation techniques
Steroids and anabolics	GC-MS, GC-MS/MS, HPLC-MS, HPLC-MS/MS	GC-MS, GC-MS/MS, HPLC-MS, HPLC-MS/MS
Stimulants	GC, GC-MS, GC-MS/MS, HPLC, HPLC-MS, HPLC-MS/MS	GC-MS, GC-MS/MS, HPLC-MS, HPLC-MS/MS
Diuretics and masking agents	GC, GC-MS, GC-MS/MS, HPLC, HPLC-MS, HPLC-MS/MS	GC-MS, GC-MS/MS, HPLC-MS, HPLC-MS/MS
Opioids	IA, GC-MS, GC-MS/MS, HPLC-MS, HPLC-MS/MS	GC-MS, GC-MS/MS, HPLC-MS, HPLC-MS/MS
Marijuana	IA, GC-MS	GC-MS
Synthetic Cannabinoiods	GC-MS/MSHPLC-MS, HPLC-MS/MS	HPLC-MS, HPLC-MS/MS
Peptide hormones	IA	IA
Alcohol	IA, GC, Breath analyzers	IA, GC, Breath analyzer
Beta blockers	GC-MS, HPLC-MS, HPLC-MS/MS	GC-MS, HPLC-MS, HPLC-MS/MS
Beta-2-Agonists	GC-MS, GC-MS/MS, HPLC-MS, HPLC-MS/MS	GC-MS, GC-MS/MS, HPLC-MS, HPLC-MS/MS
Glucocorticosteroids	HPLC-MS, HPLC-MS/MS	HPLC-MS, HPLC-MS/MS
Aromatase inhibitors	HPLC-MS, HPLC-MS/MS	HPLC-MS, HPLC-MS/MS
Selective Estrogen Receptor Modulators & Anti-Estrogens	HPLC-MS, HPLC-MS/MS	HPLC-MS, HPLC-MS/MS

IA immunoassay, *GC* gas chromatography, *HPLC* high performance liquid chromatography, *MS* mass spectrometry, *MS/MS* combined mass spectrometry techniques, *IR* isotope ratio mass spectrometry, *HRMS* high resolution mass spectrometry, *Other* isoelectric focusing

MS techniques shown in Table 5.2. However, there is increasing use of MS/MS analyzers and higher, or high-resolution instruments such as time-of-flight (TOF) and Orbitrap mass spectrometers. Sample preparation for confirmation is typically similar to that used for screening. Often certified reference materials are not available for use as standards, or to fortify quality control samples. Therefore, urine collected from subjects administered the suspected drug in controlled clinical studies is used as an "excretion" control. At a minimum, confirmation batches include a drug-free sample, a drug-/metabolite-fortified sample or excretion control, and the athlete's sample. For confirmation of drugs/metabolites with a quantitative cutoff or threshold, fortified calibrators are included in the batch. Sample preparation may be very similar to that used for screening. MS or MS/MS analyses often include both full-scan and SIM or selected reaction monitoring (SRM) data acquisition. Data are evaluated by retention time, the presence of characteristic ions, and the absence of interfering chromatographic peaks and extraneous ions. Data evaluation often include ion ratio calculations and comparisons.

Detection of exogenous use of (endogenous) natural steroids, such as T and the examples shown in Table 5.1 and Fig. 5.1, is far more challenging than detecting synthetic AAS use. Screening by standard GC-MS, GC-MS/MS, LC-MS, or LC-MS/MS techniques cannot distinguish steroids produced naturally from those administered exogenously. "Steroid profiling" has been used as one approach of identifying exogenous administration of a natural steroid. This approach assumes that the athlete's "normal" urinary steroid excretion profile has been characterized and that exogenous administration of a natural steroid produces detectable changes in the normal profile. A variation of this approach has been to establish population-based "normal profiles" to which an individual athlete's profile can be compared. In addition to profiling, the absolute concentrations (or SG adjusted concentrations) and the ratios of the natural steroids can be monitored as indicators of administration. T/E is the most commonly monitored ratio. The T/E ratio varies somewhat based on factors such as race, but is approximately 1 in normal males. The exogenous use of T increases urinary T concentrations, may decrease E concentrations, and results in an increased T/E ratio. Anti-doping programs use different T/E ratios (4:1 and 6:1) as evidence of T administration. Although exceeding these ratios may provide suggestive evidence of administration, there is substantial interindividual variation of T/E ratios. As stated, standard MS techniques cannot differentiate exogenous T from that naturally produced by the athlete. However, isotope ratio MS (IRMS) is an evolving and promising technique that is being increasingly used to detect the administration of endogenous steroids such as T. IRMS can distinguish between stable isotope forms such as ^{13}C and ^{12}C. Pharmaceutically prepared T is synthesized from C_3 (soy) plants that incorporate less ^{13}C, than C_4 plants. An athlete's normal diet includes both C_3 and C_4 plants. Consequently, steroids (such as T) produced in the body reflect their diet of both C_3 and C_4 plants and contain more ^{13}C than T produced for pharmaceutical use. When pharmaceutical T is administered, it lowers the $^{13}C/^{12}C$ ratio of the athlete's T and that change can be detected by IRMS. The measured $^{13}C/^{12}C$ of T is then compared to that of an endogenous steroid such as pregnanediol that is not in the anabolic pathway.

Stimulants

Stimulant use was reported in the 1952 Oslo Winter Olympics and has been implicated in the deaths of several cyclists including a Danish rider in the 1960 Rome Olympics. More recently, the use of stimulants such as ephedrine has been associated with the deaths of high school, college, and professional athletes. Research into the PE effects of stimulants has shown mixed results. Some studies have shown performance decrements, or at best performance-neutral results, while others have shown improved body composition through the loss of fat and improved focus and reaction time especially of fatigued subjects. The number of banned stimulants in most programs approaches that of AAS, and following the prevalence of AAS, stimulants are among the most frequently detected PE drugs in anti-doping programs.

As shown in Table 5.2, both GC and MS methods are used to screen for stimulants. GC with nitrogen phosphorus detection (NPD) has been used historically, but this technique is being replaced by GC-MS and HPLC-MS/MS methods. Sample preparation for screening usually involves isolation of the drug or its characteristic metabolites from urine using SPE or LLE. Derivatization may or may not follow extraction depending on the stimulant and the analytical approach preferred by the laboratory. Although GC-NPD, LC-MS, LC-MS/MS, and GC-MS/MS and full-scan MS acquisition may be used, many laboratories use GC-MS with SIM for screening. Confirmation of stimulants presumptively identified during screening may proceed by any of the variety of MS techniques shown in Table 5.2. There is growing use of MS/MS instrumentation especially HPLC-MS/MS. Sample preparation for confirmation is typically similar to that used for screening. As with the confirmation of AAS, certified reference materials may not be available for esoteric stimulants that are available only in certain regions or countries and excretion controls may be used during confirmation. At a minimum, confirmation batches include a drug-free sample and a drug-/metabolite-fortified sample or excretion control in addition to the athlete's sample. MS or MS/MS analyses often include both full-scan and SIM or SRM data acquisitions and data are evaluated by retention time, the presence of characteristic ions, ion ratio calculations, and the absence of interfering chromatographic peaks and extraneous ions.

Quantitative cutoffs, or threshold concentrations, are incorporated in many programs for some stimulants. Caffeine, ephedrine, pseudoephedrine, methylephedrine, and cathine are among the stimulants that are often banned only if their concentration exceeds the program's established cutoff concentration. Confirmation of these stimulants requires quality control (to help ensure) the quantitative accuracy of the analysis.

Because of the availability of over-the-counter (OTC) medications such as l-methamphetamine, d- and l- stereoisomer, determinations may be performed. These determinations are performed by MS using either a chromatographic column capable of chiral separations or reagents that result in derivatives that can be separated with a standard chromatographic column.

Stimulants such as amphetamine and methylphenidate may be used clinically to treat attention deficit disorders. The legitimate therapeutic use of these and other drugs such as opioids, glucocorticoids, certain beta-2 agonists, and even T creates a dilemma for sports agencies and antidoping programs. To address this problem, athletes are required (1) to have a clinically valid diagnosis of their disorder, (2) to have a legitimate prescription for the treatment drug, and (3) to pre-disclose their condition. Assuming that the diagnosis and therapy are appropriate, athletes are given a therapeutic use exemption (TUE) and can take their prescribed drug without risking disciplinary actions from the governing program. However, the topic of TUEs and its associated requirements of an appropriate clinical diagnosis and drug therapy are often controversial and the subject of substantial programmatic discussion, review, and controversy.

Diuretics and Masking Agents

Clinically, diuretic drugs are prescribed to increase urine flow and reduce edema associated with conditions such as hypertension and congestive heart failure. Athletes abuse diuretics to reduce body water and "make weight" in sports with weight classifications such as wrestling, boxing, and weight lifting. Diuretics may also be abused to increase urine volume, thereby decreasing urinary drug and metabolite concentrations (see SG discussion above). Decreasing drug and metabolite concentrations reduces the likelihood of detection. It also increases the likelihood that the drug or metabolite concentration may be less than the program's cutoff or threshold concentration. When abused in sports, diuretic drugs are often termed "masking agents." Some programs consider E a masking agent because administration of E reduces the T/E ratio and can mask exogenous T as administered. Probenecid is also considered a potential masking agent because it can extend the excretion time of some drugs effectively reducing their urine concentration.

Historically, LC, GC, or GC-MS methods have been used to detect diuretics. Sample preparation for screening usually involved LLE of the drug or its characteristic metabolites from the athlete's urine. Derivatization is followed for GC methods, but not for LC methods. Because the chemical structures and functional groups of the diuretics vary considerably, LC-MS or LC-MS/MS methods using selective reaction monitoring (SRM) acquisition are now standard screening approaches. LC-MS and LC-MS/MS analyses incorporate the formation and monitoring of positive ions, negative ions, or in some cases both positive and negative ions. Confirmation of diuretics presumptively identified during screening may proceed to any MS techniques shown in Table 5.2. However, there is growing use of LC-MS/MS. Sample preparation for confirmation is similar to that used for screening. As with the confirmation of the previously discussed PE drugs, the lack of certified reference materials for esoteric diuretics and their metabolites require the laboratories to use excretion controls. At a minimum, confirmation batches include a drug-free sample, drug-/metabolite-fortified sample or excretion control, and the athlete's sample. MS or MS/MS analyses often include both full-scan and SIM or (SRM) data acquisitions and data are evaluated by retention time, the presence of characteristic ions, and the absence of interfering chromatographic peaks and extraneous ions.

Narcotic Analgesics

Anti-doping programs ban the nonprescription use of narcotic analgesics. Many laboratories use commercial immunoassay (IA) tests to screen for analgesic drugs such as those listed in Table 5.1. These compounds may also be detected while screening for AAS using chromatographic techniques. Sample preparation for screening usually involves hydrolysis of the urine and isolation of the free drug and metabolites using SPE or LLE. Derivatization is needed for GC analyses of most banned analgesics, but it is not necessary for the analysis of meperidine, propoxyphene, pentazocine, and methadone. Confirmation of presumptive positive screening results may be by any of a number of GC-MS, GC-MS/MS, LC-MS, or LC-MS/MS techniques (Table 5.2). Confirmation batches minimally include a drug-free sample, drug-/metabolite-fortified sample or excretion control, and the athlete's sample. MS or MS/MS analyses often include both full-scan and SIM or SRM data acquisitions and data are evaluated by retention time, the presence of characteristic ions, perhaps ion ratio calculations, and the absence of interfering chromatographic peaks and extraneous ions.

Marijuana and Synthetic Cannabinoids

Marijuana (THC) is banned in most anti-doping programs because it is illegal and abused. Whether THC has specific PE effects remains a debated question. Since about 2004, synthetic cannabinoids that "mimic" the effects of THC have been incorporated into "spice" products and widely distributed as herbal incenses or household aromatics. These include the naphthoylindoles (JWH and AM series), cyclohexylphenols (CP series), tetramethylcyclopropylindoles (UR and XLR series), and indazole carboxamides (PINACA and FUBINACA-series), among others. Spice products were initially available over the counter in the United States and other counties. Over 400 of these synthetic cannabinoids have been synthesized and only a few are currently controlled by drug enforcement agencies. For most synthetic cannabinoids, the absorption, distribution, metabolism, and excretion patterns (especially in humans) have not been studied or reported in the scientific literature. Commercial immunoassay tests can be used to detect marijuana use and the literature contains numerous GC-MS and LC confirmation methods for THC-COOH which is the predominate metabolite found in urine. However, the synthetic cannabinoids are extensively metabolized and the metabolites can be conjugated. Consequently, sophisticated GC-MS/MS or LC-MS/MS procedures are needed to screen for and confirm the use of synthetic cannabinoids. Hydrolyzed urine samples may be extracted using either LLE or SPE. Because multiple hydroxylated metabolites with similar MS and MS/MS spectra may be formed, chromatographic separation of the metabolites is needed to ensure accurate identification even with MS/MS analyses.

Peptide Hormones

Human chorionic gonadotropin (hCG), luteinizing hormone (LH), erythropoietin (EPO), human growth hormone (hGH), and insulin-like growth factor (IGF-1) are among the peptide hormones banned in PE programs. All are endogenous substances; therefore, the major challenge confronting the laboratory is differentiating administered peptide from that naturally produced by the athlete. When exogenous steroids are administered, the body's natural production of T may decrease through normal endocrine feedback and hCG and LH are used by athletes to restimulate the natural production of T. Commercial IA tests are used to detect hCG and LH administration. Confirmation of elevated concentrations of the peptides found in screening tests is performed with a second immunoassay that uses alternate antibodies and usually from a different commercial source. EPO is secreted by the kidneys and is a major hormone in erythropoiesis, or red blood cell production. The PE effects of EPO are related to its stimulation of red cell production and the oxygen-carrying role of the cells. The use of EPO has been well chronicled in cycling and endurance sports such as cross-country skiing. Since the introduction of recombinant EPO in the late 1980s and subsequent release of similar drugs, various strategies have been advocated for detecting use. These included measuring blood markers of EPO use. More recently, anti-doping scientists have relied on isoelectric focusing coupled with gel electrophoresis to distinguish endogenous EPO from the various exogenous forms that may be abused. There are widespread allegations of Olympic and professional athlete's abusing growth factors such as IGF-1 and hGH. Both are naturally occurring and have anabolic effects. hGH has received the most anti-doping attention. It is secreted by the pituitary gland; affects skeletal growth, muscle development, and fat metabolism; and is required for normal growth and development. hGH promotes vertical growth in individuals who have not yet reached their natural height, increases lean body mass by promoting skeletal muscle growth, and decreases fat mass by causing lipolysis in adipose tissue. Although the performance-enhancing effects of hGH have not been demonstrated scientifically, the metabolic effects of hGH have potential benefits for the athlete's image, training, strength, endurance, and performance. During the past decade, anti-doping agencies have committed substantial resources for the development of testing strategies for the detection of exogenous hGH use. One strategy relies on monitoring changes in downstream markers of hGH administration such as IGF-1 and procollagen type 3 (P-III-P). The second strategy uses an IA testing paradigm to determine the ratio of recombinant hGH (a single epitope – 22kDa) to that of naturally occurring hGH that is present in multiple forms (22kDa, 20kDa, 17kDa, 5kDa, etc.). The paradigm detects a change in the ratio of the 22-kDa isoform to that of the other isoforms if the athlete uses recombinant hGH.

The detection and confirmation of exogenous peptide administration through IA tests has raised concern among many forensic toxicologists and forensic organization. Most forensic analyses utilize screening and confirmation methods based on differing chemical principles (e.g., IA screen and MS confirmation). Therefore, future research will likely focus on developing effective MS methods to confirm the exogenous administration of PE peptides.

Other Drugs

1. Alcohol. Alcohol (ethanol) is banned in some sports and certain competitions. Generally, it is banned only for those not of legal drinking age, or if the athlete has a history of alcohol abuse. Programs may require blood, breath, or urine testing. Enzymatic and GC methods are used for blood and urine testing; infrared and electrochemical methods are used for breath testing.
2. Beta-blockers. The use of beta-blockers is banned in specific sports and Olympic competitions. These drugs are used to control anxiety and improve performance in competitions such as golf, billiards, shooting, and archery. Historically, urine samples were hydrolyzed, extracted, derivatized, and subjected to GC-MS analyses. Currently, LC-MS and LC-MS/MS are the methods of choice.
3. Beta-2 agonists and glucocorticosteroids. In large, these two groups of drugs are used therapeutically in sports to treat symptoms of asthma or as anti-inflammatory agents. Their

therapeutic use is not banned in most sports, but abuse can result in sanctions. With the exception of salbutamol, formoterol, and salmeterol, WADA has prohibited the use of beta-2 agonists by inhalation. Salbutamol and formoterol are prohibited if present in urine above specified concentrations that are presumed to show that their use was not therapeutic. Glucocorticosteroids are prohibited when administered by oral, IV, IM, or rectal routes. However, glucocorticoids are not prohibited when inhaled. The challenge to anti-doping scientists and programs is to distinguish inhaled use from other routes of administration. The analysis of these drugs has migrated from GC-MS to HPLC-MS and HPLC-MS/MS.

4. Aromatase inhibitors (AI), selective estrogen receptor modulators (SERMS), and other anti-estrogens (AE). There are shared pathways and intermediates in the endogenous formation of T and estrogens such as estradiol (Fig. 5.1). Exogenous use of T and its precursors risks decreasing natural T production, increasing estrogen concentrations and development of unwanted feminine traits such as gynecomastia. In theory, administration of AI, SERMS, or other AE helps avoid development of the unwanted traits and increases AAS concentrations by reducing conversion of T and its precursors to estrogenic steroids. Specifically, AIs inhibit the enzyme aromatase that converts T to estradiol. SERMS bind to estrogen receptors, but have a mixture of agonist and antagonist characteristics. Administration of some SERMs has been shown to increase pituitary gonadotrophin secretion resulting in T production and increased T concentrations. After LLE or SPE extraction, LC-MS or LC-MS/MS is the method of choice for screening and confirmation of AI, SERMS, and AE.

Discussion

Testing for PE drugs is now common at all levels of sport and is increasing in safety-sensitive work environments and death investigations. PE test-ing may have both sports and workplace implications such as the testing of professional athletes. Regardless of testing indication, almost all PE testing has medicolegal implications. Anti-doping programs vary widely in the drugs tested, but usually, at a minimum, include testing for marijuana, common stimulants and narcotics, and AAS. However, programs frequently include exhaustive lists of AAS, stimulants, and narcotics as well as diuretics and masking agents, glucocorticoids, beta-2 agonists, AE, SERMS, peptide hormones, and the catchall phrase "and related substances." The phrase "and related substances" is common in banned substance lists and is used to ensure that drugs of similar chemical structure or with similar effects that are not explicitly listed are also banned.

Positive test results may have severe consequences for the athlete. A positive test may mean disqualification from competing in Olympic qualifying or Olympic events that may also mean a loss of endorsements. Positive results for college and university athletes may result in suspension from competition, loss of athletic scholarship, and loss of eligibility. Professional athletes risk disciplinary actions including suspension and expulsion and the accompanying loss of wages. Because of the diversity of drugs and metabolites tested and consequences of a positive test, sophisticated MS and MS/MS technologies are sometimes used for screening and usually used for confirmation. These technologies include growing use of HPLC-MS/MS, IRMS, and higher-resolution MS instruments. Testing reliability is important because of the forensic nature of PE analyses. Also most anti-doping programs are administered under the concept of "strict liability." In essence, strict liability means that the athlete is responsible for anything detected in his/her urine. Unknown or inadvertent ingestion of a banned substance (supplements or diet) or passive exposure (marijuana smoke) is not a viable defense.

PE drug use by athletes has become increasingly sophisticated as evidenced by the suspected use of hGH and the use of EPO and other peptide hormones. It has also expanded into the use of additional drugs such as the synthetic cannabinoids and into potential new avenues of abuse such as gene doping. Therefore, the need to expand testing, update banned substance lists, and improve testing technologies will undoubtedly continue in the future.

Further Reading

Botre F (2008) New and old challenges of sports drug testing. J Mas Spec 43:903–907

Catlin DH, Fitch KD, Ljungqvist A (2008) Medicine and science in the fight against doping in sport. J Int Med 264:99–114

Crouch DJ, Caplan YH (eds) (2011) Journal of analytical toxicology special issue on sports drug testing. J Anal Toxicol 35:9

Heltsley R, Shelby MK, Crouch DJ, Black DL, Robert TA, Marshall L, Bender C, DePriest A, Colello MA (2012) Prevalence of synthetic cannabinoids in US athletes: Initial findings. J Anal Tox 36:588–593

Karch S (ed) (2007) Drug abuse handbook, 2nd edn. Boca Raton, CRC Press

Martindale's Drugs Restricted in Sport – pocket companion (2009) Pharmaceutical Press, Grayslak

Robinson N, Saugy M, Mangin P, Veuthey J, Rudaz S, Dvorak J (eds) (2011) Fight against doping in 2011. Forensic Sci Int 213:1–114

WADA Prohibited List (and related documents) www.wada-ama.org

Drug Testing in Pain Management

6

Anne Z. DePriest

Abstract

Pain can be subdivided into two groups. Acute pain is typically caused by nociception and associated with events such as acute illness, trauma, or surgery. Chronic pain persists for long periods of time and does not serve a useful purpose. Pain from cancer and a neuropathy are examples of chronic pain. Opioids are the most common drugs used to treat pain; however, other types of medications are used to treat neuropathic or functional pain. These include skeletal muscle relaxants, antidepressants, anticonvulsants, corticosteroids, psychostimulants, capsaicin, local or regional anesthetics, and ketamine. When these drugs are prescribed chronically, pain management testing becomes a component of patient care. Urine is the specimen of choice for pain management testing. Although the testing is not used to establish dosing regimens, it monitors drug compliance and the use of other drugs that may interact with the prescribed drugs.

Keywords

Pain management · Urine · Toxicology · Opioids · Compliance · Testing

A. Z. DePriest (✉)
Janssen Scientific Affairs, Nashville, TN, USA
e-mail: adepries@its.jnj.com

Introduction

The art and science of chronic pain management is a complex process, requiring continual patient assessment for positive and negative outcomes. The goal of achieving analgesia and improving quality of life must be balanced with the risk of adverse effects and development of physical dependence or addiction. Most patients who undergo chronic treatment with opioids will develop dependence, which is a physiological adaptation to a medication characterized by a withdrawal syndrome upon abrupt discontinuation. This outcome is expected; the development of addiction is not. Hallmarks of addiction include craving, compulsive use of a drug for nonmedical reasons, aberrant behavior, and continued use despite harm. If patients undergoing pain management have an active addiction/substance abuse disorder, then treatment with controlled substances may compromise treatment and increase the risk of the unintended consequences of drug interactions, overdose, or death. Unfortunately, patients with substance abuse disorders are often difficult to identify. Some addicted patients may appear high functioning, maintaining successful careers, while projecting the illusion that they are in control of their treatment. While substance abuse is commonly recognized as a health threat, drug misuse may compromise care as well. Patients who misuse medications are departing from a practitioner's direction, but such misuse does not always constitute addiction. For example, a patient may make an unsanctioned dose increase for elevated pain without first discussing it with their provider. Although the reasons for drug misuse may be fairly benign, outcomes may still be severe, and healthcare professionals must be diligent in assessing patient compliance.

Patients commonly underreport or deny drug use, but toxicology results provide objective information regarding recent drug exposure. Over the last decade, drug testing has been adopted in clinical practice as an integral piece of the assessment of patient compliance and is used to determine if patients are taking prescribed or nonprescribed medications. As such, drug test results may identify (but not diagnose) potential substance misuse or abuse. In the clinical setting, testing must be comprehensive and include the breadth of prescription medications and illicit drugs that are encountered in pain management. Unlike federally regulated testing, testing in pain management yields a very high positivity rate and polysubstance use is common. Furthermore, false-negative test results in compliance testing are of heightened concern and can be extremely detrimental to patient care. Testing approaches vary widely in this setting and significant differences from other testing applications exist.

Pain Physiology

Approximately 100 million adults in the United States suffer from chronic pain; an estimated one-third of Americans will suffer severe chronic pain at some point in their lifetimes. The physiologic basis of pain may vary depending on the type of pain. Acute and chronic pain are often caused by different mechanisms.

Acute pain is typically caused by nociception and associated with events such as acute illness, trauma, or surgery. Nociceptors are nerve endings found in somatic and visceral tissue; nociceptive pain may therefore be further classified as somatic pain (arising from skin, bone, joint, muscle, or connective tissue) or visceral pain (arising from internal organs such as the intestine).

Nociceptors relay information from mechanical, thermal, or chemical impulses. Upon initiation of pain signals, nociceptor activation triggers the release of neurotransmitters including bradykinins, hydrogen and potassium ions, prostaglandins, histamine, interleukins, tumor necrosis factor alpha, serotonin, and substance P. Nociceptor activation then causes transmission of the pain signal along Aδ and C-afferent nerve fibers which synapse in the dorsal horn of the spinal cord. At this point, neurotransmitters including glutamate, substance P, and calcitonin-related peptide propagate the signal along the ascending spinal cord pathway to the brain.

Pain signals are modulated by the descending inhibitory pathway through a number of different mechanisms. The endogenous opiate system aids in pain relief and includes enkephalins, dynorphins, and β-endorphins, which bind to delta (δ), kappa (κ), and mu (μ) opioid receptors, respectively. These endogenous opioids are found throughout the central nervous system (CNS). N-Methyl-D-aspartate (NMDA) receptors in the dorsal horn of the spinal cord also play a role in signal modification; blockade of NMDA receptors may increase the responsiveness of mu receptors to opiates. Further modulation occurs along the descending pathway by way of neurotransmitters such as serotonin, norepinephrine, and gamma-aminobutyric acid (GABA). The number of complex systems involved in the transmission and perception of pain offer several potential targets for pharmacotherapy, beyond use of traditional pain relievers such as opioids.

Unlike acute pain, chronic pain may persist for months or years, does not serve a useful purpose, and is not always associated with a known pain-producing stimulus. Chronic pain is classified as cancer (sometimes called malignant) pain or noncancer pain. Neuropathic or functional pain syndromes are usually implicated in patients suffering from chronic pain, although nociceptive mechanisms are occasionally present as well. Neuropathic pain arises from nerve damage and can occur in a variety of chronic conditions such as diabetic neuropathy or postherpetic neuralgia. It may sometimes persist after an injury has healed, as in the case of phantom limb pain.

Functional pain syndromes are caused by abnormal operation of the nervous system and may be implicated in fibromyalgia or irritable bowel syndrome. In cases of neuropathic or functional pain, a physical exam may be normal which complicates the assessment and diagnosis of these pain syndromes. Patients suffering from chronic pain may exhibit anatomical and biochemical changes throughout the nervous system, which can increase pain signal transmission or render receptors less responsive to opioids. Consequently, chronic pain is typically more difficult to treat than acute pain. There is a significant incidence of psychiatric comorbidities such as depression and anxiety disorder in this population as well. Options for treating chronic pain may therefore be selected to target more than one disorder simultaneously (e.g., antidepressants for neuropathic pain and depression).

Non-pharmacologic and Pharmacologic Treatment

Pain management practitioners will select treatment for chronic pain depending on the etiology. Although treatment with opioids may be necessary, they are not always the first-line choice for analgesia; for example, pain caused by neuropathic mechanisms may be treated primarily by adjuvant non-opioid medications. Both non-pharmacologic and pharmacologic therapy may be recommended for some types of pain. Non-pharmacologic treatment may include physical manipulation, application of heat or cold, massage, exercise, transcutaneous electrical nerve stimulation (TENS), or psychological interventions such as relaxation, hypnosis, imagery, cognitive behavioral therapy, or biofeedback.

The medications used for pharmacologic treatment are varied and may include non-opioid analgesics, adjuvant therapies, and opioids. Non-opioid analgesics are frequently used in combination with opioids according to recommendations by the World Health Organization; these include acetaminophen, nonsteroidal anti-inflammatory drugs or NSAIDs (e.g., ibuprofen, naproxen, celecoxib), and aspirin. These medications can

be effective for mild to moderate pain and do not pose a risk for addiction. There are several types of medications used as adjuvant therapy, particularly for neuropathic or functional pain (see Table 6.1). Of the adjuvants, benzodiazepines are the most commonly detected drug class (presumably prescribed for concurrent anxiety disorders), secondary only to opioids in patients undergoing

Table 6.1 Adjuvants used in pain management

Class	Medications
Muscle relaxants/ sedatives	Baclofen
	Benzodiazepines
	Carisoprodol
	Cyclobenzaprine
	Metaxolone
	Methocarbamol
Antidepressants	Tricyclic antidepressants (TCAs)
	Amitriptyline
	Desipramine
	Imipramine
	Nortriptyline
	Serotonin norepinephrine reuptake inhibitors (SNRIs)
	Duloxetine
	Desvenlafaxine
	Milnacipran
	Venlafaxine
	Selective serotonin reuptake inhibitors (SSRIs)
	Citalopram
	Escitalopram
	Fluoxetine
	Paroxetine
	Sertraline
Anticonvulsants	Carbamazepine
	Gabapentin
	Lamotrigine
	Levetiracetam
	Oxcarbazepine
	Phenytoin
	Pregabalin
	Sodium valproate
	Tiagabine
	Topiramate
	Zonisamide
Corticosteroids	Dexamethasone
Psychostimulants	Dextroamphetamine
	Methylphenidate
Local or regional anesthetics	Bupivacaine
	Lidocaine
Others	Capsaicin
	Clonidine
	Ketamine
	Ziconotide

chronic pain treatment. In the antidepressant class, SNRIs are generally preferred to TCAs due to the risk of anticholinergic adverse effects. SSRIs are frequently prescribed for depression, which is a significant comorbidity in the pain management population; however, SSRIs are less effective for neuropathic and functional pain syndromes than TCAs or SNRIs. Of the anticonvulsants, gabapentin and pregabalin are more frequently prescribed due to the lower risk of adverse effects and reduced need for therapeutic drug monitoring compared to other agents in this class.

Although practitioners are trained to use adjuvants whenever possible, opioid analgesics are frequently the mainstay of treatment for chronic pain. They are the most frequently mentioned drug in office visits, constituting 10% of all drugs prescribed in the United States for adults in 2008. Opioids exert their analgesic effects by binding to mu opioid receptors located in the CNS, although some opioids exhibit affinity at kappa and delta opioid receptors. Multiple opioids may be prescribed for patients with chronic pain. Extended-release formulations are prescribed for around-the-clock dosing, with a short-acting immediate-release formulation used for breakthrough pain on a *pro re nata* (PRN), or as needed, basis. Opiates are drugs that are structurally related to derivatives of the opium plant, limited to the following natural and semisynthetic phenanthrenes: morphine, codeine, hydrocodone, hydromorphone, oxycodone, and oxymorphone. Synthetic opioids include methadone and propoxyphene in the diphenylheptane class, fentanyl analogues and meperidine in the phenylpiperidine class, and novel opioids such as tapentadol and tramadol.

Hydrocodone and oxycodone are the most frequently used drugs in pain management. The United States consumes 99% of the world's supply of hydrocodone, which is also the country's most commonly prescribed drug—far exceeding other medications such as antihypertensive or antihyperlipidemic drugs. Hydrocodone is the second most commonly abused prescription drug. A recent amendment to the FDA Safety and Innovation Act is currently under consideration which would reclassify hydrocodone combinations from Schedule III to Schedule II controlled substances. Oxycodone is the most frequently abused medication according to the Drug Enforcement Administration (DEA), and prevalence data have indicated that oxycodone is the most frequently prescribed drug in the pain management setting. Codeine and meperidine are rarely used for chronic pain given limited efficacy and, in meperidine's case, potential for neurotoxicity. Use of other opioids such as methadone, fentanyl, oxymorphone, and hydromorphone is significant in the pain management setting.

Tapentadol was first approved in 2008 and is available in immediate- and extended-release forms. In addition to mu opioid activity, tapentadol acts as a norepinephrine reuptake inhibitor, which is a mechanism considered to be potentially useful for treating neuropathic pain. Tramadol is a weak mu opioid receptor agonist and a norepinephrine and serotonin reuptake inhibitor. Although it is not a controlled substance at the federal level in the United States, it is subject to abuse and some states have classified it as a Schedule IV controlled substance.

Partial and mixed agonist-antagonists are sometimes encountered in the pain management setting. Buprenorphine is a partial mu opioid receptor agonist, available as a sublingual tablet and film for the treatment of opioid dependence and as a transdermal patch for use as an analgesic. Buprenorphine should not be used in combination with pure mu opioid agonists, as it may precipitate opioid withdrawal. Mixed agonists-antagonists include butorphanol, nalbuphine, and pentazocine. These medications exhibit a ceiling effect for analgesia (e.g., limiting analgesic response when doses are escalated) and carry an increased risk of psychomimetic effects. Their unique pharmacology profile comprises agonism at the kappa receptor and partial agonism or antagonism at the mu receptor, which, similarly to buprenorphine, predisposes patients to opioid withdrawal when given in combination with pure mu opioids. Although use of buprenorphine has increased, especially since the introduction of the transdermal patch in 2010, mixed agonist-antagonists are rarely prescribed for chronic pain.

While the oral route is the most common route of delivery, chronic pain patients may also take opioid medications through other routes including transdermal, oral transmucosal (sublingual and buccal), rectal, intranasal, intravenous, subcutaneous, intramuscular, and intraspinal (epidural and intrathecal) administration. The parenteral (intravenous, subcutaneous, and intramuscular) routes are not commonly used for most outpatients with chronic pain, except in hospice facilities. Intrathecal pumps may be implanted in the patient via a surgical procedure and periodically refilled with opioids, local anesthetics, baclofen, clonidine (an alpha-2 agonist), or ziconotide (an N-type voltage-gated calcium channel blocker).

Rationale for Drug Testing in Pain Management

Prescription pain reliever use is prevalent in the United States, with more than 200 million prescriptions dispensed in 2009. While these medications are necessary, they are also subject to abuse. Prescription drug abuse has become an epidemic, with 12 million people reporting nonmedical use of prescription pain relievers in 2010. Drug overdose is listed as the second leading cause of accidental death behind motor vehicle accidents. Polysubstance use is widespread, particularly with opioids and benzodiazepines; eighty percent of emergency department visits reported by the Drug Abuse Warning Network (DAWN) involve more than one drug.

The prevalence of patients with addiction in pain management and primary care clinics has been estimated to be between 3 and 31%. Doctor shopping and drug diversion are significant concerns in the pain management setting, where physicians are charged with the responsibility of monitoring compliance and taking steps to reduce medication misuse and abuse. However, physician training for substance abuse diagnosis and treatment has historically been lacking, and it is impossible to identify all cases of current or potential substance misuse or abuse on the basis of patient demographics or behavioral monitor-

ing. Given these factors, a "universal precautions" approach has been recommended to ensure adequate assessment of pain, treatment, and risk for addictive disorders for all patients. The universal precautions assessment should include drug testing, which is often called "compliance" testing because it is used to determine whether a patient is taking prescribed drugs or other, nonprescribed licit or illicit medications. Frequencies of unexpected toxicology results for chronic pain patients between 45 and 51% have been reported, with a prevalence of illicit drugs between 10.9 and 24%. Although not all patients with unexpected toxicology results will have a substance abuse disorder, these results are concerning because medication noncompliance can significantly reduce treatment efficacy or increase the risk of serious adverse effects, including death.

Systemic literature reviews have not yielded strong support for urine drug testing programs in pain management; however, implementation has been recommended by numerous organizations including the Institute of Medicine (IOM), Drug Enforcement Administration (DEA), American Pain Society (APS), American Academy of Pain Medicine (AAPM), American Society of Interventional Pain Physicians (ASIPP), most state medical boards, and numerous well-known practitioners and prolific authors in pain management. Some proposed state regulations have formally recommended drug testing, most recently in Florida, and further legislation proposals may follow. Finally, guidelines issued by third-party payers also recommend or require drug testing in pain management, such as the Official Disability Guidelines (ODG) for worker's compensation patients.

Implementation of Drug Testing Programs in Pain Management

Over the last decade, urine drug testing has become an established standard of care in pain clinics. Practitioners specializing in pain management are subjected to increased scrutiny to manage the risk of addiction, thereby improving patient outcomes and reducing their own medicolegal risk. Incorporation of drug testing as part of routine patient assessment remains sporadic in primary care clinics; only 8% of primary care physicians order urine drug tests. This known gap in risk assessment continues to be a problem, as the majority of opioid prescriptions are generated in the primary care setting.

Patients undergoing treatment for chronic pain may be asked to sign a treatment agreement during their initial visit, which explains the risks of opioid therapy and outlines behavioral boundaries for ongoing treatment. The requirement for submitting to a drug testing program is divulged in the treatment agreement. Although a free example of such an agreement is available online by the American Academy of Pain Medicine, practitioners often adapt these to their own practice. Certainly there is not a consensus regarding a standard urine drug testing protocol, as they vary depending on the needs of the patient or prescriber. A drug testing program may need to be adapted to changes in the clinical picture.

Testing frequency varies depending on physician preference but should be ordered randomly to reduce the opportunity for specimen adulteration or substitution. If an office uses a screening tool to identify the risk of substance abuse, testing frequency may be based on stratification of risk; however, these are not routinely applied in clinical practice and most providers adopt a general range for testing frequency such as 2–4 times per year. If patients present with abnormal test results or are diagnosed with a substance abuse disorder, they may be tested more frequently (every month or more). Patients found to be engaging in substance misuse may be counseled; substance abuse may lead to a referral for addiction treatment, tapering of controlled substances, and/or discharge from care.

Specimen Types

Urine is the gold standard and is the most common specimen tested in pain management. Other specimen types may be tested such as blood and oral fluid (saliva), which reflect recent drug use. Hair and sweat testing have not gained traction in this setting, although they may be used occasionally.

Urine testing is preferred because there is a wide body of literature supporting its use and it provides a substantial period of detection for drugs and their metabolites. However, the usefulness of urine testing is sometimes compromised in clinical practice by patient adulteration attempts. Testing of oral fluid and blood both yield shorter detection times; however, this is typically not a problem for most drugs prescribed in pain management, given the chronic nature of medication use. The option of collecting oral fluid or blood is advantageous in cases of shy bladder or suspected specimen tampering. The use of oral fluid in pain management has increased recently due to its ease of collection, limited invasiveness, and relative lack of opportunity for adulteration. The medications of interest in pain management are readily detected in oral fluid. Blood testing is invasive and costly and is usually not the preferred mode of testing in pain management.

Drugs Included in Testing

Toxicology testing in pain management is challenging given the large number of drugs of interest. Most panels include illicit drugs as well as numerous prescription medications which are either frequently prescribed in pain management or subject to abuse (see Table 6.2). Metabolites of prescription drugs should be included in urine testing. This is particularly true for opioids and benzodiazepines, which are extensively metabolized. In recent years, evidence regarding the prevalence of opioid normetabolites have been published, indicating that testing for these analytes may avoid the risk of false negatives (see Figs. 6.1 and 6.2 for metabolism pathways for opiates and benzodiazepines).

Many opioid normetabolites are products of cytochrome P450 3A4 (CYP3A4) metabolism, which may be affected by a host of drug-drug interactions. There have been case reports of patients taking CYP3A4-inducing drugs when upon drug testing had a normetabolite as the only detectable marker in urine (e.g., noroxycodone only was detected in a patient ingesting extended-release oxycodone and rifampin, an antibiotic

Table 6.2 Medications included in pain management testing

Drug class	Drugs/metabolites included in testing
Amphetamine-like stimulants	Amphetamine
	Methamphetamine
	MDMA
	Phentermine
Barbiturates	Butalbital
	Phenobarbital
Benzodiazepines	Alprazolam
	Alpha-hydroxyalprazolam
	Clonazepam
	7-Aminoclonazepam
	Diazepam/chlordiazepoxide/ clorazepate/oxazepam/ temazepam
	Nordiazepam
	Oxazepam
	Temazepam
	Flurazepam
	2-Hydroxy-ethyl-flurazepam
	Lorazepam
Opioids	Buprenorphine
	Norbuprenorphine
	Codeine
	Morphine
	Norcodeine
	Fentanyl
	Norfentanyl
	Hydrocodone
	Dihydrocodeine
	Hydromorphone
	Norhydrocodone
	Hydromorphone
	Meperidine
	Normeperidine
	Methadone
	EDDP
	Morphine
	Oxycodone
	Noroxycodone
	Noroxymorphone[a]
	Oxymorphone
	Oxymorphone
	Propoxyphene[b]
	Norpropoxyphene
	Tapentadol
	Nortapentadol
	Tramadol
	O-Desmethyltramadol
	N-Desmethyltramadol
Illicit drugs	Cocaine
	Benzoylecgonine
	Heroin
	6-Acetylmorphine
	6-Acetylcodeine
	Marijuana (THC)
	THCCOOH
	Synthetic cannabinoids (Spice/K2)
	Synthetic cathinones (bath salts)

(continued)

Table 6.2 (continued)

Drug class	Drugs/metabolites included in testing
Others	Carisoprodol
	Meprobamate
	Nicotine
	Cotinine
	Ethanol
	Ethyl glucuronide
	Ethyl sulfate
	Gabapentin
	Pregabalin

[a]Noroxymorphone testing has not yet become standard in the pain management setting
[b]The prevalence of propoxyphene has declined (but has not disappeared) since its removal from the United States market

with significant CYP3A4-inducing activity). Additionally, other drug markers resulting from CYP2D6 metabolism (e.g., oxymorphone from oxycodone metabolism, or morphine from codeine metabolism) may be undetectable if metabolism is impaired by pharmacogenetic poor metabolizer phenotypes or drug-drug interactions with CYP2D6 inhibitors. Finally, normetabolites typically exhibit longer elimination half-lives than their parent drugs and may accumulate with repeated use, exceeding concentrations of the parent drug or other metabolites in urine. Inclusion of normetabolites in a test panel may thus increase the detection of ingested drugs and potentially extend the period of detection of drug use. Many clinical laboratories offering testing in pain management have not yet developed methods for some of the opioid normetabolites, particularly norhydrocodone and noroxycodone.

Abuse of carisoprodol has increased over the last decade, necessitating its reclassification as a Schedule IV controlled substance in January 2012. Due to its abuse and common use as a muscle relaxant in pain management, it should be included in pain management profiles. Practitioners may test for nicotine (as cotinine) or alcohol use because addiction to these substances may increase the risk of developing other substance abuse disorders. In addition, alcohol can interact with opioids, particularly some extended-release formulations, exacerbating CNS depression. Provider attitudes regarding alcohol use vary: some require their patients to abstain, while

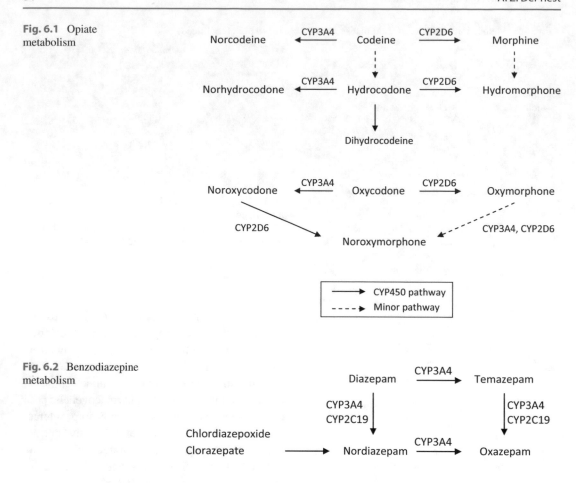

Fig. 6.1 Opiate metabolism

Fig. 6.2 Benzodiazepine metabolism

others are less concerned with occasional alcohol intake as long as a patient has been stable on chronic opioid therapy for some time. Testing for ethanol or its metabolites ethyl glucuronide (EtG) or ethyl sulfate (EtS) are primarily useful for providers who wish to ensure complete abstinence, rather than for providers who simply wish to assess whether use represents abuse/binge drinking or occasional ingestion.

Some practitioners argue against testing for marijuana and may exclude this drug from their testing profile. Studies have indicated correlation of marijuana use with misuse of opioids or other illicit drugs, and it remains to be seen if exclusion of marijuana from patient assessment increases physician liability from a legal or medical board perspective. Designer drugs, particularly synthetic cannabinoids (marketed as Spice/K2), have emerged as a significant risk in pain management

and tests for these compounds are increasingly requested. Some practices may elect to also test for antidepressants (TCAs, SNRIs, or SSRIs), methylphenidate, or anabolic steroids, although test requests for these drugs are less common. Phencyclidine is rarely tested in confirmation testing given its low prevalence.

Drug Concentrations and Testing Thresholds

Urinary concentrations of drugs in pain management occur over a dynamic range. Clinical use of drugs, particularly those administered on a PRN basis, may result in low urine concentrations. In contrast, chronic use can result in drug or metabolite accumulation and impressively high concentrations. Thus, testing methodology should be engineered to measure both very high and very low concentrations, which can be challenging for a laboratory.

Thresholds used in clinical practice must be lower than those established for workplace drug testing, or false negatives may result. This is particularly true for benzodiazepines and opiates, which are often tested to a laboratory 50 or 100 ng/mL threshold in urine. An opiate testing threshold of 2000 ng/mL is not recommended in clinical practice. Variations in laboratory-reported testing thresholds in pain management exist. Some clinicians advocate "zero-threshold" testing at low concentrations; however, this approach may complicate result interpretation. Recently, laboratories have reported increased detection of low concentrations of unexpected opiates, presumably originating from minor metabolism pathways or pharmaceutical impurities. Practitioners are often unaware of these opportunities for detection of incidental exposure, and threshold selection should consider these factors.

Specimen Collection

There are no collection or chain-of-custody requirements governing specimen collection in clinical practice, and medical personnel are not always adequately trained in proper collection procedures. Furthermore, offices may not have staff available to devote to managing a drug testing program. A laboratory may elect to place collection technicians in clinics to facilitate proper collection procedures and reduce the risk for error.

Safeguards should be instituted by clinics to prevent sample mix-up at the point of collection (e.g., patient signatures required on the requisition form and/or specimen cup label). The ordering practitioner must either sign the test request form or have a signature on file at the reference laboratory, as the requisition form is treated as a physician's order. Personnel performing specimen collections should be reminded to use a cup with a temperature strip and observe the visual characteristics of urine after the patient provides the specimen. The addition of bluing agent to toi-

lets is not a standardized practice and water is not typically turned off in pain clinics, thereby increasing the risk that a patient may adulterate a specimen by adding water. Laboratory measurements of creatinine and specific gravity are imperative to identify possible occurrences of substitution. As in nonclinical drug testing programs, adulteration attempts may be made to obscure the presence of illicit or nonprescribed licit drugs. However, there is additional risk inherent in pain management testing programs, as patients may adulterate specimens with prescription medications to appear compliant with prescribed treatment. Patients may crush a pill or tablet for addition directly to the urine specimen postcollection. Such attempts may result in obvious sediment in a urine specimen, the detection of parent drugs in the absence of metabolites in urine, and/or extremely high concentrations of parent drug. If adulteration or tampering is suspected, or if the patient has a history of a prior adulteration attempt, an observed collection may be warranted. Some practitioners are uncomfortable with the prospect of observing urine collections and may elect to obtain an alternative specimen type such as blood or oral fluid.

If a clinical practice decides to order oral fluid testing, collection practices should be thoroughly explained as they may affect the validity of results. Dry mouth, or xerostomia, is a side effect of chronic opioid therapy and drugs such as tricyclic antidepressants, tobacco, cannabis, amphetamines, antipsychotics, and antihistamines. If a patient cannot provide an adequate specimen, an alternative specimen type should be considered. Collection devices which contain buffer solution should include a volume adequacy indicator to ensure complete collection; testing of a specimen comprised mostly or entirely of buffer solution will fail to detect drug use. Stimulation of saliva production with gum or candy may increase salivary flow and affect oral fluid pH, thereby reducing drug levels in oral fluid. Medical personnel should be advised to ensure the patients' mouth is clear before providing a specimen.

Specimens collected in pain practices are usually shipped to a laboratory, either by courier or overnight shipping. Clinics that house their own on-site immunoassay screening in a physician's office laboratory (POL) may test the specimen initially before sending out for confirmation testing, thus delaying shipping to the reference laboratory. Clinics in a network may have one central location where a benchtop immunochemistry analyzer is housed; for these practices, specimens are first sent to the physician's office laboratory before being routed to the reference laboratory. Although refrigeration is recommended, in practice, specimens are sometimes left to sit on the counter for several days before shipping. Noting the date of specimen collection and receipt at the reference laboratory is critical in evaluation of potential impact of drug stability and possible degradation on analytical results, particularly for unstable analytes such as 7-aminoclonazepam or 6-monoacetylmorphine. When confronted with an adamant patient denial of drug use, practitioners may request retesting of specimens. Storage times at the laboratory should be discussed with providers, but typically these do not exceed 30 d.

Methodology

There are several similarities between testing in pain management and forensic settings, in that a large number of analytes are included. However, there are important differences as well. There are no specific requirements governing the methods used for drug testing in the clinical setting. Several testing methodologies are used in pain management, with the most common being immunoassay screening and mass spectrometry-based confirmation. However, immunoassay testing poses a challenge for the detection of some prescription drugs and their metabolites. In recent years, laboratories providing drug testing in pain management have increasingly departed from immunoassay technology in favor of testing specimens directly by gas chromatography/mass spectrometry (GC/MS) or liquid chromatography/tandem mass spectrometry (LC/MS/MS). Further driving this paradigm shift is the increasing practice of point-of-care testing in pain management clinics, wherein immunoassay screening is performed in the POL.

Testing programs may be set up as follows:

- Immunoassay screening only
- Immunoassay screening with mass spectrometry confirmation of nonnegative or unexpected results
- Immunoassay screening with mass spectrometry testing for an expanded profile of drugs and metabolites
- Mass spectrometry testing only for an expanded profile of drugs and metabolites

Testing programs that rely on immunoassay technology may exhibit an increased risk of false negatives due to reduced identification of specimens that contain only drugs or metabolites that are poorly cross-reactive (e.g., 7-aminoclonazepam, or normetabolites such as norhydrocodone, noroxycodone, or norfentanyl). Because normetabolites are frequently present in the absence of other drug markers (with a prevalence of 2–50%, depending on the opioid), the impaired detection of commonly prescribed drugs may affect the decision to rely on immunoassay as a screening technique. Because immunoassay tests yield qualitative results for a drug class, they may be marginally useful when assessing compliance of a specific prescribed drug. Furthermore, the likelihood that some drug classes such as opioids will be positive in pain management patients may reduce the cost-effectiveness of performing immunoassay as an initial screening step. Testing directly by mass spectrometry methods such as gas chromatography/mass spectrometry (GC/MS) or liquid chromatography/tandem mass spectrometry (LC/MS/MS) allows the inclusion of multiple drugs and metabolites that may not be efficiently tested by immunoassay.

The sensitivity of LC/MS/MS and ability to test small specimen volumes has made this technology a mainstay of oral fluid testing. Drug concentrations in oral fluid are 10- to 100-fold lower than urine, and testing this matrix necessitates very low testing thresholds. For example, testing thresholds for opiates such as hydrocodone and oxycodone may be 1 ng/mL, whereas carboxy-THC may be detected in the pg/mL range.

Quality of testing may vary depending on the laboratory. Most laboratories specializing in pain management are more sophisticated than POLs or hospital laboratories. There are no accreditations or certifications designed for pain management specifically, but accreditation through other agencies such as the Substance Abuse and Mental Health Services Administration (SAMHSA), the ANSI National Accreditation Board (ANAB), or the College of American Pathologists (CAP) may be evaluated as evidence of competence. Many laboratories rely exclusively on LC/MS/MS technology, with some testing all drugs in the profile in one LC/MS/MS analysis. This approach can facilitate a rapid turnaround time sometimes requested by practitioners, although such methods may introduce quality concerns.

Other testing methodologies are occasionally used in pain management, including (but not limited to) time-of-flight mass spectrometry (TOFMS) and laser diode thermal desorption/tandem mass spectrometry (LDTD/MS/MS). These methods may provide improved screening techniques over immunoassay. The landscape of instrumentation used for drug testing in the clinical setting is continually evolving.

Point-of-Care Testing (POCT)

Increasingly, practitioners are relying on point-of-care testing to provide an immediate result. A wide variety of profiles and immunoassay tests are employed in pain management clinics, including cups, dipcards, and instrumented testing with small benchtop analyzers. POCT programs vary in their effectiveness and inclusion of drugs and metabolites; many omit common drugs such as fentanyl, carisoprodol, and even oxycodone. There are varying recommendations regarding the decision to send testing to a laboratory for confirmation. Some practitioners will send only nonnegative or unexpected immunoassay results; however, following this recommendation increases the risk of false negatives due to an incomplete assessment of prescription medication use. Testing for an expanded class of prescription drugs and metabolites at a laboratory is

warranted and some authors have recommended this step on at least an annual or biannual basis. In addition, identification of illicit drugs such as marijuana and cocaine may be increased at a laboratory using lower thresholds than those employed in POCT programs. The opportunity for false positives and false negatives with POCT is frequently underestimated by practitioners. Most recommendations in pain management advise delaying changes to patient care until a result has been confirmed using a more specific method such as GC/MS or LC/MS/MS.

Clinic personnel involved in POCT programs should be trained in quality control measures and test interpretation. Laboratories which provide POCT devices to pain management practices may assist with these endeavors. Few practices have attempted POCT with GC/MS or LC/MS/MS as the expertise needed for method development, quality measures, and result interpretation is challenging, and most clinics do not have experienced or qualified personnel in this specialty. POCT at this time is generally limited to urine testing, since oral fluid devices have not achieved the desired level of sensitivity to monitor compliance with prescription medications.

Interpretation

Practitioners may struggle with how to manage patients with unexpected toxicology results. Frank discussions with the patient and/or laboratory experts are encouraged. Unexpected positive findings will indicate the need for patient evaluation. Nonnegative immunoassay test results should be confirmed by a more specific method such as mass spectrometry. Confirmed positive results should be evaluated for the medication source, keeping in mind metabolism pathways (e.g., hydrocodone metabolism to hydromorphone). Additionally, pharmaceutical impurities pose a risk for unexpected opiate positives in patients taking chronic opioid therapy or high dosages of medications. The most commonly observed impurities are codeine in morphine formulations and hydrocodone in oxycodone formulations (typically present at relatively low concentrations of 0.5 to 1% or less). The risk of detecting impurity drugs in urine or oral fluid is increased when low thresholds are used. The opportunity for pharmaceutical impurities to cause positive test results was only recently appreciated and can be a major confounding factor for test interpretation.

Unexpected negative test results can be as equally concerning as unexpected positives, as providers are tasked with determining the reason for noncompliance. Although diversion may be suspected, it is not always the reason for a negative finding; there are many clinical explanations for why a patient can test negative for prescribed drugs. A patient may have refrained from taking the drug due to concerns about side effects or fear of becoming addicted. Alternatively, if the medication is taken on a PRN basis, a patient may not have required a dose for some time prior to the test. Some patients may hoard medications for fear of running out, while others may self-escalate dosing and run out early. In rare cases, patients who have undergone gastrointestinal surgery may not absorb the medication (although under these circumstances, they are also unlikely to experience analgesia). Patients with kidney failure may test negative for some drugs in blood or oral fluid if the specimen is collected following dialysis. Medications delivered via intrathecal routes may not always be detectable in urine at routine thresholds and are extremely unlikely to be detected in blood or oral fluid.

In addition to ruling out clinical factors, testing methodology should also be considered. Inclusion of the drug in question should be checked against the ordered test profile. For example, some practitioners are unaware that fentanyl is not included in testing for opiates. If the test was performed using immunoassay, cross-reactivity to the drug or its metabolite should be evaluated. Cases of patients being fired from their pain management center for negative findings for prescribed oxycodone have been reported; the providers later discovered that oxycodone did not sufficiently cross-react to the opiate test they had ordered.

Pain management practitioners may be prone to overinterpretation of quantitative results. A common source of confusion is that urine drug concentrations do not correlate to medication dosage. Consequently, a provider cannot distinguish between a patient who is taking a dosage as prescribed or tripling their medication intake. Likewise, urine drug testing will not reveal if a patient is diverting some—but not all—of their prescription. Some laboratories may alert the prescriber if a measured drug concentration is a statistical outlier for all concentrations reported for that drug. Although these findings are not definitive indications of drug misuse, they may serve as a warning for providers to carefully assess the patient for signs of aberrancy.

Practitioners should be advised that the period of detection for each drug is a rough estimate and may be greatly impacted by medication dosing or individual differences in metabolism. Urine boasts the longest period of detection, while detection times in oral fluid and blood are relatively short. Oral fluid results may be negative for PRN drugs if these are not administered routinely; most drugs are detectable in oral fluid for a period up to 24 to 48 h.

Some practitioners have adopted blood testing in an effort to establish therapeutic drug monitoring. However, therapeutic ranges for opioids and benzodiazepines in blood or plasma have not been established and are not clinically meaningful given the impact of drug tolerance; likewise, pharmacokinetic changes and drug-drug interactions may affect blood concentrations as well. Although limited information has been published on therapeutic drug monitoring for methadone (mostly for the treatment of opioid dependence), pharmacokinetic monitoring has not been proven to be effective for monitoring dosage compliance with opioids or benzodiazepines in pain management.

Laboratory Reporting and Relationship with the Practice

Studies have repeatedly demonstrated that practitioners treating patients with chronic pain have limited understanding of drug testing methodology or results. If used indiscriminately, drug testing may harm the doctor-patient relationship, and laboratories may spend significant resources in providing guidance in result interpretation. Toxicology reports should be streamlined and easy to read and interpret. Prescription drugs may be noted on the requisition form so that reports may report compliant or noncompliant results accordingly. Laboratories are increasingly integrating reports into electronic medical record (EMR) systems used by the practice, which reduces the time spent by clinic personnel filing documentation. Additionally, laboratories providing testing in pain management must provide available consultation with qualified experts (e.g., toxicologists with clinical experience or clinical pharmacy specialists). Requests for consultation usually occur during a patient's office visit, and responses must therefore be given in a time-sensitive manner.

In patients dismissed from clinical practice, it can be extremely difficult—if not impossible—to find another clinic to reinstate care. Drug testing programs must be carefully designed to reduce the opportunity for error, with proper consideration given to the risk of false positives and false negatives.

Further Reading

Baselt RC (2020) Disposition of toxic drugs and chemicals in man, 12th edn. Biomedical Publications, Seal Beach, CA

Cone EJ, Caplan YH (2009) Urine toxicology testing in chronic pain management. Postgrad Med 121(4):91–102

Cone EJ, Huestis MA (2007) Interpretation of oral fluid tests for drugs of abuse. Ann N Y Acad Sci 1098:51–103

Gourlay DL, Heit HA, Almahrezi A (2005) Universal precautions in pain medicine: a rational approach to the treatment of chronic pain. Pain Med 6:107–112

Gourlay DL, Heit HA, Caplan YH (2012) Urine drug testing in clinical practice: the art and science of patient care, 5th edn. PharmaGroup, Stanford, pp 1–20

Heltsley R, DePriest A, Black DL et al (2011) Oral fluid drug testing of chronic pain patients. I. Positive prevalence rates of licit and illicit drugs. J Anal Toxicol 35:529–540

IOM (Institute of Medicine) (2011) Relieving pain in America: a blueprint for transforming prevention, care, education and research. The National Academies Press, Washington

Michna E, Jamison RN, Pham LD et al (2007) Urine toxicology screening among chronic pain patients on opioid therapy: frequency and predictability of abnormal findings. Clin J Pain 23(2):173–179

Moeller KE, Lee KC, Kissack JC (2008) Urine drug screening: practical guide for clinicians. Mayo Clin Proc 83(1):66–76

Nafziger AN, Bertino JS (2009) Utility and application of urine drug testing in chronic pain management with opioids. Clin J Pain 25(1):73–79

Owen GT, Burton AW, Schade CM, Passik S (2012) Urine drug testing: current recommendations and best practices. Pain Physician 15:ES119–ES133

Peppin JF, Passik SD, Cuoto JE et al (2012) Recommendations for urine drug monitoring as a component of opioid therapy in the treatment of chronic pain. Pain Med 13:886–896

Reisfield GM, Goldberger BA, Bertholf RL (2009) 'False-positive' and 'false-negative' test results in clinical urine drug testing. Bioanalysis 1(5):937–952

Starrels JL, Fox AD, Kunins HV et al (2012) They don't know what they don't know: internal medicine residents' knowledge and confidence in urine drug test interpretation for patients with chronic pain. J Gen Intern Med 27(11):1521–1527

Pharmacokinetics

7

Vina Spiehler and Barry S. Levine

Abstract

Pharmacokinetics, derived from the Greek words *"pharmakon"* (drug) and *"kinesis"* (movement), is the study of the time course of drugs in a biological system. This chapter discusses the major aspects of pharmacokinetics as it applies to drugs in humans. Absorption is the process of drugs entering the bloodstream. This may occur by diffusion, facilitated diffusion, or active transport. There are multiple routes of drug administration including oral, inhaled, intravenous, intramuscular, rectal, oral mucosal, intrathecal, dermal, ocular, and intranasal. Once in the bloodstream, drugs are distributed throughout the body. Distribution is dependent on plasma protein binding, tissue perfusion, and pH characteristics. Elimination of drugs occurs either through metabolism or excretion. Metabolism is the process of changing the chemical structure of the drug to better enable removal from the body. Metabolism may be Phase I where changes in functional groups on the drug are made, or Phase II where a drug or Phase I metabolite is conjugated with an endogenous substance. Excretion is the final removal of the drugs and/or metabolic products from the body, either into the bile, urine, or other means. Mathematical models that describe the pharmacokinetics of drugs are also included.

Keywords

Pharmacokinetics · Toxicology · Drugs of abuse

Introduction

Pharmacokinetics is defined as the study of the time course of drugs in the body. Pharmacokinetic studies investigate and characterize drug bioavailability, i.e., the amount of drug absorbed relative to the amount administered, by:

- Different routes of administration
- The rates of absorption and elimination
- The time to peak concentrations
- The relationship between dose and blood and tissue concentrations
- The rates of metabolism or biotransformation and clearance

This chapter will discuss the basic aspects of absorption, distribution, excretion, metabolism, and compartment modeling in pharmacokinetics.

V. Spiehler
Spiehler & Associates, Newport Beach, CA, USA

B. S. Levine (✉)
Office of the Chief Medical Examiner,
Baltimore, MD, USA
e-mail: blevine@som.umaryland.edu

© Springer Nature Switzerland AG 2020
B. S. Levine, S. Kerrigan (eds.), *Principles of Forensic Toxicology*,
https://doi.org/10.1007/978-3-030-42917-1_7

Absorption

Absorption is the process whereby xenobiotics enter the bloodstream. There are several mechanisms by which entry into the bloodstream can occur. The simplest mechanism is passive diffusion, the movement of a substance from an area of high concentration to an area of low concentration. Initially, at the site of absorption, there will be no xenobiotic present in the blood proximal to that site. A drug will diffuse from the site into the blood. Diffusion may also occur with the assistance of membrane proteins along a concentration gradient; this process is called facilitated diffusion.

A component common to passive and facilitated diffusion is the absence of an energy requirement. This is contrasted by active transport processes, which do require energy, act against a concentration gradient, and use carrier proteins or receptors to diffuse drug into the bloodstream. Because the concentration of these carrier proteins or receptors is finite, active transport processes can be saturable.

Drugs can enter the bloodstream through a wide variety of routes:

- *Oral.* This is one of the most common routes for drug absorption and refers to absorption through the gastrointestinal (GI) tract, i.e., the stomach and the small intestine.
- *Inhalation.* Drugs with sufficient volatility (solvents, anesthetic gases, and alkaloids with low boiling points such as nicotine) can be absorbed through the lungs.
- *Intravenous.* This is the most efficient route of administration, because the entire administered drug is placed directly into the bloodstream.
- *Intramuscular.* This is also a common route of parenteral administration of drugs, but unlike intravenous injection, it will display variable absorption.
- *Rectal.* Individuals unable to take drugs orally may be given a suppository for rectal absorption.
- *Oral mucosa.* Drugs taken by mouth that require very rapid entry into the blood may be taken sublingually. One classic example of this is the sublingual administration of nitroglycerin in patients suffering from angina pectoris.
- *Intrathecal.* Drugs requiring rapid central nervous system onset can be administered directly into the spinal fluid, thus bypassing the blood–brain barrier, a layer of cells meant to retard or prevent the entry of foreign substances into the brain.
- *Dermal.* Drugs can be absorbed through the skin. Nicotine, fentanyl, and scopolamine have been administered in this way.
- *Ocular.* Drugs used to treat eye infections or diseases may be delivered directly into the eye, usually in the form of drops.
- *Intranasal.* Drugs that are not gaseous or volatile can also be administered by insufflation. Unlike inhalation whereby drug is absorbed principally via the lungs, the substance is locally applied to the mucous membranes of the nose (e.g., via "snorting").

Unless the drug is administered intravenously, it is unlikely that all of the administered drug will be absorbed. The amount of drug absorbed relative to the amount administered, i.e., its bioavailability, can be affected by multiple factors such as the following:

- *Solubility.* In order for drugs to enter the blood, they must be in solution. For instance, a tablet, upon entry into the stomach, will disintegrate first into granules and then into particles. The rate of this disintegration will affect bioavailability. The formulation of the drug will also play a major role in the rate of this dissolution. A coated or sustained-release formulation will be absorbed more slowly than tablets or capsules. Drugs already in an aqueous medium will be more rapidly absorbed than drugs in an oily medium or in solid form. In general, salts are more water-soluble than free acids or free bases.
- *Concentration.* Because absorption frequently occurs by diffusion, the greater the concentration gradient, the faster the drug absorption rate. This means that a concentrated

formulation will be absorbed more rapidly than a diluted formulation.

- *Surface area.* The main function of the small intestine is the absorption of substances taken orally. The small intestine is made up of microvilli, which are designed to provide a large surface area to facilitate absorption. The stomach also has a large surface area, and some drugs are absorbed from the stomach.
- *Blood supply.* Increased blood flow can enhance absorption of a drug. Conversely, if an individual is in shock, then absorption is retarded.
- *pH.* Entry of drugs into the blood involves passage into membranes. Lipophilic drugs cross these membranes more easily than do hydrophilic drugs. Drugs that exist in an unionized form will be more lipophilic in the medium than drugs that exist in the ionized form. For example, suppose an acidic drug is present in the stomach, which has a pH between 1 and 3.5. This acidic drug will exist in the stomach predominantly in a nonionized (unionized) form, the degree to which this drug is in the nonionized form is a function of the drug's pK_a and can be calculated using the Henderson–Hasselbalch equation (Fig. 7.1). As this acidic drug leaves the stomach and enters the small intestine, the pH of the medium changes significantly. The pH of the upper portion of the small intestine, the duodenum, is 5–6 and increases to 8 at the lower part of the small intestine, the ileum. This means that as an acidic drug traverses the length of the small intestine, the amount of

Acid drugs:

$$pH = pK_a + \log \frac{[\text{ionized}]}{[\text{un-ionized}]}$$

Basic drugs:

$$pH = pK_a + \log \frac{[\text{un-ionized}]}{[\text{ionized}]}$$

Fig. 7.1 Henderson–Hasselbalch equations for acidic and basic drugs

drug that will be in the nonionized form will decrease. The opposite reasoning can be applied if the drug is a basic drug. In the stomach, most of the drug will be ionized, thus reducing the amount absorbed. The Henderson–Hasselbalch equation can also be used for basic drugs (Fig. 7.1). A basic drug will become increasingly nonionized as it enters the small intestine.

Because different production processes can lead to different formulations of the same active drug, the concept of bioequivalence has been developed to compare products from different manufacturers or, occasionally, lot-to-lot differences from the same manufacturer. Different formulations are said to be "biologically equivalent" if they yield similar concentrations of active drug in blood or tissues. Formulations are "therapeutically equivalent" if similar therapeutic efficacies are obtained.

Distribution

Distribution refers to the transfer of a substance from one part of the body to another part. In pharmacokinetic terms, distribution usually refers to movement from the blood into the tissues. This movement is a function of the amount of drug presented to the tissues. Highly perfused tissues such as the heart, liver, kidney, and brain initially receive the bulk of the absorbed drug, usually within minutes. Less perfused tissues, such as muscle and fat, take longer to achieve equilibrium with the blood.

Some of the factors that affect drug absorption will also affect the distribution of drugs. The more lipid-soluble the drug, the more easily the drug will move into the tissues. A sample illustration of this point would be to compare the entry into the brain of two barbiturates, thiopental and pentobarbital. The only structural difference between the two drugs is a C=S for thiopental versus C=O for pentobarbital on the barbiturate ring structure. This seemingly slight difference drastically changes the lipophilicity of the two drugs. Because thiopental is much more lipid-soluble than pentobarbital, it distributes more rapidly into the brain than does pentobarbital. This rapid onset of action explains why thiopental is used as an anesthetic agent while pentobarbital is used as a sedative hypnotic drug.

Closely related to the lipophilicity factor is the pH effect. The Henderson–Hasselbalch equation can be used to indicate the conditions under which a particular acid or basic drug will be unionized and to what degree. It is the unionized form of the drug that crosses membranes and enters tissues.

Plasma protein binding also influences the movement of drugs from blood to tissues. Albumin is the major binding protein and is present in the plasma at an approximate concentration of 40 g/L. Albumin binds preferentially to acidic drugs but may bind weakly to basic drugs. Alpha-1 acid glycoprotein is another significant plasma protein, binding preferentially to weak bases. Its plasma concentration fluctuates but is about 0.7 g/L. In addition to these major proteins, lipoproteins and globulins are available to bind drugs. Regardless of the binding protein, the extent to which a given drug binds to a plasma protein is variable. For example, warfarin, an anticoagulant, is approximately 99% protein-bound; digoxin, a cardiac glycoside used to treat congestive heart failure, is approximately 25% protein-bound.

Plasma protein binding limits drug distribution in that only unbound or free drug is able to leave the blood and enter the tissues. In turn, only free drug can interact with receptors to produce pharmacologic effects. On the other hand, drug bound to protein is restricted to the blood, because the drug–protein complex is too large to leave the capillaries. Because bound drug cannot reach the tissues, it cannot produce pharmacologic actions at the intended site. Drugs that are highly protein-bound will have a delayed onset of action and an extended duration of action relative to drugs that are not highly protein-bound.

Potential drug interactions may occur if multiple highly bound drugs are administered simultaneously. If the protein binding of a drug is reduced, then more is in the free form and is available to enter tissues. This can lead to an unexpected increase in pharmacologic activity or toxicity.

Drugs can distribute into body fluids to varying degrees. The average 70-kg male has 42 L of total body water, divided into intracellular and extracellular fluid. Intracellular fluid makes up approximately 27 of the 42 L. The remaining 15 L exists outside the cell and consists of plasma, the fluid component of blood (3 L), interstitial fluid, cerebrospinal fluid, GI fluids, and fluids of the potential spaces.

Drugs may distribute into any or all of the total body water. This has led to the concept of apparent volume of distribution (V_d), which represents the amount of fluid in which a drug dose would appear to have been distributed if the total dose had remained in the blood. The V_d is not a physiological volume, rather it is a proportionality constant that relates the mass of the drug (X) to its concentration (C) at a particular time:

$$V_d = \frac{X}{C} \qquad (7.1)$$

In order to calculate the apparent volume of distribution, the concentration of drug must be measured over time. Although it is possible to use the drug concentration at any time along with the associated quantity of drug, it is commonplace to use the initial concentration (C_0) and drug dose. A semilogarithmic plot of concentration versus time allows C_0 to be estimated by extrapolation to time zero. The V_d may be reported in units of volume (L), or volume per body weight (L/kg).

The volume of distribution is a function of the drug's lipophilicity, pK_a, and binding to plasma protein, tissues, etc. Drugs that are hydrophilic, such as alcohol, and that distribute mainly to body water or are strongly bound to plasma proteins such as salicylic acid or acetaminophen have a $V_d < 1$. Most psychoactive abused drugs are lipophilic, distribute into fatty tissue such as the brain, and have a $V_d > 1$. For example, the V_d of phencyclidine is 5.5–7.5 L/kg. Because V_d is a theoretical value, it is possible that the V_d is much greater than the total body water. This could suggest sequestration of a drug at a particular tissue site. For example, tricyclic antidepressants have very high apparent volumes of distribution because they are sequestered mainly in the liver.

The volume of distribution for a given drug can change as a function of the person's age, gender, disease, and body composition. The population average V_d for alcohol is 0.70 (range 0.62–0.79) for males and 0.60 (range 0.46–0.86) for females. The V_d of alcohol decreases with increasing age and is 10–15% lower in persons more than 60 years of age.

Although the brain is a highly perfused tissue, it has unique features that limit entry of xenobiotics. These serve as a protective mechanism for the brain. Endothelial cells of the brain capillary restrict aqueous bulk flow relative to endothelial cells in other tissues. There is also a layer of glial cells, which retards the diffusion of organic acids and bases in the brain.

Metabolism

Metabolism is the process by which the structure of a xenobiotic is altered to facilitate the removal of the foreign substance from the body. These changes occur with the assistance of enzymes or biological catalysts. Enzymatic activity occurs primarily but not exclusively in the liver. Other sites of enzyme action include the kidney, lung, GI tract, and blood. Groups of enzymes have been identified and characterized. Metabolic activity is divided into two general phases: Phase I and Phase II metabolism.

Phase I Metabolism

Phase I reactions are characterized by enzymatic transformation of functional groups (see Table 7.1). The most widely studied group of Phase I enzymes is the cytochrome P450 monooxygenases. Studies have indicated that cytochrome P450 (CYP) exists in many different forms, called isozymes, which have different physical and chemical properties as well as different affinities for different drugs. These enzymes are embedded in the lipid bilayer of the smooth endoplasmic reticulum.

In humans, there are approximately 18 families and 44 subfamilies of CYP enzymes.

Table 7.1 Examples of Phase I metabolism

Reaction	Example
N-Dealkylation	Amitriptyline
O-Dealkylation	Codeine
Desulfuration	Parathion
Sulfoxide formation	Cimetidine
Ester hydrolysis	Cocaine
Amide hydrolysis	Lidocaine
Deacetylation	Heroin
Aliphatic hydroxylation	Pentobarbital
Aromatic hydroxylation	Propranolol
Deamination	Chlordiazepoxide
Nitro reduction	Flunitrazepam
N-Oxide formation	Atropine
Epoxide formation	Carbamazepine
Reduction	Chloral hydrate

However, there are only about a dozen enzymes responsible for the metabolism of drugs. The isozyme that metabolizes the most drugs is CYP 3A4. Using CYP3A4 as an example, the nomenclature used to name these different CYP enzymes is the following: "3" represents the family, "A" represents the subfamily, and "4" represents the individual enzyme. Most hepatically cleared drugs involve the CYP enzymes from families 1, 2, or 3. CYP 3A4/5, CYP2D6, CYP2C9, CYP2C19, and CYP1A2 account for the vast majority of oxidative drug transformations.

These enzymes also have a common mode of activity. The xenobiotic to be metabolized initially binds to the ferric ion component of the CYP. This complex reduces the iron to the +2 valence state (ferrous ion). The reduced complex then binds molecular oxygen. As the oxygen is reduced, the xenobiotic is oxygenated. At this stage, NADPH is utilized. The final step is the release of the oxygenated product with regeneration of the enzyme. The net result of the process is the formation of water and $NADP^+$, the expenditure of NADPH and molecular oxygen, and the production of an oxidized xenobiotic.

A large number of CYP enzymes are selectively induced by drugs and environmental chemicals, including phenobarbital, antipyrine, rifampicin, polychlorinated biphenyls, polybrominated biphenyls, and aromatic hydrocarbons. Enzyme induction requires an increase in the number of enzyme-binding sites, which in turn require protein synthesis. Therefore, several weeks are required before significant enzyme induction is observed. These enzymes can also be selectively inhibited by a variety of drugs; examples of some P450 isozyme inhibitors include cimetidine, fluoxetine, diltiazem, and verapamil. Enzyme inhibition usually results from a competition for the active site between the drug and the inhibitor. As a result, inhibition of metabolism occurs concurrently with administration of the drug and the potential inhibitor.

The significance of CYP induction and inhibition in pharmacotherapy cannot be underestimated. Many of the compounds that have been shown either to induce or to inhibit components of the P450 system are drugs routinely prescribed for a variety of medical conditions. These drugs can profoundly influence the metabolism of other therapeutically administered drugs. These drug interactions may produce an increase in metabolism of a particular drug, leading to reduced therapeutic efficacy. Conversely, a decrease in metabolism can cause an increased amount of drug in the blood and tissues, producing unexpected toxic effects.

There are significant individual differences in the metabolism of drugs, especially the CYP enzymes. Differences in enzyme activity accounts for much of these differences. These differences can in turn be traced back to an individual's genetics. An entire field of study, pharmacogenomics has developed as a result of these genetic variants (polymorphisms). Pharmacogenomics will be discussed in a later chapter.

The body contains other oxidases in addition to the CYP monooxygenases. Monoamine oxidase, for example, is a mitochondrial enzyme that metabolizes catecholamines and tyramine. A series of flavin-containing monooxygenases, which have some similarities to the P450 system, is also present in the body. These flavin-containing monooxygenases are microsomal enzymes that use NADPH and molecular oxygen to oxidize nucleophilic nitrogen, sulfur, or phosphorus atoms.

Hydrolytic enzymes are another significant group of enzymes involved in Phase I metabolism. Cholinesterase, which takes two forms in humans,

is one such enzyme. Acetylcholinesterase, also known as true or red blood cell cholinesterase, is found in erythrocytes, lung, spleen, nerve endings, and the brain's gray matter. Acetylcholinesterase hydrolyzes acetylcholine and acetylbetamethylcholine. Pseudocholinesterase, produced in the liver but also located in the plasma, heart, pancreas, and the brain's white matter, lacks the substrate specificity of acetylcholinesterase. Pseudocholinesterase hydrolyzes acetylcholine, butyrylcholine, and benzoylcholine. Acetylcholinesterase hydrolyzes acetylcholine in the synapse; the role of pseudocholinesterase remains unclear.

Phase I metabolism is generally viewed as a detoxification process. However, this is not necessarily the case. For example, parathion, an organophosphate pesticide, is converted to paraoxon, which is the active cholinesterase inhibitor. Moreover, some drug formulations serve as "prodrugs," compounds that become activated upon entry into the body. For instance, prazepam is a benzodiazepine prescribed as a sedative, but the sedative activity is due to its conversion to nordiazepam.

Phase II Metabolism

Phase II metabolism, or conjugation reactions, involves the derivatization of a drug or Phase I metabolite with an endogenous substance. The main purpose of these reactions is to increase the water solubility of these compounds to facilitate elimination.

The most common conjugation reaction uses uridine diphosphate-glucuronic acid and reacts with hydroxyl, carboxylic acid, or amino groups to form conjugates of glucuronic acid. These reactions are catalyzed by a group of microsomal enzymes referred to as glucuronyltransferases. In general, glucuronide conjugates are inactive. One notable exception is morphine-6-glucuronide, which has a much greater analgesic potency than does morphine.

Other conjugation reactions are listed in Table 7.2. Drugs and metabolites may be conjugated with more than one substance. Both glucuronide and sulfate conjugates of morphine

Table 7.2 Examples of Phase II metabolism

Reaction	Example
Glucuronidation	Oxazepam
Sulfate formation	Morphine
Glutathione conjugation	Acetaminophen
Glycine conjugation	Salicylate
Acetylation	Procainamide
Methylation	Theophylline (neonates)

have been identified. The conjugation reaction involving acetaminophen and glutathione has been extensively studied. Acetaminophen is converted in the liver into an epoxide which is detoxified by conjugation with glutathione to form a mercapturic acid derivative. However, if too much acetaminophen is presented to the liver, as might occur in an overdose, an insufficient amount of glutathione is available for epoxide detoxification. This reactive intermediate then binds to macromolecular components in liver tissue, ultimately leading to liver necrosis and death.

Phase II metabolism is usually but not always preceded by Phase I metabolism. The structure of the xenobiotic ultimately determines whether Phase I metabolism is needed. The benzodiazepine drug diazepam is demethylated to nordiazepam, which is then hydroxylated to oxazepam (these being the Phase I reactions). Oxazepam is then conjugated with glucuronic acid. Oxazepam can also be prescribed therapeutically; when taken directly, the drug is rapidly cleared by conjugation without Phase I metabolism.

First-Pass Effect

One phenomenon that may occur when drugs are administered orally is known as the first-pass effect. Enzymes in the GI tract can metabolize drugs before they enter the bloodstream. Once absorbed from the small intestine, the drug enters the portal circulation and is transported to the liver. In the liver, metabolism may occur prior to entry into the heart and the general circulation. Drugs with a significant first-pass effect may require administration by routes other than the oral route.

Excretion

Excretion is the final removal of xenobiotics or their by-products from the body. Excretion can occur in a variety of ways. The most common routes are via the kidney and the liver, and these routes will be discussed in greater detail. Volatile substances can be eliminated through the lungs. Thus, drivers can be tested for ethanol without the invasive procedure of blood collection. Drugs can also be eliminated into breast milk and cause a breast-fed infant to be exposed to drugs. Foreign substances can also be excreted into sweat, affording drug detection in this matrix. Drugs can also be cleared into sebum and semen.

Drug elimination is discussed in terms of clearance. Clearance refers to the removal of drug from plasma. It is defined as a volume cleared of a drug per unit time. Clearance does not indicate how much drug is removed, but represents the volume of plasma from which the drug is completely removed. The total body clearance is the sum of the individual organ clearances.

Hepatic Excretion

The liver weighs 1400–1700 g and is the major site of xenobiotic metabolism. The liver receives blood from two sources: the portal vein, supplying about 1100 mL/min, and the hepatic artery, which flows at about 350 mL/min. Blood from the hepatic artery supplies the liver with the nutrients and resources that it needs to perform its functions. The functional unit of the liver is the lobule, which is constructed around a central vein and empties into the hepatic vein and the vena cava. Substances cleared by the liver form the bile that is stored in the gall bladder. The bile enters the intestines, where final elimination occurs in the feces.

One factor affecting the clearance of drugs and metabolites is the blood flow to the liver. Certain physiological, pathological, and pharmacological factors influence this flow. For example, food and a reclining posture can increase hepatic flow, while exercise, an upright posture, and dehydration can reduce blood flow. Disease states such as cirrhosis, hypertension, and congestive heart failure may decrease hepatic blood flow. General anesthetics also decrease blood flow; chronic phenobarbital administration can increase blood flow.

Another factor pertaining to the clearance of drug from the liver is the ability of the liver to remove or extract the drug from the blood. Drugs may enter the liver by diffusion or by carrier systems. Drugs cleared by the liver efficiently, such as opiates and tricyclic antidepressants, have a hepatic elimination rate not limited by processes in the liver but by the rate at which the drug in the blood gets to the liver. Conversely, elimination rates of drugs effectively removed from the blood are limited by the abilities of the liver to process the drug.

It can be difficult to assess the role of hepatic excretion. The measurement of the drug and/or metabolites in feces may indicate poor absorption rather than hepatic excretion. Moreover, drugs or their by-products excreted into the bile enter the intestine; here they can be reabsorbed into the blood. Subsequent elimination by the kidney may occur. This is known as enterohepatic circulation and can account for an increase in the time that it takes to clear a drug from the body.

Renal Excretion

To understand how the kidney clears drugs, it is necessary to understand the kidney's basic structure. The functional unit of the kidney is the nephron, and each kidney has approximately one million of them. The nephron consists of multiple components. The glomerulus is the site where the blood entering the kidney is filtered. The kidneys are perfused by about one-fifth of the total cardiac output of about 6500 mL/min. Of this, about 130 mL is filtered each minute at the glomerulus. In fact, glomerular filtration rate (GFR), which is determined by measuring creatinine clearance, is used clinically to evaluate kidney function. Creatinine is a normal by-product of muscle metabolism and is produced at a constant rate in

an individual with a stable muscle mass. Thus, an elevated serum creatinine suggests a reduced GFR and possible kidney malfunction.

Once the filtered product or ultrafiltrate is produced, it passes into the tubule component of the kidney, comprised of a proximal tubule, the loop of Henle, and the distal tubule. Changes in ultrafiltrate concentration of drugs can occur in this part of the nephron through an active secretion of drugs from the blood or a reabsorption of drugs from the ultrafiltrate into the blood. Much of the water initially filtered is reabsorbed, with the net effect being a concentration of the components in the filtrate. The remaining fluid moves into the collecting tubule, accumulates in the bladder, and is eventually excreted as urine.

The renal excretion of drugs is a function of filtration, secretion, and reabsorption. A drug will be filtered at the glomerulus if its molecular weight is less than 50,000 atomic mass units. This means that molecules such as proteins are not filtered. Therefore, any drug that is bound to plasma proteins will not be filtered. At equilibrium, a drug that is freely filtered will have the same concentration in the ultrafiltrate as appears unbound in the plasma. Drugs that are not highly protein-bound are cleared most rapidly and efficiently by filtration. The amount of free drug appearing in the ultrafiltrate is directly related to the GFR.

Highly plasma protein-bound drugs are cleared by the kidney to a greater extent by secretion, which occurs mainly in the proximal tubule. Specific carrier proteins located in the epithelium of the proximal tubule can separate bound drug from plasma proteins and carry them across the epithelium and into the tubular fluid. Secretion of drugs is an active process and requires energy.

There are separate carrier proteins for acidic and for basic drugs. These carrier proteins are saturable and subject to competition. A reduction in secretion of a particular drug can occur if another drug that is secreted with the assistance of the same carrier protein is coadministered.

Filtration and secretion increase the concentration of drugs in the tubular fluid. Reabsorption of drugs occurs mainly in the proximal and distal tubules and decreases the concentration of drugs in the tubule fluid. Reabsorption may be passive or active and is affected by factors similar to those that affect the absorption of drugs into the blood, such as the drug's lipid solubility and pH characteristics. The normal pH of urine is 4.5–7.5, which is a 1000-fold range in hydrogen ion concentrations. The pK_a of weak acids is 3–7.5, while the pK_a of weak bases is 7.5–10.5. This indicates that certain drugs can have significant differences in renal clearance depending on the pH of the urine. Agents that acidify the urine, such as ammonium chloride, can lower urine pH by 2–3 units, leading to faster elimination of basic drugs. Sodium bicarbonate, which will alkalinize the urine, will lead to faster elimination of acid drugs. This phenomenon is used when treating drug intoxications.

Compartmentalization of Drugs and Elimination Kinetics

A series of mathematical models has been developed to describe the pharmacokinetics of drugs. To minimize the complexity that rapidly develops when describing these pharmacokinetics, assumptions and generalizations are required.

One assumption is the concept of body compartments. Although each tissue or tissue substructure could be viewed individually, the body is generally described as a one-compartment or a two-compartment system. The one-compartment model assumes instantaneous distribution after administration. For this model, it is also assumed that the drug distributes evenly throughout the body. The two-compartment model, rather than assuming instantaneous distribution throughout the body, assumes different distribution rates. A more rapid distribution occurs in the more highly perfused tissues and is termed the "central compartment." Distribution continues at a slower pace in less well-perfused tissues collectively termed the "peripheral compartment."

One- and two-compartment models can be demonstrated diagrammatically by plotting the natural log (ln) of plasma concentration versus time. Figure 7.2 depicts a profile of an intravenously administered drug; in each case, the peak plasma concentration is reached instantaneously. In the one-compartment model, the decline in plasma concentration as a function of time proceeds in a linear fashion. In the two-compartment model, a rapid decline is initially observed. This consists of a combination of drug elimination and movement of drug into the peripheral compartment and is called the α-elimination phase. Once the distribution into the peripheral compartment has been completed, a slower decline from the plasma occurs and represents removal from the body. This is known as the β-elimination phase.

Most drugs follow first-order kinetics: A constant fraction of drug is removed from the blood per unit time. First-order elimination kinetics is defined by the following equation:

$$C = C_0 e^{-kt} \qquad (7.2)$$

C = concentration of drug in plasma at time, t

C_0 = the initial plasma drug concentration

k = elimination rate constant

The elimination half-life $(t_{1/2})$ is calculated using the equation

$$t_{1/2} = \frac{0.693}{k} \qquad (7.3)$$

By taking the natural log of both sides of Eq. (7.2) and rearranging, the following equation is obtained:

$$\ln C = -kt + \ln C_0 \qquad (7.4)$$

Therefore, by plotting $\ln C$ vs. t, the y-intercept is $\ln C_0$ and the slope is $-k$. In first-order elimination kinetics, the blood drug concentration is decreased by one-half every half-life. By four to five half-lives, the drug is essentially removed from the blood, assuming no additional drug is absorbed.

Some drugs are eliminated by zero-order kinetics. Rather than a constant fraction of a drug being removed from the blood per unit time, a constant amount of a drug is cleared from the blood per unit time. For instance, ethanol will display zero-order kinetics at high blood concen-

Fig. 7.2 Plot of natural log concentration (ln C) versus time plots for drugs with (**a**) one-compartment and (**b**) two-compartment pharmacokinetics

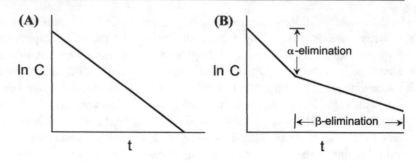

trations (this will be discussed in greater detail in Chap. 19). The equation defining a zero-order process is as follows:

$$C = C_0 - kt \qquad (7.5)$$

In this scenario, a plot of C vs. t yields a straight line with slope $-k$ and intercept C_0. The elimination half-life is also dependent on the initial drug concentration:

$$t_{1/2} = \frac{(0.5)C_0}{k} \qquad (7.6)$$

When multiple dosing occurs, the eliminated drug is being replaced by subsequent drug administration. If the amount absorbed surpasses the amount eliminated, then a net increase in plasma drug concentration will occur until equilibrium is attained. By properly setting dosing schedules, an equilibrium will eventually be realized whereby the highest blood concentration (peak) and the lowest blood concentration (trough) each becomes the same with subsequent dosing. At this point, steady state is achieved. If the drug follows first-order kinetics and the dosing interval is the elimination half-life of the drug, steady state will be reached within four to five half-life intervals. Steady-state drug concentrations may be increased either by increasing the dose but maintaining the same dosing interval or by increasing the frequency of the same dosing. The former method results in wider fluctuations between the maximum and minimum concentrations after each dose, while the latter method reduces the difference between the peak and trough concentrations.

Further Reading

Coleman MD (2010) Human drug metabolism – an introduction. Wiley-Blackwell, West Sussex

Jambhekar S, Breen PJ (2012) Basic pharmacokinetics. Pharmaceutical Press, UK

Jann MW, Penzak SR, Cohen LJ (eds) (2016) Applied clinical pharmacokinetics and pharmacodynamics of psychopharmacological agents. Springer, Switzerland

Ortiz de Montellano PR (ed) (2016) Cytochrome P450- structure, mechanism and biochemistry, 4th edn. Springer, Switzerland

Ritter JM, Lewis LD, Mant TGK, Ferro A (2008) A textbook of clinical pharmacology and therapeutics, 5th edn. Hodder Arnold, London

Zanger UM, Schwab M (2013) Cytochrome P450 enzymes in drug metabolism: regulation of gene expression enzyme activities and impact of genetic variation. Pharmacol Therapeut 138:103–141

Pharmacodynamics

8

Barry S. Levine

Abstract

Pharmacodynamics involves the effects of drugs and their mechanism of action. These effects can be described on the "macro" level, which pertains to the physiological or biochemical effects that the drugs produce. For example, a drug may lower heart rate and blood pressure or cause a reduction in the inflammatory response. These effects would often be the basis for the therapeutic use or uses of the drug. The study of pharmacodynamics also includes the effects of a drug at the molecular level that is the mechanism of action at the cellular level.

Keywords

Pharmacodynamics · Toxicology · Drugs of abuse

Receptors

To understand how a drug produces its effects, it is first necessary to understand how drugs interact at the molecular level. The molecular interaction usually involves a substrate, either endogenous or exogenous, interacting with a receptor. A receptor is a protein that these substances, called ligands, can bind. Binding can occur through a number of mechanisms, ionic, hydrogen, van der Waals, or covalent. Once bound, a cascade of biochemical processes may or may not occur, depending on the nature of the ligand.

A ligand may be a full agonist, which means that once binding to the receptor occurs, a strong physiological response ensues. The endogenous ligands would be examples of full agonists. A partial agonist is a ligand that, when bound to the receptor, produces a response that is less than that of a full agonist. Conversely, an antagonist is a substance that, when bound to the receptor, produces no response. It may block or dampen the biological response at the receptor site, rather than activating it like an agonist. An antagonist may be competitive or noncompetitive. As the name implies, a competitive antagonist can compete with an agonist for sites on the receptor. Competitive agonists are reversible. Noncompetitive antagonists bind irreversibly to the receptor, usually through covalent bonding. Noncompetitive antagonism can only be overcome through the synthesis of a new receptor.

One other interaction that a ligand may have with a receptor is as an allosteric modulator. These compounds do not bind to the same site as an agonist or antagonist, but bind to a different site. These modulators, when bound, can enhance agonist activity when the agonist is bound to the receptor.

B. S. Levine (✉)
Office of the Chief Medical Examiner,
Baltimore, MD, USA
e-mail: blevine@som.umaryland.edu

© Springer Nature Switzerland AG 2020
B. S. Levine, S. Kerrigan (eds.), *Principles of Forensic Toxicology*,
https://doi.org/10.1007/978-3-030-42917-1_8

The binding of an agonist or antagonist to a receptor follows the same laws of mass action that other chemical reactions follow. The equilibrium is between the ligand, the receptor, and the ligand-receptor complex. It is defined by the following equation:

$$[\text{ligand}] + [\text{receptor}] \underset{k_2}{\overset{k_1}{\rightleftharpoons}} [\text{ligand} - \text{receptor}]$$

where [ ] represents concentration

k_1 represents the association constant for the ligand and receptor

k_2 represents the dissociation constant for the ligand-receptor complex

At equilibrium, the rate of association of the drug to the receptor is equal to the rate of dissociation from the receptor. Putting this into an equation

$$k_1[\text{ligand}][\text{receptor}] = k_2[\text{ligand} - \text{receptor}]$$

The ratio of k_2 to k_1 is a constant and the ratio is called K_A. The parameters associated with the binding process are affinity and efficacy. Affinity is the tendency of the ligand to bind to the receptor. Efficacy is a measure of the ability of the ligand-receptor complex to produce its effect.

Receptors may be classified based on the molecular activity that is triggered when a ligand is bound to it:

- G-protein-coupled receptors (GPCR). These are the largest family of receptors and are membrane-based proteins that consist of seven transmembrane-spanning regions, an N-terminal region that extends into the extracellular space, and a C-terminal region that extends into the cell. G-proteins are signal transducers such that when an agonist is bound to the receptor, a conformational change occurs that results in the release of GDP and the binding of GTP. This in turn signals effector proteins such as adenylyl cyclase, phospholipase C, or membrane ion channels selective for Ca^{2+} and K^+ to produce the agonist's effects.
- Ionotropic receptors. These receptors cause changes in ion movement across a membrane.

- Kinase-linked receptors. These include receptors for hormones such as insulin and a variety of growth factors.
- Nuclear receptors. These receptors are located in the cytoplasm, but move into the nucleus after binding to a ligand. Steroid receptors and thyroid receptors are examples.

Neurotransmission

Ligands that bind to receptors in neurons are known as neurotransmitters. A neuron consists of a dendrite, a cell body, and an axon. Between neurons, there is a gap called the synapse. In the axon part of the synapse, there are vesicles that store neurotransmitters. When stimulated by an action potential, these neurotransmitters are released into the synapse, cross the gap called the synaptic cleft, and bind to a receptor on the dendrite of the next neuron. In this manner, activity is propagated between neurons and continues as long as the neurotransmitter remains in the synaptic cleft. Removal of the neurotransmitter from the synaptic cleft stops neuronal transmission and can occur by enzymatic breakdown of the neurotransmitter or by reuptake of the neurotransmitter back into the presynaptic neuron.

There are a number of neurotransmitters that are affected by the drug classes covered in Part III of this book:

Monoamines

There are a number of neurotransmitters that are in this group. One synthetic pathway starts with the amino acid tyrosine. Tyrosine undergoes hydroxylation through the activity of tyrosine-3-monooxygenase to form DOPA (dihydroxyphenylalanine). DOPA is decarboxylated to produce one neurotransmitter, dopamine. Dopamine may then be hydroxylated to form another neurotransmitter, norepinephrine. Norepinephrine may then be methylated to form epinephrine (adrenaline). These three neurotransmitters are collectively known as catecholamines. Numerous drugs of abuse, including the amphetamines and cocaine, interact with monoamine receptors.

In another pathway, the amino acid tryptophan is hydroxylated to form 5-hydroxytryptophan. Decarboxylation of this compound produces 5-hydroxytryptamine (5-HT) or serotonin, another neurotransmitter.

There are two broad classifications of receptors for epinephrine and norepinephrine: α- and β-adrenergic receptors. There are three subtypes of α-receptors and two subtypes of β-receptors and they have significant effects throughout the body. A listing of these effects is given in Table 8.1.

There are five dopamine receptor subtypes within two families. The D_1-like family includes D_1 and D_5 receptors, while the D_2-like family consists of receptors D_2, D_3, and D_4. In the central nervous system, dopamine receptor activity plays a role in memory, reward system, cognition, emesis, and motor function. In the heart, dopamine increases the contractile force and cardiac output of the heart without increasing heart rate. In the kidney, these receptors lead to the increase in urine output.

The 5-HT receptors have the most subclasses of the monoamine neurotransmitter group. There are seven families, numbered 1–7, and all families, except $5-HT_3$, are G-protein-coupled receptors. These receptors play a significant role in the brain, affecting aggression, anxiety, appetite, learning, memory, mood, sexual behavior, and thermoregulation. These receptors also modulate the release of other neurotransmitters and hormones. These drugs, including antidepressants, stimulants, and psychedelics, have serotonergic activity. The hallucinogenic effects of mescaline, psilocybin, and LSD are mediated via $5-HT2_A$ receptor agonism.

A complication of the coadministration of multiple drugs that interact with the 5-HT receptors is serotonin syndrome. These drugs may increase serotonin production or release, inhibit serotonin reuptake or metabolism, or serve as 5-HT agonists. The net result is a potentially life-threatening situation characterized by muscle hyperactivity, tremor, fever, altered mental status, and autonomic instability.

After release of these compounds into the synapse and binding to their specific receptors, they are removed from the synapse either by reuptake into the presynaptic vesicles by an amine pump or by metabolism. Norepinephrine and epinephrine are metabolized primarily by two enzymes. Monoamine oxidase (MAO) catalyzes an oxidative deamination followed by either a reduction or oxidation to produce 3,4-dihydroxyphenyl ethylene glycol or 3,4-dihydroxymandelic acid, respectively. Alternatively, they can be methylated through the action of catechol-O-methyltransferase to produce normetanephrine or metanephrine, respectively. Both sets of reactions ultimately occur, leading to the major urinary products of 3-methoxy-4 hydroxyphenylethylene glycol and 3-methoxy-4-hydroxymandelic acid. Serotonin also undergoes metabolism by oxidative deamination by MAO to form 5-hydroxyindole acetaldehyde which is subsequently oxidized to 5-hydroxyindole acetic acid.

Acetylcholine

There are two types of cholinergic receptors and the classification is based on drugs that specifically interact with each type. Muscarinic cholinergic receptors are located primarily in the peripheral nervous system primarily in postganglionic parasympathetic nerves. They are also located in the hippocampus, cortex, and thalamus

Table 8.1 Effects at adrenergic receptors

Receptor subtype	Primary effects
α_1	Contraction of vascular smooth muscle
	Vasoconstriction of aorta and arteries
	Cardiac growth
	Mydriasis
α_2	Platelet activation
β_1	Increased heart rate
	Increased contractile force of heart
	Increased amylase secretion
β_2	Smooth muscle cell relaxation
	Bronchodilation
β_3	Relaxation of muscle in bladder
	Increased lipolysis

Table 8.2 Effects of acetylcholine at muscarinic receptors

Cardiovascular effects
Vasodilatation
Decreased heart rate
Decreased conduction velocity of the atrioventricular node
Decreased contractile force of heart
Bronchoconstriction
Increased urination
Increased salivation
Increased defecation
Increased lachrymation

of the brain. The effects of acetylcholine at these receptors are shown in Table 8.2. There are three subtypes of muscarinic receptors, M_1, M_2, and M_3. Atropine and scopolamine are antagonists to all subtypes.

The other type of cholinergic receptor is the nicotinic receptor. It is primarily at the neuromuscular junction and at peripheral autonomic ganglia. There are two subtypes of receptors. The primary effect of receptor antagonism is muscular blockade. Curare was the classic receptor antagonist, but is not used therapeutically. Drugs that are competitive antagonists include pancuronium, vecuronium, and rocuronium. These agents vary primarily by their duration of action and are used to relax skeletal muscle during surgical anesthesia.

Unlike the monoamine neurotransmitters, there is no pump to remove acetylcholine from the synapse. Activity is stopped by hydrolyzing acetylcholine to choline and acetate. This hydrolysis is catalyzed by cholinesterase enzymes. There are two forms of cholinesterase: (1) acetylcholinesterase, found in red blood cells and in the neuromuscular junction and (2) butyrylcholinesterase, found in the plasma. Although both catalyze the hydrolysis of acetylcholine, acetylcholinesterase hydrolyzes more rapidly than butyrylcholinesterase. These enzymes also play a significant role in the metabolism of cocaine, as will be discussed in Chap. 23.

Substances that inhibit cholinesterase lead to continued cholinergic activity both at muscarinic and nicotinic receptors. Cholinesterase inhibitors have been used as pesticides and as nerve agents.

Once cholinesterase inhibition has occurred, the administration of an enzyme reactivator such as pralidoxime (2-PAM) can nullify the enzyme inhibition.

GABA

Gamma-aminobutyric acid (GABA) is the major inhibitory neurotransmitter in the central nervous system. There are two subgroups of GABA receptors, $GABA_A$, an ionotropic receptor, and $GABA_B$, a G-protein-coupled receptor. They differ in their pharmacological, electrophysiological, and biochemical properties. $GABA_A$ receptors are composed of five subunits. When GABA is bound to the $GABA_A$ receptor, the opening of chloride ion channels leads to an inhibition in the firing of a new action potential. Besides the GABA binding site, there are also allosteric sites that affect the binding of GABA to the receptor. These allosteric sites have been targets for drugs that do not bind to the GABA receptor site itself, but bind to these other sites and produce pharmacological effects in that manner. Ethanol, benzodiazepines, and barbiturates interact with GABA receptors to mediate sedative, anxiolytic, and anticonvulsant effects.

Glutamate

Glutamate is the main excitatory neurotransmitter in the central nervous system. There are three ionotropic receptors for which glutamate serves as an agonist: the N-methyl-D-aspartate (NMDA), the α-amino-3-hydroxy-5-methyl-4-isoxazolepropionic acid (AMPA), and kainate receptors. The binding of glutamate to these receptors allows cations to flow through the cell membrane. Glutamate and glycine are co-agonists for the NMDA receptor. Interestingly, glutamine in high concentrations is cytotoxic and can lead to neuronal cell death. Examples of drugs that bind to receptors of this type include ethanol and dissociative anesthetics, both of which are considered NMDA antagonists.

Endogenous Opioids

Three families of endogenous opioids have been identified: endorphins, enkephalins, and dynorphins. Each are peptides derived from large precursor proteins. These substances interact with the three opioid receptors, designated mu, delta, and kappa. The enkephalins and the β-endorphins produce strong activity when bound to the mu or delta receptors and no activity at the kappa receptor. Dynorphins and α-neoendorphins produce strong activity when bound to the kappa receptors and some activity at the mu and delta receptors. The effects produced by these agonists will be discussed in greater detail in the chapter on opioids.

Others

Other receptors are discussed in subsequent chapters. These include cannabinoids, melatonin, and orexin.

Tolerance

Whether a drug is used for therapeutic reasons or for abuse, the dose is titrated to produce the desired effect. However, over time, a phenomenon develops whereby continued administration of the same dose produces a reduced effect. This effect is known as tolerance. For a specific drug, tolerance may develop rapidly to some or all of the effects or may not develop at all. One of the classic examples of tolerance is illustrated by an opioid addict. When the abuse of the drug begins, a particular dose will produce the desired effect, euphoria. Continued abuse of opioids at the same dose will lead to less euphoric feelings in the abuser. This in turn causes an increase in dose to produce the same euphoric effects as were originally felt.

Many types of tolerances have been reported. Pharmacokinetic tolerance includes changes in distribution and elimination of the drug with continued use. A drug may induce its own metabolism, leading to reduced concentrations of the parent drug in the plasma. If the metabolites are inactive or have less activity than the parent drug, this reduces the amount of active compound at the receptor. Pharmacodynamic tolerance refers to drug-induced changes that result in changes in target receptors with repeated administration. This may be a reduction in receptor efficiency or in the number of receptors available for binding. Learned or behavioral tolerance is the ability to compensate in task performance due to the experience developed when performing the test while using the drug. Finally, acute tolerance is the tolerance that develops during one dosing session. An individual will have reduced response to each subsequent use within the session.

Tolerance to a particular drug in a class often conveys tolerance to other drugs within the class. This is referred to as cross-tolerance. Cross-tolerance may also develop between classes. For instance, there is cross-tolerance between alcohol and benzodiazepines.

With some drugs such as cocaine, a reverse tolerance or sensitization may develop during a long, single use. This is the opposite of acute tolerance and requires a longer period of time to develop.

The concept of tolerance plays a significant role in the interpretation of forensic toxicology results. The most frequently encountered drug in the field is alcohol. Alcohol displays many of the forms of tolerance discussed above. That is a primary reason why at a given blood alcohol concentration, a chronic user will demonstrate less impairment than the occasional or social drinker. This is discussed in greater detail in Chap. 19. The interpretation of drug results is also complicated by tolerance. A particular blood concentration of an opioid may be an incidental finding in a chronic user, but may account for toxicity or death in a naïve individual.

Physical Dependence

Besides tolerance, another phenomenon may occur with chronic use of a drug. This will occur after the use of the drug has abruptly stopped. During the time that a drug is being used regularly, the processes in the body make compensatory adjustments based on the regular presence of the effects caused by the drug. A physical dependence on the drug ensues. Rapid removal of this drug disrupts this "new equilibrium" and the body needs time to readjust.

The manifestation of physical dependence is the development of withdrawal symptoms. These symptoms will be the opposite of the effects that the drug produces and will often be the same symptoms that caused use of the drug in the first place. For instance, an individual being treated for anxiety with an anxiolytic drug may develop severe anxiety if taken off of the drug rapidly; the drug should be tapered gradually to prevent this from occurring. Withdrawal symptoms may not only be uncomfortable but may be life-threatening. A chronic alcoholic who abruptly stops drinking may develop an alcohol withdrawal syndrome that include anxiety, shaking, seizures, and delirium tremens (DTs) that, if untreated, can lead to death.

Further Readings

Brunton L, Hilal-Dandan R, Knollman B (eds) (2018) Goodman and Gillman's the pharmacological basis of therapeutics, 13th edn. McGraw Hill Medical, New York

Kenakin T (2015) The mass action equation in pharmacology. Brit J Clin Pharmacol 81:41–51

Mach RH (2017) Small molecule receptor ligands for PET studies of the central nervous system-focus on G protein coupled receptors. Sem Nucl Med 47:524–535

Thanacoody R (2016) Serotonin syndrome. Medicine 44:95–96

Williams J (2008) Basic opioid pharmacology. Rev Pain 1:2–5

Part II
Methodologies

Specimen Preparation/Extraction

9

Kenneth E. Ferslew

Abstract

The chapter covers the wide range of biological specimens collected in forensic cases that are submitted to the laboratory for toxicological analysis (e.g., blood, urine, vitreous, liver, kidney, hair, saliva, etc.). Specimen collection, handling, and aliquoting are covered as part of routine specimen triage for the various types of analyses that can be performed. Numerous methodologies are available for specimen preparation and/or extraction. Fundamentals of protein precipitation, bound/unbound drugs and metabolites, acidic or enzymatic hydrolysis, specimen digestion, and tissue homogenization are presented. Classic methodologies for liquid/liquid extraction (LLE), solid phase extraction (SPE), solid phase microextraction (SPME), and supported liquid extraction (SLE) are reviewed. More recently developed techniques that have been applied to forensic toxicology such as "dilute and shoot" and "QuEChERS" are presented and critiqued. Standard techniques for specimen preparation and/or extraction are presented and compared/contrasted based on their advantages and disadvantages to the toxicologist.

K. E. Ferslew (✉)
East Tennessee State University,
Johnson City, TN, USA
e-mail: ferslew@etsu.edu

Keywords

Specimen preparation · Toxicology · Protein precipitation · Extraction · LLE · SPE · SPME · SLE · QuEChERS

Purpose

Toxicologists are faced with a number of different biological specimens for drug analysis in forensic toxicology. Whether it be urine specimens in forensic urine drug testing, blood specimens with driving under the influence of drugs (DUID) cases, or the vast array of specimens (e.g., blood, urine, vitreous, tissues) in postmortem cases, they all will need some type of specimen preparation in order to analyze them for drugs. Extraction does several things for the toxicologist in preparing the biological specimens for analysis. It removes or extracts the drug from the biological matrix and thus isolates it from the normal endogenous constituents found in the specimen (e.g., lipoproteins, carbohydrates, etc.) which may interfere with the analysis. It concentrates the drug down into a smaller volume with a greater concentration for analysis. Plus, it can dissolve the drug in a solvent which can either make the drug suitable for the type analysis needing to be performed (i.e., volatile with GC or GC/MS), suitable for the derivatization required for

110 K. E. Ferslew

analysis, or dissolved in an aqueous solvent suitable for analysis by a wide array of methodologies (i.e., LC, immunoassay or spectrophotometric techniques). Some technologies do not require extraction; analytes can be tested directly in an aliquot of the specimen (i.e., immunoassays, direct injection techniques). There are a lot of different ways to prepare the specimens we are provided for analysis and each has distinct advantages and disadvantages. This chapter will summarize the different types of specimen preparation used in forensic toxicology.

Specimens

Accurate and reproducible analytical results are dependent on the proper application of validated procedures to correctly identified specimens. Good integrity and uniformity of the specimen for analysis is crucial for robust analytical results and critical to the proper interpretation of those results. Collection of sufficient specimen volume in the correct container and proper storage until analysis is essential for all testing procedures. Liquid specimens (e.g., blood, serum, plasma, urine, vitreous, amniotic fluid, oral fluid, and bile) should be collected, labeled, and separated in the proper containers or tubes indicated for the specific analysis or analyses desired. The specimens routinely collected should be homogenous by nature, and can be easily aliquoted in accurate volumes for analysis by using verified pipetting instruments. Gastric contents (i.e., stomach or bowel) as well as tissues (e.g., liver, kidney, brain, muscle, fat, placenta, skin, blood vessel, lung, spleen, hair, nails, and bone) may vary significantly in consistency and density. Gastric contents are not as homogenous as tissues. All these specimens require proper preparation and homogenization in order to achieve a high yield of extraction of the drugs and produce accurate and reproducible analysis. Specimens of greater density may even require pulverization (e.g., hair, nails, or bone) in a ball mill in order to obtain an aliquot of the specimen adequately homogenized to achieve good extraction of the drugs contained in the tissue. Special preparation techniques may also be required for certain specimens to avoid environmental contamination of the specimen in order to measure the true drug concentration in the specimen (i.e., wash and dry hair before pulverization, homogenization, and extraction). Proper collection and identification of the biological specimen is extremely important for the correct toxicological interpretation of the analytical results. The source of the specimen (e.g., femoral or cardiac blood) as well as the orientation and/or partition of the specimen (e.g., scalp versus distal segment of hair) is of toxicological significance. The source of the specimen should be noted in the report for proper interpretation of the result.

Extent of Testing

Depending on the analytical techniques used and the extent of testing needed to achieve a final result, the amount of specimen needed for analysis can vary significantly. If initial drug screening is the extent of testing to be performed, then smaller specimen volumes or weights are required. If screening and confirmation is to be performed, then more specimen is required. With the increased sensitivity of current state of the art methodologies, a toxicologist is able to detect the necessary concentrations of even some of the more efficacious drugs to the subnanogram per milliliter or gram. In today's world where resource and financial constraints must be considered, miniaturization of techniques allows us to use smaller specimen aliquots and smaller amounts of solvents, reagents, and materials. Screening specimens with immunochemistries or chromatographic techniques may require anywhere from a few microliters, to several milliliters of specimen. Focused quantitative analysis of a specific analyte or group of analytes may require a significant volume of specimen. Do not use all of a specimen unless absolutely necessary. Remember, it is always better to have additional specimen if available and collectable for repeated analyses or further testing by other laboratories.

Results

Regardless of the method of aliquoting a specimen being analyzed, the result will be reported as a quantity per volume or weight. Qualitative testing will have a positive or negative result associated with a specific cutoff concentration, decision point, or limit of detection. For quantitative testing, analyte concentrations should be associated with a known limit of detection, limit of quantitation, range of linearity, and measure of the measurement uncertainty. Units used may include milligram/liter (mg/L), microgram/milliliter (µg/mL), nanogram/milliliter (ng/mL), gram/100 milliliters (g/100 mL, g/dL or g%), milligram/kilogram (mg/kg), microgram/gram (µg/g), and nanogram/gram (ng/g). Blood ethanol concentrations can be reported with different units in different courts (e.g., mg/dL or g%). Do not use "alcohol" in place of ethanol. Correct conversion of metric units is essential for proper presentation and interpretation of results.

Analysis of Gases and Volatile Liquids

Gases and volatile liquids are particularly challenging for the toxicologist. Proper collection (e.g., full, sealed, gray top, Vacutainer® tubes for fluids and glass or plastic jars for tissues) and frozen storage are critical in order to preserve gas concentrations until analysis. Limited thawing and aliquoting of the specimen should be done. Short-chain hydrocarbons (i.e., C_{1-8}), nitrous oxide, phosgene, chlorine, trichloroethane (TCE), difluoroethane (DFE, Freon), and the inhalation anesthetic flurane derivatives all have gas solubilities in biological fluids which decrease with rising temperature and therefore allow them to degas when the specimen container is open or even when closed at room temperature. The gas/liquid partition is temperature-dependent. The absolute quantity of the gas in weight or volume is expressed as a percentage at a given temperature and pressure. Nitrous oxide, for example, is soluble in blood at a partition of 47/100 (47 volume%) at 37 °C and atmospheric pressure. This is equivalent to 0.92 gram per liter per the ideal gas law.

Gas standards in blood are achieved by saturating the fluid with the pure gas to referenced concentrations. Linear concentration ranges can then be serial diluted for comparison and quantitation of the unknown concentration in the specimen. Gas concentrations are best determined using "headspace" injection with gas chromatography and thermal conductivity, flame ionization or mass spectrometric detection. This technique utilizes the volatile nature of the analyte to our advantage. Due to the physical nature of the analyte and the difficulty in controlling gas loss from the specimen, analysis of the specimen as quickly as possible to the time of collection offers the best possibility for accurate and reproducible results that reflect the concentration when the specimen was taken.

Some gases are so water soluble that they will dissolve and ionize in blood and other biological fluids. Hydrogen sulfide and hydrogen cyanide are unionized at a pH less than 2 and can be liberated from the biological fluid with dilute sulfuric acid. Use of a Conway diffusion cell allows analysis of the gas by its liberation from an aliquot of the biological specimen with addition of dilute sulfuric acid in the outer chamber, diffusion within the sealed devise, and dissolution in a trapping solution within the inner chamber. The colorimetric reaction of the gas with the trapping solution is proportional to the concentration of the gas in the specimen. Due to their solubility in an aqueous fluid, LC and LC/MS techniques are applicable for analysis of these analytes.

Volatile liquids are just that, liquids at room temperature, readily dissolvable in biological fluids and tissues, which become gaseous with increased temperature. Ethanol determinations are the most significant, prevalent, and frequent analyses in forensic toxicology. Volatile panels will often include ethanol, acetone, isopropanol, methanol, ethyl acetate, propanol, 2-butanol, and dichloromethane. These volatiles are readily analyzed by gas chromatography with either flame ionization or mass spectrometric detectors. Direct injection and "headspace" injection techniques are utilized. Briefly, an aliquot of specimen is mixed with an appropriate internal standard such as 1-propanol, in a vial and sealed. The vial is heated to between 30 and 50 °C and a sample of the gas in the headspace above the liquid is collected and injected into the gas chromatograph. Based on Henry's law, at a constant temperature, the amount of a given gas dissolved in a given type and volume of liquid is directly proportional to the partial pressure of that gas in equilibrium with that liquid. Minimal liquid volumes (less than a microliter) of the specimen/internal standard mixture may also be injected directly into the glass liner leading to the column with direct injection techniques. In both cases, the detector response is proportional to the concentration of the analyte in the specimen. Use of a volatile internal standard such as 1-propanol normalizes all injection volumes, confirms chromatographic separation, and covers a number of analytical sins. It is essential for accurate determinations.

The volume of biological specimen is routinely mixed with much larger volumes of the internal standard in water (2 to 10 times the volume) thus relatively removing the matrix effect of the specimen. Correct measurement of specimen and internal standard volumes are critical for accurate and precise results. A distinct advantage to these techniques for volatile liquids in biological fluids is that they can be easily automated due to the physical-chemical characteristics of the analytes with the application of precise repetitive-pipettes and autosamplers. A limitation to these techniques is the potential for co-elution of interfering substances volatilized from the biological specimen. Multiple-column chromatography with flame ionization detection or single-column chromatography with mass spectrometric detection is performed to positively identify and quantitate these analytes. If it is suspected that 1-propanol is present in a specimen, reanalysis of the specimen using a different internal standard such as 2-butanol may be conducted.

Specimen Digestion for Elemental/ Inorganic Analyses

Tissues and biological fluids are predominantly organic material. In order to analyze these specimens for inorganic toxins such as the heavy met-

als (i.e., arsenic, cadmium, mercury, and lead) as well as other inorganic ions, the specimen is digested to remove the carbonaceous material. The isolated inorganic residue can then be dissolved and subjected to analysis by atomic absorption spectrophotometry, atomic emission spectrophotometry, or anodic stripping voltammetry to determine the ionic concentration without interference from the biological matrix. Digestion can be performed by either "dry" or "wet" techniques. Digestion is usually performed on milligrams to a few grams of tissue or microliters to a few milliliters of biological fluid (e.g., hair, nails, tissues, blood, or urine). Specimens are placed in either acid washed/resistant tubes or crucibles. For "wet" digestion a mixture of sulfuric, nitric, and perchloric acid is added and heated until the biological specimen is completely digested and turned into dissolved residue. For "dry" digestion the biological specimen is burned within the crucible inside a muffle furnace until reduced to a dry residue. Complete digestion is obtained when carbonaceous and sulfuric fumes are no longer emitted. Residues can then be dissolved in deionized water and analyzed.

Heavy metal analyses as well as specific inorganic elemental analyses are very specialized forensic toxicological procedures that are usually performed in larger comprehensive toxicology laboratories capable of performing the rare inorganic determinations proficiently and efficaciously. The dedicated instrumentation needed for these procedures is not routinely available in many forensic toxicology laboratories. Due to the significance and the occurrence of lead intoxication, blood lead screening programs are often the charge of state department of health laboratories. Digestion techniques for the determination of drugs in other matrices (e.g., hair) are addressed in subsequent chapters.

Specimen Preparation for Bound Drugs and Metabolites

Many drugs and metabolites in biological fluids and tissues are physically bound to proteins, lipids, and carbohydrates (i.e., glucose). This binding hinders extraction of the drug. In order to free these drugs to measure their total concentration in the specimen, different enzymatic treatments are used to liberate the analytes for detection. Subtilisin Carlsberg is a protease enzyme used to free strongly protein bound drugs that may be too acid-labile for any other chemical procedure. Enzyme is added to tissue homogenate or biological fluid, under optimized pH for enzymatic activity, and heated at a set temperature for a fixed incubation time interval. Time, temperature, and pH are set for complete liberation.

During Phase II metabolism many drugs form glucuronides, sulfates, and other conjugates. This is discussed in more detail in Chap. 7. These bound drugs and metabolites can be liberated by either chemical or enzymatic treatments. For enzymatic treatment there are several sources of sulfatase or beta-glucuronidase (e.g., bovine, bacterial, molluscan, synthetic) which are used to hydrolyze the sulfate and glucuronide bonds. Again, time, temperature, pH, and concentration are set to optimize activity and completely liberate the drug. Analysis of separate aliquots of a specimen with and without these treatments allows for determination of free, bound, and total concentration of the drug and/or metabolite in the specimen. Determination of free, bound, and total concentrations of drugs/metabolites in biological specimens can be of toxicological significance and important for forensic interpretation as to time of dosage in fatal overdose cases (i.e., opioids). Acute toxicities of opiates are correlated with unconjugated opiate parent drug.

Although chemical hydrolysis (using acid or alkali) of glucuronidated drugs can be achieved fairly rapidly (often at elevated temperature) and with limited expense, subsequent extracts may be subject to reduced cleanliness. Drug stability must also be considered due to the harsh conditions that may be used. Enzymatic treatments using beta-glucuronidases (e.g., *Helix pomatia, Patella vulgata, E. coli* Type IX) may take longer (several hours/overnight), require careful pH control, but typically produce fewer co-extractive interferences. More recently, recombinant beta-glucuronidases have become available, permitting deconjugation in as little as 30 min. However, disadvantages of enzymatic deconjugation include increased cost and limited shelf-life of reagents. When deconjugation is performed prior to extraction, the conditions used must be carefully considered prior to analysis. Chemical deconjugation may require careful pH adjustment prior to liquid-liquid or solid phase extraction. Although enzymatic reagents are removed during traditional extraction techniques, specialized cartridge and plate-based devices are also available for the removal of glucuronidase and other large biomolecules from hydrolyzed specimens.

Immunoassays

Some methods in toxicology such as immunoassays do not require a great degree of specimen preparation. Enzyme-multiplied immunoassay techniques (EMITs), enzyme-linked immunosorbent assays (ELISAs), and biochip array technology fall into this category. In most instances small volumes of specimen can be analyzed directly following dilution, centrifugation, or filtration. As long as matrix effects are evaluated as part of method validation, specimens of acceptable quality and integrity (i.e., valid as to pH and lack of adulterants) can be analyzed without extraction. This direct analysis with minimal specimen preparation is a distinct advantage and lends itself well to liquid specimens (e.g., blood, urine, vitreous, etc.) but is less applicable for more solid or semisolid specimens (e.g., decomposed blood, tissues, hair). If there is a matrix issue, then an extraction technique may be required to remove and concentrate the drug from the specimen matrix and dissolve it in an aqueous solution of the proper nature to complete the analytical determinations.

Protein Precipitation

Biological fluids and tissues vary considerably in their protein content. Serum and plasma are approximately 6% protein by weight while liver, kidney, and heart can be more than 50% protein by weight. Since there are significant concentrations of protein in these specimens, methods have been developed to precipitate the proteins so they can be separated out, allowing for better extraction and concentration of the drugs contained within the specimen. Chemicals used to precipitate proteins are listed in Table 9.1. Precipitation is followed by separation. This can be achieved by either centrifugation or filtration. The precipitant can be washed to increase recovery of drugs. Addition of an appropriate internal standard to the biological fluid or tissue homogenate prior to protein precipitation will account for drug recovery through the process. Although organic solvents (acetonitrile, acetone, methanol) are often preferred for protein precipitation, not all substances are extracted efficiently using this technique. Use of cold solvent (stored in the freezer) may improve the cleanliness and efficiency of the precipitation.

A clear aqueous solution is often needed for immunochemical or colorimetric/fluorometric analyses. This may be achieved by protein precipitation. The acidity of Trinder's reagent will precipitate protein in serum or plasma while also producing a visible purple color indicative of the presence of salicylic acid. It is an easy qualitative test for aspirin, which can also produce a quantitative result with simple spectrophotometric analysis of the supernatant. Hemolyzed blood which is often received from autopsy cases may be too dense and opaque for EMIT analysis.

Simple protein precipitation and extraction with acetone/methanol can produce an extract which can be easily concentrated and rehydrated in physiological buffer for drug screening.

The thermal and chemical stability of the analyte needs to be considered when choosing a specimen preparation and/or method of analysis with the corresponding specimen preparation and/or extraction. If the drug is heat-labile or easily hydrolyzed by aqueous or alkaline conditions then the appropriate protein precipitation method should be employed, e.g., zinc sulfate/methanol at room temperature. Alkaloids such as strychnine, quinine, various opiates, and some narcotics will be not be degraded by moderate heating and acid treatments to precipitate protein. Careful consideration must be given to the limitations of the methodology in detecting certain drugs when applied to broad spectrum screening of numerous classes of drugs versus focused analysis of a specific drug, metabolite or class of drugs. It is essential that this be addressed and determined in the validation of any toxicological method.

More recently, filter plates and cartridge-like devices for protein precipitation and specimen preparation are becoming more widespread. Proteins and biomolecules are removed using multi-layer filters of differing porosities. Numerous commercial devices are available, including some that are capable of separating proteins, lipids, and surfactant interferences from biofluids. These are particularly useful for LC-MS based applications where matrix effects and ion suppression must be closely evaluated.

Table 9.1 Protein precipitation agents

Chemical	Procedure
Organic solvents (acetone, acetonitrile or methanol)	Add 2 to 3 volumes of solvent to one volume of biological fluid.
Zinc sulfate in methanol	Dissolve 5 g of $ZnSO_4$ in 100 mL water added to 43 mL of methanol
Perchloric acid	1:10 dilution of concentrated $HClO_4$ in water
Trichloroacetic acid (TCA)	10 to 15% TCA in water
Sodium tungstate and sulfuric acid	10% Na_2WO_4 in water with 3N H_2SO_4
Ammonium sulfate and hydrochloric acid	Add solid $(NH_4)_2SO_4$ to preheated tissue homogenate, complete precipitation with 3N HCl

Tissue Homogenization

Tissue specimens obviously require a great deal of specimen preparation for analysis. Tissues are homogenized with water or buffer in order to break down the tissue matrix and facilitate the release of drug. Depending on the density of the tissue (e.g., liver versus hair, wet versus dry tissue) this process may be more complex than anticipated. Tissue homogenates are highly amenable to liquid/liquid extraction techniques, although careful attention is required to avoid the formation of an emulsion due to increased particulates. However, solid phase extraction can also be utilized, typically following a protein precipitation step. A good homogenizer with an adequate procedure to obtain a uniform homogenate is important for all toxicological procedures. Various approaches to homogenization are available, including ball mills, mechanical blades/blenders, and paddle mixer-type devices. Contamination and transfer of drug from one specimen to another must be considered if equipment comes into contact with more than one specimen (i.e., blenders).

"Dilute and Shoot"

So-called "dilute and shoot" techniques have been developed and used in forensic toxicology for a wide range of analyses. As the name implies, this methodology takes the liquid specimen and dilutes it in a favorable solvent with addition of the internal standard and then an aliquot of the diluted specimen, fortified with internal standard, is injected ("shot") onto the analytical instrument. There is really no extraction of the drug from the biological matrix, and thus from the other constituents or potential interferants. This specimen preparation technique is often used with liquid chromatography-based techniques (e.g., LC/MS, LC/MS/TOF). Using this approach, centrifugation, filtration, and the use of guard columns may be particularly important to trap constituents from the matrix. Depending on the mode of data acquisition (high-resolution mass spectrometry, targeted MS/MS), the detection method may have sufficient specificity to accommodate this type of primitive treatment. The advantage of this technique is that it is fast, inexpensive, and easy to perform. Disadvantages include additional costs associated with LC column consumables, increased routine and preventive maintenance, potential down-time associated with repairs, and increased potential for interferences. These issues must be addressed and resolved during method development and validation.

Liquid/Liquid Extraction

Liquid/liquid extraction (LLE) is a time-honored technique in forensic toxicology. Due to the aqueous nature of the biological specimens that we encounter (e.g., blood, urine, bile, vitreous, tissue homogenate) it is a logical approach as it requires very little sample pre-treatment. In some instances, a single-step LLE of the analyte from a pH-adjusted biological (aqueous) matrix into an organic solvent is conducted. Drugs and metabolites are apportioned between the aqueous and the organic solvent based partially on its polarity. Buffering or pH adjustment of the specimen will allow for selectivity in the extraction technique for ionizable (acidic or basic) drugs. Neutral drugs, which remain uncharged at all pHs, can be extracted with either an acidic or a basic extraction based on solvent solubility partitioning. Table 9.2 lists common solvents that are used by forensic toxicologists in various LLE schemes.

Solvent combinations can be used to increase recovery of select drugs and metabolites and enhance specificity. Nonpolar, organic solvents such as petroleum ether and hexane work very well extracting saturated hydrocarbons from aqueous biological matrices but do not perform well with water soluble, polar drugs. For example, caffeine is more readily extracted with chloroform than with diethyl ether since caffeine can form a hydrogen bond from a donor solvent like chloroform (Fig. 9.1a). Diethyl ether on the other hand is incapable of any hydrogen donation as with extracting phenol (Fig. 9.1b). Addition of alcohols like isopropanol, isoamyl alcohol, or butanol from 1 to 10% by volume with hexane promotes hydrogen bonding with drugs by either accepting or donating hydrogen atoms and thus increasing extraction yield. Chloroform is less preferable because it is partially converted to phosgene, a very toxic and reactive substance. Hydrogen bonding characteristics of common solvent systems are also shown in Table 9.2. Additionally, the overall tendency of a substance to partition between aqueous and lipophilic phases can be predicted by the octanol/water partition coefficient (log P).

Table 9.2 Chemical properties of organic extraction solvents

Solvent	Density (g/mL)	Boiling point (°C)	g H₂O/L saturation	Dielectric constant	H Bond donor	H Bond acceptor
n-Hexane	0.66	68	0.045	1.89	No	No
Toluene	0.87	111	0.46	2.38	No	No
1-Chlorobutane	0.89	78	0.90	7.4	No	No
Chloroform	1.49	61	1.24	4.8	Yes	No
Dichloromethane (DCM)	1.34	40	11.9	9.08	No	No
Ethyl ether	0.71	35	17.0	4.33	No	Yes
Methyl-t-butyl ether (MTBE)	0.74	55	20.3	NA	No	Yes
Ethyl acetate	0.90	77	29.4	6.0	No	Yes
1-Butanol	0.81	118	170	17.8	Yes	Yes
Isopropanol (IPA)	0.79	82	miscible	18.3	Yes	Yes
Acetone	0.79	56	miscible	20.7	No	Yes
Acetonitrile	0.79	80	miscible	37	Yes	Yes

NA, not available

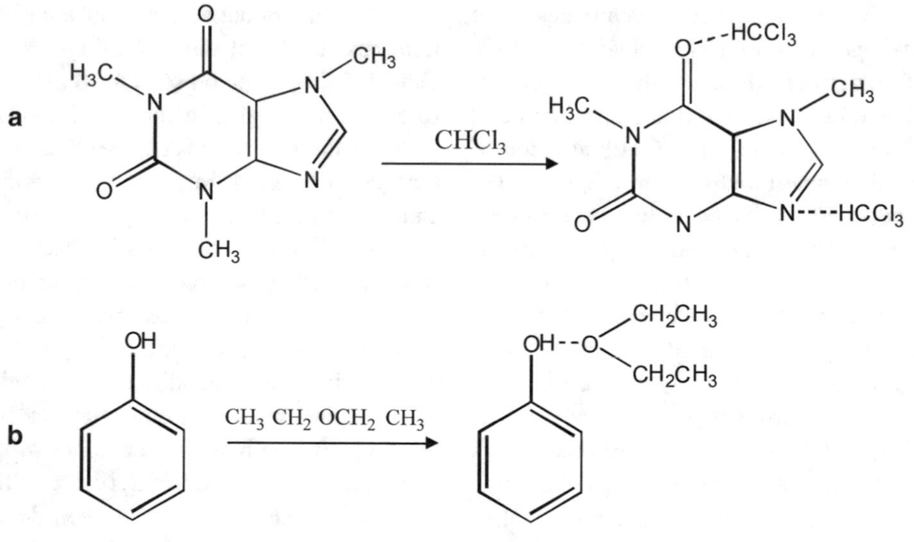

Fig. 9.1 Illustration of drug interactions with solvents. (**a**) Caffeine with chloroform (**b**) Phenol with diethyl ether

Ionizable functional groups within the molecule cause the drug to exist in either charged or uncharged states. The extent to which this occurs depends on the equilibrium association constant (K_a) as follows:

$$HA \overset{K_a}{\rightleftharpoons} H^+ + A^-$$

$$BH^+ \overset{K_b}{\rightleftharpoons} H^+ + BH$$

$$K_a + K_b = 14$$

As can be seen above, drugs bearing acidic functional groups (e.g., carboxylic acids, phenols) can exist as either uncharged (neutral) or negative species. Conversely, drugs bearing basic functional groups (e.g., amines) exist as either uncharged or positive species. The uncharged molecule, which is clearly less polar, will preferentially partition into a nonpolar solvent, whereas the charged species (positive or negative) will prefer the more polar aqueous phase. This tendency for "like dissolves like" is the basis for LLE, whereby two immiscible solvents are used to partition a substance between aqueous and organic layers. Adjustment of the specimen pH using buffer, acid, or alkali influences the percentage of drug that is either charged or uncharged in accordance with the Henderson-Hasselbalch equation:

Acidic drugs:

$$pH = pK_a + \log \frac{[charged]}{[uncharged]}$$

Basic drugs:

$$pH = pK_a + \log \frac{[uncharged]}{[charged]}$$

Ampicillin, fluoroacetic acid, ibuprofen, indomethacin, ketoprofen, probenecid, salicylic acid, and tetrahydrocannabinol metabolite all contain carboxylic acid moieties. Acidic drugs with pK_a's above a pH of 7 to 8 include barbiturates, phenytoin, acetaminophen, phenolphthalein, dicoumarol, warfarin, hydroxycoumarin, and tolbutamide. Differential extraction can be accomplished based on the classification of the analytes: strong acids (pK_a's of 1 to 5), weak acids (pK_a's of 5 to 9), neutrals (no acidic or basic moieties, extractable at any pH based on octanol/water coefficient), weak bases (neutral below pH 5 or 6), strong bases (nonionized from pH 7 and above), and amphoteric bases, which contain both acidic and basic functional groups. Buffers, which are naturally resistant to changes in pH, are frequently used in LLE. Since specimen pH can be widely variable for some matrices (e.g., urine), they ensure a more uniform extraction pH. Buffers are prepared from a mixture of a weak acid and its conjugate base, or weak base and its conjugate acid. Common buffering systems and their effective pH ranges at 25 °C are summarized in Table 9.3.

Application of a sequential extraction to separate drug groups with different chemical moieties is illustrated in Fig. 9.2. When screening specimens for multiple classes of drugs and/or metabolites as in general unknown procedures, this differential extraction will separate drugs into acidic, basic, amphoteric, and water soluble fractions from which individual drugs can be identi-

Table 9.3 Common buffers and their effective pH range in order of increasing alkalinity

Buffer	pH Range
Acetate (e.g., sodium acetate/acetic acid)	3.6–5.6
Citrate (e.g., sodium citrate/citric acid)	3.0–6.2
Phosphate (e.g., mono and dibasic sodium phosphate)	5.8–8.0
Bicarbonate (e.g., sodium carbonate/sodium bicarbonate)	9.2–10.8

fied and quantified. Examples of different drug classes based on their chemical structures are illustrated in Fig. 9.3.

Due to the large number of substances with nitrogen-bearing functional groups, the vast majority of drugs of forensic interest are basic, rather than acidic or neutral. Therefore, it is commonplace to combine acidic and neutral drugs in a single LLE. In many instances, this can be accomplished in a single step. However, LLE approaches for basic drugs often include a "back extraction", which is discussed in more detail below.

The purpose of the extraction is to remove the analytes from impurities and interfering substances in the biological matrix, while concentrating the analytes into a smaller volume which can be analyzed. Partitioning the analytes in either an aqueous or an organic phase is critical for subsequent analysis based on the methodology employed. Direct analysis of aqueous fractions is readily performed using spectrophotometric techniques (ultraviolet or fluorometric), immunochemistry (EMITs or ELISAs), or LC-based techniques. Organic fractions can be further concentrated with evaporation techniques to produce a smaller volume, or residue which can be reconstituted in another solvent. This process is particularly amenable to chromatographic techniques (e.g., TLC, GC, CE, or LC). Dried extracts can also be dissolved in various solvents and derivatized if necessary. This is discussed in more detail in Chap. 12.

The significance of the Henderson-Hasselbalch equation is to adjust the extraction pH to produce predominantly uncharged, organically soluble forms of the drug and/or metabo-

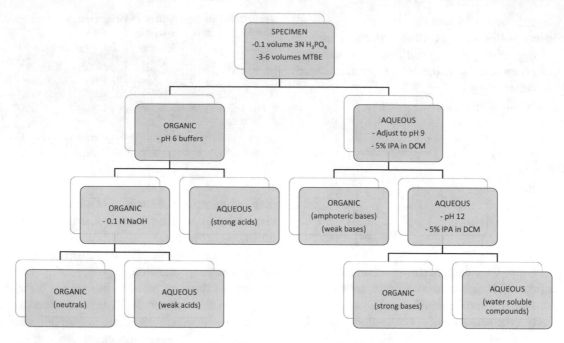

H$_3$PO$_4$ – phosphoric acid; NaOH – sodium hydroxide; DCM – dichoromethane; IPA – isopropyl alcohol

Fig. 9.2 Fractionation scheme for the separation of organic drugs according to acidity/alkalinity

lites so that they will preferentially partition into the organic solvent from the aqueous specimen. Acidic drugs (e.g., barbiturates) are uncharged in acidic solutions, while basic drugs (e.g., amphetamines) are uncharged in alkaline solutions. In accordance with the Henderson-Hasselbach equation, when the pH is adjusted two units above or below the pK$_a$, the ratio of uncharged to charged species is 100:1 for basic and acidic drugs, respectively.

Some drugs and metabolites contain two or more ionizable functional groups. Salicylic acid (Fig. 9.3) contains two acidic functional groups, a phenol (pK$_a$ 12.5) and a carboxylic acid (pK$_a$ 4.5). The functional group with the smallest pK$_a$ value will dissociate first, so it is the carboxylic acid that is most critical when determining the optimum extraction pH using LLE However, some drugs containing both an acidic and a basic functional group are considered amphoteric (e.g., morphine and benzoylecgonine, a metabolite of cocaine). Morphine has a phenolic moiety which ionizes above a pH of 10, and a tertiary amine which ionizes below a pH of 8. For drugs that carry multiple charges, the isoelectric point (isoelectric pH) is the average of the pK$_a$ values. Therefore, the optimum extraction pH for morphine by LLE is pH 9, where the positive and negative charges are balanced. Benzoylecgonine is so polar it is always ionized and therefore a "zwitterion" or internal salt between a pH of 7 and 8 (Fig. 9.3). It should be noted that although the positive and negative charges of an amphoteric drug are balanced (net zero charge) at the isoelectric point, the functional groups are still charged, potentially decreasing extraction efficiency into an organic solvent. For this reason, solid phase extraction is particularly advantageous for amphoteric drugs.

There are several issues that can cause problems with LLE. Since excessive adjustment of pH does not increase the extraction yield of acids or bases, stay within 2 pH units of the pK$_a$ of the analyte for best recovery. Substituting 2N sodium hydroxide for 0.1N, or 6N sulfuric acid for 0.1N does not further increase extraction yield. Furthermore, not all drugs are stable at extreme pH. Strong alkalization of norpropoxyphene

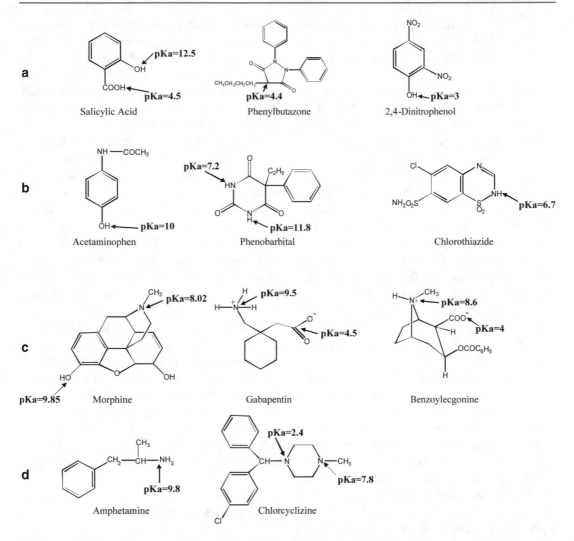

Fig. 9.3 Typical drugs by chemical class. (**a**) Strong acidic drugs (**b**) Weak acidic drugs (**c**) Amphoteric alkaline drugs (**d**) Strong alkaline drugs. Dissociation constants (pK$_a$'s) indicated for different chemical moieties

causes rearrangement to an amide and cocaine (and other drugs bearing an ester) convert into their respective carboxylic acids. Ammonium hydroxide does not alkalinize blood or other biological fluids as well as sodium hydroxide. Strong acids and bases can also cause emulsification problems when added to biological fluids.

While neutral drugs can be extracted at any pH value from 1 to 14 in an unionized form, other contaminants may also be extracted which can interfere with the analysis of the drugs. Acidic fractions will contain fatty acids from glyceride hydrolysis and neutral fractions will contain glycerides, cholesterol, and cholesterol esters.

Solvent extraction followed by "back extraction" into the aqueous phase and then re-extraction with solvent will eliminate neutral biological constituents. During the extraction of basic drugs at alkaline pH, the organic fraction containing the drug may be acidified. This forces basic drugs back into the aqueous fraction, allowing the organic layer to be discarded. Following re-alkalinization, basic drugs can be repartitioned back into the organic layer. Differential extraction/back extraction will always result in a cleaner final fraction than a single step or single phase extraction, but extraction efficiency may be reduced due to potential loss from additional steps in the procedure. Natural pigments, food additives, dyes, phthalates, and solvent impurities account for a majority of the interfering substances and extraneous peaks in chromatograms.

Hydrochloride salts of many drugs are soluble in chloroform, 1-chlorobutane, and dichloromethane. Hydrochloride salt partitioning increases proportionally with the hydrocarbon content of the solvent. Acidic extractions are best performed with methyl t-butyl ether (a proton-accepting solvent) when back extracting from chloroform or dichloromethane, followed by dilute sulfuric or phosphoric acid versus hydrochloric acid, so that the resulting salt is less soluble in the organic solvent. It is wise to note that phenothiazines such as thioridazine and other high molecular weight drugs will form hydrochloride salts that are solvent soluble. Therefore, sulfuric and phosphoric acids should be used in back extractions from solvents to produce less organically soluble salts.

There are many nuances that occur with different toxicological analytes based on the analyte's chemistry and the specifics of the LLE procedure. It is critical to follow procedures exactly as stated in the validated methodology for good analytical results. The devil is in the details.

Risk factors and cost should be considered when selecting solvents for LLE. Diethyl ether has an unpleasant odor, high volatility/flammability and can produce reactive peroxides. Known carcinogens such as benzene should not be used. Other chlorinated hydrocarbon solvents such as chloroform, dichloromethane, and butylene chloride have varying potentials for carcinogenicity. Dichloromethane with 5 to 10% isopropanol is preferable to chloroform based on contaminants in chloroform and its high degree of toxicity. Minimization of the amount of solvent used, proper storage, handling, venting, and disposal are critical for safe and economical use of these solvents in the toxicology laboratory.

The octanol/water partition coefficients for drugs indicate the degree of lipophilicity to hydrophilicity and therefore the extent of polarity for a drug. While biological fluids are not pure solvent systems, but also include carriers and molecular partitions, logP values can help predict the solubility of the drug between organic and aqueous phases. Recoveries of both very polar and nonpolar drugs using different solvents with different polarities and dielectric constants are given in Table 9.4. Selective extraction with increased yields can therefore be obtained with the optimal combination of solvents.

There are distinct advantages and disadvantages to single-step LLEs versus multi-step LLEs or extractions/back extractions. With preferential solvent to biological fluid ratios from 5:1 to 10:1, single-step LLEs may have a recovery yield of 70% or better, but there will also be extraction and concentration of soluble artifacts or matrix components/contaminants. Differential back extraction can be selective for either acids or bases and reduce the volume thus miniaturizing the procedure while concentrating desired analytes over artifacts/contaminants. While there may be loss of recovery of the analyte with each additional step, increased purity of the extract is obtained and is beneficial from the standpoint of potentially interfering substances. This should be considered with very high potency drugs, where detection of sub-nanogram per milliliter concentrations may be needed (i.e., fentanyl, buprenorphine, novel psychoactive substances (NPSs)).

Solid Phase Extraction

Limitations in LLE techniques have brought about the development of new and more convenient methodologies to extract, isolate, purify, and concentrate analytes. Solid phase extraction (SPE) is a specimen preparation process whereby the analytes that are dissolved or suspended in a liquid mixture are partitioned between a liquid and a solid (stationary) phase. Separation is still achieved based upon the distinct physical and chemical properties of the drug that dictate adsorption, solubility, binding, and electrostatic interactions. SPE can be applied to any biological fluid or tissue homogenate. The affinity of the analytes dissolved or suspended in the liquid phase for a solid stationary phase (through which the liquid passes) is the basis for separating the various analytes from the other undesirable com-

Table 9.4 Drug extraction recovery (%) using equal volumes of solvent and buffer

Drug (Extraction pH)	Hexane	1-Chlorobutane	Dichloromethane	Chloroform	Isopropyl ether	Ethyl ether	Ethyl acetate	1-Butanol
Chloramphenicol (pH 7)	0	0	22	0	15	56	58	41
Hydrochlorothiazide (pH 4)	0	4	8	0	12	30	92	84
Salicylic acid (pH 1)	0	59	83	83	100	98	98	100
Morphine (pH 9)	0	12	25	33	7	20	52	91
Caffeine (pH 7)	0	10	81	90	6	9	37	54
Procainamide (pH 11)	6	29	90	92	21	21	84	92
Pentobarbital (pH 5)	4	66	97	96	98	95	98	99
Benzocaine (pH 11)	29	82	100	100	88	88	94	94
Propoxyphene (pH 11)	48	43	96	96	71	97	-	99
Imipramine (pH 11)	35	79	88	98	84	70	99	100
Methaqualone (pH 11)	78	90	93	93	89	91	95	97
2,5-Dimethoxy-4-methylamphetamine (pH 11)	87	98	100	100	95	95	93	100
Cocaine (pH 11)	89	96	95	96	94	95	99	99
Haloperidol (pH 11)	99	99	99	100	100	100	100	100

ponents in the mixture. The stationary phase can retain either the desired analytes or the undesired artifacts/contaminants, producing the separation with either collection of the initial diluent or elution of the analytes from the stationary phase with an appropriate elution solvent. Different separation chemistries can be employed with these SPE techniques to extract various drugs and metabolites from biological specimens. These chemistries include normal phase, reverse phase, and ion exchange (both anion and cation) modalities. Some commonly employed column sorbents are listed in Table 9.5.

Several commercial companies offer manufactured SPE columns in a number of different sizes, shapes, and configurations packed with various stationary phases including ion exchange resins, XAD resins, and purified silica gel. Silica (SiO_2) is the most common stationary phase in traditional SPE columns. Advanced production processes produce a silica with uniform particle shape, size, and inactivation (e.g., spherical, 10 micron, and chemically inactivated silol sites (Si-OH)). This purified silica is covalently bonded with hydrocarbon chains (e.g., C8 or C18), phenyl groups, polar groups, as well as anionic or cationic exchange sites to create an SPE cartridge to selectively extract whatever analyte(s) is/are desired. "Mixed bed" or "copolymeric" columns can be used to extract acidic, basic, and neutral drugs and metabolites all in one procedure which is very applicable for general screening for a broad spectrum of toxicological unknowns. General steps used with SPE columns are: solvate/wet column with methanol, rinse with water and buffer, load specimen on column, wash to remove impurities/contaminants, dry column with air or nitrogen, and elute analytes with elution solvent. Multiple solvents can be used to rinse polar and nonpolar impurities from the column. Solvents can migrate through the SPE column by gravity, under vacuum, positive pressure, or by centrifugation. Although traditional silica-based SPE columns require solvation prior to the addition of a specimen, polymeric sorbents do not require this. Sorbents in polymeric SPE cartridges appear disc-like, rather than silica-based columns that contain a much larger volume of sorbent. For this reason, flow rates using polymeric SPE are often faster when using complex biological matrices, and smaller solvent volumes may be utilized.

Solid phase extraction is amenable to automation, which may be highly desirable in high throughput laboratories. Miniaturization of the SPE column to mini-columns/cartridges and even pipette tips allows for use of reduced specimen volume as well as solvents. These miniaturized techniques fit very well with ethanol and volatile analyses as well as mass spectrometric techniques (e.g., GC/MS and LC/MS). SPE plates are also available in 96-well configurations. Without sample pre-treatment (i.e., dilution, centrifugation, filtration, or protein precipitation), viscosity and density of the biological fluid can be a problem and/or limitation in application of this technique to forensic specimens. It is critical that the extraction capacity of the SPE column be confirmed in the validation of the method, especially with quantitative analyses.

Table 9.5 Sorbents for solid phase extraction (SPE)

Reverse phase/ hydrophobic	Normal phase/hydrophilic	Copolymerized	Cation exchange	Anion exchange
C_8	Silica	C_8/Benzenesulfonic acid	Propylsulfonic acid	Aminopropyl
C_{18}	Dimercaptotriazine	C_8/Aminopropyl	Carboxylic acid	Diethylamino
	Florisil		Benzenesulfonic acid	Quaternary amine
	Cyanopropyl		Triacetic acid	Polyimine
	Alumina (acidic, basic, neutral)			
	Carbon			

The overall principles by which the drug adheres to the stationary phase are similar to those described for LLE. Polar/nonpolar and ionic interactions determine the extent to which the drug interacts with the solid phase, or the liquid (mobile) phase. One notable exception between the two extraction techniques is that SPE can exploit both "like attracts like" and "opposites attract" type interactions. Incorporation of charged species on the stationary phase (e.g., sulfonic acids, quaternary amines) can be used to selectively adsorb basic or acidic species. Provided that the specimen and rinse steps are performed at a pH that maintains the charge on the functional group, the drug will be retained on the column. Conversely, an adjustment in pH to eliminate the charge can be used to elute the drug from the column. Due to the fact that ionic interactions are stronger than either hydrogen bonding or dipole-dipole interactions, careful attention to elution solvent composition (and volume) is required during method development.

Supported Liquid Extraction and Specialized Specimen Clean Up

There is a need for "better, faster, cheaper" techniques to clean up specimens for toxicological analysis. While simultaneously achieving all three characteristics may not be possible, use of multiple technologies may get toxicologists a step closer. Specimens can be quickly filtered through specialized cartridges which will remove lipids, proteins, and artifacts so that a filtrate can be directly analyzed. Cost for use of the cartridge is often offset by the ease and speed of the procedure, reduced solvents and supplies, and increased productivity. Combination of LLE chemistries with a SPE column in a supported liquid extraction (SLE) will provide specimen clean up while also increasing extraction efficiency of the analytes from the matrices. This combination eliminates emulsion formation and precipitation that may occur with standard LLE. While separation using SLE still relies upon differential solubility, the physical nature of the technique offers distinct benefits, including

potential for automation and 96-well plates for high volume testing. Other specialized specimen clean up devices are also available, including cartridge and plate-based consumables for the removal of proteins, lipids, surfactants, and enzymes. Although this increases consumable costs associated with specimen preparation, this approach is gaining in popularity.

Solid Phase Microextraction

Solid phase microextraction (SPME) is another technique that can be applied to ethanol, volatile substances, and drugs in biological specimens. The main differences between SPE and SPME are the size of the sorptive surface and the application of the biological specimen to the extracting material. SPE uses a relatively larger sorptive surface area and extraction from applied liquid samples; SPME uses a relatively smaller sorptive surface area and the sorptive fiber adsorbs analytes from gaseous, liquid, or semi-solid samples upon exposure. Analytes are adsorbed to the coating of the fiber when exposed to the specimen, either directly (e.g., urine or blood) or indirectly (e.g., head space or gas). The extent of extraction within a set time of exposure is proportional to the concentration of the analyte in the specimen. Once equilibrated, the fiber can be transferred to the sampling system for chromatographic (e.g., GC or LC) or immunochemical analysis. Analytes are desorbed from the fiber by exposing it in the injection port of the GC or in an SPME/LC interface desorption chamber. Fiber coating can be selective for specific types of analytes based on the polarity and molecular weight of the analyte. Analytes include but are not limited to gases and small molecular weight compounds, volatiles, amines/nitro-aromatic compounds, alcohols/polar compounds, polar/semi-volatiles, nonpolar large molecular weight compounds, and amines/polar compounds. The range of specificity of fibers/sorbents for analytes is given in Table 9.6. Miniaturization of the SPME is very applicable to today's GC/MS, LC/MS, and immunochemical analytical techniques, and has a distinct advantage with automation for increased efficiency and productivity.

Table 9.6 Solid phase microextraction (SPME) fibers/sorbents

Fibers/sorbents	Types of analytes best used for
Carboxen/polydimethylsiloxane	Gases, low molecular weight compounds
Polydimethylsiloxane	Volatiles
Polydimethylsiloxane/divinylbenzene	Volatiles, amines, nitro-aromatic compounds
Polyacrylate	Polar, semi-volatiles
Carbowax	Alcohols, polar compounds
Polydimethylsiloxane/divinylbenzene	Amines, polar compounds
Polydimethylsiloxane	Nonpolar, large molecular weight compounds

QuEChERS

"QuEChERS" is an acronym for *qu*ick, *e*asy, *ch*eap, *e*ffective, *r*ugged, and *s*afe sample preparation and extraction techniques. QuEChERS is pronounced "catchers". The methodology was first developed for pesticide residue analysis in foodstuffs by Anastassiades, Lehotey, et.al. in 2003 and coined QuEChERS by Schenck and Hobbs in 2004. Basics of the extraction combines a liquid extraction/partitioning from the hydrated or homogenized specimen into acetonitrile, then phase separation with addition of anhydrous magnesium sulfate and sodium chloride and centrifugation. Excessive amounts of these chemicals "salt out" matrix constituents and trap water. The primary extract is then cleaned up with addition of a dispersive (loose) solid phase extraction media (dSPE) and primary secondary amine (PSA) sorbent to further remove interferants. Centrifugation then produces a clean organic extract which can be pipetted into an appropriate vial for a wide variety of chromatographic analyses, be it GC/MS, LC/MS/MS, LC/MS/TOF or any other method of analysis (e.g., GC with NPD, FID, or ECD or LC with UV or FL).

There are a number of different modifications to the QuEChERS approach, but all methods consist of these fundamental steps. The method uses minimal reagents, disposable labware, and routine lab equipment (pipettes and centrifuge) while producing a relatively small amount of nontoxic waste. The simple solvents and dry chemicals/media/sorbent allow for commercial application and packaging of the needed supplies to perform the complete extraction from specimen to analysis on the analytical instrument. The methodology is also very easily adaptable to either low volume, hands on extractions or high volume, mechanically automated applications. Standard QuEChERS extraction methods are the basis of the Association of Analytical Communities AOAC 2007.01 and the European Standard EN 15662.2008 methods for the analysis of pesticide residues in plant foodstuffs. Modification of some buffering salts in the primary extraction with acetonitrile and addition of other sorbents with the clean up have been researched to improve the extraction of a wide range of drugs. Application of this technique has therefore been very well suited for forensic specimens of biological matrices such as whole blood and homogenates of putrefied tissues which are the foundation of many postmortem toxicology cases.

Esoteric Isolation/Extraction Techniques

Some esoteric isolation techniques such as microwave extractions, soxlet extractions, countercurrent distribution, steam distillations, vacuum distillations, and Stas-Otto procedures are beyond the scope of this basic principles chapter. A vast assortment of techniques can be used to isolate/extract various potential analytes from the large array of biological matrices. There is no single method to isolate/extract every toxicological analyte we may be faced with, but all procedures can be properly developed, validated, and applied to insure quality results.

Final Thoughts

There is no one method used to analyze all drugs or toxins. Just as there are "mutiple ways to skin a catfish", there are mutiple ways to analyze a specimen for a drug. All specimen preparation techniques have advantages and limitations. Each area of forensic toxicology has a different focus and therefore may use different methods and procedures. Regardless of the methodologies used or the extent of their application (i.e., qualitative versus quantitative, screening versus confirmation, or even stand-alone quantitation of a single analyte) proper specimen handling and extraction is essential for valid analytical results. Remember, what goes in affects what comes out.

Appendix 1

Buffer solutions[a]

Buffer	pH	pH Range	Reciepe
Acetate	4.8	3.6–5.6	4.789 g Na acetate (anhydrous) 2.498 g Acetic acid
Bicarbonate	9.9	9.2–10.6	4.35 g Na bicarbonate 5.115 g Na carbonate (anhydrous)
Citrate	6.0	3.0–5.6	12.044 g Na citrate dihydrate 11.341 g Citric acid
Phosphate	7.4	5.8–7.4	20.209 g Na phosphate dibasic 3.394 g Na phosphate monobasic

[a]All buffers 0.1 M at 25 °C Dilute in 800 mL of deionized water. Adjust pH with 1 M HCl or NaOH as appropriate

Acknowledgment A most sincere thank you to Theodore J. Siek for permitting continued use of some of his previous items and reviewing this revision of his prior contributions. Appreciate Emily Lemieux's review of the chapter.

Further Readings

Anastassiades M, Lehotey S et al (2003) Fast and easy multiresidue method employing acetonitrile extraction/partitioning and "dispersive solid-phase extraction" for the determination of pesticide residues in produce. J AOAC Int 86(2):412–431

AOAC Official Method 2007.01 Pesticide Residues in Foods by Acetonitrile Extraction and Partitioning with Magnesium Sulfate, 10.1.04.

European Standard Method EN 15662.2008 Foods of Plant Origin—Determination of Pesticide Residues Using GC-MS and/or LC-MS/MS Following Acetonitrile Extraction/Partitioning and Clean-up by Dispersive SPE – QuEChERS method

Hinshaw J (2003) Solid phase microextraction. LC/GC North America 21:1056–1061

Moffat A, Osselton M, Widdop B (eds) (2004) Clarke's analysis of drugs and poisons. Pharmaceutical Press, London

Schenck F, Hobbs J (2004) Evaluation of the quick, easy, cheap, effective, rugged and safe (QuECHERS) approach to pesticide residue analysis. Bull Environ Contam Toxicol 73:24–30

Siek T (1978) Effective use of organic solvents to remove drugs from biologic specimens. Clin Toxicol 13:205–230

Telepchak M, August T, Cheney G (2004) Forensic and clinical applications of solid phase extraction. Humana Press, Totowa, NJ

Ultraviolet-Visible Spectrophotometry

10

Kenneth Cole and Barry S. Levine

Abstract

Ultraviolet (UV) and visible spectrophotometry have been utilized in forensic toxicology for both qualitative and quantitative analysis. Lambert discovered that for monochromatic radiation, absorbance was directly proportional to the path length of the incident light through the material. Beer (1797–1850) expanded Lambert's work by studying the relationships between concentrations of a substance in solution and found that the same linear relationship existed between concentration and absorbance as Lambert had found between thickness and absorbance. The Beer-Lambert law is the basis for quantitative analysis using UV and visible spectrophotometry. Color tests involve the reaction of a specimen, a protein-free filtrate, or an extract with a reagent or a series of reagents to produce a color or change in color. Besides color tests, another use of spectrophotometry in forensic toxicology is in the detection systems of a number of commercially available immunoassays. Many immunoassays involve the conversion of a substrate by an enzyme into a product that causes either an increase or a decrease in absorbance at a particular wavelength.

Keywords

Spectrophotometry · UV-VIS · Forensic toxicology

Introduction

Ultraviolet (UV)-visible spectrophotometry is one of the most useful and widely used tools available for quantitative analysis. Characteristically, this technique has broad applicability to both organic and inorganic systems, moderate to high selectivity, sensitivities that are typically in the 10^{-4} to 10^{-5} M range, reliable accuracy with typical relative uncertainties in the range of 1–3%, and convenient methods of data acquisition.

The principle of operation for UV-visible spectrophotometry is based on two phenomena: (1) substances selectively absorb or emit electromagnetic energy at different wavelengths, and (2) the energy absorption properties of a substance

K. Cole
Annapolis, MD, USA

B. S. Levine (✉)
Office of the Chief Medical Examiner,
Baltimore, MD, USA
e-mail: blevine@som.umaryland.edu

© Springer Nature Switzerland AG 2020
B. S. Levine, S. Kerrigan (eds.), *Principles of Forensic Toxicology*,
https://doi.org/10.1007/978-3-030-42917-1_10

can be used to measure the concentration of the substance in solution. Before continuing, a review of electromagnetic radiation is in order.

Electromagnetic Radiation

Electromagnetic radiation shows both wave and particle characteristics, depending on how the radiation is observed. As a wave, electromagnetic radiation is composed of an electric field component and a magnetic field component (Fig. 10.1).

Electromagnetic radiation differs from other types of waves in several important respects. Familiar waves such as sound waves and water waves exist only by virtue of the media in which they exist, whereas electromagnetic waves can travel in a vacuum. Sound waves traveling through a gas consist of alternating zones of compression and rarefaction, and the molecular displacements that occur are in the direction that the waves travel. An electromagnetic wave is very different. Because it can travel through a vacuum, the medium is not essential. When such a wave comes in contact with matter, important interactions affect the wave and the material. The radiation couples with the medium, and how this occurs is best considered by referring to Fig. 10.1, which shows that the wave has two components: (1) an electric field and (2) a magnetic field. These components are in two planes at right angles to each other. A given point in space experiences a periodic disturbance in electric and magnetic fields as the wave passes by. A charged particle such as an electron couples its charge with these field fluctuations and oscillates with

the frequency of the wave. In other words, at the proper wavelength, an electron will interact with the electromagnetic wave and absorb energy. Conversely, an oscillating electron induces electric and magnetic fields and will also generate an electromagnetic wave or light.

Electromagnetic radiation is characterized by a wavelength (λ) and a frequency (υ). These two physical quantities are related to the velocity of light (c) by the equation $\lambda\upsilon = c$. The velocity of light is a constant in a vacuum (2.99792×10^8 m/s). Various wavelengths and the types of interactions produced in atoms and molecules are given in Table 10.1.

The wave model fails to account for phenomena associated with the absorption and emission of electromagnetic energy. These processes can be better explained with a model in which electromagnetic radiation is viewed as a stream of particles or energy packets, known as photons. The energy of a photon is proportional to the frequency of the radiation. This relationship is given by the Bohr equation $E = h\upsilon = hc/\lambda$, where E is the energy, h is Planck's constant (6.62618×10^{-34} Js), υ is the frequency of the radiation in hertz (Hz), c is the speed of light, and λ is the wavelength in meters. These dual views of electromagnetic radiation as waves and particles are

Table 10.1 Electromagnetic spectrum

Type of radiation	Frequency Range (Hz)	Wavelength range	Type of transition
Gamma-rays	10^{20}–10^{24}	$<10^{-12}$ m	Nuclear
X-rays	10^{17}–10^{20}	10^{-9}–10^{-12} m	Inner electron
Ultraviolet	10^{15}–10_{17}	400–1×10^{-9} m	Outer electron
Visible	4–7.5×10^{14}	750–450×10^{-9} m	Outer electron
Near-infrared	10^{12}–10^{14}	2.5×10^{-6}–750×10^{-9} m	Outer electron vibrations
Infrared	10^{11}–10^{12}	25–2.5×10^{-6} m	Molecular vibrations
Microwaves	10^8–10^{12}	1.0×10^{-3}–25×10^{-6} m	Molecular rotations, electron spin flips
Radiowaves	10^0–10^8	$>1 \times 10^{-3}$ m	Nuclear spin flips

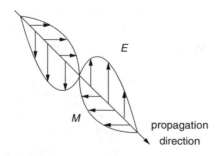

Fig. 10.1 Representation of electromagnetic radiation as a wave. (E = electric; M = magnetic)

complementary, not mutually exclusive, and this behavior has since been applied to other elementary particles such as electrons, neutrons, and protons.

The Laws of Lambert and Beer

The absorbance of light by materials was first explored by the German mathematician Johann Heinrich Lambert (1728–1777). Lambert discovered that for monochromatic radiation, absorbance was directly proportional to the path length of the incident light through the material. He formulated this discovery into Lambert's law: The proportion of radiation absorbed by a substance is independent of the intensity of the incident radiation. This means that each successive layer having a thickness of dx of a medium absorbs an equal fraction $-dI/I$ of the radiant intensity incident upon it. Mathematically this is represented as

$$-\frac{dI}{I} = bdx \qquad (10.1)$$

where b is a constant. Integration of this equation for a passage of light for a distance of l proceeds as follows:

$$\int \frac{dI}{I} = -b \int_0^l dx \qquad (10.2)$$

or

$$\ln I = -bl + g \qquad (10.3)$$

where g is an integration constant. Using the boundary condition that $I = I_0$ when $l = 0$ where I_0 is the intensity of radiation before passage through the medium, g can be evaluated as

$$g = \ln I_0 \qquad (10.4)$$

Substitution back into Eq. (10.3) gives

$$\ln I = -bl + \ln I_0 \qquad (10.5)$$

or

$$\ln \frac{I_0}{I} = bl \qquad (10.6)$$

or

$$I = I_0 e^{-bl} \qquad (10.7)$$

Using the more customary common logarithms, Eq. (10.7) is expressed as follows:

$$\log I_0 / I = bl / 2.303 = A \qquad (10.8)$$

where A is the absorbance. Absorbance has also been referred to as "extinction" or "optical density." The two terms are archaic, and their use is discouraged by the International Union of Pure and Applied Chemistry (IUPAC).

Transmittance (T) is the ratio of the intensity of the transmitted radiation to the incident radiation:

$$T \equiv \frac{I}{I_0} \qquad (10.9)$$

Substituting transmittance into Eq. (10.8) gives

$$\log \frac{I}{T} = A \qquad (10.10)$$

The German astronomer Wilhelm Beer (1797–1850) expanded Lambert's work by studying the relationships between concentrations of a substance in solution and found that the same linear relationship existed between concentration and absorbance as Lambert had found between thickness and absorbance. For a substance in solution at concentration c, Beer's law states that

$$\log \frac{I}{T} = A = \text{const} \times \text{conc} \qquad (10.11)$$

The Lambert-Beer law combines Eqs. (10.8) and (10.11) to give

$$A = \log I_0 / I = \varepsilon cl \qquad (10.12)$$

where A is the absorbance, ε is the molar absorptivity, c is the concentration of the solution in mol/L, and l is the path length of light through the solution. The molar absorptivity constant, ε, is a proportionality constant with units of L cm^{-1} mol^{-1} and is characteristic of the substance absorbing the light and of the wavelength.

This relationship indicates that the absorbance of a solution is linearly related to the concentration of the absorbing species and that quantifica-

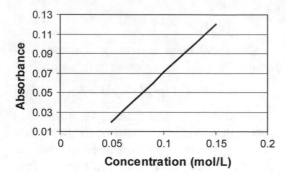

Fig. 10.2 Example of a Beer-Lambert law plot

tions may be made by plotting concentration of a solution versus absorbance (Fig. 10.2).

The linearity of the Beer-Lambert law is limited by chemical and instrumental factors. Causes of nonlinearity include deviations in absorptivity coefficients at high concentrations (>0.01 M) due to electrostatic interactions between molecules in close proximity, scattering of light due to particulates in the sample, fluorescence or phosphorescence of the sample, changes in the refractive index at high analyte concentration, shifts in chemical equilibria as a function of concentration, nonmonochromatic radiation, and stray light. Deviations can be minimized by using a relatively flat part of the absorption spectrum such as the maximum of an absorption band.

Instrumentation

Instruments for measuring the absorption of UV and visible radiation are generally composed of one or more light sources, a wavelength selector, sample container, detector, signal processor, and readout devices. Some of these components are discussed below.

Sources

It is important in UV and visible spectrometry to use a continuum source whose power does not change over a considerable range of wavelengths. For the UV range of 160–375 nm, the source is usually a hydrogen or deuterium discharge lamp.

These lamps use an electrical arc to produce excited molecules, which then dissociate into two atomic species plus UV photons. As such, these lamps require a regulated power supply to maintain a constant intensity of light.

The tungsten filament lamp is the most common source of visible and near-infrared radiation. This lamp will produce most of its energy in the infrared region, producing usable visible light in the 350–2000 nm range. The lower limit of 350 nm is usually imposed by the absorption of radiation by the glass housing of the lamp. Modern instruments commonly use a tungsten/halogen lamp as the visible light source. The lifetimes of these lamps are nearly double those of tungsten lamps. Due to the high operating temperatures of tungsten/halogen lamps (≈3200 °C), they are usually made of quartz. These lamps use a small amount of iodine that reacts with the gaseous tungsten that sublimes from the filament and assists in redepositing the tungsten onto the filament. These lamps are more efficient and have an output range well into the UV range.

Wavelength Selectors

Wavelength selection is accomplished with a monochromator. A modern monochromator consists of an entrance slit to provide a rectangular optical image from the source, a collimating lens or mirror to produce a parallel beam of radiation, a prism or a grating to disperse the radiation into its component wavelengths, a focusing element to reform the image of the entrance slit and to focus the light, and an exit slit that isolates the desired spectral band.

Two types of dispersing elements are found in monochromators: reflection gratings and prisms. In a prism monochromator, refraction at the two faces results in angular dispersion of the radiation. A reflection grating monochromator has a reflective surface onto which small grooves have been evenly etched. Light entering the monochromator strikes the grating at an angle and is dispersed. The grating offers advantages over a prism in that it gives linear wavelength dispersion along the focal plane of the light, whereas a prism gives greater dispersion at shorter wavelengths than at longer wavelengths.

Sample Cell

In any type of spectroscopy, the cells or cuvettes that hold the sample and solvent must be constructed of a material that is nearly transparent to the radiation in the spectral region of interest. For observing samples in the UV range (below 350 nm), a cuvette made of quartz or fused silica is desired. Both of these materials are transparent in the UV and visible range. Silicate glass and some plastics can be used in the visible range above 350 nm. The most common cell length for measuring absorbance in the UV and visible regions is 1 cm. Matched and calibrated cuvettes are available from several commercial sources. Cuvettes must be treated carefully: The use of unmatched cuvettes or the presence of fingerprints, grease, or other deposits on the walls of the cuvettes will dramatically decrease the quality of the absorbance data.

Detectors

For UV-visible spectrometry, the detector usually consists of a photon transducer. These detectors usually have an active surface capable of absorbing radiation that causes a photocurrent or enhances conductivity.

Several types of photon transducers are used in UV-visible spectrometry: photovoltaic or barrier-layer cells, phototubes, photomultiplier tubes, and silicon photodiodes. The photovoltaic cell usually consists of a copper or iron electrode that has a layer of a semiconducting material (e.g., selenium) and a layer of gold or silver on the outer surface of the semiconductor. Light striking the photovoltaic cell generates a current at the interface of the semiconductor layer and the metal. A typical cell has a maximum sensitivity around 550 nm, with the response falling to around 10% of the maximum around 350 and

750 nm. The photocurrent produced is directly proportional to the number of photons that strike the semiconductor surface (typically 10–100 µA). This type of detector is rugged and inexpensive and requires no external electrical source. Yet this detector also has several disadvantages. Due to the cell's low internal resistance, it is difficult to amplify its output, thus producing lower sensitivity at low levels of transmittance. In addition, the cell exhibits fatigue—its output decreases gradually during continued illumination.

The phototube is a vacuum tube that consists of a semicylindrical cathode and a wire anode. The inner surface of the cathode supports a layer of photoemissive material that ejects electrons when struck by radiation. When an electric potential is applied across the electrodes, electrons ejected from the photoemissive surface flow toward the anode, resulting in a photocurrent. The photocurrent is about one-tenth that produced by a photovoltaic cell, but because of the phototube's high electrical resistance, signal amplification is readily accomplished, accelerating the electrons that are ejected from the photoemissive surface. When an electron strikes the dynode, several electrons are ejected. This process is repeated with subsequent dynodes producing a cascade of electrons that is finally collected at the anode. It is common for a photomultiplier to generate a cascade of $>10^6$ electrons for every incident photon.

A major improvement in detector technology occurred with the photodiode array. In this detector, the photosensitive elements are small silicon photodiodes. Each diode has a dedicated capacitor and is connected to a switch register. These capacitors are charged to a specific level; when the diode is impinged by photons, the capacitors are discharged. The capacitors are then recharged at regular intervals. The amount of charge needed to recharge each capacitor is directly proportional to the light intensity.

A recent innovation in the detection system is the charge-coupled device (CCD) array. Like the diode-array detector, the CCD is capable of simultaneously measuring absorption at a range of wavelengths. CCDs are multi-channel silicon array detectors in which photosensitive semi-conducting silicon pixels collect incident light and transfer this charge in a stepwise process. Whereas a diode-array detector uses 512 or 1024 photosensitive diodes, a CCD uses 2048 pixels.

Instrument Configurations

Figure 10.3 is a schematic of a single-beam UV-visible spectrophotometer. Single-beam instruments vary widely in their complexity and performance characteristics. A very simple instrument may consist of a battery-powered tungsten bulb source, a set of glass filters to select wavelengths, test tubes for cuvettes, a phototube detector, and microammeter for readout. A more sophisticated instrument may be a computer-controlled instrument with a range of 200–1000 nm or more. These instruments consist of interchangeable tungsten/deuterium lamp sources, high-resolution grating monochromator, rectangular silica cuvettes, a photomultiplier detector, and digitized output to permit storage and presentation in a variety of forms. Single-beam instruments have the inherent advantages of greater energy throughput, superior signal to noise ratios, and less cluttered sample compartments.

Many modern spectrophotometers are based on a double-beam design. Fig. 10.4 illustrates a typical double-beam instrument. In this instrument, the beam emerging from the monochromator is split by a mirror. One beam passes through the reference solution to a detector, and the second beam simultaneously passes through the sample of interest into a second matched detector. The two detector outputs are amplified and their ratio determined electronically and displayed by the readout device. Double-beam instruments compensate for fluctuations in the output of the source and variations in source intensity and wavelength.

In addition, they continuously record absorbance or transmittance spectra.

The most recent type of spectrophotometer is a single-beam instrument using a diode-array detector. This type of instrument is illustrated in Fig. 10.5. Radiation from the source is focused on the sample and then passes into a monochromator with a fixed grating. The dispersed radiation is then reflected onto a photodiode-array transducer, which consists of a linear array of several hundred photodiodes mounted on a silicon chip. The monochromator slit is made identical to the width of one of the diodes. Thus the output of each diode corresponds to the radiation of a different wavelength. A spectrum is obtained by scanning these outputs sequentially. Because these electronic outputs are scanned rapidly, the data for an entire spectrum can be accumulated in <1 s. Moreover, the diode-array instrument is simple in design. It has few moving parts and needs no recalibration and minimal maintenance. A disadvantage of this instrument is its limited resolution of 1–2 nm.

Forensic Toxicology Applications

Color tests are one of the oldest forms of toxicology testing and can be viewed as assays using visible spectrophotometry. Color tests involve the reaction of a specimen, a protein-free filtrate, or an extract with a reagent or a series of reagents to produce a color or change in color. The biggest advantages to color tests are simplicity and ease of use. No sophisticated equipment is required and the time needed to train analysts is short. A negative result for a color test is helpful in ruling out a drug intoxication.

Two of the most commonly used color tests are for salicylate and acetaminophen, two over-the-counter non-narcotic analgesics. Salicylate, the metabolite of aspirin, reacts with an acidic

Fig. 10.3 Schematic of a single-beam spectrophotometer

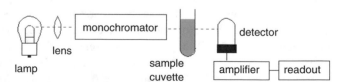

Fig. 10.4 Schematic of a double-beam spectrophotometer

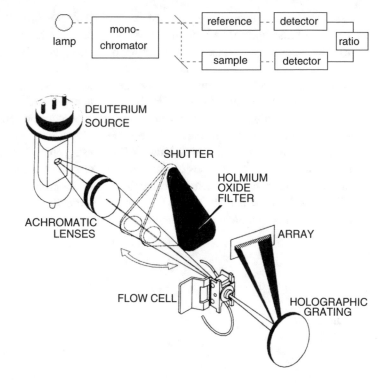

Fig. 10.5 Schematic of a single-beam spectrophotometer with a diode-array detector

solution of ferric chloride to produce a purple color. This color reaction requires the presence of both the free phenolic group and the free carboxylic acid group that appears on the salicylate molecule. Therefore, aspirin itself will not produce a positive result prior to hydrolysis to salicylate. The test for acetaminophen is performed on urine or a protein-free filtrate of blood and requires heating at 100 °C after hydrochloric acid is added. A blue color after the addition of 1% o-cresol in water and ammonium hydroxide constitutes a positive test for acetaminophen. Both of these color tests have sufficient sensitivity to detect the therapeutic use of the respective drugs. Although both color tests have a high degree of specificity, confirmation by an alternate analytical technique is necessary.

Other color tests may be used in the forensic toxicology laboratory. Some of the more esoteric color tests are listed in Table 10.2. However, for a number of reasons, these color tests are rarely used in the modern forensic toxicology laboratory. For example, they lack the necessary sensitivity to detect therapeutic concentrations of many drugs. In addition, they have low specific-

Table 10.2 Esoteric color tests

Substance identified	Color reagent(s)
Borate	Carminic acid, sulfuric acid
Bromide	Gold chloride
Iron	2,4,6-Tripyridyltriazine, thioglycolic acid
Isoniazid	Nitroprusside, sodium hydroxide
Nitrite	Sulfanilic acid, naphthylamine
Paraquat	Dithionite
Trichloroethanol	Sodium hydroxide, pyridine

ity as many drugs may have similar absorbance. Moreover, parent drugs and any active or inactive metabolites that retain the chromophore moiety will contribute to the measured absorbance.

Color reactions are also used to make visible thin-layer chromatographic spots. Ninhydrin is used to identify primary amines. Diphenylcarbazone and mercuric nitrate are used to identify barbiturates. Iodoplatinate reacts with nitrogenous bases to produce a purple color. Dragendorff's reagent produces orange, red-orange, or brown-orange color with nitrogenous bases. Carbamates can be detected by spraying with furfural and exposing to hydrochloric acid fumes. A rapid screening test for the major metabolite of marijuana uses Fast blue B.

Besides color tests, another use of spectrophotometry in forensic toxicology is in the detection systems of a number of commercially available immunoassays. Many immunoassays involve the conversion of a substrate by an enzyme into a product that causes either an increase or a decrease in absorbance at a particular wavelength. This change in absorbance can then be correlated to the amount of a drug in the specimen. For example, in EMIT®, the enzymatic activity causes the conversion of the cofactor nicotine adenine dinucleotide (NAD) to its reduced form NADH. Whereas NAD does not have any absorbance at 340 nm, NADH does; therefore, greater enzyme activity causes more production of NADH and more absorbance at 340 nm. The amount of absorbance is then used to determine the amount of drug in the specimen.

A common method in hospital laboratories to measure serum ethanol is an enzymatic method using alcohol dehydrogenase. In this reaction, the enzyme converts the ethanol to acetaldehyde and in the process, NAD is converted to NADH. The increase in absorbance at 340 nm is then used to determine the serum ethanol concentration.

Chromatography

11

Megan Grabenauer and David T. Stafford

Abstract

The molecular identification techniques used in forensic toxicology, the most significant of which is mass spectrometry (MS), are enhanced by minimizing the number of molecular species presented to the instrument at any given time. The most powerful separating technique available is chromatography, which has been in use since approximately 1900. In this chapter, fundamental principles of chromatographic separations are reviewed.

Keywords

Chromatography · Forensic toxicology · TLC · LC · GC

David T. Stafford was deceased at the time of publication.

M. Grabenauer (✉)
RTI International, Research Triangle Park, NC, USA
e-mail: mgrabenauer@rti.org

D. T. Stafford (Deceased)

Acronyms

AMU	atomic mass unit
APCI	atmospheric pressure chemical ionization
APPI	atmospheric pressure photoionization
CI	chemical ionization
EI	electron impact ionization
ESI	electrospray ionization
FID	flame ionization detector
FTIR	Fourier transform infrared
GC	gas chromatography
HETP	height equivalent to a theoretical plate
HPLC	high-performance liquid chromatography
ID	inner diameter
IR	infrared
IRD	infrared detector
LC	liquid chromatography
LLOQ	lower limit of quantification
MDQ	minimum detectable quantity
MS	mass spectrometry
NPD	nitrogen–phosphorous detector
PEEK	polyetheretherketone
PTFE	polytetrafluoroethylene
RI	retention index
rrt	relative retention time
SPME	solid-phase micro extraction
SPP	superficially porous particles
STP	standard temperature and pressure
TCD	thermal conductivity detector
TLC	thin-layer chromatography

© Springer Nature Switzerland AG 2020
B. S. Levine, S. Kerrigan (eds.), *Principles of Forensic Toxicology*,
https://doi.org/10.1007/978-3-030-42917-1_11

TN   Trennzahl number
UHPLC   ultra-high-performance liquid
        chromatography
UV   ultraviolet
WCOT   wall-coated open tubular

Definition

A nearly universal definition of chromatography is that it is a separation process based on the differential distribution of sample components between a moving and a stationary phase. This definition applies to all types of chromatography except size-exclusion chromatography, which depends on the differential diffusion of sample components in stationary phase pores of closely controlled sizes. This definition includes three very important facets:

1. Chromatography is a separation process. It is not an identification technique in the sense that infrared (IR) and MS are because it provides no molecular identification data. The fact that a component may have the same retention time as a known standard, even on several different columns, will increase the analyst's confidence that the two are the same, but identification will not have been achieved.
2. The chromatographic separation process depends on differential distribution. Distribution here refers to the relative concentrations of a component in two immiscible phases at mass transfer and temperature equilibrium, as described by Nernst in 1891. If two components do not have different distribution coefficients, they cannot be separated chromatographically.
3. The chromatographic separation process uses two immiscible phases. These may be a gas and a liquid or polymer, a gas and a solid, two liquids, or a liquid and a solid. A rather recent development uses a supercritical fluid as the mobile phase.

History

Early chromatographic separations were described by a Russian botanist, Michael S. Tswett, who published some of his work involving the separation of leaf extracts using a glass tube packed with a form of calcium carbonate as the stationary phase and petroleum ether as the mobile phase. The extract was placed at the head of the column, and then, the mobile phase was trickled through the column by gravity flow. The separation of the specimen into colored bands that could then be removed and studied gave us the term "chromatography," or color writing. This work was the genesis of liquid chromatography (LC).

Little changed in the art of chromatography until the mid to late 1930s. By that time, good-quality, small-diameter silica particles were available, and a mechanism had been developed to affix a thin layer of these particles to a glass plate. A sample placed near the bottom of the plate could then be separated by mobile phase rising through the stationary phase layer via capillary action. The small particle size and concentrated specimen spot resulted in much more efficient separations than Tswett's classical column method, and because several specimens could be processed simultaneously on a single plate, analytical time decreased. Detection was frequently by ultraviolet (UV) absorption, fluorescence, or charring with sulfuric acid spray. Thus, thin-layer chromatography (TLC) was born. Izmailov and Shraiber reported separations of a number of pharmaceuticals in 1938–1939.

In 1941, Martin and Synge elucidated the concept of partitioning, for which they later received the Nobel Prize. In 1951–1952, Martin and James reported the development of a chromatographic process using inert gas as the mobile phase, resulting in what is today called gas chromatography (GC). The first commercial GC instrumentation became available in 1954, and the analytical capabilities were so great that there was explosive growth in analytical technique and instrumentation. In the late 1950s, M.J.E. Golay reported dramatically improved column efficiency using narrow-bore columns. This discovery led to the development of capillary or wall-coated open tubular (WCOT) column chromatography. The production of the first WCOT columns was difficult and expensive, and they exhibited unstable performance. Not until the early 1970s, when the expiration of the patents on some WCOT column technology was in sight, did better-quality columns become available. The best of these were glass columns, although they were fragile and therefore tedious to handle. In 1979, fused silica was introduced as a column material, and its inertness and handling characteristics were so superior that fused silica capillary columns became, and remain today, the most widely used GC columns. For this reason, the remainder of the GC-related discussion in this chapter will focus on GC using capillary columns.

Development of the Technology

Similar to GC, both classical column LC and TLC are partitioning processes. LC changed little from Tswett's time until the mid to late 1960s. At that time, dependable mobile phase pumps and low-volume, sensitive flow-through UV detectors became available, giving rise to high-performance LC (HPLC). Subsequently, in the early to mid 2000s, smaller stationary phase particles (<2 μm) were introduced, leading to the development of ultra-high-performance LC (UHPLC), a specialized subset of HPLC.

The tremendous separating capability of chromatographic methods and their lack of capability to supply molecular identification data made it inevitable that attempts would be made to combine them with identification techniques, such as IR and MS. Because of the relative insensitivity of IR, most early work concentrated on marrying GC and MS. Since this work began in earnest in the late 1960s, the instrumentation developed was based on the GC and MS techniques in popular use at the time and was typically a combination of packed-column GC and either magnetic sector or quadrupole MS. The concurrent avail-

ability of more powerful, less expensive, and more convenient computers gave even more impetus to the development of hyphenated techniques. The first GC-MS systems provided somewhat less than routine operation; however, present-day instrumentation is powerful and reliable and allows for considerable automation. The GC-MS systems currently in analytical use are almost all capillary-column GCs directly connected to quadrupole or ion-trap MS instruments.

Compared to GC-MS, the combination of LC and MS was slower to develop, primarily because HPLC instrumentation was developed later than GC, but also because of the problems associated with handling the mobile phases, some of which contain salts, and the large volume of vapor produced when the eluent is vaporized for transfer into the MS. Perhaps the most significant advances in LC-MS came in the early 1990s when atmospheric ionization sources, such as electrospray ionization (ESI), atmospheric pressure chemical ionization (APCI), and atmospheric pressure photoionization (APPI), became commercially available. Today, these are the most widely used LC-MS interfaces.

Principles

The primary reason to subject any specimen to chromatography is to separate one or more components from the other components for identification (e.g., by MS), quantification, or pattern recognition (e.g., accelerant analysis, which is sometimes a forensic, but not toxicologic, analysis). Figure 11.1 presents a typical chromatogram of a two-component mixture, with several features indicated. This chromatogram is a graph of the detector response as a function of time of analysis from a GC or HPLC determination. If the track of a TLC plate were scanned with a densitometer, a similar plot would be expected. However, that plot would be of component density as ordinate (x-axis) versus distance from the origin or distance from the origin relative to the mobile phase front, R_f, as abscissa (y-axis).

Fig. 11.1 Typical
chromatogram

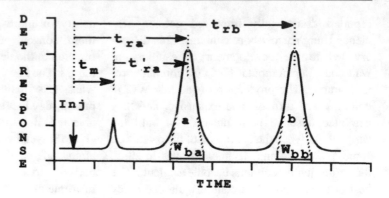

The first peak after injection, with a retention time of t_m, corresponds to an unretained component, which spent no time in the stationary phase. In the older GC literature, this time may be referred to as t_o, or the air peak. With a flame ionization detector (FID), t_m may be determined by injecting natural gas or butane from a cigarette lighter; in HPLC, it is the negative/positive response observed when the injection solvent reaches the detector. The time from injection to a peak maximum is the retention time, t_r; t_{ra} for peak **a**, and t_{rb} for peak **b**. The difference between t_r and t_m is t'_r, the adjusted retention time (e.g., t'_{ra} for peak **a**, where $t'_{ra} = t_{ra} - t_m$). The average mol-

ecule of each peak spends the same amount of time, t_m, in the mobile phase; a molecule in the mobile phase is carried through the column with the velocity of the mobile phase. Thus, because t_r represents the total time in the column, and t_m represents the time in the mobile phase, t'_r represents the time spent in the stationary phase. Separation is achieved when the molecules of two components interact differently with the stationary phase and, therefore, spend different lengths of time in the stationary phase.

In chromatography, the distribution coefficient (referred to earlier in this chapter) is designated K_d (K_{da} for analyte **a**) and is defined as:

$$K_{da} = \frac{\text{concentration of } \mathbf{a} \text{ in the stationary phase}}{\text{concentration of } \mathbf{a} \text{ in the mobile phase}} \tag{11.1}$$

The distribution coefficient for analyte **a** is a function of the temperature, pressure, stationary phase (P_s), and mobile phase (P_m):

$$K_{da} = f\left(T, P, P_s, P_m\right) \tag{11.2}$$

In GC, operating pressures are relatively low, with head pressures typically 25–30 psig for packed columns and 5–15 psig for WCOT columns. The nature of the inert gas, P_m, has little effect on K_d; therefore, K_{da} can be considered a function of T and P_s. In HPLC, operating temperatures are frequently ambient or up to a maximum of about 60 °C. Although pressures may reach up to 15,000 psig in UHPLC, the K_d values between condensed phases are only slightly

affected by pressure; therefore, K_{da} can be considered a function of P_s and P_m. Here, both the nature and concentration of P_m may have an effect. For instance, the K_{da} in 30% methanol/water may be very different than the K_{da} in 50% methanol/water or 30% acetonitrile/water. Although most analysts never measure K_d or have any knowledge of its numerical value, it is important to understand how it is affected, controlled, and manipulated because it governs chromatographic performance, and most of the parameters over which the analyst has control are set or changed to achieve differences in K_d between analytes.

As indicated previously, a primary purpose of chromatography is to separate, or resolve, the components of a specimen; therefore, it is convenient to have some way of describing this resolution. Chromatographically, the resolution, R, between two peaks is defined as the difference in their retention times relative to the peaks' average width at base, W_b. Referring to Fig. 11.1:

$$R = \frac{(t_{rb} - t_{ra})}{(1/2)(W_{ba} + W_{bb})} = \frac{(t'_{rb} - t'_{ra})}{(1/2)(W_{ba} + W_{bb})} \tag{11.3}$$

Resolution is a dimensionless number, and as a result, all factors must be in the same units. For two Gaussian peaks of the same size, complete (baseline) resolution will be achieved at approximately $R = 1.5$. At $R = 1$, the two peaks will overlap by about 10%; R for the two peaks in Fig. 11.1 is approximately 4.

Resolution is calculated using Eq. 11.3 and measurements taken from the chromatogram; however, this does not address the parameters at the analyst's disposal to control or modify R. To examine these, consider the general resolution equation:

$$R = (1/4) \quad \underbrace{\frac{(\alpha - 1)}{(\alpha)}}_{\text{Selectivity}} \quad \times \quad \underbrace{\frac{(k_b)}{(k_b + 1)}}_{\text{Capacity}} \quad \times \quad \underbrace{(N^{1/2})}_{\text{Efficiency}} \tag{11.4}$$

Equation 11.4 shows that resolution is a function of the product of a selectivity (α) term, a capacity (k) term, and the square root of an efficiency term (N). These, then, are the factors that can be altered to control or modify R.

The capacity term does not refer to volumetric or gravimetric capacity but rather to the capacity of the column to retard the passage of a component through the column. The capacity factor or partition ratio k (sometimes designated k' in older literature) is the ratio of the adjusted retention time to the time required for an unretained component to pass through the column:

$$k = t'_{ra} / t_m = (t_{ra} - t_m) / t_m \tag{11.5}$$

In GC, the partition ratio is a function of temperature; in HPLC, it is a function of the mobile phase concentration and composition. If the temperature of the GC oven is increased, k decreases because K_d decreases. As the temperature is increased, the analyte vapor pressure increases. Therefore, the analyte concentration in the stationary phase decreases, the analyte concentration in the mobile phase increases, and following Eq. 11.1, K_d must decrease. Every GC operator has observed this effect. At higher temperatures, analytes elute more quickly. Because t_r decreases and t_m remains constant, k must decrease. The retention time can be manipulated by adjusting the temperature to change K_d, and the resulting effect can be observed and measured as k, a dimensionless number.

The distribution coefficient and k are directly related through β, the phase ratio, a property of the column geometry:

$$\beta = \frac{\text{Column volume (or cross-sectional area) available to the mobile phase}}{\text{Column volume (or cross-sectional area) available to the stationary phase}} \tag{11.6}$$

β is the proportionality constant relating K_d and k:

$$K_d = \beta k \qquad (11.7)$$

Selectivity, α, describes the relative interaction of two analytes with the stationary phase and is defined as the ratio of the two analytes' adjusted retention times:

$$\alpha = t'_{rb} / t'_{ra} \qquad (11.8)$$

Substituting from Eq. 11.5 and Eq. 11.7, it can be shown that

$$\alpha = k_b / k_a = K_b / K_a \qquad (11.9)$$

In GC, temperature changes will have only a minor effect on α. The two peaks under consideration usually have very close t_r values; therefore, according to Eq. 11.9, their K_ds are nearly equal. A change in K_a will be matched by a proportional change in K_b, and the ratio will remain constant. To change α, it is necessary to change the stationary phase. In HPLC, α can be changed by changing the stationary phase or, more conveniently, by changing the mobile phase concentration or the mobile phase components. Either of these approaches can be used to manipulate the K_ds.

The column efficiency, N, in Eq. 11.4, relates the time an analyte remains in the column, t_r, to band broadening as described by W_b:

$$N = 16(t_r / W_b)^2 \qquad (11.10)$$

or using the peak width at half peak height, $W_{1/2}$:

$$N = 5.546(t_r / W_{1/2})^2 \qquad (11.11)$$

Equation 11.10 was derived from an analysis of the mass transfer in the chromatographic column, and Eq. 11.11 results from consideration of the geometry of a Gaussian peak. Column efficiency must be calculated from an *isothermal* GC or *isocratic* HPLC run. Calculating N using either Eq. 11.10 or 11.11 yields a dimensionless number, referred to as the number of theoretical plates in the total column. This is perhaps a confusing choice of nomenclature, but remember that many of the individuals who derived these relationships worked in the petroleum industry and used distillation columns that frequently contained actual plates to affect vapor/liquid contact. When the efficiency of these plates is taken into consideration, the number of theoretical plates or number of vapor/liquid equilibria can be calculated. A similar concept applies to chromatography. A more convenient indicator of column efficiency, which allows efficiency between columns of different lengths to be compared, is the *height equivalent to a theoretical plate* (HETP):

$$HETP = L / N \qquad (11.12)$$

where L is the length of the column. HETP is conveniently expressed in millimeters, and because it has a reciprocal relation to N, the smaller the HETP, the more efficient the column. In some of the chromatographic literature, HETP is simplified to H.

Consider the general resolution equation, Eq. 11.4, and notice that the chromatographer has three "handles" to control R: k, α, and N. The capacity term, $k/(k + 1)$, has a range of 0 to 1. A plot of $k/(k + 1)$ as ordinate and k as abscissa results in a hyperbolic curve that begins at 0 and is asymptotic to 1. At $k = 2$, the capacity term contributes 67% of its maximum to R, and at $k = 10$, it contributes approximately 91%. In GC, k for the first peak of interest should be ≥ 2 (≥ 1 for HPLC) and not more than about 10. When developing a method, it is desirable to have k for the first peak of interest at roughly 4–5. Examination of Eq. 11.5 reveals that k represents the ratio of the time the analyte spends in the stationary phase to the time it spends in the mobile phase. At very low k, there is too little interaction with the stationary phase, whereas at very high k, analytical time is wasted.

Examining the selectivity term of Eq. 11.4 shows that for $\alpha = 1$,

$$(\alpha - 1) / \alpha = 0 \text{ and } R = 0;$$

there is no resolution. The range of $(\alpha = 1)/\alpha$ is 0 to 1, and a plot similar to that described for k results in an identically shaped curve with the difference that the ordinate is 0 at $\alpha = 1$. Selectivity describes the ratio of the times that two analytes spend in the stationary phase, and when they elute close together, their K_ds will be nearly equal. Therefore, typical values of α are frequently in the range of 1.1 to 1.2. Values of α lower than this range make separation difficult, if not impossible, whereas higher values result in longer analysis times. When developing a method, if k is approximately 4–5 and no acceptable α is obtained, a more selective GC stationary phase may be needed, or the HPLC mobile phase composition or components may need to be changed. This recommendation assumes that the column is reasonably efficient.

Ideally, a sample is injected into a chromatograph as a bolus. As the sample travels through the column, it spreads from a single plug to a peak shaped as shown in Fig. 11.1. The longer the sample remains in the column, the broader the band will become. In 1956, van Deemter et al. described a relationship between column efficiency, diffusion, and mass transfer effects in the column. A simplified version of the van Deemter equation is given here, where efficiency is related to the average linear mobile phase velocity, $\bar{\mu}$, in cm/s:

$$HETP = A + B / \bar{\mu} + C\bar{\mu} \qquad (11.13)$$

The terms A, B, and C represent the factors that contribute most to band broadening. By minimizing each of these factors, band broadening can be minimized, and therefore, efficiency can be increased.

The A term is related to the eddy diffusion or multipath effect. In any packed column, channels are of different lengths, and diffusion and mixing occur as the mobile phase flows around the packing particles. These processes cause the analyte band to spread. Using uniformly sized, tightly packed particles with smaller diameter can minimize this effect. Once the column is packed, the eddy diffusion term is constant and independent of the mobile phase flow rate. Typical particle sizes are 100/120 mesh (0.125–0.15 mm diameter) for GC packings, 2.5–10 μm for HPLC packings, and 1.5–2.5 μm for UHPLC packings. The A term is negligible for capillary GC columns because the mobile phase travels through an open tube with stationary phase coated on the walls.

The B term in Eq. 11.13 relates to the tendency of the analyte to diffuse in the mobile phase. As a component enters the mobile phase, the analyte concentration gradient drives diffusion toward areas of lower concentration. This diffusion in the mobile phase can be minimized by using a tightly packed column of closely sized particles and a higher mobile phase flow rate. In GC, it is advantageous to use larger, heavier carrier gas molecules; for example, the diffusion rate through nitrogen is approximately one-fourth of that through helium. Diffusion rates in condensed phases are minimal compared to those in gas phases, and as a result, this term can be ignored in HPLC.

The C term in the van Deemter equation addresses band broadening caused by resistance to mass transfer in the stationary phase. If two analyte molecules enter the stationary phase at the same time, and one spends x time before re-entering the mobile phase and the other spends $2x$ time, then the first molecule will be transported down the column some distance while the second molecule is still in the stationary phase. This process spreads the analyte band. This term's effect can be minimized by using a thin, uniform film of a stationary phase with a low viscosity to promote diffusion and by decreasing the mobile phase velocity. Note that the effect of this term varies according to the square of the film thickness.

The selection of $\bar{\mu}$ is critical. To minimize the B term, it is desirable to have a high mobile phase flow rate, but to minimize the C term, it is desirable to have a low flow rate. This problem is solved by creating a van Deemter plot, as shown in Fig. 11.2, and finding the optimum flow rate, i.e., the minimum in the curve. The optimum $\bar{\mu}$ for capillary-column GC varies dramatically with carrier gas type, as shown in Fig. 11.2a. In contrast, for LC, decreasing the particle size of the stationary phase limits the effect increasing the flow rate has on the C term. As the particle size decreases, the curve becomes flatter, as shown in Fig. 11.2b, and the slope of the curve at higher rates is so low that using higher flow rates does not usually result in much loss of efficiency.

Fig. 11.2 Van Deemter curves for (**a**) WCOT-column GC using different carrier gases and (**b**) LC using different particle sizes

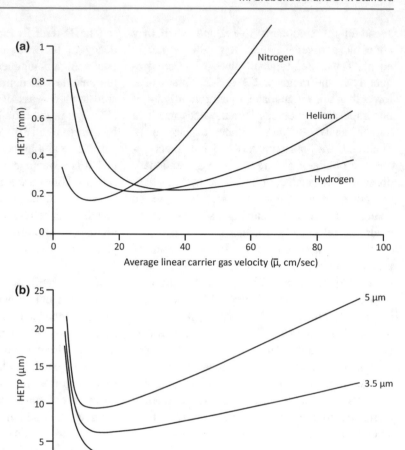

The van Deemter equation for capillary-column GC differs from that for packed-column GC and HPLC in that there is no A term because there is only one channel. However, a D $\bar{\mu}$ term must be added to account for cross-column diffusion in the mobile phase. The effect of diffusion rates through the most commonly used carrier gases is shown in Fig. 11.2a. For hydrogen and helium, the optima are much higher than for nitrogen, and the slopes of the curves at higher flows are lower. Nitrogen is a poor choice of carrier gas in capillary-column GC because analysis times are much longer than with hydrogen or helium. Another factor to consider when using capillary columns is that the analyses will almost invariably involve temperature programming, and the viscosity of gases, unlike that of liquids,

increases with increased temperature. Many capillary columns are operated at constant head pressure rather than constant flow rates. The pressure drop for flow through any channel is governed by:

$$\Delta P = (Q\mu FL)/A^2 \qquad (11.14)$$

where ΔP is the pressure drop across a column of length L and cross-sectional area A for a fluid of viscosity l at a flow rate F. The proportionality constant is Q. Examination of this equation shows that if $\bar{\mu}$ increases with increased temperature and ΔP is constant, then F must decrease, and consequently, HETP will change. The solution to this problem is to set the flow rate higher than the optimum with the oven temperature at the low point of the program. As the temperature increases, the flow will decrease, and HETP will also decrease. If conditions are selected properly, operation will never be lower than the optimum flow rate. Referring to Fig. 11.2a, with helium as the carrier gas and a temperature program of 100–300 °C, if the flow rate is set at 100 °C, $\bar{\mu}$ will be approximately 45 cm/s. This maintains efficiency and results in faster analyses.

Characterization of Separations

The simplest, least effective mechanism to describe a separation is by the absolute retention time, t_{ra}. However, this presumes that operating conditions are exactly reproducible, which is not always the case. A better method is the use of relative retention time (rrt). If one or more markers, x and y, are injected with the sample, then the retention time of an analyte a can be described relative to that of the markers. For example, $\text{rrt}_x = t_{ra}/t_{ra}$, and $\text{rrt}_y = t_{ra}/t_y$. The rrt is much less subject to change compared to the absolute retention time, and a library of rrt values can be very useful in making preliminary, or presumed, identifications.

In 1958, Kovats published a retention index (RI) system as part of his doctoral thesis. Beginning with the Clausius-Clapeyron equation, it is possible to derive a linear relation between $\log t'_r$ and molecular weight for a homologous series of compounds. Kovats plotted $\log t'_r$ as ordinate against the number of carbons number multiplied by 100 as abscissa to indicate the molecular weight for a series of normal hydrocarbons chromatographed isothermally. He called 100 multiplied by the number of carbons in the molecule the RI. The RI for n-hexane is 600, that for n-decane is 1000, and so on. Having established the RI curve for n-hydrocarbons, it is then possible to chromatograph analyte a under the same conditions, calculate $\log t'_{ra}$, and read its RI from the normal hydrocarbon line. Alternately, the RI can be calculated mathematically by linear interpolation between the two bracketing n-hydrocarbons. If $\text{RI}_a = 1250$, then analyte a chromatographs as if it were a normal hydrocarbon with 12.5 carbons. The Kovats RI is dependent on both the analyte and the stationary phase. It is independent, over a reasonable range, of column length, stationary phase film thickness, temperature, and mobile phase flow rate. Thus, analyte a will always have $\text{RI}_a = 1250$ on that stationary phase, permitting the compilation of a library of RIs that can be used by any analyst in any laboratory. A similar treatment can be applied to HPLC; however, there is no widely applicable homologous series to establish the RI curve, and it is generally not used. It should be remembered that Kovats RIs result from isothermal data. In GC applications where temperature programming is used, a similar treatment can be employed, except that the retention time, t_r, is used in place of $\log t'_r$. In this case, RI_a will be a function of the stationary phase, initial temperature, and temperature ramp.

Trennzahl

As indicated, column performance can be assessed or monitored using column efficiency, N. However, N must be calculated from isothermal data to be meaningful, and many GC separations are done under temperature-programmed conditions. In 1961, Kaiser proposed the use of the Trennzahl or separation number (TZ) to address this issue under temperature-programmed conditions. The separation number is readily calculated from the hydrocarbon data used to establish RIs, using

$$\text{TZ} = \left[\left(t_{\text{rcn}+1} - t_{\text{rcn}} \right) / \left(W_{1/2\text{cn}+1} + W_{1/2\text{cn}} \right) \right] - 1 \tag{11.15}$$

In Eq. 11.15, t_{rcn+1} and t_{rcn} represent the retention times for two adjacent normal hydrocarbons (e.g., n-C_{17} and n-C_{16}), and $W_{1/2}$ represents the corresponding peak widths at half-height. For capillary-column chromatography, TZ would be expected to be in the range 16–20. TZ represents the number of peaks, of size and shape similar to the n-hydrocarbons, that can fit evenly spaced between C_n and C_{n+1}, each with a resolution of 1.177.

By keeping a log of TZs determined periodically, the column performance can be monitored with very little effort. TZ and RI data may also be used to predict whether two compounds can be separated on a particular column without ever running them. If a column operated under a given set of conditions has a TZ of 19, then 19 peaks will fit between the bracketing n-hydrocarbons dividing this space into 20 equal segments. Two adjacent n-hydrocarbons have a ΔRI of 100 RI units; therefore, each of the theoretical peaks is separated by 5 RI units. If two analytes, a and b, have RIs that differ by 5 or more RI units, they can be separated with $R \geq 1.177$. If the RI difference is less than 5, they cannot be separated with this R.

Thin-Layer Chromatography

Tswett's classical LC was inefficient and slow, and though it was suitable for the separation of milligram quantities of natural products, it was not very useful as an analytical tool. The development of the capability to produce and classify by size adsorbents such as silica and alumina in the mid-1930s quickly led to the development of TLC. Early plates were made in the laboratory, and some were rather large, as much as 1 × 1 m. Today, plates are mass produced and usually 20 × 20 cm, 10 × 20 cm, or 2.5 × 7.5 cm. Standard analytical plates have 50- to 150-µm diameter particles in layers from 150- to 500-µm thickness. High-performance TLC plates have smaller diameter particles (≤ 10 µm) and thinner layers (100–150 µm). Plates can be purchased with the coating divided into channels about 1 cm wide that run the length of the plate to minimize lateral diffusion. Some plates also have a pre-adsorbent layer, consisting of a material different than the adsorbent, across one end of the plate. This layer allows the analyst to introduce a concentrated spot without risking disrupting the adsorbent layer, helping to present a more uniform sample front to the adsorbent.

Silica is the most widely used adsorbent, but others are available, including alumina and some reversed-phase materials. When calcium sulfate is used as a binding agent, plates are frequently designated by G for gypsum (e.g., Silica Gel G). Some plates also incorporate a fluorescent or other compound to aid in visualizing spots on the developed plates. The support material for the adsorbent is frequently glass but may be either metal or plastic.

In practice, the sample solution is spotted about 1.5–2 cm above the lower edge of the plate, either directly on the silica or near the top of the pre-adsorbent layer, if present. If samples are very dilute, then several applications may be made, with the sample solvent being allowed to dry between applications. This process results in smaller spots and less band broadening than if a larger amount of sample were applied at one time. Care must be taken not to damage the adsorbent layer if the spots are applied directly. Irregularities in the adsorbent layer can cause distorted mobile phase flow and distorted component patterns. After spotting, the sample solvent must be allowed to vaporize. It is convenient to place a piece of tape across the top of the plate, so that the identification of the sample in that lane can be designated. The tape should not come into contact with the mobile phase.

After the sample solvent has evaporated, the plate is placed in a glass developing tank containing mobile phase to a depth of approximately 1 cm in the bottom. Some time is required for the atmosphere in the tank to reach equilibrium. The plate rests nearly vertically in the tank with the lower end, near where the samples were spotted, immersed in the mobile phase. The mobile phase must contact the adsorbent or pre-adsorbent layer uniformly without touching any spot. The tank is then covered to preserve the integrity of the mobile phase vapor/liquid atmosphere during development. It is important not to make waves. Examples of mobile phases are ethyl acetate:methanol:ammonia, 90:7:3 for acid/neutral drugs and 85:13.5:1.5 for basic drugs separated on silica.

The mobile phase will rise up the adsorbent layer by capillary or wicking action, and each component will be distributed between the mobile and stationary phase according to its K_d; those with lower K_ds migrate faster and farther from the origin than those with higher K_ds. The result is separation of the components along the mobile phase path. When the mobile phase front has reached about 60–80% of the plate's height, the plate is removed from the tank, and the mobile phase front is marked for reference. The plate is then allowed to dry, typically in a 50–60 °C oven for about 5 min. Developing tanks are most commonly glass and can hold several plates.

Visualization of the separated compounds is generally done by a combination of examination under UV radiation, fluorescence, and a series of sprays and over-sprays to produce spots with colors characteristic of the drugs present. In addition to the color and, sometimes, the shape of the spots, each compound will have a characteristic retardation factor (R_f), which is the ratio of the distance the center of the spot travels from the origin relative to the distance the solvent front travels. Because the conditions under which TLC is done are not as precisely controlled as those of instrumental techniques, R_fs have more variability than t_rs or RIs. It is possible to scan the TLC channels with a densitometer, produce a chromatogram, measure retention times, do the calculations discussed previously, and even attempt quantification. However, in most cases, the imprecision of the data does not justify the effort and expense.

Gas Chromatography

Functional Division

To get an overall view of the GC process and facilitate troubleshooting, it is convenient to divide the system into five functional areas: mobile phase supply, injection, separation, detection, and data handling.

The function of the mobile phase supply system is to provide a source of pure, clean, dry carrier gas at constant pressure or constant flow rate. The function of the injector is to take the sample from atmospheric pressure, introduce it into the instrument at system pressure, vaporize it, and conduct all or part of it onto the column with minimum band broadening. Separation is achieved in the GC column, which is usually maintained in an oven for temperature control. The detector is selected to provide a signal when each of the sample components of interest elutes from the column. Under some conditions, the signal will be proportional to the concentration or amount of component passing through the detector. The primary purpose of the data-handling operation is to provide a timed record of detector response. Depending on the degree of sophistication, it may also store and manipulate data and generate reports.

Mobile Phase and Auxiliary Gas Selection, Supply, and Control

The selection of carrier gas is governed by several factors: type of chromatography, detector, operator experience and safety, and cost. For capillary-column GC, the carrier gas should be helium or hydrogen because of the shape of the van Deemter curves (Fig. 11.2a) and shorter analysis times these gasses offer. Nitrogen should not be used because of the longer analysis times and loss of efficiency at higher flow rates and under temperature-programmed conditions.

Recently, hydrogen has become more widely used as a carrier gas because of the increased cost and limited availability of helium. When hydrogen is used, an oven monitor should be used to detect any leaks. In the event of column breakage or a significant hydrogen leak, such a monitor is designed to shut off hydrogen flow and, with some designs, discontinue electrical power to the instrument. Consideration should also be given to the experience of the operator. Individuals with relatively little GC experience should be closely supervised when operating systems using hydrogen as a carrier gas. However, hydrogen diffuses rapidly, and with a single GC using about 4 mL/min for septum purge and column flow and perhaps 200 mL split vent per injection, the volume of hydrogen used per day is only about 10 L and does not represent a particular hazard under most conditions. A tank of carrier gas should last 60–90 days.

Carrier gas is frequently supplied in tanks holding about 225 cubic feet (6.3 m³) at standard temperature and pressure (STP) and a pressure of 2200–2500 psig (~150 atm). Gas is supplied to the instrument through a two-stage regulator at 30–60 psig. Further pressure and flow control are provided by the instrument's control system. Carrier gas should pass through hydrocarbon, water, and oxygen traps to remove substances that may adversely affect detector sensitivity but primarily to prolong column life. Auxiliary gases should pass through a hydrocarbon trap and, depending on the detector type, through a water trap. If high-quality gases are purchased, traps should last for about three tanks of gas. Hydrocarbon and moisture traps can be readily regenerated in-house. Some types of oxygen traps are equipped with regeneration capability, while other types must be sent back to the supplier for regeneration. Systems are also available to generate acceptable-quality hydrogen, nitrogen, and air in-house. Depending on the laboratory's requirements, investing in these systems may be justified. However, the requirements for treatment to assure carrier gas quality remain.

Traditionally, analyses were done at constant head pressure. That is, the pressure was set to give the desired pressure, and a feedback regulator was used to keep it constant. As discussed earlier (see "Principles"), as temperature increases under temperature-programmed conditions, gas viscosity increases, and at constant pressure, the flow rate will decrease. To address this problem, electronic pressure control was introduced. With this system, as the temperature and viscosity increase, the head pressure is increased to maintain constant flow and achieve more reproducible analytical conditions and column efficiency.

Auxiliary gases are required with most detectors. For example, for an FID, air at about 350–400 mL/min, hydrogen at about 30 mL/min, and perhaps a makeup gas are needed. Most thermal conductivity cells require a reference gas, usually helium, the same as the carrier gas. Electron capture detectors (ECDs) may be operated with 5% methane in argon to help produce more capturable, low-energy electrons. These gases must be clean, pure, and dry. Mass spectrometers are an exception as they require no auxiliary gas when operated in electron impact mode.

Makeup gas is required with some, though not all, detector designs. For capillary columns with inner diameters (IDs) of 0.20–0.25 mm, the carrier gas flow rate through the column will be about 1 mL/min. This rate can be calculated using:

$$F = \left[(\pi)(r^2)(L) \right] / t_m \qquad (11.16)$$

Flow, F, will be in mL/min if the column radius, r, and length, L, are in centimeters, and t_m is in minutes. With such a low flow rate, any excess empty space (dead volume) will allow mixing and, therefore, broadening of the peaks. The effect of dead volume in the detector can be reduced by supplying a makeup gas, frequently introduced with the hydrogen to increase the total gas flow through the detector and "sweep" the component peak from the system. Nitrogen works well as a makeup gas. It should be noted that for packed-column instruments that have been adapted to use 0.53-mm ID fused silica or 0.75-mm ID glass columns, whether a makeup gas is used frequently does not seem to make much difference.

Injectors

The function of the injection system is to introduce the sample, usually a measured amount, into the GC and vaporize it immediately and completely. Figure 11.3 presents a diagram of a split/splitless injector typically used in capillary-column GC. A split injector arrangement allows the operator to introduce an amount of sample

SPLIT/SPLITLESS INJECTOR

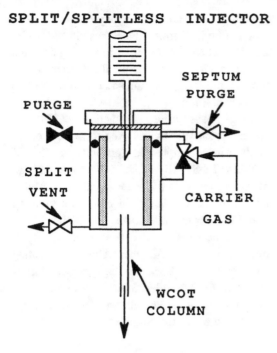

Fig. 11.3 Split/splitless WCOT-column injector with valves set for a split injection

that can be measured with reasonable accuracy (e.g., 1 μL) and have the injector conduct a portion of it (e.g., 1/50th) onto the column. The part of the sample that is injected but not taken onto the column is vented through the split vent. In splitless mode, the total amount of sample injected is conducted onto the column for the first 30–90 s after injection, and subsequently, any sample remaining in the injector is vented.

In split mode, the solenoid valves are set as shown in Fig. 11.3 for injection. The septum purge is designed to flush out any degradation products from the septum and remains open at a flow of 1–3 mL/min. Carrier flow is across the septum, down through the inside of the liner, and then through the column or out the split vent. Injected sample is vaporized in the liner, and an aliquot of it is then conducted onto the column, while the rest is vented out the split vent. With a standard 0.20–0.25-mm ID WCOT column, the flow will be about 1 mL/min. At a split ratio of 50:1, 1/51th of the sample will go onto the column, and 50/51ths will be vented. Thus, the column flow will be ~1 mL/min, and the split flow will be ~50 mL/min. Because the column and

split vent act as two resistances in parallel, the split vent can be closed 1–2 min after injection, and the column flow will remain unchanged if the column head pressure is kept constant.

The splitless mode of injection is designed to accommodate dilute samples, for which it is desirable to have most of the sample injected go onto the column. For this mode, the solenoid valves would be set as shown in Fig. 11.3, except that the split vent valve would be closed and remain that way. The sample is injected and vaporized, and the total flow goes onto the column. After a 30–90-s delay, the purge valve (not the septum purge, which remains open) is opened, and simultaneously, the carrier gas control valve is switched to cause carrier gas to flow around the outside of the liner and flush any remaining sample out through the purge valve. During splitless injection, the oven temperature is maintained at approximately 20–30 °C below the boiling point of the injection solvent. This allows 90–95% of the sample injected to be focused at the head of the column. After the 30–90-s delay, as the purge and carrier gas valves are switched, the oven temperature program is initiated. The result is that the 5–10% of sample that was not conducted onto the column is vented, and the chromatography of the sample begins. Injection solvent rushes through the column, and the analyte components are then separated. The injection solvent must be carefully selected, and the delay time must be experimentally determined. Roughly 1–2 min after the end of the delay time, the purge valve can be closed for the duration of the run. All these steps are done at constant carrier gas pressure.

Cold on-column injection may be used to circumvent some of the undesirable features of split and splitless injections. In this mode of injection, the sample is deposited directly into the head of the column, which is maintained at cryogenic conditions. After sample deposition, the injection device (needle) is removed, and the area of the column containing the sample is heated, vaporizing the sample and allowing it to be carried onto the column. The advantage of cold on-column injection is that the total sample is conducted onto the column, making this technique ideal for quantitative applications. Furthermore, there is no discrimination against higher boiling components, as can occur in split injection, and there is no solvent effect to contend with, as in splitless injection. One disadvantage is that samples must be clean to prevent column contamination and additional system maintenance.

Automated injection of gaseous samples can be done via direct transfer line or through the use of a loop injector. One advantage of using a loop injector is that a known amount of sample is injected each time. In this mode of injection, the sample is loaded into the fixed-volume loop of the injector and then flushed onto the column by the carrier gas. The valve can be thermostatically controlled. The most widely used forensic application of such an arrangement is automatic headspace analysis of alcohols and acetone in blood or urine (Fig. 11.4 shows a schematic of a headspace injector). In this type of injection, measured amounts of specimen and internal standard are contained in a septum-sealed vial and allowed to equilibrate at an appropriate temperature, typically approximately 60 °C for alcohol analyses. In standby mode, carrier flow is as indicated in Fig. 11.4, proceeding through the upper route of the tubing while also flushing through the sample loop and out the needle. After temperature equilibration of the specimen, the vial is automatically raised, the septum is punctured, and the vial contents are pressurized. When pressurization is complete, the two valves in the lower leg of the tubing are switched to stop the carrier flow through the loop and allow sample headspace vapors to flow to the left in the diagram, filling

the sample loop and venting any excess. Once the loop is filled, all four valves are switched, isolating the vial and upper leg of the tubing and closing the vent. At this point, the carrier flow is through the loop, flushing sample from the loop onto the column.

Solid-phase micro extraction (SPME) is another technique that is used to gather components from a sample and transport them for GC analysis. In SPME-GC, a syringe containing a reusable fiber with a retentive coating is inserted into a sample vial. The syringe punctures the septum, the fiber extends down into the headspace, and components in the headspace vapor are trapped on the SPME fiber. After equilibrating, the fiber is drawn back into the syringe and transported to the GC inlet. Sample components are then thermally desorbed, and the carrier gas transfers them to the column.

Separation

In GC, separation efficiency is primarily determined by the column. Four main characteristics must be considered when selecting a WCOT capillary column: the stationary phase, film thickness, column ID, and column length.

- **Stationary Phase:** As discussed under "Principles," and following Eq. 11.2, the distribution coefficient, K_{da}, for GC is nearly independent of the type of carrier gas and pressure. However, K_{da} does depend on the stationary phase and temperature. The characteristic most often used to describe a stationary phase is its "polarity." Thus, it is important to define what polarity means chromatographically. A compound in which a separation of charges results in a permanent dipole (e.g., water) is called a polar compound. However, in addition to strong permanent dipoles, a weaker dipole can be induced when a polarizable molecule is subjected to the force field of a permanent dipole, and two polarizable molecules may interact to form even weaker, mutually induced polarity. These phenomena are known as dipole–dipole, dipole–apole,

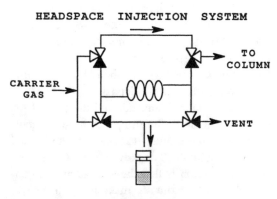

HEADSPACE INJECTION SYSTEM

Fig. 11.4 Headspace injection system

Table 11.1 Common stationary phases and applications for WCOT GC columns

Common phase designation	Stationary phase description	Polarity	Applications
X-1	100% Dimethylpolysiloxane	Non-polar	Amines, hydrocarbons, petroleum products, volatile organic compounds, environmental contaminants, amines
X-5	5% Diphenyl–95% dimethylpolysiloxane	Non-polar	Polyaromatic hydrocarbons, alkaloids, volatile organic compounds, halogenated compounds environmental contaminants, drugs of abuse
X-20	20% Diphenyl–80% dimethylpolysiloxane	Moderately polar	Aromatic compounds, compounds contain lone pairs
X-1701	14% Cyanopropylphenyl–86% dimethylpolysiloxane	Moderately polar	Pesticides, alcohols, phenols, esters, ketones
X-35	35% Diphenyl–65% dimethylpolysiloxane	Moderately polar	Pesticides, pharmaceuticals, drugs of abuse, substituted polar compounds, phenols
X-17 or X-50	50% Diphenyl–50% dimethylpolysiloxane	Moderately polar	Drug esters, ketones, plasticizers, organochloro compounds, steroids
X-200, X-210	Trifluoropropylmethylpolysiloxane, 50% Trifluoropropyl–50% dimethylpolysiloxane	Polar	Compounds with free electron pairs, steroids, esters, ketones, drugs, alcohols, freon fluorocarbons
X-225	50% Cyanopropylphenyl–50% dimethylpolysiloxane	Polar	Fatty acid methyl esters
X-WAX	Polyethylene glycol	Strongly polar	Alcohols, fatty acid methyl esters, fatty acids, solvents, amines
X-2330	90% Biscyanopropyl–10% cyanopropylphenylsiloxane	Strongly polar	Fatty acid methyl esters, dioxins, aromatic compounds

Note: "ms" at the end of the column designation often indicates a low-bleed version of the stationary phase intended for MS or high-temperature operation

and apole–apole interactions, respectively. The sum effect of these is what is referred to in chromatography as "polarity." Although the term "polarity" may oversimplify the complex interactions that occur within a columns' stationary phase, it provides a useful and succinct means by which to classify and compare different stationary phases. Table 11.1 lists some of the more common WCOT GC column stationary phases and their relative polarities.

Note that there are P_s–P_s, P_m–P_m, P_s–P_m, P_s–analyte, P_m–analyte, and analyte–analyte interactions at work, and as mentioned previously, describing this complex situation using a single term—polarity—can be misleading. To address this issue, W.O. McReynolds in 1970, following earlier work by L. Rohrschneider (1966, 1969), published the results of his characterization studies. As probes, he selected ten compounds, each

representative of a class of chemical compounds (e.g., alcohols, aromatics). He ran these compounds isothermally at 120 °C on nearly every stationary phase available and calculated their Kovats RIs. Using squalane as the least polar stationary phase known, he tabulated the McReynolds constant (i.e., the difference between the RI on a given P_s and the RI on squalene), for each probe on each P_s. Using these data, it is possible to estimate which phase might be used to separate alcohols, separate alcohols from aromatics, and so on. The data can also be used to predict elution order and compare the separation properties of stationary phases.

• **Film Thickness:** Film thickness affects the retention of analytes, sample capacity, and maximum operating temperature of the column. Thicker films cause analytes to spend more time in the stationary phase, thereby increasing their retention times. Thus, thicker films are useful for separating highly volatile compounds and also increase the column's capacity, increasing its compatibility with higher concentration samples relative to columns with thinner films. In contrast, thinner films reduce the amount of time analytes spend in the stationary phase, thereby decreasing their retention times. Additionally, thinner films are less prone to phase bleed at higher temperatures and are amenable to higher maximum operating temperatures. Common film thicknesses for 0.25-mm ID columns are 0.25 and 0.50 µm; however, the optimal film thickness varies depending on the application.

- **Column ID:** Column ID primarily affects column efficiency and sample capacity. Decreasing the column ID increases the column efficiency, enabling the separation of analytes that elute closely together. However, this increased efficiency comes at the expense of sample capacity; that is, large sample volumes or highly concentrated samples can exceed the sample capacity of narrow-bore columns, leading to peak broadening and decreased resolution. Generally, 0.25-mm ID columns are thought to provide adequate efficiency and sample capacity for most applications.

- **Column Length:** Column length affects column efficiency, carrier gas pressure, and analysis time. That is, increasing the column length increases all three of these parameters. Although increasing the column length is one option for increasing resolution, it is often more prudent to try decreasing the column ID before increasing the column length, as longer columns are more expensive and lengthen the total analysis time.

With this complex array of column options, what is the best approach to column selection? Once the separation has been defined, the fastest, easiest, and least expensive way of selecting a column is to ask someone who is doing or has done it successfully. Colleagues are a good source of information because they may be working in the same or a related area. The second most efficient way to answer this question is to look in the literature. Extensive, readily accessible electronic compilations of abstracts and online search tools (e.g., Medline, Web of Science, Google Scholar) are available. Suppliers' catalogs and websites are also excellent sources of information as major suppliers' catalogs often contain extensive sections presenting chromatograms of a wide variety of separations. Many suppliers also provide column selection guides according to intended application and application notes. These resources are all free except for the time invested. The least efficient approach to column selection is to go into the laboratory and experiment. Although this step is ultimately necessary to confirm that the separation can be performed on the chosen system, accumulating good information prior to this step will shorten the time and labor involved.

Detectors

To discuss GC detectors, it is necessary to first define some detector characteristics: sensitivity, linear dynamic range, specificity, and sample destructive or nondestructive.

- *Sensitivity* is the detector's response to the amount of analyte, which can be observed as the slope of the detector response vs. analyte amount curve. Note that there is some amount of analyte below which no discernible response is observed. Practically, this value is typically defined as the amount of analyte that produces a response twice that of the baseline noise and is referred to as the minimum detectable quantity (MDQ) or lower limit of detection. The lower limit of detection will be lower than the lower limit of quantification (LLOQ), which is the lowest concentration that will allow acceptable quantitative results according to the laboratory's criteria (e.g., a coefficient of variation of 10%).

- A portion of the response vs. amount curve will be linear up to some amount; the range over which this linear relationship exists is known as the *linear dynamic range*. Beyond this amount, which is termed the limit of linearity, the incremental increase in response will begin to decrease. Mathematically, the linear dynamic range can be described as the ratio of the limit of linearity to the MDQ. If quantification is necessary, to achieve the best accuracy and precision possible, the analysis should be done within the linear dynamic range of the detector. It is poor policy to quantify outside this range.

- *Specificity* is the ability of the detector to selectively detect a particular type of compound. A thermal conductivity detector (TCD) is nearly universal in that it will detect anything with a thermal conductivity different from that of the carrier gas. In contrast, an FID may be thought of as a carbon counter. That is, it will respond to most organic compounds, with varying degrees of sensitivity, but will not detect many fixed gases (e.g., O_2, N_2, H_2O, CO, CO_2, NH_3). An ECD is also rather selective in that it will detect only electrophilic compounds.

- Of the types of detectors that are widely in use today, nearly all but the TCD and IR detector (IRD) are *sample destructive*. That is, the sample is burned or otherwise altered and cannot be recovered intact after passing through the detector.

The most widely used detector in the early days of GC, the 1950s, was the TCD, which was initially referred to as a katharometer. In most designs, the TCD consists of two electrically heated, high-resistance filaments, typically tungsten or tungsten/rhenium, as two legs of a Wheatstone bridge circuit. One of these is in a reference channel and sees only carrier gas; the other is in the column effluent channel and sees carrier gas plus any eluting analyte. A current—usually 100–300 amps—is maintained through the filaments, which heats them, much like an incandescent light bulb filament. Heat is conducted from the filaments, most of it to the detector block, at a rate dependent on the carrier gas type and flow rate. With only carrier gas flowing through both channels, the temperatures of the filaments equilibrate, the circuit is balanced, and

a constant baseline can be established. Analyte molecules that elute and pass through the sample channel are much larger and less thermally conductive than carrier gas molecules; therefore, less heat is conducted away, and the filament temperature rises, increasing the filament's electrical resistance. This causes an imbalance in the bridge circuit and a change in the output voltage, which is monitored as the detector response.

Helium is often used as the carrier gas for GC-TCD because of its high thermal conductivity, although hydrogen, nitrogen, and argon are also used. TCDs work best when there is a large difference in thermal conductivity between the carrier gas and the analytes in the sample.

The FID, introduced in the mid to late 1950s, quickly became the most widely used detector because of its sensitivity, broad applicability, and large linear dynamic range. Figure 11.5 shows a schematic of an FID. A hydrogen/air flame burns at the jet tip, and column effluent exits through the jet into the flame. In the environment of the flame, some of the carrier gas will be ionized, and

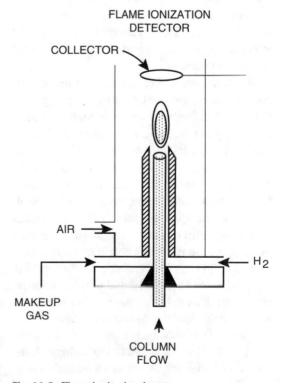

Fig. 11.5 Flame ionization detector

the analyte molecules that are eluted will also be ionized. A constant electrical potential of about 300 volts is maintained between the jet and the collector. The gap between these components acts as a variable resistance, as resistance is a function of the number of conductors (i.e., ions) in the gap. When just carrier gas is exiting from the column, the current that flows in the circuit is amplified, balanced, or nulled and monitored as baseline. As analyte molecules are ionized in the flame, the resistance decreases, and more current flows; this amplified current is the detector response.

The FID is widely applicable to most volatile organic compounds. It also has a wide linear dynamic range, typically about 10^6, and MDQs in the picogram range for many compounds. The FID, similar to other ionization detectors, is mass flow rate dependent; that is, its response is a function of the rate (i.e., mg/s) at which analyte passes through the detector. In contrast, the TCD is concentration dependent, and its response is a function of concentration over time (i.e., mg/mL/s). Thus, ionization detectors are suitable for use with capillary columns, which produce very narrow peaks with most of the mass passing through the detector over a short period of time. The TCD is not nearly so well suited to capillary-column chromatography.

Another detector widely used in forensic toxicology laboratories is the nitrogen–phosphorus detector (NPD) or thermionic detector. It is similar in design to the FID except that an alkali metal salt, typically rubidium or cesium, is positioned above the flame. The hydrogen and air flow are reduced in intensity compared to FID operation so that ionization is minimized. The hot alkali salt causes the selective ionization of compounds containing nitrogen or phosphorus. Because many drugs are nitrogen-containing compounds, using an NPD can facilitate selectively detecting drugs with good sensitivity and minimal interference from other organic compounds that are not ionized well under the operating conditions.

The ECD is constructed somewhat similarly to the FID but without a jet or flame. Instead, the source of ionization is a radioactive material, in almost all cases the nickel isotope weighing 63

atomic mass units (AMU). Within the ECD, the Ni^{63} emits β particles that result in low electrical resistance and, therefore, high current in the gap between the electrodes. This "standing current" is monitored as baseline. As analyte molecules elute from the column, very little change occurs in the electrical atmosphere of the gap unless the molecules are electrophilic. If electrophilic molecules elute, they capture electrons, decreasing the current flow across the gap. This change is amplified and monitored as the detector output. Compounds containing halogens or nitro or cyano functional groups are good candidates for detection by an ECD.

Another detector option is the atomic emission detector. This detector is capable of detecting elements contained in each component separated by the column. Note that its use in forensic toxicology has been limited because it is less sensitive than the NPD to compounds containing nitrogen and less sensitive than the ECD to halogenated compounds.

The detector most widely in forensic toxicology to collect structural information is the mass spectrometer. Chromatography is a powerful separating technique, but it does not identify anything. Conversely, MS is a very powerful molecular identification technique, but it does not separate anything. By combining these two techniques into a GC-MS system, the advantages of each are realized. By using capillary-column GC, with typical column flow rates of about 1 mL/min, the column effluent can be conducted directly into the ion source of a mass spectrometer equipped with a vacuum pump capable of handling this flow. The most common GC-MS ionization mode in forensic toxicology is electron impact ionization (EI), although chemical ionization (CI) is also used.

Mass spectra may be presented in several ways. One useful presentation is as a frequency diagram, where the signal proportional to the number of ions in a group is plotted as ordinate and the mass-to-charge ratio of the group as abscissa. Frequently, the most abundant ion in the spectrum, the "base peak," is plotted as 100, with each of the other ion abundances plotted as a percentage of the base peak. More in-depth information about GC-MS systems, ionization modes, and mass spectra is presented in Chap. 14.

IRDs are not as common as mass spectrometers in forensic toxicology, but they are being used with increasing frequency. IR spectroscopy, like MS, is valuable because it can provide identification information based on molecular structures; the other detectors mentioned do not. GC-IRD is especially useful for resolving positional isomers that may have identical fragmentation patterns in MS. However, it is rather insensitive. If an interferometer is used as the IR source, Fourier transform IR (FTIR) is possible, dramatically increasing the sensitivity of GC-IRD. In a vapor-phase IRD, the column effluent is conducted through a light pipe in the path of the IR beam. Analyte molecules in the light pipe absorb energy from the beam. Transmitted energy is detected by an IR sensor and presented as the detector output. In a solid-phase IRD, the column effluent is transferred to an IR chamber and condensed onto a slowly moving disc composed of an IR-transparent material. An IR beam is directed through the disk, producing transmission IR transmission spectra of the solid-phase material. One advantage of the IRD is that it is *sample nondestructive*; thus, the effluent from vapor-phase GC-IRD systems can be presented to another detector, such as MS, to obtain additional information. Note that because potassium bromide is used in the optics of most IRDs, the system must be purged with dry gas.

A word of caution concerning selective detectors is in order. Just because a chromatogram using a thermionic detector or ECD shows only a few peaks, it does not mean that other compounds are not present. When injected into, for example, a GC-MS system, this same sample may produce many more peaks than seen with the selective detector.

Data Systems

Data systems used with GC systems have evolved from the simple strip chart recorders used in the 1950s to onboard recorder/integrators or connected computer systems. The primary purpose of a data system is to record the separation achieved and produce a chromatogram or plot of detector response as a function of retention time. A chromatogram may be all that is required, but more frequently, it is desirable and necessary to perform additional tasks, such as calculating retention indices, quantifying one or more analytes, comparing chromatographic patterns, storing data, creating and searching libraries, controlling one or more GCs, and generating reports. Most instrument vendors have proprietary software that can accomplish all of this functionality. Additionally, third party software solutions exist that can accommodate data generated from many different vendors' instruments.

Multi-Dimensional Gas Chromatography

Multi-dimensional GC allows the use of multiple analytical columns within a single GC run. The most common incarnation of multi-dimensional GC is two-dimensional GC using columns of different polarities. In this technique, a sample is injected onto the primary column with the effluent directed to a thermal or valve modulator. In systems that use heart cuts, selected portions of the effluent from the first column are directed onto the second column in discrete portions. More complex systems direct all the effluent from the first column onto the second column in a technique known as comprehensive multidimensional GC. For comprehensive multidimensional GC, carefully controlled sample modulation is critical to generate interpretable data.

High-Performance Liquid Chromatography

Applicability

To be amenable to GC separation, a material must have at least 1 torr vapor pressure at 300 °C or below and be stable in the vapor phase. Approximately 18–20% of organic compounds meet these criteria. For those that do not, LC is available. Theoretically, any sample that can be dissolved can be separated by LC. Obviously, reactivity, suitable mobile and stationary phases, and detectors impose limitations. Even so, a much wider variety of compounds are amenable to LC than to GC separation.

Development

As described earlier, the first publication of LC separations of any note was done by Michael S. Tswett at the turn of the century. That work relied on classical LC, where the mobile phase flow was controlled by gravity, the columns were glass tubes packed with solid absorbent, and detection was frequently by visual observation. Separations were primarily confined to natural products. In the mid-1960s, materials for pump construction improved, pump designs became more reliable, controlled porosity silica with better size classification was developed, and UV detectors with small volume (100 µL) flow-through cells became available. Each of these developments contributed to the dramatic increase in interest in LC during this period. As researchers began to build systems and test and stress their capabilities, more operable instruments with increased separation efficiency were produced, and HPLC was launched. In the early to mid 2000s, stationary phases with particle sizes <2 µm were introduced, leading to dramatic increases in the speed and efficiency of HPLC and the development of UHPLC, a specialized subset of HPLC.

HPLC lags behind GC in terms of separating power, but it has other advantages, including speed, compatibility with simpler extraction procedures, and lower operating temperatures, that make it more compatible with thermally unstable compounds. Because analyte retention in LC depends largely on the compositions of both the mobile and stationary phases, LC also offers more flexibility in optimizing separations than GC. However, although LC has seen a significant rise in popularity in recent years, it does not replace GC as a universal separation technique.

HPLC separations can be based on a variety of molecular properties. The three most common types of HPLC are ion exchange, which separates compounds based on electrical charge; size exclusion, which separates compounds based on molecular size; and polarity based, which separates molecules based on their relative polarities. Polarity-based HPLC includes both normal- and reversed-phase separations and is the most widely used in forensic toxicology; therefore, it is the focus of this section.

Functional Division

The division of function in HPLC is exactly the same as in GC: mobile phase supply and control, injection, separation, detection, and data systems. There are, of course, differences in how these functions are achieved.

Mobile Phase Supply

The mobile phases used in HPLC must be compatible with the materials used to construct the system: stainless steel pump housings and tubing, sapphire pump pistons, ruby ball and ceramic check valve components, and polytetrafluoroethylene (PTFE, Teflon) or polyetheretherketone (PEEK) tubing and seal parts. Chlorinated solvents can corrode stainless steel under some conditions, and mobile phases at highly acidic or basic pHs can degrade incompatible stationary phases. In addition, the mobile phase must be free of any particulate matter and must be degassed. Particulate matter is usually removed by fitting the suction line to the pump with a metal or plastic filter with 2-µm pores. Degassing may be achieved by briefly subjecting the mobile phase to vacuum, sonication, filtering through a specially designed filter, or purging with helium (but not nitrogen). Many systems have onboard inline degassers.

Almost all pumps are reciprocating stainless steel pumps with a sapphire piston. Figure 11.6 shows a cross-section of a reciprocating piston pump. Pumps are fitted on both suction and dis-

RECIPROCATING PISTON
PUMP

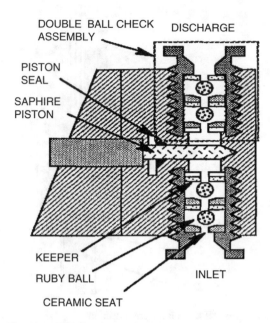

DOUBLE BALL CHECK
ASSEMBLY
DISCHARGE

PISTON
SEAL

SAPHIRE
PISTON

KEEPER

RUBY BALL
INLET

CERAMIC SEAT

Fig. 11.6 HPLC reciprocating pump cross-section

charge with single or double check valves with ceramic seats and ruby balls. The mobile phase delivery rate is controlled by either limiting the length of the piston stroke or using a fast, constant-speed suction stroke and a controlled-speed delivery stroke. Operating pressures range from several hundred to around 15,000 psi. Because the pumps use a reciprocating action, the pump delivery pressure and flow will oscillate. To minimize this oscillation, a pulse dampener is used in the delivery line.

Isocratic separations (i.e., with constant mobile phase composition) can be accomplished by preparing the appropriate solvent mixture, placing it in a reservoir, and then pumping it through the system using a single pump. Gradient elutions involve changing the mobile phase composition throughout the course of the chromatographic run. This technique requires pulling mobile phase solvents from more than one reservoir and mixing them prior to sample introduction. There are two main configurations for mixing mobile phase components in HPLC systems: high-pressure mixing and low-pressure mixing.

In systems with high-pressure mixing, each solvent reservoir is connected to a pump, and the components are independently pumped into a mixer at high pressure. These systems typically utilize binary pumps, capable of delivering mixtures of two different solvents to the column. In contrast, in systems with low-pressure mixing, a single pump is used to pull from multiple solvent reservoirs. All the solvents are simultaneously pulled into a proportioning valve that allows specified amounts of each solvent to pass through. The components are mixed at low pressure as they exit the proportioning valve and enter the high-pressure pump. An additional mixing chamber may be included to increase solvent homogeneity. Pump systems with low-pressure mixing typically include three or four solvent reservoirs and are known as ternary or quaternary pumps, respectively.

Binary pumps typically have smaller dwell volumes than ternary or quaternary pumps, and gradient changes are passed to the column quickly. Quaternary systems have larger dwell volumes to ensure adequate mixing, which can lead to longer analysis times. They are, however, more versatile and allow for more complex gradient programs, including variation of the pH as the run progresses.

Injectors

The function of the injection system is to introduce a measured volume of sample at atmospheric pressure into the mobile phase flow at high pressure, without interrupting the flow or changing the system pressure. Most injectors used in HPLC employ a six-port loop injector somewhere in the system. Figure 11.7 is a schematic of such an injector. The injector consists of a stainless steel body, a rotor, a sample loop, and six connections for tubing. In load mode, the port from the pump communicates with the port going to the column; the port where sample is introduced communicates with the fixed-volume loop and then to waste. This setup allows the loop to be filled at atmospheric pressure while maintaining flow through the column. In inject mode, the

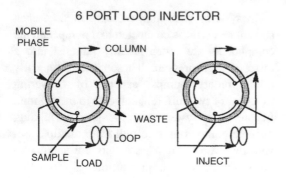

Fig. 11.7 Six-port loop injector

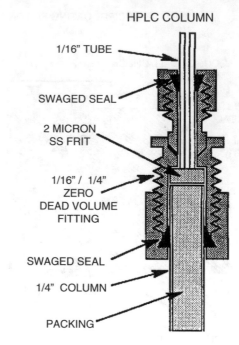

Fig. 11.8 HPLC column cross-section

rotor is rotated 60°, allowing the pump to flush the contents of the loop onto the column. These valves may be operated manually or by an actuator. Typical loop volumes are 10–20 μL. If the injector is not part of an automatic injection system, the loop is filled using a syringe. The circuit, sample injection port, loop, and waste port must be completely filled and contain no gas bubbles. If less than the full capacity of the loop is to be injected, the desired amount can be measured with the injection syringe and the remainder of the circuit filled with mobile phase. In some automatic injectors, the valve is remote and does not contact the sample. These valves are remarkably durable but must be serviced occasionally because of seal wear.

Separation

Here, we look at several factors that affect separation: the column dimensions, the column packing, and mobile phase.

- **Column Dimensions:** Efficiency is directly proportional to the column length and inversely proportional to the ID. Therefore, increasing the column length and decreasing the ID will increase the chromatographic resolution. Conventional HPLC columns are generally constructed of ¼″ outer diameter stainless steel tubing with IDs of 2–4.6 mm and are usually 3, 5, 10, 15, or 25 cm long. A typical HPLC column connection is shown in Fig. 11.8. Zero dead-volume fittings and the

shortest length of 1/16″ narrow-bore interconnecting tubing practicable are used to minimize dead volume (i.e., empty space that permits mixing). Inlet and discharge end fittings are each fitted with a 2-μm porous sintered stainless steel frit to retain the column packing. UHPLC columns have smaller IDs (<2 mm) and lengths generally in the range of 5–10 cm.

- Frequently, a guard column will be placed between the injector and analytical column inlet. The purpose of this column is to protect the analytical column from particulates and chemical impurities that may have a very high affinity for the packing and be detrimental to the life and performance of the column. Guard columns can consist of a replaceable cartridge in a holder or a very short packed column and preferably contain the same packing material as the analytical column.

- **Column Packings:** The performance characteristics of HPLC column packing materials depend largely on three main aspects: size, particle composition, and surface chemistry.

- **Size:** Early HPLC packings were nearly all porous silica or alumina of irregular shape, with sizes in the range of 45–60 μm. Today, HPLC utilizes packing particles with diameters ranging from approximately 1.5 to 10 μm. Using smaller particle sizes increases column efficiency by reducing the contributions of eddy diffusion and mass transfer to band broadening (A and C terms in the van Deemter equation [Eq. 11.13], respectively). Using smaller particles also increases the optimum linear velocity at which the minimal HETP is achieved (Fig. 11.2b), allowing for faster analysis. HPLC with column particle sizes less than 2 μm is generally considered UHPLC and results in higher backpressures compared to columns packed with larger particles.
- **Particle Composition:** Porous silica-based packings have wide applicability for a broad range of separation conditions. However, they are unstable at extreme pHs and can exhibit poor peak shapes for basic compounds. To increase column durability, several manufacturers now offer HPLC columns with hybrid organic/inorganic packing materials.
- One of the most important advances in HPLC packing materials was the introduction of small-diameter superficially porous particles (SPPs), which happened around 2006. (Note: SPPs are also known as core-shell, poroshell, fused-core, and solid-core particles.) SPPs have a solid inner core structure that is surrounded by a layer of porous material. Columns packed with SPPs have higher efficiencies than columns packed with equivalently sized, fully porous particles. The solid inner core is impenetrable to both sample analytes and the mobile phase, decreasing mass transfer and longitudinal diffusion (C and B terms in the van Deemter equation [Eq. 11.13], respectively). For small-molecule applications, SPPs have also been shown to reduce eddy diffusion (A term in the van Deemter equation [Eq. 11.13]). The mechanism underlying this reduction in eddy diffusion is currently not well understood but is often attributed to the highly uniform packing of SPPs, possibly because of their rougher surfaces, compared to fully porous particles. Columns packed with 3-μm SPPs have efficiencies similar to columns packed with <2-μm, fully porous particles but generate significantly less back pressure. Thus, they can be used on both conventional HPLC instruments and specialized UHPLC equipment.

- **Surface Chemistry:** Column packings that use unmodified silica as the stationary phase are polar, limiting the possible chromatographic separation types to what is now known as normal-phase separation. The polarity of the silica particles can be modified by bonding less-polar functional groups to the surface hydroxyl groups, creating a broad array of HPLC particles with a range of polarities and selectivities suitable for reversed-phase separations. Examples of common stationary phases used for reversed-phase separations are shown in Table 11.2.

- **Mobile Phase:** In HPLC, selectivity is a function of both the mobile and stationary phases. It is often easier and less expensive to change the mobile phase concentration and/or components than to change the stationary phase. The mobile phases used in HPLC are mixtures of buffers and solvents. Mobile phase components must be high grade and of known composition; for example, the stabilizers in many solvents may cause problems. HPLC- and UHPLC-grade solvents are available and are worth the investment to reduce pressure fluctuations, baseline drift, and system maintenance.
- In normal-phase separations, the stationary phase is polar, and the mobile phase has low polarity. A normal-phase mobile phase might be based on iso-octane and have its polarity modified with the addition of a more polar material such as chloroform. As the polarity of the mobile phase increases, the tendency of analyte molecules to adsorb on the silica

Table 11.2 Stationary phases used in reversed-phase separations

Stationary phase functional group	Applications
Octadecylsilane (C18)	Highly retentive alkyl phase for a broad range of compounds, including drugs of abuse, steroids, fatty acids, and environmental pollutants
Octylsilane (C8)	Similar to C18 but less polar
Octadecylsilane-embedded polar (C18-embedded polar)	Complementary selectivity to C18, promotes retention of polar analytes, separations based on functional group differences
Cyano	Polar compounds, suitable for normal phase also
Phenyl	Promotes retention of aromatic and moderately polar compounds
Pentafluorophenyl	Enhanced selectivity for halogenated, polar, and isomeric analytes
Amino	High retention of polar analytes, anion exchange

surface decreases somewhat. Thus, these molecules spend less time on the stationary phase and elute with shorter retention times. A more polar phase is described as a "stronger" mobile phase because it causes the analyte molecules to elute more quickly. Very polar molecules, such as organic acids, can be difficult to separate by normal-phase HPLC because they are very strongly retained on the stationary phase.

- In reversed-phase HPLC, the stationary phase is relatively non-polar, and the mobile phase is polar. Typically, a reversed-phase mobile phase is based on water and may be modified with less-polar materials such as methanol, acetonitrile, or tetrahydrofuran. A stronger reversed-phase mobile phase is one that is less polar, exactly the opposite of the situation with normal-phase HPLC. The most common organic modifiers for reversed-phase HPLC today are acetonitrile and methanol. Acetonitrile is often preferred over methanol because of its low viscosity, which leads to lower system backpressures; its low UV cutoff; and its high boiling point. However, acetonitrile/water and methanol/

water mixtures have different elution strengths, and one may be more suitable than the other for a particular application. Acetonitrile has a higher dipole moment than methanol, making it a slightly weaker mobile phase when the organic component is near 100% of the mobile phase composition. Additionally, acetonitrile is considerably more expensive than methanol.

- When a sample contains ionic or highly polar compounds, it may be necessary to add an ion pair reagent to the mobile phase to separate compounds using reversed-phase HPLC. The ion pair reagent pairs with the ionic group on the analyte molecule, allowing it to be retained by the non-polar stationary phase.
  - **Gradient elution:** The HPLC analog to temperature programming in GC is gradient elution. In a gradient elution, the strength of the mobile phase is increased by changing the mobile phase composition as the run progresses. For reversed-phase separations, this is achieved by increasing the amount of organic modifier in the mobile phase composition over the chromatographic run. Advantages of gradient elutions over isocratic elutions include the ability to separate complex samples, improved resolution, increased sensitivity, shorter analysis times, and more complete flushing of the column.
  - Gradient elutions introduce the complication that as the mobile phase composition changes, the pH may also change, affecting the charge state of ionizable analytes and, thus, their retention characteristics. Solutions to this complication include using buffered aqueous solutions and working at pH extremes to avoid slight variations having large impacts on analyte retention.
  - When selecting mobile phase components for HPLC, care must be taken to ensure that they are compatible with the intended detector. For example, low-UV-absorbing components, such as acetonitrile, should be selected for UV detection, whereas volatile buffers based on ammonium instead of potassium or sodium should be selected for MS.

HPLC Detectors

By far the most widely used detectors in HPLC are based on UV energy absorption. These detectors can be classified into three types: fixed-wavelength, variable-wavelength, and diode-array detectors. A schematic of a fixed-wavelength detector is shown in Fig. 11.9. The construction of this detector is similar to any UV spectrophotometer except that it employs a flow-through cell. To preserve peak resolution, flow cell volumes should be less than 10% of the smallest peak volume. For conventional HPLC (4.6 × 100 mm column, 3-μm particle size), flow cells typically have volumes around 8–10 μL and path lengths of 10 mm (1 cm). Under UHPLC conditions (i.e., smaller-diameter columns and <2-μm particles), an 8-μL flow cell may lead to band broadening. Specialty cells designed specifically for UHPLC applications have volumes of 0.5–3 μL while maintaining a path length of 1 cm. In most operations, the reference cell is filled with air. The energy source is usually a 254-nm lamp with higher wavelengths available through the use of filters. In a variable-wavelength UV detector, light from a broad spectrum lamp is split into multiple wavelengths, usually by a diffraction grating, and the desired wavelength, from about 180 to 300 nm, is focused through the sample cell. Specific wavelengths can be selected based on the application, and the wavelength can be changed throughout the chromatographic run. A number of attempts to produce scanning UV detectors have been made, but none has been very satisfactory. The timescale of modern HPLC conditions, where peak widths can be as narrow as 1 s, makes the use of scanning UV to acquire full UV spectra of analytes as they elute impractical. Additionally, this functionality has been achieved with advances in diode-array detectors.

A diode-array detector focuses full-spectrum energy from the source through the cell and then diffracts the beam into its component wavelengths and focuses the resultant spectrum onto an array of photodiodes. Each photodiode receives a different wavelength band, and a complete spectrum may be obtained for any point in the chromatogram. This feature enables the examination of spectra from multiple points in an eluting peak, which is particularly useful in identifying impurities. A subset of wavelengths can also be selected to generate specific-wavelength traces in a manner similar to generating extracted ion chromatograms from full-spectra LC-MS data. This mode of operation allows both targeted analysis and quantitative analysis based on multiple discrete wavelengths within a single chromatographic run.

UV detectors are widely used because many compounds exhibit appropriate UV absorption. Nevertheless, there are some limitations and precautions that must be considered. First, the solvents used in the mobile phase must have a UV cutoff below the wavelength used for detection; if this condition is not met, the mobile phase will not be transparent, and detectability will be low or nonexistent. Second, many compounds absorb at the low operating wavelengths achievable with some designs (below 200–210 nm), which increases the number of potentially interfering components and decreases selectivity.

For analytes that do not have usable UV spectral properties, the differential refractive index detector is available. A refractive index detector

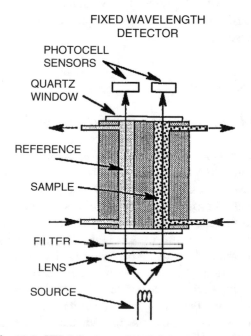

FIXED WAVELENGTH DETECTOR

PHOTOCELL SENSORS

QUARTZ WINDOW

REFERENCE

SAMPLE

FILTER

LENS

SOURCE

Fig. 11.9 HPLC fixed-wavelength detector

compares the refractive index of the mobile phase with that of the column effluent. This detector is nearly universal in that any eluting compound that has a refractive index differing from that of the mobile phase will give a response. Gradient elution is not possible because changing the mobile phase composition also changes its refractive index, and baseline drift becomes significant. Because refractive indices are temperature dependent, the system must be carefully thermostatted to control baseline drift. The differential refractive index detector was originally designed for use in the polymer industry and does not find wide use in toxicology. However, it is applicable for the analysis of sugars, starches, and similar compounds.

Fluorescence detectors offer a sensitive and selective analytical approach for those compounds that have natural fluorescence or that can be made to fluoresce by derivatization. These detectors allow the selection of excitation and detection wavelengths. However, fluorescence detectors are not widely used in forensic toxicology because of the limited number of compounds for which they are suitable.

Another detector of rather limited use in toxicological analyses is the electrochemical detector. In this detector, the flow cell contains a working electrode and reference and auxiliary electrodes. The potential between the working and auxiliary electrodes is set to a value that will selectively oxidize or reduce specific compounds. The working electrode monitors electroactivity in the cell, and the reference electrode provides a reproducible, stable voltage as a reference for the working electrode. For applicable compounds, this detector offers good sensitivity and selectivity.

The use of a mass spectrometer as a detector for HPLC has increased dramatically in recent years, concurrent with advances in LC-MS interface technologies and the development of APCI and ESI sources. The primary obstacle to overcome when interfacing LC with MS is the large volume of solvent introduced to the source of the mass spectrometer. This issue is mitigated somewhat when using UHPLC conditions, which include significantly lower flow rates than conventional HPLC. LC-MS interfaces and ionization techniques are discussed in detail in Chap. 14.

Data Systems

The same data systems available for GC can be used for HPLC.

Quantification

Objectives and Requirements

The goal of quantitative analysis is to determine with accuracy and precision how much of one or more analytes is present in a specimen or the relative amounts of two or more analytes in a specimen. Both GC and HPLC are well suited to quantitative analyses. To perform quantitative analyses satisfactorily and be able to support the results under rigorous examination in court, the analyst must be aware of, and adhere to, good analytical practices and understand what is being done and why. Details of best practices for quantitative method validation are discussed in Chap. 16. When performing quantitative analysis by GC or HPLC specifically, several factors must be considered. This section will address some of these factors.

Resolution

If using a non-mass-selective detector or collecting full-scan MS data, the resolution must be acceptable, generally 1.5 or greater, and a decision has to be made about whether to use peak area or peak height as the response to derive the result. For the quantification of a small peak in the presence of a larger, closely eluting peak, it is preferable to use peak height; otherwise, peak area should be used. When using a mass-selective detector to monitor selected ions, having coeluting peaks, while not desirable, is acceptable, providing the peaks do not interfere in each other's detection, and the final method meets all method validation parameters.

Response Factors

Equal amounts of two different analytes will not give equal detector responses. There are two approaches to handling this situation: calculating response factors and generating calibration curves. The response factor for analyte a can be defined as the response (peak area or height) per unit weight of a:

$$R_{fa} = \frac{\text{Response of } a}{\text{Weight of } a \text{ Injected}} \quad (11.17)$$

After determining response factors for each analyte of interest, the amount of each can be determined based on the magnitude of the detector response and Eq. 11.17.

Calibration Type

It is not necessary to calculate response factors if a calibration curve is generated for each analyte. An external calibration curve is determined by injecting the same volume of each of several standards of various concentrations. The response is plotted as ordinate, and the concentration is plotted as abscissa. After the line that fits these data has been determined, the same amount of analyte solution is injected, and the concentration of the material of interest is read from the curve or calculated from the equation for the curve. The precision of analyses using external standard calibration depends on injecting the same volume of standards and sample as closely as possible. Some variation in the amounts injected is unavoidable, especially if small volumes are injected with a syringe, and will affect the analytical precision. Another factor to consider when deciding whether to use external calibration is that there is no monitoring of sample recovery during extraction, derivatization, drying, or reconstitution.

The accuracy and precision of an external standard calibration can be greatly enhanced by including an internal standard. The internal standard selected should be a material that is not expected to appear in the specimen, has good sta-

bility, chromatographs satisfactorily, has a retention time reasonably close to that of the analyte, does not interfere with other peaks that may be present, and goes through the sample preparation process in a manner similar to the analyte. In practice, the same amount of internal standard is added to each specimen to be run. By plotting the ratio of the response of the analyte to that of the internal standard against concentration, for a series of calibrators at known concentrations. The use of an internal standard improves analytical precision by eliminating the effect of small variations in injection volumes. Because the internal standard peak should always give nearly the same response, this method also allows the analyst monitor method performance. If a mass-selective detector is used for quantification, a stable isotope (e.g., deuterated or ^{13}C labeled) analog of the analyte can be a good choice for an internal standard. Selected ion monitoring can be used to examine the relative magnitudes of the quantitative ions and ratios of the qualifying ions of the analyte and isotope analog.

To confidently and correctly use the techniques covered in this chapter, and to support them in court, the analyst must understand them sufficiently enough to be able to articulate their use and importance. The analyst must also appreciate the different techniques' strengths and limitations.

Further Reading

Dolan JW, Snyder LR (2018) Gradient elution chromatography. In: Myers RA (ed) Encyclopedia of analytical chemistry. Wiley, Hoboken, NJ

Ettre LS (1977) Basic relationships in gas chromatography; GCD-44. Perkin-Elmer, Norwalk, CT

Hyver KJ (1989) High resolution gas chromatography, 3rd edn. Hewlett Packard, Avondale, PA

Jonsson JA (1987) Chromatographic theory and basic principles. Marcel Dekker, New York, NY

Karger BL, Snyder LR, Horvath C (1973) An introduction to separation science. John Wiley, New York, NY

Klee MS. GC inlets – An introduction. https://www.agilent.com/cs/library/usermanuals/public/5958-9468_041007.pdf . Accessed 6 Mar 2019

Kromidas S (ed) (2017) The HPLC expert II: Find and optimize the benefits of your HPLC/UHPLC. Wiley-VCH, Weinheim, Germany

McNair HM, Miller JM (2009) Basic gas chromatography, 2nd edn. John Wiley & Sons, Hoboken, NJ

Miller JM (1975) Separation methods in chemical analysis. John Wiley, New York, NY

Perry JA (1981) Introduction to analytical gas chromatography. Marcel Dekker, New York, NY

Snyder LR (1968) Principles of adsorption chromatography. Marcel Dekker, New York, NY

Stafford DT, Brettell TA (2019) Forensic gas chromatography. In: Safferstein R, Hall AB (eds) Forensic science handbook, vol. I, 3rd edn. CRC Press, Boca Raton, FL

Synder LR, Kirlkand JJ, Dolan JW (2010) Introduction to modern liquid chromatography, 3rd edn. Wiley, Hoboken, NJ

Zadora G, Zuba D (2009) Gas chromatography in forensic science. In: Meyers RA (ed) Encyclopedia of analytical chemistry. Wiley, Hoboken, NJ

Derivatization

12

Lindsay Glicksberg and Sarah Kerrigan

Abstract

Gas chromatography-mass spectrometry (GC-MS) is still one of the most widely used analytical techniques in the forensic toxicology laboratory. Chemical derivatization is used to enhance the volatility, temperature stability, and detectability of drugs. It is an unavoidable requirement for some drugs and metabolites, particularly those with polar functional groups. Although chemical derivatization is an additional sample preparation step, chromatographic characteristics, stability, and overall improvements in detectability and specificity can be achieved. The most common derivatization techniques include silylation, acylation, and alkylation. A wide variety of derivatization reagents can be employed for this purpose. Approaches to derivatization are discussed for drugs of forensic interest, including amphetamines, benzodiazepines, cocaine metabolites, and opiates.

Keywords

Chemical derivatization · Gas chromatography · Silylation · Acylation · Alkylation · Chiral separation

Abbreviations

BF$_3$	Boron trifluoride
BSA	N,O-bis(trimethylsilyl) acetamide
BSTFA	O,N-bis(trimethylsilyl) fluoroacetamide
HFBA or HFAA	Heptafluorobutyric acid anhydride
HFBI	Heptafluorobutyrylimidazole
HFIP	1,1,1,3,3,3-hexafluoroisopropanol
l-TPC	l-N-trifluoracetyl-prolyl chloride
MBTFA	N-methyltrifluoroacetamide
MSTFA	N-methyl-N-trimethylsilyltrifluoroacetamide
MTBSTFA	N-methyl-N-($tert$-butyldimethylsilyl)-trifluoroacetamide
MTPA	(R)-(-)methoxytrifluoromethylphenylacetic acid
PFBBr	Pentafluorobenzyl bromide

L. Glicksberg (✉)
Southwestern Institute of Forensic Sciences, Dallas, TX, USA
e-mail: lindsay.glicksberg@dallascounty.org

S. Kerrigan
Department of Forensic Science, Sam Houston State Laboratory, Huntsville, TX, USA
e-mail: sarah.kerrigan@shsu.edu

© Springer Nature Switzerland AG 2020
B. S. Levine, S. Kerrigan (eds.), *Principles of Forensic Toxicology*,
https://doi.org/10.1007/978-3-030-42917-1_12

PFPA or PFAA	Pentafluoropropionic acid anhydride
PFPI	Pentafluoropropany limidazole
PFPOH	2,2,3,3,3-Pentafluoro-1-propanol
TBDMDMCS	Tert-butyldimethylchlorosilane
TFAA	Trifluoroacetic acid anhydride
TFAI	Trifluoroacetylimidazole
TMCS	Trimethylchlorosilane
TMS	Trimethylsilyl
TMSI	Trimethylsilylimidazole

Introduction

Forensic toxicologists are responsible for the identification of drugs and metabolites in biological fluids. Gas chromatography-mass spectrometry remains one of the most universally used and robust techniques in forensic toxicology. Gas chromatographic separation is particularly effective for compounds that are non-polar, thermally stable, and volatile. It has been used for the detection, identification, and quantitation of a wide range of xenobiotics. However, the presence of polar functional groups, or the introduction of such groups during biotransformation can be problematic. Under these circumstances, drugs or metabolites may exhibit poor chromatographic properties. Modification of the chemical structure of the molecule during the derivatization process can improve both separation and detection. The most frequently used derivatization techniques for GC are reviewed, including silylation, acylation, and alkylation.

Derivatization for GC-MS

If a molecule is too polar, non-volatile, thermally liable, produces insufficient diagnostic ions, or has poor chromatographic properties (e.g., peak tailing or poor separation), derivatization may be necessary. Derivatization involves the chemical modification of an existing drug or metabolite to produce a new compound, with enhanced chromatographic properties. Additionally, since the chemical structure is changed, the drug may fragment differently, potentially improving the abundance, or the diagnostic value of the resulting ions. Advantages of derivatization as it relates to gas chromatography include:

- Decreased polarity
- Increased molecular mass
- Improved detectability
- Increased specificity
- Increased volatility
- Increased thermal stability

Decreasing the polarity of a molecule is beneficial because it results in less adsorption onto the stationary phase, which can improve peak shape and enhance resolution. Derivatization, which increases the molecular mass, can also improve the specificity of ions, which is particularly important if selected ion monitoring (SIM) is being used. Some drugs of interest produce poorly diagnostic mass spectra when analyzed directly by GC-MS. For example, during electron impact (EI) ionization, methamphetamine readily fragments to produce the tropylium ion base peak at m/z 91 ($C_7H_7^+$) and the $C_3H_8N^+$ ion (m/z 58) from the phenethylamine side chain, neither of which are highly specific (Fig. 12.1). Smaller fragments are less diagnostic because of their increased abundance in nature. Therefore, the absence of the molecular ion can be a disadvantage, particularly for drugs with small molecular masses. Therefore, chemical derivatization can not only increase the molecular mass, but improve the mass spectral characteristics of the drug, yielding more specific ions with greater diagnostic value. This is depicted in Fig. 12.1, which shows EI mass spectra for underivatized and derivatized methamphetamine.

Derivatization typically involves the replacement of an active hydrogen on various functional groups. Target functional groups can include amines, alcohols, phenols, ketones, carboxylic acids, and others. The general reaction for derivatization is as follows:

$$R_1 - AH + R_2 - D \rightarrow R_1 - AD + R_2 - H$$

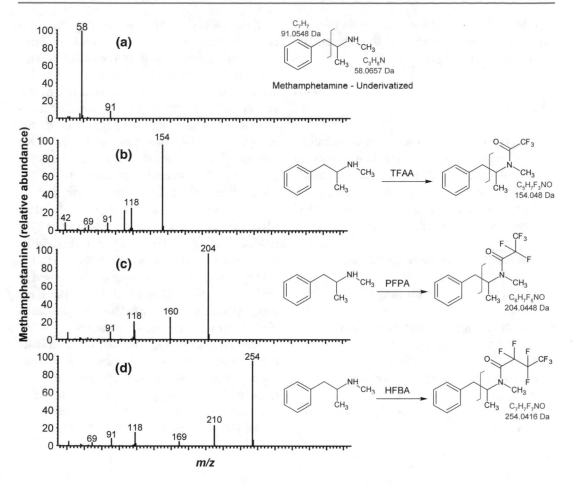

Fig. 12.1 Mass spectra of methamphetamine underivatized (**a**) and derivatized with TFAA (**b**), PFPA (**c**), and HFBA (**d**)

where "A" is an oxygen, sulfur, nitrogen, or similar atoms found in functional groups, "H" is an active hydrogen, and "D" is the functional group on the derivatization agent. There are multiple derivatization agents and a single drug may be derivatized using a variety of different approaches. Abbreviations for the most common derivatization reagents can be found at the end of the chapter. The ideal derivatization technique for a certain molecule or drug should:

- Produce a single, stable, reproducible, and high yield derivative
- Result in simple and fast reaction using straightforward laboratory techniques
- Achieve the desired modification and chemical properties

- Use non-hazardous reagents
- Not result in detector fouling

There is potential to produce more than one derivative if the molecule contains multiple functional groups. Side products may be produced during the reaction, which can change the chemical environment of the reaction (e.g., make it more acidic) and compromise the stability of the derivative product. A disadvantage of derivatization is the increased sample preparation time in the laboratory; additional post-derivatization clean-up may also be required to remove excess reagent and/or by-products prior to analysis. Failure to remove these prior to injection can result in deterioration of the stationary phase, detector fouling and increased instrument maintenance.

Once polar functional groups within the molecule have been identified, the appropriate derivatization technique can be selected.

Silylation

Silylation is one of the most universal derivatization techniques as it is applicable to numerous functional groups, including alcohols, phenols, amines, thiols, and carboxylic acids (Table 12.1). Silylation involves the introduction of a silyl moiety through substitution at the active hydrogen.

The advantages of silylation include:

- Applicability to a wide range of functional groups
- Variety of reagents commercially available
- Ease of preparation
- Thermally stable derivatives
- Excellent chromatographic characteristics
- Increased volatility
- Amenable to direct GC analysis (no clean-up)

Trimethylsilyl (TMS) are among the most common derivatives utilized, although many other alkylated silyl groups can be used. Common derivatization reagents for silylation are listed in Table 12.1. The replacement of an active hydrogen with TMS [R–Si(CH$_3$)$_3$] increases the molecular weight of the drug by 72 Da. In EI spectra the m/z 73 often features prominently and is not considered a diagnostic ion because it is not associated with the molecular structure of the drug itself. Higher alkyl homologs further increase molecular weight (e.g., t-butyldimethylsilyl or t-BDMS). They also have increased hydrolytic stability and improved mass spectral characteristics. Their EI mass spectra are often characterized by abundant [M-57]$^+$ ions due to the loss of the tert-butyl group. Despite this advantage, these bulky groups present difficulties for sterically hindered groups on some drug molecules.

While silylation is applicable to various functional groups, alcohols (primary > secondary > tertiary) are the most reactive with silyl reagents, followed by phenols, carboxylic acids, and amines (primary > secondary). N-methyl-N-trimethylsilyltrifluoroacetamide (MSTFA) and

Table 12.1 Derivatization of common functional groups

Functional group	Derivatization	Reagent	Derivatives
Alcohols/phenols	Silylation	BSTFA, BSA, HDMS, MSTFA, TMSI, TMCS (catalyst)	Trimethylsilyl (TMS)
		MTBSTFA, TMCS (catalyst)	t-Butyldimethylsilyl (t-BDMS)
	Acylation	TFAA, TFAI, MBTFA	Trifluorobutyramides
		PFPA/PFAA	Pentafluorobutyramides
		HFAA/HFBA, HFBI	Heptafluorobutyramides
	Alkylation	PFBBr	Pentafluorobenzyl ethers
Amines	Silylation	BSTFA, BSA, MSTFA, TMCS (catalyst)	Trimethylsilyl (TMS)
		MTBSTFA, TBDMCS (catalyst)	t-Butyldimethylsilyl (t-BDMS)
	Acylation	TFAA, MBTFA	Trifluorobutyramides
		PFPA/PFAA	Pentafluorobutyramides
		HFAA/HFBA	Heptafluorobutyramides
Carboxylic acids	Silylation	BSTFA, BSA, MSTFA, TMSI, TMCS (catalyst)	Trimethylsilyl (TMS)
		MTBSTFA, TMCS (catalyst)	t-Butyldimethylsilyl (t-BDMS)
	Alkylation	PFBBr	Pentafluorobenzyl ethers
		BF$_3$/Methanol	Methyl esters

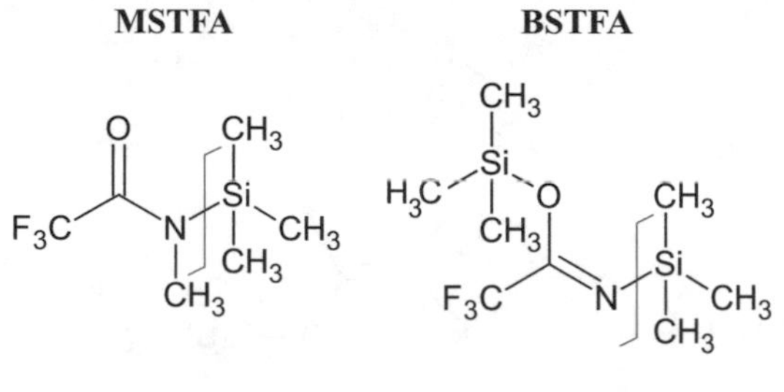

MSTFA   **BSTFA**

Fig. 12.2 Chemical structures of commonly used silylation reagents MSTFA and BSTFA with severed bond indicating the TMS group

N,O-bis(trimethylsilyl)fluoroacetamide (BSTFA) are widely utilized for this purpose (Fig. 12.2). Other silylation reagents include trimethylsilylimidazole (TMSI) and N,O-bis(trimethylsilyl) acetamide (BSA) (Table 12.1). While many of these reagents have similar silylation potencies, increased volatility of the reagent can be beneficial because it can reduce interfering peaks in the chromatogram. Silylation reactions occur through nucleophilic attack, so their efficiency depends on good leaving groups. For this reason, BSTFA is a more effective silylating reagent than BSA, because trifluoroacetamide is a better leaving group, reacting faster and more completely than BSA for most compounds.

Catalysts are often employed during silylation, particularly if sterically hindered functional groups (e.g., tertiary alcohols or steroids) are the target molecule. The most commonly used catalyst for silylation is trimethylchlorosilane (TMCS). A commonly used combination is BSTFA + 1% TMCS. Alternatively, some mixtures of silylating reagents and catalyst are used (e.g., BSA/TMSI/TMCS (1:1:1, v/v/v)). TMSI is a particularly useful derivatization reagent because it is not reactive toward amines and therefore has greater selectivity than BSTFA and MSTFA. If the drug of interest contains both hydroxyl and amine groups, TMSI could be advantageous in terms of the production of a single derivative. The use of TMSI will also preserve keto groups and prevent the formation of enols during the reaction.

It is very important when performing silylation reactions to use aprotic organic solvents, as these reagents are easily hydrolyzed when exposed to aqueous conditions and will react with any active hydrogens. GC column stationary phase should not contain any active sites as well. Pyridine is sometimes used as the solvent because it is an acid scavenger and helps drive the reaction forward. However, it can also result in peak tailing. Silylation reactions can be performed in the absence of solvent if the compounds of interest are sufficiently soluble in the reagent. Finally, silylating reagents are typically moisture sensitive, as are the derivatives themselves.

Although the reaction requires heat, most are effective at moderate temperatures (e.g., 60–80 °C), and on-column derivatization is also possible for some silylating reagents. During method development, derivatization conditions should be carefully evaluated and optimized to ensure that the reaction is either complete, or reproducible. If derivatization does not go to completion, it is important to ensure that the internal standard selected behaves in an identical fashion to the drug or interest. This can be achieved using isotopically labeled internal standards. If compounds of interest undergo derivatization, it is not acceptable to use an internal standard that does not derivatize. The completeness and reproducibility of the derivatization are particularly important when drugs contain more than one derivatization site (e.g., morphine). The trimethylsilyation of morphine is shown in Fig. 12.3, whereby both OH groups are derivatized, resulting in a di-TMS derivative.

Forensically relevant analytes that are frequently derivatized using silylation reactions include cannabinoids (e.g., Δ^9-THC, carboxy-THC, hydroxy-THC), cocaine metabolites, opiates, and benzodiazepines. Their reactivity toward so many functional groups, ease of preparation, and limited sample clean-up prior to GC injection makes silylation a popular choice in forensic toxicology applications. Advantages and disadvantages of the most common derivatization approaches are summarized in Table 12.2.

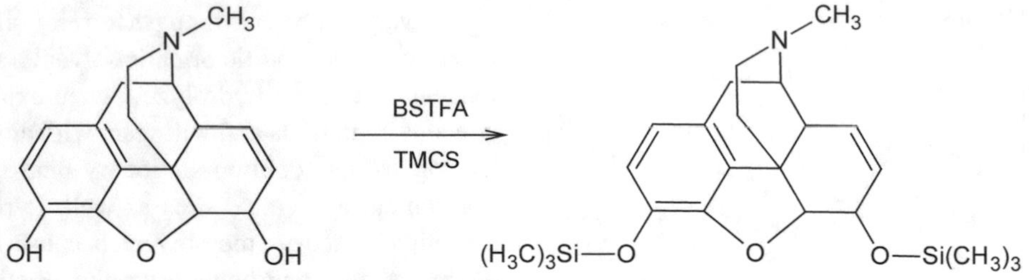

Fig. 12.3 Silylation of morphine using BSTFA + 1% TMCS

Table 12.2 Advantages and disadvantages of derivatization approaches

Derivatization type	Advantages	Disadvantages
Silylation	• Large number of silylating reagents available • Easy to prepare • No additional clean-up necessary • Reactive towards many functional groups (-CO$_2$H, NH$_2$, OH, Amide) • Useful when derivatizing drugs with more than one functional group type (e.g., –OH and –CO$_2$H, carboxy-THC)	• Must use aprotic solvents • Reagents and derivatives are moisture sensitive • Required anhydrous conditions • Potential for multiple derivatives
Acylation	• Large number of reagents available • Fluorinated derivatives with increased molecular weight and longer retention times • Derivative hydrolytically stable • Addition of halogenated carbons can increase detectability	• Acid by-products for some reagents require removal prior to GC analysis • Acylation reagents moisture sensitive • Reagents hazardous and odorous • Not reactive toward carboxylic acids
Alkylation	• Reaction conditions vary from strongly basic to strongly acidic • Some reactions possible in aqueous solution • Derivatives generally stable	• Can be used in conjunction with acylation and silylation • Reagents often toxic • Conditions may be harsh

Acylation

Another common derivatization technique is acylation, which involves the introduction of an acyl moiety (RCO–) onto a molecule through substitution of an active hydrogen. Acylation is an ideal technique for polar molecules containing hydroxyls, thiols, or amines and converts them into esters, thioesters, and amides (Fig. 12.4). The advantage of using acylation as a derivatization technique is the formation of stable derivatives that are highly volatile and have increased sensitivity with characteristic mass spectral fragmentation due to the increase in molecular weight.

Acyl derivatives can be formed using three different types of reagents: acyl halides, acid anhydrides, or reactive acyl derivatives, such as acylated imidazoles. Acetic anhydrides, particularly perfluoroacyl anhydrides, are among the most common reagents for acylation. Examples of these reagents include trifluoroacetic acid anhydride (TFAA), pentafluoropropionic acid anhydride (PFPA or PFAA), and heptafluorobutyric acid anhydride (HFBA or HFAA) (Fig. 12.5). The fluorinated acyl groups increase molecular weight and retention time significantly. This electronegativity can be further exploited if negative chemical ionization is to be used for

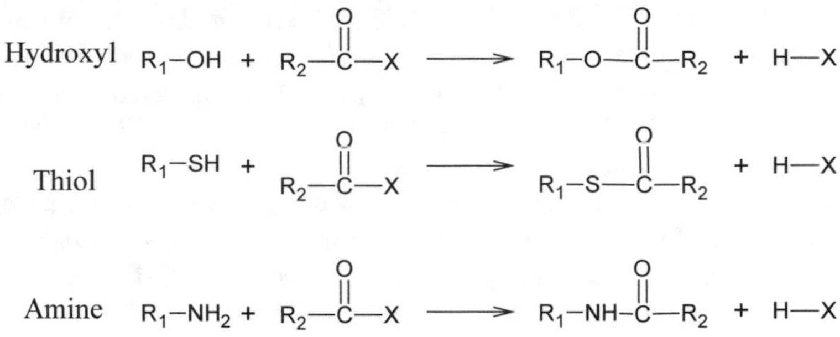

Fig. 12.4 General reaction scheme for acylation of hydroxyls, thiols, and amines

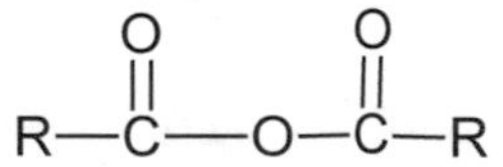

Hydroxyl $R_1{-}OH$ + $R_2{-}\overset{\displaystyle O}{\overset{\|}{C}}{-}X$ $\longrightarrow$ $R_1{-}O{-}\overset{\displaystyle O}{\overset{\|}{C}}{-}R_2$ + $H{-}X$

Thiol $R_1{-}SH$ + $R_2{-}\overset{\displaystyle O}{\overset{\|}{C}}{-}X$ $\longrightarrow$ $R_1{-}S{-}\overset{\displaystyle O}{\overset{\|}{C}}{-}R_2$ + $H{-}X$

Amine $R_1{-}NH_2$ + $R_2{-}\overset{\displaystyle O}{\overset{\|}{C}}{-}X$ $\longrightarrow$ $R_1{-}NH{-}\overset{\displaystyle O}{\overset{\|}{C}}{-}R_2$ + $H{-}X$

Fig. 12.5 General structure of perfluoroacyl acid anhydrides

$$R{-}\overset{\displaystyle O}{\overset{\|}{C}}{-}O{-}\overset{\displaystyle O}{\overset{\|}{C}}{-}R$$

Reagent	R	Additional Molecular Weight
TFAA	$O = C - CF_3$	210
PFAA	$O = C - CF_2 - CF_3$	310
HFAA	$O = C - CF_2 - CF_2 - CF_3$	410

analytes that are present at low concentration (e.g., triazolam) or if electron capture detection (ECD) is used.

While acyl halides and acid anhydride reagents produce stable and volatile acyl derivatives, they form acid by-products that must be removed prior to GC analysis. These reactions may be performed in pyridine, tetrahydrofuran, or other solvents capable of accepting the acid by-product. Even if a basic acceptor is used to neutralize them, additional steps are often necessary to remove excess derivative prior to analysis. Their removal is relatively straight-forward using simple evaporation (under nitrogen) or liquid-liquid extraction, but it does require an additional sample preparation step.

Additional common reagents include N-methyltrifluoroacetamide (MBTFA) and perfluoro-acylimidazoles, such as trifluoroacetylimidazole (TFAI), pentafluoropropanylimidazole (PFPI), and heptafluorobutyrylimidazole (HFBI). These reagents also produce highly volatile derivatives, but do not produce by-products that would need to be removed prior to analysis by GC; the by-products are inert and highly volatile. Caution is needed when using these reagents however, because they are sensitive to aqueous environments.

Acylation has been widely utilized for the derivatization of many drug classes, notably amphetamines and opiates. Since they are not reactive toward carboxylic acid groups, metabolites of cocaine and THC require an additional derivatization step (discussed later). LSD has been derivatized using trifluoroacetylimidazoles. MBTFA has been used to produce carbohydrate derivatives. Acetic anhydride can also be used for the acylation of alcohols, phenols, and amines. Although the resulting esters are more stable than silylated derivatives, the molecular weight increase is minimal.

Alkylation

While not as common as silylation or acylation, alkylation is another derivatization technique used to improve detection and chromatographic characteristics of drugs by GC analysis. Alkylation involves the substitution of an alkyl or aryl group at an active hydrogen on hydroxyls, carboxylic acids, thiols, and amines to produce ethers, esters, thioethers, thioesters, *N*-alkyl amines, and *N*-alkyl amides. It is particularly widely used for the modification of acidic hydrogens on carboxylic acids and phenols. The advantages of alkylation are the formation of stable derivatives that have higher volatility than the original molecule. However, as the acidity of the active hydrogen decreases, stronger alkylating reagents are required.

Reagents include substituted benzyl bromides, unsubstituted benzyl bromides, and alkyl halides such as aliphatic bromides and iodides. Common reagents include boron trifluoride (BF_3)/methanol and pentafluorobenzyl bromide (PFBBr).

Alkylation of carboxylic acids is also possible by esterification with alcohols. Drugs or metabolites containing a carboxylic acid can be esterified using 1,1,1,3,3,3-hexafluoroisopropanol (HFIP) or 2,2,3,3,3-pentafluoropropanol (PFPOH). These reagents convert carboxylic acids into the corresponding fluorinated ester. This approach is often used in combination with other derivatization reagents. For example, acylation and esterification of -OH and $-CO_2H$ using both PFPA and PFPOH when dealing with polyfunctional compounds (e.g., benzoylecgonine). Although silylation using a single reagent can be used to derivatize carboxylic acids and phenols, these derivatives are less stable than their alkylated counterparts.

Other Derivatization Techniques

Oximes

Some molecules contain more than one functional group; however, only one functional group may need to be transformed during derivatization reaction. This often occurs when the ketone group of a compound does not need to undergo derivatization and another more polar functional group does. An example is the silylation of the hydroxyl group on steroids. Oximes can be used to prevent the keto group from interfering with the derivatization of another functional group, essentially protecting it. Using this approach, a pentafluorobenzyl oxime can be prepared using pentafluorobenzyloxylamine. Oxime formation has been widely reported for steroids, and also for the keto-opioids (discussed later).

Cyclization

Another derivatization technique involving polyfunctional group molecules is cyclization, where there is a simultaneous reaction with two proximal active functional groups to form a cyclic derivative. In order for a cyclic derivatization to occur, there must be the appropriate amount of spatial separation between the two functional groups and the ring must be stable. Reagents using cyclization include boronic acids $[R–B(OH)_2]$ in the presence of aprotic, organic solvents such as pyridine or acetone.

The advantage of cyclization over other derivatization techniques is the potential to produce one derivative versus multiple derivatives. However, multiple derivative products could be formed if the molecule has more than two functional groups with an active hydrogen.

Chiral Derivatization

Separation of chiral compounds (e.g., *d/l* methamphetamine) presents a unique challenge using gas chromatography. If derivatization is to be avoided, stereoisomers can be separated using a chiral stationary phase. However, an alternative approach is to derivatize the molecule using an optically pure reagent, followed by separation on a traditional (achiral) chromatographic phase.

Chiral separation on GC has been achieved for multiple analytes, including methamphetamine, 3,4-methylenedioxymethamphetamine (MDMA), methadone, and a variety of anti-inflammatory medications. Fluroacyl-prolyl chlorides are commonly used: heptafluorobutyryl prolyl chloride and *l*-*N*-trifluoroacetyl-prolyl chloride (*l*-TPC) have been used to separate the two methamphetamine enantiomers and S-(-)-trifluoroacetyl prolyl chloride has been used to separate MDMA chiral forms. Additional reagents include (*R*)-(-)methoxytrifluoromethylphenylacetic acid (MTPA) for methamphetamine, (-)methyl chloroformate for methadone, and S-(-)-1-(-1-naphtyl)ethylamine for anti-inflammatory drugs.

Although chiral derivatization is more specialized and requires optically active and pure reagents of sufficient volatility, it avoids the costs associated with a chiral stationary phase.

Derivatization by Drug Class

Amphetamines

Amphetamines are frequently encountered in forensic toxicology casework. Amphetamines and structurally related analogs (e.g., cathinones) contain a primary, secondary or tertiary amine. Active hydrogens on primary and secondary amines benefit from chemical derivatization. The EI mass spectra of amphetamine and methamphetamine are each dominated by one poorly diagnostic ion, *m/z* 44 and *m/z* 58, respectively. The derivatization of these molecules improves their chromatographic and mass spectral properties. Derivatization also allows for these relatively small molecules to be better separated from structurally related endogenous compounds found in biological matrices.

Although primary and secondary amines readily undergo silylation and acylation, the latter is the most common approach. Acylation using HFBA, PFPA, or TFAA, and silylation using MTBSTFA have been reported (Fig. 12.6). Other techniques including the use of propylchloroformate, pentafluorooctanoyl chloride, and combination of acid anhydrides with organic solvents are also possible. Amphetamines bearing tertiary amines, including the pyrrolidine-type cathinones (e.g., methylenedioxypyrovalerone (MDPV), α-pyrrolidonopentiophenone (α-PVP)) do not derivatize with these techniques due to the absence of an active hydrogen. Chiral separation of amphetamines by GC is commonly achieved using the chiral derivative, *l*-TPC described earlier. A schematic for this reaction is shown in Fig. 12.7.

Benzodiazepines

While derivatization is not necessary for the analysis of most benzodiazepines by GC-MS, it can be used to improve chromatographic characteristics and improve volatility of the more polar benzodiazepines, such as oxazepam,

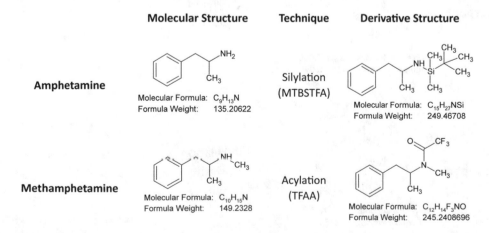

	Molecular Structure	Technique	Derivative Structure
Amphetamine	Molecular Formula: $C_9H_{13}N$ Formula Weight: 135.20622	Silylation (MTBSTFA)	Molecular Formula: $C_{15}H_{27}NSi$ Formula Weight: 249.46708
Methamphetamine	Molecular Formula: $C_{10}H_{15}N$ Formula Weight: 149.2328	Acylation (TFAA)	Molecular Formula: $C_{12}H_{14}F_3NO$ Formula Weight: 245.2408696

Fig. 12.6 Derivatization of amphetamine and methamphetamine

temazepam, and lorazepam (containing a hydroxyl group) or clonazepam (containing a nitro group). Although 1,4-benzodiazepines are most common, the drug class is extensively functionalized at many sites on the molecule. Considering the wide variety of benzodiazepine structures, derivatization has been achieved using an assortment of techniques, including silylation, acylation, and alkylation. Silylation remains one of the most popular approaches for the identification of benzodiazepines and their metabolites (Fig. 12.8).

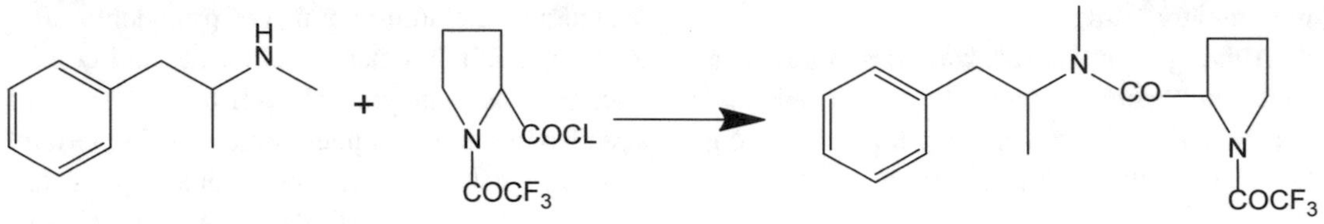

Fig. 12.7 Chiral derivatization of methamphetamine using *l*-TPC

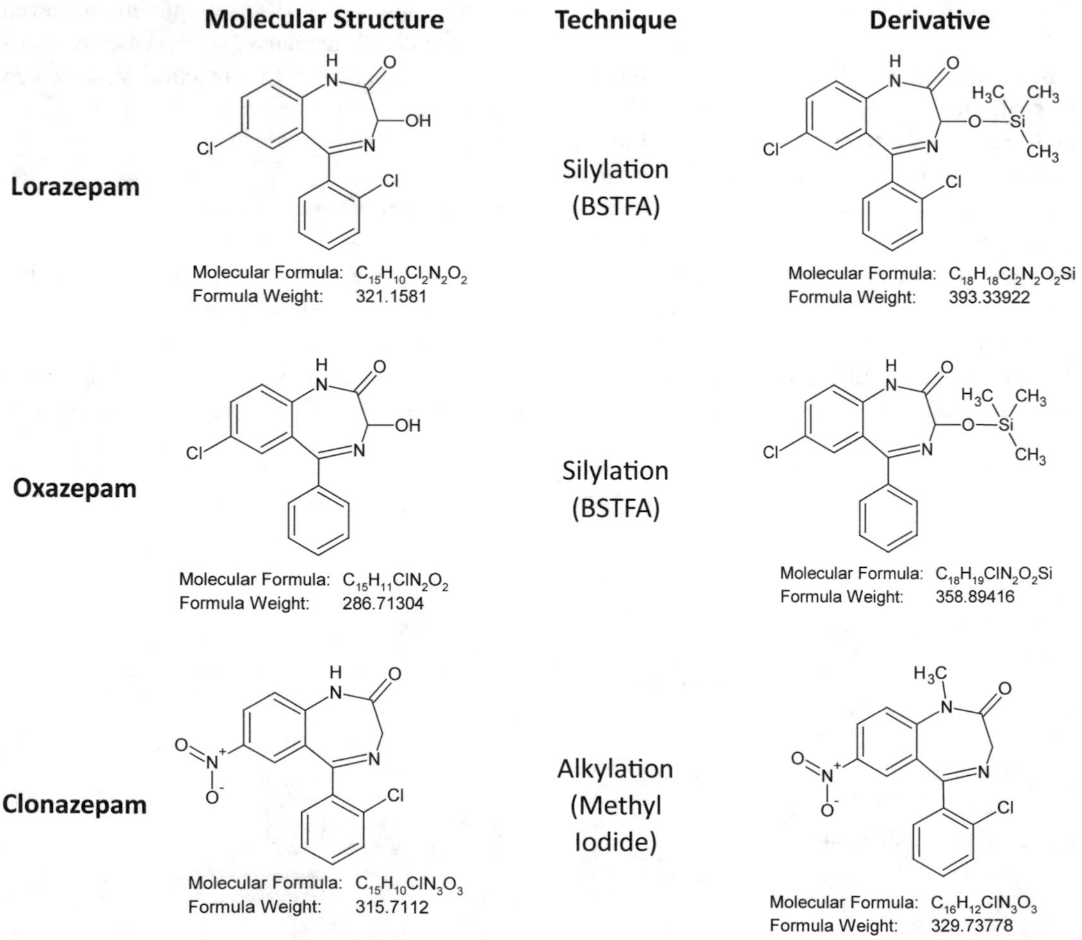

	Molecular Structure	**Technique**	**Derivative**
Lorazepam	Molecular Formula: $C_{15}H_{10}Cl_2N_2O_2$ Formula Weight: 321.1581	Silylation (BSTFA)	Molecular Formula: $C_{18}H_{18}Cl_2N_2O_2Si$ Formula Weight: 393.33922
Oxazepam	Molecular Formula: $C_{15}H_{11}ClN_2O_2$ Formula Weight: 286.71304	Silylation (BSTFA)	Molecular Formula: $C_{18}H_{19}ClN_2O_2Si$ Formula Weight: 358.89416
Clonazepam	Molecular Formula: $C_{15}H_{10}ClN_3O_3$ Formula Weight: 315.7112	Alkylation (Methyl Iodide)	Molecular Formula: $C_{16}H_{12}ClN_3O_3$ Formula Weight: 329.73778

Fig. 12.8 Derivatization of benzodiazepines by silylation and alkylation

Cannabinoids

Derivatization is necessary for the identification of THC and its metabolites in biological samples. While acylation of the hydroxy (e.g., PFPA) and esterification of the carboxylic acid (e.g., HFIP) have been reported, silylation is more convenient because it derivatizes both functional groups. Commonly used silylation reagents include BSTFA, MSTFA, and MTBSTFA (Fig. 12.9).

Opioids

Morphine and related compounds often contain multiple sites for derivatization. Silylation and acylation are the most commonly used techniques. Common reagents used for silylation of these analytes include BSTFA or MSTFA, often in the presence of a catalyst (TMCS) (Fig. 12.10).

Structurally similar to opiates, semi-synthetic opioids also require derivatization prior to analysis by GC-MS. The semi-synthetic opioids (oxycodone, oxymorphone, hydrocodone) include a keto-substituent, which decreases the volatility of these analytes. Derivatization can be achieved using silylation or acylation; however, both the enol and keto derivative may form. Protection of the ketone group by the formation of an oxime is possible. For keto-opioids this is commonly achieved using hydroxylamine or methoxylamine. This is depicted in Fig. 12.11 using hydrocodone.

Cocaine

Chromatographic properties of cocaine metabolites (particularly benzoylecgonine) are significantly improved by derivatization. This can be

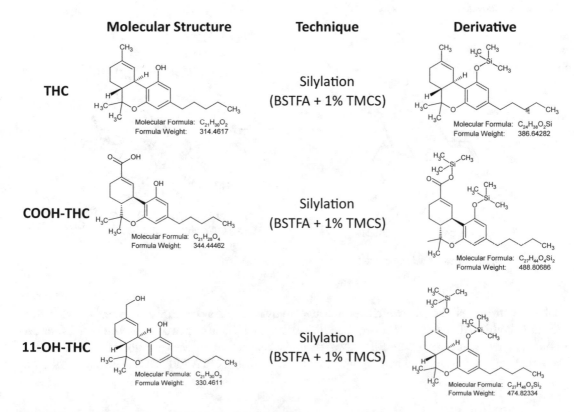

Fig. 12.9 Derivatization of cannabinoids by silylation

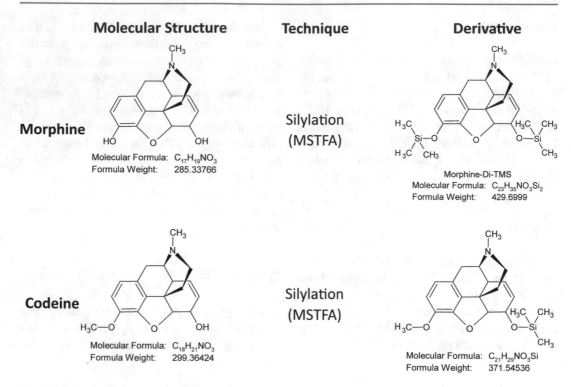

Molecular Structure　　**Technique**　　**Derivative**

Morphine

Molecular Formula: $C_{17}H_{19}NO_3$
Formula Weight: 285.33766

Silylation (MSTFA)

Morphine-Di-TMS
Molecular Formula: $C_{23}H_{35}NO_3Si_2$
Formula Weight: 429.6999

Codeine

Molecular Formula: $C_{18}H_{21}NO_3$
Formula Weight: 299.36424

Silylation (MSTFA)

Molecular Formula: $C_{21}H_{29}NO_3Si$
Formula Weight: 371.54536

Fig. 12.10 Derivatization of opiates by silylation

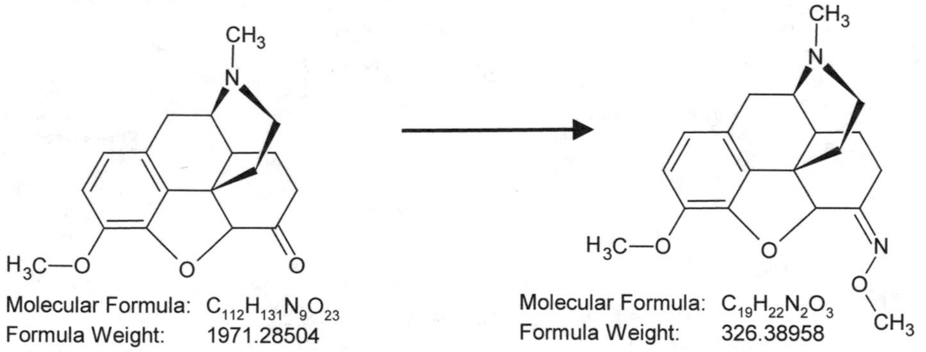

Molecular Formula: $C_{112}H_{131}N_9O_{23}$
Formula Weight: 1971.28504

Molecular Formula: $C_{19}H_{22}N_2O_3$
Formula Weight: 326.38958

Fig. 12.11 Derivatization of select opioids

achieved using silylation, which is reactive towards both –OH and –CO₂H, or by esterification. Higher abundances of BE have been reported using acylation when compared to silylation. As described earlier, esterification requires the use of two derivatization reagents. A schematic for the esterification of cocaine metabolites using PFPA/PFPOH is shown in Fig. 12.12.

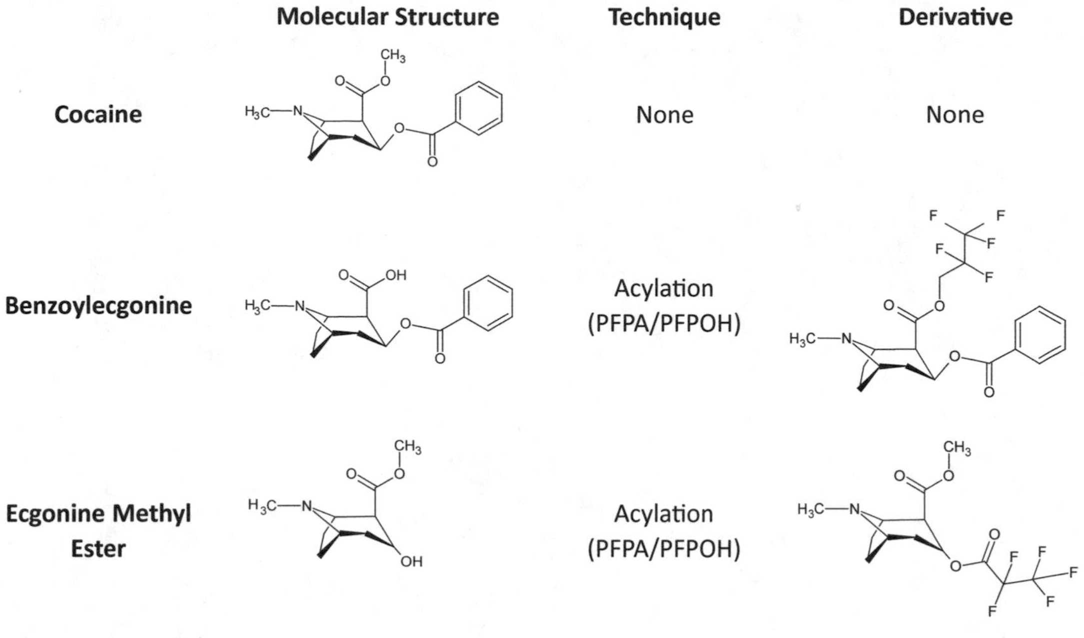

	Molecular Structure	Technique	Derivative
Cocaine		None	None
Benzoylecgonine		Acylation (PFPA/PFPOH)	
Ecgonine Methyl Ester		Acylation (PFPA/PFPOH)	

Fig. 12.12 Derivatization of cocaine and metabolites

Further Reading

Baselt RC (2020) Disposition of toxic drugs and chemicals in man, 12th edn. Biomedical Publications, Seal Beach, CA

Caplan YH, Goldberger BA (eds) (2015) Garriott's Medicolegal aspects of alcohol, 6th edn. Lawyers and Judges, Tuscon, AZ

Dinis-Oliveira RJ, Vieira D, Magalhaes T (2016) Guidelines for the collection of biological samples for clinical and forensic toxicological analysis. Forensic Sci Res 1:42–51

Dolinak D (2013) Forensic toxicology a physiologic perspective. Academic Forensic Pathology Inc, Calgary

Hulshoff A, Lingeman H (1984) Derivatzatization reactions in the gas-liquid chromatographic analysis of drugs in biological fluids. J Pharm Biomed Anal 2:337–380

Knapp D (1979) Handbook of analytical derivatization reactions. John Wiley and Sons, New York

Meatherall R (1999) GC-MS confirmation of Codeine, Morphine, 6-Acetylmorphine, Hydrocodone, Hydromorphone, Oxycodone, and Oxymorphone in urine. J Anal Toxicol 23:177–186

Moffat AC, Osselton MD, Widdop B, Watts J (eds) (2011) Clarke's analysis of drugs and poisons, 4th edn. Pharmaceutical Press, London

Segura J, Ventura R, Juardo C (1998) Derivatization procedures for gas chromatographic-mass spectrometric determination of xenobiotics in biological samples, with special attention to drugs of abuse and doping agents. J Chromatogr B 713:61–90

Smith ML, Hughes RO, Levin B, Dickerson S, Darwin WD, Cone EJ (1995) Forensic drug testing for Opiates. VI. Urine testing for Hydromorphone, Hydrocodone, Oxymorphone, and Oxycodone with Commercial Opiate Immunoassays and Gas Chromatography-Mass Spectrometry. J Anal Toxicol 19:18–26

Immunoassay

13

Michael L. Smith

Abstract

Immunoassays are still widely used for presumptive testing in forensic toxicology applications, including workplace drug testing, human performance, and medicolegal investigations. Although they cannot be used quantitatively or definitively to identify a specific substance in a forensic setting, they are widely used for screening purposes. The nature of the antibody–antigen interaction, antibody production, specificity, and cross-reactivity are described. Homogeneous and heterogeneous immunoassays are also discussed, together with the relative advantages and disadvantages of each.

Keywords

Immunoassay · Toxicology · Drugs of abuse · Cross-reactivity · Cutoff

Immunoassays are scientific tests that use antibodies to identify and measure amounts of a chemical substance. In forensic toxicology, these assays are typically used to screen biological samples for the presence of an antigen. The original immunoassays developed in the 1950s by Rosalyn Yalow and Solomon Berson were used, conversely, to quantify human antibodies themselves in the blood of diabetics who had acquired immune responses to the bovine insulin they were taking to treat their disease. The insulin antibody concentration was determined by mixing ^{131}I-labeled insulin with the patient's blood in a test tube, separating protein-bound from unbound insulin, then measuring the gamma radiation from the labeled insulin bound to immunoglobulins. The amount of bound insulin correlated to a patient's insulin antibody concentration and this laboratory result assisted physicians in prescribing insulin dosages and determining the patient's prognosis.

Using the same theoretical basis of antibody–antigen interactions, Yalow and Berson extended this technique to measure nanogram quantities of numerous human hormones. The ability to measure submicrogram quantities of hormones revolutionized the fields of endocrinology and neuroscience. The principle they exploited was called competitive binding, and Dr. Yalow received the Nobel Prize in medicine in 1977 for developing and refining the analytical method based on this principle: radioimmunoassay (RIA).

M. L. Smith (✉)
Huestis and Smith Toxicology, LLC,
Severna Park, MD, USA

© Springer Nature Switzerland AG 2020
B. S. Levine, S. Kerrigan (eds.), *Principles of Forensic Toxicology*,
https://doi.org/10.1007/978-3-030-42917-1_13

Competitive Binding Process

The generalized competitive binding process is represented in Fig. 13.1.

The antigen is represented by a drug because this is the most common analyte of interest in forensic toxicology. To generate antibodies against a drug antigen, an immunogen prepared from the drug of interest is injected into an animal, and antibodies that specifically bind the drug are produced in the serum. The serum (called antiserum) collected from the animal is mixed with labeled drug and with the drug itself. Labeled and unlabeled drug compete for the antibody binding sites; at equilibrium, the concentration of drug can be determined using the law of mass action, if the equilibrium constants, concentration of labeled drug, and concentration of antibody are known. In practice, the antigen concentration is determined by comparing the amount of labeled drug bound to antibody in a sample to that of reference standards containing known concentrations of antigen. A convenient way for readers to analyze immunoassay problems in the remainder of this chapter and in the laboratory is to remember the radioimmunoassay

(RIA) example in Fig. 13.2, which is a representation of a coated tube assay in which antibodies are attached to the bottom of test tubes.

First, the same amount of radioactive ^{125}I (γ-emitter)-labeled drug is added to each of a number of assay tubes and binds to the antibodies. Reference solutions, each containing a known concentration of drug, are then added to some of these tubes and unknown samples to the other tubes. A high concentration of drug in a reference solution or sample will displace a large amount of the labeled drug originally bound to antibodies. Samples with lower drug concentration will displace less labeled drug. The supernatant of each tube is decanted and the γ-radiation remaining in each tube (bound fraction) is measured. A calibration plot of radioactivity vs. drug concentration is constructed using data from the known solutions. The concentration of drug for each unknown sample can be determined from the standard plot by correlating its radioactivity measurement on the ordinate of the standard plot with the corresponding concentration on the abscissa.

Mathematical manipulation of the data allows one to produce a linear plot (if this is desired). One common method of converting data to a linear plot is shown in Fig. 13.2 (see the glossary for definitions). For a qualitative screening test, standard plots are not needed. Samples with bound radioactivity equal to or less than that of a selected cutoff calibrator, i.e., equal to or higher in concentration than the cutoff calibrator, would be positive for the drug and sent for confirmation by another analytical technique.

Since the introduction of the original insulin assays, there have been many new developments in immunoassay technology. For example, assays have been developed to test for molecules smaller than peptide hormones that are of more interest to toxicologists, such as drugs, organic poisons, etc. [molecular weight (MW) of many toxicants is 100–600 daltons (Da); MW of insulin is 6000 Da]. Also, methods called homogeneous assays have been developed that do not require physical separation of bound and free antigen and can be used on large-volume automated analyzers.

The RIA described above is called a heterogeneous assay and is more labor intensive. Most of

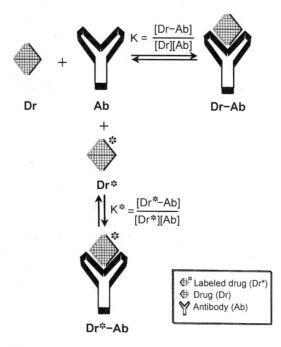

Fig. 13.1 Generalized competitive binding process

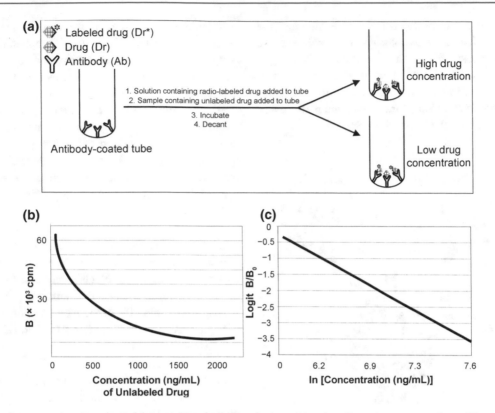

Fig. 13.2 Representation of a coated-tube RIA. (**a**) RIA procedure; (**b**) a plot of bound counts per minute (B) vs. concentration of drug; (**c**) mathematical transformation of data to produce a linear plot

the assays used by toxicologists are commercially available in kit form, have been optimized by manufacturers, and contain simple instructions for using the kit components to screen for analytes in urine, blood, and other biological fluids. Although the kits differ in many respects, the common reagents they contain are an antiserum (antibodies), labeled drug, calibrator solutions, and control solutions. Students must understand the important scientific characteristics of these components to critically evaluate the strengths and limitations of various immunoassays.

Antibodies

Production of Antibodies

Antibodies are immunoglobulins (Ig) produced by mammalian lymphocytes in response to foreign substances introduced into the body.

Scientists have taken advantage of this biological phenomenon by injecting compounds of interest into hypersensitized animals and then collecting blood serum containing antibodies specific for the compound. The antiserum can be used to construct a laboratory test that identifies the compound. The serum proteins from the animal, which specifically bind the antigen, fall into at least five classes: IgG, IgM, IgA, IgE, and IgD. About 90% of Ig in the serum of hypersensitized animals are IgG, so this form will be described and is represented in Fig. 13.3.

IgG is a monomeric form with two light peptide chains and two heavy peptide chains connected by disulfide bonds (IgG $MW = 150,000$ Da). A portion of the molecule called the Fab region contains the peptide sequences that form the antigen recognition (binding) sites. Antibodies specifically bind an antigen based on the antigen's molecular composition and spatial orientation of molecules. This is an important characteristic of antibodies to remember when evaluating the specificity of immunoassays: they will exclude many substances that are dissimilar to the antigen but will also bind others that are structurally related. Binding of structurally related compounds is called cross-reactivity and is discussed below under the subsection "Specificity."

Small molecules, i.e., those with molecular weights less than 2000 Da (e.g., amphetamine $MW = 135$ Da), are not antigenic, and scientists must "trick" an animal's immune system to produce specific antibodies. The trick is to bind the small molecule to a larger, antigenic compound before injecting it into an animal. The animal will then produce some antibodies that are specific for the small molecule. An example synthesis for preparation of such an immunogen is shown in Fig. 13.4. Note two important points in this figure:

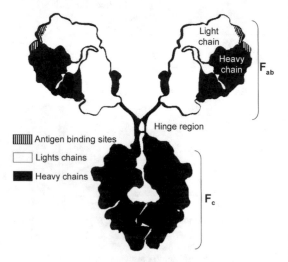

Fig. 13.3 Diagram of antibody (IgG) molecule. F_{ab} and F_c are names used by immunologists for regions of the molecule

1. Textbook diagrams of immunogens do not accurately represent the size difference between the small molecule, called a hapten by immunologists, and the attached protein. In this case, the MW of the methamphetamine hapten is 149 Da and the BGT protein is 150,000 Da.

Scientists designed the immunogen so that several bond lengths separate the hapten from the larger protein. This makes the hapten more spatially unique and causes the host animal's immune system to produce a higher concentration of antibodies that specifically bind its hapten-like struc-

Fig. 13.4 Synthesis of an immunogen

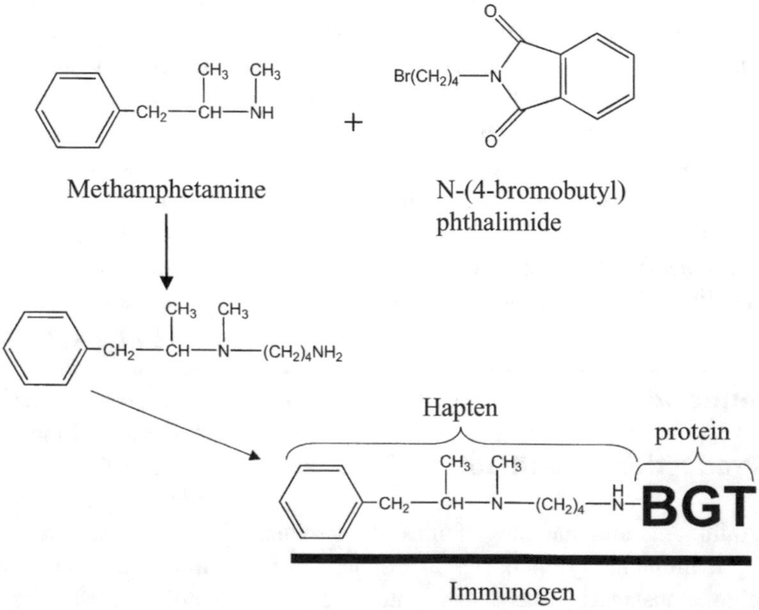

Methamphetamine

N-(4-bromobutyl) phthalimide

Hapten

protein

Immunogen

ture. Antiserum with high concentrations of specific antibodies is said to have a high titer. High titers are desirable and are typically described by the dilution factor needed in a standard binding assay; representative titers are 1:500 for small molecule antisera and 1:100,000 for protein antisera.

Polyclonal and Monoclonal Antiserum

Animals produce polyclonal antiserum in vivo. From the frame of reference of an analyst who uses the final product, this means that there are different types of antibodies in the antiserum, each with a different affinity for the compound of interest. These antibodies may also differ in which part of the compound they recognize. The distribution of antibodies usually differs between animals treated with the same antibody-producing regimen and within the same animal as time progresses after injection. Often a manufacturer will struggle to find an animal that produces the desired titer and specificity of antiserum only to discover with later blood drawings that these critical parameters have changed.

With the development of hybridoma technology, manufacturers began to produce monoclonal antibodies. The pictorial summary of the production of polyclonal and monoclonal antibodies is shown in Fig. 13.5. Production of polyclonal antiserum appears straightforward: inject an immunogen, collect blood, and then separate the serum. Variables in immune response and the time required to find the individual animal that

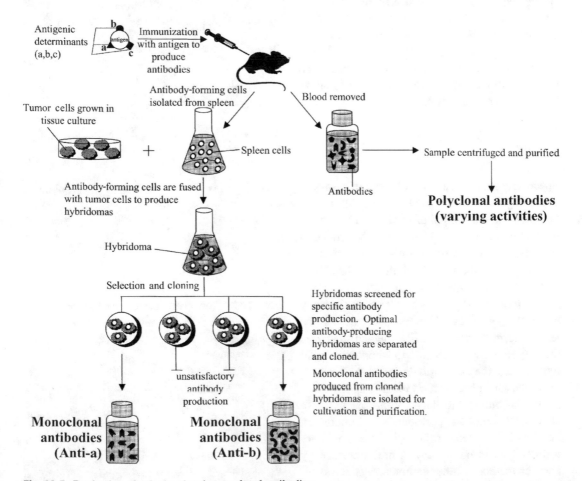

Fig. 13.5 Production of polyclonal and monoclonal antibodies

will produce antiserum with the desired properties make this a more difficult task than it appears. The host animal, usually a rabbit, sheep, or goat (not the mouse shown in the figure), must also be large enough to allow large volumes of blood to be drawn without causing harm.

Figure 13.5 also diagrams the production of monoclonal antiserum. Lymphocytes from an immunized mouse are fused to mouse myeloma cells to produce a hybridoma. The myeloma portion allows the hybridoma to propagate as long as the correct conditions are present in the culture medium. (Cancerous cells like the myeloma cells are required because normal cells die after a certain number of replications.) The lymphocyte portion of the hybridoma produces antibodies. An individual hybridoma that produces the desired type of antibody is selected by cell-sorting techniques and then reproduced in culture. Each antibody in the culture medium (serum) has identical binding properties. The antiserum is very specific for the analyte and, unlike the polyclonal antiserum produced in an animal, will have the same properties as long as the selected cell line is maintained.

Specificity

Specificity is a critical characteristic of assays. It is the degree to which an assay correctly identifies only the compound of interest. (The mathematical definition may be found in the glossary.) It is often used to describe antiserum, because in immunoassays the specific binding of the antiserum is very important, but the term specificity should more appropriately be applied to the assay using the antiserum. This is also true for the related term "cross-reactivity," which describes the degree of assay response to compounds other than the one the assay was designed to detect.

When toxicologists must identify specific toxicants in biological fluids, cross-reactivity to structurally related compounds is important, because it may lead to false-positive laboratory results if an immunoassay is not confirmed by another method. Some immunoassays and common interfering compounds are shown in

Table 13.1. Table 13.2 shows quantitative cross-reactivity figures for common interfering drugs in a representative amphetamine/methamphetamine assay.

Table 13.2 makes several important points:

1. First, samples containing substances with low cross-reactivity, such as *l*-ephedrine (0.55%), may appear to have a low probability of contamination in an amphetamine assay. However,

Table 13.1 Cross-reactants in immunoassays

Immunoassay	Common cross-reacting substances
Amphetamine, methamphetamine	MDA, MDMA, ephedrine, Pseudoephedrine, bupropion, chlorpromazine, dimethylamylamine (DMAA), promethazine, ofloxacin, tyramine, phentermine
Benzodiazepines	Efavirenz 8OH-metabolite, sertraline
Benzoylecgonine, (cocaine)	Ecgonine, ecgonine methyl ester, cocaine
Cannabinoids (THC metabolites)	Ibuprofen, naproxen, niflumic acid
LSD	Ergotamine, tricyclic antidepressants, verapamil
Morphine	Codeine, dihydrocodeine, thebaine, hydrocodone, norcodeine, levofloxacine, ofloxacine
MDMA, MDA	Trazodone metabolite (m-CPP)
PCP	Venlafaxine, diphenhydramine, dextromethorphan
Tricyclic antidepressants	Quetiapine

Table 13.2 Cross-reactivities of common drugs in an amphetamine/methamphetamine immunoassay

Compound	% Reactivity
d-Amphetamine	100
d-Methamphetamine	100
l-Methamphetamine	50
Phentermine	50
l-Amphetamine	16.7
l-Ephedrine	0.55
Tyramine	0.5
Phenylpropanolamine	0.3
Pseudoephedrine (100 mg/L)	0.15
Pseudoephedrine (1000 mg/L)	0.08

one must remember that potential ephedrine concentrations in patient urine samples (10,000–200,000 ng/mL) are typically much higher than expected amphetamine concentrations (usually <5000 ng/mL). A sample containing *l*-ephedrine at the higher end of the concentration range would produce an apparent amphetamine result of 1100 ng/mL and exceed the 500 ng/mL mandated cutoff for federally regulated workplace drug testing programs. Individuals taking ephedrine could be mistakenly identified as positive for amphetamines by this assay. For this reason, the federal program requires that immunoassay positive samples be confirmed using gas chromatography-mass spectrometry (GC/MS) or liquid chromatography-mass spectrometry (LC/MS).

2. Second, there is a lower cross-reactivity for *l*-amphetamine, the stereoisomer of d-amphetamine, than for phentermine, the structural isomer of methamphetamine. This occurs in this assay because of the nature of the antiserum, which was produced using the immunogen in Fig. 13.4. The antibodies recognize the phenyl portion of methamphetamine hapten, and the phenyl portion of phentermine is more similar to d-methamphetamine than is the phenyl portion of the *l*-amphetamine stereoisomer. This also explains why d-amphetamine and d-methamphetamine have identical reactivities. These are theoretical concepts that are primarily the province of manufacturers who design assays but are also important for toxicologists who need to apply them when evaluating immunoassay limitations.

3. Another characteristic of cross-reacting substances is that the response of assay antiserum to them is usually not parallel to the response to analyte as the concentration increases. Note that the cross-reactivity of pseudoephedrine in this amphetamine assay is 0.15% and 0.08% at 100 and 1000 µg/mL of pseudoephedrine, respectively. This indicates that the cross-reactivity of the assay is concentration dependent and quotations of the percent cross-reactivity for an assay should be accompanied by the concentration of the cross-reactant.

4. The last point can be made again using phentermine as an example. Its cross-reactivity is 50%. Expected urine concentrations can be as high as 5000 ng/mL. This means that most individuals taking an anorectic medication containing phentermine, e.g., Adipex or Ionamin, could produce urine that would screen positive in this assay. In workplace drug screening laboratories, this assay would be a nemesis since many false-positive screening results would be produced and have to be confirmed as negative by more expensive techniques. These laboratories may choose to use another immunoassay with less cross-reactivity to common over-the-counter medications such as phentermine. However, a laboratory investigating the cause of aircraft accidents, for example, may find this assay useful for detecting both amphetamines and sympathomimetic amines in the flight crew. Cross-reactivity of structurally related substances can be a boon or a bane; it is most important, in interpreting results and choosing applications, to know that it exists and how it affects immunoassay data.

Specific Immunoassay Techniques

Labeled compounds must have two important characteristics: (1) they must be immunologically similar to the compound being tested so they will successfully compete for the antibody, and (2) the labels must lend themselves to sensitive detection, free from interference by common matrices.

Labeled compounds are usually prepared by attaching a radioactive, fluorescent, enzyme, or microparticle molecule to the compound of interest. The labeled molecule is added to the reaction mixture in an assay, and the assay detects the specific energy changes associated with the label when it is bound in order to measure the amount of bound labeled compound.

Many different immunoassays that test for common toxicological substances are available, and different manufacturers usually have proprietary assays available for the same target compounds. Although the antiserum and other kit components differ between competing company's assays, the primary theoretical difference is the type of labeled compound and method of detection. The most common types of assays used by toxicologists are enzyme-multiplied immunoassay technique (EMIT®; DRI™); fluorescence polarization immunoassay (FPIA); cloned enzyme donor immunoassay (CEDIA™); kinetic interaction of microparticles in solution (KIMS®); and enzyme-linked immunosorbent assay (ELISA).

Radioimmunoassay (RIA)

RIA is rarely used in clinical and forensic laboratories due to its principal weakness, required management of radioactivity during analysis and waste disposal. A short description of this immunoassay is included here since it is a simple example of a heterogeneous assay and for historical reasons. The commonest label is ^{125}I with a 59.5-day half-life. Figure 13.2 displays the commonest method called a coated-tube assay. The supernatant containing free drug is easily

decanted leaving the bound fraction in a tube for placement in a γ-counter. RIA has a low limit of detection as evidenced by assays for LSD in urine, ricin in tissue, and THC in hair.

Enzyme-Multiplied Immunoassay Technique (EMIT)

EMIT assays use an enzyme-linked antigen. EMIT is a homogeneous assay and the basic assay theory and typical standard plot are depicted in Fig. 13.6. The label attached to drug in this assay is the enzyme glucose-6-phosphate dehydrogenase (G6P-DH) that oxidizes the substrate glucose-6-phosphate to gluconolactone-6-phosphate and also reduces the cofactor nicotinamide adenine dinucleotide (NAD) to NADH. Enzyme activity is determined by spectrophotometrically measuring the NADH produced, monitoring absorbance at the λ_{max} of 340 nm. The enzymatic activity of G6P-DH decreases when the attached drug is bound to antibody, so adding drug reduces the antibody available to bind to G6P-DH labeled drug and increases the rate of NADH production. The

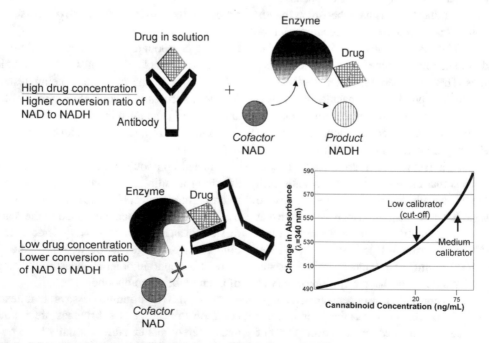

Fig. 13.6 Schematic of enzyme-multiplied immunoassay technique (EMIT®)

change in absorbance at 340 nm is directly related to the concentration of the drug in the biological fluid that is added.

Strengths
- Bound labeled drug can be measured without separation from free drug. These homogeneous assays are easy to automate since the reagents can be mixed, incubated, and have light measurements made in the original reaction container. Once samples are aliquoted and loaded, a typical high-volume analyzer can screen >500 samples/h with one operator monitoring the system. Automation improves throughput, intra-assay variability, and analyst error liability.
- Shelf lives of kits are long (usually >1 year).
- Enzyme-linked assays discriminate between concentrations over a large range.
- Enzyme-related technology is well established, which improves troubleshooting and reduces costs.
- The absorbance change of the solution is measured as a function of time, i.e., as a rate measurement. Absorbances from interfering substances do not usually change with time and their contribution is minimized.
- More specialty assays, such as LSD, are available.

Limitations
- Interference results not only from compounds that cross-react with the antibody but also from substances in the matrix that interrupt the enzyme process.
- Urinary metabolites of tolmetin and aspirin, common analgesics, can cause false-negative assay results. Scientific studies showed that salicyluric acid, the culprit aspirin metabolite, directly interferes with measurement of the NADH product by absorbing light at λ = 340 nm. This type of interference can be detected by incorporating appropriate instrument absorbance flags in the method parameter software. If not, they will go undetected.
- Interfering substances usually cause false-negative results.

- Additional sample preparation steps may be required for some biological specimens.
- The LSD assay cited above has linear characteristics in the low pg/mL range but has a high false-positive rate, probably due to cross-reacting substances.

Fluorescence Polarization Immunoassay (FPIA)

FPIA theory and a representative standard plot are depicted in Fig. 13.7. The most prevalent FPIA methods are marketed by Abbott Laboratories for operation on ADx®, AxSym®, Architect®, or Aeroset® analyzers and use fluorescein-labeled drugs as tracers. Fluorescein can absorb light at λ = 485 nm and emit light in the range of λ = 525−550 nm. If the incoming light is polarized, emitted light will remain polarized if the fluorescein molecule is fixed in space. When the fluorescein-linked drug is bound to antibody, the fluorescein label does not rotate freely and the polarized light absorbed is emitted with little loss of polarization. When the fluorescein label is free, it rotates freely in solution and the amount of polarized light emitted is reduced. Therefore, the addition of drug releases labeled drug molecules from antibody-binding sites and lowers the polarization of the light emitted. The concentration of drug in the biological fluid being measured is inversely related to the intensity of polarized light being emitted at a wavelength selected in the λ = 525−550 nm range.

Strengths
- This immunoassay is homogeneous.
- Fluorescein-labeled drug is more stable than enzyme–drug conjugates.
- Fluorescent probes provide low limits of detection. Measurement of changes in the polarization of fluorescence capitalizes on the sensitivity of fluorescence and avoids stray light interference common to measurement of direct fluorescence. Also, matrices have less effect on changes in fluorescence polarization than on changes in direct light intensity, mak-

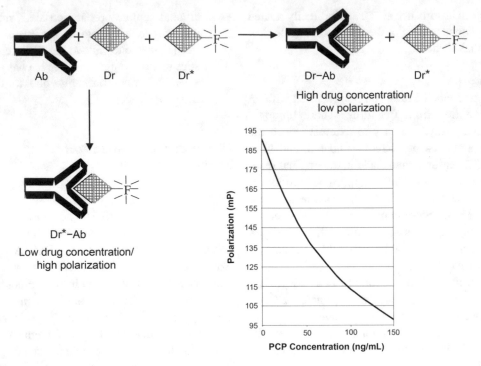

Fig. 13.7 Schematic of fluorescence polarization immunoassay (FPIA)

ing FPIA measurements in blood and older urine samples generally more accurate than those from an EMIT.

- Shelf lives of reagents are long (usually >1 year).

Limitations

- The assays are generally more expensive than comparable enzyme-linked assays.
- Fluorescent salts in bile occasionally give false-positive results.
- Currently, not many FPIAs are adaptable to common high-speed analyzers. Abbott methods must be performed on the company's own analyzers.
- Additional sample preparation steps may be required for some biological specimens.

Cloned Enzyme Donor Immunoassay (CEDIA)

The theory and a standard plot for the CEDIA are depicted in Fig. 13.8. CEDIA is a trademark method marketed by Thermo Fisher Scientific with genetically engineered fragments of *E. coli* β-galactosidase as an enzyme label. The activity of the enzyme requires assembling two fragments, termed enzyme acceptor (EA) and enzyme donor (ED) fragments. The reassociated enzyme hydrolyzes chlorophenolred-β-galactoside (CPRG) to chlorophenolred (CPR) and galactose.

CPRG does not absorb significant energy at $\lambda = 570$ nm, whereas the λ_{max} for CPR is 570 nm. Production of CPR is easily measured. A secondary wavelength (660 nm) for CPR can also be used to correct for minor changes in sample absorbance. ED is linked to the drug and will not reassociate if bound to antibody. Added drug displaces the ED-labeled drug from antibodies, reassociation occurs, and absorbance increases. The concentration of drug in biological fluid is directly proportional to the change in absorbance.

Strengths

- This immunoassay is homogeneous.
- Shelf lives of reagents are long (usually >1 year).

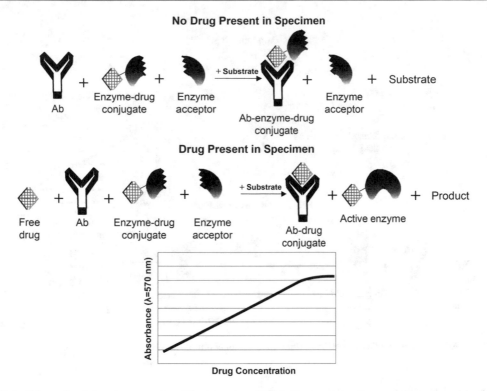

Fig. 13.8 Schematic of cloned enzyme donor immunoassay (CEDIA®)

- Enzyme activity is almost completely stopped when antibody binding blocks reassociation of the enzyme. This phenomenon makes release of labeled drug, subsequent enzyme reassociation, and production of colored product directly proportional to the concentration of the drug of interest, and the resulting standard plot is linear over a wide range of concentration values.
- Monitoring a second wavelength, 660 nm, provides some measure of security against interference from substances that may absorb light at the primary wavelength, 570 nm.
- The absorbance change of the solution is measured as a function of time, i.e., as a rate measurement. Absorbances from interfering substances do not usually change with time and their contribution is minimized.
- Additional sample preparation steps may be required for some biological specimens.
- CEDIA® has a three-component assay kit that can be used to measure LSD. The method has a large linear range and is subject to less drift than comparable immunoassays.

Limitations

Despite resistance to interference, CEDIA™ methods can be affected by urine adulterants and usually yield false-negative results.

Kinetic Interaction of Microparticles in Solution (KIMS)

KIMS theory and a typical standard plot are shown in Fig. 13.9. The method was patented by Roche Diagnostic Systems. The labeled compound is a microparticle with several drug molecules linked to it. In the absence of the drug of interest, the conjugate of microparticle and drug molecules binds several antibody molecules and forms large aggregates that scatter transmitted light. As the aggregation reaction proceeds, the change in absorbance increases. The added drug substitutes for the conjugate attached to antibodies and prevents the formation of aggregates, which diminishes the rate of absorbance increase in proportion to the drug concentration. Plotting

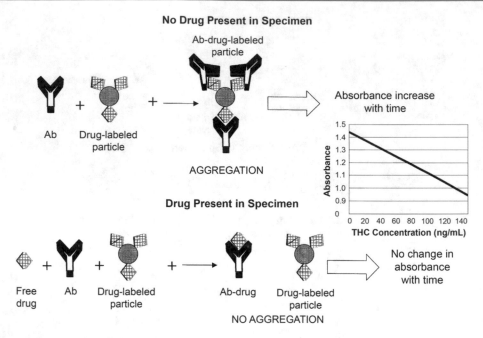

Fig. 13.9 Schematic of kinetic interaction of microparticles in solution (KIMS®)

change in absorbance vs. concentration of drug yields a negative slope. Change in transmission can also be plotted, yielding a parabolic plot with positive slopes.

Strengths

- It is an inexpensive homogeneous assay.
- Shelf lives of kits are long (usually >1 year).
- Microparticle drug conjugates are more stable than enzyme drug conjugates.
- Substances that interfere with the agglutination process in KIMS usually cause false-positive results. This is an advantage because immunoassays are screening tests for identifying samples that may contain a drug. Samples containing both a drug and an interfering substance will be identified as positive by KIMS and forwarded for confirmation testing, while other techniques, such as EMIT, will produce a false-negative result and the sample will not be identified for confirmation testing. The absorbance change of the solution is measured as a function of time, i.e., as a rate measurement. Absorbances from interfering substances do not usually change with time and their contribution is minimized.

Limitations

- The microparticle solution used in KIMS assays coats the analyzer tubing and requires special system maintenance.
- The linear range for KIMS assays is generally smaller than for EMIT and CEDIA. The microparticle technology allows a steep response plot but for a narrower range than enzyme-based assays.
- Additional sample preparation steps may be required for some biological specimens.

Enzyme-Linked Immunosorbent Assay (ELISA)

ELISA has been in use in specialty laboratories for many years, e.g., in HIV testing. Its application in drug testing is more recent; many procedures for testing oral fluid, blood, and urine have developed only within the past decade. Several companies market drug-testing methods, e.g., OraSure Technologies, Immunalysis, and others.

The theory and a representative standard plot for an OraSure method are shown in Fig. 13.10. When free in solution, the enzyme label (horse-

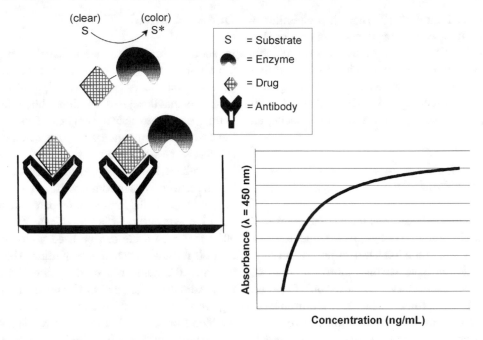

Fig. 13.10   Schematic of enzyme-linked immunosorbent assay (ELISA)

radish peroxidase) converts the substrate tetramethylbenzidine (TMB) to a colored product ($\lambda_{max} = 450$ nm). Enzyme activity is restricted when the drug portion of the enzyme–drug complex is bound to antibodies attached to the bottom of the well in a microtiter plate. Labeled drug is released from antibody-binding sites, and enzyme activity is restored in proportion to the concentration of the drug in the sample that is added.

Strengths

- ELISA has very good sensitivity.
- Being a heterogeneous assay, it is less subject to matrix effects, especially if the double-wash technique is used. Some laboratories have implemented this technique to analyze postmortem blood samples.
- Compared to RIA, ELISA is much easier to automate. Both current and traditional methods typically used 96 well microtiter plates with automated pipetting, washing, and spectrophotometric reading.
- Because the label is an enzyme, shelf lives are longer than for RIA (usually >1 year).
- Limited sample preparation due to the heterogeneous nature of the assay.

Limitations

- Being a specialized heterogeneous assay, it cannot be easily adapted to common high-speed analyzers. Analyzers currently being used are specific for this technology.
- Cost per sample is generally higher than for some of the homogeneous assays, primarily because of the special analyzer needed.
- Sodium azide, a common antimicrobial agent added to preserve urine, will block the activity of horseradish peroxidase, and the method cannot be used to test these samples.

Biochip Array Technology (BAT)

BAT is a specialized ELISA that allows a multi-analyte testing platform. A proprietary method (Randox) bonds antibodies or antigens to a 9×9 mm square on a solid chip. With this ability manufacturers can create a chip with discrete testing regions that allow a laboratory to identify a different analyte in each region. As a result, multi-analyte testing can be achieved simultaneously, and custom panels are available. The detection system is similar to that shown for the

ELISA in Figure 13.10 except that chemiluminescent light is produced and a charge-coupled device (CCD) camera simultaneously records the light intensity for each discrete testing region. The analyzer can be large enough for laboratory screening or small enough for special applications, such as screening blood during an autopsy.

Method Validation

High-quality laboratories have always ensured that their immunoassays met standards for accuracy and precision but over the past decade the standards have become more formal. The National Laboratory Certification Program (NLCP) describes specific requirements. Laboratories in this program must have documentation of an immunoassay's linearity, precision around any decision concentrations (called cutoffs), false-positive and false-negative rates, carryover detection, and interference studies. When the method is first established laboratories must also conduct a parallel study, usually on authentic specimens, showing that it is comparable to the previous screening technique. These standards apply to urine immunoassays for drugs of abuse that are under the auspices of NLCP, but are also important for tests in other biological matrices. For blood, hair, tissue, etc., it is also important to identify matrix effects on the immunoassay. This is particularly important if the immunoassay kit was initially developed for use with a different biological sample (e.g., plasma, rather than whole blood). Heterogeneous immunoassays such as ELISA can be readily adapted for use with a variety of biological samples with relatively minimal sample preparation. Due to the sensitivity of immunoassay, predilution of the specimen is often sufficient to mitigate matrix effects. Protein precipitation, filtration, centrifugation, and other techniques may be used, and these are discussed in more detail in Chap. 9. Additionally, method validation for immunoassay and other screening techniques is outlined in Chap. 16.

Quality Control

In addition to antiserum and labeled antigen, most immunoassay kits contain calibrators and control solutions. A general principle of quality control is that these two solutions should be in a matrix similar to actual samples. This is very important in immunoassays because matrix effects can be significant.

In practice, limited supplies of human urine and serum force analysts to compromise. As a compromise rule, urine that is used to prepare calibrators for urine assays should not be diluted more than 50%; synthetic urine can be used with caution; controls must be in actual human urine. These are basically the guidelines used by the Food and Drug Administration to clear kits for medical testing. Very few drug-of-abuse assays are available for blood or serum that require toxicologists to compromise further when applying urine-based kits to analysis for these fluids. Calibrators from the kits may be used if quantitative values are not important. Controls must be prepared in drug-free blood or serum, respectively. More detailed discussions of quality control requirements can be found elsewhere, but a few basic principles need to be discussed here. Calibrators should be used in consonance with analytical requirements. If the immunoassay is a screening test, then a single calibrator is sufficient. For quantitative tests, multiple calibrators with concentrations that bracket those of the samples should be included in each assay. There should be sufficient control solutions, run with the samples in each assay, to demonstrate discrimination above and below the cutoff for screening tests. For quantitative tests, these controls should demonstrate good assay performance in the low- and high-concentration region of the linear range. Prior to placing an immunoassay in service, the laboratory should establish and verify a limit of detection and linear range for the method. Cross-reactivities to common interfering substances must also be verified. Performance parameters must be reverified periodically or when reagent lots change because assay response varies greatly with changes in antiserum or components that interact with it in the assay.

Cutoffs

"Cutoff" is a term used in screening assays because these methods identify samples as either positive or negative with no quantitative results reported. A cutoff is the concentration of drug below which all specimens are considered to be negative. This can be the limit of detection of the assay or a higher concentration. For most programs using immunoassays, oversight agencies mandate administrative cutoffs well above the limit of detection of the method.

Table 13.3 lists the cutoffs for two workplace drug testing programs. A cutoff above the limit of detection is usually established to ensure that most laboratories can achieve accurate results at this concentration and to meet other special program requirements. For example, the administrative immunoassay cutoff for cannabinoids was originally set at 100 ng/mL to identify active marijuana smokers but reduce the risk of identifying as positive urine samples from individuals passively exposed to marijuana smoke.

Applications

Immunoassays have applications in postmortem investigations, workplace drug testing, and human performance investigations. In a postmortem examination, the forensic pathologist collects blood, urine, tissues, and other body fluids from the deceased for toxicological analyses. If there is no apparent anatomic cause of death, toxicology results are critical to the investigation. Analytically, urine is the specimen of choice for immunoassay screening because it usually has fewer interfering proteins and decomposition products, but other fluids or tissues may be the specimens of choice for interpretation. For example, some victims who die of acute heroin overdose have high concentrations of morphine in their blood but not in urine. An immunoassay screen of urine for opiates would give a negative result and the cause of death could be missed. This example supports screening blood but presents challenges for the toxicologist since blood assays have many more interfering substances. Proteins are usually precipitated before analysis using acetonitrile or a similar solvent to eliminate some of the interfering substances, and then the supernatant is pipetted for immunoassay. Historically, RIA was used to screen postmortem blood. With the decreased availability of RIA methods, other techniques are being implemented.

The following assorted facts about application of different immunoassay techniques to postmortem analysis illustrate some of the assay characteristics discussed above:

- Postmortem blood decomposes with time, producing biogenic amines. These amines often cross-react with the antibody in amphetamine immunoassays (regardless of the type) and produce false-positive results. For example,

Table 13.3 Immunoassay cutoffs for urine

	Drug testing programs	
	DoD (ng/mL)	HHS (ng/mL)
Amphetamines	500	500
Benzodiazepines	200	*
Cannabinoids	50	50
Cocaine metabolites	150	150
Designer amphetamines	500	500
Opiates (codeine/morphine)	2000	2000
Opioids (hydrocodone/hydromorphone)	300	300
Opioid (6-acetylmorphine)	10	10
Opioids (oxycodone/oxymorphone)	100	100
Phencyclidine	a	25
Synthetic cannabinoids	10	*
Opioid (Fentanyl/Norfentanyl)	1.0	*

*Drug class not included in program

due to decomposition, tyramine can accumulate in biological fluids and cross-react in the immunoassay (see monoclonal assay in Table 13.2).

- Salts in bile, some of which are fluorescent, can cause false-positive FPIA results.
- Some RIA and ELISA assays will give false-positive cannabinoid results in old blood. The mechanism is not well understood.
- High concentrations of diphenhydramine cause false-positive results in some urine PCP immunoassays.
- Dihydrocodeine and codeine give false-positive results in most morphine assays.
- As mentioned above, enzyme-based assays may yield false-negative results if sodium azide is present in the sample.

Most urine drug-testing programs use immunoassays. The federally regulated workplace program, for example, mandates an immunoassay screen for cannabinoids, benzoylecgonine (cocaine metabolite), PCP, opiates, opioids, and amphetamines, and establishes screening cutoffs for each class of drugs. Table 13.3 shows cutoffs for the Department of Health and Human Services and Department of Defense programs. Samples that screen positive must be confirmed by GC/MS, LC/MS, or LC/MS/MS for both programs. Some common interfering substances in urine assays for these drugs are listed in Table 13.1.

Drug testing in accident, probable cause, and similar human performance investigations use immunoassays as screening tests. Immunoassay quantifications are often used in medical testing where other clinical information about the patient is available, but forensic analysis usually requires quantification and confirmation by a technique based on a different scientific principle than the immunoassay. In a 2008 policy statement, the National Safety Council recommended that the practice of reporting only presumptive drug screen results in transportation safety cases be abolished. If both blood (or serum) and urine are collected from the subject, the urine may be screened for evidence of drug use and then the blood analyzed (usually by chromatography) for evidence of the drugs found in the urine screen. It is easier to relate impaired performance to drug concentrations in blood, serum, or plasma than in urine. Elevated blood concentration of drug also indicates more recent use of the drug, which may be important in the investigation. The relationship of blood alcohol, which is not typically measured with an immunoassay, to impairment has been investigated for many years and is well documented, but correlation of blood drug concentration to impaired performance is in its infancy. It is an active field of research.

Special Problems

Manufacturers of immunoassay kits are challenged by customers to produce a product that will test certain analytes in a class of drugs but exclude others. An excellent example is the development of a method for screening the urine of employees for amphetamines. Program directors want to identify amphetamine and methamphetamine in a donor's urine with a single immunoassay and exclude other amines such as the over-the-counter cold medication pseudoephedrine. In addition, they want to identify only the d-isomers since these are the usual illicit forms of the drugs. A first approach to assay development might be to construct an immunogen with the amino function of the hapten, either amphetamine or methamphetamine, exposed. However, antibodies produced with increased specificity for d-amphetamine will have a reduced ability to detect d-methamphetamine because the amino portions of these two molecules differ. Attempts to reduce the specificity of amphetamine antiserum by hiding the amino group to achieve increased cross-reactivity to methamphetamine usually result in the capture of other unwanted amines.

One solution offered by some manufacturers is to use a mixture of two specific antibodies, one for amphetamine and one for methamphetamine. The Roche Online Amphetamines method combined antibodies and used microparticle–amphetamine as a labeled drug. In this method, the methamphetamine antibody must have some cross-reactivity to amphetamine for the method to be effective. The ADx, EMIT, and CEDIA methods use both an amphetamine and methamphetamine labeled compound in the reaction mixture with the combined antibodies. The combined antibody approach increases specificity for just these two analytes but often introduces an analytical problem. The methamphetamine antibody binds methamphetamine in a sample more strongly than the labeled amphetamine and this binding difference may increase cooperative binding. This phenomenon occurred for the Online and ADx methods. A typical cooperative binding curve is shown in Fig. 13.11.

These assays are good screening methods, but the characteristics of their plots complicate interpretation of assay results. For example, let us consider a urine sample from a methamphetamine user that has 500 ng/mL of methamphetamine and 500 ng/mL of its principal metabolite, amphetamine. One would expect an immunoassay with reactivity to each drug of 100% to yield a response equivalent to 1000 ng/mL of amphetamines but might observe an assay result of 1500 ng/mL as a result of the cooperative binding phenomenon.

Another special problem of immunoassays involves cross-reactivity studies. Most manufacturers examine potential interfering substances and list these in package inserts before assays are approved for marketing. Independent research scientists expand these studies and publish a larger list of cross-reacting compounds. However, the human metabolites of these compounds are usually not readily available for study, are often elevated in urine, and can significantly influence urine immunoassay results. For example, fenfluramine and phentermine, two drugs used to treat obesity, each had low cross-reactivities in studies using the ADx (FPIA) amphetamine/methamphetamine assay. Norfenfluramine, a metabolite of fenfluramine in urine, was initially unavailable and not examined in studies of cross-reactivity. Laboratories were puzzled when they observed many false-positive results from testing the urine of patients who were taking diet medications containing fenfluramine since previous studies showed little cross-reactivity to this drug. However, they later discovered that norfenfluramine with high cross-reactivity in the assay had caused the false-positive results. Note in Table 13.1 that some cross-reactants are drug metabolites. It should be noted that although cross-reactivity can result in unconfirmed positive results, the general lack of specificity can also be exploited when a large number of structurally similar compounds (e.g., benzodiazepines, barbiturates) are of interest.

The concept of administrative cutoffs for assays presents a special problem. In workplace drug testing programs, specific cutoffs are mandated so that each person, regardless of which laboratory tests the sample, will be treated equally. That is, the cutoff must be easily achieved by most laboratories and must be the same

Fig. 13.11 Assay response for a solution containing 1000 ng/mL of total amphetamines in an amphetamine/methamphetamine immunoassay that exhibits cooperative binding

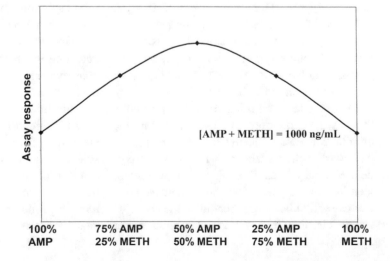

whether the employee works in California or Maryland and regardless of the immunoassay used by the laboratory. However, as we have learned, different immunoassays have different cross-reactivities to common metabolites of the target drug. For some urine samples, one manufacturer's assay may be negative and another positive even if both have the same cutoff for the target drug. The special problem is that the very nature of immunoassays defies the legal objectives of equal treatment. One solution is to make each immunoassay for these programs more specific for the drug of interest. Unlike workplace drug testing, uniform administrative cutoffs are not employed in human performance or postmortem forensic toxicology laboratories. In these settings, each jurisdiction or agency establishes its own cutoffs. Minimum cutoffs for toxicological testing in impaired driving investigations were first proposed in 2007 and were updated in 2013 and 2017. In 2019, minimum standards for the scope and sensitivity of toxicological testing (including immunoassay screening) were proposed for impaired driving investigations (ANSI/ASB 120), medicolegal death investigations (ANSI/ASB 119), and drug-facilitated crimes (ANSI/ASB 121).

Over the years, immunoassays have in general been manufactured to be more specific to address this problem. Good examples include the immunoassays for amphetamines, benzoylecgonine, cannabinoids, morphine/codeine, and PCP that are required in the large federal workplace drug testing program. This program emphasizes the reduction of false-positive screening results and equal treatment of urine donors. To satisfy customers who are responsible for drug testing programs, manufacturers have refined immunoassays to be more specific for the drug of interest.

One adverse result is that in other applications these assays miss more drug users. For example, original cannabinoid assays targeting the principal marijuana metabolite, 11-nor-9-carboxy-delta-9-tetrahydrocannabinol glucuronide, identified more users than the current methods that use antibodies more specific for the unconjugated acid that is lower in concentration. As another example, European toxicologists in the 1990s complained that available amphetamines assays no longer detected MDMA, one of their most problematic drugs of abuse, as manufactures made their immunoassays more specific for d-amphetamine and d-methamphetamine to satisfy the larger workplace drug testing market in the United States. New immunoassays that detected MDMA were not developed until the use of this drug began to increase in the United States. This problem related to specificity may be more of a lesson in marketing than science, but users must know the scientific characteristics of immunoassays to understand it.

Conclusions

Immunoassays in forensic toxicology are primarily used to screen biological samples for the presence of drugs and similar toxicants. Many commercial kit methods are available, and each kit contains an antibody reagent, labeled drug, calibrators, and controls. The assays are very sensitive, usually detecting analytes in the low ng/mL range, and many of the methods can be easily adapted to automated analyzers that test hundreds of samples per hour for several drugs. Yet cross-reactivity of structurally similar substances is a major problem with immunoassays, resulting in false-positive results. In forensic toxicology applications immunoassay results should be confirmed by a method based on a different scientific principle. The primary theoretical difference between various immunoassays is the labeled antigen used and the method of detecting it. The most common types of immunoassays are listed above as subheadings with a description beneath each. The general strengths and limitations of each method are listed and may be categorized under the following headings: specificity (cross-reactivity to unwanted substances), sensitivity, matrix interferences, stability of reagents, stability of assay components, cost and labor requirements, and problems reproducing antibodies with the same characteristics as original lots.

Glossary

Affinity (In immunology) The strength of binding between an antibody and its antigenic determinant.

Analyte A substance of interest that is being identified and measured in an assay.

Antibody A protein synthesized by animal lymphocytes in response to a foreign substance that specifically binds the foreign substance. The molecular weight of the monomeric form of an antibody is about 150,000 Da.

Antigen Any substance that stimulates an animal lymphocyte to produce an antibody that specifically binds it. Small molecules that were part of a larger immunogen when the antibodies were produced may later be referred to as antigens when they are being measured in an immunoassay but are technically called antigenic determinants by immunologists.

Antigenic determinant The portion of an immunogenic molecule that binds to an antibody-binding site.

Avidity (In immunology) The strength of binding between antiserum, or an antibody mixture, and an antigen.

Calibrator A solution containing an analyte at a known concentration that is used to establish a measured reference concentration in an assay.

CEDIA® A type of immunoassay: Cloned Enzyme Donor Immunoassay.

Competitive binding process The process of two different substances competing for the same antibody-binding sites. In immunoassays, the competing substances are an antigen and a labeled antigen.

Cross-reactivity Qualitative definition: The degree of response in an immunoassay to a substance other than the analyte of interest. Quantitative definition:

$$\%\text{cross} - \text{reactivity} = \frac{\text{Concentration reading of assay} \left(w\,/\,v\,\text{units of assay analyte} \right)}{\text{Concentration of cross reactivity analyte} \left(w\,/\,v\,\text{units} \right)} \times 100$$

Cutoff A concentration of an analyte established for a screening assay below which all measured values are identified as negative for the analyte.

Efficiency Qualitative definition: A characteristic of an assay that denotes the assay's ability to detect and correctly identify an analyte in samples. Also called accuracy of an assay in older literature. Quantitative definition:

$$\text{Efficiency} \left(\% \right) = \frac{\left[\text{True positive test results} + \text{True negative test results} \right]}{\left[\text{All test results} \right]} \times 100$$

ELISA A type of immunoassay: Enzyme-Linked Immunosorbent Assay.

EMIT® A type of immunoassay: Enzyme-Multiplied Immunoassay Technique.

FPIA A type of immunoassay: fluorescence polarization immunoassay.

Hapten A small, nonimmunogenic molecule that is attached to a larger immunogenic substance, forming a new antigen that stimulates production of antibodies specific for the small molecule.

Heterogeneous immunoassay An immunoassay that requires bound and free antigen to be separated before labeled antigen is measured.

Homogeneous immunoassay An immunoassay that allows measurement of labeled antigen without separating bound and free antigen.

Immunoassay Any assay using antibodies that specifically bind an analyte to identify and measure the amount of the analyte.

Immunogen A substance injected into an animal causing production of antibodies to the injected substance.

KIMS® A type of immunoassay: Kinetic Interaction of Microparticles in Solution.

Limit of detection (LOD) Qualitative definition: The smallest amount of analyte that can be distinguished from random assay noise.

Quantitative definition: The smallest concentration of analyte that can be distinguished from analyte-free samples in 95% of repeated measurements.

Logit B/B₀ A mathematical function used to linearize standard plots where B = bound counts per minute (cpm) of sample, B_0 = bound cpm of drug-free sample.

Monoclonal antiserum Antiserum containing antibodies that each have identical binding properties. This antiserum is produced in tissue culture by a set of selected lymphocytes (clones) that produce a single type of antibody.

Polyclonal antiserum Antiserum containing antibodies with a spectrum of affinities/specificities toward an antigen. Animals produce polyclonal antiserum.

Sensitivity Qualitative definition: An assay characteristic that denotes the assay's ability to detect an analyte in samples. Quantitative definition:

$$\text{Sensitivity}\,(\%) = \frac{\left[\text{True positive test results}\right]}{\left[\text{True positive test results} + \text{False negative test results}\right]} \times 100$$

Specificity Qualitative definition: An assay characteristic that denotes the assay's ability to correctly identify an analyte in a sample. Quantitative definition:

$$\text{Specificity}\,(\%) = \frac{\left[\text{True negative test results}\right]}{\left[\text{False positive test results} + \text{True negative test results}\right]} \times 100$$

Titer A measure of an antiserum's antibody concentration, usually expressed as the antiserum dilution that gives 50% binding of labeled antigen.

Further Reading

Collins JA (2009) Screening: Immunoassays. In: Ropero-Miller J, Goldberger BA (eds) Handbook of workplace drug testing, 2nd edn. AACC Press, Washington, DC

Hand C, Baldwin D (2004) Immunoassays. In: Moffat AC, Osselton MD, Widdop B (eds) Clark's analysis of drugs and poisons in pharmaceuticals, body fluids and postmortem material, vol 1, 3rd edn. The Pharmaceutical Press, London, UK, pp 301–312

Logan BK et al (2018) Recommendations for toxicological investigation of drug-impaired driving and motor vehicle fatalities-2017 update. *J Anal Toxicol* 42:63–68

Miller JJ, Valdes R (1991) Approaches to minimizing interferences by cross-reacting molecules in immunoassays. *Clin Chem* 37:144–153

Saitman A, Park H-D, Fitzgerald RL (2014) False-positive interferences of common urine drug screen immunoassays: A Review. *J Anal Toxicol* 38: 387–396

Mass Spectrometry

14

Shawn P. Vorce

Abstract

Mass spectrometry (MS) is the most widely used identification technique in forensic toxicology. In a mass spectrometry, the sample, usually following chromatographic separation, enters the mass spectrometer through an inlet device. Once inside the ion source, the sample components are ionized and selectively monitored by the mass analyzer. The ions that exit the mass analyzer enter the instrument's detector. Common ionization techniques for gas chromatography-MS are the electron ionization, where significant fragmentation can occur, and the softer chemical ionization. Common liquid chromatography-MS ionization techniques are electrospray ionization, atmospheric pressure chemical ionization, and collision-induced dissociation. The quadrupole, ion trap, and time of flight are common mass analyzers. Currently, multistage mass spectrometers have gained widespread use. Although an identification technique, MS coupled with its hyphenated chromatographic techniques is widely used in quantitative analysis as well.

Mass spectrometry (MS) was developed about 80 years ago and has since been applied in a wide variety of scientific disciplines. The applications of MS run the gamut from the elucidation of fundamental physical and chemical properties of substances to the study of large biological molecules. The technique has come into widespread use in the last several decades, largely because of the development of small, relatively inexpensive instruments that are easy to operate. Advances in computers and sophisticated software have reduced the need for training, because instruments can be controlled and data acquired with little analyst intervention. Moreover, various advances have made MS technology more usable for a wider variety of compounds in a diverse array of scientific endeavors, most recently in elucidating the nature of the genome and its encoded protein products. Since the previous edition of this book, the use of MS in forensic toxicology has begun to transition toward more applications that use liquid chromatography (LC), tandem MS (MS/MS), and time-of-flight (TOF) MS. The introduction of these techniques into forensic analysis promises to be an exciting area of advancement in the coming years.

Keywords

Mass spectrometry · Forensic toxicology · Ionization · Mass analyzer · Detector · MS/MS · TOF · QTOF

S. P. Vorce (✉)
Chesapeake Toxicology Resources,
Frederick, MD, USA
e-mail: svorce@ctrlabs.com

© Springer Nature Switzerland AG 2020
B. S. Levine, S. Kerrigan (eds.), *Principles of Forensic Toxicology*,
https://doi.org/10.1007/978-3-030-42917-1_14

General Theory

Mass spectral analysis is accomplished by measuring an analyte that has been converted into an ion in the gas phase. Compared with neutral molecules, ionic species are relatively easy to manipulate because they can be affected by magnetic and electrostatic fields that allow the ions to be isolated with remarkable specificity. The fundamental physical chemistry properties of a compound's mass (m) and charge (z) make its ions unique and permit separation with resolutions of <1 Dalton (a Dalton, abbreviated Da, is equal to 1 atomic mass unit, i.e., one twelfth of the mass of a carbon atom). A molecule is introduced via one of a variety of inlet devices into an "ion source," where the molecule is ionized by one of a variety of techniques. The ions of the various molecules constituting the sample are then directed through a mass analyzer to a detector system, where a signal is generated to represent the ions that have impinged on the detector. The system requires a vacuum to allow the transfer of ions from one place to another, virtually eliminating the chance for the ions to collide with other ions or molecules. Manipulation of the electrical and magnetic fields allows the isolation of ions of a single mass-to-charge ratio (m/z). The mass resolutions available range from unit mass resolution (the ability to separate ions differing by 1 Da) to the ability to differentiate ions with the same nominal mass but different exact masses.

Schematic

Figure 14.1 illustrates the basic components of the MS system. The sample enters the mass spectrometer through an inlet device. Once inside the ion source, the sample components are ionized and selectively monitored by the mass analyzer. The ions that exit the mass analyzer enter the instrument's detector. Traditionally, these three critical components of the system were under vacuum. Recent advances that permit ionization at atmospheric pressure have led to the development of a number of ion sources that operate at atmospheric pressure. The process of ion selec-

tion and detection remains under vacuum in all systems. Data are captured by the data system (computer) and manipulated to describe the analyzed sample in a meaningful way.

Sample Inlet

For mass analysis, the sample must first be introduced into the mass spectrometer. Of the several different methods that have been used for this task, the most commonly used technique in forensic toxicology remains gas chromatography (GC). In recent years, however, LC and capillary electrophoresis have become more widely used. Sample introduction by direct insertion is still an option, but this method has not gained wide use, most probably because the lack of automation for the process limits its efficiency. Each method has distinct advantages and disadvantages that influence the selection of inlet type for sample analysis. Because the molecules must be in the gas phase and the mass spectrometer must be under vacuum, introducing molecules into the system poses a significant problem. Each of the sample introduction techniques overcomes this problem differently. Likewise, each technique addresses vacuum integrity in different ways. Several of these techniques are discussed in more detail later in this chapter.

Direct Insertion Probe

Directly inserting a sample into the mass spectrometer is the simplest form of introduction. The simplicity of this approach is its appeal, because no material is lost in the process and the amount placed into the analyzer can be easily controlled. The direct insertion probe is also often referred to as a *solid probe* because it can be used to introduce solid material into the mass spectrometer. Materials that otherwise could not readily be introduced can be placed on the probe and then inserted directly into the source. Compounds that do not lend themselves to introduction through a chromatographic system can often be analyzed via direct insertion. The disadvantage of direct

Fig. 14.1 Schematic representation of the basic components of a mass spectrometer

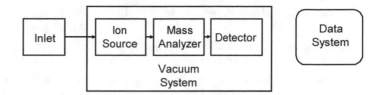

insertion is a lack of separation. A sample is typically placed into the probe, which is then inserted directly into the ion source through a vacuum interlock. The probe can then be heated to volatilize the compound(s) on the probe. If a mixture of compounds is on the probe, the only separation that can be effected is by heating the probe in such a manner that compounds with lower boiling points are volatilized, ionized, detected, and pumped out of the mass spectrometer before other compounds with higher boiling points are volatilized. Depending on the manufacturer, the probe may also be fitted with a cooling capability that allows for rapid temperature cycling of the probe from low to high and back to low again. This feature makes it possible to process samples in rapid succession.

A related technique uses a direct exposure probe. Using the same principle as the direct insertion probe, the direct exposure probe has a small filament on which a sample is placed and then inserted into the source. A liquid sample, usually 1–2 μL, is placed directly on the wire. The solvent is evaporated, thereby depositing the residue on the wire. Solid samples can be applied directly, or they can first be dissolved in a solvent and then applied to the wire. Once inside the source, the sample wire can be heated to volatilize the sample. Both electron ionization (EI) and chemical ionization (CI) can be used to ionize samples that have been introduced by either of these probes.

Gas Chromatography

The most common method of sample introduction for MS is to pass the sample through a GC instrument. GC has been used to analyze compounds for many years, and several different detector methods besides MS have been used, with flame ionization, nitrogen-phosphorus detection, and electron capture being three of the most common. Although each of these GC detector methods has its advantages, MS offers a significant advantage over other detectors. The ability of GC to separate compounds chromatographically is a tremendous advantage. Ideally, the GC instrument provides a pure compound to the mass spectrometer, facilitating spectral analysis. Because the mass spectrometer operates at low pressure, the amount of carrier gas introduced into the mass spectrometer must be limited so that the pumping system can keep up with the volume of incoming gas. Various types of GC interfaces can be used, depending to some extent on the pumping capacity of the system. Large-diameter packed columns have far too large a gas volume to allow all of the effluent to enter the source of most MS systems. Therefore, a number of devices have been designed to divert the bulk of the carrier gas away from the MS instrument, allowing only a small portion of the gas—along with the analyte(s)—to enter the mass spectrometer. Some large-bore capillary columns also carry too large a gas volume for some of the benchtop MS systems to handle, because of their relatively low pumping capacities. For such MS systems, "macro-bore" columns require some means of separating the carrier gas from the analyte. Capillary columns that have flow rates consistent with the pumping capacity of the mass spectrometer (usually 1–2 mL/min) can be inserted directly into the source. This method, commonly called *capillary direct*, provides the most efficient delivery of analyte to the mass spectrometer while still not overwhelming the pumping system. Chromatographic separations are discussed in more detail in Chap. 11.

Liquid Chromatography

Interfacing an LC instrument with a mass spectrometer is not a new technique, but recent advances in technology have made this approach a much more common method of analysis. Many different LC procedures are available, and all allow the separation of analytes, even in very complex matrices. In many ways, LC offers advantages over GC. Typically, extraction procedures can be less extensive than for GC, derivatization is not required (thus saving time and expense), and many compounds that are not stable at high temperature fare much better with LC. The main hurdle that had been associated with coupling LC with MS was the removal of the large volumes of solvent used in LC.

Recent developments in LC interfaces have made LC a very viable technique for introducing samples for MS analysis. Several different techniques [e.g., atmospheric pressure CI (APCI), atmospheric pressure photoionization (APPI), and electrospray ionization (ESI)] are available for getting the LC effluent into the mass spectrometer. These methods, along with the ability to ionize samples at atmospheric pressure, have made LC available for use with many different analytes and with far fewer difficulties than were seen with previous methods.

Ionization

Several different ionization techniques are commonly used in MS. The most common techniques are EI and CI. EI produces positive ions by causing the loss of an electron, leaving a net positive charge on the molecule or its fragment. CI can lead to the production of either positive or negative ions.

These techniques are somewhat limited by the volatility of the compounds and are typically used for compounds with a mass of approximately 1000 Da or less. For larger compounds, the energy used in the process can lead to decomposition of the molecules. An approach that helps to avoid this problem with these nonvolatile compounds often involves the use of desorption-ionization techniques, including field, chemical ionization, plasma, laser, secondary ion MS, fast atom bombardment, and laser desorption. Because this discussion is directed toward compounds of relatively small molecular weight, these desorption techniques are not discussed in detail in this chapter. Larger compounds can also be analyzed with LC-MS techniques involving multiply charged species.

Electron Ionization

EI is the most common form of ionization used in MS. This method involves a source of electrons, typically a filament, to which an electric potential is applied, causing electrons to leave the surface of the filament and move to ground. The energy potential applied to the filament is typically fixed at 70 eV. The molecules in the ion source are exposed to the beam of electrons, and the interaction between these high-energy electrons and the molecule imparts sufficient energy such that the molecule loses an electron, leaving a positively charged molecular ion (M^+). Although EI is a high-energy process, the efficiency of ionization is low, with typically only 1 of 1000 molecules being ionized. The high energy of these electrons (70 eV) commonly destabilizes the molecule, causing rearrangement, bond breaking, and, ultimately, fragmentation of the molecule. In some cases, virtually none of the intact molecular ion remains after exposure to this high-energy process. Some instruments allow the user to adjust the voltage, but many, including most benchtop instruments, do not. Lowering the voltage generally leads to less ionization and less fragmentation; such information can be useful in elucidating the chemical structure of a molecule.

The ionized fragments produced by EI are characteristic of a molecule. Therefore, the ions formed and their relative proportions are reproducible, and this information can be used for qualitative identification of the compound, thus making MS a powerful analytical tool for the identification of unknown compounds. Libraries of mass spectra are commonly used in the identification of unknown compounds through comparison of spectrum of the unknown compound with spectra of known compounds. Various algorithms are used to compare ions and their relative intensities to assist in compound identification. The net result of such analyses is the identification of spectra for known compounds that are similar to the spectrum of the analyte of interest. Such comparisons are possible because the relatively high energy of the EI process produces consistent behavior by molecules exposed to the same energy. Because most instruments use the same 70 eV potential, a molecule's behavior is remarkably similar from day to day and from instrument to instrument, thus facilitating comparisons with reference spectra generated on other instruments.

Chemical Ionization

The CI process depends on electrons as the primary source of ions, but the electrons ionize a reagent gas rather than directly ionizing the analyte molecules. The reagent gas enters the ion source and is ionized by high-energy electrons. When analyte molecules are exposed to the ionized reagent gas, the analytes themselves are ionized and give rise to molecular ions. The CI source differs slightly from the EI source in that it is more "gas tight," which allows a reagent gas to be introduced into the source and to be at a sufficiently high concentration to permit reagent ion-analyte molecule reactions to occur. Because of the added reagent gas, the vacuum in the CI source is lower than typically seen in EI, thus increasing the probability that an analyte molecule will collide with a reagent gas ion. The initial ionization of the reagent gas with electrons is a high-energy process, but the ionization of analyte molecules by the reagent gas is far less energetic. Consequently, this type of ionization causes less fragmentation of the analyte molecule than EI. Ionization is most commonly due to the transfer of a proton from the ionized reagent gas to the analyte molecule.

Several different reagent gases have been used for CI (e.g., methane, ammonia, isobutane). The reaction with methane is shown below. The first reaction is the EI of the methane molecule:

$$CH_4 + e^- \rightarrow CH_4^{+\bullet} + 2e^-$$

The electrons resulting from this process are of low energy and can play a significant role in res-

onance electron capture negative-ion CI, which is discussed later. The ion formed in this process may itself fragment in several ways, one of which is:

$$CH_4^{+\bullet} \rightarrow CH_3^+ + H^{\bullet\pm}$$

There will also be a significant number of collisions between the ions and other neutral methane molecules, which will yield the following:

$$CH_4^{+\bullet} + CH_4 \rightarrow CH_5^+ + CH_3^{\bullet}$$

$$CH_3^+ + CH_4 \rightarrow C_2H_5^+ + H_2$$

When these ions interact with the analyte molecule (M), several reactions are possible. The most common reaction for most molecules, except saturated hydrocarbons, is for the molecule to acquire a proton:

$$M + CH_5^+ \rightarrow CH_4 + M + H^+$$

Ion-molecule reactions can also lead to the formation of adduct ions, such as the following:

$$M + CH_3^+ \rightarrow M + CH_3^+$$

$$M + C_2H_5^+ \rightarrow M + C_2H_5^+$$

These ions (M+H$^+$, M+CH$_3$$^+$, M+C$_2H_5$$^+$) are referred to as molecular species or pseudomolecular ions. The actual molecular weight of the molecule is determined by subtracting the mass of the added proton or adduct ions, as the case may be.

Ammonia is another commonly used ionization gas that is ionized by an electron:

$$NH_3 + e^- \rightarrow NH_3^{+\bullet} + 2e^-$$

The radical ion created by this EI process reacts with another ammonia molecule in the following manner:

$$NH_3^{+\bullet} + NH_3 \rightarrow NH_4^+ + NH_2^{\bullet}$$

The ionization by this reagent gas depends on the kind of molecule with which it interacts. An amine-containing molecule (RNH$_2$) will generally undergo the following reaction:

$$NH_4^+ + RNH_2 \rightarrow RNH_3^+ + NH_3$$

Polar molecules without a strong basic group will generally form adduct ions. Importantly, molecules that do not have these characteristics are not readily ionized, thus making ammonia CI a selective ionization technique that eliminates much of the potential interference by other molecules.

The most commonly used form of CI is positive-ion CI. The reagent gas forms ions that, in turn, transfer a charge to analyte ions. This charge transfer is most commonly due to proton transfer, which yields a molecular ion with an additional proton attached, $[M + H]^+$, as described above. Commonly used reagent gases include methane, isobutane, and ammonia. Reagent gases are also sometimes combined to give a mixture that optimizes the ionization of the analyte molecules of interest. The ability of the reagent gas to transfer a proton to the molecules depends on the proton affinity of the molecules and the acidic properties of the reagent gas.

Negative-ion CI (NICI or NCI) is a valuable tool in the analysis of some analytes. The process involves the generation of negative ions by resonance electron capture, in which the analyte molecule captures a relatively low-energy electron. This process typically yields intact molecular anions that are readily detected. Because the energy is low, molecules with high electron affinity are the best candidates for this type of ionization. Almost all neutral molecules can yield positive ions, but negative-ion formation generally works with molecules containing a halogen, a nitro, an acidic, or similar electronegative group. Many biological molecules do not contain such groups and therefore do not become ionized by this method. This selectivity typically leads to a much cleaner baseline and cleaner chromatograms, which contribute to the sensitivity of this technique, often 100–1000 times as sensitive as positive-ion CI. Derivatization of molecules with highly electronegative reagents, such as trifluoroacetic, pentafluoropropionic, and heptafluorobutyryl groups, yields a derivatized molecule with a high electron affinity, thus facilitating the capture of an electron.

Atmospheric Pressure Ionization

The coupling of LC to a mass spectrometer requires the transition of analytes from a liquid medium at atmospheric pressure to the gaseous state under high vacuum in a mass spectrometer. To make this transition possible, the analytes of interest must be ionized before they enter the mass spectrometer. This process is commonly referred to as *atmospheric pressure ionization*(API). Specially designed interfaces connecting the LC instrument and the mass spectrometer are required to successfully facilitate the transition.

LC-MS interfaces have two main functions: (1) to remove and dispose of the liquid mobile phase and (2) to create and/or facilitate the transfer of ions into the mass spectrometer. Removal of the liquid mobile phase is a process called *desolvation*. Desolvation of the liquid mobile phase is accomplished with heaters, gas nebulizers, and the strategic positioning of the nebulized LC spray with respect to the capillary. Instrument manufacturers have moved away from aligning the spray directly in front of the capillary, which serves as the entrance into the high-vacuum region. Instead, most modern interface designs are orthogonal or perpendicular to the capillary. This positioning of the spray reduces the amount of solvent and other unwanted material from entering the mass spectrometer. By allowing only ions to enter the capillary, the background signal is reduced, thereby increasing the signal-to-noise ratio and the overall sensitivity.

Ionization is the second main function of an LC-MS interface and can be accomplished in a number of ways, depending on the chemical properties of the analyte(s). Some analytes can be ionized in solution with acid/base chemistry via adjustments in the solvent pH. Two of the most common methods are ESI and thermospray (TSP). For example, alkaline drugs containing primary or secondary amines will accept a hydrogen molecule and become positively charged in acidic solutions. A second method of ionization is the transfer of a charge from a charged gas molecule to an analyte, namely, APCI. A third method is APPI, which uses a UV lamp source to emit high-energy photons that can directly ionize vaporized analytes. Matrix-assisted laser desorption-ionization (MALDI) is an ionization technique that uses a laser to vaporize and ionize analytes within the matrices themselves. Most MALDI applications are retained for analyses of larger macromolecules, such as proteins and polypeptides. All of these ionization techniques have been used in cur-

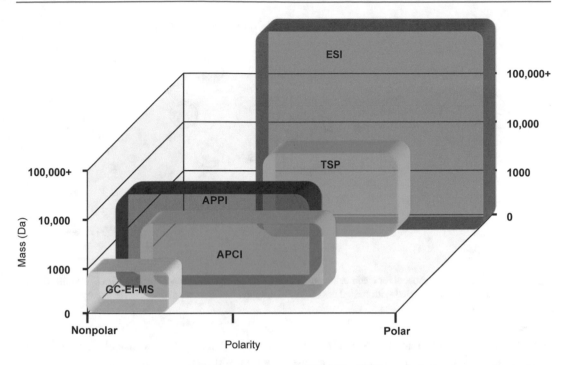

Fig. 14.2 The relative applications of the atmospheric pressure ionization techniques used in liquid chromatography-mass spectrometry, compared with gas chromatography-electron ionization-mass spectrometry (GC-EI-MS). APCI, atmospheric pressure chemical ionization; APPI, atmospheric pressure photoionization; TSP, thermospray; ESI, electrospray ionization

rent LC-MS and LC-MS/MS analyses. Their applicability depends on the polarities and molecular weights of the compounds being analyzed. Figure 14.2 illustrates a general guideline to the applicability of the different ionization techniques used in forensic toxicology.

Certain considerations are required when developing methods that use an API technique. Ion suppression is a major concern, and all LC-MS and LC-MS/MS ionization techniques are susceptible. Ion suppression is a matrix effect that can coincide with other factors (some of which are not really understood) to muffle the signal from the analyte. When excessive ions are present in the sample, the signal from the analyte of interest can be suppressed or buried in the background noise. These effects can vary greatly between samples and between different matrices, such as blood and urine. The interferences can come from the matrices, the extraction procedure, the solvents, and even the glassware or plastic tubes used in the extraction procedure. Other factors relating to the chemical properties of the analytes, such as mass, alkalinity, and concentration,

can also contribute to ion suppression. The degree of suppression can negatively affect the limit of detection, the precision, and the accuracy of quantitative results. All API methods should be examined for the presence and influence of ion suppression, and appropriate steps should be taken, if needed, to minimize their effects.

Electrospray Ionization

ESI is the most commonly used API technique and is regularly used in forensic toxicology. An electrospray interface has three main components: the nebulizer, the desolvation assembly, and the mesh electrode or repeller. Modern electrospray interfaces have pneumatically assisted nebulization, which enables larger solvent volumes and higher flow rates. Heated, highly pressurized nitrogen gas nebulizes the mobile phase as it enters the ESI interface and creates an aerosol of charged droplets. As the solvents evaporate and shrink, ions within the droplets become closer and closer to one another until the electro-

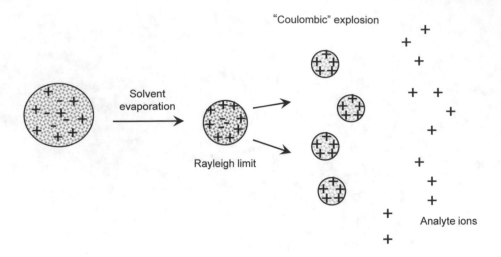

Fig. 14.3 The desolvation process for electrospray ionization (ESI) and thermospray (TSP) interfaces. Nebulized droplets containing ions are evaporated with heated gas (N_2) until only the free ions remain

static repulsion is too great for the surface tension. At this breaking point, referred to as the *Rayleigh limit*, the droplet explodes into smaller droplets (Coulombic explosion). The process of desolvation (Fig. 14.3) continues until the solvent is evaporated and only free ions remain. Ions are drawn into the capillary via a difference in electrostatic potential between the end of the capillary and the mesh electrode. This electrode is positioned across from the capillary orifice on the opposite side of the spray. Figure 14.4 is an illustration of an ESI interface.

Depending on the pK_a of the compound and the pH of the mobile phase, ions formed in solution can be either positively or negatively charged. Most modern ESI interfaces can be programmed to analyze both positive and negative ions, either separately or simultaneously. ESI is the "softest" API technique available and often produces only the [M + 1] ion of the molecule of interest. ESI is used for very polar to slightly nonpolar compounds that can be charged in solution. For all analytes, the optimal operational parameters for fragmentation are determined by a sequential series of injections of a standard solution. This process of optimization is referred to as a *flow injection analysis* (FIA). During an FIA study, such parameters as the fragmentor voltage, drying gas temperature and flow, and nebulization pressure are varied in sequential injection. Ion

abundance and intensity usually determine the optimal settings.

ESI is a valuable technique in forensic toxicology, because most drugs are plant alkaloids. Alkaline compounds are ideal for ESI because they can be easily charged in solution and typically have some polar properties. Typical ESI techniques are capable of analyzing a singly charged ion up to 3000 Da in size; however, analyses of large molecules such as proteins and enzymes make up the majority of ESI applications. The use of a high electrostatic potential in the ESI interface is thought to help charge the many functional groups found on large proteins and enzymes. Therefore, the use of ESI helps accomplish the goal of creating multiply charged ions. This capability greatly extends the dynamic mass range of an MS detector that differentiates molecules on the basis of the m/z ratio and enables LC-ESI-MS techniques to analyze molecules with masses greater than 100 kDa. Deconvolution software is used to decipher the cluster of peaks produced by multiple charges and to determine the molecular weight and structural identity of an analyte.

Some disadvantages are associated with ESI techniques. ESI operates most efficiently when flow rates are less than 1.0 mL/min, and loss of sensitivity occurs when this flow rate is exceeded. ESI does not work well for nonpolar analytes,

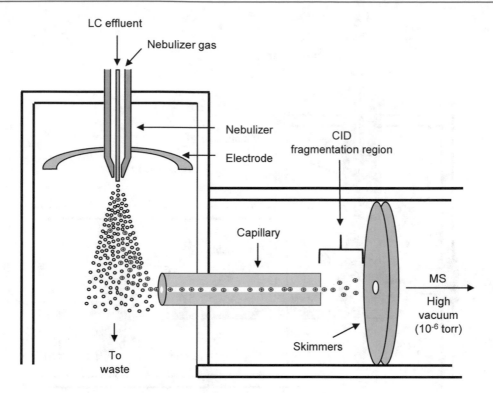

Fig. 14.4 Example of an electrospray ionization (ESI) interface for a liquid chromatography-mass spectrometry (LC-MS) system. CID, collision-induced dissociation

thereby limiting the types of analytes that can be analyzed successfully. Additionally, the formation of such adducts as [M + Na] or [M + NH₄] is common with ESI and can contribute to ion suppression effects. The formation of adducts is minimized by the use of highly pure mobile phases (HPLC grade) and low-molarity buffer solutions (<50 mmol/L).

Thermospray

TSP is an API technique very similar to ESI. Ions are created in solution with buffers that permit the analysis of polar, thermally labile, and non-volatile analytes. The pressurized mobile phase is passed through a heated tube that vaporizes the solution. The desolvation process for the mobile phase and the subsequent production of free ions are similar to the process described for ESI. With the addition of a repeller electrode, ions are transferred into the mass spectrometer for analysis. Traditional designs for TSP differ from those for ESI only in that ESI uses a high electrostatic

potential in the interface to facilitate the production and transfer of free ions. This high electrostatic potential gives ESI a significant advantage in its ability to produce multiply charged species, thus extending its mass range. Unlike ESI, for which the more efficient flow rates are lt;1.0;mL/min, TSP interfaces can sustain flow rates of up to 2.0 mL/min. TSP is a soft ionization technique and produces primarily pseudomolecular adduct ions, such as $[M + NH_4]^+$ or $[M + Na]^+$, depending on the buffer and salts used in the mobile phase. Although still used in forensic toxicology, TSP techniques have mainly been sidelined by the advances in other API techniques, such as ESI and APCI.

Atmospheric Pressure CI

An ionization method complementary to ESI is APCI. APCI is used for analyzing low- to medium-polarity molecules that are easily vaporized. Unlike ESI, for which compounds can have multiple charges, APCI usually yields a singly

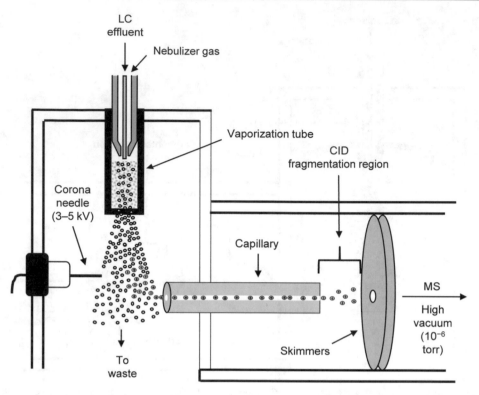

Fig. 14.5 Example of atmospheric pressure chemical ionization (APCI) interface for a liquid chromatography-mass spectrometry (LC-MS) system. CID, collision-induced dissociation

charged ion. Consequently, the mass range for APCI is limited by the mass spectrometer's mass range, which is typically <3000 Da.

APCI sample introduction is similar to that of ESI. An APCI interface has four basic components: the nebulizer, the vaporization tube, the corona needle, and the desolvation module. Figure 14.5 illustrates an APCI interface for LC-MS system. The liquid mobile phase enters the nebulizer and flows through the needle assembly. The nebulizer blows high-pressure nitrogen (approximately 60 psi) around the needle and blasts the mobile phase into a fine aerosol. The nebulizing gas then carries the aerosol containing the mobile phase and analytes through the heated (200–400 °C) vaporization tube. The temperature in this region is optimized to minimize any thermal decomposition and to maximize solvent vaporization. The vaporized mobile phase and the analytes are then ionized by a discharge from the corona needle, which is positioned at the exit of the vaporization tube. The corona needle creates a field of electrons that protonates the gas-

phase solvent as it exits the tube. The charge is then transferred to the analytes in a process similar to methane positive-ion CI in GC-MS. The corona needle can produce positively or negatively charged ions, depending on the application and the analyte. The nebulizer pressure, the vaporization temperature, and the corona current are analyte dependent and are optimized with an FIA.

APCI is best used for analytes of intermediate polarity and molecular weight that do not contain acidic or basic sites. This consideration is especially true for compounds that are sensitive to acid/base solution chemistry and exhibit a poor ESI response. Samples that contain such compounds as ketones, esters, aldehydes, alcohols, and some hydrocarbons can be analyzed with APCI. APCI tolerates higher flow rates without sacrificing sensitivity and accommodates a wider range of solvents than ESI.

Applications for APCI are more limited than for ESI, and some considerations are necessary before APCI can be developed. Compounds must be moderately volatile so that they can be vaporized and ionized. A compound must have a molecular mass <3000 Da, because APCI will produce only a singly charged ion. These two limitations rule out larger, more polar molecules, such as peptides and proteins. APCI is also less effective for analyzing thermally labile analytes. The high temperature in the vaporization tube will degrade thermally sensitive molecules such as steroids. The vast majority of compounds encountered in a forensic toxicology laboratory, including most pharmaceuticals and abused drugs, can be analyzed with APCI or ESI techniques.

Atmospheric Pressure Photoionization

APPI is an interface that uses photons emitted by a light source to ionize analytes. Figure 14.6 presents a schematic of an APPI interface. APPI uses a gas discharge lamp that emits UV photons at distinct energy levels that are specific to the type of gas used. Three gases frequently used in APPI are krypton (10.0 eV and 10.6 eV), argon (11.2 eV), and xenon (8.4 eV). Analytes will ionize if their ionization energies are lower than the energy emitted by the source lamp. Typically, nonpolar analytes will appear as a radical molecular ion ($M^{+\bullet}$), and polar compounds will appear as a protonated pseudomolecular ion ($[M + 1]^{+}$). Depending on the composition of the mobile phase and the polarity of the analyte, the $[M^{+\bullet}]$ created can accept a hydrogen from the mobile phase (MP) to produce the $[M + 1]^{+}$ ion:

$$M + h\nu \rightarrow M^{+\bullet} + e^{-}$$

$$M^{+\bullet} + MPH \rightarrow [M+1]^{+} + MP^{\bullet}$$

APPI can operate in both positive- and negative-ion modes. In positive-ion mode, the mobile phase must contain a solvent, such as methanol, that can easily donate a hydrogen mol-

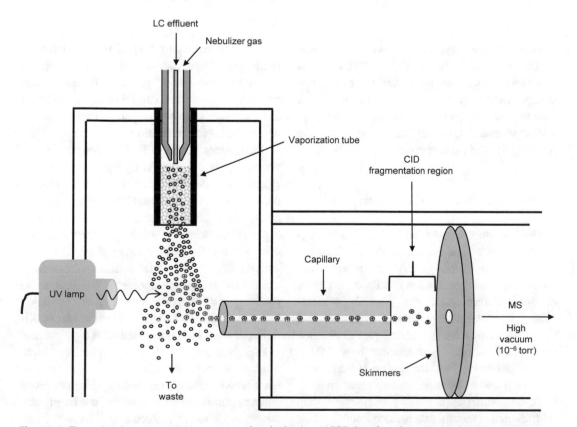

Fig. 14.6 Example of an atmospheric pressure photoionization (APPI) interface for a liquid chromatography-mass spectrometry (LC-MS) system. CID, collision-induced dissociation

ecule. In general, one of the most popular choices for the mobile phase is a combination of acetonitrile and water. This combination is not suitable for APPI, however, because there is no hydrogen that can be freely donated. Water in its gaseous state acts as a strong base and has a strong affinity for hydrogen. The compound must have a stronger affinity for the proton than for the solvent gas, or the ionization efficiency will be decreased severely. In negative-ion mode, the reagent gas must have a strong affinity for protons or be able to capture electrons.

APPI is not limited by acid/base chemistry or by the compound's volatility. APPI can be used to analyze nonpolar to moderately polar compounds that may not be amenable to analysis with either ESI or APCI. The energy used for ionization is relatively low but can generate doubly charged ions, thereby increasing the mass range of the mass spectrometer to slighter better than APCI but not as high as ESI.

Compounds can be ionized directly, or a dopant can be used to transfer the charge indirectly. Direct ionization occurs if the compound being analyzed has an ionization energy lower than that of the photon. Dopants are chemical additives used to increase the overall ionization efficiency of APPI for compounds that are difficult to ionize or that lose their ionization easily. Dopants (D) are added in the nebulizer to the mobile phase. Most dopants have very low ionization energies. This property makes them more easily photoionized and thereby more able to transfer their charge to the compounds of interest:

$$D + hv \rightarrow M^{+\bullet} + e^-$$ Photoionized analyte

$$D^{+\bullet} + M \rightarrow \rightarrow [M+1]^+ + D$$ Photoionized dopant

$$D^{+\bullet} + M \rightarrow M^{+\bullet} + D$$ Charge transfer from dopant

Toluene, acetone, and anisole have all been used successfully as dopants. Most APPI methods show increases in sensitivity and ionization efficiency when dopants are used. One drawback with the use of dopants is the potential increase in adduct formation, which can complicate the interpretation of mass spectra.

Collision-Induced Dissociation

Collision-induced dissociation (CID) is a fragmentation technique used in LC-MS, MS/MS, or ion trap MS applications. CID occurs when ionized compounds accelerated in a fixed area by an electrical charge collide with neutral gas molecules (molecular nitrogen, argon, or helium) and cause fragmentation. API techniques most often produce even numbers of electron ions. CID is analyte dependent, and the degree of fragmentation is dependent on experimental parameters. In CID, fragmentation is much less energetic than with EI, and sometimes there is no fragmentation at all. Figure 14.7 displays cocaine fragmentation patterns produced with three different ionization techniques. Note that the highly energetic EI technique produces greater fragmentation, whereas positive-ion CI and ESI have less energy and produce mostly the pseudomolecular ion with minimal fragmentation.

Two places where CID can occur are in the source and in the mass analyzer. For an LC-MS system, *in-source CID* refers to the fragmentation that occurs prior to mass detection. Applying a potential difference between the capillary endcap and the skimmer accelerates the molecules over a short distance, causing them to collide with the drying gas. These collisions cause fragmentation of the compounds. Increasing the potential difference (fragmentor voltage) increases the rate of collisions and produces differing degrees of fragmentation. The fragmentor voltages can be optimized to produce a desired fragmentation for each ion of interest. The distance between the endcap and the skimmer varies among manufacturers and affects the fragmentation of a particular molecule at a fixed voltage. Fragmentor voltages are not universal; the same

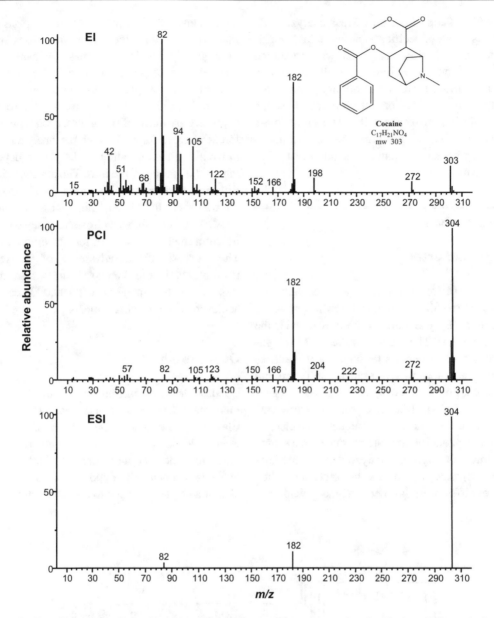

Fig. 14.7 Illustrated are the distinctly unique full-scan spectra of cocaine produced with three different ionization techniques: electron ionization (EI), positive-ion chemical ionization (PCI), and electrospray ionization (ESI)

fragmentor voltage in two instruments from different manufacturers can cause different degrees of fragmentation. In addition, the mass of the collision gas also affects the overall fragmentation. A heavy gas, such as argon, will accelerate faster and impact the molecules with more energy, causing a greater degree of fragmentation. In-source CID can take place in the octapole region by increasing the voltage applied, thereby increasing the number of collisions.

In tandem quadrupole MS, CID occurs in the second mass analyzer (collision cell) via increasing the pressure and accelerating the ions to collide with the gas molecules. Similarly, CID can occur inside an ion trap. Energy applied to the trap excites the ions and causes them to collide with helium gas, producing fragmentation. Helium also serves to cool and focus the ions inside the center of the trap by forming a buffer between the orbiting ions and the inside walls of the trap. Mass analyzer CID imparts greater specificity and has a higher efficiency of collision compared with in-source CID. The molecular ions are isolated prior to fragmentation, therefore eliminating the possibility of co-eluting ion interferences that can occur during in-source CID. Therefore, mass analyzer CID is the preferred method for studying fragmentation patterns and identifying unknowns.

Mass Analyzer

Magnetic Sector

Magnetic sector instruments are generally not used in the routine analytical, forensic, or clinical laboratory. They are most commonly found in the research arena. The recent requirement for high-resolution MS in sports testing may make these instruments more widely used in the future, but the discussion in this chapter is limited to a general description. Magnetic sector instruments separate ions by means of a magnetic and electro-static analyzer. The ions are produced in a source and travel through the analyzers. Magnetic analyzers separate ions by the principle that when ions of different mass enter a magnetic field (per-pendicular to the ion path), the smaller ions turn more quickly than the larger ones. Ions move through a slit that limits the mass that can exit the magnet. Sweeping the magnetic field from a high to a low field strength causes ions to pass through the slit from higher to lower mass. Electrostatic analyzers are made of two plates, each with a different charge. As ions enter the analyzer, they move along the curvature of the plates, depending on the energy of the ions. The ability to identify even very small differences in this manner allows ions of the same nominal mass to be separated. Magnetic and electrostatic analyzers can be combined in several different combinations. The most significant advantage of the sector instruments is the increased mass resolution. Resolution of upwards of 100,000 can be achieved with these instruments.

Quadrupole

Quadrupole mass spectrometers are the most common mass analyzers in use today (Fig. 14.8). Classically, the quadrupole is a set of four pre-cisely machined rods. Use of a combination of radio frequency and direct current voltages on the two sets of diagonally opposed rods allows only ions of a single m/z value to pass through the ana-

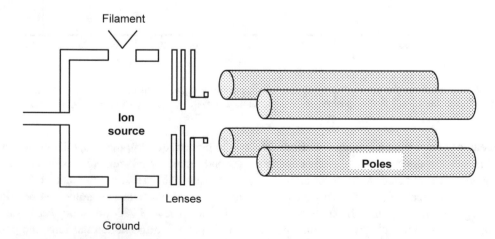

Fig. 14.8 Example of a quadrupole mass spectrometer. Note that various systems actually use more rods (octapole) or a single-shaped device that simulates four rods (e.g., Agilent Technologies 5973 mass spectrometers). Regardless of the configuration, the basic principles are the same

lyzer. Ions that enter the analyzer move toward the detector. All but those of the specific mass selected are deflected into the rods. The rods can be scanned, usually from lower to higher mass, allowing ions of successively higher mass to pass through the filter. In actual practice, the term *quadrupole* is often used to describe analyzers that have four, six, or eight rods, not just those with four.

The mass spectrum produced is referred to as a full-scan spectrum and is used when performing automated searches of mass spectral libraries. Specific masses can also be selected so that only the specified *m/z* values are detected. This process, commonly called *selected ion monitoring* (SIM), is used for qualitative and quantitative analysis of targeted analytes. Selecting a limited number of specific masses permits longer dwell times (time spent monitoring a single ion) for detecting these ions, thus increasing the sensitivity. SIM analysis provides less spectral data than a full-scan analysis but is far more sensitive. SIM analysis has better sensitivity because more time is spent monitoring fewer ions. Full-scan analysis monitors an entire range of ions over the same period of time. In SIM analysis, the loss of other *m/z* data is less important than determining the presence of a specific compound, often referred to as *target compound analysis*. With the increase in sensitivity, much lower amounts of analyte can often be identified and quantified. Typically, full-scan MS methods are used in screening analysis, and SIM methods are used in quantitative analysis.

Ion Trap

The ion trap is best considered as a unique form of a quadrupole mass analyzer. Rather than being arranged parallel to each other, the four rods form a three-dimensional sphere in which ions are "trapped" (Fig. 14.9). The trap consists of a central ring electrode and two endcap electrodes. Applying radio-frequency voltage to these electrodes causes ions to be trapped in the three-dimensional space of the trap. Ions are then ejected from the system by changing the applied radio frequency, which causes the trapped ions to destabilize and exit the trap. This process is often referred to as "scan-out" of the trap. Ions ejected from the trap enter the detector portion of the instrument. Increasing the radio-frequency voltage destabilizes ions of increasing *m/z* values until all masses within the desired range are ejected. The steps in mass analysis using an ion trap can be summarized as:

1. Ion storage
2. Ion isolation
3. Collision-activated dissociation (for MS/MS)
4. Ion scan-out

For multiple mass spectrometer (MS^n) experiments, steps 2 and 3 are repeated.

The distances in the ion trap are short, which allows the use of a lower vacuum in the system. This is because the mean free path required is much shorter than in conventional quadrupole or

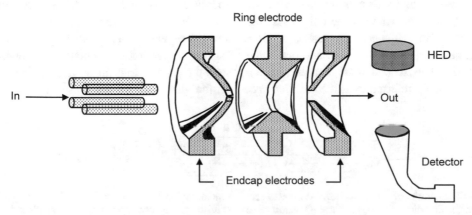

Fig. 14.9 Example of ion trap mass spectrometer. HED, high-energy dynode

sector instruments. Because the molecules are within a confined space, ion-molecule reactions are more likely than in a conventional quadrupole instrument. These ion-molecule reactions have the potential to generate atypical mass spectra. This potential problem can be minimized by sensing the number of ions in the trap and adjusting ionization times so that fewer molecules and ions are involved in a single scan, thus reducing the incidence of ion-molecule reactions. Ion traps of older design ionized the molecules inside the trap itself. In this design, all effluent from the column entered the trap, leading to a high density of molecules and ultimately to a high probability of ion-molecule reactions. Newer designs generate the ions outside the trap, and only ions enter the trap. This approach eliminates a large number of neutral molecules observed inside the trap when the ionization is accomplished within the trap.

MS/MS and MS^n

In recent years, the power of MS analysis has been greatly augmented by multistage MS analysis. The method of multistage MS depends on the instrument design. MS/MS analysis can be thought of as occurring in space or in time. The process traditionally used in many instruments is based on linking several quadrupole mass analyzers together in sequence. These types of setups are typically referred to as triple quads, owing to the presence of three quadrupole analyzers in series (Fig. 14.10); however, today's instruments are referred to as *tandem mass spectrometers* because quadrupoles are not the only mass analyzers used in sequence. Typically, modern designs have a quadrupole as the first mass analyzer (Q1). The second mass analyzer region (Q2), commonly referred to as the *collision cell*,

may contain a quadrupole, a hexapole, an octapole, or some other design. The third mass analyzer region (Q3) can contain a quadrupole or an ion trap. The instruments generate ions in the same manner as described earlier, but they usually use an ionization technique that only produces molecular ions. The most common form of MS/MS analysis that uses these instruments involves setting the Q1 region to allow only ions corresponding to the *m/z* of the ion of interest to pass. Once the ion has passed through the Q1 region, it enters the Q2 region where CID takes place. This is typically accomplished by putting a collision gas into this area, which generates frequent collisions between these gas molecules and the ion that has been selectively allowed to pass through Q1. The single ion passed through Q1 is referred to as the *precursor ion* (or, less commonly, the *parent ion*). The ions formed from the fragmentation of precursor ions are called *product ions* (or, less commonly, *daughter ions*). The Q3 analyzers can then be set to scan all ions produced or selectively allow only one or more of these product ions through to the detector. This method of MS/MS is referred to as MS/MS in space, whereas the other process uses time.

MS/MS in time is accomplished with ion trap mass spectrometers. To perform MS/MS or MS^n experiments in the ion trap, all ions are ejected from the trap except for the selected precursor ion. A voltage is then applied to the endcap electrode 180 degrees from the field generated by the radio frequency on the ring electrode. When the voltage applied to the endcap is resonant with the energy of a particular *m/z* value, ions with that value become destabilized and fragmented. The amount of energy used can be varied to yield varying degrees of fragmentation. Following this step, the product ions are scanned out of the trap to the detector. All of these separations are

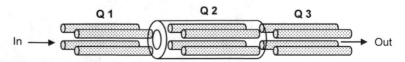

Fig. 14.10 Example of a tandem (MS/MS) mass spectrometer. Quadrupoles one (Q1) and three (Q3) are used in the traditional sense as mass filters. Quadrupole two (Q2) is actually a collision cell within which ions collide with collision gas molecules, causing collisionally induced dissociation (fragmentation)

accomplished within the confines of the trap; thus, it represents MS/MS in time.

The ability to trap ions can be a significant advantage in these experiments. When a single ion is trapped and then fragmented, the experiment can proceed to a third level by isolating a single product ion in the trap by scanning out all of the others and then fragmenting the remaining trapped ion. Such an analysis represents MS/MS/MS (MS³). Theoretically, this operation can be performed repeatedly, yielding fragments that are generated as MS/MS/MS/MS (MS⁴), MS/MS/MS/MS/MS (MS⁵), and so on. Commercially available instruments permit MS to the 10th level; however, going beyond level three or four is unlikely—and unnecessary—in most applications.

MS/MS has tremendous advantages in the analysis of compounds. Because the first ion isolated can be the molecular ion, the likelihood of interference from other compounds that may also be in the source at the same time (i.e., chromatographically co-eluting peaks) is all but eliminated. This design raises the confidence of identification and depends less on the ability of the chromatographic method to provide a single pure compound to the mass spectrometer. In addition, these methods enhance the ability to elucidate the structure of a molecule. Rather than seeing the total spectrum formed from the fragmentation of a molecule, individual ions can be isolated and their fragmentation evaluated. This ability to determine which ions come from which other fragments can be a powerful tool in the determination of chemical structure. In the case of MSn analysis, multiple levels of fragmentation can enhance the ability to elucidate chemical structure or, in the case of identification of a compound, can provide very strong analytical evidence for the presence of a compound. The elimination of other interfering ions makes the use of these techniques more sensitive and allows more rapid analysis of samples.

Other advantages of MS/MS analysis include monitoring of neutral loss for all compounds entering the mass spectrometer. This feature can be a very powerful tool in the search for metabolites of a compound or in the identification of structurally related compounds. Because this and other applications for MS/MS analysis are not commonly used in forensic toxicology, they are not discussed further.

Time-of-Flight (TOF) Mass Spectrometers

The time-of-flight (TOF) mass analyzer is a type of high resolution mass spectrometer (HRMS) capable of determining the exact mass of charged ions with an accuracy of between 1 and 3 parts per million (ppm). Like all mass spectrometers, the TOF analyzes ions based on their mass-to-charge ratio (m/z). The principles of TOF mass analyzers can be explained by two physics equations: kinetic energy and velocity. Kinetic energy (E) is the energy of motion and is equal to one half the mass (m) multiplied by the velocity (v) squared.

$$E = \frac{1}{2} mv^2$$

Velocity is a vector measurement of the direction and rate of an object's motion. Velocity (v) or speed of a given object in a vacuum is equal to the distance (d) traveled divided by the time (t).

$$v = d / t$$

Combining the two equations and solving for mass (m) explains the basic principles of the TOF and how it can be used as a mass analyzer. The mass (m) of an object in a vacuum is equal to two times the kinetic energy (E) divided by the distance (d) the object travels squared, divided by the time (t) the object traveled squared.

$$m = \left(2E / d^2 \right) t^2$$

TOF instruments are designed to apply a specific kinetic energy (E) and have a flight tube of a specific length (d). Therefore, by keeping the kinetic energy (E) and distance (d) constant (C), the mass (m) is proportional to the square root of the flight time of the ion.

$$m = Ct^2$$

Smaller molecular weight ions will travel with more velocity, thereby reaching the detector before heavier ions. Even the smallest variation in the flight time can have significant effects on the mass accuracies; therefore most instrumentation has a mechanism for infusing a reference calibrator compound into the analyzer at specific intervals throughout the analyses. This will ensure the mass corrections are performed throughout the analysis to account for the infinitesimal variations in the system.

In practice, ions are created in the source, focused through the ion optics, and accelerated into the time-of-flight tube by an electric potential. The ions travel through the flight tube in a vacuum with no electric fields. Most flight tubes have a reflectron at one end which helps focus ions of the same weight and direct them back to the detector. By reflecting the ions, the distance (d) of the flight tube is extended allowing for a longer flight time and thereby increasing the resolution. The newest flight tube designs have multiple reflectrons which double or quadruple the instrument's flight path. Advancements in electronic circuitry, computer processors, and vacuum technologies have allowed for the development of benchtop time-of-flight (TOF) instruments capable of routinely measuring an ion mass below 3 ppm. These advancements have allowed for the benchtop instruments to be smaller, efficient, and more affordable without sacrificing resolution or mass accuracy.

Quadrupole time-of-flight (QTOF) mass spectrometers have a quadrupole and collision cell prior to the flight tube (Fig. 14.11). This configuration allows for the accurate mass measurements of the parent compound and all of its fragment ions generated in the collision cell. The QTOF design allows for the simultaneous quantitative and qualitative analysis of any compound where a reference standard is available.

Typically, tandem MS-MS instruments collect specific targeted data in the form of a parent to fragment ion transitions. The only mass spectral data collected is what the user has specifically instructed the instrument to monitor. A significant benefit when using a TOF instrument is that all of the mass spectral data is collected and stored from the original analysis. Retrospective data analysis can be performed with unknown compounds not currently in the instrument library. When new drugs, metabolites, or drug analogs are discovered and reference material becomes available, old casework data files can be searched to determine if any of these compounds were present during the orginal analysis. This can save time and resources by simply reprocessing the original data with the updated library, thereby eliminating the need to re-extract and re-analyze the sample. This is especially important when there is limited sample amount or if the stability of the compound in a given matrices is unknown. This scenario becomes more important in postmortem investigations because the original analysis is performed closely after the time of death. If the specimen has to be reanalyzed months or even years later, the stability of the given compound and degradation of the sample can have negative effects on the identification and quantitation results.

TOF and QTOF are now being routinely used in forensic toxicology laboratories for screening and confirmation. TOF and QTOF MS allow data to be acquired using a wide variety of approaches. Collection of high-resolution MS and MS/MS spectra, retrospective data analysis, and the ability to perform library searching provide the forensic toxicology laboratory with a number of flexible approaches for screening, qualitative, and quantitative analyses. Standards for identification criteria and mass spectral data acceptance in forensic toxicology are described in ANSI/ASB 113 and ANSI/ASB 098, respectfully.

Others

Although not yet in wide use in the field of forensic toxicology, certain ionization MS techniques, such as direct analysis in real time (DART), desorption electrospray ionization (DESI), laser diode thermal desorption (LDTD), desorption atmospheric pressure photoionization (DAPPI), acoustic ejection mass spectrometry (AEMS), acoustic droplet mass spectrometry (ADMS), paper spray (PS), and touch spray-

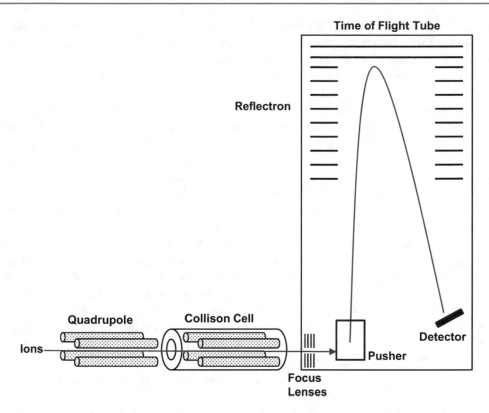

Fig. 14.11 Example of a quadrupole time-of-flight (QTOF) mass spectrometer. This basic design illustrates a simple configuration including a quadrupole mass filter, a collision cell, ion-focusing lenses, a pusher plate, a reflectron, and the detector

mass spectrometry (TS-MS), have gained popularity. Applications are being explored and developed by instrument manufacturers and in academia for use in the various forensic disciplines including forensic toxicology.

Applications

Qualitative Analysis

One of the major applications of MS is in qualitative analysis of samples to identify what compounds are present. Identification of compounds can be accomplished in several different ways, depending on the analyte. The simplest form of identification is detection of an analyte whose characteristics are well known. Identification can be as simple as monitoring several (usually three) selected ions and comparing the ratios of the

detected ions with the ratios from a known reference standard, which is typically analyzed in the same analytical batch. These ions and their ratios, combined with retention time data from a chromatographic system, are generally accepted as sufficient evidence to positively identify a compound. Another common method of identification is comparing full-scan mass spectra with a mass spectral library. Several different search algorithms can be used to help identify compounds by comparison of the acquired spectrum with spectra in the library. For determining the presence or absence of a specific analyte, the monitoring of selected ions has several advantages; however, this method is less useful for identifying an unknown compound because the approach is based on a comparison with known characteristics, as described above. When examining a sample for what compounds might be present, the use of full-scan spectra produces more information.

Coupling the spectrum with a library helps the analyst select likely candidates for the compound. Evaluation of data regarding the extraction and derivatization of the molecule can also help identify the compound. When searching for metabolites of a particular compound, the use of full-scan spectra, together with expected metabolically induced changes to the molecule (i.e., hydroxylation, demethylation), can lead to the identification of analytes of interest.

More recently the use of high-resolution mass spectrometer (HRMS), which includes QTOF analyzers, has become more prevalent as a qualitative screening instrument in forensic toxicology laboratories. QTOF instruments can collect untargeted full-scan mass spectral data and match these accurate mass fragmentation patterns to custom accurate mass libraries. This data can also be retrospectively searched when newer drug standards are discovered and reference standards become available. In some cases, reference standards may not need to be available; instead identification can be determined based on the accurate mass, the isotopic patterns, and the fragmentation patterns of the compound. Coupled to a liquid chromatography (LC) system, the QTOF mass analyzer with its accurate mass capabilities might eliminate the need for chromatographic separation, allowing for a shorter run times. Co-eluting peaks can be identified by their exact mass. LC can also minimize the need for extensive and expensive sample preparation if matrix effects are within acceptable limits.

Quantitative Analysis

Another common application of MS is quantitative analysis. Quantitative applications are found across the range of available chromatographic and ionization techniques. The most common of these applications is found in GC-MS. For quantitative purposes, the internal standard method is the most often used and is typically the most accurate of the available techniques. With the tremendous ability of the mass spectrometer to separate ions by mass, stable isotope-labeled internal standards are now in wide use for quantitative analysis. The most commonly used stable isotope is deuterium, and the incorporation of each deuterium adds one mass unit to the overall mass of the molecule or fragment observed in the mass spectrometer. A wide variety of compounds now have deuterium-labeled isotopes available for use in quantitative analysis. Isotope-labeled compounds have some very significant advantages, because the chemical and physical properties of the molecules remain almost identical to the naturally occurring compound. Therefore, the behavior of the analyte and its internal standard with respect to extraction, derivatization, and fragmentation are virtually identical. Use of stable isotope-labeled isotopes is a special form of the internal standard method of quantification, sometimes referred to as *isotope dilution MS*. When stable isotope-labeled isotopes are not available or when the procedure is designed to analyze a large number of analytes, a number of internal standards that have chemical properties sufficiently close to those of the analytes of interest are used to yield accurate quantitative information.

Examples

There are numerous examples of analytical procedures that use MS. Analysis of amphetamines and related compounds is one interesting example. The amphetamines are abused drugs commonly found in the illicit drug environment. Chemically, they are very simple yet difficult to separate from many other small, naturally occurring molecules. They are easily extracted from biological fluids, but they are often co-extracted with chemically related compounds. Amphetamine and methamphetamine can be separated from other compounds by means of several GC procedures. These molecules can be detected with most GC detectors, including the flame ionization detector, the nitrogen-phosphorus detector, and—when derivatized properly—an electron capture detector. The amphetamines can also be readily derivatized, although derivatization is not required for GC analysis. If they are not derivatized, the peaks tend to tail slightly, but identification and quantification are readily accomplished. Because of the large number of compounds often found in biological samples, the use of MS has some significant advantages for most compounds. The underivatized drugs, however, tend to yield only a single intense fragment ion at m/z 44 for amphetamine and m/z 58 for methamphetamine. Derivatization of these molecules not only improves their chromatographic behavior but also dramatically changes their mass spectra. Derivatized amphetamine and methamphetamine typically have three or more intense ions, thereby substantially increasing the confidence of identification. See Fig. 14.12 for an example of derivatized methamphetamine. An examination of the spectra of the derivatized compounds clearly demonstrates the advantage of using derivatization with MS. One of the significant powers of the mass spectrometer is to determine the ions formed from the analyte of interest. Underivatized amphetamine and methamphetamine show only a single prominent ion. Although of limited information, it is still more than is provided by other GC detectors, such as flame ionization. Nevertheless, it is not possible to monitor multiple ions and their relative proportions to provide a strong confirmation of the presence of the analyte. Use of the derivatized molecules permits monitoring of fragments of higher masses (generally considered more characteristic and less prone to interference) and monitoring of several ions that provide consistent ratios that can unequivocally confirm the presence of the compounds.

Full-scan analysis of a sample provides a simple demonstration of the power to identify an unknown compound. A peak is identified, and the spectrum is compared with a mass spectral library. As shown in Fig. 14.13, the selec-

Fig. 14.12 Derivatized methamphetamine. This example shows mass spectra from underivatized methamphetamine and methamphetamine derivatized with trifluoroacetic anhydride (TFAA), pentafluoropropionic anhydride (PFPA), and heptafluorobutyric anhydride (HFBA). Note the increase in number and uniqueness of the ions for the derivatized compounds

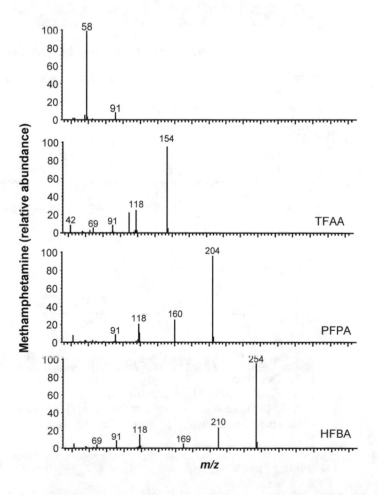

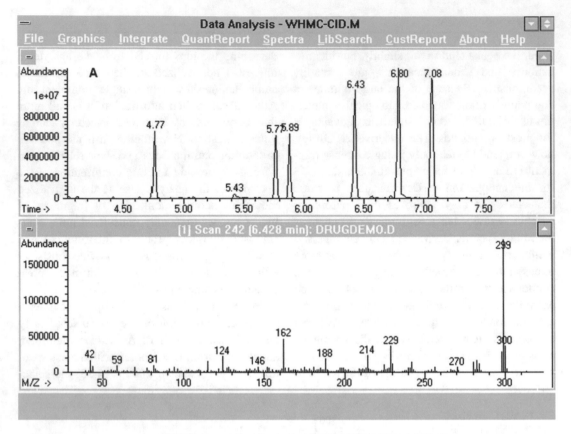

PBM Graphics Results: C:\DATABASE\NBS54K.L

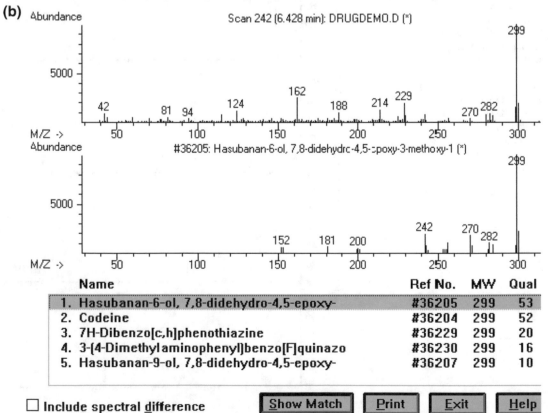

Name	Ref No.	MW	Qual
1. Hasubanan-6-ol, 7,8-didehydro-4,5-epoxy-	#36205	299	53
2. Codeine	#36204	299	52
3. 7H-Dibenzo[c,h]phenothiazine	#36229	299	20
4. 3-[4-Dimethylaminophenyl)benzo[F]quinazo	#36230	299	16
5. Hasubanan-9-ol, 7,8-didehydro-4,5-epoxy-	#36207	299	10

☐ Include spectral difference   Show Match   Print   Exit   Help

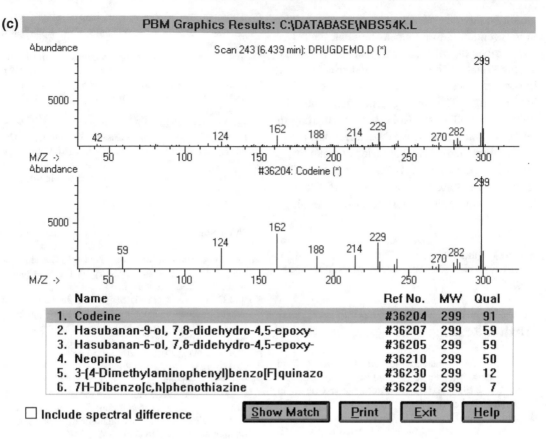

Fig. 14.13 (Continued)

tion of the spectrum can have a significant influence on the result of the library search. A peak with a retention time of 6.43 min is examined with a spectrum at 6.428 min (Fig. 14.13a), and a library search produced a result on that spectrum (Fig. 14.13b). A spectrum taken later in the same peak at 6.439 min suggests that the spectrum belongs to a different compound (Fig. 14.13c). The actual compound was codeine, not the first choice on the library search result for the peak's retention time. The message in this simple example is that full-scan mass spectral analysis is a tremendously powerful analytical tool, but competent professional judgment is needed in interpreting the analytical results.

Accurate mass databases have become a new source of positive identification of drugs and metabolites. Accurate mass data collected from a TOF MS instrument can be searched on custom and prebuilt accurate mass libraries with thousands of compounds without the need for a standard. For example, a custom accurate mass library can be set up to search for compounds with a measured mass (m/z) within 3 ppm and retention time within +/− 2%. If a peak was detected at 8.81 min with the measured mass of 243.1991, the search would match only possible chemical formulae within the expected ppm and at that retention time. In this case, the exact monoisotopic mass of phencyclidine ($C_{17}H_{25}N$) is 243.1987 m/z with a retention time of 8.80 and

Fig. 14.13 Example of a library search. (**a**) Total ion chromatogram and full-scan spectrum from single peak. (**b**) Library search results for spectrum selected at apex of chro-matographic peak. (**c**) Library search results for spectrum selected later in chromatographic peak. First result in the list of candidate molecules is correct for c but not for b

would be the only possible chemical match. The more accurate the mass measurement, the fewer the number of possible chemical formulae. By adding retention time as additional criteria, these library matches constitute a positive chemical identification. The method parameters must be tightly controlled to avoid any fluctuation in retention times, and many laboratories build their own custom methods and libraries to fit their specific needs. Accurate mass MS such as (TOF) mass analyzers are becoming a powerful screening and confirmation tool in forensic toxicology laboratories.

Acknowledgment The editors wish to acknowledge Dr. John Cody for prior contributions to the Mass Spectrometry chapter.

Further Reading

ANSI/ASB 098: Standard for Mass Spectral Data Acceptance in Forensic Toxicology.

ANSI/ASB 113: Standard for Identification Criteria in Forensic Toxicology.

Brittain R, Fiegel C (1994) Chemical ionization and MS-MS technologies for benchtop ion trap GC-MS systems. Am Lab 26:44–48

Colby JM, Thoren KL, Lynch LL (2018) Suspect screening using LC-Qq-TOF is a useful tool for detecting drugs in biological samples. J Anal Toxicol 42(4):207–213

Cole RB (ed) (1997) Electrospray ionization mass spectrometry fundamentals, instrumentation and applications. John Wiley, New York, 577 p

Dalsgaard PW, Rode AJ, Rasmussen BS, Bjork MK, Petersen DI, Madsen KA, Gammelgaard B, Simonsen KW, Linnet K (2013) Quantitative analysis of 30 drugs in whole blood by SPE and UHPLC-TOF-MS. Forensic Sci Criminol 1(1):1–7

De Hoffman E, Charette J, Stroobant V (1996) Mass spectrometry principles and applications. John Wiley, New York

Desiderio DM (ed) (1992) Mass spectrometry clinical and biomedical applications, vol 2. Plenum, New York, 269 p

Desiderio DM (ed) (1992) Mass spectrometry clinical and biomedical applications, vol 1. Plenum Press, New York, 353 p

Domin M, Cody R (2014) Ambient ionization mass spectrometry. Royal Society of Chemistry, Cambridge, UK

Habala L, Valentová J, Pechová I, Fuknová M, Devínsky F (2016) DART–LTQ ORBITRAP as an expedient tool for the identification of synthetic cannabinoids. Leg Med 20:27–31

Hoja H, Marquet P, Verneuil B, Lotfi H, Penicaut B, Lachatre G (1997) Applications of liquid chromatography-mass spectrometry in analytical toxicology: A review. J Anal Toxicol 21:116–126

Kitson FG, Larsen BS, McEwen CN (1996) Gas chromatography and mass spectrometry: A practical guide. Academic Press, New York, 381 p

Koppel C, Tenczer J (1995) Scope and limitations of a general unknown screening by gas chromatography-mass spectrometry in acute poisoning. J Am Soc Mass Spectrom 6:995–1003

Liu RH, Goldberger BA (eds) (1995) Handbook of workplace drug testing. AACC Press, Washington, DC, 380 p

Partridge E, Trobbiani S, Stockham P, Scott T, Kostakis C (2018) A validated method for the screening of 320 forensically significant compounds in blood by LC/QTOF, with simultaneous quantification of selected compounds. J Anal Toxicol 42(4):220–231

Pirro V, Jarmusch AK, Vincenti M, Cooks RG (2015) Direct drug analysis from oral fluid using medical swab touch spray mass spectrometry. Anal Chim Acta 861:47–54

Sparkman OD (1996) Evaluating electron ionization mass spectral library search results. J Am Soc Mass Spectrom 7:313–318

Thomson BA (1998) Atmospheric pressure ionization and liquid chromatography/mass spectrometry – together at last. J Am Soc Mass Spectrom 9:187–193

Wang H, Liu J, Cooks RG, Ouyang Z (2010) Paper spray for direct analysis of complex mixtures using mass spectrometry. Angewandte Chem 122(5):889–892

Quantitative Analytical Methods

15

Robert D. Johnson

Abstract

Quantitative analytical methods allow the forensic toxicologist to derive the amount of a xenobiotic present in a biological specimen. Quantitative analyses are frequently requested and commonplace in today's forensic toxicology laboratory. With proper development and implementation, numerous analytical methodologies are well-suited to provide quantitative data. These analytical techniques include but are not limited to gas chromatography (GC) and liquid chromatography (LC), which provide the chromatographic separation of chemical compounds, and are combined with numerous detector technologies including, most commonly, mass spectrometry (MS) for non-volatile compounds and flame ionization detectors (FID) for volatile organic compounds. Current mass spectrometry technology may allow for the quantitation of compounds without, in some cases, achieving chromatographic baseline resolution, which was once considered crucial. Rigorous method validation provides the analyst with confidence in the methodology being utilized to generate quantitative results, while on a day-to-day basis, the use of proper quality control ensures the accuracy of the obtained quantitative result.

Although quantitative results are generated by instrument software following the analysis of a series of samples, it is critical that the analyst within a laboratory understand how those results are obtained and have the ability to convey that understanding in court if required.

Keywords

Quantitative analysis · Forensic toxicology · Internal standards · Calibration · Reporting

Introduction to Quantitative Methods

It is often necessary to determine the amount of a specific compound, or numerous compounds, present within a biological specimen. This quantitative analysis of a specimen can be significantly more complicated than a simple qualitative analysis which only informs the toxicologist that a compound was either detected or not detected in the sample that was analyzed. Numerous factors must be considered when developing and utilizing a quantitative analytical method. Some of these factors include:

- Internal standard selection
- Calibration
- Method of standard additions
- Quality control

R. D. Johnson (✉)
Tarrant County Medical Examiner's Office,
Fort Worth, TX, USA
e-mail: rdjohnson@tarrantcounty.com

© Springer Nature Switzerland AG 2020
B. S. Levine, S. Kerrigan (eds.), *Principles of Forensic Toxicology*,
https://doi.org/10.1007/978-3-030-42917-1_15

- Limit of detection (LOD)
- Limit of quantitation (LOQ)
- Calibration range
- Accuracy
- Precision
- Reporting

Currently, the most common quantitative methodologies utilize a multipoint calibration curve prepared on the day of the analysis of the case specimen(s). However, this process may not be necessary in all cases and will be discussed in more detail. Regardless of the number of calibrators utilized or the frequency with which a calibration curve is prepared and analyzed, appropriate calibrator concentrations must be chosen based on the target analyte(s). For example, a calibration curve that spans a concentration range of 1 ng/mL to 100 ng/mL may not be appropriate for a high-dose drug that has a therapeutic concentration of 10,000 ng/mL. Since it isn't acceptable to report a quantitative value above the highest acceptable calibrator in a calibration curve, in the scenario described above, dilution, extraction, and reanalysis of case specimens that were positive for this compound would be frequently required. Prior to performing dilution and reanalysis of a sample, dilution integrity experiments would be a required part of the method validation process to demonstrate the accuracy and precision of this process. Appropriate quality control (QC) samples must be utilized. These QC samples would ideally span the range of the calibration curve and challenge the low, middle, and upper portion.

In any quantitative methodology, potential sources of variation and error should be considered. These sources may be dependent on the analytical instrumentation utilized and include analyte recovery, matrix effects, ion suppression/enhancement, carryover, interference, and compound stability. While possibly not affecting the reliability of the generated data, specimen integrity should also be considered. If a case specimen is designated as whole blood but is clear in appearance, it may in fact be plasma or serum and not whole blood. The quantitative method utilized may generate an accurate result for that specimen, but the interpretation of that result may depend on the specimen type from which it was obtained.

Obtaining Quantitative Analytical Results

Internal Standards

When the process of quantifying compounds extracted from case specimens began, numerous methods were utilized to determine the amount of the compound present in a sample. External standards, or standards of known purity and concentration, were once commonly analyzed for quantitation. A plot of the peak areas or peak heights obtained from the injection of the neat external standards was made versus concentration. A case specimen was processed, and the same volume was injected onto the instrument, and its peak area or peak height was compared to the known standards, and a quantitative amount was derived from that comparison of area or height. This method of quantitation relied heavily on the precise amount of substance injected onto the instrument. Since the area of a peak is proportional to the amount of that substance injected onto the instrument, variation in injection volume created error in the calibration curve and the subsequent quantitative result.

An internal standard is a compound that is added to samples prior to extraction and is subjected to the sample preparation steps as the analyte of interest. Ideally, an internal standard (1) is not expected to be normally present in the specimen being analyzed, (2) is close in chemical structure to the analyte of interest, (3) is stable, and (4) extracts from the specimen and elutes from the chromatographic column in a similar fashion as the analyte of interest. An internal standard is added to calibrators, QC samples, and case specimens. The amount of internal standard added is determined during method validation and may vary depending on the expected concentration of the analyte of interest; however, once that amount is determined, the same concentration is added to every sample that will be analyzed. When utilizing an internal standard, a response ratio is obtained by dividing the chromatographic area obtained from the analysis of the analyte by the chromatographic area obtained from the analysis of the internal standard. The response ratio is then plotted versus concentration to obtain a calibration curve. Once obtained, the calibration curve can then be utilized to quantify the amount of the analyte of interest in a case specimen by comparison of the response ratio obtained from the case specimen to the newly formed curve.

Utilizing an internal standard as opposed to an external standard is commonplace in the current forensic toxicology laboratory. Internal standards normalize the effects of some of the potential error in quantitative analytical methods discussed above. When deuterated analogues are employed as internal standards, sources of variation including analyte recovery, matrix effects, and ion suppression/enhancement are mitigated since the deuterated analogue reacts identically as the analyte of interest. As such, the response ratio is not affected by these factors. For this reason, deuterated analogues of analytes of interest are the internal standards of choice when they are available for purchase and not cost prohibitive.

Calibration

Just as the use of internal standards has evolved over time, so has the generation of calibration curves. Where calibration is concerned, there are several choices that a forensic toxicology laboratory must make. First, the laboratory must decide if a calibration curve will be run concurrently with every batch of case specimens analyzed or if a historic calibration curve will be utilized. The laboratory must then decide if a single-point or multipoint calibration curve will be created. Reference standards utilized to prepare calibrators should be purchased from a supplier who will certify the concentration of the material. Certified reference materials (CRMs) come with a certificate of analysis that describes the precise concentration of the standard and the uncertainty associated with that concentration. The use of CRMs also provides traceability back to the National Institute of Standards and Technology (NIST) standards.

For a single-point calibration, the response ratio of a single calibrator is plotted versus its concentration, and a line is created by forcing the curve through the origin. The generated curve is then utilized to determine the quantitative amount of an analyte of interest present in the case specimen. This method may introduce significant error in the obtained result. Any variation in the accuracy of that single calibrator is propagated to each unknown that the calibration curve is used to quantify. Error is also introduced by the inclusion of the origin as a calibration point as the origin is not the LOD for the analytical method.

Multipoint calibration curves provide inherently better quantitative data. The analysis of multiple calibrators spanning the calibration range of the instrument method, while not including the origin as a calibration point, is the soundest way to obtain quantitative results. In addition, the preparation and analysis of a new calibration curve concurrently with each batch of case specimens provides an additional level of certainty around the obtained analytical results. This practice eliminates the concern of day-to-day variations in analyte extraction and instrument operation that must be considered when comparing case samples to a calibration curve extracted and analyzed on a day in the past. As discussed in Chap. 16 (Method Validation), a minimum acceptable number of calibrators in a multipoint calibration model must be established. Five calibration points spanning the calibration range may be sufficient for a linear multipoint calibration curve. However, a non-linear model will require additional calibration points covering the calibration range due to the inherent stability and reproducibility issues associated with non-linear calibration curves.

Calibration Curve Fitting Methods

In a multipoint calibration model, a best-fit line must be utilized to generate the calibration curve. The line may be linear, where a least square linear regression is used to fit the calibration points, or quadratic, which utilizes a quadratic equation to fit a curved line. The calibration points may be weighted or unweighted. Weighting refers to the

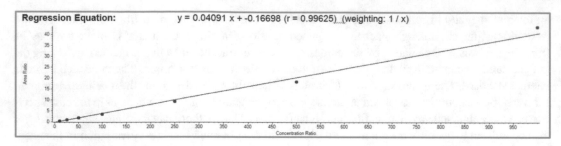

Fig. 15.1 An example of a linear, weighted (1/x) calibration curve

process of emphasizing the importance of certain calibration points in a calibration curve. Calibrators at high concentrations have more variation, so when each calibrator is equally weighted, those points tend to skew the calibration and bias it to the upper portion of the curve. Weighting linear calibration points by a factor of $1/x$ removes some of the bias at the high end of the curve and oftentimes provides better quantitative data. An example of a linear, weighted, calibration curve can be seen in Fig. 15.1.

In this example, the origin is not included as a point in the curve, and the calibration points are weighted by a factor of $1/x$ as discussed above. The equation for this linear plot can be seen in the figure and follows the $y = m(x) + b$ format utilized for all linear plots. The coefficient of linear correlation, or correlation coefficient, mathematically describes how well the calibration curve fits the calibration points that were plotted. A perfect fit with no variation would result in a r value equal to 1.00000. As can be seen in Fig. 15.1, the r value for this curve was 0.99625. The correlation coefficient can be calculated using the equation found in Fig. 15.2.

Calculation of the correlation coefficient is performed by instrument software on all modern instrument platforms. Depending on the manufacturer and the software package utilized, the correlation coefficient may be represented as r^2 or R^2, which is known as the coefficient of determination and also represents the fit of the calibration line to the calibration points. The coefficient of determination is calculated by squaring the correlation coefficient.

Laboratories must set acceptability limits for the correlation coefficient of a calibration curve.

$$r = \frac{\displaystyle\sum_{i=1}^{n} x_i\, y_i - \frac{1}{n}\sum_{i=1}^{n} x_i \sum_{i=1}^{n} y_i}{\sqrt{\displaystyle\sum_{i=1}^{n} x_i^2 - \frac{1}{n}\left(\sum_{i=1}^{n} x_i\right)^2}\sqrt{\displaystyle\sum_{i=1}^{n} y_i^2 - \frac{1}{n}\left(\sum_{i=1}^{n} y_i\right)^2}}$$

Fig. 15.2 An equation for the calculation of correlation coefficient

For some assays, a correlation coefficient of 0.98 may be acceptable, while in other analyses, a better curve fit of 0.99 may be required. In addition, laboratories must determine procedures for the dropping of a calibrator point. It isn't acceptable to drop a calibrator point that meets all identification and accuracy criteria simply to improve the fit of the line so that the correlation coefficient meets required specifications. However, it may be appropriate to drop the highest calibrator in a linear calibration curve if the mass spectrometric detector is saturated during the analysis of that point and it is no longer linear, referred to as a plateauing effect. Or it may be acceptable to drop the lowest calibrator in a calibration curve if the response on that day is below a predetermined threshold established during method validation.

Non-linear calibration curve fits, typically quadratic, are an additional option available for quantitative assays. This model is useful for sensitive mass spectrometric detectors that have a limited linear range or for assays where a larger quantitative range is beneficial. An example of a quadratic calibration curve can be seen in Fig. 15.3.

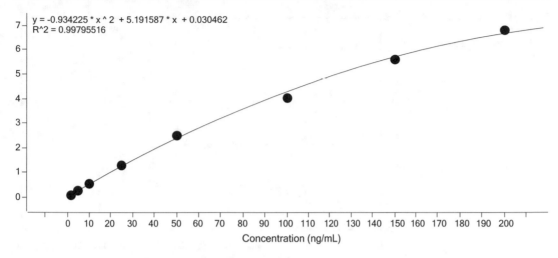

y = -0.934225 * x ^ 2 + 5.191587 * x + 0.030462
R^2 = 0.99795516

Fig. 15.3 An example of a quadratic calibration curve

As can be seen in Fig. 15.3, the linear range for this assay is very limited due to the high sensitivity of the mass analyzer. However, by using a quadratic fit, it is possible to obtain quantitative data without dilution, up to a concentration of 200 ng/mL. Choosing this calibration model expanded the useful concentration range for this assay by severalfold. Given that non-linear calibration models can be less predictable than linear models, additional calibrators may be required.

The choice of calibration model and calibrator weighting is determined through rigorous method validation. Residual plots can be useful in determining the appropriate calibration model and weighting factor. A residual is the difference between the value obtained following analysis and the target value. A residual plot is a graph that shows the residuals on the vertical axis and the target value on the horizontal axis. If the plot is random, a linear calibration model is appropriate. If the plot is u-shaped, a non-linear model may be better suited for the method. In a similar manner, larger residuals at higher concentrations indicate that weighting the calibration curve may be beneficial. Once each of these choices has been established during method validation and is found to be fit for the intended purpose, a calibration curve can be extracted, analyzed, and used to quantify analytes present in case specimens.

Method of Standard Additions

There are occasions in performing a quantitative analysis where the use of matrix-matched calibrators and controls is not practical. For example, in postmortem testing, the analysis of decomposed or embalmed specimens or the analysis of a very unusual specimen type may not lend itself to the either of the calibration methods discussed above. One way to alleviate this problem is through the use of the method of standard additions. In this method, a series of identical aliquots of the original specimen are placed in different tubes. Internal standard is then added to each tube. Increasing amounts of analyte are then added to each successive tube after the first, which is left unaltered and serves as the unknown. The samples are then analyzed, and the area ratios of the analyte to internal standard are calculated. A plot of area ratio versus concentration serves as the calibration curve. The curve is extended back until it crosses the x-axis, and this x-intercept gives the concentration of the analyte in the specimen. Note that the concentration on the x-axis will appear to be a negative number, and the absolute value of this number gives the concentration of analyte in the unknown. Assuming that detector response is linear within the range of concentrations being analyzed, the advantage of this method is that matrix effects are normalized because the same matrix is used for calibration and analysis. An example plot of a standard addition

Fig. 15.4 A graphical demonstration of the method of standard additions

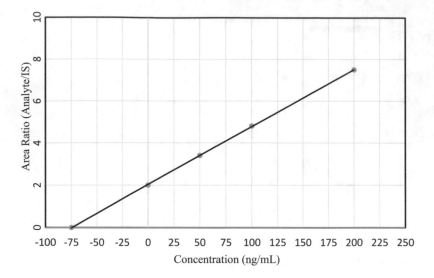

experiment can be seen in Fig. 15.4. In this figure, the result from the unaltered specimen can be seen plotted at a concentration added of zero, with successive standard additions. The concentration of the analyte in the unknown is found at the x-intercept, or 75 ng/mL.

Quality Control

Quality controls are samples that are extracted with a calibration curve to verify its accuracy and validity. The matrix chosen for the preparation of control samples is important. It is best practice to extract and analyze a control that represents each matrix type that will be quantified using either a linear or quadratic calibration model, regardless of the matrix validated for use when creating a calibration curve. This practice is relatively simple when whole blood, urine, or plasma/serum is being analyzed, but may not always be possible when esoteric tissues are being quantified in a postmortem laboratory as is discussed immediately above in the standard addition section of this chapter.

Quality control samples may contain the analyte of interest, a positive control, or consist of the calibration matrix without any added analyte of interest, a negative control. Both types of QCs are important and necessary to validate the analysis process. Negative control samples demonstrate that the matrix utilized for calibrator preparation was free of the analyte of interest. If possible, reference materials purchased for use as positive QCs should be obtained from a different manufacturer than those obtained to create calibrators. If that isn't possible, a different lot number from the same manufacturer should be utilized. The concentration of QC samples should be chosen to cover the quantitative range of the calibration curve, whether linear or quadratic. A minimum of three control concentrations are recommended so that the low, middle, and high portion of the calibration curve is challenged during each assay. For some assays, it may be beneficial to run more QC samples and space them evenly throughout the sequence.

Acceptance criteria for QC samples utilized in forensic toxicology laboratories are evolving. In the past, a set acceptability range of ± 20% from a target concentration was typical for all positive QC samples. Currently, the trend is to utilize a statistical evaluation of QC data and set the limits for acceptability at one, two, or three standard deviations from the mean. Ultimately, the acceptability of a QC sample is determined by laboratory policy, regardless of the criteria set. Laboratory policy also determines what steps are taken when a QC fails.

Analytical Considerations

Numerous analytical parameters are important when developing and utilizing a quantitative method in a forensic toxicology laboratory. Questions addressed by these parameters include:

- What is the lowest concentration the method can detect?
- What is the lowest concentration the method can quantify?
- What is the range of concentrations within which the method can quantify an analyte?
- How accurate is the method?
- How precise is the method?
- What reporting criteria will be used following the generation of a quantitative result?

Limits of Detection, Quantification, and Calibration Range

Limit of detection (LOD), limit of quantification (LOQ), and calibration range are analytical parameters determined during method validation. These parameters allow the toxicologist to confidently state the concentration of an analyte below which an analytical method cannot determine its presence, the concentration below which an analytical method cannot be used to quantify an analyte, and the range of concentrations within which analytes may be quantified if present in a biological specimen.

Limit of detection is typically defined as the lowest concentration of a compound that can be routinely detected by an analytical method. Certain criteria, e.g., Gaussian-shaped peak, retention time within 2% of the expected, signal-to-noise ratio > 3, and ion ratios within 20% of the expected, are utilized to define when a compound is or is not detected. The laboratory decides the specific criteria utilized for each individual methodology. Of note, however, there is not typically a concentration dependence associated with LOD. Limit of detection is determined during method validation through repeated analysis of specimens containing known concentrations of analyte at the lowest end of the methods' expected capability.

Limit of quantification is typically defined as the lowest concentration of a compound that can be quantified by an analytical method that both meets the criteria for LOD described above with two noted additions. First, the signal-to-noise ratio requirement is typically more stringent. Laboratories may choose to set the minimum signal-to-noise ratio for the LOQ at 10. Second, there is a concentration requirement that states the analyte of interest must be quantified at a concentration within a certain percentage of the target value, e.g., within 20%. Like LOD, the laboratory determines the specific criteria utilized for each individual methodology. When these requirements are met, the laboratory has determined the concentration, above which an analyte can be quantified and reported with an associated concentration.

Calibration range is defined as the concentration range within which a quantitative value can be confidently reported. This range is set by the calibration curve that is extracted and analyzed with case specimens. The calibration curve typically spans concentrations from the LOQ to the upper limit of linearity, where a least square linear regression is used to fit the calibration points as described above. Determined during method validation, this range establishes the concentration of an analyte that can be reported following analysis. Specimens containing analytes above the upper limit of this range must be diluted, reextracted, and reanalyzed. If the concentration found following analysis of the diluted sample is within the LDR, the concentration can be multiplied by the dilution factor and reported. If the calibration model utilized is quadratic, LDR is better described as a quantitative dynamic range and utilizes an upper limit of quantification (ULOQ) since the linear portion of the calibration curve may be small as in the example shown in Fig. 15.3.

Limit of detection, LOQ, and the calibration range may be matrix-dependent. For example, the analytical method for drug X may have an LOD of 10 ng/mL if whole blood is used as the matrix for the calibration curve and an LOD of 5 ng/mL if urine is utilized. The matrix chosen may even dictate the appropriate calibration model for the assay, i.e., linear versus quadratic.

Accuracy and Precision

Accuracy and precision are frequently demonstrated utilizing graphical representations like that seen in Fig. 15.5.

For the quantitative analytical methods utilized in a forensic toxicology laboratory, both of these factors are critically important. Generating quantitative data that is highly precise, but highly inaccurate, does a disservice to the customer.

Accuracy describes the closeness of a measurement to the true value. This concept may also be described as trueness. As depicted in Fig. 15.4, multiple quantitative analytical results can be accurate without necessarily being precise. Accuracy of a method is determined during method validation by repeated analysis of a specimen prepared at a specific concentration. The relative error between the average of the obtained results and the target concentration can be used as a tool to determine the accuracy of a quantitative method. It is often beneficial to analyze multiple controls at concentrations that span the calibration curve to determine if there is a higher degree of accuracy at low, medium, or high concentrations. The specifications for accuracy are determined by the laboratory and may differ by analysis type; however, if the mean of numerous measured concentrations is within ± 20% of a target value, the method may be considered sufficiently accurate for routine use.

Precision is defined as the degree to which repeated measurements, obtained when utilizing the same quantitative analytical method, produce the same results. As depicted in Fig. 15.4, multiple quantitative analytical results can be precise without being accurate. The precision of an analytical method is determined during method validation by repeated analysis of a specimen prepared at a specific concentration. The coefficient of variation (CV) calculated from the obtained results can be used as a tool to determine how precise a quantitative method is. It is often beneficial to analyze multiple controls at concentrations that span the calibration curve to determine if any imprecision present is concentration dependent. The specifications for precision are determined by the laboratory; however, if the CV from repeated measurements is less than 20%, the method may be considered sufficiently precise for routine use.

Reporting

When a quantitative value is obtained and the analytical results meet all requirements established during method validation, it is possible to report the results of the analysis to the customer. The reporting of quantitative analytical results can be accomplished in a variety of ways. If the obtained concentration is within the limits of an acceptable calibration curve, the identity of the substance and its associated concentration can be directly reported. This statement assumes that the compound, or an associated class of compounds, had been previously detected during a screening process, and the quantitative result is a confirmation of that positive screening test. If the concen-

Low Accuracy
High Precision

High Accuracy
High Precision

High Accuracy
Low Precision

Low Accuracy
Low Precision

Fig. 15.5 A graphical demonstration of accuracy and precision

tration of a compound is determined to be above the upper limit of the calibration curve, the specimen must be diluted and reanalyzed prior to reporting. An exception to this process may be made by laboratory policy, where compounds are reported as positive and greater than an upper concentration limit. Policies like this are particularly useful when reporting inactive drug metabolites that may be present at high concentrations and play no role in the interpretation of a case. Likewise, it may be possible based on laboratory policy to report compounds as positive and less than the lowest calibrator, provided that the concentration is above the established LOD for that compound.

It is important to note that all laboratory QA/QC requirements for the analysis must be met prior to the reporting of a quantitative result. If a specific criterion is not met, reanalysis of the specimen(s) in question may be necessary, or it may be possible to report the results qualitatively, without an associated concentration, based on laboratory policy. It is also important to consider the uncertainty of measurement (UM) when discussing the reporting of results. As discussed extensively in Chap. 17, UM is established for every quantitative analytical method during method validation. Reporting the UM for a specific compound may be dictated by statute or accreditation requirements, and it is critical that the laboratories have appropriate UM budgets for each compound that is quantified.

Conclusions

Quantitative analytical methods in the forensic toxicology laboratory are vital tools that are necessary for the thorough interpretation of a case. Whether analyzing specimens from human performance or postmortem toxicology casework, quantifying compounds from a blood specimen or other specimen types provides the toxicologist with the information necessary to appropriately interpret the toxicological results associated with a case. Qualitative results may be sufficient for specimen types that provide no interpretive value; however, when a blood specimen is available for analysis, determining the amount of a compound present in that sample is invaluable and well worth the time and effort necessary to validate an appropriate quantitative method.

Further Reading

ANSI/ASB 036: Standard Practices for Method Validation in Forensic Toxicology

Desharnais B, Camirand-Lemyre F, Mireault P, Skinner CD (2017) Procedure for the selection and validation of a calibration model I – description and application. J Anal Toxicol 41:261–268

ISO 5725-1:1994, Accuracy (trueness and precision) of measurement methods and results – Part 1. General principles and definitions

Peters FT, Maurer HH (2002) Bioanalytical method validation and its implications for forensic and clinical toxicology – A review. Accred Qual Assur 7:441–449

Scientific Working Group for Forensic Toxicology (SWGTOX): Standard Practices for Method Validation in Forensic Toxicology (2013) J Anal Toxicol 37:452–474

Method Validation

Justin M. Holler and Shawn P. Vorce

Abstract

Method validation is an important component of the quality assurance program in a forensic toxicology laboratory. The extent of validation that is required is based on the type of method being evaluated. A qualitative screening method requires less validation than a quantitative confirmation method. For example, all methods require at a minimum precision and accuracy studies, specificity studies, and carryover studies. Precision should be evaluated within a single batch and between batches. A quantitative method will also require determination of limit of detection, limit of quantitation, linearity range, selectivity, specimen stability, and extract stability. A method employing liquid chromatography-mass spectrometry or tandem mass spectrometry requires ion suppression or ion enhancement studies as well. Changes to the analytical method necessitate additional validation, the extent of which depends on the nature of the change.

Keywords

Validation · Forensic toxicology · Screening · Confirmation

J. M. Holler (✉) · S. P. Vorce
Chesapeake Toxicology Resources,
Frederick, MD, USA
e-mail: jholler@ctrlabs.com; svorce@ctrlabs.com

Method validation in forensic toxicology is a critical component to ensuring quality results. With increased media attention on the forensic disciplines, government entities identified the need for standards in forensic testing. Previously, the National Laboratory Certification Program in the Department of Health and Human Services drafted requirements for forensic toxicology testing performed under its jurisdiction. The Scientific Working Group for Forensic Toxicology (SWGTOX) also developed guidelines for method validation where the basis is ANSI/ASB 036 (Standard Practices for Method Validation in Forensic Toxicology). These documents outline the minimum requirements needed by a forensic toxicology laboratory for method validation to be acceptable. In the legal arena, method validation has become important to the overall credibility of results. The questions include general scientific acceptability, method precision and accuracy, and method reliability.

The challenge for most forensic toxicology laboratories is to decide what steps are needed to validate their methods while considering the time and expense in performing the validation. This becomes more critical as new technologies and methodologies are being implemented in laboratories such as liquid chromatography-tandem mass spectrometry (LC/MS/MS), time of flight (TOF), and direct injection analysis. The emergence of designer drugs also solidifies the importance of validating analytical procedures.

B. S. Levine, S. Kerrigan (eds.), *Principles of Forensic Toxicology*,
https://doi.org/10.1007/978-3-030-42917-1_16

Many of the drugs being detected and reported today have limited scientific literature associated with them; this in turn limits the peer-review process that accompanies published work.

The principle behind method validation is to demonstrate that the performance of the assay is scientifically acceptable within the parameters of its use. A method needs to work for the most pristine blood and tissue specimens as well as clotted blood specimens or decomposed tissues; it needs to work for urine specimens of all pH ranges. The validation batches need to be conducted in a manner consistent with how casework is analyzed. All testing aspects of the laboratory need to be validated including initial and confirmatory testing procedures. The level of validation will vary based on the type of method being evaluated. For example, an immunoassay screen requires less evaluation than a mass spectrometry (MS)-based screening method. More evaluation is required for a MS confirmation procedure involving drug extraction from a matrix followed by instrument evaluation. The more complex the testing procedure, the more validation that may be required to show the performance is scientifically acceptable.

In addition to the question of what validation is required, laboratories also must determine when validation is required. Clearly, a new method requires a full validation; however, changes in a method may not require a full validation. This would depend on the extent and significance of the modifications.

Method validation responsibility is part of the quality assurance (QA)/quality control (QC) programs in forensic laboratories. The two entities of QA and QC in the past have always been associated together; however, most laboratories today separate them into two areas. QA is responsible for ensuring a laboratory follows proper forensic procedures and is accurately reporting results. They oversee all aspects of the laboratory from the receipt of specimens to reporting results and litigation support. Proper method validation is essential to a QA program and a vital part of reporting legally defensible results. Chain of custody documentation is often the first line of attack in litigation cases but is often closely followed by

attacking the documentation for proper validation of methods used to produce results.

The following information provides laboratories an overview of what each validation step is and what is involved in those processes. Each laboratory is responsible for determining what policies will be implemented and what evaluations will be performed that will meet acceptability criteria for their respective governing bodies.

Terms and Definitions

An **analyte** is a chemical compound that is being measured or analyzed. The analyte is extracted from a **biological matrix** that is the specimen fluid or tissue such as blood, serum, urine, or liver. To accurately quantitate the drug, an **analytical reference standard** of known purity and molecular composition, often accompanied with a certificate of analysis (CoA), is required. From the analytical reference standard, a concentrated solution, the **analyte standard** is prepared. An **internal standard**, commonly a structurally related compound or deuterated analog of the analyte being measured, is also needed for accurate quantitation.

In addition to the case specimen, it is required to analyze a **blank sample**, an aliquot of the biological matrix match that contains no target analytes or internal standards. It is also necessary to analyze **positive controls** (specimen containing analyte at a known concentration used to verify calibration) and **negative controls** (specimen containing no analyte, used to verify the absence of interference with the analyte). **Interferences** are substances present in a specimen, matrix, or specimen preparation process that cause chromatography or quantitation problems with the target analyte.

From the analyte standard, a series of **calibrators** are prepared. The calibrator is a solution of known concentration prepared in the biological matrix that is used to establish the relationship between what is measured, the "response," and the analyte concentration. The **calibration model** is the mathematical model that shows a plot of response versus concentration generated by the analysis of multiple calibrators. It is often desirable to have a linear relationship between response and calibrator concentration. The linear range should include the concentrations expected in the different matrices. The linear relationship can be evaluated by calculating the line of regression by the method of least squares. The measure of the linear relationship between two variables is called the **correlation coefficient (r)**. The coefficient ranges between ±1, where +1 indicates a perfect positive linear relation between the two variables and −1 indicates a perfect negative linear relationship. A correlation coefficient of zero indicates a nonlinear relationship exists. The correlation coefficient is a useful indicator of the linearity within a certain concentration range and should be above 0.985 for an analytical method. In forensic toxicology, a minimally acceptable **coefficient of determination (r^2)** is required depending on the analytical technique. Typically, (r^2) must be greater than 0.980 for GC and LC/MS quantitative assays. The acceptance of calibration models that are nonlinear or weighted has become more prevalent. It is recommended that the simplest calibration model be adopted for the method evaluated.

Specific analyte concentrations within the calibration process must be defined during the validation process. The **limit of detection (LOD)** is the smallest amount of analyte, measured in relative concentration that can be detected with reasonable certainty for a given analytical procedure. For example, the LOD for a MS assay using a chromatographic separation must be within ±2% retention time and the ion ratios within ±20%, but the quantitative value may be outside ±20% of the target concentration. The **limit of quantitation (LOQ)** is the lowest concentration of analyte in a sample that can be measured with a defined precision and accuracy for a particular method. Using the above example, the LOQ must be within ±2% retention time, the ion ratios within ±20%, and the quantitative value within ±20% of the target concentration. The **upper limit of linearity (ULOL)** is the highest concentration of analyte in a sample that can be measured and identified. For the above example, the ULOL must be within ±2% retention time, the

ion ratios within ±20%, and the quantitative value within ±20% of the target concentration.

The **accuracy** of a method is defined as the closeness of the measured quantitative results to the actual value. The term accuracy is often interchanged with **bias** to define the measurement error of a method between a known value and the measured value. **Precision** is the measurement of agreement among test results when the method is applied repeatedly to multiple samplings of a homogeneous specimen. Repeatability is defined in two forms: intra-assay and inter-assay. **Intra-assay repeatability** is the measurement of the amount of agreement among test results when the method is applied repeatedly to multiple samplings of a homogeneous sample within the same batch. **Inter-assay repeatability** is the measurement of the amount of agreement among test results when the method is applied repeatedly to multiple samplings of a homogeneous sample between separate batches. The acceptability of these requirements is based on the **coefficient of variance (CV)**, which is defined as the measure of precision calculated by dividing the standard deviation for a series of measurements by the average measurement. The CV is also known as the percent relative standard deviation (% RSD).

There are other components of the analytical process that must be performed before a method is properly validated. **Selectivity** is the objective measurement of an analytical method to distinguish the analyte of interest from interfering components that may be expected in the sample matrices. These components commonly include metabolites, endogenous substances, breakdown products, and impurities. **Specificity** is the ability of the assay to identify an analyte from those compounds that are structurally related. This includes compounds in the same drug class or metabolites of the analyte of interest. The **robustness**, the ability of an assay to perform without failure over a wide range of conditions, must be evaluated to ensure consistent results are achieved. The **stability** of an analyte prior to extraction is a critical component and defined as the measure of an analyte's ability to remain unchanged under different storage conditions including matrix temperature and time. Another important factor to analyze is **carryover**, the measure of contamination from a previous specimen analysis to the following analysis. The amount of analyte recovered through extraction and analysis compared to the amount of the analyte measured unextracted is referred to as **recovery or extraction efficiency** of the assay. In addition to recovery for LC assays, ion suppression and enhancement must be measured as well. **Ion suppression** is a negative signal difference between the extracted blank matrix, the mobile phase, and the unextracted standard. **Ion enhancement** is the positive signal difference between the three variables. For LC analysis, a **system suitability check**, a feature used to ensure the complete testing system (LC, reagents, column, source) is operating in a sufficient manner for the intended application, is necessary.

Immunoassay Method Validation

Most forensic toxicology laboratories include immunoassays in their testing protocol. The most common types of immunoassay technologies are enzyme-linked immunosorbent assay (ELISA), cloned enzyme donor immunoassay (CEDIA), enzyme-multiplied immunoassay technique (EMIT), and kinetic interaction of microparticles in solution (KIMS). These are described in more detail in Chap. 13. The majority of the assays sold are FDA approved, and manufacturers have performed multiple parts of validation. However, laboratories should perform in-house validation of these assays as well. Any deviations from the manufacturer's guidelines, such as changes in matrix to be assayed, calibrator concentration, calibrator drug, or reagent volumes, must be validated prior to placement into service. If a laboratory purchases a new immunoassay analyzer, method validation for the analyzer is also required. Areas that need to be validated may include accuracy, precision, linearity, specificity, repeatability, and stability.

Accuracy and precision should be validated for all immunoassays being used in the laboratory. The most critical concentration range for immunoassays is around the cutoff as immunoas-

says are often employed to distinguish between positive and negative specimens. Other critical points to analyze are 0, 25, 50, 75, 100, 125, 150, and 200% of the cutoff concentration. It is recommended to analyze a minimum of three replicates at the aforementioned concentrations over five different batches; more replicates increase statistical power. Accuracy will be measured in relation to the theoretical concentrations, and precision will be measured by the coefficient of variation for both within and between runs. It is imperative for the assays to be both accurate and precise. Acceptability criteria for accuracy are minimally ±20%, but some laboratories will tighten the requirement to ±10%. Precision acceptability for CVs can vary widely between laboratories with a minimum requirement of ±5% up to ±20%. There should also be no observed overlap near the decision point when evaluating the 50 and 150% concentrations.

Repeatability will be used to measure the ability of the assay to produce the same results over time. Repeatability can be included with the precision and accuracy measurements. The assay needs to be tested both within day (intra-day) and between days (inter-day) to ensure the variability is acceptable. This may be accomplished by analyzing a minimum of three replicates per batch for a minimum of ten batches.

Linearity is certainly less important for immunoassay testing compared to confirmation analysis. Most immunoassay techniques do not possess a large linear range; the upper limits may reach 200–400% of the cutoff concentration. Although immunoassay testing is largely qualitative, it is still important to establish the linear range. This can be accomplished by analyzing, at a minimum, three replicates at each target concentration to obtain a least square linear regression model. Some laboratories use screening results to trigger automatic dilutions prior to extraction for confirmation. Most assays demonstrate a direct relationship between absorbance and concentration; however, KIMS displays an inverse relationship between absorbance and concentration. Immunoassays may also be used in a semiquantitative fashion using multiple point calibrations. Setting the calibrators to cover the linear range can allow for fairly accurate quantitations based on immunoassay testing. This can be used to trigger more accurate dilutions for confirmation testing.

Most manufacturers provide specificity information in the package inserts of their assays. However, in-house validation should be completed to verify this information; in addition, other drugs of interest that may appear frequently in a lab's casework should also be included. As mentioned previously, the primary purpose of immunoassay is to serve as a qualitative screening technique. One example of this was the emergence of dimethylamylamine (DMAA), as a weight loss supplement. DMAA is a simple aliphatic amine compound that cross-reacts with several amphetamine immunoassays. The military drug testing program saw a tremendous decrease in confirmation rates for amphetamines and was unable to determine the cause until an immunoassay vendor suggested that DMAA might be producing the positive immunoassay results to be the problem. This was subsequently verified by confirmatory testing for DMAA.

Specificity should be tested against structurally similar compounds, endogenous compounds, and common over-the-counter compounds. The increased use of monoclonal antibodies has improved the specificity of most immunoassays available. Concentrations tested for the structurally similar compounds should be pharmacologically realistic. The non-structurally similar compounds can be analyzed at much higher concentrations to show the effectiveness of the assay. If compounds are found to cross-react, then the trigger point concentration should be determined. Immunoassays for classes of drugs such as benzodiazepines use specificity to their advantage allowing a high range of cross-reactivity with multiple benzodiazepines. It is important to verify the concentration in which an analyte of interest will trigger a positive result; just as important is verifying the concentrations that cause positives for analytes you will not be monitoring.

Some kits allow for high sensitivity options which involve adding β-glucuronidase to a reagent to hydrolyze conjugated metabolites, thereby increasing the amount of drug capable of interacting with the antibody. The assays should be tested with and without the addition of β-glucuronidase with conjugated controls to validate the enzyme is working properly.

Stability of assays used should also be measured to reflect the time planned to be used at the laboratory. Most vendors provide some stability information with assays as short as 1 day and as long as 3 months. Laboratories should determine the expected time an assay will be used and verify the stability for this time period. Analysis of calibrators and controls over the period of time and comparing latter results with earlier results provides the user a good way to validate the stability of the assay.

Another important factor in the validation process is carryover. Carryover is more of a factor of instrumentation than the assay. To evaluate carryover, a specimen should be spiked at high concentrations and analyzed, followed by a blank specimen. The blank specimen will be compared to a true blank to see how much, if any, of the high specimen was carried over during analysis. One approach to address carryover has been adopted by the military drug testing program; for many years, the program implemented a second screening technique which consisted of positive screened specimens with blanks in between to verify carryover was not the cause of the initial positive result. New immunoassay analyzers have very little carryover due to improved washing techniques of sampling and reagent needles compared to older instrumentation. This step can also be used to ensure the hook effect does not occur with the assay as well. The hook effect occurs when the concentration is so high that the antigen overwhelms the antibodies and can reduce the response, therefore causing lower readings and sometimes false-negative results.

The final step in the validation of an immunoassay is the analysis of real specimens. The number of specimens analyzed should minimally be 25 positive and 25 negative specimens. The immunoassay results should be compared either to a reference immunoassay method if it is replacing an existing immunoassay or to a reference confirmation method. The specificity, sensitivity, and efficiency should be calculated. This is discussed in more detail in Chap. 13. The importance of sensitivity versus specificity is a function of the use of the desired assay. If specific drugs within a class are targeted, then fewer false-positive results are desired. If the immunoassay is used as part of a more comprehensive drug testing panel, then fewer false negatives are preferred.

Chromatographic Method Validations

Confirmation methods used to quantitate results in forensic toxicology require more extensive method validation than immunoassay and other screening techniques. The process of developing methods will be briefly discussed in this section as it is so closely linked to validation of the final method. The results from these methods could be used in criminal or civil litigation; therefore, the generation of reliable and defensible results is imperative. Validation is necessary no matter what type of confirmation method is used. Liquid chromatography (LC) methods will require some additional validation steps compared to gas chromatography (GC); similarly, mass spectrometry (MS) requires additional validation steps than other detection systems. The remainder of this section will use MS as the detector, since it requires more validation work than more general detectors.

Obviously, before a method can be validated, it must first be developed. Development of methods using MS starts by analyzing full-scan unextracted standards to determine what ions to monitor or by infusing standards into a MS/MS to determine transitions to be monitored as well as the collision energy and other source parameters. In most cases, extraction procedures need to be developed to allow efficient removal of the analyte or analytes from the biological matrix with minimal matrix interferences. Then separation techniques need to be established to allow detection of the drug without interference from co-extracted substances. This is an extremely simplistic view of method development, but all of these items are part of validating a method. The

necessary validation requirements will not be met if the development of the method is inadequate.

After completing the initial steps of development, a good starting point for validation is selectivity; this allows the analyst to determine if there are any matrix interferences present. Obviously more matrix sources increase the confidence that the method is free from interference. Minimally, six different sources of the matrix should be used for this experiment. They should be analyzed with and without the internal standard to be used. The analysis of the matrix without internal standard will determine if there is interference from the matrix. Analysis with the internal standard will allow the analyst to determine if the internal standard is free from structural interferences. When using a deuterated or isotopically labeled analog as an internal standard, it is important to note that many of these analogs are contaminated to some extent with the non-deuterated compound. Additionally, the analyte(s) should be evaluated at the high end of the expected concentration range without internal standard to evaluate if any deuterated analog is observed. If an endogenous interference is detected, then it must be resolved by either modification to the extraction procedure or through the separation technique. Some guidelines suggest for postmortem laboratories that each different source of blood must be validated. The practicality of this for most postmortem laboratories is unrealistic. However, if possible, laboratories should make an attempt to at least analyze as many different sources as they can.

The specificity of a method may be the most important factor to be assessed during validation. As stated earlier, specificity is the ability to identify an analyte from those compounds that are structurally similar, either a drug metabolite, another member of the drug class, or other structural analogs. To assess specificity, the matrix should be analyzed with and without analyte in the presence of potentially interfering compounds. Ideally the drug should be spiked at the limit of quantitation of the assay since this is the minimal concentration for accurate quantitation. The tough question is determining what compounds to use for the interference studies. Every method should be analyzed using common over-the-counter drugs and common drugs of abuse with their metabolites. Additionally, structurally similar compounds for the drug of interest should be analyzed as well. If a laboratory is located in a region where use of a certain drug or drug class is prevalent, this also should be analyzed for potential interference. The concentrations of the potentially interfering compounds to be evaluated vary. Some recommend 5 mg/L across the board regardless of therapeutic concentrations. Each laboratory should assess the concentration based on historical information of concentrations seen at their laboratory. In either case, if interferences are discovered during the selectivity or specificity experiments, more method development would be required, necessitating a new method validation process.

The linearity of the assay is another critical part of validation as it establishes the range in which accurate quantitation can be achieved. Prepare a calibration curve, and then spike a minimum of three concentrations below the lowest level of the curve and analyze in duplicate. The lowest concentration at which the established ion ratios are acceptable but quantitation is outside 20% is the limit of detection (LOD). The lowest concentration at which both the ion ratios and the quantitation are acceptable is the limit of quantitation of the assay (LOQ). Repeat this procedure for the upper end of the calibration curve to determine the upper limit of linearity. The highest concentration in which both the ion ratios and the quantitation are within 20% of the target is the upper limit of linearity (ULOL). Several factors can be changed to adjust if the desired quantitation range is not achieved. The sample volume can be adjusted, reconstitution volume can be changed, and injection volume and split ratios can also be changed to achieve the desired linearity range. However, these changes may affect LOD and/or LOQ. The laboratory must decide the critical points in which the linear range should cover. A laboratory could also administratively assign the LOD/LOQ/ULOL of an assay if they have concentrations that meet acceptability requirements and do not want to attempt to extend

the range. If they are assigned administratively, they must also meet all acceptability requirements for chromatography as if they were established experimentally. The evaluation of linearity also included establishing the calibration model to be used for the assay. The model selected (linear, weighted linear, quadratic) will be used throughout validation and in daily casework batches. Once the calibration model is established, it should not be changed to compensate for other variations during batches such as extraction efficiency or instrument variability.

The accuracy (bias) and precision of the method are necessary factors included in validation. The assay needs to be validated for both within-day and between-day acceptability. Accuracy and precision can be analyzed concurrently during validation. Minimally, the laboratory should prepare three controls in the desired matrix that cover the concentration range of the assay. The controls should be prepared from a different source than the calibrators; if a second source is unavailable, then controls should be prepared from a separate standard solution. These controls will then be analyzed over a number of batches to determine the accuracy and precision of the method. Each laboratory will need to determine the minimum number of batches they deem acceptable; ideally it would be at least five batches. The results of the three controls prepared will be used to determine the accuracy and precision of the method. Acceptability criteria should minimally be a CV less than 20 percent for precision. Accuracy should at least be within 20% of the expected result. In addition to this inter-assay statistical determination, the laboratory should also determine intra-assay variation. The three controls minimally should be analyzed five times within the batch and have less than 20 percent variation. The accuracy and precision studies will allow a laboratory to show the method's ability to reproduce results which is critical in forensic toxicology.

Carryover needs to be assessed for confirmation methods as is done with immunoassays. Some laboratories analyze a solvent in between case specimens to address carryover, but determining an experimental level can prove beneficial. Analysis of a high concentrated control followed by an extracted blank will determine what concentration carryover is observed. The analyst can adjust instrument factors to address carryover by adding more needle washes to the method or changing the wash solvent for LC analysis.

Matrix effects are a major concern for all LC/MS and LC/MS/MS techniques and must be assessed during method validation. Coeluting substances from the matrix can suppress the analyte signal, resulting in ion suppression. If not remediated during method development, matrix effects can result in quantitative bias. Ion enhancement is also possible but is less frequently encountered. These effects can vary greatly between samples and between different matrices such as blood and urine. The interferences can come from the sample matrices, the extraction procedure, the solvents, the mobile phase, and even the glassware or plastic tubes used in the extraction procedure. Other factors relating to the chemical properties of the analytes, such as mass, alkalinity, and concentration, can also contribute to ion suppression. The degree of suppression or enhancement can negatively affect LOD and the precision and accuracy of quantitative results.

Matrix effects (ME) are typically evaluated using post-column infusion and post-extraction addition techniques. Post-column infusion is a dynamic approach that allows ion suppression or enhancement to be assessed during the entire chromatographic run. It is particularly useful during method development. Continuous infusion of the analyte into the source while simultaneously injecting blank (drug-free) matrix allows regions of ion suppression or enhancement to be identified. Chromatographic separations can be optimized as a result. In contrast, post-extraction addition is a static technique, in the sense that it allows the matrix effect to be numerically determined at the retention time of interest. Matrix effects and extraction efficiency studies can be performed simultaneously. Signal intensities of analyte fortified into drug-free matrix are compared with those fortified in mobile phase for

ME. Extraction efficiency can be determined in a similar fashion by comparing signal intensity in extracts with analyte fortified into matrix post-extraction. Minimally, matrix effects should be determined at low and high concentrations, depending on the calibration range of the assay. Ion suppression can be minimized and/or accounted for by additional sample preparation, use of stable isotope-labeled internal standards, mobile phase selection, source conditions, and LC optimization.

Ion suppression experiments only measure the effects of negative matrices used in that particular laboratory. Laboratories should evaluate at a minimum ten different matrix sources. Authentic specimens are always different, and true matrix effects and variations associated with real specimens can never be measured in practical applications, only minimized through thorough method validation. This is an important fact to consider if direct injection or dilute and shoot methods are to be used.

If a laboratory routinely performs dilutions on the assay, then dilution integrity should be evaluated during validation. Dilutions may be required if sample volume is low or if concentrations are outside the acceptable limits of the assay. The evaluation of dilution integrity is by repeating accuracy and precision studies with common dilution ratios used in casework.

Analyte stability must also be evaluated during method validation. Stability can be affected by multiple variables to include storage conditions and sample handling. Areas that should be evaluated include processed sample stability and storage stability. Processed sample stability should be catered to each laboratory's standard practices. For example, if a laboratory will analyze a batch on Friday night and not process until Monday, the processed sample stability should be measured for at least 72 h. Additionally, if a sample is extracted but cannot be analyzed immediately, this time should also be evaluated for stability. Sample handling stability should include storage conditions such as samples stored for 90 days should be evaluated to ensure the analyte(s) are stable for this time period. The last stability that should be evaluated is freeze/thaw for each analyte. This should be determined by each laboratory depending on their internal procedures. It is recommended that a minimum of three freeze/thaw cycles be evaluated.

Another factor in validation of LC methods is developing a system suitability check. A system suitability test is an analysis designed to ensure that the complete analytical testing system (i.e., LC, reagents, columns, software, source, and the mass spectrometer) is operating adequately for the intended application. Regardless of whether a LC/MS/MS instrument has an automated autotune or checktune feature, a system suitability test should be performed on a daily basis. Many manufacturers do not have a built-in autotune feature that many in forensic toxicology are accustomed to with GC/MS analysis. Therefore, there is no record of instrument performance if a system suitability test is not used.

Typically, a system suitability test is analyzed before a batch is started. However, to ensure the system is operating correctly throughout the entire batch, system suitability tests can be analyzed throughout the analysis. System suitability samples should consist of compounds that are the same, structurally similar, or in the same class as the compounds being analyzed in the assay. The compounds should cover the entire retention time and mass range of the analytes of interest. Parameters that can be monitored include MRM transitions, retention time, peak area counts, peak widths at half height, and chromatography parameters such as peak resolution and capacity factor. Historical values should be established, recorded, and monitored over time to determine if any system degradation has occurred. For instance, a shift in retention times can indicate an incorrect or contaminated mobile phase. It could also be an indication of column degradation. A dramatic decrease in the area counts can indicate a dirty source, and missing peaks could indicate the instrument needs a mass calibration. Experiments during method development are used to define system suitability acceptance limits, and guidance should be provided when those limits are exceeded.

One decision left to the discretion of the laboratory is when and to what extent is a method validation required. At a minimum, a full validation is required when a new method is developed. If a change is made to instrumentation such as a new model GC/MS, an instrument validation should be completed. This should include side-by-side comparison of at least three batches of authentic specimens as well as re-establishing the linearity and sensitivity of the method. The extent of the re-validation will depend on the magnitude of the changes. If the method changes from GC to LC, then a more in-depth validation should be performed. This should include side-by-side comparison of authentic specimen batches, linearity, matrix effects, specificity, and ion suppression. The necessity of the expanded validation due to instrument change is because of the impact LC can have on an analyte. The ionization technique used is very different than GC/MS which requires the matrix effects, specificity, and ion suppression to be validated. The separation technique can lead to drugs that did not interfere by GC to be problematic with LC.

Changes made to the extraction will also require some re-validation of a confirmation method. For example, if a laboratory chooses to switch from a liquid/liquid extraction to a solid-phase extraction, they will need to analyze side-by-side batches, matrix effects, specificity, linearity, ion suppression (if LC), and recovery. If the method change is washing a column with a different buffer to enhance the clean-up process, it may require only specificity and recovery to be validated.

Mass Spectrometry Screening Method Validation

Mass spectrometry screening methods are becoming more popular as advancement in the technology of multiple quadrupole systems allows their applications to be more efficient, specific, sensitive, and practical. They are emerging as a viable replacement for immunoassays that cannot adapt fast enough to the ever-changing world of designer drugs. MS screening methods can utilize a variety of techniques for analysis such as MRM transition screen with or without LC separation and high-resolution time-of-flight (TOF) MS, capable of identifying a compound using exact mass calculations. Regardless of the technique, method validation is required to ensure the method will be reliable and accurate for the intended application. For screening procedures, the validation emphasis should be on the detection of the compounds of interests. There should be extensive specificity and selectivity experiments to ensure no compounds could interfere with the assay. Numerous negative controls for each matrix used in the assay should be investigated for possible interference and matrix effects. Recovery experiments should be performed, if the method involves LC introduction or separation, and matrix effect also needs to be addressed. Cutoffs can be established administratively or experimentally, and thus the limit of detection (LOD) must be determined and criteria for positive identification established. If a semi-quantitative method is being developed, then intra-day and inter-day precision studies need to be performed. These experiments should cover at least three separate concentrations over the proposed concentration range. Upper limits of detection can also be determined if necessary for the specific application. Carryover also needs to be evaluated to determine if and when washes are needed in a batch.

Summary

Method validation is a necessity in forensic toxicology laboratories. Governing bodies are providing guidelines for requirements of method validations but can vary greatly. Each laboratory is responsible for determining what is required for their validation based on their certifications, casework, workload, and budget. This chapter should provide laboratories with a template of what is needed based on the analysis being performed.

Appendix: Typical Method Validation Protocol

Experiments	Requirements
Selectivity	10 negatives of each matrices with ISTD
	10 negatives of each matrices without ISTD
Specificity	10 negatives of each matrices with Interference Standards
	10 negatives of each matrices with Interference Standards and LOQs
Linearity	Minimun of 6 calibration points over 10 batches
LOD	3 LOD/LOQ samples over three batches
LOQ	3 concentrations in triplicate (LOD/LOQ)
ULOL	3 concentrations in triplicate above highest calibrator over 3 batches
Accuracy	3 concentrations in triplicate over 5 batches
Precision	3 concentrations in triplicate over 5 batches
Matrix Effects	2 UNEXTRACTED concentrations injected 6 times each
	2 POST_EXT concentrations injected 6 times each
Recovery	2 UNEXTRACTED concentrations injected 6 times each
	2 EXTRACTED concentrations injected 6 times each
Carryover	Analyze ULOL, 2xULOL, 5xULOL, 10xULOL, 10xULOL, 10xULOL
SSC	20 injections to establish historical values
Dilution integrity	Repeat Accuracy or Precision studies @ 1:2, 1:5, 1:10
Robustness	Variation in extraction, pH, injection amount, etc.
Stability	Room Temp—Calibration curve and two controls in triplicate over 0 h, 24 h, 48 h, etc. (as needed)
	Refrigerator—Calibration curve and two controls in triplicate over 0 h, 24 h, 48 h, etc. (as needed)
	Freezer—Calibration curve and two controls in triplicate over 0 h, 24 h, 48 h, etc. (as needed)

Further Reading

ANSI/ASB 036: Standard Practices for Method Validation in Forensic Toxicology

Guidance for Industry, Bioanalytical Methods Validation. Center for Drug Evaluation and Research, USDA, May, 2003

Manual for Urine Laboratories. National Laboratory Certification Program (NLCP). October 2010

National Committee on Clinical Laboratory Standards (NCCLS). Gas Chromatography/Mass Spectrometry (GC/MS) Confirmation of Drugs; Proposed Guidelines. NCCLS document C43-P (ISBN 1-56238-403-1). Vol. 20(9). NCCLS, Wayne, PA, 2000

(2013) Scientific Working Group for Forensic Toxicology (SWGTOX) Standard Practices for Method Validation in Forensic Toxicology. Journal of Analytical Toxicology 37:452–474

SOFT/AAFS. Forensic Toxicology Laboratory Guidelines. Society of Forensic Toxicologist and American Academy of Forensic Sciences, Toxicology Section.

Swartz M, Krull I (2003) Validation of bioanalytical methods – Highlights of FDA's guidance. LCGC North America 21(2)

Metrological Traceability and Measurement Uncertainty

17

Laurel Farrell and Tate Yeatman

Abstract

This chapter reviews the history of measurement science, providing the foundation for the international system of measurement in place today. Information is provided on the most common paths to establish metrological traceability of forensic toxicology quantitative test results and for a general framework to evaluate the measurement uncertainty of any forensic toxicology measurement process.

Keywords

Measurement · Metrological traceability · Measurement uncertainty · Toxicology

Measurement Science

History

Metrology can be defined in very broad terms as the science of measurement; however, any

L. Farrell
ANSI National Accreditation Board, Cary, NC, USA
e-mail: lfarrell@anab.org

T. Yeatman (✉)
Palm Beach County Sheriff's Office Crime Laboratory, West Palm Beach, FL, USA
e-mail: yeatmand@pbso.org

measurement obtained is meaningless without standardization. An understanding of the history of metrology provides valuable context to the field of metrology in its current form. The first standard of measurement can be traced back to approximately 2900 BC and the royal Egyptian cubit. The Egyptian cubit was carved from black granite and defined to be the length of the Pharaoh's forearm plus the width of his hand. Replicas of this standard were given to the builders of the pyramids solidifying the cubit as the first measurement standard. Many civilizations, including the Romans and Greeks, also developed measurement standards that were generally accepted and became an integral part of their development as a civilization.

In its modern form, metrology has roots in the French Revolution when France wished to harmonize units of measurement and proposed a length standard based on a natural source. In 1791 the meter was defined, leading to the creation of the decimal-based metric system by 1795. During the period from 1795 to 1875, several countries adopted the metric system ultimately leading up to the Metre Convention which established an international measurement infrastructure through the establishment of three international organizations tasked with maintaining and standardizing metrology, a responsibility still entrusted to them today.

International Infrastructure

The three international organizations established were the General Conference on Weights and Measures (French: *Conférence générale des poids et mesures* or CGPM); the International Committee for Weights and Measures (French: *Comité international des poids et mesures* or CIPM); and the International Bureau of Weights and Measures (French: *Bureau International des Poids et Mesures* or BIPM).

The CIPM is made up of 18 individuals from a member state with high scientific standing which is nominated by the CGPM as advisors on administrative and technical matters. The BIPM oversees international definitions and agreements regarding units of measurements. The principal decision-making body is the CGPM consisting of delegates from member states and non-voting observers from associate states. Meetings are held every 4 to 6 years to receive the CIPM report and endorse developments in the International System of Units (SI) with advisement by the CIPM.

Other international organizations involved with maintaining and standardizing metrology include the International Organization of Legal Metrology (French: *Organisation Internationale de Métrologie Légale* or OIML); the Joint Committee for Guides in Metrology (JCGM); and the International Laboratory Accreditation Cooperation (ILAC).

OIML is an intergovernmental organization which promotes the harmonization of legal metrology procedures that facilitate international trade. OIML publishes recommendations for regulations establishing metrological characteristics and conformity of measuring instruments, informative documents harmonizing legal metrology, and guidelines for the application of legal metrology.

JCGM is a BIPM committee created from a collaboration of eight partner organizations to maintain and promote two metrology guides: *Guide to the expression of uncertainty in measurement* (GUM) and the *International vocabulary of metrology – Basic and general concepts and associated terms* (VIM). These documents originally published by ISO, the International Organization for Standardization, are now published in the name of all JCGM member organizations (BIPM, International Electrochemical Commission (IEC), International Federation of Clinical Chemistry and Laboratory Medicine (IFCC), ISO, IUPAC, International Union of Pure and Applied Physics (IUPAP), and OIML).

ILAC is an international organization that standardizes practices for the accreditation of conformity assessment bodies providing testing and calibration services and supports development of accreditation systems in developing countries.

National Infrastructure

Each country's measurement infrastructure is implemented and maintained by a network of testing laboratories, calibration laboratories, and accreditation bodies which makes up that country's national measurement system. The collective effort ensures the accuracy, comparability, consistency, and reliability of measurements made in that country.

The role of the national metrology institute (NMI) in a country's national measurement system is to conduct scientific research in the development of new measurement methods and, through calibration of equipment or manufacturing of certified reference material, provide traceability to international standards. Examples of centralized metrology organizations include the National Institute of Standards and Technology (NIST) in the United States and the National Research Council (NRC) in Canada. Some countries do not have a centralized metrology institute but have several designated institutes specializing in specific national standards. Such institutes operate in accordance with the metrological plan for a specific subject field and the metrological policy of the country. For a country's national measurement system to be recognized internationally by the CIPM Mutual Recognition Agreement (CIPM MRA), an NMI must participate in international comparisons of its measurement capabilities. Measurements made in member countries of the CIPM Mutual Recognition Agreement (CIPM MRA), an agreement of national metrology institutes (NMI), are recognized by other member countries and are maintained in a database by the BIPM.

Metrological Traceability

Global definitions and agreements regarding units of measurement provide the critical foundation to measurement science. Metrological traceability, as defined by the International Vocabulary of Metrology (VIM), is a "property of a measurement result whereby the result can be related to a reference through a documented, unbroken chain of calibrations, each contributing to the measurement uncertainty."

The "reference" referred to in this VIM definition is the International System of Units (SI), overseen by the BIPM. Today, the SI is made up of seven base units of length, mass, time, electric current, temperature, luminous intensity, and amount of a substance. Table 17.1 provides each SI base quantity, base unit, and symbol.

As of May 20, 2019, all SI base units are defined by fixed numerical values of seven defining constants (Table 17.2) providing a fundamen-

tal, universal reference that allows for continued advancement in measurement science.

Measurements in forensic toxicology are not made in a SI base quantity measurement unit but instead are made by use of a SI derived unit, a SI prefix, and unit conversion. SI derived units are obtained by combining base units and other derived units algebraically such as m^3 for volume. SI prefixes are measurements made in factors of 10 of base units such as milli- or micro-. Conversion is the process of multiplication or division by a numerical factor, selecting the correct number of significant digits, and proper rounding. Use of SI derived units, SI prefixes, and conversion is apparent in common units of measurement utilized in forensic toxicology such as mg/L or ng/mL.

A measurement made in a forensic toxicology laboratory can be related to the SI by an "unbroken chain of calibrations." The approach to establishing metrological traceability for a measurement in forensic toxicology is primarily through the calibrator(s) used and their preparation. Additionally, if the test method includes one or more measurements that affect the validity of the reported results, it will be important to also establish metrological traceability for those measurements.

Use of a control with established metrological traceability does not establish the metrological traceability of the test result, but the reference value of the control does allow the laboratory to evaluate both precision and bias performance of the test method.

Generally, calibrator preparation can be broken into two pathways:

Table 17.1 International System of Units (SI) base units

SI base quantity	Base unit	Symbol
Time	Second	s
Length	Meter	m
Mass	Kilogram	kg
Electric current	Ampere	A
Thermodynamic temperature	Kelvin	K
Amount of substance	Mole	mol
Luminous intensity	Candela	cd

Table 17.2 International System of Units (SI) defined constants

Defining constant	Symbol	Numerical value	Unit
Hyperfine transition frequency of Cs	$\Delta\nu_{Cs}$	9,192,631,770	Hz
Speed of light in vacuum	C	299,792,458	m s^{-1}
Planck constant	H	$6.62607015 \times 10^{-34}$	J s
Elementary charge	e	$1.602176634 \times 10^{-19}$	C
Boltzmann constant	k	1.380649×10^{-23}	J K^{-1}
Avogadro constant	N_A	$6.02214076 \times 10^{23}$	mol^{-1}
Luminous efficacy	Kcd	683	lm W^{-1}

- Prepared by multiple measurements
  - Weight to Weight
    Weight of reference material (RM) diluted with a Weight of solvent
  - Weight to Volume
    Weight of RM diluted with a Volume of solvent
  - Volume to Volume
    Volume of RM diluted with a Volume of solvent
- No preparation – certified reference material (CRM) used without dilution

The unbroken chain of calibrations, often referred to as the calibration hierarchy, that ties a measurement made by a piece of equipment (e.g., balance, pipette, or volumetric flask) in a forensic toxicology laboratory to the SI is depicted generally in Fig. 17.1. The calibration hierarchy in Fig. 17.2 has added specifics for a weight measurement.

The calibration hierarchy for a pipette or volumetric flask will look the same with the forensic

toxicology laboratory having the equipment calibrated by an appropriately accredited calibration laboratory.

Of note, the number of calibrations in this hierarchy can be increased or decreased. Levels are added or subtracted through the choice of the accredited calibration laboratory used to calibrate the equipment used by the forensic service provider. Adding or subtracting levels in the calibration hierarchy has no impact on the establishment of metrological traceability. The impact of more levels is seen in evaluating measurement uncertainty as adding levels in this hierarchy increases the measurement uncertainty in the measurement made in the forensic laboratory.

The calibration hierarchy when establishing metrological traceability using a CRM (Fig. 17.3) is very similar as the accredited reference material producer (RMP) will establish the metrological traceability of the product that you purchase in the same way.

If a forensic toxicology laboratory chooses an appropriate calibration from an appropriate

Fig. 17.1 General calibration hierarchy to establish metrological traceability

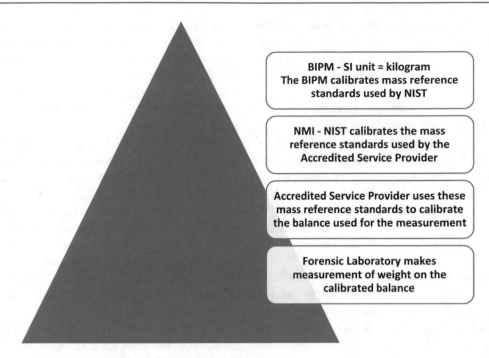

Fig. 17.2 Calibration hierarchy to establish metrological traceability for a weight measurement

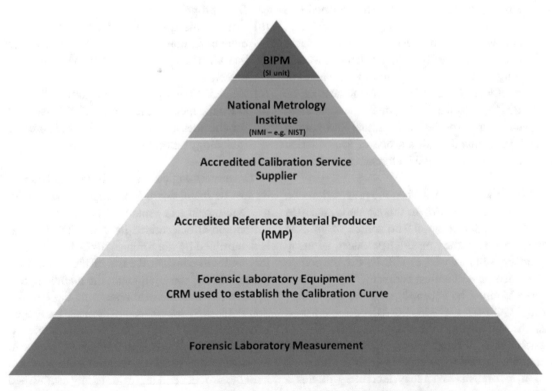

Fig. 17.3 Calibration hierarchy to establish metrological traceability using a CRM as a calibrator

calibration service provider, the upper levels of the hierarchy are deemed to be in place, and documentation by the forensic toxicology laboratory of each level in the hierarchy is not needed.

A supplier of calibration services or certified reference material must be competent. Using an NMI or an appropriately accredited supplier ensures that their competence and establishment of metrological traceability for services and products provided has already been evaluated and therefore does not need to be independently evaluated by the forensic toxicology laboratory. An appropriate service provider is either:

(a) A national metrology institute (NMI) that is a signatory to the BIPM-CIPM Mutual Recognition Arrangement with the calibration or the certified reference material listed in Appendix C of the BIPM key comparison database (KCDB), or

(b) A service supplier accredited to ISO/IEC 17025 by an accrediting body that is a signatory to the ILAC Mutual Recognition Arrangement, with the calibration listed in a scope of accreditation, or

(c) An accredited reference material producer that is accredited to ISO 17034, by an accrediting body that is a signatory to a mutual or multilateral recognition arrangement in an ILAC-recognized regional accreditation cooperation or the ILAC Mutual Recognition Arrangement, with a scope of accreditation covering the certified reference material.

There will be times when the preparation of a calibrator uses a RM. In this scenario, the RM must be fit-for-purpose. The source of the RM may be a reference material producer, as many produce RMs as well as CRMs, but the source may also be a chemical company. The purity of the RM must be acceptable for the technology (e.g., GC-FID, GC-MS, LC-MS-MS, etc.) used in the test method. Metrological traceability is established through appropriately calibrated equipment used to prepare the calibrator(s).

If a forensic toxicology laboratory dilutes a CRM to produce a concentration other than that provided, the accredited reference material producer will no longer stand behind the certified reference value. The CRM becomes an RM that is fit for purpose, and metrological traceability is established through appropriately calibrated equipment used in the preparation of the calibrator(s).

From a practical standpoint, the laboratory can reduce the volume of equipment requiring calibration if they identify the small set equipment needed only for the preparation of calibrators. Calibrator storage is separate and can be done in any appropriate vessel. A laboratory can also evaluate efficiency versus cost when determining the path for calibrator preparation. Each laboratory may come to a different decision regarding use of CRMs with no dilution versus use of an RM and associated calibrated equipment.

By utilizing calibrators that have metrological traceability, the forensic toxicology laboratory has established the calibration hierarchy up to the measurement made in the laboratory. The test method used must:

(a) Be appropriate,

(b) Specify the quantity to be measured (e.g., ethanol in antemortem blood by headspace gas chromatography with flame ionization detector),

(c) Be performed by competent staff, and

(d) Have the measurement uncertainty evaluated for the measurement made by the forensic toxicology laboratory.

Once metrological traceability is established, it must be maintained. Metrological traceability of equipment is maintained through recalibration at determined intervals. The interval is determined by the forensic toxicology laboratory and will consider the use of the equipment, the stability of the equipment, the method specifications, if intermediate checks of the calibration status are performed, and any risk associated with a failed calibration. Metrological traceability of a CRM is maintained through adherence to the storage and handling requirements provided with the product and use prior to any established expiration date.

Measurement Uncertainty

The concept of measurement uncertainty is based on the idea that when a measurement is repeated, even using the same measurement process, a different value may be obtained each time if the measuring system being used is sensitive enough. This variation in the value obtained each time a measurement is taken is due to the many variables which can affect the result including the measuring system, the measurement procedure, the person performing the measurement, and other aspects of the measurement process. Quantitative measurements are estimates of the true value and have an associated uncertainty which represents the expected dispersion around a measurement and should not be confused with error. Even when all components of error in a measurement have been evaluated and corrected for, there will still be uncertainty associated with the measurement. Since no measurement can be made with infinite sensitivity, there will always be a lack of knowledge of the true quantity value. However, knowledge of the uncertainty associated with the measurement made communicates the confidence in the validity of the measurement result being reported.

The concept of measurement uncertainty is not new to the scientific community. Albert Einstein calculated and reported measurement uncertainties in the early 1900s. The push to establish international consensus on the evaluation and expression of measurement uncertainty began in 1977 and culminated in the 1995 publication of ISO/IEC Guide 98. The current version was published in 2009 titled ISO/IEC Guide 98-1 Uncertainty of measurement—Part 1: Introduction to the expression of uncertainty in measurement. Many of the concepts of measurement uncertainty are not new to the forensic science community either, but the approach used to evaluate and express measurement uncertainty has been inconsistent. As forensic science laboratories moved to ISO/IEC 17025, an international standard for quality, as a foundation for accreditation, a more uniform approach to evaluation and reporting of measurement uncertainty has been developed in the forensic science community.

Measurement uncertainty is not only an essential element in establishing metrological traceability but also an important parameter describing the quality of a measurement. The importance of forensic science laboratories reporting test and calibration results that are reliable, accurate, and comparable cannot be overstated. Information regarding the uncertainty associated with a test or calibration result is crucial when comparing quantitative test or calibration results between laboratories or when comparing a quantitative test result to a statute specification or requirement.

Forensic toxicology laboratories should evaluate measurement uncertainty for all procedures where a quantitative measurement is reported. NIST in its Standard Operating Procedure for the Assignment of Uncertainty (SOP 29) has established a multi-step process that can be applied to evaluating measurement uncertainty in forensic toxicology. This multi-step process includes:

- Defining the measurand and measurement process,
- Identifying and characterizing uncertainty components,
- Quantifying uncertainty components,
- Converting all components to standard uncertainties,
- Calculating the combined uncertainty,
- Calculating and evaluating the expanded uncertainty, and
- Reporting the uncertainty.

In the following sections, each step in the process will be discussed in further detail to assist forensic toxicology laboratories with evaluating measurement uncertainty.

Specify the Measurement Process

The first step is to define the measurand and specify the measurement process in question. Defining the measurand can be in the form of a written statement, a visual diagram, and/or a mathematical expression (Eq. 17.1) and should be as specific as possible to clearly indicate for what

measurement process the evaluation is being calculated. A reference to the equipment used, the
SOP, etc. may be required to clearly distinguish
the measurement process from others in the
laboratory.

Equation 17.1: Measurement process mathematical expression for the concentration of ethanol in antemortem blood

$$C_{measurand} = C_{calibrators} x \frac{I_{measurand}}{I_{calibrators}} + b \quad (17.1)$$

where:

I is the instrument (GC or GC-MS) response.
C is the concentration.
b is the bias.

In forensic toxicology, the measurement process takes many steps where the measurand is
determined through a functional relationship to
the equipment used to make the measurement.
Considering a test method as a series of discrete
steps and evaluating the uncertainty for each step
may be effective. When looking at a measurement process, you will need to determine if the
measurement uncertainty evaluation needs to
encompass multiple pieces of measurement
equipment, variable process parameters, or multiple analysts. At times it is necessary to revisit
this first step in the process as the evaluation of
measurement uncertainty develops, revising the
written statement, visual diagram, and or mathematical expression as required.

Identify Uncertainty Components

Once the measurand has been defined and the
measurement process specified, laboratories
must attempt to identify all components of uncertainty. The most effective way to ensure all potential components of uncertainty are identified is to
involve all analysts who perform the measurement process in discussions. Evaluating measurement uncertainty is neither a routine task nor a
purely mathematical one but depends on detailed
knowledge of the nature of the measurand and

the measurement process. No guide or book
chapter providing a framework for assessing
uncertainty components can replace critical
thinking, intellectual honesty, and professional
skill of the analysts performing the testing.
Although a laboratory should look closely at all
possible sources of uncertainty, a preliminary
review of the measurement process will usually
identify the most significant sources of uncertainty that ultimately impacts the value obtained
for the combined uncertainty.

An excellent place to start when identifying
potential uncertainty components is the mathematical expression determined in step 1 as all
parameters in this expression will have one or
more components that contribute to uncertainty.
Possible uncertainty components to consider
include, but are not limited to:

- Transportation, storage, and handling of
  samples,
- Preparation of samples,
- Environmental and measurement conditions,
- Personnel performing the tests,
- Variation allowed in the test procedure,
- The measurement instruments and equipment
  used, and
- How measurement traceability is estab-
  lished—calibration of equipment or reference
  materials.

How a laboratory documents the uncertainty
components considered in this step can take
many forms including a simple list, a "fishbone"
diagram, or a spreadsheet, but laboratories may
find greater efficiency with some formats. From a
practical standpoint, the effort a laboratory puts
forth early in the process of evaluating measurement uncertainty can pay great dividends. The
laboratory should commit time and resources to
performing a critical evaluation of the similarities
and differences between their quantitative methods as most toxicology methods share many
uncertainty components in common. Once a laboratory identifies these common components, an
uncertainty budget template can be developed
and utilized for evaluating measurement uncertainty for all methods, all analytes with little to no

modification. Taking this concept further, developing a template that addresses all steps in the uncertainty evaluation process is highly recommended as such a template will provide a single source of both guidance and documentation.

Quantify Uncertainty Components

Once all uncertainty components have been identified, a determination will need to be made as to how components can be quantified. The GUM classifies the method of quantification as either Type A or Type B evaluation depending on whether the evaluation is performed by statistical analysis of a series of observations from the measurement process or some other means, respectively. Many of the uncertainty components that can impact a measurement process in forensic toxicology can be quantified by a Type A evaluation. This is most commonly performed by statistical analysis of quality control data, method validation data, and/or data from a measurement assurance program and quantified as a relative standard deviation. With an appropriately structured validation plan, method validation precision data can initially be utilized to evaluate and quantify a number of uncertainty components. Since toxicology measurements are often made over a concentration range, validation should investigate whether precision is constant over the range of measurements. If precision is not constant, the laboratory will need to consider quantifying the Type A evaluation uncertainty component at multiple concentrations. The laboratory has several choices as to how to proceed in this scenario including utilizing the data from the control with the largest variance; determining where the variance changes occur and using data appropriate for each concentration range in the measurement uncertainty evaluations; or evaluating measurement uncertainty at each control level and calculating the measurement uncertainty for each test result utilizing the control concentration closest to the sample concentration. Such considerations are important as data from the measurement process encompassed by one or more components is typically the largest

contributor to the overall calculated uncertainty for a measurement process.

Although a number of uncertainty components can be accounted for and quantified by a Type A method of evaluation using repeatability, intermediate precision, or reproducibility data, additional uncertainty components will remain. Common components that require a Type B evaluation include the uncertainty associated with the calibration of equipment, the reference values for certified reference material (CRM), and often the homogenization of testing items. The value for these uncertainty components can, respectively, be obtained from the calibration certificate, certificate of analysis, and by establishing administrative requirements for agreement of replicate analysis.

Convert Quantities to Standard Uncertainties

Once quantified, all components need to be converted to a standard uncertainty or one standard deviation. Keep in mind during this process that the next step combines standard uncertainties from all components quantified from both the Type A and Type B method of evaluation. Therefore, all standard uncertainties must be expressed in the same measurement units. The most common practice is to express standard uncertainties in the unit of measurement being made or as a percentage variation for each component.

Generally, statistical calculations of standard deviation based on measurement process data are expressed as one standard deviation or can be easily converted to one standard deviation. It is assumed that data used in a Type A evaluation follows a normal distribution. This can be confirmed in many ways including, but not limited to, graphing the data as a function or histogram, constructing a normal probability plot, or using a quantitative technique such as the Kolmogorov-Smirnov test.

For those components that are evaluated using a Type B method of evaluation, it is most common to use either a rectangular or triangular distribution as the probability density function to best describe the data, but at times, the information may indicate a normal distribution. The uncertainties reported on equipment calibration certificates and CRM Certificates of Analysis should be reviewed carefully. If the certificate reports an uncertainty and indicates a normal distribution at 95.45% confidence ($k = 2$), then the reported uncertainty must be divided by 2, to obtain the standard uncertainty. In the case of a laboratory administrative requirement for replicate analysis agreement or other pre-defined criteria where only the upper and lower limits are known, a rectangular distribution is used to describe the probability, and the equivalent of one standard deviation is estimated to be the upper (or lower) limit*1/SQRT(3). However, if the value near the mean is more likely than the upper or lower limit, a triangular distribution is used to describe the probability, and the equivalent of one standard deviation is estimated to be the upper (or lower) limit*1/SQRT(6).

Calculate the Combined Standard Uncertainty

Individual standard uncertainties quantified by Type A and Type B methods of evaluation are now combined to calculate the combined standard uncertainty of the measurement process. This combined standard uncertainty is an estimated standard deviation and characterizes the dispersion of the values that could reasonably be attributed to the measurement result at the equivalent of one standard deviation, a coverage probability of 68.26%.

The combined standard uncertainty is the positive square root of the variance of all components combined. The formula commonly used is the root sum of the squares or RSS (Eq. 17.2).

Equation 17.2: Root sum of the squares formula

$$u_c(y) = \sqrt{\sum (c_i u_i)^2}$$
$$u_c(y) = \sqrt{s_p^2 + u_0^2 + u_1^2 + u_2^2 + \ldots + u_i^2}$$

(17.2)

where:

s_p is the standard deviation of the measurement process (Type A evaluation).
u_i are individual uncertainty components (Type B evaluation or additional Type A evaluation).

Use of this formula assumes that the uncertainty components are independent and uncorrelated, meaning a large change in one component does not cause a large change in another component. Calculating the combined uncertainty for correlated contributions is a significantly more complex task and requires additional guidance beyond the material covered in this text.

Evaluation of Bias

Measurement accuracy encompasses both precision and bias. A measurement is more accurate when it has less bias and greater precision. When possible, an evaluation of bias should be performed to recognize all systematic effects within the measurement process and correct those effects. An evaluation of bias can be performed when one or more controls prepared with metrological traceability and having a known reference value and uncertainty are included as part of the measurement process.

The general approach to evaluating bias will:

- Determine if bias is present by comparing control data to reference values with measurement traceability; then
- Estimate the combined standard uncertainty without considering the bias; and then
- Compare the bias with the combined standard uncertainty.

When the bias is less than the combined standard uncertainty, the bias can be viewed as not significant, and the laboratory may decide whether or not to include as a component in the evaluation of uncertainty. When the bias is greater than the combined standard uncertainty, the bias is viewed as significant, and the laboratory must take appropriate actions.

The laboratory may take actions to eliminate or reduce the bias until it is not significant, correct the measurement result for the bias, or report the observed measurement result including both the MU and the bias.

Expand the Combined Standard Uncertainty by Coverage Factor (k)

As mentioned previously, the combined standard uncertainty characterizes the dispersion of the values that can be reasonably attributed to the measurement result with a coverage probability of 68.26%. To increase the coverage probability to a level fit for purpose for forensic toxicology results, the combined standard uncertainty must be expanded. The standard uncertainty is expanded by multiplying by a coverage factor, k, that is determined using a Student's distribution based on the degrees of freedom for the measurement process (number of observations $(n) - 1$). The value for k is quite large when the degrees of freedom are small, when less is known about the measurement process. As knowledge of the measurement process increases, more observations have been made, and the value of k decreases until at infinity the value for k for a coverage probability of 95.45% will be 2.000. Respectively, the value for k associated with a coverage probability of 99.73% will be 3.000. Of course, the value for k changes less and less as more observations are made; therefore, the difference in the value of k with >100 measurements and infinity is small.

Evaluate the Expanded Uncertainty

The point in the process has been reached where it is time to critically evaluate the estimated measurement uncertainty to determine if it reasonable. Steps to making this determination include:

- Identifying any calculation errors in previous steps.
- Is the uncertainty appropriate for the measurement process? Does the uncertainty meet the laboratory's limits with respect to fit for purpose?
- Does the expanded uncertainty meet the customer's needs?

If the laboratory determines that the expanded uncertainty is not acceptable, steps should be taken to identify areas of method improvement. The evaluation of measurement uncertainty will provide valuable information related to the component(s) to target to reduce the expanded measurement uncertainty. Areas of method improvement might include standardization of the measurement procedure, improved calibration of equipment, improved measuring equipment, and lowering of administrative performance requirements to name a few. Once areas of improvement have been identified, changes to the measurement process made and the method revalidated, the measurement uncertainty can be recalculated and reevaluated.

Report the Measurement Uncertainty

Once the expanded measurement uncertainty has been calculated, decisions must be made regarding when and how to report the uncertainty. Whether the laboratory reports uncertainty in a test report, in an attachment to the test report, or not at all will depend on any accreditation requirements that must be met by the laboratory, the customer requests, and the philosophy of the laboratory. One consideration that should be taken into account by the laboratory when making a decision regarding reporting of uncertainty is that from a metrological standpoint, a measurement is not complete without including uncertainty. Reporting the measurement uncertainty provides valuable information to the reader regarding the expected dispersion of measurement results made using the method and, if bias has been assessed, around the true value. Reporting the measurement uncertainty allows for comparability between measurement results made by different methods or different laboratories.

When the decision is made to report, the measurement uncertainty should be expressed as an expanded uncertainty, include the coverage probability, and be at the same level of significance as the measurement result.

Periodic Reevaluation

Evaluating measurement uncertainty is not a "one and done" process. Beyond the steps to initially evaluating measurement uncertainty, consideration should also be given to establishing an interval for the review and recalculation of measurement uncertainty. Many factors will affect the interval for such a review and whether recalculation of the uncertainty is necessary. Such factors would include the uncertainty components included in the initial calculation; frequency with which components change; magnitude of any change compared to the calculated MU; and any change in the measurement process. Additionally, the laboratory may decide to administratively establish a time interval for review and recalculation of measurement uncertainty.

Further Reading

ANSI/ASB 017: Standard Practices for Measurement Traceability in Forensic Toxicology

ANSI National Accreditation Board, ANAB ISO/IEC 17025:2017 Forensic Science Testing and Calibration Laboratories Accreditation Requirements (AR 3125). Available for download: https://anab.org

ANSI National Accreditation Board, ASCLD/LAB – International Guidance on Measurement Traceability, 2013. Available for download: https://www.anab.org

ANSI National Accreditation Board, ASCLD/LAB – International Guidance on Measurement Traceability – Measurement Assurance, 2013. Available for download: https://anab.org

ANSI National Accreditation Board, ASCLD/LAB – International Guidance on the Estimation of Measurement Uncertainty – Overview, 2013. Available for download: https://www.anab.org

ANSI National Accreditation Board, ASCLD/LAB – International Guidance on the Estimation of Measurement Uncertainty – ANNEX A Details on the NIST 8-Step Process, 2013. Available for download: https://www.anab.org

ANSI National Accreditation Board, ASCLD/LAB – International Guidance on the Estimation of Measurement Uncertainty – ANNEX D Toxicology Testing Discipline, 2013. Available for download: https://www.anab.org

Barwick V, Prichard E (eds), Eurachem terminology in analytical measurement – Introduction to VIM 3. Available for download: https://www.eurachem.org/index.php/publications/guides/terminology-in-analyticalmeasurement

Ellison SLR, Williams A (eds), Eurachem/CITAC guide: Quantifying uncertainty in analytical measurement, 3rd edn, (QUAM: 2012 P1). Available for download: https://www.eurachem.org/index.php/publications/guides/quam

International Bureau of Weights and Measures (BIPM) Key Comparison Database (KCDB), Appendix C http://kcdb.bipm.org/appendixC/

International Organization for Standardization (ISO), ISO Guide 30: 2015 Reference materials – Selected terms and definitions (Geneva, Switzerland)

International Organization for Standardization (ISO), ISO Guide 33: 2015 Reference materials – Good practice in using reference materials (Geneva, Switzerland)

International Organization for Standardization (ISO). ISO/IEC 9000:2015 Quality management systems—Fundamentals and vocabulary (Geneva, Switzerland)

International Organization for Standardization (ISO). ISO/IEC 17000:2004 Conformity assessment—Vocabulary and general principles (Geneva, Switzerland)

International Organization for Standardization (ISO). ISO/IEC 17025:2017 General requirements for the competence of testing and calibration laboratories (Geneva, Switzerland)

National Institute of Standards and Technology, Standard Operation Procedure for the Assignment of Uncertainty (SOP 29). Available for download: https://www.nist.gov/pml/weights-and-measures/laboratory-metrology/standard-operating-procedures

Statistics for Forensic Toxicology

18

Patrick Buzzini and Sarah Kerrigan

Abstract

Forensic toxicologists routinely deal with the analysis of numerical data. Statistical methods have a wide variety of applications, from initial method development and data interpretation to method validation and measurement uncertainty. In this chapter, basic concepts including data distributions, types of error, and hypothesis testing are explored. Using illustrative examples from forensic toxicology, the use of statistical tests is discussed, including the Student's t-test and some of its variants, F-tests, and analysis of variance (ANOVA). The treatment of outliers, regression analysis, and tools for the evaluation of calibration models are also discussed.

Keywords

Statistics · Forensic toxicology · Error · Uncertainty · Student's t-test · F-test · ANOVA · Outliers · Regression · Likelihood ratios

P. Buzzini (✉) · S. Kerrigan
Department of Forensic Science, Sam Houston State University, Huntsville, TX, USA
e-mail: Patrick.buzzini@shsu.edu;
Sarah.kerrigan@shsu.edu

Introduction

The analysis of numerical data is common ground for forensic toxicologists. However, applying statistical methods of analysis to actual data can be challenging. Nevertheless, these basic concepts provide the foundation for everyday functions in the laboratory, including method development, validation, measurement uncertainty, and quality control practices. Understanding error types and how data are distributed is important for measurement uncertainty, and comparing datasets under different experimental conditions can be critical during method development and validation.

In this chapter, we explore some fundamental theories associated with statistical methods and use real-world examples to explore how the statistical tests are selected and why. Hypothesis testing is a valuable tool with broad applicability. The use of independent, paired, one-tailed, and two-tailed t-tests is discussed for the comparison of means, and one-way and two-way ANOVA methods are presented for the comparison of more than two groups, with single or multiple factors. Regression is also discussed, with an emphasis on residual analysis and calibration models for quantitative analysis. Common outlier tests are also discussed, and a brief introduction to the Bayesian approach is presented, including the use of likelihood ratios. Although multiple software approaches are possible, datasets for some examples provided are presented using Microsoft Excel (Analysis ToolPak) and *R* statistical software.

Significant Figures, Uncertainty, and Reporting

The appropriate use of significant figures is critically important in forensic toxicology. Since no measurements are made with 100% precision, the use of significant figures provides valuable information concerning the precision of the answer or the uncertainty involved. A measured blood alcohol concentration (BAC) of 0.08*0* g/dL does not have the same meaning as 0.08 g/dL. When used in analytical chemistry or toxicology, trailing zeros, i.e., those appearing after the last integer, imply that the measurement is significant. For example, when weighing cocaine powder to prepare a stock solution using an analytical balance designed to read accurately within 0.1 mg, a recorded result of 0.01*00* g (10.0 mg) is not the same as 0.01 g. The trailing zeros (in italics) convey to the user that the apparatus used was capable of making a measurement to the reported number of significant figures.

Likewise, the use of spurious zeros or digits is inappropriate when performing measurements or calculations, because it implies greater precision that the data may allow. Adhering to rules associated with significant figures is important but is often overlooked. Rounding (to the nearest integer or appropriate number of significant figures) and truncating (removing a fractional measurement) are also important in forensic toxicology. For example, when measuring an evidential BAC, a laboratory may (by policy) perform arithmetic rounding on duplicate measurements or truncate results. A measured value of 0.078 g/dL conveys significance of the "8" to the client receiving the report. However, this reported value could have arisen from duplicate measurements that were rounded to this value using arithmetic (e.g., 0.0779) or truncated (e.g., 0.078*9*), whereby the last digit is removed entirely. Regardless, the appropriate use of significant figures in analytical

work and reporting results conveys meaning because it describes uncertainty.

Rounding or truncating to a nominal value is commonplace when reporting results in forensic toxicology, but when doing so, the expression of the inherent uncertainty is not conveyed. To accomplish this, the uncertainties of each contributing factor, device, or step must be known (e.g., analytical balances, volumetric pipettes, flasks, analytical reference materials). Once the *absolute uncertainty* of these factors is known, the *relative or standard uncertainty* can be expressed in the same units (i.e., %). This approach allows the *combined uncertainty* of the measurement to be calculated, by squaring the individual uncertainties (i.e., standard deviations), summing them (under the assumption that they are independent from each other), and taking the square root of the total. This approach to measurement uncertainty, which takes into account the total variance, is described in more detail in Chap. 17. ISO/IEC 17025 (General Requirements for the Competence of Testing and Calibration Laboratories) requires the estimation of measurement uncertainty for testing and calibration laboratories. Specific accrediting bodies may stipulate how this is reported to the client for measurements that matter (i.e., on the report itself, units of measurement). Tolerances for Class A volumetric glassware utilized during the preparation of controls are shown in Table 18.1.

Table 18.1 Example tolerances associated with Class A volumetric glassware

Class A volumetric flask capacity (mL)	Tolerance to contain (± mL)	Uncertainty (%)
5	0.02	0.40
10	0.02	0.20
25	0.03	0.12
50	0.05	0.10
100	0.08	0.08
250	0.12	0.04
500	0.15	0.03
1000	0.30	0.03

Data Distributions, Error Propagation, and Measurement Uncertainty

Types of Error

Errors can be categorized as *gross*, *random*, or *systematic* in nature. Gross errors are often so serious that the entire measurement must be abandoned (e.g., instrument failure, spill, or breakage of the specimen). Random errors (i.e., uncertainties) are those that cause the result to scatter on both sides of the central value, affecting the precision of the result. In contrast, systematic errors cause the results to deviate on the same side from the central value, influencing the accuracy (or proximity to the true value) of the measurement, therefore introducing bias. Systematic and random areas are sometimes referred to as *determinate* and *indeterminate* errors. Repeatability and reproducibility are both measures of precision. Repeatability refers to the variation that occurs when repeated measurements are made under identical conditions (e.g., same instrument, same examiner, same analytical method). This type of variation might be determined during the validation of an analytical method as part of the *within-run* or *intra-assay* precision. Reproducibility is a measure of the variance under different conditions (e.g., different examiners, different days, different instruments, or different laboratories). During method validation (see Chap. 16), this type of variation is described as *between-run* or *inter-assay* precision. While random errors can never be eliminated, by careful technique and proper training, they can be minimized, and they should be properly documented. Replicate measurements and statistical analysis allow us to understand their significance.

It should be noted that while random errors can be evaluated using replicate measurements, systematic errors cannot be identified unless the true value is known in advance. Therefore, bias introduced by an improperly calibrated volumetric pipette used to aliquot a specimen or an unacceptable level of ion suppression during the analysis of a sample might go undetected without proper attention to quality assurance, quality control, and rigorous method validation. Additional safeguards include the use of certified reference materials (CRMs), external controls, collaborative trials, and inter-laboratory comparisons.

Type I error and *Type II error* also play an important role in the context of hypothesis testing and particularly in cases where a *decision* needs to be made about the rejection or acceptance (or failure to reject) of a hypothesis of interest, and a cutoff point or threshold is initially set. This aspect is discussed in more detail below.

Distribution of Errors

If the error associated with the determination of a drug concentration in blood, for example, is due to relatively small random errors, the results will cluster around the central value (mean, median, or mode). Although the variance (or more practically the standard deviation) describes the spread of the results (i.e., for a normal distribution), it does not indicate the way in which the results are *distributed*. It is useful to organize the data in a frequency table (or count table) or a relative frequency table (percentages relative to the total number of observations) and plot them to appreciate their shape or distribution. The *sample* dataset is a subset of a much larger *population*. In the absence of systematic errors, the mean of this population (μ), which is unknown, is the true value. The sample mean ($\bar{x}$ is used to provide an estimate of μ. Similarly, the population has a standard deviation of σ, also most often unknown, which can be estimated from the sample standard deviation, s. In the Gaussian or normal distribution, the curve is unimodal and symmetrical about its central value μ, and the greater the spread of σ, the greater the spread of the curve. The normal distribution undergoes a characteristic property known as the Empirical Rule. According to the Empirical Rule of the normal distribution, whatever the value of μ and σ, approximately 68%, 95%, and 99.7% of the population lie within $\pm 1\sigma$, $\pm 2\sigma$, or $\pm 3\sigma$ of the mean, respectively (Fig. 18.1). This approach is often used to express the uncertainty empirically in terms of a specified *confidence interval* (CI). For example, when purchasing a certified reference material from a vendor accredited to ISO Guide 34 (General Requirements for the Competence of

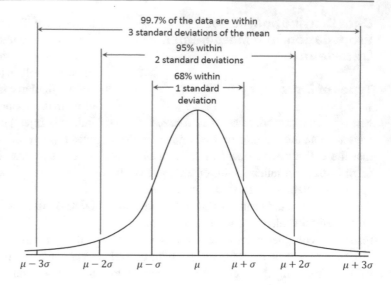

Fig. 18.1 Properties of the normal distribution

Reference Material Producers), the certificate of analysis may indicate that the concentration of methamphetamine in a methanolic solution is 1.000 ± 0.004 mg/mL. In the example provided, the manufacturer may state that the concentration is expressed as an expanded uncertainty in accordance with ISO/IEC 17025 and Guide 34, using a specified confidence interval (e.g., 95%) and *coverage factor* ($k = 2$) (see Chap. 17). The use of this information when estimating measurement uncertainty is discussed later.

Many of the statistical concepts described in this chapter assume a normal distribution and are not valid if this condition is not met. Although this is a reasonable assumption for replicate measurements made on the same sample, asymmetric or log-normal populations are also encountered; in this case, the logarithm of the concentration (or other variable) is plotted against frequency or density to give a normal distribution. Figure 18.2 depicts some of the most common distributions. The symmetry of the probability distribution can also identify if the data are skewed. If the data are perfectly Gaussian, the mean, median (middle), and mode (most frequently occurring) data all coincide. Therefore, numerical differences between these can be used to identify if the data are skewed in a positive (right) or negative (left) direction.

However, the distribution of measurements is not always unimodal. Bimodal and multimodal distributions are also possible, and when this

occurs, it may be misleading to report the mean or standard deviation of the combined populations. For example, consider a clinical study to evaluate the pharmacokinetic properties of a new drug. The frequency of peak plasma concentrations between subjects may yield a multimodal distribution, which might be attributed to slow, normal, and fast metabolizers. Elimination of subjects with specific metabolic phenotypes might yield a unimodal distribution. As the number of measurements increases (toward ∞), the appearance of normally distributed data may improve. When the frequency of the individual measurements is normalized such that the area under the curve equals 1, the frequency table or histogram becomes a *probability density distribution*.

Consider the following example. Two trainees and an experienced examiner in the laboratory perform BAC determinations on an external whole blood control reported to containing 0.08 g/dL ethanol. Table 18.2 shows the individual results for ten determinations for each individual and the summary statistics of the results. All measurements are those of the sample population (i.e., a subset) (n) of the parent population (N). The *sample mean* ($\bar{x}$) is typically reported using the same decimal places as the individual measurements, although sometimes an additional digit is added to avoid rounding errors. This is evident when comparing the *% accuracy* and *% bias* with the mean (reported to the same decimal places as the measurement) for Trainee A and the

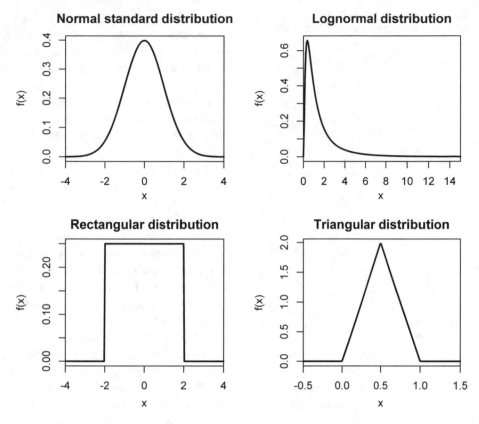

Fig. 18.2 Common probability distributions (normal, lognormal, rectangular, triangular)

Examiner. When the standard deviation is expressed relative to the mean (i.e., *relative standard deviation* (RSD) or *coefficient of variation* (CV)), the spread of the population can be effectively compared between individuals. This example shows that although both Trainee A and the Examiner perform the analysis with acceptable bias (+0.4% and −0.4%, respectively), the precision of the Examiner far outperforms Trainee A, whose individual BAC determinations range from 0.067 to 0.092 g/dL. This unacceptable variance could be attributed to random error (e.g., sloppy pipetting during volumetric manipulations). The bias is only acceptable because of the number of replicates ($n = 10$). This number far exceeds that which would be considered practical during routine forensic toxicology casework: typically, duplicate measurements ($n = 2$) for BAC determinations and often single determinations for other drugs. The *sample vari-ance* (v or s^2) is important when determining analysis of variance (ANOVA) discussed later.

As the number of replicates (n) increases, the sample standard deviation approaches the population standard deviation because the difference between n and $n−1$ is minimal. When calculating a confidence interval, the Student's t-value accounts for the size of n (discussed later). Using the example provided in Table 18.2, it can be seen that not only is the % bias much higher for Trainee B but the 95% CI (0.071–0.077) also falls outside of the true value (0.080 g/dL). Although the precision for Trainee B is far superior to Trainee A (4.3% CV compared with 9.5%), a large negative bias exists (−7.8%). This outcome might be attributed to a systematic error, for example, failure to completely eject blood from the tip of the volumetric pipette. The strip chart in Fig. 18.3 visually depicts the differences between the results obtained by the three analysts

Table 18.2 Example data for BAC determinations (g/dL) collected by an experienced examiner and two trainees

		Trainee A	Trainee B	Examiner
	1	0.067	0.070	0.081
	2	0.075	0.075	0.080
	3	0.088	0.079	0.079
	4	0.082	0.071	0.078
	5	0.078	0.073	0.078
	6	0.085	0.075	0.083
	7	0.072	0.070	0.078
	8	0.085	0.072	0.078
	9	0.080	0.078	0.080
	10	0.092	0.076	0.082
Sample mean, x		0.080	0.074	0.080
Sample standard deviation, s		0.0076	0.0032	0.0018
% RSD or CV		9.5%	4.3%	2.3%
% accuracy		100.5%	92.4%	99.6%
% bias		0.5%	−7.6%	−0.4%
Range		0.067–0.092	0.070–0.079	0.078–0.083
95% confidence interval ($t_{crit} = 1.833$)		0.076–0.085	0.072–0.076	0.079–0.081
99% confidence interval ($t_{crit} = 2.821$)		0.074–0.087	0.071–0.077	0.078–0.081

with regard to the expected (true) value of 0.080 g/dL.

Measurement Uncertainty

Quantitative measurements are used routinely in forensic toxicology (e.g., mass, volume, concentration). Estimating the uncertainty associated with these measurements is a requirement under ISO/IEC 17025. This crucial topic was explored in more detail in Chap. 17. The purpose of measurement uncertainty (MU) is to express the level of certainty (or confidence) in a given measurement. Although there are different approaches to MU, the ISO Guide to the Expression of Uncertainty in Measurement (GUM) is commonly used. A simplified eight-step approach is shown in Fig. 18.4. Measurement uncertainty simply allows the analyst to say with a given confidence level that the true value has a high probability of being within the specified range. Measurement uncertainty is not synonymous with error. Unlike error, the true value is not known in forensic casework, so MU is particularly useful when making decisions about quantitative results in forensic investigations.

An example of an uncertainty budget for the quantitative determination of methamphetamine in blood is shown in Table 18.3. This example assumes Type A uncertainty data from 30 replicate measurements obtained from historical quality control data (20 ng/mL), capturing day-to-day variations in performance over time and multiple examiners ideally. If these data were plotted using a histogram, it should show a normal distribution. In contrast, the Type B uncertainty data are not determined statistically, are assigned individually, and depend on the component steps in the standard operating procedure. A schematic of the hypothetical steps is shown in Fig. 18.5, and the associated uncertainties are depicted in Table 18.3. As can be seen from this example, Type B uncertainty cannot be eliminated from the procedure, but it can be minimized to some extent by optimizing the different steps (e.g., number of volumetric manipulations). Tolerances for Class A volumetric flasks were previously shown in Table 18.1.

In the example provided, it is assumed for simplicity that all volumetric pipettes used in the procedure (20–200 µL and 200–1000 µL) have tolerances that do not exceed 2%. Unlike the repeatability data in the first row, some of the measurements accounting for Type B uncertainties have rectangular distributions that have an equal probability of an outcome across the specified range. This assumption is appropriate when the measurement has an equal chance of being distributed anywhere within the range. Note that these distributions have different divisors in the uncertainty budget, as discussed in Chap. 17. Triangular distributions are also possible, but less common. However, if it is more realistic to expect a value near the center than at the two limits (and extreme values are less likely), a triangular distribution might be appropriate. For the purposes of measurement uncertainty, if the distribution is not known, a rectangular distribution is often

Fig. 18.3 Strip chart depicting BAC determinations by three analysts

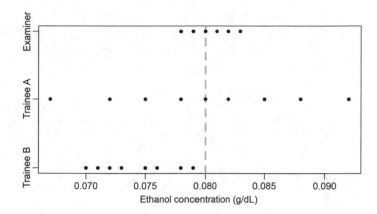

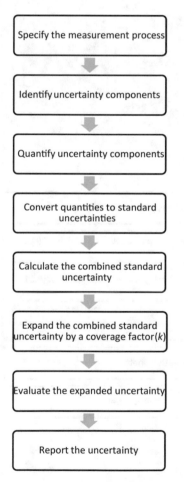

Fig. 18.4 The NIST (National Institute on Standards and Technology) eight-step approach to measurement uncertainty

selected because it is the most conservative approach. In the example provided, a 95% confidence interval is selected, rounding is used, but

the rule of thirds is not; this approach increases the reported uncertainty. Additionally, in this hypothetical example, the laboratory elected to determine the measurement uncertainty at the recommended cutoff for impaired driving (20 ng/mL methamphetamine). However, the selection of the concentration for the MU determination and the confidence interval are independently determined by the laboratory.

It should be noted that there are many acceptable approaches to the development of an uncertainty budget. Even within the discipline of forensic toxicology, one size does not fit all. Given this flexibility, decisions regarding the preferred approach should be governed by common sense and logic so that reported results for measurements that matter are fit for purpose.

Hypothesis Testing

Theoretical Concepts

Hypothesis tests are an important component of statistical inference in the sense that they are utilized to make inferences about a population of interest based on information from a sample representative of that population. A classic approach is to use tests of significance that are designed to collect evidence intended to reject, accept (or fail to reject), or support a certain claim about a population. The starting point of hypothesis testing is the definition of the question of interest to be translated into a formal hypothesis statement. Every hypothesis test includes two or more

Table 18.3 Example calculation of measurement uncertainty for methamphetamine in blood

Source of uncertainty (units)	Uncertainty (variable units)	Uncertainty (%)	Distribution	Divisor	Standard uncertainty (%)
Historical (statistical) data ($n = 30$) at 20 ng/mL (29 d.f.)		2.9	Normal	1	2.9
Purchased certified reference material (1±0.004 mg/mL)	0.004 mg/mL	0.4	Normal	2	0.2
Volumetric dilution—10 mL flask (preparation of stock standard)	0.02 mL	0.2	Rectangular	$\sqrt{3}$	0.115
Preparation of stock standard using a 200–1000 μL volumetric pipette		2	Rectangular	$\sqrt{3}$	1.155
Volumetric dilution (10 mL flask)—preparation of working standard	0.02 mL	0.2	Rectangular	$\sqrt{3}$	0.115
Preparation of working standard using a 200–1000 μL volumetric pipette		2	Rectangular	$\sqrt{3}$	1.155
Aliquot blood sample with a 200–1000 μL volumetric pipette		2	Rectangular	$\sqrt{3}$	1.155
Volume of methamphetamine standard added to sample using a 20–200 μL volumetric pipette		2	Rectangular	$\sqrt{3}$	1.155
Volume of internal standard added to sample using a 20–200 μL volumetric pipette		2	Rectangular	$\sqrt{3}$	1.155
Combined uncertainty	3.9 (rounded)				3.891
Expanded uncertainty ($t = 2.04$, 29 d.f., 95% CI)	**8.0**				

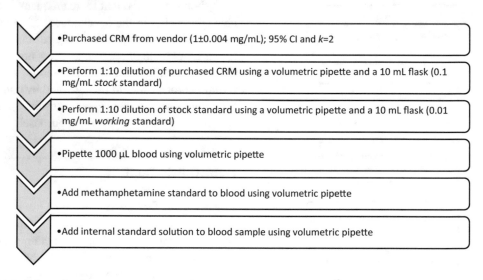

- Purchased CRM from vendor (1±0.004 mg/mL); 95% CI and k=2

- Perform 1:10 dilution of purchased CRM using a volumetric pipette and a 10 mL flask (0.1 mg/mL *stock* standard)

- Perform 1:10 dilution of stock standard using a volumetric pipette and a 10 mL flask (0.01 mg/mL *working* standard)

- Pipette 1000 μL blood using volumetric pipette

- Add methamphetamine standard to blood using volumetric pipette

- Add internal standard solution to blood sample using volumetric pipette

Fig. 18.5 Schematic of steps with associated Type B uncertainties

hypotheses: the *null hypothesis* (e.g., denoted H_0) and the *alternative or alternate hypothesis* (e.g., denoted H_a or H_1). The null hypothesis is the statement to be tested, and a statistical test is devised to assess the strength of the evidence against the null hypothesis. Typically, the null hypothesis consists of a statement of "no differ- ence" or "no effect," and this implies that any observed effect in the sample under the alterna- tive hypothesis is only due to random variation. Alternative hypotheses are statements believed to be the case instead of the null hypothesis. The claimed and observed effect in the sample is real and representative of the entire population of interest. Alternative hypotheses refer to a *one-sided* (*right-tailed* or *left-tailed*) or *two-sided* (*two-tailed*) *test*. For example, if H_0: $\mu = 0$ and H_a refers to a one-sided test, then H_a: $\mu > 0$ for a right-tailed test, or H_a: $\mu < 0$ for a left-tailed test.

If H_0: $\mu = 0$ and H_a refers to a two-sided or two-tailed test, then H_a: $\mu \neq 0$.

The subsequent step is to collect data and calculate a sample statistic aiming to estimate the parameter stated in the hypotheses. Choosing a test statistic depends on different aspects such as the question of interest (i.e., relationship or differences between variables), the types of *variables* (*categorical*, *discrete*, or *continuous*), the number of groups or populations, the number of objects or observations within a sample, the number of variables per object (i.e., *univariate* or *multivariate*), and if the data follow a distribution with known parameters and in compliance with its assumptions. Figure 18.6 shows an example of flowchart that leads to the selection of a test depending on the type of data and the overall purpose of the test.

This section primarily discusses tests regarding univariate continuous variables that are normally distributed but that are of small size ($n < 30$). In these tests, the main parameter for comparing populations of interest is their mean μ. An important property of the normal distribution is the *standardization of the values*, that is, the observed or measured values (i.e., in units such as concentrations) are standardized by means of *z-scores* where probabilities under the curve are measured *in units of the standard deviation* σ relative to the mean μ as the center:

$$z_i = \frac{x_i - \mu}{\sigma} \sim N(0,1)$$

The z-scores (or standard scores or standardized values) are said to be standardized for a normal distribution because they are centered to a mean of 0 and reduced to a standard deviation of 1, $N(0,1)$: the z-scores inform about how many standard deviations each z_i value is away from the mean and in which direction of the standard normal distribution. However, for small-sized datasets, the Student's t-distribution is used, which has a similar bell shape like the normal distribution; its parameter is the *degrees of freedom* (d.f.) defined as $n - 1$ for a sample size of n. Due to the smaller quantity of data compared to the normal distribution, the shape of the t-distribution appears flatter in the area of the tails. With the increase of n and consecutively the degrees of

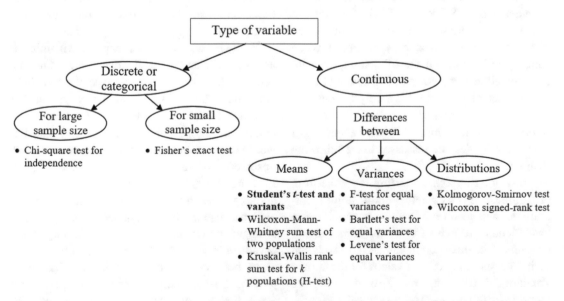

Fig. 18.6 Schematic for the selection of a hypothesis test method. The Student's t-test and its variants are highlighted in bold due to their extensive use in the evaluation of experimental results. Note that this flowchart is far from exhaustive and the emphasis in this chapter focuses on continuous variables

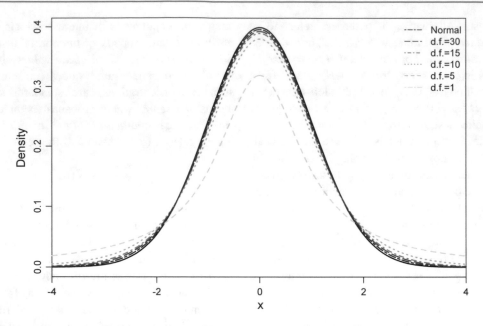

Fig. 18.7 Comparison between the normal standard distribution and *t*-distributions at different degrees of freedom. Note how the increase of the degree of freedom—the parameter of the *t*-distribution—leads to similarities to the normal distribution particularly at the level of the tail regions

freedom, the shape of the *t*-distribution tends to come closer to the normal distribution since *s* approaches *σ*. Figure 18.7 shows different *t*-distributions at different degrees of freedom and how they compare to the normal distribution.

When using a Student's *t*-distribution, the test statistic is converted to a *t*-score (or value) to be interpreted using the *t*-table (Appendix 1). When data are collected from a small dataset, the standard deviation *σ* of a normal distribution of mean *μ* of an actual population is rarely known, and therefore the *standard error of the sample mean s / √n* is used instead. Different variants of the Student's *t*-test are discussed in the following sections.

Most often hypothesis testing takes the form of significance tests where a cutoff point is initially defined according to a chosen significance level (denoted α) in the form of a *critical value* or a *p-value*. The most commonly used *α*-levels and their corresponding critical values for the normal standard distribution or Z-distribution are reported in Table 18.4. The critical values for the *t*-distribution are function of the degrees of freedom.

From Table 18.4, it can be noticed that for a two-tailed test (e.g., H_a: $\mu \neq 0$), there are two critical *z* values, a negative one and positive one. This implies that the rejection area must be split in two parts. For example, if $\alpha = 0.05$ is chosen, the rejection area is 0.025 (0.05/2) under each tail of the distribution as shown in Fig. 18.8.

While the critical value is expressed in units of normalized standard deviations away from the central zero value, the *p*-value is the rejection area under the null distribution and consists of evidence against H_0. Formally, the *p*-value is defined as the probability that the test statistic would take a value at or beyond the one actually observed, assuming H_0 to be true. The *p*-value measures the plausibility of the null hypothesis and expresses the measure of the strength of the evidence *against* it: the smaller the *p*-value, the stronger the evidence against H_0; the larger the *p*-value, the weaker the evidence against H_0.

In both cases where a critical value or a *p*-value is used in conjunction with a significance level, the observed values (i.e., calculated test statistics) that are far from the value of the parameter stated in the null hypothesis provide evidence

Table 18.4 Critical values at typical significance levels $\alpha = 0.01$, $\alpha = 0.05$, and $\alpha = 0.10$ for the Z-normal standard distribution

α-Levels	Alternative hypothesis	Critical values
0.01	>	+2.33
	<	−2.33
	≠	−2.58 and +2.58
0.05	>	+1.64
	<	−1.64
	≠	−1.96 and +1.96
0.10	>	+1.28
	<	−1.28
	≠	−1.64 and +1.64

decision on whether or not a hypothesis should be rejected. Predefining the α-level is useful if a decision has to be taken. However, the p-value offers a clear statement about the degree of evidence of the sample against the null hypothesis, without the necessity of rejecting it. In this case, the test helps gauge how much a test statistic *supports* the null hypothesis. Indeed, p-values can assume values that are close to the borderline between accepting and rejecting a hypothesis, and it may be of higher interest to rather qualify the strength of evidence against H_0: for example,

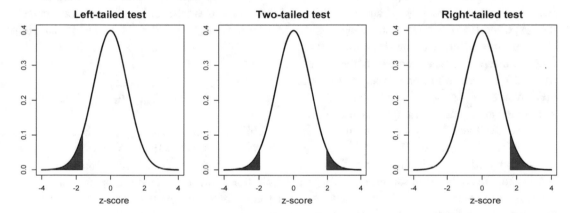

Fig. 18.8 Rejection area defined by a critical value of −1.64 for a left-tailed test (left), −1.96 and +1.96 for a two-tailed test (middle), and +1.64 for a right-tailed test (right), for a α-level of 0.05 of a normal standard distribu- tion. The area under the three distributions for the three tests is the same. However, in the two-tailed test, the rejection area is equally distributed in the two tails of the distribution

against H_0. If these values exceed or fall beyond the cutoff point, then the null hypothesis is rejected in favor of the alternative one. If the test statistic does not exceed the cutoff point, then the null hypothesis is accepted (or the test fails to reject it) at the chosen α significance level. Alternatively, if a calculated p-value is lower than the probability defined by the selected α-level (i.e., the area under the distribution characteristic of the null hypothesis), H_0 is rejected. In the case of rejection, the result is said to be *statistically significant* at that α-level in the sense that the differences are not attributed to random variation in the observations or measurements.

Hypothesis testing may not be confined to applying a significance test intended to reach a

a calculated p-value of around 0.05 consists of weak evidence against H_0 as opposed to a calculated p-value of around 0.001 or lower which, instead, offers very strong evidence against H_0.

From a practical standpoint, these tests can be used to determine if the differences between measurements can be accounted for by random variations. This approach is highly relevant in forensic toxicology when evaluating experimental results. Common examples include comparing of the mean of a single dataset against a *known* or established value, comparing the means of *two independent datasets*, comparing means from *different* samples, and comparing the mean differences of *paired data*. The application of independent and paired t-tests is explored below using practical examples from forensic toxicology.

Comparison of an Experimental Mean with a Known Value

Very frequently it is necessary to compare experimentally determined means with a known or established value. This case is also known as hypothesis testing of a population mean. For example, when a new lot of an external whole blood control containing 50 ng/mL free morphine is analyzed using a properly validated procedure, it is expected that the mean result is not significantly different from the true value ($\mu = 50$ ng/mL). Four replicate measurements of the concentrations of the new whole blood morphine control yield results of 48, 50, 51, and 54 ng/mL; the sample mean $\bar{x}$ and the sample standard deviation s are 50.8 and 2.5 ng/mL, respectively. The hypotheses to be tested are H_0: $\mu = 50$ ng/mL and H_1: $\mu \neq 50$ ng/mL. A significance level of $\alpha = 0.05$ is selected. Given the small sample size ($n = 4$), a Student's t-distribution is used with 3 degrees of freedom, or t_3. A Student's t-statistic or t-score is calculated as follows:

$$t = \frac{\bar{x} - \mu}{s / \sqrt{n}}$$

The test statistic t_3 is calculated to 0.64. From the t-table in Appendix 1, the row for 3 degrees of freedom is first located, and the critical value for $\alpha = 0.05$ is found at the 3rd column ($\alpha = 0.025$), that is, $t_{crit} = 3.18$. Since this is a two-tailed test and the table reports critical values for the upper tail only (right side of the distribution), α is split in two, that is, $\alpha/2$ or $P = 0.025$ for each tail. In this example, $t < t_{crit}$, and therefore the null hypothesis is rejected, and the measurements are not statistically different from the expected value of 50 ng/mL.

However, suppose that instead of 4 replicate QC measurements, cumulative QC data were used for the comparison (e.g., over 100 measurements of the control over the period of several months). In this situation, the z-score (described earlier) may be more appropriate.

Comparison of Two Population Means

Most often, it is necessary to compare two populations by testing whether or not they have similar properties, such as their means (e.g., the comparison of two quantitative methods between laboratories or modifying an existing procedure). A random sample is collected from each population, and their sample means $\bar{x}_1$ and $\bar{x}_2$ are considered to test the following hypotheses: H_0: $\mu_1 - \mu_2 = 0$ and H_1: $\mu_1 - \mu_2 \neq 0$.

If the population variances or standard deviations are not significantly different (i.e., *equal variances* or $\sigma_1^2 = \sigma_2^2 = \sigma^2$), the t-test statistic is:

$$t = \frac{\bar{x}_1 - \bar{x}_2}{s_p \sqrt{\dfrac{1}{n_1} + \dfrac{1}{n_2}}}$$

This statistic has a t-distribution with $n_1 + n_2 - 2$ degrees of freedom, and s_p is a pooled estimate of the standard deviation calculated from the following pooled estimator of the variance s_p^2 based on the two sample variances s_1^2 and s_2^2:

$$s_p^2 = \frac{(n_1 - 1)s_1^2 (n_2 - 1)s_2^2}{n_1 + n_2 - 2}$$

For example, a validated method was developed to quantify a new fluorinated fentanyl analog in blood. At the time the original assay was developed, no isotopically labelled internal standard (IS) for the new fentalog was available, so fentanyl-d_3 was used. Later, the deuterated fentalog became commercially available, and quantitative results using both internal standards were compared. A control sample containing 10 ng/mL was analyzed ten times using both internal standards. The results using both internal standards are shown in Table 18.5a. The question of interest is whether or not the quantitative results using the two internal standards are significantly different.

The boxplot in Fig. 18.9 shows the distribution of fentalog concentrations measured from the original and new internal standards. Although the shift between the two sample means is visually different (the central lines in the boxplot are the sample median values of 12.0 and 10.5 which are very close to the calculated sample means), there is considerable overlap between the values from the two sample sets between 9 and 11 ng/mL.

Table 18.5a Drug concentrations using two internal standards

Concentration (ng/mL) $n = 10$	
Original internal standard	New internal standard
12	13
11	11
12	10
13	9
14	11
9	10
10	11
13	8
12	10
14	11
Mean ± SD	*12.0 ± 1.6*	*10.4 ± 1.3*
CV (%)	*13.6*	*13.0*

The null hypothesis adopted is that the means using the two internal standards are not significantly different at a significance level $\alpha = 0.05$. Using the equation above, s_p^2 is 2.2, and t is 2.39 (Table 18.5b). There are 18 degrees of freedom, so t_{crit} for a two-tailed test ($\alpha = 0.05$) is 2.10 (Appendix 1). Since $t > t_{crit}$, the null hypothesis is rejected, and the results are significantly different. However, the results are not significant at the significance level $\alpha = 0.10$: $t < t_{crit}$, so the laboratory may need to carefully weigh the pros and cons of revalidating the entire procedure using the new internal standard.

The intervals of values reported in the t-table available in Appendix 1 are too large to operate using p-values. The use of statistical software is indispensable. From Table 18.5b, the p-value is reported as $P(T<=t)$ two-tail $= 0.028$. This p-value is the probability that a test statistic less than -2.39 or higher than 2.39 is observed *if* there would truly be no difference between the two compared internal standards. Hence, the p-value is the area under a t_{18} distribution to the left of -2.39 and to the right of 2.39, which account for

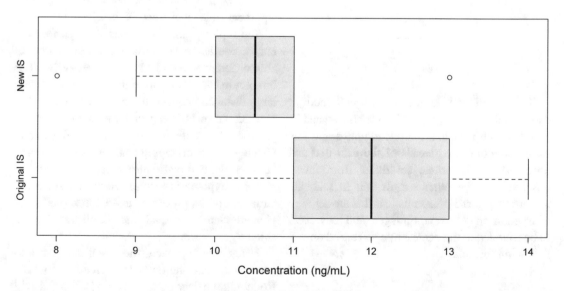

Fig. 18.9 Boxplot of the distributions of fentalog concentrations obtained from two internal standards ($n = 10$ for each sample)

Table 18.5b Two-tailed *t*-test for the comparison of two means assuming equal variances. Output obtained using MS Excel Analysis ToolPak

	Variable 1 (original IS)	Variable 2 (new IS)
Mean	12	10.4
Variance	2.666667	1.822222
Observations	10	10
Pooled variance	2.244444	
Hypothesized mean difference	0	
d.f.	18	
t-stat	2.388089	
P(T<=t) two-tail	0.028105	
t critical two-tail	2.100922	

Table 18.6a Drug concentrations using a preserved and unpreserved QC

	Concentration (ng/mL) $n = 10$	
	Preserved	Unpreserved
	97	73
	102	86
	98	93
	91	81
	105	67
	97	89
	96	79
	103	82
	98	99
	92	104
Mean ± SD	*98 ± 4.5*	*85 ± 11.4*
CV (%)	*4.6*	*13.3*

0.014 for each tail. The obtained *p*-value of 0.028 is smaller than $\alpha = 0.05$ suggesting that it is unlikely to observe such an extreme test statistic if H_0 is true. As mentioned above, the null hypothesis is rejected at the statistical level $\alpha = 0.05$. Analogously, considering the significance level $\alpha = 0.10$, the *p*-value of 0.028 is lower than 0.10.

In the example provided above, the variance between both sample sets was close enough to assume equality. Most often, this assumption does not hold, and in the case of *unequal variances* between the two sample sets, the test statistic *t* is modified as follows:

$$v = \frac{\overline{x}_1 - \overline{x}_2}{\sqrt{\dfrac{s_1^2}{n_1} + \dfrac{s_2^2}{n_2}}}$$

This *v* statistic is known as the Welch modification of the Student's *t*-test (or Welch test) and is based on the idea that the uncertainties and the errors affecting the spreads of the data that are observed for a sample set differ from those observed for the other sample set. In fact, an important aspect of this statistic is that the degrees of freedom may be a non-integer (and may need to be rounded to the nearest integer) based on the following formula:

$$\text{d.f.} = \frac{\left(\dfrac{s_1^2}{n_1} + \dfrac{s_2^2}{n_2}\right)^2}{\dfrac{1}{n_1 - 1}\left(\dfrac{s_1^2}{n_1}\right)^2 + \dfrac{1}{n_2 - 1}\left(\dfrac{s_2^2}{n_2}\right)^2}$$

For example, a quantitative urine control is prepared in-house, and the role of preservative is of interest following several QC failures. After 72 h of refrigerated storage, mean and standard deviations for preserved and unpreserved controls were 98 ± 9 ng/mL and 87 ± 19 ng/mL, respectively (Table 18.6a). Although both values may be within acceptable criteria for bias (±20%), it is important to test whether or not the results are statistically different. The null and alternative hypotheses are established as described earlier, that is, $H_0: \mu_1 - \mu_2 = 0$ and $H_1: \mu_1 - \mu_2 \neq 0$, and a significance level at $\alpha = 0.05$ is selected.

Ten replicate measurements were performed, but the coefficients of variation (CVs) are noticeably different (4.6 and 13.3%, respectively). The boxplot in Fig. 18.10 not only shows a relatively large distance between the median values of the two sample sets but especially a much wider dispersion of results in the unpreserved sample. Given that overlapping values are observed between the two distributions, it is still useful to perform hypothesis testing. However, since the variances of the preserved and unpreserved samples are clearly unequal, the Welch test is more suitable.

Using this approach, the *v* statistic is calculated to 3.3 and the degrees of freedom to 11.7. Rounding the degrees of freedom (12), t_{crit} is 2.18 ($\alpha = 0.05$), so the results are indeed statistically different (Table 18.6b). Also note that the calculated *p*-value of 0.007 is much smaller than $\alpha = 0.05$.

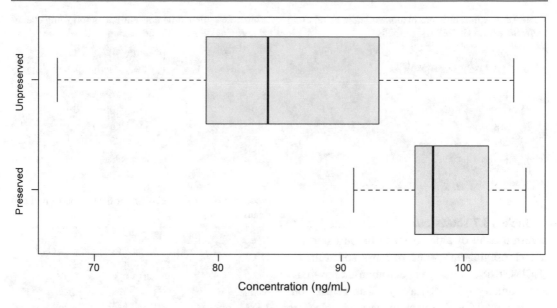

Fig. 18.10 Boxplot of the distributions of drug concentrations in preserved and unpreserved urine controls ($n = 10$ for each sample)

Table 18.6b Two-tailed Welch test for the comparison of two means assuming unequal variances

	Variable 1 (preserved)	Variable 2 (unpreserved)
Mean	97.9	85.3
Variance	20.1	129.6
Observations	10	10
Hypothesized mean Difference	0	
d.f.	12	
t-stat	3.26	
$P(T<=t)$ two-tail	0.00687	
t critical two-tail	2.18	

Paired *t*-Test

The paired t-test is used for quantitative variables when objects or individuals from the samples are "paired up," as the name suggests. This variant of the t-test may be used for evaluating the effect of a new treatment or method, when the differences between the subjects or samples themselves are substantial (e.g., to test of the effect of a new drug on blood pressure before and after treatment). Data are then collected in pairs, and the *difference between the two values for each pair* is recorded. The dataset submitted for statistical testing consists of all the recorded differences

and specifically the mean of all the differences. The null hypothesis of interest is H_0: $\mu_d = 0$, where μ_d is the mean of the paired differences. The alternative hypothesis H_a may be $\mu_d > 0$, $\mu_d < 0$, or $\mu_d \neq 0$ depending on the question of interest. If the null hypothesis is true, the average of all the differences has to be zero, meaning that there is no effect recorded before and after the two measurements on the same object. The test statistic for the paired differences is:

$$t = \frac{\bar{d} - \mu_d}{s_d / \sqrt{n}}$$

where $\bar{d}$ and s_d are, respectively, the sample mean and the sample standard deviation of all the n differences; also, $\mu_d = 0$.

If two methods of analysis are compared using case samples containing different quantities of drug, the test for comparing the means of two samples described above cannot be used because the variation due to the methods of analysis will be overpowered by the differences in concentration between the test samples. Also, the two methods are used on the same sample. In this instance, a paired t-test is used to test for a significance difference between the two methods.

Table 18.7 Concentrations of alprazolam in blood using LC/MS/MS and GC/MS test methods

| Case sample ID | Alprazolam concentration (ng/mL) | | |
	LC/MS/MS	GC/MS	Differences
2020-0056	20	17	3
2020-0081	35	41	−6
2020-0020	50	48	2
2020-0018	60	57	3
2020-0004	61	68	−7
2020-0017	71	79	−8
Mean difference, $\bar{d}$			−2.2

Table 18.7 shows quantitative results for the determination of alprazolam in blood using liquid chromatography-tandem mass spectrometry (LC/MS/MS) and gas chromatography-mass spectrometry (GC/MS) assays. The actual concentrations of alprazolam in case samples are expected to be variable, so the paired t-test is appropriate. For the six paired case samples (and 5 degrees of freedom), the differences are 3, −6, 2, 3, −7, and −8 ng/mL. The mean difference $\bar{d}$ is calculated to −2.2, and the standard deviation of the differences (s_d) is 5.3. Using these inputs in the formula above, the test statistic t is calculated to −0.99. The t_{crit} value for a two-tailed test for 5 degrees of freedom and a significance level of $\alpha = 0.05$ is 2.57 or −2.57 in this case (Appendix 1). Since the calculated t value does not fall beyond the critical value, the null hypothesis is not rejected, and it is concluded that the two test methods do not provide significantly different results. Again, the obtained p-value is 0.3663 (much larger compared to $\alpha = 0.05$).

One-Tailed and Two-Tailed Tests

The examples provided so far have used two-tailed t-tests, where significant differences between means are evaluated in *either direction*. In some cases, the sign of the significant difference is not known, in other words, it is unknown whether a specific test method would increase or decrease a measurement. When there is no preconceived idea as to the direction, all possibilities should be considered, and a *two-tailed (two-sided)* test should be performed.

Table 18.8a Free drug concentrations following chemical deconjugation for 30 and 60 min

| Final concentration of free drug (ng/mL) | |
30 min	60 min
225	256
242	280
232	240
240	245
238	249
265	263

Table 18.8b One-tailed t-test for the comparison of two means

| t-test: two-sample assuming equal variances | | |
	Variable 1 (30 min)	Variable 2 (60 min)
Mean	240.3333	255.5
Variance	184.2667	209.9
Observations	6	6
Pooled variance	197.0833	
Hypothesized mean difference	0	
d.f.	10	
t-stat	−1.87122	
$P(T<=t)$ one-tail	0.045413	
t critical one-tail	1.812461	

F-test for equal variances

However, if it is clear before the experiment that a given condition would change the measurement in one direction, then a *one-tailed (one-sided)* test should be performed. A one-sided test is used when the tested effect is expected to increase or decrease.

For example, when evaluating deconjugation efficiency, it might be reasonably assumed that increasing the incubation time for the hydrolysis step could increase the final concentration of free (unconjugated) drug. Table 18.8a shows free drug concentrations for six blood samples that were deconjugated for 30 and 60 min. The hypotheses to be tested may be defined as H_0: $\mu_1 - \mu_2 \geq 0$ and H_1: $\mu_1 - \mu_2 < 0$ where μ_1 is the population mean of the drug concentration after 30 min and μ_2 is the population mean of the drug concentration after 60 min. A significance level at $\alpha = 0.05$ is considered. Table 18.8b shows the results of the one-tailed t-test where the calculated t-statistic is -1.87 and the p-value is 0.0454. Although this is a left-tailed test (i.e., comparing negative values), the t-table in Appendix 1 only shows values for the upper tail, which are positive; hence for a one-tailed test, $|t| = 1.87$ is compared to the critical value in the column of $\alpha = 0.05$ which is 1.81 for 10 degrees of freedom. Given that the t-statistic of 1.87 falls beyond the critical value of 1.81 (also, the calculated p-value of 0.0454 is smaller than $\alpha = 0.05$), the null hypothesis can be rejected, indicating that the increased free drug concentration using the longer incubation time is statistically significant at $\alpha = 0.05$.

The significance tests provided so far have discussed the comparison of means with each other or known values to determine if there are differences between populations. However, sometimes it is also important to compare the variances or standard deviations between datasets, which allows the random errors between methods to be statistically compared.

For example, if we hypothesize that a method using an isotopically labelled internal standard is more precise than a non-isotopically labelled internal standard, then a one-tailed test could be used to evaluate statistical significance. However, if the purpose is to test whether the standard deviations of both methods differ significantly (in either direction), a two-tailed test is more appropriate. Different tests for equal variances are available such as the F-test, the Bartlett's test, or the Levene's test. The F-test is discussed here, due to its importance in ANOVA (discussed later).

The F-test is defined by the ratio of the two sample variances (or squared standard deviations) of the two populations of interest:

$$F = \frac{s_1^2}{s_2^2}$$

The F-statistic is always equal or greater than 1. Differences from 1 are attributed to random variation; however, if the difference is too large, it is attributed to a true difference between the variances or standard deviations. The null hypothesis states that the compared populations are nor-

Table 18.9 Quantitative determination of benzoylecgonine (BE) using liquid-liquid extraction (LLE) and solid-phase extraction (SPE)

Internal standard	BE concentration (ng/mL)	
	Mean	Standard deviation
LLE ($n = 8$)	72	3.05
SPE ($n = 8$)	71	1.51

mal and have equal variance. The alternative hypothesis may be stated as a one-tailed or a two-tailed test. Like for the t-statistic, if $F > F_{crit}$, then the null hypothesis is rejected. Some of the critical values for F are reported in Appendix 2 and depend on the size of both samples (i.e., their degrees of freedom) and the significance level of interest. Finally, if the null hypothesis of equal variances is true, F is close to 1; on the other hand, if the alternative hypothesis is true, then F tends to be large.

Table 18.9 lists benzoylecgonine concentrations obtained using two extraction techniques. It can be observed that the standard deviation for the LLE is higher than the one for SPE; therefore a legitimate question might be if SPE is indeed more precise than LLE or, alternatively stated, if the variance in the BE concentration is greater for LLE than for SPE. In this case a one-tailed test is used where H_0: $\sigma_1^2 / \sigma_2^2 \leq 1$ and H_1: $\sigma_1^2 / \sigma_2^2 > 1$. σ_1^2 is the variance for LLE, and σ_2^2 is the variance for SPE.

The value of the $F_{7,7}$ statistic is $3.05^2/1.51^2 = 4.08$. The critical value of F for a one-tailed test at a α-level of 0.05 is 3.79 (see F-table in Appendix 2). Therefore, because $F_{7,7} > F_{crit}$, the increased variance using LLE is significant at the chosen significance level allowing to conclude that the SPE method is more precise than the LLE method.

However, assume that the question of interest is a more general one about the precision of the two methods, that is, are there statistically significant differences in precision between the two extraction techniques? A two-tailed test is carried out, and the hypotheses become H_0: $\sigma_1^2 / \sigma_2^2 = 1$ and H_1: $\sigma_1^2 / \sigma_2^2 \neq 1$. The $F_{7,7}$ statistic remains the same, 4.08, and, considering a α-level of 0.05, it is compared to the critical value of 4.99 for $\alpha/2$ in the F-table. In this case, the calculated F-statistic

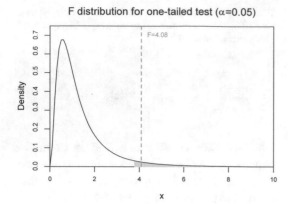

Fig. 18.11 $F_{7,7}$ distributions for one-tailed test (left) and two-tailed test (right) at a significance level $\alpha = 0.05$. The location of the critical value ($F = 4.08$) is located in the rejection area of the distribution in the case of the one-tailed test but not in the case of the two-tailed test

does not fall in the rejection region of the distribution, and therefore H_0 is retained, and a difference in precision between the two extraction methods cannot be claimed. Figure 18.11 shows the comparison between the F distribution for both one-tailed and two-tailed tests.

In general, failure to reject the null hypothesis from a F-test does not necessarily justify the assumption that the null hypothesis is true, that is, the variances of the compared sample sets are actually equal. Also, note that in this example, there were eight replicates. Should a test be carried out using ten replicates, and assuming that the same standard deviation values were obtained, the two-tailed test would have rejected the null hypothesis ($F_{\mathrm{crit}} = 4.03$) as was the case of the one-tailed test. Therefore, caution is necessary when comparing relatively small datasets, which is commonplace during method development or optimization in forensic toxicology applications.

Type I and Type II Errors

In the context of hypothesis testing, and particularly in cases where a decision needs to be made about the acceptance (or failure to reject) or rejection of a hypothesis of interest, a cutoff point or threshold is initially set. A classic approach for continuous data (e.g., BAC) would be to initially

define a desired significance level α (or cutoff point) and compute a p-value; if the calculated p-value is smaller than α then the null hypothesis is rejected. It is not possible to know if the null hypothesis or its alternative is actually true, and therefore this type of decision is not exempt from error; the choice of a significance level corresponds to how much risk one wants to take to make an incorrect decision of rejecting the null hypothesis when it is true. This rejection is known as *Type I error* and is denoted by α However, the null hypothesis could also be incorrectly accepted when it should be rejected: this error is referred as *Type II error* and is denoted by β. The decisions of correctly accepting the null hypothesis $(1-\alpha)$ and the alternative hypothesis $(1-\beta)$ are known as the *size* and *power* of a test respectively. While the amount of α is predetermined before the test, β is typically deduced from the power. The power of a test is the probability of correctly rejecting the null hypothesis when the alternative one is true or, otherwise stated, the probability that the fixed significance level α will lead to the rejection of the null hypothesis, when the specified value in the alternative hypothesis is true.

To calculate the power, a value of interest under the alternative hypothesis is first specified, then the rejection region for the null hypothesis is computed, and finally the probability that the calculated test statistic falls in the rejection region if

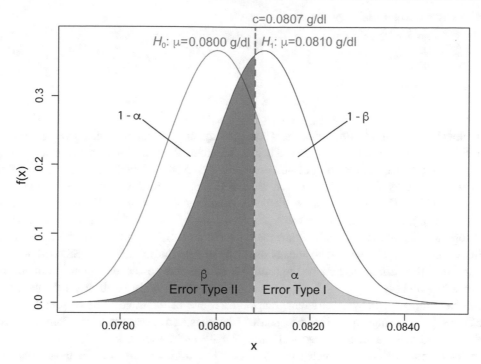

Fig. 18.12 Overlapping normal distributions for a hypothetical BAC centered at 0.080 g/dL for the null hypothesis and 0.081 g/dL for the alternative hypothesis. The critical value was set to 0.087 g/dL. The areas of the size $(1-\alpha)$, the power $(1-\beta)$, the Type I error α, and Type II error β are shown

the alternative hypothesis is true is computed. There is a compromise that needs to be made between power and size: relatively to the cutoff point, if size increases, power decreases, and vice versa or if α is increased, β is decreased, and vice versa. Figure 18.12 shows this effect for an example of a hypothesis test for a population mean from a normal distribution.

Comparison of Several Means: Analysis of Variance (ANOVA)

Analysis of variance or ANOVA is an extension of hypothesis testing and the linear model. In analytical work, it is often of interest to compare the properties of more than two groups or populations. Examples may be the comparison of the results of measurements made by different examiners using the same procedure in a laboratory or the means of samples stored under different conditions over a period of time. In instances like this, there are two sources of variation: the

first is the random variation in the measurement which causes a different result to be obtained each time the measurement is repeated under the same conditions and the second possible source of variation could be due to a *controlled* or *fixed-effect factor* (e.g., the storage conditions or different examiners). In these instances, ANOVA is a helpful method to compare more than two groups or populations on the basis of the variations of some properties and factors of interest, considering their different causes of variation. In the example provided above, ANOVA can be used to separate variation that is caused by changing the controlled factor (i.e., storage conditions) from the random errors associated with the measurement itself. ANOVA can be used when there is more than one source of random variation, for example, sampling, where homogeneity may be an issue. This is sometimes referred to as a *random effect factor*.

ANOVA methods simultaneously explain the different sources of variation that lie within a group and between different groups. The ques-

Table 18.10 Analysis of variance table for one-way ANOVA

Variation	Sums of squares	Degrees of freedom	Mean squares	F-statistic	p-value
Model	SSM	DFM	MSM	MSM/MSR	
Residuals	SSR	DFR	MSR		
Total	SST	DFT	MST		

tions of interest are "Is the difference between groups significant or is it due to chance?" These questions are formalized in the form of null and alternative hypotheses to be tested, which are typically defined as H_0, all the means are equal ($\mu_1 = \mu_2 = \ldots = \mu_i$), and H_1, not all of the μ_i are equal. Note that the different sample means may be different even if their population means are equal, and thus this difference may be the result of the sampling process.

When the comparison between different groups is made considering a single quantitative response variable grouped using a single categorical variable or factor, the method is denoted *one-way ANOVA*. On the other hand, if the measurements on a single quantitative response variable are grouped using two categorical variables, then a *two-way ANOVA* is carried out. Higher-way ANOVA approaches are possible as well.

The examined sources of variation of the individual observations y_i are partitioned in (a) between-group variation and (b) within-group variation. The total variation in the response variable y corresponds to the deviations $y_i - \overline{y}$, where y_i is the response variable for a single observation i and $\overline{y}$ is their mean. For the between-group variation, the observations y_i differ because of the different values of the explanatory variable x. The fitted value $\hat{y}_i$ estimates the mean response for specific x_i values, and therefore the differences $\hat{y}_i - \overline{y}$ describe the variation of the mean response due to the differences in the x_i values. With regard to the within-group variation, the y_i observations fluctuate around their mean due to the variation within the responses to a fixed x_i. The residuals $y_i - \hat{y}_i$ describe this variation, which corresponds to the scattering of the various observations around the fitted line for a given x_i value. The total variation is thus expressed as $(y_i - \overline{y}) = (\hat{y}_i - \overline{y}) + (y_i - \hat{y}_i)$, which can be regarded as *data = fit + residual* or *data = signal + noise*. These three deviations

are squared and then summed over all the n observations to obtain the three characteristic descriptors of the ANOVA table (Table 18.10), that is, SST = SSM + SSR, which are denoted *total sum of squares*, *sum of squares of the model*, and *sum of squares of the residuals*, respectively. The total variation (SST) is the sum of the variation due to the straight line of the model (SSM) along with variation due to the deviations from the model (SSR). From Table 18.10, it can be seen that for each one of the three sums of squares, there are three respective degrees of freedom, expressed as DFT = DFM + DFR.

The third column of the table contains the *mean squares*, which are the ratios between the sum of squares and the degrees of freedom for each of the three types of variations. The mean squares in the residual (MSR) expressed the pooled variance and is used to calculate the F-statistic (MSM/MSR) used to test the hypotheses defined above. A *p*-value is also reported in the table to gauge the strength of the evidence against the null hypothesis.

As part of the linear model, ANOVA also assumes that the population means are normally distributed and that the variance is the same for all the groups or populations. The same applies to the residuals that should be independent to each other, be normally distributed, and have a mean of zero and standard deviation σ. Some diagnostics can be run to evaluate compliance with these conditions including checking the normality of the data, the equality of the standard deviations of the groups to be compared, and the normality of their residuals.

For example, consider that during method development for a new extraction method, three organic solvents are evaluated. Drug recoveries were measured using four replicate measurements ($n = 4$) for each solvent (Table 18.11a). The question at hand is whether the results are

Table 18.11a Recovery of drug using three organic solvents

Drug recovery (%)		
Ether/toluene (1:1)	N-Butyl chloride	Hexane/ethyl acetate (9:1)
104	75	85
83	71	92
81	76	69
103	86	82

statistically significant. A one-way ANOVA is used with the solvent type as the single categorical factor and the drug recovery percentage as the continuous response variable. The hypotheses are defined as H_0, all the means are equal ($\mu_{ether/toluene} = \mu_{n\text{-}butylchloride} = \mu_{hexane/ethylacetate}$), and H_1, not all of the means are equal.

The ANOVA table (Table 18.11b) shows that the calculated F-statistic is 2.75, compared with F_{crit} of 4.25 for 11 degrees of freedom. Therefore, the differences in drug recovery between organic solvents is not statistically significant. Also, the obtained p-value of 0.1166, which is higher than 0.1, does not constitute evidence against the null hypothesis.

In the case of two-way ANOVA, the FIT part of the model includes the two factors denoted by A and B, where factor A has I levels and B has J levels. Each level of A is combined with each level of B, and the result is the comparison of $I \times J$ groups. The model is called $I \times J$ ANOVA. In addition to the factors A and B, also known as the *main effects*, their *interaction* is also evaluated.

The ANOVA table is changed accordingly by adding a row for the interaction of A and B. Also, three F-statistics are calculated, two for each one of the two factors taken individually and one for the interaction. Therefore, three null hypotheses are enunciated, and a F-test is performed for each of them.

For example, consider that the stability of a drug is evaluated at various temperatures and pH. Replicate measurements ($n = 4$) are made under each experimental condition. The two categorical factors are temperature, which has three levels (frozen, refrigerated, and RT), and pH, which has four levels (pH values of 2, 4, 6, and 8);

the continuous response variable is the drug concentration (ng/mL). Table 18.12a summarizes the concentration of drug following a specified period of storage under each of the 12 conditions. Since there are now *two factors* of interest (temperature and pH), a two-way ANOVA can be used. In the two-way ANOVA, there are three hypotheses that are tested: (1) there is no effect on drug stability due to temperature, (2) there is no effect on drug stability due to pH, and (3) there is no interaction between temperature and pH.

First, the data are inspected visually by means of boxplots (Fig. 18.13). The graph shows a clear decrease of concentration as a function of temperature. There is overlapping between concentrations for different pH values within a given group of temperatures. While it appears clear that temperature is a factor that affects storage of this drug, it is important to verify whether pH also impacts storage and more importantly if the two factors together *interact*.

The interaction between the two factors of temperature and pH can be inspected by means of an interaction plot (Fig. 18.14), which displays the mean values (connected with lines) of the drug concentration response variable of all the levels of the two factors. The lines of the mean values indicate an interaction between the two factors if they are parallel, and there is no interaction if the lines are not parallel. The interaction plot in Fig. 18.14 exhibits parallel lines. The only deviation from parallelism is observed for pH 4 and between the frozen and refrigerated temperatures. It is then useful to test if this deviation may be significant.

Tables 18.12b and 18.12c show the outputs of the two-way ANOVA using the Excel Analysis ToolPak and Rsoftware ($\alpha = 0.05$), respectively. The sum of squares (SS), degrees of freedom (d.f.), and mean square (MS) are shown. The F-test is used to determine if the estimates of variance differ significantly. Comparing the between-pH mean square with the residual or within mean square yields a calculated $F < F_{crit}$. Therefore, no significant difference between pH was observed.

However, variation between temperature yields an F value of 91.76, far exceeding F_{crit}

Table 18.11b One-way ANOVA of drug recovery results

ANOVA: single factor							
Summary							
Groups	*Count*	*Sum*	*Average*	*Variance*			
Column 1	4	3.713811	0.928453	0.015503			
Column 2	4	3.079888	0.769972	0.003898			
Column 3	4	3.275303	0.818826	0.009299			
ANOVA							
Source of variation	*SS*	*d.f.*	*MS*	*F*	*p-value*	F_{crit}	
Between groups	0.052695	2	0.026347	2.754007	0.116642	4.256495	
Within groups	0.086102	9	0.009567				
Total	0.138796	11					

Table 18.12a Drug concentrations following sample storage for 24 h at various temperatures and pH

	Concentration (ng/mL)			
	pH 2	pH 4	pH 6	pH 8
Frozen	105	95	105	110
	101	89	96	114
	110	101	90	105
	107	93	111	108
Refrigerated	87	88	85	89
	93	93	90	94
	82	83	80	84
	84	85	82	86
RT	79	81	78	79
	74	86	78	80
	85	76	83	74
	77	80	73	85

(3.26). Also note that the probability (*p*-value) of obtaining an *F*-statistic of 3.26 or greater when the null hypothesis is true is extremely small (<0.00001). Since the *p*-value is much less than the specified value ($\alpha = 0.05$), the null hypothesis is rejected confirming that storage temperature is statistically significant.

ANOVA can be a useful tool that helps detect differences between the compared groups or populations. However, additional statistical tests are sometimes warranted to further investigate the individual factors or the variables themselves or to identify which groups or populations actually differ. Subsequent methods may be linear contrasts which are linear combinations of variables whose coefficients add up to zero allowing comparisons of different factors or treatments by means of hypothesis testing (e.g., *t*-tests) or multiple comparison procedures which use hypothesis testing with confidence intervals such as the

Bonferroni's correction, the Tukey's honestly significant difference (HSD), the Fisher's protected least significance difference (LSD), the Fisher-Hayter test statistic, or the Sheffé's multiple comparison test and confidence interval.

Outliers

Statistical tests can be used to identify and remove data that appear to be outliers, that is, observations that fall far from the rest of the observations in the distribution. When the removal of data is presented as a hypothesis (i.e., the aberrant value is, or is not, an outlier), the evaluation is quantitative and objective. However, the decision on whether or not an aberrant value is actually an outlier and can be reasonably omitted depends on the specific case and on the context of the analysis. In analytical work, it is important to determine if aberrant value is due to instrumental or human factors, lack of homogeneity of the sample, inadequate sampling, or lack of control on unknown specimens. Indeed, in the case of unknown specimens submitted to the laboratory for testing, caution should be exercised when considering to omit aberrant values, especially if a low number of replicates are collected. Trusting a statistical test may be misleading in such context.

Statistical outlier detection takes the form of hypothesis testing. If one assumes that data gathered during instrumental analysis in forensic toxicology mostly follow a normal distribution, this assumption can be tested. Given that 95% of

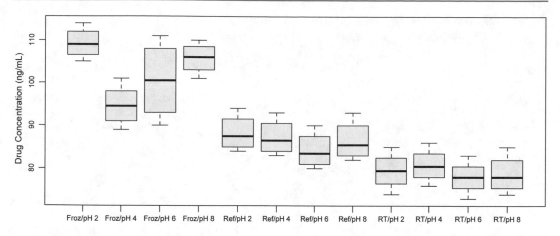

Fig. 18.13 Boxplots of drug concentrations for each combination of temperature and pH factors during a drug stability experiment ($n = 4$ for each combination); frozen (froz), refrigerated (ref), room temperature (RT)

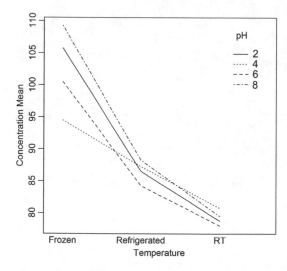

Fig. 18.14 Interaction plot of the mean values of the drug concentration for each temperature and pH

the data are within two standard deviations of the mean, 5% are expected to fall on the outside edges; although the appearance of data in this region is less prevalent, it is not unexpected. Statistical testing can help determine if a particular observation is a true outlier or an unlikely result.

The hypotheses to be tested are first stated and have a quantity with an associated calculated probability. The null hypothesis is accepted or rejected by comparing the calculated quantity with a critical value from a table of values. An associated confidence level or a significance level

must be selected (e.g., 95% or $\alpha = 0.05$, respectively). The null hypothesis takes the form of a statement that assumes that there is no difference between the calculated quantity and the expected quantity except that portion attributed to random error.

For example, in the BAC determination described earlier, suppose that both the Examiner and Trainee B obtained a value of 0.069 g/dL instead of the tenth determination listed in Table 18.2. How can these values be evaluated for both individuals, to determine if they are in fact outliers?

The null hypothesis in the example provided above assumes that the 0.069 g/dL BAC results for both the Examiner and Trainee B can be attributed to normal random error. In order for inclusion of the data point with 95% confidence, the results would need to be significant (or not significant) at the 5% level (i.e., $\alpha = 0.05$). Once the hypothesis and confidence level have been selected, a statistical test can be applied. The significance level gives the probability of rejecting the null hypothesis.

Different tests exist for testing for outliers. Examples are the Dixon's Q test and the Grubbs test for detecting a single outlier as well as the Tietjen-Moore test or the generalized extreme Studentized deviate test for more than a single outlier.

The use of the Dixon's Q test is shown for the BAC example. The Dixon's Q test must meet the

Table 18.12b Two-way ANOVA using Excel Analysis ToolPak

ANOVA: two-factor with replication					
Summary	pH 2	pH 4	pH 6	pH 8	Total
Frozen					
Count	4	4	4	4	16
Sum	423	378	402	437	1640
Average	105.75	94.5	100.5	109.25	102.5
Variance	14.25	25	87	14.25	61.2
Refrigerated					
Count	4	4	4	4	16
Sum	346	349	337	353	1385
Average	86.5	87.25	84.25	88.25	86.5625
Variance	23	18.91667	18.91667	18.91667	18.2625
RT					
Count	4	4	4	4	16
Sum	315	323	312	318	1268
Average	78.75	80.75	78	79.5	79.25
Variance	21.58333	16.91667	16.66667	20.33333	16.2
Total					
Count	12	12	12	12	
Sum	1084	1050	1051	1108	
Average	90.33333	87.5	87.58333	92.33333	
Variance	156.6061	51	131.5379	184.6061	
ANOVA					
Source of variation	SS	d.f.	MS	F	p-value	F_{crit}
Rows (temp)	4522.875	2	2261.438	**91.7574**	**7.36E-15**	**3.259446**
Columns (pH)	196.5625	3	65.52083	2.658495	0.062889	2.866266
Interaction	351.125	6	58.52083	2.374472	0.049121	2.363751
Within	887.25	36	24.64583			
Total	5957.813	47				

Table 18.12c Two-way ANOVA using R statistical software

```
Analysis of Variance Table

Response: Conc
            Df Sum Sq Mean Sq F value    Pr(>F)
Temp         2 4522.9 2261.44 91.7574 7.364e-15 ***
pH           3  196.6   65.52  2.6585   0.06289 .
Temp:pH      6  351.1   58.52  2.3745   0.04912 *
Residuals   36  887.2   24.65
---
Signif. codes:  0 '***' 0.001 '**' 0.01 '*' 0.05 '.' 0.1 ' ' 1
```

conditions that the sample size needs to be greater than 3 and that the population of interest is normally distributed. Operationally, the n observations are organized in increasing or decreasing order $(x_1,...,x_n)$; the gap between the observed aberrant value (x_1) and its closest value (x_2) is calculated, and the range of the data is determined (i.e., the difference between the maximum and the minimum). The Q statistic is then calculated as the ratio between the gap and the range as follows:

$$Q = \frac{x_2 - x_1}{x_n - x_1} \text{if} 3 < n \le 7$$

$$Q = \frac{x_2 - x_1}{x_{n-1} - x_1} \text{if} 8 \le n \le 10$$

If $Q > Q_{\text{crit}}$, then, according to the test, x_n is statistically considered as an outlier is considered for omission from the dataset.

Using the BAC example above, assuming that the tenth measurement in Table 18.2 is replaced with 0.069 g/dL, the Q statistic for Trainee B is calculated to 0.11 (0.001/0.009). From the Q table (Appendix 3), the critical value of Q for $\alpha = 0.05$ is 0.464. Therefore, the value should not be considered for rejection. However, the Q statistic for the Examiner is calculated to 0.75 (0.009/0.012) which exceeds the Q_{crit}, and therefore the Examiner should consider rejecting this aberrant value.

Regression

The linear model or simple linear regression is the most basic method for regression and is widely used in forensic toxicology. The linear model describes the existence of a linear relationship between two variables, or covariates, to make predictions of a new quantity value of a *dependent or response variable* y (e.g., concentration) after gathering measurements from a correlated *independent or explanatory variable x*. Most often, x and y are continuous variables. Their liner relationship is described by the equation of a straight line:

$$y_i = \beta_0 + \beta_1 x_i + \varepsilon_i$$

where the regression coefficients β_0 and β_1 are the *intercept* and the *slope* of the line. The term $\beta_0 + \beta_1 x_i$ corresponds to the mean response, and ε_i is called the *error* (residuals or deviations) and describes the difference between a single observation and the mean. Other ways to describe that models are again *data=fit+residual* or *data=signal+noise*. The residuals or deviations ε_i are assumed to be independent and normally distributed with mean 0 and standard deviation σ. Hence, the parameters β_0, β_1, and σ are estimated from the collected sample and are denoted b_0, b_1, and s, respectively.

The single measurements are initially visualized in a scatterplot, which is an informative way to appreciate the direction and the strength of the linear relationship. A linear relationship is strong when the plotted points lie close to a straight line and weak if they are widely scattered. A regression line is then fitted, which is a straight line that describes how the response variable y changes as the explanatory variable x changes and is used to predict a value of y for an observed value of x.

A typical measurement of the direction and the strength of the linear relationship between two quantitative variables is the *Pearson correlation* or simply *correlation*, denoted r, and is calculated using the following formula:

$$r_{x,y} = \frac{\sum_{i=1}^{n}(x_i - \bar{x})(y_i - \bar{y})}{(n-1)s_x s_y}$$

where $\bar{x}$ and $\bar{y}$ are the means of the two variables, s_x and s_y are their standard deviations, and n is the total number of observations. The numerator of this formula is the *covariance* which describes how small x values are paired with small y values and large x values are paired with large y values or vice versa. The correlation r is a number between -1 and 1, these latter values indicating that the points in a scatterplot lie exactly along a straight line, while values near 0 indicate a very weak linear relationship. However, the coefficient of *determination*, R^2 (or percentage level of variation of y is attributed to x), is considered a more representative measure of the strength of the linear relationship between the two covariates in the sense that it measures how much of the variance in one of the covariates is attributed to the other.

To construct the simple linear regression model, the parameters of the model β_0 and β_1 are estimated by means of b_0 and b_1 for the n observations (x_1,y_1), (x_2,y_2),..., (x_n,y_n) on the explanatory variable x and the response variable y. For the least squares line $\hat{y} = b_0 + b_1 x$, the slope is determined using the equations below and the intercept is derived as $b_0 = \bar{y} - b_1\bar{x}$.

$$b_1 = r\frac{s_x}{s_y} \text{ or } b_1 = \frac{\sum_{i=1}^{n}(x_i - \bar{x})(y_i - \bar{y})}{\sum_{i=1}^{n}(x_i - \bar{x})^2}$$

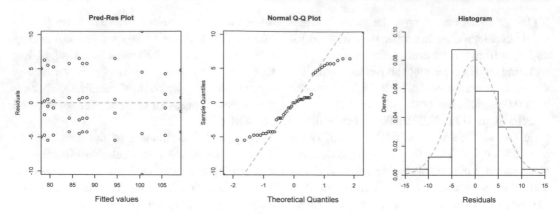

Fig. 18.15 Pred-res plot, Q-Q plot, and histogram of the residuals of the data from the two-way ANOVA study on the effects of temperature and pH on sample storage

Regression analysis is widely used in forensic toxicology, most frequently for the quantitative analysis of a substance in a biological matrix, where the mathematical relationship between signal response and concentration is of interest. However, it is also useful for the comparison of experimental methods or data to evaluate the concordance of results or establish mathematical relationships between them (so that one can be predicted from the other).

Residuals

In a real setting, there is no line that passes through all the data points, and therefore a regression line that passes as close as possible to the observed points in the scatterplot needs to be fitted. In other words, the line passes as close as possible to the points in the *vertical direction*, and given that the line is used to predict y from x, the errors in the predictions are errors in y.

Within this model, called least squares regression, the vertical distances between the observed data points and the fitted line have the smallest possible sum of squares. These distances are called residuals because they consist of the surplus of variation in the response variable y after having fitted the regression line. A residual is defined as the difference between an observed data point of the response variable and the value predicted by the regression line for a given value of the explanatory variable, denoted $y_i - \hat{y}_i$. The

residuals are useful to evaluate how well the fitted line describes the data. Their mean is always zero; just like the observed data points, they are assumed to be independent to one another, have constant scatter around the line (i.e., same variance σ^2), and are normally distributed.

Diagnostics can be performed to verify the assumptions of the residuals. A *pred-res plot* can be constructed to verify if the residuals have different variances between y values. The residuals ($y_i - \hat{y}_i$) are plotted against the fitted values over the range of x. If the residual points exhibit constant scatter around the line, then they are homogeneously distributed and centered around zero (i.e., homoscedasticity). Another useful graphical aid is the normal quantile-quantile plot (or normal Q-Q plot). The Q-Q plot compares the normality of the distribution of the residuals by plotting the empirical quantiles of the data points against the theoretical quantiles of the normal distribution. If the data points are normally distributed, they will align to the straight line defined by the theoretical quantiles. Figure 18.15 shows an illustration of these diagnostics for the two-way ANOVA example on the effects of temperature and pH on sample storage (Table 18.12a).

Selection of the most appropriate calibration model is important in forensic toxicology. Simple linear regression models are preferred when homoscedasticity is observed. When there is a notable difference in variance across the concentration range (i.e., heteroscedasticity), typically at the lowest or highest concentrations, a weighted

Table 18.13 Coefficients of determination (R^2) for linear and quadratic calibration models

Day	R^2 value	
	Linear	Quadratic
1	0.9887	0.9998
2	0.9930	1.0000
3	0.9983	0.9997
4	0.9977	0.9999
5	0.9871	1.0000
Mean	0.9937	0.9999

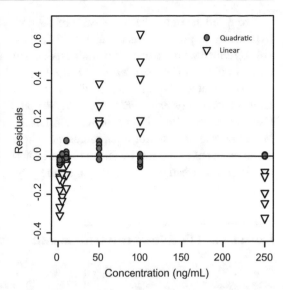

Fig. 18.16 Residual plot analysis depicting improved assay performance (homoscedasticity) using a quadratic calibration model over the concentration range of interest

or non-linear model should be explored. However, it is not sufficient to consider only the correlation coefficient or coefficient of determination when selecting the calibration model. This is illustrated in the following example.

During method validation, calibration models were explored in accordance with ANSI/ASB Standard 036 (Standard Practices for Method Validation in Forensic Toxicology). Six non-zero calibrators (2, 5, 10, 50, 100, 250 ng/mL) were evaluated over 5 days. Table 18.13 summarizes coefficients of determination obtained using unweighted linear and quadratic calibration models. R^2 values for both calibration models exceed 0.99. However, the residual plot analysis (Fig. 18.16) shows very clearly the superiority of the quadratic fit. Although unweighted calibration models are depicted for simplicity, this approach is very useful when multiple calibration models are being evaluated.

The Bayesian Approach

The Bayesian approach is a reasoning tool that allows revising or reassigning probabilities or beliefs of events of interest when new informa-

tion becomes available. In forensic science, it is appealing because it allows integrating the scientific findings into an already existing context (e.g., investigation or trial) and, as a fundamental property, it considers simultaneously opposing positions (e.g., prosecutor vs. defense). Within the structure of the Bayesian approach, the role of the forensic scientist and those of other parties (e.g., jury, attorneys, or investigators) are clearly separated and well defined. The logic and the usefulness of the Bayesian approach with emphasis on likelihood ratios has been discussed in the literature since the 1970s. Mathematically, the Bayesian approach has been proposed using the following odds form:

$$\underbrace{\frac{p\left(H_1 \mid I\right)}{p\left(H_2 \mid I\right)}}_{\substack{\text{Prior Odds} \\ \text{Domain of} \\ \text{stakeholders of justice} \\ \text{(e.g., jury, attorneys, investigators)}}} \times \underbrace{\frac{p(E \mid H_1, I)}{p(E \mid H_2, I)}}_{\substack{\text{Likelihood Ratio} \\ \text{Domain of the} \\ \text{forensic scientist}}} = \underbrace{\frac{p\left(H_1 \mid E, I\right)}{p\left(H_2 \mid E, I\right)}}_{\substack{\text{Posterior Odds} \\ \text{Domain of stakeholders} \\ \text{of justice} \\ \text{(e.g., jury, attorneys, investigators)}}}$$

From left to right, the *prior odds* of the two hypotheses or propositions of interest H_1 and H_2 are combined with the scientific findings, denoted by E, in the form of the *likelihood ratio*, to provide an updated ratio of probabilities of H_1 and H_2 in a form of *posterior odds*. The term I denotes knowledge about the relevant case circumstances. While prior and posterior odds represent beliefs about an event of interest by stakeholders of justice such as investigators, attorneys, or the jury,

the likelihood ratio (LR) constitutes the forensic scientist's domain of competence.

The likelihood ratio is defined as the probability of observing certain results given that the proposition H_1 is true, divided by the probability of observing the same results given that the proposition H_2 is true. The likelihood ratio can assume values that range between zero and infinity: if $LR > 1$, the observed results (i.e., the evidence E) support H_1; if the $LR \approx 1$, the evidence is said to be inconclusive

Appendix 1: Table of the critical values for the Student's *t*-distribution

| d.f. | α – upper tail probability p | | | | | | |
	0.10	0.05	0.025	0.01	0.005	0.001	0.0005
1	3.078	6.314	12.076	31.821	63.657	318.310	636.620
2	1.886	2.920	4.303	6.965	9.925	22.326	31.598
3	1.638	2.353	3.182	4.541	5.841	10.213	12.924
4	1.533	2.132	2.776	3.747	4.604	7.173	8.610
5	1.476	2.015	2.571	3.365	4.032	5.893	6.869
6	1.440	1.943	2.447	3.143	3.707	5.208	5.959
7	1.415	1.895	2.365	2.998	3.499	4.785	5.408
8	1.397	1.860	2.306	2.896	3.355	4.501	5.041
9	1.383	1.833	2.262	2.821	3.250	4.297	4.781
10	1.372	1.812	2.228	2.764	3.169	4.144	4.587
11	1.363	1.796	2.201	2.718	3.106	4.025	4.437
12	1.356	1.782	2.179	2.681	3.055	3.930	4.318
13	1.350	1.771	2.160	2.650	3.012	3.852	4.221
14	1.345	1.761	2.145	2.624	2.977	3.787	4.140
15	1.341	1.753	2.131	2.602	2.947	3.733	4.073
16	1.337	1.746	2.120	2.583	2.921	3.686	4.015
17	1.333	1.740	2.110	2.567	2.898	3.646	3.965
18	1.330	1.734	2.101	2.552	2.878	3.610	3.922
19	1.328	1.729	2.093	2.539	2.861	3.579	3.883
20	1.325	1.725	2.086	2.528	2.845	3.552	3.850
21	1.323	1.721	2.080	2.518	2.831	3.527	3.819
22	1.321	1.717	2.074	2.508	2.819	3.505	3.792
23	1.319	1.714	2.069	2.500	2.807	3.485	3.767
24	1.318	1.711	2.064	2.492	2.797	3.467	3.745
25	1.316	1.708	2.060	2.485	2.787	3.450	3.725
26	1.315	1.706	2.056	2.479	2.779	3.435	3.707
27	1.314	1.703	2.052	2.473	2.771	3.421	3.690
28	1.313	1.701	2.048	2.467	2.763	3.408	3.674
29	1.311	1.699	2.045	2.462	2.756	3.396	3.659
30	1.310	1.697	2.042	2.457	2.750	3.385	3.646
40	1.303	1.684	2.021	2.423	2.704	3.307	3.551
60	1.296	1.671	2.000	2.390	2.660	3.232	3.460
120	1.289	1.658	1.980	2.358	2.617	3.160	3.373
1000	1.282	1.646	1.962	2.330	2.581	3.098	3.300
z	1.282	1.645	1.960	2.326	2.576	3.091	3.291
	80%	90%	95%	98%	99%	99.8%	99.9%
	Confidence level C						

Appendix 2: Table of selected critical values for the *F* distribution for sample sets of 10 objects or 9 degrees of freedom and a significance level at α = 0.05. Refer to rows α = 0.05 for a one-tailed test and rows α = 0.025 for a two-tailed test

		d.f. in the numerator								
d.f. in the denominator	α	1	2	3	4	5	6	7	8	9
1	0.05	161.45	199.50	215.71	224.58	230.16	233.99	236.77	238.88	240.54
	0.025	647.79	799.50	864.16	899.58	921.85	937.11	948.22	956.66	963.28
2	0.05	18.51	19.00	19.16	19.25	19.30	19.33	19.35	19.37	19.38
	0.025	38.51	39.00	39.17	39.25	39.30	39.33	39.36	39.37	39.39
3	0.05	10.13	9.55	9.28	9.12	9.01	8.94	8.89	8.85	8.81
	0.025	17.44	16.04	15.44	15.10	14.88	14.73	14.62	14.54	14.47
4	0.05	7.71	6.94	6.59	6.39	6.26	6.16	6.09	6.04	6.00
	0.025	12.22	10.65	9.98	9.60	9.36	9.20	9.07	8.98	8.90
5	0.05	6.61	5.79	5.41	5.19	5.05	4.95	4.88	4.82	4.77
	0.025	10.01	8.43	7.76	7.39	7.15	6.98	6.85	6.76	6.68
6	0.05	5.99	5.14	4.76	4.53	4.39	4.28	4.21	4.15	4.10
	0.025	8.81	7.26	6.60	6.23	5.99	5.82	5.70	5.60	5.52
7	0.05	5.59	4.74	4.35	4.12	3.97	3.87	3.79	3.73	3.68
	0.025	8.07	6.54	5.89	5.52	5.29	5.12	4.99	4.90	4.82
8	0.05	5.32	4.46	4.07	3.84	3.69	3.58	3.50	3.44	3.39
	0.025	7.57	6.06	5.42	5.05	4.82	4.65	4.53	4.43	4.36
9	0.05	5.12	4.26	3.86	3.63	3.48	3.37	3.29	3.23	3.18
	0.025	7.21	5.71	5.08	4.72	4.48	4.32	4.20	4.10	4.03

Appendix 3: Table of critical values of the Q test statistic (*P* = 0.05)

Q test statistic		Significance level α		
	n	0.10	0.05	0.01
	3	0.886	0.941	0.988
	4	0.679	0.765	0.889
$Q = \dfrac{x_2 - x_1}{x_n - x_1}$	5	0.557	0.642	0.780
	6	0.482	0.560	0.698
	7	0.434	0.507	0.637
	8	0.479	0.554	0.683
	9	0.441	0.512	0.635
$Q = \dfrac{x_2 - x_1}{x_{n-1} - x_1}$	10	0.409	0.477	0.597
	11	0.517	0.576	0.679
	12	0.490	0.546	0.642
$Q = \dfrac{x_3 - x_1}{x_{n-1} - x_1}$	13	0.467	0.521	0.615
	14	0.492	0.546	0.641
	15	0.472	0.525	0.616
$Q = \dfrac{x_3 - x_1}{x_{n-2} - x_1}$	16	0.454	0.507	0.595
	17	0.438	0.490	0.577
	18	0.424	0.475	0.561
	19	0.412	0.462	0.547
	20	0.401	0.450	0.535
	21	0.391	0.440	0.524
	22	0.382	0.430	0.514
	23	0.374	0.421	0.505
	24	0.367	0.413	0.497
	25	0.360	0.406	0.489

meaning that it supports neither H_1 nor H_2; and if $LR < 1$, the observed results support H_2.

Although the likelihood ratios are widely used in many forensic disciplines, they are not commonly used in forensic toxicology. Therefore, a complete discussion of Bayesian methods is beyond the scope of this chapter. However, the Bayesian statistics are widely used for the determination of odds ratios that are applicable to forensic toxicology (e.g., crash risk).

Further Reading

ANSI/ASB 036: Standard Practices for Method Validation in Forensic Toxicology

Bell, S (2006) Statistics, Sampling, and Data Quality in Forensic Chemistry. Pearson Prentice Hall, Saddle River, NJ

Curran MJ (2011) Introduction to data analysis with R for forensic scientists. CRC Press, Taylor & Francis Group, Boca Raton, FL

ENFSI. Guideline for evaluative reporting in forensic science. Strengthening the Evaluation of Forensic Results across Europe (STEOFRAE). European Network of Forensic Sciences Institutes (2015)

Lucy D (2005) Introduction to statistics for forensic scientists. John Wiley & Sons, Chichester, UK

Miller JN, Miller JC, Miller RD (2018) Statistics and chemometrics for analytical chemistry, 7th edn. Pearson Education Ltd, Harlow, UK

Robertson B, Vignaux GA, CEH B (2016) Interpreting evidence: Evaluating forensic science in the courtroom. John Wiley & Sons, Chichester

Skoog DA, West DM, Holler FJ (1994) Analytical chemistry – An introduction, 6th edn. Saunders College Publishing, Harcourt Brace College Publishers, Philadelphia, PA

Taroni F, Bozza S, Biedermann A, Garbolino P, Aitken C (2010) Data analysis in forensic science – A Bayesian decision perspective. John Wiley & Sons, Chichester

Part III
Analytes

Alcohol

19

Barry S. Levine, Yale H. Caplan,
and A. Wayne Jones

Abstract

Ethanol is the most widely detected drug in both postmortem and human performance forensic toxicology. After ingestion, ethanol is absorbed into the body primarily by passive diffusion in the small intestine. It is distributed throughout the body according to the water content of the fluid or tissue and is eliminated mainly by metabolism in the liver by oxidation. The pharmacokinetics of ethanol is best described by Michaelis-Menten kinetics. The primary effect of ethanol is central nervous system depression, and the extent of the depression is roughly correlated with the blood ethanol concentration. Tolerance, both dispositional and cellular, plays a key role in the individual differences to the effects of alcohol. Ethanol is quantitated in blood specimens by enzymatic or gas chromatographic methods; ethanol is measured in breath specimens by infrared spectrophotometric or electrochemical methods. Testing for ethanol in

postmortem specimens may be affected by postmortem production of ethanol in blood specimens. Mandatory testing of ethanol in suspected drunk driving cases and in the workplace at established limits has been accepted as an important component of public safety.

Keywords

Alcohol · Forensic toxicology ·
Pharmacology · Effects · Analysis ·
Impairment

Alcohol, which is better known to chemists and toxicologists as ethanol (CH_3CH_2OH), is the psychoactive substance most commonly encountered in forensic toxicology casework when blood or other body fluids from living and deceased persons are analyzed. Ethanol tops the list of drugs identified in medical examiner or coroner cases, impaired drivers (traffic cases), drug-facilitated sexual assaults, as well as workplace accident investigations. Between 20 and 50% of all drivers killed in road-traffic crashes, according to various epidemiological surveys, had been drinking alcohol before the crash, and their blood alcohol concentration (BAC) at autopsy exceeded the statutory alcohol limit for driving.

B. S. Levine (✉)
Office of the Chief Medical Examiner,
Baltimore, MD, USA
e-mail: blevine@som.umaryland.edu

Y. H. Caplan
National Scientific Services, Inc.,
Baltimore, MD, USA

A. W. Jones
Magasinsgrand, Linköping, Sweden

© Springer Nature Switzerland AG 2020
B. S. Levine, S. Kerrigan (eds.), *Principles of Forensic Toxicology*,
https://doi.org/10.1007/978-3-030-42917-1_19

Ethanol is probably man's oldest psychoactive drug and is produced in nature by microbial fermentation of sugars contained in fruits, honey, or other vegetable matter. Alcohol is a legal drug and is available for purchase by adults almost without any restrictions. Moderate drinking, such as 10–20 g ethanol daily (1–2 drinks), has no detrimental effects on a person's health or well-being, and there is growing evidence that this amount, especially in the form of red wine, has a protective effect against cardiovascular diseases, such as stroke. Unfortunately, for about 10% of the population, especially among men, initial moderate drinking escalates into overconsumption and abuse of alcohol, with serious consequences for the individual, the family, and society as a whole.

Efforts to prevent alcohol-related problems have a long history, and one example is the enactment of prohibition during the first decades of the twentieth century in the USA. Examples of medical complications caused by excessive drinking are disease of the liver (hepatitis, cirrhosis), acute and chronic pancreatitis, gout, various cancers, and cardiomyopathy. The prevalence and deaths from these medical conditions are highly correlated with total alcohol consumption in society.

Classification of Alcohols

Textbooks devoted to organic chemistry classify alcohols according to their chemical structure, such as carbon chain length, the degree of branching, or the number of hydroxyl groups (-OH) contained in each molecule. Alcohols with one hydroxyl group are referred to as monohydroxy (e.g., ethanol and methanol), and two hydroxyl groups are dihydroxy (e.g., ethylene glycol), whereas glycerol is a trihydroxy alcohol and mannitol and sorbitol are polyhydroxy alcohols. The various aliphatic alcohols are also denoted as primary (ethanol), secondary (*iso*propanol), or tertiary (*t*-butanol), depending on whether one, two, or three alkyl groups are bonded to the saturated carbon atom containing the hydroxyl (-OH) radical.

Examples of the alcohols commonly encountered in clinical and forensic toxicology are shown in Table 19.1 along with their main physicochemical properties and toxic metabolites formed in the body during metabolism in the liver.

In general, the narcotic effects of aliphatic alcohols on cell membranes increase with the number of carbon atoms in the molecule, with the notable exception of methanol (CH_3OH). Methanol is commonly referred to as wood alcohol because it was originally made from the distillation of wood under vacuum. Although methanol is comparable with ethanol in terms of its acute intoxicating effects, wood alcohol is much more dangerous, owing to toxicity of its metabolites, namely, formaldehyde and formic acid (Table 19.1). Another common alcohol is isopropanol, or rubbing alcohol, widely used in clinics as an antiseptic to clean the skin before taking blood samples. The additional carbon atom in isopropanol makes it more lipid-soluble and easier to penetrate cell membranes giving a greater depression of the central nervous system. Occasionally, chronic alcoholics resort to drinking industrial alcohol products that contain more toxic alcohols, such as methanol or isopropanol, in addition to varying amounts of ethanol.

Another toxic alcohol encountered in clinical and forensic toxicology is the sweet-tasting solvent ethylene glycol, which is a major component of antifreeze. The two hydroxyl groups in ethylene glycol are oxidized successively by hepatic enzymes, first to aldehydes (-CHO) and then carboxylic acids (-COOH), and the end product of metabolism is oxalic acid (Table 19.1). Oxalic acid can react with intracellular calcium ions to produce insoluble calcium oxalate crystals, which get trapped in the kidney tubuli eventually causing renal failure and death. In a poisoned patient, the analysis of ethylene glycol and/or its metabolites in body fluids and extent of metabolic acidosis furnish proof of toxic alcohol ingestion. In medical examiner cases, ethylene glycol fatalities are often recognized from presence of calcium oxalate crystals in sections of the kidney or from presence of these crystals in the urine when examined under polarized light.

Table 19.1 Physicochemical properties of various alcohols often encountered in clinical and forensic toxicology

Property	Methanol	Ethanol	*n*-propanol	Isopropanol	Ethylene glycol
CAS number[a]	65–46-1	64–17-5	71–23-8	67–63-0	107–21-1
Molecular weight	32.04	46.07	60.09	60.09	62.07
Chemical formula	CH_3OH	CH_3CH_2OH	$CH_3CH_2CH_2OH$	$(CH_3)_2CHOH$	$(COOH)_2$
Structure	Primary aliphatic alcohol	Primary aliphatic alcohol	Primary aliphatic alcohol	Secondary aliphatic alcohol	Dihydroxy aliphatic alcohol (diol)
Common name	Wood alcohol	Beverage or grain alcohol	Propyl alcohol	Rubbing alcohol	Antifreeze
Boiling point	64.7 °C	78.5 °C	82.6 °C	82.5 °C	197 °C
Melting point	−95.8 °C	−114.1 °C	−126.5 °C	−88.5 °C	−13 °C
Density (20 °C)	0.791	0.789	0.805	0.785	1.11
Solubility in water	Mixes completely	Mixes completely	Mixes completely	Mixes completely	Mixes completely
Toxic metabolites	Formaldehyde and formic acid	Acetaldehyde and acetic acid	Propionaldehyde and propionic acid	Acetone	Glycolic, glyoxylic, and oxalic acid

[a]Chemical abstract service number

Because the boiling point of ethylene glycol (197 °C) is much higher than that of ethanol (78 °C), methanol (65 °C), and isopropanol (82 °C), this aliphatic diol is not identified in biological specimens during routine gas chromatography (GC) analysis of volatiles. Ethylene glycol is usually determined by an enzymatic method (e.g., with glycerol dehydrogenase) or after protein precipitation and direct injection into a GC instrument fitted with a flame ionization detector (FID) or by GC-FID after making a suitable chemical derivative, such as the phenyl boronate ester.

On entering the bloodstream, primary alcohols are oxidized in the liver to aldehydes, whereas secondary alcohols, such as isopropanol, are converted into ketones, such as acetone. Tertiary alcohols are resistant to oxidation and usually undergo phase II conjugation reactions forming glucuronides, which are excreted in the urine. The method used to determine ethanol in blood and other body fluids must be able to distinguish acetone, isopropanol, and methanol, which are commonly encountered together with ethanol in forensic casework.

Production of Alcoholic Beverages

The initial step in the production of alcoholic beverages is fermentation, which is one of the oldest known organic reactions dating back ~3000 years. Fermentation requires adding yeast to an aqueous solution of some carbohydrate substrate, and one molecule of a six-carbon sugar, such as glucose, is converted into two molecules of ethanol and two molecules of carbon dioxide.

$$C_6H_{12}O_6 \rightarrow 2CH_3CH_2OH + 2CO_2$$

Any natural product with sufficient amounts of starch or sugar can undergo fermentation by the enzymes contained in yeast or by other microorganism depending on appropriate conditions of temperature and time. Brewer's yeast (*Saccharomyces cerevisae*) has been around for a long time and is a type of fungus. During the fermentation process, ethanol concentrations up to 12–14 vol% are produced, whereas on reaching higher concentrations, the yeast is inactivated and the fermentation stops. Beverages with higher concentrations of ethanol are produced by distillation or by spiking fermented drinks with extra ethanol.

In addition to ethanol and water, alcoholic beverages contain small amounts of other substances broadly classified as congeners, which according to the *Oxford English Dictionary* means *one of the same kind, allied in nature or origin*. Accordingly, congeners are other types of alcohols (e.g., methyl, pentyl, or amyl), aldehydes, and ketones as well as other low-molecular-weight substances that might be produced during the fermentation process, depending on source and type of raw materials used. Other congeners are imparted when fermented or distilled beverages are stored in oak casks during the aging process prior to bottling.

The congeners contribute to the smell and taste and give color to certain types of alcoholic beverage, such as whisky or cognac. The "cleanest" alcoholic drink in terms of low congener content is vodka, which after distillation is filtered through activated charcoal to remove any trace impurities. Distilled alcoholic beverages usually contain 40–60 vol% ethanol (80–120 proof), and in some nations this alcohol content is regulated by statute. Beers might contain from 4 to 12 vol% alcohol depending on the manufacturing process, whereas table wines are 8–14 vol%, and fortified wines 14–24 vol% ethanol. The so-called alcohol-free beers, which are widely available, are usually about 1 vol% or less, which makes these drinks safe to consume by drivers and others engaged in safety-sensitive work.

Fate of Alcohol in the Body

Absorption

Absorption describes the process by which a drug or poison (e.g., alcohol) passes from outside the body into the bloodstream. The oral route of administration (by mouth or drinking) is how drinks are consumed in real-life situations. However, in emergency medicine sterile solutions of ethanol in saline (8–10 vol%) might be administered intravenously to treat patients admitted to hospital poisoned from drinking methanol or ethylene glycol. High blood alcohol concentrations can also be reached after rectal administration.

The absorption of alcohol into the portal venous blood starts already in the stomach, but the rate of uptake is much faster when the stomach contents empty into the duodenum and jejunum, owing to the much larger surface area provided by the villi and microvilli that project from the surface of the mucosa of the small intestines. Accordingly, factors influencing gastric emptying have a major influence on the rate of absorption of ethanol into the bloodstream. A more rapid rate of absorption is associated with a higher and earlier occurring peak blood concentration (C_{max}) and thus a greater impairment of the central nervous system.

Small amounts of ethanol might be absorbed into the blood via the dermal route (intact skin) or by inhalation through the lungs, although these methods are ineffective in elevating the BAC above 0.01 g/100 mL. The slow absorption through the skin is balanced by simultaneous metabolism in the liver at a rate of 7–8 g/hour. If the skin is damaged with cuts or abrasions and there are open blood vessels, this might enhance uptake, but this is still not an effective way to increase the BAC. The absorption of ethanol into the bloodstream by inhalation via the lungs depends on the concentration in the ambient air breathed and the degree of lung ventilation. However, even under extreme conditions when concentrations in the inhaled air are high, this is not a practical way to increase a person's BAC owing to ongoing metabolism of any absorbed ethanol.

Because absorption is a passive diffusion process, one can expect that ethanol contained in distilled liquors (40 vol%) is absorbed faster than ethanol in wine (10 vol%) or beer (5 vol%), as predicted by Fick's principle. However, this simple rule is offset by the fact that beers and wines, as well as fruit brandies, contain sugars and other constituents that delay gastric emptying. The type of mixer used with spirit drinks also impacts on speed of absorption by delaying gastric emptying. The ethanol in carbonated (CO_2) beverages, such as champagne, seems to be absorbed faster than decarbonated drinks with the same alcohol content, such as white wine. When neat spirits are consumed on an empty stomach, this often irritates the gastric mucosa and results in a pyloric spasm, which leads to a delayed gastric emptying and a slower rate of absorption of ethanol into the blood.

The results from hundreds of controlled drinking studies show that peak BAC occurs at between 10–120 min after end of drinking and on average after about 60 min. However, in social drinking situation, when multiple drinks are consumed over longer time periods, the absorption takes place progressively as more and more alcohol is consumed and the peak concentration in blood is reached earlier, usually within 30 min after cessation of drinking. Figure 19.1 gives examples of blood alcohol curves obtained from experiments with N = 16 healthy men after they drank a standard dose of alcohol (0.85 g/kg) as neat whisky on an empty stomach in 25 min. These BAC curves show the magnitude of intersubject variation, which is greatest during the absorption phase as reflected in variations in C_{max} and t_{max} before the post-absorptive phase starts at about 60–90 min post-drinking.

Some absorption of alcohol occurs through the mucous surfaces of the stomach, but the bulk of the dose administered is absorbed via the upper part of the small intestine. Estimates of the relative amounts of ethanol absorbed from the stomach (20%) and intestines (80%) are only approximate because much depends on stomach emptying, such as presence of food in the stom-

ach before drinking, the type of beverage consumed, and use of certain prescription drugs. Absorption of ethanol from different parts of the gastrointestinal (GI) tract depends on the concentration present in the individual structures, the blood flow (vascularity), and the absorption surface area.

Factors that increase GI motility will increase the rate of ethanol absorption into the blood, and a delayed gastric emptying (gastroparesis) decreases the absorption of ethanol. Inflammation of the GI tract, for example, increases blood flow to that region resulting in a more rapid absorption of alcohol. Prokinetic drugs increase gastric motility (e.g., cisapride or metaclopramide) and lead to a faster rate of absorption of ethanol into the portal blood. Heavy cigarette smoking delays gastric emptying and slows rate of ethanol absorption. However, the single most important factor delaying the absorption of ethanol is the presence of food in the stomach such as when alcohol is consumed immediately after eating a large meal. The amount of food eaten seems more important than its composition in terms of protein, fat, or carbohydrate content. Figure 19.2 shows blood alcohol curves obtained when the same dose of ethanol (0.8 g/kg) was consumed on an empty stomach (overnight fast) or immediately after eating a standardized breakfast.

The peak concentration of ethanol in blood was higher and occurred earlier when ethanol was consumed on an empty stomach compared with the same dose after eating a meal. Food

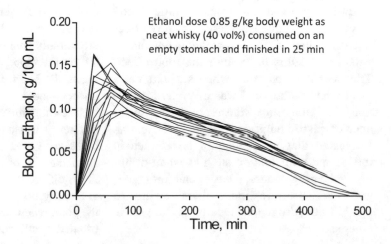

Fig. 19.1 Interindividual variations in concentration-time profiles of ethanol in 16 health men after they consumed the same dose of ethanol (0.85 g/kg body weight) as neat whisky (40 vol%) on an empty stomach (overnight fast) in a drinking time of 25 min

Ethanol dose 0.85 g/kg body weight as neat whisky (40 vol%) consumed on an empty stomach and finished in 25 min

Fig. 19.2 Blood
alcohol curves in male
subjects after drinking
the same dose of ethanol
(0.8 g/kg) either on an
empty stomach
(overnight fast) or after
eating a standardized
breakfast

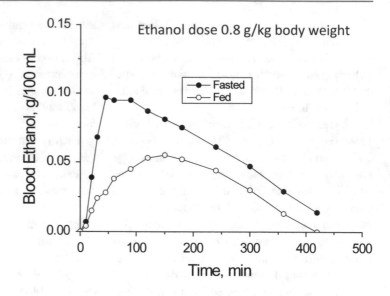

mixes with and dilutes the concentration of ethanol in the stomach so that it remains unabsorbed for a much longer time. The BAC curve obtained in the fed state gives the impression that a smaller dose of ethanol had been administered, but this was not the case (Fig. 19.2). It seems that food not only lowers the bioavailability of ethanol but also increases the rate of metabolism as reflected in a smaller area under the curve and a shorter time to reach zero BAC. For the most part, the rate of ethanol metabolism is independent of the concentration in blood provided the oxidative enzymes are saturated with substrate (BAC > 0.02–0.03 g/100 mL).

Eating a meal increases hepatic blood flow, and consequently there is a more effective clearance of ethanol, which is one mechanism that helps to explain the food effect. This was demonstrated when subjects eat a meal when the alcohol was given by intravenous infusion, thus sidestepping any influence of gastric emptying. Some investigators suggested that when alcohol is retained in the stomach for longer, such as when drinking and eating occurs, a larger amount undergoes pre-systemic metabolism owing to alcohol dehydrogenase located in the gastric mucosa.

Distribution

After absorption into the portal venous blood, ethanol is transported first to the liver, then the right side of the heart, and to the lungs, before oxygenated blood returns to the left side of the heart and transported throughout the whole body. When blood enters the pulmonary circulation, some of the ethanol in solution diffuses across the alveolar-capillary membrane and is exhaled in the breath. This forms the basis of the widely used breath alcohol test, which will be covered in more detail later in this chapter. During the absorption phase, the concentration of ethanol in alveolar air and hence in the expired air runs closer to the arterial blood concentration rather than the venous blood concentration. Tissues that are initially free of alcohol extract alcohol from the arterial blood so that the venous blood returning to the heart with deoxygenated blood has a lower concentration of alcohol.

The magnitude of the arterial-venous (A-V) difference in alcohol content is greatest when a bolus dose is consumed on an empty stomach. After the end of drinking, the magnitude of the A-V difference progressively decreases and eventually becomes zero (A = V), which marks the point when ethanol is fully absorbed and distributed in all body fluids and tissues. Studies have shown that venous blood contains a slightly higher concentration of ethanol than arterial blood during the post-absorptive elimination phase of the BAC curve.

The speed of equilibration of ethanol between blood and other body fluids and tissues depends on the ratio of blood flow to tissue mass, which means that organs with a rich blood supply, such as the brain and kidneys, rapidly equilibrate with the concentration of ethanol in arterial blood, whereas bulky skeletal muscles, with lower ratio of blood flow to tissue mass, require a longer time to equilibrate. Body fluids containing more water than blood (e.g., saliva, vitreous humor, and urine) will also have higher concentration of ethanol when equilibration is reached.

An important concept in pharmacokinetics is how a drug distributes between the blood or plasma and the other tissues of the body. Known as volume of distribution (V_d), this important pharmacokinetic parameter relates the concentration of a drug in the blood or plasma to the total amount of drug in the body. A drug's V_d depends on lipid solubility and the degree of binding to plasma proteins. From a knowledge of V_d, it is easy to calculate the amount of drug absorbed and distributed in all body fluids and tissues from the concentration determined in a sample of blood. The V_d for a water-soluble drug like ethanol depends on the person's age and gender and the proportion of fat to lean tissue in the body.

Total body water (TBW) comprises about 60% of body weight in men and 50% in women as determined by isotope dilution experiments. The V_d for ethanol varies twofold between individuals from a low of 0.4–0.5 L/kg in obese females to a high of 0.7–0.8 L/kg in lean male subjects. Results from drinking experiments show in average values of V_d of 0.7 L/kg in healthy adult men and 0.6 L/kg in healthy adult women. The water content of blood is easy to determine by desiccation or freeze-drying and is ~80% w/w with a small but statistically significant gender difference, owing to lower hematocrit (less red cells and more plasma) in female blood.

Because ethanol distributes into the water fraction of all body fluids, the distribution ratio of ethanol between the blood and the body as a whole should be similar to distribution of water, namely, 60/80 or 0.75 for men and 50/80 or 0.62 for women. In practice, much depends on body composition, especially the amount of adipose tissue in relation to fat-free mass. A clinical measure of obesity is given by body mass index (BMI) calculated as ratio of body weight in kg to height in meters squared (kg/m$_2$). A person with BMI 30 kg/m^2 can be expected to have a lower ethanol V_d than a person with normal BMI of 20–25 kg/m^2.

Blood consists of the straw-colored plasma (92 % w/w water) and red cells (erythrocytes) which are 68% w/w water. This suggests a plasma/blood distribution ratio of ethanol of 1.15:1 (92/80 = 1.15) and a red cell/blood ratio of 0.85 (68/80 = 0.85) depending in part on hematocrit and lipid content of the blood specimen. Most people can be expected to have plasma/blood distribution ratio of ethanol ranging from 1.1:1 to 1.2:1 depending on state of health. In people suffering from anemia (low hematocrit) with more plasma (and water) per unit volume of blood, the plasma/blood distribution of ethanol should be closer to 1.10:1 or lower. Plasma and serum contain the same amount of water, and therefore the same amount of ethanol and ethanol distribution ratios are the same.

If a clinical laboratory reports a serum ethanol concentration of 0.1 g%, then for forensic purposes, the expected concentration in whole blood is 0.087 g/100 mL (0.1/1.15 = 0.086) and might range from 0.083 g/100 ml (0.1/1.2) to 0.091 g/100 mL (0.1/1.1). The results from analysis of ethanol in plasma and serum done at hospital clinical chemistry laboratories cannot be used for legal purposes without making this conversion to the expected concentration in whole blood.

The distribution of ethanol between blood and other biological fluids and tissues has been extensively studied, and the values depend on water content of specimens and the time after drinking when samples are taken. Results from many such studies are summarized in Table 19.2 if samples are taken after absorption and distribution is complete. The concentrations in vitreous humor, saliva, spinal fluid, and urine are 15–20% higher than in an equal

Table 19.2 Average distribution ratios of ethanol between blood and other biological specimens at equilibrium

Specimen analyzed	Specimen/blood concentration ratio[a]
Mixed saliva (oral fluid)	1.12
Vitreous humor	1.20
Bile	1.0
Cerebrospinal fluid	1.3
Liver tissue	0.6
Kidney tissue	0.7
Brain tissue	0.8
Urine	1.3

[a]The concentration ratios show wide variation depending on, among other things, time after drinking when samples are taken and equilibration of ethanol in all body fluids and tissues

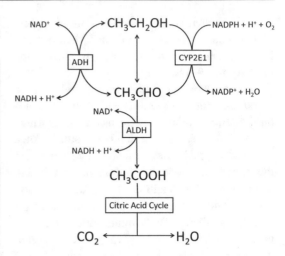

Fig. 19.3 Scheme showing the main pathway for oxidative metabolism of ethanol, where ADH is alcohol dehydrogenase, ALDH is aldehyde dehydrogenase, NAD^+ and NADH are oxidized and reduced forms of coenzyme nicotinamide adenine dinucleotide and CYP2E1 is a microsomal enzyme

volume of blood as expected from differences in water content. However, in practice the distribution ratios of ethanol between CSF and blood and urine and blood are higher (1.3:1), because of a lag time in the formation of these alternative body fluids. Concentrations of ethanol in the liver, kidney, and brain are less than in blood in part because of lower water content in these tissues and the fact some are metabolically active after death, leading to a decrease in the concentrations of ethanol.

Metabolism

More than 90% of the dose of ethanol consumed undergoes oxidative metabolism in the liver by various enzymatic reactions as shown in Fig. 19.3. The first step involves oxidation of ethanol to acetaldehyde, and this reaction is catalyzed by a cytosolic enzyme alcohol dehydrogenase (ADH). ADH is polymorphic, and various isozymes exist with slightly different amino acid sequences and kinetic properties (V_{max} and k_m), which might account for individual differences in rates of ethanol metabolism. Zinc is a necessary element for enzyme activity of alcohol dehydrogenase. During oxidative metabolism of ethanol, the cofactor nicotinamide adenine dinucleotide (NAD^+) is simultaneously reduced to NADH and the reoxidation of NADH to NAD^+ is the rate-limiting step in the overall redox reaction.

Acetaldehyde is a toxic and highly reactive substance, but luckily the primary metabolite of ethanol is rapidly oxidized to acetic acid by the action of low k_m aldehyde dehydrogenase (ALDH) located in the mitochondria. The acetate becomes transported with blood away from the liver and enters the aerobic respiration process (citric acid cycle) eventually being breakdown to end products carbon dioxide and water. The oxidative metabolism of ethanol via the ADH and ALDH pathway is the primary route of alcohol elimination from the body. However, in the early 1960s it was discovered that the smooth endoplasmic reticulum of liver cells contained an enzyme that oxidized ethanol denoted microsomal ethanol oxidizing system (MEOS). MEOS formed part of the cytochrome P450 family of enzymes, and CYP2E1 was the variant mainly responsible for oxidation of ethanol. The same P450 enzyme is responsible for metabolism of certain drugs such as acetaminophen and chlorinated and aromatic hydrocarbons. The P450 system is inducible after chronic exposure to substrate, which accounts for the finding that some alcoholics during detoxification have higher rates of metabolism of ethanol compared with occasional drinkers.

Non-oxidative Metabolism

Considerable research has focused on non-oxidative metabolites of ethanol (Fig. 19.4). A small fraction of the dose of ethanol ingested (0.1–0.2%) undergoes phase II conjugation reactions to give ethyl glucuronide (EtG) and ethyl sulfate (EtS) as metabolites via glucuronosyltransferase and sulfotransferase enzymes, respectively. EtG and EtS are detectable in blood and urine for considerably longer than ethanol itself and can serve as biomarkers to disclose recent drinking after ethanol has been eliminated from the body. However, care is needed when results of EtG are interpreted because ethanol is a constituent of many household products, such as mouthwash, cosmetics, cough medication, hand sanitizers, etc. This requires use of conservative and reasonable cutoff concentration when urinary EtG is analyzed and reported, such as 100–500 ng/mL (0.1–0.5 mg/L). Lower cutoffs are acceptable for EtS, such as 25–100 ng/mL (0.025–0.1 mg/L), before a person is accused of drinking alcoholic beverages.

Analysis of EtG and EtS finds applications in postmortem toxicology to distinguish ethanol produced during decomposition from antemortem ingestion of alcoholic beverages. If EtG and/or EtS conjugates are verified present in postmortem blood or urine, this speaks toward consumption of alcoholic beverages during life. Ethanol must undergo metabolism to produce these conjugates and must therefore have passed through the liver as opposed to being produced after death by action of bacteria or yeasts.

Another non-oxidative metabolite of ethanol is phosphatidylethanol (PEth), which is formed in a reaction between ethanol and phosphatidylcholine and the enzyme phospholipase D. PEth also remains elevated after ethanol has been cleared from the bloodstream. However a heavier drinking period is needed to produce elevated levels of PEth compared with EtG and EtS.

Ethanol undergoes an enzymatic reaction with both saturated and unsaturated fatty acids (e.g., palmitic, linoleic, stearic, etc.) to give fatty acid ethyl esters (FAEE). The incorporation of FAEE into various body organs (the heart, brain, and pancreas) has been suggested as a possible mechanism for alcohol-related tissue damage, which is often seen in chronic alcoholics. FAEE can also be determined in hair strands and used to monitor abstinence in people required to refrain from drinking for various reasons.

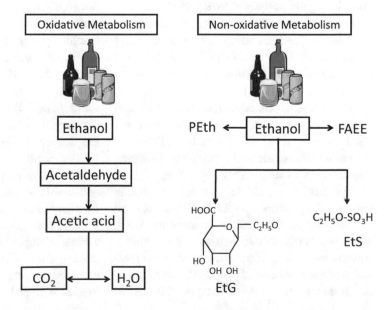

Fig. 19.4 Pathways of oxidative metabolism of ethanol via acetaldehyde, acetate, and end products carbon dioxide and water (left part) and non-oxidative metabolism to ethyl glucuronide (EtG) and ethyl sulfate (EtS) conjugates, phosphatidylethanol (PEth), and fatty acid ethyl esters (FAEE)

Excretion

Excretion refers to the removal of ethanol from the body in an unchanged form and this occurs via the lungs (in breath), the kidney (in urine), and through the skin (in sweat). However, all three routes of excretion combined account for at most 5–10% of the dose of ethanol administered. Ethanol can also be detected in the saliva, which however is usually swallowed and then reabsorbed into the blood.

Urine has a long history as a biological specimen for forensic analysis of alcohol because large volumes are available. In the past, the urine alcohol concentration (UAC) was used to estimate the BAC, but this conversion is not advisable owing to large variations in the UAC/BAC ratio depending on sampling time after end of drinking. Concentration-time profiles of ethanol in blood and bladder urine are shown in Fig. 19.5 when 0.85 g ethanol/kg body weight was consumed as neat whisky on an empty stomach. Note that after a bolus dose the concentration in urine is less than in blood during the absorption phase and higher than in blood after about 100 min and remains higher for the duration of the post-absorptive period. The insert graph shows the ethanol-induced dieresis, which is greatest (6 mL per min) during the absorption phase of the blood alcohol curve returning to normal (~1 mL per min) during the post-absorptive period.

The physiological principles of ethanol excretion in urine are well known, and as renal artery blood enters the kidney, about 20% is filtered at the glomerulus. Most of this filtrate is reabsorbed, with <1% of the filtrate being excreted as urine in the bladder. Analysis of near simultaneous samples of blood and bladder urine shows that UAC/BAC concentration ratios range from 1.2 to 1.3 after absorption of alcohol is complete. However, individual ratios vary widely depending on status of absorptive and the time of storage of urine in the bladder before voiding. Blood ethanol decrease by metabolism as urine is produced, whereas there is no metabolism in urine after it collects in the bladder. During the absorptive phase of the BAC curve, UAC/BAC ratio is <1.0, and during the post-absorptive phase, the concentration in urine is 25–30% higher than in blood. The variations in urine to blood concentration ratios for an individual in the post-absorptive phase can be so large that it is generally considered unacceptable to estimate a blood ethanol concentration from the ethanol concentration of a randomly collected urine specimen. Better correlations are obtained for ethanol in urine and blood when two consecutive urine specimens are collected. The second voided specimen, collected 30–60 min after the first, shows a closer correlation with BAC and the average UAC/BAC is about 1.3:1.

Pharmacokinetics

Pharmacokinetics is concerned with absorption, distribution, metabolism, and excretion (ADME) of drugs and how these processes can be described in quantitative terms. The Swedish scientist Erik MP Widmark (1889–1945) made extensive studies of ADME of ethanol in the 1930s when he plotted BAC time profiles and used these to derive a set of alcohol parameters for controlled drinking conditions. A Widmark-type BAC curve is shown in Fig. 19.6 along with the pharmacokinetic parameters of ethanol C_0, C_{max}, t_{max}, β, min_0, and rho.

A male subject drank a moderate dose of ethanol (0.8 g/kg) on an empty stomach in 30 min. The peak concentration in (C_{max}) and time of reaching the peak t_{max} are read directly from the graph. At about 80 min post-dosing after C_{max} is reached, the BAC decreases at a constant rate per unit time in accordance with zero-order saturation kinetics. The slope of this rectilinear elimination part of the BAC profile is determined from the dashed diagonal line in Fig. 19.6 denoted β-slope with y-intercept C_0 (g/100 mL) and x-intercept min_0 (min or h), where $C_0/min_0 = \beta$ (g/100 mL per h). In the example shown, the rate of ethanol elimination from blood (β-slope) was 0.014 g/100 mL per h. The other important pharmacokinetic parameter is distribution volume of ethanol derived from the ratio of alcohol in the entire body (g/kg) to concentration in the blood at time zero given by C_0 (g/L). This latter parameter

Fig. 19.5
Concentration-time curves of ethanol in blood and bladder urine in one subject who drank ethanol (0.85 g/kg) as neat whisky on an empty stomach. Note that the bladder was emptied before drinking started and the insert graph shows ethanol-induced dieresis at different times after end of drinking

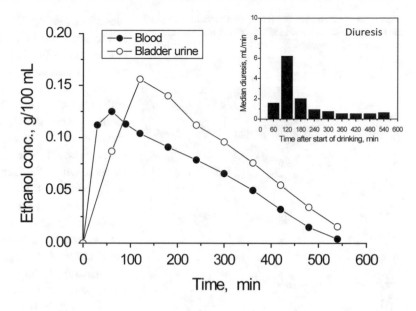

Fig. 19.6 Blood alcohol curve resulting from drinking a dose of ethanol (0.8 g/kg) on an empty stomach in 30 min. Shown on the graph is calculation of pharmacokinetic parameters including zero-order elimination rate constant (β-slope) and volume of distribution (V_d)

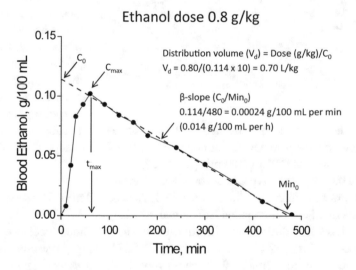

is the concentration of ethanol in blood that would be obtained if the entire dose was absorbed and distributed in the body before any metabolism occurred. In Fig. 19.6 the volume of distribution (V_d) was calculated to be 0.70 L/kg and represents a good average for male subjects.

On reaching low concentrations of ethanol in blood (< 0.01–0.02 g/100 mL), the ADH metabolizing enzyme is no longer saturated with substrate and zero-order kinetics change to first-order kinetics. The entire post-absorptive elimination phase from high to low concentrations is best described by saturation kinetics described math-

ematically by the Michaelis-Menten equation. Table 19.3 compares the properties of zero-order, first-order, and Michaelis-Menten kinetics when applied to BAC profiles.

The Michaelis constant (k_m) for human class I ADH is about 0.005–0.01 g/100 mL. Table 19.3 shows that if the Michaelis constant is much greater than the substrate concentration (BAC), the equation collapses into first-order kinetics. In contrast, if the substrate concentration (BAC) is much greater than the Michaelis constant (e.g., > 0.02 g/100 mL), elimination kinetics of ethanol are adequately described by zero-order kinetics.

Table 19.3 Examples of various pharmacokinetic models used to describe blood alcohol concentration-time profiles in blood or plasma

Pharmacokinetic model	Rate equations describing the process	Important kinetic parameters
Zero-order	$-dC/dt = kC0$ Integration gives a linear equation $C_t = C_0 - k_0 t$	$C_0 = $ y-intercept Zero-order rate constant (k_0)
First-order	$-dC/dt = kC1$ Integration gives $C_t = C_0 e^{-kt}$ Log transformation gives $Ln\, C_t = Ln\, C_0 - k_1 t$	Ln $C_0 = $ y-intercept First-order rate constant (k_1) Elimination half-life $(t_{1/2}) = 0.693/k_1$
Michaelis-Menten (saturation kinetics)	$-dC/dt = (V_{max} \times C)/(k_m + C)$ When $C >>> k_m$ then $-dC/dt = V_{max}$ (zero order) When $C <<< k_m$ then $-dC/dt = kC$ (first order) Note that $k = V_{max}/k_m$	Maximum reaction velocity (V_{max}) Michaelis constant (k_m)

The results from many alcohol dosing studies show that the average elimination rate of ethanol from blood is 0.015 g/100 mL per hour for men and 0.018 g/100 mL per hour for women. Several factors can affect this elimination rate. Enhanced rates of ethanol elimination from blood are likely in alcoholics during detoxification owing to a process of enzyme induction involving CYP2E1. Genetic factors may also be involved in controlling rates of metabolism, as seen in some ethnic groups such as Asians with slightly faster elimination rates of ethanol from blood compared with Caucasians. Because most of the ethanol consumed is eliminated in the liver, any disease state in that tissue can potentially impair the clearance of ethanol. Administration of fructose, glycine, or alanine may enhance ethanol elimination. Recent work has suggested that food, as well as affecting the absorption of ethanol, might slightly enhance the elimination of ethanol.

There is some evidence that metabolism of ethanol occurs in the gastric mucosa before the blood reaches the liver, which would contribute to the observed first-pass metabolism (FPM) of ethanol when drinking occurs after a meal. The relative importance of FPM and whether this occurs in the liver or stomach or both organs is still an open question although most investigators seem to consider it more important in part because of the greater amount of oxidative enzyme present. The area under the BAC curve is smaller when the same dose is administered orally compared with intravenously which indicates a lower systemic availability. Gastric ADH would facilitate metabolism of some of ethanol the longer it remains unabsorbed in the stomach. This implies that any drug that affects the activity of gastric ADH impacts on the FPM of ethanol. Drugs such as cimetidine and ranitidine, which inhibit the activity of gastric ADH, are therefore expected to allow more of the dose of ethanol to become absorbed into the blood, thus increasing the bioavailability. Activity of gastric ADH also varies as a function of age and gender and also between different racial groups. With all these factors to consider, it is not surprising that the absorption phase of the BAC curve shows large intersubject variations and speaks against making predictions of BAC expected after a given dose.

The Widmark Equation

Blood alcohol curves are characterized by a rising phase mainly reflecting the absorption process which initially occurs faster than elimination through metabolism and excretion. As time passes and amount of alcohol that is still unabsorbed decreases, the BAC eventually reaches a peak or maximum concentration usually at 30–90 min post-drinking. At this time the rates of absorption and metabolism are now about equal. During the post-absorptive declining portion of the BAC curve, absorption has already ended and elimination is the dominant process.

The relationship between a person's blood alcohol concentration and the amount of alcohol in the body has been thoroughly investigated and is expressed by the well-known Widmark equation:

A(g) = BAC(g/L) × body weight (kg) × Vd or rho (L/kg)

In the above equation, A is amount of alcohol (g) absorbed and distributed in all body fluids and tissues at the time of sampling blood, BAC is the blood alcohol concentration in g/L (g/100 mL × 10), and V_d is the apparent volume of distribution (rho factor = L/kg), which expresses the ratio of ethanol concentration in the whole body (g/kg) to that in the blood (g/L).

Blood alcohol calculations are commonly requested when alcohol-related crimes are investigated, such as driving under the influence of alcohol. For example, if a male person (V_d = 0.7 L/kg) with a body weight of 80 kg has a BAC of 0.1 g/100 mL, then 56 g ethanol is absorbed and distributed in all body fluids and tissues. If drinking began 6 h before the blood was taken, the total amount of ethanol consumed is easy to calculate by adding on the amount lost through metabolism. Ethanol is eliminated from the whole body in moderate drinkers at a rate of 0.1 g/kg per h, so over 6 h a person has disposed of 48 g ethanol (0.1 × 80 × 6). The total amount consumed is easy to calculate from the equation below, and this comes to 104 g (56 + 48 = 104), which if necessary, can be converted to the number of standard drinks consumed.

$$A(g) = \left[BAC(g/L) \times \text{body weight}(kg) \times V_d \text{ or rho}(L/kg) \right] + \left[0.1 \times kg \times h \right]$$

The main sources of variation are uncertainty in the distribution factor V_d or rho and the elimination rate of alcohol from the body (g/kg/h). The results from many controlled drinking studies show that average V_d for ethanol is 0.70 for men and 0.60 for women and the interindividual variation of about ± 20%. The lower average V_d of ethanol in females leads to a higher BAC for a given dose of ethanol ingested, and this gender difference needs to be considered when blood alcohol calculations are made. The ± 20% variability in V_d stems from differences in body composition, especially the proportion of fat to lean tissue in the body. There is scant evidence that menstrual cycle and female sex hormones impact on the disposition and fate of ethanol in the body.

Other Alcohols

Forensic toxicologists are often required to analyze and interpret the concentrations of other aliphatic alcohols in blood samples, such as methanol (wood alcohol), isopropanol (rubbing alcohol), and ethylene glycol (antifreeze). These alcohols are widely available in household and commercial products and are sometimes consumed as ethanol substitutes for intoxication purposes by problem drinkers and alcoholics. The acute intoxication effects of ethanol are similar to these more toxic alcohols, which means that people are initially unaware they are in danger of poisoning and therefore don't seek emergency hospital treatment.

The metabolism of methanol is blocked as long as blood ethanol concentration exceeds 0.02 g/100 mL. Below this concentration methanol is converted in the liver first to formaldehyde and then formic acid, and the elimination half-life is about 2–4 h. Formic acid is a strong organic acid (pK_a = 3.77), which causes a disordered acid-base balance and a dangerous state of metabolic acidosis. Patients complain of nausea, and they might vomit and suffer from abdominal pains after drinking methanol. A well-recognized clinical observation in methanol poisoning is blurred vision and blindness, owing to the interaction of formaldehyde with the retina or the eye. Methanol poisoning is associated with high mortality because people seek emergency treatment too late when life-threatening acidosis has already developed. Clinical diagnosis of methanol poisoning might include measuring osmolal gap and anion gap metabolic acidosis, although specificity is improved if blood methanol and serum formate are determined. When methanol poisoning deaths are investigated, fatalities often depend on whether this alcohol was consumed alone or mixed with ethanol. The presence of ethanol prevents conversion into toxic metabolites, and during this time methanol is eliminated in urine and breath.

Ethylene glycol is metabolized in the liver by the same enzymes involved in the metabolism of ethanol and methanol, and the elimination half-life of the diol is 2.5–3.5 h in the absence of antidote treatment. The first product of metabolism is glycolaldehyde, which is further oxidized to glycolic acid. Oxidation of the second hydroxyl group produces glyoxylic acid and finally oxalic acid. Glycolic, glyoxylic, and oxalic acids contribute to the metabolic acidosis seen in patients poisoned with ethylene glycol. The clinical presentation of glycol toxicity is usually considered in three stages depending on time elapsed after ingestion. The first stage occurs after 0.5–2 h when concentrations of the diol in blood are fairly leading to acute intoxication and depression of the central nervous and also a raised osmolal gap. The second stage is seen after 12–24 h when anion gap metabolic acidosis increases and osmolal gap decreases. Patients might experience difficulties breathing with hyperventilation with hypoxia. The third stage is after 24–72 h when concentration of the diol in blood is low or zero, but there is a high anion gap and patients complain of pain in the lower back. Many cannot urinate (oliguria), and victims eventually die from renal failure and metabolic acidosis.

The traditional first-aid treatment for patients poisoned with methanol or ethylene glycol was to administer ethanol (8–10 % v/v) to reach and maintain a BAC of 0.1–0.15 g% for several hours. The higher affinity of liver ADH for ethanol meant that methanol and ethylene glycol were not converted into toxic metabolites. The unchanged alcohols as well as any metabolites formed could be removed from the blood by hemodialysis. Because dialysis also removes ethanol from the bloodstream, the infusion must be continued even during treatment.

A more modern alternative to ethanol as antidote for methanol and ethylene glycol poisoning is the drug fomepizole (Antizol®), which chemically is 4-methylpyrazole. This heterocyclic molecule is a potent competitive inhibitor of liver ADH and like ethanol blocks conversion of the toxic alcohols into their more dangerous metabolites. Fomepizole also undergoes metabolism and needs to be administered as a series of i.v. injections to be an effective treatment for the poisoned patient. Unlike ethanol, fomepizole does not depress the central nervous system and is the preferred antidote for treatment of children or skid-row alcoholics, who might suffer from hepatic dysfunction (cirrhosis or other liver diseases). The disadvantage of fomepizole is the high costs of the medication compared with ethanol.

Treatment of patients poisoned with isopropanol is less complicated and requires only a general supervision to ensure they don't vomit and thus keep the airways clear and wait for the alcohol to become metabolized. The secondary alcohol is converted in the liver into acetone as the principal metabolite so patients have a sweetish smell of this ketone on the breath. The elimination half-life of isopropanol (3–5 h) is much shorter than that of acetone (15–20 h), which means that acetone can be measured in blood and breath for a lot longer than isopropanol.

Effects of Ethanol

Ethanol exerts a wide spectrum of biochemical and physiological effects on the body depending on the amounts consumed on each occasion (the dose) as well as duration (years) of exposure to this drug. The acute intoxicating effect of ethanol depends on the dose, the speed of drinking, and gastric emptying.

Metabolic Effects

A variety of metabolic disturbances occur during hepatic oxidation of ethanol as a direct result of an altered redox state of the liver, which is shifted to a more reduced potential. Acetaldehyde, the first product of oxidation, is a highly reactive chemical species which binds to proteins and other endogenous molecules, and toxicity of acetaldehyde has been incriminated in alcohol-related diseases, including development of various cancers. When ethanol is oxidized to acetaldehyde, one atom of hydrogen is transferred to the cofactor nicotinamide adenine dinucleotide (NAD), which is converted to its reduced form (NADH). Further reduction of NAD to NADH occurs when acetaldehyde is oxidized to acetate in the second stage of ethanol biotransformation. The acetate generated from ethanol metabolism is transported with the blood away from the liver and is oxidized in the citric acid cycle into end products carbon dioxide and water (see Fig. 19.3). When people were given ethanol labeled with ^{14}C, this radioactive tracer was immediately afterward detected in the expired air as $^{14}CO_2$ verifying a rapid oxidative metabolism.

The markedly raised NADH/NAD$^+$ ratio and excess of reducing equivalents associated with the hepatic metabolism of ethanol have important consequences for other NAD-dependent biochemical reactions in the liver. The lactate/pyruvate ratio increases, which leads to hyperlactacidemia and a metabolic acidosis; this diminishes the capacity of the kidney to excrete uric acid which eventually leads to hyperuricemia and attacks of gout. Furthermore, an elevated NADH/NAD ratio favors triglyceride accumulation and also promotes fatty acid synthesis and lipogenesis, hence the clinical syndrome of fatty liver. Another metabolic consequence of elevated NADH/NAD is inhibition of hepatic gluconeogenesis, which explains why heavy drinkers and alcohols often suffer from hypoglycemia. This condition is worsened by an inadequate diet in alcoholics, who obtain most of their calories from the combustion of ethanol (7.1 kcal per gram). However, these are referred to as "empty calories" because the body cannot store alcohol for later use and alcoholic drinks lack essential proteins, vitamins, and minerals contained in normal foods so many alcoholics are also malnourished.

Cardiovascular System

Moderate ethanol consumption has no significant effect on blood pressure, cardiac output, and cardiac contractile force. Moderate doses increase high-density lipoprotein, which has been associated with reduced cardiovascular disease. Ethanol does cause vasodilatation of the cutaneous vessels, which creates a feeling of warmth often associated with the consumption of alcoholic beverages. This vasodilatation does not occur uniformly over the vasculature. In fact, moderate doses of ethanol can cause vasoconstriction in the heart and the brain.

Central Nervous System

Ethanol easily crosses the blood-brain barrier to interact with nerve cell membranes and receptor proteins with the overall effect of depressing the central nervous system. At fairly low BAC (0.03–0.05 g/100 mL), people feel less inhibited; they become more talkative and social, which is often incorrectly conceived as stimulation. After higher doses and increasing BAC, depression of simpler and more basic functions occurs. At very high blood ethanol concentration (> 0.4 g/100 mL), the respiratory center in the brain is depressed and coma and death ensue. Scientific studies performed over many years have established general relationships between BAC and effects on the brain as reflected in clinical signs and symptoms of drunkenness, and one widely cited and recently updated compilation is shown in Table 19.4.

The table shows a broad overlap in the signs and symptoms of alcohol influence for different ranges of BAC. The mild euphoria at low BAC (< 0.05 g/100 mL) is actually caused by disinhibition. As the blood ethanol concentration increases (0.03–0.12 g/100 mL), judgment and decision-making abilities are influenced, and perception and reaction to events are impaired. This impairment develops prior to the onset of more overt symptoms of ethanol intoxication, such as difficulties in walking, speaking, and maintaining balance (0.09–0.25 g/100 mL). The signs and symptoms described in Table 19.4 are what might be expected for an adult person with moderate drinking habits. Habituation to alcohol alters the relationship, and some people are able to function at high BAC, especially when relatively sim-

Table 19.4 Stages of acute alcoholic influence or intoxication in relation to blood alcohol concentration (BAC)

Blood alcohol conc. g/100 mL (g%)	Stage of alcohol influence	Clinical signs or symptoms
0.01–0.05	Subclinical	Behavior nearly normal by ordinary observation Influence/effects usually not apparent or obvious Impairment detectable by special tests
0.03–0.12	Euphoria	Mild euphoria, sociability, talkativeness Increased self-confidence; decreased inhibitions Diminished attention, judgment, and control Some sensory-motor impairment Slowed information processing Loss of efficiency in critical performance tests
0.09–0.25	Excitement	Emotional instability; loss of critical judgment Impairment of perception, memory, and comprehension Decreased sensory response; increased reaction time Reduced visual acuity and peripheral vision and Slow glare recovery Sensory-motor incoordination; impaired balance; slurred speech Vomiting; drowsiness
0.18–0.30	Confusion	Disorientation, mental confusion; vertigo; dysphoria Exaggerated emotional states (fear, rage, grief, etc.) Disturbances of vision (diplopia, etc.) and of perception of color, form, motion, dimensions Increased pain threshold Increased muscular incoordination; staggering gait; ataxia Memory loss Apathy with progressive lethargy
0.25–0.40	Stupor	General inertia; approaching loss of motor functions Markedly decreased response to stimuli Marked muscular incoordination; inability to stand or walk Vomiting; incontinence of urine and feces Impaired consciousness; sleep or stupor; deep snoring
0.35–0.50	Coma	Complete unconsciousness; coma; anesthesia Depressed or abolished reflexes Subnormal temperature Impairment/irregularities of circulation and respiration Possible death
Mean, median = 0.36 90% = 0.21–0.50	Death	Death from respiratory or cardiac arrest

Copyright© 2012 by Kurt M. Dubowski, Ph.D., Oklahoma City, Oklahoma, USA

ple tasks are performed. The pattern of drinking is also important in relation to ethanol-induced impairment, which is more pronounced after rapid drinking and when the BAC is in the rising phase. When the BAC curve enters the post-absorptive phase, several hours post-dosing, one observes a marked recovery in the intoxication/impairment effects of alcohol, which does not necessarily mean that a person is a safe driver, owing to anxiety and fatigue.

Gastrointestinal Tract

Consumption of ethanol preceding or in combination with meals stimulates the production of gastric juices rich in acid and poor in pepsin. Concentrated ethanol, i.e., at concentrations above 40%, can irritate mucosal membranes, which may lead to hyperemia or gastritis. Many chronic alcoholics have chronic GI problems due to the irritating effects of ethanol on the stomach.

In general, gastric motility is not directly affected by ethanol.

Kidney

The ingestion of ethanol produces a diuretic effect in part because of an increase in volume of liquid consumed, especially in beer drinkers who frequently need to urinate. However, the main diuretic action of ethanol is by inhibition of the secretion of antidiuretic hormone (vasopressin). Antidiuretic hormone is produced by the pituitary gland and is responsible for the renal tubular reabsorption of water. In general, about 99% of the water filtered by the kidney is reabsorbed, with the remaining water (1%) entering the bladder as urine. The increased production of urine after drinking ethanol is only evident during the absorption part of the BAC curve as shown in Fig. 19.5. In the post-absorptive elimination phase of the BAC curve, the production of urine returns to normal at about 1 mL per minute.

Liver

The acute ingestion of ethanol has little effect on hepatic function. Damage to the liver will develop as a result of long-term, regular consumption of ethanol. Injury first occurs from the accumulation of fat in the liver. The amount of ethanol presented to the liver after drinking is large in comparison to the concentration of other substances. For the liver to process the ethanol, it reduces the activity of other biochemical processes. One of the processes reduced is the oxidation of fat, causing excess fat to remain in the liver. Furthermore, ethanol ingestion leads to increased acetaldehyde formation, which can also have a toxic effect on the liver by increasing lipid peroxidation. Initially, these fatty changes are reversible; however, over time, continued heavy drinking requires repair of liver damage through the deposition of collagen. This leads to fibrotic changes in the liver that eventually become irreversible, developing into liver cirrhosis, liver failure, and death.

Miscellaneous Effects

Ethanol may cause either an increase or a decrease in a variety of secretions. For example, ethanol increases the production of hydrocortisone but decreases plasma testosterone concentrations. Plasma catecholamines also increase following the consumption of ethanol.

Ethanol is also associated with teratogenic effects. These effects have been defined collectively as the "fetal alcohol syndrome" and are described by lower intelligence, slower growth, and facial abnormalities. As a result, drinking alcoholic beverages during pregnancy is not recommended.

While the vasodilatation of ethanol gives the feeling of warmth, it in fact causes increased sweating which leads to heat loss. Therefore, ethanol may cause a slight lowering of body temperature.

Tolerance

It is common knowledge that people differ in their response to the same dose of a drug and the legal drug ethanol is no exception. Ethanol's effects are biphasic with stimulation being more pronounced during the rising part of the BAC curve and sedative and depression on the declining part of the BAC curve

Tolerance is defined as a decrease in response to a given dose of a drug after repeated intake, and in pharmacology this is reflected in a shift in the dose-response curve to the right. Two main types of tolerance are recognized for ethanol, known as dispositional and cellular tolerance. Dispositional tolerance has to do with altered absorption, distribution, or elimination after repeated exposure to the drug, whereas cellular tolerance is reflected in an altered pharmacological response. Another name for dispositional tolerance is metabolic tolerance, reflected in an increased rate of metabolism owing to induction of the microsomal CYP2E1 enzyme after a period of chronic heavy drinking. The slope of the post-absorptive elimination phase in alcoholics might range from 0.02

to 0.035 g/100 mL per hour compared with 0.01–0.02 g/100 mL per hour in moderate drinkers. The dose of alcohol and frequency of drinking necessary to cause an induction of the microsomal enzyme have not been established in humans.

The cellular tolerance to alcohol has two components. One is acute tolerance, which refers to diminished effects of the drug on performance and behavior during a single exposure. Acute tolerance is sometimes referred to as the "Mellanby effect" named after a British pharmacologist, who first observed the phenomenon in dogs receiving alcohol by stomach tube. Acute tolerance is a robust finding and has been confirmed by many investigators using various behavioral measures of alcohol influence. Impairment is more pronounced on the ascending limb of the blood alcohol curve compared with the descending phase. A steeper slope on the ascending limb of the BAC curve produces greater degree of intoxication and can be reinforcing for some drinkers but aversive for others causing nausea and vomiting, especially in novice drinkers. Gulping drinks and drinking on an empty stomach are associated with a steeper rise in BAC and a greater effect on the brain. The mechanism behind the development of acute tolerance is however not completely understood.

The other aspect of tolerance is chronic or functional tolerance, reflected in diminished effects of alcohol after the same dose or the need to drink greater amounts (higher dose) to achieve the same effects before development of tolerance. Many people are capable of functioning despite an elevated BAC as exemplified by drunk drivers many of whom when examined by physicians were judged not under the influence of alcohol despite a high BAC. Apart from the smell of alcohol on the breath, when people arrested for public intoxication were admitted to emergency hospital departments for treatment they were coherent and could be interviewed despite some having a BAC of 0.3 g/100 ml or more. Whether caused by learning or previous experience, these individuals were able to compensate for the behavioral impairment effects of ethanol and in this way conceal the more overt symptoms of intoxication.

The phenomenon of cross-tolerance occurs between ethanol and other classes of drugs, such as barbiturates and benzodiazepines, which act as agonists at the $GABA_A$ receptor complex. Larger doses of these drugs might be necessary to achieve a desired effect in individuals who are tolerant to alcohol. This calls for caution when drugs such as benzodiazepines are prescribed to alcoholics and other people susceptible to abuse and dependence.

Blood Alcohol Analysis

Sampling

The proper sampling of blood for determination of ethanol and other drugs requires assistance from a registered nurse, a physician, or a phlebotomist, legally entitled to draw blood. In some jurisdictions medical laboratory technicians might also be trained and permitted to take blood samples for forensic analysis. Obviously, when ethanol is the substance analyzed in blood, an alcohol swab should not be used to disinfect the skin where the needle puncture is made. This would raise a suspicion that the blood might have been contaminated with alcohol from the swab, even through the risk of this happening is minimal when blood is drawn by venipuncture. To avoid unnecessary discussion and debate in legal cases, a non-alcohol skin disinfectant should be used, such as povidone-iodine or chlorhexidine. Simply washing the skin with soap and water would suffice, because the needle used to penetrate the skin is sterile. Many alcohol-type antiseptics contain isopropanol and not ethanol; these alcohols are easily separated when using gas chromatography for analysis. Evacuated tubes used for sampling blood intended for ethanol analysis should contain an anticoagulant (potassium oxalate or heparin) as well as sodium fluoride (1% w/v) as an enzyme inhibitor. The latter is necessary to quash any notion that ethanol was produced by the action of yeasts or bacteria on blood glucose, which is not very likely anyway because the tubes and needle are sterile.

Three principal methods are available for analysis of ethanol in biological specimens: (i) chemical oxidation and titrimetric or photometric analysis, (ii) enzymatic oxidation and measuring reduced coenzyme NADH by UV absorption at 340 nm, and (iii) gas chromatography either by liquid injection or headspace analysis after equilibration of blood at a fixed temperature.

Chemical Oxidation

Methods of alcohol analysis based on chemical oxidation methods have been used for over 100 years and the most common oxidizing agent is a mixture of potassium dichromate and sulfuric acid. Before starting the chemical reaction, it was necessary to remove ethanol from the sample by distillation, aeration, diffusion, or protein precipitation. The aqueous solution of ethanol produced was then reacted with the dichromate-acid mixture and the endpoint determined by titrimetric analysis or photometric analysis.

Wet-chemical oxidation methods of analysis were not specific for ethanol, and other volatiles, such as acetone, methanol, or ether, if also present in blood were oxidized leading to false high concentrations of ethanol. This was a particular problem in postmortem toxicology when alcohol poisonings were investigated and the deceased had consumed denatured industrial alcohol. Special preliminary tests were necessary to identify the presence of these interfering substances.

One of the most successful wet-chemical oxidation methods was described by Widmark in 1922 and was used in several countries for legal purposes. This micro-diffusion method required only 80–100 mg of capillary blood for each analysis. Widmark flasks resemble the Conway diffusion cells, which is a dish containing two concentric wells. The blood or other biological specimen (~100 mg) enters the outer well, and an excess of the dichromate oxidizing agent is added to the inner well. The flask was sealed and allowed to stand at room temperature or heated until the reaction was completed. Ethanol and any other volatile substances in the blood diffuse into the center well where the chemical reaction occurs. The amount of oxidizing agent that remained after the reaction was over was determined by iodometric titration. Crystals of potassium iodide were added to react with dichromate and liberate iodine, which was determined by volumetric analysis using standard sodium thiosulfate and starch indicator to detect the endpoint.

The dichromate ion (Cr^{+6}) is converted to the chromic ion (Cr^{+3}), which causes a change in color from yellow to green, which was observed visually providing a simple screening test of alcohol. Semiquantitative results were possible by making a series of ethanol standards and allowing them to react with dichromate in exactly the same way as case specimens. However, methods based on chemical oxidation are labor intensive and nonspecific making them more or less obsolete in modern clinical and forensic laboratories.

Enzymatic Oxidation

Enzymatic methods were first applied to blood alcohol analysis in the 1950s and coincided with the isolation of the liver enzyme alcohol dehydrogenase (ADH) in a pure crystalline form. The enzymes contained in yeast were found to be more selective for oxidation of ethanol than mammalian ADH, which was an important consideration for specificity of the method. Because the ADH-NAD$^+$ oxidative is reversible, the acetaldehyde formed must be trapped so that the reaction is driven to completion. The buffer solution of coenzyme NAD$^+$ also had semicarbazide present, which reacted with acetaldehyde to produce a stable semicarbazone. The NADH produced from NAD$^+$ is measured spectrophotometrically at 340 nm and used for quantitative analysis. Although this assay was designed for serum, it works equally well with urine and also whole blood after precipitation of proteins with perchloric acid.

Enzymatic methods had the advantage in that they were easier to automate, and several procedures became available including use of a Technicon AutoAnalyzer or an Abbott X series analyzers. In the latter method, NADH produced by the ADH-catalyzed reaction of ethanol reacts with a thiazolyl blue dye, forming a chromagen. This technique is called radiative energy attenuation (REA) and is based on the principle that the measured fluorescence intensity of a solution containing a fluorophore and a chromagen is related to the absorbance of the solution. In this assay, fluorescein is the fluorophore and has been used successfully to measure ethanol in serum, urine, as well as blood from living and deceased persons.

Gas-Liquid Chromatography

The "gold standard" method for qualitative and quantitative determination of ethanol in biological specimens in both clinical and forensic laboratories is gas-liquid chromatography (GLC) equipped with a flame ionization detector (FID). GLC is a highly sensitivity and specific and provides accurate and precision results in a minimum of time. Moreover, other volatiles that might be present in blood together with ethanol, such as other alcohols, aldehydes, and ketones, can be determined simultaneously and can be distinguished by their retention times, that is, the time after injection until the appearance of the apex of the peak on the gas chromatogram. Quantitative analysis by FID gives a linear response over a wide range of ethanol concentrations in blood from 0.01 to 0.5 g/100 mL, and the limit of quantitation in routine casework is usually 0.01 g/100 mL. The FID detector has the advantage that it is insensitive to water vapor but sensitive to substances containing carbon, hydrogen, and oxygen atoms. The analytical sensitivity can be increased by saturating the blood sample with an inorganic salt, such as sodium chloride or potassium carbonate, which might be necessary if endogenous concentrations of ethanol are of interest.

The two most widely used GLC methods are direct injection of a liquid sample (1–2 μL) and analysis of the headspace vapor in equilibrium with the blood sample in a closed glass vial. Biological specimen should first be diluted (1:10)

with an aqueous solution of internal standard (IS), such as n-propanol or t-butanol before GLC analysis. Diluting with an internal standard reduces the amount of biological substance that enters the GC instrument, which prolongs the life of the analytical column, and measuring peak area ratios helps to compensate for any variations in operating conditions. A calibration plot is constructed by plotting peak area ratio (ethanol/IS) for known strength aqueous standards and using this to deduce the ethanol concentration in blood samples.

The problem posed by making repeated injections of the biological matrix into the GC instrument is avoided when headspace GC analysis is done. The diluted blood sample is transferred to a glass vial, which is then fitted with a rubber septum and a crimped on aluminum cap. The vial is allowed to equilibrate at 50 or 60 °C, and then headspace vapor samples are removed with a gas-tight syringe and injected into the GC instrument for analysis. At a fixed temperature, the amount of any volatile in the air space is proportional to the concentration of the volatile liquid in the solution. Therefore, sampling the headspace of heated specimens and similarly treated ethanol calibrators allows calculation of the ethanol concentration in the specimen. Furthermore, aqueous calibrators can be used if the specimen is diluted ten times, which eliminates matrix effects.

The traditional gas chromatographs used packed columns measuring about 2 m long and 3 mm inside diameter containing polar stationary phases such as polyethylene glycol (Carbowax) or porous polymer materials (Porapak) which separated the volatile substances. Today capillary columns are the norm for GLC analysis of ethanol and other substances, and specialist columns are available for blood alcohol and related volatiles. These substances are separated according to the size of the molecules and their volatility. A thermal conductivity detector can be used but is not advisable because of the large response to water vapor in the sample. The flame ionization detector is the most appropriate for carbon-hydrogen molecules and has high sensitivity and good linearity. The effluent from the GC column could also be analyzed by mass spectrometry,

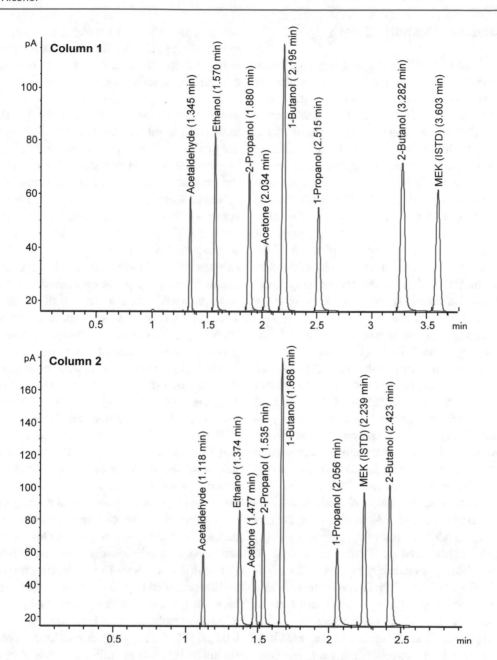

Fig. 19.7 Typical gas chromatogram obtained from analysis of a mixture of volatiles containing acetaldehyde, ethanol, acetone, isopropanol, 1-propanol, 1-butanol, and 2-butanol using 2-butanone (MEK) as the internal standard on two different columns

and the electron impact spectrum contains mass fragments at m/z 31 (base peak), m/z 45, and m/z 46 (molecular ion), which are characteristic of ethanol and "fingerprint" the molecule. The theory behind each of these detectors is explained in Chap. 11. An example of a gas chromatogram from a calibrator containing multiple volatiles is shown in Fig. 19.7.

Analysis of Alcohol in Breath

A maximum of 10% of the total amount of alcohol consumed leaves the body unchanged by excretion via the lungs (exhaled air), the kidney (urine), and the skin (sweat). The small amount eliminated via the lungs forms the basis of the use of breath analyzers in traffic law enforcement as evidence of driving under the influence of alcohol. Roadside breath alcohol tests are routinely done by police authorities worldwide to test people suspected of driving under the influence of alcohol. There are several advantages of breath alcohol analysis over sampling blood for laboratory analysis including noninvasive sampling and obtaining results immediately afterward so that decisions can be made to arrest the driver or repeat the test.

Three special characteristics of ethanol facilitate use of breath analysis: (1) ethanol is volatile; (2) the concentrations in blood and breath are highly correlated; and (3) after drinking alcohol the concentration of ethanol exhaled in breath far exceeds that of other endogenous volatile substances. However, acetone is a potential interfering substance, and high concentrations are exhaled in breath in poorly treated diabetics or after a prolonged fast or eating low-carbohydrate diets.

Two types of breath alcohol analyzer are currently available: (1) handheld electronic devices mainly intended for screening purposes and (2) highly sophisticated stationary units used at police station for evidential purposes. The handheld units are denoted PBTs (preliminary breath testers), and they capture a sample of breath as the suspect exhales through a disposable plastic mouthpiece. Ethanol content in the breath is determined by electrochemical oxidation (fuel cell). Breath alcohol analyzers intended for evidential purposes determine ethanol content of breath by infrared spectrometry and by measuring the stretching frequency of C-H bonds (3.5 microns) or the C-O bond (9.5 microns) in ethanol molecules. Some modern breath alcohol analyzers incorporate both infrared and electrochemical methods of analysis, which is highly desirable in forensic toxicology because this furnishes two independent methods of analysis. Test

subjects are required to make a prolonged end exhalation into the instrument for at least 6 seconds, and the concentration profile of exhaled ethanol is monitored as a function of time.

The physiological principles of breath alcohol testing are well founded scientifically. The distribution of ethanol between blood and alveolar air obeys Henry's law, which states that at a given temperature, a direct relationship exists between the amount of a volatile substance (ethanol) dissolved in a liquid (blood) and the amount of the substance in the vapor (alveolar air) above the solution. Commercially available evidential breath-testing devices are based on the relationship that the amount of ethanol in 2100 mL of breath equals the amount of ethanol in 1 mL of blood at 34 °C, the temperature of expired air. This 2100:1 ratio was based on early scientific studies; more recent work indicates that 2300:1 is a better representation of the actual breath-to-blood ratio. This means that breath-testing devices based on a 2100:1 ratio will underestimate the actual blood ethanol concentration for the overwhelming majority of individuals.

Several scientific safeguards are necessary when breath alcohol analyzers are used for legal purposes; the most important of which is to observe the subject for at least 15–20 min prior to taking a sample and to ensure that nothing enters the mouth. Belching or vomiting could return ethanol from the stomach, possibly leading to an erroneous result. Evidentiary tests are confirmation tests that require a 15 min deprivation period and are preceded by a blank reading. At least two breath samples should be collected and analyzed, with the replicate analyses agreeing within 0.02 g/210L for approval. Breath ethanol results should be reported in terms of a mass of ethanol per volume of breath, which avoids any assumptions about a particular blood/breath ratio. Instrument performance should be validated with the testing of each subject using either a wet bath simulator or a calibrated dry gas standard as an ethanol control sample.

Many analytical methods have been developed for forensic breath alcohol analysis including the classic Breathalyzer® instrument developed by Robert F Borkenstein in the 1950s. The sampling of breath was done in a stainless steel cylinder and piston device with a vent that allowed discarding the initially top-lung exhaled breath. The last part of the exhalation that was considered to reflect alveolar air is trapped and saved for analysis. The sample chamber was heated to 50 °C to prevent condensation of water vapor and ethanol in the breath sample. The breath sample was analyzed by mixing with a mixture of potassium dichromate and sulfuric acid and a small amount of silver nitrate catalysis, which was contained in a glass ampoule. The oxidation reaction was allowed to proceed for 90 s which was the optimal time to prevent interference from any acetone that might be present in the breaths' ample. The actual photometric measurement of ethanol was done at an absorbance of 440 nm.

Infrared (IR) Spectrophotometry

The absorption of infrared (IR) radiation is a characteristic property of a molecule depending on its structure and the types of chemical bonding. Absorption at IR light at certain wavelengths is characteristic of certain bonds, such as C-H, O-H, or C-O. Molecules can undergo stretching and bending vibrations when exposed to IR radiation, and the usual range of wavelengths span from 2.5 to 25 μM corresponding to wavenumbers 4000-400 cm^{-1}.

The use of IR technology for the analysis of ethanol in breath has become a mainstay in evidential breath-testing devices. Ethanol has several types of bonds: C-H, C-C, C-O, and O-H. Selecting a wavelength where these bonds specifically absorb IR energy allows partial identification and quantification of ethanol in breath. Because many other compounds have the same chemical bonding and absorb IR energy at the same wavelength, there is a risk for interference with analysis of ethanol in breath. This potential interference problem is mitigated by the fact that an interfering substance must be volatile enough to appear in significant concentration in human expired air. Specificity can be enhanced by using multiple wavelengths simultaneously using a series of filters 3.3–3.5 μM.

IR breath analyzers differ in certain respects, such as volume of breath sampled, wavelength monitored, number of wavelengths used, and manner in which the exhalation is controlled for time and pressure characteristics. However, the basic principle is the same, and an end-expired sample of breath enters a heated chamber cell where it is irradiated with IR energy. If ethanol is present in the sample, it will absorb some of the IR energy in relation to the amount of ethanol that is in the sample. Absorption of IR energy by ethanol means that less energy reaches the detector in comparison to an air sample not containing ethanol. By calibrating the instrument with simulator solutions of known ethanol concentration, the ethanol concentration in the subject's breath can be determined.

Electrochemical Oxidation

Electrochemical detectors oxidize ethanol in the vapor phase to acetaldehyde and further to acetic acid, and such detectors have been incorporated in a range of instruments intended for forensic breath alcohol analysis. This detector is constructed as a fuel cell, which consists of two platinum-coated conduction electrodes separated by an ion-conducting electrolyte layer, such as phosphoric acid. The conversion of ethanol present in breath to acetic acid produces a current. The flow generated is directly proportional to the amount of ethanol present in the sample. The fuel cell may react minimally with other alcohols like methanol and isopropanol but does not respond to any great extent to acetone.

Fuel cell technology has been used since the 1970s in handheld instruments for breath alcohol analysis. These devices are intended as roadside screening tests to furnish police officer with probable cause to arrest a driver for further testing. Fuel cells might also be used in evidential breath analyzers, especially in combination with an IR detector. Because the IR detector is nondestructive of ethanol, a fuel cell can be placed in series after an IR detector. The fuel cell does not oxidize acetone, which the major endogenous volatile in the breath under some circumstances.

However acetaldehyde is oxidized, but the concentrations in breath, even after drinking alcoholic beverages, are so low that this ethanol metabolite is not a serious problem as an interfering substance.

Gas chromatography has also been adapted for breath alcohol analysis, because ethanol is already in the gaseous state when exhaled in the breath. Small and compact GC instruments incorporated a pressurized cylinder containing a mixture of hydrogen and nitrogen as combustible gas for the flame detector and a sampling loop to capture a portion of the exhaled air. One such instrument was the GC Intoximeter (FID detector) and another AlcoAnalyzer (thermal conductivity detector). However, the complexity of GC analysis, the need for more intensive training of operators, and the need for more frequent recalibrations meant that GC methods, although more specific, were abandoned in favor of infrared breath alcohol analyzers.

Examples of handheld PBT instruments include Alcolmeter, Alcotest, Lifeloc, and Alco-Sensor, all of which incorporate fuel cell sensors for determination of ethanol. Electrochemistry is not completely specific for ethanol because methanol and other alcohols (but not acetone) are oxidized but at different reaction rates. The instruments used for evidential breath alcohol testing are mostly based on multiple wavelength infrared (IR) detectors at 3.4 μM and/or 9.5 μM ranges, e.g. Intoxilyzer, DataMaster, and Evidenzer. One evidential breath analyzer (Intoximeter EC/IR) uses electrochemical oxidation as the primary means of detection, whereas others use a combination of IR and electrochemistry (Alcotest).

Stability of Ethanol in Blood and Urine

Compared with many other drugs and toxicants encountered in forensic toxicology, the concentrations of ethanol in blood are remarkably stable during short- and long-term storage of specimens. A small decrease in concentration of ethanol in blood of about 0.003 g/100 mL per month occurs when specimens are stored refrigerated (4 °C) in evacuated tubes until analyzed. The loss of ethanol is higher if the tubes are opened periodically to remove aliquots for analysis. Besides a diffusion of ethanol from the liquid into the air space, exposure to room air replenishes the oxygen content in the air space above the blood, and one mechanism suggested to loss of ethanol is nonenzymatic oxidation via oxyhemoglobin. Hence ethanol concentrations might be more stable in blood samples from smokers with higher concentrations of carboxyhemoglobin compared with nonsmokers. Stability is improved if specimens are stored frozen.

The evacuated tubes used to collect blood samples for ethanol analysis should contain chemical preservatives in powder form. Use of potassium oxalate, EDTA, or heparin is suitable as an anticoagulant, and sodium fluoride (~1% w/v) is included as an enzyme inhibitor. A widely used 10 mL gray stopper evacuated tube used for collecting blood samples for ethanol analysis has potassium oxalate (25 mg) as an anticoagulant and sodium fluoride (100 mg) as an enzyme inhibitor.

Ethanol concentrations in blood from living persons are rarely found to increase during long-term storage. But the situation is different in autopsy work because the specimens might already be contaminated with bacteria when the autopsy was performed. Ethanol can be produced by fermentation of substrates such as glucose and various fatty acids or amino acids in the presence of bacteria or yeasts. It is always a challenge in postmortem toxicology to establish whether a measured BAC resulted from antemortem ingestion or postmortem synthesis (neoformation). This can be investigated in a number of ways, although knowledge of the circumstances surrounding the death, especially witness statements and police reports about possible drinking by the deceased, is important information.

In postmortem toxicology, the concentrations of ethanol in different biological specimens should be compared and contrasted because this furnishes useful information to rule out postmortem synthesis having occurred. Finding acceptable agreement in results based on known water content of the materials analyzed speaks toward antemortem ingestion of ethanol and not postmortem synthesis. If the body emits a bad smell at autopsy, this is a strong indication that decomposition has already commenced and care is needed when toxicological results are interpreted. Finding an elevated concentration of ethanol in blood but negligible concentrations in vitreous humor or urine, which are both resistant to the putrefaction process, speaks toward postmortem production of ethanol.

Low concentrations of ethanol in blood, such as 0.01 g/100 mL, are easily produced after death even when there are no obvious signs of decomposition or putrefaction. This suggests that in postmortem toxicology a blood ethanol cutoff concentration of 0.02 g/100 mL would be more appropriate when positive results are reported. Low BACs of 0.01–0.03 g/100 mL need to be verified by analysis of ethanol in alternative specimens, such as vitreous humor or urine. Occasionally, blood ethanol concentrations exceeding 0.10 g/100 mL are seen with zero concentrations in alternative specimens. On the other hand, a measurable concentration found in vitreous humor or urine specimens speaks toward antemortem ingestion of alcohol, especially if the concentration ratios VH/blood or urine/blood are in the expected range of 1.2–1.3 based on relative water content of the specimens analyzed.

Other evidence that ethanol was produced in the body after death comes from fining other volatile substances besides ethanol (e.g., acetaldehyde, acetone, n-propanol, or n-butanol). Although ethanol is the main product of bacterial activity, it is not the exclusive product. However, because acetaldehyde is a normal metabolic product of ethanol metabolism and acetone might be elevated in blood of diabetics or malnourished individuals, the presence of these substances can occur by other mechanisms than fermentation.

Recent research demonstrates the possibility to determine non-oxidative metabolites of ethanol in body fluids as evidence that ethanol has undergone metabolism in the body during life. Methods involving GC-MS or LC-MS with deuterium-labeled internal standards are widely used to determine ethyl glucuronide or ethyl sulfate in postmortem specimens, including hair strands. The analysis of EtG and EtS verifies that ethanol has undergone a phase II conjugation reaction, which points toward antemortem consumption rather than postmortem synthesis. Use of realistic cutoff concentrations for positive EtG and EtS is necessary to avoid extraneous sources of ethanol in foodstuffs, medication, and various household products.

Numerous studies show a good stability of ethanol in antemortem blood specimens when they are properly stored in evacuated tubes and contain a chemical preservative. Potassium oxalate is commonly used as an anticoagulant to prevent clotting and is used in conjunction with sodium fluoride as an enzyme inhibitor. Under these conditions, in properly sealed tubes, the blood ethanol concentration will remain stable for at least a month, even if kept at room temperature.

As alluded to earlier, ethanol is rarely produced after voiding if the urine specimens are obtained from healthy subjects. The situation is different in diabetics, who might secrete glucose in the urine and also suffer from a urinary tract or *Candida* infection. Under these circumstances after 24–48 h storage at room temperature, high urinary concentrations are produced. However, all three components sugar, microorganism or yeast, and time are necessary for the in vitro production of ethanol after sampling. Storage of samples in the cold at +4°C or better still frozen (−20°C) prevents microbial synthesis of ethanol even when there is no NaF in the tubes. However, because urinary tract infections and candidiasis are common in diabetics, the inclusion of a fluoride preservative should be mandatory if ethanol is the substance to be analyzed.

Legal and Regulatory Aspects

Driving Under the Influence

Epidemiological surveys verify that overconsumption of alcohol and drunkenness play a major role in many types of accidents in the home, at work, and on the roads. Therefore, the

Table 19.5 Threshold blood alcohol concentration (BAC) limits expressed in different units and used for regulatory and legal purposes

g/100 mL (g%)	mg/100 mL (mg%)	g/L (mg/mL)	mmol/L[a]	g/kg (mg/g)[b]	Threshold or legal standard
0.08	80	0.80	18.2	0.76	Blood alcohol limit for driving in 49 US states[c]
0.05	50	0.50	11.3	0.47	Medical standard for alcohol influence and the statutory limit for driving in most EU countries
0.04	40	0.40	9.1	0.38	Federal highway safety standard for commercial vehicle drivers and also workplace violations
0.02	20	0.20	4.5	0.19	Blood alcohol limit for novice drivers in US states and also some EU nations

[a]Molecular weight of ethanol = 46 (0.1 g/100 mL = 21.7 mmol/L)
[b]Density of blood = 1.055 g/mL
[c]As of January 2019, the per se limit in Utah was 0.05 g/100 mL

analysis of alcohol in blood and other body fluids forms a critical component in any criminal or civil investigation of alcohol-related accidents. To address this problem, state legislatures have set limits on the concentration of ethanol permitted in blood or breath when an individual operates a motor vehicle.

Most countries have enacted blood alcohol limits ranging from 0.02 to 0.08 g/100 mL depending on activity, such as driving on the highway or engaging in safety-sensitive work (Table 19.5). The blood alcohol concentrations are expressed in different concentration units, such as mg/100 mL (UK and Canada), g/L (France and Spain), and g/kg (Nordic countries and Germany). SI concentration units (mmol/L) are also given for comparison because these units are increasingly used in hospital clinical chemistry laboratories when alcohol is analyzed and reported.

As early as 1971, the US National Safety Council Committee on Alcohol and Other Drugs stated that any driver with a blood alcohol concentration of 0.08 g/100 mL or more was impaired in terms of driving performance. Subsequent statements by the Committee have emphasized that driving impairment occurs at lower concentrations in some individuals. Almost all states have moved away from "presumption" statutes where the issue of an individual's intoxication is rebuttable by other evidence, regardless of the ethanol concentration. Instead, "per se" laws have been adopted that make it a violation of the

law to have above a fixed ethanol concentration in blood or breath at time of driving.

The National Committee on Uniform Traffic Laws and Ordinances (NCUTLO) developed the Uniform Vehicle Code to be adopted by the various states and the District of Columbia. The document consists of two parts: (1) the Uniform Vehicle Code, a set of motor vehicle laws designed and advanced as a comprehensive guide or standard for the state motor vehicle traffic laws, and (2) the Model Traffic Ordinance. Within the Uniform Vehicle Code, several recommendations are important to alcohol testing:

- Revocation of license for refusal to submit to a chemical test or having a BAC of 0.08 g/100 mL or g/210 L or more, generally referred to as the "implied consent law." Any person who drives a motor vehicle on public highways shall be deemed to have given his/her consent to have a chemical test of breath, blood, or urine to determine the alcohol concentration or the presence of other drugs.
- Revocation of license for refusal to submit to a chemical test or having a BAC of any measurable and detectable amount (0.02 g/100 mL or g/210 L or more) for persons under 21 years of age.
- The administration of a preliminary breath test when a law enforcement officer has probable cause to believe the person may be impaired by alcohol.

- A driver may be compelled to submit to a chemical test if involved in a serious personal injury or fatal crash.
- The State Department of Health is authorized to approve techniques or methods for the analysis of alcohol in blood, breath, and urine and to promulgate guidelines to determine competence of individuals to conduct such analysis.
- The sample for analysis of blood may only be drawn by a physician, registered nurse, or other person qualified to withdraw blood acting at the direction of a police officer.
- The defendant may have an additional test administered in addition to the test administered at the direction of the officer.
- Alcohol concentration shall mean either grams of alcohol per 100 mL of blood or grams of alcohol per 210 L of breath.
- If alcohol concentration measured 0.08 g/100 mL or g/210 L or more, it shall be presumed that the person was under the influence of alcohol.

The Uniform Vehicle Code serves as a basis for standardizing laws and practices among the states.

As part of an ongoing effort to decrease alcohol-related injuries and fatalities, in 2013 the National Transportation Safety Board (NTSB) recommended lowering the per se limit to 0.05 g/dL. The American Medical Association and the World Health Organization have also endorsed this position. Efforts to lower the legal alcohol limit for motor vehicle operators in the USA were also supported by the National Safety Council in 2016. Utah became the first state to decrease the per se limit to 0.05 g/dL in January 2019.

Figure 19.8 shows relative frequency distributions of blood alcohol concentrations in men and women apprehended in Sweden (statutory BAC limit 0.02 g/100 mL) for drunken driving. Mean blood alcohol concentration, regardless of gender, was 0.16–0.17 g/100 mL which signifies a period of heavy drinking and suggests that many drunk drivers are problem drinkers or alcoholics. Males dominated over females among traffic delinquents by 88% to 12%, although BAC did not seem to vary much in relation to the person's age.

Alcohol in the Workplace

Some workplace activities obviously entail greater hazards than others, including significant risks to the worker, the workplace, and other individuals. In particular, the transportation workplace in all modalities presents a variety of basic safety hazards, which are increased by the effects of alcohol use by workers performing various safety-sensitive functions. Many non-transportation industries and workplaces also involve transport of persons, goods, and materials. In others, activities and operations occur that are inherently hazardous or associated with potential risks. The risk of error or adverse events is increased when tasks are performed by alcohol-impaired workers. Fundamentally, workers should be free of alcoholic influence at all times while at work. It is, therefore, recommended that:

- Employees abstain from alcohol intake for 12 to 24 hours prior to undertaking critical and safety-sensitive tasks.
- An appropriate program of on-site and off-site alcohol testing be implemented.
- Breath alcohol concentrations <0.01 g/210 L and blood and saliva alcohol concentrations <0.01 g/100 mL should be deemed alcohol-free.

The universe of alcohol testing in the workplace is readily divided into governmentally regulated and nonregulated testing (testing for alcohol that is not required by law). In addition to testing performed under federal mandates, increasing numbers of states have enacted laws that control testing for alcohol and other drugs in workers. Further, such groups as the National Football League and the National Basketball Association require testing for alcohol and other abused drugs in professional athletes.

There are several important differences between alcohol and other abused drugs. Principally, alcohol is a licit drug and consumption of alcoholic beverages by adults is lawful, with limited exceptions, such as while driving motor vehicles. The mere presence of alcohol in the body and in body fluids (breath or saliva)

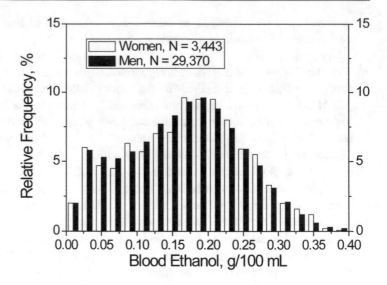

Fig. 19.8 Relative frequency distributions of blood alcohol concentration in men and women apprehended for drunken driving in Sweden where the statutory limit is 0.02 g/100 m

does not imply a violation of law. Alcohol in the body has a short half-life, meaning that its elimination from the body is significantly faster than that of other commonly abused drugs (hours rather than days or weeks). Thus the timing of specimen collection for alcohol testing is more critical and demanding.

The National Safety Council's Committee on Alcohol and Other Drugs (now the Alcohol, Drugs, and Impairment Division) in 1995 developed "A Model Program for the Control of Alcohol in the Workplace." The program was designed primarily to assist employers and other required to establish testing programs in response to the Omnibus Transportation Employee Testing Act of 1991. It suggests that the purpose of alcohol testing programs is to help prevent accidents and injuries resulting from the misuse of alcohol by employees who perform safety-sensitive functions.

Workplace alcohol testing regulated by the US Department of Transportation (DOT) is mandated by the Omnibus Transportation Employee Testing Act of 1991 (Public Law 102-143, 1991) for certain transportation modalities. Performance of safety-sensitive functions by a covered employee in a DOT-regulated entity is prohibited:

1. When such a person has an alcohol concentration of 0.04 g/210 L or greater, as indicated by a breath alcohol test, or temporarily when such person has an alcohol concentration of

0.02 g/210 L or greater but less than 0.04 g/210 L
2. While such person is using alcohol
3. Within 4–8 h after using alcohol

In addition, an employee involved in an accident may not refuse alcohol testing or consume alcoholic beverages until tested or until 8 h after an accident.

The categories for alcohol testing in the workplace are largely self-explanatory and include:

• Applicant testing
• Reasonable suspicion and reasonable cause testing
• Fitness-for-duty testing
• Post-accident testing
• Return-to-duty and follow-up testing
• Random testing

Testing for alcohol under the DOT regulations has the following features:

• Alcohol is defined as "the intoxicating agent in beverage alcohol, ethyl alcohol, or other low molecular weight alcohols including methyl or isopropyl alcohol."
• Alcohol concentration is defined as "the alcohol in a volume of breath expressed in terms of grams of alcohol per 210 liters of breath as indicated by a breath test."

- All alcohol testing is to be carried out on-site at the workplace, except in some post-accident situations.
- Breath and saliva are the only acceptable specimens for initial "screening" tests.
- "Screening" and "confirmation" tests are required in specific situations. Breath is the only acceptable specimen for "confirmation" tests, with some exceptions for post-accident testing.

Testing is categorized into two varieties:

- Initial tests, sometimes referred to as screening or preliminary tests, are intended to establish whether the tested person is alcohol-free or not. Alcohol-free individuals do not require any further testing. To be most practical, screening tests must be simple and rapidly performed with minimal training.
- Confirmatory tests are performed with evidential-grade testing devices after an initial test has indicated the presence of alcohol in the tested person. The results of the confirmatory test are relied upon for personnel actions such as removal from current safety-sensitive duties.

All testing for alcohol in breath or saliva must be carried out with testing and associated devices appearing on NHTSA Conforming Products Lists. Screening tests on breath or saliva must use approved breath or saliva-alcohol screening test devices or be performed on breath with approved evidential breath testers (EBTs). Confirmation tests must be carried out on breath and must use EBTs that:

1. Are capable of providing a printed result in triplicate
2. Are capable of assigning a unique and sequential number to each completed test and displaying same before test
3. Are capable of printing on each copy of the result the manufacturer's name for the device, the device serial number, the time of the test, the test number, and the test result

4. Are able to distinguish alcohol from acetone at an alcohol concentration of 0.02 g/210 L
5. Are capable of testing an air blank prior to each collection of breath and of performing an "external calibration check"

Confirmation tests must be carried out within 30 minutes of the completion of a screening test that reports an alcohol concentration of 0.02 g/210 L or greater. A deprivation period of not less than 15 minutes and an air blank yielding a 0.00 g/210 L result must precede the breath collection for a confirmation test. (Air blanks are not required before or after a breath screening test.) Testing must be performed by a breath alcohol technician (BAT) who has successfully completed a course of instruction equivalent to the DOT model course and who has "demonstrated competence in the operation of the specific EBT(s)" that the BAT will use. Law enforcement officers who have been certified by state or local governments to conduct breath alcohol testing with the EBT concerned are deemed by DOT to be qualified as BATs.

The following documents define the criteria for evaluation and provide notice of acceptable products that meet the established criteria:

1. Model Specifications for Evidential Breath-Testing Devices (58 FR 48705–10, September 17, 1993)
2. Conforming Products List of Evidential Breath Alcohol Measurement Devices (82 FR 50940-50944, November 2, 2017)
3. Model Specifications for Screening Devices to Measure Alcohol in Bodily Fluids (73 FR 16956-16960, March 31, 2008).
4. Conforming Products List of Screening Devices to Measure Alcohol in Bodily Fluids (77 FR 35745-35747, June 4, 2012)
5. Model Specifications for Calibrating Unit for Breath Alcohol Testers (72 FR 34742-34748, June 25, 2007)
6. Conforming Products List of Calibrating Unit for Breath Alcohol Testers (77FR 64588-64590, October 22, 2012)

Updated notices of conforming products appear periodically in the Federal Register.

Suggested Reading

Caplan YH, Zettl JR (2002) The determination of alcohol in blood and breath. In: Saferstein R (ed) Forensic science handbook, 2nd edn. Prentice-Hall, Englewood Cliffs, pp 635–695

Caplan YH, Goldberger BA (eds) (2015) Garriott's medicolegal aspects of alcohol, 6th edn. Lawyers and Judges, Tuscon

Dubowski KM (1985) Absorption, distribution, and elimination of alcohol: Highway safety aspects. J Stud Alcohol (Suppl 10):98–108

Dubowski KM (1992) The technology of breath-alcohol analysis. National Institute on Alcohol Abuse and Alcoholism, DHHS publication (ADM)92-1728

Jones AW (1990) Physiological aspects of breath-alcohol measurement. Alcohol, Drugs, and Driving 6:1–25

Jones AW (1996) Measuring alcohol in blood and breath for forensic purposes—a historical review. Forensic Sci Rev 8:14–43

Jones AW (2006) Urine as a biological specimen for forensic alcohol analysis and variability in the urine-to-blood relationship. Toxicol Rev 25:15–35

Jones AW (2010) Evidence based survey of the elimination rates of ethanol from blood with applications in forensic casework. Forensic Sci Int 200:1–20

Jones AW (2011) Pharmacokinetics of ethanol – issues of forensic importance. Forensic Sci Rev 23:91–136

Kugelberg FC, Jones AW (2007) Interpreting results of ethanol analysis in postmortem specimens: A review of the literature. Forensic Sci Int 165:10–29

O'Neal CL, Poklis A (1996) Postmortem production of ethanol and factors that influence interpretation. A critical review. Am J Forensic Med Path 17:8–20

Porter WH (2012) Ethylene glycol poisoning. Quintessential clinical toxicology, analytical conundrum. Clin Chim Acta 413:365–377

Walsham NE, Sherwood RA (2012) Ethyl glucuronide. Ann Clin Biochem 49:110–117

Benzodiazepines

20

Rebecca A. Jufer-Phipps and Barry S. Levine

Abstract

Benzodiazepines are the most widely prescribed central nervous system (CNS) depressants in the United States. They have been in use since the 1960s as anxiolytics, anticonvulsants, and muscle relaxants. The name of the class is derived from the combination of a benzene ring with a seven-membered diazepine ring. Included in the structure is a phenyl ring attached to the 5-position of the diazepine, a requirement for benzodiazepine activity. Benzodiazepines mediate their CNS-depressant activity through the neurotransmitter gamma-amino butyric acid (GABA), the major inhibitory neurotransmitter in the brain. Benzodiazepines bind to $GABA_A$ receptors and potentiate the inhibitory action of GABA. Benzodiazepines have a high therapeutic index and, as a result, rarely cause death by themselves. In addition to the widely prescribed benzodiazepines such as alprazolam, clonazepam, diazepam, and lorazepam, a number of analogs have been developed illicitly, including pyrazolam, flubromazolam, and others. Analysis of benzodiazepines often requires the inclusion of metabolites, depending on the specimen being tested. The chemistry, pharmacology, effects, and analysis of therapeutic and designer benzodiazepines are reviewed.

Keywords

Benzodiazepines · Pharmacology · Effects · Toxicology · Interpretation · Analysis

As a class, benzodiazepines are one of the most widely prescribed drugs in the world and have largely replaced barbiturates as the major class of CNS-depressant drugs. Data from 2018 indicated that five benzodiazepines rank among the top 200 drugs in the United States, as determined by the number of prescriptions dispensed. These top-ranking benzodiazepines were alprazolam (#23), clonazepam (#38), lorazepam (#55), diazepam (#91), and temazepam (#174). Currently, approximately 24 benzodiazepines, including prodrugs, are approved for use in the United States and are prescribed as anxiolytics, muscle relaxants, anesthetic adjuncts, anticonvulsants, and treatment for obsessive-compulsive disorders. The properties of selected benzodiazepines are summarized in Table 20.1.

Dr. Leo Sternbach of Hoffmann-La Roche is credited with the discovery of the benzodiazepines. During an assistantship in Poland in the 1930s, Dr. Sternbach studied a class of

R. A. Jufer-Phipps · B. S. Levine (✉)
Office of the Chief Medical Examiner,
Baltimore, MD, USA
e-mail: blevine@som.umaryland.edu

© Springer Nature Switzerland AG 2020
B. S. Levine, S. Kerrigan (eds.), *Principles of Forensic Toxicology*,
https://doi.org/10.1007/978-3-030-42917-1_20

Table 20.1 Selected properties of common benzodiazepines

Benzodiazepine	Trade name(s)	Uses	Primary metabolite(s)	Half-life	V_d	Dose	Therapeutic concentrations
Alprazolam	Xanax	Antidepressant Anxiolytic	α-Hydroxyalprazolam	11–15 h	0.7–1.3 L/kg	General anxiety: 0.75–4 mg/day Panic disorder: Up to 10 mg/day	5–50 ng/mL
Bromazepam	Lectopam Lexotan	Anxiolytic Muscle relaxant	3-Hydroxybromazepam glucuronide 2-Amino-5-bromo-3-hydroxy-benzoylpyridine glucuronide	8–19 h	0.9 L/kg	3–18 mg daily (max 60 mg daily)	0.08–0.15 mg/L
Chlordiazepoxide	Librium	Anxiolytic Alcohol withdrawal	Norchlordiazepoxide Demoxepam Nordiazepam Oxazepam	5–30 h (CDP) 30–100 h (nordiazepam)	0.3–0.6 L/kg	Anxiety: 30–100 mg daily Alcohol withdrawal: Up to 300 mg daily	0.4–4 mg/L
Clobazam	Frisium Urbanyl	Anticonvulsant Anxiolytic Panic disorder Sedative	Desmethylclobazam	10–30 h (clobazam) 2–3 d (desmethylclobazam)	0.9–1.8 L/kg	20–60 mg daily	0.1–0.4 mg/L
Clonazepam	Klonopin	Anticonvulsant Panic disorder	7-Aminoclonazepam	19–60 h	2–4 L/kg	1.5–20 mg daily	0.005–0.07 mg/L
Clorazepate	Tranxene	Anticonvulsant Anxiolytic Alcohol withdrawal	Nordiazepam Oxazepam	2 h (clorazepate) 30–100 h (nordiazepam)	0.5–2.5 L/kg	Up to 60 mg daily	0.02–0.8 mg/L nordiazepam
Diazepam	Valium	Anticonvulsant Anxiolytic Muscle relaxant	Nordiazepam	20–50 h (diazepam) 30–100 h (nordiazepam)	0.5–2.5 L/kg	2–40 mg daily	0.1–1.5 mg/L
Estazolam	ProSom Eurodin	Hypnotic	1-Oxoestazolam 4-Hydroxyestazolam	10–30 h	3 L/kg	1–2 mg	0.05–0.1 mg/L
Flunitrazepam	Rohypnol	Anesthetic induction agent Hypnotic	7-Aminoflunitrazepam	9–25 h	3.5–5.5 L/kg	0.5–2 mg	0.005–0.015 mg/L

Flurazepam	Dalmane	Hypnotic	N-1-Desalkylflurazepam N-1-Hydroxyethyl-flurazepam	1–3 h (flurazepam)	3.4–5.5 L/kg 80 h (N-1-desalkylflurazepam)	15–30 mg daily	0.0005–0.03 mg/L
Halazepam	Paxipam	Anxiolytic	Nordiazepam	14–16 h	1.0 L/kg	20–40 mg 3–4× daily	0.037–0.125 mg/L
Lorazepam	Ativan	Anxiolytic Pre-operative	Lorazepam glucuronide	9–24 h	1–2 L/kg	1–10 mg daily	0.05–0.24 mg/L
Midazolam	Versed	Anesthetic induction agent Pre-operative Sedative	α-Hydroxymidazolam	1.5–2.5 h	1.0–2.5 L/kg	0.05–0.5 mg/kg	0.08–0.25 mg/L
Nitrazepam	Mogadon	Hypnotic	7-Aminonitrazepam	16–48 h	2–5 L/kg	5–10 mg daily	0.03–0.12 mg/L
Oxazepam	Serax	Anxiolytic	Oxazepam glucuronide	4–15 h	0.5–2.0 L/kg	15–60 mg daily	0.5–2.0 mg/L
Prazepam	Centrax	Anxiolytic	Nordiazepam	1.3 h (Prazepam) 30–100 h (Nordiazepam)	12–14 L/kg	20–60 mg daily	0.02–0.8 mg/L Nordiazepam
Temazepam	Normison Restoril	Hypnotic Pre-operative	Oxazepam	5–15 h	0.8–1.4 L/kg	15–60 mg daily	0.3–0.9 mg/L
Triazolam	Halcion	Hypnotic	α-Hydroxytriazolam	1.5–5.5 h	1.1–2.7 L/kg	0.125–0.25 mg daily	0.002–0.02 mg/L

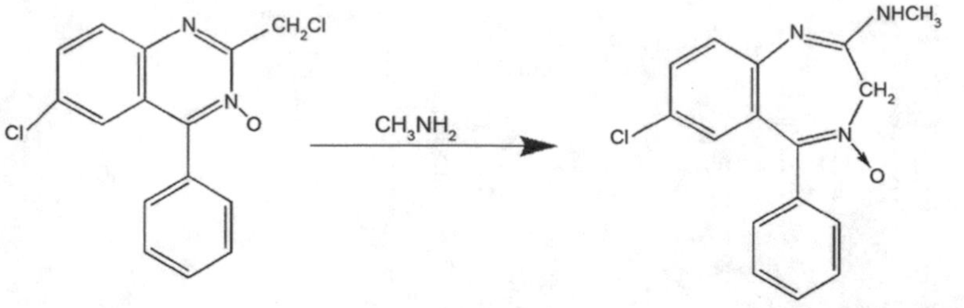

Fig. 20.1 The first
benzodiazepine was
synthesized by the
reaction of a quinazoline
N-oxide with
methylamine

compounds called heptoxdiazines. His interest in these compounds resurfaced in the mid-1950s when he began to evaluate "heptoxdiazines" as potential tranquilizers. During his investigation, he discovered that these compounds were not heptoxdiazines as previously thought, but they were quinazoline 3-oxides. After several years of synthesizing numerous quinazoline 3-oxide compounds with disappointing pharmacological test results, Dr. Sternbach initiated a "cleanup" of the laboratory and expected to complete this work with at least some publishable material. During the cleanup, a co-worker drew his attention to a compound that formed when quinazoline N-oxide was treated with methylamine. This compound was subsequently submitted for animal pharmacological testing, which yielded promising results. Further testing indicated that this compound was the product of an unusual ring enlargement, which had created a benzodiazepine derivative (Fig. 20.1). Clinical trials with this benzodiazepine compound were initiated in 1958, leading to its approval by the FDA in February 1960. One month later it was marketed as Librium (chlordiazepoxide), the first benzodiazepine approved for therapeutic use.

Chemistry and Use

The general benzodiazepine structure is shown in Fig. 20.2. The name of the class is derived from the combination of a benzene ring (A) with a seven-member diazepine ring (B). Included in the structure is a phenyl ring (C) attached to the 5-position of the diazepine ring. This phenyl group (C) appears to be a requirement for benzodiazepine activity. Moreover, the benzene component of the benzodiazepine structure needs an electron-withdrawing group present at R7 to have enhanced activity; a chlorine atom and a nitro group are the most common entities attached. Potency can be improved by adding an electron-withdrawing group in the ortho position (R2') on the phenyl ring attached to the benzodiazepine nucleus (i.e., lorazepam, clonazepam, flunitrazepam). An electron-withdrawing group at this position also produces a greater amnesic effect.

Other structural modifications are possible and can affect both potency and duration of action. Groups commonly bonded to the N1 position include hydrogen, a substituted alkyl group, or a fused triazole (triazolobenzodiazepines) or imidazole ring (imidazobenzodiazepines). Benzodiazepines with smaller substituents on position N1 tend to have higher intrinsic activity; however, some drugs with larger N1 substituents are effective (e.g., flurazepam), largely due to metabolic dealkylation to an active metabolite. Most benzodiazepines have a double-bonded oxygen attached to C2 (the exceptions are chlordiazepoxide, which has a methylamino group, and quazepam, which has a double-bonded sulfur). Replacing a hydrogen with a hydroxyl group on C3 reduces the drug's duration of action. The influence of these structural changes on the pharmacological effects can be exploited for a wide variety of clinical purposes. The addition of the hydroxyl group allows direct conjugation of the parent drug to an inactive glucuronide conjugate. An additional ring can be added to positions 1 and 2 of the diazepine ring, resulting in the highly potent imidazo- (e.g., midazolam) and triazolobenzodiazepines (e.g., triazolam). A host of analogs are possible, and this has been exploited for illicit purposes. Some of the newer ("designer") benzodiazepines involve the replacement of the phenyl ring (C) with a pyridine (e.g., pyrazolam)

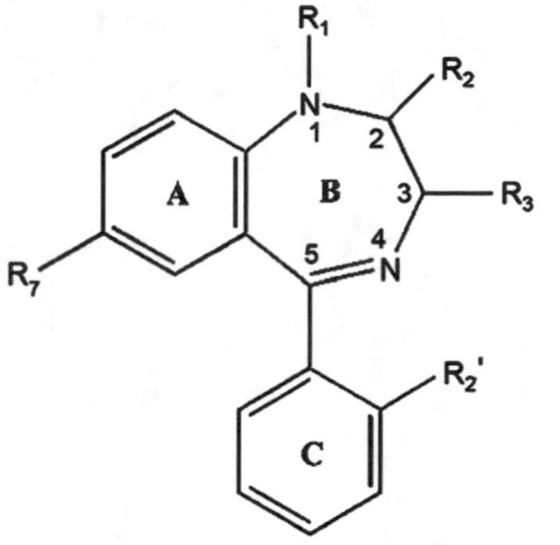

Fig. 20.2 The benzodiazepine structure

or replacement of the benzene ring (A) with thiophene ring (e.g., etizolam). Selected benzodiazepines are illustrated in Figs. 20.3 and 20.4.

As therapeutic agents, benzodiazepines have many advantages over the drugs they largely replaced, barbiturates; namely, they have fewer side effects and are much safer from the standpoint of potential overdose. Benzodiazepines display selective rather than generalized central nervous system depressant actions. This gives them a uniquely wide margin of safety. There is less liver enzyme induction with benzodiazepines, which presents fewer complications when multiple drugs are co-administered. While withdrawal effects after discontinuing benzodiazepine use do occur, the symptoms are milder than those observed with barbiturates.

Benzodiazepines have wide-ranging clinical utility. One of the most common therapeutic uses of benzodiazepines is to treat anxiety. Diazepam gained widespread use in the 1970s as an anxiolytic drug. Alprazolam was introduced in the US pharmaceutical market in the 1980s and has largely replaced diazepam for this purpose. The anxiolytic effects of benzodiazepines are likely related to their ability to produce inhibitory effects in areas of the brain that are associated with anxiogenesis. Additionally, it has been reported that benzodiazepines act to suppress noradrenergic and/or serotonergic pathways in some areas of the brain, which appears to play a role in their anxiolytic effects. The major advan-

tages of benzodiazepines as anxiolytics include their rapid onset of action and their safety. The major disadvantages of benzodiazepines as anxiolytics include the development of tolerance and/or dependence with long-term use and their potential negative effects on psychomotor performance.

Benzodiazepines are also prescribed as hypnotic agents for the treatment of insomnia. Insomnia is a fairly common condition, affecting 30–40% of the US adult population within a given year. It is more common in women and its prevalence increases with age. To be an effective hypnotic, a drug should have a rapid onset of action, assuming that it is taken at bedtime. Ideally, the duration of action should be long enough to allow a complete night's sleep but not so long that the drowsiness persists into the following day (the hangover effect). Benzodiazepines effectively treat insomnia; their use often results in a more rapid sleep onset, decreased nighttime awakenings, and an increased total sleeping time. However, benzodiazepine-induced sleep differs from natural sleep, resulting in prolonged periods of light sleep and decreased duration of (rapid eye movement) REM and slow wave sleep. The major disadvantages associated with benzodiazepine hypnotics include the development of tolerance and dependence, rebound insomnia with discontinuation of use, hangover effects, and respiratory depression that can aggravate some respiratory conditions.

The benzodiazepines are also used clinically for the management of seizure disorders. For example, diazepam has long been the drug of choice for the treatment of status epilepticus. Clonazepam can be used to treat a variety of seizures (with the exception of generalized tonic-clonic seizures). The major disadvantages of benzodiazepines as anti-epileptics are the development of tolerance in many patients and potential sedation and psychomotor impairment.

In addition to their use as therapeutic agents, benzodiazepines produce sedative and amnesic effects for brief medical procedures and are used to premedicate patients. An intravenous dose of a short-acting benzodiazepine, midazolam, assists in the induction of surgical anesthesia. Diazepam

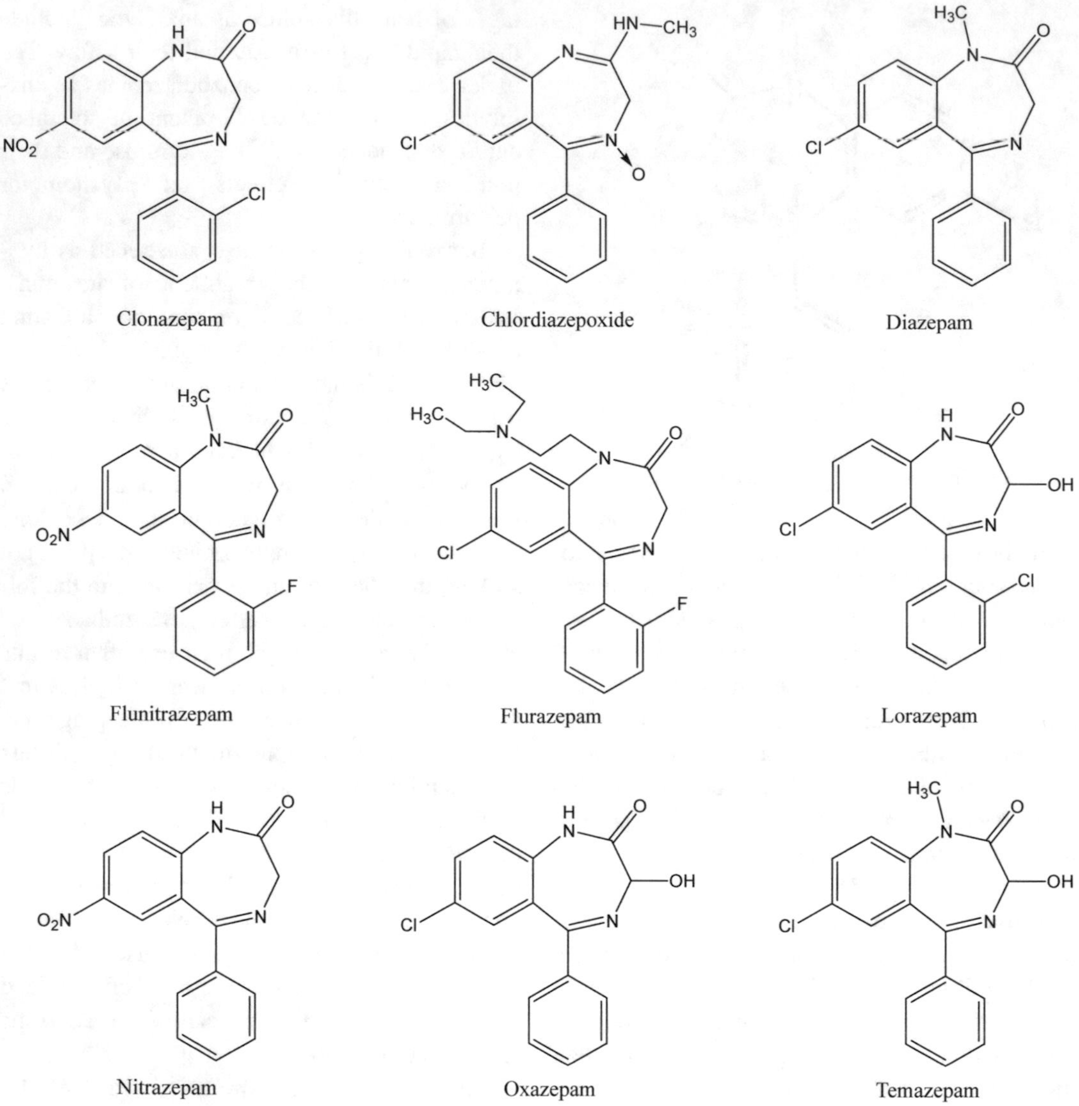

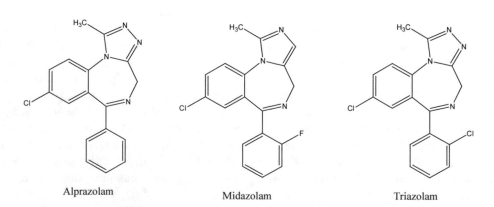

Clonazepam   Chlordiazepoxide   Diazepam

Flunitrazepam   Flurazepam   Lorazepam

Nitrazepam   Oxazepam   Temazepam

Fig. 20.3 Structures of selected 1,4-benzodiazepines

Alprazolam   Midazolam   Triazolam

Fig. 20.4 Structures of selected imidazo- and triazolobenzodiazepines

and lorazepam are also administered as preanesthetic medications. Diazepam is an effective muscle relaxant. It has been used in this capacity to treat various motion disorders. Chlordiazepoxide and diazepam have been used to treat alcohol dependence. They are administered during alcohol detoxification to prevent seizures associated with withdrawal.

Benzodiazepines are often used in combination with illicit drugs. The combination of benzodiazepines with opiates has been reported to produce an enhanced high. Benzodiazepines in combination with cocaine decrease the seizure threshold and are reported to offset the negative effects of the drug following binge use. Benzodiazepines may also reduce withdrawal symptoms associated with drugs of abuse. As a consequence, they are frequently detected in combination with illicit drugs. The most commonly encountered benzodiazepines among illicit drug users are diazepam and alprazolam.

When benzodiazepines are prescribed as therapeutic agents, they are recommended for short-term (4 weeks or less) or intermittent use in most cases, since tolerance and dependence can occur with extended use. Tolerance to the sedative effects of benzodiazepines develops rapidly, usually within a week of the initiation of benzodiazepine therapy. However, tolerance to the anxiolytic effects appears to develop more slowly and to a lesser degree. Long-term benzodiazepine use has been associated with dependence. It has been reported that approximately 35% of patients taking benzodiazepines for more than 4 weeks—regardless of whether the dosage is therapeutic or excessive—develop dependence, as evidenced by the appearance of withdrawal symptoms following dosage decrease or termination. In addition, patients who are on benzodiazepines for extended periods (without dose escalation) may exhibit withdrawal symptoms such as anxiety, agitation, irritability, increased sensitivity to light and sound, muscle cramps, myoclonic jerks, insomnia, fatigue, headache, dizziness, concentration difficulties, paresthesias, nausea, seizures, loss of appetite, weight loss, and depression. Benzodiazepines with higher potency and shorter elimination half-lives appear to be associated with an increased risk of dependence.

Although benzodiazepines are considered relatively safe drugs, overdose can produce life-threatening effects. When benzodiazepine intoxication occurs, it can be treated with a variety of measures, including generalized supportive care, monitoring of vital signs, maintenance of adequate airway, and administration of vasopressors to treat hypotension. Activated charcoal administration is most beneficial within two to four hours of ingestion and when risk of aspiration is minimal. Flumazenil, a GABA antagonist, may be administered if appropriate. However, flumazenil must be used with caution because it reduces seizure threshold and may actually precipitate seizure activity in a patient who has co-ingested a substance that induces seizures (e.g., tricyclic antidepressants) or in a patient with an underlying seizure disorder. When a patient presents with suspected benzodiazepine intoxication, it is important to identify any co-intoxicants, as they may alter the recommended course of treatment.

Although benzodiazepines can be classified according to their chemical structure (described above), they are also classified according to their pharmacological properties, namely, their duration of action and elimination half-lives.

Pharmacology

Mechanism of Action

Benzodiazepines mediate their CNS-depressant activity through the neurotransmitter gamma-amino butyric acid (GABA). GABA is the major inhibitory neurotransmitter in the brain and consists of two subtypes: (1) $GABA_A$ and (2) $GABA_B$.

$GABA_A$ receptors are a set of ligand-gated ion channels that convey GABA's effect on fast synaptic transmission. Benzodiazepines bind to $GABA_A$ receptors and potentiate the inhibitory action of GABA. Activating the $GABA_A$ receptor opens an ion channel and allows chloride ions to enter the cell. As a result, neuronal activity slows down because of hyperpolarization of the cell membrane potential. Specifically, the binding of the drug increases the amount of chloride current generated by the $GABA_A$ receptor complex, increasing inhibitory effect. Benzodiazepine binding to the $GABA_A$ receptor does not open the chloride ion channel directly, but increases the effectiveness of GABA by decreasing the concentration of GABA required to open the channel. There are also multiple subtypes of $GABA_A$ receptors, and benzodiazepines appear to interact with many of these subtypes. This accounts for the varied pharmacologic uses of the drugs.

Pharmacokinetics

Benzodiazepines may be administered orally, intravenously, or intramuscularly. When taken orally, they are completely absorbed—their high lipid solubility aids absorption. However, the rate of absorption depends on the benzodiazepine. For example, diazepam reaches peak blood concentrations within an hour after ingestion. Other benzodiazepines require several hours to reach their peak. Several benzodiazepines, such as clorazepate and prazepam, serve as prodrugs, being rapidly broken down to nordiazepam, which is the active drug.

Generally, benzodiazepines display a significant first-pass effect prior to general distribution. Their volume of distribution is around 2 L/kg and they are highly protein-bound. Typically, the fraction-bound portion is >80%. The major binding protein for benzodiazepines is albumin; however, it appears that triazolobenzodiazepines bind to all acid glycoprotein. Like barbiturates, benzodiazepines are classified according to their elimination half-lives. Midazolam and triazolam are considered short-acting because their elimination half-lives are only several hours. Many (such as alprazolam, lorazepam, oxazepam, and temazepam) have elimination half-lives of 6–24 h and are classified as intermediate-acting. Long-acting benzodiazepines, such as diazepam and quazepam, have elimination half-lives >24 h. One difficulty in the establishment of this classification is the presence of active metabolites that may have substantially different half-lives than the parent drug. For example, flurazepam has an elimination half-life of several hours, but an active metabolite has an elimination half-life of several days. Selected properties of the benzodiazepines are summarized in Table 20.1.

Benzodiazepines are extensively metabolized in the liver. Microsomal enzymes play a prominent role in this metabolism. Phase I metabolic routes include hydroxylation, dealkylation, deamination, and reduction. Substituents are usually removed from the B-ring, with larger or further removed alkyl substituents often removed more rapidly than smaller ones. Hydroxylation, a slow process that can take about 100 hours, usually occurs at position R3 of the B-ring. Structural modifications, such as the presence of a pyridine ring (e.g., bromazepam) can greatly enhance the rate of hydroxylation. The cytochrome P450 3A3 and 3A4 enzyme subtypes mediate many hydroxylation and dealkylation reactions.

Table 20.2 gives specific examples of each type of metabolic pathway. As previously stated, many of these metabolites have CNS-depressant activity that affects potency and duration of action. Once hydroxyl products are formed, phase II metabolism or conjugation with glucuronic acid then occurs. These conjugated metabolites are the major urinary products of benzodiazepines.

Performance Effects of Benzodiazepines

As central nervous system depressants, benzodiazepines can have significant impairing effects, even at prescribed doses. Such effects include prolonged reaction times, impaired judgment, impaired coordination, decreased alertness and concentration, and impaired short-term memory. Clinical studies have demonstrated that typical doses of diazepam, nitrazepam, flunitrazepam, flurazepam, lorazepam, and triazolam can impair some skills necessary for driving. Concomitant use of ethanol and benzodiazepines will increase impairment. Tolerance to some of these effects can develop with prolonged use. However, considering the scale on which benzodiazepines

Table 20.2 Examples of benzodiazepine phase I metabolism

Reaction	Precursor	Product
Dealkylation		
	Diazepam	Nordiazepam
	Temazepam	Oxazepam
	Flurazepam	N-1-desalkylflurazepam
Deamination		
	Chlordiazepoxide	Demoxepam
Hydroxylation		
	Alprazolam	α-Hydroxyalprazolam
	Diazepam	Temazepam
	Nordiazepam	Oxazepam
Reduction		
	Clonazepam	7-Aminoclonazepam
	Demoxepam	Nordiazepam

are prescribed, their effects on driving skills and potential contribution to traffic and other accidents are a major concern.

Interactions

When administered alone, benzodiazepines are relatively safe drugs. There are few reports of fatal overdoses due solely to benzodiazepine toxicity. However, benzodiazepine use in combination with other CNS depressants can increase toxicity: recent Drug Abuse Warning Network data indicated that 78% of benzodiazepine-related emergency department visits involved two or more drugs. The drugs most often combined with benzodiazepines were alcohol, illicit drugs, and opiates.

Since the cytochrome P450 3A enzyme family is involved in the metabolism of many benzodiazepines, it is important to consider the potential effects of drugs that induce or inhibit this enzyme system. Some of the more commonly encountered drugs that inhibit the CYP3A enzymes include cimetidine, diltiazem, fluoxetine, fluvoxamine, paroxetine, verapamil, antifungals, and protease inhibitors. Co-administration of some of these inhibitors and benzodiazepines has been reported to produce clinically significant effects, including increased blood benzodiazepine concentrations and increased benzodiazepine elimination half-life. Drugs that induce the CYP3A enzyme family include barbiturates, phenytoin, carbamazepine, and rifampicin. Drugs that alter glucuronyl transferase activity may also affect the metabolism of 3-hydroxy benzodiazepines.

Special Considerations

There is limited data on the effects of benzodiazepines on the fetus and nursing infants. The available data suggest that benzodiazepine administration during pregnancy does not increase the risk of congenital malformations. However, the data are insufficient to definitively state that there is no risk of injury to the fetus with benzodiazepine exposure. Withdrawal can occur in infants of mothers receiving chronic benzodiazepine therapy, especially if benzodiazepines are administered near term or during delivery. Although benzodiazepines are not contraindicated in lactating mothers, there is evidence that some benzodiazepines are excreted into breast milk, at concentrations about 10–20% of plasma concentrations. If benzodiazepines are administered to mothers who breastfeed, their infants should be closely watched for lethargy, sedation, and weight loss.

Benzodiazepines are widely administered to the elderly. It has been estimated that elderly patients receive 50% of all benzodiazepine prescriptions, although they account for less than 13% of the population. Studies have indicated that the elderly show increased sensitivity to the effects of some benzodiazepines. This is partially due to the decrease in the rate at which the elderly oxidize some benzodiazepines. The decreased rate of metabolism is a result of the decreased CYP3A4 activity that occurs with age. The pharmacokinetic profiles of benzodiazepines that are metabolized primarily by conjugation, including temazepam and oxazepam, are not significantly altered in the elderly. These benzodiazepines may be more suitable choices for benzodiazepine therapy in elderly patients.

Renal disease can significantly affect benzodiazepine elimination. Because most parent benzodiazepines are highly protein-bound, glomerular filtration is low and their metabolism is less affected by renal disease. However, metabolites such as glucuronide conjugates can accumulate, because the kidney's ability to excrete these substances is compromised. Another consequence of renal disease is decreased plasma protein binding of benzodiazepines, which increases the concentrations of circulating free drug.

Conditions that cause hypoalbuminemia can increase the concentrations of free active drug. Hypoalbuminemia can occur as a result of liver disease (decreased synthesis of albumin), renal disease (extravascular protein loss), ascites and congestive heart failure (hemodilution), and severe burns (direct loss of albumin from the skin, a major site for albumin storage).

Individual Benzodiazepines

Alprazolam

Alprazolam is an intermediate-acting triazolobenzodiazepine that is primarily used to treat anxiety and depression. Its potency is about 20 times that of diazepam. A white powder with a pK_a of 2.4, alprazolam is soluble in methanol and ethanol and insoluble in water. Following oral administration, alprazolam is well absorbed, with a bioavailability of approximately 90%. Alprazolam is metabolized to α-hydroxyalprazolam and 4-hydroxyalprazolam by cytochrome P450 3A4. Both metabolites are less active than alprazolam and are typically detected in plasma at concentrations <10% of alprazolam concentrations. Almost all of a single dose of alprazolam is excreted within 72 h, with 80% excreted in urine and 7% in feces; twenty percent is excreted as unchanged alprazolam.

Clonazepam

Clonazepam is a long-acting benzodiazepine indicated for the treatment of seizure disorders and panic disorder. Clonazepam is a white to light yellow crystalline powder that is soluble in acetone, chloroform, and methanol. Following oral administration, clonazepam is well absorbed, with a bioavailability close to 100%. Clonazepam is primarily metabolized by reduction of the nitro group to form 7-aminoclonazepam, which is detected in plasma at concentrations similar to clonazepam. Cytochrome P450 3A4 mediates the formation of 7-aminoclonazepam. Up to 70% of a dose is eliminated in the urine over 7 days, mainly as 7-aminoclonazepam and 7-acetamidoclonazepam. Clonazepam is relatively unstable in postmortem specimens due to bacterial and thermal degradation.

Diazepam

Diazepam is a long-acting 1,4-benzodiazepine that is commonly prescribed for the management of anxiety, as an adjunct for the treatment of skeletal muscle spasm and status epilepticus, and as a minor tranquilizer or sedative. It is also used to reduce the effects of alcohol withdrawal. Diazepam is a white or yellow crystalline powder with a pK_a of 3.3 that is soluble in ethanol and chloroform and slightly soluble in water. Its oral bioavailability is about 100%. Following administration, diazepam is demethylated to form its primary active metabolite, nordiazepam, which accumulates in plasma with repeated administration. The CYP2C19 and CYP3A4 enzymes mediate the demethylation of diazepam; the CYP3A4 enzyme is involved in the formation of 3-hydroxy metabolites of diazepam, oxazepam, and temazepam. Following oral administration, much of a diazepam dose is eliminated in the urine as oxazepam glucuronide and conjugates of nordiazepam and temazepam.

Estazolam

Estazolam is an intermediate-acting triazolobenzodiazepine that is structurally related to both alprazolam and triazolam. It is prescribed orally in doses of 1–2 mg nightly for the treatment of insomnia, and its duration of action is approximately 6–8 hours. It is extensively metabolized in the liver to 4-hydroxyestazolam (by the CYP3A family of isoenzymes), followed by glucuronidation. Although the 4-hydroxy and 1-oxoestazolam metabolites have some pharmacological activity, their low potencies and abundance preclude significant contribution to the overall hypnotic effect of the drug.

Flurazepam

Flurazepam is a white crystalline hypnotic agent, soluble in chloroform, that is used to treat insomnia. Following oral administration, flurazepam is rapidly metabolized to N-1-desalkylflurazepam and N-1-hydroxyethylflurazepam, which may be responsible for much of flurazepam's observed effects. N-1-desalkylflurazepam accumulates in blood with repeated administration, achieving steady-state concentrations after 7–10 days of dosing. Steady-state N-1-desalkylflurazepam plasma concentrations are generally five to six times the concentrations observed following a single dose. Up to 60% of a flurazepam dose is eliminated in the urine within 48 h, and about 9% of a dose is eliminated in the feces. The primary urinary metabolite of flurazepam is conjugated N-1-hydroxyethylflurazepam.

Lorazepam

Lorazepam is an intermediate-acting benzodiazepine that is indicated for the treatment of anxiety. It is also used as a pre-anesthetic to alleviate anxiety, produce sedation, and decrease the ability to recall events related to a procedure. Following oral administration, lorazepam is well absorbed, with a bioavailability of 95% and a primary metabolic pathway of inactive glucuronide

conjugate formation. Lorazepam glucuronide accumulates in plasma and attains concentrations greater than lorazepam. Approximately 75% of a lorazepam dose is eliminated over 5 days as lorazepam glucuronide in the urine; only a very small amount of lorazepam is eliminated as unchanged drug. Lorazepam can be difficult to detect, as most commercially available immunoassay screening tests do not have high cross-reactivity to this benzodiazepine.

Temazepam

Temazepam is a hypnotic agent indicated for the short-term treatment of insomnia. It is a white crystalline powder that is slightly soluble in water and freely soluble in methylene chloride. Temazepam is well absorbed following oral administration with a bioavailability close to 100%. The major metabolic pathway for temazepam is glucuronidation; smaller amounts of oxazepam and oxazepam glucuronide are formed. Approximately 80% of a dose is eliminated in the urine and 12% in the feces. Because the primary metabolic route is conjugation, temazepam pharmacokinetics are not significantly altered by changes in CYP3A4 activity.

Benzodiazepine Antagonist: Flumazenil

Flumazenil is an imidazobenzodiazepine derivative that acts as a competitive GABA antagonist in humans. The structure of flumazenil is illustrated in Fig. 20.5. Flumazenil does not antagonize the action of drugs binding to the GABA receptor at sites other than the benzodiazepine binding site (i.e., barbiturates, ethanol, and general anesthetics). Flumazenil can be used to reverse benzodiazepine effects such as sedation, respiratory depression, memory impairment, and psychomotor impairment. The duration and degree of antagonism are related to the dose administered and to the concentrations of flumazenil in plasma. Flumazenil is administered intravenously, and its actions are usually observed

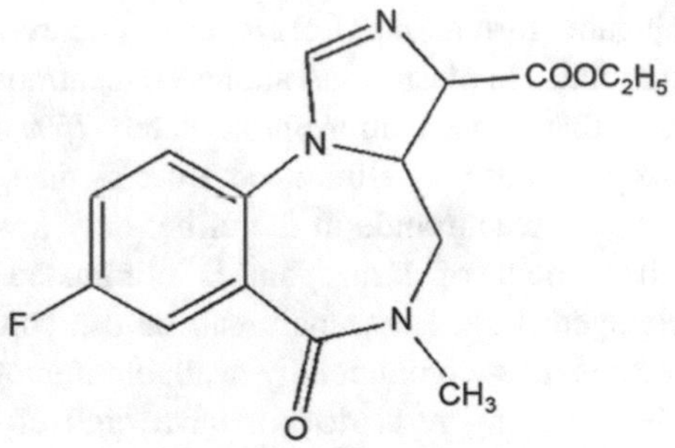

Fig. 20.5 Structure of flumazenil, a benzodiazepine antagonist

within minutes of administration. The complications associated with flumazenil administration are related to the reversal of benzodiazepine effects: flumazenil has been reported to precipitate withdrawal in patients who have been on benzodiazepine therapy long enough to develop tolerance and/or dependence. In addition, seizure activity can occur with flumazenil administration, especially if the patient has co-ingested a substance that causes seizure activity.

Flumazenil is not as highly protein-bound as most benzodiazepines, with only about 50% of the drug protein-bound. Following intravenous administration, flumazenil is rapidly distributed and eliminated; its half-life is 40 to 80 minutes. When flumazenil is administered as an antidote for benzodiazepine intoxication, the patient must still be monitored for signs of benzodiazepine intoxication, because the flumazenil may be eliminated more rapidly than the ingested benzodiazepine. Up to 95% of a dose of flumazenil is eliminated in the urine in 3 days and about 5–10% is eliminated in the feces. Flumazenil is excreted mainly as a desethyl carboxylic acid derivative and its glucuronide conjugate; less than 1% of unchanged drug is excreted in the urine.

Benzodiazepine Analogs

Illicit benzodiazepine use is common. As a consequence, clandestinely produced benzodiazepines have emerged, sometimes referred to as designer benzodiazepines. Many of these analogs involve variations of the 1,4-benzodiazepine skeleton

Table 20.3 Chemical classification of selected benzodiazepine analogs

1,4-benzodiazepines
Desalkylflurazepam (norflurazepam)
Desmethylflunitrazepam (norflunitrazepam, fonazepam)
Diclazepam
Flubromazepam
Meclonazepam
Nifoxipam
Nimetazepam
Phenazepam
Triazolobenzodiazepines
Adinazolam
Bromazolam
Clonazolam
Flubromazolam
Flunitrazolam
Nitrazolam
Pyrazolam
Thioenotriazolodiazepines
Deschloroetizolam
Etizolam
Metizolam
Oxazolobenzodiazepines
Flutazolam

based upon known structure-activity relationships, synthesis of active metabolites (e.g., desalkylflurazepam), as well as triazole, oxazole, pyridine, and thiophene analogs of these compounds. Although some were initially approved outside of the United States for medical use (e.g., phenazepam, etizolam, adinazolam), others are illicitly manufactured to circumvent drug legislation. Due to their relatively recent emergence, the pharmacological properties of some of these analogs are not yet well understood. However, their chemical classification (Table 20.3) provides some insight into their structure-activity relationships and relative potencies. The structures of some of these analogs are shown in Fig. 20.6 and selected drugs are discussed below.

Etizolam

Etizolam is a thienotriazolodiazepine analog that is approved for clinical use outside of the United States as a sedative-hypnotic drug. Doses of

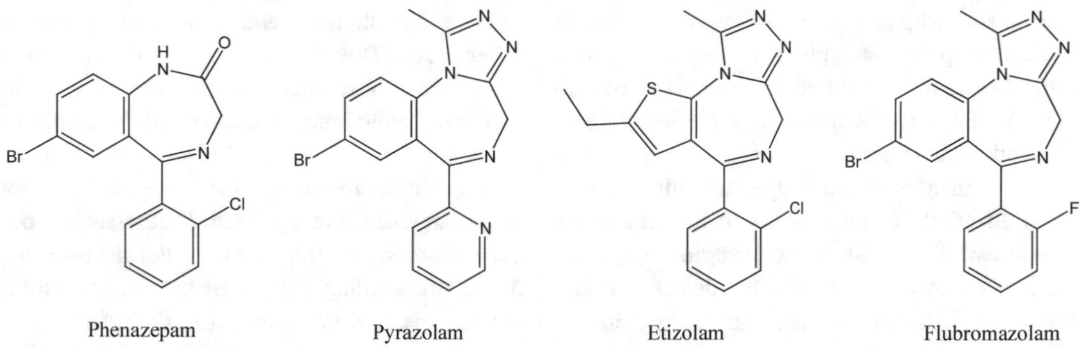

Phenazepam   Pyrazolam   Etizolam   Flubromazolam

Fig. 20.6 Structures of selected benzodiazepine analogs

0.5–3 mg daily are administered orally. Single oral doses of 1 mg produced peak plasma concentrations of approximately 0.02 mg/L at 1 hour. The half-life is reported to be 7–15 hours and the drug is extensively metabolized by hydroxylation and glucuronidation. The major phase I metabolite (α-hydroxyetizolam) significantly contributes to the CNS-depressant effects of the drug, due to its approximately equipotent pharmacological activity and longer half-life.

Flubromazolam

Flubromazolam is a triazole analog of flubromazepam containing a fluorine atom, a bromine atom, and a methylated triazole moiety on the benzodiazepine backbone. It is a very potent benzodiazepine with only 0.25 mg needed to produce a sedative-hypnotic effect. It is metabolized primarily by hydroxylation and conjugation with glucuronic acid. Serum concentrations around 0.01 mg/L have been reported in forensic samples.

Phenazepam

Phenazepam is a benzodiazepine that was developed in the former Soviet Union in the 1970s and has been used in Russia to treat insomnia, anxiety, alcohol withdrawal, and seizures. It is not approved for use in the United States. It is a relatively potent benzodiazepine, and doses of 0.5 to 1.0 mg can produce significant central nervous system depression. After oral ingestion, the peak plasma concentration occurs at 4 hours. It has a

longer half-life than most benzodiazepines, approximately 60 hours. It undergoes phase I metabolism by hydroxylation to produce 3-hydroxyphenazepam which is also psychoactive. The metabolite then undergoes phase II metabolism and is excreted as a glucuronide. Two other metabolites have also been reported, 5-bromo-(2-chlorophenyl)-2-aminobenzophenone (ABPH) and 6-bromo-(2-chlorophenyl) quinazoline-2-one.

Pyrazolam

In 2012, another designer benzodiazepine, pyrazolam, began appearing on the illicit drug market. Pyrazolam is structurally similar to alprazolam, with pyrazolam having a bromine atom on the benzene ring of the benzodiazepine nucleus instead of chlorine and a pyridine ring instead of a benzene ring on C-6 of the diazepine ring. The presence of the strong electron-withdrawing groups again leads to the potency of pyrazolam and small doses prescribed. Ingestion of 1 mg produced a peak blood concentration of around 0.05 mg/L. Surprisingly, no expected hydroxylation, dealkylation, or dehalogenation phase I or phase II metabolites have been identified.

Analysis

Many difficulties are associated with the attempt to take a comprehensive approach to benzodiazepine analysis. A large number of benzodiazepines with different functional groups exist on the benzodiazepine nucleus. Many metabolites of benzodiazepines are pharmacologically active and should be quantified to assess the overall effects of benzodiazepines in a particular case. Benzodiazepine potencies may vary by several orders of magnitude, so analytical methodologies need different detection limits to identify therapeutic use. Low-dose benzodiazepines (e.g., triazolam) may be difficult to detect without specialized instrumentation. With many benzodiazepines, establishing a simultaneous method for blood and urine specimen analysis is difficult, because the target compound is often different. Moreover, urinary benzodiazepine products are conjugated and a hydrolysis step is required to improve detectability.

There are many commercially available screening tests for benzodiazepines. Some are designed to test urine, while others test a wide range of matrices, making them applicable to postmortem toxicology. Often the target analyte is oxazepam or nordiazepam, and good cross-reactivity to a number of benzodiazepines can be achieved. More recently, specific assays for flunitrazepam have been developed. Typically, no specimen pretreatment is necessary; however, sensitivity of these assays may be enhanced by an enzymatic hydrolysis step, because the predominant urinary products are conjugated species. One limitation to the use of immunoassays is that certain benzodiazepines, such as lorazepam, do not have sufficient cross-reactivity with the assay antibody to identify that benzodiazepine's therapeutic use.

Benzodiazepines can be separated from biological specimens by liquid-liquid extraction or by solid-phase extraction. When analyzing urine specimens, hydrolysis is necessary to cleave the glucuronide conjugate. Enzymatic hydrolysis is preferred over acid hydrolysis; some benzodiazepines are unstable in acid and rearrange to form benzophenones. Adjusting the pH to 9–10 allows extraction of benzodiazepines into an immiscible organic solvent. Solid-phase extraction procedures also rely on pH adjustment, with the final pH dependent on the type of solid phase being used. After application of the pH-adjusted specimen to the column, buffers and solvents are used to wash the column of endogenous substances or other drugs. This is followed by solvent elution of the benzodiazepines from the column.

Chromatographic separation of benzodiazepines can be accomplished using either gas or liquid chromatography. Gas chromatography (GC) can analyze many benzodiazepines without derivatization, among them chlordiazepoxide, diazepam, nordiazepam, flurazepam, and alprazolam. Disadvantages to using GC analysis of benzodiazepines include the thermal instability of chlordiazepoxide, which can degrade during operating temperatures. The most significant drawback to using GC is that some of the more polar drugs within the class have poor chromatographic properties. Some of the diazolobenzodiazepines and triazolobenzodiazepines require high temperatures for elution from a GC column; these compounds are also very sensitive to chromatographic conditions, and less than optimal results may be obtained if regular instrument maintenance is not performed. Drugs with a hydroxyl group (such as oxazepam, temazepam, and lorazepam) or a nitro group (such as clonazepam and nitrazepam) can display poor chromatographic characteristics. Derivatization by gas chromatography is often necessary for the analysis of these compounds. Because of this requirement, liquid chromatography is the preferred chromatographic separation technique to detect individual benzodiazepines and their metabolites. A reverse-phase C_8 or C_{18} column is commonly used to provide analytical separation. Isocratic mobile phases can provide adequate separation for most applications. After chromatographic separation, mass spectrometry (MS) is used to provide definitive identification of the benzodiazepines.

Analytical sensitivity is another consideration. Low-dose benzodiazepines may require specialized analytical approaches, such as GC-MS with chemical ionization (CI). The electrophilic halogen present can be exploited for this purpose when negative CI is utilized. However, not all laboratories have CI capability with GC-MS. As a result, targeted LC-MS-based approaches (e.g., LC-MS/MS) provide sufficient sensitivity for single-dose or therapeutic drug concentrations.

Interpretation

Therapeutic ranges for benzodiazepines reflect their differences in potency. Many drugs, like diazepam and chlordiazepoxide, have therapeutic concentrations around 2 mg/L. Others, like alprazolam and lorazepam, have therapeutic concentrations in the 0.05–0.1 mg/L range. In contrast, low-dose benzodiazepines (e.g., triazolam) may be present at low ng/mL concentrations. Active metabolites are also a factor to be considered when evaluating the amount of active benzodiazepine in the blood.

Although the presence of benzodiazepines is a relatively common finding in postmortem cases, few intoxication cases due exclusively to benzodiazepines have been reported due to their high therapeutic indices. However, there have been some studies that suggest alprazolam is relatively more toxic in overdose situations than other benzodiazepines. Generally, benzodiazepines are involved in drug deaths as a result of being combined with alcohol or other drugs, with the cause of death attributable to alcohol and drug or multiple drug intoxication.

One complication in the interpretation of postmortem benzodiazepine concentrations is that some display in vitro instability. For instance, chlordiazepoxide is broken down in the blood to demoxepam and nordiazepam. Drugs with a nitro group, such as clonazepam and nitrazepam, can be reduced in vitro to their respective amino products. Chlordiazepoxide standards are unstable in water or methanol and should be prepared fresh or in aprotic solvents such as acetonitrile. Stability issues must also be considered during specimen storage and transport.

The instability of the nitrobenzodiazepines should also be considered for some of the newer nitro-analogs (e.g., clonazolam, diclazepam, flunitrazolam, fonazepam, nifoxipam, nimetazepam, nitrazolam, meclonazepam).

A negative result of a benzodiazepine screen must be interpreted in the context of the methodology used. The discussion of benzodiazepine analysis in the previous section clearly indicated that different methodologies have different abilities to identify certain benzodiazepines. If the case history indicates the presence or involvement of a particular benzodiazepine, then a method must be selected that would identify the drug or metabolite of interest. This is of particular importance when benzodiazepines are implicated in drug-facilitated sexual assault, where a single dosage may be administered, and significant delays between the time of the alleged incident and specimen collection may exist.

Suggested Reading

Baselt RC (2020) Disposition of toxic drugs and chemicals in man, 12th edn. Biomedical Publications, Seal Beach, CA

Hoiseth G, Skogstad S, Karinen R (2016) Blood concentrations of new designer benzodiazepines in forensic cases. Forensic Sci Int 268:35–38

Howard P, Twycross R, Shuster J, Mihalyo M, Wilcock A (2014) Therapeutic reviews – Benzodiazepines. J Pain Symp Mngt 47:955–967

Kurko TAT, Saastamoinen LK, Tahkapaa S, Tuulio-Henriksson A, Taiminen T et al (2015) Long-term use of benzodiazepines: Definitions, prevalence and usage patterns-a systematic review of register-based studies. Euro Psychiatry 30:1037–1047

Licata SC, Rowlett JK (2008) Abuse and dependence liability of benzodiazepine-type drugs:GABA$_A$ receptor modulation and beyond. Pharmacol, Biochem Beh 90:74–89

Manchester KR, Lomas EC, Waters L, Dempsey FC, Maskell PD (2018) The emergence of new psychoactive substance (NPS) benzodiazepines: A review. Drug testing and analysis 10:37–53

Persona K, Madej K, Knihnicki P, Pikoszewski W (2015) Analytical methodologies for the determination of benzodiazepines in biological samples. J Pharm Biomed Anal 113:239–264

Miscellaneous Central Nervous System Depressants

21

Barry S. Levine and Marc LeBeau

Abstract

Central nervous system (CNS) depressants remain a frequently encountered class of drugs in forensic toxicology. The most commonly encountered group, the benzodiazepines are discussed in Chap. 20. The oldest group of CNS depressants, the barbiturates, are still used therapeutically, principally as anesthetic agents and anticonvulsants. Barbiturates are classified based on their chemical structure, duration of action, and pharmacological properties. Gamma-hydroxybutyric acid (GHB) is a simple hydroxylated, short-chain fatty acid with a very short duration of action. However, its detection in biological specimens is complicated by the fact that it is also produced endogenously from the metabolism of the neurotransmitter gamma-aminobutyric acid (GABA) and is produced in postmortem blood specimens. Zolpidem, zopiclone, and zaleplon, collectively known as "z-drugs," all interact with the GABA receptor in different ways to produce their CNS depressant effects. Some of the newer CNS depressants that are used to manage sleep disorders include melatonin agonists such as ramelteon and tasimelteon, and dual orexin receptor antagonists such as suvorexant. Other sedative-hypnotics, muscle relaxants, and drugs with CNS depressant activity are also discussed.

Keywords

CNS depressants · Barbiturates · GHB · Sedative-hypnotics · Muscle relaxants · Toxicology · Pharmacology · Analysis · Interpretation

This is publication 19–20 of the FBI Laboratory Division. Names of commercial manufacturers are provided for identification purposes only, and inclusion does not imply endorsement of the manufacturer or its products or services by the FBI. The views expressed are those of the authors and do not necessarily reflect the official policy or position of the FBI or the US Government.

B. S. Levine (✉)
Office of the Chief Medical Examiner,
Baltimore, MD, USA
e-mail: blevine@som.umaryland.edu

M. LeBeau
FBI Laboratory, Quantico, VA, USA
e-mail: malebeau@fbi.gov

Gamma-Hydroxybutyric Acid (GHB)

GHB is a simple hydroxylated, short-chain fatty acid composed of four-carbon, eight-hydrogen, and three-oxygen atoms (Fig. 21.1). It has a molecular weight of 104.1 g/mol and is usually supplied as the sodium salt with a molecular weight of 126.1 g/mol. The salt is typically a white or off-white powder that is readily soluble in water. When in solution, GHB coexists in a

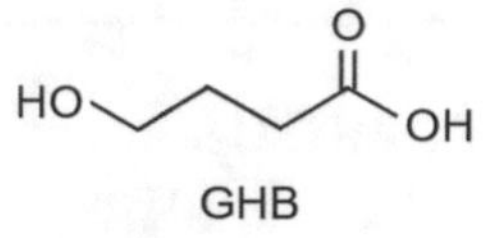

Fig. 21.1 Structure of gamma-hydroxybutyric acid (GHB)

state of equilibrium with its lactone, gamma-butyrolactone (GBL). The conversion of GHB to GBL is dependent upon the matrix it is in, as well as the pH and temperature of the matrix. Because GHB has a pK_a of 4.72, it will predominate when the pH of the matrix is greater than 4.72; GBL will predominate if the pH is below 4.72. The presence of the enzyme lactonase in plasma will also affect the equilibrium because it converts GBL to GHB.

Use and Abuse

GHB was first introduced in Europe in the 1960s as an intravenous general anesthetic agent that lacked analgesic properties. A short time later this use diminished due to difficulties in determining the proper dose, as well as reported side effects of vomiting, seizures, and coma. GHB has also been studied for its ability to suppress the symptoms of alcohol dependence and opiate-withdrawal syndrome and for the management of narcoleptic patients. In 2002, the US Food and Drug Administration (FDA) approved GHB for clinical use in patients suffering from cataplexy. In its prescription form, GHB is a Schedule III substance; however, street formulations of GHB and illegal trafficking of the prescription formulation carry Schedule I penalties.

The history of GHB abuse shows that it has been a popular drug within different populations. One group includes bodybuilders who believe it to be a steroid alternative for building muscle mass based on reports indicating that GHB increases the release of human growth hormone. Other GHB abusers include those who use it for the strong CNS depressant effect that leads to euphoria, reduced inhibitions, and sedation. As with other CNS depressants, the effects largely depend upon the amount consumed and the individual's tolerance to the drug. Thus, an individual consuming GHB may experience any variety of effects, ranging from wakefulness and euphoria to deep sleep or coma.

GHB is nearly always abused orally, most often diluted in an aqueous matrix where it can be disguised as bottled water, a sport drink, or juice. As law enforcement agencies have recognized these attempts to conceal GHB, sellers and abusers have disguised it in other containers such as hair sprays, eye drop bottles, or mouthwashes. Usually consumed by the capful or by the teaspoon, a dose of GHB is usually 0.5 to 3 grams. It should also be noted that there are precursors of GHB [e.g., GBL and 1,4-butanediol (1,4-BD)] that, once ingested, are metabolized into GHB. Since GBL and 1,4-BD have industrial and cosmetic uses, they are not easy to classify as controlled substances. Table 21.1 includes common street names for these analogs.

GHB, GBL, and 1,4-BD can cause the user to pass from a completely alert state to deep unconsciousness within 10 to 15 min after ingestion. Additionally, GHB demonstrates an amnesiac effect upon the individual under its influence. As a result, GHB has been implicated in a number of drug-facilitated crimes (DFC). Since GHB is naturally present in the body, the evaluation of its role in these cases can be complicated. Further, its rapid elimination after ingestion leaves only low concentrations of GHB in the body, concentrations that often cannot be readily differentiated from what is considered endogenous. While the time will vary based on dose and interindividual differences, in general it may not be possible to differentiate between exogenous and endogenous concentrations of GHB if a blood or urine sample is collected later than 6 h or 12 h, respectively, after ingestion. Another factor that makes GHB, GBL, and 1,4-BD attractive to perpetrators of these crimes is that the drugs are all readily available; it is simple to make GHB in an ordinary kitchen, and these drugs remain relatively easy to buy on the Internet, on the street, in numerous fitness facilities, and in dance clubs.

Table 21.1 Chemical Synonyms and Street Names for GHB, GBL, and 1,4-BD

Compound	Chemical Synonyms	Street Names and Trade Names
γ-Hydroxybutyrate (GHB)	γ-Hydroxybutyric acid	Cherry Menth
	4-Hydroxybutyrate	Easy lay
	Sodium 4-hydroxybutyrate	Energy drink
	Sodium oxybate	Everclear
	Sodium oxybutyrate	Fantasy
		G
		G juice
		GBH
		G-Riffick
		Gamma 10
		Gamma hydrate
		Gamma OH
		Georgia home boy
		Gook
		Great hormones at bedtime
		Grievous bodily
		Harm
		Liquid ecstasy
		Liquid E
		Liquid G
		Liquid X
		Nature's Quaalude
		Organic Quaalude
		Salty water
		Scoop
		Soap
		Somsanit
		Somatomac
		Somatomax PM
		Vita G
		Water
		Xyrem ®
		Zonked
γ-Butyrolactone (GBL)	Dihydro-2(3H)-furanone	BLO
	Butyrolactone	Blow
	1,2-Butanolide	Blue moon
	1,4-Butanolide	Blue nitro
	γ-Hydroxybutyric acid lactone	Firewater
	3-Hydoxybutyric acid lactone	G3
	4-Hydroxybutanoic acid lactone	Gamma G
		G.H. revitalizer
		Insom-X
		Invigorate
		Longevity
		N-force
		Pure Raine
		Regenerize
		Remedy GH
		Remforce
		Renewtrient

(continued)

Table 21.1 (continued)

Compound	Chemical Synonyms	Street Names and Trade Names
		Revivarant
		Thunda
		Verve
		X-12
1,4-Butanediol (1,4-BD)	Butanediol	Enliven
	Butane-1,4-diol	Diol 14B
	Butylene glycol	Dormir
	1,4-butylene glycol	FX
	1,4-Dihydroxybutane	GHRE
	1,4-Tetramethylene glycol	Inner G
	Tetramethylene 1,4-diol	NRG3
		One comma four
		One four B
		One four B-D-O
		Revitalize plus
		Serenity
		Soma
		SomatoPro
		Sucol B
		Thunder II
		Thunder nectar
		Weight Belt cleaner
		White magic

Effects

Although GHB affects nearly every organ system, its primary effect is as a CNS depressant from perturbations of several neurotransmitter systems. Within the CNS, GHB mediates sleep cycles, temperature regulation, cerebral glucose metabolism and blood flow, memory, and emotional control. After typical doses, GHB levels in the CNS increase 100- to 500-fold. The neurodepressant effect of GHB may be mediated by its affinity for two receptor sites in the CNS: a GHB-specific receptor and the $GABA_B$ receptor. The GHB receptors appear to be localized to neuronal cells and, more specifically, to the synaptosomal membrane. Following exogenous administration of GHB, these GHB receptors are saturated. In human brain, the pons and hippocampus exhibit the highest density of GHB receptors, followed by the cerebral cortex and caudate. GHB binds to the $GABA_B$ receptor at a much lower affinity than to the GHB receptor. Physiological levels of GHB would not bind this receptor sufficiently to cause a pharmacological effect. However, supra-physiological levels that are achieved following exogenous administration could cause significant binding of the $GABA_B$ receptor, leading to membrane hyperpolarization and CNS depression.

Experimental findings indicate that some dopaminergic activity is mediated by the GHB receptor following GHB administration. GHB administration increases dopamine concentrations in the striatum and cortex in a dose-dependent fashion. The increase occurs due to stimulation of tyrosine hydroxylase, the enzyme necessary for dopamine synthesis, and is not related to a decrease in the catabolism of dopamine. A dose-dependent effect of GHB has been reported, in which lower doses inhibit and higher doses stimulate the release of dopamine. Further, GHB inhibits dopamine release in awake animals, while it stimulates dopamine release in anesthetized animals. The cholinergic and serotonergic systems also seem to be affected by GHB.

Both behavioral and neurological effects are observed in subjects who have ingested GHB. Low doses of GHB (approximately 0.5–1.5 g) induce a state of relaxation and tranquility, placidity, sensuality, mild euphoria, a tendency to verbalize, emotional warmth, and drowsiness. Higher doses, such as those probably involved in drug-facilitated crimes (1.5 grams or more), can induce more obvious clinical manifestations and adverse effects including confusion, dizziness and drowsiness, nausea and vomiting, agitation, nystagmus, loss of peripheral vision, hallucinations, short-term amnesia, somnolence, uncontrollable shaking or seizures, combativeness, bradycardia, respiratory depression, apnea, and coma. One study found that blood concentrations exceeding 260 mg/L were associated with deep sleep, levels of 156–260 mg/L with moderate sleep, 52–156 mg/L with light sleep, and < 52 mg/L with wakefulness. In animal experiments, the median lethal dose is 5 to 15 times the coma-inducing dose.

There have been reported cases of physical dependence on GHB, with symptoms attributed to GHB withdrawal that include hallucinations, tremors, tachycardia, hypertension, sweating, anxiety, agitation, paranoia, insomnia, confusion, and aggression. Additionally, there have been numerous fatalities resulting from GHB overdose, sometimes in combination with other drugs.

Since GBL and 1,4-BD are rapidly metabolized to GHB after oral ingestion, the pharmacological effects of these drugs are analogous to those observed when GHB is ingested.

Pharmacokinetics

Due to its highly hydroscopic nature, GHB is usually administered as an oral solution and is rapidly absorbed, with plasma concentrations peaking within about 30 min and urinary concentrations peaking at about 1 h. Research suggests that GHB absorption is capacity-limited and may be enhanced when the drug is consumed on an empty stomach. Oral bioavailability of GHB in rats is 59–65%. Initial clinical effects occur 15–20 min after oral administration, with peak effects occurring 30–60 min after ingestion. Extensive first-pass metabolism of GHB occurs following oral administration.

The lipid-soluble nature of GHB allows it to readily cross the blood-brain barrier where it exerts its primary effect. No appreciable plasma protein binding occurs with GHB. Distribution to target tissues occurs rapidly and follows a two-compartment model with apparent volumes of distribution (V_d) of 0.4 L/kg and 0.6 L/kg.

The primary pathway for GHB metabolism involves conversion to succinic semialdehyde before it is converted to succinic acid (Fig. 21.2). After succinic acid enters the Krebs cycle, it is ultimately expired as carbon dioxide. A small amount of GHB may be metabolized to succinic acid via a beta-oxidation pathway in the liver

Fig. 21.2 GHB synthesis and metabolism

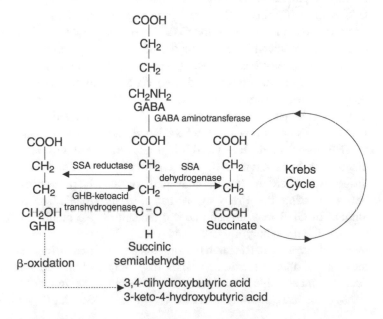

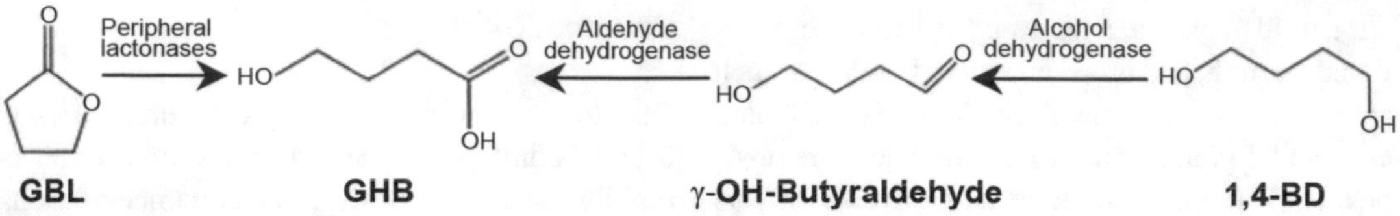

Fig. 21.3 Metabolism of 1,4 BD and GBL

before entering the Krebs cycle. Due to the extensive biotransformation of GHB, less than 5% of an oral dose is excreted unchanged in the urine. It should also be noted that a GHB-glucuronide metabolite has been identified in urine samples.

Pharmacokinetic studies demonstrate capacity-limited, nonlinear, and dose-dependent elimination of GHB with a half-life of 20–53 min in healthy human subjects. As mentioned previously, GBL and 1,4-BD are both metabolized to GHB following their ingestion (Fig. 21.3). The conversion to GHB is rapid and can be complete within 10 min of ingestion. Once this has occurred, GBL and 1,4-BD mimic the pharmacokinetics and pharmacodynamics of GHB.

Interpretation

The endogenous nature of GHB in the body results, in part, from the normal metabolism of GABA in the CNS (Fig. 21.2) and from its production outside the CNS. In the CNS, GABA is converted into succinic semialdehyde (SSA) via GABA aminotransferase. Most of the formed SSA is oxidized to succinic acid (SA) via SSA dehydrogenase, where it enters the Krebs cycle and is converted to water and carbon dioxide. However, a small amount of the SSA is reduced to GHB via SSA reductase. GHB is typically oxidized back to SSA via GHB ketoacid transhydrogenase, where it, too, is converted to SA before entering the Krebs cycle, but a small amount of GHB may instead undergo oxidation to 3,4-dihydroxybutyric acid and 3-keto-4-hydroxybutyric acid. Research has suggested that these metabolites of oxidized GHB may only occur at measurable levels when the ketoacid transhydrogenase pathway is blocked.

There is evidence that there are sources of endogenous GHB in the body other than GABA. For example, GHB is present in extraneural sites (e.g., the heart, lung, liver, skeletal muscle, kidney, and hair) that have either no or very little amounts of GABA present. Research has also shown that 1,4-BD is an endogenous product from fatty acids and may be a source of GHB in peripheral tissues.

A number of published cases reported urinary GHB concentrations following ingestion of the chemical. In one study, a driver found asleep in his car and unable to stand unassisted had a urinary GHB concentration of 1975 mg/L approximately 2 h post-ingestion. Another study found GHB in the urine of two impaired drivers at concentrations of 1086 and 1041 mg/L, respectively. A third case reported a comatose emergency room patient with a urine GHB concentration of 141,000 mg/L 1 h after ingestion of ethanol and GHB. It should be emphasized that the subjects were still under the influence of the drug when the urine specimens were collected in all three reports. This is not likely to be the case when dealing with instances of drug facilitated crimes. In one such case, a 27-year-old female was invited to a male friend's home for dinner and to watch a movie. After dinner, she agreed to have a cocktail but did not remember any of the events that followed. She awoke a couple of hours later, confused and completely nude in the man's bed. She left his house and got immediate medical attention. Approximately 4 h after consuming the cocktail, she provided blood and urine specimens for testing. The results identified GHB in both the blood and urine specimens at concentrations of 47 and 308 mg/L, respectively.

The endogenous nature of GHB makes interpreting results in clinical and forensic specimens difficult at times. Most investigators agree that GHB concentrations exceeding 10 mg/L in urine samples are evidence of exogenous GHB exposure. Findings in blood specimens from living patients, however, can be complicated because it has been reported that the use of citrate-buffered specimen collection tubes may cause a falsely elevated amount of GHB in these tubes. Generally, GHB concentrations that exceed 2 mg/L in a blood sample stored in a non-citrate-buffered tube provide additional evidence of exogenous GHB exposure. Whenever interpreting GHB findings in clinical specimens, it should be remembered that in most cases the maximum detection time of GHB after ingestion is 6 h in blood and 12 h in urine. Further, it is entirely possible that blood and urine concentrations of GHB will drop to endogenous concentrations in much less time than this.

Postmortem samples provide an additional challenge to the interpretation of GHB results. It is now well documented that GHB concentrations will artificially increase in postmortem blood specimens within a very short period of time. To minimize this increase, postmortem blood specimens should be preserved with sodium fluoride and stored at temperatures <5 °C. One study found that GHB concentrations in blood samples remained stable for several years if preserved with sodium fluoride and stored at -20 °C. Generally, in vitro increases in GHB concentrations have not been observed in postmortem vitreous humor specimens. A good rule of thumb for interpreting GHB findings in postmortem blood is that a GHB concentration >50 mg/L suggests the ingestion of GHB. However, as with all death investigations, the blood findings should be complemented by findings in other specimens and must be consistent with the case history.

Endogenous concentrations of GHB in hair are more complex and are still the subject of investigation. Therefore, interpretation of GHB concentrations in hair should be undertaken with caution.

Barbiturates

Chemistry, Classification, and Use

Barbiturates are one of the oldest classes of general CNS depressants. A wide variety of barbiturates are available today; they are primarily indicated for use as sedative-hypnotics, as anticonvulsants, in migraine therapy, and for reduction of cerebral edema secondary to head injury. The first barbiturate to be used therapeutically dates back to the early 1900s when diethylbarbituric acid (or barbital) was introduced. Shortly thereafter, phenobarbital was approved for use as a hypnotic agent. Barbituric acid results from the reaction of urea and malonic acid, with the resulting loss of water. The general formula of barbiturates (as well as the structural components of commonly used barbiturates) is shown in Fig. 21.4.

Modification of the general barbiturate structure to produce the various therapeutic barbiturate analogs can occur at multiple sites. For example, most barbiturates have a double-bonded oxygen attached to C_2, but some have a double-bonded sulfur at that position. Hydrogen is usually bonded to the N_3 position, but some barbiturate analogs substitute a methyl group at that position. However, the major structural modifications for barbiturates occur at the C_5 position, where two groups can be changed. One group, the C_{5a} position, may have an ethyl or an allyl group. The other position, C_{5b}, may have a variety of aliphatic or aromatic side chains.

Since barbiturates have been around for approximately 100 years, numerous structural modifications have been attempted. The result is a great deal of information regarding the structure-activity relationships of barbiturates. For instance, increasing barbiturates' lipid solubility increases the potency but decreases the drugs' duration of activity. Lipid solubility can be increased by increasing the length of the aliphatic chain at the C_{5a} or C_{5b} position. Lipid solubility is also increased by substituting sulfur for oxygen at the C_2 position. However, once the carbon chain

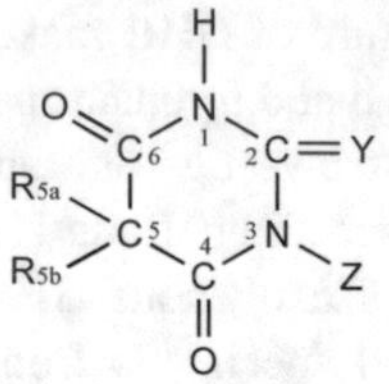

Fig. 21.4 The general barbiturate structure and structures of common barbiturates

DRUG	R_{5a}	R_{5b}	Y	Z
amobarbital	ethyl	isopentyl	O	H
butabarbital	ethyl	sec-butyl	O	H
butalbital	allyl	isobutyl	O	H
methohexital	allyl	1-methyl-2-pentynyl	O	CH_3
pentobarbital	ethyl	1-methylbutyl	O	H
phenobarbital	ethyl	phenyl	O	H
secobarbital	allyl	1-methylbutyl	O	H
thiamylal	allyl	1-methylbutyl	S	H
thiopental	ethyl	1-methylbutyl	S	H

length on the C_{5b} position reaches or exceeds seven, CNS stimulation and not CNS depression results. Adding polar groups on the alkyl side chains, such as a hydroxyl group, removes hypnotic activity. Moreover, alkylating the N_3 position with a methyl group increases potency and decreases duration of activity. These methylated barbiturates are rapidly demethylated in vivo, resulting in active desmethyl metabolites.

A classification system for barbiturates based on their duration of action has been developed. The ultrashort-acting barbiturates act with great potency for a short period of time. Thiopental, thiamylal, and methohexital fall within this classification. The short-acting barbiturates include pentobarbital and secobarbital. The intermediate-acting barbiturates, as the name implies, act for a longer period of time than the previously grouped drugs; amobarbital, butalbital, and butabarbital are classified as such. Phenobarbital is the most commonly prescribed drug in the long-acting barbiturate group.

The therapeutic uses of barbiturates are developed from this classification system. The ultrashort-acting barbiturates are used to induce surgical anesthesia. The short- and intermediate-acting barbiturates have been prescribed as sedative-hypnotic agents. Pentobarbital has also been used to relieve intracranial pressure in head trauma cases. Butalbital has been prescribed to treat migraine headaches. Phenobarbital is used to control seizures.

The use of barbiturates as sedative-hypnotic agents has declined over time. Because barbiturates have general CNS depressant activity, they have significant impairing effects. Moreover, tolerance occurs to a greater extent with barbiturates than with other CNS depressant drugs. Barbiturates have largely been replaced as sedative-hypnotic agents by other drugs, mainly benzodiazepines, which have a shorter duration of action and a higher therapeutic index, thus providing a greater margin of safety when administered.

Pharmacokinetics

Barbiturates may be administered either orally or parenterally. The oral route is preferred when the drug is prescribed as a sedative-hypnotic or as an anticonvulsant drug. Barbiturates as sodium salts are well absorbed orally. Despite the pH characteristics of the drugs (weak acids with pK_a values ranging from 7 to 8), the small intestine is the major site for oral absorption. The intravenous route is used to administer ultrashort-acting barbiturates during the induction of anesthesia. Seizure emergencies may also be handled through the intravenous administration of phenobarbital. Sodium salts of barbiturates are not usually administered intramuscularly because of alkalinity, which results in poor absorption of the drugs from muscle depots.

Barbiturates distribute throughout the major tissues of the body. Binding to plasma proteins is variable, depending on the drug. Ultrashort-acting thiobarbiturates show a biphasic distribution within the brain. A rapid initial distribution of the drug into the gray matter occurs within seconds of intravenous administration; this is the reason for their utility as anesthetic agents. Subsequently, the drug redistributes into other components of the brain.

Elimination half-lives vary with the particular barbiturate and form the basis for the classification system. The short-acting barbiturates have a half-life of about 1 day, while the intermediate-acting barbiturates have a half-life of about 2 days. The elimination half-life of long-acting barbiturates is 2–5 days.

Barbiturates are extensively metabolized in the liver. Except for phenobarbital, less than 10% of a dose appears in the urine as unchanged drug. Hydroxylation at the C_{5b} constituent is a common metabolic route. Oxidation of the end carbon of the C_{5b} constituent to a carboxylic acid can also occur in barbiturates with an aliphatic structure at that position. In addition, a ring nitrogen can form a glucoside metabolite by reacting with glucose.

One of the most important characteristics of barbiturates is their ability to induce microsomal enzymes in the liver. This can significantly influence the therapeutic action of drugs that are metabolized via this mechanism when they are coadministered with barbiturates. Doses of these drugs may need adjustments to correct for this increased metabolism.

Interpretation

The therapeutic ranges of barbiturates in blood have been well established. The short-acting barbiturates have a therapeutic range of 0.5–2 mg/L. The intermediate-acting barbiturates have an expected range of 1–5 mg/L. When phenobarbital is used as a sedative-hypnotic, targeted blood concentrations are 5–15 mg/L. To treat seizures, a phenobarbital concentration of 15–40 mg/L is considered therapeutic. These ranges can be subject to exceptions. Occasionally with epileptics, higher phenobarbital concentrations are necessary to control seizures. When an apparently elevated phenobarbital concentration is measured, a review of the history is in order before deciding that a drug intoxication has occurred. Patients being treated with pentobarbital to relieve intracranial pressure may reach blood concentrations of an order of magnitude above the generally reported therapeutic range. Hospital record analysis should clarify this and thcus prevent an erroneous interpretation of the analytical results.

"Z" DRUGS

Besides the fact that the generic names of the drugs in this grouping all begin with a "z," they all interact with the GABA receptor to produce their CNS depressant effects (Fig. 21.5).

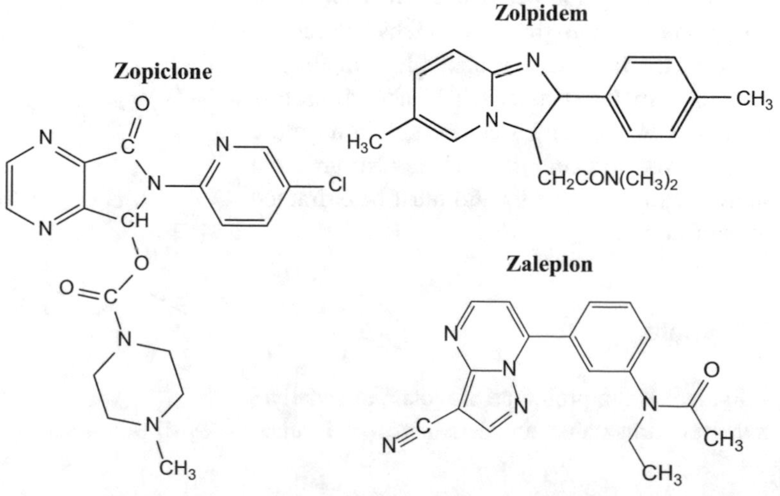

Fig. 21.5 Structure of "z" drugs

Zaleplon

Zaleplon is a pyrazolpyrimidine derivative that has been used to treat insomnia since 1999. Like the structurally similar zolpidem, zaleplon is a selective agonist at the benzodiazepine type I receptor subtype on the $GABA_A$ receptor complex in the brain. The recommended dose is 5–20 mg per night. Neither tolerance nor withdrawal effects have been reported from drug use. Although administered orally, zaleplon undergoes significant first-pass metabolism, leading to a bioavailability of approximately 30%. It is extensively metabolized to inactive products, including N-desethylzaleplon and 5-oxozaleplon. Peak plasma concentrations following a 20 mg dose are in the range of 0.05 mg/L.

Zopiclone

Zopiclone has a cyclopyrrolone structure and is structurally unrelated to barbiturates, benzodiazepines, or other previously marketed CNS depressant drugs. It is a short-acting CNS depressant used to treat insomnia and anxiety, but also has muscle relaxant and anticonvulsant activities. The drug binds to the same site on the $GABA_A$ receptors as the benzodiazepines. Zopiclone is metabolized by decarboxylation, oxidation, and demethylation. The N-oxide metabolite has CNS depressant activity. Blood concentrations of about 0.1 mg/L are seen following therapeutic use. The analysis of zopiclone in biological specimens is complicated by the fact that it is unstable in methanol, forming a methoxy adduct. To make calibrators for analysis, the stock standard solution should be prepared in acetonitrile. It is also unstable in acidic or basic media and must be extracted at neutral pH.

Zolpidem

Zolpidem is the prototype of a class of sedative-hypnotic drugs that are derivatives of imidaz-

opyridine. Although not considered a benzodiazepine, zolpidem does possess some structural similarities to this class of drugs. Whereas benzodiazepines bind nonspecifically to many $GABA_A$ receptor subtypes, zolpidem binds specifically to the $GABA_A$ receptor responsible for sedative activity. Thus, zolpidem is used for the short-term management of insomnia. It has an elimination half-life of several hours. Following therapeutic use, blood zolpidem concentrations are in the 0.1–0.2 mg/L range.

Melatonin Receptor Agonists

Melatonin or N-acetyl-5-methoxytryptamine is an endogenous substance derived from the amino acid L-tryptophan and is produced by the acetylation of serotonin followed by the methylation of the hydroxyl group. Melatonin has a number of functions in the body, including regulation of circadian rhythm, contribution to hormonal homeostasis and antioxidant effects. There are two primary melatonin receptors in humans, designated MT_1 and MT_2. The effect of melatonin on the biological clock in the suprachiasmatic nuclei of the hypothalamus is the main effect that has led to the development of this class of drugs. Figure 21.6 displays the structures of several of these drugs.

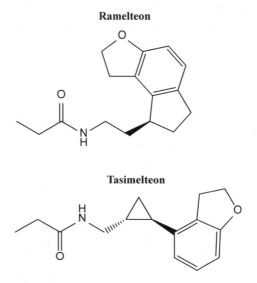

Fig. 21.6 Structures of melatonin agonist drugs

Ramelteon

Ramelteon was approved by the FDA in 2005 for the treatment of insomnia. It binds to MT_1 and MT_2 receptors in the brain with no affinity for other receptors. It has greater affinity for the MT_1 receptors. After oral ingestion, it has low bioavailability, approximately 1–2 %, and has a short half-life of about 2 h. It is extensively metabolized by furan ring oxidation, side-chain hydroxylation, and ketone formation. Although the side-chain hydroxylated product has less activity than parent drug, its longer half-life means that it makes a significant contribution to the overall drug effect.

Tasimelteon

Approved by the FDA in 2014, tasimelteon is used to treat non-20-h sleep-wake disorder, a condition that affects blind people. It has affinity for both MT_1 and MT_2 receptors. Its oral bioavailability is approximately 38% and has an elimination half-life of about an hour. It is metabolized by hydroxylation of the furanyl portion of the dihydrobenzofuran ring.

Other CNS Depressants

Additional CNS depressant drugs are described below (Fig. 21.7).

Buspirone

Buspirone is an azapirone drug approved for use in the United States in 1986. Unlike benzodiazepines and zolpidem, the drug does not mediate its CNS depressant activity through GABA. Instead, buspirone acts as a partial agonist at the $5HT_{1A}$ receptor site. Buspirone does not have any anticonvulsant or muscle relaxant activity.

One advantage to using buspirone to treat anxiety is its relatively short half-life (<6 h). It is metabolized to 5-hydroxybuspirone and to 1-(2-pyrimidinyl)piperazine (1-PP). This latter metabolite appears in higher concentrations in the blood than does the parent drug, and it is pharmacologically active. Blood buspirone concentrations <0.01 mg/L result from therapeutic administration.

Carisoprodol/Meprobamate

Carisoprodol (N-isopropyl meprobamate) is a carbamate derivative used as a muscle relaxant. It has a half-life of approximately 1–2 h and is metabolized by dealkylation to meprobamate. Meprobamate is also an older CNS depressant originally marketed as an alternative to barbiturates without the risk of abuse or overdosage. The safety that was advertised failed to develop, because meprobamate produced toxic effects similar to other sedative-hypnotic drugs. Meprobamate is further metabolized by hydroxylation to an inactive product and is excreted as a glucuronide conjugate. The average elimination half-life of meprobamate is about 12 h. After therapeutic use of carisoprodol, serum concentrations of both parent drug and meprobamate are in the range of 2–5 mg/L. When meprobamate was used as a sedative-hypnotic, concentrations of 5–25 mg/L range were observed.

Chloral Hydrate

Chloral hydrate is the oldest sedative-hypnotic still in use today. Although not widely prescribed for adults, it is used to reduce agitation in neonates and infants requiring mechanical ventilation. Spontaneous extubation in chronically ventilated infants occurs less often when they are treated with chloral hydrate. One advantage over other CNS depressant drugs in these patients is that there appears to be no depression in respiratory drive. Chloral hydrate serves as a prodrug, as it rapidly loses water to form trichloroethanol, the active metabolite of chloral hydrate. Trichloroethanol may be excreted as a glucuronide conjugate or be oxidized to trichloroacetic acid, conjugated, and cleared. A general therapeutic range for trichloroethanol is 2–12 mg/L.

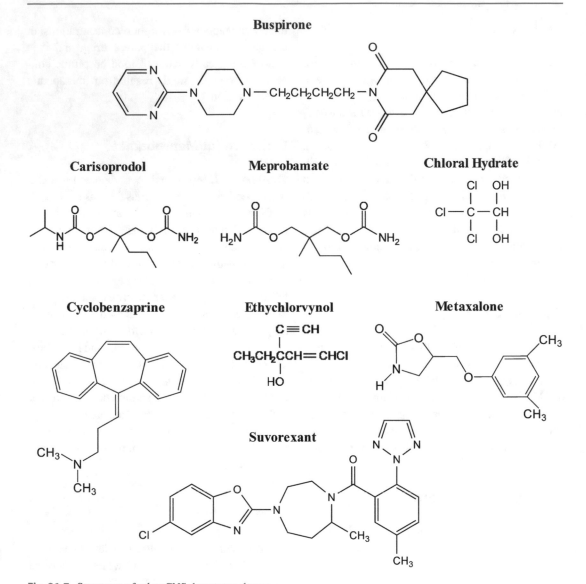

Fig. 21.7 Structures of other CNS depressant drugs

Cyclobenzaprine

Cyclobenzaprine is structurally similar to amitripty-line, with a double bond in the cycloheptane ring as opposed to a single bond with amitriptyline. Despite the structural similarities, it lacks the antidepressant properties possessed by amitriptyline and is used therapeutically as a muscle relaxant. Like amitripty-line, it is metabolized by demethylation, hydroxyl-ation, and N-oxide formation; unlike amitriptyline, hydroxylation occurs on the phenyl ring. A diol on

the cycloheptane ring has also been identified as a metabolite. Therapeutic concentrations are in the range of 0.01–0.03 mg/L.

Ethchlorvynol

Ethchlorvynol was approved for use in the 1950s as a sedative-hypnotic drug with a shorter duration and more rapid onset of action than barbiturates. Its rapid onset of action is related to its high lipophilicity. In fact, it is one drug that has significant distribution into fat. As such, ethchlorvynol shows biphasic elimination from the blood. There is a rapid α-elimination half-life of several hours, which represents rapid distribution. This is followed by a β-elimination half-life of approximately 1 day. Ethchlorvynol is metabolized to hydroxyethchlorvynol, which is the major urinary metabolite. A blood concentration of 2–8 mg/L is expected after therapeutic use.

Metaxalone

Metaxalone is an oxazolidine derivative that acts centrally as a skeletal muscle relaxant, marketed either as alone or as components of combination products. At lower doses, they depress polysynaptic reflexes as measured by the loss of the righting reflex. At high doses, they produce depression of monosynaptic reflexes. Metaxalone does not directly relax "tense" skeletal muscle since it has no direct effect on the contractile mechanism of striated muscle, the motor endplate, or the nerve fiber. The onset of action is 1 h with a duration of action of 4–6 h and a half-life of 2–3 h. Plasma concentrations following a single 400–800 mg dose are in the range of 1–4 mg/L. Metaxalone is extensively metabolized to at least three products that are primarily excreted in the urine. One metabolite is formed by the oxidation of one of the methyl groups to the carboxy analog and appears in the urine as the glucuronide conjugate. Drowsiness is the most frequently reported adverse effect of the drug.

Suvorexant

Suvorexant has been used in the United States since 2014 to treat insomnia. It is a Schedule IV drug as classified by the DEA. It is the first dual orexin receptor antagonist (DORA) to be approved for therapeutic use in the United States. Unlike traditional sedative-hypnotic drugs,

suvorexant has no effect on GABA receptors, but instead inhibits orexin A and B in the lateral hypothalamus to control the transition from wakefulness to sleep. It is administered orally and has a half-life of approximately 12 h. It is extensively metabolized to inactive products.

Suggested Reading

Baselt RC (2020) Disposition of toxic drugs and chemicals in man, 12th edn. Biomedical Publications, Seal Beach, CA

Borgen LA, Okerholm RA, Lai A, Scharf MB (2004) The pharmacokinetics of sodium oxybate oral solution following acute and chronic administration to narcoleptic patients. J Clin Pharmacol 44:253–257

Brailsford AD, Cowan DA, Kicman AT (2012) Pharmacokinetic properties of gamma-hydroxybutyrate (GHB) in whole blood, serum, and urine. J Anal Toxicol 36:88–95

Brenneisen R, Elsohly MA, Murphy TP, Passarelli J, Russmann S, Salamone SJ et al (2004) Pharmacokinetics and excretion of gamma-hydroxybutyrate (GHB) in healthy subjects. J Anal Toxicol 28:625–630

Brunton LL, Lazo JS, Parker KL, Gilman AG (eds) (2006) Goodman and Gilman's The pharmacological basis of therapeutics, 11th edn. McGraw-Hill, New York

Busardo FB, Jones AW (2015) GHB pharmacology and toxicology: Acute intoxication, concentrations in blood and urine in forensic cases and treatment of the withdrawal syndrome. Current Neuropharm 13:47–70

Dooley M, Plosker GL (2000) Zaleplon-A review of its use in the treatment of insomnia. Drugs 60:413–445

Fieler EL, Coleman DE, Baselt RC (1998) Gammahydroxybutyrate concentrations in pre- and postmortem blood and urine. Clin Chem 44:692

Kavanagh PV, Kenny P, Feely J (2001) The urinary excretion of gamma-hydroxybutyric acid in man. J Pharm Pharmacol 53:399–402

Kerrigan S (2002) In vitro production of gammahydroxybutyrate in antemortem urine samples. J Anal Toxicol 26:571–574

Langtry HD, Benfield P (1990) Zolpidem: A review of its pharmacodynamic and pharmacokinetic properties and therapeutic potential. Drugs 40:291–313

LeBeau MA, Montgomery MA, Jufer RA, Miller ML (2000) Elevated GHB in citrate-buffered blood. J Anal Toxicol 24:383

LeBeau MA, Miller ML, Levine B (2001) Effect of storage temperature on endogenous GHB levels in urine. Forensic Sci Int 119:161–167

LeBeau MA, Christenson RH, Levine B, Darwin WD, Huestis MA (2002) Intra- and interindividual variations in urinary concentrations of endogenous gamma-hydroxybutyrate. J Anal Toxicol 26:340–346

Mahmood I, Sahajwalla C (1999) Clinical pharmacokinetics and pharmacodynamics of buspirone, an anxiolytic drug. Clin Pharmacokinet 36:277–287

Palatini P, Tedeschi L, FrisonG PR, Zordan R, Orlando R et al (1993) Dose-dependent absorption and elimination of gamma-hydroxybutyric acid in healthy volunteers. Eur J Clin Pharmacol 45:353–356

Rohrig TP, Moore CM (2005) Zolpidem-Forensic Aspects for the toxicologist and pathologist. Forensic Sci Med Path 1:81–90

Srinivasan V, Brezinski A, Oter S, Shillcutt SD (eds) Melatonin and melatonin drugs in clinical practice. Springer, New Dehli

Torres R, Dressman MA, Kramer WG, Baroldi P (2015) Absolute bioavailability of tasimelteon. Amer J Therapeutics 22:355–360

Opioids

22

Sarah Kerrigan and Bruce A. Goldberger

Abstract

Opioids are one of the most important drug classes in forensic toxicology, due to their widespread medical and illicit use. While *opiates* are naturally derived, the term *opioid* encompasses all natural, semi-synthetic, and synthetic derivatives. While most of the naturally occurring and semi-synthetic derivatives share a morphine-like structure, synthetic opioids encompass a wide variety of chemical classifications. Despite their structural differences, they all exhibit opioid receptor activity at various receptor sub-types. More recently, the emergence of novel synthetic opioids (NSOs) has significantly complicated the landscape of opioid use. The United States is in the midst of an opioid epidemic due to irresponsible prescribing practices, the availability of diverted pharmaceutical products, and illicitly manufactured drugs. Increases in opioid use disorder and fatal overdoses nationwide have significantly impacted forensic toxicology. In this chapter, the chemistry, pharmacology, uses, and effects of opioids are discussed, in addition to their analysis and interpretation.

Keywords

Opioids · Pharmacology · Toxicology · Analysis · Interpretation · Fentalogs

Introduction

Used for more than 2000 years, opiates are naturally occurring alkaloid analgesics obtained from the opium poppy, *Papaver somniferum*. The milky exudate obtained upon incision of the unripe seed contains several pharmacologically active compounds, including morphine and codeine. Morphine, the principal alkaloid of opium, is named after Morpheus, the ancient Greek god of dreams.

First isolated in 1806, morphine was the primary building block in the subsequent development of many semi-synthetic opioid analgesics. The term *opioid* is used to describe natural and semi-synthetic alkaloids prepared from opium, as well as synthetic surrogates whose pharmacologic effects, rather than their structures, mimic those of morphine. This term also includes the natural

S. Kerrigan (✉)
Department of Forensic Science, Sam Houston State University, Huntsville, TX, USA
e-mail: sarah.kerrigan@shsu.edu

B. A. Goldberger
Department of Pathology, Immunology and Laboratory Medicine, Forensic Medicine Division, University of Florida College of Medicine, Gainesville, FL, USA
e-mail: bruce-goldberger@ufl.edu

endogenous neuropeptides (opiopeptins), such as enkephalins, endorphins, and dynorphins, which are not within the scope of this discussion.

The semi-synthetic derivative heroin was first synthesized from morphine in 1874 and was made available as a pharmaceutical preparation in 1898. Heroin is unavailable in the United States for therapeutic use, but widespread illicit use of the drug has persisted since the 1970s. The first fully synthetic opioid without a morphine-like structure was meperidine (prepared serendipitously in 1939). Another fully synthetic opioid, methadone, was synthesized shortly thereafter, in 1946.

Nalorphine was first synthesized in 1942. A significant pharmacotherapeutic advancement, nalorphine is able to reverse the respiratory depression produced by opioid agonists such as morphine and facilitate abstinence in drug-dependent individuals. This capability, in combination with its analgesic properties, is due to its mixed agonist–antagonist effect. Further discoveries led to the development of other drugs, such as naloxone, that possess an almost exclusive antagonistic binding behavior. The design of new synthetic opioids is concomitant with investigations into interactions with opioid receptors, in the hope that enhanced understanding in this area will facilitate the development of potent analgesics with fewer side effects.

The landscape of opioid use has changed dramatically on a global scale. According to the Centers for Disease Control and Prevention (CDC), the United States is in the midst of an opioid epidemic. They attribute the rise in opioid-related deaths to three distinct waves. The first wave began in the 1990s, due to increased prescribing practices and copious therapeutic opioid use. A sharp increase in heroin-related deaths marked the start of the second wave in 2010. This was followed by a third wave in 2013, where fatal overdoses were largely attributed to an influx of illicitly manufactured synthetic opioids, including fentanyl analogs (fentalogs). Synthetic opioid deaths increased by more than 70% from 2014 to 2015 and doubled from 2016 to 2017. The CDC estimated that in 2017 as many as 130 Americans died each day from an opioid overdose. More recently, atypical opioids, which have both opioid and non-opioid effects, have also emerged (e.g., mitragynine). In this chapter, licit and illicit opioids are reviewed.

Chemistry and Mechanism of Action

The characteristic pharmacologic effects of opioids are due to the somewhat selective receptor binding at several sites in the central nervous system (CNS). The limbic system, a region rich in opioid-binding sites, is primarily involved in the arousal of human emotion. Opioids produce an analgesic effect by blocking the transmission of painful stimuli. The interaction between the opioid and specific receptors at terminal nerve endings impedes the release of neurotransmitters, thus interrupting the pain. This prevents the recognition of painful sensations, inhibits the negative emotional component of pain, and can produce euphoria.

Opioid Receptors

The pharmacologic profile of different opioids is characterized by their interaction with certain receptors (Table 22.1), of which there are at least three major types: μ (mu), κ (kappa), and δ (delta).

- μ receptor interactions produce central nervous system depression, which clinically manifests as supraspinal (μ_1) and spinal (μ_2) analgesia, respiratory depression, miosis, euphoria, reduced gastrointestinal motility, hypothermia, bradycardia, and physical tolerance and dependence.
- κ receptor interactions produce spinal analgesia, sedation, miosis, diuresis, mild respiratory depression, and low addiction liability.
- δ receptors are the binding sites for most endogenous opioid peptides. Interactions at these sites mediate spinal analgesia, dysphoria, delusions, hallucinations, and respiratory and vasomotor stimulation.

Table 22.1 Mode of action and analgesic potency of opioids

Drug	Mode of action	Analgesic potency morphine = 1
Buprenorphine	Partial μ agonist, κ antagonist	25–50
Butorphanol	Strong κ agonist, μ antagonist	4–8
Codeine	Weak μ agonist, weak δ agonist	0.1
Dihydrocodeine	μ agonist	0.3
Fentanyl	Strong μ agonist	100–200
Heroin	Strong μ agonist	1–5
Hydrocodone	μ agonist	1–2
Hydromorphone	Strong μ agonist	7–10
Levorphanol	Strong μ and κ agonist	4–5
Meperidine	Strong μ agonist	0.1
Methadone	Strong μ agonist	1
Morphine	Strong μ agonist, weak κ and δ agonist	1
Nalbuphine	Strong κ agonist, σ agonist, μ antagonist	0.5–1.0
Oxycodone	μ agonist	1–2
Oxymorphone	Strong μ agonist	8–15
Pentazocine	Mixed κ, μ, and σ agonist	0.2
Propoxyphene	μ agonist	<0.1
Tapentadol	μ agonist, norepinephrine reuptake inhibition	0.05
Tramadol	μ agonist, norepinephrine, serotonin reuptake inhibition	0.1–0.2

The analgesic effect of morphine and several of its congeners is mediated through the μ opioid receptor (MOR). κ receptor interactions can also produce analgesia, but this effect is sometimes accompanied by psychomimetic effects that limit their clinical utility. Opioids may also bind to σ (sigma) receptors to produce central excitation, causing tachycardia, hypertension, tachypnea, mydriasis, and hallucinations.

Agonist and Antagonist Behavior

Opioids are broadly classified into three groups, depending on their mode of action. The term *full agonist* refers to compounds that have an affinity for opioid receptors of a certain type and produce a response. *Full antagonists*, which inhibit agonist binding, tend to have reduced analgesic effects and are primarily indicated for the treatment of opioid intoxication. Drugs with an agonistic effect at one class of receptor and an antagonistic effect at another are called *mixed agonist–antagonists*.

An antagonist can preferentially displace another opioid from a receptor's binding site because of an increased affinity or competitive potency. For example, substitution of the N-methyl group in morphine with an allyl moiety tends to produce antagonistic binding behavior. Naloxone, an extremely potent antagonist with high opioid receptor affinity, has no analgesic effect when administered alone. Consequently, the properties of these drugs have been exploited clinically for the treatment of opioid intoxication and overdose, including the rapid reversal of opioid-induced respiratory depression. After naloxone administration, the reversal of opioid effects occurs within a few minutes and effectively normalizes respiration.

The pharmacologic profile of an agonist–antagonist opioid analgesic is generally consistent with the type of opioid receptor involved. Pentazocine interacts preferentially with κ receptors, which advantageously mediate analgesia with limited respiratory depression, whereas its interactions with σ receptors may produce behavioral and dysphoric side effects.

In some instances, multiple modes of action are responsible for an array of pharmacologic responses. When drugs have multiple mechanisms of analgesic action beyond the opioid receptors themselves, they are sometimes referred to as "atypical opioids." Buprenorphine is one such drug, because in addition to its opioid receptor activity, there are other contributory mechanisms involving the ORL-1 receptors and others. The analgesic effect of tramadol is also mediated via non-opioid pathways involving inhibition of noradrenaline and serotonin reuptake. More recently, tapentadol was specifically engineered to exploit dual mechanistic features through activation of the μ opioid receptor and inhibition of norepinephrine reuptake. This "directed poly-pharmacology" approach is a valuable tool in drug discovery. Natural products also have mul-timechanistic opioid features. Mitragynine, the principal alkaloid in *Mitragyna speciosa* known as kratom, also has both opioid and non-opioid (monoamine neurotransmitter) contributions. Study of these atypical opioids and their mecha-nisms has provided understanding of the different classes of receptors and their pharmacologic characteristics which facilitates the design of potent narcotic analgesics with reduced side effects and addiction liability.

Structure–Activity Relationships

Opioids exert their pharmacologic effects by mimicking the activities of enkephalins and endorphins, which are the body's own analgesic resource. Structural modification of the polycy-clic framework of morphine can considerably alter the pharmacology of the drug and its potency as an analgesic. Major qualitative and quantitative changes in pharmacologic response are brought about by variations in conformation, rigidity, and the nature of the moieties substituted into the ring system of morphine. The degree of complement, or goodness of fit, between the receptor binding site and the drug determines the extent of analge-sia and the duration of effects. Consequently, drugs within this class exhibit a wide range of potencies relative to morphine (Table 22.1).

The pharmacodynamics of a particular opioid are largely predetermined by the steric and elec-tronic characteristics of the drug. An opioid's bind-ing interactions with the receptor, which are responsible for the pharmacologic effect, are deter-mined by both its molecular structure and stereo-specificity. For example, only the levorotatory isomer of morphine, which occurs in nature, is a potent analgesic. The dextrorotatory enantiomer of morphine does not have mu-opioid receptor (MOR) affinity or produce any pharmacologic effects asso-ciated with MOR binding. Within the drug mole-cule, one region is responsible for the goodness of fit, and another region facilitates the conforma-tional changes necessary for receptor binding.

These factors ultimately determine whether the drug behaves as an agonist or an antagonist.

Despite the wide variation in size and func-tionality, opioids are characterized by their aro-matic core and basic nature. Typical pK_a values (approximately 7.6–8.9) ensure some degree of protonation at physiological pH, which is believed to facilitate the binding interaction with receptors. Various conformations and molecular structures promote the initial pharmacophoric interaction between the drug and the opioid receptor, and aspects of secondary structure may enhance or impede their association.

The evolution of drug design to optimize ther-apeutic analgesic effects has led to the production of a number of useful natural, semi-synthetic, and synthetic opioids, which are broadly classi-fied as:4,5-Epoxymorphinans: e.g., morphine, codeine, dihydrocodeine, hydrocodone, hydro-morphone, oxycodone, oxymorphone, buprenor-phine, nalbuphine

- Morphinans: e.g., butorphanol, levorphanol
- Phenylheptylamines: e.g., methadone, propoxyphene
- Phenylpiperidines: e.g., meperidine, fentanyl
- Benzomorphans: e.g., pentazocine
- Cyclohexanols: e.g., tramadol
- Phenols: e.g., tapentadol

The 4,5-epoxymorphinans include the major opiate alkaloids obtained from the opium poppy. Structural modification of these natural alka-loids has expanded this class, which is now the largest and best characterized group of opioids. Their general structure is shown in Fig. 22.1. In addition to the three-membered phenanthrene core (rings A, B, C), they contain a six-mem-bered nitrogen ring (D) and an epoxy ring between C4 and C5 (E). Structural alterations of the basic morphine framework include the methylation or acetylation of the C3 and C6 hydroxyl groups, saturation of the C7-C8 dou-ble bond (dihydro derivatives), oxidation to a ketone at position 6 (hydro derivatives), and subsequent hydroxylation of the C14 atom (oxy derivatives). Chemical structures of selected opioids are shown in Fig. 22.2.

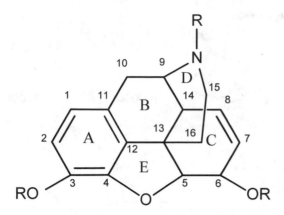

Fig. 22.1 General structure of 4,5-epoxymorphinans

Relatively minor changes in molecular structure can profoundly affect the pharmacologic properties of a drug. For example, replacement of the C3 hydroxyl group of morphine can substantially reduce the affinity for μ opioid receptors, as is the case for both heroin and codeine. Substitution of the N-methyl in morphine with a larger group can result in antagonistic binding activity, as in nalbuphine. Replacing the C3 and C6 hydroxyl groups of morphine alters the pharmacokinetics of the opioid. Methylation of these groups (e.g., codeine, oxycodone) decreases susceptibility to first-pass metabolism and significantly increases the potency of orally administered drugs. Similarly, acetylation of morphine produces diacetylmorphine (heroin), and its increased lipophilicity facilitates penetration of the blood–brain barrier.

Simplification of the morphine structure by removing the furan bridge (in morphinans) or by ring exclusion to yield a bridged naphthalene (in benzomorphans) can produce congeners that retain analgesic activity. In addition to these semi-synthetic analogs, relatively simple synthetic opioids, such as the piperidines, may have analgesic properties that exceed the effectiveness of the principal alkaloid, morphine. The lipophilicity of the opioids varies considerably, due to the differences in their chemical scaffolds and individual substituents. Log P values for the opioids range from <1 (e.g., morphine) to 4.0 (e.g., methadone).

In addition to the chemical drug classes listed above, other novel synthetic opioids have emerged as illicit drugs. These are discussed in more detail later.

Use and Effects

Therapeutic uses of opioids include indications in surgical and medical emergencies where anesthetic and sedative supplements are needed such as myocardial infarction, trauma, burns, orthopedic pain, and postoperative pain. Management of chronic pain associated with cancer and terminal illness is another use case. Opioids are also used clinically for their antitussive and antidiarrheal properties as well as for detoxification of patients after opioid intoxication. Table 22.2 summarizes specific uses of individual opioids.

Opioids exert their major pharmacologic effects on the CNS. Their clinical importance lies in their ability to provide analgesia without the loss of consciousness. Analgesia is often accompanied by euphoria, sedation, and mental clouding. In addition, opioids may produce pulmonary and gastrointestinal effects, including respiratory depression, nausea, vomiting, and constipation. Other risks associated with opioid toxicity are coma, hypothermia, seizure, and hypotension. Table 22.3 provides a more thorough description of the therapeutic and adverse effects of opioids, which act both centrally and peripherally.

The major disadvantages associated with the use of opioid analgesics include the risk of respiratory failure, which is the major cause of death in intoxication cases, and addiction liability, which can cause physical dependence. Associated with these disadvantages is the increasing tolerance of the drug with sustained use, which necessitates the administration of a higher dose to produce an equivalent therapeutic effect.

Opioid tolerance is initiated after the first dose but is not usually clinically significant until the second or third week of chronic use. Depending on the drug, the degree of tolerance may necessitate a 35-fold increase for an equipotent analgesic dose. Cross-tolerance also exists between opioids that have the same mode of action, e.g., μ

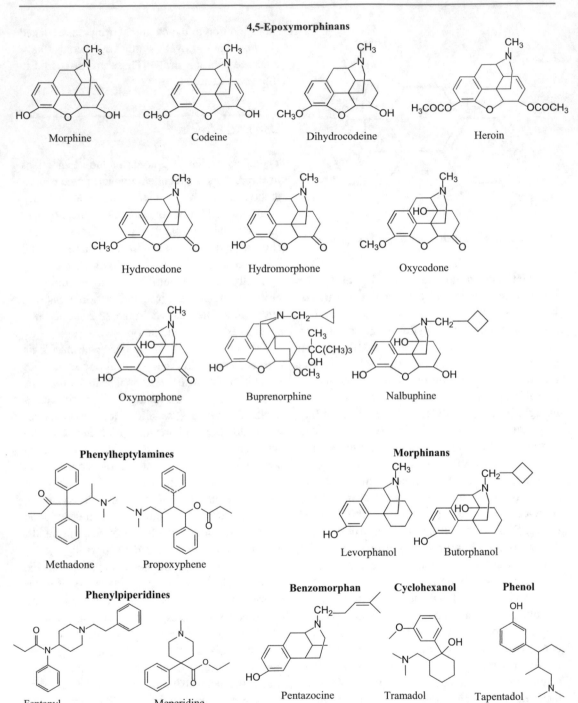

Fig. 22.2 Chemical structures of the opioid analgesics

Table 22.2 Therapeutic uses, effectiveness, and abuse potential of opioids

Drug	Uses	Pain relief	Abuse potential
Buprenorphine	MI, anesthetic supplement, orthopedics, obstetrics	Moderate to severe	Low
Butorphanol	Migraine, obstetric, musculoskeletal, postoperative, and cancer pain	Moderate to severe	Low
Codeine	Injuries, musculoskeletal, neuralgia	Mild to moderate	Moderate
Dihydrocodeine	Injuries, musculoskeletal, neuralgia	Mild to moderate	Moderate
Fentanyl	Pre−/postoperative medication, anesthetic supplement	Moderate to severe	High
Hydrocodone	Postoperative, pulmonary disease	Moderate to severe	Moderate
Hydromorphone	Cancer, surgery, trauma, biliary and renal colic, MI, burns	Moderate to severe	High
Levorphanol	Cancer, biliary and renal colic, MI, anesthetic supplement	Moderate to severe	High
Meperidine	Postoperative pain, anesthesia, obstetrics	Moderate to severe	High
Methadone	Detoxification, maintenance	Severe	High
Morphine	Cancer, preoperative sedation, anesthetic supplement, obstetrics	Moderate to severe	High
Nalbuphine	Pre−/postoperative anesthesia, childbirth	Moderate to severe	Low
Oxycodone	Bursitis, injuries, neuralgia, postoperative, obstetrics	Moderate to severe	Moderate
Oxymorphone	Preoperative, obstetric analgesia, anxiety, dyspnea	Moderate to severe	High
Pentazocine	Pre−/postoperative analgesia, surgical anesthesia	Moderate to severe	Low
Propoxyphene	Detoxification	Mild to moderate	Low
Tapentadol	Postoperative, dental	Moderate to severe	Low
Tramadol	Postoperative, gynecologic, obstetric, cancer	Moderate to severe	Low

MI, myocardial infarction

receptor agonists such as morphine, methadone, and meperidine. Habituation and drug dependence are related to the analgesic potency of the drug. Repeated administration of opioid analgesics that act as μ receptor agonists invariably leads to drug dependence even with normal, compliant treatment involving opioids. Mixed agonist–antagonists, such as buprenorphine, pentazocine, or nalbuphine, have the lowest potential for addiction and subsequent misuse (Table 22.2). Opioid use disorder can result as a consequence of chronic administration.

Discontinuation of opioid use or administration of an opioid antagonist following overdose can produce characteristic withdrawal symptoms known as abstinence syndrome, the features and chronology of which are described in Table 22.4. Typical effects include increased heart rate, irritability, profuse sweating, and piloerection, as well as uncontrollable muscle spasm and pain. Physiological withdrawal manifests itself clinically 6–8 h after the last dose and becomes heightened at 36–72 h. The severity of symptoms varies, depending on the frequency and duration of drug use. Physiological effects generally subside within 7–10 days, whereas psychological dependence may last for prolonged periods. Intense drug craving, which may prove unbearable, is a common cause of recidivism among recovering individuals. Withdrawal is not life-threatening, but it can be excruciating and avoidance behaviors spur continued drug use.

Table 22.3 Therapeutic and adverse effects of opioids

Central nervous system effects	
Nervous	Euphoria
	Analgesia
	Sedation
	Mental clouding
	Mood swings
	Vertigo
	Decreased responsiveness
Pulmonary	Respiratory depression
Gastrointestinal	Nausea
	Vomiting
Other	Cough suppression
	Miosis
	Truncal rigidity
	Flushing and warming of the skin
	Sweating
	Itching
Peripheral effects	
Cardiac	Bradycardia
	Orthostatic hypotension when system is stressed
	Stroke
Gastrointestinal	Constipation
	Decreased motility
	Increased tone
	Decreased gastric secretions
	Biliary tract constriction of smooth muscle
Genitourinary	Decreased renal plasma flow
	Increased urethral and bladder tone
	Prolongation of labor
	Menstrual abnormalities
	Sexual dysfunction
Neuroendocrine	Increased release of antidiuretic hormone

Table 22.4 Chronology of opioid abstinence syndrome in humans

8–12 h	Lacrimation
	Yawning
	Rhinorrhea
	Perspiration
12–14 h	Irritability
	Piloerection ("goose flesh")
	Restless sleep
	Weakness
	Mydriasis
	Tremor
	Anorexia
	Muscle spasm
48–72 h (peak of syndrome)	Increased irritability
	Increased heart rate
	Insomnia
	Hypertension
	Marked anorexia
	Hot and cold flashes
	Sneezing
	Sweating and flushing
	Nausea and vomiting
	Piloerection
	Hyperthermia
	Hyperpnea
	Abdominal cramps
	Aching muscles
7–10 days	Symptoms persist

Opiate intoxication is treated with a variety of antidotal and supportive measures that include ventilation alongside cardiac and respiratory monitoring, oxygen and anticonvulsants to combat seizures, intravenous fluids and vasopressors to normalize blood pressure, and naloxone to reverse CNS and respiratory depression (Table 22.5).

Reversal of opioid intoxication with naloxone is carried out at the risk of precipitating severe withdrawal symptoms. Additional care including continued naloxone dosing is necessary for the reversal of effects caused by opioids with long half-lives. Careful monitoring and treatment over several days may be necessary for the complete reversal of effects and clinical support during withdrawal.

Methadone has been used for detoxification and maintenance of opioid-dependent persons; the withdrawal effect of methadone is milder but longer lasting than that of morphine. Tolerance and physical dependence to methadone develop more slowly than with morphine. During maintenance therapy, daily oral methadone doses of 80–120 mg substantially reduce the severity of withdrawal symptoms, thus minimizing the likelihood of drug craving and resumption of compulsive use. This response is due to the cross-tolerance that exists between methadone, morphine, and heroin, which allows addiction-reinforcing effects to be blocked. While the individual is receiving methadone treatment,

Table 22.5 Clinical treatment for symptoms of opioid overdose

1. Monitoring of cardiovascular and respiratory status
2. Ventilation for reestablishment of respiratory exchange
3. Oxygen for seizure
4. Naloxone to counteract CNS and respiratory effects
5. Intravenous fluids for hypotension
6. Therapeutic intervention
a. Doxapram as a respiratory stimulant
b. Vasopressors for hypotension
c. Anticonvulsants for seizure
7. Other supportive measures
a. Rewarming (<90 °F) for hypothermia
b. Mechanical ventilation

Table 22.6 Opioids and human performance

Psychological effects
Drowsiness, sedation, lethargy, dizziness, mental clouding, mood swings, euphoria, dysphoria, depressed reflexes, altered sensory perception, stupor, coma
Physiological effects
Analgesia, headache, dry mouth, facial flushing, nausea, constipation, respiratory depression, muscle flaccidity, pupil constriction (nonreactive to light stimulus), low blood pressure, low pulse, droopy eyelids, low body temperature
Driving effects
Slow driving, weaving, poor vehicle control, poor coordination, slow response to stimuli, delayed reactions, difficulty following instructions, falling asleep at the wheel

self-administered opioids fail to produce the desired euphoric effect. Buprenorphine is also a detoxification alternative to methadone. Unlike methadone, buprenorphine is more convenient for the treatment of opioid dependency because it is available by prescription.

Other treatments that can alleviate symptoms include increased electrolyte and fluid intake, antispasmodics (propantheline), sedative-hypnotics (phenobarbital), antiadrenergics (clonidine), and nitrous oxide. The effectiveness of maintenance therapy in drug detoxification is highly dependent on the individual. During recovery, abstinence may be due to morphine-like analgesia following regular maintenance dosing, abatement of withdrawal symptoms, or the blocking effect against self-administered drugs. Although treatment of opioid abstinence syndrome requires clinical management, the atypical opioid mitragynine, also known as kratom, has become popular for the nonmedically supervised treatment of opioid addiction.

Opioids have the potential to impair human performance because of their depressant effects on the CNS. The indications of impairment are mixed and frequently complicated by tolerance and concurrent use of other drugs (polypharmacy). Opioids have an additive effect when combined with other CNS-depressant drugs and may greatly increase the deleterious effects of alcohol on driving competence. Manufacturer warnings on prescription opioids typically state that the drug may impair the mental and/or physi-

cal abilities required for the performance of potentially hazardous tasks. Table 22.6 summarizes common psychological and physiological effects that may be important in impaired driving cases. Although significant psychomotor impairment may not be evident in tolerant individuals, opioids have the potential to increase subjective feelings of sedation, to decrease consciousness, and to impair reaction time, visual acuity, and information processing in a dose-dependent fashion. More pronounced effects are expected in naïve users. Observations of drivers apprehended for driving under the influence have included slow driving, weaving, poor vehicle control, poor coordination, slow response to stimuli, delayed reactions, difficulty following instructions, and falling asleep at the wheel.

General Pharmacokinetics

Absorption and Distribution

Most opioids are absorbed readily after subcutaneous or intramuscular injection. Gastrointestinal absorption is generally good, although the bioavailability and pharmacologic effects of opioids vary considerably, depending on the extent of first-pass metabolism. Lipid-soluble opioids are effectively absorbed via the nasal or buccal mucosa in addition to the usual routes. Highly lipid-soluble drugs can be absorbed transdermally and act quickly after subcutaneous administration because of their accelerated absorption and entry into the CNS.

Intravenous administration is common in opioids consumed illicitly due to the rapid onset of effects; however, because of the increasing purity of street drugs and a greater concern about the spread of infectious diseases including human immunodeficiency virus, alternative routes such as smoking, insufflation (snorting), and inhalation of vapors ("chasing the dragon") have become popular for some illicit drugs, such as heroin. These routes of administration may not provide the same euphoric "rush" that is typical after intravenous injection.

Opioids are bound to plasma proteins in the blood at varying degrees (Table 22.7). Subsequent localization in highly perfused organs such as the lungs, liver, brain, kidneys, and spleen may also occur. Accumulation in fatty tissues becomes important for highly lipophilic opioids, which can also accumulate in skeletal muscle reservoirs and cross the placental barrier. Transfer across the blood–brain barrier is impeded for highly amphoteric opioids such as morphine but is easier for less polar congeners, such as codeine and diamorphine.

Metabolism and Excretion

Some opioids undergo significant first-pass metabolism, which decreases the efficacy of orally administered drugs. Metabolism takes place primarily in the liver to form mainly polar metabolites, which are eliminated via enterohepatic or renal recirculation. Metabolites are excreted primarily in the urine, with relatively small amounts of the glucuronidated drug eliminated in the feces.

Table 22.8 lists metabolites for individual opioids that, despite structural variations, share a number of common biotransformations, including oxidation, hydroxylation, O-demethylation, and N-demethylation. The N-demethylation pathway yields a nor-derivative, which frequently undergoes conjugation before elimination. Glucuronidation is the major metabolic route for opioids that contain available hydroxyl groups, such as morphine and levorphanol. After conjugation, these products undergo principally biliary and urinary excretion.

Drug Interactions

Opioids should be administered with caution to patients who have reduced metabolic capability or certain medical conditions, particularly pulmonary or hepatic diseases. Prudent administration of opioids is also advised because many other centrally acting drugs can initiate adverse reactions or additive effects when coadministered. Such drugs include CNS depressants, alcohol, general anesthetics, tranquilizers, sedative-hypnotics, tricyclic antidepressants, dextroamphetamine, and monoamine oxidase inhibitors. Monoamine oxidase inhibitors are a specific contraindication due to the increased risk of seizures, hyperpyrexic coma, and hypertension. Because of tramadol's dual mode of action, patients receiving selective serotonin reuptake inhibitors or other antidepressants may experience serotonin toxicity. Other dangers arise from the coadministration of opioids with drugs such as carbamazepine, phenobarbital, tricyclic antidepressants, and warfarin because of significantly reduced metabolic capability.

Novel Synthetic Opioids

The term novel synthetic opioid (NSO) generally refers to substances with opioid receptor activity that have recently surfaced in the illicit drug market. This includes fentalogs and other synthetic opioids that have gained notoriety as clandestine drugs. Although the landscape of designer drugs continues to change at a frightening pace, fentanyl derivatives are at the forefront, due to their prevalence and potency. Furthermore, these substances are often incorporated into illicit drug preparations to enhance their effects, often without the knowledge of the individual. The National Forensic Laboratory Information System (NFLIS) provides valuable information on current drug use trends. Toxicology laboratories must keep abreast of controlled substance trends in order to collect and provide relevant data. This presents a significant challenge for operational laboratories, due to the prolifera-

Table 22.7 Pharmacokinetic parameters of opioids

Drug	Half-life (h)	V_d (L/kg)	Duration of analgesia (h)	Protein binding (%)	Common routes of administration
Buprenorphine	2–4[a] 18–49[b]	1.4–6.2	4–8	96	PO, IM, IV, SL, TR
Butorphanol	2.9–8.4	5–10	3–4	83	IM, IV, SC, IN
Codeine	1.2–3.9	2.5–3.5	3–4	7–25	PO, SC
Dihydrocodeine	3.4–4.5	1.0–1.3	3–4 12d	20	PO
Fentanyl	3–12	3–8	1–1.5[c] >12[e]	79	IM, IV, IN, SL, TR
Heroin	0.03–0.10	25	3–5	<5	PO, IM, IV, SC, IN
Hydrocodone	3.4–8.8	3.3–4.7	3–5 12[d]	25	PO
Hydromorphone	3–9[c] 10–22[d]	2–4	4–5 12–24[d]	19	PO, IM, IV, SC, PR
Levorphanol	11–16	10–13	4–5	40	SC, PO
Meperidine	2–5	3.7–4.2	2–4	45–64	PO, IM, IV, SC
Methadone	15–55	4–7	4–6	87	PO, IM, IV, SC
Morphine	1.3–6.7	2–5	4–5 8-24[d]	35	PO, IM, IV, SC, E
Nalbuphine	1.9–7.7	2.4–7.3	3–6	25–40	IM, IV, SC
Opium	2–4	3–4	4–5	35	PO, PR, N
Oxycodone	3–6	1.8–3.7	4–6[c] 12[d]	45	PO, IM, IV, SC, PR
Oxymorphone	4–12	2–4	4–6[c] 12[d]	10–12	PO, IM, IV, SC
Pentazocine	2.1–3.5	4.4–7.8	3–4	61	PO, IM, IV, SC
Propoxyphene	8–24	12–26	4–5	78	PO
Tapentadol	3–5	6–9	4–6	20	PO
Tramadol	4.3–6.7	2.6–2.9	4–6 12–24[d]	15–20	PO, IM, IV, SC PO, IM, IV, SC

[a]Parenteral;
[b]Sublingual;
[c]IV and immediate release;
[d]Extended release;
[e]Transdermal;
V_d = volume of distribution;
PO = oral;
PR = rectal;
IM = intramuscular;
IN = intranasal;
IV = intravenous;
SC = subcutaneous;
SL = sublingual;
TR = transdermal

tion of new psychoactive substances in recent years.

At the present time NSOs fall into four chemical subclasses: phenylpiperidines (i.e., fentalogs), cyclohexylbenzamides, acetamides, and piperazines. The cyclohexylbenzamides include several "U-series" drugs, many of which were developed in the 1970s by The Upjohn Company. These include U-47700, U-48800, U-49900, and AH-7921 (developed by Allen and Hanburys). The structurally related acetamides include U-51754 and U-50488. Finally, the piperazine family of NSOs include MT-45 and AD-1211.

Table 22.8 Metabolism of opioids

Drug	Major metabolites
Buprenorphine	Norbuprenorphine,[a] buprenorphine[a]
Butorphanol	3-Hydroxybutorphanol, norbutorphanol[a]
Codeine	Codeine,[a] morphine,[a] norcodeine[a]
Dihydrocodeine	Dihydromorphine,[a] nordihydrocodeine,[a] dihydrocodeine[a]
Fentanyl	Despropionylfentanyl, norfentanyl, hydroxyfentanyl, hydroxynorfentanyl
Heroin	6-Acetylmorphine,[a] morphine,[a] normorphine
Hydrocodone	Hydromorphone,[a] norhydrocodone, hydrocodol, hydromorphol[a]
Hydromorphone	Hydromorphol,[a] hydromorphone[a]
Levorphanol	Norlevorphanol,[a] levorphanol[a]
Meperidine	Normeperidine, meperidinic acid,[a] normeperidinic acid[a]
Methadone	EDDP,[a,b] EDMP,[a,c] methadone,[a] methadol, normethadol
Morphine	Morphine,[a] normorphine[a]
Nalbuphine	Nornalbuphine,[a] nalbuphine[a]
Oxycodone	Noroxycodone, oxymorphone,[a] oxycodone[a]
Oxymorphone	6-Oxymorphol,[a] oxymorphone[a]
Pentazocine	Pentazocine,[a] cis- and trans-hydroxypentazocine,[a] trans-carboxypentazocine[a]
Propoxyphene	Norpropoxyphene,[a] dinorpropoxyphene,[a] cyclic dinorpropoxyphene
Tapentadol	Tapentadol,[a] N-desmethyltapentadol
Tramadol	O-Monodesmethyltramadol,[a] N,O-didesmethyltramadol,[a] N-desmethyltramadol

[a]Conjugation occurs prior to elimination
[b]EDDP, 2-ethylidene-1, 5-dimethyl-3, 3-diphenylpyrrolidine; [c]EMDP, 2-ethyl-5-methyl-3, 3-diphenylpyrroline

Representative drugs within each subclass are shown in Fig. 22.3, and the fentalogs, which have attracted widespread attention, are discussed in more detail below.

Fentalogs

The US federal government has taken considerable steps to regulate synthetic opioids and other new psychoactive substances (NPSs) that have

emerged. The Drug Enforcement Administration (DEA) has exercised its emergency scheduling authority to control their use and distribution. In February 2018 the DEA placed fentanyl analogs that were not already regulated by the Controlled Substances Act into Schedule I on a temporary basis. Schedule I substances include those with no currently accepted medical use and high abuse potential. However, licit drugs with approved therapeutic uses (e.g., fentanyl, sufentanil) remain in Schedule II.

The analgesic potency of the fentalogs is considerably greater than that of morphine, ranging from 15-, 100-, and 1,000- to 10,000-fold for alfentanil, fentanyl, sufentanil and carfentanil, respectively. These differences are attributed to structural modifications on the fentanyl scaffold, principally at the N-propionyl group, phenethyl moiety, piperidine ring, and N-phenyl (Fig. 22.4). Chemical structures of selected fentalogs are shown in Fig. 22.5; however due to their transient nature, the analogs of toxicological interest are constantly changing. The structural similarity among fentalogs has advantages and disadvantages from an analytical standpoint. Similarities in structure can be exploited during immunoassay-based screening to detect drug classes (e.g., benzodiazepines, barbiturates), rather than a specific compound. However, structural isomers with the same molecular weight can complicate mass spectrometry-based detection methods, requiring special attention to chromatographic resolution and molecular fragmentation. These issues are discussed later.

Although the pharmacologic and physicochemical properties of the fentalogs are still under investigation, they share much of the lipophilic and basic character of the parent compound. They undergo rapid diffusion through membranes and are widely distributed. Although the subject of ongoing research, fentalog metabolism has both similarities and differences relative to the parent compound. Therefore, much work is needed to fully understand the biotransformation pathways involved for such a large drug subclass. While many analogs undergo predictable N-dealkylation

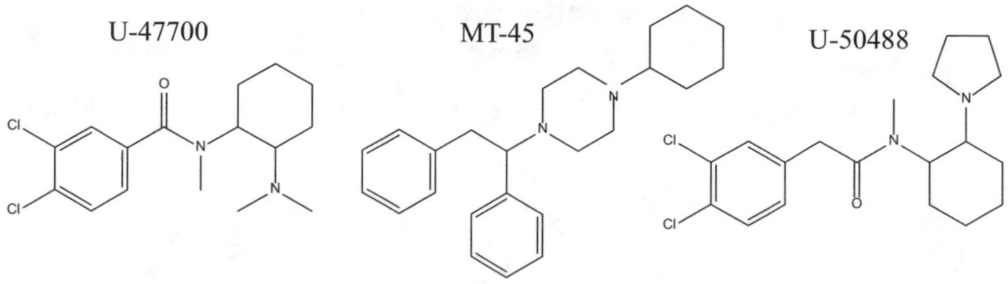

Fig. 22.3 Chemical structures of selected novel synthetic opioids

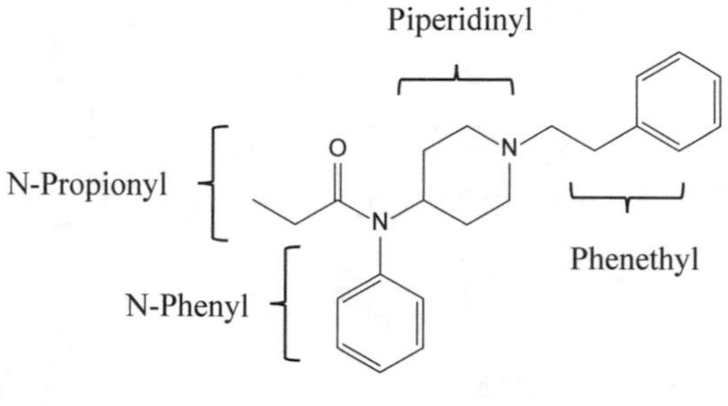

Fig. 22.4 Fentanyl scaffold

reactions, there have been reports of hydroxylation at multiple sites, carboxylation, amide hydrolysis, N-oxidation, and O-dealkylation. There are also variations in cytochrome P450 enzyme involvement in metabolism. While CYP3A4 is the predominant isoform responsible for fentanyl metabolism, 2D6, 3A5, and 2C19 are involved in the metabolic transformations of some of its analogs. To date only the readily accessible ester of remifentanil is metabolized principally by non-CYP enzymes and is most likely hydrolyzed by circulating blood esterases.

Specific Opioids

Buprenorphine

Buprenorphine is a derivative of thebaine that has mixed agonist–antagonist properties. Its high receptor affinity produces prolonged morphine-like analgesia and is used in detoxification and maintenance of opioid dependence. Its long duration of action is due to its slow dissociation from μ receptors. Therefore, reversal of respiratory depression with naloxone is not an effective mea-

sure. Biotransformation occurs via N-dealkylation to form the pharmacologically active metabolite norbuprenorphine, which is subsequently glucuronidated. The drug is eliminated primarily in the feces with only a small amount excreted in the urine and usually is detectable only within 1–3 days of use. Buprenorphine is available in a number of formulations, including transmucosal products, sublingual tablets, and buccal films. Unlike methadone in opioid treatment programs, buprenorphine can be prescribed. The drug is also available in formulations with naloxone, to decrease diversion and misuse. When buprenorphine/naloxone is taken sublingually, the opioid effects of buprenorphine dominate, mitigating opioid withdrawal; if crushed or injected, the naloxone dominates, blocking the euphoric effect. Drug detection is hampered by stability concerns, even in preserved blood. However, the addition of ascorbic acid is reported to improve buprenorphine's overall stability.

Butorphanol

Butorphanol is a synthetic benzomorphan agonist–antagonist that has been used since 1978 to treat pain. A widely used analgesic, butorphanol is absorbed rapidly and effectively via the transnasal route with a bioavailability of 60%–70%, which is several times greater than that of oral administration. Extensive first-pass metabolism occurs primarily by hydroxylation of the cyclobutyl ring and N-demethylation with subsequent conjugation. Approximately 70% of the drug is excreted in the urine within 5 days, 5%–10% of which is excreted within 24 h as the unchanged

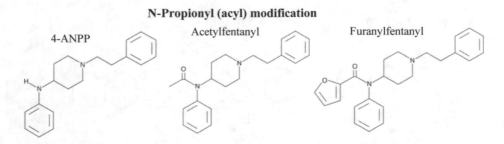

Fig. 22.5 Chemical structures of selected fentalogs

drug. Butorphanol should not be used in opioid-dependent patients who are incompletely detoxified because it can initiate withdrawal symptoms.

Codeine

A semi-synthetic agonist obtained by the methylation of morphine, codeine is a moderately low-potency analgesic that is incorporated into a number of proprietary formulations, including some over-the-counter remedies. It is often used in combination with non-opioid analgesics, such as acetaminophen or aspirin. Illicit synthesis of morphine and heroin from commercially available codeine products has been reported.

Following a typical dose, approximately 10%–20% of the drug is excreted in the urine within 24 h as unchanged codeine. N- and O-demethylation followed by glucuronidation and sulfation are the primary metabolic routes. Approximately 10% of the administered dose is metabolized to morphine, accounting for most of the analgesic effect. Further metabolism can produce the active metabolite morphine-6-glucuronide (M6G), which is more potent than morphine itself. Initially during excretion, codeine conjugates predominate, but morphine conjugates become the major products over a period of 20–40 h. Approximately 3 days after codeine use, the composition of urine metabolites is similar to that of morphine or heroin use; however, the presence of norcodeine in the urine is indicative of codeine use.

Dihydrocodeine

Hydrogenation of codeine in the C7–C8 position yields a semi-synthetic agonist which has increased potency relative to the parent compound. The drug is frequently combined with either aspirin or acetaminophen in pain-relief formulations. The metabolic fate of dihydrocodeine is analogous to codeine, with N- and O-demethylation followed by conjugation being the most likely route. Approximately 20%–60% of the drug is excreted in the urine within 24 h, depending on urinary pH and route of administration, and is principally (30%–45%) excreted in the conjugated form.

Fentanyl and Approved Derivatives

Fentanyl is an extremely fast-acting, potent synthetic agonist that was originally introduced in 1963 as an anesthetic supplement. Despite an increased analgesic potency relative to morphine, it has comparable tolerance and physical dependence liability. Because of their lipophilicity, fentanyl and its derivatives quickly cross the blood–brain barrier, where they have a pronounced effect on the CNS, including severe respiratory depression and heightened euphoria.

Transdermal fentanyl is used for managing chronic pain, although therapeutic concentrations may not be reached for 12–24 h. Transmucosal lozenges, sublingual sprays and tablets, and nasal sprays are also available in addition to injectable formulations. Misuse of this drug among healthcare workers has been a long-standing concern due to its euphoric effects and availability. However, illicit fentanyl use is now more widespread than pharmaceutical diversion.

Rapid metabolism to inactive metabolites takes place in the liver. N-Demethylation accounts for 26%–55% of the total dose, with less than 6% eliminated in the urine as the unchanged drug over 3–4 days. Although a minor urinary metabolite, despropionylfentanyl (4-ANPP) is also encountered as an illicit fentalog precursor.

Several other fentanyl analogs are used in human and veterinary medicine. The naming convention for some of these derivatives is fent-a*nil*, rather than *yl*. Sufentanil, which is used as an analgesic and anesthetic in cardiac surgery, is five to seven times more potent than fentanyl. Alfentanil has a very short duration of action, is less potent than fentanyl, and is reserved for minor surgeries. Remifentanil, an analog approximately 200–300 times more potent than morphine, is also used to control postsurgical pain. Additional derivatives include lofentanil, an analog used in trauma patients with potency 6000 times that of morphine, and carfentanil, an immobilizing agent in veterinary medicine that is 3200-fold more potent than morphine.

Heroin

Diamorphine, also known as heroin, is obtained via the morphine acetylation. Its two acetyl groups allow for better penetration across the blood–brain barrier and result in analgesic potency two to three times that of morphine. Heroin itself is rarely present in body fluids in detectable quantities. With a half-life of only a few minutes, the drug undergoes rapid deacetylation to 6-acetylmorphine (6-AM), which is about four times as potent as morphine. Heroin is different from most other opioids in that it has little or no affinity for opioid receptors. Therefore, the analgesic effects of the drug are attributed to the combined effect of 6-AM, which has a half-life of 0.6 h, and its subsequent biotransformation to morphine. Peak plasma concentrations are achieved within a few minutes of drug administration, and the prolonged duration of its effects is due to its active metabolites.

The presence of 6-AM is conclusive evidence of heroin use, because 6-AM is not a product of either morphine or codeine metabolism; however, it is detectable in urine only up to about 8 h after administration. Approximately 80% of the drug is eliminated in the urine within 24 h, mostly as morphine-3-glucuronide; only about 0.1% is eliminated as the free drug.

The clinical use of diamorphine in the United States is prohibited, although it is used in Canada and the United Kingdom for the management of chronic pain in terminal illness.

Heroin is one of the most pervasive opioids in the illicit market. Heroin produced in clandestine laboratories may contain several related opium alkaloids and synthetic artifacts, including acetylmorphine, acetylcodeine, codeine, papaverine, and morphine, among others. Subsequent adulteration at the street level uses various common diluents, such as sugars, talc, baking soda, flour, or other drugs. The average purity of illicit heroin in the United States depends on the geographic location and can range from <10% to >80%. Death following administration of heroin is typically due to profound respiratory depression, which can be rapidly reversed by naloxone administration.

Hydrocodone

Hydrocodone is a semi-synthetic analgesic agonist derived from codeine. Despite its increased toxicity and addiction liability, it is widely used in cough syrup. Approximately 26% of the drug is excreted in the urine within 72 h, 12% as the unchanged drug. Principally metabolized by demethylation to hydromorphone and reduction of the 6-keto group, the unconjugated metabolites are believed to be pharmacologically active and therefore thought to contribute to the analgesic effect of the drug. Hydromorphol and hydrocodol may be present as stereoisomers of the drug.

Hydromorphone

Hydromorphone, a metabolite of hydrocodone, is a hydrogenated ketone derivative of morphine, and it exhibits increased potency relative to morphine. This semi-synthetic agonist undergoes rapid first-pass metabolism following oral administration, with only about 6% of the unmetabolized drug being excreted in the urine after 24 h. The primary metabolic route is believed to pro-

duce active metabolites via reduction of the 6-keto group and formation of 6α- and 6β-hydroxy derivatives.

Levorphanol

A synthetic analgesic agonist with properties similar to morphine, levorphanol provides increased potency and longer-lasting effects. Data on humans is lacking, but animal studies indicate that levorphanol is metabolized primarily by 3-glucuronidation. Approximately 7% of the drug is eliminated unchanged in the urine of rats.

Meperidine

Meperidine is a synthetic narcotic agonist and is commonly diverted and misused by healthcare professionals. Less potent than morphine, it has a shorter duration of action and is slightly faster-acting. Following oral administration, meperidine is readily absorbed and extensively distributed in the tissue. Only about 7% of the total drug is excreted in the urine unchanged, although this percentage increases with decreasing urinary pH and in women taking oral contraceptives. In addition to the usual N-demethylation and conjugation, de-esterification occurs to produce acidic metabolites. Normeperidine, which is about half as potent as the parent drug, is several times more toxic than meperidine itself and has a longer half-life.

Clandestine production of the meperidine derivative MPPP (1-methyl-4-phenyl-4-propionoxypiperidine) may produce the highly neurotoxic by-product MPTP (1-methyl-4-phenyl-1,2,3,6-tetrahydropyridine), which poses a significant hazard to the drug user.

Methadone

Methadone is a synthetic analgesic agonist that, because of its oral effectiveness and moderately long-lasting effects, is largely used for detoxification and maintenance of individuals with opioid use disorder. Methadone is also used in pain management programs to treat moderate to severe pain. Only the levorotatory isomer is pharmacologically active in small doses. When administered acutely, the duration of analgesia is 3–6 h; however, long-term use can extend the pharmacokinetic and pharmacodynamic profile of methadone to alleviate drug craving over a 24-h dosing interval. It can be administered orally for relief of opioid withdrawal symptoms during detoxification and induction therapy. After initial stabilization, the full treatment dose for maintaining dependent patients is typically 80–120 mg/day. Despite the acute toxicity of methadone, doses of 200 mg/day may be tolerated after prolonged administration (>21 days).

Methadone is rapidly absorbed after oral administration and is widely distributed in the tissue, particularly the liver, lungs, and kidney. Following mono- and di-N-demethylation, cyclization of the unstable intermediates produces the inactive metabolites 2-ethylidene-1,5-dimethyl-3,3-diphenylpyrrolidine (EDDP) and 2-ethyl-5-methyl-3,3-diphenylpyrroline (EMDP). Hydroxylation and glucuronidation occur, but approximately 75% of the drug remains unconjugated. As much as 33% of the drug may be excreted unchanged within 24 h in the urine of a patient receiving methadone maintenance treatment.

Morphine

The principal alkaloid of opium, morphine, is rapidly absorbed after parenteral administration. Considerable first-pass metabolism following oral administration significantly reduces the effectiveness of the drug, which becomes widely distributed, mainly in the kidneys, liver, lungs, and spleen. Major metabolic routes are 3- and 6-glucuronidation and sulfation, N- and O-demethylation, and N-oxide formation. Both morphine-3-glucuronide and normorphine are pharmacologically active metabolites. The analgesic potency of M6G is approximately twice that of morphine. In addition, an equianalgesic dose of M6G instead of morphine has decreased potential for respiratory depression and therefore can be effective in its own right as an analgesic for the management of chronic pain.

Surprisingly, the glucuronidated metabolite has been shown to cross the blood–brain barrier despite its increased polarity. A theoretical explanation for the unexpectedly high lipophilicity of glucuronidated morphine is that intramolecular folding takes place to minimize the surface area of the polar moieties. Another issue is whether the major metabolite morphine-3-glucuronide, which has a very low affinity for opioid receptors, can antagonize the analgesic effect of morphine and therefore have a mechanistic role in the development of tolerance.

Following parenteral administration, up to 90% of morphine is excreted in the urine, and 10% is eliminated in the bile. About 10% is excreted as free morphine, but this fraction increases with decreasing urinary pH. The presence of free or conjugated morphine may also be indicative of either codeine or heroin use, because it is the principal active metabolite of both these drugs.

Nalbuphine

A synthetic opioid of the phenanthrene type, nalbuphine has agonistic and antagonistic properties. As an antagonist, nalbuphine has one quarter the potency of nalorphine and ten times that of pentazocine. It has been successfully used for the treatment of respiratory depression after postsurgical opioid administration. Approximately equivalent to morphine in analgesic potency, nalbuphine acts within 2–15 mins of injection and its effects last 3–6 h. Following N-demethylation and conjugation, approximately 71% of the administered dose is excreted in the urine, with the remainder eliminated in the feces via biliary excretion.

Opium

Opium is a complex mixture of more than 20 alkaloids obtained from the dried exudate of *P. somniferum*. The composition of opium varies from one geographic region to another, but the major constituents are morphine (10%), noscapine (6%), papaverine (1%), codeine (0.5%), and thebaine (0.2%). Replaced by synthetic opioids such as fentanyl and meperidine, opium itself is no longer used medically as an analgesic, but it is used as the starting material for the extraction and purification of other alkaloids. Morphine and codeine are the major active constituents of opium. The remaining components do not produce morphine-like euphoria. Noscapine (narcotine) and papaverine have antitussive and vasodilator properties, respectively, and thebaine is an important reactive starting material for the synthesis of other drugs.

Oxycodone

Frequently used in combination with non-opioid analgesics such as acetaminophen or aspirin, oxycodone is a semi-synthetic opioid agonist derived from thebaine. It is as potent as morphine when administered parenterally but has a higher oral-to-parenteral efficacy ratio. N- and O-demethylation occur, and the latter produces the active metabolite oxymorphone, which contributes to the analgesic potency of the drug. Metabolites undergo glucuronidation before elimination, with 13%–19% typically excreted as the unchanged drug within 24 h of an oral dose.

Oxymorphone

Oxymorphone is a semi-synthetic opiate agonist derived from thebaine. It has an increased analgesic potency relative to morphine and is a metabolite of oxycodone. It is extensively metabolized by conjugation and reduction of the keto group, and only about 2% of the unchanged drug is excreted in the urine after 5 days. It is used therapeutically in a sustained release form; because of

the increased amount of drug in this formulation, nonmedical use employing alternative administration methods has been documented.

Pentazocine

A synthetic benzomorphan derivative with agonist and antagonist activity, pentazocine is used in combination with acetaminophen or aspirin to increase the analgesic effect. Having only about 2% of the potency of nalorphine, pentazocine only weakly antagonizes morphine.

Metabolism of pentazocine principally involves the oxidation of the dimethylallyl group to produce *cis*- and *trans*-hydroxypentazocine; the latter is carboxylated to form *trans*-carboxypentazocine. After an oral dose, up to 13% of the drug may be excreted unchanged in the urine within 24 h; however, the rate of metabolism is variable and may be significantly increased up to 40% in smokers. Administration of pentazocine in combination with tripelennamine produces heroin-like effects that increase the risk of death. Pentazocine can also initiate withdrawal symptoms in opioid-dependent patients.

Propoxyphene

A mild analgesic structurally and pharmacologically similar to methadone, propoxyphene has been used clinically since 1957 and is often formulated with acetaminophen. The dextrorotatory and levorotatory isomeric forms of the drug have different uses—the former as an analgesic, the latter as an antitussive. Propoxyphene napsylate (800–1400 mg/day) has been used successfully for the treatment of opioid withdrawal and maintenance. Following N-demethylation, the active metabolite norpropoxyphene can become harmful, with effects exacerbated by its longer half-life. The drug is rapidly distributed and accumulates in the brain, lungs, liver, and kidneys. Further demethylation and dehydration of dinorpropoxyphene results in cyclization. De-esterification, hydroxylation, and conjugation also occur. Approximately 35% of the total drug is excreted in the urine within 24 h, 5% as the unchanged drug. Cardiotoxicity of the parent drug and its metabolites is a drawback, and there have been a number of fatalities associated with propoxyphene use. As a result, it has been removed from the market in a number of countries.

Tapentadol

Tapentadol is the most recent synthetic opioid to become available; it was approved for use in the United States in 2008. In addition to its μ opioid receptor activity, it is also a norepinephrine reuptake inhibitor. Unlike tramadol, which also exhibits serotonergic activity, tapentadol is more potent and has no pharmacologically active metabolites. It undergoes phase I metabolism by N-demethylation and alkyl hydroxylation. The primary urinary metabolite is tapentadol O-glucuronide.

Tramadol

Tramadol has an analgesic potency similar to that of codeine but with reduced respiratory effects. It is also a serotonin–norepinephrine reuptake inhibitor (SNRI). It is extensively metabolized and is excreted primarily through the kidneys. About 90% of an oral dose is excreted in the urine after 3 days, 30% as the unchanged drug. N- and O-demethylation of the drug are followed by conjugation with glucuronic acid and sulfate. O-Desmethyltramadol is an active metabolite with twice the potency of the parent drug and a longer half-life; it is believed to contribute to the toxicity of the drug.

Analysis

Sample Preparation

Polar opioids and their metabolites tend to undergo conjugation before elimination, so sample pretreatment is often necessary to measure the total amount of drug in a sample. Acid or enzyme hydrolysis with hydrochloric acid, β-glucuronidase, or sulfatase can be used to cleave the conjugate, allowing the "total" opioid concentration to be determined. Caution is needed when chemical hydrolysis is used. Acidic hydrolysis, which is generally faster, has the potential to degrade acid labile drugs (e.g., 6-AM). Enzymatic methods use milder conditions but proceed at a slower rate. Numerous β-glucuronidase and sulfatase preparations are available. Reactions are typically performed at 37°C, although the reaction pH must be optimized for efficient enzymatic activity. *Helix pomatia*, *Patella vulgata*, and *E. coli* (type IX) are among the most common glucuronidases used for this purpose. Some enzyme preparations have both glucuronidase and sulfatase activity, which can be beneficial when phase II metabolites include both sulfates and glucuronides. More recently, recombinant glucuronidases have become available. Some contain highly purified forms and deconjugate opioids in as little as 15 min. Recombinant glucuronidase and sulfatases can significantly improve efficiency if free and total opioid concentrations are required. Deconjugation can be avoided altogether if liquid chromatography (LC)-based techniques are used. As liquid chromatography–mass spectrometry (LC-MS) gains more widespread use, simultaneous identification of free and conjugated drug is possible because LC is amenable to both polar and nonpolar species.

Opioids may be extracted from biological matrices by either liquid–liquid extraction (LLE) or solid-phase extraction (SPE). Organic solvents, such as chloroform modified with 2-propanol, *n*-butanol, or isoamyl alcohol, are commonly used to extract opioids from aqueous mixtures in the pH range of 8–10. Increasing the sample pH prevents ionization of the unconjugated drug, because the pK_a of an opioid's basic nitrogen is about 8. However, since many of the phenanthrenes exist as zwitterions, optimum extraction efficiencies are achieved at the isoelectric pH of the drug (e.g., 8.9 for morphine). This concept is discussed further in Chapter 9. Even at the isoelectric pH, the drug still bears two charges: a negative charge at the phenol and a positive charge at the tertiary amine. Therefore, although the charges are balanced, the molecule itself is more polar. As a result, extraction efficiencies of zwitterionic opioids using liquid–liquid extraction can be compromised.

Solid-phase extraction using a copolymeric bonded phase can be used to adsorb analytes of interest via a combination of hydrophobic and cation-exchange mechanisms. All opioids have strongly basic character. Analytes can usually be isolated after column conditioning and washing steps with mixtures of basic solvents, such as methylene chloride/2-propanol/ammonium hydroxide (volume ratio, 78:20:2). This method generally produces cleaner extracts with fewer interferences than LLE, but it is more expensive.

Screening Techniques

Immunoassays are a common screening technique in forensic toxicology because of their high sample throughput, ease of automation, and lack of sample preparation. A variety of immunochemical tests are available, such as the enzyme-multiplied immunoassay technique (EMIT), kinetic interaction of microparticles in solution (KIMS), cloned enzyme donor immunoassay (CEDIA), fluorescence polarization immunoassay (FPIA), and enzyme-linked immunosorbent assay (ELISA). A variety of manufacturers produce numerous class- and analyte-specific ELISA products for phenanthrene-type drugs, buprenorphine, fentanyl, methadone, meperidine, oxycodone, oxymorphone, propoxyphene, and tramadol. Immunoassay-based screening is discussed further in Chapter 13.

Most opiate immunoassays are not specific. Cross-reactivity among structurally related compounds and various metabolites is common. The overall specificity of the assay is dependent on the antibody reagent's characteristics and the assay methodology. Heterogeneous immunoassay formats may provide fewer nonspecific interferences than their homogeneous counterparts, but the former may take longer to perform. Typically, morphine or M3G is used as the target molecule, but cross-reactions between the antibody and dihydrocodeine, hydrocodone, and hydromorphone commonly occur. Synthetic opioid immunoassays tend to be more specific and undergo fewer cross-reactions; however, methadone immunoassays may cross-react with l-α-acetylmethadol (LAAM), which is a long-acting methadone analog.

The proliferation of novel synthetic opioids, including the fentalogs and others, presents more of a challenge for immunoassay-based approaches. Although commercial ELISAs are available for fentanyl and some fentanyl analogs used clinically (e.g., remifentanil, carfentanil), their cross-reactivity with the broader class of illicit fentalogs is variable. Although some have sufficient cross-reactivity between drugs with structural modifications at either the N-propionyl or piperidine groups, no single immunoassay has proven effective for broad-spectrum fentalog screening. Other approaches include targeting a common metabolite, such as 4-ANPP. However, this approach is also limited by the subset of fentalogs that produce the metabolite. For this reason, mass spectrometry-based screening is increasing in popularity. However, the prevalence of isobaric compounds and structural isomers can complicate identification, particularly for the fentalogs. Challenges due to common precursor ions [M+H$^+$] and fragmentation characteristics in electrospray ionization must be overcome by chromatographic resolution using LC-MS-based screening.

Gas chromatography (GC) coupled with flame ionization, nitrogen–phosphorus, or mass spectrometry (MS) detection is also used by some laboratories for drug screening. Many opioids and their metabolites separate well without derivatization. Blood and urine concentrations for common opioids except buprenorphine and fentanyl analogs are sufficiently high for this approach.

Confirmatory Procedures

The initial screening technique yields only presumptive positive results, which must be confirmed with a highly specific technique. The most frequently used confirmatory methods include GC-MS and LC-MS. These protocols are labor intensive and require sample pretreatment as well as extraction of the drug from the biological matrix prior to analysis. When using LC-MS, approaches to sample preparation are variable and include SPE, LLE, simple dilution, and protein precipitation. The latter approaches are undertaken at the expense of matrix effects, assay performance, and increased instrument maintenance.

GC-MS, GC-MS/MS, and LC-MS/MS techniques are highly effective for opioid detection. Advantages of LC methods include the ability to separate both the free and conjugated drug simultaneously, improved sensitivity, and avoidance of time-consuming derivatization steps.

Opioids with polar functional groups may require derivatization prior to GC-MS analysis to increase volatility and improve chromatography. Although many of the opioids are sufficiently nonpolar, chemical derivatization is necessary for several of the phenanthrene-type opioids (e.g., morphine). Silylation and acylation are among the most common derivatization approaches for opioids and are discussed further in Chapter 12.

Although MS is preferred in most laboratories for opioid detection, electron capture, nitrogen–phosphorus, or flame ionization methods are also used. Detection limits using targeted GC-MS analysis (i.e., selected ion monitoring) are typically between 1 and 25 ng/mL. This may not be sufficient for some opioids, including buprenorphine and potent fentalogs. Targeted LC-MS-based approaches are preferred where low to sub ng/mL concentrations are common.

diagnosis, treatment, and death investigations. Depending on the drug detected, many laboratories will quantify free and total concentrations. Free and total data are particularly useful after overdoses containing morphine. For example, rapid deaths are often characterized by a higher ratio of free morphine to total morphine concentrations because there was less time for metabolism to occur.

The interpretation of opioid-related deaths is often complicated by other findings. These include prior exposure to opioids, potential pharmacologic tolerance, and the presence of other centrally acting drugs, including ethanol. For example, drug concentrations found in opioid-related deaths often overlap with those encountered among living patients. These factors also complicate the interpretation of drug concentrations in cases of impaired driving. Blood concentrations must be interpreted within the context of the case, considering driving performance, observed effects, and the assessment of impairment.

Novel synthetic opioids are now routinely encountered in forensic toxicology investigations. The pharmacology and toxicology of these drugs is still being investigated. Although their effects are mediated principally via μ opioid receptor activity, their potencies vary by orders of magnitude. Their concentration, metabolism, and distribution throughout the body are not fully understood. This is particularly important in postmortem investigations, where postmortem redistribution (PMR) must be considered. Although lipophilic basic drugs can be susceptible to PMR, this phenomenon is influenced by many other factors, including protein binding and site- and time-dependent variables.

Interpretation

Blood

Cases of suspected drug impairment or overdose are frequently investigated for the presence of opioids and their metabolites. The identification of drugs and their metabolites is essential for

Urine

The detection window for morphine and codeine is usually 48 h, but varies according to individual differences in metabolism, excretion, route of administration, and frequency of drug use. Illicit drug use must sometimes be distinguished from inadvertent exposure to opioids through ingestion of certain foodstuffs or prescription medications. A number of opioids, such as codeine, hydromorphone, hydrocodone, and oxycodone, are widely available analgesics and cough medicines that can be misused intentionally or unintentionally. These and other factors may produce results that are difficult to interpret. In some instances, it may not be possible to distinguish between heroin, morphine, and codeine use, particularly if illicit heroin preparations are contaminated with acetylcodeine, which metabolizes to codeine. The presence of morphine alone in the urine can indicate heroin, morphine, and/or poppy seed exposure, whereas detection of codeine with low concentrations of morphine is consistent with codeine use. Unequivocal identification of heroin exposure is indicated by the presence of 6-AM; however, the short urinary half-life of this metabolite may limit the detection time to 2–8 h after exposure.

Poppy seeds may contain morphine and codeine at concentrations of up to 300 µg/g and 5 µg/g, respectively. Therefore, ingestion of poppy seeds may expose the unwitting individual to a significant quantity of opiates. Urinary concentrations of morphine and codeine peak within 2–4 h of ingestion. These opiates may remain detectable for up to 72 h, posing a particular problem for employment or rehabilitation drug-testing programs. Thebaine, which is also present in poppy seeds, has been used as a marker for poppy seed ingestion. After the consumption of certain foods, thebaine was present in the urine at concentrations of 2–81 ng/mL. Because of its short half-life, however, thebaine may be difficult to detect more than 12 h after ingestion. Urine drug screening cutoff concentrations for the workplace have been adjusted to differentiate poppy seed ingestion from opiate ingestion.

Although 85% of an intravenous dose of fentanyl is eliminated in the urine over 3–4 days, only 0.4–6% is excreted as unchanged drug. Norfentanyl is the major urinary metabolite. Novel synthetic opioids present more of a challenge due to the large number of substances, differences in their metabolism, and the limited availability of commercial reference materials for analytical confirmation. With the exception of 4-ANPP, parent drugs are typically targeted for NSO screening. Since 4-ANPP is a common metabolite, its presence can be attributed to several fentalogs.

Other Matrices

Although blood (serum or plasma) and urine are generally the preferred specimens, opioids can be detected in a variety of other matrices. The concentration of opioids in sweat typically accounts for about 1–2% of the total dose administered. Sweat contains mostly the parent opioid and lipophilic metabolites, e.g., heroin and 6-AM following heroin use. Such findings differ from the metabolic profile of heroin in other matrices. For example, oral fluid contains mainly free morphine, while conjugated morphine is prominent in blood and urine.

Though its minimal sample preparation is favorable, oral fluid typically contains low concentrations of drug that decline rapidly. Oral fluid measurements may be used to estimate the amount of circulating drug, but its quantitative significance has not yet been established. Conversely, cerebrospinal fluid concentrations of morphine and M6G have been shown to correlate with those found in blood. Morphine and its conjugates can also be detected in vitreous humor, typically at concentrations lower than those found in either blood or cerebrospinal fluid.

The detection of opioids in hair may provide useful information regarding patterns of drug use over a period of months to years. This method has been applied in employment drug testing, investigation of drug overdoses, and prenatal exposures. Widespread use of hair testing has been hampered by sample preparation requirements and the difficulty interpreting the quantitative significance of results.

Hair tends to accumulate higher concentrations of lipophilic parent drugs rather than polar metabolites. Consequently, hair may be useful for the detection of drugs that are rapidly metabolized, such as heroin. The presence of 6-AM is considered conclusive evidence of heroin use and has successfully been detected in hair, typically at greater concentrations than morphine.

Opioids and other drugs are incorporated into the hair internally via the blood that circulates at the root or externally via contamination, passive deposition, or perspiration. Hair samples, ideally collected from the posterior vertex, should be thoroughly decontaminated, and the washing solutions should be analyzed. After digestion or extraction, opioids are assayed using analytical techniques described previously. Sample preparation methods that involve strong acid or alkali treatment may be unsuitable for the detection of hydrolyzable opioids such as 6-AM.

There is some controversy regarding the substantive value of hair analysis, and whether it should be viewed only in a supportive context. There are still no Federally-mandated cutoff values for hair analysis; however, according to quantitative findings in the literature, a 6-AM cutoff value of 0.5 ng/mg has been suggested as indicative of heroin use.

Suggested Reading

Baselt RC (2020) Disposition of toxic drugs and chemicals in man, 12th edn. Biomedical Publications, Seal Beach, CA

Brunton LL, Knollmann B, Hilal-Dandan R (eds) (2017) Goodman & Gilman's the pharmacological basis of therapeutics, 13th edn. McGraw-Hill, New York

Concheiro-Guisan M, Chesser R, Pardi J, Cooper G (2018) Postmortem toxicology of new synthetic opioids. Frontiers in pharmacology 9:1210

Couper FJ, Logan BK (2004) Drugs and human performance fact sheets. National Highway Traffic Safety Administration, United States Department of Transportation, Washington, DC. DOT HS 809 725

Katzung BG (ed) (2018) Basic and clinical pharmacology, 14th edn. McGraw-Hill, New York

Moffat AC, Osselton MD, Widdop B, Watts J (eds) (2011) Clarke's analysis of drugs and poisons, 4th edn. The Pharmaceutical Press, London

National Forensic Laboratory Information System (NFLIS). n.d. US Drug Enforcement Administration. https://www.nflis.deadiversion.usdoj.gov/NFLISHome.aspx

Nelson LS, Howland MA, Lewin NA, Smith SW, Goldfrank LR, Hoffman RS (eds) (2019) Goldfrank's toxicologic emergencies, 11th edn. McGraw-Hill, New York

Nowlan R, Cohen S (1977) Tolerance to marijuana: heart rate and subjective "high". Clin Pharmacol Ther 22(5 Pt 1):550–556

Prekupec MP, Mansky PA, Baumann MH (2017) Misuse of novel synthetic opioids: A deadly new trend. Journal of addiction medicine 1(4):256–265

Solimini R, Pichini S, Pacifici R, Busardò FP, Giorgetti R (2018) Pharmacotoxicology of non-fentanyl derived new synthetic opioids. Frontiers in Pharmacology 20(9):654

Cocaine

23

Daniel S. Isenschmid

Abstract

Cocaine is one of the most popular drugs of abuse and is considered to be the most abused major stimulant in the United States. It is classified by the Drug Enforcement Administration as a Schedule 2 drug because it may be used medicinally as a topical local anesthetic. Unlike other local anesthetics, cocaine has additional actions, including its ability to block reuptake of the neurotransmitters norepinephrine, dopamine (DA), and serotonin (5-HT). Norepinephrine is responsible for the classic adrenergic effects seen with cocaine use, while the desirable effects are mediated primarily by DA. Cocaine is well absorbed by intravenous, intranasal, and smoking routes of administration, but the time course and extent of absorption differ among them. Cocaine contains two ester moieties that are hydrolyzed in vitro and in vivo. The alkyl ester of cocaine is hydrolyzed to benzoylecgonine via spontaneous hydrolysis as well as liver methylesterases, and the phenyl ester is hydrolyzed to ecgonine methyl ester by plasma cholinesterase and liver benzoylesterases. Combined use of ethanol and cocaine causes the production of cocaethylene. Cocaine use can produce impairment consistent with its pharmacologic effects. Cocaine can also account for death by a number of mechanisms, including excited delirium, cardiac arrhythmias, and overstimulation of the central nervous system.

Keywords

Cocaine · Toxicology · Pharmacology · Analysis · Interpretation

Introduction

History

Cocaine is an alkaloid found in *Erythroxylum coca*, which grows principally in the northern South American Andes. The plant favors higher elevations (up to 6000 feet) because at lower elevations (below 1500 feet), the alkaloid content is significantly diminished because of more rapid growth. Coca leaves may be harvested about 2 years after planting. Then, depending on the altitude, the leaves may be harvested up to three times a year. The leaves are dried and converted into a coca paste made by macerating coca leaves in an organic solvent and sulfuric acid. Further treatment of coca paste with hydrochloric acid

D. S. Isenschmid (✉)
NMS Labs, Horsham 19044, PA, USA
e-mail: dan.isenschmid@nmslabs.com

B. S. Levine, S. Kerrigan (eds.), *Principles of Forensic Toxicology*,
https://doi.org/10.1007/978-3-030-42917-1_23

yields cocaine hydrochloride. The yield from 100 kg of coca leaves is about 1 kg of coca paste or 800 g of cocaine hydrochloride.

Cocaine is a psychotropic drug that has been used for 2000 years. The Incas of Peru chewed the leaves of the coca plant in their religious ceremonies. Later, during the Spanish conquest, the Spaniards found that the Peruvian Indians could not perform their heavy labor in the mines when deprived of the plant. Today, coca leaves (containing about 0.7% to 1.5% of total alkaloids) are still used by the indigenous populations of the high Andes, who chew them mixed with lime to cope with the rigors of life at high altitude.

In the mid-nineteenth century, Carl Wöhler, the chemist who synthesized urea, had coca leaves imported to Germany and presented them to his graduate student, Albert Niemann, to analyze. Niemann was the first to successfully isolate cocaine from the coca plant. From the 1860s through the turn of the century, cocaine appeared in various elixirs and tonics purported to have "magic" properties. Some of the more famous preparations included Vin Mariani, a mixture of wine and cocaine, and the original Coca-Cola® recipe developed by John Pemberton.

The Italian physician Paolo Mantegazza was the first to spark interest in the medicinal uses of cocaine. Several papers had been written in the 1870s about cocaine's potential use for treating morphine addiction, but not until Sigmund Freud popularized the drug in his famous 1884 treatise "Über Coca" did it become well known in the scientific community. In 1884, Carl Koller became the first physician to use cocaine as a topical anesthetic in ophthalmologic surgery. It was popularly reported to be a wonder drug that would satiate the hungry, give strength to the fatigued, and cause people to forget their misfortune.

Despite numerous early reports of cocaine toxicity, including cardiac arrhythmias and fatalities, cocaine-containing products became ever more popular. By 1903, the Coca-Cola Company agreed to use (solely as a flavoring agent) only coca leaves from which cocaine had been removed. In 1914, as cocaine abuse began to be viewed as a problem, the drug was labeled a narcotic (albeit incorrectly) under the Harrison Narcotic Act, and over-the-counter sales were discontinued. In 1970, under the Controlled Substances Act, cocaine was scheduled as a drug with some medicinal value but with a high potential for abuse (Schedule II). It continues to have some medical use, which is almost exclusively limited to topical administration as a local anesthetic in ear, nose, and throat surgery (as the hydrochloride salt in 10–20% solutions) and in ophthalmologic procedures (as a 1–4% solution). The usual maximum recommended dose for intranasal local anesthesia is 100–200 mg (1–2 mL of 10% solution). Older preparations of cocaine include tetracaine, adrenaline, and cocaine (TAC), a topical anesthetic solution used in suturing extremity wounds, in which cocaine was included because of its rapid onset of action. Topical adrenaline-and-cocaine gel is still sometimes used in pediatrics for anesthetizing children's lacerations. Cocaine is one of the most popular drugs of abuse and is considered to be the most abused major stimulant in the United States exceeding methamphetamine nationally, although the predominance of one drug over the other depends on regional differences. It has acquired numerous street names including bazooka, blow, coke, crack, dust, flake, gold dust, happy dust, lady, nose, nose candy, rock, snow, speedball (when mixed with heroin and injected), stardust, tick (when smoked with phencyclidine), toot, and white. In a 2016 National Survey on Drug Use and Health, it was reported that 14.4% of the surveyed US population between the age of 12 and 17 have used cocaine in their lifetimes, and 16.6% of those over the age of 26 used cocaine at least once. The greatest mention of lifetime use was for the 55–59 age group at 26.4% reflecting the popularity of the drug back in the 1980s and 1990s. Despite this, recent reports show that cocaine-related deaths in 2015 was the highest since 2006 according to the Substance Abuse and Mental Health Services Administration and first time use from 2013 to 2015 increased 61%. The increase in use has been correlated to the increase in cocaine trafficking and cultivation. Cocaine also is frequently seen in combinations with fentanyl and/or heroin in seized drug exhibits.

Cocaine is sold on the street in two forms: the hydrochloride salt and crack. The salt varies considerably in purity. It can be as low as 30%, but recently, exhibits have shown the purity to be much higher, in some cases exceeding 90% with greater than 80% typical. Historically, the salt form is typically diluted ("cut") with agents such as mannitol, lactose, and sucrose to add bulk. In addition, readily available central nervous system stimulants such as caffeine and ephedrine and other local anesthetics such as lidocaine, procaine, and benzocaine had been commonly used as diluents to simulate the actual drug. More recently, diphenhydramine and levamisole have been reported as cutting agents, the latter having been described widely in the literature to cause severe deleterious effects including agranulocytosis and vasculitis. The cocaine powder supplied by dealers is often clumpy and first needs to be chopped. This is usually done using a mirror and a razor blade. Then the cocaine is arranged into thin lines about 30–60 mm long and 2 mm wide (resulting in an average dose of 25 mg) and then snorted through a straw or "tooter." Alternatively, cocaine may be snorted from a "coke spoon" or "bullet" (a vial containing cocaine is inverted over a closed chamber and the chamber is rotated for convenient snorting). A single long fingernail may serve as a natural coke spoon. Alkaloidal cocaine base, known as *free base*, is made by dissolving cocaine hydrochloride salt in an aqueous alkaline solution and then extracting the free basic form with a solvent such as ether. "Crack" is a free base form of cocaine produced by using sodium bicarbonate to create the alkaline aqueous solution, the extract of which is then dried by heating (the name coming from the "crackling" sound made by the heated extract). After heating, the mixture is cooled and filtered, and the free-base cocaine precipitates into small pellets or "rocks." A typical "rock" weighs about 20 mg and costs US$5.00. These "rocks" can then be smoked in a crack pipe. Crack pipes range from elaborate glass pipes to a soda can with a hole. The heat generated from these pipes can be very high, and chronic crack users may show stigmata of thermal injuries on the fingers.

Chemistry

Cocaine (methylbenzoylecgonine), an ester of benzoic acid and the amino alcohol methylecgonine, which contains a tropine moiety, is chemically but not pharmacologically related to atropine. The ecgonine portion of the molecule has four chiral carbon atoms and can exist as four racemates (eight optically active isomers).

Cocaine is structurally different from other local anesthetics by virtue of its tropine moiety. However, like other local anesthetics, cocaine consists of a hydrophobic region and a hydrophilic region. The hydrophobic region contains a benzene ring, whereas the hydrophilic region consists of a secondary or tertiary amine. Cocaine is also similar to other local anesthetics in that it contains ester linkages which allow the body to hydrolyze and deactivate the drug. The ester group is also susceptible to in vitro hydrolysis.

Pharmacology

Effects and Toxicity

Cocaine is used medicinally as a topical local anesthetic. Clinically, its most important mechanism of action lies in its ability to block initiation and conduction of nerve impulses by decreasing axonal membrane permeability to sodium ions in fast sodium channels and thereby increase the threshold required to generate an action potential. Cocaine has additional actions, however, that make it unique among local anesthetics, including its ability to block reuptake of the neurotransmitters norepinephrine, dopamine (DA), and serotonin (5-HT). Norepinephrine is responsible for the classic adrenergic effects seen with cocaine use, including mydriasis, vasoconstriction, hypertension, and tachycardia. The desirable effects of cocaine, mediated primarily by DA, include intense euphoria, psychic energy, heightened sexual excitement, and self-confidence (elevation of mood). Potential undesirable effects include paranoia, hallucinations, and dysphoria.

After an acute dose of cocaine, brain concentrations of DA increase briefly and then decrease markedly to below normal concentrations, corresponding to the central stimulatory effects ("rush") and depression ("crash") that the cocaine user experiences. Cocaine prevents the reuptake of DA into the presynaptic dopaminergic neuron by binding to receptors on the DA transporter located on the dopaminergic nerve terminal. This DA reuptake, which is mediated by sodium, chloride, and energy-dependent active transport, is inhibited when cocaine binds to the sodium-binding site on the transporter and alters the chloride-binding site, thus preventing the binding of both ions. Because translocation of DA across the membrane of the presynaptic neuron is inhibited, increased extracellular DA concentrations chronically stimulate the DA receptor in the postsynaptic neuron.

For equivalent plasma cocaine concentrations and DA transporter blockade, smoked cocaine induces significantly greater self-reports of "high" than intranasal (IN) cocaine and shows a trend for a greater effect than intravenous (IV) cocaine. Such reports and the fact that the time to reach peak subjective effects is significantly faster for smoked cocaine (1.4 min) than for IV cocaine (3.1 min) and IN cocaine (14.6 min) demonstrate the importance of speed of cocaine delivery into the brain for its reinforcing effects.

Chronic cocaine administration alters the DA transporter in the mesolimbic regions of the brain. Increased densities in the DA transporter have been observed postmortem in the brains of cocaine abusers and in vivo in acutely abstinent cocaine users. Upregulation of cocaine-binding sites in the brain produces a need for additional cocaine to continue experiencing its rewarding effects. Chronic cocaine users repeatedly administer cocaine, increasing the synaptic levels of DA. This process becomes cyclical and demonstrates how a cocaine binge or "run" is followed by a crash and why the temptation to self-medicate is so strong.

Cocaine-excited delirium, which is associated with hyperthermia, delirium, agitation, cardiorespiratory arrest, and sudden death, may be due to an inability of the DA transporter to upregulate as it does in most chronic cocaine users. In these individuals, increased densities of DA receptors are not observed, and the lack of increased receptor sites has been postulated to produce insufficient DA reuptake, leading to excessive DA concentrations in the synapse. The extreme hyperthermia in these individuals may be related to the observed downregulation in DA-2 receptors in the hypothalamus, which are responsible for decreasing body temperature. DA-1 receptors, which are responsible for increasing the body temperature, are not affected. Individuals with a high body mass index appear to be at highest risk because they generate the most heat through skeletal muscle activity. Cocaine also binds to the 5-HT transporter and inhibits 5-HT reuptake. Acutely, 5-HT would be expected to partially antagonize the stimulatory effects of cocaine in the naive user (this expectation was the basis for investigating the use of 5-HT reuptake inhibitors for the treatment of cocaine dependence). Withdrawal from cocaine after chronic use produces a decrease in synaptic 5-HT concentrations by altering the function of the presynaptic 5-HT receptor that controls the amount of 5-HT available for release. Alterations in the sensitivity of postsynaptic receptors to 5-HT also occur. These alterations have been implicated in the depression and craving seen after cocaine withdrawal.

Repeated doses of cocaine have been shown to produce both diminished effects (tolerance) and increased effects (sensitization). Acute tolerance to cocaine typically occurs during a binge in which the users dose themselves repeatedly, leading to an acute depletion of DA and a diminished response. Sensitization tolerance, or reverse tolerance, typically occurs with chronic cocaine use and longer dosing intervals and does not appear to be related to brain catecholamine concentrations. Such observations support theories that sensitization to cocaine may occur via changes to receptors that make them more sensitive to cocaine or its action at other receptors.

The most common clinical manifestations following acute cocaine intoxication include profound central nervous system stimulation, with psychosis and repeated grand mal convulsions, ventricular arrhythmias, respiratory dysfunction with Cheyne–Stokes breathing, and, ultimately, respiratory paralysis. Other symptoms include mydriasis, hypertension leading to hypotension, and small-muscle twitching. The ability of cocaine to cause increased muscular activity and vasoconstriction may produce extreme hyperthermia. The patient may also lapse into a coma.

Symptoms of chronic cocaine use, other than psychiatric disturbances, include rhinitis (with possible nasal septum perforation), shortness of breath, cold sweats, tremors, violent protective behavior, distorted perception, tachycardia, tachypnea, dyspnea, and hyperkinetic behavior. The drug can injure cerebral arteries, and an acute hypertensive episode following a single dose in a chronic user can cause cerebral vessels to rupture. Acute myocardial infarctions have occurred after even therapeutic doses of cocaine. Chronic cocaine use accelerates the development of atherosclerosis and can also cause aortic dissection, myocarditis, and cardiomyopathy which are frequent findings at autopsies in chronic cocaine abusers. Cardiovascular toxicity resulting from cocaine use may be related to individual sensitivity and therefore may not be predictable on the basis of dose, route of administration, or underlying heart disease.

In a 2015 review of cocaine-related deaths from medical examiner and coroner data, the mean and median age of the decedents was 42 ($N = 3151$). The common sequelae associated with chronic cocaine in patients over the age of 30 include heart disease, myocardial infarction, and exacerbation of chronic disease, strokes, and renal failure. Cocaine use is often associated with violence. This may be due to violent acts caused by the pharmacological effects of cocaine (psychopharmacological model), violent interactions resulting from involvement with an expensive but illicit commodity (systemic model), and violence as an instrumental act to obtain resources to purchase/obtain cocaine (economic-compulsive model). A large percentage of homicide cases are cocaine related. In 1990–1991, 31.3% of homicide cases were positive for cocaine and/or benzoylecgonine in New York City. Detroit reported a 28% positive rate for the parent drug in blood of homicide victims in 2000.

Pharmacokinetics

Absorption

Cocaine is well absorbed from all routes of administration, but the time course and extent of absorption differ among them. The intravenous (IV) route of administration, sometimes called "mainlining," is the only route that consistently produces 100% drug bioavailability. The bioavailability of cocaine by insufflation (IN) or smoked (SM) administration is quite variable; however, the convenience of these two routes of administration and the latter's rapid, intense onset of effects make them the most commonly used.

The time course for the high in humans parallels that of the cocaine concentration in the striatum, a region in the brain implicated in control of motivation and reward. For equivalent plasma cocaine concentrations and DA transporter blockade, SM cocaine induced significantly greater self-reports of "high" than IN cocaine and showed a trend for greater effect than IV cocaine. After either IV or SM administration, the subjective euphoric response occurs in 1–5 min, with a cardiovascular response peaking in 8–12 min and lasting approximately 30 min. After IN administration, a euphoric effect occurs within 15–30 min, cardiovascular changes and plasma concentrations peak within 20–60 min, and effects last several hours but the euphoric effects are attenuated compared to the SM route despite the extended effects.

Metabolism

Cocaine contains two ester moieties, rendering it susceptible to hydrolysis in vitro and in vivo. The alkyl ester of cocaine is hydrolyzed to benzoylecgonine via spontaneous hydrolysis as well as liver methylesterases, and the phenyl ester is hydrolyzed to ecgonine methyl ester by plasma cholinesterase and liver benzoylesterases (Fig. 23.1). Benzoylecgonine and ecgonine methyl ester are both further metabolized to ecgonine which is infrequently analyzed but has

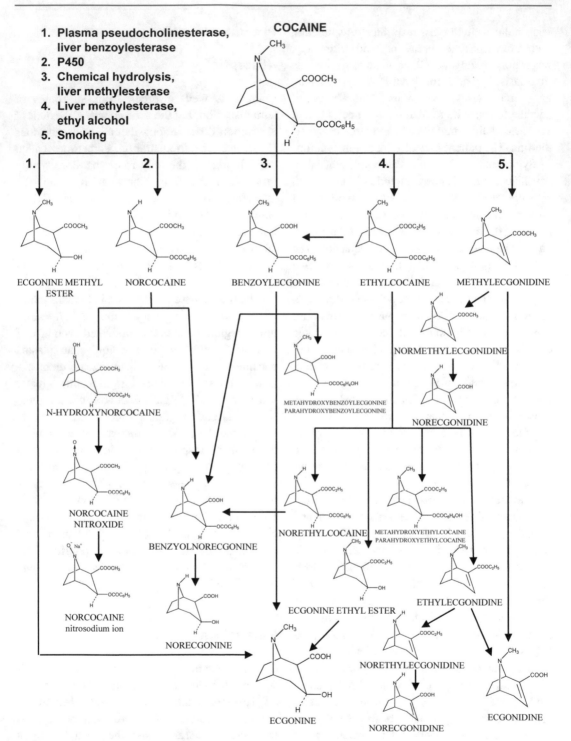

1. **Plasma pseudocholinesterase, liver benzoylesterase**
2. **P450**
3. **Chemical hydrolysis, liver methylesterase**
4. **Liver methylesterase, ethyl alcohol**
5. **Smoking**

Fig. 23.1 Pathways in the metabolism of cocaine

been reported to be a useful marker of cocaine use, especially in urine. If cocaine is used with ethanol, cocaethylene (or ethylcocaine), pro-duced by the transesterification of cocaine with ethanol, may also be observed. Unlike benzoy-lecgonine and ecgonine methyl ester which are inactive metabolites, cocaethylene is an active compound that has been shown to produce even greater euphoria than cocaine itself. The conversion of cocaine to cocaethylene occurs about 3.5 times faster than the conversion of cocaine to benzoylecgonine, thereby potentially increasing the toxicity of cocaine when used with ethanol. Other minor metabolites of cocaine include nor-cocaine, hydroxylated metabolites, and methylecgonidine, which has been associated primarily with smoked crack cocaine as a thermal decomposition product. Methylecgonidine is further metabolized to ecgonidine which may be a more useful indicator of crack smoking. When smoking cocaine and using ethanol, ethylecgonidine may be produced.

Plasma Concentrations

Many pharmacokinetic studies have been performed with cocaine. Although considerable interindividual variation between subjects has been reported, several observations can be made. When bioequivalent doses of cocaine were administered by the IV and SM routes, similar absorption and elimination curves for cocaine were obtained with dose-related mean peak plasma concentrations. After IN administration, the dose and mean peak plasma concentration showed a poor correlation due to dose-dependent bioavailability by that route. Typical peak plasma cocaine concentrations in most single-dose pharmacokinetic studies by the SM (up to 100 mg), IV (up to 64 mg), and IN (up to 100 mg) averaged between 200 and 400 ng/mL.

For IV and SM routes, the average half-life for cocaine, based on the literature, is about 60 min with a somewhat longer half-life after IN administration (up to 84 min). Benzoylecgonine appears in the plasma within 15–30 min following cocaine administration by the IV, SM, and IN routes of administration. Peak plasma benzoylecgonine concentrations usually occurred within 90 min after SM and IV cocaine administration and were about half the peak cocaine concentrations. After IN administration of cocaine, peak benzoylecgonine concentrations were not reached until 3 h and were about twice that of

cocaine and remained elevated for the next 5 h. The rate of benzoylecgonine elimination was slow compared to its rate of formation, accounting for its accumulation in plasma, while cocaine concentrations were decreasing. The elimination half-life for benzoylecgonine was between 5 and 6 h after IV and SM administration and about 3.5 h after IN administration. Ecgonine methyl ester concentrations are usually much lower than those of benzoylecgonine but are present at significant concentrations after oral cocaine administration, suggesting a possible first pass effect of liver benzoylesterase for this metabolite. Ecgonine methyl ester may also form in vitro in blood collected without or with insufficient sodium fluoride preservative as an inhibitor of plasma cholinesterase.

When cocaine is co-administered with ethanol, the appearance of cocaethylene in the blood is delayed by 10–30 min. Mean peak plasma cocaine concentrations were higher when human subjects were given 100 mg of cocaine HCl IN followed by 1 gm/kg of vodka (352 ng/mL) than after 100 mg of cocaine IN alone (258 ng/mL). The mean peak cocaethylene concentration in the subjects receiving both ethanol and cocaine was 55 ng/mL. The average half-life of cocaethylene based on various reports is about 120 min (range 100–148 min). The altered pharmacokinetics in simultaneous cocaine and ethanol use may contribute to increased risk of toxicity.

Excretion

Cocaine and its metabolites are excreted into the urine almost exclusively by simple filtration. Thus, the urinary excretion rates and plasma concentrations of cocaine and benzoylecgonine parallel one another, indicating that the elimination rate of the drug is proportional to the plasma concentration. After a single cocaine dose, 64–69% is recovered in the urine within 3 days, regardless of the route of administration, and 86% of this amount is recovered within the first day. Only a small fraction of an administered dose of cocaine is excreted as parent drug with a majority of the metabolites detected as benzoylecgonine (26–54%) and ecgonine methyl ester (18–41%).

Postmortem data suggest that with chronic use, cocaine concentrations in the urine are much higher than would be expected on the basis of pharmacokinetic data. Urine concentrations of ecgonine, initially thought to be a minor urinary metabolite, have been shown to significantly exceed those of benzoylecgonine in certain situations. In 104 of 139 urine samples in which ecgonine was present at ≥ 50 ng/mL, the mean ecgonine concentration was approximately five times the comparable benzoylecgonine concentration. On the basis of the benzoylecgonine concentrations, this scenario appears to be most likely during the late stages of urinary excretion of a cocaine dose. No pharmacokinetic studies have yet measured this metabolite, however, and its presence may be due to hydrolysis of benzoylecgonine and/or ecgonine methyl ester.

Direct Methods of Analysis

Immunoassay

Immunoassays are commonly used for screening purposes because they are readily amenable to large-batch analysis, are relatively sensitive, and require little or no sample preparation. Because immunoassays are targeted to detect benzoylecgonine, they are particularly well suited for screening urine samples. Several types of immunoassays are on the market; depending on the product selected, immunoassays use the principle of enzyme immunoassay (EIA), microparticle immunoassay (KIMS), cloned enzyme donor immunoassay (CEDIA), or enzyme-linked immunosorbent assay (ELISA). Although all immunoassay techniques are targeted to benzoylecgonine, cross-reactivities to cocaine and other metabolites vary considerably by manufacturer and analytical principle. Immunoassays that possess substantial cross-reactivity to cocaine are particularly useful for screening oral fluid, hair, and postmortem blood, where significant concentrations of the parent drug might be found. Depending on the immunoassay selected, analysis of postmortem blood and tissue homogenates may be performed directly or after protein precipitation and/or solvent extraction.

ELISA is especially well suited to postmortem analyses of whole blood because these assays generally do not require any sample preparation other than dilution. These assays can also be used successfully with tissue homogenates. Although the cutoff concentration for benzoylecgonine in US federal workplace drug testing is 150 ng/mL, most immunoassays can reliably detect far lower concentrations. Immunoassay-based approaches are discussed in more detail in Chap. 13.

Indirect Methods of Analysis

Sample Preparation

Before cocaine and its metabolites can be analyzed with chromatographic techniques, the drugs generally must be separated from the biological matrix. This may be accomplished using a variety of techniques such as liquid–liquid extraction, solid-phase extraction (SPE), and solid-phase microextraction procedures. These are explored in more detail in Chap. 9. SPE and solid-phase microextraction can be readily adapted to laboratory-automation devices. Several important issues must be considered before choosing an extraction procedure, however. Cocaine and many of its metabolites are esters that are susceptible to hydrolysis under alkaline conditions and at high temperatures. In addition, plasma and liver esterases contribute to their hydrolysis. In unpreserved specimens, this should be considered. During sample preparation, the amount of time the biological sample remains in conditions unfavorable for cocaine stability must be minimized; otherwise, esters may hydrolyze in vitro and complicate the interpretation of the analytical results (see "Interpretation of Results"). For this reason, isotopically labelled internal standards are often favored. Consideration must also be given to the targeted analytes because the polarities of cocaine and its metabolites vary considerably.

Other than stability concerns, extraction of cocaine and cocaethylene is straightforward. These compounds are readily extracted into n-butyl chloride at pH 8–9. A chloroform–2-

propanol mixture (9:1) is also commonly used. These conditions will also extract benzoylecgonine and ecgonine methyl ester, although not with optimal recoveries. SPE procedures, also used for these analytes, commonly use a protein-precipitation step before applying the buffered supernatant to the extraction column. Elution is typically accomplished with a strongly basic organic solvent (e.g., methylene chloride, 2-propanol, and ammonium hydroxide, 78:20:2). Methodologies for SPE and the different chromatographic supports are discussed in Chap. 9. This approach works well for cocaine and the majority of metabolites of interest (benzoylecgonine, cocaethylene, ecgonine methyl ester). Extraction of the most polar analyte, ecgonine, presents a unique challenge. Because it is both a carboxylic acid and an alcohol, it extracts poorly using conventional approaches.

Thin-Layer Chromatography

Thin-layer chromatography (TLC) is a simple technique that can be used to analyze for both cocaine and benzoylecgonine, but its lack of sensitivity generally limits it to the analysis of urine or bile samples, if it is used at all. Due to a lack of specificity for forensic purposes, it is rarely used today.

Gas Chromatography

Gas chromatography (GC) was the sample introduction technique most frequently used for the analysis of cocaine and its metabolites until use of liquid chromatography (LC) techniques became more frequently employed. Cocaine and cocaethylene can be readily assayed without derivatization by means of nitrogen–phosphorus detection and by mass spectrometry (MS) detection in both the electron ionization and positive chemical ionization modes. Detection by flame ionization may also be used but is not as sensitive. Ecgonine methyl ester and related compounds can be detected without derivatization but tend to tail on most analytical columns because

of free hydroxyl moieties. Benzoylecgonine and related compounds must be derivatized prior to analysis. For this reason, in addition to greater sensitivity, LC has largely replaced GC for sample introduction.

When GC is utilized, various derivatization procedures have been used. Acylation procedures (e.g., pentafluoro) and silylation (e.g., trimethyl-silyl) derivatize both benzoylecgonine and ecgonine methyl ester. Alkylation procedures (e.g., n-propyl) will derivatize N-desmethyl metabolites in addition to benzoylecgonine. Sequential derivatization allows the simultaneous detection of multiple analytes. For example, ecgonine, ecgonine methyl ester, benzoylecgonine, and norcocaine can be derivatized with 1-propyl iodide followed by p-nitrobenzoyl chloride to yield p-nitro-n-propylcocaine, p-nitrococaine, n-propylcocaine, and N-propylcocaine, respectively. Derivatization techniques are explored in more detail in Chap. 12.

If GC analysis is performed, detection by MS provides the highest degree of specificity of all GC detectors and is virtually a requirement for forensic confirmation of cocaine and its metabolites. A particular advantage with MS detection is that isotopically labelled analogues of cocaine and its metabolites are available for use as internal standards permitting excellent reproducibility and accurate analysis. If other detectors are used, the selection of internal standards should be carefully considered so that they undergo the same chemistry as the analyte.

Liquid Chromatography and Others

Liquid chromatography (LC) has become the most frequent sample introduction technique for the analysis of cocaine and its metabolites due to the need for minimal sample preparation, no need for derivatization, a variety of extremely sensitive and specific detectors, and the ability to use isotopically labeled internal standards. The use of MS and MS/MS detectors along with high resolution MS detectors has created many new approaches for the analysis of xenobiotics including cocaine and metabolites and has resulted in the virtual elimination older LC-based detectors, such as ultraviolet and diode array detectors.

The newest techniques using MS detectors bypass LC chromatographic sample introduction altogether using ionization sources such as laser diode thermal desorption (LDTD) and matrix-assisted laser desorption/ionization (MALDI) high-resolution mass spectrometry (HRMS). These techniques result in much shorter analysis times, less sample preparation, and the potential for applications to nonstandard matrices. The main disadvantage for the moment is cost.

Interpretation of Results

Pathology

Many pathologic conditions may predispose an individual to cocaine toxicity that may cause death at cocaine concentrations lower than expected. The diagnosis of such conditions will ultimately affect toxicological interpretation. Chronic cocaine use may also contribute to the development of pathologic conditions that may cause sudden death. Excellent texts on the pathology of drug abuse are available, so only the most important conditions will be considered here.

A significant number of deaths have been associated with a cocaine-induced psychosis now commonly known as cocaine-induced excited or agitated delirium. This syndrome is characterized by severe hyperthermia (104° F–108° F), extreme agitation and delirium, respiratory arrest, and sudden death. These individuals exhibit bizarre and violent behavior and extreme strength, and they frequently can be seen running around—sometimes naked—shouting, fighting, breaking things, and causing injury to themselves and others. Death may occur from these injuries, but death more frequently occurs suddenly after agitation has ceased. Unfortunately, the police have usually intervened by this time, and the restrained individual then dies in police custody. At autopsy, minor injuries, especially head injuries that may occur during attempts to restrain an individual, may lead to overinterpretation and litigation. Other autopsy findings are relatively nonspecific,

but cardiomegaly is a consistent finding. In these cases, the stress from restraint may produce catecholamine surges on an already sensitized myocardium, producing a terminal arrhythmia. The use of Tasers to try to subdue these individuals further complicates interpretation. In a multiyear review of 75 Taser-related deaths, cardiovascular disease was found in 54.1% of the cases with available autopsy reports. Illegal substances were found in 78.4% of the cases, of which 86.2% involved stimulant drugs and 75.7% had a diagnosis of excited delirium. In 27% of the cases, the use of a Taser was considered a potential or contributory cause of death. This topic remains very controversial, however.

In noncustody excited-delirium cases, decedents are frequently found in places where they may have attempted to cool themselves, such as the bathroom. Other evidence of attempts at cooling (e.g., wet towels and ice cube trays) may also be present at the scene. Toxicology results in excited-delirium cases have demonstrated cocaine-to-benzoylecgonine ratios similar to those found for other accidental deaths due to cocaine toxicity. A large percentage of excited-delirium victims die after they have survived 1–12 h. When the survival time is <6 h, cases featuring high cocaine concentrations also tend to have high benzoylecgonine concentrations, and cases with low cocaine concentrations tend to have low benzoylecgonine concentrations. Because the half-life of benzoylecgonine exceeds that of cocaine, these findings suggest that the development of excited delirium is associated with binge cocaine use.

Although chronic cocaine use may produce toxicity in a variety of organ systems, cardiovascular diseases are most commonly associated with sudden death due to cocaine. Coronary artery disease with or without myocardial infarction, myocardial diseases including myocarditis, hypertrophy, dilated cardiomyopathy, and contraction band necrosis due to catecholamine toxicity, valvular heart disease, and aortic dissection have all been attributed to complications of cocaine abuse. Unfortunately, few features distinguish cocaine-induced disease from naturally occurring pathology. Neurologic disorders have frequently been associated with chronic cocaine use and may be related to sensitization. Subarachnoid and intracerebral hemorrhages, berry aneurysms, cerebral infarction, and cocaine-induced seizures have all been reported in addition to cocaine-induced excited delirium. At autopsy, chronic cocaine users have a statistically significant decrease in body mass index compared with nonusers, an observation consistent with cocaine's anorectic properties. Interestingly, cocaine users who die after cocaine-induced excited delirium tend to have a high body mass index. Physical signs of cocaine or drug use are also important (e.g., puncture wounds, needle tracks, a perforated nasal septum, evidence of seizures such as lip bites, and drug paraphernalia at the scene or with the individual).

Occasionally, it may be possible to attribute cocaine toxicity or death to "body packing." Body packers may try transporting cocaine by swallowing a cocaine-filled condom (or other container) or concealing it rectally or vaginally. These containers have occasionally ruptured, releasing a large dose of the drug. Blood cocaine concentrations in postmortem cases are usually huge, sometimes >100,000 ng/mL, making interpretation straightforward.

Blood

Many factors must be considered when interpreting cocaine and metabolite concentrations in the blood. Adult (single) doses of cocaine, whether for medical or abuse purposes, are typically in the range of up to 100 mg producing a plasma or blood concentration of 200–400 ng/mL. Toxic doses are highly variable, depending on degree of individual tolerance, route of administration, presence of other drugs, and other factors. In simultaneous ethyl alcohol and cocaine users, cocaethylene concentrations should also be considered when interpreting results. Plasma cocaine concentrations >1000 ng/mL have been reported without adverse effects in some studies after chronic oral dosing and after repeated doses of smoked cocaine. Concentrations of >5000 ng/mL

have generally only been reported in fatal cases, although concentrations in fatalities are usually much lower.

A search of the literature suggests that cocaine concentrations of <300 ng/mL are generally considered clinically therapeutic; however, clinical and postmortem studies have clearly shown that therapeutic, toxic, and lethal cocaine concentrations overlap. Tolerance and sensitization may play a significant role in the poor correlation observed. In a study of 130 patients who presented to an emergency room with acute cocaine toxicity, the mean plasma cocaine concentration was 340 ng/mL (range, 0.00–3920 ng/mL). The median cocaine concentration in these patients was only 70 ng/mL; however, the mean and median benzoylecgonine concentrations in these patients were 1570 ng/mL and 1060 ng/mL, respectively. There was no correlation of the cocaine and metabolite concentrations in these patients with their clinical state or outcome, but the degree of symptoms of toxicity—most notably hyperthermia, heart rate, and psychosis—was a better predictor of patient outcome.

Given that cocaine is typically used in a binge of multiple doses over the course of many hours, blood concentrations of cocaine and its metabolites are usually not useful for estimating the dose or time of administration. Because the half-life of benzoylecgonine is considerably longer than that of cocaine, one would expect benzoylecgonine concentrations to increase out of proportion to the cocaine concentration during a cocaine binge. High blood benzoylecgonine concentrations with significant cocaine concentrations (>100 ng/mL) may indicate binge cocaine use, whereas similar cocaine and benzoylecgonine concentrations are more typical of a recent single dose or multiple doses within a very short period of time.

As previously discussed, cocaine stability after collection and during analysis may create analytical artifacts that may alter interpretation of the results. Blood samples collected in the hospital, in particular, are usually collected in containers without preservative and may not have been stored in refrigerated conditions. In unpreserved blood, in vitro stability studies have shown that cocaine is hydrolyzed almost exclusively at the phenyl ester by plasma pseudocholinesterase to yield ecgonine methyl ester. The rates of hydrolysis of both esters have been shown to be temperature and pH dependent, with higher temperatures and pH increasing the rate of hydrolysis. The loss of cocaine in unpreserved blood can be dramatic with 50% losses in a matter of hours at room temperature. Ideally blood samples should be preserved with 1–2% sodium fluoride w/v. Many fluoridated gray-top tubes do not contain sufficient sodium fluoridate for adequate long-term preservation. Additionally, while sodium fluoride minimizes pseudocholinesterase-mediated hydrolysis to ecgonine methyl ester, it does not prevent pH and temperature-dependent conversion of cocaine to benzoylecgonine, so refrigeration or freezing of preserved samples is still recommended.

For postmortem cases, heart blood should be collected only during the autopsy to ensure that the hypodermic syringe is aspirating blood directly from the heart. If no autopsy is performed, only peripheral blood should be collected because samples collected by "blind stick" are prone to contamination. In addition, trauma may yield contaminated blood samples. Ideally, both peripheral blood and heart blood should be collected.

Ultimately, history and investigation, laboratory findings, witness reports and field sobriety tests or drug recognition expert evaluations for human performance cases, clinical presentations, or autopsy results must all be considered together because any factor taken out of context may produce an incorrect interpretation.

Urine

Most clinical tests for cocaine, whether for hospital drug testing or workplace drug testing, are performed on urine using immunoassays. These drug screens are designed to detect benzoylecgonine. Benzoylecgonine cutoffs on urine toxicology screens under the US federal drug testing program are 150 ng/mL with a 100 ng/mL confirmation cutoff. Hospital toxicology screens may use different cutoff concentrations.

Urine is suitable only for determining an exposure to cocaine. Quantitative measurements of benzoylecgonine (especially if corrected for creatinine) in serial urine samples may be useful in substance-abuse treatment programs to detect a relapse during a period of abstinence, but single samples cannot be similarly interpreted because only a randomly collected urine sample is typically analyzed. Benzoylecgonine is typically detected for as long as 1–3 days after a single use; however, chronic cocaine use can increase this significantly. Prolonged positive immunoassay results for 5–10 days have been reported after compulsive cocaine use, with continuous positive results for up to 16 days with a longer terminal half-life after chronic, heavy cocaine use. With chronic and/or binge cocaine use, urine benzoylecgonine concentrations can exceed 100,000 ng/mL, while low-dose, single-use concentrations are much lower.

Issues concerning the stability of benzoylecgonine have been raised, particularly with regard to retesting a sample previously reported as positive. Benzoylecgonine, although relatively stable in urine when frozen, is susceptible to hydrolysis in alkaline conditions and at higher temperatures. An additional concern is that cocaine in urine can hydrolyze to benzoylecgonine in alkaline conditions and higher temperatures.

In human performance and pediatric exposure testing, issues are frequently raised regarding unknowing exposure or ingestion of cocaine. Passive exposure to cocaine smoke under extreme conditions can produce detectable benzoylecgonine in urine but at concentrations below the threshold used in workplace drug testing. If testing at lower concentrations, data should be interpreted carefully. Another issue often raised is that cocaine ingestion was unknowing because the cocaine had been added to a beverage. Studies have been performed with ingestion of coca-containing teas from South America and cocaine-fortified beverages. These studies demonstrate that very small amounts of cocaine (<5.0 mg or about one-fifth of a typical IN dose or line) added to or contained in a beverage are sufficient to produce a positive result in a drug test for cocaine metabolites in urine in an unsuspecting individual. In such cases, the detection of unique cocaine metabolites, such as methylecgonidine or ecgonidine, which are produced after smoking crack cocaine, may prove to be useful for refuting alleged oral ingestion of cocaine after a positive drug-test result for benzoylecgonine.

Concern has also been raised regarding passive exposure to cocaine in personnel who come in frequent contact with the drug. The issue of dermal exposure to cocaine has been investigated in several studies, all of which demonstrated that with appropriate personal protective equipment, casual exposure to cocaine is not likely to produce a benzoylecgonine concentration greater than the 150 ng/mL US federal workplace drug-testing cutoff concentration.

Tissues

Brain may be a useful specimen for the measurement of cocaine and its metabolites because cocaine is relatively stable in the brain and is not subject to postmortem redistribution. Because cocaine rapidly crosses the blood–brain barrier, brain cocaine concentrations in cases of acute cocaine intoxication have been shown to be much higher than concentrations in the blood. In addition, because benzoylecgonine probably does not cross the blood–brain barrier, the presence of this metabolite in the brain has been attributed to cocaine that entered the brain. Thus, the brain may be particularly helpful in estimating the pattern of cocaine use before death. In a study of 34 acute cocaine deaths, the mean brain-to-blood ratio of cocaine concentration was 9.6 (median ratio, 3.8), compared with a mean ratio of 2.5 in 14 incidental cases in which both analytes could be detected. Cocaine was also detected in the brain in 11 incidental cases in which only benzoylecgonine was detected in the blood. The mean cocaine-to-benzoylecgonine ratio was also higher in the brain than in the blood, both in acute cases (14.7 vs 0.64) and in incidental cases (0.87 vs 0.27). These observations have been replicated in other studies. The main disadvantage of the brain is the difficulty of working with fatty homogenates, although SPE technology has simplified sample handling to some degree.

Other tissues may be useful when biological fluids are not available, but they do not provide additional interpretive information. In the few cases studied, kidney and spleen have been found to have the highest cocaine concentrations.

Hair

Cocaine and metabolites may be detectable in hair for longer periods of time than urine. For this reason, analysis of hair may be useful in determining a past history of cocaine use. It takes 4–5 days for ingested cocaine to begin to appear in the hair. The ability to detect cocaine in hair is based more on the concentration than on a pharmacologic "time window," because as long as the hair is not cut, the incorporated drug will remain in it. However, the utility of hair is limited to obtaining historical information about drug use and is not useful for determining an acute use, such as in post-accident testing. As such, hair testing may be extremely useful in postmortem cases in which no other specimen is available. Hair has even been used to identify cocaine use in ancient Peruvian mummies.

Although appropriate forensic methodologies exist for the analysis of cocaine and metabolites in hair, their use for employment-related drug testing is controversial because of a lack of the data required for accurately interpreting the results. Still under study are many important issues related to hair testing, including environmental contamination, washing techniques, racial bias in hair due to the concentration of certain types of melanin, sex bias, sample adulteration, quality-control procedures, proficiency testing, and the establishment of cutoff concentrations.

The primary analyte detected in hair after cocaine use is the parent cocaine, but to minimize environmental-contamination issues and to demonstrate cocaine ingestion, the proposed guidelines for hair testing in federal workplace drug-testing programs require a benzoylecgonine/cocaine ratio of ≥ 0.1 in the confirmatory testing process in order to report a positive result. Still, some studies suggest that benzoylecgonine arises primarily from hydrolysis of cocaine in hair, not from biological incorporation. Other possible target analytes in hair for demonstrating in vivo cocaine use include norcocaine and cocaethylene.

Oral Fluid

Oral fluid may be a useful specimen for detecting recent cocaine use in human performance and workplace drug testing. There is generally a good correlation between saliva and plasma cocaine concentrations. Saliva cocaine concentrations have also been correlated to behavioral effects. In addition, saliva may be collected by direct observation without any invasive procedure.

Appropriate sample-collection procedures are critical for minimizing contamination from the oral cavity, especially after SM and IN administration. The use of benzoylecgonine as a target analyte in workplace testing should help minimize this issue. Despite cocaine being the predominant analyte in saliva after acute cocaine use, benzoylecgonine is detected more frequently and at higher concentrations than cocaine after cessation of chronic cocaine use. Detection times for benzoylecgonine after chronic oral cocaine administration were comparable for saliva and plasma (45 h vs 47 h, respectively; cutoff, 10 ng/mL) but were far less than for urine, which had a mean *minimum* detection time of 165 h for the same low cutoff concentration. On the other hand, cocaine could be detected for nearly twice as long in saliva than in plasma (15 h vs 9 h; cutoff, 10 ng/mL). The saliva/plasma cocaine ratio can also be affected by saliva pH and saliva flow rate after stimulation. For this reason, it is important to develop standardized collection protocols.

Sweat

Sweat may be a useful, noninvasive specimen for monitoring drug use. Sweat may be collected by means of a collection patch placed on the skin for a predetermined period. This collection procedure allows a continuous period of monitoring or accumulation of any excreted drug. In sweat, cocaine is excreted primarily as the parent drug, offering the added advantage of simple GC analysis. Depending on the device used to collect sweat, any attempt at tampering with the collection device would be evident. Although wearing a sweat patch for monitoring cocaine use may provide a wider detection window than for urine, any correlation between the accumulated sweat cocaine concentration with the degree of impairment or time of use is not likely. Because trace amounts of cocaine can be detected in sweat after IV administration of as little as 1 mg cocaine, some concerns regarding passive exposure have been raised.

Effect of Cocaine on Driving

Apart from the effects of cocaine, driving performance entails many factors that may affect driving, including coordination skills, reaction time, risk-taking, emotional state (e.g., anger, fear, stress, hostility), personality style (relaxed, tense, aggressive), fatigue, physical and mental health, and distractions (radio, cell phone, smoking, thoughts, conversation, children). Whether a crash could have been prevented in the absence of a drug(s) given the inherent driving performance variables is difficult to determine.

Relatively few scientific studies have evaluated the effects of cocaine on driving performance. The euphoric effects of cocaine during acute intoxication may give a driver the feeling of increased mental and physical abilities, and this optimism has been suggested to prompt increased risk-taking behavior and perhaps increase the probability of crashes, particularly in conjunction with ethyl alcohol use. In one study, 62% of cocaine smokers reported symptoms of suspiciousness, distrust, and paranoia. These effects have led to high-speed chases with police. It is not surprising that the use of stimulants has also been associated with road rage.

These findings appear consistent with an examination of 253 motor vehicle fatalities that occurred in metropolitan Detroit (Wayne County, Michigan) over a 3-year period. Cocaine and/or its metabolites were detected in the blood of 25 (10%) of these cases. An analysis of the histories confirmed that aggressive driving (as determined by high speed and loss of control) was the most common finding in all of the crashes and occurred in all but three cases. Ethyl alcohol was detected in 14 of the 25 cases, ten of which were also positive for parent cocaine and/or cocaethylene in the blood, confirming the high incidence of acute combined cocaine and ethanol use. However, although high-risk driving appeared to be associated with cocaine use (with or without ethyl alcohol), fault is more likely to occur when ethyl alcohol is present, indicating that alcohol may play a larger role in crash occurrence than cocaine. This fact is consistent with other studies that compared crash responsibility with drug and alcohol use and may be related to the combined effects of a stimulant drug with a drug that depressed inhibitions. There was no evidence to suggest that the concentration of cocaine and its metabolites was related to crash occurrence.

In a study of more than 25,000 drivers in Sweden arrested for driving under the influence of drugs, 795 were positive for cocaine and/or benzoylecgonine in the blood (in the absence of alcohol). In the 20 cases with the highest cocaine concentrations in the blood, drivers were observed to be driving dangerously, including weaving, speeding, and ignoring red lights. Typical findings reported by police officers included increased pupil diameters, bloodshot eyes, agitation, difficulty standing or sitting, incoherent speech, and increased pulse rate. However, a review of 44 reports by drug-recognition experts in cocaine-related driving-under-the-influence cases in Washington state showed that although increased pupil diameter (especially in a dark room) and pulse rate were frequently observed, the magnitude of these changes did not appear to be related to cocaine concentration.

The ability of cocaine to produce mydriasis appears to have significant effects in self-reported observations. After IN cocaine use, 43% of individuals reported increased sensitivity to light, halos around bright objects, and difficulty focusing. More than 34% of cocaine smokers reported blurred vision, often accompanied by glare-recovery problems. Hallucinations were reported by 50% of cocaine smokers and 18% of IN users.

"Snow lights," flashes or movements of light in the peripheral field of vision, were the most commonly reported hallucination. Reaction to snow lights included moving in their direction or trying to avoid or evade them.

When self-reported driving behaviors were compared for individuals in treatment for cocaine or cannabis abuse, individuals reported reckless driving 29.7% of the time when driving under the influence of cocaine, compared with only 2.4% of the time when driving under the influence of cannabis. Conversely, individuals driving under the influence of cannabis reported that they were more likely to attempt to drive carefully or cautiously (27.9%) than when driving under the influence of cocaine (11.8%).

Because the effects of cocaine are brief, the crash that follows cocaine use may be a particularly dangerous time for driving; however, samples collected from individuals in such a state may be positive only for cocaine metabolites, making assessment difficult. The presence of cocaine metabolites suggests past use and cannot be used to determine impairment or withdrawal without additional information, such as witnessed driving and/or observations by a trained drug-recognition expert. This is particularly the case when only a urine sample is available. Of 150 individuals arrested for reckless driving and who tested negative for alcohol, 13% tested positive for cocaine metabolites, 33% were positive for cannabinoids, and 12% were positive for cannabinoids and cocaine metabolites in the urine. Nearly half of the drivers testing positive for prior cocaine use performed normally on field-sobriety tests, including two individuals who were stopped for driving directly into oncoming traffic. Of those testing positive for cocaine, 21% were sleepy or slow; 39% were happy, carefree, and talkative; and 39% were combative, argumentative, and paranoid.

Double-blind laboratory studies have demonstrated that low doses of cocaine may actually improve driving performance and counteract some of the performance decrements of ethyl alcohol and other depressant drugs. In a study of more than 4000 individuals, an increased risk of injury was associated with the use of psychoactive substances, but the risk was lower when cocaine was used with other depressant drugs. Although stimulants (amphetamines or cocaine) may acutely enhance performance of simple tasks, this enhancement may disappear as the complexity of the task increases. For example, cocaine-induced hyperexcitability has led to rapid steering or braking reactions in response to sudden sounds, such as horns or sirens.

The current data suggest that it is very difficult to predict driving impairment on the basis of the presence of cocaine and or its metabolites in biological samples alone. Witnessed driving behavior and examination by a drug-recognition examiner, coupled with laboratory studies, is the triad that appears most appropriate for determining driving impairment.

Further Reading

Ambre J (1985) The urinary excretion of cocaine and metabolites in humans: A kinetic analysis of published data. J Anal Toxicol 9:241–245

Ambre J, Ruo T, Nelson J, Belknap B (1988) Urinary excretion of cocaine, benzoylecgonine, and ecgonine methyl ester in humans. J Anal Toxicol 12:301–306

Barnett G, Hawks R, Resnick R (1981) Cocaine pharmacokinetics in humans. J Ethnopharmacol 3:353–366

Baselt RC, Chang R (1987) Urinary excretion of cocaine and benzoylecgonine following oral ingestion in a single subject. J Anal Toxicol 11:81–82

Bertol E, Trigano C, Di Milia MG, Di Padua M, Mari F (2008) Cocaine-related deaths: An enigma still under investigation. Forensic Sci Int 176:121–123

Blaho K, Logan B, Winbery S, Park L, Schwilke E (2000) Blood cocaine and metabolite concentrations, clinical findings, and outcome of patients presenting to an ED. *Am J Emerg Med* 18:593–598

Brogan WC, Lange RA, Glamann DB, Hillis RD (1992) Recurrent coronary vasoconstriction caused by intranasal cocaine: Possible role for metabolites. Ann Intern Med 116:557–561

Brookoff D, Cook CS, Williams C, Mann CS (1994) Testing reckless drivers for cocaine and marijuana. N Engl J Med 331:518–522

Brzezinski MR, Abraham TL, Stone CL, Dean RA, Bosron WF (1994) Purification and characterization of a human liver cocaine carboxylesterase that catalyzes the production of benzoylecgonine and the formation of ethylcocaine from ethanol and cocaine. *Biochem Pharmacol* 48:1747

Byck R (1987) The effects of cocaine on complex performance in humans. Alcohol Drug Driving 3:9–12

Clouet D, Asghar K, Brown R (eds) (1988) Mechanisms of cocaine abuse and toxicity. Department of Health and Human Services, National Institute on Drug Abuse research monograph nr 88. Rockville, MD

Cone EJ (1995) Pharmacokinetics and pharmacodynamics of cocaine. J Anal Toxicol 19:459–478

Cone EJ, Yousefnejad D, Hillsgrove MJ, Holicky B, Darwin WD (1995) Passive inhalation of cocaine. J Anal Toxicol 19:399–411

Dean RA, Christian CD, Sample RHB, Bosron WF (1991) Human liver cocaine esterases: Ethanol-mediated formation of ethylcocaine. FASEB J 5:2735–2739

Ellenhorn M, Barceloux D (eds) (1988) Medical toxicology. Elsevier, New York

Grabowki J (ed) (1984) Cocaine: Pharmacology, effects and treatment of abuse. Department of Health and Human Services, National Institute on Drug Abuse research monograph nr 50. Rockville, MD

Hornbeck CL, Barton KM, Czarny RJ (1995) Urine concentrations of ecgonine from specimens with low benzoylecgonine levels using a new ecgonine assay. J Anal Toxicol 19:133–138

Isenschmid DS (2002) Cocaine: Effects on human performance and behavior. Forensic Sci Rev 14:61–100

Isenschmid DS, Levine BS, Caplan YH (1989) A comprehensive study of the stability of cocaine and its metabolites. J Anal Toxicol 13:250–256

Isenschmid DS, Fischman MW, Foltin RW, Caplan YH (1992) Concentration of cocaine and metabolites in plasma of humans following intravenous administration and smoking of cocaine. J Anal Toxicol 16:311–314

Isenschmid DS, Hepler BR, Kanluen, S (2001) Patterns in drugs of abuse deaths in metropolitan Detroit. Presentation – American Academy of Forensic Sciences, Seattle, WA. Updated data.

Jackson GF, Saady JJ, Poklis A (1991) Urinary excretion of benzoylecgonine following ingestion of Health Inca Tea. Forensic Sci Int 49:57–64

Jatlow PI (1988) Cocaine: Analysis, pharmacokinetics and metabolic disposition. *Yale J Biol Med* 61:105

Jones AW, Holmgren A, Kugelberg FC (2008) Concentrations of cocaine and its major metabolite benzoylecgonine in blood samples from apprehended drivers in Sweden. Forensic Sci Int 177:133–139

Jufer RA, Walsh SL, Cone EJ (1998) Cocaine and metabolite concentrations in plasma during repeated oral administration: Development of a human laboratory model of chronic cocaine use. J Anal Toxicol 22:435–444

Jufer RA, Wstadik A, Walsh SL, Levine BS, Cone EJ (2000) Elimination of cocaine and metabolites in plasma, saliva, and urine following repeated oral administration to human volunteers. J Anal Toxicol 24:467–477

Karch S (1997) A brief history of cocaine. CRC Press, Boca Raton, FL

Karch S (ed) (2002) The pathology of drug abuse, 3rd edn. CRC Press, Boca Raton, FL

Karch S (ed) (2007) Drug abuse handbook, 2nd edn. CRC Press, Boca Raton, FL

Klette KL, Poch GK, Czarny R, Lau CO (2000) Simultaneous GC/MS analysis of meta- and para-hydroxybenzoylecgonine and norbenzoylecgonine: A secondary method to corroborate cocaine ingestion using nonhydrolytic metabolites. J Anal Toxicol 24:482–488

Kump D, Matulka R, Edinboro L, Poklis A, Holsapple M (1994) Disposition of cocaine and norcocaine in blood and tissues of B6C3F1 Mice. J Anal Toxicol 18:342–345

Logan BK (1998) Considerations when trying to determine the role of cocaine in death. Presentation – California Association of Toxicologists Quarterly Meeting, San Francisco, CA, February 1998.

Logan BK (2002) CNS stimulants. Is the driver impaired by drugs? Can blood drug concentrations and DRE evaluation answer this question? Workshop nr 27. American Academy of Forensic Sciences Annual Meeting, Atlanta, GA, American Academy of Forensic Sciences.

Logan BK, Peterson KL (1994) The origin and significance of ecgonine methyl ester in blood samples. J Anal Toxicol 18:124–125

Logan BK, Smirnow D, Gullberg RG (1997) Lack of predictable site-dependent differences and time-dependent changes in postmortem concentrations of cocaine, benzoylecgonine, and cocaethylene in humans. J Anal Toxicol 20:23–31

Logan BK, Blaho K, Mandrell T, Berryman HE, Goff ME, Goldberger BA, et al. (1998) Effects of death and decomposition on concentrations of cocaine and metabolites in juvenile swine [abstract]. American Academy of Forensic Sciences Annual Meeting, San Francisco, CA, American Academy of Forensic Sciences. Abstract nr K54.

MacDonald S, Mann R, Chipman M, Pakula B, Erickson P, Hathaway A, MacIntyre P (2008) Driving behavior under the influence of cannabis or cocaine. Traffic Inj Prev 9:190–194

Majewska M (ed) (1996) Neurotoxicity and neuropathology associated with cocaine abuse. Department of Health and Human Services, National Institute on Drug Abuse research monograph nr 163. Rockville, MD

McCane-Katz EF, Kosten TR, Jatlow P (1998) Concurrent use of cocaine and ethanol is more potent and potentially more toxic than use of either alone – a multiple dose study. *Biol Pharmacol* 44:250

Rapaka R, Chiang N, Martin B (eds) (1997) Pharmacokinetics, metabolism, and pharmaccutics of drugs of abuse. Department of Health and Human Services, National Institute on Drug Abuse research monograph nr 173. Rockville, MD

Regidor E, Barrio G, de la Fuente L, Rodriguez C (1996) Non-fatal injuries and the use of psychoactive drugs among young adults in Spain. Drug Alcohol Depend 40:249–259

Romberg RW, Past MR (1994) Reanalysis of forensic urine specimens containing benzoylecgonine and THC-COOH. J Forensic Sci 39:479–485

Saady JJ, Bowman ER, Aceto MD (1995) Cocaine, ecgonine methyl ester, and benzoylecgonine plasma profiles in rhesus monkeys. J Anal Toxicol 19:571–575

Siegel RK (1978) Cocaine hallucinations. Am J Psychiatry 135:309–314

Siegel RK (1982) Cocaine smoking. J Psychoactive Drugs 14:271–359

Siegel RK (1987) Cocaine use and driving behavior. Alcohol Drugs Driving 3:1–8

Smirnow D, Logan BK (1996) Analysis of ecgonine and other cocaine biotransformation products in postmortem whole blood by protein precipitation-extractive alkylation and GC-MS. J Anal Toxicol 20:463–467

Spiehler VR, Reed D (1985) Brain concentrations of cocaine and benzoylecgonine in fatal cases. J Forensic Sci 30:1003–1011

Stewart DJ, Inaba T, Tang BK, Kalow W (1977) Hydrolysis of cocaine in human plasma by cholinesterase. *Life Sci* 20:1557

Stewart DJ, Inaba T, Lucassen M, Kalow W (1979) Cocaine metabolism: Cocaine and norcocaine hydrolysis by liver and serum esterases. *Clin Pharmacol Ther* 25:464

Strote J, Range HH (2006) Taser use in restraint-related deaths. Prehosp Emerg Care 10:447–450

Substance Abuse and Mental Health Services Administration (2016) https://www.samhsa.gov/data/sites/default/files/NSDUHmrbSampleExperience2016.pdf

Cannabis

24

Marilyn A. Huestis

Abstract

In the past 35 years, scientists discovered the endogenous cannabinoid system that mediates critical human physiological functions including planning and control of movement, emotional behavior, cognitive function, cardiovascular responses, pain, feeding, and reward. Long-term adverse effects occur to the developing brain when cannabis is used during pregnancy and during breastfeeding and when adolescents begin intake before the age of 17. The most critical short-term adverse effects are driving impairment and decreased perception of risk by young adults. This chapter reviews the chemistry, mechanisms of action, pharmacodynamics, pharmacokinetics, and the development of cannabinoid tolerance. Also included are methods for analysis and expected cannabinoid concentrations in blood, urine, oral fluid, sweat, breath, and hair. Use of synthetic cannabinoids, potent cannabinoid receptor agonists, can lead to driving impairment, drug dependence, and death.

M. A. Huestis (✉)
Institute on Emerging Health Professions, Thomas Jefferson University, Philadelphia, PA, USA

Keywords

Cannabis · Toxicology · Pharmacology · Effects · Analysis · Impairment · Interpretation

Introduction

Cannabis (marijuana), hashish, sinsemilla, dabs, wax, and edibles are psychoactive products of the *Cannabis sativa* plant ingested for its euphoric effects for over 4000 years. Cannabis is self-administered for its mood-altering properties, is dependence producing, and is characterized by reversible psychological impairment. Individuals can also develop tolerance to cannabis after frequent use for an extended period and may experience an abstinence syndrome after cessation of chronic frequent drug use. A mixture of depressant and stimulant effects occurs at low doses, and cannabis is a central nervous system (CNS) depressant at high doses. Cannabinoids share effects with other psychoactive drugs yet have a distinct pattern of effects distinguishing this unique pharmacologic drug class.

Interest in the therapeutic effects of cannabis grew as cannabinoid pharmacology advanced over the last 30 years. There is great potential for cannabinoid pharmacotherapies, as the abnormalities in the endogenous cannabinoid system play an important role in the pathology of many diseases, as well as offering new mechanisms of action and interventions for patients with unmet clinical needs. In National Academies of Sciences, Engineering, and Medicine 2017, the National Academies of Sciences, Engineering, and Medicine published an important document on the results of an extensive literature search on the "Health effects of cannabis and cannabinoids (January 2017)." All of the available research on the safety and effectiveness of cannabinoids to treat a wide variety of diseases was evaluated and a determination made on whether the research adequately or inadequately supported the use of cannabinoids to treat the illness. Except for a few indications, e.g., chronic pain, uncontrolled seizures, and sleep, the conclusion was that additional research was critically needed. However, throughout the United States, legalized cannabis for recreational use and medical cannabis for therapeutics were approved in 11 states, with some form of medical cannabis available in all but four states. This trend follows changes to legalize cannabis in Uruguay first and Canada second. These changes resulted in increased cannabis exposure at all ages with consequential exposure to the developing brain in utero, during breastfeeding, passive exposure in the home when parents smoke cannabis, and, of course, during adolescence when self-administration may begin. There are long-term consequences that accompany exposure in the young, most critically with nerve connections in the developing brain. It is clear that the endogenous cannabinoid system, which consists of cannabinoid neurotransmitters, receptors, metabolic enzymes, and transporters, plays a critical role in physiological and behavioral processes and that cannabis ingestion disrupts normal biological functions.

Cannabis is also the most commonly abused drug in the world, the drug with the highest prevalence in cases involving driving under the influence of drugs, and the source of more positive results in workplace drug tests than any other drug of abuse. For these reasons, it is essential that toxicologists understand cannabis' cognitive, physiological, biochemical, and behavioral effects, as well as the disposition of the drug and its metabolites in biological fluids and tissues.

Chemistry

Cannabis preparations include loose cannabis, kilobricks (the classic Mexican-produced material), buds, sinsemilla, Thai sticks, hashish (cannabis resin), and hash oil. Butane and other solvent extractions of cannabis produce wax characterized by high tetrahydrocannabinol (THC) concentrations reaching 80–90% and contain dangerous residual solvents that are particularly harmful to the lung and liver. A wide variety of edible cannabinoids are available as well, many leading to accidental ingestions by children due to their bright and colorful packaging and an increase in emergency room admissions of children and adults due to a lack of understanding of the pharmacokinetics and doses of oral cannabis products.

Δ^9-Tetrahydrocannabinol (THC), the primary psychoactive analyte, is found in the plant's flowering or fruity tops, leaves, and resin. The various parts of the plant differ in their chemical composition. Sinsemilla, a seedless and more potent form of cannabis produced from the unfertilized flowering tops of female cannabis plants, first appeared in 1977 and is usually produced in the United States. Figure 24.1 shows the structure of THC, its active and inactive metabolites, the enzymes responsible for its metabolism, and minor cannabinoids cannabinol (CBN) and cannabidiol (CBD). About 95% of the THC in cannabis is a mixture of monocarboxylic acids that readily decarboxylate upon heating. It was originally believed that a person who orally ingested cannabis without heating would absorb little THC but that if one heated the cannabis prior to ingestion, e.g., baked in marijuana brownies, significant quantities of THC would become available. Later research demonstrated that an individual also can absorb THC from cannabis that was dried in the sun because decarboxylation releases variable amounts of THC.

Cannabis contains >500 different chemicals, including >109 cannabinoids, nitrogenous compounds, amino acids, hydrocarbons, sugars, terpenes, and simple and fatty acids. Pyrolysis of the drug during smoking yields >2000 compounds, including those that contribute to cannabis'

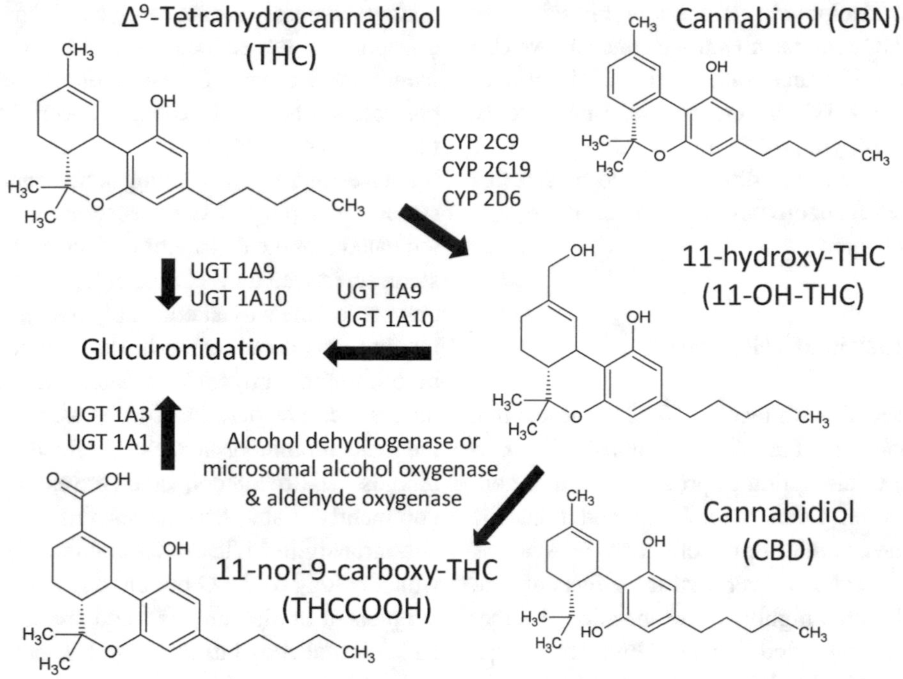

Fig. 24.1 Major metabolic routes for Δ⁹-tetrahydrocannabinol (THC), the primary psychoactive component of cannabis, its equipotent metabolite 11-hydroxy-THC (11-OH-THC), and its primary inactive metabolite, 11-nor-9-carboxy-THC (THCCOOH). Also note phase II glucuronidation pathways, enzymes responsible for phase I and II pathways, and minor cannabis plant cannabinoids, cannabinol (CBN) and cannabidiol (CBD)

known pharmacologic and toxicologic properties. CBD was the first cannabinoid other than THC to become an FDA-approved cannabinoid pharmacotherapy (Fig. 24.1). CBD was shown to significantly reduce the number of seizures in children with Dravet and Lennox-Gastaut syndromes. Cannabis that contains less than 0.3% THC was recently approved by the US Congress as legal hemp. CBD oils and tinctures are ubiquitous now in the United States, with no FDA oversight and little to no efficacy data for the dozens of proposed illnesses that are claimed to be cured by cannabidiol. Other cannabinoids include CBN (Fig. 24.1), which is approximately 10% as psychoactive as THC, cannabigerol (CBG), tetrahydrocannabivarin, and many more. There also is great interest in the therapeutic potential of the terpenes and flavonoids present in cannabis.

THC decomposes when exposed to air, heat, or light; exposure to acid can oxidize the compound to CBN. CBN is essentially a chemical-degradation product, and its relative abundance increases as samples age. The ratios of these unique cannabinoids depend on the age of the sample, its geographic origin, and the plant strain. The potency of a preparation is described by its THC concentration, usually as the percentage of THC per dry weight of material. Selective cultivation over the years steadily increased its potency, and there are hydroponic farms capable of growing cannabis with a THC content as high as 40% and dabs containing >90% THC. A cane-like variety that is devoid of psychoactive effects provides an important source of hemp fiber.

Nomenclature

The structure of THC was elucidated in 1964 by Raphael Mechoulam. Consisting of a tricyclic 21-carbon structure, THC is a volatile, viscous oil that is insoluble in water but highly soluble in lipids. THC contains no nitrogen and has two chiral centers in trans configurations. The pK_a of THC is 10.6. Two different numbering systems, the dibenzopyran (Δ^9) and monoterpene (Δ^1) nomenclatures, are commonly used to describe THC; the dibenzopyran system is used throughout this chapter.

Mechanisms of THC Action

Early research with racemic THC suggested that its mechanisms of actions were nonspecific, perhaps due to disruption of protein structures contained within lipids of cellular and organelle membranes, similar to the effects of anesthetics. It is now clear, however, that the effects of cannabinoids are highly stereospecific. Another hypothesis suggested that THC and the endogenous cannabinoids interacted with specific cannabinoid receptors. Cannabinoids are natural (−) enantiomers with (3R,4R) stereochemistry. Structure–activity investigations demonstrated that the tricyclic structure, the aromatic ring, and the phenolic group are required for THC's central activity. In addition, animal studies showed that a C5 hydroxyl group confers potent peripheral activity. Delineating mechanisms of action was difficult because initially THC demonstrated activity at many sites, including the opioid and benzodiazepine receptors, and in prostaglandin synthesis, DNA, RNA, and protein metabolism. Cannabinoids inhibit macromolecular metabolism in a dose-related manner and have a wide range of effects on enzyme systems, hormone secretion, and neurotransmitters. These numerous and diffuse effects lent support to the nonspecific-interaction hypothesis.

In the last 35 years, our knowledge of cannabinoid pharmacology increased tremendously. The discoveries included the identification of central and peripheral (CB1) receptors and primarily peripheral (CB2) cannabinoid receptors, multiple endogenous ligands termed *eicosanoids* (anandamide, 2-arachidonoyl glycerol, and others), enzymes for inactivating anandamide (fatty acid amide hydrolase, or FAAH) and 2-arachi-donoyl glycerol (monoacylglycerol lipase), and transporters of endocannabinoids across cell membranes. Many of these findings were made possible by the development of specific cannabinoid receptor antagonists, pharmacologic tools for investigating the endogenous cannabinoid system. Mapping of CB1 receptors in the brain indicated that the distribution of the high-affinity, stereoselective, and pharmacologically distinct brain receptors was anatomically selective. Dense binding was documented in the cerebral cortex, hippocampus, amygdala, striatum, and cerebellum, which are functional areas associated with the most prominent behavioral effects of cannabinoids. CB1 receptors, which are expressed predominantly at nerve terminals, mediate neurotransmitter release. Cannabinoid receptors, which belong to the G protein class of receptors, are present in high amounts and are desensitized and internalized during chronic exposure. The distinct CB2 cannabinoid receptor is involved in immunomodulation. Low concentrations of CB2 cannabinoid receptors are also found in the microglia of the brain and appear to be upregulated during inflammation in this organ. Endogenous and exogenous cannabinoids bind to additional G-protein-coupled receptors termed orphan receptors including GPR18, GPR55, and GPR119 and a wide variety of ion channel receptors including transient receptor potential (TRP) receptors that are found throughout the body.

The endogenous cannabinoid system is involved in the control of locomotion, emotional behavior, cognitive function, cardiovascular responses, pain, feeding behavior, and addiction. THC acts on dopaminergic projections in the brain in a fashion similar to that of noncannabinoid drugs of abuse. THC stimulates reward circuits in the brain and acts as a direct or indirect dopamine agonist in the projections of the medial forebrain bundle. Stimulation of the brain's reward circuits is an essential characteristic of drugs of abuse. Cannabis produces substantial changes in human behavior that are linked to physiological and biochemical changes. Subjective responses and performance effects are interrelated with other bodily functions, behavior being the highest level of human response. It is the integration of all of cannabis' pharmacologic effects that modifies behavior.

Effects

Cannabis' behavioral effects include feelings of euphoria and relaxation, altered time perception, lack of concentration, impaired learning and memory, and mood changes such as panic reactions and paranoia. This spectrum of behavioral effects is unique and prevents the drug's classification as a stimulant, sedative, tranquilizer, or hallucinogen. Subjective effects of cannabis, such as drug "liking" and "feeling drug effects," appear after the first puff of a cigarette. Cannabis smoking produces rapid changes in physiological effects, including increased heart rate, conjunctival suffusion, dry mouth and throat, and increased appetite. Although tachycardia is an expected cannabis effect, less well known is the pronounced hypotension and dizziness that we observed throughout our controlled cannabis research in approximately 30% of participants approximately 17–22 min after the start of smoking. Individuals who experienced symptomatic hypotension had peak plasma THC concentrations that were about two-thirds higher than those who did not. Also underappreciated is the substantial paranoia that many cannabis smokers experience. Most behavioral and physiological effects of THC return to baseline levels within 3–8 h. We showed that Rimonabant, the first specific CB1 cannabinoid receptor inverse agonist, could significantly reduce the subjective effects of smoked THC (Fig. 24.2) and tachycardia (Fig. 24.3) (Huestis et al. 2001). This was the first time in humans that the cardiovascular and behavioral effects of cannabis were documented to be mediated through CB1 cannabinoid receptors (Hirvonen et al. 2012).

The most common neurocognitive deficit observed during acute intoxication is impairment of short-term memory. Individuals who are acutely intoxicated during memory encoding demonstrate deficits in spontaneous recall; however, information processed prior to intoxication is unaffected. Memory impairment corresponds well with the distribution of CB1 receptors in brain regions associated with memory, such as the hippocampus and the anterior cingulate. Research studies indicated that cannabis may decrease accuracy in cognitive and psychomotor tests, impair time estimation, and reduce learning and memory functions. Deficits in motor inhibition, decision-making, and inhibitory control were documented for up to 6 h after smoking a high dose (13%) of THC. Less consistent results were obtained with respect to risk taking after cannabis use.

The acute toxic effects of cannabis include behavioral effects (e.g., panic attacks and psychosis), increased heart rates, and CNS depression (Huestis et al. 1992c). The increase in potency of cannabis in the United States over the last two decades led to an increased demand for emergency care in hospitals. Serious CNS depression may be observed in children after they inadvertently ingest cannabis; however, with supportive care, such cases resolve successfully with few residual effects. Although cannabis does not cause death directly, owing to its few effects on respiratory function, the drug is a major contributing factor to motor-vehicle crashes and other impairment related to the operation of complex machinery. There are both short- and long-term effects of chronic cannabis exposure; the immediate short-term effect on public health and safety is cannabis impaired driving (Hartman and Huestis 2013), while the greatest long-term effect is the effects of THC on brain development (Jacobus et al. 2016, Gnofam et al. 2019). Previously, it was believed that the brain was fully developed by 18–20 years, but now, it is clear that the brain does not fully develop until the late 20s. THC interferes with the connections that are formed between neurons. In utero drug exposure, perinatal exposure through THC in breast milk, and passive cannabis smoke exposure can influence the connections of dendrites that form and become permanent changes in the connectivity and functions of neurons that do not change if abstinence is initiated later. In addition, breastfeeding by women who use cannabis, passive exposure to smoked cannabis vapors by children living in

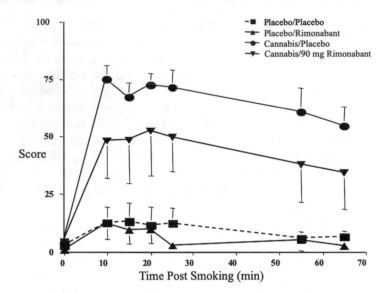

Fig. 24.2 Time course of the first CB1-cannabinoid receptor antagonist, Rimonabant, blockade of smoked cannabis' Visual Analog Scale Composite Score of "How high do you feel right now," "How stoned are you right now," and "How strong are the drug effects right now." Groups included (1) placebo cannabis-placebo Rimonabant, (2) placebo cannabis-active Rimonabant, (3) active cannabis-placebo Rimonabant, and (4) active cannabis-active Rimonabant. Cannabis smokers were pretreated with 90 mg oral Rimonabant 2 h prior to smoking a 2.64% THC cigarette. These data documented that human THC effects were mediated through the CB1-cannabinoid receptor. Reprinted from Huestis et al. (2001) with permission from the American Medical Association

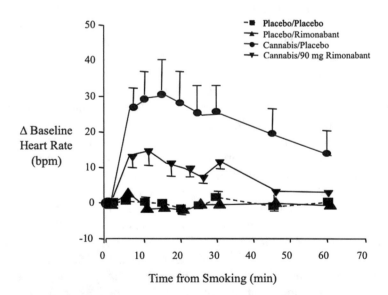

Fig. 24.3 Time course of the first CB1-cannabinoid receptor antagonist, Rimonabant, blockade of heart rate increase. Groups included (1) placebo cannabis-placebo Rimonabant, (2) placebo cannabis-active Rimonabant, (3) active cannabis-placebo Rimonabant, and (4) active cannabis-active Rimonabant. Cannabis smokers were pretreated with 90 mg oral Rimonabant 2 h prior to smoking a 2.64% THC cigarette. These data documented that human THC effects were mediated through the CB1-cannabinoid receptor. Reprinted from Huestis et al. (2001) with permission from the American Medical Association

homes with cannabis-using guardians, accidental ingestion of cannabis-infused foods, and self-administered cannabis by adolescents all increase exposure of children to cannabis, and all exposures affect the developing brain. The earlier that cannabis use begins prior to the age of 17 years, the greater the effects.

Simultaneous collection of pharmacodynamic and pharmacokinetic data during controlled cannabis administration provided insight into the relationship of THC-induced effects and THC concentrations in blood. THC is rapidly absorbed and distributed to tissues; the initial changes in blood concentration are out of phase with accompanying physiological and behavioral changes. This results in a counterclockwise hysteresis in plots of cannabis' effects including increased heart rate and subjective "high" assessment and plasma THC concentrations (Fig. 24.4). A counterclockwise hysteresis is generally indicative of a prominent distribution phase, i.e., extended distribution of drug from the vascular compartment to the drug's site of action, the brain. This hysteresis makes it difficult to interpret cannabinoid concentrations. For example, the effects observed at the same plasma concentration (e.g., 100 μg/L) are different, depending on whether the sample was collected during the absorption phase, when effects and concentrations are rapidly increasing, or during the distribution phase after the end of smoking, when concentrations are dropping rapidly. Effects remain high despite rapidly dropping THC concentrations. To demonstrate the hysteresis concentration–effect relationship, we continuously collected samples from the start of smoking until approximately 20 min after the end of smoking and collected samples frequently thereafter. These data were the first to demonstrate that peak THC concentrations occur before the end of smoking, suggesting that individuals titrate their inhaled dose to their own comfort level of physiological and behavioral effects (Desrosiers et al. 2014). Fortunately, most collections of cannabinoid samples in forensic investigations occur after the end of smoking and in many cases after the initial distribution phase is completed, approximately 45–60 min after the start of smoking. Multiple controlled cannabis administration studies documented that cannabis users titrate their THC dose during ad lib smoking and also during vaporization (Hartman et al. 2015a).

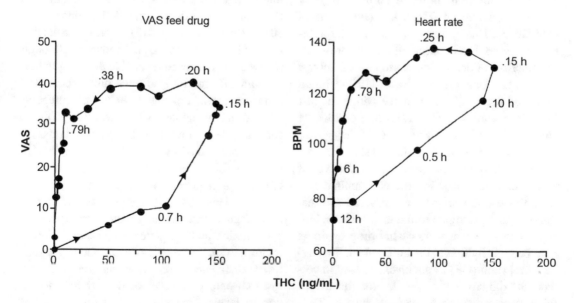

Fig. 24.4 Visual analog scale (VAS) results for "How strongly do you feel the drug now?" and heart rate in beats per minute (BPM) and THC plasma concentrations for a study participant after smoking a 3.55% Δ9- tetrahydrocannabinol (THC) cigarette. The results (time in hours) illustrate a counterclockwise hysteresis for the concentration–effect curves. Reprinted from Huestis MA, Smith ML (2007)

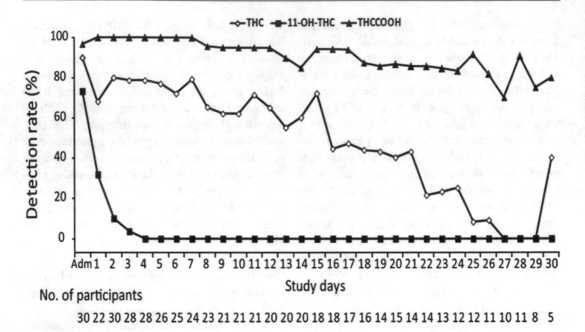

Fig. 24.5 Cannabinoid detection rates in chronic daily cannabis smokers on the basis of the method's limits of quantification, 0.25 µg/L for THC and THCCOOH and 0.5 µg/L for 11-OH-THC, documenting the long-term detection of cannabinoids in blood in this population. Reprinted from Bergamaschi et al. (2013) with permission from the American Association for Clinical Chemistry

Additional research after chronic frequent cannabis use documented identification of low THC concentrations in blood up to 30 days of sustained abstinence (Fig. 24.5) (Bergamaschi et al. 2013). This finding changed the interpretation of blood THC concentrations. Prior to this manuscript, toxicologists, including ourselves, would state that the finding of THC in blood indicated recent cannabis intake within the last 6–12 h, but after finding THC in the blood of chronic, frequent cannabis users 30 days after last use, it is no longer possible to state that low blood THC concentrations are predictive of recent cannabis use. For driver examinations, we believe it is necessary to first establish that the individual is impaired and then collect a biological sample that shows what drug or drugs may be contributing to the impairment. We suggest oral fluid (OF) as noninvasive, easy to collect at the roadside sample for onsite or laboratory screening for the presence of THC (Desrosiers et al. 2019).

In fact, in these same chronic, frequent cannabis users, significant downregulation of CB1 cannabinoid receptors in the brain for up to 28 days (Fig. 24.6) and residual psychomotor impairment for 21 days after last cannabis use (Fig. 24.7) were demonstrated (Hirvonen et al. 2012, Bosker et al. 2013). Chronic cannabis smoking can result in drug dependence. Although rodent studies showed reversible downregulation of brain CB1 receptors after chronic exposure to cannabis, it was unknown whether downregulation occurs in humans who chronically smoke cannabis. We showed with positron emission tomography imaging reversible and regionally selective downregulation of brain cannabinoid CB1 receptors in humans who chronically smoke cannabis (Fig. 24.6) (Hirvonen et al. 2012). Downregulation correlated with years of cannabis smoking and was selective to cortical brain regions. After ~4 weeks of continuously monitored abstinence from cannabis on a secure research unit, CB1 receptor density returned to normal levels. This was the first direct demonstration of cortical CB1 receptor downregulation as a neuroadaptation that may promote cannabis dependence in human brain.

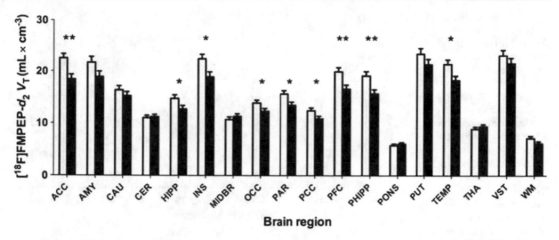

Fig. 24.6 Distribution volume (VT) of [18F] FMPEP-d2 in cortical regions is lower at baseline in chronic daily cannabis smokers (black bars, n = 30) than in control subjects (gray bars, n = 28). Values are estimated marginal means from the repeated measures analysis of variance that controls for body mass index (BMI). Values are adjusted to an average BMI of 24.8 kg m^{-2}. Error bars are s.e.m. Abbreviations: ACC, anterior cingulate cortex; AMY, amygdala; CAU, caudate nucleus; CER, cerebellum; HIPP, hippocampus; INS, insula; MIDBR, midbrain; OCC, occipital cortex; PAR, parietal cortex; PCC, posterior cingulate cortex; PFC, prefrontal cortex; PHIPP, parahippocampal gyrus; PUT, putamen; TEMP, lateral temporal cortex; THA, thalamus; VST, ventral striatum; WM, white matter; *P < 0.05; **P < 0.005, two-tailed t-test. Reprinted from Hirvonen et al. (2012) with permission from Springer Nature

We assessed psychomotor function in the same chronic, daily cannabis smokers who had measurable blood THC for as long as 33 days and whose CB1 cannabinoid receptors were downregulated following chronic exposure. We hypothesized that psychomotor performance would improve during sustained abstinence in this population of chronic, frequent cannabis smokers who resided on a closed research unit for approximately 4 weeks (Bosker et al. 2013). Performance on the critical tracking task (CTT) and divided attention task (DAT) was assessed in 19 male chronic, daily cannabis smokers at baseline and after 8, 14–16, and 21–23 days. Psychomotor performance was compared to a control group of non-intoxicated occasional drug users. We showed that chronic cannabis smokers' performance on the CTT (p < 0.001) and DAT (p < 0.001) was impaired during baseline relative to the comparison group (Fig. 24.7). Psychomotor performance in the chronic cannabis smokers improved over 3 weeks of abstinence but did not recover to equivalent control group performance. Sustained cannabis abstinence moderately improved critical tracking and divided attention performance in chronic, daily cannabis smokers, but impairment was still observable compared to controls after 3 weeks of abstinence.

Controversy exists as to whether long-term exposure produces irreversible changes in brain function. Short-term (24 h) neurocognitive impairment of verbal memory, language function, and processing speed compared with controls were reported, and impairment of memory, executive function, inhibitory control, and psychomotor speed was documented in frequent cannabis users after 28 days of abstinence (Pope et al. 2001, Pope et al. 2002). In one of our investigations of cognitive function in frequent cannabis users, we compared 45 former heavy users (>5000 occasions in lifetime, <12 occasions in the preceding 90 days), 63 current heavy users (>5000 occasions in lifetime), and 72 nonusers (<50 occasions in lifetime) on tests of neurocognitive ability (Pope et al. 2001). The battery of tests assessed executive function, abstract reasoning, sustained attention, verbal fluency, and learning and recall. Assessments occurred on days 0, 1, 7, and 28 after last reported use. Current heavy users performed more poorly than controls

Fig. 24.7 Mean (SE) (a) critical frequency (λc) and (b) tracking errors in the critical tracking task as a function of time of abstinence in chronic daily cannabis smokers. {++ indicates significant difference (p, 0.05) from baseline; ∗ indicates significant difference (p, 0.05) from control group. N = 19 at baseline, N = 18 on day 8, N = 19 on days 14–16, N = 12 on days 21–23, and N = 30 for controls. Doi:https://doi.org/10.1371/journal.pone.0053127.g001. Reprinted from Bosker et al. (2013)

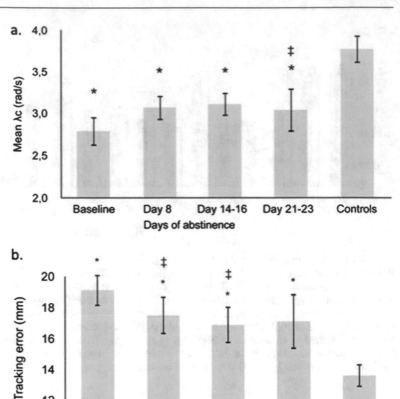

on verbal memory tests at baseline and for 7 days of abstinence. By day 28 of abstinence, there were no longer any differences in neurocognitive performance.

The cognitive effects of long-term cannabis use are insufficiently understood. Most studies concur that cognitive deficits persist at least several days after stopping heavy cannabis use. But studies differ on whether such deficits persist long term or whether they are correlated with increasing duration of lifetime cannabis use. We administered neuropsychological tests to 77 chronic, frequent cannabis users who had smoked cannabis at least 5000 times in their lives and to 87 control subjects who had smoked no more than 50 times in their lives (Pope et al. 2002). The chronic, frequent smokers showed deficits on memory of word lists on days 0, 1, and 7 of a supervised abstinence period. By day 28, however, few significant differences were found

between users and controls on the test measures, and there were few significant associations between total lifetime cannabis consumption and test performance. Although these findings may be affected by residual confounding variables, as in all retrospective studies, we suggest that cannabis-associated cognitive deficits are reversible and related to recent cannabis exposure rather than irreversible and related to cumulative lifetime use. There are discrepancies between studies, and these may be due in part to differences in experimental protocols, types and potencies of the cannabis materials, schedules and lengths of exposure, characteristics of study participants, and defined endpoints of effect.

Impaired health consequences, including lung damage, behavioral changes, and reproductive, cardiovascular, and immunologic effects, are associated with cannabis use. The condensate yield of cannabis smoke, including potential mutagens, was >50% higher than that of cigarette tobacco smoke, although usually fewer cannabis cigarettes are smoked daily (Tashkin et al. 2019). Long-term studies of chronic, frequent cannabis users indicated that odds ratios for increased risk of mouth, throat, and lung cancers were not significantly increased. Endogenous cannabinoids modulate immune functions via cannabinoid receptors. Cannabinoids alter immune function and decrease host resistance to microbial infections in experimental animal models and in vitro. Given this important immunomodulatory role, cannabinoids may be therapeutic for conditions involving pathologic immune responses (Hall et al. 2019). Cannabinoids readily cross placental membranes and expose the developing fetus (Carlier et al. 2019). Cannabinoids affect sperm fertilization of the released eggs, embryo implantation, child development, and potentially increased vulnerability to substance-abuse problems later in life.

Driving Impairment

Driving under the influence of drugs is a serious and preventable problem worldwide. Cannabis is the most prevalent illicit drug identified in impaired drivers (Hartman et al. 2013). Historically, delays in sample collection, evaluating the inactive 11-nor-9-carboxy-THC (THCCOOH), and polydrug use complicated epidemiologic evaluations of driver impairment after cannabis use. We reviewed the literature on cannabis' effects on driving, highlighting the epidemiologic and experimental data. Epidemiologic data show that the risk of involvement in a motor vehicle crash with fatal or major injury consequences increases approximately twofold after cannabis intake. The adjusted risk of driver culpability also increases substantially, particularly with increased blood THC concentrations (Drummer et al. 2004). Studies that used urine as the biological matrix did not show an association between cannabis and crash risk. Experimental data show that drivers attempt to compensate by driving more slowly after smoking cannabis, but control deteriorates with increasing task com-

plexity. Cannabis smoking increases lane weaving and impaired cognitive function. Critical-tracking tests, reaction times, divided-attention tasks, and lane-position variability all show cannabis-induced impairment. Despite purported tolerance in frequent smokers, they are still impaired performing complex tasks. Combining cannabis with alcohol enhances impairment, especially lane weaving. Differences in study designs frequently account for inconsistencies in results between studies. Evidence suggests recent smoking and/or blood THC concentrations 2–5 ng/mL are associated with substantial driving impairment, particularly in occasional smokers.

Epidemiologic Studies

Epidemiologic studies examine the effects of drugs on driving skills under authentic conditions. In case-study analyses (e.g., the 1974 Grand Rapids study of the effects of alcohol on driving), large numbers of drivers are stopped, performance is evaluated, and biological samples are collected. These types of data provide definitive information about impaired driving performance but are expensive and difficult to conduct, especially if a more invasive collection of samples is required. An important advantage of studying alcohol's effects on driving is that breath concentrations of alcohol, which are less invasive than venipuncture, are suitable for estimating blood concentrations.

Unfortunately, many of the studies that examined the frequency of crashes or fatalities among individuals who consume drugs lack proper control groups. The value of these studies in predicting possible impairment and linking drug use to increased rates of crashes or fatalities is weakened because the incidence rates of cannabis use in control populations are frequently unknown. An exciting new opportunity available to the field of traffic safety is the advent of sensitive and noninvasive monitoring of OF for drugs. The introduction of on-site OF tests provides the opportunity for roadside testing and large case–control studies for drugs of abuse. Despite the limitations of earlier work, a number of conclusions can be drawn from them. Cannabis is almost always the most common illicit drug noted in epidemiologic driving studies, and blood THC concentrations are generally low, <5 µg/L. Such low values are due to the rapid decline in THC concentration after smoking and to the time required to obtain blood samples from drugged drivers. In a high percentage of cases, THC is found in combination with ethanol or other drugs. Driving impairment is frequently evident in THC-positive cases, as witnessed by failures in roadside sobriety checks and by police stops for erratic driving.

Other approaches include responsibility analyses that statistically prove that drivers under the influence of a drug have a higher odds ratio for having a crash than drivers who are on the same road at the same time and who are not under the influence of a drug. Investigators blind to the drug status of each party assign responsibility for the accident under the conditions present at the time of the accident. If a statistically greater number of drivers with cannabis-positive samples are judged responsible for the accident than drivers without cannabis, cannabis is considered to significantly increase the odds for an accident. Many attempts were made to prove that cannabis increases the odds ratio for driving crashes; however, none of these studies were successful until Drummer et al. (2004) demonstrated that individuals with measurable THC in the blood were significantly more likely to die in a car crash than those without THC in the blood. Moreover, the odds ratio increased to 6.6 if the THC concentration was >5 µg/L. There were many reasons why this proof of cannabis-caused driving impairment was difficult to achieve. First, analysis of cannabinoids is challenging, and a low limit of quantification (LOQ) is difficult to obtain for blood. Second, early investigations did not differentiate between THC and THCCOOH and thus included measurement of the inactive THCCOOH metabolite as an indicator of impairment. Finally, THC concentrations in live drivers frequently fell below the LOQ before sample collection, which was often more than 4 h after the accident.

The Driving Under the Influence of Drugs, Alcohol and Medicines (DRUID) European Union project evaluated the risks for motor vehicle injuries and fatalities when driving following intake of licit pharmacotherapies and illicit drugs (DRUID 2011). They found that the risk associated with driving after cannabis use was similar to the risk when driving with a low alcohol concentration (between 10 and 50 mg/dL), which is slightly increased about one to three times that of sober drivers. For cannabis, data from Belgium, Denmark, and Italy could be merged, with a combined odds ratio estimate significantly higher than 1, which was also the case for the crude odds ratio estimate based on data from all countries, but not the adjusted estimate based on data from all countries. Some of the estimates based on the single countries' data were significantly above 1, while others were not. The crude and adjusted odds ratios including confidence intervals of getting killed when driving with cannabis based on data from all countries were not significant for cannabis at 1.8 (0.73–4.44) and 1.3 (0.48–3.67), respectively. In this study, the crude odds ratios of a driver of getting seriously injured with cannabis in the blood varied tremendously across countries from 0.49 (Netherlands) to 51.02 (Finland), and the odds ratio of getting killed varied from 0.19 (Portugal) to 29.17 (Sweden).

The US National Roadside Surveys showed a remarkable increasing trend in cannabis use from the 2007 survey (8.6%) (Compton and Berning 2009) to the most recent in 2013–2014 (12.6%) (Kelley-Baker et al. 2017). This represents a large 48% increase in the prevalence of drivers testing positive for cannabinoid use. These surveys raised the issue of increasing cannabis impaired driving in the United States as cannabis medicalization and legalization moves forward.

The National Highway Traffic Safety Administration (NHTSA) conducted the first large-scale case-control crash risk study in Virginia Beach, VA, that included drugs other than alcohol to estimate the risk associated with alcohol- and drug-positive driving (Compton 2017). Data were collected from more than 3000 crash-involved drivers and 6000 control drivers. Breath alcohol measurements were obtained from a total of 10,221 drivers, OF samples from 9285 drivers, and blood samples from 1764 drivers. Research teams responded to crashes 24 h a day, 7 days a week over a 20-month period. Control drivers were matched to each crash-involved driver. The drug most frequently detected in the OF and blood of drivers was THC, detected in 7.6% of the crash-involved drivers and 6.1% (n = 379) of the control drivers. The unadjusted odds ratio for THC was 1.25, representing a significantly elevated risk of crashing by about 1.25 times or 25%. These unadjusted odds ratios do not account for other factors that may contribute to increased crash risk. Male drivers and younger drivers have a higher crash rate than female and older drivers. When the odds ratios were adjusted for demographic variable of age, gender, and race/ethnicity, the significant increased risk of crash involvement was no longer significant. The adjusted odds ratio for THC-positive drivers was 1.05 (95% confidence limit of 0.86–1.27). This adjusted odds ratio was not statistically significant.

Performance Studies

A review of the literature requires careful evaluation of the study design, including appropriate placebo controls, double-blind dose presentation, dosage and route of drug administration, inclusion of more than one dose to demonstrate a dose–response effect, performance task difficulty, and individuals' experience with the task. Generally, the more complex the task, the more sensitive the task is to cannabis impairment. In addition, tasks that are well practiced, such as driving, tend to be more resistant to drug effects. Therefore, laboratory tests that require a divided attention and response to stressful, demanding situations are more likely to demonstrate performance impairment. Another key factor in evaluating reported effects is the availability of simultaneously collected blood samples for measuring THC concentrations. Few performance studies included measurement of drug concentrations in the blood. Measurements of drug concentration are important because of the difficulty in delivering a specified THC dose via the smoking route. Clinical studies with strict controls on smoking dynamics (e.g., number of puffs, time between puffs, hold time, and inhalation time) reported wide intra- and interindividual variation in blood THC concentrations because of an individual's ability to titrate their drug dose (Fig. 24.8).

The Drug Evaluation and Classification Program (DECP) is commonly utilized in driving under the influence (DUI) cases to help determine category(ies) of impairing drug(s) present in drivers. Cannabis, one of the categories, is associated

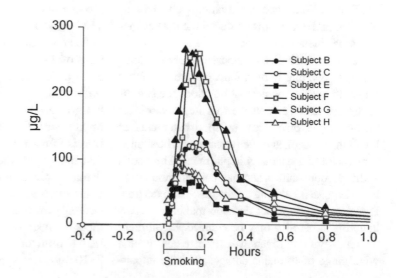

Fig. 24.8 Individual plasma Δ^9-tetrahydrocannabinol (THC) time course by gas chromatography–mass spectrometry for six individuals after controlled administration by smoking of a single 3.55% THC cigarette. Reprinted from Huestis et al. (1992a) with permission from Oxford University Press

with approximately doubled crash risk. We wanted to identify the most reliable DECP metrics for identifying cannabis-driving impairment (Hartman et al. 2016a). We evaluated 302 toxicologically confirmed (blood THC ≥1 µg/L) cannabis-only DECP cases, wherein examiners successfully identified cannabis, compared to data from 302 non-impaired individuals. Physiological measures, pupil size/light reaction, and performance on psychophysical tests (one leg stand [OLS], walk and turn [WAT], finger to nose [FTN], Modified Romberg Balance [MRB]) were included. Cases significantly differed from controls (p < 0.05) in pulse (increased), systolic blood pressure (elevated), and pupil size (dilated). Blood collection time after arrest significantly decreased THC concentrations; no significant differences were detected between cases with blood THC <5 µg/L versus ≥5 µg/L. The FTN best predicted cannabis impairment (sensitivity, specificity, positive/negative predictive value, and efficiency ≥87.1%) utilizing ≥3 misses as the deciding criterion; MRB eyelid tremors produced ≥86.1% for all diagnostic characteristics. Other strong indicators included OLS sway, ≥2 WAT clues, and pupil rebound dilation. Requiring ≥2/4 of ≥3 FTN misses, MRB eyelid tremors, ≥2 OLS clues, and/or ≥ 2 WAT clues produced the best results (all characteristics ≥96.7%). Blood specimens should be collected as early as possible to identify cannabis-impaired drivers. The frequently debated 5 µg/L blood THC per se cutoff showed limited relevance. Combined observations on psychophysical and eye exams produced the best cannabis-impairment indicators.

In general, studies of laboratory performance demonstrated that sensory functions are not highly impaired but that perceptual functions are significantly affected. Perceptual errors are the most frequently cited errors leading to driving crashes involving ethanol, and such errors could be significant factors in cannabis impairment. The user's ability to concentrate and maintain attention may be decreased during cannabis intoxication. Perceptual motor skills, decision-making, and car-handling skills also may be reduced. Impairment of hand–eye coordination is dose related over a wide range of cannabis dosages, and the impairment effects of cannabis and ethanol exposures are additive. Coordination and body-sway decrements are documented. Stability of stance and deficits in information processing decrease in a dose-related manner after cannabis use. Impairment in immediate and delayed free recall was observed, but not in recognition memory. The most consistently reported cognitive effect following cannabis use is a disruption of short-term memory.

Ramaekers et al. (2006) defined performance impairment as a function of THC concentration in serum and OF in order to provide a scientific framework for the development of limits per se for driving under the influence of cannabis. Twenty adults who smoked high-potency THC (up to 500 µg THC/kg) demonstrated impaired executive function in the Tower of London problem-solving task, impaired motor control in the critical-tracking task, increased stop-reaction time in the stop-signal task, and increased commission and omission errors in a choice reaction-time task. THC-induced impairments were still present in the last test period 6 h after smoking. A strong and linear correlation between the THC concentrations in serum and OF was shown, but there was no linear relationship between the magnitude of performance impairment and THC concentrations in OF and serum. The proportion of observations showing impairment or no impairment was evaluated at different THC concentrations to define threshold levels of impairment. Impairment increased progressively in all tasks as a function of the serum THC concentration. The critical-tracking task indicated impairment at serum THC concentrations of 2–5 µg/L, and all tasks were affected at 5–10 µg/L. These investigators suggested that serum THC concentrations between 2 and 5 µg/L establish the lower interval of THC impairment. The impairment of executive function is consistent with the general observation that the greater the multitasking and reasoning demands placed on a driver, the greater the cannabis-induced impairment. Furthermore, Grotenhermen et al. (2007) concluded from a meta-analysis of existing performance studies that a limit on serum THC concentrations of 7–10 µg/L was appropriate.

Jones et al. (2008) reported blood THC concentrations for individuals who had driven under the influence of cannabis in Sweden for cases from the previous 10 years. Eighteen percent and 30% of individuals suspected of driving under the influence of drugs had THC concentrations ≥ 0.3 µg/L alone or with other drugs, respectively. The median THC concentration for 8794 cases was 1.0 µg/L. Even when THC was the only identified drug, the individuals in 41% of the cases had THC concentrations <2.0 µg/L. The authors stated that even if a 2.0 µg/L limit were enacted, the rapid decrease in THC concentrations would allow many individuals to evade prosecution for impaired driving. They suggested that zero tolerance or LOQ laws are a more pragmatic approach to enforcing legislation for driving under the influence of drugs.

Driving Simulator Studies and Closed-/Open-Course Driving Studies

In general, cannabis use impairs performance in driving-simulator tasks and on open and closed driving courses. Cannabis decreases car-handling performance, increases reaction times, impairs time and distance estimation in a dose-related manner, and affects decision-making that relies on these skills. Cannabis use reduced the number of attempts at passing cars or other risky behavior, in contrast to ethanol use, which increased risk taking. As previously mentioned, the more difficult the task, the more apparent is the impairment in performance.

In 1998, Robbe conducted a series of driving-simulator and on-the-road driving tests of individuals after they had smoked cannabis. The task most consistently altered was the standard deviation of lateral position, or weaving. The impairment at the highest study dose, 300 µg/kg (approximately 21 mg THC), was equivalent to that of a blood alcohol concentration of ≥ 0.05 g ethanol/100 mL of blood. In less experienced cannabis users, 100–200 µg/kg (about 7–14 mg THC) impaired fundamental road tracking in a dose-related manner and reduced the individual's

ability to maintain a constant headway with the preceding vehicle for 2.5 h. Combining cannabis with alcohol had an additive effect on impairment of headway maintenance and reaction time.

We wanted to determine how blood THC concentrations related to driving impairment, with and without concurrent alcohol. Current occasional ($\geq 1 \times$/last 3 months, ≤ 3 days/week) cannabis smokers drank placebo or low-dose alcohol and inhaled 500 mg placebo, low (2.9%)-THC, or high (6.7%)-THC vaporized cannabis over 10 min ad libitum in separate sessions (within-subject design, six conditions) (Hartman et al. 2015b). Participants drove simulated drives (~ 0.8 h duration) in the National Advanced Driving Simulator, University of Iowa. Blood and breath alcohol samples were collected before (0.17 h, 0.42 h) and after (1.4 h, 2.3 h) driving that occurred 0.5–1.3 h after inhalation. We evaluated standard deviations of lateral position (lane weaving, SDLP) and steering angle, lane departures/min, and maximum lateral acceleration. In N = 18 completers (13 men, ages 21–37 years), cannabis and alcohol increased SDLP. Blood THC concentrations of 8.2 and 13.1 µg/L during driving increased SDLP similar to 0.05 and 0.08 g/210 L breath alcohol concentrations, the most common legal alcohol limits, at the time of driving. Cannabis-alcohol SDLP effects were additive rather than synergistic, with 5 µg/L THC + 0.05 g/210 L alcohol showing similar SDLP to 0.08 g/210 L alcohol alone. Only alcohol increased lateral acceleration and the less-sensitive lane departures/min parameters. SDLP was a sensitive cannabis-related lateral control impairment measure.

In driving-under-the-influence cases, blood typically is collected approximately 1.5–4 h after an incident, with unknown last intake time. This complicates blood THC interpretation due to the rapidly decreasing concentrations immediately after inhalation. We evaluated how decreases in blood THC concentration before collection may affect interpretation of toxicological results in the driving simulator study cited above. Blood THC concentrations were determined before and up to 8.3 h post dose (limit of quantification 1 µg/L; Hartman et al. 2016c). In 18 participants,

observed maximum concentration (Cmax; at
0.17 h) for active (2.9 or 6.7% THC) cannabis
was [median (range)] 38.2 µg/L (11.4–137) without alcohol and 47.9 µg/L (13.0–210) with alcohol. THC Cmax concentration decreased
approximately 74% and 90% without and with
alcohol in the first 30 min and 1.4 h after active
cannabis. During-drive THC concentrations previously associated with impairment (≥8.2 µg/L)
decreased to median < 5 µg/L by 3.3 h post dose
and < 2 µg/L by 4.8 h post dose. Forensic blood
THC concentrations may be lower than common
per se cutoffs despite greatly exceeding them
while driving. Concentrations during driving
cannot be back-extrapolated because of unknown
time after intake and interindividual variability in
rates of decrease.

We also evaluated cannabis' effects on driving
longitudinal control with and without alcohol
(drivers' most common drug combination), relative to psychoactive THC blood concentrations.
Current occasional (≥1 time in the last 3 months,
≤3 days per week) cannabis smokers drank placebo or low-dose alcohol and inhaled 500 mg
placebo, 2.9%, or 6.7% THC vaporized cannabis
over 10 min ad libitum in separate sessions
(Hartman et al. 2016b). Cannabis-smoking participants performed simulated drives at the
National Advanced Driving Simulator, University
of Iowa 0.5–1.3 h post-inhalation. Blood and
breath alcohol samples were collected before
(0.17 and 0.42 h) and after (1.4 and 2.3 h) driving. We evaluated mean speed relative to the road
limit, standard deviation (SD) of speed, percent
time spent >10% above/below the speed limit,
longitudinal acceleration, and ability to maintain
headway relative to a lead vehicle against blood
THC and breath alcohol concentrations (BrAC).
In N = 18 completing drivers, THC was associated with a decreased mean speed, increased percent speed low, and increased mean following
distance during headway maintenance. BrAC
was associated with increased SD speed and
increased percent speed high, whereas THC was
not. A less-than-additive THC∗BrAC interaction
was detected in percent speed high, suggesting

cannabis mitigated drivers' tendency to drive
faster with alcohol. Cannabis was associated with
slower driving and greater headway, suggesting a
possible awareness of impairment and attempt to
compensate. Individuals who consume concurrent cannabis and alcohol may experience more
elevated or rising alcohol concentrations longer
than with alcohol alone, thereby increasing the
driving risk.

In summary from on-road and simulator
studies, driving under the influence of cannabis
is an important public health and safety concern
that requires the development of an evidence-
based policy and legislation targeted at drugs
and driving. Impaired driving endangers individuals inside and outside the vehicle.
Consuming cannabis before driving, with or
without alcohol, is a common occurrence that
produces substantial morbidity and mortality on
the roadway. It would be helpful if drug concentrations in biological samples could be linked to
performance impairment, as is the case with
ethanol; however, the interpretation of data for
drugged driving is complicated by such factors
as the lack of a linear concentration–effect relationship (hysteresis), drug tolerance, the age
and health of the driver, driving experience,
drug interactions, road and weather conditions,
and, of course, intra- and interindividual differences. The specific effects of cannabis on driving include decreased car-handling performance,
increased reaction times, impaired time and distance estimation, inability to maintain headway,
lateral travel, subjective sleepiness, lack of
motor coordination, and impaired ability to sustain vigilance. These operational effects are
consistent with the described behavioral effects.
Evaluations of cannabis' effects on driving are
three approaches: epidemiologic studies of cannabis use and rates of crashes or fatalities, laboratory studies of cognitive or psychomotor
impairment, and driving/flying simulator or
closed- or open-course driving tests. Each of
these approaches offers a valuable and unique
perspective on cannabis's effects on driving
performance.

Development of Tolerance

Hunt and Jones (1980) evaluated the development of tolerance to THC's effects during oral 30-mg THC administrations every 4 h for 10–12 days. Subjective ratings of intoxication after 9 days on the maximum daily dose were significantly lower than ratings on the first day of dosing. The heart rate increase produced by smoking a cannabis cigarette also was reduced significantly. Significant loss of tolerance occurred within 24 h, and full recovery to pre–drug tolerance levels still had not occurred by 12 days after the last oral THC dose. Few pharmacokinetic changes were noted during chronic administration, although the mean total metabolic clearance and the mean initial apparent volume of distribution increased from 605 to 977 mL/min and from 2.6 to 6.4 L/kg, respectively. The finding that the pharmacokinetic changes observed after chronic oral THC administration could not account for the observed behavioral and physiological tolerance suggested that tolerance was due to pharmacodynamic adaptation.

In general, multiple THC exposures throughout the day are needed to develop tolerance to the behavioral and physiological effects of cannabis. Smoking a single cigarette of 1% or 2% THC each day for 28 days did not produce tolerance to cannabis-induced tachycardia. Another study found a possible "reversal" of tolerance in 16 participants who smoked two to six cannabis cigarettes per day ad libitum (125–190 mg THC/day) over 3 days. In 1977, Nowlan and Cohen induced tolerance to subjective "high" ratings and heart rate changes in 30 moderate and heavy users who were exposed to 33.7–198.7 mg THC/day for 64 days. Participants smoked 1.7 to 10 cigarettes/day, but only between 4:00 pm and midnight and with 9–12 h of abstinence between days. Subjective "high" ratings and mean heart rates after smoking during the first week were significantly greater than during weeks 5 and 9. After 1 week of abstinence, tolerance recovered only partially to these measures.

In another study in 1976, Jones et al. established substantial cannabinoid dependence and tolerance in participants via administration of 30 mg THC every 4 h (total daily dose, 210 mg) for up to 21 days. The heart rate increase produced by smoking a cannabis cigarette was reduced by >50%. The intensity of subjective effects diminished by 60–80% after 10 days of consuming 10 or 30 mg THC every 3–4 h. Tolerance developed to many other physiological effects, such as on heart rate, orthostatic hypotension, skin and body temperature, salivary flow, intraocular pressure, electroencephalograms, sleep duration and quality, eye tracking, and psychomotor performance. Increasing the single THC dose by 30–50% usually produced a prompt and temporary return of the drug's subjective effects. In addition, tolerance developed more rapidly with a dosing schedule of 20 mg THC every 3 h than with 30 mg every 4 h.

Mild tolerance to the effects of oral THC was achieved over shorter periods. Twenty or 30 mg THC was administered four times a day for 4 days, and the development of tolerance was monitored using visual analog scales (Haney et al. 1999). Three of 50 items on the visual analog scale ("good drug effect," "high," and "stimulated") showed a statistically significant change (50% decrease) from the first to the fourth day of dosing.

Six adult male daily cannabis smokers resided on a closed clinical research unit. Oral THC capsules (20 mg) were administered every 4–8 h in escalating total daily doses (40–120 mg) for 7 days (Schwilke et al. 2009). Free plasma THC, 11-hydroxy-THC (11-OH-THC), and THCCOOH concentrations 19.5 h after admission (before controlled oral THC dosing) were mean 4.3 (SE 1.1), 1.3 (0.5), and 34.0 (8.4) μg/L, respectively. During oral dosing, free 11-OH-THC and THCCOOH increased steadily, whereas THC did not. Mean peak plasma free THC, 11-OH-THC, and THCCOOH concentrations were 3.8 (0.5), 3.0 (0.7), and 196.9 (39.9) μg/L, respectively, 22.5 h after the last dose. *Escherichia coli* β-glucuronidase hydrolysis of 264 cannabinoid specimens yielded statistically significant increases in THC, 11-OH-THC, and THCCOOH concentrations ($P < 0.001$), but conjugated concentrations were underestimated owing to incom-

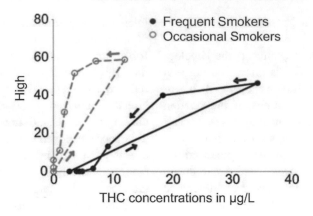

Fig. 24.9 Counterclockwise hysteresis plot demonstrating higher blood concentrations of Δ⁹-tetrahydrocannabinol (THC) required for chronic, frequent cannabis users to achieve effects similar to those of occasional smokers. Reprinted from Desrosiers et al. (2015a) with permission from Oxford University Press

plete enzymatic hydrolysis. Plasma THC concentrations remained >1 μg/L for at least 1 day after daily cannabis smoking and also after cessation of multiple oral THC doses.

Desrosiers et al. (2015a) demonstrated tolerance in chronic, frequent cannabis users as compared to occasional users on subjective effects. Chronic, frequent cannabis users had to attain much higher THC blood concentrations to achieve the same or slightly lower subjective "high" (Fig. 24.9). Occasional smokers reported significantly longer and more intense subjective effects compared to frequent smokers. This suggests that there can be substantial tolerance to subjective effects of cannabis. This is due to the downregulation of the density of CB1-cannabinoid receptors following constant exposure and stimulation (Hirvonen et al. 2012).

Therapeutic Uses

Historically, there was hope that cannabinoids might provide novel approaches to treating human diseases and disorders. The therapeutic usefulness of oral cannabinoids is now investigated for medicinal applications, including analgesia, treatment of acquired immunodeficiency syndrome (AIDS) wasting disease, counteracting spasticity of motor diseases, antiemetic agents following chemotherapy, and antispasmodics in

multiple sclerosis. Despite active research into the therapeutic uses of cannabis, the intoxicating effects are not yet successfully separated from therapeutic effects, except for CBD. Synthetic analogs and cannabis itself are used. Dronabinol (Marinol®; Solvay Pharmaceuticals), a synthetic THC, was available in the United States since 1986. Dronabinol is licensed for the treatment of nausea and vomiting associated with cancer chemotherapy. Some oncologists indicated that smoked cannabis is more effective than the synthetic oral medication because of dronabinol's low and less reliable bioavailability, some patients' inability to tolerate the oral medication, and the absence of other active compounds found in cannabis plant material.

More recently, research focused on the other cannabinoids present in cannabis, specifically cannabidiol. Productive pharmacological research on CBD occurred in the 1970s and intensified recently with many discoveries about the endocannabinoid system. Cannabidiol does not produce THC's well-known behavioral effects, and evidence exists for its efficacy as an analgesic, anti-inflammatory, antitumor, and antiepileptic medication. In 1999, the National Institutes of Health Institute of Medicine acknowledged the therapeutic potential of cannabinoids and encouraged well-designed clinical trials to document efficacy. The dangers and health risks associated with cannabis smoking were deemed inappropriate for pharmacotherapies; however, the development of less toxic forms of delivery was requested. The Volcano Vaporizer delivers THC and other cannabinoids from cannabis plant material without requiring the high pyrolytic temperatures obtained during cannabis smoking. The THC concentrations and pharmacodynamic effects are similar to those obtained after cannabis smoking. Potential therapeutic applications and the passage of medicinal-cannabis laws in multiple states complicate the interpretation of cannabis test results and drugged-driving laws.

In 2017, the National Academies of Sciences, Engineering, and Medicine released an important report entitled "The Health Effects of Cannabis and Cannabinoids: The Current State of Evidence and Recommendations for Research." They reviewed the published literature on cannabinoid pharmacotherapy and report the current evidence on the safety and efficacy of cannabinoids for different diseases. Their findings and recommendations guide the future development of medicinal cannabis. They stated that at this point, our knowledge about the biology of marijuana and cannabinoids allows us to make some general conclusions:

- Cannabinoids likely have a natural role in pain modulation, movement control, and memory.
- The natural role of cannabinoids in immune systems is multifaceted and remains unclear.
- The brain develops tolerance to cannabinoids.
- Animal research demonstrates the potential for dependence, but less so than with benzodiazepines, opiates, cocaine, or nicotine.
- Withdrawal symptoms can be observed in animals but appear to be mild compared to opiates or benzodiazepines.
- The different cannabinoid receptor types play different roles in normal human physiology.
  - Some effects of cannabinoids are independent of cannabinoid receptors.
  - The mechanisms through which cannabinoids influence human physiology underlie the potential therapeutic uses for drugs that act selectively on different cannabinoid systems.
- Scientific data indicate the potential therapeutic value of cannabinoid drugs, primarily THC, for pain relief, control of nausea and vomiting, and appetite stimulation.
- Smoked marijuana is a crude THC delivery system that also delivers harmful substances.
  - Studies suggest marijuana smoke is an important risk factor in the development of respiratory disease.
- The psychological effects of cannabinoids, such as anxiety reduction, sedation, and euphoria, influence their potential therapeutic value.
- A distinctive marijuana withdrawal syndrome is identified, but it is mild and short lived and includes restlessness, irritability, mild agitation, insomnia, sleep disturbance, nausea, and cramping.
- Present data on drug use progression neither support nor refute the suggestion that medical availability would increase drug abuse.
- Research should continue into the physiological effects of synthetic and plant-derived cannabinoids and the natural function of cannabinoids found in the body.
- Clinical trials of cannabinoid drugs for symptom management should be conducted with goal of developing rapid-onset, reliable, and safe delivery systems.
- Psychological effects of cannabinoids such as anxiety reduction and sedation, which can influence medical benefits, should be evaluated in clinical trials.
- Studies to define the individual health risks of smoking marijuana should be conducted.

Multiple preclinical and clinical studies led to FDA approval of Epidiolex®, a purified CBD medicine formulated for oral administration for treatment of infantile refractory epileptic syndromes, by the US Food and Drug Administration in 2018 (Huestis et al. 2019b). The World Health Organization is considering rescheduling cannabis and cannabinoids in 2020. CBD use around the world is expanding for diseases that lack scientific evidence of the drug's efficacy. Preclinical and clinical studies also report adverse effects (AEs) and toxicity following CBD intake. CBD is not risk-free. In animals, CBD AEs included developmental toxicity, embryo–fetal mortality, central nervous system inhibition and neurotoxicity, hepatocellular injuries, spermatogenesis reduction, organ weight alterations, male reproductive system alterations, and hypotension, although at doses higher than recommended for human pharmacotherapies. Human CBD studies for epilepsy and psychiatric disorders reported CBD-induced drug–drug interactions, hepatic abnormalities, diarrhea, fatigue, vomiting, and somnolence. CBD has therapeutic efficacy for serious conditions such as Dravet and Lennox-Gastaut syndromes and is likely to be recommended off label by physicians for other conditions. However, AEs and potential drug–drug interactions must be taken into consideration by clinicians prior to recommending off-label CBD.

Pharmacokinetics

Absorption

Smoked Administration

The smoking route, the principal means of cannabis administration, provides a rapid and highly efficient method of drug delivery, although oral use is not uncommon. Smoked drugs are highly abused in part because of the efficiency and speed of drug delivery from the lungs to the brain. Intense pleasurable and strongly reinforcing effects may be produced, owing to the almost immediate exposure of the CNS to the drug. Prior to harvesting, cannabis plant material contains little active THC. When smoked, the THC carboxylic acids spontaneously decarboxylate to produce THC, with nearly complete conversion upon heating. Pyrolysis during smoking destroys approximately 30% of the THC. Drug availability is further reduced via loss of the drug in the sidestream smoke and that remaining in the unsmoked cigarette butt. The number, duration, and spacing of puffs, the hold time, and the inhalation volume or smoking topography greatly influence the degree of drug exposure. These factors contribute to the high variability (18–50%) in drug delivery by the smoked route; the actual dose is much lower than the amount of THC and THC precursor present in the cigarette.

THC can be measured in the plasma within seconds of inhalation of the first puff of cannabis smoke (Fig. 24.10). Mean (±SD) THC concentrations of 7.0 ± 8.1 µg/L and 18.1 ± 12.0 µg/L were observed after the first inhalation of a low-dose (1.75% THC) and high-dose (3.55% THC) cigarette, respectively (Huestis et al. 1992c). Concentrations continued to increase rapidly, reaching mean peaks of 84.3 µg/L (range, 50–129) and 162.2 µg/L (range, 76–267) for the low-dose and high-dose cigarette, respectively. Peak concentrations occurred at 9.0 min, prior to initiation of the last puff sequence at 9.8 min. Intra- and interindividual variation in smoking dynamics or topography contributes to the uncertainty in dose delivery and to the actual peak THC concentration achieved, even when the drug is administered under controlled conditions. Mean peak plasma concentrations of 11-OH-THC were 6.7 µg/L and 7.5 µg/L for the low and high doses, respectively. THCCOOH concentrations gradually increased and peaked between 0.54 h and 4 h (mean, 1.9 h) at mean concentrations of 24.5 µg/L (range, 15–54) and 54.0 µg/L (range, 22–101), respectively.

We directly characterized, for the first time, free and glucuronidated THC and THCCOOH, 11-OH-THC, CBD, and CBN in cannabis smokers after a single smoked cannabis cigarette (Schwope 2011). Authentic whole blood and plasma samples were simultaneously collected before and after smoking. These data provide an accurate and comprehensive cannabinoid metabolic profile in humans following cannabis smoking, yielding further insight into cannabinoid metabolism and documenting windows of drug detection for novel markers of recent cannabis smoking. Participants (nine men, one woman) resided on a closed research unit and smoked one 6.8% THC cannabis cigarette ad libitum. We quantified THC, 11-OH-THC, THCCOOH, CBD, CBN, THC-glucuronide, and THCCOOH-glucuronide directly in whole blood and plasma

Fig. 24.10 Mean plasma concentrations (n = 6) of Δ^9-tetrahydrocannabinol (THC, ●), 11-hydroxy THC (11-OH-THC, ■), and 11-nor-9-carboxy-THC (THCCOOH, ▲) by gas chromatography–mass spectrometry during smoking of a single 3.55% THC cigarette. Each arrow represents one inhalation or puff on the cannabis cigarette

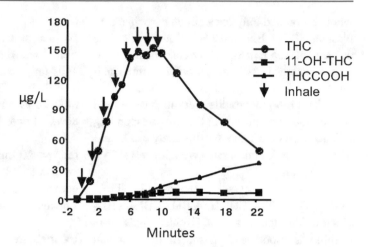

by liquid chromatography/tandem mass spectrometry (LC–MS/MS) within 24 h of collection to obviate stability issues. Median whole blood (plasma) observed Cmax were 50 (76), 6.4 (10), 41 (67), 1.3 (2.0), 2.4 (3.6), 89 (190), and 0.7 (1.4) μg/L 0.25 h after starting smoking for THC, 11-OH-THC, THCCOOH, CBD, CBN, and THCCOOH-glucuronide, respectively, and 0.5 h for THC-glucuronide. Minor cannabinoids (CBD, CBN, and THC-glucuronide) were not detected in all participants' whole blood or plasma after cannabis smoking; when they were detected, however, maximum whole blood (plasma) concentrations were 2.1 (3.4), 2.9 (4.7), and 0.8 (2.3) μg/L, respectively. At observed Cmax, whole blood (plasma) detection rates were 60% (80%), 80% (90%), and 50% (80%) for CBD, CBN, and THC-glucuronide, respectively. CBD and CBN were not detectable after 1 h in either matrix (LOQ 1.0 μg/L).

After Tmax, whole blood and plasma concentrations decreased rapidly for all analytes except THCCOOH-glucuronide; concentrations for this analyte remained increased for approximately 3–4 h after smoking. From 6 h post smoking, median whole blood and plasma THCCOOH-glucuronide concentrations decreased gradually, returning to baseline by 22 h. Within 1 h, median whole blood concentrations for CBD, CBN, and THC-glucuronide were < LOQ, and median plasma concentrations were < 2 μg/L for these analytes. Twenty-two h after smoking, whole blood concentrations (n = 6) for THC,

11-OH-THC, CBD, CBN, and THC-glucuronide were < LOQ for all but one male participant, who had residual THC and 11-OH-THC concentrations of 5.0 and 1.7 μg/L, respectively. Similar results were obtained in plasma, although a second participant also was positive for THC and 11-OH-THC at this time. THCCOOH and THCCOOH-glucuronide concentrations were variable in these extended samples, ranging from 4.4–43 μg/L to 15–190 μg/L in whole blood and 7.0–59 μg/L to 36–180 μg/L in plasma, respectively.

We determined molar glucuronide/free cannabinoid ratios for THC and THCCOOH in both matrices. Throughout the study, THC molar glucuronide/free ratios across participants ranged from 0.006 to 0.019 (median 0.013) in whole blood and 0.006 to 0.041 (median 0.019) in plasma, indicating minimal THC-glucuronide formation relative to free THC. THCCOOH molar ratios were markedly different, ranging from 0.43 to 5.30 (median 2.05). THCCOOH and THCCOOH-glucuronide were quantified in all samples. THC and 11-OH-THC were quantified in all whole blood and plasma samples for at least 2 h; after this time, detection rates decreased, with 10% detection in whole blood and 30% detection in plasma 22 h after smoking. In whole blood, CBD, CBN, and THC-glucuronide were detected 0.25 h after smoking in 60%, 80%, and 20% of samples, respectively (LOQs 1.0, 1.0, and 0.5 μg/L). By 1 h after smoking, however, CBN was the only minor cannabinoid detected in whole blood and only for a single participant. In plasma, CBD, CBN, and THC-glucuronide were detected at 0.25 h in 80%, 90%, and 70% of samples, respectively, with detection of all three analytes for at least one participant at 1 h. Detection rates for THC-glucuronide were highest in both whole blood and plasma at 0.5 h, corresponding with the observed Tmax for this analyte, whereas other analyte detection rates were highest 0.25 h after smoking.

We also compared cannabinoid (THC, 11-OH-THC, THCCOOH, CBD, CBN, THC-glucuronide, and THCCOOH-glucuronide) disposition in blood and plasma of frequent and occasional cannabis users after smoking ad libitum a single 6.8% THC cigarette (Desrosiers et al. 2014). Cannabinoids were quantified on admission (approximately 19 h before), 1 h before, and up to 15 times (0.5–30 h) after smoking. Cannabinoid blood and plasma concentrations were significantly higher in frequent smokers compared with occasional smokers at most time points for THC and 11-OH-THC and at all time points for THCCOOH and THCCOOH-glucuronide. CBD, CBN, and THC-glucuronide were not significantly different at any time point. For blood THC >5 µg/L, median (range) time of last detection was 3.5 h (1.1–>30 h) in frequent smokers and 1.0 h (0–2.1 h) in 11 occasional smokers, although two individuals had no samples with THC >5 µg/L. Cannabis smoking history plays a major role in cannabinoid detection. The presence of CBN or THC-glucuronide indicates recent use in both populations, but their absence does not exclude it.

There is increasing interest in markers of recent cannabis use because following frequent cannabis intake, THC may be detected in blood and plasma (Karschner et al. 2016) for up to 30 days. We expanded our search for recent cannabinoid use markers by adding minor cannabinoids CBG and Δ9-tetrahydrocannabivarin (THCV) and its metabolite 11-nor-9-carboxy-THCV (THCV-COOH) to our LC–MS/MS analytical marker (Scheidweiler et al. 2016). We characterized blood pharmacokinetics of THC, its phase I and phase II glucuronide metabolites (Fig. 24.11), and minor cannabinoids (Fig. 24.12)

in occasional and frequent cannabis smokers for 54 (occasional) and 72 (frequent) h after controlled smoked ad lib administration of a 6.9% THC (approximately 50.6 mg THC) (Newmeyer et al. 2016). CBG and CBN were frequently identified after smoking with short detection windows. Implementation of a combined THC ≥5 µg/L plus THCCOOH/11-hydroxy-THC ratio < 20 cutoff produced detection windows <8 h after all routes for frequent smokers; no occasional smoker was positive 1.5 h following smoked cannabis.

Vaporized Administration

While smoking is the most common cannabis administration route, vaporization and consumption of cannabis edibles are common. A survey showed that 29.8% of US adults aged ≥18 years ever consumed cannabis via "edibles or drinks" and 9.9% used a "vaporizer or other electronic device," respectively (Schauer et al. 2016), indicating the importance of characterizing multiple cannabis administration routes. We employed the Volcano® Medic vaporization device for cannabis administration in our studies in the National Advanced Driving Simulator (NADS) because smoking was not permitted on the University of Iowa campus. Although simultaneous THC and alcohol use is frequent, potential pharmacokinetic interactions are poorly understood. We studied blood and plasma vaporized cannabinoid disposition, with and without simultaneous oral low-dose alcohol (Hartman et al. 2015a). Nineteen adult cannabis smokers (>1 time/3 months, <3 days/week) drank placebo or low-dose alcohol (target approximately 0.065% peak breath alcohol concentration) 10 min before inhaling 500 mg placebo, low-dose (2.9%) THC, or high-dose (6.7%) THC vaporized cannabis. Blood and plasma were obtained before and up to 8.3 h after ingestion. Median (range) maximum blood concentrations (Cmax) for low and high THC doses (no alcohol) were 32.7 (11.4–66.2) and 42.2 (15.2–137) µg/L THC, respectively, and 2.8 (0–9.1) and 5.0 (0–14.2) µg/L 11-OH-THC. With alcohol, low- and high-dose Cmax values were 35.3 (13.0–71.4) and 67.5

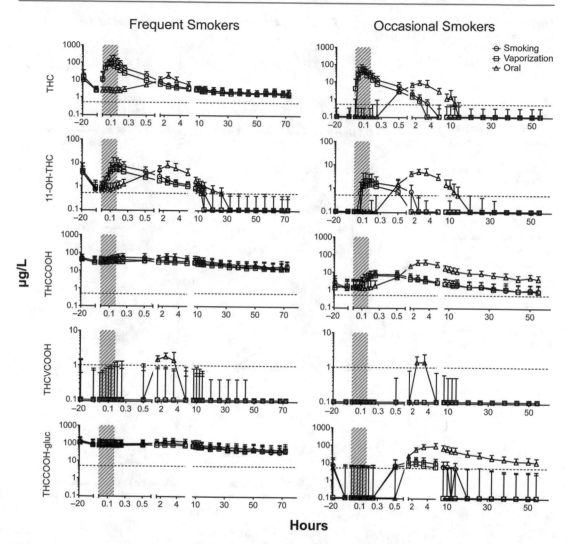

Fig. 24.11 Mean + SD blood cannabinoid concentrations from 11 frequent and nine occasional cannabis smokers following administration of cannabis containing 6.9% THC via smoked, vaporized, and oral routes. Shaded area designates 10-min smoking time. Dotted line is LOQ. Data presented on a log scale. Reprinted from Newmeyer et al. (2016) with permission from the American Association for Clinical Chemistry

(18.1–210) µg/L THC and 3.7 (1.4–6.0) and 6.0 (0–23.3) µg/L 11-OH-THC, significantly higher than without alcohol. With a THC detection cutoff of ≥1 µg/L, ≥16.7% of participants remained positive 8.3 h post dose, whereas ≤21.1% were positive by 2.3 h with a cutoff of ≥5 µg/L. Vaporization is an effective THC delivery route producing similar cannabinoid concentrations following smoked cannabis (Schwope et al. 2011, Desrosiers et al. 2014). The significantly higher blood THC and 11-OH-THC Cmax values with alcohol possi-

bly explain increased performance impairment observed from cannabis–alcohol combinations. We also directly compared vaporized cannabis to smoked cannabis in the same individuals smoking or vaporizing approximately 50.6 mg THC (Fig. 24.11) (Newmeyer et al. 2016). Few differences were observed between smoked and vaporized blood cannabinoid pharmacokinetics, with CBG and CBN frequently identified after both inhalation routes with short detection windows. Vaporization and smoking provide comparable cannabinoid delivery.

Fig. 24.12 Mean + SD blood concentrations of minor cannabinoids from 11 frequent and nine occasional cannabis smokers following administration of cannabis containing 6.9% THC via smoked and vaporized routes. Shaded area designates 10-min smoking time. Dotted line is LOQ. Data presented on a log scale. These analytes' concentrations did not exceed the LOQ after oral THC administration. Reprinted from Newmeyer et al. (2016) with permission from the American Association for Clinical Chemistry

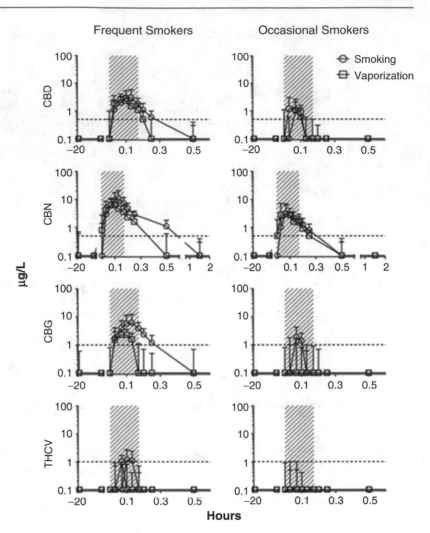

Oral Administration

After oral and sublingual administration of THC, THC-containing food products, or cannabis-based extracts, blood THC concentrations are much lower than after smoked administration. Bioavailability is reduced to 6–18% after oral use, partly because of degradation of the drug in the stomach and significant first-pass metabolism in the liver to active and inactive metabolites. Two THC peaks may be observed because of the enterohepatic circulation. We recently studied the oral administration of THC-containing hemp oils (in liquid and capsules) and dronabinol (synthetic THC). Six volunteers ingested liquid hemp oil (0.39 and 14.8 mg THC/day), hemp oil in capsules

(0.47 mg THC/day), dronabinol capsules (7.5 mg THC/day), and placebo for five consecutive days (Goodwin et al. 2006). THC and 11-OH-THC concentrations were low and never exceeded 6.1 µg/L. Concentrations of THC and equipotent 11-OH-THC were similar, unlike the low 11-OH-THC/THC ratio observed following smoking. Analytes were detectable 1.5 h after initiating dosing with the regimen of 7.5 mg THC/day and 4.5 h after starting the sessions of 14.8 mg THC/day. Tests results for plasma THC and 11-OH-THC were negative for all participants and all doses by 16 h after the last THC dose. THCCOOH was generally detected 1.5 h after the first dose. Plasma THCCOOH concentrations peaked at 3.1 µg/L during dosing with the low-dose hemp oils, whereas the much higher concentrations (up to 43.0 µg/L) found after the higher doses persisted for at least 39.5 h after the end of dosing. These data demonstrate that individuals who use hemp oil with a high THC content (347 µg/g) as a dietary supplement have THC and metabolite concentrations in the plasma comparable to those of patients who use dronabinol for appetite stimulation. Body mass index, maximal drug concentration, and the number of samples positive for THC and 11-OH-THC showed significant correlations.

In a study by Newmeyer et al. (2017), participants also ingested approximately 50.6 mg THC in a brownie. Blood THC Cmax were higher in frequent [17.7 (8.0–36.1) µg/L] cannabis users compared to occasional [8.2 (3.2–14.3) µg/L] users (Fig. 24.13). Minor cannabinoids THCV, CBN, and CBG were never detected in blood. Significantly greater THCCOOH and THCCOOH-glucuronide concentrations were observed following oral cannabis. Implementation of a combined THC ≥ 5 µg/L plus THCCOOH/11-hydroxy-THC ratio < 20 cutoff produced detection windows <8 h after all routes for frequent smokers; no occasional smoker was positive 12 h following oral cannabis.

After eating brownies containing approximately 10, 25, or 50 mg THC, blood Cmax were 1.0 (0.0–3.0), 3.5 (3.0–4.0), and 3.3 (1.0–5.0) µg/L for THC; 1.0 (0.0–2.0), 3.3 (2.0–5.0), and 3.2 (2.0–4.0) µg/L for 11-OH-THC; and 7.2 (5.0–14.0), 21.3 (12.0–39.0), and 29.3 (16.0–44.0) µg/L for THCCOOH, respectively; cannabinoid detection times were 0–22, 0–12, and 3–94 h, respectively (Vandrey et al. 2017). Quantitative cannabinoid concentrations in blood were low compared with concentrations observed following inhalation of cannabis.

Compared with THC administered by the smoking route, the onset, magnitude, and duration of pharmacodynamic effects generally occur later with the oral route, and the effects are lower in magnitude and have a delayed return to baseline. The pharmacodynamic effects of cannabis taken orally are due to both THC and its equipotent metabolite, 11-OH-THC.

Oromucosal Administration

Because of the chemical complexity of cannabis plant material compared with synthetic THC, cannabis extracts are being explored as therapeutic medications. Reproducible extracts of *C. sativa* plants containing high percentages of THC and cannabidiol are combined in different ratios to target specific diseases or illnesses. The efficacies of these extracts are being evaluated in clinical trials for chronic pain, antiepileptic, antipsychotic, post-traumatic stress disorder (PTSD), migraine, and treatment of spasticity and related complications in affected patients. THC–CBD extracts are administered sublingually to avoid first-pass metabolism by the liver. Sativex® (GW Pharmaceuticals), a cannabis-based medicinal extract, contains equivalent amounts of CBD and THC and was approved in Canada and multiple European and South American countries to treat neuropathic pain and spasticity associated with multiple sclerosis and related syndromes. THC and 11-OH-THC concentrations peak at about 120 and 160 min, respectively, after a 20-mg dose and are low, approximately 3–7 µg/L and 6–8 µg/L, respectively (Guy et al. 2003).

We evaluated cannabis users in a within-subject randomized, controlled, double-blind, double-dummy study where they received 5 and 15 mg synthetic oral THC, low-dose (5.4 mg THC and 5.0 mg CBD) and high-dose (16.2 mg THC and 15.0 mg CBD) Sativex, and placebo over five sessions (Karschner et al. 2011). CBD, THC, 11-OH-THC, and THCCOOH were quantified in plasma by two-dimensional gas chromatography–mass spectrometry (GC–MS) with an LOQ of 0.25 µg/L. Significant differences (P < 0.05) in Cmax and areas under the curve from 0 to 10.5 h post dose were found for all analytes found between low and high doses of synthetic THC and Sativex. Mean time to first CBD detection was 2.5 ± 0.4 h for low- and 2.0 ± 0.3 h for high-dose Sativex. CBD mean plasma C_{max} after low-dose and high-dose Sativex were 1.6 ± 0.4 and 6.7 ± 2.0 µg/L (Fig. 24.14) and occurred 3.7 ± 0.5 and 4.0 ± 0.5 h post dose, respectively. There were no statistically significant differences in Cmax and time to maximum

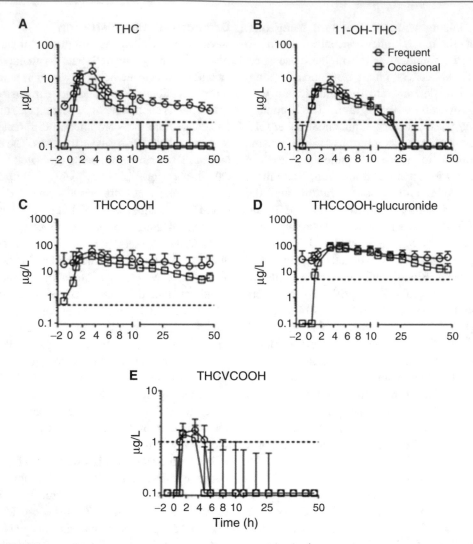

Fig. 24.13 Mean + SD blood cannabinoid concentrations from nine frequent and seven occasional cannabis smokers following administration of an oral cannabis dose containing approximately 50.6 mg THC. Dotted line is LOQ. Data presented on a log scale. Reprinted from Newmeyer et al. (2017) with permission from the American Association for Clinical Chemistry

concentration or in the $AUC_{0 \to 10.5h}$ between similar oral THC and Sativex doses. Relative bioavailability was calculated to determine the relative rate and extent of THC absorption; 5- and 15-mg oral THC bioavailability was 92.6% ± 13.1% and 98.8% ±11.0% of low- and high-dose Sativex, respectively. These data suggest that CBD modulation of THC's effects, if it occurs, is not due to a pharmacokinetic interaction at these therapeutic doses, nor at a 1:1 ratio of THC and CBD. Mean THC Cmax values were

not significantly different for 5 mg oral THC (4.7 ± 0.9 µg/L) and low-dose Sativex (5.1 ± 1.0 µg/L) (Fig. 24.15). Similarly, mean THC plasma Cmax values were not significantly different for 15 mg oral THC (14.3 ± 2.7 µg/L) and high-dose Sativex (15.3 ± 3.4 µg/L). At the higher doses, the mean 11-OH-THC Cmax values were 11.1 ± 2.0 (oral) and 8.4 ± 1.2 µg/L (Sativex), respectively. 11-OH-THC Cmax occurred 1.0–5.6 h after oral THC and 1.0–7.5 h after Sativex doses. THCCOOH Cmax were

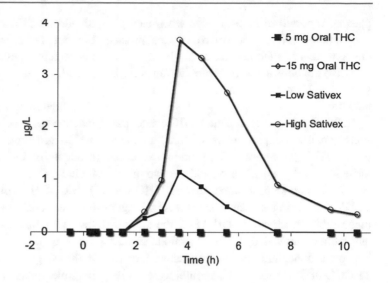

Fig. 24.14 Median (n = 9) CBD following controlled administration of placebo, 5 and 15 mg oral THC, and low-dose (5.4 mg THC and 5 mg CBD) and high-dose (16.2 mg THC and 15 mg CBD) oromucosal Sativex. Reprinted from Karschner et al. (2011) with permission from the American Association for Clinical Chemistry

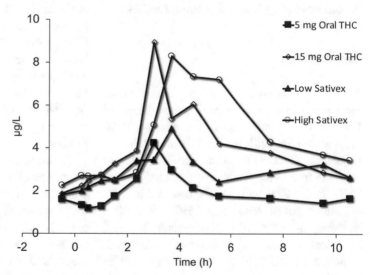

Fig. 24.15 Median (n = 9) THC concentrations following controlled administration of placebo, 5 and 15 mg oral THC, and low-dose (5.4 mg THC and 5 mg CBD) and high-dose (16.2 mg THC and 15 mg CBD) oromucosal Sativex. Reprinted from Karschner et al. (2011) with permission from the American Association for Clinical Chemistry

attained 1.2–7.5 h post dose, and THCCOOH Cmax values were 69.3 ± 17.6, 134 ± 36.3, 108 ± 30.5, and 127 ± 25.9 µg/L after 5 and 15 mg oral THC and low- and high-dose Sativex, respectively.

Distribution

THC has a large volume of distribution of approximately 4 L/kg, and 97–99% of the drug is bound to proteins in the plasma, primarily albumin and lipoproteins. Highly perfused organs, including the lung, heart, brain, and liver, are rap-idly exposed to the drug. Tissues that are less highly perfused accumulate the drug more slowly as the THC redistributes from vascular into peripheral compartments. The high solubility of THC in lipids promotes the concentration and prolonged retention of the drug in fat. Detectable concentrations of THC were found in fat biopsies obtained >4 weeks after smoking (Johansson et al. 1989). The formation of fatty acid conjugates of THC and 11-OH-THC was suggested, and such conjugates may increase the stability of the compounds in fat. Slow release of the drug from fat and significant enterohepatic recirculation contribute to THC's long drug half-life in plasma, reported to be >4.1 days when isotopically labeled THC and sensitive analytical procedures were used (Johansson et al. 1988). Less sensitive methods and shorter monitoring periods yield much lower estimates of the terminal half-life.

In 2005, Mura et al. reported THC concentrations in paired samples of postmortem blood and brain. THC concentrations in brain exceeded those in blood in all 12 cases, and the two matrices showed no significant correlation. THC was still detectable in the brain when it was no longer measurable in blood. 11-OH-THC, the equipotent metabolite, was found in the brain at similar but lower concentrations, and concentrations of THCCOOH, the inactive metabolite, were equivalent to or slightly higher than those for THC.

Metabolism

Figure 24.1 summarizes THC's primary metabolic route and metabolites. Hydroxylation of THC at C9 by the hepatic cytochrome P450 enzyme system yields the equipotent metabolite, 11-OH-THC, which early investigators believed to be the true psychoactive analyte. Cytochrome P450s 2C9, 2C19, and 2D6 are involved in THC oxidation. More than 100 THC metabolites including di- and trihydroxy compounds, ketones, aldehydes, and carboxylic acids were identified. Although 11-OH-THC predominates as the first oxidation product, significant amounts of 8β-OH-THC and lower amounts of 8α-OH-THC also are formed. Much lower plasma 11-OH-THC concentrations (approximately 10% of the THC concentration) are found immediately after cannabis smoking than after oral administration (50–100% lower). Mean peak 11-OH-THC concentrations occur approximately 13 min after the start of smoking. Other tissues, including lung, may contribute to THC metabolism, although alternative hydroxylation pathways may be more prominent. Cytochrome P450 2C9 is believed to be primarily responsible for the formation of 11-OH-THC, whereas P450 3A catalyzes the formation of 8β-OH-THC, epoxy-hexahydrocannabinol, and other minor metabolites. Excretion of 8β,11-dihydroxy-THC in urine was proposed as a good biomarker of recent cannabis use, although other investigators have not validated use of this compound. To our knowledge, it is not used in forensic or clinical investigations.

Oxidation of active 11-OH-THC produces the inactive metabolite, THCCOOH. THCCOOH and its glucuronide conjugate are the major end products of biotransformation in most species, including humans. Phase II metabolism of THCCOOH involves addition of glucuronic acid and, less commonly, other moieties (such as sulfate, glutathione, amino acids, and fatty acids) via the C11 carboxyl group. The phenolic hydroxyl group may also be a target. It is also possible to have two glucuronic acid moieties attached to THCCOOH, although steric hindrance at the phenolic hydroxyl group may be a limiting factor. THC glucuronidation is low after both oral and smoked administration, while THCCOOH-glucuronide is more prominent in blood than free THCCOOH. There is no indication that the glucuronide conjugates are active, although data to support this supposition are lacking.

Addition of the glucuronide group improves water solubility, thereby facilitating excretion, but renal clearance of these polar metabolites is low because of their extensive binding to proteins. No significant differences between males and females were reported with respect to metabolism of these compounds. Owing to the rapid decrease in THC concentrations, THCCOOH concentrations gradually increase and surpass concurrent THC concentrations shortly after the completion of smoking. The time course of THCCOOH detection in blood is much longer than for either of the active analytes.

Elimination

Total mean THCCOOH amounts of 93.9 ± 24.5 μg and 197.4 ± 33.6 μg were measured in urine over a 7-day period following the smoking of 1.75% and 3.55% THC cigarettes containing approximately 18 and 34 mg THC, respectively (Huestis et al. 1996). These amounts represented a mean of only 0.54% ± 0.14% and 0.53% ± 0.09% of the original amount of THC in the low- and high-dose cigarettes, respectively. The small percentage of total dose found in urine as THCCOOH is not surprising, considering the many factors that influence THCCOOH excretion after smoking. Most of the THC dose is excreted in the feces (30–65%) rather than in urine (20%). Another factor affecting the low amount of recovered dose is the measurement of a single metabolite, THCCOOH, in urine. Humans produce numerous cannabinoid metabolites, most of which are not measured or included in the calculation of percent dose excreted.

Eighty percent to 90% of the urinary elimination of a single THC dose occurs within 5 days, and the excreted products are primarily hydroxylated and carboxylated metabolites. Approximately 20% of acidic urinary metabolites are conjugated and unconjugated THCCOOH. Nearly all of the THCCOOH excreted in urine is THCCOOH-glucuronide, with free THCCOOH not detected in the urine of some cannabis users (Desrosiers 2014). The acid-linked THCCOOH-glucuronide conjugate has an excretion half-life of 3–4 days. Urinary THCCOOH concentrations generally decrease rapidly until a concentration of about 20–50 μg/L is reached, even in the most frequent cannabis smokers. At this point, the concentration decreases at a much slower rate. The subsequent slow release of the THC stored in the tissues extends the window of drug detection.

Interestingly, in almost all cases after smoked or oral THC administration and near the end of drug's elimination in the urine, negatively and positively testing samples become interspersed. This phenomenon appears to be due to several factors, including variable release of THC from the tissues and inconsistent dilution in the urine. The presence of a positive result in a urine test after one or more negative test results may be misinterpreted as new cannabis use. Creatinine normalization of urinary cannabinoid concentrations offers some help with this phenomenon by accounting for the individual's state of hydration, resulting in a smoother excretion curve (Fig. 24.16). No significant pharmacokinetic dif-

ferences between chronic and occasional cannabis users are substantiated.

Terminal Elimination Half-Lives of THCCOOH

The elimination of THC and THCCOOH is described with models of two or more compartments. Initially, THC and THCCOOH are eliminated rapidly to highly perfused organs, followed by much longer terminal elimination half-lives. Accurately determining terminal half-lives requires sensitive procedures for quantifying low cannabinoid concentrations and a monitoring period of four to five half-lives. Many investigations used short sampling intervals of 8–72 h, which underestimate terminal half-lives. Slow release of THC from lipid storage compartments and significant enterohepatic circulation contribute to THC's long terminal half-life in the plasma, which was reported as >4.1 days in chronic cannabis users. A plasma elimination half-life of up to 12.6 days was observed in a chronic cannabis user when THCCOOH concentrations were monitored for 4 weeks (Johansson et al. 1988). Elimination half-lives for plasma THCCOOH were measured with isotopically labeled THC and sensitive analytical procedures, yielding mean values of 5.2 ± 0.8 days and 6.2 ± 6.7 days for frequent and infrequent cannabis users, respectively. Similarly, the terminal urinary-excretion half-life of THCCOOH was estimated as 3–4 days.

Recent research on chronic, frequent cannabis users participating in our studies over the last 15 years showed quantifiable THC in the blood and plasma for >7 days during sustained cannabis abstinence (Karschner et al. 2009). Of 28 daily cannabis users residing on a closed research unit with no access to drug, 15 tested positive for >24 h for whole blood THC concentrations greater than the method LOQ of 0.25 μg/L. The whole blood samples of six participants had THC concentrations that were still greater than this limit after 7 days of monitored abstinence, with three of the six participants having THC concentrations >1 μg/L. We stress that these concentra-

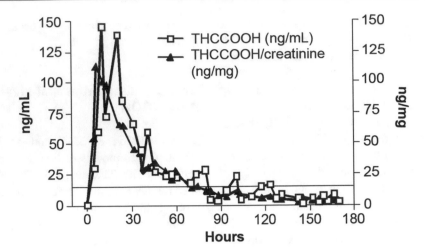

Fig. 24.16 Urinary excretion profile of 11-nor-9-carboxy-Δ^9-tetrahydrocannabinol (THCCOOH, □) as measured by gas chromatography–mass spectrometry (GC–MS) in one study participant following the smoking of a single 3.55% THC cigarette. The horizontal line at 15 ng/mL represents the current GC–MS cutoff used in most testing programs. The urinary THCCOOH concentrations (nanograms per milliliter) normalized to urine creatinine concentrations (milligrams per milliliter) are illustrated (▲). Reprinted from Huestis MA and Cone EJ (1998) with permission from Oxford University Press

tions were found only in individuals who were long-term daily cannabis smokers; individuals who smoked less frequently than daily produced negative results in tests of whole blood within about 8–12 h of cannabis use. In addition, the 0.25-μg/L LOQ that was achieved via two-dimensional gas chromatography–mass spectrometry (2D-GC–MS) with cryofocusing is much lower than the limit of most analytical procedures and lower than the cannabinoid-reporting threshold of most laboratories.

Whole and Plasma Blood Cannabinoid Concentrations

Almost all past and current cannabis studies begin blood collections after the end of smoking. We were interested in characterizing the pharmacokinetics of THC during cannabis smoking. This was a paced smoking procedure with a 2-sec inhalation, a 10-sec hold period, and a 72-sec exhalation and rest period. A total of eight puffs were inhaled in 11.2 min. We employed a continuous blood withdrawal pump that collected blood at 5 mL/min for 20 min, 1 mL/min for the next 40 min, and 0.2 mL/min up to 2 h. THC was detected in the plasma immediately after the first cannabis puff (Fig. 24.10) (Huestis et al. 1992a). Concentrations continue to increase rapidly during absorption from the lungs. After the smoking of one cannabis cigarette of 1.75% (~15.8 mg) or 3.55% (~33.8 mg) THC, peak concentrations were 50–129 μg/L (mean, 84.3 μg/L) and 76–267 μg/L (mean, 162.2 μg/L), respectively. Mean THC concentrations 15 and 30 min after smoking were approximately 60% and 20% of peak concentrations, respectively. Within 2 h, plasma THC concentrations were ≤ 5 μg/L. The time of detection of THC (GC–MS LOQ, 0.5 μg/L) was 3–12 h after the low THC dose (1.75%) and 6–27 h after the high-dose cigarette (3.55% THC).

Peak plasma concentrations of 11-OH-THC were approximately 6–10% of concurrent peak THC concentrations. Peak 11-OH-THC concentrations were noted at a mean of 13.5 min (range, 9.0–22.8 min) after smoking initiation. 11-OH-THC concentrations decreased gradually, with mean detection times of 4.5 h and 11.2 h after the two doses. THCCOOH concentrations in the plasma increased slowly and plateaued for up to 4 h. This inactive metabolite was detected in the plasma of all participants by 8 min after the start of cannabis smoking. Peak concentrations were consistently lower than peak THC concentrations but were higher than peak 11-OH-THC concentrations. Mean peak THCCOOH concentrations were 24.5 µg/L (range, 15–54 µg/L) and 54.0 µg/L (range, 22–101 µg/L) after the low- and high-dose cannabis cigarettes, respectively. Following the smoking of a 1.75% THC cigarette, THCCOOH was detected from 48 to 168 h (mean, 84 h). Detection times ranged from 72 to 168 h (mean, 152 h) after the smoking of a 3.55% THC cigarette.

Interpretation of Blood and Plasma Cannabinoid Concentrations

Scientific advances improved our ability to identify and quantify cannabinoids in body fluids; however, the interpretation of results remains a difficult task. Forensic toxicologists receive frequent requests to interpret the significance of cannabinoid concentrations in blood samples from individuals involved in crashes, criminal investigations, and traffic violations. Relevant facts, such as the amount of drug used, the route of administration, and history of use, are generally unknown. Unlike the situation with blood ethanol concentrations, practical presumptive concentrations of blood THC are more difficult to relate to measurable impairment. Because of the chemical and pharmacokinetic differences between cannabis and ethanol, we cannot use ethanol as a model for relating drug concentrations to effects. Consequently, the patterns of distribution to and elimination from active sites are quite different for these two molecules. Pharmacokinetic and pharmacodynamic models that account for the dispositional differences of THC may be more successful in defining blood concentrations that can be associated with THC's psychoactive effects.

THC and THCCOOH are found predominantly in the plasma fraction of blood, where 95% to 99% of these cannabinoids are bound to albumin and lipoproteins. Cannabinoid concentrations in whole blood are estimated at one-half the concentrations in plasma, due to the low partition coefficient of drug into erythrocytes (Fig. 24.17). The time of last THC exposure is often important in clinical, workplace, and forensic applications, and the models for calculating time of last exposure are based on plasma concentrations. When whole blood concentrations are provided, one typically employs a theoretical 0.5 whole blood-to-plasma (WB/P) ratio in order to use the models. No studies previously evaluated predictive models utilizing empirically derived WB/P ratios or whole blood cannabinoid pharmacokinetics after subchronic THC dosing until that published by Karschner et al. (2012). THC, 11-OH-THC, THCCOOH, CBD, CBN, THC-glucuronide, and THCCOOH-glucuronide were quantified directly in whole blood and plasma by 2D-GC/MS within 24 h of collection to obviate stability issues. Ten male chronic, daily cannabis smokers received escalating around-the-clock oral THC (40–120 mg daily) for 8 days. Maximum whole blood THC occurred 3.0 h after the first oral THC dose and 103.5 h (4.3 days) during multiple THC dosing. Median WB/P ratios were THC 0.63 (0.3–1.7) (n = 196), 11-OH-THC 0.60 (0.1–1.3) (n = 189), and THCCOOH 0.55 (0.2–1.5) (n = 200). Analyte WB/P ratios did not significantly differ (P > 0.05) during the initial smoked cannabis abstinence, 1–5 h post first oral THC dose, during multiple THC dosing, and after the last THC dose. Predictive models utilizing these WB/P ratios accurately estimated last cannabis exposure in 96% and 100% of specimens collected within 1–5 h after a single oral THC dose and throughout multiple dosing, respectively. Models were only 60% and 12.5% accurate 12.5 and 22.5 h after the last THC dose, respectively. Predictive models estimating time since last cannabis intake from whole blood and plasma cannabinoid concentrations were inaccurate during abstinence but highly accurate during active THC dosing. THC redistribution from large cannabinoid body stores and high circulating THCCOOH concentrations create different pharmacokinetic profiles than those in less than daily cannabis smokers that were used to derive the models. Thus, the models

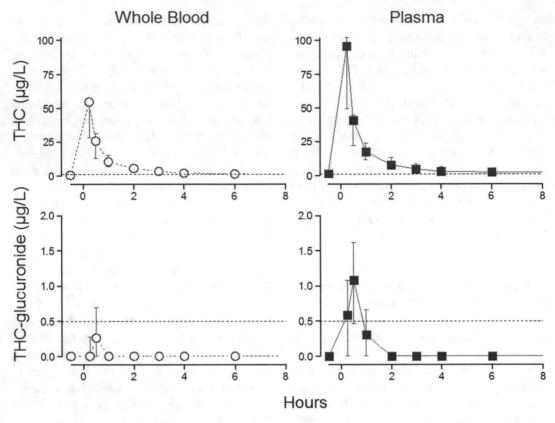

Fig. 24.17 Median (interquartile range) whole blood (E) and plasma (F) concentrations following smoking of a 6.8% THC cannabis cigarette. Dotted lines indicate limits of quantification: 1 µg/L for THC and 0.5 µg/L for THC- glucuronide (THC-gluc). Reprinted from Schwope et al. (2011) with permission from the American Association for Clinical Chemistry

do not accurately predict time of last THC intake in individuals consuming THC daily and then becoming abstinent.

We also evaluated WB/P cannabinoid ratios in frequent and occasional smokers who resided on our closed research unit and smoked one 6.8% THC cannabis cigarette ad libitum. Blood and plasma cannabinoids were quantified on admission (approximately 19 h before), 1 h before, and up to 15 times (0.5–30 h) after smoking (Desrosiers et al. 2014). Cannabinoid blood and plasma concentrations were significantly higher in frequent smokers compared with occasional smokers at most time points for THC and 11-OH-THC and at all time points for THCCOOH and THCCOOH-glucuronide. CBD, CBN, and THC-glucuronide were not significantly different at any time point. For blood THC >5 µg/L,

median (range) time of last detection was 3.5 h (1.1–>30 h) in frequent smokers and 1.0 h (0–2.1 h) in 11 occasional smokers (two occasional smokers had no samples with THC >5 µg/L). THCCOOH had the highest detection rate, followed by THCCOOH-glucuronide, THC, and 11-OH-THC. When present, CBD, CBN, and THC-glucuronide were detected for only 0.5–4 h. Overall median (range) blood-to-plasma ratios were 0.68 (0.31–1.1) for THC, 0.63 (0.38–1.1) for 11-OH-THC, 0.59 (0.41–1.2) for THCCOOH, 0.84 (0.47–1.3) for CBN, and 0.47 (0.24–1.1) for THCCOOH-glucuronide. Too few positive samples occurred for accurate CBD and THC-glucuronide ratio calculation. Cannabis smoking history plays a major role in cannabinoid detection. These differences may impact clinical and impaired driving drug detection. The presence of CBN or THC-glucuronide indicates recent use, but their absence does not exclude it.

Finally, we evaluated WB/P ratios in the controlled vaporized cannabis administration study, with and without simultaneous oral low-dose alcohol, for 32 adult occasional cannabis smokers described previously (Hartman et al. 2015a). Median (range) blood/plasma ratios were 0.71 (0.13–1.5) for THC (n = 684), 0.73 (0.42–1.4) for 11-OH-THC (n = 409), 0.65 (0.39–1.5) for THCCOOH (n = 1112), 0.55 (0.40–1.3) for THC-glucuronide (n = 12), 0.80 (0.13–7.9) for THCCOOH-glucuronide (n = 926), 0.73 (0.48–1.0) for CBD (n = 31), and 0.86 (0.49–1.3) for CBN (n = 71). THC and metabolite blood/plasma ratios did not vary by time or dose.

The interpretation of blood cannabinoid results continues to be controversial. We showed that there is no dose–response relationship for smoked THC and the THC concentrations in blood and plasma (Hartman et al. 2016a). It is well established that THC concentrations begin to decline before the occurrence of peak effects, although THC effects begin to appear rapidly after initiation of smoking. We found peak cannabis effects occur at the time of equivalent THC and THCCOOH concentrations, within 30–45 min after initiation of smoking. We evaluated 302 Drug Evaluation and Classification Program cannabis-only cases with blood THC ≥1 μg/L. All drivers were judged to be impaired by cannabis, but there were no significant differences between cases with blood THC <5 μg/L versus ≥5 μg/L. Accurate prediction of the time of cannabis exposure would be helpful in establishing the role of cannabis as a contributing factor to crashes.

Interpretation of Postmortem Blood Cannabinoids

Based on THC's lipophilicity and large volume of distribution, postmortem redistribution was expected to be a major factor in interpretation of postmortem cannabinoid results. Postmortem redistribution can occur, but surprisingly to date, the increase in concentrations appears to be generally twofold or less for THC, 11-OH-THC, and THCCOOH, with only a limited relationship between increasing THC concentrations and postmortem interval (Holland et al. 2011; Lemos and Ingle 2011). There are few data available that compare antemortem to postmortem cannabinoid data. Additional research on postmortem redistribution of THC is clearly needed, leading toxicologists to conservatively interpret postmortem cannabinoid concentrations. For instance, the prediction models that follow are usually not recommended for postmortem cannabinoid data.

The presence of THC and 11-OH-THC, equipotent cannabinoid compounds, in postmortem blood cannot automatically indicate recent cannabis use. Chronic frequent cannabis use can result in measurable THC and 11-OH-THC concentrations in blood for as long as 24 days and 2–3 days of sustained abstinence (Bergamaschi et al. 2013).

As for all postmortem blood collections, peripheral blood is preferred over central heart blood draws. This is especially important for cannabinoids that are generally inhaled, resulting in high THC concentrations in the lung and in the highly infused organs, including the heart and liver. If an individual's death is due to central torso trauma, for instance, in a motor vehicle crash, there could be THC release from tissues into the surrounding blood, suggesting the need for conservative opinions.

Mathematical Models for Predicting Elapsed Time since Last Cannabis Use

We presented two mathematical models for predicting the elapsed time after smoking using cannabinoid measurements of single plasma samples from individuals who smoke cannabis less frequently than daily (Fig. 24.18) (Huestis et al. 1992b). The models were derived from cannabinoid data obtained from a controlled clinical study of acute smoking and were validated with cannabinoid data from the literature. Model I is based on the plasma THC concentration, and model II is based on the ratio of the

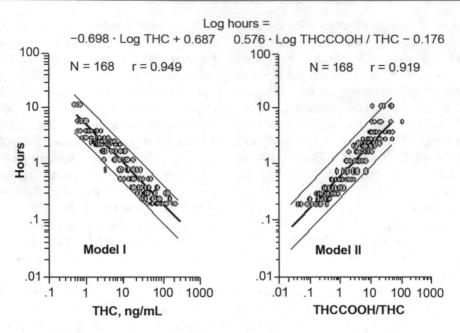

Fig. 24.18 Predictive mathematical models for estimating the elapsed time in hours (h) of last cannabis use from plasma Δ⁹-tetrahydrocannabinol (THC) and 11-nor-9-carboxy-THC (THCCOOH) concentrations measured by gas chromatography–mass spectrometry. Reprinted from Huestis et al. (1992b) with permission from Oxford University Press

concentration of plasma THCCOOH to THC. The models were applied to all published studies at the time that included plasma concentrations; both models correctly predicted times of cannabis exposure within 95% confidence intervals (CIs) for >90% of the samples evaluated. Initially, plasma THC concentrations <2.0 μg/L were excluded for two reasons: the possibility of residual THC concentrations in frequent smokers and concerns at the time about accuracy of quantification at low concentrations. In the following formulas, T represents the elapsed time in h between the beginning of cannabis smoking and blood collection, and CI represents the 95% CI for the estimate of T. Subscripts 1 and 2 refer to models I and II, respectively, and brackets denote the concentrations of THC or THCCOOH in μg/L.

Model I: $\log T = -0.698 \log[\text{THC}] + 0.687$

$$\log\text{CI}_1 = \log T \pm 1.975\sqrt{0.030\left\{1.006 + \frac{\left(\log[\text{THC}] - 0.996\right)^2}{89.937}\right\}}.$$

Model II: $\log T = (0.576 \log[\text{THCCOOH}] / [\text{THC}]) - 0.176$

$$\log\text{CI}_2 = \log T \pm 1.975\sqrt{0.045\left\{1.006 + \frac{\left(\log[\text{THCCOOH}]/[\text{THC}] - 0.283\right)^2}{123.420}\right\}}.$$

The models predict last cannabis use within a specified interval of time. The magnitude of the interval is smaller when the elapsed time between cannabis use and blood collection is shorter.

More recently, the validation of these predictive models was extended to include the estimation of the time of use after multiple THC doses and at low THC concentrations (0.5–2 µg/L), situations that were not included in the development of the original models (Huestis et al. 2005). Model I was less accurate with primarily overestimates that benefit the accused. After single doses, model II had primarily underestimates that are less favorable in forensic testing because they tend to predict earlier cannabis use that could be misinterpreted as a period of impaired performance. Model II was more accurate and had no underestimates for multiple doses. The most accurate approach applied a combination of models I and II by predicting a single time interval defined by the lowest and highest 95% confidence limits of the two models. For all 717 plasma samples, 99% of the predicted times of last use were within this combination interval, 0.9% were overestimated, and none were underestimated. For 289 plasma samples collected after multiple doses, 97% were correct with no underestimates. All time estimates were correct for 77 plasma samples with THC concentrations between 0.5 µg/L and 2 µg/L, a low concentration interval not previously examined.

These models also appeared to be valuable when they were applied to the small amount of data from published studies of oral ingestion that were available at the time the models were developed. Additional studies were performed to determine if the predictive models could estimate last use after multiple oral doses, a route of administration more popular with the advent of cannabis therapies (Huestis et al. 2006). Eighteen study participants received oral THC as Marinol or as hemp oil containing THC. The actual times between THC ingestion and blood collection spanned 0.5 to 16 h. Use of the combined CI yielded correct predicted times 96.7% of the time, with one overestimate (0.65 h) and two underestimates (0.13 h, 0.57 h). When used in combination, the models correctly predict the time of cannabis use within a 95% CI for more than 95% of cases involving a single smoked cannabis cigarette, two smoked cannabis cigarettes, or multiple oral doses of THC-containing preparations in individuals who use cannabis less than daily. Most controlled studies of cannabis administration indicated impairment of tasks related to normal driving functions for up to 6–8 h after use. A small number of studies extended this time interval to 24 h for complex, multitasking operations. The predictive models provide an objective means of estimating recent cannabis use within the 95% CI. Such estimation can be combined with evidence derived from the known pharmacodynamic effects of cannabis to develop a case of impairment. Karschner et al. (2012) evaluated the models' accuracy in ten male chronic, frequent cannabis users during round-the-clock administration of 40–120 mg oral THC/day and during abstinence. Maximum whole blood THC occurred 3.0 h after the first oral THC dose and 103.5 h (4.3 days) during multiple THC dosing. Median whole blood/plasma ratios were THC 0.63 (n = 196), 11-OH-THC 0.60 (n = 189), and THCCOOH 0.55 (n = 200). Predictive models utilizing these WB/P ratios accurately estimated last cannabis exposure in 96% and 100% of specimens collected within 1–5 h after a single oral THC dose and throughout multiple dosing, respectively. Models were only 60% and 12.5% accurate 12.5 and 22.5 h after the last THC dose, respectively. Predictive models estimating time since last cannabis intake from whole blood and plasma cannabinoid concentrations were inaccurate during abstinence, but highly accurate during active THC dosing. THC redistribution from large cannabinoid body stores and high circulating THCCOOH concentrations create different pharmacokinetic profiles than those in less than daily cannabis smokers that were used to derive the models. Thus, the models do not accurately predict time of last THC intake in individuals consuming THC daily. The models should not be used in postmortem cases because the many changes that can occur postmortem may affect the model's accuracy.

Urine Cannabinoid Concentrations

The interpretation of positive results in urine tests requires an understanding of the excretion pattern of cannabinoid metabolites in humans; however, there are limited urinary-excretion data available from controlled clinical studies to aid in such interpretation. Substantial interindividual and inter-dose variation exists in the patterns of THCCOOH excretion. The THCCOOH concentration in the first sample collected after smoking is indicative of how rapidly the metabolite appears in urine. Mean THC concentrations in the first urine sample were 47 ± 22.3 µg/L and 75.3 ± 48.9 µg/L after smoking one 1.75% THC cigarette and one 3.55% THC cigarette, respectively (Huestis et al. 1996). Approximately 50% of the study participants' first urine samples after the low dose and 83% of the first urine samples after the high dose were positive by GC–MS analysis (THCCOOH cutoff concentration, 15 µg/L). THCCOOH concentrations in the first urine sample are dependent on the relative potency of the cigarette, the elapsed time following drug administration, smoking efficiency, and individual differences in drug metabolism and excretion. Mean peak urine THCCOOH concentrations were 89.8 ± 31.9 µg/L (range, 20.6–234 µg/L) and 153 ± 49.2 µg/L (range, 29.9–355 µg/L) following the smoking of approximately 15.8 mg and 33.8 mg THC, respectively. Mean times of peak urine concentration were 7.7 ± 0.8 h after the 1.75% THC dose and 13.9 ± 3.5 h after the 3.55% THC dose. Although peak concentrations appeared to be dose related, individual values varied by as much as 12-fold.

Establishing the drug detection window in a specific biological matrix, i.e., the time after drug administration that a test is first positive until the last time a test is positive, is important since obtaining a positive test result then indicates that use most likely occurred within the specified drug detection window (Huestis 1995). Detection time is dependent on pharmacologic factors (e.g., drug dose, route of administration, rates of metabolism and excretion) and analytical factors (e.g., assay sensitivity,

specificity, accuracy). Mean detection times in urine following smoking vary considerably among individuals, even in controlled smoking studies in which cannabis dosing is standardized and smoking is paced by computer. During the terminal elimination phase, consecutive urine samples may fluctuate between testing positive and testing negative as the THCCOOH concentrations approach the cutoff concentration. After smoking a 1.75% THC cigarette, three of six study participants had additional positive urine samples interspersed among negatively testing samples. This intermittent pattern had the effect of producing much longer detection times for the last positive sample. When the 15 µg/L confirmation cutoff for THCCOOH currently required for federally mandated workplace drug testing is applied, mean GC–MS THCCOOH-detection times for the last positive urine sample following the smoking of a single 1.75% or 3.55% THC cigarette were 33.7 ± 9.2 h (range, 8–68.5 h) and 88.6 ± 23.2 h (range, 57–122.3 h), respectively. GC–MS detection times were shorter than those obtained with less specific immunoassays.

Significant differences exist between the available immunoassay products, and these differences affect the efficiency of detection of cannabinoid use. Therefore, knowledge of the sensitivity and specificity of an immunoassay is essential for proper interpretation. Reports of prolonged drug excretion are the basis for the common assumption that cannabinoid metabolites can be detected in the urine for a week or more. The accuracy, sensitivity, and specificity for detecting cannabinoids and their metabolites are unique to a particular immunoassay, and the assay may change over time. It is important that individuals who select assays and those who interpret the test results be aware of the qualitative and quantitative changes that can and do occur. In general, the detection times of cannabinoid metabolites in urine decreased as the specificities of the various immunoassays increased. This decrease improved not only the correlations between immunoassays but also the correlations between immunoassays and confirmation procedures; however, the increase in specificity also contributed to the noted decrease in the time course of detection of acute cannabis use.

Detection times for urinary cannabinoids vary substantially across assays, individuals, doses, and cutoff concentrations. Immunoassays that detect cannabinoids in addition to THCCOOH would be expected to have longer detection times, but cutoffs are usually set higher than for more specific confirmation methods to make them more consistent. GC–MS detection times with the federally mandated 15 µg/L cutoff were approximately twice as long as mean detection times with a 50-µg/L immunoassay cutoff (1–2 days). Mean detection times were longer (1–6 days after smoking) with an immunoassay with a 20-µg/L cutoff. Consecutive urine voids may produce positive or negative results as drug concentrations approach the cutoff concentration due to variation in excretion and changes in urine dilution. Quantitative results adjusted for creatinine concentration or specific gravity can reduce the effect of dilution and make estimation of detection times more consistent.

Interpretation of Urine Cannabinoid Concentrations

The detection of cannabinoids in urine is indicative of prior cannabis exposure, but the long excretion half-life of THC in the body, especially in chronic cannabis users, makes it difficult to predict the timing of past drug use. In a single extreme case, the individual's urine was positive by immunoassay for up to 57 consecutive days after the last drug exposure with a 20-µg/mL immunoassay cutoff (Ellis et al. 1985). This individual used cannabis frequently for >10 years. Urine samples from a naive user, however, may test negative by immunoassay only a few h after smoking of a single cannabis cigarette. A positive result in a urine test for cannabinoids indicates drug exposure occurred but no information on the route of administration, the amount of drug exposure, when drug exposure occurred, or the degree of impairment.

Normalization of Urine Cannabinoid Concentrations to the Urine Creatinine Concentration

Normalization of the cannabinoid drug concentration to the urine creatinine or specific gravity concentration aids in distinguishing new cannabis use from prior cannabis use because it reduces the variation in drug measurements from variable dilution of the urine. Given the long half-life of drug in the body, especially in chronic cannabis users, toxicologists are frequently asked to determine whether a positive result in a urine test represents a new episode of drug use or continuing excretion of residual drug. The excretion of creatinine into urine is relatively constant providing a mechanism for controlling for dilution of other constituents. In 1983, Hawks first suggested creatinine normalization for urine test results to account for variation in the urine volume in the bladder. Whereas urine volume is highly variable because of changes in liquid, salt, and protein intake, exercise, and age, creatinine excretion is much more stable. In 1984, Manno et al. recommended that a ratio of the creatinine-normalized cannabinoid concentration (U2) above that of the previous sample (U1) of 1.5 or greater be considered indicative of a new episode of drug exposure. If the increase is greater than or equal to the selected threshold, then new use is predicted. This approach had received wide attention for potential use in treatment and employee-assistance programs, but there was limited evaluation of the usefulness of this ratio under controlled-dosing conditions.

We conducted a controlled clinical study of the excretion profile of creatinine and cannabinoid metabolites in cannabis smokers. Figure 24.16 shows that normalization of the urinary THCCOOH concentration to the urinary creatinine concentration produces a smoother excretion pattern and facilitates determining if a subsequent urine concentration indicates new use (Huestis et al. 1998). A receiver operating characteristic (ROC) curve was constructed from sensitivity and specificity data for 26 different cutoffs that ranged from U2/U1 ratios of 0.10 to 2.0 using creatinine-normalized urine cannabinoid concentrations. The most accurate ratio was 0.50 in cannabis users who smoked less than daily (sensitivity, 80.1%; specificity, 90.2%; false-positive prediction, 5.6%; false-negative prediction, 7.4%). When the previously recommended ratio of 1.5 was applied as the threshold for new use, the sensitivity of detecting new use was only 33.4%, the specificity was high at 99.8%, and the overall accuracy of prediction was 74.2%. To further substantiate the validity of the derived ROC curve, we evaluated urine cannabinoid metabolite and creatinine data from another controlled clinical trial that specifically addressed water dilution as a means of sample adulteration. Values for sensitivity, specificity, accuracy, percent false positives, and percent false negatives were 71.9%, 91.6%, 83.9%, 5.4%, and 10.7%, respectively, when the 0.50 criterion was applied. These data indicate that selecting a threshold to evaluate sequential creatinine-normalized drug concentrations in urine can improve the ability for distinguishing residual excretion from new drug use.

A ratio $\geq$ 0.5 in the creatinine-normalized cannabinoid concentration sample is considered indicative of a new episode of drug exposure in individuals who are less-than-daily users. In long-term daily cannabis users, THCCOOH concentrations initially drop off rapidly, with the 0.5 criterion proving accurate for predicting new cannabis use, according to cannabis treatment providers; however, chronic, frequent users have smaller decreases in urinary cannabinoid excretion later in the elimination time course. Increases of >150% in creatinine-corrected concentrations for urine samples collected from chronic users were suggested as an indicator of new cannabis use.

The time course of THCCOOH elimination in urine for 60 chronic, frequent cannabis users during 24-h monitored abstinence on a closed research unit for up to 30 days was reported (Goodwin et al. 2008). We screened 6158 urine samples by immunoassay. Samples with values $\geq$50 μg/L were classified as positive, and results were confirmed by GC–MS for measurements $\geq$15 μg/L. The maximum creatinine-normalized THCCOOH concentration occurred in the first urine sample in 60% of the individuals; in 40%, peaks occurred as long as 2.9 days after admission. The creatinine-corrected initial THCCOOH concentrations were divided into three groups (0–50 μg/g, 51–150 μg/g, and > 150 μg/g). There were statistically significant correlations between groups and the number of days until the first negatively and the last positively testing urine samples (mean number of days were 0.6 and 4.3 days, 3.2 and 9.7 days, and 4.7 and 15.4 days for the three groups, respectively). These data provide guidelines for interpreting the results of urine tests for cannabinoids and suggest appropriate detection windows for differentiating new cannabis use from residual drug excretion.

In all but sports anti-doping testing, normalization to urine creatinine concentrations is the norm, but in anti-doping testing, drug concentrations may be normalized to the specific gravity of urine. All urine voids were individually collected from eight frequent and eight occasional cannabis users for up to 85 h after each received on separate occasions 50.6 mg THC by smoking, vaporization, and oral ingestion in a randomized, within-subject, double-blind, double-dummy, placebo-controlled protocol (Huestis et al. 2019a). Each urine void was analyzed for 11 cannabinoids and phase I and II metabolites by LC–MS/MS, and for specific gravity, and creatinine. The concentrations of urine specimens from the two normalization methods were compared to see if the degree of association differed by frequent or occasional cannabis use, or route of administration after adjusting for gender and time since dosing. Of 1880 urine samples examined, only THCCOOH, THCCOOH-glucuronide, THC-glucuronide, and THCVCOOH had concentrations greater than the method's LOQs. Associations between specific gravity- and creatinine-normalized concentrations exceeded 0.90. Repeated-measures regression analysis found small but statistically significant differences in the degree of association between normalization methods for THCCOOH and THCCOOH-glucuronide in frequent vs occasional smokers and in THCVCOOH and THC-glucuronide by route of administration. Both normalization methods reduced variability, improving the interpretation of urine cannabinoid concentrations, and methods were strongly correlated.

Models to Identify New Cannabis Use between Two Urine Specimens in Occasional Cannabis Users and Chronic, Frequent Cannabis Users

Identifying New Cannabis Use with Urine Creatinine-Normalized THCCOOH Concentrations and Time Intervals between Specimen Collections for Occasional Cannabis Users

A previously recommended method for detecting new cannabis use with creatinine-normalized THCCOOH urine concentrations in periodically collected specimens for treatment, workplace, and judicial drug testing applications is refined by considering the time interval between urine collections. All urine specimen concentrations from the study described above (Huestis 1998) were reevaluated taking into consideration the time between specimen collections. Ratios (n = 24,322) were calculated by dividing each creatinine-normalized THCCOOH concentration (U2) by that of a previously collected specimen (U1) (Smith et al. 2009). Maximum, 95% limit, and median U2/U1 ratios with 15 and 6 ng THCCOOH/mL cutoff concentrations, with and without new use between specimens, were calculated for each 24-h interval after smoking up to 168 h. These ratios decreased with increasing interval between collections providing improved decision values for determining new cannabis use. For example, with a 15-ng THCCOOH/mL cutoff concentration and no new use between specimens, the maximum, 95% limit, and median U2/U1 ratios were 3.05, 1.59, and 0.686, respectively, when the collection interval was ≤24 h and 0.215, 0.135, and 0.085 when it was 96–119.9 h. This refinement of the previously published creatinine-normalized urinary THCCOOH new use prediction guidelines takes into consideration specific intervals after cannabis smoking rather than grouping all data into a single week after

drug use. This improves the accuracy of prediction within each 24-h period. The most conservative method for reporting new cannabis use between collections would apply a U2/U1 decision ratio equal to the maxima. A more realistic decision ratio with reasonable certainty would be the 95% limits. These specific decision ratios improve detection of new cannabis use and support claims of abstinence and residual urinary drug excretion in drug testing programs.

Differentiating New Cannabis Use from Residual Urinary Cannabinoid Excretion in Chronic, Daily Cannabis Users

Development of a model to identify new cannabis use in chronic, frequent cannabis users was much more difficult than a model in occasional users because of the excretion of cannabinoids in urine from residual THC stored in the body. Models were based on urinary creatinine-normalized (CN) cannabinoid excretion in chronic cannabis smokers who resided on a secure research unit for 30 days without access to cannabis (Schwilke et al. 2011). For model validation, participants were abstinent with daily observed urine specimens for 28 days. A total of 48 (model development) and 67 (model validation) daily cannabis smokers participated. All voided urine was collected and analyzed for THCCOOH by GC–MS (LOQ = 2.5 ng/mL) and creatinine (mg/mL), and urine THCCOOH was normalized to creatinine, yielding ng/mg CN-THCCOOH concentrations. Urine concentration ratios were determined from 123,513 specimen pairs collected 2–30 days apart. A mono-exponential model (with two parameters, initial urine specimen CN-THCCOOH concentration and time between specimens), based on the Marquardt–Levenberg algorithm, provided a reasonable data fit. Prediction intervals with varying probability levels (80, 90, 95, 99%) provide upper ratio limits for each urine specimen pair. Ratios above these limits suggest cannabis reuse. Disproportionate numbers of ratios were higher than expected for some participants, prompting development of two additional rules that avoid misidentification of reuse in participants with unusual

CN-THCCOOH excretion patterns. This validated model is available to aid in the differentiation of new cannabis use from residual creatinine-normalized THCCOOH excretion in chronic, frequent cannabis users. These models are valuable for clinicians, toxicologists, and drug treatment staff and workplace, military, and criminal justice drug-testing programs.

Measurement of THC and 11-OH-THC in Urine as Indicators of Recent Cannabis Use

For many years, THC and 11-OH-THC were believed to be absent in urine samples after cannabis administration. Kemp et al. (1995) discovered that THC and 11-OH-THC could be detected if urine was hydrolyzed with β-glucuronidase from *Escherichia coli* rather than from *Helix pomatia* (a snail) prior to GC–MS analysis. The authors proposed that the presence of THC and 11-OH-THC in urine indicated recent cannabis use; however, urine samples were collected for only 8 h after controlled THC administration. Recently, we monitored urinary cannabinoid excretion in 33 chronic cannabis smokers, who all resided on our secure research unit under 24-h continuous medical surveillance (Abraham et al. 2007). All urine samples were collected individually ad libitum for up to 30 days, hydrolyzed with a tandem *E. coli* β-glucuronidase/base procedure, and analyzed for THC, 11-OH-THC, and THCCOOH with an LOQ of 2.5 µg/L. Although many of the chronic cannabis users had no detectable THC in their urine, extended THC excretion of greater than 72 h was observed in seven individuals during monitored abstinence (Lowe et al. 2009). THC was detected in urine for up to 24 days after cessation of cannabis use. 11-OH-THC and THCCOOH were detectable in samples from these individuals for up to 30 days. This study was the first time that extended urinary excretion of THC and 11-OH-THC had been documented. These results negated their effectiveness as biomarkers of recent cannabis exposure and substantiated the long terminal elimination times for urinary cannabinoids following chronic cannabis smoking.

Cannabinoids in OF

OF also is a suitable sample for monitoring cannabinoid exposure and achieved major acceptance with the Substance Abuse and Mental Health Services Administration (SAMHSA) publication of the 2019 Mandatory Guidelines for Workplace Drug Testing in October, 2019. OF will be accepted shortly for regulated workplace drug testing, but approximately one-third of nonregulated urine drug testing moved to OF. Alabama, California, Oklahoma, Wisconsin, Michigan, Kansas, and other law enforcement agencies conducted studies with OF for roadside drug testing. Many US states' laws allow OF testing, but currently Alabama is the only law enforcement laboratory routinely offering mass spectrometry confirmation testing for OF screening devices. Slowly the United States is moving toward OF testing for criminal justice programs, and the pain management and treatment drug testing programs are accepting this alternative matrix (Desrosiers and Huestis 2019). Random OF roadside testing is the norm in Australia, and many EU countries use OF roadside testing as a deterrent to drugged driving and as evidentiary tests for court. OF offers many advantages for driving under the influence of drugs, drug treatment, workplace drug testing, pain management, and clinical trials.

OF advantages include ease and noninvasiveness of sample collection, possible use as an indicator of recent cannabis smoking (depending on the cutoff employed), eliminating the need for specialized bathroom collection facilities or same sex collectors, and analysis of newly published recent use markers (Swortwood et al. 2017), a closer relationship to blood concentrations than urine, and reduced potential for sample adulteration because of observed collection procedures. Other advantages include potential for on-site collection and screening, lower biohazard risk during collection (compared to blood), and ease of multiple sample collections. Based on our controlled cannabis administration studies collecting OF, cannabinoid detection windows should be shorter in OF than urine. However, according to the Quest Diagnostics Workplace Drug Testing Index (Quest 2019), there is a higher positivity rate for cannabinoids in OF than urine. According to Quest, the only explanation is the easier adulteration of urine samples. OF collection is fully observed, and the mouth is checked prior to collection, with a 10-min waiting period. All of these measures make it much more difficult to adulterate.

Proponents of this matrix for roadside drug testing in Europe initially advanced the development of OF technologies. The Roadside Testing Assessment studies (ROSITA and ROSITA II) evaluated the best biological matrices (urine, OF, or sweat) for monitoring drugged driving. Although police, toxicologists, and policy personnel selected OF as the most promising matrix, the available OF collection devices and assays did not perform with acceptable sensitivity, specificity, and reliability. One of the major problems of measuring cannabinoids in OF is the low recovery from the collection device. Investigators reported that THC recoveries from many of these collection devices were < 50%. Unfortunately, manufacturers initially just adapted urine screening methods that targeted THCCOOH with cutoffs that were too high and detection rates that were too low. These technical problems were addressed by manufacturers, and OF testing procedures for cannabinoids target THC, the parent compound, that is the primary cannabinoid in OF. Identifying minor cannabinoids CBN, THCV, and cannabigerol (CBG) in OF was suggested to document past-day intake in occasional and chronic, frequent cannabis smokers, although various cannabis strains were not evaluated (Desrosiers et al. 2015a). Manufacturers invested in developing the best elution solvent for removing THC from the collection pad and stabilizing it in OF. The OF elution solvents are proprietary and account for the improved recovery, stability, and precision of the best OF collection devices today.

THC, rather than 11-OH-THC or THCCOOH, is the primary cannabinoid analyte in OF after cannabis use. The oral mucosa is coated by high concentrations of THC during smoking, vaporization, and ingestion of edible cannabinoids and is the major source of THC found in OF. After intravenous administration of radiolabeled THC, no radioactivity could be demonstrated in OF at an LOQ of 0.5 µg/L (Hawks et al. 1982). Despite these reports, we found that THC concentrations in OF correlated well with blood/plasma concentrations after the initial coating of the oral mucosa by smoking was cleared. After smoking a 3.55% THC cigarette, one individual had a THC concentration of 5800 µg/L in the first OF sample collected at 0.2 h after the start of cannabis smoking and a concentration of 81 µg/L in the sample collected at 0.33 h. Initially, THC OF concentrations easily are in the multi-thousand µg/L due to the deposition of THC in the oral mucosa (Lee et al. 2015). OF collected with the Salivette collection device (Sarstedt) was positive for THC in 14 of 22 participants after smoking cannabis. Although no 11-OH-THC or THCCOOH was identified, CBN and CBD were present as well. THC concentrations in OF correlate temporally with plasma cannabinoid concentrations and behavioral and physiological effects, but wide intra- and interindividual variation precludes the use of OF concentrations as indicators of drug impairment. We later learned that the Salivette collection device, well established in the OF testing field, has poor recovery for cannabinoids and many other drugs due to their adherence to the cotton pad.

Serum samples were collected from ten individuals who smoked cannabis containing 18 mg and 36.5 mg THC (Kauert et al. 2007). Mean concentrations at the end of smoking (47.8 ± 35.0 µg/L and 79.1 ± 42.5 µg/L, respectively) decreased to <1 µg/L at 6 h. The highest THC concentrations in OF occurred in the first collection at 0.25 h (900 ± 589 µg/L and 1041 ± 652 µg/L for the low and high doses, respectively). THC concentrations decreased in OF to 18 µg/L over 6 h. The interpretation of OF cannabinoid results depends on the assay LOQ, the cannabinoid analyte of interest, and cutoff concentrations.

2D-GC–MS (Milman et al. 2010a), GC–MS/ MS (Barnes et al. 2014), LC–MS/MS (Scheidweiler et al. 2013), and high-resolution mass spectrometry (HRMS, Concheiro et al. 2013) procedures with LOQs of 10 ng/L were developed for THCCOOH in OF. These low detection limits permitted investigators to quantify THCCOOH in OF for longer periods after cannabis smoking, vaporization, or eating. One report identified THCCOOH-glucuronide in OF and noted that THCCOOH-glucuronide constituted 64.5% of the total THCCOOH concentration $\geq$ 48 h after smoking (Coulter et al. 2012). Identifying THCCOOH-glucuronide in OF offers longer detection windows and an absence of passive contamination by cannabis smoke (Anizan et al. 2013). THCCOOH is found in much higher concentrations in chronic, frequent cannabis users with a longer detection time in this population, but its prevalence in occasional cannabis users is low (Lee et al. 2012). Additionally, THCCOOH is not found in cannabis smoke, substantiating drug intake, metabolism, and transfer into oral fluid from blood (Lee et al. 2013). Another advantage of monitoring THCCOOH in oral fluid is the identification of Marinol or dronabinol intake. Because the oral mucosa is not coated during ingestion of the synthetic THC capsules, there is no measurable THC in OF, although THCCOOH is readily quantified during oral administration of this FDA-approved medication (Milman et al. 2010b).

Current practice is to measure only THC in OF, but sidestream cannabis smoke under excessive exposure conditions can coat the oral mucosa with THC that is present in OF for up to 3 h after exposure with a 4-µg/L screening and 2-µg/L confirmation cutoff (Cone et al. 2015b). The peak THC concentration reported for oral-fluid samples collected from passively exposed individuals was 7.5 µg/L. Studies of passive cannabis exposure appear to indicate that positive THC results in tests of OF can occur shortly after cannabis smoke exposure, but results become negative within several hours (Moore et al. 2011). Consequently, when recent passive exposure to cannabis smoke can be ruled out, one can conclude that a positive result in an OF test provides credible evidence of active cannabis use.

OF collection and data describing the distribution of drugs in OF dramatically increased over the last two decades. Validated chromatographic methods to quantify multiple analytes in OF at low concentrations are available. Controlled drug administration studies and prevalence data improved interpretation of OF test results. OF offers many advantages over other matrices, but it is important to consider drug-specific characteristics, variability, and limitations in any interpretation of OF drug findings. Significant correlation was frequently observed between matrices (i.e., between OF and plasma or blood concentrations); however, high intra- and intersubject variability precludes prediction of blood concentrations from OF concentrations.

OF pharmacokinetics are available for controlled smoked cannabis, but few data exist for vaporized and oral routes. Frequent and occasional cannabis smokers were recruited as participants for four dosing sessions including one active (6.9% THC) or placebo cannabis-containing brownie, followed by one active or placebo cigarette, or one active or placebo vaporized cannabis dose. Only one active dose was administered per session. OF was collected before and up to 54 (occasional) or 72 (frequent) h after dosing from cannabis smokers. THC, 11-OH-THC, THCCOOH, THCV, CBD, and CBG were quantified by LC–MS/MS. OF cannabinoid Cmax occurred during or immediately after cannabis consumption due to coating of the oral mucosa. Significantly greater THC C_{max} and significantly later THCV, CBD, and CBG t_{last} were observed after smoked and vaporized cannabis compared to oral cannabis in frequent smokers only (Fig. 24.19). No significant differences in THC, 11-OH-THC, THCV, CBD, or CBG tmax between routes were observed for either group. For occasional smokers, more 11-OH-THC and THCCOOH-positive specimens were observed after oral dosing than after inhaled routes, increasing % positive cannabinoid results and

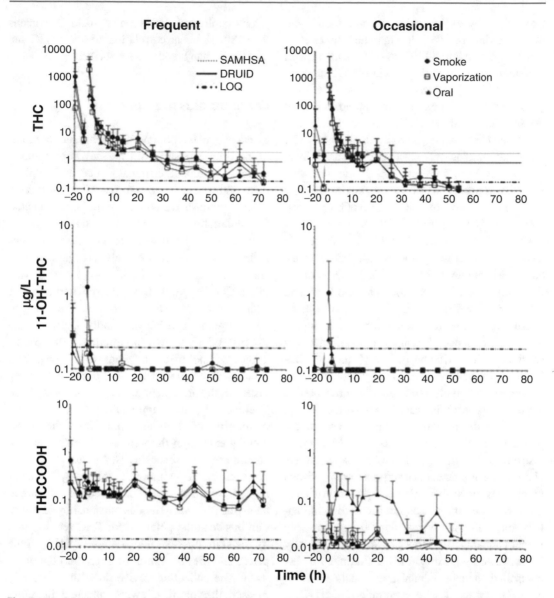

Fig. 24.19 Mean + standard deviation (SD) oral fluid concentrations on a log-scale for Δ9-tetrahydrocannabinol (THC), 11-hydroxy-THC (11-OH-THC), and 11-nor-9-carboxy-THC (THCCOOH) in n = 11 frequent (left) and n = 9 occasional (right) smokers up to 72 and 54 h, respectively, after smoked, vaporized, and oral cannabis (6.9% Δ9-tetrahydrocannabinol, THC; ~50.6 mg THC) administration (0 h). Horizontal lines present at the limits of quantification (LOQ, 0.2 µg/L for all, except 15 ng/L for THCCOOH) and OF THC cutoffs for DRUID (1 µg/L) and SAMHSA (2 µg/L). Reprinted from Swortwood et al. (2017) with permission from Wiley

widening metabolite detection windows after oral cannabis consumption. Utilizing 0.3 µg/L THCV and CBG cutoffs resulted in detection windows indicative of recent cannabis intake. OF pharmacokinetics after high potency CBD cannabis are not yet available precluding its use currently as a marker of recent use.

Cannabinoids in Breath

There is a major ongoing effort to develop a breathalyzer for cannabis. Efforts include colorimetric measurement to miniaturized mass spectrometers. We collected exhaled breath from chronic (>4 times per week) and occasional

(<twice per week) cannabis smokers before and after smoking a 6.8% THC cigarette (Himes et al. 2013). We extracted THC and THCCOOH with methanol from breath pads, solid-phase extraction (SPE), and LC–MS/MS quantification (LOQ 1 pg/pad). THC was the major cannabinoid in breath; no sample contained THCCOOH and only one contained CBN. Among chronic smokers (n = 13), all breath samples were positive for THC at 0.89 h, 76.9% at 1.38 h, 53.8% at 2.38 h, and only one sample was positive at 4.2 h after smoking. Among occasional smokers (n = 11), 90.9% of breath samples were THC positive at 0.95 h and 63.6% at 1.49 h. One occasional smoker had no detectable THC. Analyte recovery from breath pads by methanolic extraction was 84.2–97.4%. Limits of quantification were 50 pg/pad for THC and CBN and 100 pg/pad for THCCOOH. Breath may offer an alternative matrix for testing for recent driving under the influence of cannabis but is limited to a short detection window (0.5–2 h) and requires highly sensitive mass spectrometry detection.

Quantification of THC in breath is an important approach to controlling cannabis impaired driving. Multiple instrumentation companies around the world are attempting to produce a roadside breath instrument. Currently, different manufacturers claim to have a device, but no data are published on the sensitivity, specificity, and precision of such a device. The presence and concentration of cannabinoids in breath were shown to correlate with recent cannabis use (Himes et al. 2013) and may be correlated with impairment, although no new controlled cannabis administration data are available. Given the low concentration of THC in human breath, sensitive analytical methods are required to further evaluate its utility and window of detection. One promising approach for the OF confirmation assay was published by Luo et al. (2019). They describe a novel derivatization method based on an azo coupling reaction that significantly increases the ionization efficiency of cannabinoids for LC–MS/MS analysis and does not require further sample clean-up after derivatization. LOQs are sub-pg/mL to pg/mL for the five cannabinoids in breath samples, i.e., only 5–50 femtograms of an analyte was required for quantification. Cannabinoids were quantified in breath

samples collected within 3 h of smoking cannabis (n = 180). A linear correlation between THC and CBN in human breath was observed.

Cannabinoids in Sweat

Sweat testing is a noninvasive technique for monitoring drug exposure over a 7-day period and is useful in treatment, criminal justice, and employment settings. The advantages of sweat testing include noninvasive collection, reduced potential for adulteration, and continuous monitoring during the sweat patch wear period. Disadvantages include the availability of only a single commercially available sweat-collection device (the PharmChek™ patch from PharmChem), minor allergic reactions to the patch, variable sweat production within and between individuals, and the paucity of data for interpreting test results. Typically, the patch is worn for 7 days and exchanged for a new patch once each week during visits to the treatment clinic or parole officer. Theoretically, this approach permits constant monitoring of drug use throughout the week, thereby extending the window of drug detection and improving test sensitivity. As with OF testing, however, the development of this analytical technique is ongoing, and much needs to be learned about the pharmacokinetics of cannabinoid excretion in sweat, the potential for THC reabsorption by the skin, possible degradation of THC on the patch, and the adsorption of THC onto the patch itself. The collection device does not accurately measure the volume of sweat collected; therefore, the amount of drug collected per patch is reported, rather than the concentration of the drug in sweat. Furthermore, the amount of sweat excreted and collected varies, depending on the amount of exercise and the ambient temperature.

THC is the primary analyte detected in sweat, with little 11-OH-THC and THCCOOH (Huestis and Smith 2018). THC concentrations ranged from 4 to 38 ng/patch in 20 heroin abusers who wore the PharmChek patch for 5 days during detoxification (Kintz et al. 1996). Sweat was extracted with methanol and analyzed by GC–MS.

The SAMHSA guidelines proposed for testing of cannabinoids in sweat with the PharmChek patch are a screening cutoff of 4 ng THC/patch and a confirmation cutoff of 1 ng THC/patch. Only one study on the excretion of cannabinoids in sweat following controlled THC administration was published. We tested daily and weekly sweat patches from seven individuals who were administered oral doses of up to 14.8 mg THC/day for five consecutive days (Huestis et al. 2008). In this study of oral THC administration, no daily or weekly patches had THC concentrations above the LOQ; concurrent plasma THC concentrations were all <6.1 µg/L. Oral ingestion of up to 14.8 mg THC daily does not produce a THC-positive sweat patch. No similar studies that followed the controlled smoking of cannabis were reported.

We had the opportunity to monitor THC excretion from previously self-administered cannabis in 11 daily smokers after initiation of abstinence (Huestis et al. 2008). Participants resided on our secure research unit under continuous medical monitoring. PharmChek sweat patches worn for 7 days were analyzed for THC by GC–MS, with an LOQ for THC of 0.4 ng THC/patch. Sweat patches worn the first week of abstinence had THC amounts greater than the SAMHSA-proposed 1-ng THC/patch cutoff concentration for federal workplace testing. The mean (±SE) amount of THC detected was 3.9 ± 0.9 ng THC/patch. Eight of 11 individuals had negatively testing patches by the second week, and one study participant produced THC-positive patches for 4 weeks of monitored abstinence (Fig. 24.20). With the proposed federal cutoff concentrations, most daily cannabis users will have a positive sweat patch in the first week after ceasing cannabis use and a negative patch in subsequent weeks, although patches may remain positive for 4 weeks or more in chronic, frequent cannabis users.

Cannabinoids in Hair

Tests of drugs in hair are frequently used in forensic investigations, drug-treatment research, and drug testing in nonfederal workplaces, although SAMHSA is considering hair testing requirements for the Mandatory Guidelines for Workplace Drug Testing. There are multiple mechanisms for the incorporation of cannabinoids in hair. THC and its metabolites may diffuse from the blood into the hair bulb from the surrounding capillaries, from sebum secreted onto the hair shaft, and/or from sweat excreted onto the skin surface. Drug may also be incorporated into hair from the environment. Cannabis is primarily smoked providing an opportunity for contamination of hair by THC in the air. Controlled experiments showed that drugs in solution applied to hair strands can be incorporated. Environmental contamination of hair remains a controversial subject, with most investigators having demonstrated drug incorporation despite extensive washing procedures. Others contend that the use of a combination of polar and nonpolar washing solvents and comparisons of drug concentrations in wash solutions and hair extracts account for external contamination. A concern for reducing the possibility of external contamination motivated SAMHSA to propose guidelines for screening cutoffs for cannabinoids in hair at 1 pg/mg for cannabinoids and 0.05 pg/mg for THCCOOH for confirmation testing.

Hair testing is utilized in Europe for regranting of the drivers' license after suspension for driving under the influence of cannabis. Hair testing is also an important matrix for criminal investigations including drug-facilitated crimes. All reputable hair testing laboratories monitor THCCOOH in hair to avoid contamination from THC in the environment. The Society of Hair Testing guidelines for drugs in hair recommends a 0.2-pg/mg cutoff for THCCOOH in hair.

Monitoring drug use with hair testing has distinct advantages, including a wide window of drug detection, a less invasive procedure for sample collection, and the ability to collect a similar sample at a later time; however, one of the weakest aspects of testing for cannabinoids in hair is the low sensitivity of THCCOOH detection in this alternative matrix. Basic drugs such as cocaine and methamphetamine concentrate in hair because of ionic bonding to melanin, the pigment in hair that determines hair color. The more

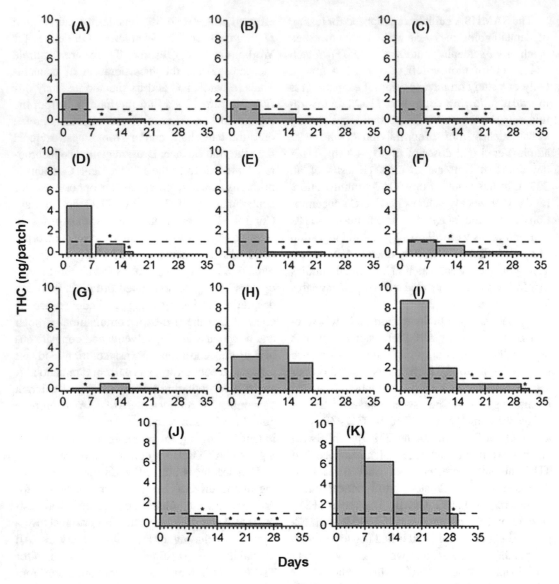

Fig. 24.20 Δ^9-Tetrahydrocannabinol (THC) excreted in the sweat of 11 tested individuals. Dashed line indicates the cutoff concentration of 1.0 ng/patch proposed by the Substance Abuse and Mental Health Services Administration. Asterisk indicates a THC amount less than the assay's limit of quantification (0.4 ng/patch). Reprinted from Huestis et al. (2008) with permission from Elsevier

neutral and lipophilic THC does not preferentially bind to melanin, thus producing much lower THC concentrations in hair compared with other drugs of abuse. Usually, THC is present in hair at a higher concentration than its THCCOOH metabolite (usually in low concentrations in the range of picograms per milligram). The advan-

tage of measuring THCCOOH is its absence in cannabis smoke; the issue of passive THC exposure from the environment can thus be avoided.

The analysis of cannabinoids in hair is challenging because of the high analytical sensitivity that is required. Tandem GC–MS and 2D-GC–MS are the most common analytical techniques. A novel approach to screening hair samples for cannabinoids uses a rapid, simple GC–MS screening method for THC, CBN, and CBD without derivatization (Cirimele et al. 1996). The method is a sensitive screen for cannabis detection, with GC–MS identification of THC recommended as a confirmatory procedure.

It is difficult to conduct controlled cannabinoid-administration studies on the disposition of cannabinoids in hair because of the inability to differentiate administered drug from previously self-administered cannabis and the low rates of incorporation of cannabinoids into hair. We studied THC and THCCOOH in 53 hair samples from 38 documented cannabis users: 18 daily users and 20 who smoked cannabis 1–5 days/week (Huestis et al. 2007). History of cannabis use was documented by questionnaire, urinalysis, and controlled, double-blind administration of smoked or oral THC. All participants had tested positive for urine cannabinoids at the time of hair collection. Additional hair samples were collected after the participants had smoked two 2.7% THC cigarettes or taken multiple oral THC doses. Cannabinoid concentrations in hair were measured by enzyme-linked immunosorbent assay (ELISA) and GC–MS/MS. Positive ELISA screening results (5 pg cannabinoids/mg hair) occurred in only 65% of daily smokers and 35% of nondaily smokers. Detection rates before and after the smoked or oral doses were not significantly different. Thirty-six percent of the participants had no detectable THC or THCCOOH at the LOQs of 1.0 pg/mg and 0.1 pg/mg of hair, respectively. THC only, THCCOOH only, and both cannabinoids were detected in 3.8%, 26%, and 34% of the study participants, respectively. GC–MS/MS detection rates for daily cannabis users and nondaily users were significantly different (85% and 52%, respectively). Detection rates in hair samples from African Americans (n = 40) and Caucasians (n = 13) were not significantly different. For samples with detectable cannabinoids, the concentration ranges were 3.4–>100 pg THC/mg and 0.10–7.3 pg THCCOOH/mg of hair. THC and THCCOOH concentrations were positively correlated. Eighty-three percent of the samples that screened positive were confirmed by GC–MS/MS at a cutoff concentration of 0.1 pg THCCOOH/mg of hair.

Hair grows at a rate of about 1 cm/month, providing an opportunity to segment hair to determine periods of drug use over time. Studies that tried to relate time of drug use with its presence in specific hair segments had inconsistent results, with positive evaluation of segmental hair analysis to indicate the time of drug exposure in drug-facilitated sexual assault, and others measured antibiotics in hair to monitor hair growth and to tie the presence of drugs to known times of drug administration. Other investigators administered deuterated cocaine and showed that the drug can be found throughout the hair shaft (Henderson et al. 1996). These data are consistent with the theory that drugs in sweat may bathe the hair shaft and deposit drug along the length of the hair follicle. Despite these issues, it does appear that higher and more frequent drug use is usually reflected in higher hair concentrations. Most of our knowledge of drug concentrations in hair is derived from basic drugs such as cocaine, amphetamines, and opiates. There are almost no data from research with controlled cannabinoid administration to help interpret the results of cannabinoid hair tests. The lack of findings can be attributed to the fact that THC is neutral and not bound to hair via ionic mechanisms that are important to the incorporation of basic drugs.

Passive Inhalation

Environmental exposure to cannabis smoke can occur through passive inhalation of sidestream and exhaled smoke. Several research studies indicated that it is possible to produce detectable concentrations of cannabis metabolites in the urine and plasma after passive inhalation of cannabis smoke, although the conditions required to produce such positive results were unrealistic and extreme (Cone et al. 1986). It is generally agreed that passive exposure is not a valid explanation for a positive result in a urine test, although this conclusion remains commonly used in workplace and forensic settings. More recently, passive inhalation was studied under extreme conditions again with higher potency cannabis cigarettes and variable air-flow conditions. The ability to produce positive blood, OF, and urine tests was shown to vary based on the potency of cannabis smoked and the amount of air flow (Cone et al. 2015a, b).

Analysis

THC binds readily to glass and plastic. This fact must be taken into consideration throughout all analyses, including preparation and storage of cannabinoid calibrators and quality-control materials. THC adsorption from solutions can be minimized with storage in amber silylated glassware at a basic pH or in an organic solvent.

Screening

The objective of the initial screening test is to identify true positive samples with a minimum number of unconfirmed positive results. To accomplish this goal, high immunoassay sensitivity must be balanced with high specificity to reduce the number of samples that require expensive and time-consuming GC–MS or LC–MS/MS confirmation. Selecting an appropriate testing methodology requires knowledge of the type of available sample, the analyte's metabolic profile, and the assay's characteristics. The nature and abundance of specific metabolites in different biological matrices must be known. Initial testing or screening methodologies for cannabinoids in body fluids include immunoassays, GC–MS, and LC–MS/MS. A wide variety of immunoassays are available, including enzyme immunoassays, cloned enzyme donor immunoassays, kinetic interaction of microparticles in solution, and recently introduced biochip assays (Randox) that screen for multiple drug classes simultaneously in a single sample.

Urine is usually tested without sample preparation because of the high concentrations of drug and/or metabolites and the low concentrations of other interfering components, such as proteins and lipids. The cross-reactivity of the immunoassay's antibodies to drug metabolites, including glucuronides, is important in method selection. Most immunoassays contain antibodies directed against THCCOOH, the primary urinary metabolite, although cross-reactivities vary considerably for THC, 11-OH-THC, CBD, CBN, and the glucuronides. This specificity toward THCCOOH makes these assays appropriate for urinalysis because little free THC or 11-OH-THC is present in urine; however, a much greater percentage of the cannabinoids in OF, sweat, and hair is parent THC. Glucuronide metabolites constitute a high percentage of the cannabinoid metabolites excreted in urine, but the combined cross-reactivity of glucuronide metabolites and the abundance of free carboxy metabolites provide adequate sensitivity to obviate hydrolysis of urine before screening. Cutoff values for initial screening tests of urine include 20, 50, and 100 μg/L. In April 1988, Department of Health and Human Services (DHHS) guidelines for testing urine for the federal sector established the initial test (screen) cutoff for cannabinoids at 100 μg/L but subsequently lowered the cutoff to 50 μg/L. We conducted a controlled study of cannabis administration via smoking and collected individual urine samples for evaluating multiple immunoassays at three cutoff concentrations and for GC–MS confirmation (Gustafson et al. 2003, 2004). The advantages of the use of authentic samples instead of fortified samples supplemented to contain only the target analyte include the presence of a variety of conjugated and nonconjugated human cannabinoid metabolites. A further advantage is the information gained from urine samples collected over an extended period after smoking. The nature and relative concentrations of cannabinoid metabolites change over time, and a controlled clinical study provides the opportunity to evaluate urine samples with distinct metabolic patterns. Lowering the cutoff concentration to 50 μg/L increased sensitivity in all immunoassays (sensitivity range, 57.0–79.5%) with minimal loss in specificity (Huestis et al. 1994). Specificity, or the true-negative rate, decreased slightly when the cutoff concentration was lowered to 50 μg/L with a confirmation cutoff of 15 μg/L for the specific THCCOOH metabolite. Unconfirmed positive screening results (false-positive tests) increased from 1.0% to 2.6%. The correlation between screening and confirmation also is important, considering the high labor and instrumentation costs of the confirmation assay. Thus, we demonstrated that lowering the cutoff to 50 μg/L greatly increased the identification of true-positive samples with little increase in false-positive screening results.

Additional challenges arose with immunoassay tests for cannabinoids in urine. The introduction of nonsteroidal anti-inflammatory drugs initially increased the number of nonconfirmed positive results in immunoassays, but manufacturers rapidly changed antibodies to eliminate the source of cross-reactivity. Another challenge arose with the widespread popularity of THC-containing foodstuffs. Hemp oil, a health food product prepared by crushing hemp seeds, was found to contain up to 300 μg/g THC in some US products and up to 1500 μg/g in Swiss hemp oil (Gustafson et al. 2003). THC content is dependent on the effectiveness of cannabis seed cleaning and oil-filtration processes. Ingestion of these materials could produce positive results in immunoassay and confirmatory cannabinoid tests. Government pressure to eliminate the illicit THC in these products was successful in reducing the probability of a positive result in a urine test from this source. New challenges will continue to occur. Currently, the therapeutic usefulness of oral cannabinoids is being investigated for various medicinal applications, as mentioned above. Use of these products could produce positive results in urine drug tests, depending on the potency, route of administration, and magnitude and chronicity of use. We demonstrated with a controlled oral-administration protocol that low-concentration hemp oils (total daily dose, 0.39–0.47 mg/day) taken in accordance with the manufacturer's recommendations produced few positive results in cannabinoid immunoassay screens, whereas high-concentration hemp oils

(total daily dose, 14.8 mg/day) and synthetic THC in the form of Marinol (7.5 mg/day) produced frequent and long-lasting positive results in urine tests.

OF also is a suitable specimen for screening for the presence of cannabinoids. SAMHSA proposed a screening cutoff for OF of 4 μg/L for cannabinoids and a confirmation cutoff of 2 μg/L for THC. OF contains much higher concentrations of parent THC than THCCOOH, which is present in the range of pg/mL. OF screening kits generally adapted urine assays to function for OF, in some cases limiting assay sensitivity. Another common difficulty encountered in oral-fluid testing is the adsorption of cannabinoids to the OF collection device. Different manufacturers resolved this problem by developing buffers that free cannabinoids from the device; however, these buffers dilute the cannabinoid concentrations in OF and frequently interfere with LC–MS/MS analysis because of the salts and proteins in the buffer.

Whole blood, plasma, and tissues also are screened for the presence of cannabinoids, generally in postmortem and human-performance laboratories (for drugged driving). Cannabinoid concentrations in whole blood are approximately one-half the concentrations in plasma samples, because of the low partition coefficient of the drug into erythrocytes. Simple preparation steps, such as dilution, protein precipitation, and single-step solvent extraction, may be required with some methodologies; more extensive extraction and concentration schemes may be required for other immunoassays. It is essential that calibrator and quality-control samples be prepared in the same matrix as the samples to be tested in order to account for matrix effects. The cutoff concentration of the immunoassay also may require adjustment for adequate screening of cannabinoid concentrations in different matrices. Method validation is essential for each matrix to instill confidence in the accuracy of the screening process. THC cross-reacts poorly with the antibodies found in most of the commercially available reagents, and a small number of cases featuring high THC concentrations and low THCCOOH concentrations (e.g., samples collected immediately after smoking) may produce negative results when assayed with THCCOOH-specific reagents. However, THCCOOH concentrations begin to rise during smoking, increase over time, and have a much longer time course of detection than the parent compound.

Drugs that eluted from sweat patches may also be screened with appropriate immunoassay reagents. The cutoff concentrations for THC, the primary analyte in sweat, are much lower than for cannabinoids in urine screening. It is essential that immunoassays be validated for the sweat matrix. Sweat contains many additional compounds, including various oils that may interfere with some immunoassays. Only a single commercial laboratory offers sweat collection and testing; sweat testing in research settings generally involves analyzing sweat directly via confirmation procedures, bypassing the screening step.

Drug testing of hair is increasing in workplace drug testing and in forensic investigations. The screening assay is highly important because of the high cost of confirmatory testing with this matrix. Sample-preparation steps are necessary, including carefully washing the hair to reduce external contamination and to remove natural oils and hair-care products. Extraction of drugs from the hair sample is necessary before screening, and a wide variety of methods were applied, from simple organic extractions to full dissolution of the hair matrix with enzyme mixtures or strong base. Many times, a hair sample is cut into small segments before or after hair washing or reduced to a powder by grinding in a ball mill after hair washing to improve homogenization of the sample and analyte-extraction efficiency. The extract may require neutralization of the pH and buffering before the immunoassay or radioimmunoassay. One of the most difficult aspects of hair testing is verifying that the extraction of the drugs from the complex matrix is complete. Fortification of hair segments or samples of powdered hair do not ensure that analytes are incorporated into hair in the same manner as after drug consumption in vivo. Thus, quality-control and proficiency tests frequently include hair samples from authenticated drug users to compare performance within and between laboratories. Sensitive immunoassays that are capable of measuring the low

ng/mg concentrations of cannabinoids in hair and that have good cross-reactivity to THC are preferred for hair testing. Method validation and preparation of calibrators in the hair matrix are critical for adequate performance.

Confirmation

Confirmation of cannabinoid results requires a chemical technique based on a scientific principle that is different from that of the initial test (e.g., immunoassay for screening and chromatography for confirmation). Routine confirmation methodologies include GC–MS, GC–MS/MS, LC–MS/MS, and HRMS. Ideally, the sensitivity of the confirmation assay should be equal to or greater than the sensitivity of the initial test method. Selected ion monitoring, full-scan ion monitoring, chemical-ionization methods, and multiple transitions from precursor to product ion LC–MS/MS are common cannabinoid confirmations. Sample preparation for GC–MS cannabinoid testing frequently includes a hydrolysis step to free cannabinoids from their glucuronide conjugates, while cannabinoid glucuronides are directly quantified in LC–MS/MS. Most GC–MS confirmation procedures for urine measure total THCCOOH after either enzymatic hydrolysis with β-glucuronidase or, more commonly, alkaline hydrolysis with sodium hydroxide. Alkaline hydrolysis appears to efficiently hydrolyze the THCCOOH–glucuronide ester linkage, and β-glucuronidase efficiently hydrolyzes the ether glucuronide.

GC–MS confirmation of THC, 11-OH-THC, and THCCOOH provides adequate sensitivity and specificity for a wide variety of biological tissues. Several deuterated THCCOOH materials are available as internal standards and are recommended to obtain results of the highest accuracy. Also available are compounds with multiple deuterium ions, which provide adequate resolution of deuterated ions from native ions for use in full-scan ion-monitoring techniques. Carboxyl and hydroxyl groups on the THC, 11-OH-THC, and THCCOOH molecules require derivatization to increase their volatility and improve chromatographic performance. Trimethylsilyl and methyl derivatizing reagents are frequently used to achieve acceptable gas chromatography analysis and sensitivity. Electron-ionization MS of cannabinoids after alkaline hydrolysis and derivatization with one of a wide variety of derivatization reagents was made achievable for most forensic toxicology laboratories by the availability of low-cost, bench-top GC–MS instruments. The increased selectivity of chemical-ionization techniques also became readily available with the release of several bench-top instruments. One of the most sensitive methods for THCCOOH detection uses negative-ion chemical-ionization MS of the methyl ester trifluoroacetate derivative. Sensitivity limits of 10 ng/L THCCOOH in blood, plasma, or urine matrices can be achieved because of the high ionization efficiency and selectivity. Metastable ion–detection techniques are also available for applications that require highly sensitive methods, e.g., pharmacokinetic studies.

Compared with other drugs of abuse, the analysis of cannabinoids presents difficult challenges. THC and 11-OH-THC are highly lipophilic and are present in low concentrations in body fluids and tissues. Complex sample matrices, i.e., blood, sweat, and hair, require multistep extractions to separate cannabinoids from endogenous lipids and proteins. Care must be taken to avoid low cannabinoid recoveries caused by their high affinities to glass and plastic containers and to collection devices for alternative matrices. Cannabinoid-extraction techniques include liquid–liquid extractions and solid-phase extraction with multiple single- and mixed-mode polymeric and ion-exchange columns. Sample preparation for urine cannabinoid testing may include enzymatic hydrolysis with β-glucuronidase or, more commonly, alkaline hydrolysis to free THCCOOH from the glucuronide conjugate. Most GC–MS procedures used for confirmation of urine results use a 15-µg/L cutoff and are specific for THCCOOH. Assays may include a hydrolysis step before the analysis of cannabinoids in blood or plasma, but this step is rarely used. The importance of glucuronide derivatives of cannabinoids in blood and plasma remains a contested issue. The efficiency of glucuronide hydrolysis in cannabinoid-extraction methods should be routinely evaluated by inclusion of a THCCOOH-glucuronide quality-control sample. This sample can be prepared from a pool of cannabinoid-positive samples or from samples spiked with THCCOOH-glucuronide.

2D-GC–MS with cryofocusing is superior to one-dimensional systems in the separation of analytes from interfering substances, as in the detection of drugs in complex matrices (Lowe et al. 2007, Milman et al. 2010a). The technology frequently yields improved sensitivity and reduces labor and time-intensive extraction procedures. Enhanced resolution is achieved by means of a pneumatically controlled switch (Deans switch) and cryofocusing with the cryotrap. The Deans switch diverts column flow from a primary (1°) column to a secondary (2°) column of different stationary phase. A short section (<1 m) of capillary column (restrictor) connects the 1° column to the primary detector. The choice of primary detector is selected according to the analytes of interest. Restrictor dimensions vary depending on the dimensions of the 1° and 2° columns, column pressures, and flow rates. Sections (heart cuts) of the chromatogram containing analytes from the 1° column are rerouted to the 2° column for further chromatographic separation and final detection by mass analysis without exposing the 2° detector to compounds with shorter and longer retention times. Cryofocusing sharpens the chromatographic signal by decreasing the signal band width of the target analytes. Compounds eluting off the 1° column are trapped in a 10-cm region at the head of the 2° column, which is maintained at low temperature. Analytes are released for further chromatographic separation on the 2° column by rapidly increasing the cryotrap temperature.

In many procedures, sensitivity is the limiting factor in cannabinoid analysis. The measurement of THCCOOH in OF and hair represents two of the most challenging confirmation assays. THC is present in OF and hair in higher concentrations but also can be deposited via passive exposure of OF to THC in environmental smoke and external contamination of hair from environmental sources of THC. The advantage of measuring THCCOOH in OF and hair is that it is a biomarker of in vivo ingestion of cannabis and eliminates the concern of passive exposure and environmental contamination. GC–MS/MS was required in most cases to accurately quantify low THCCOOH concentrations, although 2D-GC–MS offers a lower-cost alternative, and with equipment currently available in most toxicology laboratories.

The past 15 years includes a movement from GC–MS techniques to LC–MS/MS methodology due to the much wider molecular weight and polarity ranges capability of LC–MS/MS. A major force propelling this movement is the large number of analytes that can be identified and quantified in a single analytical run. Our laboratory at the National Institute on Drug Abuse developed and validated ever more sensitive and versatile analytical methods for cannabinoids in blood (Scheidweiler et al. 2016), oral fluid (Desrosiers et al. 2015b), and urine (Andersson et al. 2016) by LC–MS/MS. These are the latest methods that include many parent cannabinoids (THC, CBD, CBN, THCV, CBG) and metabolites in a single assay.

Synthetic Cannabinoids

Synthetic cannabinoids (SCs) are a heterogeneous group of compounds developed to probe the endogenous cannabinoid system or as potential therapeutics (Castaneto et al. 2014). Clandestine laboratories subsequently utilized published data to develop SC variations marketed as abusable designer drugs. In the early 2000s, SC became popular as "legal highs" under brand names such as Spice and K2, in part due to their ability to escape detection by standard cannabinoid screening tests. The majority of SC detected in herbal products have greater binding affinity to the cannabinoid CB1 receptor than THC. In vitro and animal in vivo studies show SC pharmacological effects 2–100 times more potent than THC, including analgesic, anti-seizure, antiinflammatory, and anticancer growth effects. SCs produce physiological and psychoactive effects

similar to THC, but with greater intensity, resulting in medical and psychiatric emergencies. Stimulation of the central CB1 receptors produces the desired euphoria and relaxation effects sought by natural and SC users, while CB2 receptors, primarily located in the periphery, are critical for immune functions and represent a potential therapeutic opportunity.

Determining SC activity includes binding studies to determine if the compound binds to the CB1 and/or CB2 receptors, and in vitro functional assays provide preliminary evidence of receptor agonism. In general, in vitro assays evaluate the ability of a compound to illicit a chemical response from the receptor. Three different assays were reported in studies evaluating SC: (i) guanosine triphosphate (GTP) binding assay measuring G-protein-mediated release of guanosine diphosphate (GDP) and binding of GTP at the CB1 receptor, (ii) measurement of CB1 receptor-mediated activation of G-protein-regulated inwardly rectifying potassium channels (GIRKs), and (iii) cyclic adenosine monophosphate (cAMP) accumulation assays. All three assays compare an investigational compound to a known CB1 receptor agonist, such as CP 55,490 or WIN 55,212. Finally, in vivo functional assays, such as the characteristic mouse tetrad that evaluates analgesia, hypothermia, catalepsy, and mobile activity in an open and drug discrimination studies compare the activity of new compounds to THC, the primary pharmacologically active component of cannabis.

In general, synthetic cannabinoids are chemically classified based on a structure consisting of core, linker, linked group, and tail sections. The newest generations of synthetic cannabinoids no longer have a ring in this section of the compound. The naming convention of synthetic cannabinoids, like many NPS, is not consistent. Some compounds, such as JWH-018, AM-2201, and HU-210, are named based on the individual or institution where they were first synthesized. Newer compounds are often named based on an abbreviation of their chemical name or structural similarity to a previously named compound. As a result, there are often several names for the same compound. For example, N-[1-(aminocarbonyl)-

2,2-dimethylpropyl]-1-(cyclohexylmethyl)-1H-indazole-3-carboxamide is commonly called MAB-CHMINACA and ADB-CHMINACA. Synthetic cannabinoids refer to the class of drugs targeting endogenous CB receptors.

SC consumption is widespread, despite law enforcement and regulatory control measures. Epidemiological data suggest that the majority of SC users are young adults who perceive SC as safer than non-cannabinoid illicit drugs and a favorable cannabis alternative eliciting cannabis-like "high" while avoiding detection by standard drug screens. However, data suggest that many SC users prefer cannabis over SC due to the drugs' negative effects. SCs are readily accessible, sold under several names and packaging with smoking as the most common route of administration. Most SC smokers are men from 13 to 59 years old, many with a history of polydrug use such as cannabis, alcohol, and nicotine. SCs were investigated in animals to characterize THC effects and evaluate their therapeutic benefits. Acute SC administration in rodents produced the cannabinoid tetrad of effects with dose-dependent anxiolytic and anxiogenic properties. Chronic SC administration was anxiogenic and produced more pronounced behavioral deficits in rodents exposed during adolescence, but no significant physiological effects in animals exposed in utero. SC substituted for THC in animal (rats and monkeys) discrimination studies and also attenuated antagonist-elicited withdrawal in monkeys previously exposed to THC. Recreational SC intake arose in the 2000s, and many adverse effects were reported. Acute SC intoxication can lead to emergency department (ED) presentation and hospitalization, requiring supportive care, benzodiazepines, and fluids. While most patients were released within 24 h of admission, severe adverse effects such as cardiotoxicity, acute kidney injuries, and psychosis resulted in hospitalization for as long as 2 weeks. Deaths directly linked to SC use were quite rare. Some chronic SC users experienced withdrawal symptoms when they stopped drug intake. Most SCs have greater binding affinity to CB1 receptors than does THC, suggesting a pos-sible mechanism for the severity of acute clinical reactions that result in emergency department presentation. However, SC intrinsic activity data are limited, with few direct comparisons to THC, making it premature to draw any conclusions about mechanisms.

Novel psychoactive substances (NPS) including SC represent significant analytical and interpretive challenges to forensic and clinical toxicologists. Timely access to case reports and reports of adverse incidents of impairment or toxicity is imperative to clinical diagnosis and treatment, as well as to interpretation of forensic results. Delays in identifying the presence of a novel intoxicating agent have significant consequences for public health and public safety. Adverse effects of intoxications with novel cannabinoids spanning January 2013 through December 2016 as reported in emergency departments, death investigations, impaired driving cases, and other forensic contexts were reviewed (Logan et al. 2017). Adverse effects or symptoms associated with SC ingestion were summarized in tables, including demographics, case history, clinical or behavioral symptoms, autopsy findings, and drug confirmations with quantitative results when provided. A wide range of adverse effects are associated with SC use including toxicity to multiple organ systems, gastrointestinal, cardiovascular, pulmonary, and CNS effects. XLR-11 was specifically linked to acute kidney injury (AKI). Outbreaks of SC exposure investigated by the Centers for Disease Control and Prevention between August 2011 and April 2015 included AKI produced by XLR-11, agitated delirium associated with ADB-PINACA, and severe illness and death following exposure to MAB-CHMINACA (ADB-CHMINACA). Reports from emergency rooms, poisons centers, and psychiatric clinics detailed adverse events predominantly of renal, pulmonary, gastrointestinal, and psychiatric effects. However, more concerning health threatening symptoms of seizures, psychosis, and cardiovascular effects also were noted. Unlike cannabis, SCs are implicated in deaths.

A cluster of AMB-FUBINACA (FUB-AMB) intoxications was reported in New York in July

2016. A total of 33 people were exposed to an unknown drug and reported to have altered mental status described by bystanders as "zombie-like." Toxicology testing was reported for eight patients, all of whom tested positive for a metabolite of AMB-FUBINACA. Based on the lack of fatalities associated with THC overdose, medical examiners were initially hesitant to include exposure to synthetic cannabinoids as cause of death. The number of cases where SCs are identified as the cause of death increased reflecting a greater appreciation among pathologists and medical examiners of the cardiovascular, seizure-inducing, and behavioral effects of the drugs, the availability of more comprehensive testing procedures by laboratories to confirm the presence of the drugs, and the increasing potency of SC drug classes, including the indazole carboxamides. In addition, SCs impair driving. APINACA, 5FAPINACA, UR-144, XLR-11, AB-CHMINACA, and AB-PINACA were identified as producing significant driving impairment. Drug Recognition Examiner (DRE) examination found that SC significantly increased frequency of confusion, disorientation, incoherence, slurred speech, and horizontal gaze nystagmus (HGN) compared to cannabis.

We conducted a comprehensive systematic review covering in vivo and in vitro animal and human pharmacokinetics (Castaneto et al. 2015). Of two main phases of SC research, the first investigated therapeutic applications, and the second abuse-related issues. Administration studies showed high lipophilicity and distribution into brain and fat tissue. Analytical methods are critical for documenting intake, with different strategies applied to adequately address the continuous emergence of new compounds. Immunoassays have different cross-reactivities for different SC classes but cannot keep pace with changing analyte targets. GC–MS and LC–MS/MS assays – first for a few, then numerous analytes – are available but constrained by reference standard availability and must be continuously updated and revalidated. In blood and oral fluid, parent compounds are frequently present, albeit in low concentrations. For urinary detection, metabolites must first be identified, and

interpretation of results is complex due to shared metabolic pathways between closely related SC. A new approach is non-targeted HRMS screening that is more flexible and permits retrospective data analysis. We suggest that a streamlined assessment of new SC's pharmacokinetics combined with advanced HRMS screening will lead to a promising strategy to detect new SC.

At the National Institute on Drug Abuse, we conducted controlled drug administration studies to better understand the pharmacodynamics and pharmacokinetics of drugs of abuse and licit pharmacotherapies. Despite the critical need to gain this knowledge about SC, we were unable to conduct these studies on SC because of the unknown toxicity of the compounds. In a search to determine how we could best respond to this serious novel psychoactive substance problem, we focused on identifying the best SC urinary metabolite targets. This enabled laboratories to tie specific SC to drug overdoses and deaths and focused the attention of reference standard manufacturers on production of the most relevant SC metabolite standards. Examples of the many metabolite characterizations that we completed are the non-fluoropentylindole/indazole SC and their 5-fluoro analogs.

The non-fluoropentylindole/indazole SCs are preferentially metabolized at the pentyl chain though without clear preference for one specific position (Wohlfarth et al. 2015). Their 5-fluoro analogs' major metabolites usually are 5-hydroxypentyl and pentanoic acid metabolites. We determined metabolic stability and metabolites of N-(1-amino-3-methyl-1-oxobutan-2-yl)-1-pentyl-1H-indazole-3-carboxamide (AB-PINACA) and 5-fluoro-AB-PINACA (5F-AB-PINACA), two new synthetic cannabinoids, and investigated if results were similar. For metabolic stability, 1 µmol/L of each compound was incubated with human liver microsomes for up to 1 h, and for metabolite profiling, 10 µmol/L was incubated with pooled human hepatocytes for up to 3 h. Also, authentic urine specimens from AB-PINACA cases were hydrolyzed and extracted. All samples were analyzed by LC-HRMS on a TripleTOF 5600+ (SCIEX) with gradient elution (0.1% formic acid in water and acetonitrile). HR full-scan MS and information-dependent acquisition MS/MS data were analyzed with MetabolitePilot (SCIEX) using different data processing algorithms. Both drugs had intermediate clearance. We identified 23 AB-PINACA metabolites, generated by carboxamide hydrolysis, hydroxylation, ketone formation, carboxylation, epoxide formation with subsequent hydrolysis, or reaction combinations. We identified 18 5F-AB-PINACA metabolites, generated by the same biotransformations and oxidative defluorination producing 5-hydroxypentyl and pentanoic acid metabolites shared with AB-PINACA. Authentic urine specimens documented the presence of these metabolites. AB-PINACA and 5F-AB-PINACA produced suggested metabolite patterns. AB-PINACA was predominantly hydrolyzed to AB-PINACA carboxylic acid, carbonyl-AB-PINACA, and hydroxypentyl AB-PINACA, likely in the 4-position. The most intense 5F-AB-PINACA metabolites were AB-PINACA pentanoic acid and 5-hydroxypentyl-AB-PINACA.

It is highly challenging to identify which SC was consumed by the drug abusers, a necessary step to tie adverse health effects to the new drug's toxicity. Two intrinsic properties complicate SC identification, their often rapid and extensive metabolism, and their generally high potency relative to THC. Additional challenges are the lack of reference standards for the major urinary metabolites needed for forensic verification, and the sometimes differing illicit and licit status and, in some cases, identical metabolites produced by closely related SC pairs, i.e., JWH-018/AM-2201, THJ-018/THJ-2201, and BB-22/MDMB-CHMICA/ADB-CHMICA that each produce similar N-5-hydroxylated and carboxylated metabolites. We contrasted the advantages and disadvantages of multiple metabolic approaches to identify SC metabolite targets (Diao et al. 2019). The human hepatocyte incubation model for determining a new SC's metabolism is highly recommended after comparison to human liver microsomes incubation, in silico prediction, rat in vivo, zebrafish, and fungus *Cunninghamella elegans* models. We evaluated SC metabolic patterns and devised a practical strategy to select optimal urinary marker metabolites for SCs. New SCs are incubated first with human hepatocytes, and major metabolites are identified by high-resolution mass spectrometry. Although initially difficult to obtain, authentic human urine samples following the specified SC exposure are hydrolyzed and analyzed by high-resolution mass spectrometry to verify identified major metabolites. Since some SCs produce the same major urinary metabolites, documentation of the specific SC consumed may require identification of the SC parent itself in either blood or oral fluid. An encouraging trend is the recent reduction in the number of new SCs introduced per year. With global collaboration and communication, we can improve education of the public about the toxicity of new SC and our response to their introduction.

The emergence of SC will pose continuous challenges to clinical and forensic laboratories. With each new compound, the forensic community must address three major issues: (1) identification of suitable biomarkers via in vitro studies to detect intake, (2) reference standard synthesis, and (3) continuous updating and validation of analytical methods, which is a time-consuming, cost- and labor-intensive process. Improvements are apparent: faced with logistic and analytical limitations, laboratories are applying unconventional approaches with non-targeted HRMS, permitting retrospective data inquiry after library updates. SC metabolite identification is becoming faster and more comprehensive but should be further streamlined and complemented. Laboratories need to respond quickly, adapt to the new emerging drug market, and be innovative with new HRMS technology. Therefore, we expect to see additional technological and logistic advancements and improved analytical methods for SC identification in the near future.

Conclusions

Cannabinoids are one of the most important classes of illicit drugs, and now a medicinal drug as well, for the toxicologist. Understanding its pharmacodynamic effects and pharmacokinetics in a wide variety of matrices is critical for the analysis and interpretation of cannabinoid concentrations in biological fluids and tissues. Therapeutic drug monitoring of cannabinoids will be more important in the future as efficacy in treating different disease syndromes with medicinal THC, CBD, and whole plant cannabis extracts is established. With the approval of Epidiolex (98% pure CBD), a new era of medicinal cannabis is underway, making the sensitive and specific analysis of cannabinoids critical. The data collected over the last 40 years of controlled cannabis administration guide the interpretation of cannabinoid concentrations in a wide variety of biological matrices.

References

Abraham T, Lowe RH, Pirnay SO, Darwin WD, Huestis MA (2007) Simultaneous GC/EI-MS determination of Δ9-tetrahydrocannabinol, 11-hydroxy-Δ9-tetrahydrocannabinol, and 11-nor-9-carboxy-Δ9-tetrahydrocannabinol in human urine following tandem enzyme – alkaline hydrolysis. J Anal Toxicol 31:477–485

Andersson M, Scheidweiler KB, Sempio C, Barnes AJ, Huestis MA (2016) Simultaneous quantification of 11 cannabinoids and metabolites in human urine by liquid chromatography tandem mass spectrometry using WAX-S tips. Anal Bioanal Chem 408(23):6461–6471

Anizan S, Milman G, Desrosiers N, Barnes AJ, Gorelick DA, Huestis MA (2013) Oral fluid cannabinoid concentrations following controlled smoked cannabis in chronic frequent and occasional smokers. Anal Bioanal Chem 405(26):8451–8461

Barnes AJ, Scheidweiler KB, Huestis MA (2014) Quantification of 11-Nor-9-Carboxy-Δ9-Tetrahydrocannabinol in human Oral fluid by gas chromatography-tandem mass spectrometry. Ther Drug Monit 36(2):225–233

Bergamaschi MM, Karschner EL, Goodwin RS, Scheidweiler KB, Hirvonen J, Queiroz RHC, Huestis MA (2013) Impact of prolonged cannabinoid excretion in chronic daily cannabis smokers' blood on "per se" drugged driving laws. Clin Chem 59(3):519–526

Bosker WM, Karschner EL, Lee D, Goodwin RS, Hirvonen J, Innis RB, Theunissen EL, Kuypers KPC, Huestis MA, Ramaekers JG (2013) Psychomotor function in chronic cannabis smokers during sustained abstinence. PLoS One 8(1). Epub 2013 Jan 2

Carlier J, Huestis MA, Zaami S, Pichini S, Busardo FP (2019) Monitoring perinatal exposure to cannabis and synthetic cannabinoids. Therapeutic Drug Monitoring Epub Jun 28

Castaneto MS, Gorelick DA, Desrosiers NA, Hartman RL, Pirard S, Huestis MA (2014) Synthetic cannabinoids: epidemiology, pharmacodynamics, and clinical implications. Drug Alcohol Dependence 144C:12–41

Castaneto MS, Wohlfarth A, Desrosiers NA, Hartman RL, Gorelick DA, Huestis MA (2015) Synthetic cannabinoids pharmacokinetics and detection methods in biological matrices. Drug Metab Rev 47(2):124–174

Cirimele V, Sachs H, Kintz P, Mangin P (1996) Testing human hair for cannabis. II. Rapid screening procedure for the simultaneous identification of delta 9-tetrahydrocannabinol, cannabinol, and cannabidiol. J Anal Toxicol 20(1):13–16

Compton R (2017, July) Marijuana-Impaired Driving – A Report to Congress. (DOT HS 812 440). Washington, DC: National Highway Traffic Safety Administration

Compton R, Berning A (2009) Results of the 2007 National Roadside Survey of Alcohol and Drug Use by Drivers (Report No. DOT HS 811 175). Washington, DC: National Highway Traffic Safety Administration. www.nhtsa.gov/DOT/NHTSA/Traffic%20Injury%20Control/Articles/Associated%20Files/811175.pdf

Concheiro M, Lee D, Lendoiro E, Huestis MA (2013 Jul 5) Simultaneous quantification of Δ9-tetrahydrocannabinol, 11-nor-9-carboxy-tetrahydrocannabinol, cannabidiol, cannabinol in oral fluid by microflow-liquid chromatography-high resolution mass spectrometry. Journal Chromatography A 1297:123–130

Cone EJ, Johnson RE (1986) Contact highs and urinary cannabinoid excretion after passive exposure to marijuana smoke. Clinical Pharmacology & Therapeutics 40:247–256

Cone EJ, Bigelow GE, Herrmann ES, Mitchell JM, LoDico C, Flegel R, Vandrey R (2015a) Nonsmoker exposure to secondhand cannabis smoke. I. Urine screening and confirmation results. J Anal Toxicol 39(1):1–12

Cone EJ, Bigelow GE, Herrmann ES, Mitchell JM, LoDico C, Flegel R, Vandrey R (2015b) Nonsmoker exposure to secondhand cannabis smoke. II. Oral fluid and blood drug concentrations and corresponding subjective effects. Journal Analytical Toxicology 39(7):497–509

Coulter C, Garnier M, Moore C (2012) Analysis of tetrahydrocannabinol and its metabolite, 11-nor-Δ9-tetrahydrocannabinol-9caroxylic acid, in oral fluid using liquid chromatography with tandem mass spectrometry. J Anal Toxicol 36(6):413–417

Desrosiers NA, Huestis MA. 2019. Oral fluid drug testing: Analytical approaches, issues & interpretation of results Journal of Analytical Toxicology Epub 2019 Jun 28

Desrosiers NA, Himes SK, Scheidweiler KB, Concheiro-Guisan M, Gorelick DA, Huestis MA (2014) Phase I and II cannabinoid disposition in blood and plasma of occasional and frequent smokers following controlled smoked cannabis. Clin Chem 60:631–643

Desrosiers NA, Ramaekers JG, Chauchard E, Gorelick DA, Huestis MA (2015a) Smoked cannabis' psychomotor and neurocognitive effects in occasional and frequent smokers. Journal Analytical Toxicology 39(4):251–261

Desrosiers NA, Scheidweiler KB, Huestis MA (2015b) Quantification of six cannabinoids and metabolites in oral fluid by liquid chromatography-tandem mass spectrometry. Drug Testing Analysis 7(8):684–694

Diao XX, Huestis MA (2019) New synthetic cannabinoids metabolism and strategies to best identify optimal marker metabolites. Front Chem 7:109

DRUID 2011 Website https://biblio.ugent.be/publication/1988746/file/. Accessed 6 Nov 2019

Drummer OH, Gerostamoulos J, Batziris H, Chu M, Caplehorn J, Robertson MD, Swann P (2004) The involvement of drugs in drivers of motor vehicles killed in Australian road traffic crashes. Accid Anal Prev 36:239–248

Ellis GM Jr, Mann MA, Judson BA, Schramm NT, Tashchian A (1985) Excretion patterns of cannabinoid metabolites after last use in a group of chronic users. Clin Pharmacol Ther 38(5):572–578

Gnofam M, Allshouse AA, Stickrath EH, Metz TD (2019) Impact of Marijuana Legalization on Prevalence of Maternal Marijuana Use and Perinatal Outcomes. American Journal of Perinatology. Epub 2019 Sep 6

Goodwin RS, Gustafson RA, Barnes A, Nebro W, Moolchan ET, Huestis MA (2006) Δ^9-tetrahydrocannabinol, 11-hydroxy-Δ^9-tetrahydrocannabinol and 11-nor-9-carboxy-Δ^9-tetrahydrocannabinol in human plasma following controlled oral administration of cannabinoids. Ther Drug Monit 28:545–551

Grotenhermen F, Leson G, Berghaus G, Drummer OH, Krüger HP, Longo M et al (2007) Developing limits for driving under cannabis. Addiction 102:1910–1917

Gustafson RA, Levine B, Stout PR, Klette KL, George MP, Moolchan ET, Huestis MA (2003) Urinary cannabinoid detection times following controlled oral administration of Δ^9-tetrahydrocannabinol to humans. Clin Chem 49:1114–1124

Gustafson RA, Kim I, Stout PR, Klette KL, George MP, Moolchan ET et al (2004) Urinary pharmacokinetics of 11-nor-9-carboxy-Δ^9-tetrahydrocannabinol after controlled oral Δ^9-tetrahydrocannabinol administration. J Anal Toxicol 28:160–167

Guy GW, Robson P (2003) A phase I, open label, four-way crossover study to compare the pharmacokinetic profiles of a single dose of 20 mg of a cannabis based medicine extract (CBME) administered on 3 difference areas of the buccal mucosa and to investigate the pharmacokinetics of CBME per oral in healthy male and female volunteers. Journal of Cannabis Therapeutics 3:79–120

Hall W, Stjepanović D, Caulkins J, Lynskey M, Leung J, Campbell G, Degenhardt L (2019) Public health implications of legalising the production and sale of cannabis for medicinal and recreational use. Lancet 394(10208):1580–1590

Haney M, Ward AS, Comer SD, Foltin RW, Fischman MW (1999) Abstinence symptoms following oral THC administration to humans. Psychopharmacology 141:385–394

Hartman RL, Huestis MA (2013) Cannabis effects on driving skills. Clin Chem 59(3):478–492

Hartman RL, Brown TL, Milavetz G, Spurgin A, Gorelick DA, Gaffney G, Huestis MA (2015a) Controlled cannabis vaporizer administration: blood and plasma cannabinoids with and without alcohol. Clin Chem 61(6):850–869

Hartman RL, Brown TL, Milavetz G, Spurgin A, Pierce RS, Gorelick DA, Gaffney G, Huestis MA (2015b) Cannabis effects on driving lateral control with and without alcohol. Drug Alcohol Depend 154:25–37

Hartman RL, Richman JE, Hayes CE, Huestis MA (2016a) Drug recognition expert (DRE) examination characteristics of cannabis impairment. Accid Anal Prev 92:219–229

Hartman RL, Brown TL, Milavetz G, Spurgin A, Pierce RS, Gorelick DA, Gaffney G, Huestis MA (2016b) Cannabis effects on driving longitudinal control with and without alcohol. J Appl Toxicol 36(11):1418–1429

Hartman RL, Brown TL, Milavetz G, Spurgin A, Gorelick DA, Gaffney G, Huestis MA (2016c) Effect of blood collection time on measured Δ^9-Tetrahydrocannabinol concentrations: implications for driving interpretation and drug policy. Clin Chem 62(2):367–377

Hawks RL (1982) The constituents of cannabis and the disposition and metabolism of cannabinoids. In Hawks R. Analysis of cannabinoids research monograph 42. National Institute on Drug Abuse

Henderson GL, Harkey MR, Zhou C, Jones RT, Jacob P 3rd. (1996) Incorporation of isotopically labeled cocaine and metabolites into human hair: 1. dose-response relationships. J Anal Toxicol 20(1):1–12

Himes SK, Scheidweiler KB, Beck O, Gorelick DA, Desrosiers NA, Huestis MA (2013) Cannabinoids in exhaled breath following controlled administration of smoked cannabis. Clin Chem 59(12):1780–1789

Hirvonen J, Goodwin RS, Li CT, Terry GE, Zoghbi SS, Morse C, Pike VW, Volkow ND, Huestis MA*, Innis RB* (2012, June) Reversible and regionally selective downregulation of brain cannabinoid CB1 receptors in chronic daily cannabis smokers. Molecular Psychiatry. 17(6):642–9. Epub 2011 Jul 12. *(authors contributed equally to manuscript)

Holland MG, Schwope DM, Stoppacher R, Gillen SB, Huestis MA (2011) Postmortem redistribution of Δ9-tetrahydrocannabinol (THC), 11-hydroxy-THC (11-OH-THC), and 11-nor-9-carboxy-THC (THCCOOH). Forensic Sci Int 212(1–3):247–251

Huestis MA, Cone EJ (1998) Differentiating new marijuana use from residual drug excretion in occasional marijuana users. J Anal Toxicol 22:445–454

Huestis MA, Smith ML (2007) Human cannabinoid pharmacokinetics and the interpretation of cannabinoid concentrations. In: MA ES (ed) Marijuana and the cannabinoids. Humana Press, Totawa, NJ, p 215

Huestis MA, Smith ML (2018) Cannabinoid markers in biological fluids and tissues: revealing intake. Trends Mol Med 24(2):156–172

Huestis MA, Henningfield JE, Cone EJ (1992a) Blood cannabinoids. I. Absorption of THC and formation of 11-OH-THC and THCCOOH during and after smoking marijuana. J Anal Toxicol 16:276–282

Huestis MA, Henningfield JE, Cone EJ (1992b) Blood cannabinoids. II. Models for the prediction of marijuana exposure from plasma concentrations of Δ^9-tetrahydrocannabinol (THC) and 11-nor-9-carboxy-Δ^9-tetrahydrocannabinol (THCCOOH). J Anal Toxicol 16:283–290

Huestis MA, Sampson AH, Holicky BJ, Henningfield JE, Cone EJ (1992c) Characterization of the absorption phase of marijuana smoke. Clin Pharmacol Ther 52:31–41

Huestis MA, Mitchell J, Cone EJ (1994) Lowering the federally mandated cannabinoid immunoassay cutoff increases true-positive results. Clin Chem 40:729–733

Huestis MA, Mitchell JM, Cone EJ (1995) Detection times of marijuana metabolites in urine by immunoassay and GC/MS. J Anal Toxicol 19(6):443–449

Huestis MA, Mitchell JM, Cone EJ (1996) Urinary excretion profiles of 11-nor-9-carboxy-Δ9-tetrahydrocannabinol in humans after single smoked doses of marijuana. J Anal Toxicol 20(6):441–452

Huestis MA, Gorelick DA, Heishman SJ, Preston KL, Nelson RA, Moolchan ET, Frank RA (2001) Blockade of smoked marijuana effects in humans by the oral CB1-selective cannabinoid receptor antagonist SR141716. Arch Gen Psychiatry 58:322–328

Huestis MA, Barnes A, Smith ML (2005) Estimating the time of last cannabis use from plasma Δ^9-tetrahydrocannabinol and 11-nor-9-carboxy-Δ^9-tetrahydrocannabinol concentrations. Clin Chem 51:2289–2295

Huestis MA, Elsohly M, Nebro W, Gustafson RA, Smith ML (2006) Estimating time of last oral ingestion of cannabis from plasma THC and THCCOOH concentrations. Ther Drug Monit 28:540–544

Huestis MA, Gustafson RA, Moolchan ET, Barnes A, Bourland JA, Sweeney SA, Hayes EF, Carpenter PM, Smith ML (2007) Cannabinoid concentrations in hair from documented cannabis users. Forensic Sci Int 169(2–3):129–136

Huestis MA, Scheidweiler KB, Saito T, Fortner N, Abraham T, Gustafson RA, Smith ML (2008) Excretion of Δ^9-tetrahydrocannabinol in sweat. Forensic Sci Int 174:173–177

Huestis MA, Blount BC, Milan DF, Newmeyer MN, Schroeder J, Smith ML. 2019a. Correlation of creatinine- and specific gravity-normalized free & glucuronidated urine cannabinoid concentrations following smoked, vaporized and oral cannabis in frequent and occasional cannabis users. Drug testing and analysis. Epub Feb 12

Huestis MA, Solomini R, Pichini S, Pacifici R, Carlier J, Busardo FP. 2019b Cannabidiol Adverse Events and Toxicity. Current Neuropharmacology. June 3 Epub ahead of print

Hunt CA, Jones RT (1980) Tolerance and disposition of tetrahydrocannabinol in man. J Pharmacol Exp Ther 215:35–44

Jacobus J, Castro N, Squeglia LM, Meloy MJ, Brumback T, Huestis MA, Tapert SF (2016) Adolescent cortical thickness pre- and post marijuana and alcohol initiation. Neurotoxicology Teratology 57:20–29

Johansson E, Agurell S, Hollister L, Halldin M (1988) Prolonged apparent half-life of Δ^1-tetrahydrocannabinol in plasma of chronic marijuana users. J Pharm Pharmacol 40:374–375

Johansson E, Norén K, Sjövall J, Halldin MM (1989) Determination of delta 1-tetrahydrocannabinol in human fat biopsies from marihuana users by gas chromatography-mass spectrometry. Biomed Chromatogr 3(1):35–38

Jones RT, Benowitz N, Bachman J (1976) Clinical studies of cannabis tolerance and dependence. Ann N Y Acad Sci 282:221–239

Jones AW, Holmgren A, Kugelberg FC (2008) Driving under the influence of cannabis: a 10-year study of age and gender differences in the concentrations of tetrahydrocannabinol in blood. Addiction 103:452–461

Karschner EL, Schwilke EW, Lowe RH, Darwin WD, Herning RI, Cadet JL, Huestis MA (2009) Implications of plasma Δ^9-Tetrahydrocannabinol (THC), 11-Hydroxy-THC and 11-Nor-9-carboxy-THC concentrations in chronic cannabis smokers. Journal Analytical Toxicology 33(8):469–477

Karschner EL, Darwin WD, Goodwin RS, Wright S, Huestis MA (2011) Plasma cannabinoid pharmacokinetics following controlled oral Δ^9-tetrahydrocannabinol and oromucosal cannabis extract administration. Clin Chem 57(1):66–75. Epub 2010 Nov 15

Karschner EL, Schwope DM, Schwilke EW, Goodwin RS, Kelly DL, Gorelick DA, Huestis MA (2012) Predictive model accuracy in estimating last $\Delta(9)$-tetrahydrocannabinol (THC) intake from plasma and whole blood cannabinoid concentrations in chronic, daily cannabis smokers administered subchronic oral THC. Drug Alcohol Depend 125(3):313–319. Epub 2012 Mar 29

Karschner EL, Swortwood MJ, Hirvonen J, Goodwin RS, Bosker WM, Ramaekers JG, Huestis MA (2016) Extended plasma cannabinoid excretion in chronic frequent cannabis smokers during sustained abstinence and correlation with psychomotor performance. Drug Test Anal 8(7):682–689

Kauert GF, Ramaekers JG, Schneider E, Moeller MR, Toennes SW (2007) Pharmacokinetic properties of Δ^9-tetrahydrocannabinol in serum and oral fluid. J Anal Toxicol 31:288–293

Kelley-Baker T, Berning A, Ramirez A, Lacey JH, Carr K, Waehrer G, Compton R (2017) 2013–2014 National Roadside Study of alcohol and drug use by drivers: drug results (report no. DOT HS 812 411). National Highway Traffic Safety Administration, Washington, DC

Kemp PM, Abukhalaf IK, Manno JE, Alford DD, McWilliams ME, Nixon FE et al (1995) Cannabinoids in humans. II. The influence of three methods of hydrolysis on the concentration of THC and two metabolites in urine. J Anal Toxicol 19:292–298

Kintz P, Tracqui A, Mangin P, Edel Y (1996) Sweat testing in opioid users with a sweat patch. J Anal Toxicol 20(6):393–397

Lee D, Karschner EL, Milman G, Barnes AJ, Goodwin RS, Huestis MA (2013) Can oral fluid cannabinoid testing monitor medication compliance and/or cannabis smoking during oral THC and oromucosal Sativex® administration? Drug Alcohol Depend 130(1–3):68–76

Lee D, Schwope DM, Milman G, Barnes AJ, Gorelick DA, Huestis MA (2012) Cannabinoid disposition in oral fluid after controlled smoked cannabis. Clin Chem 58:748–756.

Lee D, Vandrey R, Mendu DR, Murray JA, Barnes AJ, Huestis MA (2015) Oral fluid cannabinoids in chronic frequent cannabis smokers during ad libitum cannabis smoking. Drug Test Anal 7(6):494–501

Lemos NP, Ingle EA (2011) Cannabinoids in postmortem toxicology. Journal Analytical Toxicology 35(7):394–401

Logan BK, Mohr ALA, Friscia M, Krotulski AJ, Papsun DM, Kacinko SL, Ropero-Miller JD, Huestis MA (2017) Reports of adverse events associated with use of novel psychoactive substances, 2013–2016: a review. Journal Analytical Toxicology 41(7):573–610

Lowe RH, Karschner EL, Schwilke EW, Barnes AJ, Huestis MA (2007) Simultaneous quantification of Δ⁹-tetrahydrocannabinol (THC), 11-hydroxy-Δ⁹-tetrahydrocannabinol (11-OH-THC), and 11-nor-Δ⁹-tetrahydrocannabinol-9-carboxylic acid (THCCOOH) in human plasma using two-dimensional gas chromatography, cryofocusing, and electron impact-mass spectrometry. J Chromatogr A 1163:318–327

Lowe RH, Abraham TT, Darwin WD, Herning R, Cadet JL, Huestis MA (2009) Extended urinary delta 9 Tetrahydrocannabinol excretion in chronic cannabis users precludes use as a biomarker of new drug exposure. Drug Alcohol Depend 105:24–32

Luo YR, Yun C, Lynch KL (2019) Quantitation of cannabinoids in breath samples using a novel derivatization LC-MS/MS assay with ultra-high sensitivity. J Anal Toxicol 43(5):331–339

Milman G, Barnes AJ, Lowe RW, Huestis MA (2010a) Simultaneous quantification of cannabinoids and metabolites in oral fluid by two-dimensional gas chromatography mass spectrometry. J Chromatogr A 1217(9):1513–1521

Milman G, Barnes AJ, Schwope DM, Schwilke EW, Darwin WD, Goodwin RS, Kelly DL, Gorelick DA, Huestis MA (2010b) Disposition of cannabinoids in oral fluid following controlled around-the-clock oral THC administration. Clin Chem 56(8):1261–1269

Moore C, Coulter C, Uges D, Tuyay J, van der Linde S, van Leeuwen A, Garnier M, Orbita J Jr (2011) Cannabinoids in oral fluid following passive exposure to marijuana smoke. Forensic Sci Int 212(1–3):227–230

Mura P, Kintz P, Dumestre V, Raul S, Hauet T (2005) THC can be detected in brain while absent in blood. J Anal Toxicol 29:842–843

National Academies of Sciences, Engineering, and Medicine (2017) The health effects of cannabis and cannabinoids: the current state of evidence and recommendations for research. The National Academies Press, Washington, DC.

Newmeyer MN, Swortwood MJ, Barnes AJ, Abulseoud OA, Scheidweiler KB, Huestis MA (2016) Free and glucuronide whole blood cannabinoids' pharmacokinetics after controlled smoked, vaporized and oral cannabis administration in frequent and occasional cannabis users: identification of recent cannabis intake. Clin Chem 62(12):1579–1592

Newmeyer MN, Swortwood MJ, Andersson M, Abulseoud OA, Scheidweiler KB, Huestis MA (2017) Cannabis edibles: blood and oral fluid cannabinoid pharmacokinetics and evaluation of oral fluid screening devices for predicting Δ⁹-Tetrahydrocannabinol in blood and oral fluid following cannabis brownie administration. Clin Chem 63(3):647–662

Nowlan R, Cohen S (1977) Tolerance to marijuana: heart rate and subjective "high". Clin Pharmacol Ther 22(5 Pt 1):550–556

Pope HG Jr, Gruber AJ, Hudson JI, Huestis MA, Yurgelun-Todd D (2001) Neuropsychological performance in long-term cannabis users. Arch Gen Psychiatry 58:909–915

Pope HG Jr, Gruber AJ, Hudson JI, Huestis MA, Yurgelun-Todd D (2002) Cognitive measures in long-term cannabis users. J Clin Pharmacol 42(11 Suppl):41S–47S. Review

Quest Diagnostics Drug Testing Index accessed November 10, 2019. https://www.questdiagnostics.com/home/physicians/health-trends/drug-testing

Ramaekers JG, Moeller MR, van Ruitenbeek P, Theunissen EL, Schneider E, Kauert G (2006) Cognition and motor control as a function of Δ⁹-THC concentration in serum and oral fluid: limits of impairment. Drug Alcohol Depend 85:114–122

Scheidweiler KB, Himes SK, Chen X, Liu H-F, Huestis MA (2013) 11-Nor-9-Carboxy-Δ9- Tetrahydrocannabinol quantification in human oral fluid by liquid chromatography- tandem mass spectrometry. Anal Bioanal Chem 405(18):6019–6027

Scheidweiler KB, Newmeyer MN, Barnes AJ, Huestis MA (2016) Quantification of cannabinoids and their free and glucuronide metabolites in whole blood by disposable pipette extraction and liquid chromatography tandem mass spectrometry. J Chromatogr A 1453:34–42

Schwilke EW, Schwope DM, Karschner EL, Lowe RH, Darwin WD, Kelly DL, Goodwin RS, Gorelick DA, Huestis MA (2009) Δ⁹-Tetrahydrocannabinol (THC), 11-Hydroxy-THC and 11-nor-9-Carboxy-THC plasma pharmacokinetics during and after continuous high-dose Oral THC. Clin Chem 55(12):2180–2189. Epub 2009 Oct 15

Schwilke EW, Gullberg RG, Darwin WD, Chiang N, Cadet JL, Gorelick DA, Pope HG, Huestis MA (2011) Differentiating new cannabis use from residual urinary cannabinoid excretion in chronic, daily cannabis users. Addiction 106(3):499–506

Schwope DM, Karschner EL, Gorelick DA, Huestis MA (2011) Identification of recent cannabis use: whole blood and plasma free and glucuronidated cannabinoid pharmacokinetics following controlled smoked cannabis administration. Clin Chem 57(10):1406–1414. Epub 2011 Aug 11

Smith ML, Barnes AJ, Huestis MA (2009) Identifying new cannabis use with urine creatinine-normalized THCCOOH concentrations and time intervals between specimen collections. J Anal Toxicol 33(4):185–189

Swortwood MJ, Newmeyer MN, Abulseoud OA, Scheidweiler KB, Huestis MA (2017) Cannabinoid disposition in oral fluid after controlled smoked, vaporized and oral cannabis administration. Drug Test Anal 9(6):905–915

Tashkin DP, Roth MD (2019) Pulmonary effects of inhaled cannabis smoke. American Journal of Drug Alcohol Abuse 12:1–14

Vandrey R, Herrmann ES, Mitchell JM, Bigelow GE, Flegel R, LoDico C, Cone EJ (2017) Pharmacokinetic profile of oral cannabis in humans: blood and oral fluid disposition and relation to pharmacodynamic outcomes. J Anal Toxicol 41(2):83–99

Wohlfarth A, Castaneto M, Zhu M, Pang S, Scheidweiler KB, Kronstrand R, Huestis MA (2015) Pentylindole/pentylindazole synthetic cannabinoids and their 5-fluoro analogs produce different primary metabolites: metabolite profiling for AB-PINACA and 5F-AB-PINACA. AAPS Journal 17(3):660–677

25 Amphetamines/Sympathomimetic Amines

Michele M. Crosby and Karla A. Moore

Abstract

Amphetamines and sympathomimetic amines mimic the actions of the endogenous neurotransmitters that stimulate the sympathetic nervous system. Amphetamine and methamphetamine are used therapeutically to treat narcolepsy, attention-deficit disorder, and obesity. Sympathomimetic amines that are available therapeutically include phentermine, ephedrine, and pseudoephedrine. Phentermine is used as an appetite suppressant, and ephedrine is used as a vasopressor during resuscitation. Pseudoephedrine is used as an over-the-counter cough and cold medication. These drugs are well-absorbed orally and are generally excreted primarily as unchanged drug in the urine. Because it is easy to synthesize, methamphetamine remains a frequently encountered clandestinely produced controlled substance in the United States. Besides methamphetamine, analogs such as methylenedioxymethamphetamine, methylenedioxyamphetamine, and synthetic cathinones (bath salts) have also appeared on the illicit drug market. These analogs have greater hallucinogenic activity than the amphetamines and sympathomimetic amines. One difference between this class of compounds and other drug classes is that many of these drugs have chiral centers that lead to differences in pharmacologic activity. Therefore, chiral separation of enantiomers may be a component to the analysis of these compounds.

Keywords

Amphetamines · Sympathomimetic amines · Toxicology · Pharmacology · Analysis · Interpretation · Designer drugs

The original version of this chapter was revised. The correction to this chapter is available at https://doi.org/10.1007/978-3-030-42917-1_41

Karla A. Moore was deceased at the time of publication.

M. M. Crosby (✉)
University of Tampa, Tampa, FL, USA
e-mail: mmcrosby@ut.edu

K. A. Moore (Deceased)

Introduction

The compound "amphetamine" has come to represent a class of phenethylamine compounds that have varying degrees of sympathomimetic activity. Sympathomimetic drugs mimic the actions of the endogenous neurotransmitters that stimulate the sympathetic nervous system. This growing class of structurally related compounds may also

B. S. Levine, S. Kerrigan (eds.), *Principles of Forensic Toxicology*,
https://doi.org/10.1007/978-3-030-42917-1_25

stimulate the sympathetic nervous system by many other mechanisms of action such as affecting the release of endogenous neurotransmitters or inhibiting their reuptake.

Amphetamine was first synthesized in 1877. During the 1930s, amphetamines were first used clinically as a central nervous system (CNS) stimulant for the treatment of narcolepsy and depression. Their abuse potential quickly became evident. Since that time, the ability of amphetamines to alleviate fatigue, improve performance of simple mental and physical tasks, elevate mood, increase confidence, and produce euphoria has led to their misuse and abuse.

Amphetamine use, including amphetamine, methamphetamine, phenmetrazine, methylphenidate, diethylpropion, and propylhexedrine, reached epidemic proportions during World War II, notably by soldiers, factory workers, and prisoners of war in Japan. After World War II, a surplus on the Japanese market permitted sales without a prescription, with peak use occurring in about 1954. In the 1960s, methamphetamine abuse became a social problem in the United States. By 1970, 50% of legally manufactured amphetamine and related compounds were being sold on the black market.

Increasing abuse of these drugs eventually led to their classification as a Schedule II controlled substance under the Controlled Substances Act (Public Law 91–513) of 1970. Schedule II substances have a high abuse potential with severe psychic or physical dependence liability. This classification limited the acquisition of these compounds through legitimate channels. This Act stringently regulated the manufacture of these stimulants and forced manufacturers to decrease sales to retail pharmacies. Because methamphetamine is easily synthesized even in crude laboratories, it quickly became the "stimulant of choice." Illicit production of methamphetamine hydrochloride remains a significant drug abuse problem. Endemic areas include the Pacific Coast states, Hawaii, and other Pacific Rim countries such as Japan and Korea.

Methamphetamine is one of the most frequently encountered clandestinely produced controlled substances in the United States. Unlike d-amphetamine, d-methamphetamine is easy to synthesize. Laboratories producing methamphetamine accounted for more than 50% of all laboratories seizures by the Drug Enforcement Administration (DEA) during a 45-month period ending in September 1981. In 2006, a National Association of Counties survey identified methamphetamine as the top drug problem.

In the 1970s, the most popular method of synthesis was reductive amination using phenyl-2-propanone (P2P), methylamine, aluminum foil, mercuric chloride (catalyst), and alcohol. In a second popular method, the product of an acetaldehyde/methylamine reaction was refluxed with benzylmagnesium chloride. A third method used the Leuckart reaction, refluxing P2P with either methylamine and formic acid or N-methylformamide with hydrochloric acid. An important precursor in these syntheses was P2P, which, until 1981, was available commercially. Because of its importance in illicit synthetic methods, it is now a listed Schedule II controlled substance. As a result of its control, some clandestine laboratories now synthesize only P2P.

During the late 1970s and early 1980s, the conversion of ephedrine to methamphetamine by reductive cleavage of the hydroxyl group using either thionyl chloride or hydroiodic acid (HI) and red phosphorus was relatively uncommon; only ten of the laboratories seized used this synthetic method. In fact, through the late 1980s, the DEA reported that significantly more laboratories were synthesizing methamphetamine using one of the reductive amination methods or synthesizing P2P. However, with the growing difficulty in obtaining precursors for the reductive amination routes and with the increasing availability of (-)-ephedrine and (+)-pseudoephedrine, methamphetamine synthesized from ephedrine flooded the market in both the United States and the Far East. From 1991 to 1993, the DEA seized more than 500 illicit methamphetamine laboratories mostly from the West Coast and Houston, Texas. The ephedrine (EPH) reduction method was used in 81% of these laboratories, whereas the P2P method was used in only 16%. This represented a direct reversal of trends noted in the 1980s. Forensic laboratories in New Mexico also reported that in the first 6 months of 1994, there was a decided increase in the number of methamphetamine sei-

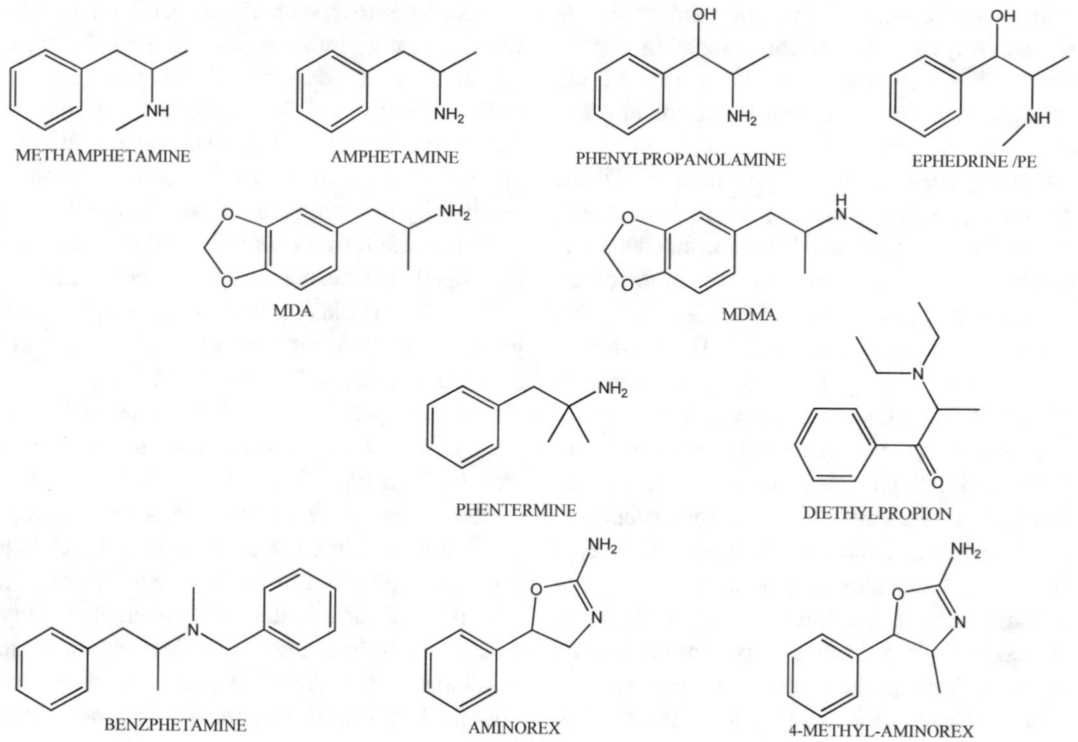

Fig. 25.1 Structures of sympathomimetic amines

zures, all using the EPH process. Additionally, the California Bureau of Narcotic Enforcement reported that the use of the precursor chemical EPH in California had rapidly increased with the availability of the chemical from Mexico. The value of ephedrine as a precursor in methamphetamine manufacture spread quickly in the Mexican drug community, causing it to become a significant smuggling commodity, resulting in a significant price drop in the US market.

In March 1994, the *Federal Register* documented a DEA proposal to make all regulated transactions of EPH, regardless of size, subject to the reporting and record-keeping requirements of the Chemical Diversion and Trafficking Act of 1988 (CDTA). This proposal was intended to subject all transactions involving bulk EPH and single-entity EPH drug products to the applicable provisions of the CDTA. In 2006, the United States passed into law the Combat Methamphetamine Epidemic Act of 2005. This law attempted to limit the availability of pseudoephedrine (PE) and phenylpropanolamine (PPA)

as well as EPH. All purchases of products containing these drugs were to be recorded and the records kept for 2 years. In addition, proof of identity was required prior to purchase them. Solid dosage forms containing these drugs were to be sold only in unit-dose packaging, and these products were to be stored in locked cabinets behind the retail counter. There were also limits in daily and monthly purchases of these drugs.

Structures of some of the most common drugs in this class are shown in Fig. 25.1.

Analogs

Almost since the inception of the pharmaceutical industry, slight changes in molecular structure of various classes of compounds have been used to circumvent patent restrictions and allow various drug manufacturers to gain a share of the lucrative drug market. This concept has not been lost on the chemists who provide materials for the illicit drug market. Their primary impetus, however, in molecular redesign and modification is finding ways to circumvent scheduling restrictions. This has been particularly true of the "designer" group of compounds in the amphetamine/methamphetamine class, especially 3,4-methylenedioxymethamphetamine (MDMA; "Ecstasy"; "Adam"; "XTC") and its N-demethyl metabolite, 3,4-methylenedioxyamphetamine (MDA). MDMA and MDA are two of the oldest so-called designer drugs. MDMA is a derivative of methamphetamine; whereas, MDA is a derivative of amphetamine. It is also important to note that MDA is a metabolite of MDMA.

Newer designer drugs with stimulant, entactogenic, and hallucinogenic properties continue to emerge in today's culture, either from recent synthesis or reintroduction of drugs discovered almost a century ago. In general, minor changes to the chemical structures of phenethylamines, piperazines, piperidines, and tryptamines provide similar effects on the central nervous system as their more traditional counterparts, although their potency may be altered. Furthermore, some of these derivatives are biotransformed into other pharmacologically active substances. With such a large, complex, and ever-changing assortment of compounds, it is often difficult for lawmakers to control manufacturing, distributing, selling, and using of these compounds designed as "legal highs." With global access through the Internet, many new compounds can be available as older ones become controlled. With this in mind, it can be challenging for researchers to elucidate the pharmacological and toxicological properties of these newer drugs within the current cultural context. Complexity of this research increases especially with the concept of drug–drug interactions. Many of these designer drugs may be ingested in combination with other drugs with the intent to enhance euphoric effects; however, these interactions may also increase the risk of toxicity.

Aside from classical phenethylamine derivatives like MDMA, MDEA, and MBDB, a number of psychoactive phenethylamines that include mescaline-derived compounds like DOM, DOET, DOI, and DOC emerged as drugs of abuse in the early 2010s. Following the DO series, the 2C series (2C-B, 2C-I, 2C-E, etc.,) of designer drugs

produced pronounced hallucinogenic effects and variable affinity for subtypes of the $5-HT_2$ receptor. 2C-T series designer phenethylamines are sulfur derivatives of the 2C analogs. Known for their psychedelic and hallucinogenic effects, these drugs are characterized by either serotonergic toxicity or a sympathomimetic toxidrome.

Some naturally occurring alkaloids can also be targets for recreational use. For example, *Catha edulis* (Celastraceae family) is a plant that grows in certain parts of East Africa and the Arabian Peninsula. The leaves of the plant are chewed by people from these areas and have deep-seeded cultural and religious traditions that date back to the Middle Ages. The use of this product, also known as "khat," has social acceptance similar to the use of alcohol in the United States. Despite its use for hundreds of years, it was not until the middle of the twentieth century when the psychoactive constituents of khat were elucidated. In 1930, Wolfes identified *d*-norpseudoephedrine [(+)-threo-2-amino-1-phenylpropanol] or cathine. However, since cathine did not explain the extent of central nervous system stimulation observed with khat usage, research continued. In 1975, l(s)-(-) aminopropiophenone or cathinone was identified. A third phenethylamine, norephedrine was also identified. Cathine and norephedrine have two chiral centers and are diastereomers. Cathinone has one chiral center. Cathinone is highly unstable in the plant material. When cathinone begins to degrade, the breakdown products are cathine and norephedrine. The fresh plant may contain 100-fold higher dose of cathinone than dried plant material. This further explains why not only young plants but fresh plants are preferred for chewing to achieve the desired effects.

The use of cathinone analogs, also known as synthetic cathinones or designer cathinones, has increased significantly since 2009. They are available from "head shops" and from the Internet. They are often distributed under alternative names such as bath salts, stain removers, plant foods, or insect repellants and are labeled as "not for human consumption." In this way, the manufacturers of these products attempt to circumvent drug laws. Nevertheless, the efficacy of these products for plant nutrition or personal hygiene has not been established. In 2010 when initially tracked, approximately 300 calls pertaining to the cathinone analogs were received by Poison Centers throughout the United States. By the following year, the number of calls received increased by over an order of magnitude. As with other drugs of abuse, cathinone analogs are administered in a variety of ways. In one method, the material is wrapped in cigarette paper and swallowed ("bombing"). The material may also be snorted, smoked, or injected intravenously or intramuscularly.

Although abuse of this drug class has skyrocketed in recent years, the synthesis of these analogs is not a recent development. Methcathinone was synthesized in 1928, and 4-methylmethcathinone or mephedrone was synthesized in 1929. Bupropion or 1-(3-chlorophenyl)-2-[(1,1-dimethylethyl)amino]-1-propanone is a cathinone derivative that is used therapeutically. It is used as an antidepressant and as a drug to assist with smoking cessation.

The so-called bath salt products contain cathinone analogs that are derived from four basic chemical backbones: (1) cathinone, (2) pyrrolidinocathinones, (3) methylendioxycathinones, and (4) methylenedioxypyrrolidinocathinones. Figure 25.2 provides the structures of many cathinone analogs. Although the synthetic cathinones can be analyzed using techniques that are amenable to other amphetamines, some derivatives (including some of the fluorinated analogs) are known to be particularly unstable.

Effects

Methamphetamine stimulates the CNS by displacing dopamine from nerve terminal storage vesicles. This release causes the hyperstimulation of dopaminergic receptor neurons in the synaptic cleft. Amphetamine and methamphetamine are substrates for serotonin (5-HT), norepinephrine (NE), and dopamine (DA) transporters and lead to transmitter release by a process of transport-mediated exchange. Upon entry to the cytoplasm, the amphetamines further reduce accumulation of NE/DA in the synaptic vesicles. Catecholaminergic vesicles use an interior-acidic proton gradient for transmitter uptake. These drugs compete for protons with neurotransmitter already present in the granules. The resulting uncharged neurotransmitter then diffuses out of the granules down its concentration gradient. This mechanism causes a continuous release of neurotransmitter at low doses of stimulant, accounting for the locomotor stimulant and reinforcing effects of these compounds. Direct peripheral and organ stimulation at the various α- and β-adrenergic receptors also occur, resulting in elevation of systolic and diastolic blood pressures and weak bronchodilator and respiratory stimulant action. At therapeutic doses, the heart rate may be reflexly slowed; large doses may produce cardiac arrhythmias.

D-Methamphetamine has greater CNS efficacy than d-amphetamine, most likely because of its greater ability to penetrate the CNS. The euphoric effects produced by methamphetamine, cocaine, and designer sympathomimetic amines are difficult to distinguish clinically. The only notable exception being the differences in half-life; for example, methamphetamine has a significantly longer half-life than cocaine, sometimes as much as ten times longer.

PPA, EPH, and PE are members of the class of sympathomimetic amines with primarily peripheral effects. These compounds stimulate α-adrenergic receptors of vascular smooth muscle, producing vasoconstriction, changes in blood pressure, and nasal decongestion. Although EPH and PE retain some β-adrenergic properties (it is this effect of EPH that leads to its occasional use in cardiac resuscitation procedures), a large part of the peripheral action of PPA is due to NE release stimulated through β-adrenergic receptors. This β-agonist effect of PPA can produce elevated blood pressure due to vasoconstriction and cardiac stimulation. Systemically, the products have muted α-effects, allowing decongestion without drastic changes in blood pressure, vascular redistribution, or cardiac stimulation. Constriction of the vessels in the mucous membranes results in their shrinkage, thus promoting drainage and improving ventilation. Other minor α-effects include con-

Cathinone backbone

Substitution Sites	R$_1$	R$_2$	R$_3$	R$_4$	Compound Name	Acronym	Mol. Wt (g/mol)
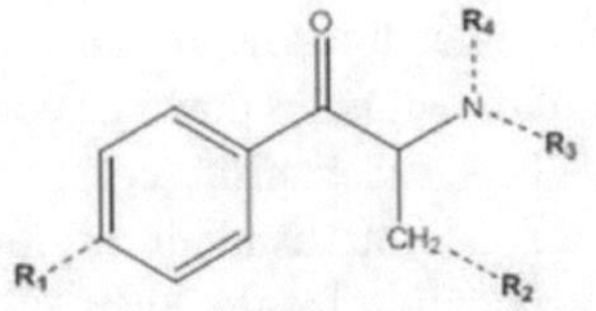	H	H	CH$_3$	H	Methcathinone	-	163.22
	H	H	CH$_3$	CH$_3$	N,N-Dimethylcathinone	-	177.25
	H	H	CH$_3$CH$_2$	H	Ethcathinone	-	177.25
	H	H	CH$_3$CH$_2$	CH$_3$CH$_2$	N,N-Diethylcathinone	-	205.30
	CH$_3$	H	CH$_3$	H	Mephedrone	-	177.25
	H	CH$_3$	CH$_3$	H	Buphedrone	-	177.25
	H	CH$_3$CH$_2$	CH$_3$	H	Pentedrone	-	191.27
	CH$_3$	H	CH$_3$CH$_2$	H	4-Methyl-ethcathinone	4-MEC	191.27
	F	H	CH$_3$	H	Flephedrone	-	181.27
	CH$_3$O	H	CH$_3$	H	Methedrone	-	193.25
	CH$_3$	H	C$_6$H$_5$CH$_2$	H	Benzedrone	4-MBC	253.34

Pyrrolidinocathinone backbone

Substitution Sites	R$_3$	R$_4$	Compound Name	Acronym	Mol. Wt (g/mol)
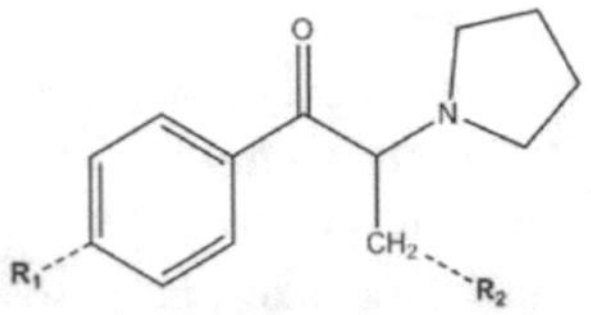	H	H	α-Pyrrolidinopropiophenone	α-PPP	203.28
	H	CH$_3$	α-Pyrrolidinobutiophenone	α-PBP	217.31
	H	CH$_3$CH$_2$	α-Pyrrolidinopentiophenone	α-PVP	231.33
	CH$_3$		4-Methyl-α-pyrrolidinopropiophenone	MePPP	217.31
	CH$_3$	CH$_3$	4-Methyl-α-pyrrolidinobutiophenone	MPBP	231.33
	CH$_3$	CH$_3$CH$_2$	4-Methyl-α-Pyrrolidinopentiophenone	Pyrovalerone	245.36
	CH$_3$	CH$_3$CH$_2$CH$_2$	4-Methyl-α-Pyrrolidinohexiophenone	MPHP	259.39
	CH$_3$		4-Methoxy-α-Pyrrolidinopropiophenone	MOPPP	233.31
	CH$_3$O	CH$_3$	4-Methoxy-α-Pyrrolidinobutiophenone	MOPBP	247.33
	CH$_3$O	CH$_3$CH$_2$	4-Methoxy-α-Pyrrolidinopentiophenone	MOPVP	261.36
	*Naphthyl	CH$_3$CH$_2$	Naphthylpyrovalerone	Naphyrone	281.39

Methylenedioxycathinone backbone

Substitution Sites	R$_2$	R$_3$	Compound Name	Acronym	Mol. Wt (g/mol)
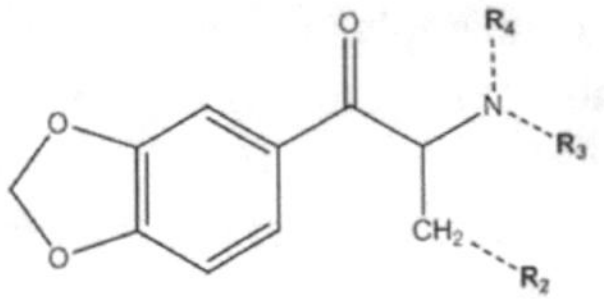	H	CH$_3$	1-(3,4-Methylenedioxyphenyl)-2-methylamino-1-propanone	Methylone	207.23
	H	CH$_3$CH$_2$	1-(3,4-Methylenedioxyphenyl)-2-ethylamino-1-propanone	Ethylone	221.25
	CH$_3$	CH$_3$	1-(3,4-Methylenedioxyphenyl)-2-methylamino-1-butanone	Butylone	221.25
	CH$_3$	CH$_3$CH$_2$	1-(3,4-Methylenedioxyphenyl)-2-ethylamino-1-butanone	Eutylone	235.27
	CH$_3$CH$_2$	CH$_3$	1-(3,4-Methylenedioxyphenyl)-2-methylamino-1-pentanone	Pentylone	235.27

Methylenedioxypyrrolidinocathinone backbone

Substitution Sites	R$_2$	Compound Name	Acronym	Mol. Wt (g/mol)
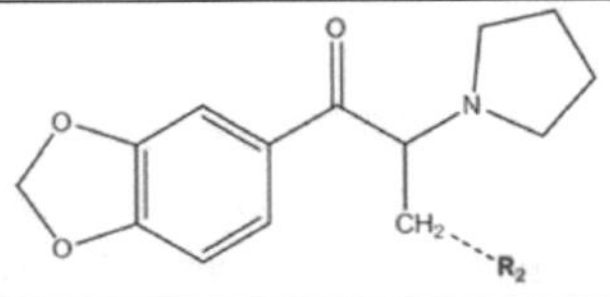	H	3,4-Methylenedioxy-α-pyrrolidinopropiophenone	MDPPP	247.28
	CH$_3$	3,4-Methylenedioxy-α-Pyrrolidinobutiophenone	MDPBP	261.31
	CH$_3$CH$_2$	3,4-Methylenedioxy-α-Pyrrolidinovalerophenone	MDPV	275.34

Fig. 25.2 Structures of synthetic cathinones

traction of gastrointestinal (GI) and urinary sphincters, mydriasis, and decreased pancreatic beta-cell secretion. EPH is a potent stimulator of the CNS but less so than amphetamine. PPA has the weakest CNS effects of this class of drugs. This is probably due to its decreased lipid solubility because of the lack of an alkyl group on the nitrogen.

Phentermine has a spectrum of pharmacological effects similar to that of the amphetamines with weaker CNS stimulation. This drug increases the concentrations of NE and DA in the brain but with less potency than amphetamines. It has no effect on 5-HT.

MDMA and MDA display marked sympathomimetic activity as demonstrated by peripheral vasoconstriction, tachycardia, pupillary dilatation, and effects on other smooth muscles. CNS stimulatory effects also mimic those of amphetamine, and, in cases of overdose, convulsions, hyperthermia, and behavioral changes may occur. Other severe complications, such as rhabdomyolysis, intravascular coagulation, acute renal failure, and hepatonecrosis, have been reported with MDMA overdose. Furthermore, both MDMA and MDA produce perceptual distortions and pronounced subjective effects including intensification of feelings, an apparent facilitation of self-insight, an overwhelming desire to communicate, profound empathy, and euphoria.

Following doses of 150–225 mg in conjunction with psychotherapy sessions, MDMA users reported experiencing positive mood changes; improvements in attitude, beliefs, relationships, occupation, and spiritual–physical condition; and a transient decrease in substance abuse. However, MDMA ingestion has also been reported to cause tachycardia, an occasional "wired" feeling, jaw clenching, nystagmus, a nervous desire to be in motion, transient anorexia, panic attacks, nausea and vomiting, ataxia, urinary urgency, diplopia, insomnia, and, rarely, transient hallucinations.

The pharmacologic effects of cathinone analogs are similar to the effects of cathinone or amphetamine. At the molecular level, their mechanisms of action are to inhibit the reuptake of norepinephrine, dopamine, and/or serotonin in varying proportions and/or increase the release of one or more of these neurotransmitters. However, cathinone analogs have different selectivities for each transporter. For instance, mephedrone and methylone are relatively nonselective in their effects on the transporter systems but have a greater affinity for the dopamine system. Cathinone and methcathinone inhibit dopamine and norepinephrine uptake and dopamine release.

The pyrovalerone cathinones are potent and selective catecholamine uptake inhibitors, especially dopamine, but do not cause release of these neurotransmitters. Adverse effects for these types of drugs can include tachycardia, hypertension, insomnia, hyperthermia, nausea, vomiting, anxiety, paranoia, and hallucinations.

Therapeutic Uses

Pharmaceutical dosage forms for amphetamine and methamphetamine include 5-, 10-, and 15 mg tablets or sustained-release capsules. Amphetamine is also available as a 5 mg/mL elixir. Clinical indications for amphetamine and methamphetamine include narcolepsy, attention-deficit disorder, and appetite suppression in the treatment of exogenous obesity where they function as a short-term adjunct to a regimen of weight reduction based on caloric restriction. In the Department of Defense (DoD), stimulants, particularly amphetamines, were once used in "go/no go" packs as countermeasures to fatigue induced by circadian desynchronosis (disruption of the natural day/night circadian rhythms) and extended flight operations. However, because of the tight DEA control of these substances and the advent of newer drugs with fewer side effects and less abuse potential, these compounds are currently rarely prescribed. The DoD has also discontinued the use of these substances in "go/no go" packs. However, studies are still being conducted to make recommendations concerning the use of dextroamphetamine for some operational tasks and flying requirements.

PE is primarily used as a decongestant, administered directly to swollen membranes (e.g., via sprays and drops) or systemically via the oral route. It is commonly found in over-the-counter cold and allergy medications in combination with antihistamines and analgesics. Until November 2000, PPA was also used as a decongestant and as an anorexiant in many over-the-counter diet aids. On November 3, 2000, the FDA announced a decision to initiate rulemaking to classify PPA as not generally safe and effective, because of an association between PPA and hemorrhagic stroke.

At the urging of the FDA, drug companies voluntarily ceased marketing over-the-counter products containing this compound. In 2005, the FDA removed PPA from over-the-counter products.

One of the common uses of drugs in this class is appetite suppression. At one time, fenfluramine was used as an anorexiant but was voluntarily removed from the United States market in 1997 by the manufacturer due to concerns of cardiac toxicity. Phentermine and diethylpropion are two amphetamine analogs that are still commonly prescribed for this purpose. In addition, there are nonamphetamine anorexiants that are indirect-acting sympathomimetic amines, including mazindol, phenmetrazine, and phendimetrazine.

Unlike other types of designer drugs, MDMA and MDA were legally synthesized in the early decades of the twentieth century intended for therapeutic use. MDMA was first synthesized by Merck in 1914 as an appetite suppressant but never marketed as such. In the 1970s and 1980s, MDMA gained brief popularity as an adjunct to psychotherapy but was never officially approved for that use. MDA was first synthesized in 1910 and had been used variously as an antitussive, as an ataractic, and as an anorexiant.

Abuse

Because of its ease of manufacture and availability, methamphetamine has become the sympathomimetic amine of choice among many stimulant abusers. Illicit methamphetamine is available as a water-soluble, white, crystalline powder (methamphetamine hydrochloride) known as "speed," "crank," "go," "crystal," or simply "meth." This compound is adulterated with a variety of substances such as dimethyl sulfone, sugars (usually added to give more volume to the final product), or cheaper stimulants (e.g., caffeine, PPA, or EPH/PE). Methamphetamine in this form can be used for intravenous injection, oral consumption, smoking, or (rarely) insufflation. Moreover, a form of methamphetamine hydrochloride called "ice" is one of the forms that can be smoked. The term "ice" originated in the Far East and refers to the large crystals of methamphetamine hydro-

chloride produced through the ephedrine reduction method. The popularity of ice is due to the immediate clinical effects of euphoria resulting from the drug's rapid absorption from the lungs.

Both MDMA and MDA can also be drugs of abuse. While both isomers of MDMA are mild hallucinogens, the S(+)-isomer of MDA is thought to be more amphetamine-like, whereas R(-)-MDA is hallucinogenic. MDA became widely abused in the 1960s and 1970s because of its reported hallucinogenic and psychoactive properties. From 1978 to 1981, 16 clandestine MDA laboratories were seized. More than 65% of these labs used the reaction of isosafrole with hydrogen peroxide and formic acid followed by formamide/ammonium formate and hydrochloric acid. The synthetic methods used for amphetamine analogs have been extensively reviewed by legitimate researchers. Some methods, including very sophisticated processes, have also been described in many "underground" publications. Regardless of the source, all of the methods result in the synthesis of racemic mixtures. While these syntheses can be modified to allow for the resolution of racemates, such modifications are rarely used in the illicit labs due to the unavailability of optically pure precursors or lack of sophistication/interest on the part of the "garage" chemist.

On July 1, 1985, the DEA placed MDMA in Schedule I on an emergency basis. Because of its structural similarity to MDA, which by that time had been shown to selectively damage 5-HT nerve terminals in the rat, dangerous side effects to MDMA's abuse were considered likely. They cited that its widespread use was proof of its abuse. Despite this scheduling, the recreational use and abuse of MDMA increased significantly in the 1990s, especially on college campuses. Partly as a result of this resurgence in popularity, numerous studies have been initiated to explore the neurochemical effects.

These studies indicate that MDMA is a selective 5-HT neurotoxin, causing retrograde destruction of 5-HT neurons following large doses. The S(+)-isomer of MDMA has been reported to be a more potent neurotoxin than the R(-)-isomer. Additionally, the S(+)-isomer of MDMA is preferentially metabolized, resulting in the stereoselective formation of the S(+)-isomer of MDA. Unlike MDMA, however, both isomers of MDA cause long-term 5-HT neurotoxicity. In fact, much of the neurotoxicity originally attributed to MDMA may actually be a result of its more potent neurotoxic metabolite, MDA.

It has been demonstrated that both enantiomers of MDMA caused an acute depletion of cortical 5-HT, but only S(+)-MDMA resulted in significant depletions of 5-HT and 5-HT uptake sites. It was later reported that the S(+) isomers of both MDA and MDMA were more potent at depleting 5-HT and in depressing tryptophan hydroxylase (TPH), the rate-limiting enzyme in 5-HT synthesis. It has since been shown that while S(+)-MDMA was more potent than R(-)-MDMA in eliciting some stereotyped behaviors, S(+)-MDA was more potent than both of its parent enantiomers in eliciting these behaviors and produced "wet dog shake" behavior as well. This may indicate that S(+)-MDA has additional harmful effects on other CNS systems in addition to the serotonergic system.

S(+)-MDA stereoselectively accumulates in the blood of animals following a racemic dose of MDMA. This is due to the stereoselective metabolism of S(+)-MDMA to S(+)-MDA, resulting in peak plasma concentrations approximately three times that of R(-)-MDA and almost twice as much S(+)-MDA being excreted in the urine as compared to R(-)-MDA.

Occasional reports of abuse have surfaced about another member of this class of drugs, 4-methylaminorex (4-MAX; "u4euh"). 4-MAX was described in 1963 as an indirect-acting sympathomimetic drug with anorectic properties. 4-MAX is similar in structure to pemoline (a Schedule IV CNS stimulant) and aminorex, an anorectic marketed in Europe in 1965 but withdrawn in 1968. Users have described the effects of 4-MAX to be like those of amphetamine and cocaine.

As mentioned previously, synthetic analogs are becoming more recognized for their abuse potential due to their stimulatory, entactogenic, and/or hallucinogenic effects. The types of effects that each one exhibits may be partially explained by which traditional sympathomimetic amines is most similar in structure. Since the goal of recreational users seems to be to create "legal highs," addressing this growing problem of abuse continues to be a challenge. Most notably, analogs seem to be introduced into the market strategically to stay ahead of legislation. For example, many are labeled with the statement "not for human consumption" and marketed nontraditionally (e.g., bath salts, stain removers, plant foods, or insect repellants).

Pharmacokinetics

Amphetamine and methamphetamine display essentially the same pharmacokinetic profile. Methamphetamine is highly lipid soluble and well absorbed orally with a bioavailability of approximately 67% and a volume of distribution of 3–7 L/kg. A single oral methamphetamine dose of 0.125 mg/kg given to human male volunteers produced a peak plasma concentration of 0.020 mg/L at 3.6 h with an average elimination half-life of approximately 10 h. In another study that evaluated the effect of d-methamphetamine on circadian rhythms, ten male volunteers were given 0.43 mg/kg d-methamphetamine during two test sessions, 1 week apart. Peak serum concentrations ranged from 0.06 to 0.3 mg/L at 3.6 h after administration during the day session and 0.03–0.08 mg/L at 4.8 h during the night session. After oral administration of 30 mg amphetamine base to eight adults, an average peak plasma level of 0.11 mg/L was observed at 2.5 h, decreasing to 0.08 mg/L by 4.5 h.

In one study, the bioavailability of an average inhaled dose of 21.8 mg was approximately 90%. The mean half-life was 11.1 h, compared to 12.2 h for an intravenous injection of 15.5 mg. The volume of distribution was 3.24 L/kg for the smoked dose and 3.73 L/kg for the intravenous dose. Because of the more rapid and intense drug effect, patients describe a "high" distinct from that produced by snorting or ingesting the drug.

Methamphetamine is excreted in the urine largely as unchanged parent drug, under normal conditions, up to 45% of a dose in a 24-h period. Approximately 7% of an administered dose

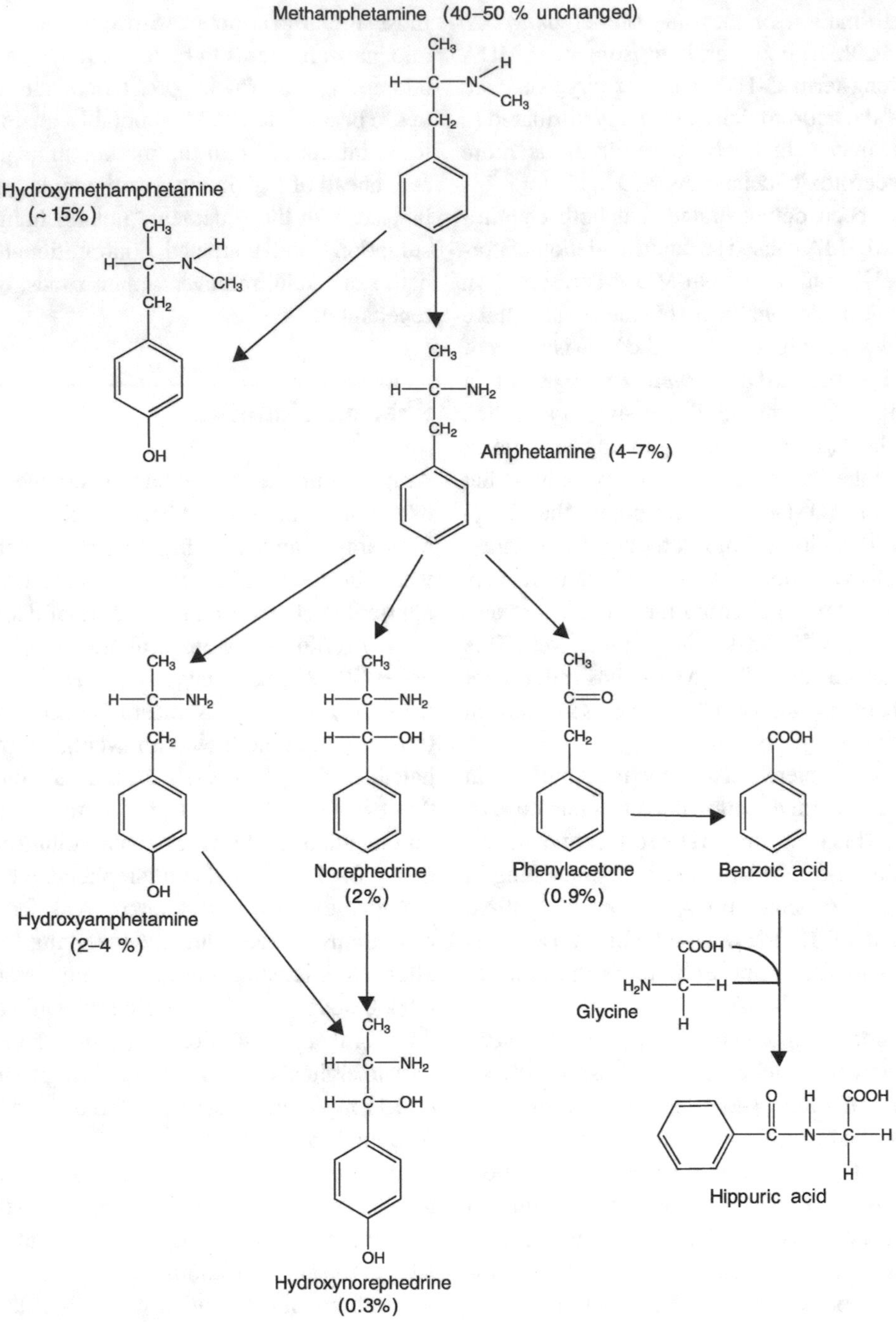

Fig. 25.3 Metabolism of methamphetamine

undergoes N-demethylation to amphetamine (Fig. 25.3). Amphetamines are also metabolized in the liver via aromatic hydroxylation. Accumulated hydroxylated metabolites have been implicated in the development of amphetamine psychosis. Elimination of the sympathomimetic amines is highly dependent on urinary pH. Urinary acidification to a pH <5.6 decreases the plasma half-life from 11–12 h to 7–8 h. Alkalization increases the half-life to 18–34 h. For every one-unit increase in urinary pH, there is an average 7 h increase in plasma half-life. In acidic urine, up to 76% of a dose can be found as unchanged drug, whereas in alkaline urine, <2% of a given dose will be detected as unchanged drug and <0.1% as amphetamine. Approximately 15% of a dose is excreted as p-hydroxymethamphetamine. After ingestion of 10 mg of methamphetamine, urine concentrations of methamphetamine can range from 0.5 to 4.0 mg/L during the first 24 h. Long-time abusers, who may be using 5000–15,000 mg per day, can have urinary methamphetamine concentrations >20 mg/L and amphetamine concentrations >10 mg/L.

EPH, PE, and PPA are all well absorbed orally. EPH, when used as a vasopressor in resuscitation, is administered parenterally—intravenous, subcutaneous, or intramuscular—where it is completely and rapidly absorbed. Onset of action by the intramuscular route is more rapid than by the subcutaneous route. Pressor and cardiac responses to EPH last about 60 min. EPH and PE are not stored to any significant extent in the body, both having a volume of distribution of 3–4 L/kg. Readily absorbed from the GI tract, PPA reaches peak plasma concentrations in 1–2 h with a plasma half-life of 3–4 h. Its volume of distribution is approximately 4 L/kg. All of these compounds are excreted primarily unchanged in the urine. EPH and PE are metabolized to a small extent (<10% of a given dose) in the liver by N-demethylation to PPA. Small amounts of PPA are metabolized in the liver to active hydroxylated metabolites with 80–90% excreted unchanged. Much like amphetamine and methamphetamine, the excretion of these compounds is highly urine pH-dependent, resulting in increased elimination with acidification of the urine. Elimination half-life can be increased from 3 h to 6 h with a pH change of 5 to 6.

Phentermine is well absorbed from the small intestine. Peak plasma concentrations occur within 8 h following oral administration, with therapeutic concentrations lasting for approximately 20 h ($t_{1/2}$ = 20–24 h). In one study of 21 individuals, once-daily dosing for 14 days with 30 mg extended-release phentermine produced mean plasma concentrations of 0.08–0.142 mg/L.

Diethylpropion is well absorbed from the GI tract, with peak plasma concentrations occurring approximately 2 h after administration. It is metabolized in the liver to numerous active metabolites that have an elimination $t_{1/2}$ of 8 h. It is likely that these metabolites contribute significantly to the efficacy of this compound. Both diethylpropion and its active metabolites readily cross the blood–brain barrier and the placenta. One of the minor metabolites of diethylpropion that is pharmacologically active is cathinone. As mentioned previously, cathinone is key constituent of khat.

Like many other drugs, the metabolism of MDMA is complex and involves multiple enzymatic pathways. Research suggests the half-life of MDMA is 5–9 h. MDMA has the potential to exhibit nonlinear pharmacokinetics as well as inhibit its own metabolism at various concentrations. MDMA metabolizes to 3,4-dihydroxymethamphetamine (HHMA) primarily through CYP 450 2D6, and HHMA is then metabolized to 4-hydroxy-3-methoxymethamphetamine (HMMA) using the catecholamine-O-methyltransferase pathway. Less than 5% of MDMA is metabolized to MDA, an N-demethylation of MDMA via the cytochrome P450 pathway. Further demethylation occurs to form 3,4-dihydroxyamphetamine (HHA) and then O-methylation to form 4-hydroxy-3-methoxyamphetamine (HMA). These multiple pathways also result in many sulfate and glucuronide conjugates.

Cathinone and its derivatives have β-keto functional groups that decrease their lipophilicity. Therefore, they are generally less potent than their amphetamine counterparts. With this in mind, larger doses of these drugs may be required to achieve similar euphoric effects. Research indicates cathinone has a half-life of 2.7–6.0 hr and is primarily biotransformed to norephedrine with one of its minor metabolites as norpseudoephedrine. Similarly, methcathinone metabolizes to ephedrine and then norephedrine. Analogous to other drugs, cathinone and its derivatives extensively metabolize through various Phase I and Phase II pathways via demethylation, hydroxylation, oxidation, reduction, O-methylation, glucuronidation, and sulfation. Excretion of these drugs and their metabolites is dependent on the pH of the urine. Potency among the synthetic cathinones varies considerably between analogs. This presents a challenge to illicit cathinone users, who may inadvertently administer a higher-than-expected dose of an unknown derivative.

Metabolic profiles of synthetic cathinones have been studied indirectly without controlled administration in humans. For example, rats were administered mephedrone, and urine was collected over a 24-h period. Suspected metabolites based on known metabolic patterns of these drugs were synthesized as standards. These urine specimens were then tested for the suspected metabolites by a combination of GC/MS and LC/MS. Finally, human urine specimens from suspected synthetic cathinone users were also tested to ascertain which of these metabolites could be identified in humans. Based on these studies, the following routes of metabolism have been postulated: N-demethylation, reduction of the keto group to an alcohol, and oxidation of the tolyl moiety to the corresponding alcohol. The total hydroxylation products undergo Phase II metabolism with glucuronic acid.

The Phase I metabolism of MDPV was investigated in a manner similar to methods described above for mephedrone. Two initial steps were postulated: (1) the methylenedioxy ring opens up and loses a methyl group to form a diol, and (2) a ketone group is added on the pyrovalerone ring. From these two initial products, methylation of one of the hydroxyl groups, hydroxylation on the alkyl chain, and dealkylation of the pyrovalerone ring occur. These reactions are catalyzed by CYP2D6, CYP2C19, and catecholamine-O-methyl transferase.

Analysis

Immunoassay

Since the introduction of the Syva enzyme-multiplied immunoassay technique drug abuse (EMIT-dau®) assays in the mid-1970s, immunoassays based on the competitive binding of labeled drugs and specimen drugs for specific drug antibody binding sites have proved successful for rapid screening for amphetamines and other drugs of abuse. This is particularly useful for screening purposes in many types of forensic toxicology laboratories, including, but not limited to, postmortem, human performance, and urine drug testing-based laboratories. With this in mind, many types of immunoassay products are available to meet the needs of such a diverse industry. Some products provide minimal cross-reactivity to target specific drugs monitored by the federal government in urine drug testing laboratories. Other products offer a wide range of cross-reactivity in diverse biological matrices to aid postmortem and human performance investigations. There are even products designed to give instant results, which may prove helpful in clinical or roadside settings that require immediate action.

The historical basis of the EMIT-dau® technique was the detection of a change in ultraviolet (UV) absorbance (340 nm) as the coenzyme NAD is reduced to NADH. The EMIT-dau amphetamine class assay (EC) contained polyclonal antibodies and had a cutoff calibrator of 300 ng/mL d-amphetamine. The assay readily cross-reacted with ephedrine, pseudoephedrine, phentermine, and other phenylisopropylamines. The EC was indicated when low detection limits for amphetamines or high cross-reactivity to other structurally related stimulants was desired. Thus, EC was used in athletic drug testing and in screening patients in substance abuse rehabilitation programs. In an effort to further confront the issue of cross-reactivity of these assays with EPH, PE, and PPA, Syva Co. also supplied an optional amphetamine confirmation kit. The kit contained sodium hydroxide and sodium periodate which were added to the specimen before testing. These reagents eliminated cross-reacting compounds with a hydroxyl group in the α-position such as PPA and PE/EPH through oxidative cleavage of the $\alpha-$ and $\beta-$ carbon bonds.

Due in part to workplace testing requirements and needs, the EMIT-dau monoclonal amphetamine/methamphetamine assay (EM) was developed with a cutoff calibrator of 1000 ng/mL d-methamphetamine. The assay displayed much less cross-reactivity with phenylisopropylamine derivatives than the EC. However, the assay readily detected low concentrations of MDA and MDMA. This was subsequently upgraded to the EMIT-II amphetamine/methamphetamine assay (EII). EII contained monoclonal antibodies with a cutoff calibrator of 1000 ng/mL *d*-methamphetamine. Unlike the EM assay, EII required 1000 ng/mL *d*-amphetamine to produce a positive response. The EII assay had low cross-reactivity to phenylisopropylamine derivatives and was configured for high-volume, high-speed analyzers and high selectivity for amphetamine, methamphetamine, MDMA, and MDA.

Besides EMIT products that are now supplied by Siemens Healthcare Diagnostics, Inc., there are a number of other immunoassay technologies available for the rapid detection of sympathomimetic amines in blood, urine, and/or alternative biological specimens. Such a variety of products have been designed to meet the needs of many forensic applications. One challenging aspect of product design for postmortem toxicology is the cross-reactivity of decomposition amines such as phenethylamine and tyramine. Many companies are designing products to cost-effectively improve efficiency and selectivity for the wide range of chemical structures that compose the amphetamine class of drugs. Among the immunoassay technologies are KIMS, CEDIA®, and ELISA, which provide a diverse range of cross-reactivity.

Kinetic interaction of microparticles in a solution (KIMS) is a homogenous assay used in many immunoassay products designed by Roche Diagnostics Corporation. Its technology has been used to create products with different target analytes. For example, Roche Diagnostics has created at least three different assays with amphetamine, methamphetamine, and MDMA as the primary target analytes. However, there is a range of cross-reactivity to related structures such as MDA, MDEA, and N-methyl-1-(3,4-methylene-dioxyphenyl)-2-butanamine (MBDB).

CEDIA®, a homogenous assay manufactured by Thermo Fisher Scientific, can be an alternative tool for screening purposes. Currently there are two CEDIA® products designed to detect amphetamines. The target analyte for one of the products

is *d*-amphetamine, but there is significant cross-reactivity to structures such as *d*-methamphetamine and MDMA. The second product has cross-reactivity with several compounds such as *d*-amphetamine, *d*-methamphetamine, MDA, MDEA, MDMA, p-methoxymethamphetamine (PMMA), and N-methyl-1-(3,4-methylene-dioxyphenyl)-2-butanamine (MBDB).

ELISA, a heterogenous assay, is used by multiple manufacturers. Assays targeted toward *d*-amphetamine, *d*-methamphetamine, and MDMA are widely available. Additional assays that target cathinones are also available, but due to the large number of drugs within this class and the structural modifications present, broad-spectrum screening of cathinones using immunoassay is problematic.

An alternative immunoassay technique supplied by Randox is the Biochip Array System. It uses a drug-labeled horseradish peroxidase and chemiluminescent detection system that offers detection of amphetamine and related compounds including cathinones. Each of these products has different target analytes with a range of selectivity for similar chemical structures.

One of the newer challenges is addressing the need to detect the ever-growing number of synthetic analogs. The concept of cross-reactivity has allowed immunoassays to play an important role in this endeavor. Many companies are creating detection systems to combat the problem; and many new products or modifications of older ones are being introduced into the market. Immunoassay is discussed in more detail in Chap. 13.

Chromatographic Separation

Amphetamines and other structurally related compounds can be separated by gas chromatography (GC) using dimethyl silicone and phenylmethyl silicone analytical columns without derivatization. They elute very early, prior to other drugs such as narcotic analgesics, antidepressants, benzodiazepines, and antihistamines. Using nonpolar or slightly polar columns, the elution order of some of the more common ones is typically as follows: amphetamine, phentermine, methamphetamine, PPA, pseudoephedrine, MDA, MDMA, mephedrone, methylone, and MDPV.

Although not required, derivatization offers a number of advantages for qualitative and quantitative analysis of stimulant amines by gas chromatography. One advantage is that peak tailing is reduced by forming a derivative. Reducing peak tailing improves peak shape which allows for better peak integration and consequently more accurate quantitations. Derivatization also reduces the volatility of these compounds, increasing their retention time and enhancing their separation from potentially interfering endogenous compounds. While many derivatives are available for GC/MS use, those most commonly used with primary and secondary amines include heptafluorobutyric anhydride (HFBA), pentafluoropropionic anhydride (PFPA), trifluoroacetic anhydride (TFAA), and 4-carbethoxyhexfluorobutyryl chloride (4-CB). As an example, Table 25.1 provides GC/MS ion characteristics for HFBA derivatives of amphetamine, methamphetamine, and other amines.

Liquid chromatography (LC) is also a useful analytical tool in the separation of amphetamines and other similar compounds. The polarity of the stationary phase in the LC column compared to the liquid mobile phase plays a key role in this separation and helps to determine elution order and retention times. Additionally, LC technology lends itself to a variety of compatible sample preparation techniques, including, but not limited to, dilution, liquid–liquid extraction, and solid-phase extraction.

Mass Spectrometry

Mass spectrometry (MS) is the most common for the detection of amphetamine and other sympathomimetic amines. However, caution should always be taken when interpreting the mass spectral data because many of the compounds are very similar in size and structure resulting in similar mass spectra. Retention time is helpful in the identification process. Furthermore, amphetamine and many other structurally similar compounds are volatile, and precautions may need to be taken to increase recovery of these compounds in the sample preparation steps. For example, an acidic methanolic solution may be added to extracts prior to evaporating away the excess solvent in preparation for GC/MS or LC/MS analysis.

There are several advantages in using LC/MS versus GC/MS in the analysis of amines including minimal sample extraction/preparation and greater specificity in the resultant MS data. A protein precipitation with methanol or acetonitrile may be all of the specimen preparation required for LC/MS analysis, as opposed to liquid–liquid extraction or solid-phase extraction for GC/MS. Furthermore, the more gentle ioniza-

Table 25.1 GC/MS ion characteristics for HFBA derivatives of sympathomimetic amines

Compound	Retention time (min)[a]	Ions monitored	Comments
β-Phenethylamine	4.6	10,411,899,149/150	
d,l-Amphetamine	4.7	24,011,891	
Phentermine	4.8	25,491	No 210 ion
Phenylpropanolamine	5.4	240,160,330,275	
d,l-Methamphetamine	5.5	254,118,210	
Ephedrine	5.7	254,210,344	No 118 or 91 ions
Pseudoephedrine	6.0	254,210,344	No 118 or 91 ions
Phenylephrine	6.5	240,169	No 91 ion
MDA	7.1	135,162,240,169	No 91 ion
MDMA	7.7	162,254,210,162	No 118 or 91 ions
Benzphetamine	7.9	1,489,165,149	Not derivatized

[a]HP-1 capillary column [12 m × 0.2 mm(id) × 0.33 μm] initial oven temperature, 100 °C; injection port, 250 °C; ramped from an initial temperature of 100 °C (held for 2 min) to 280 °C at 20 °C/min

tion of electrospray ionization (ESI) or atmospheric pressure chemical ionization (APCI) typically allows for the identification of the parent ion, which is useful with structurally similar compounds like the amphetamines and sympathomimetic amines.

Chiral Separations

Many of the drugs in this class of compounds contain a chiral carbon and therefore exist as enantiomers. In many cases, pharmaceutical companies in the development of drugs have exploited the presence of the chiral carbon and its ability to bind with chiral receptors. Examples include methamphetamine, amphetamine, EPH/ PE, and fenfluramine/dexfenfluramine. *d*-Methamphetamine and *d*-amphetamine are used therapeutically for narcolepsy, attention-deficit disorder, and weight loss. *l*-Methamphetamine has one-tenth the CNS stimulation effect of the *d*-isomer but has greater peripheral vasoconstrictive properties and thus has been used in over-the-counter nasal inhalers. As a result, the *d*-forms of amphetamine and methamphetamine are the primary abused drugs and often the target analytes for forensic and urine drug testing laboratories. Since standard GC/MS procedures are unable to distinguish between enantiomers, special testing may be necessary.

Chromatographic identification of *d*- and *l*-isomers depends on the enantiomers reacting with optically active substrates to form diastereomers. This can be accomplished in one of two ways: (1) a chiral, optically active stationary phase can be used to form transient diastereomers with the optically active drug causing different partition coefficients, or (2) a chiral derivatizing reagent may be used to achieve separation on an achiral stationary phase.

Chiral stationary phases are available for both GC and LC systems. However, chiral derivatizing reagents have gained popularity since they allow chiral analysis on the same instrument used for other routine analyses. The main disadvantage of using a chiral derivatizing reagent is the difficulty

in ensuring the optical purity of the derivatizing reagent; four possible isomers can result from the reaction of an asymmetric sample with an asymmetric reagent rather than the two desired. The four derivative isomers consist of two diastereomeric pairs of chromatographically unresolvable enantiomers. Experiments must also be done to demonstrate both that racemization is not occurring during the derivatizing process and that stereoselective formation of one pair of diastereomers is not occurring.

Amines have been converted to diastereomeric amides with several chiral acid chloride reagents for GC analysis, such as *O*-methylmandelyl chloride, α-phenylbutyryl chloride or anhydride, and *N*-trifluoroacetyl-L-prolyl chloride (L-TPC). L-TPC is the most popular of this type of reagent. First used as a chiral derivatizing reagent for the separation of amino acids, it has since become popular for both the on-column and preinjection derivatization of amphetamine and methamphetamine. There have been some reports of racemization with the use of L-TPC. Amide derivatives can also be prepared with acyclimidazole reagents and with chiral acids in the presence of *N*,*N'*-carbonyldiimidazole. Diastereomeric sulfonamide derivatives have been created using (+)-camphor-10-sulfonyl chloride and menthyl carbamates, such as menthyl chloroformate. These reagents have been used for sympathomimetic amines and amino acid analysis.

Interpretation

Impairment

At low doses, methamphetamine-induced CNS stimulation manifests clinically as euphoria, increased alertness, intensified emotions, increased feeling of self-esteem and well-being, sensations of extreme physical and mental power, and allegedly increased sexuality. Most abusers begin by taking amphetamines orally, usually 150–250 mg/day. Doses in this range generally produce plasma concentrations of 0.1– 0.2 mg/L. Progression to intravenous use usually results from the need to intensify euphoric feelings that often accompany the use of these drugs.

Intravenous use of amphetamines typically begins with 20–40 mg doses, three to four times a day. As tolerance develops, the dose and frequency of injection increase considerably, and sleep cycles may be affected. For example, if the drug is injected every 2–3 h around the clock, the user never sleeps. A wide range of injection patterns exist, but there is a potential for some drug abusers to inject repeatedly over several days, possibly up to 10–12 days. Following a run, users "fall out," i.e., become so exhausted, disorganized, tense, or paranoid, that they cease using the drug and go to sleep. This sleep could last 12–18 h following a 3–4-day run. Upon awakening, the paranoid state is diminished, but lethargy may persist. At this point, a new run terminates the lethargy. When use becomes well-established, individual injections range from 100–300 mg. Long-time abusers may use as much as 5000–15,000 mg/day.

Smoked doses of approximately 20 mg methamphetamine hydrochloride produce peak plasma concentrations of 0.04 mg/L in less than 1 h. Although methamphetamine levels peak rapidly after smoking, they remain high for a considerable time, declining with a half-life of 11–12 h. This long plateau effect and much longer half-life of smoked methamphetamine (vs. oral or intravenous use) suggest significant danger in repeated smoking of methamphetamine, because if the dose is repeated, even at fairly long intervals, markedly higher plasma concentrations would be expected.

In toxic doses, amphetamine and drugs with similar structures begin to produce unpleasant CNS symptoms such as anxiety, agitation, hallucinations, delirium, seizures, and death. Long-term, high-dose use of stimulants can induce an acute psychotic state in previously healthy individuals or precipitate a psychotic episode in those with psychiatric illness. Hyperthermia may result from CNS-induced abnormalities, seizures, or muscular hyperactivity. Secondary rhabdomyolysis may also be seen.

Cardiovascular manifestations of amphetamine use include hypertension, tachycardia, atrial and ventricular arrhythmias, and myocardial ischemia. Cerebrovascular accidents may also be seen, precipitated by elevated blood pressures or drug-induced vasospasms.

Evidence suggests that the neurochemical basis underlying the behavioral effects and increased motor activity associated with sympathomimetic amines involves dopaminergic systems. By enhancement of neurotransmitter release/blockade of reuptake, stimulants facilitate catecholaminergic neurotransmission. One of the defining characteristics of psychomotor stimulants (methamphetamine, amphetamine, cocaine, etc.) is their ability to elicit increases in spontaneous motor activity. At low doses, these drugs produce an alerting response characterized by increases in exploration and locomotion. As the dose increases, locomotor activity decreases, and the behavioral patterns become more stereotyped (i.e., a continuous repetition of one or several types of behavior). The "rewarding effects" (those responsible for psychomotor stimulant abuse) are also thought to result from enhanced DA release in the limbic regions such as the nucleus accumbens.

This mechanism causes a continuous release of neurotransmitter at low doses of stimulant, accounting for the locomotor stimulant and reinforcing effects of these compounds. As the dose increases, the cytoplasmic concentrations of neurotransmitter continue to increase, and the phenomenon of intracellular oxidative stress becomes prominent. Ultimately, this results in neurotoxicity and selective degeneration of DA neuron terminals. When the monoamine neurotransmitters are redistributed from the reducing environment of the synaptic vesicle to extravesicular oxidizing environments, generation of oxygen radicals and reactive metabolites by monoamine oxidase within the neuron may trigger selective terminal loss. Similar effects are believed to occur with other weakly basic drugs (including fenfluramine, MDMA, and phencyclidine) that are toxic to monoamine systems. Chronic cocaine abusers also have been shown to have decreased neurofilament proteins in midbrain DA regions, suggesting that cocaine may also selectively damage neuronal processes.

Clinically, damage to or complete loss of these neurons would present as Parkinson-like symptoms, choreoathetoid disorders (irregular, writhing/spasmodic, involuntary movements of the limbs or facial muscles, especially the fingers and hands), memory loss, irregular moods, anxiety, aggression, and changes in sleep patterns.

Impairment caused by designer amphetamines seems to manifest in similar ways to their more traditional counterparts. However, potency may be affected because of the minor modifications in the chemical structures that alter their physico-chemical properties. In other words, the dose required to achieve the desired euphoric effect may be vastly different from one compound to the next. With this in mind, some of the packaging may have dosing listed in creative ways, especially if the product states that it is "not for human consumption." Purity of the products may also be of concern since many of these compounds are not manufactured and distributed in a regulated manner.

Postmortem

As is true with most abused drugs, tolerance makes it very difficult to use blood and tissue concentrations as predictors of cause or contribution to death. Steady-state amphetamine blood concentrations of 2–3 mg/L have been seen in tolerant addicts, while methamphetamine/ amphetamine concentrations in fatal cases have ranged from <1 mg/L to >14 mg/L. Since the degree of tolerance for any drug is impossible to determine at autopsy, attributing significance to isolated postmortem concentrations or attempting to back-calculate to a dose is unwise. Furthermore, the redistribution of drugs within various postmortem tissues may also affect interpretation.

Fatalities have been reported after ingestion of as low as 1.5 mg/kg. Low blood concentrations, thought to be incidental findings, are hard to interpret. Very low concentrations (<0.5 mg/L) have been observed in patients dying of what is now described as "classic stimulant toxicity" with agitation, hypertension, tachycardia, and hyperthermia. In the absence of any other pathological or anatomical causes of death, the detection of any amount of methamphetamine or amphetamine in the blood could be significant and may have contributed to the cause of death. Recently, there has been an increase in reports of fatalities due to synthetic amphetamines and other designer drugs with similar structures. Since little is known about the pharmacology of these newer synthetic amphetamine counterparts, interpretation of their concentrations found in biological matrices is more challenging. As with any drugs of abuse, interpretation of findings should be done in the context of the entire investigation.

Seizures, while also often associated with stimulant abuse, tend to occur only at very high doses. Convulsions are a common sequel to long-term, high-dose use of stimulants such as cocaine, the amphetamines, amphetamine analogs (MDMA, MDA, etc.), pemoline, aminorex, and 4-MAX. The mechanisms of seizure induction appear to be as varied as the drugs themselves; however, 5-HT depletion has been implicated in several models of convulsions, neurotoxicity, and clinical syndromes such as depression, multiple sclerosis, schizophrenia, and "stimulant psychosis." Depletion of the amine in the brain increases susceptibility to seizures, whereas agents that increase 5-HT concentration decrease susceptibility.

Stimulants achieve this final common pathway to seizurgenesis/5-HT reduction through a variety of mechanisms, including decreased synthesis, decreased release, increased metabolism, or death of serotonergic neurons. Chronic or subacute administration of amphetamine or methamphetamine produces prolonged decreases in regional tryptophan hydroxylase activity and concentrations of 5-HT.

4-MAX also has potent convulsant actions. 4-MAX produces a substantial reduction in neostriatal TPH activity. Dramatic decreases in TPH activity have also been noted in other brain regions (hippocampus and frontal cortex) following 4-MAX administration.

Therapeutic Drugs Converted to Amphetamine/Methamphetamine

A number of drugs are metabolized to amphetamine and methamphetamine. This group includes benzphetamine, clobenzorex, deprenyl, famprofazone, fenethylline, fenproporex, and lisdexamfetamine. There are several ways to document the use of these drugs as an explanation for a positive urinalysis result. Examination of medical history is a straightforward approach. Alternatively, it may be possible to identify parent drug in the urine specimens. Unfortunately, this is not a guarantee given the short half-lives of many of these drugs. Instead, the identification of a metabolite unique to these drugs may provide analytical verification that these drugs were ingested.

Enantiomer analysis can be used to document selegiline use. Prescription selegiline is the *l*-enantiomer; it is converted in the body exclusively to *l*-methamphetamine and *l*-amphetamine. Therefore, any findings of the *d*-isomers of these compounds would be inconsistent with selegiline use. Conversely, fenethylline is a racemic for the amphetamine portion of the molecule, which would most likely cause the detection of equal amounts of the *d* and *l* isomers in urine.

Summary

Amphetamine and compounds with similar chemical structures represent a key class of drugs that stimulate the sympathetic nervous system. In various forms, a selective few of these drugs have become important therapeutic agents, while many are targeted by recreational users. Additionally, this class has been targeted by the designer drug movement. Extensive research has been conducted to better understand the pharmacokinetic and pharmacodynamic properties of this class of drugs. A lot of resources have been invested by laboratories to optimize methods for detecting such compounds in various biological matrices.

Further Reading

Baselt RC (2020) Disposition of toxic drugs and chemicals in man, 12th edn. Biomedical Publications, Seal Beach, CA

Caldwell J (1976) The metabolism of amphetamines in mammals. Drug Metab Rev 5(2):219–280

Cook CE (1991) Pyrolytic characteristics, pharmacokinetics, and bioavailability of smoked heroin, cocaine, phencyclidine, and methamphetamine. NIDA Res Mon 115:6–23

Cook CE, Jeffcoat AR, Hill JM, Pugh DE, Patetta PK, Sadler BM et al (1993a) Pharmacokinetics of methamphetamine self-administered to human subjects by smoking S-(_)-methamphetamine hydrochloride. Drug Metab Dispos 21:717–723

Cook CE, Jeffcoat AR, Sadler BM, Hill JM et al (1993b) Pharmacokinetics of oral methamphetamine and effects of repeated daily dosing in humans. Drug Metab Dispos 20(6):856–862

Kalix P (1991) The pharmacology of psychoactive alkaloids from Ephedra and Catha. J Ethnopharmacol 32:201–208

Kelly JP (2011) Cathinone derivatives: A review of their chemistry, pharmacology and toxicology. Drug Test Anal 3:439–453

Kolbrich EA, Goodwin RS, Gorelick DA, Hayes RJ, Stein EA, Huestis MA (2008) Plasma pharmacokinetics of 3,4-methylenedioxymethamphetamine after controlled oral administration to young adults. Ther Drug Monit 30(3):320–332

Levine B, Holler JM, Vorce SP (2014) Quick guide to designer drugs. AACC Press, Washington, DC

Moffat AC, Osselton MD, Widdop B, Watts J (eds) (2011) Clarke's analysis of drugs and poisons, 4th edn. Pharmaceutical Press, London, UK

Negrusz A, Cooper G (eds) (2013) Clarke's analytical forensic toxicology, 2nd edn. Pharmaceutical Press, London, UK

Samanin R, Garattini S (1993) Neurochemical mechanism of action of anorectic drugs. Pharmacol Toxicol 73:63–68

Silverstone T (1992) Appetite suppressants: A review. Drugs 43(6):820–836

Westfall TC (2011) Westfall DP adrenergic agonists and antagonists. In: Brunton LL, Chabner BA, Knollman BC (eds) Goodman and Gilman's pharmacological basis of therapeutics, 12th edn. McGraw Hill Medical, New York, NY, pp 187–220

Hallucinogens and Psychedelics

26

Amanda J. Jenkins and Madeleine J. Gates

Abstract

Hallucinogens are drugs that alter perception of reality. In high-enough doses, these psychedelic or psychomimetic drugs can induce illusions, hallucinations, or delusions. The hallucinogenic state is characterized by heightened awareness of sensory input, a sense of a divided self, and feelings not experienced outside of dreams or religious experiences. Most hallucinogens are plant alkaloids and function as 5-HT_{2A} receptor agonists. Hallucinogens can be divided into indolylalkylamines and phenylalkylamines. This chapter encompasses the history, synthesis, drug abuse patterns, pharmacology, metabolism, detection and analysis, and toxicological interpretation of classic hallucinogenic compounds, including phencyclidine (PCP), lysergic acid diethylamide (LSD), mescaline, psilocybin, and ketamine. More recently, synthetic analogs have also emerged in the illicit drug market as novel psychoactive substances, including analogs of PCP, mescaline (2C and NBOMe types), and ketamine. While PCP may be considered a dissociative anesthetic and ketamine is used as another anesthetic, they are abused for their hallucinogenic properties and are therefore discussed in detail in this chapter.

Keywords

Hallucinogens · Pharmacology · Effects · Synthesis · Analysis · Interpretation

Introduction

Hallucinogen is a term commonly applied to a group of drugs that are capable of altering perception of reality. These are also known as psychedelic, psychotomimetic, or psychotogenic drugs. According to the most recent drug use survey in 2017, there are more than 1.4 million people (12 years or older) in the United States who currently use hallucinogens, including 1.7% of young adults (18–25 years).

Under certain conditions, or at toxic doses, several classes of drugs can induce illusions, hallucinations, or delusions. These include anticholinergics, bromides, antimalarials, opioid antagonists, cocaine, corticosteroids, certain volatile solvents, and some novel psychoactive substances. There is no distinct line dividing

A. J. Jenkins (✉)
UMass Memorial Medical Center/UMASS Medical School, Worcester, MA, USA
e-mail: amanda.jenkins@umassmemorial.org

M. J. Gates
Department of Forensic Science, Sam Houston State University, Huntsville, TX, USA
e-mail: GatesM@SHSU.edu

psychedelic compounds from other centrally acting drugs. Most hallucinogens are 5-HT_{2A} receptor agonists, which accounts for cognitive alterations. However, one feature that distinguishes the psychedelic agent is the capacity to reliably induce states of altered perception, thought, and feeling that are not experienced otherwise except in dreams or at times of religious exaltation. Historically, there have been several attempts to define the term "hallucinogenic." Hollister defined hallucinogens by the following criteria:

1. Changes in thought, perception, and mood should dominate among the effects of the drug.
2. Memory or intellectual impairment should be minimal.
3. Stupor or excessive stimulation should not be a major effect.
4. Autonomic nervous system adverse effects should be minimal.
5. Addictive craving should be absent.

Most descriptions of the hallucinogenic state include several major effects, including a heightened awareness of sensory input and diminished control over what is experienced. There may be a feeling that the self is divided in two, with one part a passive observer while the other part participates in the sensory experience. Frequently, the attention of the individual is turned inward, with mild sensations having deep meaning. The user may experience a diminished capacity to differentiate the boundaries of one object from another and also of the user from the environment.

Most hallucinogens are New World alkaloids of plant origin. Although only 60 of the hundreds of thousands of plant species in existence have been used as hallucinogens, approximately 20 are considered clinically important. More recently, synthetic analogs have also emerged in the illicit market as "legal alternatives." Hallucinogens have been classified generally into nitrogen-containing and non-nitrogen-containing compounds. Marijuana is an example of the latter and is discussed in Chap. 24. An alternate classification system also divides hallucinogens into two

categories: the indolealkylamines and the phenylalkylamines. The indolealkylamines are subdivided as follows:

1. β-Carbolines, e.g., harmala alkaloids
2. Ergolines, e.g., lysergic acid diethylamide
3. α-Methyltryptamines, e.g., 5-methoxy-α-methyltryptamine
4. Tryptamines, e.g., N,N-dimethyltryptamine, psilocin

Phenylalkylamines may be subdivided as follows:

1. Phenylalkylamines, e.g., mescaline
2. Phenylisopropylamines, e.g., 1-(2,5-dimethoxy-4X-phenyl-)-2-aminopropane

This chapter will discuss several examples of hallucinogens and also phencyclidine, which, although classified as a dissociative anesthetic, is primarily abused for its hallucinogenic properties. Ketamine, another anesthetic agent, is also included in the list of abused hallucinogenic substances. As with many drugs of abuse, synthetic analogs of these hallucinogens have emerged into the drug market as novel psychoactive substances and are also included in this chapter.

Phencyclidine

Phencyclidine [PCP, 1-(1-phenylcyclohexyl) piperidine] is an arylcyclohexylamine with a chemical formula of $C_{17}H_{25}N$ and a molecular weight of 243.4 (Fig. 26.1). It is structurally similar to ketamine. PCP was first synthesized in 1926, but its utility as an anesthetic was not discovered until 1956, when Victor Maddox of the Product Development Department of Parke-Davis and Co. in Detroit, Michigan, investigated chemical reactions to Grignard reagents with nitriles. Maddox submitted several compounds to a pharmacologist at Parke-Davis, Graham Chen, for pharmacological testing. Experiments with laboratory animals (cats) led Chen to categorize this new compound as a "cataleptoid anesthetic." Further experiments with rhesus monkeys dem-

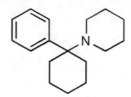

Fig. 26.1   Structure of phencyclidine

onstrated its ability to produce serenity, tranquility, and peace.

Clinical trials in 1957 demonstrated phencyclidine's usefulness as an anesthetic in individuals with compromised cardiac function. In 1960 and 1963, the UK and US governments, respectively, permitted the use of PCP (under the trade name Sernyl™) as a short-acting analgesic or general anesthetic in humans. Shortly thereafter, adverse psychological reactions were observed in humans following surgery. These included delusions, delirium, hallucinations, muscle rigidity, and seizures. In 1963, Parke-Davis and Co. discontinued marketing PCP for human use. PCP continued to be used, however, as a large-animal veterinary tranquilizer under the trade name Sernylan™. The legal manufacture of PCP continued until 1979.

PCP first appeared illicitly in 1967, when it was sold in the Haight-Ashbury district of San Francisco. At that time it was known as the "peace pill" and was self-administered orally. The adverse psychological effects of PCP use resulted in a brief decrease in use in the late 1960s. Because illicit synthesis is relatively easy and inexpensive, abuse became widespread in the 1970s and early 1980s. Today, the use of PCP tends to be highly regionalized in the United States, apparent particularly in Los Angeles, New York, and the Baltimore–Washington, DC, corridor. According to National Survey Results on Drug Use from the Monitoring of the Future Study, 1975–1994, PCP use among high school seniors fell sharply between 1979 and 1982, from an annual prevalence of 7.0–2.2%. It reached a low in 1988 of 1.2%, rising slightly thereafter to 1.6% in 1994, but was no longer included in the survey after 2013 (1.3%). In the same study, the prevalence rate was reported as 0.3% for young adults (19–32 years of age). More recent data suggests a continued decline in PCP use, with past year initial use declining from 123,000 in 2002 to 45,000 in 2010. However, these figures do not reflect the use of marijuana cigarettes laced with PCP. According to the 2011 report from Drug Abuse Warning Network (DAWN) of the US Department of Health and Human Services, of the more than five million drug-related emergency department visits, approximately 1.25 million involved illicit drugs. PCP was involved in 24.2 ED visits/100,000 population of persons 21 or older, compared with 162.1 visits/100,000 for cocaine. In 2017, PCP was among the top 25 most frequently identified drugs submitted to US laboratories (4910 or 0.31%).

Drug Abuse Patterns

PCP has many street names, including angel dust, killer weed, crystal, PeaCe Pill, hog, horse tracks, embalming fluid, and busy bee. It may be sold as flakes or "angel dust" of high (80%) purity or in a less pure form (10–30%), resulting from soaking a tobacco or marijuana cigarette in liquid PCP or mixing with vegetable matter such as mint or parsley leaves. A single dose is approximately 5 mg, with a range of 1–10 mg.

Experimental and chronic abuse patterns have been described. First-time users are introduced to PCP by friends; these friends may misrepresent the drug as a more desirable hallucinogen such as lysergic acid diethylamide (LSD). Many first-time users do not continue experimentation with PCP, disliking the sensory isolation PCP produces. Those who continue to use PCP are most likely polydrug abusers, already experienced with ethanol, marijuana, and sedatives. To these individuals, the disassociation and perceptual distortions that occur with PCP use are welcomed. PCP use may also result in feelings of power and strength, which users find attractive. Chronic use increases the likelihood of undesirable and unpredictable side effects.

Synthesis

PCP is controlled under Federal Schedule II of the Controlled Substances Act of 1970. Its salts,

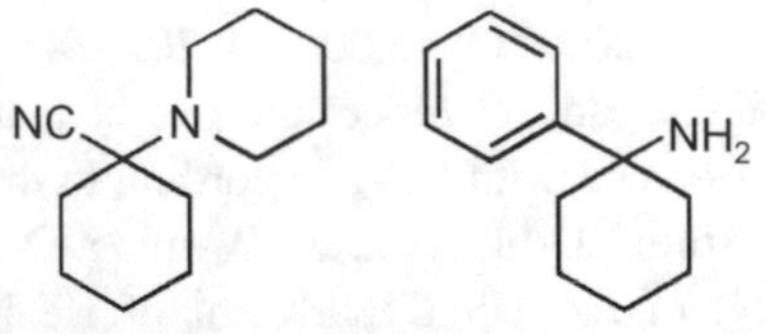

PCC   **PCH**

Fig. 26.2 Structure of phencyclidine precursors: 1-phenylcyclohexylamine (PCH) and 1-piperidinocycloh exanecarbonitrile (PCC)

TCP

PHP

PCE

Fig. 26.3 Structure of phencyclidine analogs: 1-(1-thiophenecyclohexyl) piperidine (TCP); 1-(1-phenylcyclohexyl) pyrrolidine (PHP); and 1-(1-phenylcyclohexyl) ethylamine (PCE) or cyclohexamine

isomers, and salts of isomers are also controlled. Two of the precursors are also controlled: 1-phenylcyclohexylamine (PCH) and 1-piperidin ocyclohexanecarbonitrile (PCC) (Fig. 26.2).

To synthesize PCP, PCC is prepared by adding potassium cyanide and sodium bisulfite to piperidine and cyclohexanone. A Grignard reaction between phenylmagnesium bromide and PCC gives PCP as the product, with a yield of approximately 65% if care is exercised to remove water during synthesis. Several analogs of PCP have been clandestinely manufactured, including a thiophene analog, an n-ethyl analog, and a pyrrolidine analog, all controlled under Schedule I (Fig. 26.3). 1-(1-Thiophenecyclohexyl)piperidine (TCP) is prepared as above, except that bromothiophene is used in the Grignard reagent. In the synthesis of 1-(1-phenylcyclohexyl) ethylamine (PCE) or cyclohexamine, ethylamine replaces piperidine. For the pyrrolidine analog PHP or 1-(1-phenylcyclohexyl) pyrrolidine, pyrrolidine is used in place of piperidine.

Organic solvents, such as diethyl ether, are used during this procedure for extraction purposes. PCP may be converted to the hydrochloride salt by the addition of concentrated hydrochloric acid followed by air evaporation or by passing anhydrous hydrochloric acid into an ether solution of the base. Typically, the salt is sold on the street but the base is also available. Unreacted PCC is not completely removed during this procedure and therefore will appear in the final product unless further cleanup is conducted. The colorless crystalline base has a melting point of 46 °C and a boiling point of 135–137 °C. Ultraviolet (UV) maxima in 0.1N hydrochloric acid occur at 252, 257.5,

262, and 268.5 nm. The octanol/water partition coefficient is 6600 at 25 °C. The hydrochloride salt of PCP has a molecular weight of 279.9 amu and is a stable white crystalline powder with a melting point of 233–235 °C. UV maxima in ethanol occur at 254, 258, 262.5, and 269 nm.

Mechanism of Action

PCP is classified pharmacologically as a dissociative anesthetic but exhibits stimulant, depressant, hallucinogenic, and analgesic properties. These effects appear to depend upon the dose, the route of drug administration, the personality of the individual, and also, possibly, the genetic predisposition.

PCP interacts with many neurotransmitter systems, including the cholinergic, adrenergic, and dopaminergic systems. The relationship between specific receptor binding and the signs and symptoms observed in PCP users is unclear. PCP interacts with the *N*-methyl-D-aspartate (NMDA) receptor in the brain cortex, hippocampus, basal ganglia, and limbic system. Binding of excitatory amino acids such as glutamate and aspartate to the NMDA receptor permits cations to move across cell membranes. PCP binds to the glutamate receptor, blocking the channel, thus preventing the flux of cations such as calcium.

The actions of PCP on the dopaminergic system are thought to account for the principal effects on behavior (via the mesolimbic pathway) and on motor control (via the nigrostriatal pathway). PCP is thought to inhibit dopamine (DA) presynaptic uptake, promote the spontaneous release of DA, and stimulate the enzymes adenylate cyclase and tyrosine hydroxylase. PCP also increases glucose metabolism in those areas of the brain responsible for regulating or controlling emotional behavior, namely, the frontal cortex, the hippocampus, and the caudoputamen.

PCP receptors have been described in the rat brain. Specific [^{3}H]PCP binding was highest in the hippocampus, and binding in the cervical spinal cord was approximately one-third that of the hippocampus. Intermediate binding was observed in the hypothalamus, caudate nucleus, frontal cortex, and cerebellum, followed by the medulla/pons and amygdala. [^{3}H]PCP binding was also found in hepatic and renal homogenates. This binding did not correlate with binding in the central nervous system or with behavioral tests. Therefore, specific binding sites may exist in the human brain and also to a lesser extent in other organs such as the liver and kidney. PCP may interact with non-cAMP-mediated DA_2 dopamine receptors rather than DA_1 receptors. In addition, PCP interacts with central sigma opiate receptors and affects endorphin-mediated behavior in laboratory animals. Sigma receptors are found in the central nervous system and also in endocrine, immune, and peripheral tissues. Stimulation of sigma receptors is thought to be responsible for several adverse effects of opiate use. Interaction with sigma receptors may explain similarities in the behavioral effects of different drugs that bind to them.

PCP may also bind to cholinergic receptors and potentially interact with cholinesterase enzymes. Mild anticholinergic effects are observed. For example, in the periphery, the antimuscarinic effects of PCP are several orders of magnitude less than atropine, resulting from action upon the ion channel of the motor endplate. PCP blocks nicotinic receptors.

PCP is an adrenergic agonist, elevating blood pressure and causing a pressor response at low doses. At high doses, PCP is a direct myocardial depressant. PCP reduces norepinephrine concentrations in the brain by causing the release of stored catecholamines. It also blocks certain sensory inputs, such as pain. PCP interferes with the sensory association pathways, thereby diminishing the user's ability to integrate sensory input into meaningful behavior.

Pharmacokinetics

The most common form of PCP encountered is the water-soluble hydrochloride salt. The base form is insoluble in water. PCP is a lipophilic weak base with a pK_a of 8.5. When produced for use as an anesthetic, PCP was administered intravenously. Illicit use as a "peace pill" was by oral ingestion. More recently, PCP has been self-administered by smoking. Flakes of crystalline PCP may be sprinkled on marijuana ("lovely"). Conversely, marijuana cigarettes or regular tobacco cigarettes may be "dunked" in liquid PCP ("Sherman") and then smoked. Alternatively, vegetable matter, such as parsley flakes, may be mixed with liquid PCP and then rolled into cigarettes. Powdered PCP may also be mixed with cocaine ("tick"). Smoking as a route of drug administration has the advantage of allowing the smoker to control the dose by varying the frequency and depth of puffs. The pharmacokinetic characteristics of absorption vary depending upon the route of administration. Several pharmacokinetic parameters of PCP are listed in Table 26.1.

PCP is typically self-administered by the oral, intravenous, or smoked routes. After oral administration to healthy human volunteers, the bio-

Table 26.1 Pharmacokinetic parameters of common hallucinogens

Drug	$T_{1/2}$ (h)	Duration of effect (h)	Protein binding (%)	V_d (L/kg)	pK_a (base)	Blood/plasma ratio	Unchanged in urine (%)	Primary metabolites
PCP	7–46	2–4	65	5.3–7.5	8.5	0.9–1.0	3–50	4-Phenyl-4-piperidinocyclohexanol; 1-(1-phenylcyclohexyl)-4-hydroxypiperidine
LSD	3–4	8–12	90	0.28	7.8	0.5–0.6	<1	2-Oxo-3-hydroxy-LSD; 2-oxo-LSD; norLSD
Mescaline	6	–	<5	–	9.6	–	55–60	3,4,5-Trimethoxyphenylacetic acid
Psilocybin	1.8–4.5[a]	–	–	2.5–5[a]	8.5[a]	–	<1	Psilocin[b]; 4-hydroxyindole-3-acetic acid
Ketamine	3–4	0.5–2	30–35	3–5	7.5	1.6–1.7	2–5	Norketamine[b], dehydronorketamine[b]

$T_{1/2}$ elimination half-life, V_d volume of distribution

[a]Indicated for psilocin

[b]Pharmacologically active

availability was found to vary between 50% and 90%. In this study, peak plasma concentrations were achieved after 1.5 h and appeared to correlate with the time to reach maximum pharmacological effects. However, because there have been no comprehensive clinical controlled studies of phencyclidine, correlation between PCP blood concentrations and pharmacological effects has not been definitively documented. Maximum serum PCP concentrations ranged between 2.7 and 2.9 ng/mL after 1 mg PCP administered orally.

PCP is commonly self-administered by the smoked route. Upon smoking, PCP is partially volatilized to 1-phenylcyclohexene (PC). One study found that 69 ± 5% of the PCP available in the cigarette was inhaled, 39% as PCP, and 30% as PC. Losses of drug also occurred in main and sidestream smoke. The pharmacological and toxicological properties of PC have not been established. Peak plasma concentrations of PCP were reached within 5–20 min. In 80% of the subjects, a second peak was observed in plasma PCP concentrations, occurring 1–3 h after the end of smoking. This may have been due to trapping of PCP in the mouth, where it could be released and absorbed by the gastrointestinal tract, or alternatively, it could be due to absorption by the lung and bronchial tissue with slower release into the systemic circulation. Long-term users of PCP report feeling the effects of the drug within 2–5 min of smoking, with a peak effect after 15–30 min and residual effects for 4–6 h.

Plasma protein binding of PCP in healthy individuals remains relatively constant between 60 and 70% over the concentration range of 7–5000 ng/mL. PCP binding to serum albumin accounts for only 24% of the binding; this suggests that binding to another protein may occur to a significant extent. When studied in vitro, $\alpha 1$-acid glycoprotein was also found to bind PCP. The volume of distribution has been shown to be large (5.3–7.5 L/kg), providing evidence of extensive distribution to extravascular tissues.

The pharmacokinetics of PCP have been described by a two-compartment model with a plasma half-life for PCP of 7–16 h or a more complex three-compartment pharmacokinetic model with reported half-lives for each compartment of 5.5 min, 4.6 h, and 22 h. The specific tissues and organs represented by the multicompartment model were not identified. Half-lives >3 days have been reported in cases of PCP overdose.

PCP is metabolized by the liver through oxidative hydroxylation. Unchanged PCP and one dihydroxylated and two monohydroxylated metabolites have been identified in urine after oral and intravenous administration. The monohydroxylated metabolites have been identified as 4-phenyl-4-(1-piperidinyl)-cyclohexanol (PPC) and 1-(1-phenylcyclohexyl)-4-hydroxypiperidine (PCHP). These metabolites are pharmacologically inactive in humans, and PPC is present in both cis- and trans-isomeric forms. The cis/trans ratio was found to be 1:1.4 in human urine. The dihydroxylated metabolite was identified as 4-(4-hydroxypiperidino)-4-phenylcyclohexanol (HPPC). These metabolites are present in urine as glucuronide conjugates, as well as in their unconjugated forms.

Approximately 30–50% of a labeled intravenous dose was excreted over a 72-h period in urine as unchanged drug (19.4%) and 80.6% as polar metabolites, PPC. Only 2% of a dose is excreted in feces. After 10 days, an average of 77% of an intravenous dose is found in the feces and urine. Urine PCP concentrations of 40–3400 ng/mL have been reported in ambulatory users.

Urine pH is an important determinant of renal elimination of PCP. In a study in which urine pH was uncontrolled (6.0–7.5), the average total clearance of PCP was 22.8 ± 4.8 L/h after intravenous administration. In the same study, renal clearance was 1.98 ± 0.48 L/h. When the urine was made alkaline, the renal clearance of PCP was found to decrease to 0.3 ± 0.18 L/h. If the urine was acidified (pH 6.1) in the same subjects, renal clearance increased to 2.4 ± 0.78 L/h. There is disagreement about the utility of urine acidification in the treatment of PCP overdose, even though excretion may be increased by as much as 100-fold. It should be noted that acidification may increase the risk of metabolic complications.

Effects

Pollack noted that PCP intoxication is "a clinical condition that is defined by clinical signs and symptoms, ranging from 'mild, moderate to severe,' with coma and eventual death." Intoxication is influenced by several variables mentioned previously, such as preparation, route of administration, dose, age, personality, and medical, drug, and behavioral history. These factors result in variable responses to given doses and poor correlation between blood concentrations and behavior. However, generalized statements can be made.

The effects of PCP administration are observed within a few minutes after smoking or intravenous administration and within 1 h after oral ingestion. The typical high from PCP lasts 4–6 h, with a "come-down" period of 6–24 h. A dose of 1–5 mg generally produces feelings of euphoria and numbness. At this stage an observer may liken the effect to alcohol intoxication. Disinhibition and emotional liability may also be observed in the user. A dose of 5–10 mg will likely produce an excited but confused individual who may exhibit repetitive motor movements, fever, diaphoresis, myoclonus, vomiting, decreased peripheral sensations, and horizontal and vertical nystagmus. At these doses, catatonia and paranoid schizophrenia may occur. Coma and death from respiratory depression caused by seizure activity may occur at doses ≥20 mg. Table 26.2 lists the pharmacological effects of PCP according to approximate dose. Generally, impaired thought or psychotic reactions are more likely to occur with phencyclidine use than with LSD or mescaline. In one study, despite adverse effects 72% of individuals continued to use PCP due to its powerful psychological effects, availability, and relatively low cost.

A PCP abuse syndrome has been described. It is distinguished by four behavioral phases, namely, acute toxicity, toxic psychosis, PCP-precipitated psychotic episodes, and PCP-induced depression. Acute PCP toxicity is characterized by the four cs: combativeness and catatonia at low doses and convulsions and coma at higher doses. Toxic psychosis includes

Table 26.2 Pharmacological effects of phencyclidine

Physiological	Psychological
Low dose (<5 mg)	
Increased blood pressure	Agitative behavior
	Euphoria
Increased deep tendon reflexes	Disorganization of thought
Perspiration	Body image changes
Facial grimacing	Apprehension/anxiety
Tremors	Dissociation
Incoordination	
Moderate dose (5–10 mg)	
Spontaneous nystagmus	Feelings of inebriation
	Insomnia
Hypersalivation	Loss of appetite
Nausea and vomiting	Rage
Repetitive motor movements	Amnesia
	Hypnotic state
Muscle rigidity	Fever
High dose (>10 mg)	
Hypertension	Catatonia
Arrhythmias	Eyes open or closed
Tonic-clonic seizures	Cerebral bleeding
Absent peripheral sensations	Coma
	Death

impaired judgment, paranoid delusions, visual and auditory hallucinations, and agitations. This may occur from 24 h to 7 days. The PCP toxic psychosis is typically observed in chronic users. Toxic psychosis may be followed by the psychotic episode, which may last 7–30 days. PCP-induced depression may occur after any of the preceding three stages and may last from 1 day to several months. During this time, the individual is at high risk of suicide.

Additional medical complications of PCP intoxication include generalized tonic–clonic seizures, elevation of systolic and diastolic blood pressure, hyperthermia, and rhabdomyolysis with or without renal failure due to myoglobinuria. There is no antidote for PCP overdose. Seizures and respiratory depression are more frequently observed in children. Treatment of the PCP-intoxicated individual involves stabilization, such as maintaining airway and ventilatory adequacy. This is followed with supportive care to correct medical complications only and not to restrain individuals unnecessarily. Therefore, if body temperature is elevated above 105 °F, the individual is rapidly cooled. Hypertension is observed in approximately 50% of PCP intoxications. Complications are unusual even with systolic pressures of 250 mm Hg. Once agitated or violent behavior is controlled, blood pressure typically drops. However, if the diastolic blood pressure remains above 140 mm Hg or symptoms related to hypertension occur, treatment with sublingual nifedipine or intravenous nitroprusside should be administered. The agitated state or any violent behavior may be treated with 5–10 mg (in adults) of diazepam, administered intravenously. Psychoses may be treated with haloperidol or chlorpromazine. Response appears to be better with haloperidol, a specific DA_2 receptor antagonist, than with chlorpromazine, a mixed DA_1 and DA_2 antagonist. Airway hyperactivity may be treated with aminophylline while dystonic reactions respond to diphenhydramine. Rhabdomyolysis is the main complication of PCP intoxication; it is thought to result from the use of restraints in agitated people. Therefore, it is recommended that restraints not be used but that the individual be placed in a quiet room with minimal stimuli. Rhabdomyolysis is treated with fluid replacement and monitoring of urinary output. Retention of the urine may require catheterization. Generally, elimination enhancement procedures are not recommended treatment for the PCP-intoxicated patient.

Analysis

PCP has been measured in drug seizures using the techniques of colorimetry, UV spectrophotometry, thin-layer chromatography (TLC), gas chromatography (GC), and gas chromatography/mass spectrometry (GC/MS). PCP has also been detected on US paper currency in microgram quantities using GC/MS technology. Similarly, PCP, its analogs, and metabolites are commonly determined in biological specimens using immunoassay, gas chromatography/mass spectrometry (GC/MS), or liquid chromatography-based techniques.

A presumptive color test has been described for PCP in urine using tetrabromophenolphtha-lein ethyl ester reagent after buffering the sample to pH 6–7. The limit of detection is 1000 ng/mL. TLC was the first analytical technique used for detecting PCP in urine although it is less widely used today. Biological specimens are routinely screened for PCP by immunoassay. Numerous immunoassay-based approaches are described in Chap. 13. Commercial kits intended for urine generally provide reagents using the federally mandated cutoff for workplace drug testing of 25 ng/mL. On-site drug testing or point-of-care testing devices are also typically based on competitive binding immunoassay technology. Commercial immunoassays for PCP cross-react to a varying degree with several analogs such as TCP. In addition, false-positive results have been reported for venlafaxine and metabolite, tramadol and metabolite, dextromethorphan, ibuprofen, 3,4-methylenedioxypyrovalerone (MDPV), and methoxetamine.

PCP may be extracted from biological specimens by traditional liquid–liquid extraction procedures or by solid-phase extraction. Solid-phase extraction techniques typically exhibit recoveries >85%. Many of these assays, especially those analyzed by GC/MS, use a deuterated internal standard (d_5-PCP). Classic liquid–liquid extraction procedures alkalinize the biological matrix, add an organic solvent such as n-butyl chloride, and back-extract by adding acid followed by another base and then an organic solvent such as methylene chloride. This solvent is evaporated to dryness and the extract is reconstituted with isopropanol or an alternate organic solvent. Solid-phase extraction procedures typically buffer the matrix to pH 4–6, precondition the column, and elute the analyte with a basic organic solvent such as 2% ammonium hydroxide in ethyl acetate or methanol. PCP may be analyzed qualitatively and quantitatively by GC with capillary columns. Flame ionization detection has been used with limits of detection of 50 ng/mL. Several procedures have been described using nitrogen phosphorus detection with limits of quantification around 10 ng/mL. PCP exhibits good chromatographic characteristics without the need for derivatization. However, methods described in the literature include derivatization with hepta-fluorobutyric anhydride.

High-performance liquid chromatographic procedures for the analysis of PCP in biological specimens have been described. One procedure used a C_{18} reversed-phase column, a buffered mobile phase containing 65% methanol and 1% triethylamine, and UV detection at 254 nm. Several GC/MS procedures have been described to measure PCP and its hydroxylated metabolites in biological matrices using electron impact ionization. Full-scan and selected ion-monitoring (SIM) modes have been used. When performing SIM analysis, m/z 200, 242, and 243 ions are commonly monitored. Reported limits of detection for these assays are 1–5 ng/mL. Chemical ionization GC/MS has also been used to quantify PCP and its metabolites. In one report, ions selected for monitoring were m/z 159 and 243 for PCP and m/z 164 and 248 for the pentadeuterated PCP internal standard. LC/MS/MS procedures have been developed for the measurement of PCP using deuterated internal standards. These methods typically involve little sample preparation while achieving lower limits of quantification close to 5 ng/mL. More novel techniques using microfluidic chip-based nano-liquid chromatography-tandem mass spectrometry and capillary zone electrophoresis with ultraviolet detection have also been described.

Interpretation of PCP Concentrations

As previously discussed, no controlled pharmacokinetic studies have been performed in humans using psychoactive doses. In 26 individuals arrested for driving under the influence of drugs or exhibiting disorderly behavior in public, blood phencyclidine concentrations were 7–240 ng/mL, with an average of 75 ng/mL. In a study reporting PCP blood concentrations in Drug Recognition Expert (DRE) cases, blood concentrations were measured in 259 people over a 2-year period. The mean PCP concentration for those cases in which only PCP was identified by both the DRE and toxicology was 51 ng/mL, with a range of 12–118 ng/mL. No correlation

was found in this study between PCP concentration and behavior.

Another study described the incidental intoxication of a 62-year-old woman who lived above a clandestine PCP laboratory and visited a hospital emergency room complaining of odors in her bathroom that made her dizzy. A serum PCP concentration of 8 ng/mL was determined by GC with nitrogen phosphorous detection (NPD) and later confirmed by GC/MS. On admission, the woman appeared fully oriented, alert, and cooperative but depressed. GC-NPD was also used to measure phencyclidine in blood and urine specimens obtained from two law enforcement personnel who handled confiscated PCP preparations. One individual had a blood PCP concentration of 28 ng/mL that declined to 4 ng/mL after 2 weeks, during which time he continued to handle PCP cases. The second individual had a blood PCP concentration of 70 ng/mL, declining to <1 ng/mL after 2 weeks. PCP was detected in the urine of the first individual but not the second.

PCP has been measured in saliva obtained from 100 emergency room patients. Paired serum and saliva samples were measured by RIA. Seventy-four of the 100 saliva samples and 75 of the paired serum samples were positive for PCP. PCP protein binding in saliva is approximately 7%. Saliva concentrations usually exceed plasma concentrations with a saliva/plasma concentration ratio of 2.4. PCP has also been detected in cerebrospinal fluid, usually exceeding serum concentrations. PCP has been identified in human hair at 0.1–23 ng/mg of hair. This drug has also been measured in sweat. In one study, radiolabeled PCP was detected in axilla perspiration for 54 h following intravenous administration. The appearance of PCP has been studied in cord blood, amniotic fluid, and breast milk. PCP was detected in 12% of cord blood samples in a large urban teaching hospital with concentrations of 0.1–5.8 ng/mL. In the same study, PCP was identified in amniotic fluid on the 36th day of pregnancy in one individual. The PCP concentration in the maternal blood was 0.77 ng/mL with a concentration of 3.42 ng/mL reported in the amniotic fluid. In the same case, PCP was identified in the breast milk 5 days later at a concentration of 3.9 ng/mL.

The majority of PCP-related deaths occur due to the behavioral toxicity of the drug. This includes jumping from high buildings and drowning. In a Los Angeles County study in 1983 of 104 PCP-related fatalities, only 15 deaths were determined to be due to PCP overdose. The deaths were usually accidental or homicidal. Individuals who commit suicide while under the influence of PCP typically choose very violent methods, such as leaping from a building or a freeway overpass or plunging a large knife into the chest or running into a wall. Death by direct PCP toxicity is usually due to respiratory arrest, hyperpyrexia with cardiovascular collapse, status epilepticus, or coma with multiple organ failure. Death has been reported after the ingestion of 120 mg of PCP.

In a study in Maryland, PCP was detected in 37 cases in a Medical Examiner population over a 2-year period in the mid-1970s. However, in only two cases was death a result of acute PCP toxicity. Blood PCP concentrations in these cases were 1500 and 25,000 ng/mL. In the other 35 cases, blood concentrations ranged from 20 to 700 ng/mL with a median concentration of 100 ng/mL. Individuals were typically white males age 16–42 (mean age, 21). Causes of death in these cases included gunshot wounds, asphyxia, stab wounds, smoke and soot inhalation, drowning, multiple injuries, and intravenous narcotism. The manner of death in 38% of the PCP positive cases in this study was suicide. In another study in California, nine fatal cases attributed to PCP overdose had blood PCP concentrations of 300–12,000 ng/mL and liver concentrations of 999–80,000 ng/g. Two of the cases were determined to be suicides. These investigators compared blood and tissue concentrations in deaths due to PCP toxicity vs. deaths due to other causes. They determined that the two groups could not be separated based upon PCP concentrations.

In a 5-year retrospective study, 2003–2007, conducted by the Office of Chief Medical Examiner, New York City, PCP was identified in postmortem blood [in 95% of cases, the heart was site of collection] in 138 cases. The concentration of PCP in blood in mixed drug intoxications [$N = 52$, 38%] ranged from <1 to 598 ng/mL. Of the 80 violent deaths, concentrations were <1 to 581 ng/mL. Similar to the study in Maryland, 30 years earlier, these deaths included sharp force injuries, firearm injuries, smoke inhalation, drownings, falls from a height, and asphyxia. Blood PCP concentrations in five nonviolent deaths ranged at 53–361 ng/mL. It was concluded that underlying medical conditions could have contributed to the death of these individuals.

In cases of PCP intoxication, there are no specific pathologic findings. At autopsy, pulmonary congestion is often found in probable acute PCP intoxication. In addition, acute posterior lobar pneumonia, or bronchopneumonia, or numerous alveolar macrophages have been reported in several cases. No neuropathologic changes have been documented from autopsy studies of PCP intoxications.

Precursors and Analogs

Contamination of street samples of PCP with the precursor PCC is not uncommon. During synthesis, incomplete reaction with the Grignard reagent results in the presence of PCC in the finished product. PCC is present in approximately 20% of street samples and is approximately equipotent to PCP in producing lethality in mice. Its toxicity is reported to be three times greater than PCP, with a lethal synergism between PCC and PCP. The mechanism of toxicity appears to be different with the labile cyano group resulting in the in vivo release of hydrogen cyanide. Toxic symptoms include vomiting, abdominal pain, and diarrhea. Upon degradation, PCC produces piperidine that has a fishlike smell.

The analog cyclohexamine (PCE) has similar pharmacological properties as PCP, with a potency in rats six times greater than PCP. It is usually available as a powder or tablet in a range of colors from off-white to pink to brown. It may be self-administered by routes similar to those for PCP. Two fatalities resulting from PCE use have been documented in the literature. The first, a 24-year-old male, had a blood PCE concentration of 3100 ng/mL. The cause of death was determined to be drug overdose. The second individual, also a young male in his twenties, had a blood PCE concentration of 1000 ng/mL and a liver concentration of 1900 ng/g. In the latter case, the cause of death was determined to be drowning. In both cases, no other drugs, including ethanol, were detected.

The physiological properties of the analog TCP appear to be similar to PCP in humans. In rats, TCP may be slightly more active. Approximately 9% of PCP seizures also contain TCP. The analog PHP produces similar pharmacological effects as PCP. The presence of PHP was reported in specimens obtained from the autopsy of an individual shot while acting in a bizarre manner and resisting police arrest.

Other PCP analogs have been reported: TCM or 1-[1-(2-thienyl)cyclohexyl] morpholine; PCM or 1-(1-phenylcyclohexyl) morpholine; and PCDEA or N,N-diethyl-1-phenyl-cyclohexylamine. More recently, 3-methoxy-PCP, 4-methoxy-PCP, and 3-methoxy-PCE emerged as analogs and elicit similar effects in humans to ketamine and PCP. Studies demonstrate that these analogs are also ligands for the glutamate NMDA receptor.

Lysergic Acid Diethylamide

d-Lysergic acid diethylamide (LSD; 9,10-Didehydro-N,N-diethyl-6-methylergoline-8B-carboxamide) is an indolealkylamine (Fig. 26.4) discovered by Albert Hofmann of Sandoz Laboratories in 1943 after he inadvertently ingested the compound. It may be synthesized from lysergic acid and diethylamine. Lysergic acid, a naturally occurring ergot alkaloid, is present in grain parasitized by the fungus *Claviceps purpurea* which may grow on certain rye plants. A closely related alkaloid, lysergic acid amide, is present in morning glory seeds and the Hawaiian baby wood rose.

LSD is a colorless, odorless, tasteless liquid that is very potent. As a result, it is almost always diluted and self-administered in low doses. It is available illicitly as a powder, tablet, gelatin capsule, or impregnated in sugar cubes, gelatin squares, blotter paper, or postage stamps.

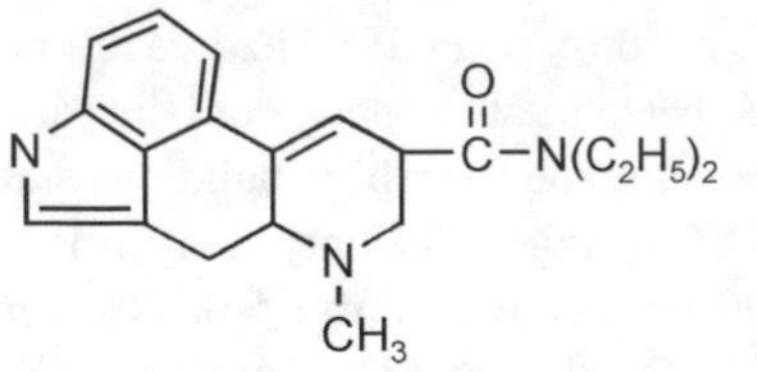

Fig. 26.4 Structure of LSD

Impregnation is achieved by pouring an aqueous solution of LSD evenly over the absorbent. Blotter paper is typically perforated into squares that are often imprinted with figures, logos, and other designs. Clandestine laboratories may manufacture tablets that are usually small and colored. They are often referred to by their color, such as orange sunshine, purple haze, and yellow microdots. One tablet typically contains 0.05–0.1 mg LSD. Another form of LSD known as windowpanes was popular in the 1970s and consisted of small (1 × 2 mm) gelatin rectangles.

Like many drugs of abuse, synthetic analogs of LSD have also emerged. LSD analogs, including 1P-LSD, AL-LAD (N(6)-allyl-norLSD, "Aladdin"), LSZ (2S,4S-dimethylazetidine), and ETH-LAD (N(6)-ethyl-norLSD), are 5-HT$_{2A}$ receptor agonists. LSD derivative use is reported in nightclubs. Some analogs, including 1P-LSD and LSZ, are prohibited in several regions, including the United Kingdom. In an online survey of psychoactive drug use, duration and time to peak effects were reported comparable to those of LSD but not as strong in their effects. Little pharmacological data is available for analog activity. However, LSZ was determined to be almost 40% more potent than LSD in a mouse model. Many LSD analogs are reported in the form of blotters with sub-milligram dosages.

Synthesis

LSD may be synthesized by adding cold trifluoroacetic anhydride in acetonitrile to a cold solution of lysergic acid. After standing for a few hours, a solution of diethylamine in acetonitrile is added, the mixture is allowed to stand for 2 h, and then the acetonitrile is removed by vacuum. The crude LSD should be dissolved in chloroform and washed with water. Purification may be achieved by evaporating the chloroform and then pouring on an alumina column with a 3:1 benzene/chloroform solution. The resulting mixture contains d-LSD and d-iso-LSD that may be separated using a carbonate column.

Drug Abuse Patterns

In the 1950s, LSD was used in medicine as an aid in the treatment of alcoholism, opioid addiction, psychoneurosis, and sexual disorders. Currently it is classified under Schedule I of the Federal Controlled Substances Act of 1970, with no accepted medical use in the United States. Despite status as a controlled substance, clinical research interest in LSD and other psychedelics has reemerged in Europe in order to assess potential therapeutic effects on depression and anxiety. Its precursor, lysergic acid, is controlled under Schedule III, which restricts distribution. According to the National Institute on Drug Abuse's Monitoring the Future Study, LSD lifetime use in eighth, tenth, and twelfth graders peaked during 1997 (9.1%) but later decreased to a steady rate between 2006 and 2017 (2.5–3.1%). According to the most recent DAWN data, LSD-related emergency room episodes have remained relatively stable since 1988, at 3000–5000 annually. More recently, among youths [ages 12–17], the number of lifetime users of LSD has remained fairly stable since 2004, with a prevalence estimate in 2017 of 0.8%. Current trends suggest that more than 794,000 individuals aged 12 or older will initiate LSD use within a given year, up from 358,000 in 2011. In 2017, LSD was among the top 25 most frequently identified drugs submitted to US laboratories (4287 or 0.27%).

Of all illicit drugs, LSD is probably the least adulterated. More than 90% of alleged LSD street samples are genuine with diethylamine present as a contaminant. The typical street dose is 50–300 µg (average, 100 µg) with a minimum effective dose of about 25 µg. The optimal psychedelic dose is considered 100–1000 µg. LSD is approximately 3000 times more potent on a per-weight basis than mescaline. It is typically self-administered orally, with intermittent use (a "binge") more common than intense and sustained use. LSD users are typically polydrug users, experimenting with ethanol, marijuana, and amphetamines. Concurrent sedative-hypnotic and opiate use is uncommon in this group of drug users. Tolerance to the effects of LSD does occur, but physical withdrawal symptoms upon discontinuation do not occur although a user may be psychologically dependent. Development of tolerance depends upon the dose and frequency but typically develops after three to four daily doses. Tolerance disappears 4–5 days after drug withdrawal. Cross-tolerance develops between LSD, psilocybin, and mescaline but not d-amphetamine.

Mechanism of Action

LSD is a potent centrally acting drug. The d-isomer is pharmacologically active, while the l-isomer is apparently inactive. Neuropharmacological studies have shown that LSD exerts a selective inhibitory effect on the brain's raphe system by causing cessation of the spontaneous firing of serotonin-containing neurons of the dorsal and median raphe nuclei. In this way, LSD acts as an indirect serotonin antagonist. However, inhibition of raphe firing is not sufficient to explain the psychotomimetic effects of LSD, because the compound lisuride is a more potent inhibitor of the raphe system yet does not demonstrate hallucinogenic potential in humans. Therefore, other postsynaptic mechanisms such as action on glutamate or serotonin receptors may be involved. In addition, there is evidence that LSD indirectly exerts effects on the cytoskeleton by reducing the amount of serotonin released by the raphe system.

Effects

The effects of LSD may be divided into physiological, psychotomimetic, and psychiatric.

Physiological effects are primarily sympathomimetic, parasympathomimetic, and neuromuscular such as mydriasis, lacrimation, tachycardia, piloerection, hyperglycemia, and elevated body temperature. Pupil dilation of 3–5 mm is the most frequent and consistent sign of LSD use. After large doses, salivation, tremor, nausea, vomiting, hyperactivity, and hyperreflexia may occur. Rhabdomyolysis has been reported after LSD ingestion.

Psychological experiences include perceptual alterations such as visual illusions and alterations in sound or in intensity of colors. Misrepresentation of sensory cues is the most notable and consistent alteration. Fixed objects undulate and flat surfaces assume depth. Amplification of background noise may occur with an overflow of sensory input such that colors are heard and music is palpable. Thought processes are affected to the degree that body image changes with depersonalization. Typically, orientation is preserved, but judgment may be poor due to paranoia or ideas of persecution. Behavioral patterns after LSD use are difficult to predict because they depend upon the setting, expectations, the individual's underlying personality, and emotional stress in addition to the dose. Individuals tend to be quiet, passive, self-centered, and withdrawn. However, the mood may be labile.

No single factor guarantees a pleasurable LSD experience. An acute panic attack is the most common side effect of LSD use and frequently accompanies accidental consumption. Other psychiatric effects include flashbacks (the recurrence of drug effect without drug use), acute psychotic reactions, and behavior-induced trauma. Flashback experiences include visual alterations, time distortions, and body image changes after a period of abstinence. Flashbacks may be precipitated by physiological and emotional stress and occur in approximately 15% of users for several years following ingestion. The etiology of flashbacks is unknown. Acute psychotic reactions include superimposed visual alterations and spatial and depth distortions. The occurrence of acute mania after LSD use is suspected but not proven. LSD-induced suicide and accidental trauma are more common than homicide. Amnesia for the events is rare.

Life-threatening reactions to LSD are rare but do occur. Death resulting from pharmacologic overdose has been reported in one case in which antemortem serum contained 14 ng/mL LSD. Death resulting from trauma or dangerous activities experienced during hallucinations with altered perceptions is more common.

Pharmacokinetics

LSD may be self-administered orally, nasally, or by injection. However, the oral route is the most common. Absorption is rapid and complete regardless of the route of administration. Food in the stomach slows absorption when ingested. Effects are observed within 5–10 min, with psychosis evident after 15–20 min. Peak effects have been reported 30–90 min after dosing, with effects declining after 4–6 h. The duration of effects may be 8–12 h. Several pharmacokinetic parameters of LSD are listed in Table 26.1.

Pharmacokinetic studies in humans are limited, and most of the data are from the 1960s. In one study, a peak plasma LSD concentration of 5 ng/mL was observed 1 h after intravenous administration of 2 µg/kg. At 8 h, the plasma concentration had declined to 1 ng/mL.

Plasma protein binding of LSD is >80%. As the drug penetrates the CNS, it is concentrated in the visual brain areas and the limbic and reticular activating systems, correlating with perceived effects. LSD is also found in the liver, spleen, and lungs. The volume of distribution is reported to be low at 0.28 L/kg. A two-compartment open model for LSD has been described, with an elimination half-life of 3 h.

The metabolism and elimination of LSD in humans have received limited study. Animal studies demonstrated extensive biotransformation via N-demethylation, N-deethylation, and hydroxylation to inactive metabolites. In humans, demethylation and aromatic hydroxylation occur resulting in N-desmethyl-LSD and 13- and 14-hydroxy-LSD. A recent study indicates that less than 1% of LSD is eliminated unchanged in the urine and approximately 13% as 2-oxo-3-hydroxy-LSD within 24 h. Hydroxylated metabolites undergo glucuronidation to form water-soluble conjugates. Excretion into the bile accounts for approximately 80% of a dose. Concentrations of unchanged drug range from 1 to 55 ng/mL in the 24-h urine after ingestion of 200–400 μg LSD in humans. LSD or its metabolites have been detectable for 34–120 h after a 300-μg oral dose in seven human subjects. The clearance of LSD in humans is unknown.

Analysis

LSD is often difficult to analyze due to the low doses required to produce psychoactive effects. One tablet or one square of blotter paper may contain 0.1 mg LSD. In addition, LSD is relatively unstable and is sensitive to UV light and heat. LSD in biological specimens is considered stable when the samples are stored frozen. Losses during analysis may also occur due to irreversible absorptive processes especially when using GC.

Color tests are often used to screen possible LSD samples. These include Ehrlich's test that uses p-dimethylaminobenzaldehyde (DMBA) to produce a purple color in the presence of LSD. TLC may also be used to analyze samples. Common mobile phases for normal-phase silica gel plates include chloroform/methanol (9:1), toluene/dimethylformamide (6:1), and acetone/ammonium hydroxide/methanol (18:1). Ergot alkaloids are highly fluorescent, and therefore fluorescence technologies are ideal for qualitative and quantitative analysis of LSD. Its fluorescence maxima are approximately 320 nm (excitation) and 400 nm (emission).

Immunoassay-based techniques have been described for the analysis of LSD in biological specimens. Enzyme-linked immunosorbent assay (ELISA) is particularly commonplace in forensic toxicology laboratories because it can be adapted to a variety of matrices.

LSD may be isolated from biological specimens by liquid–liquid and solid-phase extraction procedures. Liquid–liquid methods may use methysergide as an internal standard, rendering the sample basic with ammonium carbonate and sodium

hydroxide followed by extraction into petroleum ether/dichloromethane/isoamyl alcohol (70:30:0.5). Alternative extraction methods have added 0.5 M disodium hydrogen phosphate to urine followed by extraction with chloroform, evaporation to dryness, reconstitution in methanol, and analysis by HPLC using an RP-2 column and a methanol–water (70:30) mobile phase. A luminescence spectrometer may be used for detection. HPLC methods may use lysergol as internal standard, target LSD only, and therefore do not detect LSD metabolites, often present in urine specimens.

Electron ionization (EI) and chemical ionization mass spectrometric techniques have been described for the analysis of LSD in biological samples. EI GC/MS with SIM analysis of the trimethylsilyl derivative of LSD permits detection of LSD in urine at concentrations as low as 29 pg/mL. Quantification of LSD was linear over the concentration range 50–2000 pg/mL. A negative-ion CI GC/MS assay for LSD in plasma and urine has been described using deuterium-labeled LSD as internal standard and derivatizing with trifluroacetylimidazole to produce a N-trifluoroacetyl derivative. A linear response was achieved over the concentration range of 0.1–3.0 ng/mL. Liquid chromatographic mass spectrometric techniques, including ultra-performance technology, have been described for the analysis of LSD in biological specimens. Deuterated internal standards are utilized to measure parent drug, achieving a lower limit of quantification <10 pg/mL. More recently, a method was developed utilizing liquid chromatographic tandem mass spectrometry for the identification of parent drug and several metabolites (LAE, lysergic acid LEO, 2-oxo-LSD, trioxylated-LSD, and 13- and 14-hydroxy-LSD) in plasma samples collected in a clinical trial with low limits of detection (0.01 ng/mL) and quantification (0.05–0.1 ng/mL).

Mescaline

Introduction

Mescaline (3,4,5-trimethoxyphenethylamine) is an alkaloid (Fig. 26.5) with hallucinogenic properties, isolated from the peyote cactus, *Lophophora williamsii*. It is controlled under Schedule I of the Controlled Substances Act and is often referred to as peyote, mescal button, or mescal. The cactus is small (3–10 cm diameter) and blue-green with well-defined ribs, pink flowers, and a large cylindrical rootstock. The dome-shaped heads are removed and dried as peyote buttons. Each button contains approximately 45 mg mescaline. Gelatin capsules may be sold on the street and contain powdered buttons with approximately 6% mescaline. Native to southern Texas and northern Mexico, peyote buttons have been found in Mexican burial caves dating back to 810–1070 B.C.

Mescaline is commonly self-administered orally in doses of 200–500 mg as the hydrochloride or sulfate salt. It may be macerated and mixed with flavorings such as cocoa. Effects of a single administration may persist for 12 h. Mescaline may also be synthesized from 3,4,5-trimethoxybenzaldehyde by refluxing with nitromethane, ammonium acetate, and glacial acetic acid. The precipitate is reduced by refluxing with lithium aluminum hydride in ether. After drying, mescaline may be precipitated as the sulfate salt from ether by adding sulfuric acid.

Pharmacokinetics

Mescaline is rapidly absorbed after oral administration with peak blood concentrations averaging 3.8 mg/L at 2 h in 12 subjects after a 500-mg dose. At 7 h after ingestion, the concentration had declined to 1.5 mg/L. The half-life of mescaline was estimated to be 6 h. After intravenous administration of 5 mg/kg in one study, average peak blood mescaline concentrations of 14.8 mg/L were achieved at 15 min, declining to 2.1 mg/L by 2 h. Maximum physiological effects occurred at 2 h in this study. Approximately 87% of an oral dose is excreted in the 24-h urine, with mescaline accounting for 55–60% of the excretion products. Mescaline is metabolized to four known pharmacologically inactive metabolites. The main metabolite, 3,4,5-trimethoxyphenylacetic acid,

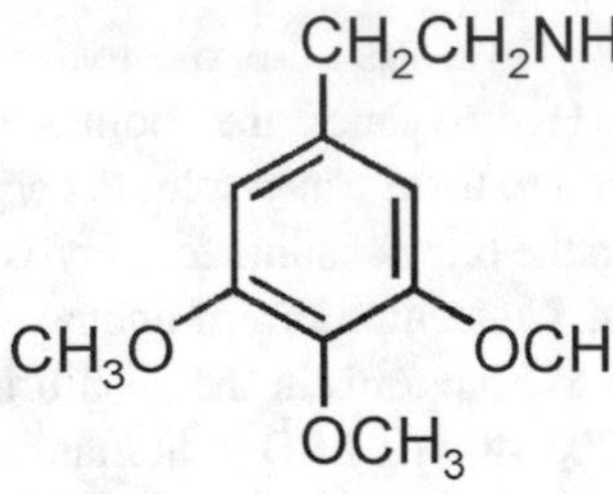

Fig. 26.5 Structure of mescaline

accounts for 27–30% of the urinary excretion products. The other metabolites are formed by n-acetylation, hydroxylation, and demethylation. A summary of mescaline pharmacokinetic parameters is listed in Table 26.1.

Effects

After oral absorption, mescaline produces a period of mild intestinal distress. This may include nausea, vomiting, and occasionally diarrhea. These effects may occur 30–60 min after eating peyote. Thereafter, sympathomimetic effects dominate with mydriasis, tachycardia, hypertension, and diaphoresis. Nystagmus and hyperreflexia may also be observed. The sensory phase of mescaline-induced effects occurs after the gastrointestinal effects subside and typically peak 4–6 h after ingestion. Sensory effects are similar to those occurring after LSD ingestion and include visual hallucinations and perceptual distortions that may be very vivid. Emotional instability, anxiety, and panic reactions may result in accidental trauma following consumption. Sensory effects usually subside 12 h after ingestion. In some cases, hallucinogen persisting perception disorder (HPPD) may result in the form of flashbacks. Mescaline doses of >20 mg/kg may result in significant bradycardia, hypotension, and respiratory depression, but death due to toxicity is rare. Violent deaths while under the influence of mescaline have been reported. One case described the death of an adult male who jumped from a height of 600 ft. Postmortem mescaline concentrations were 9.7 mg/L in the blood and 71 mg/kg in liver. As with other hallucinogens discussed above, the effects of mescaline can be attributed to its 5-HT$_{2A}$ receptor agonist activity.

Analysis

Mescaline may be extracted from peyote by macerating the dried buttons in a blender with absolute ethanol. The mixture should be heated over a steam bath, filtered, and dried. The dry filtrate is then dissolved in 0.1 N HCl and washed with ether. The acid is rendered alkaline and the alkaloid extracted with ether. The ether solution may be back-extracted with acid and washed with chloroform. The solution is then adjusted to pH 8 with bicarbonate and hydroxide and extracted with chloroform. The chloroform layer is then evaporated to dryness, resulting in a tan-colored mescaline powder.

Mescaline may be presumptively analyzed with color tests such as Marquis reagent (orange) or Mecke's (orange to brown spots). Microcrystalline tests have also been described, such as the bismuth iodide test. Mescaline may be assayed by TLC with visualization using potassium iodoplatinate. Procedures have also been described for the analysis of mescaline in urine with GC and flame ionization detection. Fluorimetry and GC/MS of trifluoroacetyl derivatives have been used for the quantitative determination of mescaline in plasma and urine. Positive chemical ionization mode has been used for the analysis of mescaline in hair by GC-MS/MS.

Analogs

The mescaline structure served as a backbone for many analogs or novel psychoactive substances over the past few decades. First, α-methylmescaline (3,4,5-trimethoxyamphetamine or TMA) was investigated and determined to be similar to mescaline's effects but without the feelings of empathy. Later, the "2C" family of hallucinogens were synthesized as phenethylamines with methoxy groups at the 2 and 5 positions, often with halo-

gens substituted at the 4 position (Fig. 26.6). Dozens of the 2C compounds were described in terms of synthesis and effects by Alexander Shulgin in his 1991 book entitled *PiHKAL (Phenethylamines I Have Known and Loved): A Chemical Love Story*. With rising popularity and cause for concern, many 2C compounds were established as Schedule I controlled substances, including 2C-B, 2C-C, 2C-D, 2C-E, 2C-H, 2C-I, 2C-P, 2C-T-4, and 2C-T-7. These drugs are available for oral consumption or insufflation. The onset of action and duration of action vary for each compound (minutes to hours). The 2C compounds have affinity for 5-HT$_2$ but may be agonists or antagonists. The effects are hallucinogenic at moderate doses and stimulating at low doses. Signs and symptoms of use include hallucinations, empathy, agitation, hypertension, respiratory depression, and often seizures. Like cocaine and other potent stimulants, 2C compounds have been linked to excited delirium or serotonin syndrome which have been fatal in several published reports. Drugs in the 2C class are infrequently detected in casework.

More recently, *N*-benzylmethoxy derivatives of the 2C compounds were developed and are known as "NBOMes" or "N-bombs" (Fig. 26.7). These NBOMe structures have significantly higher affinity for the 5-HT$_{2A}$ receptors and are extremely potent. The naming of these compounds are shorted to 25-*X* or 25*X*-NBOMe, where *X* indicates the halogen like in the 2C family. These potent drugs can produce effects with low sub-mg sublingual doses, although a few cases cite insufflation or intravenous administration. In 2013, the United States classified 25B-NBOMe, 25C-NBOMe, and 25I-NBOMe as

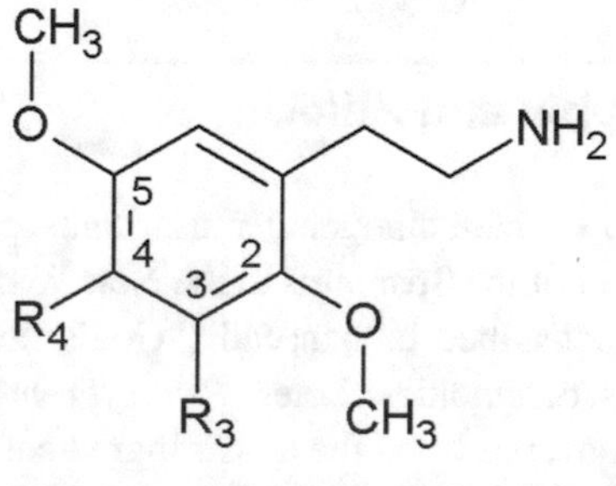

Fig. 26.6 Structural backbone of 2C compounds

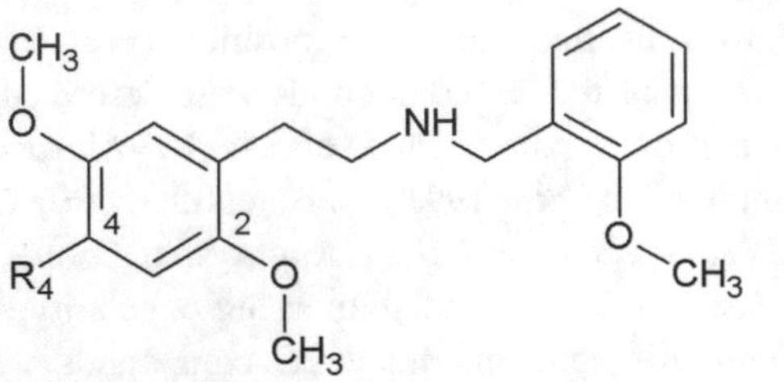

Fig. 26.7 Structural backbone of NBOMe compounds

Schedule I controlled substances. Acute and fatal toxicities are reported in literature. Undesirable effects include agitation, tachycardia, hypertension, delirium, aggression, hallucinations, seizures, and hyperthermia. In some cases, subjects believed they had ingested LSD blotter paper so the identity of the drug, like many novel psychoactive substances, is unknown to the user. Users report peak effects after 2 h (oral) or 45 min (insufflation) with effects lasting 3–13 h. As the compounds are highly potent, sensitive instrumentation is necessary to detect these compounds at pg/mL concentrations in urine and serum. Published analytical methods are available that utilize high-performance liquid chromatography with mass spectrometry or tandem mass spectrometry for analysis of NBOMe in serum, urine, and postmortem specimens. Prevalence of these drugs is somewhat unknown. However, there were no NBOMe listed in the top 15 phenethylamine-type substances submitted to forensic laboratories in 2017. In a 2013 study of night club attendees ($N = 22,289$), only 2.6% admitted to ever using a NBOMe. No human pharmacological data exist, although metabolism has been investigated in vitro. NBOMe compounds are identified as potentially unstable, and samples should be refrigerated or frozen before analysis.

Psilocybin and Psilocin

The use of hallucinogenic mushrooms predates the arrival of the Spaniards to the New World. The Aztecs consumed teonanacatl ("God's flesh") in religious ceremonies. Later, *Psilocybe mexicana* was discovered to be the active ingredient in teonanacatl. Indole derivatives of tryptamine, psilocy-

bin (4-phosphoryloxy-*N,N*-dimethyltryptamine) (Fig. 26.8), and the less stable psilocin were isolated in 1958 from mushrooms used in Indian ceremonies in Mexico. *Psilocybe* is one genus of the three principal hallucinogenic mushrooms in North America. It has long, thin stalks with a conical- or bell-shaped cap and dark brown to purple brown spores. The stalk turns blue upon handling due to bruising. It is commonly known as the liberty cap, blue legs, and magic mushroom and is found in the Pacific Northwest, Hawaii, Texas, and Florida. Psilocybin is the primary psychoactive component of these mushrooms (0.1–1.5% by weight), with only trace amounts of psilocin found. However, psilocin is almost twice as potent as psilocybin in producing hallucinogenic effects. In 2017, psilocin/psilocybin was among the top 25 most frequently identified drugs submitted to US laboratories (42,107 or 0.26%).

Synthesis

Psilocybin may be extracted from mushrooms by repeated methanol trituration of the dried plant material for approximately 20 h. The methanol is then evaporated until the psilocybin crystallizes out. Psilocybin may be prepared in the laboratory using psilocin as the starting material. If psilocybin is synthesized completely, 4-benzoyloxyindole and oxalyl chloride are mixed and allowed to stand for 1 h. Cool dimethylamine is added and this intermediate recrystallized, purified, and reduced with lithium aluminum hydride and then elemental palladium. Psilocin then crystallizes. Psilocybin is prepared from this by dissolving in *tert*-amylalcohol and adding a solution of dibenzyl phos-

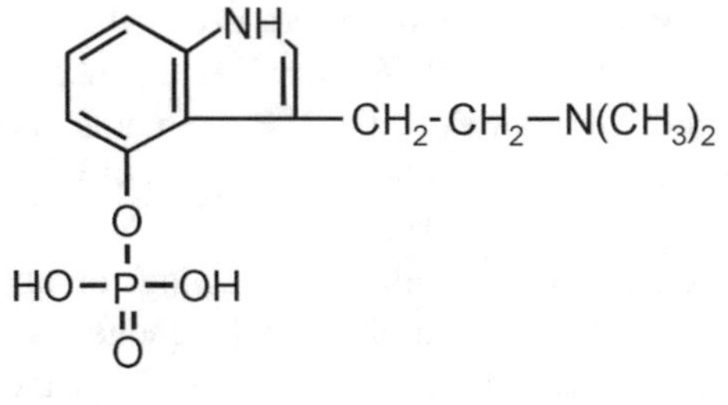

Fig. 26.8 Structure of psilocybin

phorochloridate and shaking for 2 h. The residue is recrystallized in chloroform/ethanol (9:1) and then reduced with hydrogen on an aluminum oxide carrier using palladium as a catalyst.

Pharmacology

Psilocybin is usually ingested as the mushroom without prior extraction. Occasionally, brown-white psilocybin may be sold on the street, but in many instances, samples turn out to be another substance, such as PCP. There is a wide variation in clinical response to mushroom ingestion. Agitation and hallucinations may occur after consuming ten mushrooms (approximately 10 mg psilocybin per gram of mushroom). Typically, individuals may experience lightheadedness, muscle weakness, and anxiety approximately 30–60 min after ingestion. These symptoms may persist for about 4 h. In addition, individuals may engage in unmotivated laughter and compulsive movements. Hallucinations are usually visual, with perceptual alterations occurring in most individuals. These may involve distortion of shapes and colors. Drowsiness and dreamless sleep may follow the perceptual alterations. Other effects include mydriasis, blurred vision, dysphoria, disorientation, aggressive behavior, and antisocial behavior. Suicidal thoughts are infrequently encountered after psilocybin ingestion. The persistence of dysphoric symptoms after 12 h is rare. Persistent neurologic symptoms composed primarily of flashback phenomena do occur after the use of psilocybin, but they are uncommon complications of ingestion. In some instances, flashback symptoms have been experienced for up to 4 months. Limited pharmacokinetic data exist, but some parameters for psilocin are summarized in Table 26.1. Psilocin is also metabolically formed in vivo after psilocybin consumption.

Adverse reactions after ingestion of psilocybin-containing mushrooms may occur with a frequency of 13%. Cases of serious complication have usually occurred in small children. Coma, convulsions, and a death from status epilepticus have been described. In adults, seizures have been described as a serious complication. In very preliminary evaluations of psychedelics, psilocybin has been investigated as a therapeutic agent to treat obsessive compulsive disorder, addiction, and depression.

Analysis

Psilocybin may be detected using spot tests such as the Marquis (yellow) and Mandelin's (green). Psilocybin is thermally labile and therefore not amenable to GC analysis without derivatization. Conversion to trimethylsilyl (TMS) derivatives permits accurate quantification of psilocybin and psilocin by GC. HPLC techniques have been described using UV detection at 268 nm. The detection of psilocin in urine after glucuronide hydrolysis by LC-MS and LC-MS/MS and the measurement of psilocybin in oral fluid with a limit of quantification <5 ng/mL by LC-MS/MS have been described. Both psilocin and the inactive metabolite HIAA (4-hydroxyindole-3-acetic acid) are considered unstable in aqueous solutions, so biological samples should be preserved, frozen, and stored away from light when possible.

Phenylethylamine was identified in the mushroom *Psilocybe semilanceata*, a wild mushroom growing in Sweden. It was present in amounts varying from 1 to 146 µg/g wet weight of mushroom. HPLC analysis of psilocybin was performed on mushroom extracts using reversed-phase chromatography with fluorescence detection (excitation at 270 nm and emission at 339 nm). GC and GC/MS of phenylethylamine were performed using nitrogen phosphorus detection and selected ion monitoring, respectively. The pharmacological role of this substance is unclear, but it has been reported to exert amphetamine-like activity and to have peripheral sympathomimetic effects. Therefore, its presence in mushrooms may contribute to the pharmacological effects of ingestion and may play a role in producing adverse reactions.

Ketamine

Ketamine, 2-(2-chlorophenyl)-2-(methylamino) cyclohexanone, an analog of PCP, has a chemical formula of $C_{13}H_{16}ClNO$ and a molecular weight of 237.7 (Fig. 26.9). The hydrochloride salt is available as an injectable for induction of anesthesia. It has been utilized for this purpose in human and veterinary medicine since 1972. Ketamine possesses the ability to activate bronchodilators and therefore has also been utilized in the emergency treatment of individuals in status asthmaticus. Its clinical usefulness has been limited due to incidence of hallucinations upon waking after ketamine-induced anesthesia, so-called emergencereactions, and also due to its cardiovascular stimulating properties. At subanesthetic doses, ketamine is an effective analgesic and may have a role in the treatment of chronic neuropathic pain and ischemic pain. In addition, ketamine may have a role as an antidepressant for individuals with unipolar or bipolar depression. It is structurally and pharmacologically related to PCP (Fig. 26.1).

The most common licit form of ketamine is an injectable for intravenous administration. More recently, ketamine has been utilized as a drug of abuse for its hallucinogenic properties and as a drug to facilitate sexual assault. When ingested illicitly, common routes of administration include intravenous, subcutaneous, intramuscular, nasal insufflation of the powder, smoking, or oral ingestion of a tablet. When used as an agent of sexual assault, a tablet may be slipped into the victim's drink at a bar or party. Slang names for this drug include Special K, Bump, and Vitamin K.

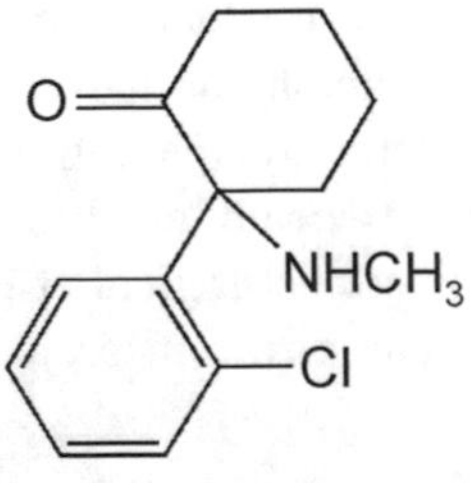

Pharmacokinetics

Ketamine is a weakly basic compound with a pK_a of 7.5. After intravenous administration of 175 mg, peak serum concentrations average 1.0 mg/L within 12 min after injection. Continuous infusion of 41 μg/kg/min after a bolus of 2 mg/kg produced steady-state plasma concentrations of 2.2 mg/L. As with PCP, blood concentrations of ketamine do not correlate with clinical findings. Blood concentrations observed in overdose are generally >3 mg/L. The plasma half-life of ketamine is 3–4 h. This basic drug has a large volume of distribution, 3–4 L/kg, with plasma protein binding of 30%.

Ketamine undergoes *N*-demethylation to form norketamine, followed by dehydrogenation to dehydronorketamine. The metabolites may reach similar blood concentrations to the parent drug and at a minimum the nor-metabolite possesses pharmacologic activity. Ketamine and metabolites undergo hydroxylation and conjugation. These conjugates comprise approximately 80% of a single dose eliminated in urine over 72 h. Urine ketamine concentrations have been reported to range from 6 to 7744 ng/mL, with a mean of 1083 ng/mL (*N* = 33) in individuals tested by the US Department of Defense. In the same individuals, metabolite concentrations ranged from 7 to 7986 ng/mL for norketamine and 37–23,239 ng/mL for dehydronorketamine.

Effects

Ketamine may produce hallucinations in addition to effects that include irrational behavior, gastrointestinal distress such as nausea and vomiting, and blurred vision. More severe adverse effects include cardiac arrhythmias and seizures. Effects on respiration, heart rate, and blood pressure may be to increase or decrease these physiological measures.

As a dissociative anesthetic, ketamine produces effects desirable as a potential drug for drug-facilitated sexual assault. The use may result in CNS depression with impairment of

Fig. 26.9 Structure of ketamine

speech, thought processes, and amnesia. Ketamine produces these effects by interacting with similar receptors as PCP. Ketamine possesses some μ agonist activity, but most of the pharmacological effects of this compound are due to noncompetitive binding of NMDA receptors. Ketamine also binds to sigma-1 receptors.

Analysis

Presumptive immunoassay-based screening for ketamine in biological matrices typically involves ELISA. This basic drug may be easily detected using basic liquid–liquid or solid-phase extraction techniques followed by chromatographic analysis. Gas chromatographic techniques utilizing flame ionization, nitrogen phosphorus, or electron impact mass spectrometric detection have been described. The drug may be readily detected with these techniques without derivatization. However, electron ionization GC analysis may be conducted on heptafluorobutyryl derivatives. More recently, chemical ionization techniques with deuterated internal standards have been reported that measure picogram concentrations of ketamine and norketamine in biological specimens. HPLC and LC-MS procedures have also been described. For example, one assay achieved separation with an XDB C8 column at 35 °C, a mobile phase of 20 mM ammonium formate; pH 4.3 and acetonitrile at an isocratic elution of 25:75, respectively; and electrospray ionization. The limit of quantification was 4 ng/mL.

Methoxetamine (Fig. 26.10) is a 3-methoxy, N-ethyl analog of ketamine and abused as a novel psychoactive substance. With a rise in abuse and reported fatalities, methoxetamine was listed as a Schedule II compound by the United Nations. However, it is not federally scheduled in the United States although some individual states consider it a Schedule I controlled substance. It is also a dissociative anesthetic with a similar pharmacodynamic profile to ketamine although also structurally similar to PCP. It has a chemical formula of $C_{15}H_{21}NO_2$ and a molecular weight of 247.3. Like PCP and

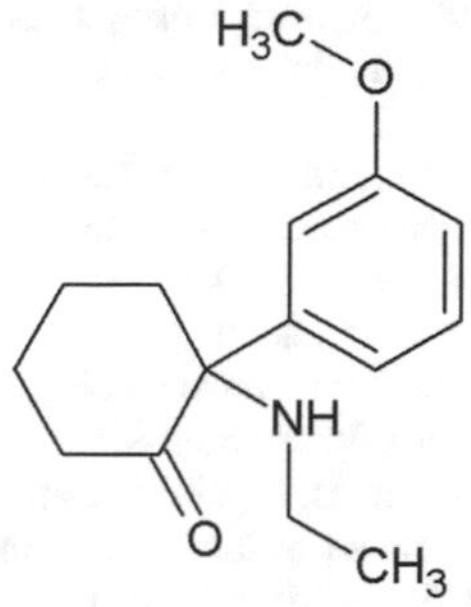

Fig. 26.10 Structure of methoxetamine

ketamine, methoxetamine is a potent NMDA glutamate receptor antagonist. Methoxetamine is metabolized in the liver to normethoxetamine (pharmacological activity unknown) as well as several other phase I (O-demethylation and hydroxylation) and phase II metabolites. This compound may produce a false-positive result with immunoassays for PCP. Methoxetamine may be recovered from biological specimens with alkaline extraction procedures followed by GC-NPD or electron impact GC/MS detection. Prominent ions are observed at m/z 190, 219, and 134. The deoxy-analog of methoxetamine, 3-methoxy-eticyclidine (3-MeO-PCE), is also considered a structural analog of PCP, as discussed earlier in this chapter.

Further Reading

Annual Medical Examiner Data 1993 (1995) Data from the Drug Abuse Warning Network, Statistical Series I Number 13-B, DHHS Publication No. (SMA) 95-3019. U.S. Dept. of Health and Human Services, Substance Abuse and Mental Health Services Administration, Rockville, MD

Aronow R, Miceli JN, Done AK (1978) Clinical observations during phencyclidine intoxication and treatment based on ion-trapping. In: Petersen RC, Stillman RC (eds) Phencyclidine (PCP) abuse: an appraisal (Research Monograph Series #21). National Institute on Drug Abuse, Rockville, MD, pp 218–228

Axelrod J, Brady RO, Witkop B, Evarts EV (1956) Metabolism of lysergic acid diethylamide. Nature 178:143–144

Bailey DN, Shaw RF, Guba JJ (1978) Phencyclidine abuse: plasma levels and clinical findings in casual users and in phencyclidine-related deaths. J Anal Toxicol 2:233–238

Baselt RC (2020) Disposition of toxic drugs and chemicals in man, 12th edn. Biomedical Publications, Seal Beach, CA

Bertron JL, Seto M, Linsley CW (2018) DARK classics in chemical neuroscience: phencyclidine (PCP). ACS Chem Neurosci 9:2459–2474

Bey T (2007) Phencyclidine intoxication and adverse effects: a clinical and pharmacological review of an illicit drug. Cal J Emerg Med 8(1):9–14

Budd RD, Lindstrom DM (1983) Characteristics of victims of PCP-related deaths in Los Angeles County. J Toxicol Clin Toxicol 19:997–1004

Burns RS, Lerner SE (1978) Causes of phencyclidine-related deaths. Clin Toxicol 12(4):463–481

Caplan YH, Orloff KG, Thompson BC, Fisher RS (1979) Detection of phencyclidine in medical examiner's cases. J Anal Toxicol 3:47–52

Cassels BK, Sáez-Briones P (2018) DARK classics in chemical neuroscience: mescaline. ACS Chem Neurosci 9:2448–2458

Coney LD, Maier LJ, Ferris JA, Winstock AR, Barratt MJ (2017) Genie in a blotter: a comparative study of LSD and LSD analogues' effects and user profile. Hum Psychopharmacol Clin Exp 32:e2599

Cook CE, Brine DR, Jeffcoat AR, Hill JM, Wall ME (1982) Phencyclidine disposition after intravenous and oral doses. Clin Pharmacol Ther 31:625–634

Cook CE, Brine DR, Quin GD, Perez-Reyes M, DiGuiseppi SR (1982) Phencyclidine and phenylcyclohexene disposition after smoking phencyclidine. Clin Pharmacol Ther 31:635–641

Coppola M, Mondola R (2012) Methoxetamine: from drug of abuse to rapid-acting antidepressant. Med Hypotheses 79:504–507

Cravey RH, Reed D, Ragle JL (1979) Phencyclidine-related deaths: a report of nine fatal cases. J Anal Toxicol 3:199–201

Dean BV, Stellpflug SJ, Burnett AM, Engebretsen KM (2013) 2C or not 2C: phenethylamine designer drug review. J Med Toxicol 9:172–178

deRoux SJ, Sgarlato A, Marker E (2011) Phencyclidine: a 5-year retrospective review from the New York city medical examiner's office. J Forensic Sci 56(3):656–659

Domino EF (1980) History and pharmacology of PCP and PCP-related analogs. J Psychedelic Drugs 12(3–4):223–227

Domino SE, Domino LE, Domino EF (1982) Comparison of two- and three-compartment models of phencyclidine in man. Subst Alcohol Actions Misuse 2:205–211

Done AK, Aronow R, Miceli JN (1978) The pharmacokinetics of phencyclidine in overdosage and its treatment (Research Monograph 21). National Institute on Drug Abuse, Rockville, MD, pp 210–217

Ellenhorn MJ, Barceloux DG (1988) Medical toxicology, diagnosis, and treatment of human poisoning. Elsevier Science Publishing Company, Inc., New York, NY

Geiger H, Wurst MG, Daniels RN (2018) DARK classics in chemical neuroscience: psilocybin. ACS Chem Neurosci 9:2438–47.19

Glennon RA (1994) Classical hallucinogens an introductory overview. In: Lin GC, Glennon RA (eds) Hallucinogens: an update (Research Monograph Series, #146). National Institute on Drug Abuse, pp 4–32

Goldberger BA (1993) Lysergic acid diethylamide. AACC Ther Drug Monit Toxicol 14(6):99–100

Brunton LL, Lazo JS, Parker KL (eds) (2006) Goodman & Gilman's: the pharmacological basis of therapeutics, 11th edn. McGraw-Hill Co., New York, NY

Hollister LE, Thomas CC (ed) (1968) Chemical psychoses. Springfield, IL, pp 17–18

Jenkins AJ (2001) Drug contamination of U.S. paper currency. Forensic Sci Int 121:189–193

Johnson K, Jones S (1990) Neuropharmacology of phencyclidine: basic mechanisms and therapeutic potential. Annu Rev Pharmacol Toxicol 30:707–750

Johnston LD, Miech RA, O'Malley PM, Bachman JG, Schulenberg JE, Patrick ME (2018) Monitoring the future national survey results on drug use: 1975–2017: overview, key findings on adolescent drug use. Institute for Social Research, The University of Michigan, Ann Arbor, MI

Karch SB (2009) Karch's pathology of drug abuse, 4th edn. CRC Press, Boca Raton, FL

Kaufmann KR, Petrucha RA, Pitts FN, Weeks ME (1983) PCP in amniotic fluid and breast milk: case report. J Clin Psychiatry 44:269

Kunsman GW, Levine B, Costantino A, Smith ML (1997) Phencyclidine blood concentrations in DRE cases. J Anal Toxicol 21:498–502

LeBeau MA, Mozayani A (eds) (2001) Drug-facilitated sexual assault: a forensic handbook. Academic Press, London UK, pp 27–147

Liu R (1995) Evaluation of commercial immunoassay kits for effective workplace drug testing. In: Liu R, Goldberger B (eds) Handbook of workplace drug testing. AACC Press, Washington, DC

McCarron MM, Schulze BW, Thompson GA (1981) Acute phencyclidine intoxication: clinical patterns, complications, and treatment. Ann Emerg Med 10:290–297

McCarron MM, Walberg CB, Soares JR, Gross SJ, Baselt RC (1984) Detection of phencyclidine usage by radioimmunoassay of saliva. J Anal Toxicol 8:197–199

Menzies EL, Hudson SC, Dargan PI, Parkin MC, Wood DM, Kicman AT (2014) Characterizing metabolites and potential metabolic pathways for the novel psychoactive substance methoxetamine. Drug Test Anal 6:506–515

Moffat AC, Jackson JV, Moss MS, Widdop B (eds) (1986) Phencyclidine. In: Clarke's isolation and identification of drugs. The Pharmaceutical Press, London, UK, pp 874–876

Moore KA, Sklerov J, Levine B, Jacobs AJ (2001) Urine concentrations of ketamine and norketamine following illegal consumption. J Anal Toxicol 25:583–588

Nichols DE (2018) DARK classics in chemical neuroscience: lysergic acid diethylamide (LSD). ACS Chem Neurosci 9:2331–2343

Noguchi TT, Nakamura GR (1978) Phencyclidine-related deaths in Los Angeles County, 1976. J Forensic Sci 23:503–507

Papac DI, Foltz R (1990) Measurement of lysergic acid diethylamide (LSD) in human plasma by gas chromatography/negative ion chemical ionization mass spectrometry. J Anal Toxicol 14:189–190

Perez-Reyes M, DiGuiseppi S, Brine DR, Smith H, Cook CE (1982) Urine pH and phencyclidine excretion. Clin Pharmacol Ther 32:635–641

Ropero-Miller JD, Goldberger BA (2009) Handbook of workplace drug testing, 2nd edn. AACC Press, Washington, DC

Roth BL, Gibbons S, Arunotayanun W, Huang X-P, Setola V, Treble R, Iversen L (2013) The ketamine analogue methoxetamine and 3- and 4-methoxy analogues of phencyclidine are high affinity and selective ligands for the glutamate NMDA receptor. PLoS One 8:e59334

Saferstein R (1988) Phencyclidine. In: Forensic science handbook, vol II. Prentice Hall, Englewood Cliffs, NJ, pp 101–104

Substance Abuse and Mental Health Services Administration (2013) Drug Abuse Warning Network 2011: National Estimates of Drug-Related Emergency Department Visits. HHS Publication No. SMA 13-4760, DAWN Series D-39. Substance Abuse and Mental Health Services Administration, Rockville, MD

Substance Abuse and Mental Health Services Administration (2018) Results from the 2017 National Survey on Drug Use and Health. NSDUH Series H-53, HHS Publication No. SMA 18-5068. Substance Abuse and Mental Health Services Administration, Rockville, MD

Sunshine I (1989) Phencyclidine. AACC Ther Drug Monit Toxicol 10(7):7–13

Suzuki J, Dekker MA, Valenti ES, Arbelo Cruz FA, Correa AM, Poklis JL, Poklis A (2015) Toxicities associated with NBOMe ingestion—a novel class of potent hallucinogens: a review of the literature. Psychosomatics 56:129–139

U.S. Drug Enforcement Administration (2018) Diversion Control Division: National Forensic Laboratory Information System: NFLIS-Drug 2017 Annual Report. U.S. Drug Enforcement Administration, Springfield, VA

Antidepressants

27

William H. Anderson

Abstract

Antidepressants, as the name implies, are drugs used to treat depression and are widely used therapeutic agents. They are also some of the most frequently encountered drugs in forensic and clinical toxicology. Antidepressants are often characterized based on when they were developed: first-generation antidepressants, second-generation antidepressants, selective serotonin reuptake inhibitors, and third-generation antidepressants. All of the antidepressants are well absorbed and reach peak serum concentrations within 2–12 h, but there is considerable first-pass metabolism with most of these drugs. They are rather lipophilic and have large volumes of distribution. In general, these drugs are extensively metabolized by cytochrome P450 isoenzymes to demethylated and hydroxylated metabolites, many of which are active. Analysis of these compounds in biological specimens requires specimen preparation either by liquid–liquid extraction or solid-phase extraction. Chromatographic separation by gas or liquid chromatography allows simultaneous analysis of most antidepressants and their major metabolites. First-generation antidepressants are associated with greater toxicity, primarily due to anticholinergic effects, central nervous system effects, and cardiovascular effects. Interpretation of postmortem concentrations of these drugs is complicated by postmortem redistribution; therefore, the use of therapeutic ranges established for antemortem serum is inappropriate.

Keywords

Antidepressants · Pharmacology · Toxicology · Analysis · Interpretation

Introduction

Depression and schizophrenia are two of the most common and most debilitating mental disorders. Depression is a mood disorder characterized by sadness, depressed mood, inactivity, loss of interest or pleasure, and a reduced ability to enjoy life. Depression in the absence of mania is referred to as unipolar disorder; in the presence of mania, it is bipolar disorder. Schizophrenia is a disorder characterized by abnormal perceptions, delusions, hallucinations, illusions, and, sometimes, bizarre behavior. Complete diagnostic criteria for depression and schizophrenia have been developed and published by the American Psychiatric Association in the fifth edition of the Diagnostic and Statistical Manual of Mental Disorders (DSM-5).

W. H. Anderson (✉)
NMS Labs, Horsham, PA, USA
e-mail: William.anderson@nmslabs.com

© Springer Nature Switzerland AG 2020
B. S. Levine, S. Kerrigan (eds.), *Principles of Forensic Toxicology*,
https://doi.org/10.1007/978-3-030-42917-1_27

According to the World health Organization, 350 million people worldwide suffer from depression. Consequently, drugs used to treat depression (antidepressants) are widely used therapeutic agents and are the focus of much research and development. They are also some of the most frequently encountered drugs in forensic and clinical toxicology. This is not surprising considering the patient population for which the drugs are designed, the frequency with which these drugs are prescribed, and their high potential for serious side effects, toxicity, and drug–drug interactions. This chapter provides an overview of the pharmacology, toxicology, and analysis of antidepressants.

Pharmacologic Actions

Antidepressants, psychotherapy, and, in some circumstances, electroconvulsive therapy, are the primary treatments for clinical depression. Various compounds classified as antidepressants are also used in the treatment of other disorders or conditions, e.g., obsessive-compulsive disorder, chronic pain, eating disorders, panic disorders, peptic ulcer disease, and childhood enuresis.

The exact mechanism of action of the antidepressants is not entirely understood, although it has been an area of intense research for the last 50 years. A thorough discussion of the topic is beyond the scope of this chapter, but it appears that an increase in monoamine transmission, especially serotonergic transmission, is an essential element.

The earliest (first-generation) antidepressants comprised the tricyclic antidepressants (TCAs) and the monoamine oxidase inhibitors (MAOIs). The TCAs inhibit the reuptake of either norepinephrine (NE), dopamine (DA), or serotonin (5-HT) to varying degrees, and the MAOIs block their metabolism; both mechanisms produce increased amounts of neurotransmitter in the synapse. These observations led to the monoamine hypothesis of depression, which held that a deficit of either NE, DA, or 5-HT at certain sites in the brain was responsible for depression. However, it was recognized early on that the mechanism of action of antidepressant drugs had to be more complicated than merely increasing the concentration of monoamine. There is a well-recognized time delay of several weeks before the therapeutic effect of the first-generation antidepressants emerges, although the inhibition of reuptake or blockage of metabolism is acute. In addition, other compounds (e.g., cocaine) that block the reuptake of neurotransmitters do not function as antidepressants. The detection and characterization of a plethora of 5-HT receptors (5-HT_{1A}, $5\text{-HT}_1\text{D}$, 5-HT_{2A}, 5-HT_{2C}, 5-HT_3, 5-HT_4), DA receptors (D1, D2, D3, D4, D5), and NE receptors (α_1, α_2, β_1) located on pre- and postsynaptic neurons have led to many current areas of research and to the development of new antidepressant compounds. Many of the new antidepressants do not effectively block the reuptake of NE or 5-HT or hinder their metabolism. Areas under current investigation concerning the mechanism of action of antidepressants include the direct effects of neurotransmitter binding to a variety of receptors, the subsequent downregulation of receptors, and the possibility that continued use of antidepressants produces adaptations in post-receptor signaling pathways, including regulation of neural gene expression.

Mechanism of Action

Antidepressants are often characterized as first-, second-, and third-generation antidepressants, depending on when they were developed. This discussion will address

- First-generation TCAs
- Second-generation compounds amoxapine, maprotiline, trazodone, and bupropion
- Compounds that selectively block the reuptake of 5-HT, which are referred to collectively as selective serotonin reuptake inhibitors (SSRIs)
- Third-generation compounds venlafaxine, nefazodone, mirtazapine, and duloxetine

Though the definitive mechanism leading to an antidepressant effect remains elusive, the inhibition of the reuptake of 5-HT, DA, or NE is still regarded as an important action and apparently initiates the subsequent antidepressant effect for many drugs.

First-Generation Antidepressants

The structures of the TCAs are presented in Fig. 27.1. They obviously derive their name from the three-ring structure common to all members of this group. Most TCAs affect the reuptake of 5-HT and/or NE, but they are not equal in their action, and some have substantial specificity. In general, the secondary TCAs are relatively selective inhibitors of NE reuptake, while the tertiary TCAs are less selective except for clomipramine, which is a relatively selective inhibitor of 5-HT reuptake. Trimipramine has little or no effect on reuptake of monoamine. Amitriptyline, doxepin, and nortriptyline also have high affinity for and antagonize the 5-HT_{2A} receptor. The TCAs have many other pharmacologic actions that apparently do not contribute to their therapeutic effect but do contribute to the considerable side effect profiles of these drugs. These interactions include the blockade of α_1 adrenoreceptors (hypotension, dizziness, and sedation), H_1 histamine receptors (weight gain and sedation), and M_1 muscarinic receptors (dry mouth, blurred vision, constipation, and urinary retention). Sinus tachycardia and short-term memory impairment may also be a result of M_1 blockade. TCAs are also known to lower the seizure threshold.

Second-Generation Antidepressants

The structures of specific second-generation drugs are presented in Fig. 27.2. Amoxapine and maprotiline have effects on reuptake of monoamines that are similar to the secondary amine TCAs. These two drugs also have antihistamine, anticholinergic, and a1 antagonist properties similar to the TCAs. Trazodone is a weak inhibitor of 5-HT reuptake and has little effect on NE reuptake, but it is a potent antagonist of the 5-HT_{2A} and α_1 receptors. Although it is not an antihistamine, trazodone is quite sedating in vivo. Priapism has been reported to be a risk in patients taking trazodone. Bupropion is unique among the antidepressants in that it has no known effect on the serotonin system. Bupropion blocks the reuptake of NE and DA. This property probably contributes to the use of bupropion in attention-deficit disorder and as an aid to stop smoking. The adrenergic stimulation also probably accounts for the agitation, insomnia, and nausea that have been reported with bupropion. Seizures have also been encountered with bupropion, especially in former dosage units and in doses higher than recommended.

Selective Serotonin Reuptake Inhibitors

The SSRIs have become the most widely prescribed group of antidepressants in the United States; their structures are presented in Fig. 27.3. In addition to inhibiting the reuptake of 5-HT, they interact with a variety of serotonin receptors (5-HT_{1A}, 5-HT_2, and

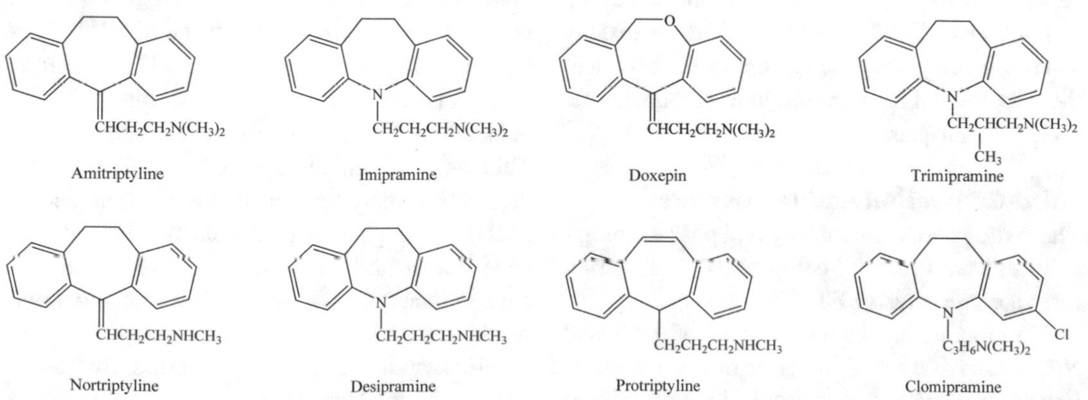

Fig. 27.1 Structures of the tricyclic antidepressants

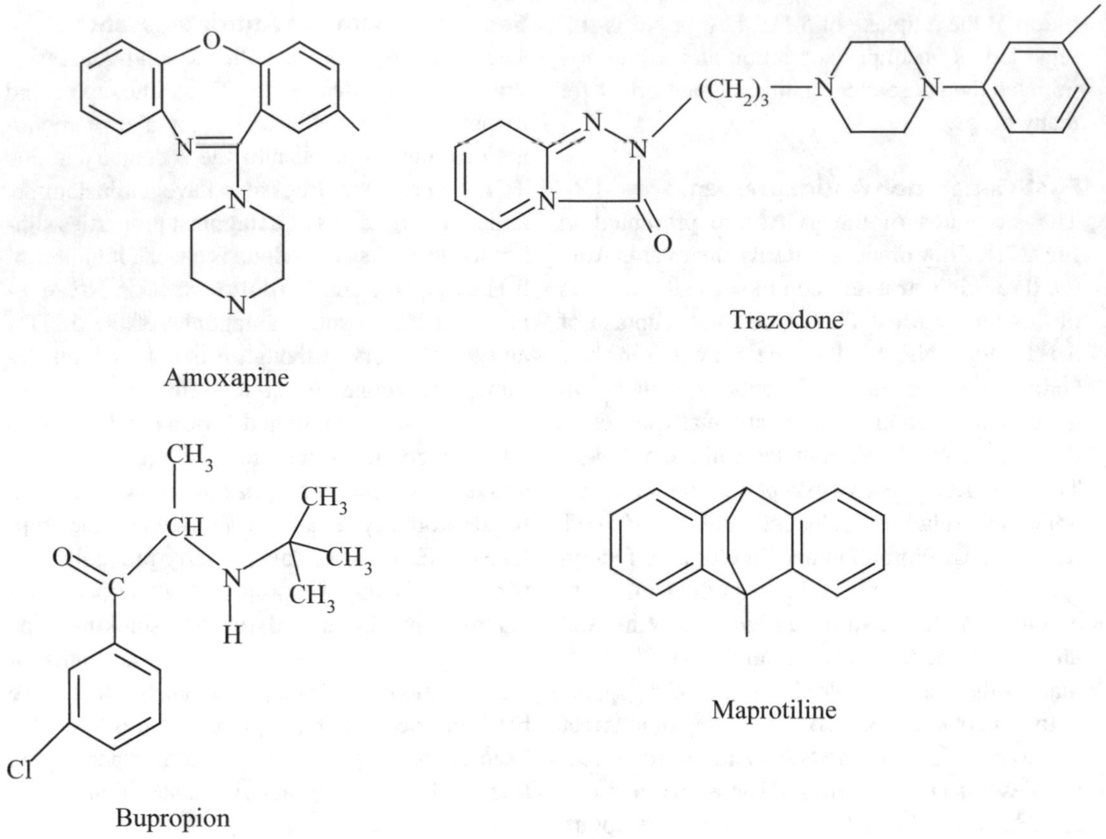

Amoxapine

Trazodone

Bupropion

Maprotiline

Fig. 27.2 Structures of selected second-generation antidepressants

5-HT$_3$). The significance of these interactions is not fully understood. These drugs lack the major adrenergic, antihistaminic, and anticholinergic side effects of the TCAs, are generally much better tolerated, and are safer. However, anxiety, sleep disturbances, sexual dysfunction, and insomnia are common side effects. These drugs also have toxicity and proven drug–drug interactions that can be fatal; these topics will be discussed in a subsequent section of this chapter.

Third-Generation Antidepressants

These drugs are a chemically and pharmacologically diverse group of compounds. Their structures are presented in Fig. 27.4.

Venlafaxine blocks the reuptake of 5-HT and NE; it is also a weak inhibitor of dopamine. At low doses, venlafaxine may function primarily as an SSRI. It lacks affinity for H$_1$, α_1, and M$_1$ receptors. Common adverse effects include headache, nausea, somnolence, dry mouth, and sexual dysfunction. Sustained hypertension is a potentially dangerous side effect.

Nefazodone is similar in structure to trazodone but has a different pharmacologic profile. It is similar to the SSRIs in blockage of 5-HT reuptake, and it interacts with the 5-HT$_2$ receptors. However, the 5-HT$_2$ receptor is blocked with nefazodone and is stimulated with the SSRIs. This may explain the improved profile of nefazodone for anxiety and insomnia as compared to SSRIs, although anxiety, dizziness, and insomnia have been reported as adverse reactions. Nefazodone also interacts with α_1 receptors and weakly inhibits the reuptake of NE.

Mirtazapine has been referred to as a "designer" antidepressant. It is an α_2 antagonist, a 5-HT$_2$ antagonist, a 5-HT$_3$ antagonist, and a

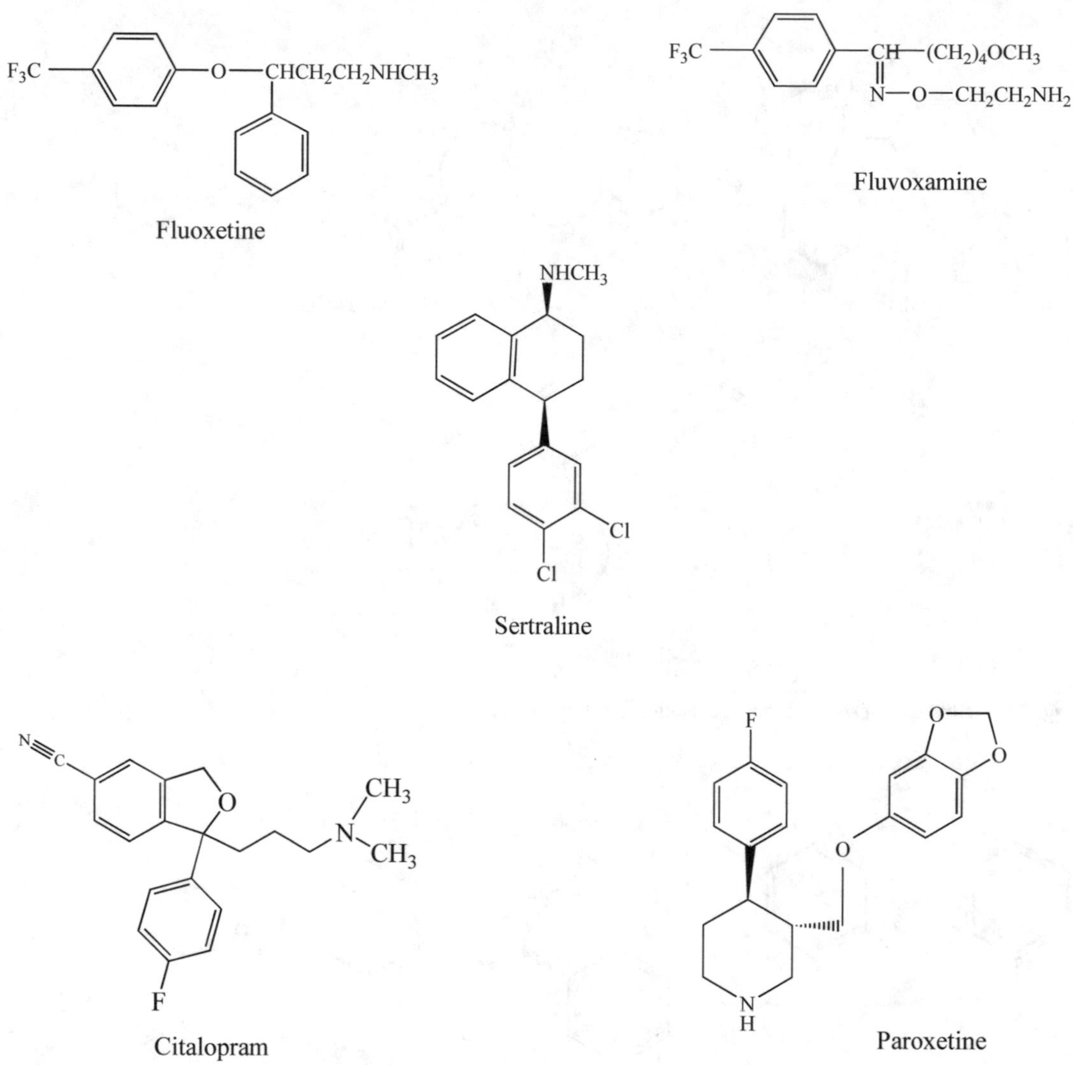

F_3C — [benzene ring] — O — CHCH_2CH_2NHCH_3

Fluoxetine

F_3C — [benzene ring] — CH — (CH_2)_4OCH_3
                        ‖
                        N — O — CH_2CH_2NH_2

Fluvoxamine

NHCH_3

Sertraline

N≡C ... CH_3 / N—CH_3 ... F

Citalopram

F ... O ... N—H

Paroxetine

Fig. 27.3 Structures of the selective serotonin reuptake inhibitors

potent H_1 antagonist. Predictable side effects are weight gain and sedation.

Duloxetine was approved as an antidepressant in the United States in 2004. It is a potent inhibitor of both 5-HT and NE reuptake but only weakly affects DA reuptake. Common side effects include drowsiness, nausea, a slight increase in blood pressure, and a slight decrease in heart rate.

Newer Antidepressants

Several newer antidepressants are also discussed below, and their chemical structures are shown in Fig. 27.5.

Vortioxetine is an atypical antidepressant with multimodal activity. It was approved for medical use in the United States in 2013. It functions as an SSRI, a 5-HT_{1A} agonist, a 5-HT_{1B} partial agonist, and an antagonist at 5-HT_{1D}, 5-HT_7, and 5-HT_3. Vortioxetine is reported to have procognitive effects. Side effects include nausea, vomiting, diarrhea, dry mouth, headache, and abnormal dreams.

Vilazodone has dual action as an SSRI and a 5-HT_{1A} partial agonist. It was approved for medical use in the United States in 2011. Side effects include diarrhea, nausea, insomnia, and vomit-

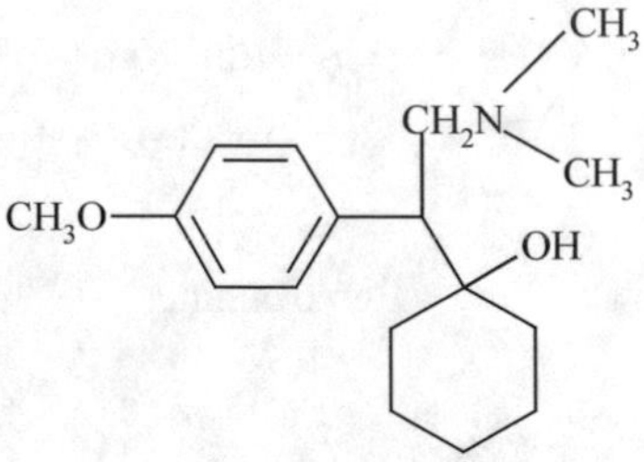

Venlafaxine

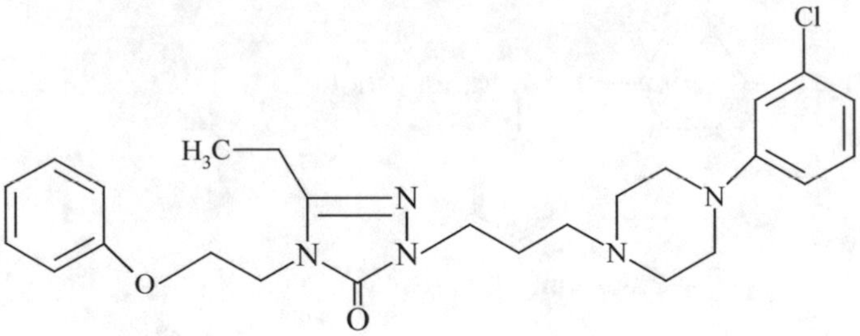

Nefazodone

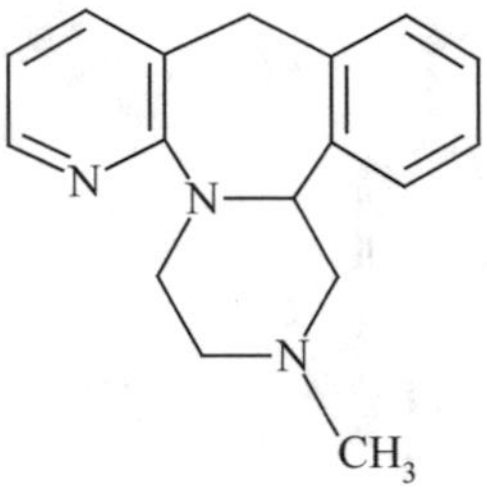

Mirtazapine

Fig. 27.4 Structure of selected third-generation antidepressants

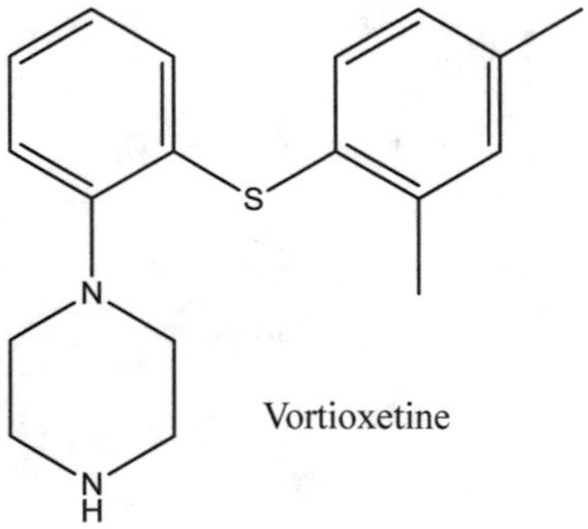

Vortioxetine

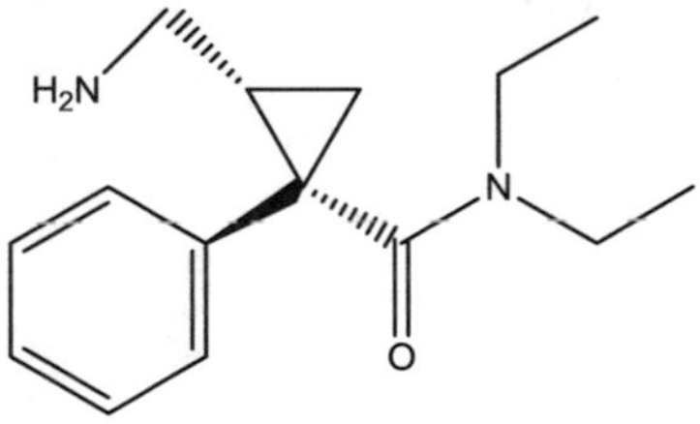

Levomilnacipran

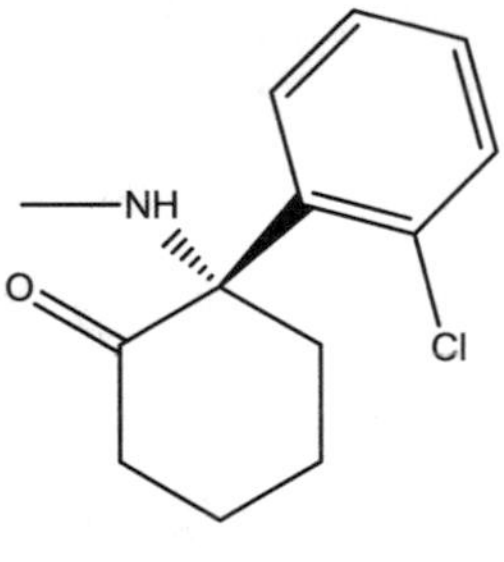

Esketamine

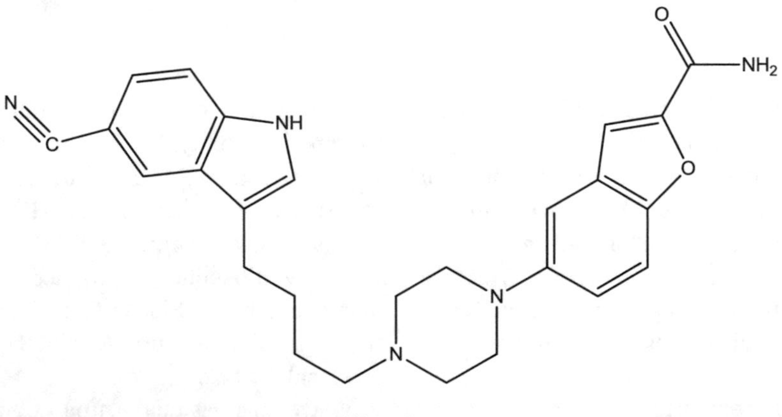

Vilazodone

Fig. 27.5 Newer antidepressants

ing. Other adverse effects included dizziness, dry mouth, fatigue, abnormal dreams, decreased libido, arthralgia, and palpitations.

Racemic milnacipran is used to treat depression in many countries. Levomilnacipran was approved for treatment of depression in the United States in 2013. Levomilnacipran (1S, 2R-milnacipran) is the more potent of the enantiomers found in racemic milnacipran. It inhibits the reuptake of serotonin and norepinephrine and has little effect upon other receptors. It appears to be a more potent inhibitor of the NE transporter than the 5-HT transporter. Side effects include anxiety, weakness, dizziness, somnolence, headache, nausea, insomnia, tremor and orthostatic hypotension, tachycardia, and serotonin syndrome.

In 2019, a drug nasal spray formulation of esketamine was approved by the FDA for treatment-resistant major depression. The drug is the S-enantiomer of ketamine, a dissociative anesthetic. It must be used in conjunction with an oral antidepressant. Esketamine is a noncompetitive NMDA receptor antagonist. The exact mechanism of esketamine action is unknown but is under rigorous investigation. Esketamine seems to work quickly to relieve depression and then a second action is to trigger reactions that enable connections in the brain to regrow. Typical doses are 56–84 mg. Side effects require close patient monitoring and include sedation, anxiety, dissociation, abuse and misuse, cognitive impairment, ulcerative or interstitial cystitis.

Many drugs developed for other purposes are being used as adjuncts for treatment of depression. Included are **lurasidone**, aripiprazole, quetiapine, and olanzapine, and brexpiprazole.

Pharmacokinetics

All of the antidepressants are well absorbed and reach peak serum concentrations within 2–12 h, but there is considerable first-pass metabolism with most of these drugs. They are rather lipophilic and have large volumes of distribution. In general, these drugs are extensively metabolized by cytochrome P450 isoenzymes to demethyl-ated and hydroxylated metabolites, many of which are active.

Table 27.1 lists pharmacokinetic properties and the suggested therapeutic ranges of various antidepressants. Several caveats are associated with any such compilation of data. The half-life and volume of distribution for these drugs and their active metabolites are quite variable; average or median values may not be assumed to apply to an individual. The therapeutic ranges for many of these drugs either have not been established or are controversial. The ranges listed in Table 27.1 are taken from a large number of standard references that have different study designs, patient populations, and dosing regimens. However, a growing amount of evidence indicates that a curvilinear relationship exists between serum concentration and efficacy. In many cases, therapeutic effect may be enhanced by lowering the dose of antidepressant and consequently lowering the serum concentration. For the newer antidepressants, the listed "therapeutic ranges" may be more accurately considered as the concentrations observed in early clinical trials.

There is considerable debate about the necessity of performing therapeutic drug monitoring for antidepressants. Critics of routine monitoring claim that the therapeutic ranges are so ill-defined that the expense and effort of determining the serum concentration are unwarranted. Proponents believe that, for many drugs, enough information concerning target concentrations is available to warrant the procedure and that toxicity due to increased serum concentration can be averted. There seems to be consensus that therapeutic ranges are well established for imipramine, desipramine, and nortriptyline.

The metabolism of the TCAs is illustrated in Fig. 27.6, with amitriptyline and imipramine as examples. The hydroxylated metabolites are further metabolized by glucuronidation. As is the case with amitriptyline and imipramine, the metabolism of a parent antidepressant may produce an active metabolite(s). It is common knowledge that any therapeutic monitoring program for these two drugs should include nortriptyline and desipramine; this is also true for other, less well-understood antidepressants.

Table 27.1 Selected pharmacokinetic information for antidepressants

Drug	$t_{1/2}$ (h)	V_d (L\kg)	Active metabolite	Therapeutic range (mg/L)
Amitriptyline	9–46	6.4–36	Nortriptyline	0.11–0.25[a]
Amoxapine	9–14	–	8-Hydroxy amoxapine	0.20–0.60[a]
Bupropion	10–21	27–63	Hydroxy-bupropion	0.025–0.10
Citalopram	25–35	12–16	Desmethylcitalopram	0.04–0.10
Clomipramine	15–62	9–25	Desmethylclomipramine	0.20–0.80[a]
Desipramine	12–28	24–60	–	0.115–0.25
Doxepin	9–25	9–33	Nordoxepin	0.15–0.25
Duloxetine	9–19	20–24	–	0.01–0.2
Fluoxetine	26–220	12–42	Norfluoxetine	0.20–0.90[a]
Fluvoxamine	23	25	–	0.02–0.40
Imipramine	6–28	9–23	Desipramine	0.20–0.35[a]
Maprotiline	27–50	16–32	–	0.20–0.60
Mirtazapine	13.1–33.6	4.5	N-desmethyl mirtazapine	–
Nefazodone	2–5	0.51	M-chlorophenylpiperazine hydroxynefazodone	0.30–0.50
Nortriptyline	18–56	15–23	–	0.05–0.15
Paroxetine	7–37	3–28	–	–
Protriptyline	54–198	15–31	–	0.10–0.20
Sertraline	26	25	Desmethylsertraline	–
Trazodone	6–13	0.8–1.5	M-chlorophenylpiperazine	0.80–1.60
Trimipramine	16–40	17–48	Desmethyltrimipramine	0.10–0.30
Venlafaxine	5	7.5	O-desmethyl venlafaxine	0.25–0.50[a]
Vortioxetine	66	26–34	–	0.004–0.031
Vilazodone	17–36	7–17	–	0.028–0.15
Milnacipran	7–8	3–8	–	0.039–0.157[b]
L-milnacipran	10–16	5.5–6.8	–	0.12–0.39[c]

[a]Total of antidepressant and active metabolite
[b]Trough concentration at steady state
[c]Peak plasma concentration at steady state

There is considerable indication that the hydroxylated metabolites are also active, but these compounds are infrequently incorporated into monitoring programs. In the case of amitriptyline, the 10-hydroxy compounds exist as E and Z isomers. They are difficult to determine without highly targeted procedures.

The metabolism of amoxapine and maprotiline proceeds via demethylation and hydroxylation in a manner analogous to the TCAs (Fig. 27.6). The metabolism of trazodone is depicted in Fig. 27.7. The major active metabolite is m-chlorophenylpiperazine (m-CPP), which has a reported half-life of 4 h or greater. An inactive carboxylic metabolite is also produced but is not considered in most analytical schemes. The metabolites of bupropion that are usually encountered in analytical toxicology are presented in Fig. 27.8. The hydroxybupropion ($t_{1/2}$ = 15–22 h) and threobupropion ($t_{1/2}$ = 9–27 h) are pharmacologically active; erythrobupropion ($t_{1/2}$ = 22–43 h)

is inactive. Hydroxybupropion is usually present in the highest concentration after therapeutic dosing, followed by threobupropion and bupropion. Bupropion is reported to be unstable in biological specimens. Suspected cases should be analyzed as quickly as possible or the specimens should be frozen if immediate analysis is not possible.

The SSRIs are extensively metabolized, mostly to inactive metabolites, with very little unchanged drug excreted in the urine. The major metabolic route for the production of active metabolites is demethylation. Fluoxetine, sertraline, and citalopram are metabolized into norfluoxetine, desmethylsertraline, and desmethylcitalopram, respectively. The metabolism of fluoxetine is illustrated in Fig. 27.9. Fluvoxamine and paroxetine have no demethylated or other active metabolites. The half-life of norfluoxetine is quite long: 7–15 days for short-term administration and up to 21 days for patients who have been taking the drug for extended peri-

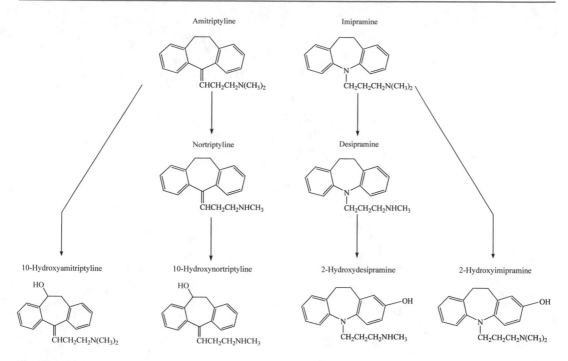

Fig. 27.6 Major metabolic pathways for amitriptyline and imipramine

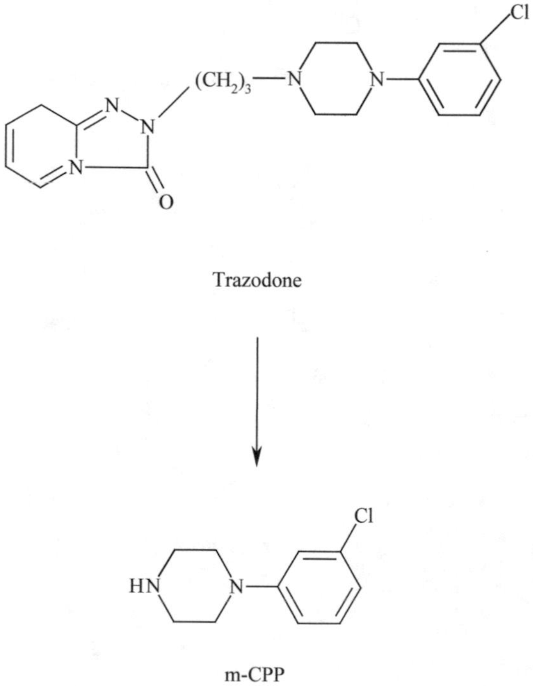

Trazodone

m-CPP

Fig. 27.7 Selected metabolites of trazodone

ods. The extremely long half-life of fluoxetine and norfluoxetine is an important consideration when dose adjustments of fluoxetine are attempted, especially if fluoxetine is discontinued and another antidepressant initiated. Similarly, the half-life of desmethylsertraline is 3–10 days. Therapeutic ranges for the SSRIs have not been established with certainty. In clinical dosing, the total fluoxetine and norfluoxetine concentration is usually less than 1.0 mg/L with a drug/metabolite ratio near unity. Sertraline concentrations are usually 0.1–0.2 mg/L and desmethylsertraline 0.15–0.3 mg/L. Paroxetine and fluvoxamine steady-state concentrations are usually less than 0.2 mg/L. Steady-state citalopram concentrations range from 0.04 to 0.1 mg/L.

The metabolism of venlafaxine is presented in Fig. 27.10. O-desmethylvenlafaxine (ODV) is the major metabolite; it is active and has pharmacologic properties similar to venlafaxine. ODV has a half-life of 11 h and a volume of distribution of 5.7 L/kg. N-desmethylvenlafaxine may have some NE and 5-HT reuptake inhibi-

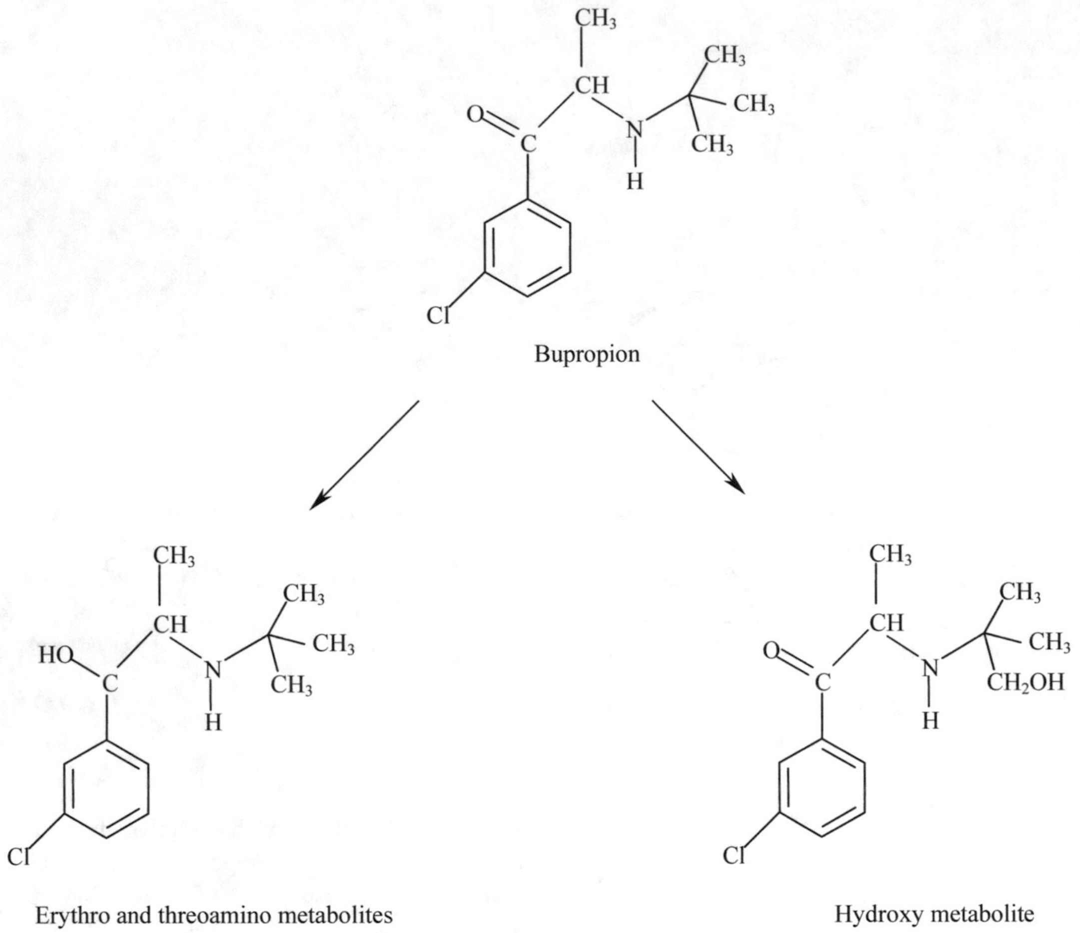

Fig. 27.8 The metabolic pathway for bupropion

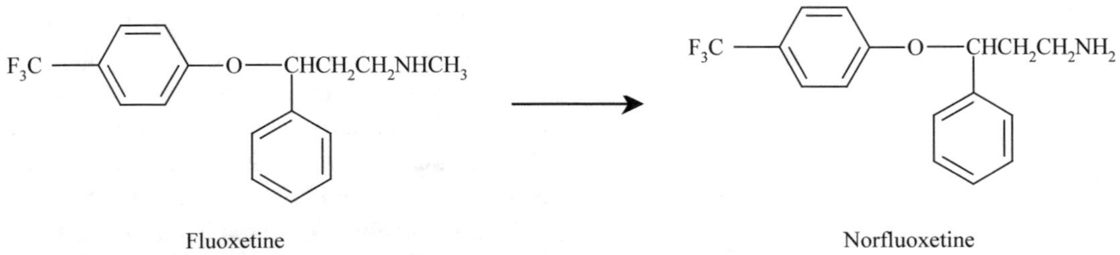

Fig. 27.9 The major metabolic pathway for fluoxetine

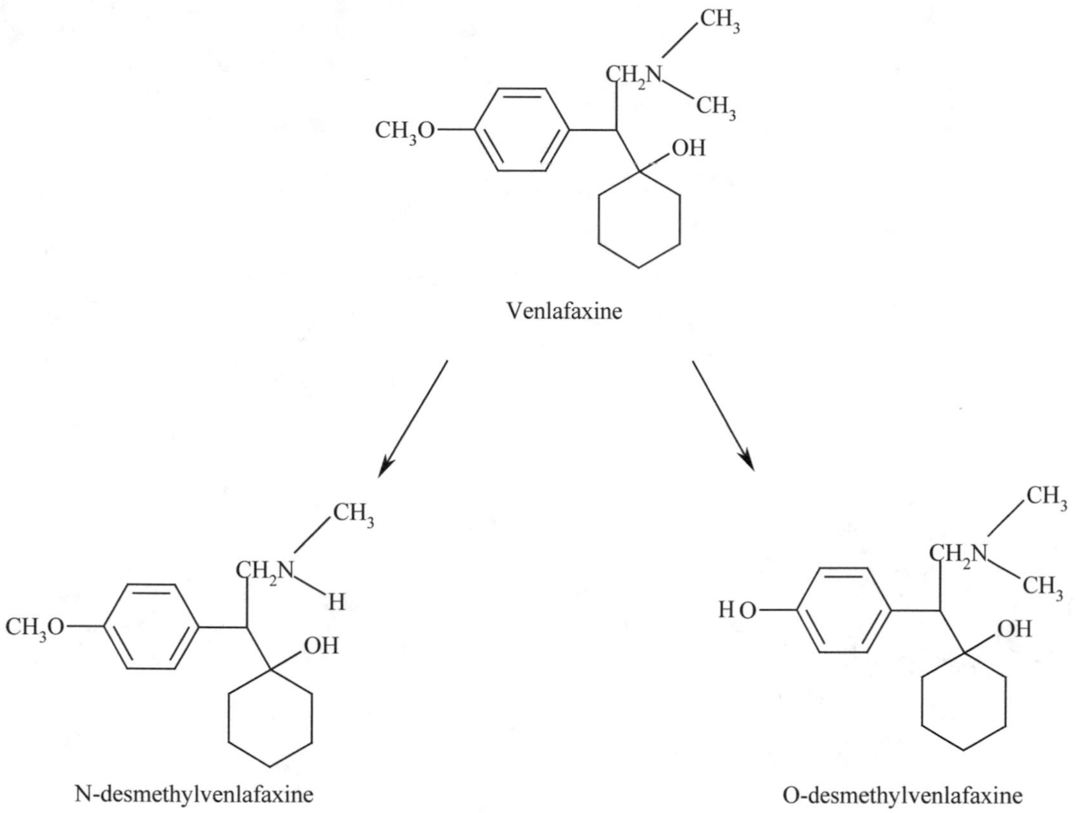

Venlafaxine

N-desmethylvenlafaxine   O-desmethylvenlafaxine

Fig. 27.10 The metabolic pathway for venlafaxine

tion, but it is a minor metabolite. Concentrations of venlafaxine and ODV at steady state have been reported to be near 0.15 and 0.4 mg/L, respectively. Venlafaxine and ODV are approximately 30% bound to plasma proteins; this characteristic is unique among the antidepressants discussed in this chapter. All other antidepressants are extensively bound, usually 90% or more.

Nefazodone is metabolized to three active metabolites, hydroxynefazodone, triazoledione, and m-CPP, as illustrated by Fig. 27.11. The half-lives of hydroxynefazodone, triazoledione, and m-CPP are on the order of 2.5–10.5, 7–12, and 5–9 h, respectively. The concentrations after nefazodone administration are quite variable. Average maximum serum concentrations (ng/mL) after a single 100-mg dose have been reported

within these ranges: nefazodone, 0.25–0.4 mg/L; hydroxynefazodone, 0.09–0.11 mg/L; triazoledione, 0.58–0.71 mg/L; and m-CPP, 0.01–0.025 mg/L. When two 300-mg tablets are taken daily, average maximum concentrations have been reported within these ranges: nefazodone, 2.8–3.86 mg/L; hydroxynefazodone 0.8–1.2 mg/L; and m-CPP, 0.07–0.11 mg/L. Nefazodone exhibits nonlinear pharmacokinetics, resulting in greater-than-expected serum concentrations with increasing doses. Plasma concentrations per dose are greater in the elderly, especially elderly women.

Mirtazapine is metabolized to the active metabolite N-desmethylmirtazapine, as illustrated in Fig. 27.12. The N-desmethyl metabolite has pharmacologic activity of one-third to one-fourth that of mirtazapine. Inactive N-oxide and 8-hydroxy metabolites have also been

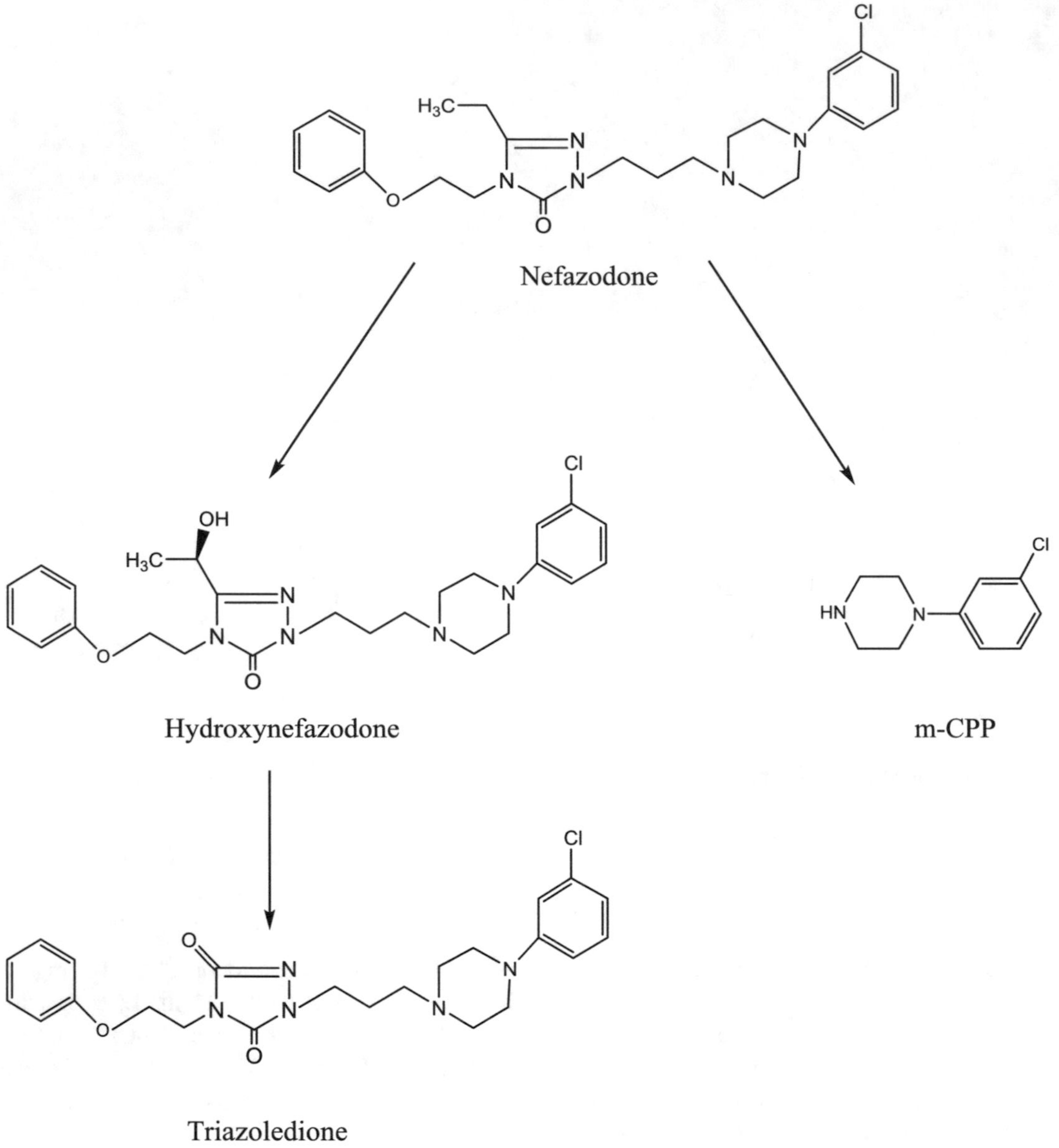

Fig. 27.11 The metabolic pathway for nefazodone

reported. Little pharmacokinetic information has been published to date concerning the metabolites of mirtazapine. The drug itself displays linear kinetics over the usual therapeutic dosing range. Maximum steady-state plasma concentrations are reached within 2–3 h after dose. After a once-per-day 15-mg dose and a once per day 75-mg dose, the concentration of mirtazapine is approximately 0.03 mg/L and 0.15 mg/L, respectively.

Duloxetine is well absorbed orally with peak plasma concentrations occurring 6–10 h after use. Phase I metabolism involves hydroxylation. The primary metabolite in plasma is the glucuronide conjugate of 4-hydroxyduloxetine. Two other conjugated metabolites, 4,6-dihydroxyduloxetine

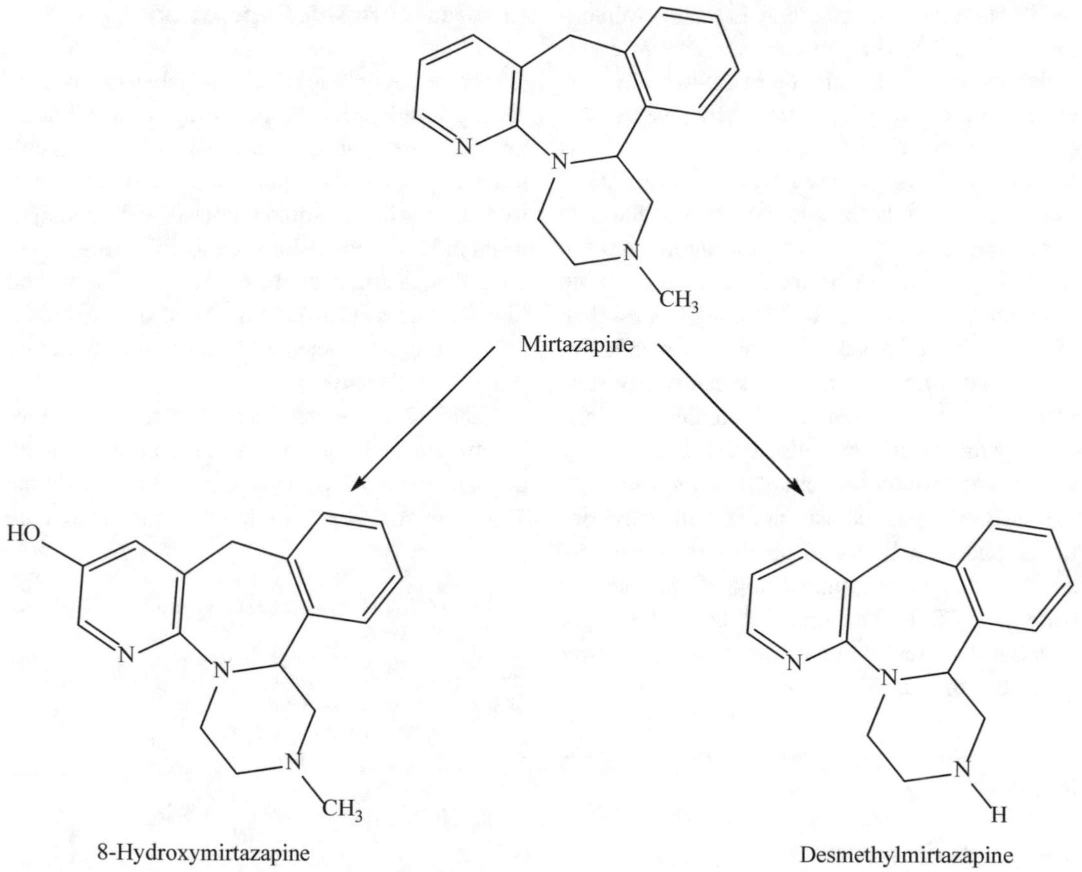

Fig. 27.12 The metabolic pathway for mirtazapine

sulfate and 6-hydroxy-5-methoxyduloxetine sulfate, have also been identified in plasma. The conjugated metabolites form rapidly and are inactive.

Vortioxetine is well absorbed with a bioavailability of 75%; peak plasma occurs in 7–11 h. The drug is extensively metabolized to inactive metabolites. Only traces are eliminated as free drug in the urine.

Vilazodone is well absorbed with a bioavailability of 72% with food; bioavailability is considerably less without food. There are no know active metabolites of vilazodone. Only 1% of the dose excreted in the urine as free drug. CYP3A4 is primarily responsible for its metabolism among CYP pathways, with minor contributions from CYP2C19 and CYP2D6.

Milnacipran is rapidly absorbed with a bioavailability of 85–90% with peak concentration 2–4 h post-dose. It is primarily metabolized to oxidized and conjugated metabolites. A significant portion of the dose, 50–60%, is excreted unchanged in the urine.

Levomilnacipran is absorbed from its extended-release capsule with a bioavailability of 80–90% with peak plasma levels occurring in 6–8 h. It is metabolized to inactive metabolites. Approximately 60% of the dose is excreted in the urine as unchanged drug.

Esketamine as a nasal spray has a bioavailability of 48%. The time to reach maximum esketamine plasma concentration is 20–40 min after the last nasal spray of a treatment session. No accumulation of esketamine in plasma was observed following twice-a-week administration. The drug is metabolized to the active metabolite noresketamine. Plasma concentrations on the fourth day of treatment taken 2 h after a 56-mg dose ranged from 0.014 to 0.142 mg/L. Less than 1% of a dose of nasal esketamine is excreted as unchanged drug in urine. The mean steady-state volume of distribution of esketamine administered by the intravenous route is 709 L. After C_{max} was reached following intranasal administration, the decline in plasma esketamine concentrations was biphasic, with rapid decline for the initial 2–4 h and a mean terminal half-life that ranged from 7 to 12 h. The elimination of the major metabolite, noresketamine, from plasma is slower than esketamine.

Analysis

Specimen Pretreatment

An examination of the structure of the antidepressants indicates that they are organic bases with moderate pK_a and sufficient lipophilic character to make them amenable to a variety of extraction techniques. Although single-step liquid–liquid extractions have been used with success, double or back extractions are more common in forensic toxicology *for gas chromatographic procedures*. One common procedure uses chlorobutane as the extraction solvent and is prototypical of those schemes that use back extraction. Common modifications to this procedure include addition of polar compounds to the extraction solvent and substitution of heptane/isoamyl alcohol or other nonchlorinated solvent mixtures for chlorobutane. Solid-phase extraction is also widely utilized for this class of drug and can be adapted for use with a variety of biological specimens. Specimen preparation is discussed in more detail in Chap. 9.

Chromatographic Separation

Gas chromatography (GC) is widely used for separating antidepressants in biological specimens. Columns are typically fused silica capillary columns with bonded nonpolar to intermediate polarity methyl silicone liquid phases (0–50% phenyl); usual column dimensions are as follows—length 10–30 m, internal diameter 0.20–0.53 mm, and film thickness 0.25–1.5 μm. Most of the antidepressants can be detected in routine temperature programmed analyses.

Table 27.2 presents the relative retention times (relative to amitriptyline) of the common antidepressants on a 5% phenyl-methyl silicone column. The retention time of amitriptyline under these con-

Table 27.2 Relative retention time (RRT) of antidepressants

RRT	Compound
0.43	Bupropion
0.52	Erythrobupropion
0.53	Threoaminobupropion
0.55	m-CPP
0.65	Hydroxybupropion
0.67	Norfluoxetine
0.69	Fluoxetine
0.70	Fluvoxamine
0.89	Venlafaxine
0.92	N-desmethylvenlafaxine
0.95	O-desmethylvenlafaxine
1.00	Amitriptyline (RT = 10.25 min)
1.01	cis-Doxepin
1.02	Imipramine
1.02	Nortriptyline
1.03	Trimipramine
1.03	trans-Doxepin
1.04	Mirtazapine
1.04	Desipramine
1.05	Protriptyline
1.05	Nordoxepin
1.13	Desmethylsertraline
1.14	Sertraline
1.14	Citalopram
1.14	Clomipramine
1.15	Desmethylcitalopram
1.16	Desmethylclomipramine
1.20	Duloxetine
1.30	Paroxetine
1.85	Trazodone
2.67	Nefazodone

ditions is 10.25 min. The detection of trazodone and especially nefazodone requires a high elution temperature and may persuade some analysts to use an alternate technique to detect these analytes.

One does not usually encounter chromatographic difficulties with the antidepressant drugs in overdose quantities. However, with low concentrations or in certain chromatographic systems, the secondary amines or hydroxylated metabolites may have asymmetrical peak shapes. This can be overcome by preparing acyl, fluoracyl, or silane derivatives. The use of derivatives may also allow the separation of closely eluting pairs of antidepressants or other drugs. Derivatization is discussed in more detail in Chap. 12.

Liquid chromatography (LC)-based separations are also an attractive separation technique for the analysis of antidepressants due to the polarity of the secondary amines and hydroxy metabolites. LC/MS/MS is widely utilized, does not require derivatization, and offers excellent sensitivity. For trazodone and nefazodone and their metabolites, methods are available that obviate the problems associated with their analysis by GC. Numerous stationary and mobile phases have been described for the various classes of antidepressants. Some antidepressants are not readily amenable to analysis by gas chromatography; therefore, LC-based methods are gaining popularity. Chromatographic separations and mass spectrometry are discussed in more detail in Chaps. 11 and 14. It should be noted that many chromatographic methods do not separate stereoisomers of antidepressants.

Toxicity and Postmortem Findings

The subject of antidepressant toxicity is evolving. New compounds are being introduced at a rapid rate. As a group, the newer drugs exhibit less inherent toxicity than do their predecessors; however, many have properties that can lead to toxic or fatal drug–drug interactions. The ability of many antidepressants to affect hepatic metabolism is an important factor in understanding the potential toxicity of this class of therapeutic agents. These concepts figure significantly in the following discussion.

The TCAs are compounds with well-known toxicity. They are among the leading causes of drug-related deaths throughout the world. There is no evidence of significant differences in toxicity among the TCAs. Amoxapine and maprotiline are so similar to TCAs in their toxicity that they are included in this discussion. The major toxicity associated with overdose of these compounds is due to anticholinergic effects, central nervous system effects, and cardiovascular effects. Effects include flushing, mydriasis, delirium, confusion, lethargy, fever, seizures, tachycardia, coma, and, most important, cardiac arrhythmia. Hypertension can occur early in the toxicity due to an anticholinergic effect; hypotension, probably due in part to alpha-adrenergic blockade, can also occur and can be a major contributor to morbidity. Seizures and cardiac arrhythmias are the most likely conditions to cause death in TCA overdose. Although any type of arrhythmia may be observed, the prolongation of the QRS interval in the electrocardiogram is often a diagnostic tool in overdose by TCAs. In the living patient, concentrations of TCA and active metabolite above 0.45 mg/L have been associated with toxicity. Concentrations of TCAs and their active metabolite in excess of 1.0 mg/L are often associated with life-threatening toxicity. In contrast, concentrations in postmortem blood are often much higher.

In postmortem specimens, the interpretation of postmortem blood concentrations is not as simple as applying the concentrations in Table 27.1 to the postmortem blood. Blood concentrations in postmortem specimens are much higher than expected from clinical data and in comparison to concentrations in specimens taken near or at the time of death. This is a result of the well-established concept of postmortem redistribution. The premise of postmortem redistribution is that drug concentrations are not static after death; they tend to rise, especially for basic drugs with high volumes of distribution. It is common for TCA blood concentrations to rise by a factor of 2–8 during the postmortem interval from death to specimen collection. Typically, concentrations of TCAs rise faster and to higher concentrations in blood specimens from the central cavity as compared to more peripheral sites.

Several implications of this are obvious. The exact dose taken by an individual cannot be estimated by a pharmacokinetic calculation that depends on the concentration measured in a postmortem blood specimen, especially if obtained from the central cavity. Postmortem redistribution also plays a role in defining what constitutes a toxic concentration in postmortem specimens. A concentration of TCA plus metabolite of 1.0 mg/L in clinical specimens would be considered potentially toxic. The same concentration in postmortem specimens is often observed in cases where it is clear that the drugs played no role in the death. Postmortem blood concentrations of 2.0 mg/L are considered to be potentially toxic; however, in the absence of clear and convincing evidence of the role of a TCA in death, interpretations of concentrations in this range that are based solely upon the analysis of a blood specimen should be undertaken with extreme caution.

The analysis of peripheral blood specimens and tissues can often provide the necessary information to successfully interpret a case. A liver specimen is a most useful complement to blood specimens in the interpretation of TCA-related cases. In acute TCA overdose cases, the concentration of drug and metabolite is much higher in the liver than in the blood. Liver concentrations in cases related to TCA toxicity can be quite high and are typically greater than 35 mg/kg. The drug-to-metabolite ratio is typically greater than unity. In certain situations, toxic concentrations of TCAs, and especially their active metabolites, may arise from chronic dosing because of a genetic deficiency of metabolizing enzyme or because of enzyme inhibition by coadministered medications. If the TCA in question is a tertiary amine, and a high desmethyl metabolite-to-drug ratio is observed, the toxicologist should be alerted to the possibility of a chronic poisoning. For secondary amine TCAs and other compounds, which have no routinely detected metabolites, the problem is even more vexing. If the circumstances surrounding a death are not clear, it is imperative to consider all possibilities before the manner of death is determined. Enzyme inhibition will be addressed in more detail in the discussion of toxicity of the SSRIs.

Trazodone appears to be safer in overdose situations than TCAs. Symptoms observed after trazodone overdose include drowsiness, vomiting, respiratory arrest, seizures, and EKG changes. Most reported trazodone-related deaths have involved trazodone and other medications. The concentration of trazodone in reported fatal overdose cases has been 15–30 mg/L in blood and 50–80 mg/kg in liver. These blood values overlap with those reported for nonfatal outcomes; however, concentrations of this magnitude clearly indicate an overdose situation. Trazodone has been reported to be much less susceptible to postmortem redistribution than the TCAs. In contrast to therapeutic cases, significant amounts of trazodone may be detected in the urine in overdose cases.

Symptoms related to bupropion overdose include hallucinations, tachycardia, and seizures, with seizures being the most significant event. The concentrations of bupropion and metabolites in reported overdose cases have been in the ranges: bupropion, 4 mg/L or greater; hydroxybupropion, 3–5.1 mg/L; threoamino metabolite, 4.6–11.6 mg/L; and erythron-metabolite, <1 mg/L. For those cases in which liver values were reported, bupropion concentrations were 1–14 mg/kg. As mentioned previously, bupropion is unstable in biological specimens; this must be taken into account not only during the analysis but also in the interpretation of analytical results.

The SSRIs have become the most widely prescribed group of antidepressants. Their efficacy in treating other disorders such as obsessive-compulsive disorder and bulimia nervosa have added to their popularity. They exhibit fewer troublesome side effects and are better tolerated than the first-generation antidepressants. Moreover, they are safer in overdose situations, primarily because they do not demonstrate the cardiovascular toxicity associated with the TCAs. Unfortunately, their relative safety in overdoses compared to TCAs has led many to believe that there is little to no potential for a fatal outcome with these drugs. This is not the case. These drugs can cause serious toxicity, especially when taken with serotonin-enhancing drugs, and they can affect the metabolism and clearance of a variety of drugs.

All of the SSRIs exhibit similar toxicity. They have been noted to cause nausea, vomiting, mydriasis, tachycardia, tremor, seizures, and coma when taken in overdose. Serotonin syndrome, a potentially fatal condition caused by a sudden systemic excess of serotonin, has been reported after SSRI ingestion. Symptoms of serotonin syndrome include hyperthermia, diaphoresis, excitement or confusion, shivering, tremors, hypotension, and seizure. This condition can be caused by the ingestion of SSRIs alone but occurs more often when SSRIs are ingested with other drugs that have serotonergic-enhancing properties. Serotonin syndrome is commonly seen with MAOIs, but it has been reported to occur with TCAs, tramadol, administration of more than one SSRI, lithium, dextromethorphan, and others.

The development of serotonin syndrome is often delayed as much as 12 h after ingestion. The long half-life of some of the SSRIs, such as fluoxetine, makes the development of a serotonin syndrome possible for long periods after the drug is discontinued. Another major complication of all SSRIs is their effect on the hepatic cytochrome P450 (CYP) isoenzymes. These enzymes are involved in the metabolism of many drugs. The systems primarily involved in drug metabolism are CYP 1A2, 2C, 2D6, and 3A4. The most studied of the isoenzymes is CYP2D6. This isoenzyme exhibits polymorphism; a percentage of the population (5–10% for Caucasians, other races vary) lacks it entirely or has less than normal amounts. These individuals (poor metabolizers) are in contrast to those with normally functioning CYP2D6 (extensive metabolizers). When a compound inhibits CYP2D6, an extensive metabolizer can functionally become a poor metabolizer. The CYP2D6 isoenzyme catalyzes many important hydroxylation reactions, including hydroxylation of antidepressants, antipsychotics, analgesics, and cardiovascular drugs, among others. When CYP2D6 is inhibited, it can strongly affect the concentration and clearance of any drug dependent on it for metabolism. Clinically significant interactions arising from CYP2D6 inhibition have been reported for imipramine, methadone, alprazolam, and haloperidol, among others. The other isoenzymes primarily involved

in drug metabolism do not naturally exhibit polymorphism to the degree of CYP2D6, but they can be inhibited by drugs or drug metabolites. It is not necessary for a drug to be a substrate for an isoenzyme to cause inhibition. The SSRIs vary in the isoenzymes that they inhibit and in the magnitude of their inhibition. Pharmacogenomics is discussed in more detail in Chap. 36. However, it is now clear that significant drug–drug interactions can occur with the ingestion of SSRIs and these interactions may have significance in forensic toxicology.

There are more data in the literature about fluoxetine and norfluoxetine concentrations after self-poisoning than for the other SSRIs. In one clinical study of 87 patients who had taken overdose quantities of fluoxetine, serum concentrations, when measured, were 0.23–1.39 mg/L of total fluoxetine (fluoxetine + norfluoxetine); none of the 87 patients died. A postmortem case in which fluoxetine is the only ingested agent is rare, and only a few are found in the literature. In non-fluoxetine-related postmortem cases, the total fluoxetine concentration is typically less than 2 mg/L, with a fluoxetine/norfluoxetine ratio less than or near 1.0. Liver total fluoxetine in non-fluoxetine-related cases is typically less than 20–50 mg/kg, and the fluoxetine concentration is usually less than the norfluoxetine concentration. Fluoxetine exhibits considerable postmortem redistribution.

Sertraline concentrations averaged 0.25 mg/L in a series of nonfatal overdose cases. The concentration of sertraline in non-sertraline-related deaths is generally less than 0.8 mg/L in the blood and less than 20 mg/kg in the liver. Desmethylsertraline is generally less than 1.5 mg/L in the blood and less than 50 mg/kg in the liver; a majority of the liver values are expected to be less than 20 mg/kg. One unique aspect to therapeutic sertraline use is that very low or even non-detectable concentrations of parent drug and metabolite are found in urine specimens. This is contrasted to other antidepressants where urine concentrations usually exceed blood concentrations. Therefore, blood or bile specimens are better postmortem specimens to screen for the use of sertraline than is urine. In addition, several groups of investigators have reported a lack of significant differences in postmortem heart and femoral blood concentrations in sertraline cases.

Therapeutic use of paroxetine and citalopram is indicated when the postmortem heart blood concentration is <1.0 mg/L. Concentrations of these drugs in intoxication cases are generally several times higher than this. Like most other antidepressants, the liver concentration of these drugs is generally an order of magnitude higher than the blood concentration.

Of the third-generation antidepressants, venlafaxine has the most data concerning its toxicity. Overdose symptoms include tachycardia, convulsions, somnolence, and coma. The concentrations of venlafaxine in overdose deaths have varied widely. Concentrations of 6.6–89.7 mg/L have been reported for venlafaxine and 3.44–50 mg/L for O-desmethylvenlafaxine (ODV). The ratio of venlafaxine to ODV was not consistent in these cases.

Symptoms reported as a result of nefazodone overdose include nausea, vomiting, and somnolence. Because nefazodone inhibits the reuptake of 5-HT, serotonin syndrome can be produced by the coadministration of a MAOI or another serotonin-enhancing drug. Such reactions have been reported for nefazodone and paroxetine. Nefazodone is a weak inhibitor of CYP2D6 but is a potent inhibitor of CYP3A4. It has the potential to increase the concentration of drugs metabolized by this enzyme. Very little information is available concerning the concentration of nefazodone in overdose situations. No fatal cases have been reported in which nefazodone was thought to be sole cause of death.

Symptoms of mirtazapine toxicity include drowsiness, disorientation, tachycardia, and impaired memory. A number of postmortem studies involving mirtazapine indicate that blood concentrations <0.5 mg/L are associated with therapeutic use. Postmortem concentration in overdose cases were generally between 1.0 and 3.0 mg/L.

In cases where death was due was due to duloxetine and other drug(s), duloxetine concentrations ranged from 0.32 to 2.5 mg/L. Deaths due to duloxetine have occurred at concentrations of 6.1 and 7.5 mg/L.

Patients who accidently or intentionally consumed 40–75 mg of vortioxetine had increased rates of nausea, dizziness, abdominal discomfort, generalized pruritus (skin irritation), somnolence, and flushing. Little information is available concerning the toxicity of vortioxetine in overdose cases, especially in death cases.

Little is known about vilazodone concentrations in overdose situations. During clinical trials overdose with serotonin syndrome, lethargy, restlessness, hallucinations, and disorientation were noted. A concentration of 0.36 mg/L was observed in a pediatric patient who survived an overdose.

Milnacipran concentrations in two nonfatal overdose cases were 3.0 and 8.4 mg/L. Two deaths due to milnacipran had blood concentrations of 22 and 40 mg/L.

There have been no reported deaths due to esketamine. Deaths due to racemic ketamine have been reported from 1.8 to 27 mg/L. Esketamine is more potent than racemic ketamine.

Further Reading

Apter JT, Greenberg WM (1994) New drug development in psychiatry. J Clin Res Drug Dev 8:87–100

Balant-Gorgia AE, Balant LP (1992) Therapeutic drug monitoring of antidepressants. Clin Ther 14(4):612–614

Cole JO, Bodkin JA (1990) Antidepressant drug side effects. J Clin Psychiatry 51(suppl):21–26

Devane CL (1987) Monitoring cyclic antidepressants. Clin Lab Med 7(3):551–566

Devane CL (1994) Pharmacokinetics of the newer antidepressants: clinical relevance. Am J Med 97(6A):13S–23S

Duman RS, Heninger GR, Nestler EJ (1977) A molecular and cellular theory of depression. Arch Gen Psychiatry 54(7):597–606

Ereshefsky L, Riesenman C, Lam YWF (1996) Serotonin selective reuptake inhibitor drug interactions and the cytochrome P450 system. J Clin Psychiatry 57(suppl 8):17–25

Frazer A (1997) Pharmacology of antidepressants. J Clin Psychopharmacol 17(suppl 1):2S–8S

Furlanut M, Benetello P, Spina E (1993) Pharmacokinetic optimisation of tricyclic antidepressant therapy. Clin Pharmacokinet 24(4):301–318

Hebb JH, Caplan YH, Crooks CR, Mergner WJ (1982) Blood and tissue concentrations of tricyclic antidepressant drugs in postmortem cases: literature survey and a study of forty deaths. J Anal Toxicol 6:209–216

Hyman SE, Nestler EJ (1996) Initiation and adaptation: a paradigm for understanding psychotropic drug action. Am J Psychiatry 153(2):151–162

Jones GR, Pounder DJ (1987) Site dependence of drug concentrations in postmortem blood—a case study. J Anal Toxicol 11:184–190

Joron S, Rogert H (1994) Simultaneous determination of antidepressant drugs and metabolites by HPLC. Design and validation of a simple and reliable analytical procedure. Biomed Chromatogr 8(4):158–164

McIntyre IM, King CV, Skafidis S, Drummer OH (1993) Dual ultraviolet wavelength high-performance liquid chromatographic method for the forensic or clinical analysis of seventeen antidepressants and some selected metabolites. J Chromatogr 621(2):215–223

Nemeroff CB, Devane CL, Pollock BG (1996) Newer antidepressants and the cytochrome P450 system. Am J Psychiatry 153(3):311–320

O'Toole SM, Johnson DA (1997) Psychobiology and psychopharmacotherapy of unipolar major depression; a review. Arch Psychiatr Nurs 6:304–313

Owens MJ (1996) Molecular and cellular mechanisms of antidepressant drugs. Depress Anxiety 4:153–159

Preskorn SH (1997) Clinically relevant pharmacology of selective serotonin reuptake inhibitors. Clin Pharmacokinet 32(suppl 1):1–21

Preskorn SH (1993) Pharmacokinetics of antidepressants: why and how they are relevant to treatment. J Clin Psychiatry 54(suppl:14–34):55–56

Prouty RW, Anderson WH (1990) The forensic science implications of site and temporal influences on postmortem blood-drug concentrations. J Forensic Sci 35(2):243–270

Richelson E (1997) Pharmacokinetic drug interactions of new antidepressants: a review of the effects on the metabolism of other drugs. Mayo Clin Proc 72:835–847

Stahl SM (1998) Basic psychopharmacology of antidepressants, Part 1: antidepressants have seven distinct mechanisms of action. J Clin Psychiatry 59(suppl 4):5–14

Spina E, Santoro V, D'Arrigo C (2008) Clinically relevant pharmacokinetic drug interactions with second-generation antidepressants—a review. Clin Ther 30(7):1206–1227

Swanson JR, Jones GR, Krasselt W, Denmark LN, Ratti F (1997) Death of two subjects due to imipramine and desipramine metabolite accumulation during chronic therapy: a review of the literature and possible mechanisms. J Forensic Sci 42(2):335–339

Neuroleptics

28

James H. Nichols

Abstract

Neuroleptics are antipsychotic drugs that are used to treat schizophrenia and bipolar disorder. They are subdivided into "typical" and "atypical" drug classes, based on chemical structure and associated pharmacological properties. Typical neuroleptics include phenothiazines, thioxanthenes, butyrophenones, dihydroindoles, dibenzoxapines, diphenylbutylpiperidines, and benzamides. Atypical neuroleptics include clozapine, risperidone, ziprasidone, sertindole, and benzothiazepine derivatives. Typical neuroleptics are believed to have dopamine antagonism as their mechanism of action; clozapine and the other atypical antipsychotic drugs have a different mechanism of action that possibly involves dopamine receptors, the serotonin 5-HT$_2$ receptors, or both. Neuroleptics are extensively metabolized by various cytochrome P450 isozymes. These drugs produce both neurologic and non-neurologic side effects; the most severe toxic effects are the extrapyramidal effects that include dystonia, tardive dyskinesia, and akathisia. Plasma concentrations of neuroleptic agents do not correlate well with clinical signs and symptoms. The chemistry, pharmacology, analysis, and interpretation of these drugs in forensic toxicology investigations are discussed.

Keywords

Neuroleptics · Antipsychotics · Chemistry · Pharmacology · Interpretation

Introduction

There are many indications for antipsychotic medications. Originally used for the treatment of psychotic symptoms in schizophrenia, the use of antipsychotics has been expanded to include treatment of specific aspects of bipolar disorder and has been applied with varying degrees of success for the treatment of psychosis, regardless of cause. Of note, the US Food and Drug Administration (FDA) has not approved antipsychotics for dementia and should not be used in the withdrawing alcoholic. The focus of this chapter is antipsychotics for the treatment of schizophrenia.

Schizophrenia

The DSM 5 outlines the following criterion to make a diagnosis of schizophrenia.

J. H. Nichols (✉)
Vanderbilt University School of Medicine,
Nashville, TN, USA
e-mail: james.h.nichols@vumc.org

© Springer Nature Switzerland AG 2020
B. S. Levine, S. Kerrigan (eds.), *Principles of Forensic Toxicology*,
https://doi.org/10.1007/978-3-030-42917-1_28

Two or more of the following for at least a 1-month (or longer) period of time, and at least one of them must be 1, 2, or 3:

- Delusions
- Hallucinations
- Disorganized speech
- Grossly disorganized or catatonic behavior
- Negative symptoms

1. Impairment in one of the major areas of functioning for a significant period of time since the onset of the disturbance: work, interpersonal relations, or self-care.
2. Some signs of the disorder must last for a continuous period of at least 6 months. This 6-month period must include at least 1 month of symptoms (or less if treated) that meet criterion A (active phase symptoms) and may include periods of residual symptoms. During residual periods, only negative symptoms may be present.
3. Schizoaffective disorder and bipolar or depressive disorder with psychotic features have been ruled out.

The negative symptoms of schizophrenia include alogia (inability to speak), avolition (lack of will), anhedonia (absence of pleasure), and affective flattening (lack of emotional expression). In addition to these positive and negative symptoms, schizophrenia may also be associated with the impairment of cognition or mood and with social or occupational dysfunction (Table 28.1). Schizophrenia commonly has an early age of onset (15–25 years of age) with a peak age of onset of the first psychotic episode in the early to mid-twenties for males and late twenties for females and unfolds in a chronic, relapsing course. Although less than 1% of the population develops schizophrenia at some point in their lives, schizophrenia is the most frequently occurring chronic major mental illness in people under 65 years of age.

For many patients, psychiatric drugs offer a degree of stability that enables them to remain in relationships, participate in the workplace, or tolerate insight-oriented psychotherapy. Social factors and support systems also play a role in the rehabilitation of psychiatric patients.

Table 28.1 Clusters of symptoms in schizophrenia

Positive symptoms	Cognitive symptoms
Delusions	Attention-deficit disorder
Hallucinations	Memory
Disorganized speech	Executive functions (such
Catatonia	as abstractions)
Negative symptoms	**Mood symptoms**
Affective flattening	Dysphoria
Alogia	Suicidality
Avolition	Hopelessness
Anhedonia	
Social and occupational dysfunction	
Work	
Interpersonal relationships	
Self-care	

Chemistry of Neuroleptic (Antipsychotic) Drugs

Antipsychotic compounds are traditionally subdivided according to their chemical structure. In this classification scheme, conventional or typical antipsychotic drugs can be divided into seven different groups (Fig. 28.1):

1. Phenothiazines have a tricyclic aminophenothiazine molecule with different side chains joined at the nitrogen atom of the middle ring. These side chains may be aliphatic (e.g., in chlorpromazine), piperazine (e.g., in fluphenazine), or piperidine chains (as found in thioridazine).
2. Thioxanthenes, which are chemically and pharmacologically similar to phenothiazines, have a carbon atom substituted for the nitrogen atom in the middle ring. This class of typical antipsychotics can also possess piperazine or aliphatic side chains (as chlorprothixene and thiothixene do, respectively).
3. Dibenzoxazepines are derived from phenothiazine. The only available dibenzoxazepine in the United States is loxapine, which has a piperazine side chain. Loxapine is structurally similar to clozapine (Fig. 28.2) but has different pharmacokinetic properties.
4. Dihydroindoles are structurally related to serotonin, melatonin, and indole hallucino-

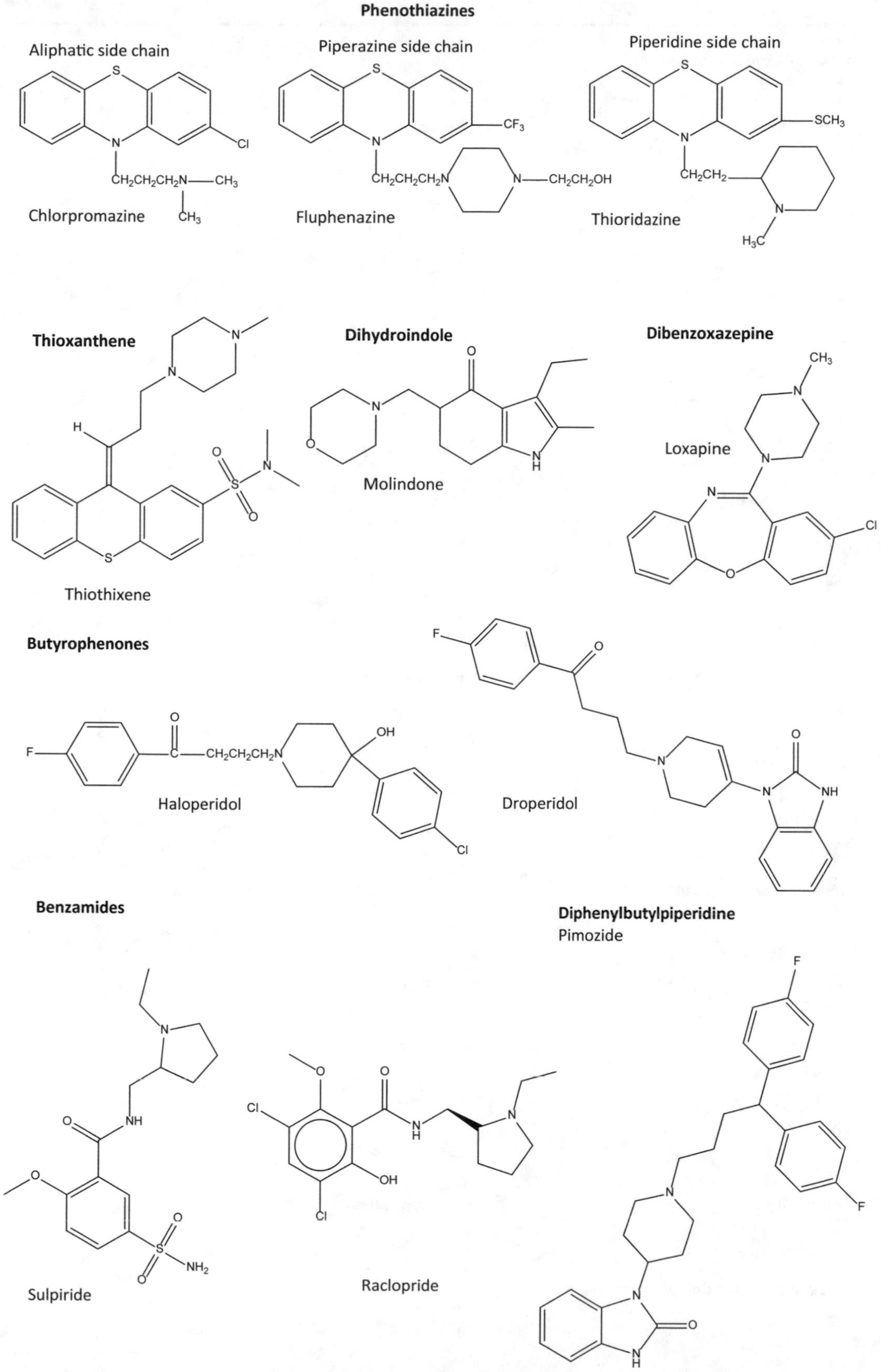

Fig. 28.1 Typical antipsychotic drugs

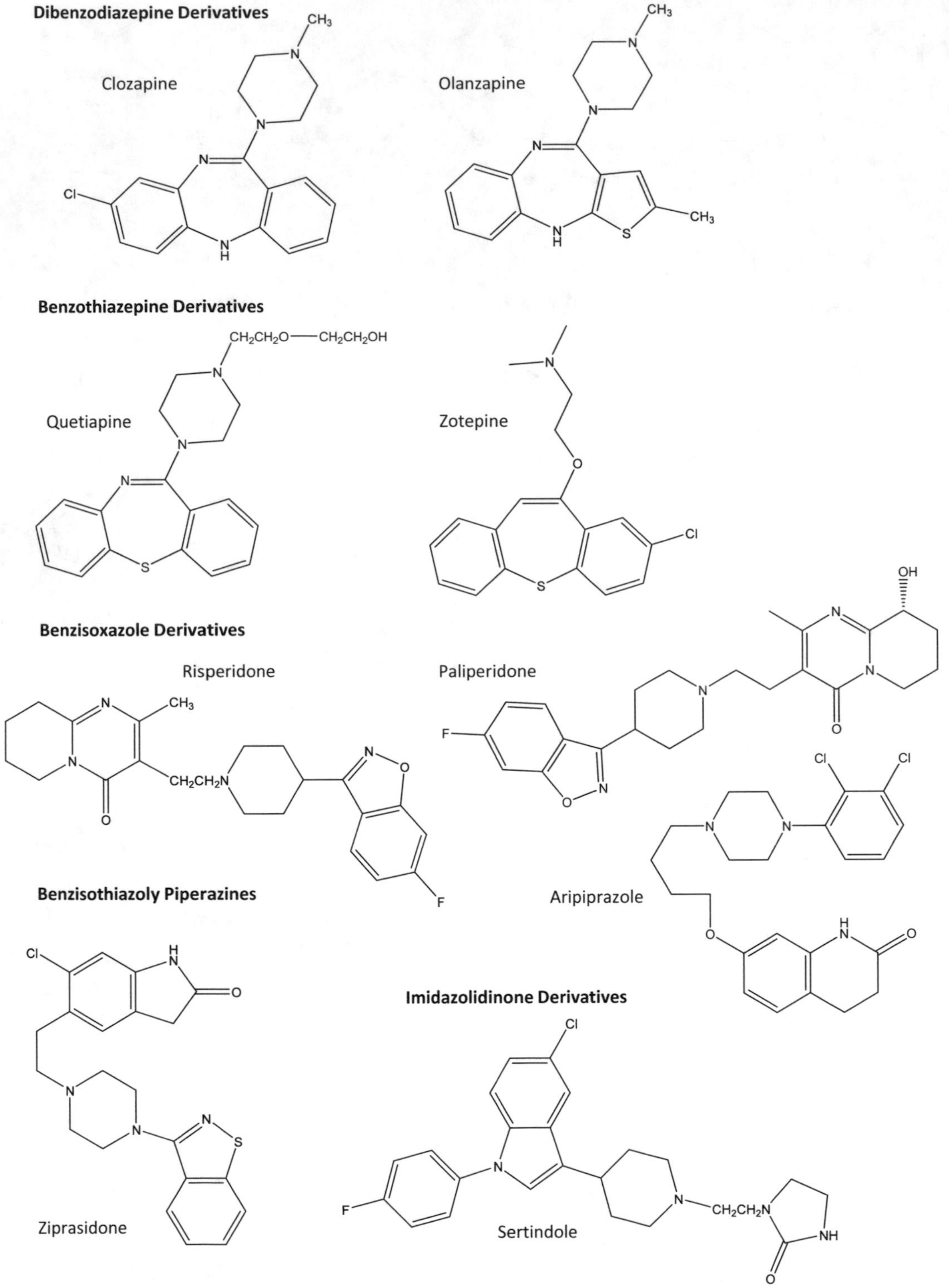

Fig. 28.2 Atypical antipsychotic drugs

gens. One member of this subgroup, molindone, has the unusual clinical property of not inducing weight gain and perhaps being less epileptogenic than other dopamine receptor antagonists.

5. Butyrophenones are derived from pethidine-type analgesics but lack their morphine-like activity. This group, containing haloperidol and droperidol, are potent dopamine receptor antagonists.

6. Diphenylbutylpiperidines are structurally similar to butyrophenones. The only available diphenylbutylpiperidine drug in the United States is pimozide.

7. Benzamides, as sulpiride and raclopride, are available in some countries outside of the United States.

The atypical antipsychotic drugs (Fig. 28.2) represent a chemically diverse group of drugs:

1. Clozapine is a dibenzodiazepine derivative. Olanzapine was derived from clozapine by substitution of a thieno ring for clozapine's carbonyl ring.

2. Benzothiazepine derivatives, including quetiapine and zotepine, make up a new chemical class of antipsychotic drugs. As a group, benzothiazepines are structurally related to dibenzodiazepine. Zotepine is a substituted dibenzothiepine tricyclic agent.

3. Risperidone belongs to another new chemical class of antipsychotic drugs, the benzisoxazole derivatives. Paliperidone is the primary active metabolite of risperidone, 9-hydroxyrisperidone. Aripiprazole is also a benzisoxazole derivative.

4. Ziprasidone is a benzisothiazolyl piperazine.

5. Sertindole is an imidazolidinone derivative.

Pharmacokinetics

It is beyond the scope of this chapter to completely discuss the pharmacokinetics of all antipsychotic agents. Rather, a number of drugs have been selected to illustrate aspects of the pharmacokinetics of this class of drugs.

Absorption and Distribution

The typical antipsychotic drugs discussed below include chlorpromazine, fluphenazine, thioridazine, and haloperidol:

- *Chlorpromazine* is readily absorbed from the gastrointestinal tract; however, its bioavailability varies, owing to considerable first-pass metabolism by the liver. Liquid concentrates may have greater bioavailability than tablets. Food does not appear to affect bioavailability consistently. Intramuscular (IM) administration bypasses much of the first-pass effect, and higher plasma concentrations are achieved. The onset of action usually occurs 15–30 min after IM administration and 30–60 min after oral administration. Rectally administered chlorpromazine usually takes longer to act than with oral administration. Chlorpromazine is highly bound to plasma proteins (>90%), principally albumin. It is not dialyzable. Distributed widely throughout the body, chlorpromazine crosses the blood–brain barrier and the placenta and is distributed into milk. The volume of distribution is about 20 L/kg.

- *Fluphenazine* is rapidly hydrolyzed by blood esterases with no attenuation of its antipsychotic action. Esterification of fluphenazine slows the rate of release of drug from fatty tissues. The onset of action for fluphenazine hydrochloride is about 1 h, while administration of fluphenazine decanoate has a delayed onset of action between 24 and 72 h after injection of a single dose, and the effects of the drug on psychotic symptoms become significant within 48–96 h. The primary metabolites are 7-hydroxyfluphenazine and conjugates.

- *Thioridazine* is rapidly and completely absorbed from the gastrointestinal tract. Maximum plasma concentrations are reached 2–4 h after ingestion. The average systemic bioavailability is approximately 60%. The relative distribution volume is about 10 L/kg, and binding to protein is high (>95%). Thioridazine crosses the placenta and passes into breast milk.

- *Haloperidol* is the most widely used butyrophenone. Peak plasma concentrations are reached within 2–6 h after oral administration and within 20 min after IM administration. It has a half-life of approximately 20 h.

Atypical antipsychotic drugs are all available for oral administration. All of the drugs, however, are incompletely absorbed after they are administered orally. Ziprasidone and aripiprazole are also available for parenteral administration and can be given IM in short-acting injections (e.g., in emergency rooms). This route of administration allows for attaining therapeutic plasma concentrations more rapidly and reliably than what is possible with oral administration. For all of the atypical antipsychotic drugs except sertindole, peak plasma concentrations are usually reached 1–5 h after oral administration. Sertindole's peak plasma concentration is reached 10 h after oral administration.

The atypical antipsychotic drugs have high binding affinity to plasma proteins (83–99% bound). Olanzapine, sertindole, and quetiapine have higher volumes of distribution than clozapine, risperidone, ziprasidone, and aripiprazole. Most of the atypical antipsychotic drugs have relatively high solubilities in lipids.

Elimination

The typical antipsychotic drugs addressed below include chlorpromazine, thioridazine, and haloperidol:

- *Chlorpromazine* is metabolized extensively, and at least 12 different metabolites are known. Less than 1% is excreted unchanged. Most metabolites are excreted in the urine as unconjugated or conjugated forms. The terminal half-life of chlorpromazine is approximately 30 h but is variable.
- *Thioridazine* is metabolized in the liver, and some of its metabolites (e.g., mesoridazine, sulforidazine) possess pharmacodynamic properties similar to those of the parent compound. Excretion is mainly via the feces (50%) but also occurs via the kidney (<4% as the unchanged drug, about 30% as metabo-

lites). The plasma elimination half-life is approximately 10 h.

- *Haloperidol* is extensively metabolized; the C-N bond is cleaved, leading to the production of two inactive acid metabolites. In addition, the ketone is reduced, forming reduced haloperidol, which possesses about one-fifth the activity of the parent drug.

Atypical antipsychotic agents are metabolized in the liver and reach steady-state plasma concentrations within 2–10 days. Isoenzymes of the cytochrome P-450 (CYP) system metabolize atypical agents. These enzymes are listed below and are summarized in Table 28.2.

- *Clozapine* appears in the urine or feces primarily (80%) as the N-desmethyl (norclozapine) and N-oxide metabolites. These metabolites have low pharmacologic activity and clear more quickly than the parent compound. Clozapine appears to be metabolized primarily by CYP1A2 and CYP3A4, with additional contributions by CYP2C19 and CYP2D6. In addition, clozapine may inhibit the activity of CYP2C9 and CYP2C19 and induce CYP1A, CYP2B, and CYP3A.

Table 28.2 Elimination of atypical antipsychotics by the cytochrome P-450 (CYP) system

Drug	Primary enzyme	Other contributors
Clozapine[a]	CYP1A2	CYP2C19
	CYP3A4	CYP2D6
Risperidone	CYP2D6	
Quetiapine	CYP3A4	
Olanzapine	CYP1A2	CYP2D6
		CYP2C19
Sertindole	CYP2D6	
	CYP3A	
Ziprasidone	CYP3A4	
	CYP1A2	
Zotepine	CYP3A2	CYP1A2
		CYP2D6
Aripiprazole	CYP3A4	
	CYP2D6	
Paliperidone	CYP3A4	
	CYP2D6	

[a]Clozapine inhibits CYP2C9 and CYP2C19. Clozapine induces CYP1A, CYP2B, and CYP3A

- *Risperidone* is extensively metabolized in the liver, producing 9-hydroxyrisperidone as the major active metabolite. Risperidone demonstrates metabolic changes consistent with the CYP2D6 polymorphism (there is a bimodal distribution of extensive and poor metabolizers). Because 9-hydroxyrisperidone is an active metabolite, CYP2D6 polymorphism may be of limited importance.
- *Quetiapine* is metabolized into approximately 20 inactive compounds, mainly by sulfoxidation and hydroxylation. CYP3A4 is believed to play an active role in quetiapine metabolism.
- *Olanzapine* is metabolized into multiple inactive compounds, mostly by N-glucuronidation, CYP1A2, and flavin-containing monooxygenase 3, with additional support by CYP2D6 and CYP2C19.
- *Sertindole* is metabolized by CYP2D6 into dehydrosertindole and by CYP3A into norsertindole. The pharmacologic activity of dehydrosertindole appears to be less than that of sertindole, possibly increasing the clinical significance of polymorphism and drug interactions at CYP2D6.
- *Ziprasidone* is metabolized primarily hepatically by aldehyde oxidase; less common pathways involve CYP3A4 and CYP1A2.
- *Zotepine* is primarily metabolized via N-demethylation by CYP3A2, producing the active metabolite norzotepine. Other minor metabolic pathways include formation of 2- and 3-hydroxyzotepine by CYP1A2 and CYP2D6, respectively.
- *Aripiprazole* is metabolized by CYP3A4 and CYP2D6 to its active metabolite, dehydroaripiprazole. N-dealkylation is catalyzed by CYP3A4.
- *Paliperidone* is also metabolized by CYP3A4 and CYP2D6.

The metabolism of atypical antipsychotic drugs can be affected by age (the elderly have decreased clearance of clozapine and olanzapine), sex (women have higher plasma concentrations of clozapine, risperidone, and sertindole), genetics (polymorphism at CYP2D6 and CYP2C19), ethnic differences, medical conditions, changes in binding proteins, and drugs that interfere with the metabolism. Inhibitors of CYP1A (furafylline, fluvoxamine) significantly increase the plasma concentrations of clozapine and olanzapine, whereas cigarette smoking induces CYP1A2 and significantly decreases the plasma concentrations of these drugs. Carbamazepine and phenytoin induce CYP3A and thereby increase the metabolism of sertindole and, to a lesser extent, clozapine and olanzapine. The inhibition of CYP3A by ketoconazole, erythromycin, and itraconazole significantly increases the plasma concentrations of clozapine and olanzapine. Ethanol decreases the plasma concentration of olanzapine by inducing CYP enzymes. CYP2D6 is induced by fluoxetine and inhibited by quinidine and paroxetine.

Mechanism of Action

The exact mechanism of action of antipsychotic drugs is not known. Typical antipsychotic drugs have been proposed to act primarily as dopamine receptor antagonists. This idea stems from studies that have shown that the ability of typical antipsychotic drugs to reduce psychotic symptoms is most closely correlated with the affinity of these drugs for dopamine D_2 receptors. The therapeutic actions of typical antipsychotic drugs are presumed to be in the limbic system, whereas extrapyramidal symptoms result from their action in the nigrostriatal region of the basal ganglia. Inhibition of the tubuloinfundibular tract is responsible for the endocrine effects of these drugs.

Clozapine and the other atypical antipsychotic drugs have a different mechanism of action that possibly involves other dopamine receptors, the serotonin 5-HT_2 receptors, or both. No single hypothesis can explain why a particular drug behaves as an atypical antipsychotic drug. In the case of clozapine, for example, three hypotheses have evolved to explain its potential mechanism of action.

The regional neuroanatomic specificity hypothesis postulates that clozapine's unique effects involve selective affinity for the anatomic regions that are pathologically involved in schizophrenia (the mesolimbic and mesocortical dopamine receptor neuronal system). Thus, clozapine alters dopamine receptor function where the disease is present but leaves other brain regions that dopaminergic neurons innervate (the nigrostriatal system in the basal ganglia and tuberoinfundibular system of the pituitary gland) relatively undisturbed. This pattern of action would account for clozapine's lack of unwanted side effects, such as extrapyramidal effects, galactorrhea (spontaneous flow of milk from the nipple), and oligomenorrhea (abnormal menstrual flow).

A second hypothesis postulates that the novel effects of clozapine are produced by the combined effects of the drug on the dopaminergic system and one or more additional neurotransmitter systems (including the serotoninergic, adrenergic, cholinergic, and glutaminergic systems) or on specific behaviorally active neuropeptides. Supporters of the second hypothesis put the greatest emphasis on the actions of clozapine on the serotoninergic system.

The third hypothesis postulates that clozapine exerts its effects by its selective affinity for specific dopaminergic receptor subtypes. Specifically, the hypothesis refers to the actions of clozapine on the dopamine D_1 and dopamine D_4 receptor subtypes, individually or in combination with its dopamine D_2 affinity.

At the present time, the individual significance of these three hypotheses remains unclear. Despite this uncertainty, it can be generally stated that the antipsychotic efficacy of clozapine is due to its central dopamine D_2 activity or a combination of dopamine D_1 and D_2 receptor antagonism with supplementary serotonin 5-HT$_2$ receptor antagonism and potent blockade of serotoninergic, adrenergic, and cholinergic receptors.

Like clozapine, the effects of many of the atypical antipsychotic agents can be explained by using one or a combination of the three hypotheses. Aripiprazole is different from the other atypical antipsychotics, however, because it is a partial agonist at the dopamine D_2 and serotonin 5-HT$_{1a}$ receptors and also shows serotonin 5-HT$_2$ receptor antagonism.

Adverse Reactions

The adverse effects associated with the treatment of schizophrenia vary from mild to life-threatening. They are one of the major reasons for the constant search for new, better antipsychotic drugs. In general, the adverse effects of typical antipsychotic drugs are primarily non-neurologic in low doses and neurologic in high doses. Atypical antipsychotic drugs have a low risk of causing serious neurologic side effects; however, they may cause some serious non-neurologic adverse reactions. The non-neurologic and neurologic side effects are discussed below.

Non-neurologic Side Effects

1. Cardiac effects. Low-potency typical antipsychotic drugs are more cardiotoxic than are high-potency drugs. Chlorpromazine prolongs QT and PR intervals, blunts T waves, and depresses the ST segment. Thioridazine, on the other hand, has marked effects on T waves and is associated with malignant arrhythmias, such as torsade de pointes. Prolonged QT intervals >0.44 milliseconds may lead to sudden death, possibly secondary to ventricular tachycardia or ventricular fibrillation. Among the atypical antipsychotic drugs, sertindole and ziprasidone have shown some prolongation of the QT interval. Patients on these drugs must have frequent electrocardiography examinations.

2. Orthostatic (postural) hypotension. Orthostatic hypotension is mediated by adrenergic blockade. It is most common with chlorpromazine, thioridazine, chlorprothixene, clozapine, and olanzapine. Orthostatic hypotension occurs within the first few days of treatment, and tolerance to its adverse effects rapidly develops. The major danger of orthostatic hypotension is injuries. The patient's blood pressure should be monitored (lying and standing) before and after the first dose and during the first few days of treatment. Patients should avoid caffeine, drink ≥2 L of fluid per day, and add salt

to their food, unless they are already hypertensive. They should be instructed on how to manage possible orthostatic hypotensive attacks.

3. Hematologic effects. A transient leukopenia is the most common hematologic problem. A more serious drop of leukocyte counts, agranulocytosis, is observed with chlorpromazine, thioridazine, and clozapine. Agranulocytosis (marked leukopenia and neutropenia) is a major drawback of clozapine treatment. It occurs in 1–2% of patients, usually within the first 6 months of treatment. Several fatalities have been attributed to agranulocytosis; however, the death rate is decreasing significantly, likely because of improved recognition, management, and treatment. The incidence of agranulocytosis is associated with an older age and female sex. Ashkenazi Jews with a specific human leukocyte antigen haplotype (B38, DR4, DQW3) appear to be at increased risk. The pathophysiology underlying clozapine-induced agranulocytosis has not been fully elucidated, but genetic factors, dose-related factors, and immunologic components may play a role. The frequent monitoring of blood counts made necessary by the risk of agranulocytosis increases the cost of treatment, reduces patient acceptance, and excludes from treatment significant numbers of patients who cannot tolerate the medication.

4. Peripheral anticholinergic effects. Anticholinergic effects of both the typical and atypical drugs usually cause dry mouth and nose, blurred vision, constipation, urinary retention, mydriasis, nausea, and vomiting.

5. Endocrine effects. Blockade of dopamine receptors in the tubuloinfundibular tract may cause increased secretion of prolactin, thus leading to breast enlargement, galactorrhea, impotence in men, and inhibited orgasm in women. The vast majority of atypical antipsychotic drugs do not produce these disturbances.

6. Other side effects. Other non-neurologic side effects involve weight gain, jaundice, and dermatologic and ophthalmologic effects.

Neurologic Side Effects

The neurologic side effects are the most serious side effects associated with the typical antipsychotic drugs. This drawback contrasts with the benefits of the atypical antipsychotic agents that lack these side effects. Neurologic side effects generally correlate with the potency of the antipsychotic agent. High-potency agents (those with higher affinity for dopamine D_2 postsynaptic receptors) are usually associated with extrapyramidal effects, Parkinsonism, neuroleptic malignant syndrome, epileptogenic effects, sedation, and central anticholinergic effects. The first three effects mentioned above will be discussed in greater detail.

1. Extrapyramidal effects. These effects include dystonia, tardive dyskinesia, and akathisia side effects.

   Dystonia. Acute dystonic reactions involve involuntary muscle contraction, especially of the head and neck. These reactions usually occur within hours to days after initiation of treatment or an increase in dose. They occur in as many as 10% of the patients treated with typical antipsychotic drugs, with young males being at greater risk for developing this syndrome. Dystonic movements result from a slow, sustained muscular contraction or spasm that can lead to involuntary movement. The symptoms can be episodic, lasting from minutes to hours, and may involve trismus (lockjaw), dystonia of the tongue, dystonia of the neck (typically arching the neck backwards), and oculogyric crisis in which extraocular muscles fix in the gaze position. Fortunately, the potentially fatal involvement of respiratory muscles is rare. Partial prophylaxis against acute dystonic reaction is achieved by the use of an anticholinergic agent with the initiation of a high-potency neuroleptic. Treatment of acute dystonic reactions consists of the administration of benztropine (1–2 mg intramuscularly), diphenhydramine (50 mg intramuscularly), or diazepam (5 mg by slow intravenous injection).

Tardive dyskinesia. A late-developing extrapyramidal effect of neuroleptic therapy, tardive dyskinesia causes abnormal, involuntary, and irregular choreoathetoid muscle movements. The most common movements affected are perioral movements. The risk of tardive dyskinesia is greater in women, in patients older than 50 years, and in those with affective illness or brain injury. Management of tardive dyskinesia may include discontinuation of the neuroleptic drug, and this discontinuation may cause a transient worsening of the movements of tardive dyskinesia. Tardive dyskinesia may appear late in treatment with antipsychotic medication and is treated with the anticholinergic effects of benzodiazepines.

Akathisia. This subjective feeling of muscular discomfort can cause patients to appear agitated, pace relentlessly, alternately sit and stand, and feel generally dysphoric. It may appear at any time of the treatment. Treatment of akathisia involves either reducing the dose of the antipsychotic drug or changing to a lower-potency drug, as well as pharmacologic intervention with a β-blocker (e.g., propranolol, 30–120 mg/day), a benzodiazepine (e.g., lorazepam, 0.5–1 mg three times a day), an anticholinergic agent (e.g., benztropine, 0.5–2 mg twice daily), or an α-adrenergic agonist (e.g., clonidine, 0.1 mg three times daily).

2. Parkinsonism. Parkinsonism, which is associated with high-potency antipsychotic medication and is dose related, usually appears within the first days to weeks after initiation of treatment. This effect occurs in approximately 15% of patients treated with dopamine receptor antagonist drugs (typical antipsychotic drugs) and is caused by the blockade of dopaminergic transmission in the nigrostriatal tract. Symptoms of Parkinsonism include muscle stiffness (lead pipe or cogwheel rigidity), pill rolling or coarse tremor, shuffling gait, stooped posture, drooling, mask-like faces, and akinesia. These effects are frequently seen in children receiving high-potency drugs. Women are more often affected than men. Management of Parkinsonism includes reducing the dose of the antipsychotic drug, changing to a lower-potency drug, administration of an anticholinergic drug (usually benztropine, 0.5–2 mg twice daily), and/or treatment with the dopamine agonist amantadine (100 mg, one to three times a day).

3. Neuroleptic malignant syndrome. This syndrome, the etiology of which is unknown, is the most toxic complication of neuroleptic use. It evolves over 24–72 h and presents with fluctuating levels of consciousness from agitation to stupor and autonomic dysregulation, including fever, increased heart rate, labile blood pressure, sweating, and muscle rigidity. Laboratory findings consist of leukocytosis, increased creatine kinase concentrations, and myoglobinuria. Neuroleptic malignant syndrome is seen more frequently in men and may occur at any age. The mortality rate is 10–25%. Treatment of the syndrome consists of immediate withdrawal of neuroleptic drugs in conjunction with supportive care, including hydration and cooling.

Mortality

In 2005, the FDA issued a public health advisory stating that elderly patients taking atypical antipsychotic drugs for the treatment of dementia-related psychosis are at an increased risk of death. A second warning issued in 2008 added typical antipsychotic drugs to this advisory. The current FDA warning claims an increased mortality risk for elderly patients taking typical or atypical antipsychotic drugs for the treatment of dementia-related psychosis.

The use of typical or atypical antipsychotic drugs for dementia-related psychosis is not FDA approved. It is recommended that healthcare professionals use other treatment options; however, no other medication options are available for dementia-related psychosis. The FDA warning does not apply to the use of antipsychotic drugs for other mental health diagnoses. In situations other than dementia-related psychosis, the mortality rate is typically higher in patients not taking any medications than in patients taking an antipsychotic drug. Five to 6% of people with schizophrenia die from suicide, and about 20% make suicide attempts on more than one occasion. Many more have suicidal thoughts, and suicidal behavior is often in response to hallucinations. Pharmacologic treatment of schizophrenia, despite the drug side effects, can reduce risk of injury from psychotic episodes.

Interpretation

In general, plasma concentrations of neuroleptic agents do not correlate well with clinical signs and symptoms. Therapeutic serum reference intervals have been established for many of the typical and atypical antipsychotic medications (Table 28.3). Therapeutic drug monitoring has been found to be appropriate in determining compliance with neuroleptic regimens, changing neuroleptic medications, documenting the concentration that is therapeutic in any given patient, and evaluating patients who exhibit signs of neuroleptic toxicity.

One problem in the interpretation of antipsychotic drug concentrations is the significant overlap between therapeutic and toxic drug concentrations. For instance, postmortem studies have reported blood thioridazine concentrations of 0.3–8.5 mg/L and blood chlorpromazine concentrations of 1–44 mg/L in fatalities directly related to the drugs. However, because most of the signs and symptoms of neuroleptic toxicity are clinical changes in electrocardiograms and extrapyramidal symptoms, it is very difficult to determine toxic overdose of neuroleptic drugs without antemortem clinical information.

Table 28.3 Therapeutic serum antipsychotic drug concentrations[a]

Drug name		Serum drug concentration, ng/mL	
		Therapeutic	Potentially toxic
Typical antipsychotic drugs			
	Haloperidol	5–20	>42
	Thioridazine	250–1250	NE
	Mesoridazine	150–1000	NE
	Chlorpromazine	30–300	750
	Thiothixene	10–30	NE
	Loxapine	5–30	NE
	Perphenazine	Low dose, 0.6–2.4	>12
		High dose, 5–30	
	Fluphenazine	Low dose, 0.5–2.0	NE
		High dose, 1–10	
Atypical antipsychotic drugs			
	Clozapine	350–600	>1500[b]
	Risperidone	20–60[b]	NE
	Quetiapine	70–170[c] (100–1000)[d]	>1000–1500
	Olanzapine	10–80	NE
	Ziprasidone	50–200	NE
	Aripiprazole	150–500	NE
	Paliperidone	20–60	NE

[a]Reference intervals obtained courtesy of ARUP Laboratories, Salt Lake City, UT; Laboratory Corporation of America, Burlington, NC; and MedTox Laboratories, St. Paul, MN
[b]Total parent and metabolites
[c]Predose trough
[d]Steady-state peak
NE, not established

Further Reading

American Psychiatric Association (2013) Diagnostic and statistical manual of mental disorders (DSM-5), 5th edn. American Psychiatric Association, Washington, DC

Andrès E, Maloisel F (2008) Idiosyncratic drug-induced agranulocytosis or acute neutropenia. Curr Opin Hematol 15:15–21

Baselt RC (2020) Disposition of toxic drugs and chemicals in man, 12th edn. Biomedical Publications, Seal Beach, CA

Brunton LL, Hilal-Dandan R, Knollman BC (2018) Goodman and Gilman's the pharmacological basis of therapeutics, 13th edn. McGraw-Hill, New York

Hoffman RS, Howland MA, Lewin NA, Nelson LS, Goldfrank LR (eds) (2015) Goldfrank's toxicologic emergencies, 10th edn. McGraw-Hill, New York

Klaassen CD (ed) (2013) Casarett & Doull's toxicology: The basic science of poisons, 8th edn. McGraw-Hill, New York

Pierre JM (2008) Deconstructing schizophrenia for DSM-V: Challenges for clinical research and research agendas. Clin Schizophr Relat Psychoses 2:166–174

Vuica M, Ross AE, Nichols JH (2000) Atypical antipsychotic drugs. AACC Ther Drug Monit Toxicol 22:66–75

Wetli CV, Mittleman RE, Rao VJ (1999) An atlas of forensic pathology. American Society of Clinical Pathologists Press, Chicago

Miscellaneous Therapeutic Drugs

29

Barry S. Levine

Abstract

This chapter discusses four classes of therapeutic drugs often encountered in forensic toxicology: antiepileptic drugs, antiarrhythmic drugs, antihistamines and non-narcotic analgesics. Seizures are classified based on three components: (1) where seizures begin in the brain, (2) level of awareness during a seizure, and (3) other features of seizures. The type of seizure determines which drug is appropriate for treatment; three generations of antiepileptic drugs are discussed. A cardiac arrhythmia is defined as the loss of rhythm in the heartbeat and may occur due to malfunctions in the initiation and/or propagation of the cardiac action potential. Antiarrhythmic drugs are classified according to their mechanism of action: sodium channel blockade, beta-adrenergic blockade, potassium channel blockade, and calcium channel blockade. Examples of each type of antiarrhythmic drug are provided. Histamine produces a number of physiological effects, the most prominent of which is an allergic response producing redness, swelling, and increased secretions. H_1 antagonists counteract this effect. Histamine also stimulates the secretion of acid, pepsin, and intrinsic factor in the stomach. H_2 antagonists counteract these effects of histamine. The final group of drugs discussed in this chapter are the non-narcotic analgesics and include aspirin, nonsteroidal anti-inflammatory agents, and acetaminophen.

Keywords

Antiepileptics · Antiarrhythmics · Antihistamines · Non-narcotic analgesics · Effects · Interpretation

Introduction

Therapeutic drug monitoring may be defined as the measurement of therapeutic drugs in biological specimens in an attempt to optimize the therapeutic and limit the toxic effects of the drug. The need to adjust dosage regimens according to patient response has been known for a long time. For many drug classes, these adjustments are made as a result of clinical measurements. For example, an individual with high blood pressure is treated with antihypertensive medication such as a diuretic, beta-blocker, or calcium channel blocker. To assess the effectiveness of this treatment, the patient's blood pressure is monitored. If the dosage regimen controls the blood pressure, then no changes in the treatment are

B. S. Levine (✉)
Office of the Chief Medical Examiner,
Baltimore, MD, USA
e-mail: blevine@som.umaryland.edu

© Springer Nature Switzerland AG 2020
B. S. Levine, S. Kerrigan (eds.), *Principles of Forensic Toxicology*,
https://doi.org/10.1007/978-3-030-42917-1_29

necessary; if an elevated blood pressure persists, then the treating physician modifies the therapy by increasing the dose of the prescribed drug, supplementing the drug treatment with another drug or changing the drug. The need to measure antihypertensive drugs is usually not necessary since the ultimate target of the treatment, blood pressure, can be measured.

Besides clinical measurements, drug efficacy can be monitored using clinical chemistry measurements. For instance, measuring prothrombin time may check the effectiveness of anticoagulant therapy with heparin or warfarin. Moreover, measuring serum glucose can monitor oral hyperglycemic treatment. Again, measuring the concentration of drugs in plasma would usually not be necessary.

The individualization of dosing is more difficult for drugs whose effects cannot be measured either with clinical measurements or with routine laboratory tests. For example, drugs used to prevent the onset of disease states, such as seizure disorders and cardiac arrhythmias, cannot be monitored in this way. Nevertheless, the need for optimizing treatment is still present. For these conditions, the best way to optimize drug therapy is to measure the amount of drug present in biological fluids such as serum or saliva.

Additionally, therapeutic drug monitoring may be necessary to confirm patient compliance, that is, to ensure that the patient is in fact taking the drug as prescribed. In general, a lack of compliance is not a major factor when the patient is suffering from the acute effects of an illness or a disease. However, once these symptoms dissipate and the patient is required to continue drug treatment for prophylaxis, the urgency in maintaining the prescribed dosing regimen is removed. Noncompliance may be easily detected by measuring the amount of drug in the blood; however, variable or intermittent compliance is more difficult to verify.

Assuming that the patient complies with the prescription regimen, there are other reasons why different individuals may have different blood concentrations of a drug despite taking the same dose. In Chap. 7, the pharmacokinetic factors of absorption, distribution, and elimination were discussed in great detail. Individual differences associated with all of these factors can account for differences in drug concentrations for a given dose. For example, bioavailability varies not only between individuals but between different dosage forms of the same drug. Drug forms that have increased bioavailability can lead to increased blood concentrations and, potentially, to toxic effects. Other pharmacokinetic factors that may contribute to different blood concentrations at a given dose include first-pass effect, plasma protein binding, and regional blood flow.

Differences in drug metabolism are another significant factor in the justification of therapeutic drug monitoring. A tremendous amount of work has been done documenting polymorphism in drug metabolism. For example, procainamide, an antiarrhythmic drug, is metabolized by acetylation to N-acetyl procainamide. There are genetically determined differences whereby some individuals are slow acetylators and other individuals are rapid acetylators. Therapeutic drug monitoring can be used to monitor both parent drug and active metabolite to ascertain the individual's phenotype.

Drug interactions also play a role in causing changes in the plasma concentration of certain drugs. A number of psychoactive drugs either inhibit or induce the cytochrome P450 metabolizing system. This can either increase or decrease drug concentration and lead to either toxic effects or reduced therapeutic efficacy, respectively.

In summary, drugs that are good candidates for therapeutic drug monitoring have some or all of the following characteristics:

1. Absence of clinical or laboratory measurements to evaluate efficacy. When possible, it is preferable to ascertain drug effectiveness by monitoring the desired effect. However, this is not desirable in disease states where drug treatment is intended for prophylaxis.
2. Poor correlation between dose and effect. If the dose could be correlated to the effect, then there would be no need to make plasma drug measurements.
3. Good correlation between plasma concentration and effect. Unless a range of plasma

concentrations has been established for drug efficacy, then measurement of drug concentrations would only be useful to identify noncompliance. A therapeutic range has been established for a large number of drugs. This range has two components: (a) a lower limit, which constitutes the minimum effective concentration for the drug, and (b) an upper limit, which represents the maximum safe concentration.

4. Narrow therapeutic index. The therapeutic index is defined as the ratio of the dose that causes toxic effects to the dose that produces the desired therapeutic effects. Drugs that have a high therapeutic index are relatively safe in that slight changes in drug concentration are unlikely to produce toxicity. These drugs do not ordinarily require therapeutic drug monitoring. Conversely, drugs with a narrow therapeutic index need therapeutic drug monitoring to make certain that the plasma concentration remains in the therapeutic range and out of the toxic range.

It is beyond the scope of this book to review all of the drugs for which therapeutic drug monitoring has become a recognized component in patient care. However, there are several classes of drugs that are routinely encountered in postmortem forensic toxicology laboratories. In general, it is the function of the postmortem forensic toxicology laboratory to measure these concentrations as it relates to one of the following:

1. Drug intoxication cases. Clearly, it is necessary to measure drug concentrations in the blood if a drug overdose or intoxication is indicated by investigation or by autopsy. All drugs will have toxicity associated with them if taken in excess. Even drugs not routinely monitored, such as antihypertensive agents, can require drug quantitation if an intoxication is suspected. The results for these drugs are usually interpreted in light of concentrations reported in the pharmacological literature following therapeutic administration.

2. Compliance issues. Issues related to patient compliance may also be important in postmortem cases. Individuals who committed suicide may not have been taking their prescribed medication. The measurement of antidepressants, even if unrelated to the cause of death, may be a significant component to the overall case investigation. In cases where anatomic findings related to a disease state may be limited, the failure of the patient to have an adequate amount of therapeutic drugs in the body may bolster the medical examiner's final assessment that the cause of death was due to that disease state. For instance in deaths caused by a seizure disorder, a specific site of seizure activity in the brain is often not identified. The absence of therapeutic concentrations of antiepileptic drugs supports the hypothesis that a fatal seizure had occurred.

This chapter will initially discuss two drug classes where therapeutic drug monitoring has been a component of patient care—the antiepileptic drugs and the antiarrhythmic drugs. This will be followed by a discussion of two drug classes where therapeutic drug monitoring has not been employed in patient care: antihistamine drugs and non-narcotic analgesic drugs.

Antiepileptic Drugs

A seizure is an abnormal, excessive firing of neurons in the gray matter of the brain. A seizure may cause violent, involuntary muscular contractions known as convulsions. Staring or subtle movements characterize nonconvulsive seizures, also known as absence seizures. The clinical manifestations of seizures depend on the usual function of the part of the brain where the abnormal activity is occurring. No single feature is characteristic of all forms of seizures.

Seizures may be due to natural abnormal activity in brain function. Epilepsy is a disease of the brain in which an individual experiences recurrent seizures. Seizures may also be a secondary manifestation of another disease process. Children may develop seizures as a result of a fever, referred to as febrile seizures. Alcoholics who are going through ethanol withdrawal may also develop seizures. Seizures may also develop as a result of injury to the brain. Treatment of seizures is usually based on the type of seizure experienced.

In 2017, the International League Against Epilepsy established new guidelines for the classification of seizures. This classification is based on three components: (1) where seizures begin in the brain, (2) level of awareness during a seizure, and (3) other features of seizures.

If a seizure starts on one side of the brain, it is called a *focal* seizure. This was called a partial seizure in earlier classifications. A *generalized* seizure initially involves both sides of the brain. If the site of origin is unknown, the seizures are classified as *unknown onset*. A seizure that begins on one side and spreads to both lobes is called a *focal to bilateral* seizure. Awareness in focal seizures can range from "aware" to "impaired awareness" to "unknown awareness." Generalized seizures will all affect an individual's awareness.

The other features of seizures are based on movement. A *focal motor seizure* will involve movement such as twitching and jerking or automatic movements such as licking the lips and rubbing the hands. A *focal non-motor seizure* includes changes in sensation, emotion, and thinking. Generalized seizures may also be classified as motor or non-motor. Subclassifications of generalized motor seizures include the following: (1) *tonic–clonic*, major convulsions, tonic spasms followed by clonic jerking; (2) *tonic*, loss of consciousness and notable autonomic manifestations; (3) *clonic*, rhythmic clonic contractions of all muscles; (4) *myoclonic*, isolated chronic jerks or *atonic*—loss of postural tone. Generalized non-motor seizures are also known as absence seizures and may be subdivided into typical, atypical, myoclonic, or eyelid myoclonia.

First-Generation Antiepileptic Drugs

The structures of the classical or first-generation antiepileptic drugs are given in Fig. 29.1.

Carbamazepine. Carbamazepine is one of the drugs used to treat generalized tonic–clonic and focal seizures. It inhibits sodium channels and exerts a stabilizing effect on excited membranes. Carbamazepine is metabolized to carbamazepine-10,11- epoxide; this metabolism is induced by the drug itself. Therefore, the plasma half-life decreases with chronic use. The therapeutic range is 6–12 mg/L. One significant toxic effect of the drug is aplastic anemia. As a result, blood counts are recommended while on drug therapy.

Ethosuximide. Ethosuximide is used to treat absence seizures; it is not effective in the treatment of motor seizures. The plasma half-life is approximately 2 days, which means that fluctuations in concentration across the dosing interval are small. The drug is metabolized in the liver to a hydroxylated product. The therapeutic range is 40–100 mg/L. The use of this drug has decreased with the advent of valproic acid.

Phenobarbital. Phenobarbital was the first drug used to treat seizures, dating back to the early years of the twentieth century. Although still in use, it has become a second choice to phenytoin or carbamazepine for use in treating patients with generalized seizures. It is also used as prophylaxis for febrile seizures. Its mechanism of action involves the reduction of the excitatory effects of glutamate and the lengthening in the inhibitory effects of gamma-aminobutyric acid (GABA). After oral administration, peak plasma concentrations do not occur until several hours after a dose. It distributes throughout the whole body water and has a long plasma half-life, approximately 4 days. When phenobarbital is used as an anticonvulsant drug, the therapeutic range is 15–40 mg/L.

Phenytoin. Phenytoin is used for the prevention and treatment of generalized tonic–clonic and focal seizures. It is ineffective against absence seizures. Phenytoin inhibits voltage-gated sodium channels and reduces the spiral of excitation from epileptic foci. It is slowly absorbed after oral administration, but its bioavailability is approximately 90%. The drug is approximately 90% bound to plasma proteins. It is metabolized in the liver by the cytochrome P450 system, but its metabolism is saturable. The main metabolic product is p-hydroxyphenyl phenylhydantoin (HPPH), which is inactive. The therapeutic range is 10–20 mg/L.

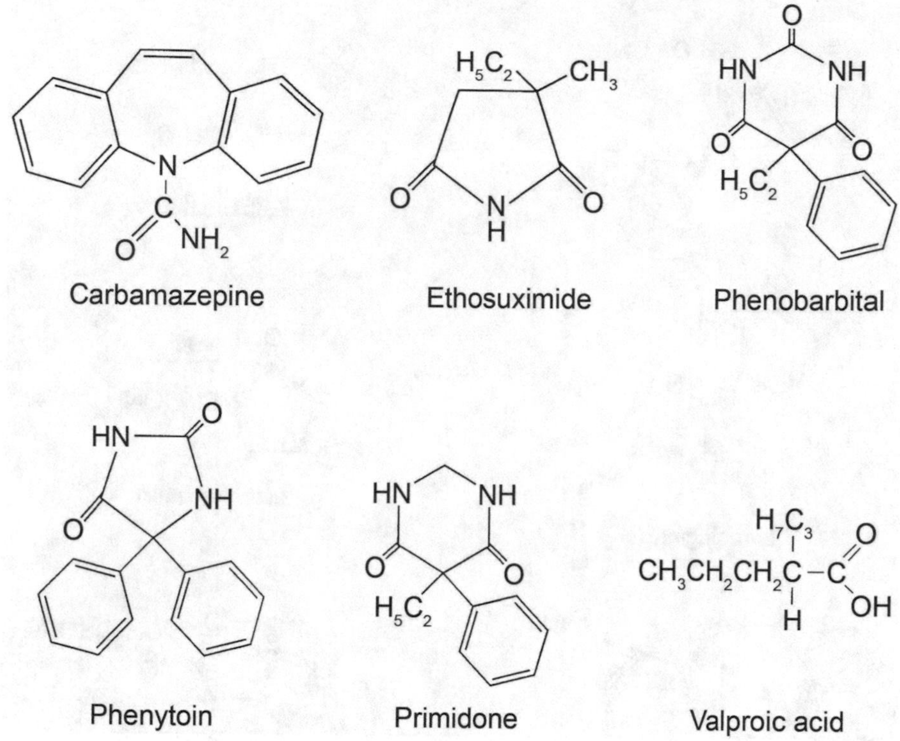

Fig. 29.1 Structures of classical anticonvulsant drugs

Primidone. Primidone is used to a number of types of seizures. Much of its pharmacologic activity is derived from its metabolism to two active metabolites, phenobarbital and phenyle-thylmalonamide (PEMA). Primidone has a much shorter plasma half-life than its metabolites: 6–8 h. Optimal therapeutic range for seizure control is 8–12 mg/L.

Valproic acid. Valproic acid has become the drug of choice for the treatment of myoclonic seizures and generalized absence seizures. It has also been used for the prevention of febrile seizures. The mechanism of action is believed to be involved with increasing the total brain concentration of GABA, either by increasing the synthesis or reducing the breakdown of this inhibitory neurotransmitter. Valproic acid is rapidly and completely absorbed after oral administration. It is highly protein-bound. A plasma half-life of 7–15 h accounts for widely fluctuating plasma concentrations. The therapeutic range is 50–100 mg/L.

Second-Generation Antiepileptic Drugs

The structures of the second-generation antiepileptic drugs are shown in Fig. 29.2.

Felbamate. Felbamate is structurally similar to meprobamate. It is used as adjunctive therapy and monotherapy to treat focal seizures with or without generalization in adults and as adjunctive therapy for the treatment of focal seizures, generalized seizures and Lennox–Gastaut syndrome in children. Its mechanism of action is related to its ability to raise the seizure threshold and to prevent the electrical spread of seizure activity in the brain. Felbamate is well absorbed orally. It is metabolized by the cytochrome P450 enzyme system in the liver, nevertheless, the parent drug is the major urinary metabolite. Following therapeutic usage, plasma concentrations in the range of 30–80 mg/L are observed.

Gabapentin. Gabapentin has structural similarities to GABA. Its mechanism of action is

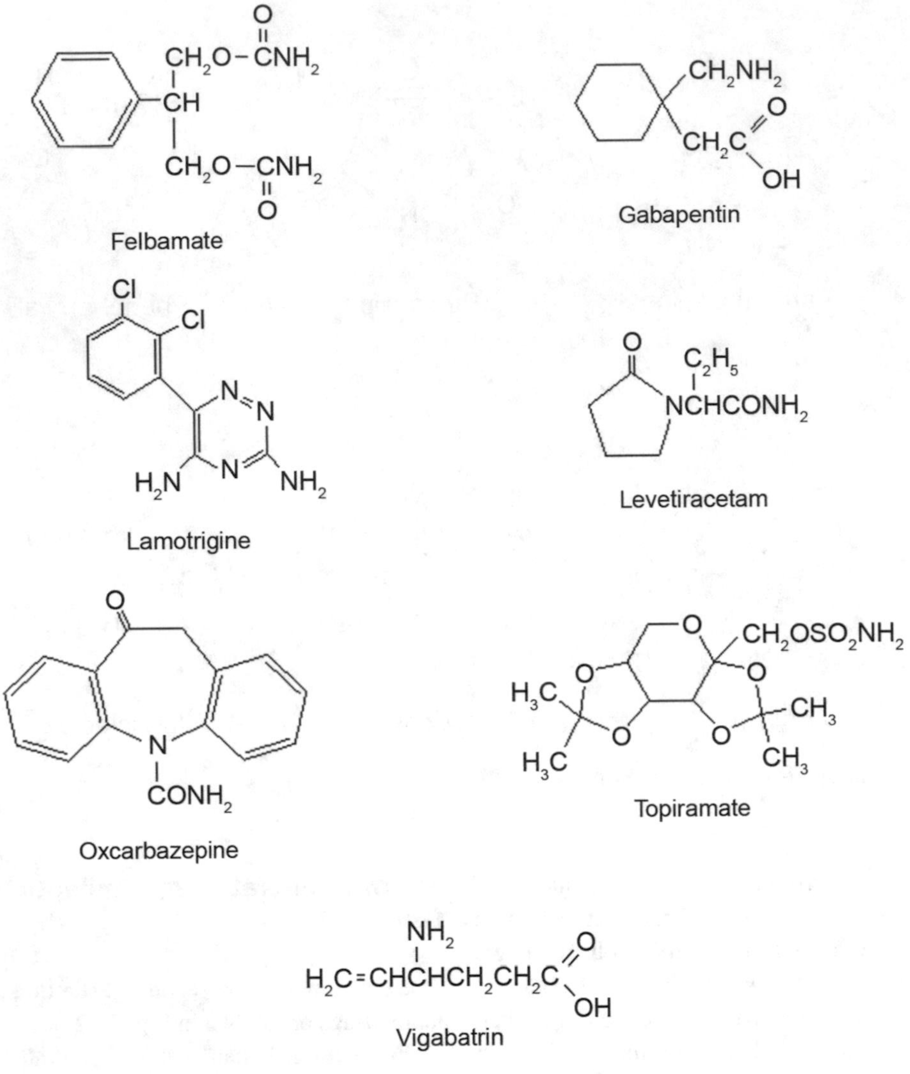

Fig. 29.2 Structures of second generation anticonvulsant drugs

believed to be related to an effect on GABA synthesis and release. It is used as adjunct therapy for partial seizures and for partial seizures with secondary generalization in patients not controlled by other antiepileptic drugs. It is absorbed orally with the assistance of an l-amino acid active transport system. It has a short elimination half-life, approximately 5–7 h. It is not metabolized to any great extent, with mostly parent drug appearing in the urine. The effective concentration is 2–20 mg/L.

Lamotrigine. Lamotrigine is used as adjunctive therapy for focal seizures and generalized tonic–clonic seizures that are not controlled with more commonly prescribed seizure medications. Good efficacy has also been demonstrated for patients with absence, atypical absence, myoclonic, and atonic seizures and for patients with Lennox–Gastaut syndrome. Lamotrigine has been used successfully to treat seizures in children. Its mechanism of action involves the inhibition of the release of excitatory amino acid neurotransmitters. Following oral ingestion, lamotrigine is rapidly and completely absorbed. It has an apparent volume of distribution of 1.2 L/kg. It is metabolized to a glucuronide conjugate and is excreted in the urine. Its plasma half-life is reduced by coadministration of phenytoin or carbamazepine while its plasma half-life is increased by coadministration of valproic acid. As a result, dosage regimens must be adjusted accordingly. The most common side effect associated with lamotrigine use is a rash. A therapeutic range of 3–15 mg/L is used; however, the need for therapeutic drug monitoring has not been established.

Levetiracetam. A pyrrolidine derivative, levetiracetam, exists as enantiomers; the S isomer is used as the anticonvulsant drug. It is used clinically to treat focal and secondarily generalized tonic–clonic seizures. It is excreted primarily as the unchanged drug. Plasma concentrations of 10–40 mg/L are seen following therapeutic use.

Oxcarbazepine. Oxcarbazepine is a keto analog of carbamazepine and functions as a prodrug. It is rapidly converted to a 10-monohydroxy derivative, which accounts for the drug's anticonvulsant activity. Oxcarbazepine is used to treat generalized tonic–clonic and focal seizures, either alone or in combination with other drugs. Its mechanism of action is similar to that of carbamazepine but causes less enzyme induction than carbamazepine. The plasma half-life of the parent drug is 1–3 h, whereas the plasma half-life of the active metabolite is 8–15 h. Following therapeutic use, serum concentrations of hydroxycarbazepine are in the range of 10–35 mg/L.

Pregabalin. Pregabalin is an analog of GABA and is structurally similar to gabapentin. Unlike other antiepileptic drugs, it is scheduled by the Drug Enforcement Agency as a Schedule V drug. Besides its use to treat seizures, it is also used to treat fibromyalgia and neuropathic pain. It undergoes little metabolism and 90% is excreted as unchanged drug. Its therapeutic range is 2–5 mg/L.

Topiramate. Topiramate is a naturally occurring monosaccharide derived from D-fructose. The precise mechanism of action is unknown but may be related to three factors: (1) blocking of sodium channels, (2) potentiation of GABA, or (3) blocking of a subtype of glutamate receptor. It is rapidly absorbed with peak plasma concentrations occurring approximately 2 h post-dose.

Topiramate is 13–17% plasma protein bound and distributes into the total body water. It is not extensively metabolized, with approximately 70% appearing in the urine as unchanged drug. After therapeutic use, concentrations ranging from 2 to 10 mg/L are observed.

Zonisamide. Zonisamide is used as adjunct therapy in adults with refractory focal seizures. It is metabolized by acetylation and by glucuronidation of a ring fusion product. Its therapeutic range is 10–40 mg/L.

Third-Generation Antiepileptic Drugs

The third generation of antiepileptic drugs began around 2008 with the approval of lacosamide. A number of drugs from this generation are discussed below. The structures of the third generation antiepileptic drugs are shown in Fig. 29.3.

Clobazam. Clobazam is a benzodiazepine approved for the treatment of patients with Lennox–Gastaut syndrome. Like other drugs in its class, it binds to the GABA-A receptor and potentiates the inhibitory activity of GABA. It is metabolized by demethylation to an active metabolite. The therapeutic range for clobazam is 0.03–0.3 mg/L, and the therapeutic range for desmethylclobazam is 0.3–3.0 mg/L.

Lacosamide. Lacosamide is used as adjunct therapy for the treatment of focal seizures but has also been approved as monotherapy. It acts by enhancing slow inactivation of voltage-gated sodium channels. It has a half-life of 10–15 h and is metabolized by O-demethylation to an inactive metabolite, designated SPM 12809. The therapeutic range is 1–10 mg/L.

Eslicarbazepine acetate. Like lacosamide, eslicarbazepine acetate was originally approved for adjunct therapy of focal seizures but subsequently gained approval as monotherapy. It competitively binds to the inactive state of voltage-gated sodium channels to inhibit neuronal firing. The prodrug undergoes hydrolysis to eslicarbazepine which is the active compound. It is further metabolized to oxcarbazepine and a diol. The therapeutic range of eslicarbazepine is 10–35 mg/L.

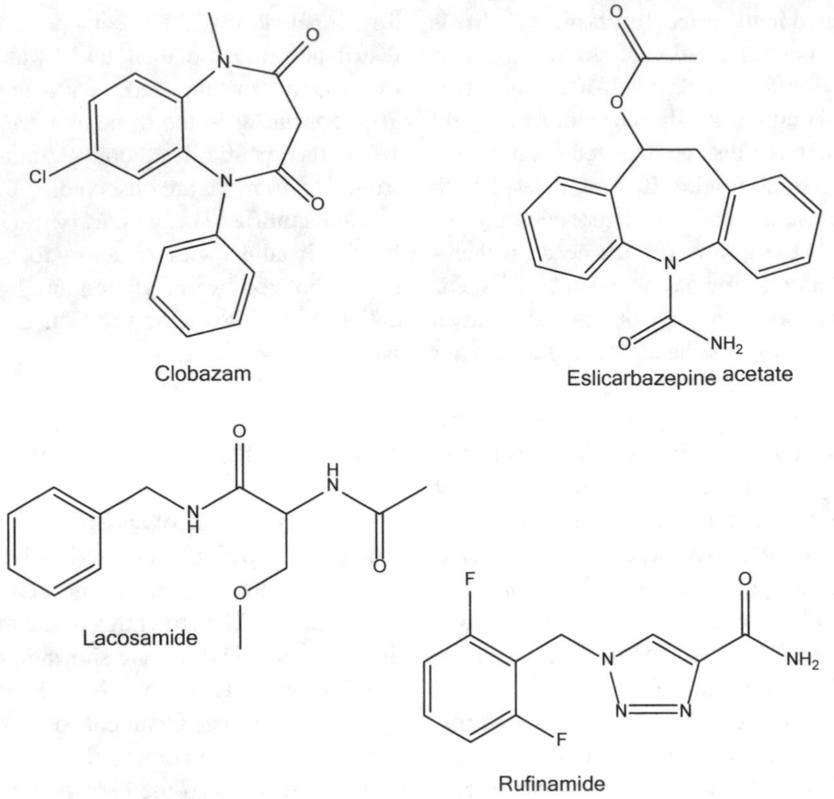

Fig. 29.3 Structures of third generation anticonvulsant drugs

Rufinamide. Rufinamide is used to treat Lennox–Gastaut syndrome in children above 4 years old and in adults. A unique aspect to the drug is that it is not metabolized by the CYP enzyme system, but instead, is hydrolyzed by carboxylesterases to the inactive CGP 47292. Its therapeutic range is 5–30 mg/L.

Vigabatrin. Vigabatrin is used to treat seizures not controlled by more common drugs. It is a structural analog of GABA, and its mechanism of action is to inhibit GABA transferase, the enzyme responsible for the metabolism of GABA. The drug exists as a racemic mixture with the S(+) isomer possessing the anticonvulsant activity. Metabolism is minimal and the major urinary product is unchanged drug.

Concentrations seen after therapeutic use range from 2 to 10 mg/L.

Anti-arrhythmic Drugs

Cardiac Function and Arrhythmias

The conduction system of the heart has two basic functions. One function is to produce an electrical signal that ultimately causes the heart muscle to contract on a regular basis. The sinoatrial (SA) node provides this signal and is known as the pacemaker site. The second function of the conduction system is to facilitate the orderly propagation of the electrical signal generated by this pacemaker throughout the cells of the heart. Once the electrical signal begins in the SA node, it spreads rapidly through the atrial muscle. The atrial conduction system transports the electrical signal toward the atrioventricular (A-V) node. From the A-V node, it arrives at the ventricular conduction system.

The basic cell that comprises the cardiac conduction system is an electromagnetic structure that depends on the movement of ions through channels to produce an electrical signal known as an action potential. This action potential is responsible for the mechanical function of the heart. There are five phases of the action potential in the ventricular myocardium:

- Phase 0: Sodium ions rapidly move inward, leading to a rise in intracellular voltage from −90 to 20 mV. The primary inward current in the SA and A-V nodes is the calcium ion.
- Phase 1: After a few milliseconds, potassium ions leave the cell, causing the membrane potential to become closer to 0 mV.
- Phase 2: The membrane potential remains at 0 mV and the cell is in the refractory state.
- Phase 3: A second rapid depolarization occurs and is caused by a maximal outward potassium flux and a minimal calcium flux.
- Phase 4: Once the resting potential of −90 mV is reached, there is a slow intracellular voltage drift in the positive direction.

Cardiac arrhythmia is defined as the loss of rhythm in the heartbeat. Arrhythmias may occur due to malfunctions in the initiation and/or propagation of the cardiac action potential. Causes of arrhythmias include ischemia, heart failure, metabolic abnormalities, or drugs. Cardiac arrhythmias are treated mechanically with pacemakers or defibsrillators or pharmacologically with antiarrhythmic drugs. These drugs can act in at least one of the following three ways:

- Increase the membrane potential threshold or slow the rate of diastolic depolarization.

- Decrease the inward sodium current at Phase 0.
- Prolong the effective refractory period.

Antiarrhythmic drugs are classified according to their mechanism of action:

1. Class I: Sodium channel blockade
   IA. Prolongs the action potential duration
   IB. Shortens the action potential duration
   IC. No effect on action potential duration
2. Class II: Beta-adrenergic blockade
3. Class III: Potassium channel blockade
4. Class IV: Calcium channel blockade

Drugs

The structures of the antiarrhythmic drugs are shown in Fig. 29.4.

Quinidine. Quinidine is the oldest drug still in use to treat arrhythmias. It is classified as a type IA drug; however, it also blocks potassium channels that prolong the action potential. It is administered orally with peak plasma concentrations occurring 1–5 h after ingestion, depending on the salt form. It is extensively metabolized by hydroxylation and N-oxide formation. Approximately 20% appears in urine as unchanged drug. The therapeutic range is 2–5 mg/L.

Procainamide. Procainamide is a type IA antiarrhythmic drug used in the treatment of ventricular and supraventricular arrhythmias. It may be administered orally, intramuscularly, or intravenously. It is metabolized by acetylation to N-acetylprocainamide (NAPA); NAPA has similar pharmacologic activity as the parent drug. The rate of acetylation is bimodal with patients being classified as slow or fast acetylators. The therapeutic range for procainamide is 4–10 mg/L; the therapeutic range for procainamide plus NAPA is 5–30 mg/L.

Disopyramide. Like procainamide, disopyramide is a type IA antiarrhythmic drug. It is used to treat ventricular and supraventricular tachycardia and suppression of premature depolarizations. Disopyramide is not used as often as quinidine or procainamide. Oral bioavailability is approximately 80% with peak

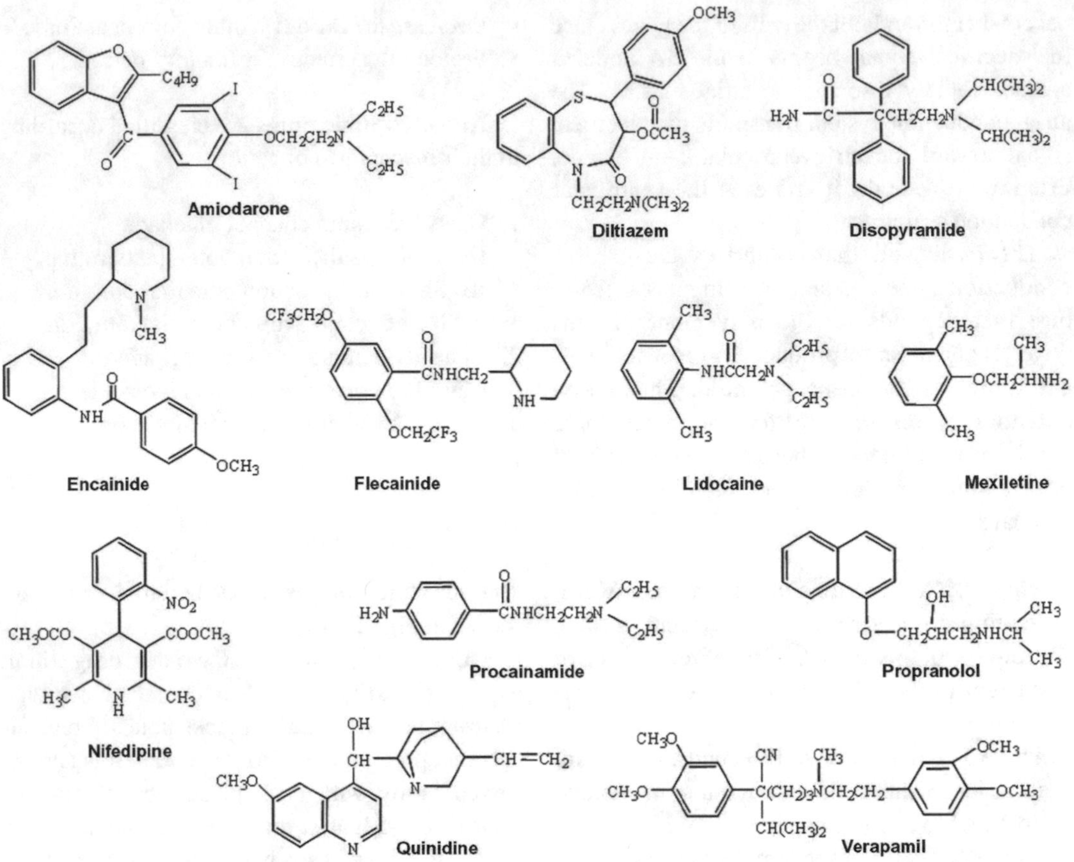

Fig. 29.4 Structures of antiarrhythmic drugs

plasma concentrations occurring at 2 h. It is metabolized by mono-N-dealkylation, forming nordisopyramide, which has about half of the cardiac activity as the parent drug. The therapeutic range for disopyramide is approximately 2–5 mg/L.

Lidocaine. Lidocaine is a class IB antiarrhythmic drug that shortens the action potential duration and refractoriness. In addition to its cardiac activity, lidocaine also acts as a local anesthetic. Lidocaine is one antiarrhythmic drug that is not administered orally because it has a significant first-pass effect and it also causes abdominal discomfort. Instead, lidocaine is administered intravenously for its antiarrhythmic activity and topically for its local anesthetic activity. This drug has two primary metabolites: monoethylglycinexylidide (MEGX) and glycinexylidide (GX). MEGX is eliminated hepatically with a

half-life of 2 h. GX is eliminated hepatically and renally with a half-life of 10 h. Less than 10% of a dose of lidocaine is recovered in the urine as unchanged drug. Lidocaine is the drug of choice for treating life-threatening ventricular arrhythmias and is often used in resuscitative efforts. The therapeutic range of lidocaine is 1–5 mg/L. Concentrations greater than 5 mg/L are associated with central nervous system toxicity, including coma, seizures, light-headedness, disorientation, and dizziness. Cardiac toxicity including heart block and increased ventricular rate may also be observed.

Mexiletine. Mexiletine is a class IB antiarrhythmic drug that is structurally similar to lidocaine and reduces the rate of the action potential. It may be administered orally, intramuscularly, or intravenously. It has a high volume of distribution (5–12 L/kg), suggesting tissue sequestration of the drug. It is extensively metabolized in the liver to inactive hydroxymethylmexiletine, p-hydroxymexiletine, and their respective alcohols. The therapeutic range is approximately 0.7–2.0 mg/L. Concentrations above 2 mg/L are associated with side effects such as tremor, ataxia, diplopia, drowsiness, nausea, and vomiting.

Flecainide. Flecainide is classified as a IC antiarrhythmic, a drug that blocks sodium and delayed rectifier potassium currents. It is well absorbed orally and is metabolized by CYP2D6 to m-O-desalkylflecainide, which is pharmacologically inactive. It is further metabolized by conjugation or lactam formation. The therapeutic range is 0.2–1.0 mg/L. The drug is prescribed when other antiarrhythmic drugs have been ineffective.

Propafenone. Propafenone is a class IC antiarrhythmic drug used to treat life-threatening supraventricular tachyarrhythmias and ventricular arrhythmias. Although administered orally, it has poor oral bioavailability. An intravenous formulation is also available. It is metabolized by hydroxylation and dealkylation to form 5-hydroxypropafenone and norpropafenone, respectively; both are active. Concentrations of propafenone in the range of 0.2–2.0 mg/L are seen when the drug is effective therapeutically.

Propranolol. Propranolol is a nonspecific, first-generation beta-adrenergic receptor blocker that is classified as a group II antiarrhythmic drug. In addition to this use, propranolol is used to treat hypertension and certain coronary artery diseases. Propranolol is completely absorbed after oral administration but undergoes significant first-pass metabolism. Approximately 80% of the dose is subjected to this effect. The drug, which is 90–95% plasma protein bound, has a plasma half-life of 4–6 h. It is metabolized by hydroxylation to 4-hydroxypropranolol, which is equipotent to the parent drug. The major urinary products are propranolol glucuronide and an oxidation product, naphthoxylactic acid. The therapeutic ranges for propranolol and 4-hydroxypropranolol are 0.05–0.1 mg/L and 0.005–0.03 mg/L, respectively.

Metoprolol. Metoprolol is a second-generation beta-blocker, with specific blockade of the β_1 receptors in the heart. As a result, it decreases contractility, heart rate, and conduction velocity. It is well absorbed orally and is metabolized to an active metabolite, α-hydroxymetoprolol. The major urinary product found after metoprolol use is formed by O-demethylation and oxidation. Following therapeutic use, metoprolol concentrations around 0.1 mg/L are observed.

Sotalol. Sotalol is both a Class II and Class III antiarrhythmic drug used to treat atrial flutter and fibrillation. It may be administered both orally and intravenously. It undergoes limited metabolism and is excreted primarily unchanged in the urine. Concentrations in the range of 1–6 mg/L are found after therapeutic usage.

Amiodarone. Amiodarone is a Class III antiarrhythmic drug that is approved for use in the treatment of life-threatening ventricular tachyarrhythmias. It is poorly absorbed from the gastrointestinal tract with bioavailability ranging from 31 to 65%. Peak serum concentrations are reached within 3–10 h. It is metabolized by deiodination, O-dealkylation, N-dealkylation, hydroxylation, and glucuronidation. Mono-N-desalkylamiodarone is the major metabolite. Amiodarone demonstrates an extremely long terminal half-life; different studies list this half-life anywhere from 26 to 107 days. An apparent therapeutic range of 0.5–2.5 mg/L has been offered for amiodarone. The use of amiodarone is restricted because of some potentially serious side effects, including alveolitis, pulmonary fibrosis, neuromuscular weakness, and tremor.

Verapamil. Verapamil is a derivative of phenylalkylamine and was the first calcium antagonist drug to receive a great deal of clinical use. It is approved for use in the prophylaxis of repetitive paroxysmal supraventricular tachycardia and the control of atrial flutter. A group IV antiarrhythmic drug, greater than 90% of a dose, is absorbed, but due to substantial first-pass metabolism, bioavailability is about 30%. Verapamil is metabolized by N-dealkylation to norverapamil; it is also metabolized by O-demethylation and oxidative cleavage of the C N C linkage. Of these metabolites, only norverapamil has pharmacologic activity (approximately 20% of parent). Following therapeutic use, plasma concentrations of verapamil are in the 0.1–0.3 mg/L range. Therapeutic drug monitoring of verapamil is not commonly performed.

Diltiazem. Diltiazem is a benzothiazepine structurally unrelated to other calcium channel blockers available in the United States. It is used to treat angina, supraventricular arrhythmias, and hypertension. Adult daily doses range from 60 to 420 mg. Diltiazem is deacetylated to a metabolite that is approximately one-half as potent as the parent drug as a vasodilator. It is also metabolized by N-demethylation and by O-demethylation; the N-desmethyl metabolite has about 20% of the activity of diltiazem. Steady-state plasma concentrations following therapeutic use are in the range of 0.1–0.3 mg/L.

Nifedipine. Nifedipine is a calcium channel blocker used to treat angina, hypertension, and arrhythmias. It is rapidly and almost completely absorbed after oral or sublingual administration. The plasma half-life is 2–6 h. It is extensively metabolized to inactive compounds; dehydronifedipinic acid is the major serum and urinary metabolite. Peak serum concentrations after oral ingestion of 10–60 mg are <0.3 mg/L.

Antihistamines

Histamine (Fig. 29.5) consists of an imidazole ring and a chain moiety consisting of a dimethylamino group. It is synthesized by the decarboxylation of the amino acid histidine through the enzymatic activity of L-histidine decarboxylase. Histamine is metabolized by two pathways; the final products are N-methylimidazoleacetic acid and imidazoleacetic acid riboside. It is stored in basophils in the blood and in mast cells in tissues.

Histamine produces a number of physiological effects, the most prominent of which is an immediate allergic response after it is released from storage through the involvement of immunoglobulin E. The allergic response includes redness,

Histamine

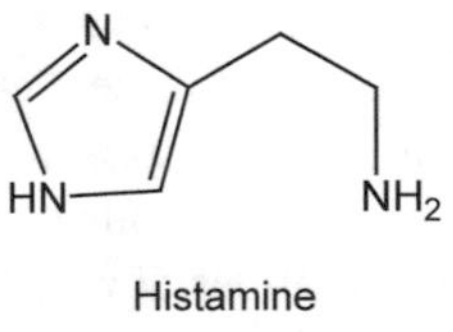

Fig. 29.5 Structure of histamine

swelling, and increased secretions. Histamine also stimulates the secretion of acid, pepsin, and intrinsic factor in the stomach. In the central nervous system, histamine acts as a neurotransmitter. This action may lead to increased wakefulness and decreased appetite, among other things. It also causes the contraction of smooth muscle cells in the lungs and the gastrointestinal tract but causes the relaxation of small blood vessels.

Four distinct histamine receptors have been classified. Therapeutic agents have been developed as antagonists to the H_1 and H_2 receptors, however, and the discussion in this chapter is limited to effects on these receptors. Bronchial constriction and gastrointestinal contraction are mediated through the H_1 receptor. Gastric secretions occur with the involvement of the H_2 receptor. Vasodilatation is mediated through both the H_1 and H_2 receptors. The edema associated with the allergic response is due primarily to interaction with the H_1 receptor. Activation of the H_2 receptor leads to increased contractile force of the heart and increased automaticity, but activation of the H_1 receptor leads to a decrease in atrioventricular velocity.

H_1 Antagonists

A number of different structures with H_1 antagonist activity have been developed. These compounds are subdivided into first-generation H_1 antagonists and second-generation H_1 antagonists. First-generation H_1 antagonists include the following (examples are in parentheses):

1. Alkylamines (brompheniramine, chlorpheniramine)
2. Ethanolamines (diphenhydramine, clemastine)
3. Ethylenediamines (pyrilamine, tripelennamine)
4. Phenothiazines (promethazine)
5. Piperidines (cyproheptadine)
6. Piperazines (cyclizine, hydroxyzine, meclizine)

Figure 29.6 illustrates structures of first-generation H_1 antagonists.

Second-generation H_1 antagonists include the following:

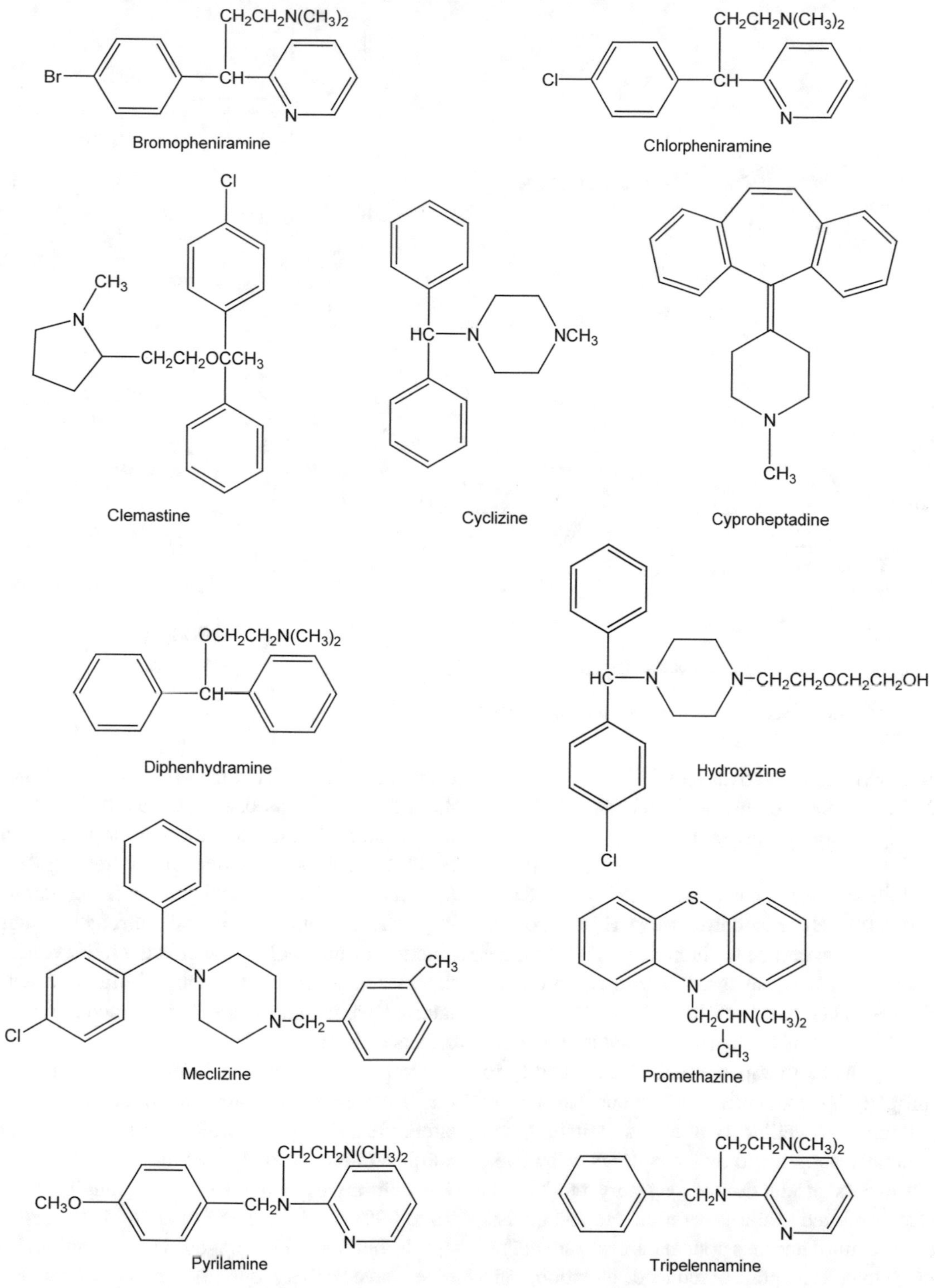

Fig. 29.6 Structures of first-generation H_1 antagonists

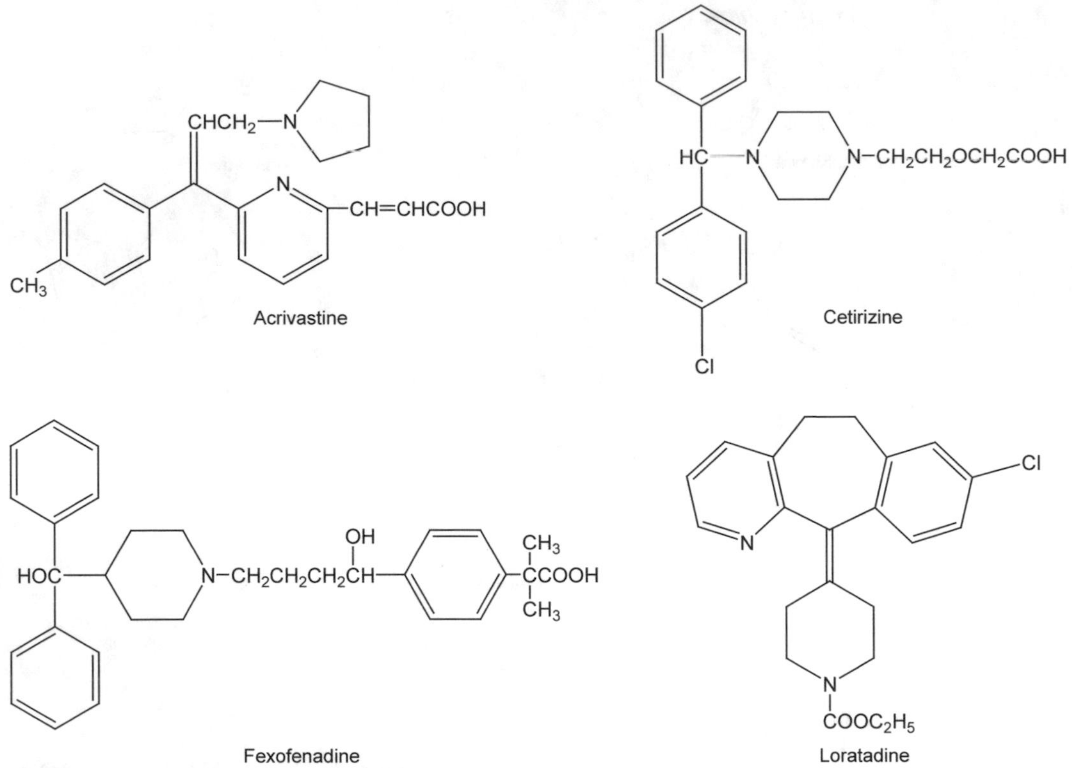

Fig. 29.7 Structures of second-generation H_1 antagonists

1. Alkylamines (acrivastine)
2. Piperidines (loratadine, fexofenadine)
3. Piperazines (cetirizine)

Figure 29.7 shows structures of second-generation H_1 antagonists. Most H_1 antagonists have the ethylamine chain moiety that histamine has, but most H_1 antagonists have two aromatic rings attached to this chain.

The effect of H_1 antagonists that accounts for their primary therapeutic use is their ability to mitigate hypersensitivity reactions caused by histamine. Swelling, redness, and itching are generally suppressed by these drugs. Moreover, the excess production of secretory products is also inhibited. First-generation H_1 antagonists cause central nervous system depression, including slowed response, reduced attention, and drowsiness. In fact, some of these drugs are marketed as over-the-counter sleep aids. Conversely, second-generation H_1 antagonists do not cross the blood–brain barrier and consequently do not cause drowsiness. This major advantage allows these drugs to be used without adversely affecting regular daytime activities. First-generation H_1 antagonists are also useful for treating vertigo, motion sickness, and postoperative vomiting. This effect occurs through their antimuscarinic cholinergic effects on the vestibular system and the brainstem. Within the vasculature, H_1 antagonists inhibit the vasoconstrictive effects of histamine.

Despite significant differences in structure, the H_1 antagonists share some pharmacokinetic similarities. They are well absorbed after oral administration, usually within several hours. They are highly bound to protein, ranging from 78 to 99%. Their duration of action is generally 4–6 h, but some H_1 antagonists, such as loratadine, have activity durations of approximately 24 h.

Many H_1 antagonists are extensively metabolized by the cytochrome P450 enzyme system. Table 29.1 shows the major metabolic products

Table 29.1 Metabolic products of selected H_1 antagonists

Drug	Metabolites
Chlorpheniramine	Norchlorpheniramine
	Dinorchlorpheniramine
Diphenhydramine	Nordiphenhydramine
	Dinordiphenhydramine
	Diphenylmethoxyacetic acid
Hydroxyzine	Norhydroxyzine
	Cetirizine
Loratadine	Descarboethoxyloratadine
Promethazine	Desmethylpromethazine
	Promethazine sulfoxide
Tripelennamine	4-Hydroxytripelennamine
	α-Hydroxytripelennamine
	Tripelennamine-N-oxide

of representative H_1 antagonists. For instance, chlorpheniramine is N-demethylated to norchlorpheniramine and dinorchlorpheniramine. Diphenhydramine undergoes an analogous demethylation process, which is followed by a deamination to produce diphenylmethoxyacetic acid. In addition to dealkylation, hydroxyzine, a first-generation H_1 antagonist, is oxidized to cetirizine, a second-generation H_1 antagonist. A less common route of metabolism is N-oxide formation: tripelennamine is converted to tripelennamine N-oxide. Fexofenadine, cetirizine, and acrivastine are excreted primarily as the unchanged drug.

The concentrations of H_1 antagonists in the serum following therapeutic use are in the range of 0.02–0.3 mg/L, depending on the specific drug, route of administration, and frequency of use. Urine concentrations are generally greater than blood concentrations, and urine would be the specimen of choice for identifying drug use. Diphenhydramine is the most cited H_1 antagonist in intoxication cases, with blood concentrations >8 mg/L having been reported in fatal cases. Liver concentrations will also be greater than blood concentrations. In one study, blood and liver concentrations of H_1 antagonists were summarized in cases in which the cause of death was unrelated to these drugs. The antihistamines included were diphenhydramine, chlorpheniramine, and doxylamine. From the data, heart blood concentrations <1.0 mg/L were generally

associated with therapeutic use of diphenhydramine; the median blood concentration in these cases was 0.2 mg/L. The median liver concentration of diphenhydramine associated with therapeutic use was 1.2 mg/kg, and the median liver-to-blood concentration ratio was 8.0. Moreover, the median "postmortem therapeutic" heart blood and liver concentrations of chlorpheniramine were 0.3 mg/L and 2.9 mg/kg, respectively.

H_2 Antagonists

Figure 29.8 illustrates the structures of H_2 antagonists available in the United States. As stated earlier, histamine stimulates the secretion of acid in the stomach, and this action is accomplished via the H_2 receptor. The binding of histamine to the H_2 receptor activates adenylate cyclase, leading to an increase in intracellular cyclic AMP concentrations. This increase activates the proton pump in the parietal cells to secrete protons against the concentration gradient. H_2 antagonists competitively inhibit the binding of histamine to H_2 receptors, thus preventing acid secretion. H_2 antagonists are selective for the H_2 receptor and do not significantly affect activity at the H_1 receptor. Therapeutic use of H_2 antagonists is related to its effect on gastric acid secretion. They are used to promote healing of gastric and duodenal ulcers, reduce the formation of stress ulcers, and treat gastroesophageal reflux disease.

Like H_1 antagonists, H_2 antagonists are rapidly absorbed after oral ingestion, usually within several hours. Unlike their H_1 counterparts, however, H_2 antagonists are only slightly bound to proteins. They are not extensively metabolized in the liver, but routes of metabolism include hydroxylation, sulfoxide formation, and conjugation. Potential drug interactions are more significant with these drugs. For example, cimetidine inhibits cytochrome P-450 enzymes CYP1A2, CYP2C9, and CYP2D6, leading to increased concentrations of coadministered drugs that are metabolized by these enzyme systems. The other drugs are much safer than cimetidine in this respect; consequently, cimetidine has seen

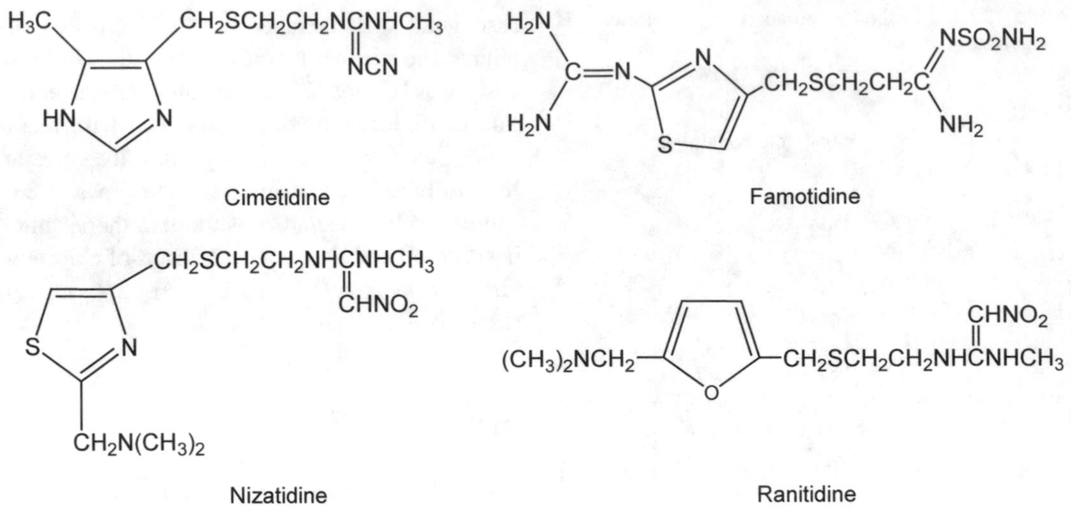

Fig. 29.8 Structures of H_2 antagonists

reduced use as a therapeutic agent. Ethanol consumed while taking H_2 antagonists will produce a slight increase in blood ethanol concentration, compared with the blood ethanol concentration attained without drug use.

Although these drugs are widely used and are available without a prescription, they are not frequently encountered in forensic toxicology laboratories. These drugs have little abuse potential. Consequently, they are not tested in workplace drug screening, and no commercial immunoassays are available for their detection. Furthermore, they have few central nervous system effects and are not included in drugged-driver testing. Therapeutic concentrations of these drugs in the blood range from 0.5 to 5 mg/L, with the exception of famotidine, which has a slightly lower therapeutic range of 0.1–1 mg/L.

Non-narcotic Analgesics

The treatment of pain involves a number of classes of therapeutic agents. Narcotic analgesic drugs or opioids are described in Chap. 22. Non-narcotic analgesics are among the most widely used therapeutic agents. The agents discussed in this chapter are acetaminophen and the anti-inflammatory drugs, such as aspirin (salicylates), traditional nonsteroidal anti-inflammatory drugs

(tNSAIDs), and cyclooxygenase-2 (COX-2) inhibitors. Besides their ability to treat pain, these drugs have several other uses. These drugs have antipyretic properties, and all of these drugs except acetaminophen have anti-inflammatory effects as well. Inflammation is the body's response to a potentially injurious stimulus. This stimulus may be a physical injury, an allergen, or an infection. The classic inflammatory response involves pain, redness, and swelling at the site of injury. This response is followed by the entry of white blood cells into the area, leading to tissue fibrosis.

Anti-inflammatory Drugs

The mechanism by which anti-inflammatory drugs exert their pharmacologic activity has been known for decades. These drugs inhibit the synthesis of prostaglandins, a group of compounds known as eicosanoids and derived from arachidonic acid. Arachidonic acid either is ingested directly from the diet or is derived from dietary linoleic acid. Prostaglandins cause a number of effects associated with the inflammatory response. For example, prostaglandin E_2 causes vasodilation and a decrease in blood pressure. It also enhances platelet aggregation. Another prostaglandin, designated D_2, causes flushing, nasal stuffiness, and hypotension.

The first step in prostaglandin synthesis is the conversion of arachidonic acid into prostaglandin G2 and prostaglandin H2, two unstable intermediates. This reaction is catalyzed by the enzyme prostaglandin G/H synthase, also known as cyclooxygenase (COX). There are two main forms of this enzyme, COX-1 and COX-2. COX-1 is the primary constitutive isozyme and is found in most normal cells and tissues. COX-2 is induced by cytokines and inflammatory mediators. One significant difference between the two isoenzymes is that COX-1 is the primary isoenzyme found in gastric epithelial cells, where prostaglandins provide cytoprotective effects. Salicylates and tNSAIDs inhibit both COX isoenzymes. As a result, these drugs inhibit prostaglandin synthesis in the gastrointestinal tract, accounting for the gastrointestinal distress that these drugs produce. Conversely, COX-2 inhibitors do not affect prostaglandin synthesis in the gastrointestinal tract and do not cause the gastric upset caused by the tNSAIDs.

Aspirin. Aspirin is one of the most widely used nonprescription drugs in the United States. The structure of aspirin (acetylsalicylate) and salicylate are shown in Fig. 29.9. It is used primarily as an analgesic and as an antipyretic. In addition, its ability to prolong bleeding time makes it a useful drug in the prevention of thromboemboli. Specifically, it prevents platelet aggregation by irreversibly acetylating platelet COX, thereby reducing the formation of thromboxane A_2 and increasing the bleeding time.

Aspirin serves as a prodrug. After oral ingestion, it is rapidly hydrolyzed by liver and blood esterases to salicylic acid, the drug form that

accounts for aspirin's pharmacologic activity. The half-life of aspirin is approximately 15 min, whereas the half-life of salicylate is dose-dependent, ranging from 3 to 20 h. In plasma, salicylate is highly bound to protein, but this binding is also concentration-dependent. Ninety percent of salicylate is bound to protein at concentrations up to 100 mg/L, and binding decreases to 50% at 400 mg/L.

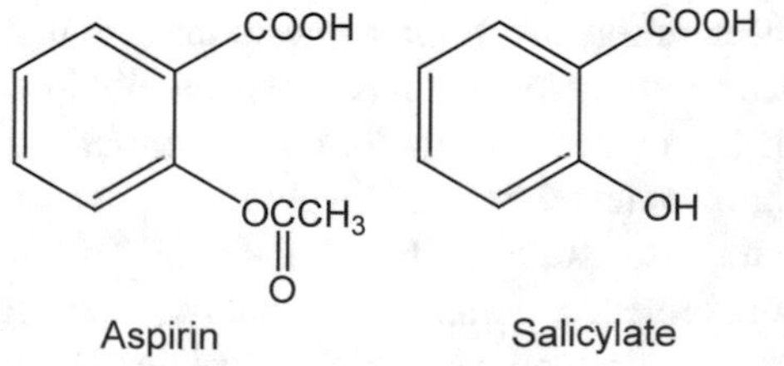

Salicylate concentrations of up to 350 mg/L may be seen in the plasma, depending on the therapeutic use. Higher concentrations are seen in the treatment of arthritis patients than would be seen in the treatment of pain or hyperthermia. Salicylate is metabolized primarily through phase II metabolism. Approximately 80% of the dose is conjugated with glycine to form salicyluric acid. Small amounts of the acyl and phenolic glucuronide conjugates are also formed.

The toxic effects of salicylate generally occur at plasma concentrations >300 mg/L. Salicylate stimulates respiration by causing an uncoupling of oxidative phosphorylation, leading to increased carbon dioxide production. It also acts directly as a stimulant to the respiratory center in the medulla. The increased carbon dioxide produces a respiratory acidosis that leads to increased bicarbonate excretion as the body tries to compensate for the acidosis. On top of this compensated respiratory alkalosis is a metabolic acidosis caused by the presence of the acidic salicylate, which displaces bicarbonate, impairs the excretion of sulfuric and phosphoric acids, and inhibits various enzymes.

Salicylates produce other toxic effects beside the respiratory and pH abnormalities mentioned above. A group of these effects occurs with chronic, mild salicylate intoxication and is termed *salicylism*. Such intoxication is characterized by headache, dizziness, ringing in the ears, dimness of vision, and mental confusion. These effects subside within several days after withdrawal from the drug.

Central nervous system effects associated with high doses of salicylate include stimulation that leads to seizures, followed by central nervous system depression. Salicylates may also trigger the chemoreceptor trigger zone in the

Fig. 29.9 Structure of aspirin and salicylate

medulla, leading to nausea and vomiting. Salicylate characteristics of inhibiting platelet aggregation and prolonging bleeding time can lead to hemorrhage, especially in individuals predisposed to excess bleeding. Large doses of salicylates may also cause hyperglycemia, glycosuria, and aminoaciduria.

There is a classic color test for the detection of salicylate in biological samples. Salicylate reacts with Trinder reagent to produce a purple color. Trinder reagent is an acidic solution of ferric chloride prepared by mixing mercuric chloride, concentrated hydrochloric acid, and ferric nitrate. For the color reaction to occur, the free carboxylic acid and the free phenolic group are required. Neither aspirin nor methyl salicylate will produce a positive test. The color test has sufficient sensitivity to measure therapeutic concentrations of salicylate. The test can be performed directly on samples, but centrifugation may be necessary to make the purple color readily apparent.

Traditional nonsteroidal anti-inflammatory drugs (tNSAIDs). tNSAIDs constitute a number of different structures that have similar mechanisms of action. These drugs are subdivided as follows (examples in parentheses):

1. Acetic acid derivatives (indomethacin, sulindac)
2. Enolic acid derivatives (piroxicam, meloxicam)
3. Propionic acid derivatives (ibuprofen, naproxen)
4. Fenamates (mefenamate, meclofenamate)
5. Heteroaryl acetic acid derivatives (tolmetin, ketorolac)

Figure 29.10 illustrates the structures of these drugs.

Despite their differences in structure, the tNSAIDs have many pharmacokinetic characteristics in common. All of these drugs are well absorbed after oral ingestion, and peak plasma concentrations are reached within 1–2 h after ingestion. Ketorolac is one of the few tNSAIDs that is administered parenterally. These drugs are highly bound to plasma proteins, usually >90%. This property has the potential to lead to drug interactions with coadministered drugs that are also highly bound to proteins.

The plasma half-life of these drugs is variable, even within a structurally similar group. For instance, ibuprofen has a half-life of 2–4 h, whereas naproxen has a half-life of about 14 h. The enolic acid derivatives generally have the longest plasma half-lives, 1–2 days.

Routes of phase I metabolism also vary between groups. Table 29.2 gives the phase I metabolic route of many of the commonly used tNSAIDs. The metabolic products are generally inactive, with the exception of sulindac, which is a prodrug (the sulfide metabolite of sulindac is a much more potent inhibitor of COX than the parent drug). The metabolites of tNSAIDs are then conjugated, usually with glucuronic acid, and are excreted in the urine.

Selective COX-2 inhibitors. Although efficacious, the tNSAIDs have the disadvantage of causing gastrointestinal distress. Gene research identified a second COX enzyme, designated COX-2, that was believed to be the major cause of prostaglandin formation in inflammation. In addition, the "original" COX enzyme, designated COX-1, was the predominant enzyme in the gastrointestinal tract. Therefore, the rationale was that developing drugs that were more specific for the COX-2 enzyme could achieve the desired anti-inflammatory effect while minimizing gastrointestinal distress. The "coxibs" were the first class of drugs developed with specific COX-2 inhibition.

Three members of this class were approved for use in the United States, celecoxib, valdecoxib, and rofecoxib; however, concerns over cardiovascular toxicity caused the latter two drugs to be removed from the market, leaving celecoxib as the only COX-2 inhibitor available (Fig. 29.11). Celecoxib reaches its peak plasma concentration 2–4 h after ingestion. It is highly bound to proteins and has a plasma elimination half-life of about 11 h. Serum concentrations of approximately 0.5 mg/L are observed after therapeutic use. Celecoxib is metabolized to a hydroxymethyl compound, which is then converted to a carboxylic acid derivative. The car-

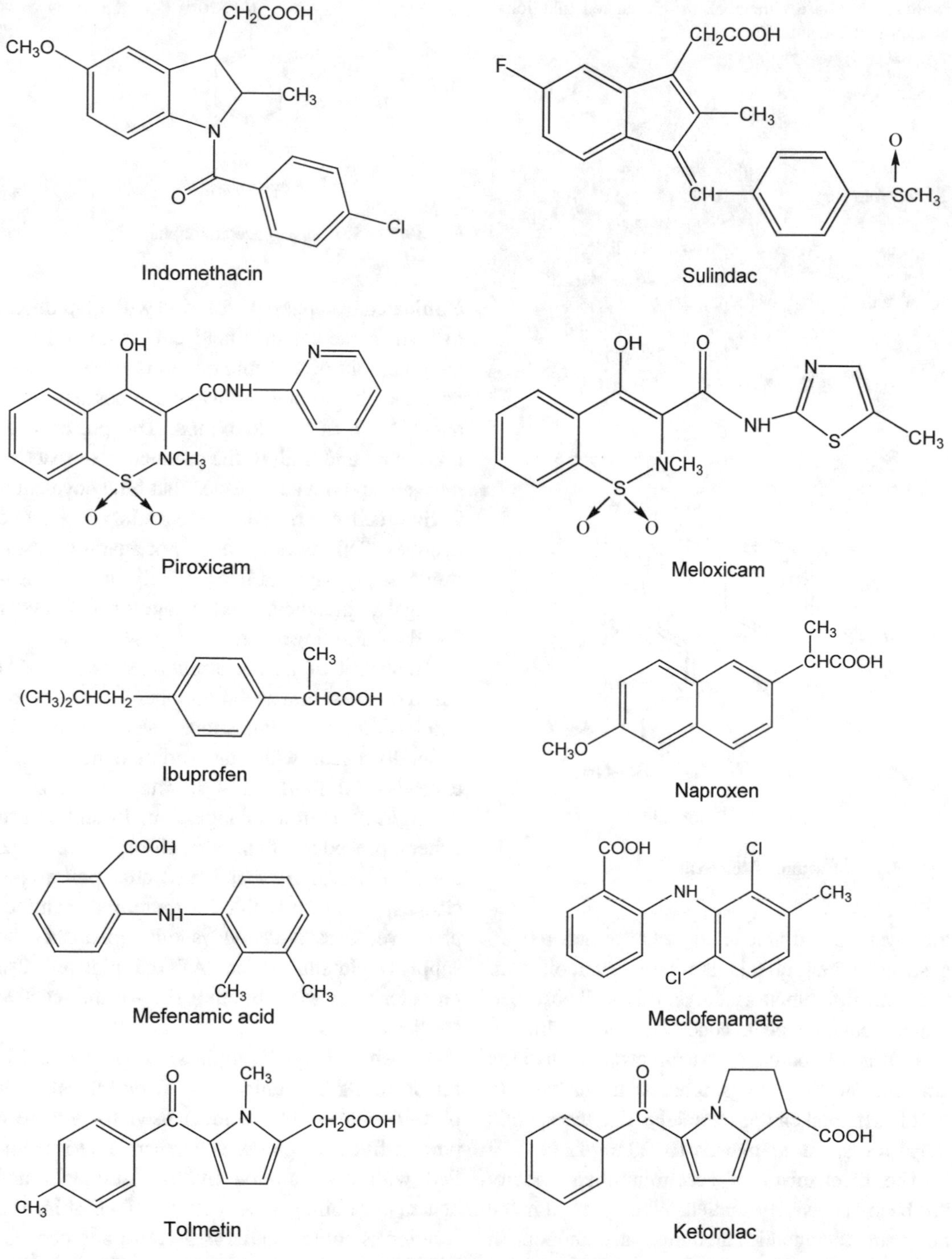

Fig. 29.10 Structures of traditional nonsteroidal anti-inflammatory drugs

boxylic acid derivative is glucuronidated and is excreted primarily in the feces.

Acetaminophen. As stated above, acetaminophen (Fig. 29.12) has analgesic and antipyretic effects similar to the anti-inflammatory drugs; however, it has minimal anti-inflammatory activity. When taken therapeutically, it also has little effect on the cardiovascular system, the respira-

Table 29.2 Phase I metabolism of selected traditional nonsteroidal anti-inflammatory drugs

Drug	Route of phase I metabolism
Indomethacin	O-Demethylation
	N-Demethylation
Sulindac	Sulfone formation
	Sulfide formation
Mefenamic acid	3-Methyl hydroxylation
	3-Methyl carboxylation
Tolmetin	p-Methyl carboxylation
Ketorolac	None
Ibuprofen	Hydroxylation
	Carboxylation
Naproxen	6-Demethylation
Piroxicam	Pyridyl ring hydroxylation

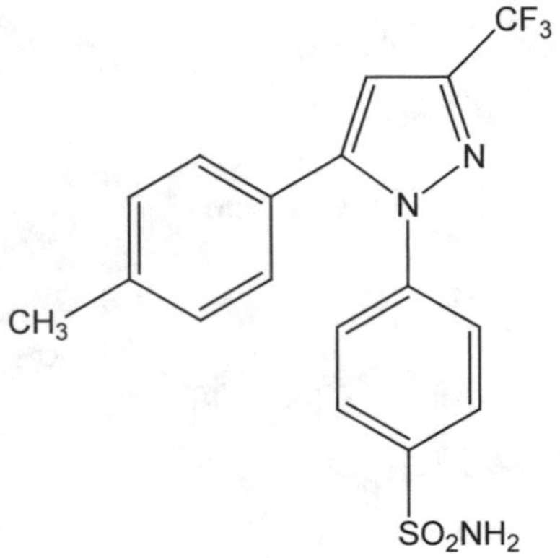

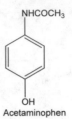

Fig. 29.12 Structure of acetaminophen

Celecoxib

Fig. 29.11 Structure of celecoxib

tory system, and platelet aggregation. Moreover, gastrointestinal effects are less common than with anti-inflammatory drugs. It is well absorbed orally, reaching peak concentrations within an hour. It is less bound to plasma proteins than the anti-inflammatory drugs. It has a plasma half-life of 2 h when taken appropriately. The therapeutic range for acetaminophen is 10–20 mg/L.

The mechanism of acetaminophen toxicity has been extensively studied. When present in the body in therapeutic amounts, acetaminophen undergoes phase II metabolism with glucuronic acid and sulfuric acid to form conjugated products that are excreted in the urine. Acetaminophen also undergoes phase I metabolism to form N-acetyl-p-benzoquinone (NAPQI), which is

eliminated by a phase II reaction with glutathione to form a mercapturic acid conjugate. When a large amount of acetaminophen is present, however, the glutathione pathway becomes saturated, and NAPQI is not detoxified. The presence of this compound leads to the production of reactive nitrogen and oxygen species that bind covalently to liver cell macromolecules, leading to hepatic necrosis. This toxicity does not manifest itself immediately; signs of liver toxicity such as hepatomegaly, jaundice, and coagulopathy occur 2–4 days after ingestion.

Treatment of an acetaminophen overdose is based on the serum acetaminophen concentration and the time since ingestion. Liver damage will generally occur when the serum concentration exceeds 300 mg/L at 4 h after ingestion or 45 mg/L at 15 h after ingestion. In addition to general procedures to prevent absorption, such as the administration of activated charcoal, a specific antidote is available for treating acetaminophen overdoses. N-acetylcysteine replenishes the supply of glutathione for NAPQI to bind and also provides a nontoxic binding site for the reactive species.

As with salicylate, a classic color test exists for detecting acetaminophen in biological samples. Trichloroacetic acid is used to prepare a protein-free precipitate. The supernatant is acidified with concentrated hydrochloric acid and heated in a boiling water bath for 10–15 min. The solution is cooled, and 1% o-cresol and concentrated ammonium hydroxide are added. A blue color indicates the presence of acetaminophen. Unlike many color tests, this method has the sensitivity to identify therapeutic and toxic concentrations of acetaminophen.

Further Reading

2017 Revised Classification of Seizures/Epilepsy Foundation. https://www.epilepsy.com/article/2016/12/2017 revised-classifications-seizures. Accessed 24 March 2018

Baselt RC (2020) Disposition of toxic drugs and chemicals in man, 12th edn. Biomedical Publications, Seal Beach, CA

Bialer M (1993) Comparative pharmacokinetics of the newer antiepileptic drugs. Clin Pharmacokinet 24:441–452

Chong DJ, Lerman AM (2016) Practical update: review of anticonvulsant therapy. Curr Neurol Neurosci Rep 16:39

Clarke W, Dasgupta A (eds) (2017) Clinical challenges in therapeutic drug monitoring-special populations, physiological conditions, and pharmacogenomics. Elsevier, Amsterdam

Feldman M, Burton ME (1990) Histamine$_2$-receptor antagonists. Standard therapy for acid-peptic diseases. 1. N Engl J Med 323:1672–1680

Hammett-Stabler CA, Dasgupta A (eds) (2007) Therapeutic drug monitoring data-a concise guide. AACC Press, Washington

Heimke C, Bergemann N, Clement HW, Coca A, Deckert J et al (2018) Concensus guidelines for therapeutic drug monitoring in neuropsychopharmacology-update 2017. Pharmacopsychiatry 51:9–62

Klabunde RE (2012) Cardiovascular Physiology Concepts-second edition. Lippincott, Williams and Wilkins, Baltimore

LaPenna P, Tormoehlen (2017) The pharmacology and toxicology of third-generation anticonvulsant drugs. J Med Toxicol 13: 329–342

Krishna DR, Klotz U (1988) Newer H$_2$-receptor antagonists. Clinical pharmacokinetics and drug interaction potential. Clin Pharmacokinet 15:205–215

Paton DM, Webster DR (1985) Clinical pharmacokinetics of the H$_1$ receptor antagonists (the antihistamines). Clin Pharmacokinet 10:477–497

Simons FER, Simons KJ (1997) The pharmacology and use of H$_1$ receptor antagonists drugs. N Engl J Med 330:1663–1670

Simons FER, Simons KJ (1999) Clinical pharmacology of new histamine H$_1$ receptor antagonists. Clin Pharmacokinet 36:329–352

Verbeeck RK, Blackburn JL, Loewen GR (1983) Clinical pharmacokinetics of non-steroidal anti-inflammatory drugs. Clin Pharmacokinet 8:297–331

Carbon Monoxide/Cyanide

30

Jamie McAllister, Gary W. Kunsman, and Barry S. Levine

Abstract

Carbon monoxide (CO) poisoning is the leading cause of both accidental and intentional poisoning deaths in the United States. Carbon monoxide produces its toxic effects primarily by reducing the oxygen availability to tissues (anoxic anoxia) in two ways: CO binding to hemoglobin (Hb) reduces the amount of Hb available to carry oxygen to tissues and prevents the release of some of the oxygen from Hb binding sites at the low oxygen tension present in the tissues (leftward shift in the oxygen-Hb dissociation curve). The signs and symptoms of CO intoxication are relatively nonspecific; treatment of CO poisoning is primarily supportive. Evaluation of the extent of CO exposure is based on a determination of the percentage of Hb bound with CO (%COHb) in the blood. Fatalities due to CO exposure are typically characterized by %COHb >50%. The presence of a bright cherry-red coloration of the blood, fingernails, mucous membranes, and skin may indicate CO poisoning. Cyanide is a fast-acting, lethal poison, with death occurring within minutes after inhalation and more slowly following oral ingestion. Cyanide inhibits the electron transport process of cellular respiration at the cytochrome c oxidase step, binding to the heme ion of cytochrome c oxidase. Hydrogen cyanide (HCN) is more rapidly absorbed than salts of cyanide. Detoxification of cyanide to thiocyanate occurs via two enzyme systems: rhodanese and beta-mercaptopyruvate-cyanide sulfurtransferase. The onset of symptoms in cyanide poisoning is dependent on the type of exposure; HCN vapor acts more quickly than cyanide salts. The signs and symptoms of cyanide poisoning are relatively nonspecific, with rapid onset of coma, metabolic acidosis, and symptoms of anoxia without cyanosis as noteworthy indicators. Cyanide deaths have occurred from both accidental and intentional exposure. The findings at autopsy are generally nonspecific. Blood cyanide concentrations of 2–3 mg/L are consistent with death in the absence of other findings.

J. McAllister
FireTox, LLC, New Market, MD, USA

G. W. Kunsman
Broward County Medical Examiner,
Fort Lauderdale, FL, USA

B. S. Levine (✉)
Office of the Chief Medical Examiner,
Baltimore, MD, USA
e-mail: blevine@som.umaryland.edu

Keywords

Carbon monoxide · Cyanide · Toxicity · Analysis · Interpretation

Carbon Monoxide

Carbon monoxide (CO) is an odorless, colorless, and tasteless gas that readily mixes with air; its density is slightly less than that of air ($d = 0.968$, $d_{air} = 1$). It is produced as a result of the incomplete combustion of organic compounds. The concentration of CO produced during the combustion process is largely driven by the efficiency of the fuel/air mixture, e.g., more carbon monoxide is produced when the fuel/air mixture falls outside of the stoichiometric ratio. CO is present in the environment from cigarette smoke, vehicle exhaust, fossil fuel-powered heating and cooking appliances, and other combustion processes. Accidental and incendiary fires are also a major source of exogenous exposure to CO. CO is also produced endogenously from heme catabolism (0.4 mL/h) and results from exposure to and metabolism of dihalomethanes, such as methylene chloride, a chemical compound used in paint removers, metal cleaning products, degreasers, and manufacturing of some pharmaceutical products. Exposure to 0.4% (v/v) CO in air can be fatal in <1 h. The American Conference of Governmental Industrial Hygienists (ACGIH) Threshold Limit Value (TLV)-Time Weighted Average (TWA) for an 8-h workday is 25 ppm of CO; however, exposure to higher concentrations can occur along expressways or in smoke-filled rooms.

Pathophysiology

CO is a relatively inert chemical. Its toxicity results when it combines with hemoglobin (Hb) in the red blood cells. Oxygen is inspired from the air, transported from the lungs through the alveoli and into the blood stream where it binds with Hb. Bound to the Hb, oxygen is then transported throughout the body to the vital organs. Cells within the organs need oxygen for respiration; respiration is the biochemical process that manufactures high-energy molecules, such as adenosine triphosphate (ATP), which are needed to keep the organs functioning and sustain life. Hb contains an iron atom in the +2 valence state (ferrous ion), and CO readily binds to the ferrous ion, forming carboxyhemoglobin (COHb). When blood is exposed to a combination of CO and oxygen, binding occurs in proportion of one mole of CO or oxygen per mole of ferrous ion. However, the partial pressure required for CO binding is 1/200 to 1/300 of the partial pressure required for oxygen binding. In other words, CO has approximately 200–300 times greater affinity for Hb than oxygen.

CO binding to Hb produces its toxic effect through two facets of the same mechanism. One obvious effect is that the portion of Hb that is bound to CO is no longer available to bind oxygen, thus reducing the body's oxygen-carrying capacity. This leads to a shortage of oxygen where it is needed and produces anoxia. This mechanism of toxicity is referred to either as anoxic anoxia or anemic hypoxia. The second, less obvious effect is the result of a leftward shift in the oxygen–Hb saturation curve due to the binding of CO to Hb. This shift means that the presence of CO causes an increase in the affinity of oxygen for Hb, thereby decreasing the release of oxygen from Hb binding sites and further exacerbating the CO-induced anoxia. Those tissues with the greatest oxygen demand (e.g., heart and brain) are most susceptible to the toxic effects of CO.

The percentage of Hb saturated with CO (%COHb) does not completely account for all of the pathologies associated with CO exposure. For example, there is a poor correlation between the COHb saturation following exposure and the degree of neurological injury that follows many nonfatal CO exposures. There are also some studies that suggest there are physiological effects at low COHb saturations as well as continued CO effects after COHb levels have returned to normal. In an effort to account for these and other findings, a histotoxic mechanism of CO toxicity has been proposed. This mechanism has not been completely elucidated but essentially involves the binding of CO to intracellular hemoproteins such as cytochrome c oxidase, myoglobin, catalase, and cytochrome P450, resulting in an inhibition of cellular respiration and other cellular functions. This postulation of such a mechanism does not reduce the role of anoxic anoxia in CO toxicity.

Disposition

Carbon monoxide is readily absorbed through the lungs, and its primary route of elimination is also through the lungs through exhalation. Less than 1% undergoes metabolism to carbon dioxide. After absorption, CO rapidly distributes into the blood. The binding of CO to Hb is reversible, but, due to the greater affinity of CO as compared to oxygen, CO is not readily displaced at normal oxygen concentrations. This can lead to a gradual increase in the percentage of COHb with prolonged CO exposure; CO is not spontaneously displaced from Hb but is displaced by the mass action of oxygen. The half-life of CO is described as the time period over which the quantity of CO in the blood decreases by half its original value. The half-life of CO at normal, room air, oxygen concentration (21%) is 3–5 h. The half-life of CO at 100% oxygen is 30–90 min, but under hyperbaric conditions, the half-life can be reduced to 20–30 min. Of importance with pregnant women is that the fetus reaches higher COHb concentrations with longer elimination times when compared to the mother.

Analysis

One of the early methods of CO analysis involved microdiffusion using a Conway cell. The specimen is placed in the outer well, and sulfuric acid is added to release the CO from the Hb. A solution of palladium chloride is added to the center well. The cell is sealed and incubated at room temperature for 1–2 h. As the reaction proceeds, the palladium chloride is reduced to metallic palladium, forming a black or a silver mirror in the center well, and the CO is converted to carbon dioxide. This method can be made semiquantitative by measuring the amount of unreacted palladium chloride and the Hb in the blood specimen. This technique is useful for screening specimens with COHb saturation values >10%. Another qualitative technique that is effective as a preliminary screen is diluting 1 mL blood with 20 mL 0.01M ammonium hydroxide. Elevated COHb will result in a pink or bluish-red color as compared to a yellowish-red color in the absence of COHb.

Gas chromatography has been used successfully for the analysis of COHb in biological specimens. CO must first be separated from Hb to permit gas chromatographic analysis. This separation can be accomplished by adding the blood to a stoppered container and injecting a releasing agent, commonly a dilute solution of potassium ferricyanide, through the stopper. A sample of the headspace is collected with a gas syringe and injected into the gas chromatograph using a molecular sieve column to achieve the analytical separation. Two types of detectors can be used for this analysis. A thermal conductivity detector can be used to quantify the amount of CO directly. A flame ionization detector provides greater sensitivity but requires the conversion of CO to methane. This can be accomplished with a post-column nickel catalyst and hydrogen gas.

The actual calculation of %COHb may be accomplished in two ways. Blood calibrators can be prepared by saturating blood with 100% CO and subsequently making dilutions of the blood to generate a calibration curve. This necessitates the measurement of Hb in the specimen to correct for the differences in the Hb concentration between the calibration blood and the test blood. An alternative method is to saturate the test blood with 100% CO and measure the CO released from that saturated sample. The area ratio of CO in the unsaturated sample (untreated blood) to that in the saturated sample produces a ratio of CO content to CO capacity. This ratio is the percent saturation of the blood and removes the need for measuring the amount of Hb in the specimen. This Hb-independent method is very useful for determining the CO content of low-Hb specimens such as purge fluid from decomposed bodies. This technique can also be used to measure %COHb in tissue specimens such as the spleen.

Spectrophotometry is commonly used to measure COHb in blood specimens. Hb, COHb, oxyhemoglobin, and methemoglobin have unique visible absorption spectra. In methemoglobin, the iron is in the +3 (ferric) valence state. In normal (living) individuals, no more than 1–2% of total hemoglobin is in the form of methemoglobin. The simultaneous measurement of multiple species in the blood is based on the concept that at each wavelength, absorption of separate components is additive. This means that the quantification of n components in a solution can be performed by measuring n wavelengths. If the molar absorptivity of each compound at each wavelength is known, a series of n equations with n unknowns can then be solved simultaneously. Typically, the wavelengths selected are absorption maxima, minima, or isosbestic points, i.e., points where absorption spectra of two species intersect. After exposure to CO, a blood specimen would predominantly contain three Hb species: Hb, COHb, and oxyhemoglobin. In postmortem specimens, a significant amount of methemoglobin is typically present at amounts well above the normal 1–2%. The amount of methemoglobin (MetHb) continues to increase in a variable manner after death. Theoretically, this would require the measurement of absorbance at four wavelengths to quantify each species. However, the addition of sodium hydrosulfite (dithionite, $Na_2S_2O_4$) reduces oxyhemoglobin and methemoglobin to Hb while leaving COHb unaffected:

$$HbCO + Na_2S_2O_4 \rightarrow No\,reaction$$

$$HbO_2 / MetHb + Na_2S_2O_4 \rightarrow Hb$$

This technique allows for the COHb measurement to be accomplished using only two wavelengths based on the spectral differences between Hb and COHb. The Tietz method is a classic example of this technique.

Several instrument companies have developed automated spectrophotometric systems for the simultaneous analysis of multiple forms of Hb, including COHb. These instruments have a visible light source with interference filters for specific and precise wavelength selection. Whole blood is introduced into the system and is chemically hemolyzed. It then passes through a flow cell where the absorbance measurements are made. Based on these measurements and the appropriate molar extinction coefficients, the microprocessor is able to simultaneously solve the equations and either display or print out the amounts of the different Hb species present within a specimen.

Preserved whole blood, especially blood preserved with ethylenediaminetetraacetic acid or served with ethylenediaminetetraacetic acid or EDTA (purple-top tubes), is the preferred specimen for carbon monoxide analysis in living patients. Sodium fluoride-preserved blood, spleen, and tissue fluid rich in Hb are also acceptable specimens for analysis in postmortem cases.

Poisoning and Autopsy Findings

Carbon monoxide poisoning is the leading cause of both intentional and accidental poisoning deaths in the United States. Exposure to automobile exhaust is the most common mechanism for intentional CO poisoning. Smoke inhalation is the most common source of accidental CO exposure; approximately 80% of fire deaths result from smoke inhalation. The toxic and potentially lethal effects of the smoke have been known since man first built fires in enclosed dwellings. However, awareness that CO was the principal asphyxiant gas in smoke followed much later. C. Bernard in the late 1800s and J.B.S. Haldane in the early 1900s were among the first scientists to thoroughly study and report on the uptake and effects of CO. In the 1960s, Coburn, Forster, and Kane made considerable advances in the understanding of CO absorption, distribution, metabolism, and excretion including the development of a physiological-based model for CO uptake. This research was furthered in the 1970s by Peterson and Stewart and in the 1980s and 1990s by Tikuisis.

The symptoms of CO toxicity are dependent upon the concentration of CO in the inspired air, the state of activity of the exposed person, the individual's weight (correlating to their blood volume), and the duration of exposure; all of these factors affect the rate of accumulation of CO in the blood and the resultant COHb level in the blood. The percentage of Hb in the COHb form is used as a measure of the extent of CO exposure and the degree of CO toxicity. Because CO is produced endogenously and all individuals are exposed to some exogenously produced CO, COHb saturations of ≤3% are considered normal levels for nonsmokers, and saturations of <10% are considered normal levels for smokers. In general, COHb saturations of <10% are not considered to be toxicologically significant in healthy

Table 30.1 Normal carboxyhemoglobin saturation

COHb (% saturation)	Population
0.4–0.7	Endogenous production
0.4–2.6	Pregnant women
0.5–4.7	Normal infants
0–3	Nonsmokers
0–6	Hemolytic anemia
3–8	Smokers
>10	Significant toxicology

Table 30.2 Symptoms associated with various %COHb

COHb (% saturation)	Clinical symptoms
0–10	Normal, shortness of breath with vigorous exercise
10–20	Headache, flushed skin, shortness of breath with moderate exercise
20–30	Headache, throbbing temples, irritability, emotional instability, impaired judgment, memory impairment, rapid fatigue
30–40	Dizziness, weakness, nausea and vomiting, severe headache, visual disturbances, confusion
40–50	Intensified symptoms, hallucinations, severe ataxia, tachypnea
>50	Syncope, coma, tachycardia with weak pulse, incontinence of urine and feces, convulsions, loss of reflexes, cyanosis, respiratory paralysis, death

individuals although a finding of low but above normal levels of CO may provide important data to the death investigator, e.g., establishing if a victim was alive and breathing before an incendiary fire was set or establishing if a victim was smoking prior to the onset of an accidental fire. Table 30.1 provides ranges of normal COHb saturation levels in selected populations.

Prolonged exposure to low levels of CO or gradually increasing levels of CO as may result from a faulty combustion appliance in a home will result in a slow increase in the individual's %COHb. This typically results in more serious long-term sequelae and lower risk of fatality than does exposure to high CO concentrations, such as from fires, that result in a rapid increase in the %COHb level.

It is suspected that many nonlethal exposures to CO are neither detected nor suspected due to the nonspecific symptomatology that develops. Many individuals that have been diagnosed with low levels of CO exposure present with flulike symptoms. Exposure to CO appears to most significantly affect the blood, central nervous system (CNS), cardiovascular system, and respiratory system. The mechanism of toxic action is tissue hypoxia due to the reduced oxygen-carrying capacity of Hb and the rightward shift of the oxygen–Hb dissociation curve and inhibition of cellular respiration. The signs and symptoms of acute CO poisoning include frontal headache, ataxia, tremor, nausea, vomiting, blurred vision, visual field constriction, mydriasis, nystagmus, dementia, atrioventricular block, arrhythmias, bradycardia, hypotension, dyspnea with hyperventilation, seizures, disorientation, hypothermia, tinnitus, drowsiness, coma, and ultimately death. Carbon monoxide exposure to the pregnant woman may result in fetal neurological abnormalities, malformations, and fetal death. Table 30.2 lists clinical symptoms associated with varying amounts of COHb saturation.

Nonfatal exposures to CO can be divided into three categories based on the existence and degree of residual effects:

1. Mild poisoning: The exposure to CO produces no measurable long-term effects.
2. Immediate disability: More severe exposure than mild poisoning; the patient regains consciousness after removal from the CO-containing environment, but neurological deficits are immediate (e.g., dementia, drowsiness, seizures, headache, confabulation, deafness, peripheral neuropathies, etc.). Some of the neurological deficits may improve over time.
3. Delayed neurological syndrome: A period of CO-induced unconsciousness follows removal from the environment. Upon the return to consciousness, there is a period of apparent recovery with no impairment; this may last from a few days (typically at least 5 days) to a few weeks. This period of pseudo-recovery is followed by a slow deterioration resulting in long-term disabilities such as disorientation, chorea, equilibrium disturbances, cogwheel rigidity, aphasia, incontinence of urine and feces, chronic headaches, personality changes, and most frequently Parkinsonism. The

mechanism(s) of this delayed toxicity may be a result of mitochondrial dysfunction, brain lipid peroxidation, direct neuronal damage leading to neuronal death, and demyelination of white matter. This syndrome occurs in approximately 10–30% of CO-poisoned patients.

There is technically no chronic CO poisoning in the sense that CO does not accumulate in the body over prolonged periods of exposure. The %COHb will eventually return to normal levels after nonfatal acute exposures. There is then no increased susceptibility to the toxic effects of CO upon subsequent exposures. Repeated anoxic episodes due to CO exposure, or any other agent or event producing anoxia, can cause a gradually worsening degree of damage to the CNS, e.g., loss of sensation in the fingers, positive Romberg's sign, memory loss, persistent headache, neuropathies, and psychomotor defects. Routine exposure to CO from smoking or occupation, e.g., firefighters, has been shown to result in higher incidences of heart disease which is believed to be the result of chronic anoxia.

Deaths related to CO exposure have been noted over a wide range of %COHb. Most fatalities in which CO intoxication is considered to be the ultimate cause of death are associated with %COHb >50%, with most values falling between 50 and 70%. Due to the extremely high concentration of CO that can result in the fire environment and the inhalation dose that results, COHb levels as high as 90% have been found in some fire victims. Although death may be associated with either lower or higher %COHb, values above 50% are typically considered to be incompatible with life. Lower %COHb may be associated with fatalities secondary to CO intoxication if there is some preexisting pathology (e.g., pulmonary insufficiency or cardiovascular disease), administration of other CNS depressants, physical exertion that would increase the body's oxygen demand, or the presence of other intoxicating substances such as cyanide gas in fire-related deaths. The most significant postmortem characteristic in fatal CO intoxications is the presence of a bright cherry-red coloration of the blood, fin-

Table 30.3 Blood/spleen %COHb correlation

Spleen (%COHb)	Blood (%COHb)
<10	<10
10–30	Inconclusive
>30	Toxic/lethal

gernails, mucous membranes, and skin. This coloration, however, may also be present in cases of cyanide intoxication or exposure to cold and in the early stages of decomposition.

The specimen most frequently analyzed for COHb in the postmortem forensic toxicology laboratory is blood. Other useful postmortem specimens for CO analysis are spleen and Hb-containing fluid from within any of the solid organs. The difficulty with analysis of Hb-containing fluid is that it often has very low Hb levels that may yield unreliable results with spectrophotometric methods or other Hb-dependent methodologies. Spleen CO values do not always correlate well with blood %COHb but may be interpreted using the generalizations detailed in Table 30.3.

Treatment

Treatment for CO poisoning is a complicated issue due to the nonspecific symptomatology associated with CO exposure. For this reason the diagnosis of CO intoxication is frequently missed. In cases of obvious exposure (house fire, intentional exposure to automobile exhaust, etc.), removal from the environment is the first step in treatment. Following decontamination, 100% oxygen is administered for at least 120 min ($t_{\frac{1}{2}CO}$ = 30–90 min at 100% oxygen). In cases in which the %COHb exceeds 15% in pregnant women or 30% in asymptomatic patients, hyperbaric oxygen may be considered although there is little evidence to suggest that this treatment is more effective than normobaric oxygen; some studies suggest hyperbaric oxygen may be effective in poisoned patients with acute neurotoxicity, metabolic acidosis, angina, or other cardiac abnormalities. Normal supportive measures should also be instituted. These include maintenance of normal vital signs, administration of mannitol or prednisolone to reduce cerebral edema, administration of diazepam in the event of seizures, administration of N-acetylcysteine and allopurinol to reduce the risk of lipid peroxidation, and administration of insulin in cases of CO-induced hyperglycemia and hypothermia. The patient should be given bed rest for at least 2 weeks for observation and to possibly reduce the risk of late-developing sequelae. Complete recovery is possible, but long-term disability due to CNS damage may occur if a high %COHb saturation persists for several hours. Another complicating issue in the treatment of CO poisoning is that %COHb does not correlate well with neurologic damage or the risk of late-developing effects. Therefore, rapid reduction of %COHb levels is no guarantee that a delayed neurological syndrome will not result.

Fire-Related Deaths

Carbon monoxide is one of the main products of combustion and is the most impactful asphyxiant gas present in most fires. The major lethal factors in uncontrolled fires are asphyxiant gases and heat. The majority of fire-related deaths are due to CO exposure and injuries related to smoke inhalation as compared to thermal injuries. Fire creates a complex environment involving flame, heat, oxygen depletion, smoke, and a variety of toxic and irritant gases. Materials have different gas yields under different fuel and ventilation conditions, but CO is the predominant asphyxiant gas generated from the incomplete combustion of wood and other cellulose materials.

Most fire-related deaths are associated with an elevated COHb saturation. Lower COHb levels (20–50%) may be associated with rapid death due to thermal injuries when victims are intimate with the fire or from trauma occurring before the fire. Higher COHb levels are commonly found in individuals that are remote from the room of fire origin and thereby protected from heat but exposed to the toxic gases and smoke which spread beyond the fire enclosure. Ethanol and drug intoxication has also been shown to be a sig-

nificant factor in fire-related deaths. The psychomotor impairment associated with an elevated blood alcohol concentration has been shown to hinder escape from a fire environment and impact one's ability to awaken to a sounding smoke alarm. Berl and Halpin found that over 50% of all fire victims over 20 years of age had a blood alcohol level in excess of 0.10 g/dL. Grace reported that benzodiazepines have a similar effect to alcohol in limiting the ability of an occupant to awaken to a smoke alarm, and Lykiardopoulos found that psychotropic drugs, specifically sedatives, had a profound impact on both awakening and human behavior in fires. Escape may also be hindered by the CNS depression resulting from both ethanol and asphyxiant gases such as CO present in the fire environment, although Levine found that this did not impact or lower the COHb level necessary to cause death.

Because a fire is a complicated environment comprising many toxicants and irritants, it is difficult to fully evaluate the role of any single component in fire-related deaths. In terms of asphyxiant gases, CO and cyanide are present in the highest concentrations in most fires (dependent on the types of materials present). Therefore, the combined exposure to these two gases may also be implicated in fire-related deaths. In a study of fire-related deaths in Maryland, more than 50% of the cases had CO levels above 30% and abnormal cyanide levels (suggestive that both gases were significant contributors in the death); approximately 10% of the cases had CO levels above 30% and normal cyanide levels (cyanide possibly enhanced the toxicity of CO or else was not significant in the death); approximately 20% of the cases had CO levels below 30% and normal cyanide levels (the gases were either not a significant factor in the death or acted in a synergistic manner to cause the death); and less than 10% of the cases had CO levels below 30% and abnormal cyanide levels (the low number of cases makes interpretation difficult). Animal studies have confirmed that simultaneous exposure to sublethal concentrations of both gases can cause death based on additive and even synergistic effects, possibly at cytochrome c oxidase.

Storage and Stability Considerations

One of the most significant factors affecting the measurement of %COHb and the subsequent interpretation of CO toxicity is the ability to accurately measure the CO content of the blood. Postmortem alterations in %COHb concentration have been documented in a number of studies. In general, the %COHb saturation decreases as storage time increases.

There is no evidence that CO is produced in stored blood as a result of putrefaction. Unpreserved specimens have been documented to lose up to 60% of their CO content when stored in uncapped containers at room temperature. Reduction of %COHb was dependent on the surface area of the specimen exposed to air (the greater the surface area, the greater the loss of CO), the temperature of storage (increased temperatures result in greater CO loss), and the initial %COHb saturation (higher initial %COHb results in greater and more rapid loss of CO). When containers are capped, the volume of headspace over the blood specimen is a significant factor in the amount of CO lost, because some CO will equilibrate between the blood and the headspace. The loss of CO will cease once the equilibration point has been reached; therefore, the larger the volume of headspace, the greater the loss of CO into that headspace. Storage temperature and initial %COHb also affect the rate of loss. Although loss of CO occurs in all stored specimens, this loss may be minimized by preserving blood specimens with EDTA or sodium fluoride, minimizing the headspace above the specimen, and storing specimens at reduced temperature; storage under frozen conditions minimizes CO loss more effectively than does refrigeration.

Summary

Carbon monoxide reduces the oxygen availability to tissues (anoxic anoxia) in two ways: CO binding to Hb reduces the amount of Hb available to carry oxygen to tissues and prevents the release of some of the oxygen from Hb binding sites at the low oxygen tension present in the tissues (leftward shift in the oxygen-Hb dissociation curve). The other mechanism of CO toxicity is through the binding of CO to intracellular hemoproteins inhibiting cellular respiration and other intracellular functions (a histotoxic mechanism).

CO poisoning is the leading cause of both accidental and intentional poisoning deaths in the United States. The signs and symptoms of CO intoxication are relatively nonspecific, and for this reason, a substantial percentage of poisonings are incorrectly diagnosed. Treatment of CO poisoning is primarily supportive along with the administration of 100% oxygen. If patients survive, they may fully recover, but a substantial percentage of poisoned patients suffer from long-term neurological sequelae.

Fatalities due to CO exposure are typically characterized by %COHb >50%. Lower COHb percentages may be associated with fatalities in the presence of some preexisting pathology, physical exertion, or other asphyxiant gas, such as hydrogen cyanide. The presence of a bright cherry-red coloration of the blood, fingernails, mucous membranes, and skin may indicate CO poisoning.

Evaluation of the extent of CO exposure is based on a determination of the percentage of Hb bound with carbon monoxide (%COHb). These determinations are typically performed using either a spectrophotometric or gas chromatographic technique. Proper storage of specimens is important to minimize the loss of CO, which could adversely affect the interpretation based upon the analytical results. Blood specimens should be preserved with EDTA or sodium fluoride and kept frozen.

Cyanide

Cyanide is a rapidly acting and lethal poison, with death occurring within minutes after ingestion. Cyanide and cyanogenic products are used in a wide variety of ways. Hydrogen cyanide (HCN), also referred to as hydrocyanic acid or prussic acid, is used as a fumigant, for executions using the "gas chamber," and in the production of resin monomers such as acrylates and methacrylates.

HCN, a weak acid, is a colorless volatile liquid with a boiling point of 26.5 °C—and therefore presents an inhalation hazard. The density of cyanide vapor is similar to that of air and will consequently permeate an area in which it is released. The vapor has the characteristic odor of bitter almonds at an air concentration ranging from 0.2 to 5 ppm; beyond this concentration, olfactory fatigue occurs and the odor is no longer detectable. Cyanide gas is also released as a by-product of incomplete combustion in blast furnaces, coke ovens, cigarettes, and house fires, and also from the pyrolysis of nitrogen-containing materials such as wool, silk, acrylonitriles, polyurethane, and other polyacrylic fibers and materials. The potassium and sodium salts of cyanide readily hydrolyze in aqueous solutions, making them strong bases that can cause skin ulceration upon contact and congestion and corrosion of the gastric mucosa upon ingestion. These salts also give off the characteristic bitter almond smell associated with cyanide and are used in the processes of metal hardening, metal cleaning, electroplating, and gold and silver recovery and refining. Potassium cyanide may also be used in the illicit manufacture of phencyclidine, resulting in a final product contaminated with cyclohexane carbonitrile.

Some of the other forms and uses of cyanide are calcium cyanamide, used in the production of melamine resins in laminated tabletops, dishware, shrink- and wrinkle-resistant fabrics, and high-strength paper; acrylonitrile, an intermediate in the production of acrylic fibers and synthetic rubber; adiponitrile, an intermediate in the manufacture of Nylon 6-6; cyanoacetic acid, an intermediate in the production of pharmaceuticals; production of the synthetic amino acids methionine, glycine, and alanine; production of lactic acid, a food acidifier also used in the leather tanning process and in antiperspirants; cyanuric chlorides, the trimerization product of cyanogen chloride, used in the manufacture of herbicides, optical brighteners, and dyes; acetonitrile and proprionitrile, used in the manufacture of pharmaceuticals; cyanoacetic acid, an intermediate

product used in the manufacture of phenylbutazone and barbiturates; nitroprussides, used in chemical synthesis and as hypotensive agents; potassium ferricyanide, used in photography, blueprints, and manufacturing of pigments; and sodium thiocyanate, used in the printing and dyeing of textiles and in color film processing.

Several plants have also been found to contain cyanogenic glycosides. Amygdalin, the active component of laetrile, is probably the most commonly encountered cyanogenic glycoside and is found in bitter almonds; apricot, pear, and apple seeds and peach and plum pits. Laetrile has been purported to be an antineoplastic agent and gained popularity in the 1970s. Enzymatic degradation of amygdalin or the other cyanogenic glycosides such as prunasin (the primary metabolite of orally administered amygdalin also found in cherry laurel) and linamarin (from cassava and some lima beans) releases hydrogen cyanide and can be a significant source of poisonings. Cyanide is found in measurable levels in most people as a result of vitamin B_{12} (cyanocobalamin) metabolism and also in smokers; cyanide levels <0.26 mg/L are generally considered to be normal levels and are nontoxic.

Pathophysiology

The molecular toxicity of cyanide is well understood. Cyanide stops cellular respiration by inhibiting electron transport at the cytochrome c oxidase step. Cytochrome c oxidase is the last step of the electron transport scheme, where molecular oxygen and two protons are converted into water, with an associated production of high-energy ATP molecules. When this process is inhibited, oxidative phosphorylation stops. This in turn stops the Krebs cycle and leads to an accumulation of pyruvic acid, which is produced during glycolysis. Pyruvic acid is then processed anaerobically to lactic acid, causing a metabolic acidosis. Molecular oxygen, because it is not reduced, also builds up in the tissues and alters the gradient for release of oxygen from Hb. This produces hypoxia in the tissues. This inability of cells to use oxygen is referred to as histotoxic anoxia. In this way, the cellular impact of cyanide is different from carbon monoxide in that it affects the utilization of oxygen rather than the binding and release of oxygen.

The binding of cyanide to cytochrome c oxidase is a two-step process. Initially, cyanide penetrates into the protein structure of the cytochrome. Once inside, it is able to bind to the heme iron. It has been demonstrated that HCN binds to both the oxidized and the reduced forms of the cytochrome a_3 component of cytochrome oxidase. However, it is believed that the kinetically relevant toxic effect of cyanide is at the reduced cytochrome a_3. The binding of cyanide produces an oxidized enzyme–cyanide complex, which is stable but can be reversed in the presence of reducing equivalents.

Because it is rich in cytochrome c oxidase, the primary target organ of cyanide is the brain. There is also evidence that cyanide toxicity impacts the heart. Cyanide is a very potent protoplasmic poison. It is estimated that the lethal dose of HCN is 100 mg and the lethal dose of NaCN is 200 mg. This difference is probably related to the relative ability of each to enter the brain.

Disposition

The absorption of cyanide depends on the chemical nature of the substance absorbed as well as the route of administration. HCN, being nonionized and readily diffusable, is rapidly absorbed through biological membranes and diffuses throughout the body. Therefore, absorption is more efficient through inhalation than through dermal contact. Salts of cyanide are readily absorbed after oral ingestion but, being ionized, are absorbed at significantly lower rates. Oral ingestion of cyanide also allows entry into the portal circulation prior to its passage into the systemic circulation. The liver is capable of detoxifying a significant amount of cyanide (first-pass metabolism), meaning that less cyanide ultimately enters the circulation.

The major pathway of detoxification of cyanide is by enzymatic conversion to thiocyanate (SCN) and subsequent excretion by the kidney.

Two enzymes that facilitate this transsulfuration process have been identified: rhodanese and beta-mercaptopyruvate-cyanide sulfurtransferase. The first enzyme identified was rhodanese or thiosulfate-cyanide sulfotransferase. It is a mitochondrial enzyme that catalyzes the transfer of a sulfur atom from a donor, usually thiosulfate, to an acceptor such as cyanide. Rhodanese activity is greatest in the liver and kidney. The mechanism of action is well understood: rhodanese cleaves an S-S bond, producing a rhodanese–sulfur complex with the subsequent regeneration of rhodanese by the transfer of the sulfur atom to cyanide, producing SCN. The second enzyme identified was beta-mercaptopyruvate-cyanide sulfurtransferase, which is present in the liver, kidney, and blood. These reactions are detailed below:

$$CN^- + S_2O_3^{2-} \xrightarrow{(1)} SCN^- + SO_3^{2-}$$

$$HSCH_2COCOO^- + CN \xrightarrow{(2)} SCN^- + CH_3COCOO$$

(1) = Rhodanese
(2) = Beta-mercaptopyruvate-cyanide sulfurtransferase

Analysis

Many methods for the identification and quantification of cyanide in biological specimens have been published over the past 40 years. The initial step in the analysis is the separation of cyanide from the biological matrix. The most common initial step is acidification to convert cyanide to the more volatile HCN. If this reaction is performed in a sealed container at an elevated temperature, the HCN will enter the gaseous phase above the biological layer. This gas can then be sampled directly. One other technique is to perform a microdiffusion reaction using a Conway cell. A dilute base, such as sodium hydroxide, that serves as a trapping agent for the released HCN is added to the center well of the cell. In a two-reservoir cell, the blood or tissue specimen is added to the outer well, followed by a releasing agent. This releasing agent may be a dilute mineral acid such as sulfuric acid or an organic acid such as tartaric acid. The reaction is allowed to proceed at room temperature for several hours. Alternatively, a three-well cell may be used. The sample and acid are added to the middle well, while a more dilute acid is added to the outer well to serve as a sealing agent. After the reaction is complete, the center well contains the trapped cyanide and is available for detection.

A number of colorimetric reactions have been developed to detect cyanide from the trapping agent. One classical color reaction uses chloramine-T to convert cyanide to cyanogen chloride. A color reagent containing pyridine and barbituric acid is then added to produce a red color. This assay can be qualitative or quantitative using spectrophotometric measurement at 580 nm. Several fluorescent derivatives of cyanide have been produced to enhance the sensitivity of spectrophotometric methods.

Various gas chromatographic methods for the analysis of cyanide are also available. The fact that cyanide contains a nitrogen atom and is an electron-withdrawing group makes it amenable to both nitrogen-phosphorus and electron capture detection. One method is based on the conversion of cyanide to cyanogen chloride by chloramine-T. The cyanogen chloride is extracted with hexane, and an aliquot of the hexane layer is injected into the gas chromatograph with a Halcomid column and an electron capture detector. This method requires initial cyanide separation from the biological matrix by Conway cell microdiffusion. A simpler procedure uses headspace gas chromatography of cyanide itself. The specimen is placed in a container with a solution of acetonitrile, which serves as an internal standard. Acid is added to the headspace vial immediately prior to sealing and is heated for 10 min at 60 °C. The vapor containing HCN and acetonitrile is sampled. A Poropak column separates HCN from acetonitrile, and detection can be achieved with a nitrogen-phosphorus detector.

Microdiffusion separation has also been combined with direct potentiometric measurement of cyanide in biological specimens. An ion-specific electrode originally designed for aqueous solutions has been used. A very rapid semiquantitative screening test for cyanide uses a commercially available paper impregnated with substances that turn blue in the presence of HCN.

Poisoning and Autopsy Findings

Cyanide is an extremely fast-acting poison. The onset of symptoms is dependent on the type of exposure. HCN vapors act rapidly, with symptoms appearing in seconds and death within minutes. Cyanide salts act more slowly, with symptoms appearing in minutes and death within hours. This exposure-dependent symptomatology is the result of the rate and degree of production of histotoxic hypoxia. When the tissue cyanide concentration rises rapidly, as seen with inhalation exposure, the signs and symptoms of poisoning are more acute, and the amount of cyanide required to produce toxicity is small, whereas oral or dermal exposure leads to a slower cyanide buildup in the tissue. Tissue concentrations of cyanide and the rate of increase are dependent on the cyanide compound, dose, and extent, rate, and site of absorption.

The signs and symptoms of acute cyanide exposure are relatively nonspecific and reflect cellular hypoxia due to the inability of cells to use oxygen. This cellular hypoxia generally results in cell death and also stimulates carotid and aortic bodies, causing an initial hyperpnea followed by dyspnea. Other symptoms include headache, tachypnea, and dizziness within the first few seconds following exposure. These symptoms progress toward slowed respiration, gasping breaths, lactic acidosis, bradycardia, erratic cardiac rhythms including ischemic changes on an electrocardiogram, hypotension, coma, opisthotonus, seizures, and death. Because only oxygen utilization and not oxygen saturation is affected, venous blood reaches an oxygen saturation approximating arterial blood, and cyanosis is usually not present. Cyanide poisoning should thus be considered in the differential diagnosis of patients with rapid onset of coma, metabolic acidosis, and symptoms of severe anoxia without cyanosis.

The prognosis in acute cyanide poisoning is dependent on the amount, form, and route of exposure and on the rapid support of respiration and circulation. Survival for 4 h is usually followed by recovery without sequelae, although hypoxic and hemodynamic brain damage may occur. Rapid initiation of supportive care is essential for survival. Oxygen (100%) should be used routinely even in cases of moderate exposure or where pO2 is normal. Hyperbaric oxygen has been used but does not appear to significantly contribute to recovery. Removal from a contaminated atmosphere and external decontamination should be accomplished as soon as possible to limit continued exposure to cyanide. In cases of ingested cyanide, gut decontamination should follow (not precede) antidote therapy due to the rapid onset of toxicity. Hemodialysis and hemoperfusion have been shown to be ineffective in enhancing cyanide elimination.

In some cases of cyanide poisoning, the above steps, including correction of acidosis and seizure control, can be sufficient to ensure survival without antidote therapy. In cases of severe poisonings, the primary goal of treatment after supportive measures and decontamination is to decrease the amount of cyanide available to bind to ferric iron by administering an antidote. A number of antidotes have been suggested over the years; these antidotes produce methemoglobinemia, replenish depleted stores of reducing sulfur substrates (e.g., administer thiosulfate), or chelate cyanide. One antidote combines an amyl nitrite inhalant and solutions of sodium nitrite and sodium thiosulfate. The amyl nitrite is administered by inhalation followed by intravenous sodium nitrite. This combination results in the formation of methemoglobin, which has a greater binding affinity for cyanide than does cytochrome oxidase; a methemoglobin level of approximately 40% is most effective. The last step is administration of sodium thiosulfate, which binds the cyanomethemoglobin and, in the presence of rhodanese, forms the nontoxic compound thiocyanate. The kidneys subsequently excrete thiocyanate. Care must be taken

with these types of antidotes because excessive methemoglobin formation (>70%) is life-threatening, as methemoglobin cannot bind to oxygen. In addition nitrites induce vasodilation, which may drastically lower blood pressure and result in cardiovascular collapse. Because of the potentially negative side effects of the three-component (e.g., amyl nitrite, sodium nitrite, and sodium thiosulfate) antidote kit, some emergency medical service providers have implemented a cyanide poisoning treatment protocol which utilizes CYANOKIT, an antidote approved for use in the United States in 2006. The CYANOKIT utilizes a single antidote, hydroxocobalamin, which binds with cyanide to form inactive cyanocobalamin which is subsequently excreted through the urine. Additionally, some countries utilize dicobalt edetate (Kelocyanor) which is used to chelate cyanide and facilitate its excretion.

The signs and symptoms of chronic cyanide poisoning are also diverse and pervasive. Initial signs of poisoning are CNS excitation and hyperpnea. Chronic and subchronic exposure to cyanide may result in weakness, dizziness, headache, nausea, and vomiting. Mild abnormalities of vitamin B_{12}, folate, and thyroid function have been noted in some cases of chronic exposure, as well as psychosis and thyroid enlargement without alteration in function. A number of disease states have been associated with chronic cyanide exposure or disordered cyanide detoxification: tobacco amblyopia (reduction of vision probably due to elevated thiocyanate levels secondary to tobacco smoking), Leber's hereditary optic atrophy, and Nigerian nutritional ataxic neuropathy (segmental demyelination leading to peripheral sensory neuropathy resulting from increased thiocyanate levels secondary to the consumption of large amounts of cassava and other nutritional factors). Smokers exhibit elevated blood cyanide levels as well as elevated blood thiocyanate levels. The actual role of cyanide and cyanide exposure in these disease states has not been well established.

Deaths from cyanide have been reported from a variety of sources. Accidental poisoning can result from occupational exposure in agriculture or in the laboratory. These exposures are usually avoidable by taking reasonable safety precautions. Accidental exposure may also occur in the home, with children being the most susceptible. The burning of nitrogen-containing materials might also provide an unexpected source of cyanide. An insidious unintentional poisoning with cyanide has occurred when medicinal products are tampered with by replacing the therapeutic agent with cyanide. This has been reported in Chicago and in the state of Washington, among other places.

Intentional ingestion of cyanide has also been well documented. The Jonestown massacre was the most extreme example of massive numbers of fatalities resulting from the known ingestion of a cyanide-containing drink. However, the worst case of mass cyanide poisoning was the use of prussic acid to exterminate millions of prisoners in Nazi concentration camps during the 1930s and 1940s. Cyanide has also been used throughout time by politicians and spies to escape the ramifications of capture. HCN has also been used to perform the judicially ordered execution of criminals.

Autopsy findings following cyanide intoxication are generally nonspecific. There are no gross or microscopic findings unique to cyanide poisoning. Findings often include visceral congestion and edema and petechial hemorrhages in the brain, pleura, lungs, and myocardium. Although the hypoxia produced by cyanide would be expected to produce a bright red color of the blood, this is not a consistent finding. The most characteristic finding that can lead the pathologist to suspect cyanide poisoning is the odor of the blood and tissues. This smell has been described as being similar to bitter almonds, but those familiar with the smell believe that it is unique to cyanide. Unfortunately, not all individuals can detect the odor of cyanide. There clearly is a genetic component to this ability, but it appears to be more complicated than simple Mendelian genetics.

The specimen most frequently analyzed for cyanide in the postmortem forensic toxicology laboratory is blood. Other useful postmortem specimens for cyanide analysis are the spleen,

Table 30.4 Interpretation of blood cyanide concentrations

Range (mg/L)	Effect
≤0.25	Normal
0.25–2	Potentially toxic
>2–3	Potentially fatal

liver, and brain. Blood cyanide concentrations <0.25 mg/L are considered normal. Blood concentrations >0.25 mg/L but <2–3 mg/L are considered elevated but ordinarily would not cause death. Blood cyanide concentrations above 3 mg/L are consistent with death in the absence of other relevant autopsy and toxicology findings (Table 30.4).

Fire-Related Deaths

Fire creates a complex environment involving flame, heat, oxygen depletion, smoke, and a variety of toxic and irritant gases. The nature of that environment is dependent upon the circumstances surrounding the fire, the immediate location of the fire relative to the occupant, the fire source, and the materials burning, e.g., fuels. Fuels have different toxic gas yields under different fuel and ventilation conditions. Like carbon monoxide, the yield of hydrogen cyanide increases as combustion inefficiency increases; however, the yield of HCN is also dependent upon the percentage of nitrogen within the fuel. Fuels with high nitrogen content, such as polyurethane foams found in mattresses, couches, loveseats, etc., are ubiquitous in households and often the primary source of hydrogen cyanide production in fires.

CO is the predominant asphyxiant gas that is generated from the incomplete combustion of wood and other cellulose materials, but hydrogen cyanide is also a key factor in deaths in fires which involve nitrogen-containing fuels. As previously mentioned, in a study of fire-related deaths in Maryland, more than 50% of the cases had CO levels above 30% and abnormal cyanide levels (suggestive that both gases were significant contributors in the death). Several landmark fires, such as the 1990 Happy Land Social Club fire in New York City, the 1986 Dupont Plaza Hotel fire in Puerto Rico, and the 1977 Maury County Jail fire in Tennessee, have shown the devastating impact of exposure to lethal concentrations of CO and HCN. Purser hypothesized that HCN may play a substantial role in smoke inhalation deaths by quickly incapacitating fire victims, thereby preventing them from escaping. Purser theorizes that these victims, once incapacitated, then die as a result of CO inhalation, in combination with the HCN. While a heavily validated, physiological-based model does not exist to correlate the inhaled cyanide dose with resultant blood concentrations, the finding of cyanide in fire victims is still useful to the investigator. At minimum assuming proper treatment of the sample, an indication of cyanide exposure provides a positive indication that a nitrogen-containing fuel was burning prior to the victim's death. This information could be useful for the investigator as they establish first fuels ignited, fire spread scenarios, and origin and cause hypotheses.

When a positive indication of cyanide is found in a fire victim, however, one must consider the route of absorption of the toxicant, specifically when the presence of cyanide and/or carbon monoxide is used in establishing cause and/or manner of death, e.g., homicide with subsequent incendiary fire, aviation accident resulting in blunt force trauma and subsequent fire, aviation accident resulting from combustion engine malfunction, and crew exposure to carbon monoxide. In a study where pooled blood was exposed to atmospheric carbon monoxide and hydrogen cyanide, researchers found that COHb levels were 4.3–11% after 30–60 min of exposure to significantly high concentrations of CO (~5000 to over 30,000 ppm), whereas cyanide concentrations increased to 1.43–5.01 µg/mL after 15–60 min of exposure to 100–200 ppm of hydrogen cyanide. The findings indicate that increases in blood cyanide and blood carbon monoxide concentrations, above those normally found in healthy adults, can occur when pooled blood is continuously exposed to high concentrations of these gases for at least 15 min (cyanide) and 30 min (carbon monoxide).

Storage and Stability Considerations

The role that cyanide played in the death can be challenging due to the inherent instability of the compound in the biological specimen. One factor that complicates the analysis of cyanide in biological specimens is that in vitro changes in concentration have been well documented. A recent review on the stability of cyanide in postmortem specimens indicated that the rate of change in cyanide concentrations is dependent on four criteria: (1) the initial sample concentration at the time of death, (2) the length of time that the sample remains in the body after death, (3) the length of time that the sample remains in storage before analysis, and (4) the conditions of sample preservation and storage, i.e., temperature, pH, and sodium fluoride addition. When cyanide is present at or above toxicologically significant concentrations, a subsequent decrease in concentration occurs over periods of hours to months. The greatest rate of cyanide decrease occurs in intact bodies, and to a slightly lesser extent in blood samples, at ambient or elevated temperatures. Under conditions where cyanide decreases occur, these decreases tend to be greater with higher initial blood cyanide concentrations. When blood is frozen, a small increase tends to occur upon thawing (approximately 0.2 mg/L), which is considered to be due to the formation of small amounts of cyanide resulting from acidification of plasma or serum thiocyanate in the presence of hemoglobin.

Although most studies show a decrease in cyanide concentration in postmortem specimens, there are a limited number of reports from studies of cyanide-negative transfusion blood and a small number of cases considered not to have involved cyanide exposure in which very high concentrations of cyanide have been measured in blood samples stored under room temperature, refrigerated, or frozen conditions for periods of a month or more. In several of these cases, measured cyanide concentrations were more than 30 times the lethal concentration. No obvious reasons have been identified for the very high levels of cyanide formation in these samples, although microbiological contamination is a possible consideration.

The lack of reports of similar exceptionally high blood levels in several major blood cyanide studies of fire fatalities and survivors indicates that such instances are relatively uncommon.

Cyanide instability can be reduced by taking samples of blood and other tissues as soon as possible after death and analyzed for cyanide as soon as possible after collection. In instances where collected samples cannot be immediately analyzed, it is research has shown that storage at 4 °C increases stability with the best results found by deep freezing (−20 °C). The addition of 2% sodium fluoride was also found to enhance cyanide stability over a longer period of time by preventing microorganism activity. Those samples treated with 2% sodium fluoride showed a reduction in blood cyanide variability with virtually no overall change, over a 25–30 day period when compared to control samples.

Summary

Cyanide is a fast-acting, lethal poison, with death occurring within minutes after inhalation and more slowly following oral ingestion. Cyanide and cyanogenic compounds are abundant in a variety of applications, making the possibility of exposure or poisoning extensive. Cyanide inhibits the electron transport process of cellular respiration at the cytochrome c oxidase step, binding to the heme ion of cytochrome c oxidase. HCN is more rapidly absorbed than salts of cyanide. Detoxification of cyanide to thiocyanate occurs via two enzyme systems: rhodanese and beta-mercaptopyruvate-cyanide sulfurtransferase.

The analysis of cyanide may begin with Conway microdiffusion to separate cyanide from the biological matrix. Several reagents are available to enable spectrophotometric or spectrofluorometric analysis. Gas chromatography can also be used with either electron capture or nitrogen-phosphorus detection. Direct potentiometric determination of cyanide is another analytical option.

The signs and symptoms of cyanide poisoning are relatively nonspecific, with rapid onset of coma, metabolic acidosis, and symptoms of anoxia without cyanosis as noteworthy indicators. The primary goals in treatment are supportive measures, decontamination, and administration of an antidote to decrease the amount of cyanide available to bind ferric iron.

Cyanide deaths have occurred from both accidental and intentional exposure. The findings at autopsy are generally nonspecific. Blood cyanide concentrations of 2–3 mg/L are consistent with death in the absence of other findings. Fires in which nitrogen-containing natural and synthetic polymers are consumed can also be a source of cyanide production. Cyanide may contribute to the incapacitation of fire victims, preventing their escape from the fire environment after which point they die from lethal CO exposure. Another complicating factor in determining the role of cyanide in death cases is that both increases and decreases in cyanide concentrations have been reported during specimen storage.

Further Reading

Ball M, Bruck D (2004) the effect of alcohol upon response to fire alarm signals in sleeping young adults, human behavior in fire. Proceedings of the Third International Symposium, September 1–3, 2004, Belfast, N. Ireland, Interscience Communications Ltd., London, England

Ballantyne B, Marrs T, Turner P (eds) (1993) General and applied toxicology, 2nd edn. Stockton Press, New York, NY

Barrillo DJ, Goode R (1996) Fire fatality study: demographics of fire victims. Burns 22(2):85–88

Baselt RC (2020) Disposition of toxic drugs and chemicals in man, 12th edn. Biomedical Publications, Seal Beach, CA

Benignus V, Hazucha M, Smith M, Bromberg P (1994) Prediction of carboxyhemoglobin formation due to transient exposure to carbon monoxide. J Appl Physiol 76(4):1739–1745

Berl WG, Halphin BM (1980) Human fatalities from unwanted fires. John Hopkins APL Technical Digest 1(2)

Birky M, Paabo M, Brown J (1979/80) Correlation of autopsy data and materials involved in the Tennessee jail fire. Fire Saf J 2:17–22

Caplan YH (1982) Pathology and pathophysiology of the systemic toxicants carbon monoxide and cyanide. In: Trump BF, Cowley RA (eds) Cell injury in shock, anoxia, and ischemia. Williams and Wilkens Co., Baltimore, MD, pp 270–279

Coburn RF, Forster RE, Kane PB (1965) Considerations of the physiological variables that determine the blood carboxyhemoglobin concentration in man. J Clin Invest 44:1899–1910

DiPalma JR (ed) (1971) Drill's pharmacology in medicine, 4th edn. McGraw-Hill, New York, NY

Dreisbach RH, Robertson WO (eds) (1987) Handbook of poisoning, 12th edn. Appleton and Lange, Norwalk, CT

Ellenhorn MJ (ed) (1997) Ellenhorn's medical toxicology: diagnosis and treatment of human poisoning, 2nd edn. Williams & Wilkins, Baltimore, MD

Gill J, Goldfeder L, Stajic M (2003) The happy land homicides: 87 deaths due to smoke inhalation. J Forensic Sci 48:161–163

Gossel TA, Bricker JD (eds) (1990) Principles of clinical toxicology, 2nd edn. Raven Press, New York, NY

Grace T (1997) Improving the waking effectiveness of fire alarms in residential areas. Master's thesis, University of Canterbury

Leiken JB, Paloucek FP (1995) Poisoning and toxicology handbook, 2nd edn. Lexi-Comp Inc., Hudson, OH

Levin BC, Rechani PR, Gurman JL, Landron F, Clark HM, Yoklavich MF, Rodriguez JR, Droz L, Mattos de Cabrera F, Kaye S (1990) Analysis of carboxyhemoglobin and cyanide in blood from victims of the Dupont Plaza Hotel fire in Puerto Rico. J Forensic Sci 35:151–168

Levine B, Moore KA, Fowler D (2001) Interaction between carbon monoxide and ethanol in fire fatalities. Forensic Sci Int 124:115–116. https://doi.org/10.1016/S0379-0738(01)00583-7

Lykiardopoulos C (2014) Psychotropic drug usage and human behavior during fire emergencies. PhD thesis, Victoria University, Melbourne, Australia

McAllister J et al (2018) Guide to human behavior in fire, 2nd edn. Society of Fire Protection Engineering, Gaithersburg, MD

McAllister JL, Roby RJ, Levine B, Purser D (2011) The effect of sodium fluoride on the stability of cyanide in postmortem blood samples from fire victims. Forensic Sci Int 209:29–33

McAllister JL, Carpenter DJ, Roby RJ, Purser D (2014) The importance of autopsy and injury data in the investigation of fires. Fire Technol 50(6):1357–1377

McAllister JL, Roby RJ, Levine B, Purser D (2008) Stability of cyanide in cadavers and in postmortem stored tissue specimens, a review. J Anal Tox 32:612–620

Penney DG (ed) (1996) Carbon monoxide. CRC Press, New York, NY

Peterson J, Stewart R (1975) Predicting the carboxyhemoglobin levels resulting from carbon monoxide exposures. J Appl Physiol 39:633–638

Prockop L, Chichkova R (2007) Carbon monoxide intoxication: an updated review. J Neuro Sci 262:122–130

Purser D, McAllister J (2016) Assessment of hazards to occupants from smoke, toxic gases, and heat. In: SFPE handbook of fire protection engineering, 5th edn. National Fire Protection Association, Quincy, MA

Reay DT, Insalaco SJ, Eisele JW (1984) Postmortem methemoglobin concentrations and their significance. I Forensic Sci 4:1160–1163

Ryan RP, Terry CE (eds) (1997) Toxicology desk reference, 4th edn. Taylor and Francis, Washington, DC

Tikuisis P, Madill HD, Gill BJ, Lewis WF et al (1987) A critical analysis of the use of the CFK equation in predicting COHb formation. Am Ind Hyg Assoc J 48(3):208–213

Thoren T, Thompson K, Cardona P, Chaturvedi A, Canfield D (2013) In vitro absorption of atmospheric carbon monoxide and hydrogen cyanide in undisturbed pooled blood. J Anal Tox 37:203–207

Inhalants

Larry Broussard

Abstract

"Inhalants" is a term used to describe volatile compounds that may be inhaled accidentally or intentionally. This includes the following groups of compounds: aliphatic hydrocarbons, aromatic hydrocarbons, halogenated hydrocarbons, oxygen-containing compounds, and alkyl nitrites. Products preferred by inhalant users include hair spray or aerosols, airplane glue, gasoline, paint or solvents, marker pens or correction fluid, and amyl or butyl nitrates (poppers); these products are legal and easily obtained. Inhalants are primarily eliminated by inhalation, either as unchanged compound or as metabolites. The primary effects of these compounds are euphoria and loss of inhibitions, but toxic effects such as hallucinations, confusion, nausea, vomiting, and ataxia may develop after abuse. Inhalant abuse may lead to death from asphyxiation, suffocation, dangerous high-risk behavior, or cardiac arrhythmias leading to cardiac arrest. Urine drug screens do not detect the chemicals that are commonly abused, and blood is the specimen of choice for inhalant analysis. The most common method for detecting volatile substances in blood and other samples is headspace gas chromatography with flame-ionization, electron-capture, or mass spectrometer detection devices.

Keywords

Inhalants · Abuse · Toxicology · Pharmacology · Analysis · Interpretation

Classification and Abuse

Classification

The terms "inhalants" and volatile organic compounds (VOCs) are used to describe a wide range of volatile chemicals that may be inhaled accidentally or intentionally. There is no classification system based on clinical effect or chemical structure. Solids and liquids, as well as gases, contain volatile substances. The common feature is volatility, the property of existing in or being able to be converted to a form that may be inhaled. Compounds having this property include:

- Aliphatic hydrocarbons (e.g., butane, hexane, propane)
- Aromatic hydrocarbons (e.g., benzene, toluene)
- Halogenated hydrocarbons (e.g., chloroform, carbon tetrachloride), including ozone-depleting chlorofluorocarbons (CFCs) (e.g., Freon 11,

L. Broussard (✉)
Louisiana State University Health Sciences Center, New Orleans, LA, USA
e-mail: lbrous@lsuhsc.edu

Table 31.1 Some of the commercial products containing inhalant substances

Air fresheners
Contact adhesives
Computer/electronic cleaning equipment
Correction fluid
Felt-tip pens
Fire extinguishers
Lighter fluid
Liquid aroma, incense
Paint thinner
Polish remover
Refrigerants
Room deodorizers
Spray paint

Freon 12) and alternative fluorocarbons (e.g., difluoroethane)

- Oxygen-containing compounds (e.g., acetone, ethyl acetate)
- Alkyl nitrites (e.g., isobutyl nitrite, butyl nitrite, propyl nitrite)

With the exception of the gaseous anesthetics such as ethyl chloride, halothane, isoflurane, and nitrous oxide, these chemicals are not used pharmaceutically. Moreover, their commercial uses are too diverse to be discussed individually. Table 31.1 lists some of the commercial products where inhalants are found.

Abuse

The extensive availability and low cost of inhalants have contributed to an increased incidence of intentional inhalation of volatile substances (inhalant abuse, volatile-substance abuse, glue sniffing) in younger adolescents, even though legislation has been enacted to limit accessibility and to make their use by adolescents illegal. There are many more reported incidences of deaths due to inhalant abuse than deaths due to accidental exposure in the workplace or home. Worldwide, inhalants continue to be one of the most dangerous classes of abused substances because of their high prevalence in underdeveloped countries.

Products preferred by inhalant users include hair spray or aerosols, airplane glue, gasoline, paint or solvents, marker pens or correction fluid,

and amyl or butyl nitrates (poppers). These products are generally relatively inexpensive and easy to obtain, and they contain volatile substances free of large quantities of toxic components. Some of the volatile substances in these products include toluene, chloroform, butane, propane, acetone, and many halogenated hydrocarbons. One of the most commonly abused halogenated hydrocarbons is 1,1-difluoroethane which is found in computer and electronic cleaning equipment. This has replaced the ozone-depleting CFCs that have largely been removed from the market. Abuse of many of these substances has also been reported.

Depending on the product, volatile substances may be inhaled directly from the container (snorting or sniffing), from a plastic bag ("bagging")—particularly if the product is an aerosol or a viscous liquid such as glue—or from a saturated cloth ("huffing"). Of these routes of administration, bagging usually produces the highest concentration, snorting the lowest, and huffing an intermediate concentration. Products containing toxic nonrespirable compounds, such as antiperspirants containing aluminum chlorohydrate, may be bubbled through water in an attempt to separate the volatile substance from the toxic chemical. Adolescents have drowned in bath water while attempting this separation. Inhalation includes deep breathing through the mouth and nose and often involves rebreathing exhaled air when a bag is used.

Clues to inhalant abuse include chronic sore throat, cough, and runny nose; unexplained listlessness; moodiness; weight loss; bloodshot eyes or blurred vision; and chemical odors on breath, hair, bed linen, and clothes. Oral and nasal ulceration or a rash around the mouth ("glue sniffer's or huffer's rash") may be observed. Sometimes the products themselves may be discovered in the room of the abuser.

Pharmacology

Pharmacokinetics

The physical and pharmacokinetic properties of these substances are based on animal studies and are available for most inhalants. Chemicals used for anesthesia and those used in occupations leading to long-term exposure have been studied extensively. Unfortunately, most of the available data for situations of inhalant abuse are postmortem distributions and concentrations. In almost all situations (occupation, anesthesia, and abuse), exposure is chronic (repeated), although the dosage is variable. Some pharmacokinetic properties and principles apply to all inhalants.

Pulmonary uptake of a volatile substance is influenced by many factors. The individual's general health (respiratory rate, blood flow), proportion of body fat, and metabolic clearance rate are major factors. Properties of the substance, such as the partition coefficients (e.g., air–blood and blood–tissue), interaction with other inhaled compounds, and concentration in the inspired air also affect the pharmacokinetics of the inhalant. The distribution of inhaled compounds within the body generally follows a pattern of initial high concentrations in well-perfused organs such as the brain, liver, heart, and kidney, followed by slow accumulation in tissues (muscle, fat) with lesser blood supply as the chronic exposure continues. When exposure ceases, the compounds are released, with those in muscle and fat being slowly released, leading to bi- or multiphasic elimination half-lives. In situations of acute fatal exposure, the inhalant may be found only in the well-perfused organs, producing a monophasic elimination pattern.

The metabolism of volatile substances includes elimination unchanged in the exhaled air and elimination as metabolites in exhaled air and urine. As with many compounds, a primary site of metabolism is the liver, with the metabolism often including oxidation or reduction followed by conjugation to produce a more polar and water-soluble compound. These more polar metabolites generally do not pass through biological membranes as easily as the parent compound. The metabolites of some volatiles are more toxic than the parent compound itself. Some examples of toxic metabolites include carbon monoxide, a metabolite of dichloromethane; phenol, a metabolite of benzene; 2,5-hexanedione, the neurotoxic metabolite of hexane; and trichloroacetic acid, the metabolite of tetrachloroethylene. Some volatiles have multiple toxic metabolites; one such volatile is carbon tetrachloride, which is metabolized to chloroform, carbon dioxide, and the hepatotoxic trichloromethyl free radical.

Effects

The abuse appeal of these inhaled substances is that they produce effects similar to those caused by ethanol, i.e., euphoria and loss of inhibition, which may be followed by hallucinations, confusion, nausea, vomiting, and ataxia. Convulsions, coma, or death may result from larger doses. Causes of death associated with inhalant abuse include asphyxiation, suffocation, dangerous high-risk behavior, and cardiac arrhythmias leading to cardiac arrest when an intoxicated subject becomes alarmed or frightened ("sudden sniffing death syndrome"). The mechanism of action for cardiac arrest has been postulated to be either sensitization of the myocardium to epinephrine by the hydrocarbon inhalants or a depressant effect on sinoatrial, atrioventricular, and ventricular conduction systems, allowing other ectopic foci to cause arrhythmias.

Problems caused by chronic inhalant abuse include central nervous system (CNS) damage characterized by loss of cognitive and other higher functions, gait disturbance, and loss of coordination. Other features of chronic abuse include nosebleed and rhinitis, halitosis, oral and nasal ulceration, conjunctivitis and bloodshot eyes, anorexia, thirst, lethargy, weight loss, and fatigue. Another frequent complication of solvent abuse is renal tubular acidosis, characterized by decreased arterial pH and serum bicarbonate, hyperchloremia, and a normal anion gap in the presence of an abnormally high urine pH. These solvents literally dissolve brain cells, as shown by the loss of brain mass and white matter degeneration detected by computed tomography and magnetic resonance imaging. Associations between specific chemicals and effects have been shown. For example, toluene abuse causes deafness and metabolic acidosis, and hexane abuse produces peripheral neuropathy.

Management of patients experiencing acute intoxication caused by volatile substances begins with the removal of the source or removal of the patient from the contaminated area. Administration of oxygen and cardiopulmonary resuscitation may be necessary. Initial laboratory support includes assessment of acid–base and electrolyte status and subsequent monitoring of treatment to correct any disturbances. Concurrent rapid identification or confirmation of suspected inhalants by analysis for the compound or metabolite(s) is desirable. Additional laboratory testing may include screening (with conventional tests, including organ-specific profiles and complete blood count) for hematologic, hepatic, renal, and muscular complications associated with specific compounds. Treatment in general includes conventional supportive measures to stabilize potential cardiac arrhythmias and manage possible hepatic, renal, and respiratory complications, including organ system failure.

Common Inhalants

Toluene

Toluene is the solvent with the most documentation of abuse, possibly because of its relative low risk of sudden death and the ease of detection in blood. It is found in many products including paint and contact adhesives. The principal metabolite of toluene is benzoic acid (approximately 80% of the dose), which is conjugated with glycine to form hippuric acid for excretion in the urine (half-life, 2–3 h). Chronic exposure to toluene causes hepatic, renal, cardiac, respiratory, and CNS problems. Toluene abuse can cause high anion gap acidosis (possibly due to accumulation of benzoic acid) and electrolyte imbalances (hypokalemia, hypophosphatemia, hypercalcemia, hypercalcuria). Renal complications include renal tubular acidosis, renal calculi formation, and glomerulonephritis, with at least one report of renal failure. Cardiorespiratory system complications of chronic toluene abuse include emphysema, reduced lung capacity, pulmonary hypertension, cardiomyopathy, and myocardial degeneration. CNS problems attributed to chronic toluene abuse include cerebellar degeneration, acute encephalopathy, cortical atrophy, peripheral neuropathy, and optic nerve atrophy. Symptoms associated with these CNS problems include tremor, amnesia, ataxia, altered mental state, hearing loss, nystagmus, convulsions, and coma. Sustained abstinence often leads to reversal of symptoms, but residual effects have been documented.

Halogenated Hydrocarbons

Halogenated hydrocarbons include not only chlorinated hydrocarbons used as solvents but also CFCs and non-ozone-depleting CFC-replacement hydrocarbons used as solvents, aerosols, refrigerants, and foams. Volatile chlorinated hydrocarbons used as solvents include chloroform, carbon tetrachloride, methylene chloride, 1,1,1-trichloroethane (correction fluid), and trichloroethylene (dry cleaning). All of these compounds may be abused, although exposure to carbon tetrachloride is usually due to ingestion or accidental exposure rather than to voluntary abuse. Chloroform inhalation has been involved in fatalities including accidents, suicides, and homicides. The primary concern associated with acute exposure is cardiac arrhythmias leading to sudden death. Trichloroethylene was formerly used as an anesthetic, and it was well-known for its ability to cause cardiac arrhythmias. Signs and symptoms of chronic exposure to chlorinated hydrocarbon solvents are similar to those described for toluene. Detection and monitoring of these compounds often include analysis for the parent compound and its metabolite(s). Examples include carbon tetrachloride (metabolites—chloroform and carbon dioxide), chloroform (metabolite—carbon dioxide), and trichloroethylene (metabolites—2,2,2-trichloroethanol and trichloroacetic acid). Ingestion of large amounts of known hepatotoxins such as carbon tetrachloride and chloroform may warrant early administration of acetylcysteine (as used for acetaminophen intoxication) as a preventive measure. The association of phosgene, the highly toxic chloroform metabolite, with hepatic glutathione depletion is the rationale for use of acetylcysteine for chloroform ingestion.

The widespread use of CFCs as propellants and components in cooling systems and fire extinguishers makes them readily available for abuse. These chemicals are identified by various nomenclatures, including the chemical name or a CFC number, which may be preceded by the words *Halon* or *Freon*. For example, trichlorofluoromethane is also identified as CFC number 11 and as Halon 11 or Freon 11. Often these chemicals are referred to as "the freons," although Freon is a DuPont trade name. Because of the ozone-depleting properties of the CFCs, replacement products have been developed, particularly for use as aerosol propellants and refrigerants. The replacement CFCs have at least one halogen replaced with a hydrogen atom. Although these replacement compounds can also deplete the ozone layer, they do so at a much lower rate. The nomenclatures for these replacement products include the chemical name or a number (HFC or HCFC). For example, difluoroethane (CH_3CHF_2) is also referred to as HFC-152a and has been referred to as Freon 152a. The names and chemical formulas of the previously used and replacement compounds are given in Tables 31.2 and 31.3. Some products contain more than one such compound as propellants, which can affect the laboratory analysis as well as possibly produce multiple/synergistic effects on the user.

The distribution half-life of inhaled fluorocarbons is rapid, a mean of 13–14 s, with a plateau effect within 5–20 min. Blood clearance is rapid, usually <3 min, with tissue uptake and release inversely proportional to the fat content of the tissue. The elimination half-life for the total body is approximately 1.5 h, with most of the fluorocarbon being eliminated unchanged via the respiratory system. The primary complication of exposure is cardiovascular toxicity, including arrhythmias, myocardial depression, and reduction in peripheral vascular resistance. These compounds also produce CNS depression leading to cognitive impairment, confusion, and muscular incoordination. This effect is caused by an increased affinity of the inhibitory neuron GABA for the $GABA_A$ receptor. This depression can lead to injuries or a traumatic death.

Butane

Butane is a component of aerosol propellants and the fuel gas used in cigarette lighters, camping stoves, and small blowtorches. It consists of *n*-butane and small amounts of isobutane and propane. Small containers such as cigarette lighters may be abused by clinching the nozzle between the teeth and pressing to release the contents. This rapid release of a fluid cooled to below −20 °C may cause burning of the throat and lungs and lead to death from cardiac arrest due to vagal stimulation of the larynx. As with other inhalants, the primary concern from butane is sudden death due to cardiac arrest. Ventricular tachycardia and ventricular fibrillation have been documented in abusers of butane.

Nitrous Oxide

Nitrous oxide is a colorless, odorless gas used therapeutically as an anesthetic agent. The general public knows nitrous oxide as "laughing gas" because it produces euphoric and anxiolytic (anxiety-reducing) effects. It enters the body by

Table 31.2 Previously used chlorofluorocarbons (CFCs)

Name	Number	Chemical formula
Trichlorofluoromethane	CFC 11	CCl_3F
Dichlorodifluoromethane	CFC 12	CCl_2F_2
Trifluorochloromethane	CFC 13	$CClF_3$
Trichlorotrifluoroethane	CFC 113	CCl_2FCClF_2
Dichlorotetrafluoroethane	CFC 114	$CClF_2CClF_2$
Chloropentafluoroethane	CFC 115	$CClF_2CF_3$
Bromochlorodifluoromethane (BCF)	FC12B1	$CBrClF_2$

Table 31.3 Replacement CFCs

Name	Number	Chemical formula
Chlorodifluoromethane	HCFC 22	$CHClF_2$
Trifluoromethane	HFC-23	CHF_3
1,1,1,2,2-Pentafluoroethane	HFC-125	CF_3CF_2H
1,1,1,2-Tetrafluoroethane	HFA-134a	CF_3CH_2F
1,1-Difluoroethane	HFC-152a	CH_3CHF_2
1-Chloro-2,2-difluoroethane	HFC-142b	CH_3CClF_2
1,1,1,2,3,3,3-Heptafluoropropane	HFC-227ea	CF_3CHFCF_3
1,1,1,3,3-Pentafluoropropane	HFC-245fa	$CF_3CH_2CHF_2$

inhalation and leaves the body through the lungs without being metabolized. It is a weak anesthetic agent, but has significant analgesic (pain reducing) effects.

The main complication of nitrous oxide inhalation is hypoxia. This has pronounced effects on the heart and the brain. Clinically, decreased blood pressure, cardiac arrhythmias, headache, dizziness, anoxic brain injury, cerebral edema, and permanent mental deficit are symptoms that may be observed. Nitrous oxide inactivates vitamin B12 and folate metabolism. This ultimately leads to a reduction in DNA synthesis. This has the greatest effect on rapidly dividing cells such as bone marrow. Chronic use of nitrous oxide may produce a decrease in fertility, kidney and liver disease, and a decrease in the immune response. Deaths due to recreational use of nitrous oxide are caused by asphyxia, either from inadequate ventilation of the area or from insufficient oxygen intake.

Butyl Nitrite

Butyl nitrite is an abused, inhalant drug, commonly referred to as "poppers." The effects of butyl nitrite inhalation occur rapidly and are very intense for a period of minutes. Effects include a rush of blood to the head leading to light-headedness sensation. They also relax smooth muscle and blood vessels and result in an increased blood flow and an increased heart rate. Excessive use of butyl nitrite may lead to a headache, and skin contact can cause burns to the skin. With repeated inhalation, irritation may develop around the mouth and nose.

Analysis

In rare instances, suspicion or detection of chronic use may result from nontoxicologic laboratory results. Chronic users may have abnormal results for aspartate aminotransferase, alanine aminotransferase, prothrombin time, and partial thromboplastin time because of an impaired liver function. Toluene abuse may produce low potassium and phosphorus concentrations and increased creatine kinase values, which help explain the symptom of muscle weakness. Abnormal electrolyte and blood gas results may also occur as the consequence of proximal and distal tubular acidosis caused by toluene abuse. Chronic inhalation abuse may also cause bone marrow depression, causing leukopenia, anemia, thrombocytopenia, leukemia, and hemolysis.

Urine drug screens do not detect the chemicals that are commonly abused. The likelihood of detecting recent use is influenced by the dose, the length of the sampling time relative to the exposure time, and conditions of sample collection and storage. Blood is the specimen of choice, although analysis of urine for metabolites sometimes extends the time frame for detecting exposure. Proper collection techniques include the use of a glass tube with minimal headspace remaining after sample collection, an anticoagulant such as lithium heparin or EDTA, and a cap that ensures a tight seal. Soft rubber stoppers are permeable to toluene and other VOCs. Samples should be collected and stored in containers with minimal headspace, and addition of an internal standard after collection will minimize errors due to evaporation during storage or tissue homogenization. Samples should be stored, transported, and handled at temperatures between $-5\,°C$ and $4\,°C$. For fatalities in which inhalant abuse is suspected, tissues (brain, lung, fat, liver, heart, kidney) should be analyzed in addition to blood. The highest concentrations are typically found in blood and brain tissue. For cooperative, conscious patients, it may be possible to collect and analyze expired air. The most common method for detecting volatile substances in blood and other samples is headspace gas chromatography with flame-ionization, electron-capture, or mass spectrometer detection devices. Flame-ionization and mass spectrometer detectors have wider applicability for detecting inhalants; virtually all inhalants can be detected. Much greater sensitivity can be achieved for halogenated compounds by using an electron-capture detector. Partition coefficients and phase ratios (headspace volume relative to sample volume) affect method sensitivity as well as analyte loss. In general, the concentrations of volatile analytes in the headspace are higher when conditions are adjusted to produce the lowest values for both the partition coefficient and the phase ratio. Practical applications to achieve these results include increasing the temperature, agitation, adding inorganic salts (e.g., sodium chloride, ammonium chloride, ammonium sulfate, potassium carbonate, sodium citrate) to decrease the solubility of polar organic volatiles in aqueous matrices, and the use of sample containers with minimal headspace.

A variety of polar and nonpolar column phases have been used for the separation and quantification of volatiles. Capillary columns are more frequently used today, but packed columns can be used. The headspace capillary gas chromatographic procedures for ethanol and other volatiles used by many laboratories can often be modified for preliminary qualitative screening for particular suspected volatiles. Variations of headspace techniques used to increase sensitivity include solid-phase microextraction sampling and concentration, cryogenic focusing or cryogenic oven trapping to lower the temperature of the injection port or oven, and purge and trap dynamic analysis. Acceptable forensic practice recommends that the detection of an analyte (drug) be confirmed by a second or definitive method. For VOCs, two acceptable gas chromatographic confirmation procedures are reanalysis with a different column or use of mass spectrometry for absolute identification.

Interpretation

The detection of some volatile substances in the blood does not always indicate inhalant abuse or occupational exposure. For example, acetone and other volatile compounds may be found in ketoacidotic patients, and some inborn errors of metabolism lead to the accumulation of volatile compounds. Even though many studies and case reports have described concentrations of volatile substances in the blood, definitive correlations between these blood concentrations and the clinical features of toxicity have not been demonstrated for any of these compounds. In postmortem cases, the identification of these compounds as a cause or contributor of death will be a diagnosis of exclusion based on the absence of other findings to account for death. The identification of inhalants in drugged driving cases will be based on the observations of a drug recognition expert consistent with the use of inhalants and the presence of an inhalant in a biological specimen.

The detection of urinary metabolites has also been used to confirm inhalation of volatile substances. Urinary metabolites that have been measured include phenol (benzene metabolite), trichloroacetic acid (tetrachloroethylene), hippuric acid (toluene), and methylhippuric acid (xylene). Results are often expressed as a ratio to the urine creatinine concentration in order to normalize results with respect to urine volume and fluid intake. These urinary metabolites may also be used to detect occupational exposure, but caution must be used when interpreting results. For example, urinary hippuric acid may be due to ingestion of benzoate preservatives in foods and not to exposure to toluene.

The toxicologist should also be aware that the presence of some volatile substances may interfere with other toxicologic analyses. The volatile substances toluene, m-xylene, o-xylene, methanol, and 2-propanol have been shown to be capable of inducing false-positive readings for ethanol on the evidential infrared-based breath-testing device, the Intoxilyzer 5000.

Further Reading

Avella J, Wilson JC, Lehrer M (2006) Fatal cardiac arrhythmias after repeated exposure to 1,1-difluoroethane (DFE). Am J Forensic Med Path 27:58–60

Avella J, Kunaparaju N, Kumar S, Lehrer M, Zito SW, Barletta M (2010) Uptake and distribution of the abused inhalant 1,1-difluoroethane in the rat. J Anal Toxicol 34:381–388

Backstrom B, Johansson B, Eriksson A (2015) Death from nitrous oxide. J Forensic Sci 60:1662–1665

Baselt RC (2020) Disposition of toxic drugs and chemicals in man, 12th edn. Biomedical Publications, Seal Beach, CA

Broussard L (2000) The role of the laboratory in detecting inhalant abuse. Clin Lab Sci 13:205–209

Broussard L (2007) Chromatographic measurement of volatile organic compounds (VOCs). In: Bertholf RL, Winecker RE (eds) Chromatographic methods in clinical chemistry and toxicology. Wiley, Chichester

Caldwell JP, Kim ND (1997) The response of the Intoxilyzer 5000® to five potential interfering substances. J Forensic Sci 42:1080–1087

Cox D, DeRienz R, Jufer-Phipps R, Levine B, Jacobs A, Fowler D (2006) Distribution of ether in two postmortem cases. J Anal Toxicol 30:635–638

Dehon B, Humbert L, Devisme L, Stievenart M, Mathieu H, Lhermitte M (2000) Tetrachloroethylene and trichloroethylene fatality: case report and simple headspace SPME-capillary gas chromatographic determination in tissues. J Anal Toxicol 24:22–26

Espeland K (2000) Inhalant abuse. Lippincotts Prim Care Pract 4:336–340

Fonseca CA, Auerbach DS, Suarez RV (2002) The forensic investigation of propane gas asphyxiation. Am J Forensic Med Pathol 23:167–169

Jones HE, Balster RL (1998) Inhalant abuse in pregnancy. Obstet Gynecol Clin N Am 25:153–167

Kurtzman TL, Otsuka KN, Wahl RA (2001) Inhalant abuse by adolescents. J Adolesc Health 28:170–180

Litovitz TL, Klein-Schwartz W, Rodgers GC Jr, Cobaugh DJ, Youniss J, Omslaer JC et al (2002) 2001 Annual report of the American Association of Poison Control Centers Toxic Exposure Surveillance System. Am J Emerg Med 20:391–452

Musshoff F, Junker H, Madea B (2000) Rapid analysis of halothane in biological samples using headspace solid-phase microextraction and gas chromatography-mass spectrometry—a case of a double homicide. J Anal Toxicol 24:372–376

Sharp ME (2001) A comprehensive screen for volatile organic compounds in biological fluids. J Anal Toxicol 25:631–636

Tranthim-Fryer DJ, Hansson RC, Norman KW (2001) Headspace/solid-phase microextraction/gas chromatography-mass spectrometry: a screening technique for the recovery and identification of volatile organic compounds (VOC's) in postmortem blood and viscera samples. J Forensic Sci 46:934–946

Vance C, Swalwelt C, McIntyre IM (2012) Deaths involving 1,1-difluoroethane at the San Diego County Medical Examiner's Office. J Anal Toxicol 36:626–633

Xiang Z, Avella J, Wetli CV (2004) Sudden death caused by 1,1-difluoroethane inhalation. J Forensic Sci 49:627–629

Metals

32

Joseph J. Saady

Abstract

Although less commonly encountered than more traditional (organic) drugs and poisons, metals are an important consideration in forensic toxicology investigations. Environmental, occupational, and industrial exposures are considered for some of the most common metals. The pharmacokinetics, effects, and toxicity associated with metals are discussed, in addition to methods of analysis.

Keywords

Metals · Exposure · Toxicity · Pharmacology · Aluminum · Arsenic · Iron · Mercury · Lithium · Lead · Thallium

Introduction

Previous chapters have dealt primarily with organic compounds: abused drugs, therapeutic drugs, and volatile substances. This chapter deals primarily with inorganic compounds containing metals, i.e., those elements in the periodic table that, when ionized, lose electrons to form cations. Some metals are essential for life; others are nonessential or are not known to have any biological function. Even those metals required to sustain life can produce toxic effects if present in high enough concentrations. The increased industrialization of the world has caused an increased use of metals and metallic compounds and therefore has increased the potential for human exposure to these substances. Individuals can be exposed to metals via their occupation, their living environment, or their consumption of food and beverages, including water. The following is a discussion of some of the most commonly encountered metals in forensic toxicology, as well as a brief discussion of the techniques used to assay metals in biological specimens.

Aluminum

Aluminum is a ubiquitous metal that presents analytical and interpretive challenges in forensic toxicology. Aluminum does not occur naturally as the metal but is found as ores of aluminum and includes oxygen, fluorine, and silicone, among others. It is the third most abundant element of the earth's crust (8%). The most important raw material for the production of aluminum is bauxite, which contains 40–60% aluminum oxide. The Romans and Greeks used alum as an astringent and also in the dyeing process. In 1761, de Morveau proposed the name "alumine" for the base in alum, and Davy proposed "aluminum" in 1807. The electrolysis method of obtaining

J. J. Saady (✉)
Saady Consulting Inc., Richmond, VA, USA

© Springer Nature Switzerland AG 2020
B. S. Levine, S. Kerrigan (eds.), *Principles of Forensic Toxicology*,
https://doi.org/10.1007/978-3-030-42917-1_32

aluminum from cryolite was used in 1886, and the Bayer process is commonly used to refine bauxite.

In the industrial setting, humans are exposed to aluminum and related compounds through dust, pyro products, welding fumes, and aluminum alkyl compounds. Portions of inhaled aluminum are retained and become bioavailable over a period of time, thus lengthening the time for excretion. The Occupational Health and Safety Administration has set a limit of 15 mg/m^3 total dust and 5 mg/m^3 responsible fraction of aluminum in dust for an 8 h workday.

Food is the primary source of aluminum. Aluminum compounds may be added to flour, baking powder, coloring agents, or anticaking agents. Daily exposure for adults in the United States is 7–9 mg. Some aluminum may appear in drinking water, but the concentrations generally do not exceed 0.1 mg/L. The EPA recommended a secondary maximum level of 0.05–0.2 mg/L for aluminum in drinking water. Other consumer items that contain the metal include antiperspirants, cosmetics, internal analgesics, anti-ulcer and anti-diarrhea medications, some vaccines, and food packing materials. Highest exposures to the metal appear to come from antacids, buffered aspirin, and certain vaccines.

Pharmacokinetics

Aluminum is poorly absorbed by the oral or inhalation routes; about 0.1–0.6% of ingested aluminum is absorbed in the small intestine and 1.5–2% of a dose is absorbed through the lungs. Aluminum accumulates in bone and lung tissue with most of the body burden residing in bone. The total body burden is 30–50 mg. The half-life of this metal in the urine of an occupational worker can vary from 8 h to 8 years and is directly proportional to the length of exposure years. The half-life in retired aluminum powder workers is 1–8 years.

The American Conference of Governmental Industrial Hygienists (ACGIH) has determined that aluminum oxide (Al_2O_3), containing no asbestos and <1% crystalline silica, has minimal effects on the lungs and is not a significant health risk when exposure is reasonably controlled. The kidney can eliminate 0.5 mg aluminum per 24 h, but in cases of renal insufficiency or end-stage renal disease, high concentrations accumulate in the body. The brain is the target organ in this instance. Urinary excretion is the primary route of absorbed aluminum. Unabsorbed aluminum is eliminated in the feces. Aluminum is distributed throughout the body, with the highest concentrations found in bone and lung tissue. In vivo, aluminum may appear in four forms: Al^{3+}, low molecular weight complexes, physically bound macromolecular complexes, or covalently bound macromolecular complexes.

Toxicity

The molecular mechanism of action of aluminum is unknown, but is believed to be related to its ability to compete with other cations, especially magnesium. It can also bind to transferrin and citrate in the blood. It may also affect calcium availability. Bone tissue and the central nervous system (CNS) are the target organs. Bone toxicity involves the development of osteomalacia or bone softening. Two different forms may develop. One develops in normal individuals who use antacids and is related to a reduction in phosphate. The other develops in dialyzed uremic patients exposed to aluminum. The aluminum is present between the junction of calcified and noncalcified bone. There is evidence of impairment of cognitive function or effects on the nervous system in aluminum workers. Patients receiving long-term dialysis are susceptible to a fatal neurological syndrome possibly caused by aluminum toxicity. This disorder affects speech and causes dementia, convulsions, and myoclonus.

Arsenic

Arsenic is present in all living organisms, plant and animal. It can be called a semi-metal because it has chemical properties of both metals and nonmetals. Forms of this substance have been known and used since ancient times for therapeutic uses and for poisonings, both overt and covert. The medicinal effects of arsenic are extolled by Hippocrates, Aristotle, and Pliny the Elder. The name was derived from the Arabic *az-zernik*. During the Middle Ages, when arsenic was used frequently as a poison to eliminate royalty, bezoar stones were used to detoxify wine and other drinks. "Bezoar" is derived from Persian words meaning "to protect" and "against poison." It was recently determined that arsenic binds to the sulfur in these stones, which are found in the alimentary tracts of mountain goats, llamas, and other ruminant animals. Arsenic is ubiquitous and can be found as a contaminant in soil, water, and air. It is the third most common element and is typically not mined but is a recoverable by-product of the smelting process of various metals such as copper, lead, zinc, and iron.

Arsenic has been used in wood preservatives, insecticides (e.g., calcium and lead arsenates), herbicides (arsenites), sheep dips, fly paper, arsenical soaps, germicides, and rat poisons. Arsenicals are also used as growth promoters in poultry and other livestock. The major source of occupational exposure to arsenic is herbicide and pesticide production. Fruits and vegetables sprayed with these substances may present another source of exposure. Lewisite is an arsenic-containing blister agent that has been used in chemical warfare.

Chromated copper arsenate and ammoniacal copper arsenate are used as wood preservatives. The metal is used in special solders and as a doping agent in silicon and germanium solid-state products; lead-antimony-arsenic alloys are used in making lead-acid storage batteries. In the computer chip industry, arsine and arsenic trioxide provide another occupational source of exposure. Gallium arsenide is used in the production of semiconductors. Arsenic can be leached from mineral-spring waters and geothermal power plant effluent coming into contact with soil and rock that contain high concentrations of the metal. Exposure to arsenic by these sources and extensive pesticide use can result in high concentrations of arsenic in runoff water, which eventually makes its way to streams, rivers, and the ocean, whereby many species of fish and seafood may be exposed.

Elemental arsenic [As^0 or As (0)] is relatively nontoxic. Common forms of arsenic exist as the arsenate [As^{+5} As(V)] and as arsenite [As^{+3} or As(III)]. Arsine (AsH_3) is a gas formed when hydrogen is generated in the presence of trivalent arsenic. It is used in industrial organic synthesis, in lead-acid storage battery manufacture, and as a doping agent for solid-state electronic compounds. The relative toxicity for these species is as follows: $As^0 < As^{+5} < As^{+3} <$ arsine.

Pharmacokinetics

Arsenic compounds are primarily absorbed via the respiratory and gastrointestinal (GI) tracts. Breathing is the major route of exposure in the workplace; percutaneous exposure may occur depending on the skin permeability of the compound. Airborne arsenic is frequently deposited in the respiratory tract and, because of mucociliary clearance, is eventually swallowed and presented to the GI tract. The degree of absorption depends on the solubility of the arsenic compound, but in general, >90% of orally consumed arsenic is absorbed. Organic arsenic compounds in seafoods are readily absorbed after ingestion. Arsenic is absorbed by diffusion, enters the portal system, and circulates to the liver prior to entering the general circulation. The half-life of inorganic arsenic in blood is approximately 10 h; the half-life of methylated arsenic is 30 h. Arsenic binds the sulfhydryl groups and concentrates in hair and nails. Arsenic is excreted to a minor extent in sweat and skin. It can also be transferred to the fetus via placental transfer. The muscle tissue accumulates a large amount of this metal. Smaller amounts distribute into the liver, lungs, intestinal wall, spleen, and bone. Nails (fingernails or toenails) and hair accumulate the metal and provide another means of determining if and when exposure occurred.

Trivalent arsenic can be oxidized in vivo to the pentavalent species, and there is evidence that pentavalent arsenic can be reduced to the trivalent species. Arsenite methyltransferase was recently discovered to be an enzyme responsible for arsenic methylation. Urine is the major elimination pathway and accounts for approximately 60% of the amount absorbed. The metabolic pathway at low arsenic concentration is first order, with the major metabolite being dimethyl arsinic acid (DMA). If oral intake exceeds 0.5 mg, then the methylation process is saturated. Organoarsenicals are present in seafood and will not appear as inorganic arsenic or DMA.

Toxicity

Poisonings are less common than in the past, but they still occur due to the availability of arsenic-containing herbicides and pesticides. As with any poisoning, the chemical form of the arsenic compound, the age and physical condition of the individual exposed, and the dose are critical issues. Intentional poisonings frequently involve the use of arsenic-containing rodenticides or pesticides. Arsine poisonings occur in occupational settings but do not result from the manufacture or use of the gas. Poisonings occur when arsine is formed as a by-product of a chemical reaction typically involving a base metal, an arsenic impurity, and an acid or strong base.

Acute symptoms of exposure include GI symptoms such as pain, vomiting, discomfort, diarrhea, and inflammation and can occur within minutes to hours after exposure. Rice-water and/ or bloody stools can occur. Renal damage may result in proteinuria, oliguria, and hematuria. Cardiovascular effects may be evident by prolongation of the QT interval and abnormal T-wave pattern on the ECG. Complaints of skeletal muscle pain and severe thirst are common. Encephalopathy and peripheral neuropathy are common in both acute and chronic exposure. If the dose is sufficiently high, spasms, stupor, convulsions, and death will result.

Chronic arsenic poisoning can result after weeks or years of exposure. Symptoms may be subtle and mimic other conditions. Muscle weakness, hyperkeratosis (especially on the palms of the hands and soles of the feet), garlic breath, Mee's lines, and neuropathy can result. The neu-

ropathy has sometimes been confused with Guillain-Barré syndrome. Hematological changes result in anemia and other blood abnormalities.

Arsine toxicity produces different symptoms than listed above because of the differing mechanism of action. Arsine gas binds to hemoglobin, producing lysis of red blood cells, hemoglobinuria, anemia, and kidney damage following the severe hemolysis.

Iron

Iron has been used by humans since ancient times. There is evidence that iron from meteorites was used and formed in predynastic times in Egypt. Iron may have been smelted accidentally at first, and fragments of smelted iron date back to 2700 BC. A regular production of useful objects by smiths occurred by 1200 BC, as evidenced by the unearthing of iron hoes, sickles, plowshares, and smelting furnaces. Iron, particularly when alloyed with carbon to make steel, is perhaps the most important metal of an industrial economy. Various salts of iron are used extensively in occupational settings and in some pharmaceutics:

Fe Cl_3: Sewage and waste treatment, engraving, textiles, photography

Fe(NO_3)$_3$: Textile dyeing, tanning, weighting silt

Fe$_2$(SO$_4$)$_3$: Water treatment, textile dyeing

Fe Cl_2: Metallurgy, pharmaceutical industry, sewage treatment

Fe SO$_4$: Fertilizer, food or feed additive, herbicides, process engraving, iron-deficiency anemia

Pharmacokinetics

Iron is an essential metal required by the body for routine biochemical processes. Iron is orally consumed in the normal dietary intake, but only a small portion is biologically available. Therefore, iron deficiency is more common than iron intoxication. The largest portion of the 5–15% of absorbed iron is stored in hemoglobin, which

Table 32.1 Stages of iron toxicity by ingestion (From: Jacobs J, Green H, Grendel B. Acute iron intoxication. N Engl J Med 1965;273:1124–1127)

Phase	Time after ingestion	Symptoms
I	0.5–2 h	Lethargy, restlessness, bloody vomiting, diarrhea, abdominal pain (iron has a corrosive effect on the mucosa of the GI tract)
II	Variable	Apparent recovery
III	2–12 h	Shock, metabolic acidosis, cyanosis, fever
IV	2–4 days	Hepatic necrosis
V	2–4 weeks	GI obstruction secondary to gastric or pyloric scarring

contains two-thirds of the body burden. Approximately 25% is storage iron contained in ferritin and hemosiderin, with the remaining iron stored in myoglobin. Pathologic conditions exist where too much iron is absorbed and transferred to the liver and other organs where accumulation occurs. Stores of iron are conserved by the body, with small portions excreted in stool and urine. Only 1 mg per year is lost in males, with more losses in females due to menstruation.

Toxicity

Poisonings with this metal are rare and almost always involve children. The typical scenario involves a toddler "discovering" the mother's prenatal iron supplements or vitamins and then consuming the contents. Acute toxicity has been divided into five phases (Table 32.1). The overall mortality rate from acute poisonings is about 1%. In the industrial setting, inhalation of ferric salts can cause irritation to the respiratory tract and skin. Inhalation of fumes can produce deposition of particles within the lung, sometimes determined by X-ray and termed "arch welders lung."

Lead

Lead has been one of the most studied metals, and controversy still surrounds the effect of low concentrations in newborns. The most common ore of lead (galena or lead sulfide) was used as early as 4000 BC. Metallic lead objects have been discovered among ancient ruins dating to that period, and the Bible has several references to lead. The Romans used lead frequently for transporting water and for cooking. It has often been stated that the fall of the Roman Empire was due to lead poisoning because the more affluent Romans had a form of running water plumbed to their domiciles using lead pipes.

It was recognized in ancient times by Greek, Roman, and Arabic physicians that orally consumed lead would cause colic and paralysis, and that lead fumes caused the same disorder. Galena was used as an eye salve in early West African cultures and as an eye cosmetic in India. Symptoms of toxicity were later described by Hippocrates (370 BC), Nicander (second century BC), and Pliny (first century BC). Lead-contaminated products have been used for centuries for dispensing liquids and foods (e.g., ceramic pottery, clay and cooking vessels, paints and glazes).

This metal is distributed throughout the world; there have always been "background" concentrations of lead in living creatures, caused by natural lead ores occurring worldwide. The Industrial Revolution and the use of tetraethyl lead in gasoline caused a redistribution of lead throughout the environment, thus leading to various degrees of exposure in humans and wildlife.

Many different products are produced with lead. Most water supplies in the United States are controlled for lead concentration. Acidic foods and beverages have a tendency to leach lead from the container or from the solder used on the can (e.g., orange juice, cider, pickles). Therefore the foods we consume contain various concentrations of lead.

Many forms of lead are used in paint pigments (e.g., lead carbonate and lead oxide), with lead composing up to 38% of the dry weight. Lead paint has been favored due to its durability, but US regulations banned lead-based paints from use in residences in 1978. Leaded paint continues to be used on industrial surfaces (e.g., bridges and street surfaces). Individuals who display pica (a habitual hand to mouth action) are particularly vulnerable to lead poisoning from paint chips and dust.

Lead is also a major component of solder, brass, and many bronzes. It is used in lead storage batteries, glass, plastic, and ceramics, as well as smelting, refining, scrap recovery, automobile radiator repair, construction, demolition, and firing range operations. Lead arsenate continues to be used in insecticides.

Organic lead in the form of tetraethyl lead has been used since 1923 to increase the octane rating of fuels, but this has been stopped in many industrialized countries. Tetramethyl lead has been a combustion control additive of premium gasoline and aviation fuels since 1960.

Pharmacokinetics

In adults, typically 5–15% of ingested lead is absorbed, but up to 50% may be absorbed if the adult is fasting. Infants absorb approximately 50% of ingested lead. Iron deficiency enhances intestinal absorption of lead. Approximately 40–50% of inhaled lead is absorbed, with most of the remainder exhaled. Portions trapped in the upper respiratory tract are eventually swallowed. Of the lead that is eventually absorbed, 99% of the lead portion retained in the blood compartment is bound to hemoglobin in red blood cells, with 1–3% found in serum. Absorbed lead gradually is deposited in soft tissues, especially the tubular epithelium of the kidney and the liver. Eventually there is redistribution to bone, teeth, and hair, with 95% of the body burden in bone. Unabsorbed lead is eliminated in the feces. Absorbed lead is eliminated in the urine (76%); as GI secretions (16%); in hair, nails, and sweat (8%); and in breast milk. Lead is transferred to the fetus via placental transfer and correlates with maternal concentrations.

Lead is deposited into bone in the form of tertiary lead phosphate in the same manner that calcium is deposited into bone. The half-life of lead in bone has been estimated from 10 years to >20 years. In blood, the half-life is 1–2 months. Factors that affect distribution of calcium similarly affect lead.

Toxicity

Acute lead poisoning is an infrequent occurrence, but may occur from ingestion of acid-soluble lead salts or lead vapor inhalation. Local actions in the mouth may be apparent, with the victim having abnormal thirst and metallic taste. Nausea, vomiting, abdominal pain, and black stools from lead sulfide may occur, which is followed by shock resulting from a loss of fluid. CNS symptoms include pain, paresthesia, and muscle weakness; kidney effects include oliguria; and hematological effects due to acute hemolytic crisis may cause anemia and hemoglobinuria.

The primary concern with lead toxicity is the effects caused by chronic exposure to the metal. As a result, lead concentrations in the environment are regulated by a number of national and international organizations. The World Health Organization sets cutoffs of 0.5 µg/m³ and 0.01 mg/L for air and drinking water, respectively. In the United States, the thresholds are 1.5 µg/m³ and 0.015 mg/L, respectively. OSHA limits air exposure for lead workers to 50 µg/m³ for an 8 h period. There are also limits established by the FDA for lead concentrations in food utensils and flatware.

Blood lead concentrations are used to monitor exposure to lead. Over time, the CDC has set limits for the maximum lead concentration in children. In the 1960s, that limit was 60 µg/dL. That limit has been reduced over time and, in 2012, was lowered to 5 µg/dL.

The hematological effects of lead arise from the combination with and inactivation of several enzymes in the heme system pathway. A simplified schematic representation of how lead affects enzymatic activity in the heme system pathway is shown in Fig. 32.1. As indicated by the sequence of steps in Fig. 32.1, lead poisoning eventually causes elevated urinary delta-aminolevulinic acid and coproporphyrin III concentrations and also increases in (zinc) protoporphyrin in the blood. These blood and urine enzymes are diagnostic tests that can be used along with blood lead in assessing lead poisoning. The resultant effect is anemia due to impaired heme synthesis and shortened erythrocyte lifespan. Red blood cells are microcytic and hypochromic with increased basophilic stippling.

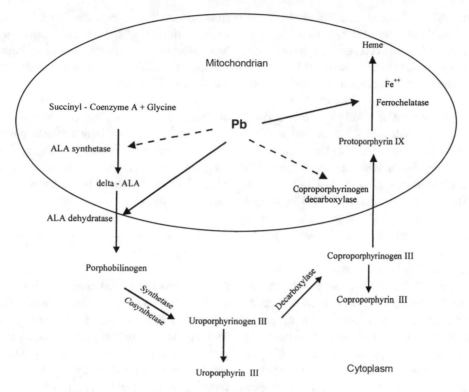

Fig. 32.1 Schematic representation of the effects of lead on the heme system pathway. Simplified schematic representation of lead's effects on mitochondrial and cytoplasmic enzymatic activity in the heme system pathway.

Strong inhibition of enzyme activity by lead is indicated by solid arrows, with less intense inhibition indicated by dotted arrows

Lead neuropathy has long been recognized as an adverse health effect of lead. Kidney damage is three times more likely in lead workers than in controls. The damage is usually manifested as glomerulonephritis developing over a 20- to 30-year exposure. The kidney damage is likely to cause hypertension in lead-exposed workers. In the production of "moonshine" liquor, lead is a source of contamination in the distillation process and at times in the transport of the liquid in automobile radiators. The reversible proximal renal tubular damage may manifest itself as aminoaciduria and glycosuria.

Another manifestation of poisoning is lead palsy, characterized by muscle weakness, fatigue, wrist drop, and foot drop. Lead encephalopathy, particularly on the developing CNS (i.e., in children), results in lethargy, ataxia, headache, irritability, loss of appetite, and projectile vomiting. Visual disturbances, delirium, and seizures fol-

low. Metallic lead in the eye has been a cause of concern due to mechanical injury or inflammatory damage rather than lead toxicity. Other signs of plumbism include a bright color of the face, pallid lips, stooped posture, and lead line (a black or gray line along the gums due to lead sulfide).

In children, the developing CNS is much more susceptible to the effects of lead than the adult CNS. Exposure to lead by children causes irreversible damage to their health, and chronically elevated concentrations may cause decreased intelligence, impaired neurobehavioral development, decreased stature and growth, and impaired acuity.

Lithium

Lithium is the lightest of metals, with an atomic number of 3, and one of the alkali metals. It was discovered in 1817 by J. Arfuedson, a Swedish chemist, and is obtained from minerals. Small amounts of the substance have been found in meteorites, soils, tobacco, grains, coffee, seaweed, and milk. Lithium has been used therapeutically since the nineteenth century as an anticonvulsant, a sedative (including for manic patients), and a treatment for gout. In late 1940, its use as a table salt substitute resulted in many poisonings and deaths, and that unfortunate use was eventually discontinued. In 1949, Cade discovered that lithium carbonate (Li_2CO_3) was useful in the treatment of mania. This substance remains responsible for a significant improvement in the lives of patients with bipolar disorder.

Industrially, no health-related problems were reported prior to the 1950s because lithium was rarely used. Lithium hydride is used as a high-performance desiccant, a source of hydrogen, a nuclear shielding material, and a condensing agent in organic synthesis. Lithium hydride workers have the potential for dermal contact or inhalation of lithium fumes in welding and brazing operations.

Pharmacokinetics

There is rapid and nearly complete absorption of lithium from the GI tract, which distributes into the total body water. It has a volume of distribution of 0.8 L/kg and is not bound to plasma protein. The concentration in the cerebrospinal fluid is 40–50% of plasma concentration. Approximately 95% is eliminated in the urine (half-life 20–24 h). Lithium is freely filtered, but about 80% is reabsorbed in the proximal renal tubules. Less than 1% is eliminated in the feces and 4–5% in sweat. Saliva concentrations are two times plasma concentrations, and lithium is secreted in human milk. When used therapeutically to treat bipolar disorder, the serum therapeutic range is 0.6–1.2 mM.

Toxicity

Lithium hydride is intensively corrosive and may produce skin burns. Eye injuries have developed from an explosion, and the inhalation of dust causes strictures of the larynx, bronchi, trachea, and esophagus. In atmospheres containing 0.5 mg/m^3 lithium, the skin becomes inflamed and lacrimation occurs.

Patients taking $LiCO_3$ for manic-depressive disorders sometimes develop thyroid enlargement. Acute exposure may produce polydipsia, polyuria, sedation, tremor, vomiting, diarrhea, ataxia, confusion, coma, and seizures. Other side effects include cardiac arrhythmias, hypotension, and albuminuria.

Mercury

Mercury has been used since prehistoric times; the drawings on cave walls were made with cinnabar, a red stone made of mercury sulfide. Mercury is also mined and produced as a byproduct of gold and bauxite mining. Other processes involving mercury include cyanide leaching of low-grade gold and silver which collects mercury in the ore and amalgamation where mercury is recovered for reuse. The metal has been used therapeutically since the sixteenth century for treatment of syphilis and as a diuretic, antiseptic, skin ointment, and laxative. Mercury occurs naturally through degassing from the earth's crust and is usually produced from volcanic action and hot springs. The name and chemical symbol (Hg) are derived from the Greek "hydrargyros," meaning "water silver" and referring to the appearance of the metal, which is liquid at ambient temperature. In fact, mercury is the only metal that is liquid at room temperature. Metallic or elemental mercury (Hg^0) is the main volatile form occurring in air. Inorganic and organic mercury compounds are formed in the +1 (mercurous) valence state and +2 (mercuric) valence state. Organic forms of mercury include methyl mercury and phenyl mercury.

Humans may be exposed to mercury from the naturally occurring amount in the environment. More commonly, humans may be close to or in contact with a site where mercury was disposed of in an industrial process. This metal is used extensively in industry because of its unique properties. Because its expansion is proportional to temperature, it is used in thermometers, manometers, barometers, gauges, and valves. It is used heavily in industries making dry-cell batteries, lamps, wiring, switching devices, and electronic equipment, as well as in the production of chlorine and caustic soda. Compounds of mercury are also used in pigments, refining, lubricating oils, heat transfer, water-based paint (as mildewcide), and paint preservative. Dental professionals use the metal in dental amalgams. Alkyl mercury compounds are used as fungicides and preservatives for wood, paper pulp, textiles, and leather.

Pollution of water by mine tailing is significant. Mercuric salts and organic mercury are readily absorbed by organisms in the water. Fish accumulate and retain the metal in tissue, primarily as methyl mercury. There is evidence that microorganisms cause methylation of inorganic mercury in aquatic species. Individuals who consume fish from contaminated lakes have higher than average mercury concentrations.

Pharmacokinetics

Mercurous salts have poor water solubility and therefore are poorly absorbed in the small intestine. Mercuric salts are also poorly absorbed orally, but the corrosive action on the gastrointestinal tract may lead to greater absorption. Most of the metallic mercury vapor that gets to the lungs is readily absorbed and quickly transported to other organs in the body. Mercurous and mercuric salts that are sufficiently volatile will be similarly absorbed. Methyl mercury is also well absorbed via inhalation. However, methyl mercury is also absorbed efficiently in the intestines and through the skin.

After entering the blood, the majority of the mercury is taken up by erythrocytes and then oxidized to the divalent mercuric ion (Hg^{2+}). Mercury in plasma is also oxidized to Hg^{2+}. Organic mercury is also converted to mercuric ion in tissues. About 80% of the body burden of inorganic mercury is deposited in the proximal tubules in the kidneys and is bonded to metallothionein. Methyl mercury is also found in highest concentration in the kidney. Both metallic and methyl mercury can also accumulate in the brain and placenta.

Routes of elimination include the feces (due to biliary excretion and intestinal secretion) and urine, which accounts for more than 50% of elimination. Excretion also occurs by sweat, by exhalation, and in hair. The estimated half-life approximates a two-compartment model with a rapid phase ($t_{1/2}$ = 3–5 days) and a slow phase (45 days).

Toxicity

Except for dermatitis, skin contact with mercury poses little, if any, danger. Orally consumed mercury poses more problems from the internal mechanical abrasions than from systemic toxicity. Most of the orally consumed mercury will be eliminated in the feces. There has been marginal effect when large quantities were released into the GI tract.

On a molecular level, both metallic mercury and organic mercury bind to sulfhydryl groups. This disrupts protein structure and thus can interfere with the function of any tissue or organ system. Acute toxicity can result from inhalation of high vapor or dust inhalation. Flu-like symptoms and symptoms of interstitial pneumonitis, bronchitis, and metal fume fever result (e.g., chills and aching muscles with dry mouth and throat). Oral consumption of mercuric chloride can produce GI symptoms, burning mouth and throat, nausea, vomiting, severe gingivitis, and esophageal destruction.

Chronic poisoning almost always manifests itself as neurological symptoms with tremors of the arms and hands at lower concentrations and lower limb involvement as concentration increases. Acrodynia (pink disease) can develop with erythema of the extremities, chest, and face, with photophobia, diaphoresis, anorexia, and rapid heart rate. Chronic effects lead to renal tubular injury. Classic chronic symptoms include tremor, loss of memory, excitability, gingivitis, and hallucinations (mad hatter's disease).

Thallium

Thallium was named from the Greek word "thallos," meaning green twig, because the metal produced a bright green spectral line. The metal was isolated in 1862 by Crooks and Lamy and is present naturally in a number of ores. It is recovered mainly from sulfide minerals in the smelting process of lead and zinc. Thallium sulfate has been used in the past as a household rodenticide and ant poison, but it was banned for residential use in 1975. It was used in the 1930s as a cosmetic depilatory cream, which unfortunately caused many cases of chronic exposure. Thallium is used in the semiconductor industry and is an alloy along with mercury in some switches. It is used in mineralogical solutions, optic systems, and photoelectric cells, in the production of cement, and in pyrites and flue dusts.

Pharmacokinetics

Thallium is almost 100% absorbed from the GI tract, and, like potassium, it distributes throughout the body. In the blood compartment, thallium can be found mainly in red blood cells. It also appears in the brain, lung, gut, skeletal and cardiac muscle, salivary gland, spleen, pancreas, and testes, with accumulation in the kidney, liver, and bone. There is some evidence for enterohepatic circulation. Thallium is secreted during glomerular filtration, with some 50% being reabsorbed in the tubule. The metal half-life of elimination in the urine is 4 weeks.

Toxicity

Thallium is regulated in many countries because of its toxicity. Acute poisoning involves GI distress, paralysis, and respiratory failure. Characteristic chronic poisoning causes alopecia and lobster-red skin. Paresthesia of the hands and feet, psychosis, delirium, and convulsions can occur. The most characteristic symptom of intoxication in patients whose death is delayed at least 20 days is alopecia. Optic cataracts and neuritis result from exposure. The oral lethal dose of thallium acetate is 12 mg/kg in humans. In chronic poisonings, symptoms of incoordination, paralysis of extremities, hepatic and renal involvement, endocrine disorders, and psychoses may develop. Death may result from respiratory and cardiovascular collapse.

Treatment of Metal Poisonings

Assuming that poisoning by a particular metal is properly diagnosed, treatment by chelation therapy may be in order. Chelation is the formation of a complex between the metal and a charged or uncharged electron donor molecule known as a ligand. Specific ligands are used to treat a given metal poisoning. The first clinically useful ligand was dimercaprol (2,3-dimercaptopropanol) or British Anti-Lewisite (BAL). This compound was developed during World War II to offset the toxicity of arsenic in Lewisite, an arsenic-containing war gas. Using arsenic's affinity for sulfhydryl groups, BAL's two sulfur atoms compete for arsenic with the body's sulfhydryl groups. The arsenic-BAL complex is excreted in the urine.

Other chelation agents have been successfully used to treat other metal poisonings and diseases as well. For example, transfusional iron overload in thalassemia or copper overload in Wilson's disease may require daily chelation therapy. Deferiprone, deferoxamine, and deferasirox are chelating agents used to treat thalassemia. Most recently, the need for decorporation or removal of internally deposited radionuclides from the body has become more apparent following the Fukushima Daiichi nuclear event in Japan. Diethylenetriaminepentaacetic acid is the only approved chelation agent for radioactive metals such as plutonium and uranium.

Table 32.2 lists some common chelating agents. In general, some caution is required when administering chelating agents; along with the target metal, essential metals may also be bound and removed from the body requiring essential metal supplementation to correct the imbalance.

Table 32.2 Commonly used chelating agents

Chelating agent	Primary target metal (other target metals)
Calcium disodium ethylenediaminetetraacetate (CaNa₂EDTA)	Lead
Deferasirox	Iron
Deferiprone	Iron
Desferoxamine	Iron
Diethylenetriaminepentaacetic acid	Plutonium, uranium
Dimercaprol (2,3-dimercaptopropanol or BAL)	Arsenic (mercury, lead)
Dimercaptosuccinic acid (DMSA, succimer)	Lead, arsenic, mercury
Dimercapto-propane sulfonate (DMPS)	Mercury (arsenic)
D-Penicillamine	Copper (gold, arsenic, lead)

Analysis of Metals

The analysis of tissues for metal concentrations presents an interesting and challenging responsibility for the forensic toxicologist. Numerous techniques can be applied to metal determinations in biological tissues. Currently, the most common analytical methods for metals are atomic absorption spectrophotometry and inductively coupled plasma (ICP) combined with mass spectroscopy (ICP-MS). Several variations of each technique exist, but they are not routinely available in most forensic toxicology laboratories. The purpose of this section is to present a brief overview of methods used in metal analysis for each of the metals previously discussed.

Preanalytical Considerations

One of the main concerns of the forensic toxicologist is extraneous metal contamination of the sample. For example, there have been several instances where exhumations occur in order to collect tissue to be analyzed for possible metal poisoning. In these cases, analysis of the surrounding soil for the metal or metals of interest should be performed to exclude external contamination of the specimens. Furthermore, contami-

nation during the analytical procedure must also be considered (specimen containers, reagents, glassware, etc.). Acid-washing containers in 10% nitric acid removes the metal contamination.

For specimens other than blood or urine, digestion of the sample by acid is required. Sometimes this requires boiling the tissue in acid, and other times this can be accomplished by allowing the specimen to remain in contact with the acid overnight. The acid itself may contain excessive amounts of the metal being tested, and doubly distilled quality acid is frequently used.

Atomic Absorption Spectrophotometry (AAS)

This technology was simplified by Massman in 1968 and is the basis of current commercial instrumentation. A pyrolytically coated graphite tube, referred to as a graphite furnace, is placed within an inert gas atmosphere, and 1 μL of sample is applied within the tube. The tube temperature is increased in a controlled fashion, first to dry and vaporize the sample, then to burn off the organic material, and finally to atomize the metal. The absorption of the spectral line is measured by the electronics (which must be rapid); excellent optics and background correction techniques are very necessary. This system is best automated, because pipetting microliter amounts into the graphite furnace requires skill.

Once the metal in the sample is atomized, the process becomes similar to molecular absorption spectrophotometry. The light source for atomic absorption is a hollow cathode lamp consisting of a cathode and anode sealed within a glass tube with a low pressure of the inert gas, neon or argon. When a current is applied to the gas atoms, they become ionized and collide with the cathode, causing atoms to come off of the cathode. If the cathode is made from the metal of interest, those atoms in the excited state will emit energy at wavelengths that correspond to the specific metals' absorption spectrum. Using the graphic furnace technology, the sensitivity required for the analysis of metals in biological tissue can be achieved.

ICP-MS

This system is presently considered the state of the art in metal analysis because multiple metals can be simultaneously determined. A liquid sample is pumped into a nebulizer, and a flow of gas converts the liquid to an aerosol. The smaller droplets are ionized by a plasma torch, forming positive ions. These ions are passed through the interface into the mass spectrometer. ICP is a multielement technique that presents a large number of ionized atoms to the MS, which scans the mass range of interest.

Other Techniques

There are additional ways to test for metals, some very simple and some very complex. The simple Reinsch test methodology was developed by the German chemist Reinsch and is still used today in forensic toxicology. The Reinsch test is used as a qualitative screening test for an overdose of arsenic, antimony, bismuth, or mercury. This method involves boiling a small copper coil in an acidified solution. Arsenic (or antimony, bismuth, or mercury) replaces the copper on the coil as a dark film. This method lacks sensitivity but can usually determine an overdose. A positive test requires confirmation of the metal in question.

Arsenic can be quantitatively determined by colorimetry using the Gutzeit method or a modification thereof. It can also be determined electrochemically using anodic stripping voltammetry. When arsenic is determined using AAS, because of the metal's low volatility, arsenic is converted to arsine within a closed system, and the arsenic is then carried to the special hydrogen flame. Mercury is another volatile metal for which the technique of cold vapor generation is needed. Typically, the specimen is digested with potassium permanganate and sulfuric acid overnight. Then the excess oxidizing agent is hydrolyzed by hydroxyl amine, and mercury is liberated with stannous chloride. The mercury vapor is measured in the flow cell.

Both iron and lithium are metals routinely tested in clinical chemistry laboratories. Iron determinations are routinely included in chemistry profiles and are offered in most clinical laboratories, using large analyzers. Lithium is of sufficient concentration in therapeutic amounts to be measured by flame AAS, or flame emission using a flame photometer.

Neutron activation analysis is a very sensitive and specific technique that preserves the original specimen for additional testing. Thermal neutrons bombard the specimen of interest, which induces radioactivity in some of the metal atoms; then the emitted radiation is measured. Thus, qualitative and quantitative nondestructive analysis is possible. This nonroutine method requires a nuclear reactor, which is too large and too costly for most laboratories. Magnetic resonance imaging (MRI) has been used as a tool for monitoring excess iron in various organs and for monitoring chelation therapy progress.

Metal Speciation

Currently in metal analysis, it is becoming important to determine each species of the metal in question, rather than measuring the total metal in a tissue. Speciation concerns the identification and quantitation of specific forms of an element. For example, as opposed to measuring total arsenic, one instead measures As(III), As(V), monomethylarsonic acid (MMA), and dimethylarsinic acid (DMA). Similarly, one will measure Cr (III) and Cr(VI) or Hg (0), Hg(II), and methyl mercury instead of total chromium and mercury, respectively. In many instances, a chemical method separates the species from one another, followed by instrumental analysis.

Further Reading

ATSDR Toxicological Profile for Aluminum (2008) U.S. Department of Health and Human Services, Public Health Service, Agency for Toxic Substances and Disease Registry, Atlanta

ATSDR Toxicological Profile for Arsenic (2007) U.S. Department of Health and Human Services, Public Health Service, Agency for Toxic Substances and Disease Registry, Atlanta

ATSDR Toxicological Profile for Lead (2007) U.S. Department of Health and Human Services, Public Health Service, Agency for Toxic Substances and Disease Registry, Atlanta

ATSDR Toxicological Profile for Mercury (1999) U.S. Department of Health and Human Services, Public Health Service, Agency for Toxic Substances and Disease Registry, Atlanta

ATSDR Toxicological Profile for Thallium (1992) U.S. Department of Health and Human Services, Public Health Service, A 1992

Bernhoft RA (2012) Mercury toxicity and Treatment: a review of the literature. J Environ Pub Health 2012:460508. https://doi.org/10.1155/2012/460508

Buchet J, Lauwerys R, Roels H (1981) Urinary excretion of inorganic arsenic and its metabolites after repeated ingestion of sodium meta-arsenite by volunteers. Int Arch Occup Environ Health 48:111–118

Cade J (1949) Lithium salts in the treatment of psychotic excitement. Med J Aust 2:349–352

Hunter R (1988) Steady-state pharmacokinetics of lithium carbonate in healthy subjects. Br J Clin Pharmac 25:375–380

Jacobs J, Green H, Grendel B (1965) Acute iron intoxication. N Engl J Med 273:1124–1127

Klaassen C (2006) Heavy metals and heavy-metal antagonists. In: Brunton LL, Lazo JS, Parker KL (eds) Goodman and Gillman's the pharmacological basis of therapeutics. McGraw-Hill, New York

Schroeder H, Balassa J (1966) Abnormal trace metals in man: arsenic. J Chron Dis 19:85–106

TLV (2001) Documentation for the threshold limit values, 7th edn. American Conference of Governmental Industrial Hygienists, Cincinnati, OH

Part IV
Special Topics

Drug Stability in Biological Specimens

33

Barry S. Levine, Daniel S. Isenschmid, and Michael L. Smith

Abstract

Drug stability is an important consideration that is sometimes overlooked. However, changes in drug concentration can occur after specimen collection, during storage, shipping, transport, and evidence handling. Although environmental conditions, such as temperature and exposure to light, can play an important role, drug stability is analyte dependent and is largely determined by physicochemical properties of the molecule. The stability of common drug classes in biological matrices is reviewed within the context of proper specimen preservation and storage. Differences between antemortem and postmortem specimens are also addressed.

Keywords

Drugs · Stability · Postmortem · Antemortem Blood · Urine · Preservative · Storage

B. S. Levine (✉)
Office of the Chief Medical Examiner, Baltimore, MD, USA
e-mail: blevine@som.umaryland.edu

D. S. Isenschmid
NMS Labs, Horsham19044, PA, USA

M. L. Smith
Huestis and Smith Toxicology, LLC, Severna Park, MD, USA

Introduction

Biological specimens are analyzed for drugs for many reasons. An analysis may be performed to indicate exposure to or use of a particular drug, to correlate the presence of a drug with physiological or behavioral effects, or to assist in the treatment of disease or other medical conditions. Analysis of postmortem specimens for drugs indicates whether drugs were responsible for or otherwise involved in the fatality.

In general terms, drug stability is influenced by many factors. Physicochemical properties of the drug such as labile functional groups (e.g., esters) or low boiling points (e.g., alcohols or volatile bases) can contribute to changes in drug concentration over time. Specimen collection technique, storage, use of preservative and other additives, and container selection can help mitigate changes mediated by microorganisms, chemical or enzymatic means.

Stability in postmortem specimens can be more complex because conditions prior to collection may be less controlled. Degradation of analytes can be accelerated during putrefactive decomposition, microbial invasion, and increased presence of bacteria. Following collection, enzymes within the specimen may remain active and continue to transform the drug in vitro. This is particularly important for esterases, which may hydrolyze drugs post-collection unless they are inhibited with a chemical preservative such as sodium fluoride.

© Springer Nature Switzerland AG 2020
B. S. Levine, S. Kerrigan (eds.), *Principles of Forensic Toxicology*,
https://doi.org/10.1007/978-3-030-42917-1_33

Chemical instability arises due to functional groups within the molecule that are susceptible to transformation. Notably, these may include esters (e.g., cocaine, 6-acetylmorphine, acetylsalicylic acid), sulfur-containing drugs, photolabile drugs (e.g., lysergic acid diethylamide, phenothiazines, midazolam), and functional groups that are readily oxidized or reduced. Although instability typically reduces the concentration of analytes of interest, this is not always the case. For example, some glucuronidated drugs are susceptible to hydrolysis and may deconjugate under some conditions (increasing the concentration of free drug).

Thermal instability is another consideration. Drugs may be subjected to elevated temperatures during the administration of the drug (e.g., smoking) or during the analytical process itself (e.g., gas chromatography/mass spectrometry or GC/MS). Pyrolysis of the drug during smoking may identify products in biological matrices that are indicative of this route of administration (e.g., anhydroecgonine methylester or AEME following crack cocaine use, 1-phenyl-cyclohexane following PCP use, or trans-phenylpropene following methamphetamine use). However, identification of biomarkers associated with smoking must take into consideration potential pyrolysis (in situ) during analysis. Alternative analytical methods (e.g., liquid chromatography-based techniques) may be required for substances that are known to be thermally labile.

Ideally drug stability should be evaluated short and long term in the biological matrix of interest. This may include freeze-thaw cycles during long-term storage, short-term refrigerated storage, and ambient temperatures during routine specimen handling and sample preparation/processing. Appropriate use of isotopically labelled internal standards can mitigate changes in concentration during the analytical process. Processed sample stability should also be addressed during method validation. Although drug instability is predominantly analyte-dependent, the kinetic variables are typically temperature-, matrix-, and pH-dependent.

Because toxicological tests are frequently performed a period of time after specimen acquisition and because the results of these tests may be used in criminal or civil litigation, it is important that the test results accurately reflect the drug quantity present at the time of interest: Therefore, knowledge about the in vitro stability of drugs is important for the proper interpretation of test results. Much of this information has been provided in the individual chapters covering the analytes. This chapter will either summarize or expand these discussions.

Amphetamines

Methamphetamine and amphetamine were stable in preserved urine during long-term (frozen) storage for at least a year. Although both drugs are considered moderately stable in blood and urine, storage of blood or tissue samples at room temperature should be avoided due to the production of interfering substances. The overall stability of the amphetamines extends to many of the designer amphetamines, such as methylenedioxymethamphetamine (MDMA) and methylenedioxyamphetamine (MDA). However, there are some notable exceptions, particularly among the ketone-containing derivatives and newer designer drugs. Several beta-keto amphetamines are known to be unstable. Bupropion has been shown to degrade in biological samples in a temperature- and pH-dependent manner. The half-life of bupropion in plasma (pH 7.4) was approximately 11 h at 37 °C. It is therefore not surprising that many of the synthetic cathinones are also unstable, particularly at alkaline pH. Although most synthetic cathinones were found to be stable in preserved acidic (pH 4) urine for at least 6 months when refrigerated or frozen, half-lives were as short as 9 h in alkaline urine (pH 8) at ambient temperature. Similar temperature- and pH-dependent stability has been observed in blood. Unsubstituted and ring-substituted secondary amines were among the least stable synthetic cathinones, notably the fluorinated derivatives (e.g., 3-fluoromethcathinone). In contrast, those bearing a tertiary amine (pyrrolidone moiety) were the most stable. The methylenedioxy group was also found to exert a significant stabilizing effect on the secondary and tertiary amines. Instability has also been observed for some of the N-benzylmethoxy derivatives (NBOMes). Although storage at low temperature can mitigate degradation, significant decreases in concentration can exacerbate detection efforts, particularly for analytes that may be present at low concentrations initially.

Barbiturates

Since barbiturates have been prescription drugs for approximately 100 years, a number of studies on stability of these drugs in biological specimens have been published. Many of the earlier studies produced conflicting results on drug stability in blood and tissue specimens. However, recent studies suggest that there are minimal changes in barbiturate concentrations in blood, plasma, or liver stored at room temperature or at 4 °C over a 2- to 3-month period. These small changes would not affect interpretation based on drug concentrations obtained at the time of collection or after a short period of storage.

Benzodiazepines

Two functional groups appearing on the benzodiazepine backbone have been associated with in vitro instability. Chlordiazepoxide is an N-oxide compound and has been shown in numerous studies to be unstable in blood. One of the coauthors found that a blood chlordiazepoxide concentration of 5 mg/L rapidly disappeared when the blood was stored at room temperature; by day 8, no chlordiazepoxide was detected. Norchlordiazepoxide, the desmethyl metabolite of chlordiazepoxide, demonstrated similar instability. When the blood was stored at 4 °C, a substantial decrease was also observed, but the drug was still detectable after 2 months. The presence of sodium fluoride and potassium oxalate did retard the degradation of chlordiazepoxide at room temperature to the extent that about 40% of the amount originally present was still detected after 2 months. Two breakdown products, demoxepam and nordiazepam, were identified and accounted for some, but not all, of the lost drug.

Benzodiazepines with a nitro group, such as nitrazepam, flunitrazepam, and clonazepam, also decrease in concentration during storage. These drugs are converted to their analogous amino compounds. Robertson and Drummer performed a comprehensive study on the stability of three nitrobenzodiazepines, clonazepam, nitrazepam, and flunitrazepam, and their respective amino metabolites in postmortem blood. Nitrazepam and clonazepam were stable in sterile, preserved fresh blood at 22 °C and at 4 °C over 28 days. Over the same time period, a 25% reduction in flunitrazepam was observed. In the absence of the preservative, 25–50% of the drugs were lost at 22 °C after 10 days. In non-sterile blood, all three drugs were converted to the corresponding amino compounds within 8 h at 22 °C. All three drugs were stable at −20 °C up to 2 years and for 10 months at 4 °C. Surprisingly, the amino compounds also demonstrated instability, with greater instability occurring at higher temperatures. At 22 °C, a 10–20% decrease was observed in nonpreserved blood over 45 h. At 4 °C, a 21% loss occurred after 1 month and at −20 °C, a 29% loss occurred after 2 months.

Benzodiazepines without the N-oxide or nitro groups appear to display greater stability in biological specimens. Drugs that have been studied in blood include diazepam, flurazepam, N-1-desalkylflurazepam, and temazepam. In general, these drugs have shown decreases less than 25% in blood stored at room or refrigerated temperatures over a several month period.

The stability of the designer benzodiazepines is less studied. These newer drugs may contain the 1,4-benzodiazepine, triazolobenzodiazepine, thienotriazolodiazepine, or oxazolobenzodiazepine skeleton. Inferences concerning their stability can be drawn from studies involving other well-established benzodiazepines. For example, given that the nitrobenzodiazepines are among the most unstable within this class, it is perhaps not surprising that clonazolam, nifoxipam, and meclonazepam (all containing the nitro functional group) were unstable in urine at refrigerated and ambient temperatures. Instability of flubromazepam has also been reported.

Instability has been documented for some of the atypical antipsychotics (e.g., olanzapine and quetiapine) which are sulfur-containing benzodiazepines (benzothiazepines). These are discussed under neuroleptics below.

Cannabinoids

Whole blood and plasma delta-9-tetrahydrocannabinol (THC), 11-hydroxy THC (11-OH-THC), 11-nor-delta-9 THC-9 carboxylic acid (THCACOOH), cannabidiol, cannabinol, and THC-glucuronide concentrations are stable after 4 weeks at −20 °C and 4 °C and for at least 1 week at room temperature. THCCOOH-glucuronide was stable for 4 weeks at −20 °C, unstable at 4 °C over 4 weeks (mean whole blood decrease > −20%; mean plasma > −66%), and very unstable at room temperature losing more than −40% over a week for whole blood. When plasma is stored for longer periods, THC and THCCOOH concentrations can decrease with THC showing more loss than its metabolite. One study found that THC and THCCOOH plasma concentrations stored at −20 °C decreased more than 15% by 1 year. THC and 11-OH-THC concentrations in blood at room temperature were stable for 1 month, had decreased significantly after 2 months, and at 6 months decreased 90% and 44%, respectively. Blood total THCCOOH concentrations had not changed significantly after 6 months at room temperature.

Both THC and THCCOOH have been examined in oral fluid. Earlier collection devices had problems with both analytes binding to the containers during storage causing large decreases in concentration. This occurred due to their hydrophobic nature and also for THCCOOH its low concentration in oral fluid, i.e., in the pg/mL range. Many manufacturers have designed current collection devices with buffers that minimize this loss. One study found that cannabinoids in oral fluid collected with a Quantisal™ device were much more stable than when expectorated. THC, THCCOOH, cannabidiol, and cannabinol concentrations in Quantisal™ devices were stable (i.e., within ±20% of initial concentration) for 1 week at 4 °C. After 4 weeks at 4 °C, 4 weeks at −20 °C, and 24 weeks at −20 °C, THC was stable in 90%, 80%, and 80% of Quantisal™ samples, respectively. THCCOOH was stable in 89%, 40%, and 50% of the samples. Cannabidiol and cannabinol concentrations decreased more than 20% in over 56% of samples after 24 weeks at −20 °C.

THCCOOH concentrations are reasonably stable in urine when the method of analysis hydrolyzes the glucuronide. THCCOOH-glucuronide is stable at −20 °C for up to 10 days but at higher temperatures and longer periods of storage breaks down to form THCCOOH. When urine specimens are stored for longer periods, total THCCOOH concentration may decrease even at −20 °C in selected specimens. A number of reasons for this loss have been proposed: adsorption to the container or to solid matter, concentration of this amphipathic molecule in the foam created during mixing, or urine pH. The extent of the degradation is variable. In one study, 85 urine specimens positive for THCCOOH that were stored frozen for up to 1 year following the initial analysis were retested. The average decrease in concentration of the retested specimens was 24%. A normal bell-shaped distribution was observed, with a range of concentration changes between 30 and − 80%.

Cocaine

The ester linkage on the cocaine molecule makes the drug susceptible to chemical and enzymatic hydrolysis. In fact, the two major metabolites of cocaine, benzoylecgonine (BE) and ecgonine methyl ester (EME), are hydrolytic products of cocaine. Conversion to BE occurs chemically, especially under alkaline conditions, and enzymatically by a liver methyltransferase; conversion to EME occurs enzymatically by pseudocholinesterase in the plasma and by a benzoyl esterase in the liver.

In unpreserved blood, in vitro stability studies have shown that cocaine is hydrolyzed almost exclusively at the phenyl ester by plasma pseudocholinesterase to yield EME. The addition of sodium fluoride while inhibiting enzymatic hydrolysis of cocaine to EME does not prevent spontaneous chemical hydrolysis of cocaine to BE. The rates of hydrolysis of both esters have been shown to be temperature- and pH-dependent, with higher temperatures and pH increasing the rate of hydrolysis. The loss of cocaine in unpreserved blood can be dramatic. In antemortem blood fortified with cocaine at 2000 ng/mL, cocaine concentrations decreased to 640 ng/mL after storage at room temperature for 24 h, with corresponding increases in EME concentrations. Even after the addition of 2% sodium fluoride, a 25% decrease in cocaine concentrations was observed at room and refrigerated temperatures within 5 and 80 days, respectively, with corresponding increases in BE concentrations. A small amount of EME also formed, indicating that the action of 2% sodium fluoride was not obsolete. Acidifying blood to pH 5 to inhibit chemical hydrolysis in conjunction with adding 2% sodium fluoride to inhibit enzymatic hydrolysis produced no cocaine loss after 200 days at refrigerated (4 °C) and frozen (−15 °C) temperatures and for at least 60 days at room temperature.

Both BE and EME have ester moieties and are also subject to temperature- and pH-dependent hydrolysis. Benzoylecgonine is considerably more stable than EME in unpreserved blood (pH 7.4) at room temperature. A 50% loss of EME occurred over a 35-day period, compared with a 25% loss for BE. Little loss of either compound was observed when the blood sample was refrigerated for the same period of time.

In another study, the stability of cocaine, BE, EME, and ecgonine in blood preserved with 0.25% potassium fluoride at 4 °C and 20 °C over a 15-day period was examined. At 4 °C and 20 °C, BE and EME could be detected from cocaine 1 day after storage. Ecgonine was detectable after 2 days of storage. At 4 °C, approximately 25% of the initial cocaine concentration was still detected at day 14. The relative amount of hydrolytic products was EME > BE > ecgonine. At 20 °C, no cocaine was detected by the end of the study. BE and EME concentrations increased, but decreased after 6 and 7 days of storage, respectively. The concentration of ecgonine increased steadily. Ecgonine was stable at

4 °C and at 20 °C over the 2-week period. At 4 °C, BE was converted to ecgonine by day 3, and the concentration of ecgonine was less than 10% of the initial BE concentration. At 20 °C, about 40% of the initial BE concentration had been converted to ecgonine by day 14. At 4 °C, the EME concentration decreased by about 90% by day 14, while at 20 °C, no EME was detected by the end of the observation period. The conversion of cocaine to BE, EME, and ecgonine appeared to be stoichiometric at all time intervals at both storage temperatures.

Cocaethylene or ethylcocaine is produced in vivo following the simultaneous ingestion of alcohol and cocaine. Cocaethylene was found to break down more slowly in the blood than cocaine. About 25% of cocaethylene was still detected in blood by the third day when stored at 20–25 °C. Conversely, no cocaine was detected after the first day.

Stability studies have indicated that some hydrolysis of cocaine to EME is expected during the postmortem period, with the rate of hydrolysis decreasing as the pH of the blood sample falls. Cocaine fortified into decomposed human blood and tissues (pH 4.2–5.2) has been shown to be stable when the sample is stored at 20–37 °C for 24 h. In a study of juvenile swine, cocaine and metabolite concentrations were relatively stable in serial blood samples that had been collected from animals and allowed to decompose for 3 weeks in cool weather. The results are less predictable in humans, however. Properly collected and preserved heart and peripheral blood samples that were obtained at the scenes of suspected cocaine deaths (t_1) and at autopsy (t_2) were analyzed for cocaine, BE, and ethylcocaine. There was no consistent pattern in the magnitude or direction of change in concentration for any of the analytes with respect to the time of collection, suggesting that competing processes of hydrolysis and tissue release of the drug were occurring. The study showed a net decrease in cocaine concentrations and a net increase in benzoylecgonine concentrations in samples between t_1 and t_2, but the decrease in the cocaine concentration was not statistically significant and was not necessarily accompanied by increases in the BE concentration. The mean concentration of cocaine in the ventricular blood was higher than in the femoral blood at both t_1 and t_2, but the mean differences were not statistically significant. The lack of predictability in postmortem cocaine and metabolite concentrations after death calls their usefulness into question, especially given that therapeutic, toxic, and fatal cocaine concentrations overlap.

The stability of BE in urine specimens can have significant forensic implications. Any urine testing positive under the Department of Health and Human Services guidelines must be frozen for at least 1 year. During that year, the specimen is eligible for retesting upon request. In one study of 61 retested urine specimens containing BE, an average decrease of 19% was measured. However, distribution of the percentage of change suggested a bimodal distribution, with one distribution around 10% and a second distribution around 80%. No explanation for these changes was provided. However, it has also been shown that decreases in BE concentrations can occur at neutral or alkaline pH and at room temperature. The growth of microorganisms may also be a factor.

Like BE, EME in urine has been shown to be susceptible to alkaline hydrolysis. At pH 3 to pH 5, EME is stable for up to 3 years, but at pH 9 no EME remained after 30 days of storage at 4–5 °C. Very rapid hydrolysis of EME occurs in buffers at higher pHs, but these nonphysiological conditions are not likely to be found. Ecgonine methyl ester in postmortem urine is stable for at least 6 months under frozen (−20 °C) and refrigerated (4 °C) conditions.

Other factors, such as microbial growth or in vitro adulteration with alkaline materials such as bleach, also affect the stability of cocaine and its metabolites in urine.

To summarize, the instability of cocaine in untreated blood or plasma is well documented. Loss of cocaine can be minimized by adding pseudocholinesterase inhibitor immediately after collection, reducing the pH to 5, and storing the sample frozen. The stability of cocaine in urine is pH dependent, similar to cocaine stability observed in aqueous solutions. Benzoylecgonine exhibits greater stability in blood and urine, but decreases over time have been observed. EME also displays greater stability in urine, especially at neutral or slightly acidic pH.

Ethanol

Undoubtedly, the drug most frequently studied for in vitro stability in biological specimens is ethanol. Studies have been performed using specimens from living individuals and from autopsy cases. Both increases and decreases in ethanol concentration during storage have been reported. Mechanisms of ethanol loss include evaporation, chemical oxidation to acetaldehyde, and microbial consumption. The most common source of in vitro ethanol production is microbial conversion of glucose, fatty acids, or amino acids to ethanol.

The vast majority of studies performed on ethanol stability have been on blood specimens. Autopsy specimens have been used to monitor ethanol production at room temperature. In an early study from the 1960s, 50 autopsy blood specimens were collected and stored with and without preservatives. In 34 cases, there was no significant production of ethanol after 10 days; the remaining 16 specimens showed significant ethanol production. The average increase in ethanol concentration after 2–3 days was 0.030 ± 0.028 g/dL; but the average increase after 6–10 days was 0.048 ± 0.036. g/dL. The maximum increase over 10 days was 0.13 g/dL. The presence of 1% sodium fluoride prevented in vitro ethanol formation after 10 days. In contrast, 0.1% mercuric chloride failed to prevent ethanol formation, and 1% mercuric chloride in many specimens produced a solid that precluded ethanol analysis. A subsequent study reported seven cases in which storage of the blood at room temperature produced increases greater than 0.05 g/dL. A maximum blood concentration of 0.14 g/dL was measured after 7 days in blood that initially contained no ethanol.

To ascertain whether the ethanol measured in postmortem specimens was present due to alcohol consumption prior to death or due to postmortem ethanol formation, vitreous humor is often measured for alcohol in conjunction with the postmortem blood. Vitreous humor, because of its isolated location, is more resistant to the decomposition process than are other fluids and tissues in the body. One study looked at the change in alcohol concentrations in 32 paired postmortem blood and vitreous humor specimens. The blood was collected and stored in 50 mL polypropylene tubes containing sodium fluoride and potassium oxalate. The vitreous humor specimens were stored in 10 mL Vacutainer® tubes containing 25 mg of potassium oxalate and 25 mg of sodium fluoride. The specimens were stored under refrigeration and reanalyzed 5–6 years later. Decreases in ethanol concentration in both blood and vitreous humor specimens were observed. The average loss of ethanol in the blood was 0.06 g/dL, a 35% loss. The average loss of ethanol in the vitreous humor was 0.01 g/dL, a 6.1% loss. They concluded that vitreous humor may be a more reliable specimen for reanalysis of ethanol after prolonged refrigeration.

In addition to postmortem blood ethanol analysis, testing of suspected intoxicated drivers is also commonly performed. In these cases, the integrity of the blood sample tested can be critical to successful prosecution. It is standard to collect these blood in gray top tubes that contain a preservative, sodium fluoride, and an anticoagulant, potassium oxalate. Many studies have been published discussing the stability of ethanol in these samples. The general consensus of these studies is blood collected under standard conditions into fluoride/oxalate tubes will be stable for weeks, even at room temperature. Moreover, any changes that occur in alcohol concentrations are likely to be decreases as opposed to increases in concentration.

Ethanol demonstrates greater stability in urine specimens than in blood specimens. Several studies have demonstrated that ethanol production is unlikely even when the specimens are stored at room temperature. However, under the right conditions, in vitro production of ethanol in some urine specimens can occur. In one study, 14 random urine specimens testing negative for ethanol and containing variable amounts of glucose were stored at room temperature for up to 3 weeks. Five specimens produced ethanol at concentrations ranging from 0.036 to 2.327 g/dL. In each case, yeast was identified in the urine specimen.

Conversely, in the six glucose-positive specimens in which no yeast was found, no in vitro production of ethanol was observed. Ethanol production in the presence of yeast and glucose can be prevented by refrigeration or by the addition of sodium fluoride at a strength of 1 or 2% (w/v).

A large amount of literature data exists indicating that under certain storage conditions, ethanol can be produced in blood in vitro. These conditions include higher temperatures, contamination with certain microorganisms, and the absence of chemical preservatives. When blood is preserved with fluoride, the ethanol concentration remains essentially unchanged for short periods of time, regardless of the storage temperature. Long-term storage of fluoridated blood samples will usually cause decreases in ethanol concentration. Ethanol is less likely to be produced in urine specimens, except in the rare instance of high glucose concentrations and the presence of certain microorganisms. Changes in ethanol concentration in biological fluids can be minimized if the specimens are preserved with sodium fluoride and stored at as low a temperature as possible.

Gamma-Hydroxybutyric Acid

Changes in the concentration of gamma-hydroxybutyric acid (GHB) in biological samples have also been documented postmortem. GHB interpretation is further complicated by the fact that it is an endogenous substance. The most notable differences in GHB concentration have been observed in unpreserved postmortem blood. Concentrations of 100 mg/L were documented following refrigerated storage for 4 months. Increases in concentration were much less pronounced in postmortem urine, even in the absence of preservative. For this reason, urine, vitreous humor, and cerebral spinal fluid are preferred postmortem specimens for quantitative GHB analysis. Antemortem specimens are less susceptible to concentration changes, although refrigeration and addition of sodium fluoride as preservative are recommended. Under strongly acidic conditions, GHB lactonizes to form gamma-butyrolactone. This transformation is exploited analytically for some quantitative determinations. This is discussed in more detail in Chap. 21.

Lysergic Acid Diethylamide

Lysergic acid diethylamide (LSD) is photolabile, and specimens containing the drug should be protected from light. Concentrations of LSD in blood and urine have been shown to decrease with light exposure, even in the presence of sodium fluoride. Use of transparent containers should be avoided. Specimens stored in amber glass or non-transparent polyethylene showed no decrease in concentration. When exposed to ultraviolet radiation, LSD is believed to undergo photocatalytic hydration. Under acidic conditions, LSD is also reported to epimerize to iso-LSD.

Neuroleptics

Several neuroleptic drugs are known to be unstable. These include the atypical antipsychotics quetiapine and olanzapine. These sulfurcontaining neuroleptics are known to be unstable, particularly at room temperature. Quetiapine is a benzothiazepine and olanzapine is a dibenzothiazepine. Phenothiazines can also exhibit pH-dependent photosensitivity. Additionally, increases in chlorpromazine and thioridazine concentrations have been reported among patient samples, attributed to the conversion of metabolite back to the parent drug during storage.

Opioids

The in vitro instability of heroin in blood or plasma has been well documented; it is rapidly deacetylated to 6-acetylmorphine. However, 6-acetylmorphine and morphine display greater stability in blood and plasma. In one study, morphine was added to blood that was then stored at room temperature, refrigerated, or frozen. Aliquots of blood at each temperature were removed at 2, 4, 6, and 8 weeks and 3, 6, 9, and 12 months. Under all conditions and times tested,

more than 80% of the morphine initially present was measured. Morphine has also been shown to be stable in postmortem blood, liver, and urine specimens over a 10-day period at temperatures ranging from 4 °C to 37 °C.

Although free concentrations of morphine, codeine, and methadone were moderately stable in preserved frozen urine for over a year, total morphine concentrations were less predictable. Important differences in stability exist between free and conjugated species. This is of importance because ratios of free to total morphine are sometimes used for interpretive purposes. Differences in glucuronide stability have been observed between antemortem and postmortem blood. Hydrolysis of glucuronidated species increases with temperature, storage time, and degree of putrefaction. While morphine-3-glucuronide (M3G) was stable in preserved refrigerated antemortem blood, instability was observed in postmortem blood under the same conditions. M3G was not converted to free morphine in blood and urine specimens stored from 4 °C to 37 °C over a 10-day period. M3G was hydrolyzed completely to free morphine in liver specimens stored at 18 °C and 37 °C over 10 days, but was stable at 4 °C over the same time period.

Stability issues have been reported for buprenorphine during long-term storage. Buprenorphine concentrations in blood decreased by half over 12 weeks, even when frozen. Significant decreases were observed, even in the presence of sodium fluoride preservative. Stability was improved using sub-zero (−80 °C) storage or the addition of an antioxidant. Instability of buprenorphine in frozen blood was eliminated with the addition of ascorbic acid (30 mM) prior to storage. As mentioned previously, instability is of particular concern for drugs like buprenorphine that have low therapeutic drug concentrations.

Phencyclidine (PCP)

PCP is stable in blood and urine specimens. In one study of 41 blood specimens obtained from arrested individuals, the specimens were stored at room temperature for up to 18 months after an initial quantitation. In 30 of the 41 specimens, the difference between the original and the subsequent analysis was less than 10%; in the remaining specimens, the difference was ≤30%. The regression line correlating the original blood concentration and the reanalyzed blood concentrations had a slope of 1.00. Most of the observed differences were attributed to variations in the method. Other studies have demonstrated similar results with PCP in blood specimens for periods up to 5 years when the blood was stored in the refrigerator or freezer.

Further Reading

Al-Hadidi KA, Oliver JS (1994) Stability of buprenorphine and morphine in whole blood stored at different conditions. In: Mueller RK (ed) Contribution to forensic toxicology. Molina Press, Leipzig, p 255

Al-Hadidi KA, Oliver JS (1995) Stability or temazepam in blood. Sci Justice 35:105

Barrett DA, Dyssegaard P, Shaw PN (1992) The effect of temperature and pH on the deacetylation of diamorphine in aqueous solution and in human plasma. J Pharm Pharmacol 44:606

Carroll FT, Marraccini JV, Lewis S, Wright W (2000) Morphine-3-D-glucuronide stability in postmortem specimens exposed to bacterial enzymatic hydrolysis. Am J Forensic Med Pathol 21:323

Christopoulos G, Kirsh ER, Gearien JE (1973) Determination of ethanol in fresh and putrefied postmortem tissues. J Chromatogr 87:455

Clardy DO, Ragle JL (1981) Stability of phencyclidine in stored blood. Clin Toxicol 18:929

da Cunha KF, Eberlin MN, Huestis MA, Costa JL (2019) NBOMe instability in whole blood. Forensic Toxicol 37:82

Isenschmid DS, Levine B, Caplan YH (1989) A comprehensive study of the stability of cocaine and its metabolites. J Anal Toxicol 13:250

Johnson JR, Jennison TA, Peat MA, Foltz RL (1984) Stability of delta-9-tetrahydrocannabinol (THC), 11-hydroxy-THC and 11-nor-9-carboxy-THC in blood and plasma. J Anal Toxicol 8:202

Jones AW, Hylen L, Svensson E, Helander A (1999) Storage of specimens at 4oC or addition of sodium fluoride (1%) prevents formation of ethanol in urine inoculated with Candida albicans. J Anal Toxicol 23:333

Kerrigan S (2011) In: Moffat AC, Osselton MD, Widdop B (eds) Sampling, storage and stability in Clarkes analysis of drugs and poisons, 4th edn. Pharmaceutical Press, London

Lee D, Milman G, Schwope DM, Barnes AJ, Gorelick DA, Huestis MA (2012) Cannabinoid stability in authentic oral fluid after controlled cannabis smoking. Clin Chem 58:1101–1109

Levine B, Blanke RV, Valentour JC (1984) Postmortem stability of barbiturates in blood and tissues. J Forensic Sci 29:131

Levine B, Blanke RV, Valentour JC (1983) Postmortem stability of benzodiazepines in blood and tissues. J Forensic Sci 28:102

Levine B, Ramcharitat V, Smialek JE (1996) Stability of ecgonine methyl ester in postmortem urine specimens. J Forensic Sci 41:126

Melo P, Lourdes Bastos M, Teixeira HM (2012) Benzodiazepine stability in postmortem samples stored at different temperatures. J Anal Toxicol 36:52–60

Moody DE, Monti KM, Spanbauer AC (1999) Long-term stability of abused drugs and antiabuse chemotherapeutical agents stored at −20 degrees C. J Anal Toxicol 23:535–540

Moriya F, Hashimoto Y (1997) Distribution of free and conjugated morphine in body fluids and tissues in a fatal heroin overdose: is conjugated morphine stable in postmortem specimens? J Forensic Sci 42:736

Olsen T, Hearn WL (2003) Stability of ethanol in postmortem blood and vitreous humor in long-term refrigerated storage. J Anal Toxicol 27:517

Peters FT (2007) Stability of analytes in biosamples – an important issue in clinical and forensic toxicology? Anal Bioanal Chem 388:1505–1519

Plueckhahn VD, Ballard B (1968) Factors influencing the significance of alcohol concentrations in autopsy blood samples. Med J Australia 1:939

Plueckhahn VD (1970) The significance of alcohol and sugar determinations in autopsy blood. Med J Australia 1:46

Robertson MD, Drummer OH (1998) Stability of nitrobenzodiazepines in postmortem blood. J Forensic Sci 43:5

Romberg RW, Past MR (1994) Reanalysis of forensic urine specimens containing benzoylecgonine and THC-COOH. J Forensic Sci 39:479

Saady JJ, Poklis A, Dalton HP (1993) Production of urinary ethanol after sample collection. J Forensic Sci 38:1467

Skopp G, Potsch L, Mauden M, Richter B (2002) Partition coefficient, blood to plasma ratio, protein binding and short-term stability of 11-nor-Δ9-carboxy tetrahydrocannabinol glucuronide. Forensic Sci Int 126:17

Skopp G, Potsch L (2002) Stability of 11-nor-Δ9-tetrahydrocannabinol glucuronide in plasma and urine assessed by liquid chromatography-tandem mass spectrometry. Clin Chem 48:301

Skopp G, Potsch L (2004) An investigation of the stability of free and glucuronidated 11-nor-Δ9-tetrahydrocannabinol-9-carboxylic acid in authentic urine samples. J Anal Toxicol 28:35

Skopp G, Klingsmann A, Potsch L, Mattern R (2001) In vitro stability of cocaine in whole blood and plasma including ecgonine as a target analyte. Ther Drug Monit 23:174

Sørensen LK, Hasselstrøm JB (2019) Ascorbic acid improves the stability of buprenorphine in frozen whole blood samples. J Anal Toxicol 43:482

Stevens HM (1984) The stability of some drugs and poisons in putrefying human liver tissues. J Forensic Sci Soc 24:577

Vasiliades J (1993) Long term stability of ecgonine methyl ester in urine. J Anal Toxicol 17:253

Winek CL, Paul L (1983) Effect of short-term storage conditions on alcohol concentrations in blood from living human subjects. Clin Chem 29:1959

Postmortem Redistribution of Drugs

34

Fred S. Apple

Abstract

Postmortem redistribution is a phenomenon that complicates the interpretation of postmortem forensic toxicology findings. It refers to changes in drug concentration that can occur after death. This can be attributed to the movement of drugs from tissue compartments or solid organs into the blood. The tendency of a drug to redistribute in this fashion is influenced by its physicochemical properties, notably its basicity (pK_a), lipophilicity, volume of distribution, protein binding, and energy-dependent transport processes across membrane. The physiological processes and tendency of drugs to exhibit postmortem redistribution are discussed, highlighting the need for careful interpretation of results.

Keywords

Postmortem redistribution · Toxicology · Interpretation

F. S. Apple (✉)
Hennepin Co. Medical Center, University of Minnesota, Minneapolis, MN, USA
e-mail: Apple004@umm.edu

Introduction

The topic of postmortem redistribution (PMR) has been extensively reviewed over the past several years. Several investigators have described multiple mechanisms that can be responsible for the release of tissue-bound drugs from anatomic sites of high drug concentration to sites of lower concentration (concentration gradient), creating an artificially increased blood/fluid concentration postmortem that differs from the blood concentration that would have been present at the time of an individual's death. Therefore, for drugs or classes of drugs that have been described in the literature that demonstrate increases in blood concentrations over a postmortem (PM) interval, the degree of certainty and confidence that the autopsy (which can be hours to days after death) plasma/serum/blood concentration of a drug reflects the drug concentration at the time of death diminishes.

PMR of drugs can be defined as the physiologic process of drug release and/or mixing of drugs from one compartment (organ tissues) into another compartment (blood fluid) after death. For the past 30 years, practicing forensic toxicologists have encountered death investigation cases where postmortem blood concentrations are inconsistent with the case history of drug or medication use. Specifically, drug concentrations were found to be substantially greater than anticipated in a decedent's blood in which the cause of death was

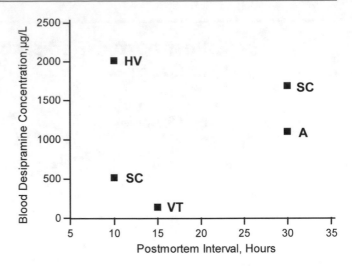

Fig. 34.1 Findings of tricyclic antidepressant suspected toxicity case demonstrating serum desipramine concentrations collected at different times from varying anatomic sites. *HV* heart ventricle, *SC* subclavian, *VT* vitreous humor, *A* atrial

clearly unrelated to drug. Pharmacokinetic calculations of expected steady-state concentrations by the toxicologist, based on dosing records and witnessed medication use, were found to show five-fold to tenfold lower concentrations than the measured PM blood level in the blood obtained at autopsy. These disparities initially became recognized in the 1970s, which led to the early observational studies of site-to-site variations of drug concentrations measured at autopsy. Figure 34.1 shows findings for a representative medical examiner case involving a cancer-related death, in which the patient was treated for depression with the antidepressant medication, desipramine. The figure demonstrates (a) a large variation in desipramine concentrations over time between two subclavian blood specimens (10 h vs. 30 h), (b) a large variation in desipramine concentration by anatomic location at the same time (10 h between subclavian and heart ventricle blood), and (c) variations between atrial and vitreous humor concentrations.

This chapter will address the interpretation of PM drug concentrations by forensic toxicologists and pathologists in assigning the cause of death (COD) and manner of death (MOD). Specifically, the chapter will review the following: clarification of the definition of PMR, physiologic processes that occur after death that result in PMR, drug characteristics that have been identified to suggest PMR, literature review of drugs that have been shown to result in PMR, and the role of the toxicologist in providing the evidence-based lit-

erature findings to the forensic pathologist to assist in the COD and MOD determinations. Postmortem forensic toxicology is discussed in more detail in Chap. 1.

Definition of PMR

The scientific fact is that PMR occurs both in central (heart) blood and in peripheral (femoral) blood. One misconception associated with PMR is based on the assumption that a PM heart blood to peripheral blood ratio greater than 1.0 is defined as PMR and that the greater the heart blood to peripheral blood ratio, the greater the PMR. In reality, this ratio represents an anatomic site-to-site difference and may or may not be related to PMR. Whether or not the blood concentration of a drug observed at autopsy is the steady-state concentration following stable, therapeutic dosing or represents an acute toxic drug exposure resulting in death that has not distributed throughout the body will have a substantial impact on the PM heart blood to peripheral blood ratio. What has been reported frequently is that central (heart) blood is more prone to PMR compared to peripheral blood and is related to the diffusion of drugs from the stomach, liver, lungs, and heart tissues; these tissues often contain two- to tenfold greater drug concentrations (mg per kilogram of tissue) than that found in blood. However, one cannot rule out that skeletal muscle tissues are prone to drug release back into the blood. At best all one can accurately state is that there is an anatomic site location difference between heart blood and peripheral blood drug concentration, which may or may not be an accurate representation of PMR in either location.

It is not easy to design a scientific experiment to study PMR. Ideally, blood would be drawn serially from a vessel over time without disruption of the body. Whether a blood vessel would need to be ligated or clamped is not clear. Drawing blood from a blood vessel after death may be contaminated with fluids released from surrounding tissue. While not hampered by sound, analytical techniques that toxicologists use to quantitate drug concentrations (i.e., mass spectrometry), the inexact science of postmortem toxicology is affected by many known and unknown effects that occur postmortem. Care must be taken by scientists reporting findings in the peer-reviewed and non-peer-reviewed literature that better represents whether site-to-site differences in drug concentrations are found or whether serial samples from the same blood vessel were obtained which better indicate whether PMR occurs.

PM Physiological Processes Causing PMR

Numerous articles have reviewed the processes that occur in the body from the time of death to the time blood is drawn at autopsy that cause a redistribution of drugs from an area of high concentration (e.g., tissues) to an area of low concentration (e.g., blood). PMR can result in an inaccurate representation of what blood concentration was at the time of death compared to the higher blood concentration found at autopsy. The impact of PMR is that a falsely high blood concentration can lead to an inappropriate COD determination by forensic pathologists.

The general thought process has been that since PMR occurs less frequently in peripheral blood compared to heart blood, that peripheral blood drug concentrations are a reliable indication of a drug concentration at the time of death.

Using fentanyl as a representative case example, the biochemical and physical mechanisms responsible for increasing fentanyl concentrations in femoral/peripheral and heart blood over the postmortem interval are complex and likely vary from case to case. Fentanyl is a lipophilic drug, which is highly bound to proteins at physiological pH (7.4). A broad tissue uptake of fentanyl creates a large steady-state volume of distribution. Fentanyl distribution can be described to occur in a three-compartment model: (a) the circulatory system (blood) plus vessel-rich highly perfused tissue (liver, lung, heart) compartment; (b) peripheral compartment comprised of skeletal muscle; and (c) peripheral compartment comprised of adipose (fat) tissue. High partitioning of fentanyl into skeletal muscle occurs rapidly, with tissue concentrations fourfold to tenfold higher than in plasma. There is also a high tissue to blood concentration gradient for liver, 3- to 35-fold, and heart, 2- to 5.3-fold. Small decreases in plasma pH that can occur within minutes following death result in substantial decreases in protein binding of fentanyl. At death there is a decrease in plasma pH, from the physiological pH of 7.4 in the living to as low as 5.6 within 24 h postmortem. The pH decrease results in an increased permeability of tissue cell membranes, which results in a shift of drug concentrations to move along a concentration gradient (from the high tissue levels to the lower plasma levels). Postmortem fentanyl concentrations, both in the peripheral and central (heart) blood, may not stay static. Whether heart or peripheral blood is collected, it is more likely a reflection not of the blood concentration at the time of death but rather a combination of tissue-bound drug that has been released into the blood/fluid that is drawn at autopsy hours after death. Peripheral blood, such as femoral blood, is also subject to PMR influences from local tissues, skeletal muscle, and fat. Figure 34.2 demonstrates the dynamic changes that can occur in fentanyl-related death investigations. In four of the seven cases, significant increases in PB fentanyl concentrations were observed over the PM interval between blood draws.

Fig. 34.2 Findings of postmortem redistribution of peripheral blood fentanyl concentrations in seven cases with specimens collected over two postmortem times. (From Olson 2010)

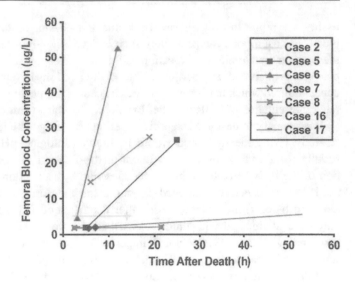

Assessing the role of drugs in "marginally toxic" cases involves understanding of the timing of collection, method of collection, and site of sample collection, all of which may influence the interpretation of toxicological analysis. Leading up to and following death, several physiological processes occur that lead to cell death and disintegration of cell structure and integrity. This results in release of cellular contents into surrounding blood/fluids as noted earlier. Cellular aerobic metabolism decreases and stops, energy (ATP) productivity declines, and anaerobic metabolism begins. This leads to an intracellular decrease in pH, predominantly due to lactic acid accumulation. Progressive cellular alterations occur that results in degradation of cellular integrity, with leakage of cellular contents into the extracellular space, including protein-bound drugs. Irreversible cell damage has been observed within 30–60 min after ischemia. The rate and extent of the movement of drugs PM varies unpredictably and can be influenced by several factors. These include the nature of the drug and the time interval between death and PM specimen collection. Typically lipophilic basic drugs concentrate in solid tissues such as liver, lung, and heart muscle. These drug-enriched tissues would therefore provide a concentration gradient for passive diffusion after death, resulting in PMR. Furthermore, as cells are largely aqueous and become increasingly acidic after death, basic

drugs will be more ionized in a lower pH environment, and after cell membrane lysis, basic drugs will tend to redistribute more readily.

Changes that occur in the body after death also have been attributed to the position of the body after death and subsequent movement of the body from the site of death to the site of autopsy; both may have an effect on PMR. In addition, purification of the body can also contribute to changes in blood drug concentrations after death.

Drug Characteristics Suggesting Potential PMR

Individual drug characteristics will determine the extent to which a drug undergoes PMR. The drug distribution involves the delivery of drug by way of the circulation to the rest of the body and involves passage of the drug through cell membranes. This depends on binding of the drug to plasma protein and tissue receptors as well as drug polarity or ionization. The rate of distribution depends upon the rate of tissue perfusion. For drugs which permeate membranes readily, their distribution will be perfusion limited. For example, perfusion rates can vary 500-fold between the lung (higher) and resting skeletal muscle or fat. The volume of distribution (Vd) measures a drug's ability to distribute throughout the body. Drug distribution is affected by protein binding since only drugs that are not bound to plasma proteins are free to cross all membranes. Other factors include lipid solubility, pK_a, tissue affinity, and energy-dependent transport processes across membranes.

Drugs Displaying PMR

When a forensic pathologist or toxicologist attempts to estimate the amount of drug present at the time of death or the number of tablets consumed, the assumption is often made that the drug concentration found PM is a reliable estimate of that present at the time of death. We have learned from the evidence-based literature for many drugs that the pharmacokinetic concept that a concentration (C) equals the dose (D) of a drug divided by the volume of distribution (Vd) does not often pertain to PM toxicology. Pounder once described PMR as a "toxicological nightmare." Examination of the postmortem to antemortem drug concentration ratio has been studied to provide information pertaining to PMR. In one study Cook examined seven drugs in peripheral blood obtained antemortem and postmortem. The PM to antemortem ratio was found to be unreliable in estimating antemortem concentrations from postmortem levels. They concluded that PMR was an important contributor to the substantial differences found at autopsy, with increased concentration found over the time period after death. The mechanisms Cook propose underlying PMR of drugs derived from drug release from the gastrointestinal tract, lungs, liver, heart, body, and skeletal muscle. Cook noted that drugs are sequestered in organs during life and act as drug reservoirs. After death, they are redistributed to the surrounding tissues and blood fluids. Table 34.1 proposes queries that both forensic pathologists and toxicologists should ask when interpreting drug concentrations measured in blood obtained postmortem.

As shown in Table 34.2, there are numerous case reports and series of cases reported for drugs that clearly demonstrate that PMR does occur in peripheral and heart blood. The following drugs have been identified as being affected by PMR: citalopram, desethylamiodarone, dextropropoxyphene, digoxin, dothiepin, fentanyl, flecainide,

Table 34.1 Questions which should be asked when interpreting drug concentrations measured in blood obtained postmortem

1.	What blood vessel and anatomic location was the specimen drawn from?
2.	If peripheral blood was obtained, was the vein ligated or clamped prior to sampling?
3.	Was the blood obtained after drawing into a single tube mixed before aliquoting into multiple tubes?
4.	If blood was drawn from more than one anatomic site, i.e., heart and femoral, how does one interpret differences in blood levels found between sites?
5.	What was the PM interval before blood was drawn?
6.	How was the body handled and stored between the time of death and blood/tissue collection?
7.	Were tissue specimens, i.e., liver, obtained?
8.	Was there evidence of decomposition?
9.	Is there antemortem or perimortem blood available for analysis?
10.	Has the literature been thoroughly reviewed to determine whether studies document PMR for the drug of interest?

Table 34.2 Published studies of drugs demonstrating postmortem redistribution

Drug	Blood source
Citalopram	Heart
Desethylamiodarone	Heart, peripheral
Dextropropoxyphene	Peripheral
Digoxin	Heart, peripheral
Dothiepin	Peripheral
Fentanyl	Heart, peripheral
Flecainide	Heart
Haloperidol	Heart
MDMA/MDA	Heart, peripheral
Propoxyphene	Heart, peripheral
Quetiapine	Heart, peripheral
Sotalol	Heart, peripheral
Tetrahydrocannabinol	Heart, peripheral
Thioridazine	Heart
Tricyclic antidepressants	Heart, peripheral

haloperidol, MDMA/MDA, propoxyphene, quetiapine, sotalol, tetrahydrocannabinol, thioridazine, and tricyclic antidepressants. This is not considered to be an inclusive list, because the tendency for any drug to exhibit PMR is largely determined by its physicochemical properties. Furthermore, PMR has not been studied for all drugs, particularly new psychoactive substances and emerging drugs of abuse.

Role of Toxicologist

PMR needs to be carefully considered in COD determinations when interpretation of PM drug concentrations is backed by literature in support of PMR. This information known by the toxicologist must be fully disclosed to their forensic pathology partners to allow them to make educated COD and MOD decisions. This is especially true in death cases in which blood concentrations may be erroneously interpreted as the COD based on the assumption that the peripheral PM blood concentration is an accurate record of the perimortem blood concentration at the time of death. To assist the forensic toxicologist in interpretation of these difficult cases, some laboratories have moved to measuring PM tissue concentrations, primarily liver that are minimally affected by PMR. For example, the history of tricyclic antidepressant (TCA) monitoring of liver concentrations, differentiating between toxic/fatal and therapeutic ingestions, has been established since 1970. Studies in postmortem cases have reported that liver TCA concentrations (total of parent drug and active metabolite) <15 mg/kg are not indicative of toxicity while concentrations reported as >30 mg/kg were considered indicative of toxicity. A ratio of parent drug to metabolite concentration greater than 1.0 was indicative of a recent or acute exposure to a TCA. Recently several investigators have proposed and utilized the measurement of fentanyl liver concentrations to differentiate therapeutic from toxic or fatal fentanyl concentrations. Liver concentrations <31 µg/kg have been shown to be therapeutic or non-toxic, while concentration >69 µg/kg was potentially toxic and fatal. Studies need to be performed to better address how and from where blood should be drawn for all drugs potentially prone to PMR. Moreover, PM blood concentrations from multiple sites should be tabulated in cases where the cause of death was not drug related, so as to develop "postmortem therapeutic" ranges for drugs. Furthermore, larger databases are also needed to best optimize liver tissue cutoff concentrations. Just as important are studies that have already shown that drugs, such as cocaine and morphine, are not significantly prone to PMR; this means that either central or peripheral blood are acceptable samples for postmortem quantitation and interpretation for COD assistance.

PMR is a complicated phenomenon that is influenced by time-dependent and site-dependent variables, in addition to the physicochemical properties of the drug. As a result, published literature on this topic is sometimes inconsistent, particularly for relatively small populations of cases. Differences in postmortem interval, environmental factors, sampling of postmortem specimens, and other factors such as disruption of the compartments caused by blunt force trauma significantly complicate the issue. These topics are discussed in more detail in Chap. 1.

Summarizing, the overriding goal is to provide quality and dependable forensic toxicology results that can be reliably used for interpretation by all forensic scientists and pathologists. A better understanding of PMR of drugs can go a long way to improving the field of forensic toxicology and assisting in the appropriate determination of cause of death investigations.

Further Reading

Anderson DT, Muto JJ (2000) Duragesic transdermal patch: postmortem tissue distribution of fentanyl in 25 cases. J Anal Toxicol 24:627–634

Andresen H, Gullans A, Veselinovic M, Anders S, Schmoldt A, Iwersen-Bergmann S, Mueller A (2012) Fentanyl: toxic or therapeutic? Postmortem and antemortem blood concentrations after transdermal fentanyl application. J Anal Toxicol 36:182–194

Apple FS, Bandt CM (1988) Liver and blood postmortem tricyclic antidepressant concentrations. Am J Clin Pathol 89:794–796

Apple FS (2011) A better understanding of interpretation of postmortem blood drug concentrations. J Anal Toxicol 35:381–383

Baselt RC (2020) Disposition of toxic drugs and chemicals in man, 12th edn. Biomedical Publications, Seal Beach, CA

Cook DS, Braithwaite RA, Hale KA (2000) Estimating antemortem drug concentrations from postmortem blood samples, the influence of postmortem redistribution. J Clin Pathol 53:282–285

Hilborg T, Rogde S, Morland J (1999) Postmortem drug redistribution—human cases related to results in experimental animals. J Forensic Sci 44:3–9

Moriya F, Hashimoto Y (1999) Redistribution of basic drugs into cardiac blood from surrounding tissues during early-stages postmortem. J Forensic Sci 44:10–16

Olson K, Luckenbill K, Thompson J, Middleton O, Geiselhart R, Mills K, Kloss J, Apple F (2010) Postmortem redistribution of fentanyl in blood. Am J Clin Pathol 133:447–453

Pelissier-Alicot AL, Gaulier JM, Champsaur P, Marquet P (2003) Mechanisms underlying PMR of drugs: a review. J Anal Toxicol 27:533–544

Pounder DJ, Jones GR (1990) Postmortem drug redistribution—a toxicological nightmare. Forensic Sci Int 45(3):253–263

Prouty RW, Anderson WH (1990) The forensic science implications of site and temporal influences on postmortem blood-drug concentrations. J Forensic Sci 35:243–270

Postmortem Clinical Testing

35

Barry S. Levine

Abstract

Testing of postmortem specimens for clinical analytes may be important in the determination of certain causes of death. Because of changes that occur after death, postmortem blood specimens may not be appropriate for testing. For example, clinical chemistry assays performed on vitreous humor can provide more meaningful information in deaths due to diabetes (glucose) and dehydration (urea nitrogen, sodium). Mast cell tryptase is a test that can be performed on postmortem serum to assist in the diagnosis of anaphylactic deaths. The blood is also a useful specimen in identifying metabolic disorders that produce functional abnormalities without corresponding structural anomalies. Thyroid function tests may also be performed on postmortem blood specimens but are best interpreted in combination with histological findings. Postmortem clinical testing and the selection of appropriate postmortem specimens are reviewed for some of the most common conditions of interest, including anaphylaxis, dehydration, diabetes, metabolic disorders, and thyroid function.

Keywords

Postmortem · Toxicology · Clinical testing · Anaphylaxis · Dehydration · Diabetes · Electrolytes · Urea nitrogen · Glucose · Tryptase

Introduction

Clinical tests to diagnose natural disease states are an important component of clinical medicine. These tests may identify both structural and functional abnormalities in the vasculature, tissues, and organs. However, after death, the performance of an autopsy, with both gross and microscopic examinations, can detect many conditions that require clinical testing for diagnosis during life. Nevertheless, there are disease states that are not identifiable without postmortem clinical testing. Since some of these conditions may account for death, the ability to perform these tests on postmortem specimens is critical to the ultimate cause of death ruling.

Many endogenous compounds have been studied for their potential utility in postmortem investigations. Among the more common ones used are electrolytes (sodium, potassium, and chloride), urea nitrogen, creatinine, glucose, and tryptase.

B. S. Levine (✉)
Office of the Chief Medical Examiner,
Baltimore, MD, USA
e-mail: blevine@som.umaryland.edu

© Springer Nature Switzerland AG 2020
B. S. Levine, S. Kerrigan (eds.), *Principles of Forensic Toxicology*,
https://doi.org/10.1007/978-3-030-42917-1_35

Specimens

Blood. Although similar in color to a blood specimen from a living individual, a postmortem blood specimen is often quite different. The blood pH drops during the early postmortem interval, so movement of substances based on their degree of ionization may also occur. Cells lose their structural integrity rapidly after death. For example, red blood cells hemolyze, making the collection of serum or plasma more difficult. The loss of integrity allows movement of substances in and out of the cell, depending on the concentration gradient. During life, potassium is kept in the cell against a concentration gradient by an active process. After death, this active process stops, and potassium leaves the cell. Similarly, blood sodium and chloride concentrations decrease rapidly after death. Due to the stress of death or cardiopulmonary resuscitation, glucose concentrations increase rapidly during the perimortem period. Attempts have been made, largely unsuccessful, to correlate these postmortem concentrations to their concentrations at death. Variables such as postmortem interval, disease state, and environmental conditions have all contributed to this failure.

Vitreous humor. The vitreous is a chamber of the eye that is located between the lens and the retina and fills the center of the eye. It constitutes 80% of the eye and has a volume of about 4 mL. The vitreous is filled with a transparent, delicate connective tissue gel called the gel vitreous or a transparent liquid called the liquid vitreous. The gel vitreous is a collagen gel that is water insoluble. The liquid vitreous is present only in the adult eye. Together, they constitute the vitreous humor.

The vitreous humor weighs approximately 4 g. It consists of 99% water and has a specific gravity of 1.0050–1.0089. Its viscosity is approximately two times that of water but with an osmotic pressure close to that of aqueous humor. The pH of the vitreous humor is 7.5. The osmolality of the vitreous humor ranges from 288 to 323 mOsm/kg, slightly higher than the osmolality of serum, 275–295 mOsm/kg.

Collagen is the major structural protein of the vitreous humor. Although similar to cartilage collagen, there are some distinct differences as well. Another major component of the vitreous humor is hyaluronic acid (HA). HA is a glycosaminoglycan, a polysaccharide composed of repeating disaccharide units; each unit contains a hexosamine linked to uronic acid. The vitreous humor is composed of interpenetrating networks of HA molecules and collagen fibrils. In addition to collagen and HA, there are six specific noncollagenous proteins and two types of glycoproteins in the human vitreous humor.

The movement of molecules in and out of the vitreous occurs by a number of mechanisms: diffusion, hydrostatic pressure, osmotic pressure, convection, and active transport. Water movement is significant, as approximately 50% of the water is replaced every 10–15 min. High molecular weight substances and colloidal particles travel by convection. Low molecular weight substances move in and out of the vitreous primarily by diffusion; however, there is evidence that bulk flow also contributes to their movement.

There are a number of low molecular weight substances that are found in the vitreous humor. Vitreous humor concentrations of sodium and chloride will approximate the serum concentrations of these ions in healthy adults, especially in the early postmortem period. Potassium concentrations in the vitreous humor increase rapidly after death as potassium leaves the cells into nearby fluids. Urea nitrogen and creatinine are also present in concentrations similar to serum and are stable during the early postmortem period. Because of this general stability, the measurement of vitreous humor sodium, chloride, urea nitrogen, and creatinine has become standard as indicators for the serum concentrations of these substances at death.

The vitreous humor should be collected using a syringe and a 20 gauge needle. The needle is placed against the eye at the lateral aspect just above the junction between the upper and lower eyelids. The needle is inserted into the eye approximately 2 cm, and the vitreous humor is gradually withdrawn. It is recommended that the vitreous humor from both eyes should be

Table 35.1 Normal vitreous humor concentrations

Analyte	Range
Chloride	115–125 mM
Creatinine	0.6–1.3 mg/dL
Glucose	<200 mg/dL
Sodium	135–145 mM
Urea nitrogen	10–20 mg/dL

collected. No preservatives need to be added to the specimen; however, it should be stored in the refrigerator until analyzed.

Other specimens. Other fluids such as cerebrospinal fluid (CSF) or pericardial fluid have been investigated as viable specimens for postmortem clinical chemistry testing. Postmortem CSF urea nitrogen and creatinine concentrations are generally similar to antemortem serum concentrations. As with postmortem blood, CSF sodium and chloride concentrations rapidly decrease after death, while CSF potassium concentrations increase, albeit slower than in postmortem blood.

The current consensus is that vitreous humor is the specimen of choice for electrolytes, urea nitrogen, creatinine, and glucose. Normal vitreous humor concentrations for these substances are provided in Table 35.1.

Anaphylaxis

Anaphylaxis is a serious allergic reaction that occurs rapidly and can lead to death. It results from the release of histamine from mast cells and basophils triggered by either immunologic or non-immunologic mechanisms. In the immune response, immunoglobulin E (IgE) binds to a foreign substance that ultimately leads to the release of histamine. The increase in histamine concentration leads to a number of physiological changes that are described in Chap. 29. The life-threatening symptoms include bronchial smooth muscle cell contraction leading to difficulty in breathing and vasodilatation that can lead to hypotension and shock.

A variety of substances can trigger the immune response that leads to anaphylaxis. Allergies to food such as shellfish and peanuts can be trig-

gers. Medications such as penicillins, cephalosporins, and narcotics have also been known to initiate an immune response. Venoms from bee or wasp stings can also cause a potentially fatal immune response.

The postmortem diagnosis of anaphylaxis has generally relied on a combination of history and autopsy findings. Known allergies to a particular substance and a report of a rapid death are initial clues that an anaphylactic death has occurred. If the allergen entered the body through an insect bite, the site of the bite may be observable during the external examination of the body. Internal examination may identify laryngeal or epiglottic swelling and mucous plugging of the airways. Microscopically, mucosal edema with mast cell infiltration and tissue eosinophilia may be observed. If the triggering substance was food or medication, examination of the stomach contents may identify the specific source.

However, none of the above findings are sufficient to make an unequivocal diagnosis of anaphylaxis. Thus, the identification of a clinical marker to support the diagnosis of anaphylaxis was important to raise the level of certainty for the ruling. Since histamine is released during the immune response, it would be the obvious choice to investigate as a clinical marker. Unfortunately, histamine has a very short half-life in the blood, and its release may occur for non-allergy reasons. Moreover, IgE, the immunoglobulin that binds to the allergen and begins the process, has unknown stability postmortem.

Tryptase is a serine protease that, along with histamine, is released by mast cells during the immune response. Unlike histamine, tryptase is found only in mast cells and basophils, but not eosinophils or platelets. As a result, its detection in elevated concentrations would provide greater evidence that an immune response had occurred. During anaphylaxis, tryptase is detectable 15–30 min after mast cell degranulation and peaks between 30 min and 2 h. In addition, it has a half-life of several hours as opposed to several minutes for histamine. There are two forms of tryptase, α and β. The β form is released as a result of a challenge by an allergen. Studies suggest that in deaths clearly unrelated to anaphylaxis, a "postmortem normal" serum concentration is up to 10 ng/mL. In deaths due to anaphylaxis, serum tryptase concentrations are usually several times greater than this.

Although postmortem serum tryptase concentrations are useful in making the ultimate diagnosis of anaphylaxis, it is not 100% specific for the diagnosis. Tryptase concentrations greater than 10 ng/mL have been reported in cardiac deaths and trauma deaths. One study indicated that a specificity of 90% can be attained using a threshold of 10 ng/mL. Therefore, although serum tryptase measurements are useful to support other facts and observations consistent with anaphylaxis, it should not be used by itself for the diagnosis.

Dehydration

Dehydration occurs when the individual loses more water than is taken in. Physiological conditions that can lead to dehydration include vomiting and diarrhea, fever, and excessive sweating. Dehydration may also occur when an individual does not consume an adequate amount of water or fluids. The extent of dehydration is variable, but severe dehydration can be life-threatening and can actually lead to death. At autopsy, observations of dried organs and sunken eyes may indicate dehydration. The diagnosis of dehydration is aided by the analysis of sodium, chloride, urea nitrogen, and creatinine in the vitreous humor. Normal vitreous humor sodium concentrations are similar to antemortem serum sodium concentrations and range from 135 to 145 mM. A vitreous humor sodium concentration greater than 155 mM may indicate dehydration. Similarly, normal chloride concentrations range from 115 to 125 mM with a chloride concentration greater than 135 mM suggesting dehydration. A vitreous humor urea nitrogen concentration ranges between 10 and 20 mg/dL in normal individuals; concentrations above 40 mg/dL are consistent with dehydration. A urea nitrogen to creatinine concentration ratio greater than 20 is typical for "prerenal" dehydration. If dehydration has occurred, all of these analytes would be elevated.

If the urea nitrogen is elevated and the electrolytes are normal, kidney malfunction may explain the elevated urea nitrogen. In kidney disease, the vitreous humor creatinine would also be elevated.

Diabetes Mellitus

Diabetes is a disease where an individual has elevated blood glucose concentrations. It exists in two forms; type 1 is the less common form and is caused by the destruction of pancreatic beta cells that are responsible for the production of insulin. Insulin is the hormone responsible for lowering blood glucose when it becomes elevated. Type 2 diabetes is the more common form and occurs when the body does not produce enough insulin or is unable to utilize the insulin that is produced. People with type 1 diabetes, because of the imbalance of insulin with hormones that cause an increase in blood glucose concentrations, break down fat to a larger extent than normal individuals, leading to increased production of free fatty acids. The subsequent metabolism of free fatty acids leads to an increased production of ketone bodies. The most prominent ketone bodies in man are beta-hydroxybutyrate (BHB), acetoacetate, and acetone. Patients with type 2 diabetes, because there is some functioning insulin, produce hyperglycemia without the increased breakdown of fat. As a result, an increased in ketone bodies does not occur. However, there is a hyperosmolar hyperglycemic state that leads to increased diuresis and dehydration.

Generally, there are no obvious gross or microscopic findings associated with deaths caused by diabetic ketoacidosis. Therefore, it is important to measure glucose and ketone bodies in cases where death due to diabetes is suspected. As stated previously, because postmortem blood glucose concentrations do not reliably reflect the individual's sugar status during life, vitreous humor has become the specimen of choice for this determination. In his review of postmortem chemistries, Coe stated that a vitreous humor glucose concentration greater than 200 mg/dL will only be seen in diabetics. He further stated that even when the postmortem peripheral serum glucose concentration was greater than 500 mg/dL in nondiabetics, the corresponding vitreous humor glucose concentration was never greater than 100 mg/dL.

Unlike postmortem blood glucose concentrations, postmortem blood ketone body concentrations are a reliable indicator of ketone body concentrations at death. Of the three common ketone bodies, acetone is the easiest to measure. Acetone is detected by headspace gas chromatography at the same time that ethanol is measured (see Chap. 19). In fact, in the absence of a history of diabetes, the detection of acetone during the ethanol analysis may be the first indication that the death was caused by diabetic ketoacidosis. Subsequent measurement of glucose in the vitreous humor would indicate whether the measured acetone was caused by a diabetic ketoacidosis or alcoholic ketoacidosis. This latter condition may be seen in alcoholics and is attributed to a combination of large alcohol consumption and malnutrition. Normal vitreous glucose concentrations are observed in people with alcoholic ketoacidosis.

Although acetone is the easiest ketone body to detect, BHB is the ketone body found in the highest concentrations in diabetics. BHB is the ketone body most responsible for acidosis. BHB concentrations less than 50 mg/L are considered normal, while concentrations greater than 250 mg/L are considered significant.

In addition to blood glucose, another substance used to monitor glucose control is glycated hemoglobin. In healthy adults, hemoglobin (Hb) consists of three forms: HbA1, HbA2, and HbF. HbA constitutes approximately 97% of the total hemoglobin in the blood and consists of three subgroups: HbA1a, HbA1b, and HbA1c. HbA1c comprises about 80% of HbA1. Glycated hemoglobin is produced by the nonenzymatic addition of sugars to amino acids on the protein; specifically, glucose binds to the N-terminal valine amino acids of the beta chain of hemoglobin. The more glucose that is present in the blood, the more glycated hemoglobin is present. Since the life span of a red blood cell is approximately 4 months, the percentage of HbA1c that is glycated represents an average measure of blood glucose concentrations over this time period. In theory, this percentage would not be susceptible to the wild changes in glucose concentration that may occur around death. "Normal glycated HbA1c" is generally less than 7% in living patients, but this expected concentration has not clearly been established in postmortem cases. Several postmortem studies have indicated that glycated HbA1c is elevated in diabetic individuals, but the results have generally been used in conjunction with vitreous humor glucose and blood ketone body concentrations to conclude that the death was caused by diabetes.

Metabolic Disorders

Unexpected deaths in infants and children qualify for a medicolegal investigation. Since deaths due to sudden infant death syndrome (SIDS) or sudden unexpected death in infancy (SUDI) are diagnoses of exclusion, a complete investigation, autopsy, and toxicology testing are required prior to making these rulings. Deaths caused by structural abnormalities would be identified during the gross internal examination of the body. Functional abnormalities without corresponding structural deficits would not be observable and require clinical testing for a diagnosis. A number of inborn errors of metabolism have been identified, and a number of these can lead to death:

Acute intermittent porphyria (AIP). This disorder affects the production of heme, the iron-containing component of hemoglobin. The specific enzyme that is deficient is porphobilinogen deaminase, leading to an increase in porphobilinogen concentrations.

Glycogen storage diseases. This results from the inability to produce or breakdown glycogen. Any single enzyme involved in the process of glycogen synthesis or metabolism can be the cause of the disease.

Lysosomal storage diseases. This disease is a series of disorders that have as their common characteristic a deficit in lysosome function. The lysosome breaks down unwanted material in the cell; the malfunctioning of this process leads to the buildup of these unwanted substances. There are a number of processes that can be defective, each leading to a specific disease.

Medium-chain acyl-CoA dehydrogenase (MCAD) deficiency. This disorder in fatty acid oxidation is caused by reduced activity of this enzyme system. Fatty acids of varying lengths combine with glycerol to form triglycerides. Fatty acids with 6–12 carbon atoms are metabolized with this enzyme system. This condition is diagnosed by measuring elevated concentrations of medium-length acylcarnitines caused by the buildup of fatty acids. Carnitine is the molecule that transports fatty acids from the cytoplasm to the mitochondria for incorporation into triglycerides.

Organic acidemia. This disorder disrupts normal metabolism of amino acids. One example of this disease is maple syrup urine disease; a malfunctioning branched-chain α-keto acid dehydrogenase complex causes an increased concentration of leucine, valine, isoleucine, and alloisoleucine. Other examples of this disease are propionic acidemia and methylmalonic acidemia.

Phenylketonuria. This disorder results from a deficiency in hydroxylase, the enzyme that catalyzes the conversion of phenylalanine to tyrosine. This leads to an elevation in phenylalanine concentrations with a corresponding decrease in tyrosine concentrations.

Thyroid Function

Available clinical measurements for assessing thyroid function include thyroxine (T_4), triiodothyronine (T_3), and thyroid-stimulating hormone (TSH). The normal ranges for T_4, T_3, and TSH in living individuals are 9–24 pM, 3–9 pM, and 0.4–4.0 mU/L, respectively. In general, blood T_4 concentrations will decrease after death, but not in a consistent manner. It has been suggested that in the early postmortem period, T_4 is converted to T_3. Nevertheless, T_4 concentrations above 24 pM may be associated with normal histology, and an elevated T_4 concentration in the absence of other history or anatomic findings should be interpreted cautiously. T_3 concentration changes are more variable but appear to remain in the normal range when histological findings are unremarkable. T_3 is elevated in cases where focal epithelial hyperplasia is observed microscopically. T_4 and T_3 enter the vitreous humor and are generally present in much lower concentrations that in the blood. It appears that thyroid function tests are most properly utilized when measured in postmortem blood and combined with histological findings.

Further Reading

Chase DH, Kalas TA, Naylor EW (2002) The application of tandem mass spectrometry to neonatal screening for inherited disorders of intermediary metabolism. Annu Rev Genomics Hum Genet 3:17–45

Coe J (1993) Postmortem chemistry update—emphasis on forensic applications. Am J Forensic Med Pathol 14:91–117

Edston E, Druid H, Holmgren P, Ostrom M (2001) Postmortem measurements of thyroid function in blood and vitreous humor combined with histology. Am J Forensic Med Pathol 22:78–83

Hockenhull J, Dhillo W, Andrews R, Peterson S (2012) Investigation of markers to indicate and distinguish death due to alcoholic ketoacidosis, diabetic ketoacidosis and hyperosmolar hyperglycemic state using post-mortem samples. Forensic Sci Int 214:142–147

Horn KD, Halsey JF, Zumwalt RE (2004) Utilization of serum tryptase and immunoglobulin E assay in the postmortem diagnosis of anaphylaxis. Am J Forensic Med Pathol 25:37–42

Palmiere C, Comment L, Vilarino R, Mangin P, Bonetti LR (2014) Measurement of β-tryptase I postmortem serum in cardiac deaths. J Forensic Legal Med 23:12–18

Palmiere C, Mangin P (2012) Postmortem chemistry update Part I. Int J Legal Med 126:187–198

Palmiere C, Mangin P (2012) Postmortem chemistry update Part II. Int J Legal Med 126:199–215

Pourfarzam M, Zadhoush F (2013) Newborn screening for inherited disorders; new and views. J Res Med Sci 18:801–808

Randall B, Butts J, Halsey JF (1995) Elevated postmortem tryptase in the absence of anaphylaxis. J Forensic Sci 40:208–211

Tse R, Wong CX, Kesha K, Garland J, Tran Y, Anne S, Elstub H, Cala AD, Palmiere C, Patchett KL (2018) Post mortem tryptase cut-off level for anaphylactic death. Forensic Sci Int 284:5–8

Yunginger JW, Nelson DR, Squillace DL, Jones RT, Holley KE, Hyma BA, Biedrycki L, Sweeney KG, Sturner WQ, Schwartz LB (1991) Laboratory investigation of deaths due to anaphylaxis. J Forensic Sci 36:857–865

Pharmacogenomics

36

Thomas Kupiec

Abstract

Pharmacogenomics is the study of the association between an individual's genotype and the disposition of drugs in the body. The phenotype or external manifestations are mediated by an individual's genotype. One prominent example of genotypic differences leading to phenotypic differences in pharmacokinetics is with drug-metabolizing enzymes. Differences in the cytochrome P450 (CYP) genes can lead to enzymes that have either reduced or increased enzyme activity. Three CYP enzymes where genotypic differences have been observed are CYP2D6, CYP2C9, and CYP3A. In addition to drug-metabolizing enzymes, genotypic differences in transport proteins can impact transporter-mediated drug interactions. Drug receptor genotypic differences can lead to altered effects of drugs. Several examples are provided as to how pharmacogenomics may be used in the interpretation of forensic toxicological findings.

Dr. Vishnu Raj is acknowledged for his contribution to research and assistance with this chapter.

T. Kupiec, Ph.D. (✉)
ARL Bio Pharma, Oklahoma City, OK, USA
e-mail: tkupiec@arlok.com

Keywords

Pharmacogenomics · Forensic toxicology · CYP450 · Interpretation

Introduction

Pharmacogenomics can prove to be a useful tool to the forensic toxicologist. The consideration of genetic variation and its contribution to pharmacokinetics should be examined in the interpretation of drug concentrations. Understanding the potential effect of pharmacogenomics can be beneficial in evaluating postmortem drug concentrations, workplace drug testing, or drugs and driving cases. In addition to age, physical condition, diet, or co-administered drugs, genetic variation can affect drug metabolism and efficacy. Large inter-individual variations can occur in drug concentration, toxicity, and drug response when given the same dosage.

Pharmacogenomics is the study of the association between an individual's genotype and the disposition of drugs in the body. The first association between adverse drug reactions and inherited variations was recognized in the 1950s, linking peripheral neuropathy with isoniazid and apnea with succinylcholine. However, genetic influence on drug disposition has existed for centuries dating back to Pythagoras and his observation that the ingestion of fava beans triggered a potentially fatal hemolytic anemia in some but not all individuals. Variations in drug response are basically because of differences in individual genetic makeup. Genes are made of DNA sequences, and if these sequences are disrupted (i.e., deletions, insertions, transpositions, etc.), it may lead to discernible differences in form or function of gene products.

An individual's phenotype corresponds to observable characteristics such as their eye and hair color or their rate of drug clearance. The phenotype, or external manifestation, is modulated by the individual's genotype (i.e., their genetic makeup) and other factors such as age, gender, and health. Inter-individual differences in phenotype are often caused by genetic polymorphisms. The most prevalent type of polymorphism involves a single base pair variant in a DNA sequence, which is referred to as a single-nucleotide polymorphism (SNP). Millions of SNPs have been identified in the human genome. The effect of only one change in the base pair can change the amino acid. A change in the amino acid may result in a change in the protein folding or structure, thus culminating in a change in the drug-metabolizing enzyme activity (Fig. 36.1). Other applications of SNPs include new drug development, prediction of drug efficacy and toxicity, optimization of clinical trials, and individualization of drug therapy.

Most drug effects are determined by the interaction of several gene products (drug targets, enzymes, and transporters) that influence the pharmacokinetics and pharmacodynamics of medications.

Polymorphisms have been observed in genes encoding for drug-metabolizing enzymes, drug transport proteins, and drug targets/receptors. Polymorphic gene products can affect drug disposition, thereby causing adverse effects. For example, the enzyme thiopurine S-methyltransferase (TPMT) metabolizes the drugs azathioprine and mercaptopurine. Individuals with the genes for reduced TPMT activity must be treated with substantially different doses of the affected drugs (i.e., about 5–10% of the standard dose) to prevent toxicity.

Pharmacogenomics is an additional parameter along with pharmacodynamics and pharmacokinetics, all of which influence drug response, metabolism, and toxicity (Fig. 36.2). Pharmacokinetics and pharmacodynamics are discussed in more detail in other chapters in this book.

Drug-Metabolizing Enzymes

The majority of drugs undergo hepatic metabolism to water-soluble compounds, which are subsequently excreted. Drug metabolism typically results in drug detoxification and elimination or, in some cases, may lead to the activation of a prodrug to the active form. Drug-metabolizing enzymes (DMEs) may exhibit inter-individual variations in protein expression or catalytic activity, thus resulting in unique drug metabolism phenotypes. These variations can be attributed to transient causes such as enzyme inhibition and induction or to a permanent cause such as genetic mutation or gene deletion. Mutations in the cytochrome P450 (CYP) genes can lead to enzyme products with absent, reduced, or increased enzyme activity. Metabolism in the liver is primarily carried out by two groups of enzymes: phase I and phase II enzymes. Phase I enzymes, including CYP oxidative enzymes, modify functional groups on drugs via hydrolysis, oxidation, reduction, or hydroxylation. The CYP enzyme system is responsible for the metabolism of the majority of drugs and has been a major focus of pharmacogenomic research.

CYP2D6. Pharmaceutical drugs are frequently found in drug-related deaths, and some of these drugs include benzodiazepines, antide-

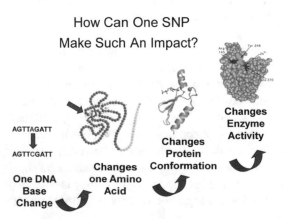

How Can One SNP Make Such An Impact?

AGTTAGATT
↓
AGTTCGATT

One DNA Base Change

Changes one Amino Acid

Changes Protein Conformation

Changes Enzyme Activity

Fig. 36.1 Effect of base pair change on enzyme

Fig. 36.2 Determinants of drug metabolism

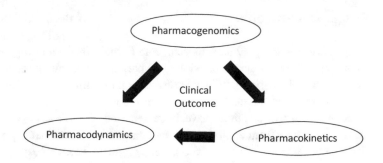

pressants, amphetamines, and opioids. CYP2D6 metabolizes a number of opioid drugs such as codeine, tramadol, oxycodone, and hydrocodone and is one of the most widely researched cytochrome enzymes. CYP2D6 is the most polymorphic CYP enzyme, with polymorphisms resulting in the absence of enzyme, reduced enzyme, or enzyme with increased activity. Based on genetic polymorphisms of CYP2D6, three metabolizer types are currently recognized: ultra-extensive metabolizers (UMs), extensive metabolizers (EMs), and poor metabolizers (PMs).

Individuals with a UM phenotype generally have multiple copies of a gene and will metabolize drugs faster and, as a result, do not achieve therapeutic plasma drug concentrations at ordinary drug dosages. In contrast, individuals with a PM genotype may require substantial dose reduction to prevent toxicity. For instance, in the case of the tricyclic antidepressant, nortriptyline, poor metabolizers have zero copies of the CYP2D6 enzyme, intermediate metabolizers have one copy, extensive metabolizers have two copies, and ultra-extensive metabolizers have more than two copies. These drug metabolism profiles exhibit clinical manifestations ranging from therapeutic inefficacy to toxicity for the same dose of a drug. Thus, CYP2D6 deficiency can lead to manifestations of drug overdose and intensified drug effects when CYP2D6 is the major inactivation pathway as with tricyclic antidepressants or to depreciated therapeutic effect when CYP2D6 is the activator, like in the case of the prodrug codeine. Genetic inactivity of CYP2D6 has been known to affect opioid analgesics in different ways; it renders codeine inactive, slightly

decreases the clearance of methadone, and slightly reduces the efficacy of tramadol.

CYP2C9. The CYP2C9 enzyme metabolizes warfarin, phenytoin, and several nonsteroidal anti-inflammatory drugs (NSAIDs). Small variations in warfarin and phenytoin dosage may be clinically relevant because of their narrow therapeutic range. CYP2C9 polymorphisms have been associated with significant reductions in the metabolism and dosage of selected CYP2C9 substrates. Individuals with these genotypes also appear to be significantly more susceptible to adverse events during the inception of warfarin and phenytoin therapy. Subjects with reduced clearance of oral anticoagulants such as warfarin are more susceptible to adverse bleeding events. CYP2C9 polymorphisms have been reported to occur in greater frequency among individuals who experienced acute gastric bleeding complications after NSAID use.

CYP3A. CYP3A represents a group of enzymes that are abundant in the liver and intestine. CYP3A4 is a very important enzyme in human drug metabolism, and it is known to metabolize the largest number of drugs. CYP3A4 accounts for 20–40% of the total hepatic cytochrome enzymes in humans and mediates the dealkylation of fentanyl to norfentanyl. Several drugs of toxicological significance, including buprenorphine, benzodiazepines, fentanyl, and methadone, are metabolized by CYP3A4. Both CYP3A4 and CYP3A5 are polymorphic, thus resulting in variable fentanyl metabolism. Although fentanyl abuse may lead to toxicity, adverse effects due to fentanyl may also be attributable in part to CYP3A4 or CYP3A5 variant alleles.

Transport Proteins

Transport proteins play an important role in the absorption of drugs across physiological barriers such as the blood-brain, biliary, intestinal, tubular, and renal epithelia. Significant transporter-mediated drug interactions have been reported and may range from inhibitory to inductive or both. For example, the P-glycoprotein (P-gp) efflux pump belongs to the ATP-binding cassette (ABC) family transporters and is encoded by the MDR1 gene (or ABCB1). In humans, P-gp is present in several tissues that are important for drug absorption, distribution, and elimination. Due to the broad substrate specificity of P-gp, inhibitors or inducers of P-gp may produce significant drug-drug interactions. Another important group are the organic anion (protein) transporters encoded by the solute carrier (SLC) gene family. These sodium ion-independent transporters partly rely on co-transport and are responsible for the transport of a wide range of endogenous compounds as well as drugs. Organic cation transporter interactions, as well as peptide transporter and nucleoside transporter interactions, have also been described.

Drug Targets

Most drugs exert their pharmacologic effect by interaction with specific targets (i.e., receptors, enzymes, or proteins). These targets include the $\beta2$-adrenoceptors, insulin receptors, angiotensin-converting enzyme, etc. Polymorphisms in genes encoding these targets may influence the sensitivity to selected drugs, and these polymorphisms may be significant in cases where inter-individual variations in plasma-drug concentrations are minimal, but major pharmacodynamic differences are observed. For example, a greater frequency of the Gly16 polymorphism of the $\beta2AR$ gene has been identified within a patient population of asthmatics, leading to an increased risk of morbidity and mortality from asthma. Another example of a drug target polymorphism is the anticancer drug 5-fluorouracil (5-FU), which acts by the inhibition of the enzyme thymidylate synthase (TS). TS is a critical element in DNA synthesis and repair, and clinical resistance to 5-FU and other folate-based antimetabolites has been linked to overexpression of TS.

Pharmacogenomics in Forensic Toxicology

Forensic toxicology contributes substantially to the determination of the cause and manner of death and provides valuable information regarding the interpretation of circumstances surrounding a fatal event. Particularly in overdose cases, it is essential to determine the drug(s) responsible for the intoxication, both for providing evidence in the particular case and for identification of drugs that could, over time, prove especially dangerous. Much effort has been put on the estimation of fatal concentrations of various drugs in postmortem material. Many fatal intoxications involve suicidal overdoses, but during recent years, chronic high dosage has attracted increased interest. In order to differentiate between an acute overdose and a chronic poisoning, the distribution of the drug in different specimens can be of assistance, since in an acute overdose death, the drug may not have reached high levels in less proximate samples like vitreous humor, cerebrospinal fluid, or hair. For a number of drugs, the parent drug to metabolite ratio (higher concentrations anticipated in acute overdose cases) may provide even more convincing evidence. However, the parent drug to metabolite ratio may provide misleading information; a low ratio may be encountered in acute overdoses, preceded by a high chronic dosage of the same drug. Conversely, a high parent drug to metabolite ratio could also be due to a reduced metabolism of the parent drug, either because of interaction with other drugs or because of genetically low metabolic capacity.

The following are examples of case studies where pharmacogenomics may play an important role in the interpretation of toxicological results:

Case Study: Oxycodone

A 49-year-old Caucasian male with a history of prescription drug abuse, depression, and post-traumatic stress disorder was found dead. The decedent had been prescribed OxyContin® and Percocet® for his chronic back pain. A postmortem oxycodone concentration of 0.437 mg/L was found in subclavian blood. Autopsy showed hepatic cirrhosis which might have impaired his drug metabolism. CYP2D6 is the polymorphic enzyme responsible for the metabolism of oxycodone. Whereas a majority of the population exhibit high CYP2D6 activity, 5–10% of Caucasians and 1–4% of most other ethnic groups have decreased CYP2D6 activity, leading to an increased risk of toxic effects and possible fatality from routine doses of oxycodone. Pharmacogenomic testing (i.e., molecular autopsy) indicated that he was CYP2D6∗4 homozygous, thus corresponding to the poor metabolizer phenotype. This deficiency might have contributed to impaired metabolism of oxycodone, along with hepatic cirrhosis. The cause of death was ruled as oxycodone intoxication, and manner of death was ruled as an accident.

Case Study: Methadone

A 51-year-old Caucasian male with a history of heroin addiction was enrolled in a methadone maintenance program. He was found dead on a Monday at 8 AM. His girlfriend confirmed that he was alive at 7 AM on Sunday. The decedent had hepatitis C and hepatic cirrhosis. A postmortem iliac blood methadone concentration of 1.6 mg/L was reported. Although there is a significant overlap between quoted therapeutic methadone concentrations and the concentrations reported in fatalities, an acute ingestion was considered likely. Postmortem redistribution was assumed to be minimal since the postmortem interval was less than 24 h. However, polydrug interactions also play a role in methadone fatalities. For example, concurrent administration of CYP3A4 inhibitors such as ketoconazole and erythromycin increases the risk of methadone toxicity. Molecular autopsy showed CYP2D6∗3 and CYP2D6∗4 compound heterozygosity, corresponding to a poor metabolizer of methadone. Other drugs found included benzoylecgonine, propoxyphene, and diazepam. Autopsy findings also included end-stage alcoholic liver disease. Cause of death was ruled as mixed drug toxicity, and manner of death was ruled as an accident.

Case Study: Fentanyl

A 44-year-old Caucasian female, with a history of drug abuse, suicidal ideation, and psychiatric disorders, was found dead. One fentanyl patch was attached to her arm, and another was adhered to a blanket. Postmortem subclavian blood concentrations of 19 and 7.6 µg/L were reported for fentanyl and norfentanyl, respectively. Other drugs found included cyclobenzaprine, tramadol, diphenhydramine, citalopram, and olanzapine. Molecular autopsy indicated heterozygosity of CYP3A4∗1B and CYP3A5∗3. This genotype corresponded with a reduced rate of fentanyl metabolism. Therefore, the cause of death was ruled as mixed drug toxicity, and manner of death was ruled as an accident.

Case Study: Fluoxetine

A 9-year-old boy, diagnosed with attention-deficit hyperactivity disorder, obsessive-compulsive disorder, and Tourette's syndrome, was treated with methylphenidate, clonidine, and fluoxetine. Over a 10-month period, he developed gastrointestinal toxicity, incoordination and disorientation, and seizures. He eventually died from a cardiac arrest. Postmortem toxicology showed high fluoxetine and norfluoxetine concentrations, and pharmacogenomic analysis revealed a poor CYP2D6 metabolizer genotype, resulting in fluoxetine accumulation and toxicity. Subsequently, the boy's parents were absolved from involvement in fluoxetine intoxication. (See Sallee, et al. of the Further Reading.)

Case Study: Doxepin

Doxepin is predominantly metabolized to the active metabolite N-desmethyldoxepin (nordoxepin) by CYP2C19. CYP2D6 appears to be involved in another important pathway catalyzing 2-hydroxylation of (E)-doxepin but also that of (E)-nordoxepin. A case was reported of a 43-year-old male alcoholic with suicidal tendencies who was found dead; the cause of death was doxepin intoxication. The doxepin concentration was 2.4 mg/L, the concentration of nordoxepin was 2.9 mg/L, and the doxepin/nordoxepin ratio was 0.83, the lowest found among the 35 nordoxepin-positive postmortem cases analyzed during the same year. No alcohol or other drugs were detected in the case. The manner of death remained unclear (suicide/accident). The postmortem DNA analysis indicated a CYP2C19 genotype that was determined to be that of an extensive metabolizer. However, it also revealed two CYP2D6 alleles, which were both not functional (CYP2D6*3/CYP2D6*4). Therefore doxepin could only be metabolized to nordoxepin, but not to 2-hydroxydoxepin or 2-hydroxynordoxepin. Correspondingly high doxepin and especially high nordoxepin concentrations were found with a ratio of 0.83. In suicidal poisonings, a ratio greater than one is expected; therefore an accidental chronic intoxication could be assumed. (See Koski, et al. of the Further Reading.)

Case Study: Codeine

Codeine is metabolized to the active drug morphine by CYP2D6. A healthy male infant presented with intermittent difficulties in breast-feeding and lethargy, starting on day 7. On day 12, he presented with gray skin and decreased milk intake. The infant was deceased on day 13. The autopsy revealed no anatomical cause of death; however, a blood morphine concentration of 70 ng/mL was found. Neonates breastfed by mothers receiving codeine typically have morphine serum concentrations of 0–2.2 ng/mL. The mother received a combination preparation of codeine 30 mg and paracetamol, which she took for 2 weeks. She stored milk at day 10 that had a morphine concentration of 87 ng/mL (normally 1.9–20.5 ng/mL). The investigation into the reason for the intoxication (accidental/homicidal) led to genotyping that revealed that the mother was an ultrarapid metabolizer of CYPD6, thus leading to an increased formation of morphine from codeine. Thus, cause of death was ruled as accidental morphine intoxication. (See Koren, et al. of the Further Reading.)

Summary

Emerging evidence suggests that the underlying cause of death in many postmortem cases is genetic and that both heart and liver abnormalities can play a role. The dilemma is that death from a wide variety of genetic defects may leave no histological markers. The ability to identify these "invisible diseases" with postmortem genetic testing has become a reality far more quickly than anyone had ever imagined. In the medicolegal system, pharmacogenetic testing has the potential to significantly reduce errors and increase the accuracy of toxicological interpretations used in establishing the cause and manner of death. The cost savings and legal ramifications of this technology are vast and will continue to grow as ongoing research supplements our understanding of individual differences in drug disposition.

Further Reading

Carlsson B, Holmgren A, Ahlner J, Bengtsson F (2009) Enantioselective analysis of citalopram and escitalopram in postmortem blood together with genotyping for CYP2D6 and CYP2C19. J Anal Toxicol 33(2):65–76

Druid H, Holmgren P, Carlsson B, Ahlner J (1999) Cytochrome P450 2D6 (CYP2D6) genotyping on postmortem blood as a supplementary tool for interpretation of forensic toxicological results. Forensic Sci Int 99(1):25–34

Jannetto PJ, Wong SH, Gock SB, Laleli-Sahin E, Schur BC, Jentzen JM (2002) Pharmacogenomics as molecular autopsy for postmortem forensic toxicology: genotyping cytochrome P450 2D6 for oxycodone cases. J Anal Toxicol 26:438–447

Jin M, Gock SB, Jannetto PJ, Jentzen JM, Wong SH (2005) Pharmacogenomics as molecular autopsy for forensic toxicology: genotyping cytochrome P450 3A4*1B and 3A5*3 for 25 fentanyl cases. J Anal Toxicol 29(7):590–598

Jones AW, Holmgren A, Ahlner J (2012) Blood methadone concentrations in living and deceased persons: variations over time, subject demographic, and relevance of coingested drugs. J Anal Toxicol 36(1):12–18

Jortani SA, Stauble E, Wong S (2012) Pharmacogenetics in clinical and forensic toxicology: opioid overdoses and deaths. In: Mozayani A, Raymon L (eds) Handbook of drug interactions: a clinical and forensic guide. Springer

Karch SB (2007) Changing times: DNA resequencing and the "nearly normal autopsy." J Forensic Legal Med 14(7):389–397

Kingbäck M, Karlsson L, Zackrisson AL, Carlsson B, Josefsson M, Bengtsson F, Ahlner J, Kugelberg FC (2012) Influence of CYP2D6 genotype on the disposition of the enantiomers of venlafaxine and its major metabolites in postmortem femoral blood. Forensic Sci Int 214(1–3):124–134

Koren G, Cairns J, Chitayat D, Gaedigk A, Leeder SJ (2006) Pharmacogenetics of morphine poisoning in a breastfed neonate of a codeine-prescribed mother. Lancet 368:704

Koski A, Ojanpera I, Sistonen J, Vuori E, Sajantila A (2007) A fatal doxepin poisoning associated with a defective CYP2D6 genotype. Am J Forensic Med Pathol 28:259–261

Kupiec TC, Raj V, Vu N (2006) Pharmacogenomics for the forensic toxicologist. J Anal Toxicol 30(2):65–72

Musshoff F, Stamer UM, Madea B (2010) Pharmacogenetics and forensic toxicology. Forensic Sci Int 203(1–3):53–62

Dinis-Oliveira RJ (2016) Metabolomics of methadone: clinical and forensic toxicological implications and variability of dose response. Drug Metab Rev 48(4):568–576

Sallee FR, DeVane CL, Ferrell RE (2000) Fluoxetine-related death in a child with cytochrome P-450 2D6 genetic deficiency. J Child Adolesc Psychopharmacol 10(1):27–34

Shi Y, Xiang P, Li L, Shen M (2011) Analysis of 50 SNPs in CYP2D6, CYP2C19, CYP2C9, CYP3A4 and CYP1A2 by MALDI-TOF mass spectrometry in Chinese Han population. Forensic Sci Int 207(1–3):183–187

van der Weide J, van Baalen-Benedek EH, Kootstra-Ros JE (2005) Metabolic ratios of psychotropics as indication of cytochrome P450 2D6/2C19 genotype. Ther Drug Monit 27(4):478–483

Watanabe J, Suzuki Y, Fukui N, Sugai T, Ono S, Inoue Y, Someya T (2008) Dose-dependent effect of the CYP2D6 genotype on the steady-state fluvoxamine concentration. Ther Drug Monit 30(6):705–708

Wong SH, Happy C, Blinka D, Gock S, Jentzen JM, Donald Hon J, Coleman H, Jortani SA, Lucire Y, Morris-Kukoski CL, Neuman MG, Orsulak PJ, Sander T, Wagner MA, Wynn JR, Wu AH, Yeo KT (2010) From personalized medicine to personalized justice: the promises of translational pharmacogenomics in the justice system. Pharmacogenomics 11(6):731–737

Wong SH, Wagner MA, Jentzen JM, Schur C, Bjerke J, Gock SB, Chang CC (2003) Pharmacogenomics as an aspect of molecular autopsy for forensic pathology/toxicology: does genotyping CYP2D6 serve as an adjunct for certifying methadone toxicity? J Forensic Sci 48(6):1406–1415

Hair Drug Testing

37

Robert Kronstrand

Abstract

The rationale for drug analysis in hair is that drugs circulating in the bloodstream will be incorporated into the hair cells when they are formed, trapped when they are keratinized, and subsequently moved further out from the scalp as new hair is formed. In theory, the hair will form a calendar of previous drug use. Drugs are deposited in the hair through active or passive diffusion from the blood vessels in the dermal papilla, through diffusion from sweat and other secretions into the growing or mature hair, or through external drugs from vapor or solids that diffuse into the mature hair. Head hair is the dominant matrix even though alternative collection sites may be tested. The recommendation is to obtain samples from the posterior vertex which has the most consistent growth rate. Hair has been used in investigations of drug-related deaths, drug-facilitated crimes, and child protection cases. It has also been used in the monitoring of drug abuse in rehabilitation programs, the workplace, and driver's license reinstatement. This chapter will provide an overview into the basic features of drug deposition into the hair, the analysis, and the interpretation of results.

R. Kronstrand (✉)
National Board of Forensic Medicine,
Dep. Forensic Genetics and Forensic Toxicology,
Linköping, Sweden
e-mail: Robert.kronstrand@rmv.se

Keywords

Hair · Drug incorporation · Melanin · Extraction recovery · Interpretation

Introduction

Over the past 30 years, the analysis of drugs in hair has become a component of forensic toxicological testing. The rationale for drug analysis in hair is that drugs circulating in the bloodstream will be incorporated into the hair cells. Once in the hair cells, they are trapped when the hair is keratinized and subsequently move further out from the scalp as new hair is formed. In theory, the hair will form a calendar of previous drug use. In reality, it is more complicated, and drugs may also be deposited on the hair via sweat and secretions as well as from external sources such as smoke and powders. Incorporation rate may depend on pigmentation, and the temporal pattern of use will depend on the individual growth rate. Therefore, even though the analysis of hair is straightforward, the interpretation of results is less definitive. The Society of Hair Testing (SoHT), founded in 1995, has over the years provided guidance to toxicologists performing analysis of drugs in human hair. In their latest publication, they acknowledge the use of hair drug testing in a variety of applications, including drug-related deaths, drug-facilitated crimes,

© Springer Nature Switzerland AG 2020
B. S. Levine, S. Kerrigan (eds.), *Principles of Forensic Toxicology*,
https://doi.org/10.1007/978-3-030-42917-1_37

child protection cases, drug use monitoring in rehabilitation programs and the workplace, and driver's license reinstatement. In particular they give advice on how to perform hair analysis in drug-related deaths, drug-facilitated crime, child custody cases, and chronic excessive alcohol consumption. The SoHT has also published additional guidelines regarding the analysis and interpretation of alcohol markers in the hair. In addition to SoHT, the European Workplace Drug Testing Society (EWDTS) and United Nations Office on Drugs and Crime (UNODC) have published guidelines for the use of the hair as matrix. In the United States, there is still no guidance available, but the analysis of drugs in hair may serve as an alternative matrix to urine in workplace drug testing and as a complementary matrix in forensic toxicology in general. This chapter provides an insight into the basic features of drug deposition into the hair, the analysis, and the interpretation of results.

Hair Physiology

Hair is mainly composed of proteins, lipids, and pigments. Proteins are the main components of hair (65–95%), with the remainder being lipids (1–9%), pigments (0.1–5%), and minor amounts of trace elements, polysaccharides, and water. The outer part of the hair fiber, the *cuticle*, consists of a sheath of overlapping scale cells protecting the *cortex*, the bulk of the hair fiber. The cortex is mainly composed of spindle-shaped keratin-containing cells. In the center of the cortex, human scalp hair may have a *medulla* that can be continuous or fragmented. A schematic cross-sectional view of the hair structure is shown in Fig. 37.1. Hair is formed in a follicle 3–5 mm beneath the epidermis. The high mitotic activity in the follicle results in a flow of cells that forms the hair fiber, pushing it further away from the surface of the scalp. During formation, melanin pigments are introduced into the hair fiber. These pigments are produced in organelles called melanosomes in melanocytes situated at the base of the follicle. The pigments can be classified into four different classes, eumelanin,

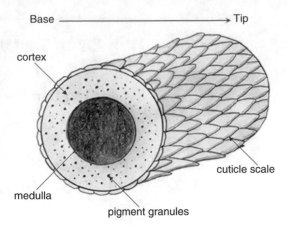

Fig. 37.1 Cross section of a hair. (Source: Reprinted with permission from Ecobyte Pty Ltd. Australia)

oxyeumelanin, pheomelanin, and oxypheomelanin The amount and type of pigments determine the color of human hair. Black and dark brown hair contains only eumelanin. Lighter brown hair also contains the oxidized eumelanin, whereas red hair contains pheomelanin and/or its oxidized products. Even though melanin only represents a few percent of the hair matrix, its ability to attract and bind chemicals may be important in hair analysis. Many studies in vitro and in vivo have shown that substances bind to melanin and influence the rate of incorporation of drugs into hairs of different pigmentation. Unlike many animals that have synchronously growing hair, human hair grows in a mosaic pattern where each follicle has its own growth cycle. The human hair life cycle consists of three major phases: the anagen or growth phase, the catagen or transition phase, and the telogen or resting phase. Hair growth, as well as the proportion of the hair that is in any of the three phases, varies in different parts of the body and between individuals. Head hair grows at a rate of about 0.35 mm/day, while chest, underarm, and leg hair grow at a rate of 0.4, 0.3, and 0.2 mm/day, respectively. The anagen phase lasts from 48 to 72 months for head hair, 5–7 months for chest hair, 6–7 months for underarm hair, and 4–5 months for leg hair. The telogen phase lasts from 4–6 months for head hair, 2.5 months for chest hair, 2.5 months for underarm hair, and

2–3 months for leg hair. The differences in hair growth between individuals complicate temporal interpretation of hair analysis results.

Drug Disposition into the Hair

There are numerous publications that discuss the pathways for incorporation of drugs into hair and that investigate the mechanisms by which drugs bind to the hair matrix. Three routes for incorporation have been suggested:

1. Active or passive diffusion from the blood vessels in the dermal papilla
2. Diffusion from sweat and other secretions bathing the growing or mature hair
3. External drugs from vapor or solid that diffuse into the mature hair

Systemic Incorporation from the Blood

Rapid cell division requires a good blood supply to the hair follicle and results in the ready delivery of circulating drug molecules to the growing hair. For the drugs to enter the matrix, they first have to diffuse across the cell membrane. The rate of this passive transport is related to the lipid solubility of the drug. In addition, the difference in pH between the blood and the cell is important for the transport since weak bases or weak acids are ionized by protonation or deprotonation. The pH of plasma is 7.4, whereas the pH of the keratinocytes and melanocytes is much lower, favoring the incorporation of basic drugs. Basic drugs may accumulate in keratinocytes and melanocytes as the diffusion into the cell is favored by the pH gradient. Once in the cell cytosol, the molecule will be protonated and not able to diffuse back into the blood. Instead the drugs will bind to negatively charged proteins or pigments. Animal studies have shown that even though the blood concentration of benzoylecgonine was four times higher than that of cocaine, the cocaine concentration in hair was ten times higher. This may be explained by the psychochemical differences between the weak base cocaine and the zwitterion benzoylecgonine. Studies on human subjects and patients have shown that basic drugs such as codeine, methamphetamine, and amphetamine preferably incorporate into pigmented hair. However, studies also demonstrate that amphetamines are readily incorporated into nonpigmented hair, but to a lower extent, up to eight times less than in pigmented hair.

Incorporation from Sweat and Other Secretions

Administered drugs or metabolites will excrete in sweat or sebum and therefore are potential routes for drug incorporation into the hair. Studies have shown that drugs such as codeine and cocaine can be detected in hair shortly after administration, suggesting deposition on the already mature hair. Even though incorporation from sweat can be regarded as deposition of ingested drugs, it complicates the interpretation from multiple segments of hair as it tends to broaden the band of positive hair. However, a more serious complication can be the transfer of drugs into hair from another person's sweat.

Incorporation from External Contamination

Because of the exposure of hair to the environment, external contamination should be considered an alternative explanation for a positive result. Experimental studies investigating the deposition of drugs and dyes from internal and external sources have shown differences in incorporation. The in vivo deposition was mainly in the medulla and the cortex as compared to the cuticle junctions observed when soaking the hair. Independent of the route of deposition, the compounds could not be removed by extensive washing. Similar deposition results have been shown for zolpidem with soaked hair resulting in accumulation of zolpidem in the cuticle junctions. However, in contrast to earlier work with cocaine, fentanyl, and dyes, zolpidem could be completely removed from the hair by washing. Even though the endogenous and exogenous deposition can be distinguished, the analytical result after extraction still remains difficult to interpret.

Drug Analysis

Sampling

Both in research and in case work, head hair is the primary matrix collected and analyzed. The recommendation is to obtain samples from the posterior vertex which has the most consistent growth rate. Then, the analytical work begins with obtaining an appropriate and representative aliquot of the hair to be used for extraction and analysis.

Sample Preparation

Segmentation
The first thing to consider is what portion of the hair to analyze. One or several segments of the hair sample may be used for the analysis. Commonly, the proximal 3 cm portion, representing hair grown during the last 3 months, is used for both screening and confirmatory analysis. However, depending on the case, different strategies for segmentation may apply. Using the same total length of hair for screening and confirmation facilitates interpretation. Short segments can provide a detailed profile of an individual's drug exposure, but the accuracy of segmental analysis depends on both the sampling and laboratory procedures and the individual hair growth rate. The SoHT recommends that only hair cut from the scalp with the root end identified should be segmented. Even in experimental settings, results from segmental analyses are difficult to interpret as discussed later in this chapter.

Washing
Washing of hair samples has several purposes. It removes hair care products, sweat, or sebum that may interfere with the analysis or that may affect

extraction recovery. A reproducible recovery is important if comparing concentrations between segments or individuals. Washing also removes drugs deposited from sweat and sebum. Drugs or medications are deposited into the hair not only from the bloodstream but from sources including sweat, sebum, and other secretions. This means that a drug user or patient, in addition to incorporating drugs through the bloodstream, also exposes the hair to an "internal/external contamination" that may obscure changes in drug intake unless extensive washing is part of the testing protocol. Furthermore, washing removes drugs that externally contaminate the hair from the environment. The risk of contamination from the environment resulting in false positive results is a major concern in hair analysis. To lower this risk, washing of the hair is important. However additional steps, e.g., detection of metabolites, should be part of the strategy to rule out false positives due to external contamination. The SoHT recommends that laboratories use a procedure for washing hair that has been validated for removing surface contamination. It is recommended that the procedure includes washing steps with both organic solvent and aqueous solutions. An initial wash with an organic solvent that doesn't penetrate the inner structure of the hair will remove surface contamination, whereas subsequent washes with aqueous solutions also remove drugs incorporated from sweat into the hair matrix.

Homogeneity and Sample Amount
The SoHT recommends that hair samples should be cut into smaller pieces or powdered to ensure that a representative sample aliquot is used for analysis. An aliquot of 10–50 mg is recommended for analysis. Similar to all tissues, homogenization will increase the chance of analyzing a representative aliquot. Powdering of hair is the best way to ensure a representative aliquot, and it also decreases variation due to differences in extraction recovery, especially if extraction is performed using incubation rather than dissolving/disintegrating the hair matrix. When incubating hair, the ratio between the matrix and solvent is important. In a series of experiments with authentic hair samples using solvent extraction

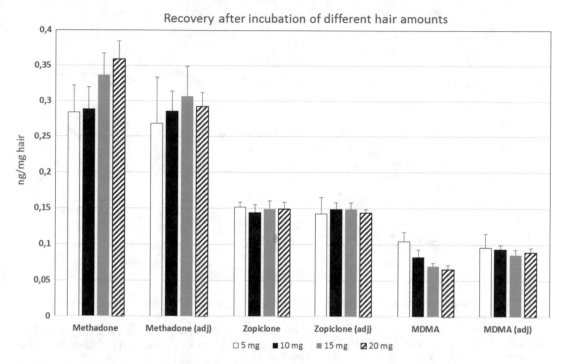

Fig. 37.2 The effect of sample weight on analyte recovery from intact hair. The standard procedure was 10 mg hair and 500 µL extraction medium (methanol/acetonitrile/formate buffer pH 3 (10:10:80)). The samples were incubated in an orbital shaking water bath at 37 °C for 18 h ($N = 10$). The adjusted procedure kept a hair/extraction medium ratio of 1:50

with different amounts of hair, the recovery differed between analytes. In Fig. 37.2 the results from 5 to 20 mg hair samples are shown with and without adjustment of sample/solvent ratio. Methylenedioxymethamphetamine (MDMA) shows a decreasing trend, whereas methadone shows an increasing trend; zopiclone has no significant difference between 5 and 20 mg of hair used for incubation. Interestingly, when adjusting extraction solvent volume to keep a 1:50 ratio, the difference between sample weights becomes less apparent. During validation, the variation in recovery from different sample weights should be investigated, and ranges for allowed weights should be established.

Extraction

Extraction recovery is important for any analytical method, but for hair testing, it must be evaluated using authentic hair from patients or users, rather than fortified matrix. The reason for this is that it is impossible to mimic incorporated drugs by adding them to the hair in the same manner as one can fortify a urine sample with drug. A complication is that the true concentration is unknown. Therefore, recovery studies will be relative rather than absolute. The recovery of analytes depends on physical and chemical properties of solvents and analytes and extraction conditions in general. For hair, factors such as surface area, incubation time, and the degree of hair disintegration will greatly affect recovery. During extraction of drugs from the hair, one must also consider the potential degradation of drugs and metabolites. Therefore, incubations in organic solvents or mixtures of buffers and organic solvents are commonly used. In addition, they are usually good for screening procedures where drugs with quite different chemical properties are extracted at the same time. However, the extraction of drugs from the solid hair fiber is not uncomplicated. In Fig. 37.3, the recovery of MDMA from an authentic hair sample is shown using intact hair

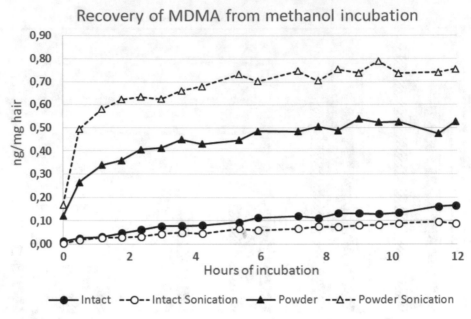

Fig. 37.3 Recovery curve of MDMA from an authentic hair sample incubated in methanol over 12 h. Four conditions were used: Incubation at 37 °C in an orbital shaking water bath using either intact (●) or powdered (▲) hair and sonication at approximately 60 °C using either intact (○) or powdered (△) hair

snippets or hair milled into a powder. The hair was incubated in methanol for over 12 h, with or without sonication. With sonication, the temperature reached approximately 60 °C, whereas the incubation of intact hair was kept at 37 °C in an orbital shaking water bath. Powdering of the hair increased recovery three times from 0.17 ng/mg at 12 h to 0.53 ng/mg. Sonication on the powdered hair again increased final concentration to 0.76 ng/mg. Also, the extraction kinetics show a steeper incline in the beginning when using powdered hair. An apparent drawback with incubation methods is the poor recovery, but as shown above, recovery can be increased using powdered hair, sonication, and long extraction times. Methods that involve the disintegration of the hair and the liberation of the analytes into liquid phase are more efficient and can be performed with enzymatic hydrolysis or using strong base. However, other complications may arise. Depending on the chemical properties of the analyte, care is needed to keep the analyte intact during hair disintegration. As examples, cocaine, 6-acetylmorphine, and zopiclone are unstable at high pH, and several ben-

zodiazepines and their metabolites are unstable at both high and low pH. During alkaline hydrolysis using sodium hydroxide, the hair structure is disintegrated, and the analytes are liberated into the aqueous medium. Thus, alkaline hydrolysis ensures a high recovery for stable analytes such as amphetamines, but the conditions make it unsuitable for methods where cocaine, heroin, and benzodiazepines are investigated. Enzymatic hydrolysis at close to neutral pH, on the other hand, has been proven successful but is more expensive than chemical hydrolysis. The SoHT recommends that laboratories investigate the efficiency of extraction procedures so as to minimize breakdown of labile drugs.

Screening and Confirmation

A well-established concept in forensic toxicology is the use of two different techniques and two different sample aliquots to verify a positive result. Hair analysis should be no exception to this. Usually, there is no need to wash samples prior to screening since only negative results are reported. Depending on the type of cases analyzed, different approaches to screening can be applied. Immunoassays are useful when many samples are analyzed for the same panel of analytes and especially when the expected positive rate is low. However, chromatographic screening methods are increasingly used.

The most common immunoassay for screening is enzyme-linked immunosorbent assay (ELISA). Microplates are coated with an antibody specific for a particular drug, and then horseradish peroxidase-linked antigen and sample are combined in the wells; after incubation, the wells are washed and substrate are added, usually followed by acidic stopping solution which also changes the color from blue to a higher-intensity yellow. In hair testing, it is often the parent compound that is present in the highest amount, similar to the composition in the subject's blood, and the antibodies for hair assays therefore need to be directed to the parent compounds. For the cocaine group, cocaine is primarily detected, with benzoylecgonine at usually 10% or less. For heroin use detection, the antibody may be morphine specific or also react readily with 6-monoacetylmorphine (6-MAM). When extracting opiates from the hair, it has been observed that morphine is more difficult to recover than other analytes. Since the hair of heroin users is likely to be contaminated with 6-MAM, less effective extraction procedures benefit from an assay antibody that recognizes 6-MAM as well as morphine. This will help to avoid false negatives near the cutoff. For the amphetamines group, methamphetamine will be in the hair at about a 10:1 ratio with its metabolite amphetamine; MDMA and MDEA will show a similar ratio with MDA. Antibodies for screening assays are selected to either minimize cross-reactivities if a specific drug is targeted or to maximize cross-reactivities if a broader screening of related compounds is required. For example, cocaine assays are primarily specific for cocaine and benzoylecgonine to differing degrees. Opiate assays, on the other hand, can be designed to detect numerous opiates, including codeine, hydrocodone, hydromorphone, oxycodone, and oxymorphone in addition to morphine

and 6-MAM. If these pain medications are not of interest in a particular setting, then a morphine-specific assay is preferred. Likewise, amphetamine antibodies are usually reactive either with methamphetamine and amphetamine or with methamphetamine, MDMA, and MDEA. It is rare for a methamphetamine antibody to detect methamphetamine, amphetamine, MDMA, MDA, and MDEA, with adequate sensitivity; therefore, to detect the range of amphetamines, two assays utilizing two different antibodies are generally required.

Even though immunoassays have dominated screening procedures in the hair, the use of chromatographic techniques for the screening of drugs in the hair has increased, and methods using gas chromatography-mass spectrometry, liquid chromatography-tandem mass spectrometry (LC-MS/MS), and more recently high-resolution mass spectrometry with time-of-flight technology (TOF) have been published. LC-MS/MS methods are almost exclusively targeted and operating in multiple reaction modes measuring a set of predefined transitions for the analytes. This is contrasted with data acquisition using TOF which is comprehensive and analyte independent. All ions are recorded over the chromatographic run. This means that additional analytes can be validated into a method without changing the acquisition parameters. This is an increasingly important advantage since new abused and therapeutic drugs are constantly developed.

Independent of the screening methodology used, thresholds should be used to define a presumptive positive result. Recommended thresholds for the most common drug groups have been published by the SoHT and the EWDTS as shown in Table 37.1.

The screening assays identify negatives and presumptive positives for various drug classes. To confirm the positive screening results, a new sample aliquot is used. Prior to the confirmation analysis, the new aliquot of hair should be segmented and washed. Confirmation should be performed with techniques that unequivocally identify the analyte responsible for the screening result(s). The confirmation process should also include quantitation of appropriate compounds.

Table 37.1 Recommended cutoffs (ng/mg hair) to detect chronic use of drugs

	Screening		Confirmation		
	SoHT	EWDTS	Target analyte	SoHT	EWDTS
Amphetamines	0.2	0.2	Methamphetamine	0.2	0.2
			Amphetamine	0.2	0.2
			MDMA	0.2	0.2
			MDA	0.2	0.2
			MDEA		0.2
Cannabinoids	0.1	0.1	THC	0.05	0.05
			Carboxy-THC	0.0002	0.0002
Cocaine	0.5	0.5	Cocaine	0.5	0.5
			BE, EME, CE, NC	0.05	0.05
Opiates	0.2	0.2	6-acetylmorphine	0.2	0.2
			Morphine	0.2	0.2
			Codeine	0.2	0.2
Methadone	0.2	0.2	Methadone	0.2	0.2
			EDDP	0.05	0.05
Buprenorphine	0.01	0.01	Buprenorphine	0.01	0.01
			Norbuprenorphine	0.01	0.01
Ketamine		0.5	Ketamine		0.5
			Norketamine		0.1
Benzodiazepines and Z-drugs		0.05			0.05

SoHT Society of Hair Testing, *EWDTS* European Workplace Drug Testing Society, *MDMA* methylenedioxymethamphetamine, *MDA* methylenedioxyamphetamine, *MDEA* methylenedioxyethylamphetamine, *THC* tetrahydrocannabinol, *BE* benzoylecgonine, *EME* ecgonine methyl ester, *CE* cocaethylene, *NC* norcocaine, *EDDP* 2-ethylidene-1,5-dimethyl-3,3-diphenylpyrrolidine

In addition, it is important to look for metabolites, as the presence of metabolites may provide evidence of ingestion of the drug. Accordingly to the SoHT, laboratories must ensure that confirmation techniques have sufficient sensitivity and are targeted to reflect the drug profile in the hair. Today, most confirmatory analyses are performed either with LC-MS/MS or gas chromatography-tandem mass spectrometry. Table 37.1 shows the recommended analytes for confirmation methods together with thresholds that should be met to detect chronic drug use.

Interpretation of Results

Drug-Related Deaths

In opiate-related deaths, tolerance or the lack of tolerance may play a role. Blood concentrations of opiates overlap between the living and the dead, an observation pointing toward tolerance being important. Although there is no way to measure tolerance, the careful analysis of hair may be useful to show a period of abstinence prior to death. Changes in opiate concentrations over the length of the hair may indicate periods of limited or no drug use, with potential loss of tolerance. Making at least three short segments (5 mm each) should be sufficient to provide an answer. As mentioned before, drugs from sweat and sebum can obscure the timeline, and therefore extensive washing of each segment separate is recommended. Figure 37.4 shows the segmental results from the analysis of morphine in a suspected heroin-related death and a patient 3 months into substitution treatment with buprenorphine. In the autopsy case, the negative inner segment suggests a decrease or termination of use shortly prior to death, providing some evidence for abstinence. In the patient, the two inner segments are negative for morphine indicating that no heroin (or morphine) has been used.

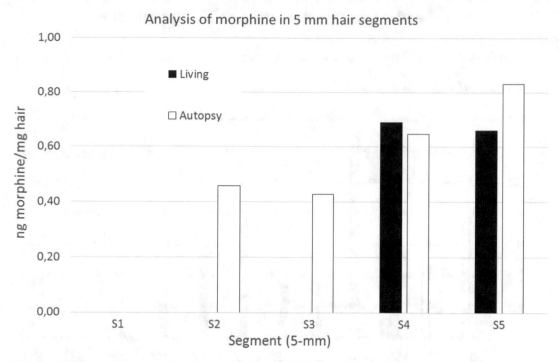

Fig. 37.4 Hair morphine concentrations in five 5 mm segments from a suspected heroin-related death (white bars) and a patient 3 months into heroin substitution treatment with buprenorphine (black bars). In the patient, the two inner segments are negative for morphine indicating that no heroin has been used. In the autopsy case, the negative inner segment suggests a decrease or termination of use shortly prior to death

Drug-Facilitated Crimes

Blood and urine are the most common specimens in drug-facilitated crimes. Provided that the samples are obtained shortly after the incident, these specimens are sufficient to investigate an involuntary drug intake. However, sometimes the incident is not revealed until later, and a blood or even urine sample may not provide relevant information. The rationale for using hair as a matrix in drug-facilitated crimes is that even a single exposure can be detected and the time of exposure can be estimated. Today, with sensitive instrumentation and methodology, it has been demonstrated that a single dose of a few milligrams of many sedatives as well as other drugs can be detected. According to the SoHT guidelines, a hair sample should be collected 4–6 weeks after the alleged incident. This is to allow the hair containing the drug to emerge from the scalp. Longer delay times are not disqualifying, and the

SoHT also recommends a second sample to verify an initial positive result. However, the temporal pattern may be less apparent as the time between ingestion and hair collection increases. Even in experimental settings, results from segmental analyses are difficult to interpret. Figure 37.5 depicts the results from the analyses of samples taken 1, 2, and 4 months after a single intake of 10 mg zopiclone. Each sample was analyzed in 5 mm segments including 6 segments from the 1-month sample, 8 from the 2-month sample, and 12 from the 4-month sample. Using a nominal growth rate of 10 mm per month, segment S2 (sample 1), S4 (sample 2), and S8 should represent the time of intake. For the samples obtained 1 and 2 months after zopiclone administration, the corresponding segment contains the highest concentration of zopiclone, but the neighboring segments were also positive. In the 4-month sample, segment S7, rather than S8, contains the highest concentration. Multiple seg-

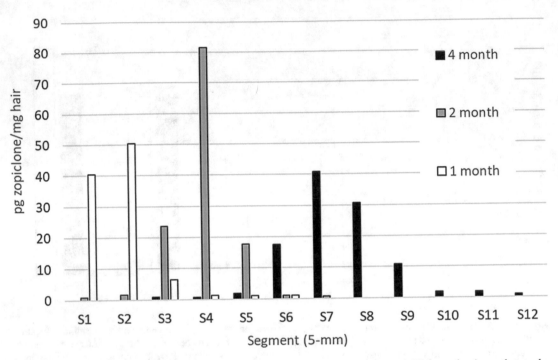

Fig. 37.5 Hair zopiclone concentrations 1 (white squares), 2 (gray squares), and 4 (black squares) months after a single intake of 10 mg zopiclone. Each segment is 5 mm with 6 segments from the 1-month sample, 8 from the 2-month sample, and 12 from the 4-month sample. Using a nominal growth rate of 10 mm per month, S2, S4, and S8 should represent the time of intake in the 1-, 2-, and 4-month sample, respectively

ments being positive even after a single dose are commonly seen and may be explained by physiological factors. Hair strands may go from the anagen phase to catagen phase at different times, and the drug-positive segment is not pushed further out resulting in several positive segments. As the time between ingestion and sample collection increases, the likelihood that the hair strand has stopped growing also increases. Cutting hair strands at different lengths from the scalp or hairs shifting during transport and handling may also result in a broadening of the timeline. Taking this into consideration, the hair can provide valuable information about past drug intake when other matrices cannot be used.

Dose-Concentration Relationships

Many studies have investigated the relationship between the dose and the concentration found in the hair. Indeed, there is evidence of such relationships, and the more variables that are controlled, the higher is the correlation between dose and what is found in hair. As an example, we can use the drug clozapine. Clozapine is a weak base favoring incorporation into pigmented hair through its association with melanin. In Fig. 37.6, the correlation between dose and concentrations in hair is shown for an outpatient population ($r = 0.142$) and an inpatient population ($r = 0.364$), with an additional graph where a correction for hair melanin has been made ($r = 0.622$). When controlling for compliance by using inpatients with supervised dosing, the correlation increases. The correlation increases further by correcting for the melanin content. However, one can clearly see that at a certain dosage, there is a wide range of individual concentrations. Although the estimation of a dose from a hair concentration should not be attempted, population data might provide

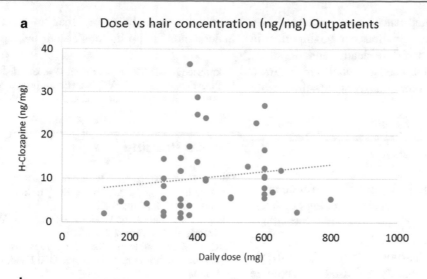

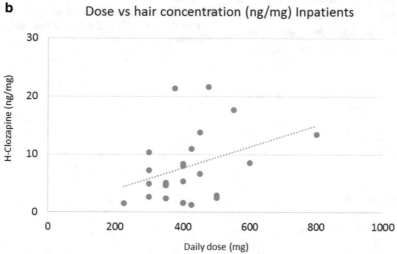

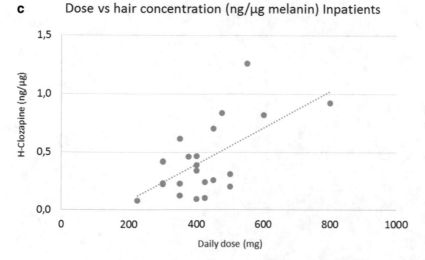

Fig. 37.6 The correlation between clozapine dose and hair concentrations in (**a**) outpatient population ($r = 0.142$, $N = 42$), (**b**) inpatient population ($r = 0.364$, $N = 23$), and (**c**) the inpatient population corrected for hair melanin ($r = 0.622$, $N = 23$)

insight into compliance. As described above, quantitative determinations can be important in both the drug overdose deaths and the drug-facilitated crimes. The individual is his/her own control when comparing concentrations from different segments.

should be taken to ensure that the customer understands the limitations of hair testing.

Acknowledgment The editors wish to acknowledge Dr. Michael Schaffer and Ms. Virginia Hill for prior contributions to the Hair Drug Testing chapter.

Summary

In summary, the hair can be a useful complementary matrix in forensic toxicology to determine past drug use or to investigate drug-facilitated crimes long after drugs have vanished from the blood or urine. Quantitative results should mainly be used to compare results within an individual to find changes in drug use. The use of hair analysis results should be interpreted with caution, and care

Further Reading

Cooper GAA, Kronstrand R, Kintz P (2012) Society of Hair Testing guidelines for drug testing in hair. Forensic Sci Int 218:20–24

European Guidelines for Workplace Drug and Alcohol Testing in Hair Version 2.0 (2015)

UNODC (2014) Guidelines for testing drugs under international control in hair. Sweat and Oral Fluid, United Nations

Kintz P, Salomone A, Vincenti M (eds) (2015) Hair analysis in clinical and forensic toxicology. Science, Elsevier

Oral Fluid Testing

38

Dayong Lee

Abstract

Oral fluid is a specimen that has gained popularity over the past 20 years as an alternative matrix for drug testing. Although the terms oral fluid and saliva are often used interchangeably, they are physiologically different. Saliva is a fluid secreted from granules in the acini (small sacs lined with secretory cells) of the salivary glands. Oral fluid encompasses not just saliva but also gingival crevicular, nasal, and bronchial secretions and other components such as bacteria, cellular elements, electrolytes, immunoglobulins, proteins, and food debris. There are a number of factors that influence the transfer of drugs into the oral fluid, including oral fluid composition, flow rate, pH, the drug's pK_a, protein binding, lipophilicity, spatial configuration, and molecular size. Oral fluid testing has been used in drug abuse, pain management, and drugged driving testing. Oral fluid differs from urine drug testing in that parent drugs are often the targeted analytes. Several collection devices are commercially available to collect oral fluid. Screening of oral fluid for drugs can be performed simply by immunoassay either on-site or in the laboratory. A more broad-based screening or confirmation can be performed using mass spectrometry or by hyphenated chromatography-mass spectrometry techniques. When interpreting oral fluid test results, the following factors unique to oral fluid should be considered: appropriate cutoff concentrations of screen and confirmation tests; medical conditions affecting oral fluid flow or composition and drug transfer to oral fluid; analyte stability during storage; oral cavity contamination from smoked, unencapsulated oral, insufflated, vaporized, or inhaled administration of drugs; and the detection times of drugs in oral fluid.

Keywords

Oral fluid · Physiology · Collection · Analysis · Toxicology · Interpretation

Introduction

Oral fluid has been proposed as an alternative test matrix since as early as the 1970s. Mandel in 1990 wrote that saliva is not as emotionally attractive as other biological fluids because it "lacks the drama of blood, the sincerity of sweat and the emotional appeal of tears." From the utilitarian perspective, however, oral fluid offers safer collection than blood and more interpretative

D. Lee (✉)
Houston Forensic Science Center, Inc.,
Houston, TX, USA
e-mail: dlee@houstonforensicscience.org

© Springer Nature Switzerland AG 2020
B. S. Levine, S. Kerrigan (eds.), *Principles of Forensic Toxicology*,
https://doi.org/10.1007/978-3-030-42917-1_38

value than urine, demonstrating its merit as a viable alternative biological matrix for forensic drug testing. Collectors can obtain oral fluid samples in a simple, noninvasive manner under direct observation while significantly reducing biohazard risk during the process. They can also easily collect multiple samples in one setting. Oral fluid further offers minimal potential for sample adulteration and substitution as well as a stronger correlation with blood than urine concentrations. The main obstacle to fully exploring the utility of oral fluid testing has been the need for highly sensitive analytical methods. The volume of oral fluid samples is typically smaller than that of blood samples and even more so than the volume of urine samples. Depending on analytes, oral fluid drug concentrations can be 10- to 100-fold lower than urine concentrations. The advances in analytical technologies in the past decade, most notably the widespread availability of liquid chromatography-mass spectrometry systems, have led to the increase in research on drug disposition in oral fluid and broader applications of oral fluid testing.

The private sector workplace programs embraced oral fluid drug testing first in the early twenty-first century as they have more flexibility to accept novel technologies than forensic institutions. The Substance Abuse and Mental Health Services Administration (SAMHSA) proposed oral fluid testing in 2004, but it was not until 2015 when the agency published the proposed Mandatory Guidelines for Federal Workplace Drug Testing Programs Using Oral Fluid. These regulatory guidelines are discussed in more detail in Chap. 4. The guidelines recommend allowing the US federal agencies to test oral fluid specimens for their drug testing programs and to establish standards and technical requirements of oral fluid collection and analysis processes. Within the United States, most states (82%) permit some forms of oral fluid drug testing in their workplace programs. Australia, Canada, and European countries have also established standards/guides to employ oral fluid in the workplace drug testing programs. While urine has been the conventional drug testing for clinical practices such as drug

treatment centers and pain management clinics, oral fluid has gained the popularity here as well, serving as a more convenient matrix to monitor compliance of prescribed drugs and to detect use of illicit or non-prescribed drugs.

Oral fluid more lately began to expand its applicability to forensic practice. The type of biological matrix that law enforcement officers are authorized to collect for driving under influence of drugs (DUID) investigations varies by state. While roadside drug testing has not gathered much acceptance in the United States, oral fluid testing is permitted in six states and "other bodily substances" in nine additional states and Puerto Rico as of December 2008. In Canada, the federal criminal code stipulates oral fluid collection to evaluate the presence of drugs in a person's body while operating a vehicle/vessel/aircraft/ railway equipment. Several other countries permit either oral fluid screening and confirmation (Belgium, Australia, and Spain) or oral fluid screening and blood confirmation (France, Germany, Norway, the United Kingdom, and Canada) for DUID investigations. Logan et al. in 2017 updated the 2007 report describing the National Safety Council's recommendations for the toxicological investigation of suspected alcohol and drug-impaired driving cases and motor vehicle fatalities to include oral fluid cutoff concentrations. Table 38.1 lists oral fluid analytes and their cutoff concentrations defined or recommended by selected entities for workplace, clinical, and DUID drug testing programs. Theoretically, the cutoff criteria reflect the difference in the purpose of each drug testing program; workplace and clinical drug testing would require lower cutoff concentrations to increase analyte detection windows, because the goal is to detect and deter drug use versus identifying recent use and impairment in DUID investigations. However as shown in Table 38.1, the currently proposed cutoff concentrations are similar among different drug testing programs. This suggests that the oral fluid cutoff criteria are still driven by the analytical constraints. The subsequent section further discusses the analytes prevalently detected in oral fluid.

Table 38.1 Proposed or studied cutoff concentrations of major analytes in oral fluid for driving under the influence of drugs (DUID), clinical, and workplace drug testing programs

Drug group	Analytes in oral fluid[a]	Screen[b], ng/mL			Confirmation, ng/mL		
		Workplace[c]	Clinical[d]	DUID[e]	Workplace[c]	Clinical[d]	DUID[e]
Amphetamines	Amphetamine	25; 40	25, 50	20	15; 15	5, 10	20
	Methamphetamine						
	MDA						
	MDEA						
	MDMA						
Benzodiazepines	Alprazolam	—; 10	5, 10	5	—; 3 (10 for temazepam)	0.5–1	1
	Chlordiazepoxide						
	Clonazepam, 7-aminoclonazepam						
	Diazepam > nordiazepam						
	Flunitrazepam, 7-aminoflunitrazepam						
	Flurazepam						
	Lorazepam						
	Nitrazepam, 7-aminonitrazepam						
	Oxazepam						
	Temazepam						
Cannabinoids	THC > THCCOOH	4; 10	4	4	2; 2	2	2
Carisoprodol	Meprobamate > carisoprodol	—	50	100	—	10, 50	100
Cocaine	Cocaine ≈ benzoylecgonine	15	20	20	8	2, 8	8
Opioids	6-Acetylmorphine	3; 4	10, 20	—	2; 2	1, 10	2
	Codeine > norcodeine	30; 40		—	15; 15		5
	Morphine						
	Hydrocodone > norhydrocodone	30; —			15; —		
	Hydromorphone						
	Oxycodone > noroxycodone > oxymorphone						
	Methadone > EDDP	—	10, 50	25	—	2, 20	10
	Buprenorphine > norbuprenorphine	—; 5	2, 5	1	—	0.5, 2	0.5
	Tramadol > O-desmethyltramadol ≈ N-desmethyltramadol	—	50	50	—	20, 25	10
	Fentanyl > norfentanyl	—	1	1	—	0.1, 0.5	0.5
Phencyclidine	Phencyclidine	3; —	10	—	2; —	10	—
Zolpidem	Zolpidem	—	10	10	—	5	10

MDA 3,4-methylenedioxyamphetamine, *MDMA* 3,4-methylenedioxymethamphetamine, *THC* delta-9-tetrahydrocannabinol, *THCCOOH* 11-nor-9-carboxy-THC, *and EDDP* 2-ethylidene-1,5-dimethyl-3,3-diphenylpyrrolidine

[a]Order of concentration when applicable as indicated by the greater than (>) and almost equal to (≈) symbols

[b]Cutoff may not target the specific analyte

[c]Proposed cutoff concentrations for federal workplace drug testing programs from Federal Register Vol. 80, No. 94, 2015; recommended cutoff concentrations from European Guidelines for Workplace Drug Testing in Oral Fluid, Drug Test Anal 2018;10:402–415

[d]Cutoff concentrations described in the literature for clinical studies (Conermann et al. Pain Physician 2014;17:63–70, Heltsley et al. J Anal Toxicol 2011;35:529–540)

[e]Recommended cutoff concentrations for DUID investigations from Logan et al. J Anal Toxicol 2018;42:63–68

Physiology

The terms saliva and oral fluid are often interchangeably used in practice and in the literature. Saliva is a fluid secreted from granules in the acini (small sacs lined with secretory cells) of the salivary glands. Oral fluid encompasses not just saliva but also gingival crevicular, nasal, and bronchial secretions and other components such as bacteria, epithelia cell, erythrocytes, leukocytes, and food debris. Therefore, for the purpose of defining a drug testing matrix, oral fluid is a more accurate term.

Oral fluid is a clear, slightly acidic, mucous/serous fluid. It consists of >99% water, various electrolytes (e.g., sodium, potassium, calcium, magnesium, bicarbonate, and phosphates), immunoglobulins (e.g., IgA, IgG), proteins (e.g., mucins, amylases, cystatins, histatins, statherins, and proline-rich proteins), and nitrogenous compounds (e.g., urea and ammonia). Three major salivary glands (parotid, submandibular, and sublingual) contribute over 90% of the total unstimulated salivary secretion, and less than 10% comes from 450 to 750 minor salivary glands. Upon stimulation, the contributing proportions of the glands change (e.g., parotid contribution increases from 20% to over 50%). While the non-water components take up a small portion of the total composition, they can significantly affect the oral fluid condition and subsequently disposition of drugs in the matrix: bicarbonates, phosphates, and urea alter pH and the buffering function of oral fluid, which can either widen or tighten its pH difference from the blood. Proteins (e.g., mucins, enzymes, macromolecule proteins) and immunoglobulins affect aggregation and antibacterial action, which can change how drugs accumulate in oral cavity.

White and Moore noted in their 2018 book that the conditions of different neat oral fluid samples considerably vary; some may form a solid precipitation, produce proteinaceous fibers, or be gelatinized, while others remain clear and watery. This is not surprising as oral fluid exhibits significant inter- and intrapersonal variability in salivary secretion and its composition, particularly protein contents. Salivary glands are innervated by both parasympathetic and sympathetic nervous systems. Parasympathetic stimuli lead to salivary secretion with low protein contents, whereas sympathetic stimuli lead to salivary secretion with high protein contents; viscosity also changes with different nervous stimuli. Additionally, salivary glands produce different types of secretion; the parotid gland mainly produces serous secretions, while secretions from the minor glands are mucous. It is, however, an overly simplified description of variations in oral fluid constituents. Other factors such as the circadian and circannual cycles, sensory stimuli (e.g., taste, pain), hormonal changes, mechanical stimulation, psychological conditions (e.g., anger, fear), genetic makeup, oral hygiene, anticholinergic and parasympathomimetic drugs (decreasing and increasing salivary flow, respectively), and systemic diseases (e.g., cystic fibrosis, diabetes, kidney dysfunction) affect salivary flow rate and composition, not to mention the variations of other components in oral fluid. This multifaceted variability in oral fluid composition also explains the difficulty in finding biomarkers to normalize oral fluid sample volume, similar to creatinine for urine samples. Oral fluid creatinine and IgG concentrations exhibited large intra- and intersubject variability. Several compounds (amylase, serum lactate dehydrogenase, IgA, albumin) were tested to validate specimen integrity for oral fluid testing, which showed different potential values as biomarkers. Since oral fluid collection can be observed directly, the cost of developing and performing specimen validity tests to identify dilution, adulteration, and substitution is debatable.

Oral fluid serves a number of important functions. It preserves oral health via lubricating, cleaning, and buffering of oral issues; protecting against physical, chemical, and microbial attacks; and maintaining tooth integrity via mineralization. It also initiates digestion and heightens taste via forming and lubricating food bolus and maintaining taste buds. Healthy adults produce approximately 0.5–1.5 L of oral fluid per day. The average unstimulated salivary flow rate is 0.3 mL/min, which increases up to 7 mL/min upon stimulation; the unstimulated flow rate of <0.1 mL/min is considered hypofunction. Many oral fluid collection devices with a pad collect around 1 mL; considering the minimum flow rate of stimulated oral fluid of 0.2 mL/min (and the pad induces mechanical stimulation), the collection would take about 5 min or less in normal conditions. Approximately 30% of the US population reportedly experience some form of dry mouth (xerostomia), which can make oral fluid collection difficult; salivary dysfunction is also a side effect of many drugs (e.g., anticholinergic drugs, antidepressants, antipsychotics, antihypertensives).

Oral fluid pH ranged from 6.2 to 7.4. Because it typically has a lower pH than blood pH of 7.4, ion trapping of basic drugs may occur. In this phenomenon, unionized basic drugs readily transfer from the blood to oral cavity and subsequently, due to the pH difference, become ionized and accumulated in oral fluid. Gray et al. reported higher concentrations of methadone and EDDP as pH of oral fluid samples decreased. If based exclusively on pH, basic drugs would have oral fluid to blood ratio greater than one, whereas acidic drugs would have the ratio less than one. However, drugs may not be distinctly classified as acidic, neutral, and basic compounds (e.g., benzoylecgonine, gabapentin).

Drug Disposition

The oral cavity is exposed to multiple internal regions and to the external environment. Therefore, when evaluating the sources of drugs in oral fluid, one must consider not just the salivary fluids but also other secretions from the nasal cavity and esophagus as well as the contamination from oral, transmucosal, smoked, inhaled, and insufflated administrations. Intravenous injection or oral administration via coated tablets, in contrast, does not contaminate the oral cavity, and thus the oral fluid concentrations would represent the amount transferred from the blood. Drugs and drug metabolites of interest to forensic practice typically are small molecules with molecular weight less than 500 g/mol. Owing to their small size, the drugs/metabolites are passively diffused from capillary blood

to saliva and then to the oral cavity via the salivary ducts passing through lipophilic layers of cellular membranes. To achieve the simple passive diffusion, a drug must not be ionized or bound to proteins in addition to being small, unless the drug is bound to a protein actively transferred (using energy) to saliva.

Besides aforementioned oral fluid composition, flow rate, and pH, multiple other factors affect drug transfer into oral fluid, including:

1. The drug's pK_a—unionized and weakly basic drugs more easily diffuse than acidic drugs.
2. Protein binding—drug fraction bound to plasma proteins cannot diffuse to oral fluid.
3. Lipophilicity—lipophilic drugs more easily diffuse than hydrophilic drugs; lipophilic parent drugs tend to diffuse more easily than metabolites, and hence the predominant analytes for oral fluid testing tend to be parent drugs.
4. Spatial configuration—rod-shaped molecules more easily diffuse than globular molecules.
5. Molecular size—the diffusion coefficient decreases as the molecular radius increases; consequently peptide hormones would be too large (e.g., angiotensin II with molecular weight of 1046 g/mol) for oral fluid testing.

Table 38.2 gives an overview of oral fluid disposition of drugs commonly detected in forensic settings. Unlike urine testing, the predominant analytes for oral fluid testing tend to be parent drugs. For the nitrobenzodiazepines and carisoprodol, however, the 7-amino metabolites and meprobamate are more prevalently detected at higher concentrations, respectively. The predominant metabolites may also differ from urine testing; in oral fluid, the demethylated metabolites (nor-) of oxycodone, hydrocodone, and codeine are present at higher concentrations than oxymorphone, hydromorphone, and morphine, respectively. The workplace and clinical laboratories commonly performing urine tests should consider sensitivity of their methodology in addition to changing the analyte panel of the test when incorporating oral fluid analysis. Overall the concentrations found in oral fluid samples

Table 38.2 Oral fluid disposition of common drugs of abuse and their feasibility to the oral fluid testing

Dosed Drug[e]	Route administration	Analytes detected (C_{max} estimate[a])	t_{max}[b], h	$t_{1/2}$[b], h	OF-B ratio[c]	pK_a[d]	Protein binding[d], F_b	Feasibility	Reference
Alprazolam[e]		Alprazolam (##)			<1	2.4	0.80	Challenging due to low concentrations	Heltsley et al. (2011)
Clonazepam[e]		Clonazepam (#)			<1	1.5, 10.5	0.85		
Diazepam	PO	Diazepam (#)	0.3		<1	3.4	0.96		Laloup et al. (2007)
Flunitrazepam	PO	Flunitrazepam (0.#)	3		<1	1.8	0.85		Samyn et al. (2002)
		7-AF (0.#–#)	3						
Lorazepam	PO	Lorazepam (##)	0.3		<1	1.3, 11.5	0.80		Kintz et al. (2004)
Oxazepam	PO	Oxazepam (##)	2–6		<1	1.7, 11.6	0.87–0.94		Smink et al. (2008)
		Oxazepam glucuronide (#)	2–6		<1				
Cannabis	SM, PO (brownie), vaporization, oromucosal spray	THC (###–####)	0.2–0.4	0.8	>1	10.6	0.97	Challenging due to oral cavity contamination and low concentrations of THCCOOH and THC after oral THC dose	Swortwood et al. (2016)
		THCCOOH (0.0#–0.#)	0.2–26		<1				
THC	PO (pill)	THC (0.#–#)	0.3–0.6						Milman et al. (2010)
			5–8						
		THCCOOH (0.#)							
Carisoprodol	PO	Carisoprodol (###)			<1	4.2	0.58	Feasible	Coulter et al. (2012)
		Meprobamate (####)			<1		0.20		
Cocaine	IN, IV, SC, SM	Cocaine (###–####)	0.2–1	0.9–3	>1	8.6	0.92	Feasible	Cone et al. (1997); Ellefsen et al. (2016)
		Benzoylecgonine (###)	0.5–2	4–9					
		EME (###)	2	3–6					
MDMA	PO	MDMA (####)	3	5–7	>1	8.7	0.65	Feasible	Barnes et al. (2011)
		MDA (##–###)	5	8					

Methamphetamine	PO	Methamphetamine (###)	5–6	7–8	>1	9.9	0.10–0.20	Feasible	Schepers et al. (2003)
		Amphetamine (#·##)	8–9	7–25	>1	9.9	0.16		
Methylphenidate	PO	Methylphenidate (##·###)	0.5		>1	8.8	0.15	Feasible	Marchei et al. (2010)
		Ritalinic acid (#)	2		<1				
Buprenorphine[e]		Buprenorphine (##)			~1	8.5, 10.0	0.96	Feasible	Heltsley et al. (2011)
		Norbuprenorphine (#)							
Codeine	PO	Codeine (### ####)	1.6–1.7	2–3	>1	8.2	0.07–0.25	Feasible	Kim et al. (2002)
		Norcodeine (##)	2.1–2.4	5–8	>1				
Fentanyl[e]		Fentanyl (#)			>1	8.4	0.79	Challenging due to low concentrations	Heltsley et al. (2011)
		Norfentanyl (#)							
Heroin	SM, IV	Heroin (SM: ### ·#####, IV: #)	0.03	0.1–10	SM:>1, IV: <1	7.6	<0.05	Challenging due to oral cavity contamination after smoking and rapid elimination of heroin and 6-AM	Jenkins et al. (1995)
		6-AM (SM: ### ·####, IV: ##)	0.03–0.25						
		Morphine (SM: ##, IV: # ·##)	1						
Hydrocodone	PO	Hydrocodone (###)	1	4	>1	8.9	0.25	Feasible	Cone et al. (2015)
		Norhydrocodone (##)	3	6	~1				
		Dihydrocodeine (#)	5	6					
Methadone[f]	PO	Methadone (###)			>1	8.6	0.87	Feasible	Gray et al. (2011)
		EDDP (##)							
Morphine[e]	PO	Morphine (##)			~1	7.9, 9.6	0.35	Feasible	Heltsley et al. (2011)
Oxycodone	PO	Oxycodone (###)	3	5	>1	8.5	0.45	Feasible	Cone et al. (2015)
		Noroxycodone (##)	5	8	~1				
		Oxymorphone (#)	4						
Poppy seeds	PO	Morphine (##)	0.5					Feasible	Concheiro et al. (2015)
		Codeine (#)	0.5						

(continued)

Table 38.2 (continued)

Dosed Drug	Route administration	Analytes detected (C_{max} estimate[a])	t_{max}[b], h	$t_{1/2}$[b], h	OF-B ratio[c]	pK_a[d]	Protein binding[d], F_b	Feasibility	Reference
Phencyclidine[g]		Phencyclidine (#.##)				8.5	0.65	Feasible	Fritch et al. (2009)
Zolpidem	PO	Zolpidem (##)	2–3			6.2	0.93	Feasible; the metabolite present at low concentrations	Feng et al. (2017)
		ZPCA (0.#)	2		<1				

6-AM 6-acetylmorphine, *7-AF* 7-aminoflunitrazepam, *EDDP* 2-ethylidene-1,5-dimethyl-3,3-diphenylpyrrolidine, *EME* ecgonine methyl ester, F_b fraction of drug bound to plasma proteins of the predominate analyte, *IN* intranasal administration, *IV* intravenous administration, *MDA* 3,4-methylenedioxyamphetamine, *MDMA* 3,4-methylenedioxymethamphetamine, *OF-B* oral fluid to blood, *PO* oral administration, *SC* subcutaneous administration, *SM* smoking, *THC* delta-9-tetrahydrocannabinol, *11-OH-THC* 11-hydroxy-THC, *THCCOOH* 11-nor-9-carboxy-THC, *ZPCA* zolpidem phenyl-4-carboxylic acid

[a]Magnitude of the average peak concentrations in ng/mL found in the literature; the concentration depends on the dose, route of administration, dosing regimen, collection times, and study subjects; "#" represents a number

[b]The average values found in the literature

[c]Rough valuation of oral fluid to blood ratios

[d]The values from Baselt. Disposition of Toxic Drugs and Chemical in Man. 11th Edition. 2017

[e]No controlled dosing study; pain patients' median concentration

[f]Oral fluid samples collected during daily methadone treatment for opioid dependence

[g]No controlled dosing study; drug treatment patients' concentrations ($n = 3$)

would be 10- to 100-fold lower than those in urine samples, especially after dissipation of drug contamination in the oral cavity. The analyte profile in blood samples is similar to that in oral fluid samples. But the concentrations in the two matrices can differ due to the aforementioned factors. The drugs with acidic nature and/ or high protein binding such as benzodiazepines and THCCOOH show low oral fluid to blood ratios with concentrations at low or sub-ng/mL in oral fluid; similarly, carisoprodol also shows oral fluid to blood ratio less than 1. Basic drugs including amphetamines, cocaine and opioids, and THC have higher or comparable concentrations in oral fluid compared to those in the blood. Using the blood and oral fluid data from the ROSITA-2 (Roadside Testing Assessment) project collected from drivers suspected of DUI or randomly stopped, Wille et al. observed median (range) oral fluid to blood ratios of 13.4 (0.5–182.1) for amphetamine, 0.9 (0.2–10.6) for benzoylecgonine, 9.6 (0.8–39.0) for codeine, 21.8 (3.8–119.4) for cocaine, 0.02 (0.01–0.15) for diazepam, 5.6 (0.9–88.2) for MDMA, 5.2 (2.2–23) for methamphetamine, 2.3 (0.8–5.7) for morphine, and 15.4 (0.01–568.9) for THC. The wide distribution of the ratios prohibits converting oral fluid concentrations to blood concentrations. Basic drugs like cocaine and codeine may show lower oral fluid to blood ratios in stimulated oral fluid than in unstimulated oral fluid. O'Neal et al. examined the effects of four collection methods: expectoration (control), acidic stimulation (lemon drop), nonacidic stimulation (sugarless gum), and collection devices. The average control codeine concentration was 3.6 times higher than the acidic stimulation concentrations, 2.0 times higher than the nonacidic stimulation concentrations, and 1.3 times higher than the collection device concentrations. As previously described, stimulation alters oral fluid composition including higher bicarbonate concentrations, which in turn increases oral fluid pH and lowers the concentrations of basic drugs in oral fluid. It should be noted that even the control group was subjected to a degree of mechanical stimulation. Thus, oral fluid to blood ratios should be examined in consideration of the inter-

twined variables of stimulation, oral fluid pH, and collection technique.

The detection windows of commonly abused drugs in oral fluid are generally within 24 h at ng/mL concentrations but may extend to 2–3 days; the values depend on analyte, cutoff concentrations, dose, and duration of sample collection. This characteristic of oral fluid testing is valuable in identifying recent drug exposure. Contamination of the oral cavity is another major consideration for drugs administered via smoking like cannabis and heroin. It can increase detection rates as the initial concentrations can be over 1000 ng/mL. The concentrations can decline sharply after a few hours and be present at low levels. THC concentrations become less than 10 ng/mL within 24 h after smoking. Furthermore, the parent drugs may be present at high concentrations at the initial drug intake, but the metabolites can be present at much lower concentrations. The analytical methods for such drugs should cover a wide concentration range to encompass potential concentrations seen in case samples. Fig. 38.1 shows median cannabinoid concentration curves after smoking one cannabis cigarette for 22 h illustrating the initial high concentrations due to oral cavity contamination, their rapid decline within 2 h, and the concentration difference between the parent compounds and the metabolite THCCOOH.

Given the relatively recent introduction of oral fluid as a drug testing matrix compared to blood and urine, it is not surprising that more research is needed to elucidate the kinetics and disposition of drugs in oral fluid. A few studies have investigated half-lives of drugs in oral fluid, and the values vary by dose, collection times, and collection devices. Research on drug disposition in a variety of population groups (e.g., different age, sex, drug use history) after different routes of administration (e.g., smoked or insufflated cocaine), controlled administration, or high recreational doses is limited. After ad libitum smoking sessions where participants smoked up to 40 cannabis cigarettes over 13 h, the peak THC concentration was as high as over 10 µg/mL, and its detection window extended. Controlled administration studies evaluating concentrations

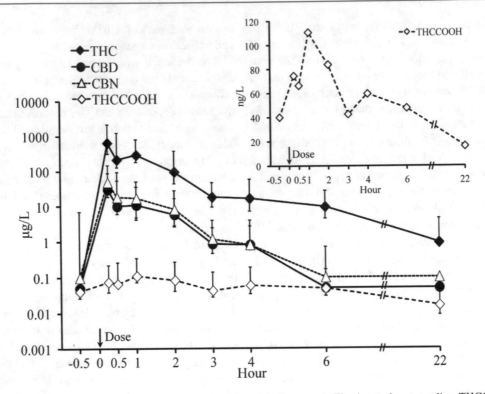

Fig. 38.1 Median (up to 6 h, n = 10; at 22 h, n = 6) oral fluid delta-9-tetrahydrocannabinol d (THC), cannabidiol (CBD), cannabinol (CBN), and 11-nor-9-carboxy-THC (THCCOOH) concentrations after smoking one cannabis cigarette (6.8% THC). Error bars indicate inter-quartile ranges. The inset shows median THCCOOH concentrations over time at a lower scale for more details (Lee et al. 2012, Reproduced with permission from the American Association for Clinical Chemistry)

in oral fluid are yet to be conducted for many drugs including novel psychoactive substances.

Collection Methods

Oral fluid can be collected by using a commercial collection device or passive drool or expectoration without using a collection device. Each collection method has advantages and limitations, which affect stability, recovery, and disposition of drugs in oral fluid specimens. The proposed 2015 SAMHSA guidelines recommend collecting a minimum of 1 ± 0.1 mL of undiluted (neat) oral fluid with a device that has an indicator displaying the volume adequacy of collected specimen and that offers ≥90% (but no more than 120%) drug recovery.

Passive drool is to drain oral fluid naturally pooled in the mouth into a plastic or glass con-tainer without stimulation. Hence, drug concentrations in passively drooled specimens may more closely represent the concentrations from salivary glands than those collected by expectoration or a collection device that induces mechanical stimulation. Expectoration is to spit into a container. Both techniques are more cost-efficient than collection devices and have simpler collection procedures. They also collect neat oral fluid not diluted by buffer common in collection devices; thus, correction for dilution factor is not necessary and may enhance analytical sensitivity. On the other hand, the collection is slow and unhygienic. The specimens can be frothy and viscous, containing food particles and other mouth debris that may require additional centrifugation prior to analysis. In the absence of stabilizing buffer and possible drug adsorption to the container, some analytes (e.g., THC and cocaine) have shown lower stability in expectorated oral fluid samples compared to oral fluid samples collected using commercial devices. There are commercial products that facilitate collection of expectorated oral fluid with a funnel (e.g., RapidEASE®) or a straw (e.g., Salicule™) with a marker to indicate sample volume.

Commercial collection devices typically use a pad or sponge made of cotton or synthetic fibers to absorb oral fluid. In addition to mechanical stimulation induced by inserting a pad into the mouth, some devices may utilize chemical stimulation by applying additives like citric acid to the pad (e.g., Intercept®) to further increase saliva production. Most contain a buffer solution that includes preservatives, surfactants, and/or stabilizing salts. The devices commonly collect 1 mL of oral fluid (e.g., Certus®, Cozart®, Intercept®, Oral-Eze™, Quantical™, StatSure™, Saliva-Sampler™), often equipped with a volume adequacy indicator; the volume of buffer varies from 0.8 mL (Intercept®) to 1 mL (StatSure™), 2 mL (Oral-Eze™), and 3 mL (Certus® and Quantisal®). Langel et al. found that % recovery of oral fluid from eight different collection devices ranged from 67 to 99%. Such commercial devices allow more consistent, convenient, and hygienic collection. Pads filter food debris and other particulates. Buffers can reduce sample viscosity by dilution and stabilize drugs during storage. However, recovery of drugs from the pads may vary within and among collection devices. THC tends to show lower recovery than other drugs. For instance, Langel et al. reported >80% recovery of all studied drugs collected with Quantisal®, Salicule™, and plastic tube except THC, which showed 46–75% recovery; StatSure™ was the only device among the eight study devices with >80% THC recovery. In a later study, Wille et al. observed >73% THC recovery from StatSure™ and Quantisal®. The poor recovery of THC suggests that the drug recovery from the collection device may relate to lipophilicity of the drug. The volume and composition of the buffers, the time that the pad remained in the buffer, and transportation/storage conditions (temperature, duration, position of the pad) affect drug recovery, which also differs by analytes. For accurate and reliable test results, it is important to follow the manufacturer's instructions and evaluate drug stability of the particular collection device used.

Additionally, buffers may interfere with the analysis and increase matrix effects, so more extensive extraction techniques (e.g., SPE rather than dilute and shoot) are recommended.

Some devices may not contain buffer (e.g., OraTube™ and Salivette®) and recover oral fluid via compression of the pad or centrifugation. Yet another type of collection devices (e.g., Greiner Bio-One) utilizes a rinsing solution that collects oral fluid as individuals rinse their mouth for a few minutes. The solution contains a dye to estimate the volume of collected oral fluid via spectrophotometry. The method eliminates the need for the pad that can reduce drug recovery from the collection device. However, there is a risk of the individuals swallowing the rinsing solution.

It should be noted that commercial collection devices can be modified or out of the market over time. As the proposed SAMHSA guidelines recommend a split sample collection, manufacturers may redesign their products to facilitate simultaneous collection of two specimens (e.g., UltraSal-2™ and Quantisal® II). If composition of buffer or pad changes, it can affect recovery, stability, and analysis of target drugs. The collection method should be adequately validated for those parameters to ensure accurate and reliable test results.

Drug Analysis

Oral fluid drug testing generally consists of on-site screening test devices, laboratory-based immunoassay screening, and laboratory-based gas/liquid chromatography (GC/LC) interfaced with mass spectrometry (MS) confirmation. Laboratories may also perform screening tests using GC-MS, LC-MS/MS, and more recently LC with high-resolution mass spectrometry (HRMS, e.g., time-of-flight, Orbitrap) rather than immunoassay. Analytical challenges to detect and quantify drugs and metabolites in oral fluid include (1) low sample volume; (2) low concentrations of metabolites necessitating low limits of detection for the analytes (e.g., THC metabolite present at pg/mL); (3) wide concentration ranges of parent compounds for drugs that cause extensive contamination of oral cavity (e.g., smoking, oromucosal spray, inhalation) due to highly concentrated samples immediately after consumption and a sharp decline after contamination clears, posing difficulty maintaining linear calibration and potentially validating carryover and dilution procedures; (4) low concentrations of analytes that do not transfer well from the blood to oral fluid (e.g., benzodiazepines); and (5) buffer in collection devices that can interfere with analysis. Highly sensitive analytical techniques that can quantify multiple drugs in a single test are necessary; it is more challenging for laboratories with only GC-MS systems to incorporate oral fluid testing because they typically require larger sample volume and are less versatile than LC-MS/MS systems.

Screening

Oral fluid drug screening tests are usually immunoassay-based. They can be portable on-site devices or laboratory-based immunologic methods. These are discussed in more detail in Chap. 13. Immunoassays offer a rapid turnaround time, relatively low cost of installation, large workload capacity, ease of automation, and simple operation procedure. On the other hand, immunoassays may cross-react with non-targeted compounds to cause false positive results. It can also have low cross-reactivity with drugs of interest leading to false negative results. Another drawback is the difficulty to add more drugs to the screen panel because laboratories need to rely on available test kits. Alternatively, oral fluid samples can be screened using GC-MS, LC-MS/MS, or LC-HRMS. Higher sensitivity and specificity offered by GC/LC-MS systems are especially suitable for oral fluid testing, with lower sample volumes and lower analyte concentrations than blood or urine testing. It is also easier to add more analytes to the existing screen panel. Disadvantages of GC/LC-MS systems include more extensive method development and validation procedures, costly installation, and complex and more labor-intensive operation.

On-site screening devices utilize lateral flow immunoassay technology where the presence or absence of a color line indicates a negative or positive result through competitive drug binding. It further allows generation of test results almost in real time; in combination with its small size, the technology has been widely applied to workplace and clinical settings (pain management, drug dependence, general physician's offices) for urine specimens and more recently for oral fluid specimens. With improvements in sensitivity and technology, its oral fluid application lately has expanded to roadside testing for DUID investigations. Roadside drug tests can serve as a deterrent to DUID by increasing the perceived risk of being caught and by more efficiently targeting drug-impaired cases.

Evaluation of applicability of roadside oral fluid testing started two decades ago. The ROSITAproject supported by the European Commission (Directorate-General Transport) first investigated on-site screening device performance during 1999–2000 in eight European countries. Initially, three on-site screening devices (DrugWipe®, ORALscreen™, and Rapiscan™) were evaluated, comparing results with confirmatory blood concentrations and oral fluid collected with the Intercept® device. The proposed acceptance criteria for screening tests were accuracy ≥95%, sensitivity ≥90%, and specificity ≥90% with device failure rate of 5–10%. The testing panel included amphetamines, benzodiazepines, cannabis, cocaine, and opiates. None of the on-site screening devices met the criteria. Compared to oral fluid GC-MS confirmation, sensitivity ranged from 25% (cannabis) to 87% (amphetamines); specificity ranged from 26% (opiates) to 100% (cocaine). The performance could not be evaluated fully due to a small number of positive results.

The ROSITA-2 project in 2003–2005 further evaluated nine on-site oral fluid devices including DrugWipe®, Impact®, OraLab®, OraLine®, OralStat®, Oratect™ II, Rapiscan™, SalivaScreen™ 5, and Dräger/OraSure DrugTest®/Uplink®. Again, none of the on-site screening devices met the criteria. Compared to oral fluid GC-MS confirmation, the total sensitivity ranged from 46% (cannabis) to 79% (amphetamines); the total specificity ranged from 89% (benzodiazepines) to 99% (opiates). Subsequently, the European integrated project DRUID (Driving Under the Influence of Drugs, Alcohol and Medicine) continued the evaluation of on-site oral fluid devices in 2007–2009. DRUID lowered the recommended sensitivity, specificity, and accuracy to ≥80%. Eight devices (BIOSENS® Dynamic, Cozart® DDS 806, DrugWipe® 5+, Dräger DrugTest® 5000, OraLab® 6, OrAlert™, Oratect® III, and RapidSTAT®) were evaluated with oral fluid samples collected from drivers suspected of DUID, patients at drug treatment facilities, and patrons at Dutch coffee shops. As with the previous studies, significant difference in performance among the on-site devices was observed. The results also differed by the study populations. None of the devices met the target sensitivity, specificity, and accuracy of 80% for all tests. The average sensitivity ranged from 36% (cocaine) to >80% (opiates); the average specificity was >90%. The device limitations documented during the ROSITA and DRUID projects include long collection time, insufficient sample volume (often due to dry mouth), frequent device failure, difficulty in reading results, poor performance in cold/rainy weather, long/complicated operation procedure, and high cutoff concentrations compared to those of confirmation tests. Despite the limitations, both subjects and operators favored oral fluid as a drug testing matrix. High sensitivity targeting analytes predominant in oral fluid (parent drugs as opposed to metabolites), test panel covering the prevalent drugs important for traffic safety, short and simple collection and operation procedures, sturdy and easily transportable device, and clearly distinguishable outcome are key characteristics for on-site screening devices.

As technology continually develops, devices available on the market are expected to improve. More recent studies focused on three devices, DDS2®, Dräger DrugTest® 5000, and DrugWipe®, which showed overall greater sensitivity, specificity, and accuracy. As with the earlier studies, however, a small number of positive findings compared to the number of negative findings in roadside studies made sensitivity evaluation a challenge. Logan et al. tested DUI-suspected drivers in Florida with Dräger DrugTest® 5000

and DrugWipe® in 2014. Compared to the oral fluid confirmation results using GC-MS and LC-MS/MS, sensitivity was still around 40–60% (except for cocaine at 90%), whereas specificity was above 90% for all drug groups. Researchers evaluating DDS2® in Wisconsin, Oklahoma, and Kansas in 2013–2016 also showed low sensitivity of benzodiazepines but concluded that the device can be a beneficial tool to aid law enforcement in identifying drug-impaired drivers when combined with observed signs of impairment. Dräger DrugTest® 5000 produced overall satisfactory sensitivity, specificity, and efficiency (>80%) to identify cannabis use following controlled administration of smoked cannabis. Dräger DrugTest® 5000 and DDS2® also demonstrated satisfactory performance after administration of an oral cannabis dose in a brownie. The device performance considerably changed with the different confirmation cutoffs, oral fluid collection devices, time interval between collection and smoking, and study groups (occasional vs. frequent smokers). Dräger DrugTest® 5000 likewise performed well with sensitivity and specificity of >80% to detect cocaine intake after 25 mg intravenous cocaine administration. The manufacturer developed the test strip for the device that can cross-react with both cocaine and benzoylecgonine rather than cocaine only, which increased detection window of cocaine use. De Castro et al. showed cross-reactivity of several synthetic cathinones and piperazines with the methamphetamine test strip of Dräger DrugTest® but at high concentrations (10 or 100 µg/mL).

On the whole, the cutoff concentrations of the on-site screening devices should be lowered, especially for benzodiazepines; the current cutoff concentrations (10–20 ng/mL) are too high to account for the limited benzodiazepines' transfer from the blood to oral fluid caused by their strong protein binding and weak acidity. Laboratories can consider adjusting the confirmation cutoff concentrations to optimize the performance of the on-site screening devices. For cannabis, confirmation of THC at ≥5 ng/mL performed better than THC at 1 or 2 ng/mL. However, the researchers noted that while increasing the screening cutoff improved analytical sensitivity of the on-site device, it reduced the detection window. This can be beneficial for roadside testing to identify acute intake, but lower cutoff concentrations would be more appropriate for clinical applications. Future on-site devices should also expand the test panel to include more illicit and prescription drugs other than amphetamine/methamphetamine, benzodiazepine, opiates, cocaine, methadone, and cannabinoids.

Laboratory-based screening tests using immunoassay can be adapted from urine screening tests by enhancing sensitivity, changing target analytes from metabolites to parent drugs for certain drug classes (THC in oral fluid vs. THCCOOH in urine), and minimizing matrix effects from buffers in the oral fluid collection devices. While the fundamental principle is the same, laboratory-based immunoassays offer larger test panels (e.g., buprenorphine, carisoprodol, fentanyl, tramadol, antidepressants, and even synthetic cannabinoids) and generate more reliable results compared to the on-site screening devices. Presently Immunalysis, Neogen, and OraSure provide enzyme-linked immunosorbent assay (ELISA) designed for oral fluid testing; as a heterogeneous assay, ELISA has good sensitivity and is less susceptible to matrix effects. However, it cannot easily accommodate high-speed analyzers and thus is less suitable for high-volume laboratories than homogenous immunoassays. Immunalysis also provides homogenous enzyme immunoassay (HEIA®), and Thermo Fisher Scientific provides cloned enzyme donor immunoassay (CEDIA™); both are homogenous assays that offer longer shelf lives of reagents and easier adaptation to automation. Researchers found that existing immunoassay kits are not suitable for detecting 30 designer amphetamine drugs (cross-reactivity ≤0.1%). In response to the expansion of designer drugs of abuse and their limited cross-reactivity with the existing kits, the immunoassay manufacturers provide a few kits specifically targeting such newer drugs.

GC/LC-MS screening methods can either test for a broad spectrum of drugs and metabolites or target a specific drug class. GC/LC-MS methods allow lower cutoff concentrations and more easily expandable test panels apt to address contin-

ual shifting of the drug use market. They are additionally more flexible in being applied to other biological matrices. Allen et al. compared the performance of immunoassay and LC-MS/MS in routine drug screening in oral fluid samples; the authors concluded that LC-MS/MS can provide more flexible, specific, and sensitive screening methods for oral fluid samples. Dresen et al. developed a LC-MS/MS method that can identify 700 drugs via multi-target screening and library searching. One thing to keep in mind is that GC/LC-MS systems are also prevalently used for confirmatory tests. Thus, before implementation of GC/LC-MS systems for screening purposes, laboratories should ensure that the reporting of analytes is supported by two different analytical techniques (e.g., GC-MS for screening and LC-MS/MS for confirmation, two different GC or LC columns). Alternatively, laboratories may explore a more advanced option of HRMS measuring accurate masses within <5 ppm mass error, which can be especially effective in detecting and identifying ever-increasing new psychoactive substances. HRMS platforms collect full scan MS and MS/MS data. They can be operated in data-dependent (triggering full scan MS/MS events based on the precursor ions satisfying established criteria from the preceding MS survey scan) or data-independent (triggering full scan MS/MS events for all precursor ions detected in the MS scan) modes. HRMS allows identification of a compound even when a reference material is not available by evaluating mass spectra to generate its molecular formula and other structural data. In turn, HRMS heavily relies on data processing software, which can be complex, time-consuming, and subsequently dependent on the operator's proficiency. Both GC and LC separation techniques can be interfaced with HRMS although coupling with LC is more common. Griswold et al. developed a LC-QTOF-MS method for detecting fentanyl, fentanyl analogues, and other synthetic opioids in oral fluid. Whether using GC/LC-MS/HRMS or immunoassay, laboratories should fully assess expertise and availability of the staff, training, installation/operational needs (ventilation, electricity, space), budget, and workload.

Validation of immunoassay and GC/LC-MS screening (qualitative) methods can be designed according to the Standard Practices for Method Validation in Forensic Toxicology issued by the Scientific Working Group for Forensic Toxicology (SWGTOX) in 2013 or the more recent document, ANSI/ASB Standard 036, First Edition, Standard Practices for Method Validation in Forensic Toxicology by the AAFS Standards Boards in 2019. For immunoassay methods, the limit of detection and precision around the decision point should be evaluated. Sensitivity and specificity can also be calculated. For GC/LC-MS qualitative methods, evaluations of interference from matrix, internal standard, drug standard, and potentially interfering other compounds and carryover are recommended in addition to the limit of detection. Validation and optimization of data processing parameters would be particularly important for HRMS methods. Furthermore, evaluations of the parameters specific to the oral fluid collection devices used, including interference from buffer solution, stability of analytes in the devices, and recovery of analytes from the collection pads, are recommended.

Confirmation

Confirmatory tests typically utilize GC-MS or LC-MS/MS and target specific drug classes. The number of the published methods has been increasing over the past two decades as oral fluid testing gains acceptance in clinical and forensic settings. As described in the previous sections, analytical sensitivity is critical in oral fluid testing because of the limited sample volume and low concentrations of many analytes in oral fluid samples. Samples can be diluted and injected directly onto the instrument with or without filtration, protein precipitation, and/or centrifugation. However, to enhance sensitivity and minimize the interference from the buffer solution, it is recommended to perform a more extensive sample preparation. Analytes can be extracted from the samples via solid-phase extraction (SPE), liquid-liquid extraction (LLE), or supported liquid extraction (SLE). More

recently, LC-MS/MS methods using micro-SPE and automated SPE or SLE have been published. The use of 96-well plates rather than test tubes for sample preparation facilitates automation and significantly lowers the sample volume needed for analysis. In addition to conventional GC-MS and LC-MS/MS systems, methods using two-dimensional GC-MS, GC-MS/MS, and micro-flow LC-MS/MS have been published. Typically, 0.5 mL or less of oral fluid mixed with the collection buffer solution is used for analysis. Limits of quantification can be at sub-ng/mL, which is necessary for certain analytes like THCCOOH and benzodiazepines present at low concentrations in oral fluid. Table 38.3 shows selected methods in the literature. The purpose of the table is not to list all the available methods but rather to demonstrate the variety of instrumentation, extraction techniques, and oral fluid collection devices used by different analytical methods for various drugs and metabolites. It shows that laboratories have a wide range of analytical choices when developing a method. On the other hand, laboratories should take into account that changing those variables would affect performance of the method. Validation of quantitative confirmation methods may include sensitivity (LOD/LOQ), bias and precision, linearity, carryover, interferences, matrix effects, dilution integrity, and stability studies. As technology improves, newer methods test for more analytes including novel psychoactive substances, use smaller sample volume, and/or have more convenient sample preparation.

Stability

Stability of drugs and metabolites in biological matrices during sample transfer, analysis, and storage can significantly change the detected concentrations. Potential causes leading to loss of analytes in oral fluid specimens include adsorption to container/collection pad surfaces, pH of samples, chemical reactions, microbial actions, thermal decomposition, photosensitivity, sample handling (recovery from the collection device), analytical method (extraction recovery, in-process stability, autosampler stability), and for-

Table 38.3 Selected quantitative methods for oral fluid testing for difficult analytes using various collection methods, extraction techniques, and instrumental platforms

Instrument	Collection	Sample Prep	Analytes	LLOQ, ng/mL	Reference
LC-MS/MS	Quantisal®, Oral-Eze™	SPE, chiral derivatization	d,l-AMP, MAMP	1	Newmeyer et al. (2014)
LC-MS/MS	Quantisal®	LLE	25 benzodiazepines, zolpidem	0.1–0.5	Jang et al. (2013)
2D-GC-MS	Oral-Eze™, saliva-sampler™	SPE	Cocaine, BE	1	Ellefsen et al. (2016)
LC-MS/MS	Quantisal®	SPE	12 opioids/metabolites	1	Tuyay et al. (2012)
LC-MS/MS	Quantisal®	SPE	10 opioids, novel synthetic opioids	10	Truver and Swortwood (2018)
Microflow LC-MS/MS	Neat oral fluid	Filtration	THCCOOH	0.0075	He et al. (2012)
2D-GC-MS	Quantisal®	SPE	THC, 11-OH-THC, CBD, CBN, THCCOOH	0.5, 1 (CBN), 0.0075 (THCCOOH)	Milman et al. (2010)
LC-MS/MS	Quantisal®	SPE	THC, 11-OH-THC, CBD, CBG, THCV, THCCOOH	0.2, 0.015 (THCCOOH)	Desrosiers et al. (2015)
GC-MS	Rapiscan™	SPME	9 drugs/metabolites of abuse (AMP, COC, OPI, THC)	10–50	Fucci et al. (2003)
GC-MS	Salivette®	SPE	30 drugs/metabolites of abuse (AMP, COC, OPI, DEP, PSY, HIS, HYP, COV)	1–21	Pujadas et al. (2007)
GC-MS	Saliva-sampler™	LLE, SPE	50 drugs/metabolites of abuse (AMP, BDZ, COC, OPI, PCP, THC, COV, DEP, HIS, HYP, PSY)	0.5–50	Langel et al. (2011)
LC-MS/MS	Saliva-sampler™	SPE	29 drugs/metabolites of abuse (AMP, BDZ, COC, OPI)	0.5 µg/kg	Badawi et al. (2009)
LC-MS/MS	Expectoration	Filtration	16 drugs/metabolites of abuse (COC, OPI, NIC)	0.5, 1	Concheiro et al. (2010)
LC-MS/MS	Intercept®	SPE	21 drugs/metabolites of abuse (AMP, COC, OPI, PCP)	0.4–5	Fritch et al. (2009)
LC-MS/MS	Passive drool	Protein precipitation	44 drugs/metabolites of abuse (AMP, BDZ, COC, OPI, DEP, PSY, COV)	0.1–10	Di Cordia et al. (2013)
LC-MS/MS	Passive drool	SPME	20 drugs/metabolites of abuse (AMP, COC, OPI, PCP, HAL)	0.5–30	Montesano et al. (2015)
LC-MS/MS	Intercept®	Auto-SLE	21 drugs/metabolites of abuse (AMP, BDZ, COC, OPI, THC)	0.014–1.2	Valen et al. (2017)
LC-MS/MS	Salivette®	US-DLLME	20 drugs/metabolites of abuse (OPI, COC, CAT)	0.25–50	Fernández et al. (2018)
LC-MS/MS	Dräger DCD 5000	LLE	30 synthetic cannabinoids	0.15–3	Kneisel et al. (2013)
LC-MS/MS	Expectoration	Protein precipitation	32 Bath salts	2.5	Williams et al. (2017)

AMP amphetamine, *MAMP* methamphetamine, *BDZ* benzodiazepines, *BE* benzoylecgonine, *CAT* synthetic cathinones, *CBD* cannabidiol, *CBG* cannabigerol, *CBN* cannabinol, *COC* cocaine/metabolites, *COV* anticonvulsants, *DEP* antidepressants, *HAL* hallucinogens, *HIS* antihistamines, *HYP* hypnotics, *OPI* opioids, *PCP* phencyclidine, *PSY* antipsychotics, *THC* delta-9-tetrahydrocannabinol, *11-OH-THC* 11-hydroxy-THC, *THCCOOH* 11-nor-9-carboxy-THC, *THCV* tetrahydrocannabivarin

mation of conjugates and/or aggregation with proteins, mucus, and other oral cavity debris. Therefore, the risk of analyte loss should be carefully considered for accurate interpretation of test results, especially for forensic and clinical purposes. Storage issues of analytes in all specimens include storage container, temperature, and duration; the storage conditions specific to oral fluid samples include collection methods and the composition of buffer/preservative solution in commercial collection devices. When using commercial collection devices, it is essential to follow the manufacturer's recommended sample handling procedure and storage condition for consistency and preservation of analytes.

Langel et al. evaluated the stability of eight drugs (amphetamine, MDMA, THC, cocaine, morphine, codeine, diazepam, and alprazolam) in fortified oral fluid samples collected with nine different collection devices (Cozart®, Greiner Bio-One, Intercept®, OraCol, OralTube™, Quantisal®, Salicule™, Saliva-Sampler™, and Salivette®) and in polypropylene tubes; drug stability was examined after 0, 14, and 28 days of storage at −18 °C except Greiner Bio-One at 4 °C. The study demonstrated marked difference in stability among the analytes and the oral fluid collection devices. Subsequently Langel et al. investigated the long-term stability of 50 illicit and prescription drugs including amphetamine, benzodiazepines, cocaine, opioids, THC, antidepressants, and others in fortified oral fluid samples collected with Saliva-Sampler™; the samples were stored for 378 days at −18 °C. Most analytes showed some decrease in concentration over time but were still more than 62% of the day 1 concentration. A number of analytes exhibited a concentration decrease even on day 1 from the normal concentration, which can be attributed to absorption to the collection pad. Valen et al. examined 21 drugs of abuse in fortified oral fluid samples collected with Intercept® and Quantisal® after 1-, 7-, and 30-day storage at 18, 4, and −20 °C. Most analytes were stable (within 15% loss) for 30 days at −20 °C except the 7-amino metabolites of clonazepam, flunitrazepam, and nitrazepam, to be discussed in a later paragraph.

Ventura et al. evaluated the stability of four drugs during the sample transfer using Cozart® and Intercept® collection devices; 19 laboratories analyzed oral fluid samples fortified with 6-AM, cocaine, THC, and THCCOOH 48–72 h after sending out the samples at ambient temperature. As expected, some analyte loss was observed, and the drug % recovery varied between the devices and among the analytes. Drug instability at room temperature even for a short period as observed in the study should be considered when transferring evidence and evaluating external proficiency test performance. Furthermore, conversion of 9–12% 6-AM to morphine and conversion of 26–41% cocaine to benzoylecgonine were observed. The researchers noted that buffering oral fluid at acidic pH can reduce the formation of the hydrolyzed metabolites. For a longer storage of 30 days at 18 °C, approximately 40% increase in morphine concentration was observed. This can be an important consideration when adding basic drugs like amphetamines and opioids to an unbuffered solution that also contains cocaine and 6-AM; increased pH in the solution may hydrolyze cocaine and 6-AM. On the other hand, lowering pH below 4 can lead to loss of THC from isomerization to delta-8-tetrahydrocannabinoid. White and Moore remarked in their 2018 book that pH of 6.5 in the collection medium sufficiently stabilizes 6-AM. Another principal drug group to consider is benzodiazepines. Jang et al. studied stability of 25 benzodiazepines and zolpidem in fortified oral fluid samples after three freeze/thaw cycles and after 30-day storage at 4 and −20 °C. The samples were diluted with the Quantisal® buffer solution. All analytes were stable (84–105% recovery) except nitrobenzodiazepines (clonazepam, flunitrazepam, and nitrazepam), which showed 44–79% recovery at 4 °C. Their 7-amino metabolites exhibited satisfactory stability. The nitrobenzodiazepines were stable at −20 °C (86–103%) indicating that the freezing temperature is recommended for analysis of benzodiazepines. Valen et al. presented contradictory stability results where the 7-amino metabolites showed significant instability (approximately 50% loss) in both the Intercept® samples (at low and high concentrations) and the Quantisal® samples (at low concentrations). The discrepancy could be due to low recovery (27–37%) of the metabolites from the collection devices in the Valen et al. study and/or difference in the preparation of the stability samples between the two studies. Using authentic patient samples from drug treatment practices, two other researcher groups (Vindenes et al. and Melanson et al.) showed lower detection rates of nitrobenzodiazepines than their 7-amino metabolites. This suggests that unlike many oral fluid analytes, which tend to be parent drugs, the 7-amino metabolites could be better analytes for detection of nitrobenzodiazepine use. Conversely, the studies found the presence of the parent drugs only in some cases, suggesting that analysis of both parent drugs and metabolites may be needed for accurate detection of the drug intake.

Stability studies for novel psychoactive substances have also been studied. Kneisel et al. studied the stability of 30 synthetic cannabinoids in oral fluid collected with Dräger DCD 5000/Salivette® tubes after 3 days at room temperature (22–27 °C). The drug recovery ranged from 43 to 88% after stabilizing the pads with ethanol. Coulter and Moore examined the stability of six synthetic cannabinoids in fortified oral fluid mixed with Quantisal® buffer after 7 days at room temperature and 4 °C; the analyte loss at room temperature was up to 25% (JWH-073), but refrigeration reduced degradation to approximately 10%. Miller et al. evaluated the stability of ten synthetic cathinones in fortified neat oral fluid samples and oral fluid samples mixed with Quantisal® and Oral-Eze™ buffers for up to 1 month at room temperature, 4 °C, and −20 °C and after three freeze/thaw cycles. The synthetic cathinones were more stable in Quantisal® samples than Oral-Eze™ samples, and neat samples showed most instability; the drugs were more stable as the temperature decreased. All synthetic cathinones were stable in the Quantisal® samples at −20 °C (−13 to 15%) except naphyrone (−22%). In the Oral-Eze™ samples, all synthetic cathinones were stable at −20 °C (−18 to 19%) except cathinone (−30%) and PVP (22%). The most stable analyte was MDPV, stable under all storage conditions; having tertiary amines may improve drug stability. Acidic conditions may also improve stability of cathinones as the researchers observed that the Quantisal® samples

had pH 6, lower than the neat samples (pH 8) and the Oral-Eze™ samples (pH 7).

Drug stability in authentic oral fluid samples collected after use could be different from drug stability in fortified oral fluid samples. The microenvironment around analytes in oral fluid of different individuals varies as oral fluid flow rate, pH, and composition of other compounds including electrolytes, proteins, and enzymes may differ. Indeed, studies employing authentic oral fluid samples showed varied drug stability among participants. After the stability study following controlled cannabis administration, THC concentration of one participant decreased to only 17% of the baseline concentration after 4 weeks at −20 °C where the % baseline median of the study group was 89%. The researchers recommended analysis of cannabinoids within 4 weeks at 4 °C storage when using Oral-Eze™, StatSure™, and Quantisal® collection devices. Cannabinoids in expectorated oral fluid samples exhibited less consistent results and analyte loss over 20% even after 1 week at 4 °C. The buffer solution in the collection devices may reduce loss of cannabinoids by stabilizing oral fluid pH, inhibiting degradative enzymatic activities, preventing adsorption of drugs to collection tube surfaces and/or precipitants, and/or decreasing viscosity that can improve drug recovery during the same preparation. The subsequent long-term stability study demonstrated stability of THC, THCCOOH, THCV, CBD, and CBG for up to 2 months at 4 °C. Fucci and De Giovanni reported stability of methadone for up to 2 months at 4 °C with authentic oral fluid samples collected from drug treatment patients using Cozart® RapiScan. It is, therefore, important to evaluate the relevant storage parameters fully before implementing a new test for oral fluid samples to ensure the test is fit for purpose.

Interpretation of Test Results

Multiple factors should be considered when interpreting oral fluid test results with a major consideration specific to oral fluid testing being sample collection. The pre-collection variables influencing drug transfer from the blood to oral fluid comprise pK_a, protein binding, and lipophilicity of the analyte as well as flow, composition, and pH of oral fluid. Weakly acidic and highly protein-bound analytes like benzodiazepines require sensitive methodology that allows sub-ng/mL cutoff concentrations. Weakly basic drugs such as cocaine are detected in oral fluid at higher concentrations because a lower pH in oral fluid compared to the blood traps the drugs in oral fluid.

Oral Cavity Contamination

Contamination of the oral cavity resulting in extremely high concentrations of the parent drugs and high oral fluid to blood ratios during the first 2 h of the drug intake has been observed for cocaine, codeine, heroin, and THC. Administrations via smoking, intranasal, oral (without coating), oromucosal spray, vaporization, and insufflation routes can cause such contamination, leading to artificially elevated drug concentrations in oral fluid. After oral cavity contamination is cleared, oral fluid concentrations rapidly decrease and more closely correlate with blood concentrations. Metabolites are minimally affected by oral cavity contamination. However, metabolite concentrations could be much lower and sporadically detected that they may pose a challenge in achieving reliable detection.

Several studies demonstrated the oral cavity contamination leading to high THC concentrations up to >900 ng/mL in the initial oral fluid samples collected immediately after cannabis smoking, oromucosal spray (Sativex®), vaporization, and oral (brownie) cannabis. Unlike cannabis-fortified brownie, THC concentrations in oral fluid after oral administration of encapsulated THC (dronabinol) were low and reflected residual excretion because oral cavity contamination was minimal; even during 36 doses of 20 mg THC 4–8 h around the clock, the median THC concentration remained ≤2.0 ng/mL. For detection of encapsulated THC use, THCCOOH would be a better analyte. However, highly sensitive instrumentation is necessary as THCCOOH is present at pg/mL concentrations in oral fluid; following a single smoked cannabis dose, the peak median THCCOOH concentrations were 168 pg/

mL in frequent smokers and 40 pg/mL in occasional smokers. Detection of THCCOOH in oral fluid can also be intermittent, and thus it may not be as a reliable analyte as THC. Similar to THC, cocaine concentrations in oral fluid also exhibited a significant effect of oral cavity contamination. Cone et al. found cocaine concentrations up to >7000 ng/mL after smoking and > 100,000 ng/mL after intranasal administration, which rapidly decreased within 4–6 h. Following intravenous administration, which did not contaminate the oral cavity, the peak concentrations were much lower (≤1303 ng/mL). Once the contamination was cleared 2 h after doing, the ratios of all three routes were comparable. The metabolites, benzoylecgonine and ecgonine methyl ester, were present at low concentrations after smoked and intranasal doses, similar to the concentrations after intravenous administration (mostly <50 ng/mL).

Multiple controlled cannabis administration studies collectively revealed several factors affecting oral fluid cannabinoid concentrations, which could also apply to other drugs that contaminate oral cavity:

1. Higher-potency cannabis leading to more extensive oral cavity contamination, resulting in higher initial THC concentrations—smoking a higher (27.5–44.5 vs. 13.8–22.3 mg) THC dose cigarette resulted in a higher mean THC concentration (1041 vs. 900 ng/mL) 15 min post-smoking.
2. The composition of cannabinoids in the cannabis product—after using Sativex® that contains approximately 1:1 ratio of THC and CBD per actuation, CBD to THC concentration ratios were correspondingly about 1 with both CBD and THC initial concentrations over 1000 ng/mL.
3. Self-titration of cannabis—Swortwood et al. reported significantly higher mean THC peak concentrations in frequent smokers compared to occasional smokers after smoked (2789 vs. 837 ng/mL) and vaporized (1874 vs. 545 ng/mL) cannabis. The difference was not significant after consumption of oral cannabis, which cannot be titrated. Chronic smokers may inhale more drug-laden smoke as they

develop tolerance to the drug and also more efficient smoking topography.

4. Large interpersonal variability in drug disposition—the controlled administration studies reported standard deviations about the same or even higher than the mean values and wide concentration ranges. Study participants had THC concentrations as low as 68 ng/mL and as high as 10,284 ng/mL after smoking one cannabis cigarette.

Passive Exposure

Whereas other test matrices are also susceptible to being positive for the drugs passively (second-handedly) consumed, this issue becomes more critical in oral fluid testing because of the oral cavity's inherent vulnerability to environmental contamination. Drugs that contaminate the oral cavity can potentially induce positive test results in non-users via environmental intake. The size of the enclosed space, potency of drug smoke, duration of the exposure, collection procedure and frequency, and ventilation of the room substantially affect the extent of the exposure and consequently oral fluid concentrations in non-users. Hence, when examining the effect of passive drug exposure, it is important to closely review the study design. One way to minimize the possibility of positive test results due to passive exposure is detecting metabolites. However, it will not completely remove the possibility because secondhand inhalation of extreme drug-laden smoke may mimic active smoking and the amount of a parent drug can be large enough to produce a detectable concentration of its metabolite. The possibility is marginal because as previously discussed, metabolite concentrations in oral fluid are low even after active use. It is important to note that the studies tend to establish extreme exposure scenarios. Therefore, when applying a research finding to casework interpretation on passive exposure, one should carefully consider comparability between the study condition and the case condition.

While the research assessing the effects of passive exposure on oral fluid samples is limited, it has been more extensively done for cannabis smoke than for other drugs. The first study on the passive cannabis exposure was conducted as early as 1985. Gross et al. set up a closed room (3 × 3 m) where eight smokers and non-smokers seated alternatively in a circle. Each of the smokers smoked one cannabis cigarette (27 mg THC). The average THC concentration in oral fluid samples of non-smokers was 18 ng/mL at 15 min, and all were negative at 30 min after the smoke exposure. Subsequently Niedbala et al. used an unventilated eight-passenger van where four non-smokers sat next to four smokers who each smoked a cannabis cigarette (39.5 mg THC in Session 1 and 83.2 mg THC in Session 2). The mean THC concentration in the Session 1 non-smokers was 5.3 ng/mL immediately after the smoke exposure, and all were negative by 6 h; the collection occurred inside the van for 1 h and afterward outside for up to 72 h. In Session 2 where the oral fluid collection occurred outside of the van, THC concentrations were ≤1.1 ng/mL in non-smokers right after the smoke exposure, and all were negative by 2 h. Moore et al. had ten non-smokers in one of two Dutch coffee shops for 3 h. Oral fluid collection occurred outside the shops. Shop 1 contained 4–16 smokers in the 5 × 7 × 3.5 m smoking area. All five non-smokers were positive for THC at 0.5–6.8 ng/mL after 0.5–3 h of exposure; two were still positive even after 12–22 h post-exposure (1.0 and 1.1 ng/mL). Shop 2 contained 0–6 smokers in the 2 × 7 × 3 m smoking area. Non-smokers were not positive for THC until 1 h post-exposure, but by 3 h, all were positive at 1.3–17 ng/mL.

More recently, Cone et al. examined the effects of extreme cannabis smoke exposure conditions. The study consisted of three sessions with different THC potencies (5.3% THC in Session 1 and 11.3% THC in Sessions 2 and 3) and ventilations (no ventilation in Sessions 1 and 2 and ventilation in Session 3). Each session had six non-smokers and six smokers seated alternatively in the 3 × 4 × 2 chamber; the smokers smoked cannabis ad libitum for 1 h, and oral fluid samples were collected after the 1-h exposure. Without and with ventilation, THC concentrations at 0.25 h post-smoking ranged from 4.9 to 308 ng/mL and 1.7–75 ng/mL, respectively. The concentrations quickly declined by 3 h to

≤2.9 ng/mL. The amount of THC delivered to non-smokers was <5–18% of smokers' doses. Non-smokers also reported experiencing some extent of drug effects, which suggests that the passive exposure effects mirror the active smoking effects albeit to a lesser degree. THCCOOH was not detected in any of the oral fluid samples from non-smokers even at the low detection limit of 0.02 ng/mL. All smokers were positive for THCCOOH in oral fluid, and the concentrations after smoking ranged from 0.065 to 3.349 ng/mL. This indicates that THCCOOH would be a valid analyte to differentiate passive exposure from active smoking.

Cocaine is another drug commonly abused via smoking. While its effects on oral fluid testing have not been investigated, Cone et al. reported the peak concentrations of benzoylecgonine at 22–123 ng/mL and cocaine at 1.5–64 ng/mL in urine samples from participants passively exposed to the vapor of 100/200 mg freebase cocaine in an unventilated room for 1 h. The finding raises the possibility that oral fluid samples may also be positive from the passive exposure of cocaine smoke. Lately the increased popularity of highly potent opioids like carfentanil and fentanyl has elicited the concern of possible exposures to airborne drugs for law enforcement officers and first responders. The medical profession noted, contrary to the sensationalized media reports, that the risk of individuals experiencing acute opioid toxicity from environmental exposure is extremely low. On the other hand, the trace levels of anesthetics including fentanyl, propofol, and nitrous oxide in the air samples of operating rooms may cause positive results in oral fluid of anesthetists and operating room staff. Further studies on the secondhand effects of inhalable drugs and reliability of their metabolites to identify active use are warranted.

solution; and (3) recovery and stability of analytes in the collection devices described in the prior sections. Low sample volume, interference from the buffer solution, low analyte recovery, and poor analyte stability reduce detection rates and increase the possibility of false negative results. If the collection devises lack efficiency, then analytical methods with greater sensitivity are required; this may then necessitate a more extensive sample preparation procedure. Analytical results are inherently associated with analytical limitations. Therefore, the interpretation of results, especially for interpreting the time of last use, must consider the analytes' detection limits. In general, the oral fluid detection limits should be lowered by 10–100-fold relative to urine concentrations to attain comparable clinical sensitivity. If a subject is taking flunitrazepam and the test result comes back negative for flunitrazepam, one needs to confirm whether the detection limit is too high and if the test includes the 7-amino metabolite that may be present at a higher concentration. One should also confirm that the test panel includes relevant analytes. Although parent drugs generally predominate, metabolites that may be prevalent in oral fluid should be considered (e.g., norcodeine, noroxycodone, and norhydrocodone for codeine, oxycodone, and hydrocodone rather than morphine, oxymorphone, and hydromorphone, respectively). Oral cavity contamination of analytes increases detection rates but reduces the correlation between oral fluid and blood concentrations. Testing for metabolites can minimize the possibility of testing positive due to oral cavity contamination or passive exposure. However, detecting metabolites in oral fluid poses an analytical challenge, because metabolites in oral fluid are likely present at low or sub-nanogram per milliliter concentrations.

Collection and Analytical Variables

The variables associated with oral fluid sample collection consist of (1) stimulation, pH, and volume of oral fluid collected and recovered; (2) composition of stabilizing/preservative buffer

Correlations

Correlation of oral fluid concentrations with the concentrations in other biological matrices is another important consideration for determining whether oral fluid test results can replace, supplement, or translate into more conventional test results (e.g., blood testing in DUI investigations and urine testing in workplace and clinical settings). Furthermore, its correlation with impairment aids in determining to what extent oral fluid concentrations can be used to assess impaired signs and symptoms from drug use. The short answer to both questions unfortunately is that oral fluid concentrations cannot be directly translated to blood or urine concentrations nor can they be used to estimate the degree of impairment. The interpersonal and even intrapersonal variations in oral fluid concentrations are too large because of many variables that affect the drug disposition in oral fluid samples. Nonetheless, the study of these relationships contributes to the informed interpretation of the oral fluid test results.

Blood

Oral fluid concentrations tend to show a stronger correlation with blood concentrations than urine concentrations. Blood concentrations are more closely associated with drug effects at the central nervous system than other biological matrices. Moreover, since only unbound (free) drugs in the blood are transferred to oral fluid, excluding oral cavity contamination, oral fluid concentrations generally better reflect recent drug use and offer a stronger temporal correlation with impaired symptoms than urine concentrations. Coupled with safe and convenient sample collection, oral fluid testing can be advantageous in impaired driving and accident investigations to establish impairment, substituting, or complementing blood tests. In clinical practice, oral fluid testing can be beneficial to monitor compliance of prescription drugs for patients whose blood cannot be easily collected (e.g., children, those with psychological symptoms or vascular diseases). Generally, the drugs with the oral fluid to blood ratios above 1 are detected longer in oral fluid if the cutoff concentrations are similar for oral fluid and the blood. As previously noted, drug detection rates and windows significantly depend on cutoff concentrations. The relationship between

oral fluid and blood concentrations can be causal, leading to a stronger correlation with the weakly protein-bound drugs (e.g., amphetamine) being more easily transferred from the blood to oral fluid. Or the correlation can be temporal because the elimination curve of a drug like THC in oral fluid follows its elimination curve in the blood. Oral cavity contamination may weaken the both types of correlations.

After smoking cannabis cigarettes (250 and 500 μg/kg THC), the relationship between oral fluid and serum THC concentrations was significantly linear ($r = 0.84$, $p < 0.001$). After subcutaneous administration of cocaine (75 and 150 mg/70 kg), oral fluid and plasma cocaine, benzoylecgonine, and ecgonine methyl ester concentrations exhibited significant but weak correlations ($r^2 = 0.27$, 0.49, and 0.35, respectively, $p < 0.0001$). Zopiclone also showed a significant but weak correlation ($r^2 = 0.30$, $p = 0.01$) between oral fluid and blood concentrations following 5 or 10 mg dosage. Oral fluid and plasma samples from cancer patients on oral morphine, oral oxycodone, or transdermal fentanyl showed moderate correlations between oral fluid and plasma concentrations for morphine ($r^2 = 0.584$) and fentanyl ($r^2 = 0.667$) but not for oxycodone ($r^2 = 0.267$). Fisher et al. evaluated six antipsychotics from 90 patients and observed oral fluid concentrations being lower than plasma concentrations except amisulpride, which showed comparable values, and poor correlations ($r^2 = 0.34$ for risperidone to 0.71 for quetiapine) between oral fluid and plasma concentrations. Following two oral doses of the fast-release 10 mg methylphenidate, oral fluid methylphenidate concentrations showed a weak correlation with plasma concentrations ($r = 0.22$, $p < 0.05$), which increased to a value of $r = 0.47$ ($p < 0.01$) when the concentrations at the first time point (0.5 h) were removed. The correlation was much stronger ($r = 0.79$, $p < 0.01$) after one dose of the extended-release 20 mg methylphenidate. Huge fluctuations in oral fluid concentrations were observed at the peak time after administration of the fast-release formulation. Oral cavity contamination was suggested as the cause; the fast-release drugs were tablets, whereas the extended-release drugs were capsules, minimizing oral cavity contamination and leading to more homogeneous oral fluid concentrations. Agreement between oral fluid and blood concentrations from field studies can be lower than controlled administration studies due to more uncontrolled variables. Using 112 pairs of blood and oral fluid samples from psychiatric patients and suspected drugged drivers, Gjerde et al. found strong correlations for amphetamine ($r = 0.95$), methamphetamine ($r = 0.96$), nordiazepam ($r = 0.95$), and morphine ($r = 0.85$), a moderate correlation for diazepam ($r = 0.61$), and a weak correlation for THC ($r = 0.15$). Another field study using the ROSITA-2 project data also showed a weak correlation for THC ($r = 0.46$). Based on 100 oral fluid and blood sample pairs from Norwegian-suspected DUID drivers, Vindenes et al. also documented overall poor or moderate correlation coefficient (r^2) values ranged from 0.005 (cocaine) to 0.767 (n-desmethyldiazepam); THC again showed a poor correlation ($r^2 = 0.122$), but amphetamine exhibited a stronger correlation ($r^2 = 0.97$). In a larger study comparing 4080 paired oral fluid and whole blood samples from drivers, Langel et al. reported significant correlations between oral fluid and blood concentrations of 21 drugs ($p < 0.05$) with r^2 values ranged from 0.305 (clonazepam) to 0.850 (amphetamine); THC showed a weak correlation ($r^2 = 0.030$), which was still significant, but lorazepam correlation was not ($r^2 = 0.031$, $p = 0.293$). To estimate equivalent cutoff concentrations in oral fluid and the blood for comparable prevalence of drug detection, Gjerde et al. presented formulas using prevalence regression curves. As expected based on oral fluid to blood ratios, estimated oral fluid cutoff concentrations were higher than blood cutoffs for all drugs except benzodiazepines. The authors also examined oral fluid and blood amphetamine, methamphetamine, cocaine, and THC concentrations of 4080 mostly randomly stopped drivers to determine comparability of oral fluid detection rates to blood detection rates. The optimized cutoff concentrations in oral fluid were significantly higher than analytical cutoffs as more positive results were found in oral fluid when the same cutoff concentrations were used for both matrices.

Urine

Acceptable agreement between oral fluid and urine concentrations can support the laboratory's decision to replace or supplement urine testing with oral fluid testing. Drugs tend to be detected longer in urine than oral fluid as urine samples can be positive for several days after last use. Shorter detection windows of drugs in oral fluid compared to those in urine would contribute to somewhat higher detection rates in urine samples shown in the comparison studies. The difference in prevalent analytes in oral fluid and urine additionally contributes to the different detection rates in these two biological matrices, depending on the time interval between drug use and sample collection. The samples collected shortly after drug use may have negative urine results but positive oral fluid results, because analytes for urine testing (metabolites) need to be metabolized and excreted prior to being detected in urine samples. In contrast, the samples collected long after drug use may have positive urine results but negative oral fluid results, because analytes for oral fluid testing (parent drugs) exhibit shorter detection windows due to shorter half-lives of parent drugs and lower metabolite concentrations. Yet studies still found comparable correlations between oral fluid and urine detection rates suggesting that qualitative determination of results will be similar between oral fluid and urine tests. Considering large variations between oral fluid and urine concentrations along with different analyte profiles, however, urine concentrations should not be converted to or from oral fluid concentrations.

Heltsely et al. examined 1544 urine and oral fluid paired test results for 34 drugs/metabolites from 133 pain patients and reported an overall agreement of 85%; among discrepant results, 9.6% were negative in oral fluid but positive in urine, many for hydromorphone and oxymorphone. The authors noted the greater polarity and lower lipophilicity of the drugs that can reduce their transfer from the blood to oral fluid leading to their lower detection rates in oral fluid. Not surprisingly benzodiazepines were also often not detected in oral fluid when they were positive in urine. In another pain patient study where 153 paired oral fluid and urine samples were analyzed, an overall agreement was 92%; urine samples had a slightly higher number of positive results (191 vs. 176) than oral fluid samples. Oral fluid and urine detection rates were further compared among 100 suspected drugged drivers. Once more, urine samples had a slightly higher number of positive results (348 vs. 336) than oral fluid samples. Oxazepam (cutoff 0.6 ng/mL in oral fluid and 143 ng/mL in urine) and cannabinoids (cutoff THC at 0.6 ng/mL in oral fluid and THCCOOH at 10 ng/mL in urine) were the two most missed analytes in oral fluid. When 70 matched urine and oral fluid samples from 13 participates were compared for cannabis, amphetamine, benzodiazepines, cocaine, opiates, and synthetic cannabinoids, the agreement ranged from 76% (cocaine) to 94% (amphetamine); there was only one case positive for a synthetic cannabinoid (AB-FUBINACA) in both urine and oral fluid samples. PB-22, 5-fluoro-PB-22, or UR-144 was detected in urine samples but negative in paired oral fluid samples. The authors speculated the possibility of 4-hydroxyl UR-144 metabolite being more prevalent in oral fluid than the parent drug and being missed in the study as the analytical method did not include the metabolite.

Impairment

Even if oral fluid concentrations are closely correlated with blood concentrations for particular analytes under certain conditions, their quantitative correlation with the magnitude of performance impairment is minimal. The temporal relationship between oral fluid concentrations and impairment can be weakened by oral cavity contamination and the difference in time profiles of oral fluid drug disposition and impairment; oral fluid concentrations decrease sharply after dissipation of the contamination, whereas impaired signs may last for several hours. For the drugs needing to be transferred from the blood to be present in oral fluid (e.g., those administered in encapsulated oral or intravenous routes), oral fluid concentrations may peak after maximum drug effects as the transfer delays the time of maximum concentrations. However, while oral fluid concentrations cannot estimate the degree of impairment, they can be utilized to identify recent drug intake and capture the window of a drug's acute impairing effects by adjusting cutoff concentrations and consequently detection times.

Ramaekers et al. documented a nonsignificant relationship between oral fluid THC concentrations and performance in the critical tracking task of 20 participants after 250 and 500 µg/kg THC cigarettes ($r = -0.18$) and a significant but weak correlation with the Tower of London task ($r = -0.35$, $p = 0.006$). Vandrey et al. also observed the effects of oral cavity contamination on oral fluid THC concentrations following oral administration of cannabis brownie (10, 25, and 50 mg THC). Correlations between oral fluid THC/THCCOOH concentrations and pharmacodynamic outcomes including subjective drug effect ratings and computerized cognitive/psychomotor performance measures were not significant or orderly by dose. After intravenous cocaine administration, out of 100-mm visual analogue scales, significant but weak correlations were observed between oral fluid cocaine concentrations and the ratings for "rush," "good drug effects," "stimulated," "high," and "strong effect" ($r = 0.29$–0.44, $p < 0.05$). The relationship between the subjective measures and oral fluid concentrations exhibited clockwise hysteresis. The authors further observed peak subjective effects occurring before peak oral fluid cocaine concentrations. Following 25–100 mg MDMA after a night of sleep loss, a significant association ($p < 0.05$) between impairment in the road-tracking task and oral fluid MDMA concentration ranges (0–100, 100–500, and > 500 ng/mL), compared to placebo standard deviation of lateral position (SDLP), was found. The correlations between changes in SDLP and oral fluid MDMA concentrations were, however, marginal ($r^2 = 0.0291$ before the sleep loss and $r^2 = 0.0206$ after the sleep loss). In a field study that examined 21 ketamine-positive participants from discos, oral fluid ketamine concentrations >300 ng/mL led to 90% impairment detection rate using field impairment tests consisted of vital sign measurements, eye examinations, and four divided attention tests. On the other hand, the authors observed one participant showing no impairment with oral fluid ketamine at 4144 ng/mL and noted oral cavity contamination after drug use via nasal insufflations causing a drastic elevation of ketamine concentrations for 1–2 h, which may not reflect detection times of observable impairment signs.

Conclusion

Advantages to oral fluid drug testing include convenience, easily performed direct observation, and less invasive specimen collection. Conversely, it is associated with various limitations including limited sample volume and low analyte concentrations that require highly sensitive methodology, inadequate samples due to collection device failure or conditions causing dry mouth, collection buffer solutions that may require more extensive sample preparation steps, large variability in drug recovery and stability among collection devices, and non-standardized collection procedures among published studies. Additionally, the following factors should be considered when interpreting oral fluid test results: (1) appropriate cutoff concentrations of screen and confirmation tests (e.g., benzodiazepine cutoff above 10 ng/mL may result in many false negative findings); (2) analyte panels of screen and confirmation tests including prevalent parent drugs/metabolites in oral fluid (e.g., designing oral fluid screening based on urine cannabinoid immunoassay targeting THCCOOH would result in false negative findings); (3) impurities of drug formulation (e.g., <1% of codeine in morphine medication) or different compositions of the drug (e.g., varied cannabinoid contents in cannabis products); (4) medical conditions affecting oral fluid flow or composition and drug transfer to oral fluid (e.g., dry mouth, chronic gingivitis which has been associated with higher salivary pH); (5) dose of the consumed drug (i.e., the lower the dose, the lower the drug concentration in oral fluid and the shorter the detection window); (6) analyte stability during storage; (7) oral cavity contamination

from smoked, unencapsulated oral, insufflated, vaporized, or inhaled administration of drugs; (8) secondhand exposure of inhalable drugs; (9) interpersonal variability in drug metabolism; (10) time since the last drug intake (e.g., administered drugs may not have appeared in oral fluid or have already been eliminated); and (11) short detection time in oral fluid. Broadly, the illicit and prescription drugs of interest to forensic applications are detected in oral fluid within 24 h at ng/mL levels. The detection window, however, can be shortened or expanded depending on dose, route of administration, analyte, and cutoff concentration of the testing. Individuals' drug use history may also affect the detection times for self-titratable drugs like smoked cannabis. Oral fluid's short detection window allows identification of recent drug exposure and acute impairment, a beneficial characteristic for DUI and post-accident investigations. While oral fluid offers many advantages as an alternative matrix for monitoring drug use, further research on drug disposition in oral fluid and the effects of different oral fluid testing variables should continue. The interpretation of oral fluid test results must be limited to the existing scientific knowledge. The applicability of oral fluid testing expands as its scientific foundation develops with more standardization and research studies.

Further Reading

Allen KR, Azad R, Field HP, Blake DK (2005) Replacement of immunoassay by LC tandem mass spectrometry for the routine measurement of drugs of abuse in oral fluid. Ann Clin Biochem 42:277–284

Alere. State by state legal status guide. May 2017 Update. http://www.aleretoxicology.com/support/lab_resources/; Quest Diagnostics. Guide for drug testing laws. December 2015 Update. https://blog.employersolutions.com/wp-content/uploads/2015/12/quest-diagnostics-guide-drug-testing-laws-Dec2015.pdf

Anizan S, Bergamaschi MM, Barnes AJ, Milman G, Desrosiers N, Lee D, Gorelick DA, Huestis MA (2015) Impact of oral fluid collection device on cannabinoid stability following smoked cannabis. Drug Test Anal 7:114–120

Aps JKM, Martens LC (2005) Review: the physiology and saliva and transfer of drugs in to saliva. Forensic Sci Int 150:119–131

Baselt RC (2020) Disposition of toxic drugs and chemicals in man, 12th edn. Biomedical Publications, Seal Beach, CA

Blandino V, Wetzel J, Kim J, Haxhi P, Curtis R, Concheiro M (2017) Oral fluid vs. urine analysis to monitor synthetic cannabinoids and classic drugs recent exposure. Curr Pharm Biotechnol 18:796–805

Blencowe T, Pehrsson A, Lillsunde P, Vimpari K, Houwing S, Smink B, Mathijssen R, Van der Linden T, Legrand SA, Pil K, Verstraete A (2011) An analytical evaluation of eight on-site oral fluid drug screening devices using laboratory confirmation results from oral fluid. Forensic Sci Int 208:173–179

Bosker WM, Kuypers KP, Conen S, Kauert GF, Toennes SW, Skopp G, Ramaekers JG (2012) MDMA (ecstasy) effects on actual driving performance before and after sleep deprivation, as function of dose and concentration in blood and oral fluid. 222:367–376

Brcak M, Beck O, Bosch T, Carmichael D, Fucci N, George C, Piper M, Salomone A, Schielen W, Steinmeyer S, Taskinen S, Weinmann W (2018) European guidelines for workplace drug testing in oral fluid. Drug Test Anal 10:402–415

Carpenter GH (2013) The secretion, components, and properties of saliva. Annu Rev Food Sci Technol 4:267–276

Cheng WC, Ng KM, Chan KK, Mok VK, Cheung BK (2007) Roadside detection of impairment under the influence of ketamine—evaluation of ketamine impairment symptoms with reference to its concentration in oral fluid and urine. Forensic Sci Int 170:51–58

Cone EJ, Yousefnejad D, Hillsgrove MJ, Holicky B, Darwin WD (1995) Passive inhalation of cocaine. J Anal Toxicol 19:399–411

Cone EJ, Oyler J, Darwin WD (1997) Cocaine disposition in saliva following intravenous, intranasal, and smoked administration. J Anal Toxicol 21:465–475

Cone EJ, Huestis MA (2007) Interpretation of oral fluid tests for drugs of abuse. Ann N Y Acad Sci 1098:51–103

Cone EJ, Bigelow GE, Herrmann ES, Mitchell JM, LoDico C, Flegel R, Vandrey R (2015) Nonsmoker exposure to Secondhand cannabis smoke. III. Oral fluid and blood drug concentrations and corresponding subjective effects. J Anal Toxicol 39:497–509

Conermann T, Gosalia AR, Kabazie AJ, Moore C, Miller K, Fetsch M, Irvan D (2014) Utility of oral fluid in compliance monitoring of opioid medications. Pain Physician 17:63–70

Coulter C, Garnier M, Moore C (2011) Synthetic cannabinoids in oral fluid. J Anal Toxicol 35:424–430

Crouch DJ (2005) Oral fluid collection: the neglected variable in oral fluid testing. Forensic Sci Int 150:165–173

de Castro A, Lendoiro E, Fernández-Vega H, Steinmeyer S, López-Rivadulla M, Cruz A (2014) Liquid chromatography tandem mass spectrometry determination of selected synthetic cathinones and two piperazines in oral fluid. Cross reactivity study with an on-site immunoassay device. J Chromatogr A 1374:93–101

Desrosiers NA, Milman G, Mendu DR, Lee D, Barnes AJ, Gorelick DA, Huestis MA (2014) Cannabinoids in oral fluid by on-site immunoassay and by GC-MS using two different oral fluid collection devices. Anal Bioanal Chem 406:4117–4128

Dresen S, Ferreirós N, Gnann H, Zimmermann R, Weinmann W (2010) Detection and identification of 700 drugs by multi-target screening with a 3200 Q TRAP LC-MS/MS system and library searching. Anal Bioanal Chem 396:2425–2434

Edwards LD, Smith KL, Savage T (2017) Drugged driving in Wisconsin: oral fluid versus blood. J Anal Toxicol 41:523–529

Ellefsen KN, Concheiro M, Pirard S, Gorelick DA, Huestis MA (2016) Cocaine and benzoylecgonine oral fluid on-site screening and confirmation. Drug Test Anal 8:296–303

Ellefsen KN, Concheiro M, Pirard S, Gorelick DA, Huestis MA (2016) Pharmacodynamic effects and relationships to plasma and oral fluid pharmacokinetics after intravenous cocaine administration. Drug Alcohol Depend 163:116–125

European Monitoring Centre for Drugs and Drug Addiction Driving Under the Influence of Drugs, Alcohol and Medicines in Europe—findings from the DRUID project. http://www.emcdda.europa.eu/system/files/publications/743/TDXA12006ENN_402402.pdf

Fisher DS, van Schalkwyk GI, Seedat S, Curran SR, Flanagan RJ (2013) Plasma, oral fluid, and whole-blood distribution of antipsychotics and metabolites in clinical samples. Ther Drug Monit 35:345–351

Fucci N, De Giovanni N (2008) Stability of methadone and its main metabolite in oral fluid. Drug Metab Lett 2:125–129

Gjerde H, Mordal J, Christophersen AS, Bramness JG, Mørland J (2010) Comparison of drug concentrations in blood and oral fluid collected with the intercept sampling device. J Anal Toxicol 34:204–209

Gjerde H, Verstraete AG (2011) Estimating equivalent cutoff thresholds for drugs in blood and oral fluid using prevalence regression: a study of tetrahydrocannabinol and amphetamine. Forensic Sci Int 212:e26–e30

Gray TR, Dams R, Choo RE, Jones HE, Huestis MA (2011) Methadone disposition in oral fluid during pharmacotherapy for opioid-dependence. Forensic Sci Int 206:98–102

Griswold MK, Chai PR, Krotulski AJ, Friscia M, Chapman BP, Varma N, Boyer EW, Logan BK, Babu KM (2017) A novel oral fluid assay (LC-QTOF-MS) for the detection of fentanyl and clandestine opioids in oral fluid after reported heroin overdose. J Med Toxicol 13:287–292

Gross SJ, Worthy TE, Nerder L, Zimmermann EG, Soares JR, Lomax P (1985) Detection of recent cannabis use by saliva delta 9-THC radioimmunoassay. J Anal Toxicol 9:1–5

Heiskanen T, Langel K, Gunnar T, Lillsunde P, Kalso EA (2015) Opioid concentrations in oral fluid and plasma in cancer patients with pain. J Pain Symptom Manag 50:524–532

Heltsley R, DePriest A, Black DL, Robert T, Marshall L, Meadors VM, Caplan YH, Cone EJ (2011) Oral fluid drug testing of chronic pain patients. I. Positive prevalence rates of licit and illicit drugs. J Anal Toxicol 35:529–540

Heltsley R, Depriest A, Black DL, Crouch DJ, Robert T, Marshall L, Meadors VM, Caplan YH, Cone EJ (2012) Oral fluid drug testing of chronic pain patients. II. Comparison of paired oral fluid and urine specimens. J Anal Toxicol 36:75–80

Hjelmeland K, Gustavsen I, Øiestad EL, Øiestad ÅML, Høiseth G, Mørland J (2017) Zopiclone concentrations in oral fluid and blood after, administration of therapeutic doses of zopiclone. Forensic Sci Int 278:177–183

Humphrey SP, Williamson RT (2001) A review of saliva: normal composition, flow, and function. J Prosthet Dent 85:162–169

Kneisel S, Auwärter V, Kempf J (2013) Analysis of 30 synthetic cannabinoids in oral fluid using liquid chromatography-electrospray ionization tandem mass spectrometry. Drug Test Anal 5:657–669

Jang M, Chang H, Yang W, Choi H, Kim E, Yu BH, Oh Y, Chung H (2013) Development of an LC-MS/MS method for the simultaneous determination of 25 benzodiazepines and zolpidem in oral fluid and its application to authentic samples from regular drug users. J Pharm Biomed Anal 74:213–222

Langel K, Engblom C, Pehrsson A, Gunnar T, Ariniemi K, Lillsunde P (2008) Drug testing in oral fluid-evaluation of sample collection devices. J Anal Toxicol 32:393–401

Langel K, Gunnar T, Ariniemi K, Rajamäki O, Lillsunde P (2011) A validated method for the detection and quantitation of 50 drugs of abuse and medicinal drugs in oral fluid by gas chromatography-mass spectrometry. J Chromatogr B Analyt Technol Biomed Life Sci 879:859–870

Langel K, Gjerde H, Favretto D, Lillsunde P, Øiestad EL, Ferrara SD, Verstraete AG (2014) Comparison of drug concentrations between whole blood and oral fluid. Drug Test Anal 6:461–471

Lee D, Schwope DM, Milman G, Barnes AJ, Gorelick DA, Huestis MA (2012) Cannabinoid disposition in oral fluid after controlled smoked cannabis. Clin Chem 58:748–756. https://doi.org/10.1373/clinchem.2011.177881

Lee D, Huestis MA (2014) Current knowledge on cannabinoids in oral fluid. Drug Test Anal 6:88–111

Logan BK, Mohr AL, Talpins SK (2014) Detection and prevalence of drug use in arrested drivers using the Dräger drug test 5000 and Affiniton DrugWipe oral fluid drug screening devices. J Anal Toxicol 38:444–450

Logan BK, D'Orazio AL, Mohr ALA, Limoges JF, Miles AK, Scarneo CE, Kerrigan S, Liddicoat LJ, Scott KS, Huestis MA (2018) Recommendations for toxicological investigation of drug-impaired driving and motor vehicle fatalities—2017 update. J Anal Toxicol 42:63–68

Marchei E, Farré M, Pardo R, Garcia-Algar O, Pellegrini M, Pacifici R, Pichini S (2010) Correlation between

methylphenidate and ritalinic acid concentrations in oral fluid and plasma. Clin Chem 56:585–592

Melanson SE, Griggs D, Bixho I, Khaliq T, Flood JG (2016) 7-Aminoclonazepam is superior to clonazepam for detection of clonazepam use in oral fluid by LC-MS/MS. Clin Chim Acta 455:128–133

Miller B, Kim J, Concheiro M (2017) Stability of synthetic cathinones in oral fluid samples. Forensic Sci Int 274:13–21

Moore C, Coulter C, Uges D, Tuyay J, van der Linde S, van Leeuwen A, Garnier M, Orbita J Jr (2011) Cannabinoids in oral fluid following passive exposure to marijuana smoke. Forensic Sci Int 212:227–230

Moore C, Crouch D (2013) Oral fluid for the detection of drugs of abuse using immunoassay and LC-MS/MS. Bioanalysis 5:1555–1569

Newmeyer MN, Desrosiers NA, Lee D, Mendu DR, Barnes AJ, Gorelick DA, Huestis MA (2014) Cannabinoid disposition in oral fluid after controlled cannabis smoking in frequent and occasional smokers. Drug Test Anal 6:1002–1010

Newmeyer MN, Swortwood MJ, Andersson M, Abulseoud OA, Scheidweiler KB, Huestis MA (2017) Cannabis edibles: blood and oral fluid cannabinoid pharmacokinetics and evaluation of oral fluid screening devices for predicting Δ9-Tetrahydrocannabinol in blood and oral fluid following cannabis brownie administration. Clin Chem 63:647–662

Niedbala S, Kardos K, Salamone S, Fritch D, Bronsgeest M, Cone EJ (2004) Passive cannabis smoke exposure and oral fluid testing. J Anal Toxicol 28:546–552

Niedbala RS, Kardos KW, Fritch DF, Kunsman KP, Blum KA, Newland GA, Waga J, Kurtz L, Bronsgeest M, Cone EJ (2005) Passive cannabis smoke exposure and oral fluid testing. II. Two studies of extreme cannabis smoke exposure in a motor vehicle. J Anal Toxicol 29:607–615

Nieddu M, Burrai L, Baralla E, Pasciu V, Varoni MV, Briguglio I, Demontis MP, Boatto G (2016) ELISA detection of 30 new amphetamine designer drugs in whole blood, urine and oral fluid using Neogen® "amphetamine" and "methamphetamine/MDMA" kits. J Anal Toxicol 40:492–497

Øiestad EL, Øiestad ÅM, Gjelstad A, Karinen R (2016) Oral fluid drug analysis in the age of new psychoactive substances. Bioanalysis 8:691–710

O'Neal CL, Crouch DJ, Rollins DE, Fatah AA (2000) The effects of collection methods on oral fluid codeine concentrations. J Anal Toxicol 24:536–542

Ramaekers JG, Moeller MR, van Ruitenbeek P, Theunissen EL, Schneider E, Kauert G (2006) Cognition and motor control as a function of Delta9-THC concentration in serum and oral fluid: limits of impairment. Drug Alcohol Depend 85:114–122

Rohrig TP, Moore CM, Stephens K, Cooper K, Coulter C, Baird T, Garnier M, Miller S, Tuyay J, Osawa K, Chou J, Nuss C, Collier J, Wittman KC (2018) Roadside drug testing: an evaluation of the Alere DDS® 2 mobile test system. Drug Test Anal 10:663–670

SAMHSA. Notice of proposed mandatory guidelines for Federal Workplace Drug Testing Programs, 94 FR

28054, Oral fluid, 2015. https://www.gpo.gov/fdsys/pkg/FR-2015-05-15/pdf/2015-11523.pdf

Scheidweiler KB, Spargo EA, Kelly TL, Cone EJ, Barnes AJ, Huestis MA (2010) Pharmacokinetics of cocaine and metabolites in human oral fluid and correlation with plasma concentrations after controlled administration. Ther Drug Monit 32:628–637

Scheidweiler KB, Andersson M, Swortwood MJ, Sempio C, Huestis MA (2017) Long-term stability of cannabinoids in oral fluid after controlled cannabis administration. Drug Test Anal 9:143–147

Swortwood MJ, Newmeyer MN, Andersson M, Abulseoud OA, Scheidweiler KB, Huestis MA (2017) Cannabinoid disposition in oral fluid after controlled smoked, vaporized, and oral cannabis administration. Drug Test Anal 9:905–915

Valen A, Leere Øiestad ÅM, Strand DH, Skari R, Berg T (2017) Determination of 21 drugs in oral fluid using fully automated supported liquid extraction and UHPLC-MS/MS. Drug Test Anal 9:808–823

Vandrey R, Herrmann ES, Mitchell JM, Bigelow GE, Flegel R, LoDico C, Cone EJ (2017) Pharmacokinetic profile of oral cannabis in humans: blood and oral fluid disposition and relation to pharmacodynamic outcomes. J Anal Toxicol 41:83–99

Ventura M, Pichini S, Ventura R, Leal S, Zuccaro P, Pacifici R, de la Torre R (2009) Stability of drugs of abuse in oral fluid collection devices with purpose of external quality assessment schemes. Ther Drug Monit 31:277–280

Veitenheimer AM, Wagner JR (2017) Evaluation of oral fluid as a specimen for DUID. J Anal Toxicol 41:517–522

Verstraete AG (2004) Detection times of drugs of abuse in blood, urine, and oral fluid. Ther Drug Monit 26:200–205

Verstraete AG, Raes E (eds). Rosita-2 project: final report. https://ec.europa.eu/transport/road_safety/sites/road-safety/files/pdf/projects_sources/rosita2_final_report.pdf

Vindenes V, Lund HM, Andresen W, Gjerde H, Ikdahl SE, Christophersen AS, Øiestad EL (2012) Detection of drugs of abuse in simultaneously collected oral fluid, urine and blood from Norwegian drug drivers. Forensic Sci Int 219:165–171

Vindenes V, Strand DH, Koksæter P, Gjerde H (2016) Detection of Nitrobenzodiazepines and their 7-amino metabolites in oral fluid. J Anal Toxicol 40:310–312

White RM, Moore CM (2018) Detection of drugs and their metabolites in oral fluid, Emerging Issues in Analytical Chemistry. Elsevier, Cambridge

Wille SM, Raes E, Lillsunde P, Gunnar T, Laloup M, Samyn N, Christophersen AS, Moeller MR, Hammer KP, Verstraete AG (2009) Relationship between oral fluid and blood concentrations of drugs of abuse in drivers suspected of driving under the influence of drugs. Ther Drug Monit 31:511–519

Wille SM, Ramírez-Fernandez Mdel M, Samyn N, De Boeck G (2010) Conventional and alternative matrices for driving under the influence of cannabis: recent progress and remaining challenges. Bioanalysis 2:791–806

Wille SM, Di Fazio V, Ramírez-Fernandez Mdel M, Kummer N, Samyn N (2013) Driving under the influence of cannabis: pitfalls, validation, and quality control of a UPLC-MS/MS method for the quantification of tetrahydrocannabinol in oral fluid collected with StatSure, Quantisal, or Certus collector. Ther Drug Monit 35:101–111

Meconium Drug Testing

39

Teresa Gray

Abstract

Meconium is the first neonatal feces and is often chosen over other maternal and/or neonatal matrices to identify neonatal drug exposure. Meconium is primarily composed of mucopolysaccharides, water, bile salts, bile acids, epithelial cells, and other lipids. Meconium is usually excreted within the first 1–3 days of life, and specimens are easily and non-invasively collected from soiled diapers. Contamination by neonatal urine is possible if urine collection devices are not employed. Drugs, metabolites, and other exogenous agents are theorized to deposit in meconium through biliary excretion following fetal hepatic metabolism and by swallowing contaminated amniotic fluid. Because accumulation begins around the 12th week of gestation, meconium is assumed to reflect drug exposure in the second and trimesters, representing the longest window of drug detection among neonatal matrices. Meconium testing is performed in a common forensic manner, involving screening and confirmation (if the screening results are above a pre-determined cutoff). However, due to the nature of the matrix, more expensive specimen preparation is required before analysis.

Keywords

Meconium · Gestational drug exposure · Analysis · Interpretation

Introduction

Alcohol, tobacco, and drug use by pregnant women is associated with adverse cognitive, physical, and psychological outcomes in their exposed children, but identifying affected children can be challenging. Maternal self-reports may be unreliable because of feelings of guilt, embarrassment, or fear of prosecution; therefore, toxicological testing of the mother or neonate is preferred. Meconium, the first neonatal feces, is often chosen over other maternal and/or neonatal matrices (Table 39.1) to provide objective evidence of prenatal drug exposure. While meconium testing is usually initiated in a clinical setting, results can extend beyond informing diagnosis and guiding medical treatment into more traditional forensic contexts. Depending on the jurisdiction, positive meconium results could result in maternal referral to drug treatment and/or social service programs or mandatory reporting of child abuse and neglect, potentially leading to removal of the child from the mother's care,

T. Gray (✉)
Harris County Institute of Forensic Sciences, Houston, TX, USA
e-mail: Teresa.Gray@ifs.hctx.net

Table 39.1 Advantages, limitations, detection windows, and expected concentration ranges for maternal and neonatal biological fluids and tissues used in gestational drug exposure monitoring

Matrix	Collection	Detection window	Analyte concentration	Notes
Maternal fluids and tissues				
Urine	Noninvasive; easy to adulterate	1–3 days, except for frequent cannabis use	ng–μg/mL	Standardized urine cutoff concentrations; immunoassay and chromatographic analytical procedures available
Hair	Easy, noninvasive; collected under direct observation	Months to years, depending on hair length	pg–ng/mg	Frequently requires enzymatic digestion, cutting, or pulverization before analysis; segmental analysis may reflect time of use; basic drugs preferentially bind to melanin in the hair, generating a color bias; potential for external contamination
Oral fluid	Easy, noninvasive; collected under direct observation	0.5–36 h, depending on drug	pg–μg/mL	Parent drug generally more prevalent than metabolites; higher concentrations of basic drugs in oral fluid than plasma due to ion trapping; stimulation of salivary flow generally decreases drug concentrations; analyte recovery dependent on collection device
Blood/ plasma	Invasive; requires trained personnel; risk of infection, pain, and swelling	1–3 days	ng–μg/mL	Most closely reflects drug exposure of the fetus
Sweat	Easy, noninvasive	A few days before patch application through removal	pg–ng/patch	Results considered qualitative rather than quantitative
Neonatal fluids and tissues				
Urine	Requires special collection device that often fails to adhere or may irritate neonatal skin	1–3 days prior to delivery	ng–μg/mL	
Hair	Easy, noninvasive; however, consent may be difficult to obtain for cosmetic or cultural reasons	Third trimester	pg–ng/mg	Often, insufficient quantities are available; can be collected within first 3 months, after which time neonatal hair replaces fetal hair; may be contaminated by drug-containing amniotic fluid; basic drugs preferentially bind to melanin in the hair
Fingernails/ toenails	Easy, noninvasive	Unknown	ng/mg	Few published reports specifically identifying prenatal drug exposure; pulverization required prior to extraction; all clippings over first 3 months required for adequate sensitivity

(continued)

Table 39.1 (continued)

Matrix	Collection	Detection window	Analyte concentration	Notes
Vernix caseosa	Easily removed from a newborn's skin with gauze prior to first bath	Unknown	Qualitative assessment	Thick, white lipid, and cell mixture covering the fetus starting at about 24 weeks of gestational age, protecting fetal skin from amniotic fluid; limited quantities available; weighing difficult; therefore, quantitative analysis not possible
Shared fluids and tissues				
Umbilical cord tissue	Easy, noninvasive	Unknown	ng/g	Available immediately after birth; little data to define detection window; analyte disposition along cord length unknown
Umbilical cord blood	Easy, noninvasive	Unknown, but presumed to be similar to maternal blood	ng–μg/mL	Available immediately after birth
Amniotic fluid	Possible, but safety risk to sample during pregnancy; may be available as excess specimen from other medical procedures; at birth, non-invasively collected if under medical observation prior to rupture of membranes	Presumed to have long window of detection, but unproven	ng/mL	Consists of a maternal blood filtrate in early pregnancy, mostly fetal urine in later gestation; fetus may be re-exposed to drug and metabolites by continuously swallowing amniotic fluid; transdermal exposure from amniotic fluid possible early in pregnancy before skin fully develops or late in pregnancy when vernix caseosa production decreases; rarely collected for prenatal drug exposure detection
Placenta	Easy, noninvasive, and adequate specimen amount; waste material after birth	Unknown	ng/g	Few published reports of placenta analysis following prenatal exposure; in vitro transplacental studies have analyzed placenta tissue perfused with drug-containing media

monetary fine, or imprisonment. In addition, postmortem investigations of stillborn fetuses have used meconium testing to assist cause of death determinations. Given the serious consequences, it is imperative that the advantages and limitations of meconium testing are understood, the chosen analytical techniques are scientifically sound, and results are properly interpreted.

Meconium is primarily composed of mucopolysaccharides, water, bile salts, bile acids, epithelial cells, and other lipids. The color ranges from dark green to brown-black, and the texture is highly viscous. Previously thought to be sterile, recent findings suggest bacterial colonization, yet meconium remains odorless. The complex composition and need to aliquot by weighing make meconium analysis challenging and laborious as compared to other matrices.

Meconium is usually excreted within the first 1–3 days of life, and specimens are easily and non-invasively collected from soiled diapers. Contamination by neonatal urine is possible if urine collection devices are not employed; these devices frequently irritate delicate neonatal skin and do not adhere properly. Defecation may be delayed in some infants. Decreased gestational age is associated with delayed meconium passage, as is postnatal morphine treatment, which many premature infants receive. Delayed passage hampers exposure determination and related diagnoses, such as opioid-elicited neonatal abstinence syndrome. Additionally, meconium is released into amniotic fluid prior to birth in ~12% of deliveries, possibly precluding meconium testing.

Drug Disposition

Drugs, metabolites, and other exogenous agents are theorized to deposit in meconium through biliary excretion following fetal hepatic metabolism and by swallowing contaminated amniotic fluid. Because accumulation begins around the 12th week of gestation, meconium is assumed to reflect drug exposure in the second and trimesters, representing the longest window of drug detection among neonatal matrices. However, few studies have attempted to objectively determine drug detection windows in meconium. Meconium specimens from terminated human fetuses as young as 17 weeks of gestation had detectable drug concentrations. Yet, other, more recent human data suggest that second trimester drug exposure is poorly documented in meconium from term or near-term infants and the time between last exposure and birth is critical for detection of prenatal exposure. Meconium testing more reliably reflected third trimester drug use, particularly if use occurred in the last few weeks of pregnancy, in a population of women whose drug use was monitored by thrice weekly urine drug screens.

Additional studies are necessary to corroborate the third trimester drug exposure detection window, although these results are consistent with known maternal-fetal physiology. Greater transplacental drug diffusion occurs in term placentas, as compared to preterm placentas, and the expression of P-glycoprotein, a drug efflux transporter, decreases as pregnancy progresses. Additionally, it is thought that meconium formation increases with fetal weight; thus more meconium is produced at the end of pregnancy than during the second trimester. If the window of drug detection in meconium is limited to the last trimester, earlier exposures could only be identified if the mother self-reported substance use, maternal biological specimens were positive earlier in gestation, or maternal hair was positive at birth.

Drug Analysis

Like most forensic drug testing, meconium analysis generally entails a two-stage approach. First, specimens are screened for a variety of drug classes, most often by immunoassay. If the screening result falls below a pre-determined cutoff concentration, the specimen is considered negative, and no further testing is required. Conversely, if the result exceeds the cutoff, a second analysis, based on a different scientific principle, is performed to confirm the identity of the reactive substance and quantify the amount present.

Screening

Urine immunoassay techniques were modified for meconium, many times without extensive validation or confirmation. Specimens are liquefied with water or buffer prior to analysis; some assays require more involved specimen preparation, such as precipitation with organic solvent to remove particulates, to improve testing results. Immunoassay techniques include enzyme-multiplied immunoassay technique (EMIT), fluorescence polarization immunoassay (FPIA), radioimmunoassay (RIA), and enzyme-linked immunosorbent assay (ELISA). These are discussed in more detail in Chap. 13. Direct comparison of ELISA and EMIT for cannabinoids, amphetamines, methadone, propoxyphene, cocaine, phencyclidine, barbiturates, benzodiazepines, and opioids found fair agreement between the two screening techniques, but ELISA required half the time of EMIT. A recent publication describes a screening procedure by LC coupled with a time-of-flight (TOF) MS that was able to detect over 70 compounds including illicit drugs, local anesthetics, antidepressants, and antipsychotics in meconium.

Confirmatory Analysis

Positive immunoassay results should be confirmed by a more specific method, generally a chromatographic method, such as GC-MS, liquid chromatography-mass spectrometry (LC-MS), or tandem mass spectrometry (MS/MS), as false positive immunoassay results are possible. Meconium concentrations are typically in the ng/g to mg/g range, so confirmatory techniques should be sufficiently sensitive.

Meconium preparation is more complex than traditional matrices because of its semisolid composition. Meconium is not homogenous; therefore, specimens should be mixed well before sampling. As with other solid tissues, meconium specimens are aliquoted by weighing. Specimen preparation generally includes homogenization with an aqueous buffer or solvent prior to liquid/liquid or solid-phase extraction (SPE). Homogenization with methanol or acetonitrile offers the added advantage of precipitating matrix proteins that could otherwise clog SPE columns or interfere with drug adsorption. Sample preparation techniques, including those suitable for meconium, are extensively reviewed in Chap. 9.

Often the amount of meconium is limited; therefore, prioritizing testing may be warranted. Most confirmatory analyses use a relatively large amount of meconium (0.5–1.0 g) and target a single drug class, yet many neonates are exposed to multiple drugs. As LC-MS/MS analysis gains popularity, these problems may be alleviated; newer published methods evaluate multiple drug classes (i.e., opiates, cocaine, and amphetamines) in a single method using smaller specimen amounts without sacrificing sensitivity.

Most importantly, confirmatory analyses should include appropriate drug targets to minimize false positives and maximize identification of drug-exposed children. Adult and fetal metabolism can differ, and thus, the metabolites needed in meconium testing may be different than analytes ordinarily evaluated in postmortem or workplace drug testing. For example, a large portion of cocaine-exposed neonates would not be identified if only cocaine, benzoylecgonine, and cocaethylene were included in confirmatory analyses. m-Hydroxybenzoylecgonine (mOHBE), a minor urinary cocaine metabolite in adults, is the primary cocaine metabolite present in meconium. Additionally, the extent of phase II metabolic products deposited in meconium is not well established, so hydrolysis or direct analysis of drug conjugates may be necessary to improve

confirmation rates. For example, initial research indicates that cannabinoid detection improves nearly twofold following alkaline hydrolysis of 11-nor-9-carboxy-Δ^9-tetrahydrocannabinol glucuronide. Table 39.2 lists the most common biomarkers for drugs in meconium using published confirmatory methods. In addition to drugs of abuse and pharmaceuticals, meconium testing can also be used to determine exposure to selenium, phthalates, pesticides, herbicides, and other environmental agents.

Interpretation of Results

Meconium testing offers objective evidence of maternal drug use. In most studies, detection rates with meconium are comparable or greater than maternal self-report or toxicological testing in other matrices. Yet, meconium's ability to reflect drug use early in pregnancy is limited by known maternal-fetal physiology as previously described. Furthermore, women often, after discovering their pregnancy, dramatically reduce or cease drug and/or tobacco use; thus identifying early drug exposure would be dependent on maternal admission. When drug use in early pregnancy is suspected, maternal interviews must be carefully constructed to elicit more truthful and accurate recall.

Most confirmatory assays are quantitative, yet the significance of meconium concentrations is not clear. Controlled administration studies in animals demonstrate positive correlations between maternal dose and meconium concentration for some drugs of abuse; however, extrapolating animal results to humans would be imprudent. Obvious safety and ethical concerns prohibit controlled illicit drug administration to pregnant women to evaluate dose-concentration relationships. Determining maternal dose by self-report has several limitations, so for illicit drugs, the dose is rarely, if ever, known. Monitoring pharmacotherapeutics, however, offers a unique opportunity to evaluate concentration dependence on maternal dose. Two studies followed women maintained on methadone or buprenorphine during pregnancy, but there was no apparent relationship between total dose during pregnancy or

Table 39.2 Common drugs and metabolites analyzed in meconium

Amphetamines	Cannabinoids	Ethanol
Amphetamine	Δ^9-Tetrahydrocannabinol	Fatty acid ethyl esters
Methamphetamine	(THC)	Ethyl laurate
3,4-Methylenedioxymethamphetamine	11-hydroxy-THC	Ethyl myristate
(MDMA)	11-nor-9-carboxy-THC	Ethyl palmitate
Benzodiazepines	Cocaine	Ethyl palmitoleate
Alprazolam	Cocaine	Ethyl stearate
α-Hydroxyalprazolam	Benzoylecgonine (BE)	Ethyl oleate
Clonazepam	Cocaethylene	Ethyl linoleate
7-Aminoclonazepam	*m*-Hydroxy-BE	Ethyl linolenate
Diazepam	Opiates	Ethyl arachidonate
Nordiazepam	Morphine	Ethyl glucuronide
Flurazepam	Codeine	Ethyl sulfate
Desalkylflurazepam	Hydrocodone	Other
α-Hydroxyethyl-flurazepam	Hydromorphone	Tobacco related
Lorazepam	Oxycodone	Nicotine
Midazolam	Methadone and cyclic	Cotinine
Oxazepam	metabolite	
Temazepam	Buprenorphine	3'-*trans*-
α-Hydroxytriazolam	Norbuprenorphine	hydroxycotinine
		Phencyclidine

the third trimester and methadone, buprenorphine, or their respective metabolite concentrations in meconium.

Several factors may contribute to the lack of a dose-concentration correlation. First, maternal plasma concentrations often are not related to the dose received due to highly variable pharmacokinetic and pharmacogenetic influences. Secondly, placental permeability changes over pregnancy; thus, inconsistent exposure to the fetus may result in unpredictable meconium concentrations. Maternal, placental, and fetal metabolism may contribute to differing extents to the final spectrum of analytes and concentrations deposited in meconium. Also, the timing of meconium collection may influence quantitative relationships. Multiple researchers have shown decreasing concentrations in meconium passages as time from birth increases, with concentrations often falling below quantification limits within 48 h. The relative proportion of metabolites found in sequential meconium passages can differ, presumably after induction of metabolic processes at birth. Furthermore, dose-concentration relationships could be obfuscated by contributions from extracorporeal urine contaminating meconium in the diaper.

Given the state of knowledge at this time, meconium concentrations should not be employed to infer the degree of maternal drug use. Some laboratories report meconium results as positive or negative using an administratively set cutoff, likely based on analytical capability. This conservative approach appears to be reasonable as reporting meconium concentrations may result in the requesting agency, possibly a clinician, researcher, or child protective services agent, erroneously concluding that higher concentrations indicated a higher degree of maternal substance use. The end user should also be aware of drugs administered during labor before interpreting meconium results. A recent publication screening meconium samples with TOF-MS observed a high prevalence of local anesthetics and vasopressors administered intrapartum. Therefore, caution should be used when interpreting results for drugs, like opioids, routinely used during delivery.

While a linear dose-concentration relationship may not exist, it may be possible to differentiate active maternal use from passive exposure by defining a cutoff concentration in meconium, particularly for ethanol and tobacco. Detecting ethanol use poses a challenge, as ethanol itself is extensively metabolized and not likely to deposit unchanged in meconium. Minor non-oxidative ethanol metabolites, fatty acid ethyl esters (FAEE) (Table 39.2), ethyl glucuronide (EtG), and ethyl sulfate (EtS), have been investigated in meconium as evidence of maternal ethanol use. Using populations abstaining from alcohol use for cultural and/or religious reasons, several investigators have attempted to define "baseline" levels to account for endogenous ethanol or passive exposure to ethanol-containing foods or medicines. Individual FAEE, various combinations of FAEE, EtG, and EtS have been evaluated; however, to date, there is not a universally accepted cutoff to differentiate ethanol abstainers, moderate users, and heavy abusers.

Using meconium results to differentiate active smokers from non-smokers and those passively exposed has been more successful. Nicotine is metabolized to cotinine which is further metabolized to trans-3′-hydroxycotinine, the latter being the most prevalent and abundant biomarker found in meconium. Concentrations of nicotine, cotinine, or trans-3′-hydroxycotinine greater than 10 ng/g indicated active maternal smoking in two study groups, but meconium results were not able to distinguish non-smokers from women passively exposed to tobacco smoke.

Conclusion

Identification of prenatal drug exposure through meconium testing or other means is important for understanding and mitigating potential consequences of exposure. Meconium is a unique analytical matrix, with many characteristics still unknown or only partially understood. Therefore, it is imperative that the meconium testing results are interpreted cautiously.

Further Reading

Concheiro M, Huestis MA (2018) Drug exposure during pregnancy: analytical methods and toxicological findings. Bioanalysis 10(8):587–606

Gareri J, Klein J, Koren G (2006) Drugs of abuse testing in meconium. Clin Chim Acta 366(1–2):101–111

Gray T, Huestis M (2007) Bioanalytical procedures for monitoring in utero drug exposure. Anal Bioanal Chem 388(7):1455–1465

Lozano J, Garcia-Algar O, Vall O, de la Torre R, Scaravelli G, Pichini S (2007) Biological matrices for the evaluation of in utero exposure to drugs of abuse. Ther Drug Monit 29(6):711–734

Moore C, Negrusz A, Lewis D (1998) Determination of drugs of abuse in meconium. J Chromatogr B 713(1):137–146

Ostrea EM, Brady M, Gause S, Raymundo AL, Stevens M (1992) Drug screening of newborns by meconium analysis: a large-scale, prospective, epidemiologic study. Pediatrics 89(1):107–113

Drugs in Embalmed Tissues

40

Erin A. Spargo

Abstract

In postmortem forensic toxicology, there are instances when the only specimens available for testing are embalmed tissues. The embalming process infuses formalin throughout the body as a means of preservation. Formalin is prepared by saturating 40% formaldehyde with water. Methanol is added to formalin to act as a stabilizing factor. Formaldehyde is a highly reactive substance and may react with drugs present in tissues by hydrolysis, degradation, or methylation. Formalin-fixed tissues are prepared for toxicological analysis in a similar manner to fresh tissues; both liquid-liquid extraction and solid-phase extraction may be used. Drug concentrations in embalmed specimens may be affected not only by typical processes affecting postmortem concentrations but also by a reaction with formaldehyde. In addition, the introduction of embalming fluid to the body can dilute specimens, resulting in reduced concentrations. As a result, analyte concentrations in embalmed specimens, formalin-fixed tissues, and formalin solutions generally cannot be considered representative of concentrations present at death. However, qualitative information

regarding the presence of drugs may be helpful in assigning the cause and manner of death.

Keywords

Embalmed tissues · Forensic toxicology · Analysis · Stability · Interpretation

Introduction

Typical postmortem specimens may be unavailable in the absence of a request for toxicology testing at the time of death. An autopsy may not have been performed, specimens may not have been collected at autopsy, or the request may occur after specimen disposal. In these situations, toxicologists have to rely on alternative specimens for analysis. Tissue specimens preserved in formalin (formalin-fixed tissues) for the purpose of histological examination may be available as these specimens often have lengthy retention schedules. Formalin solution in which tissues are preserved may be another viable option. Alternatively, specimens may be collected from the body at the time of the request. If burial has occurred, it is likely that the decedent has undergone the embalming process; embalmed tissues or fluids can be collected and used for analysis.

E. A. Spargo (✉)
Southwestern Institute of Forensic Sciences, Dallas, TX, USA

Formaldehyde

Formaldehyde is a highly reactive substance used both as a component in the embalming process and in chemical fixation as a part of the formalin solution. When water is saturated with ~40% formaldehyde, the solution is considered 100% formalin; therefore, a 20% formalin solution would contain ~8% formaldehyde. Formalin solutions often contain 5–20% formaldehyde, with <15% methanol included as a stabilizing agent to prevent polymerization; when unbuffered, the pH of the solution is acidic at ~3.5. The activity of formaldehyde can be affected by factors including concentration, pH, temperature, formic acid or methanol content, water purity, and metal ions. Formaldehyde will produce formic acid when oxidized and methanol when reduced. Formalin is a reducing agent, particularly in basic conditions. Acidic drugs tend to be more stable in formaldehyde than basic drugs. Formalin-fixed tissues are generally stored at room temperature.

Formaldehyde may react with a drug by hydrolysis, degradation, or methylation. The Eschweiler-Clarke conversion describes the methylation of primary and secondary amines via formaldehyde and formic acid. Formaldehyde and a primary amine will produce an imine; this reaction is favored to occur at basic pH. Carbon dioxide released from formate ions causes production of a secondary amine. The reaction of a secondary amine with formaldehyde forms a quaternary ammonium salt, and ultimately a tertiary amine is produced. No reaction between a tertiary amine and formaldehyde occurs.

Analytical Considerations

Fresh and formalin-fixed tissues often can be extracted via the same procedure. After homogenization, samples commonly are buffered, extracted via liquid-liquid extraction (LLE) or solid-phase extraction (SPE), dried down, and reconstituted with a solvent suitable for analysis. Formalin solutions can be extracted following the same process or may simply be dried

down and reconstituted prior to injection. Typical analytical techniques, including gas chromatography with various detectors, UV spectrophotometry, and liquid chromatography tandem-mass spectrometry, have been used to analyze these specimens. Sample preparation techniques including LLE and SPE are described in detail in Chap. 9.

As previously described, products formed from the reaction of drugs with formaldehyde may be present. Additionally, embalming fluid has numerous components beyond formaldehyde including modifying agents, germicides, dyes, and masking agents; methanol is often present and would be expected to be present in a volatile analysis. Compounds may interfere with a method, or alternatively, a drug can react with formaldehyde to form a compound present at higher concentrations than the drug of interest, making the reaction products more suitable targets for analysis.

Drugs in Embalmed Specimens

Drug concentrations in embalmed specimens may be affected not only by typical processes affecting postmortem concentrations but also by reaction with formaldehyde. In addition, the introduction of embalming fluid to the body can dilute specimens, resulting in reduced concentrations. Fentanyl concentrations in the liver were shown to decrease by 26% after a 2-week embalmment. Other studies have not obtained pre-embalmment concentrations but have used data from embalmed specimens in case determinations (Table 40.1). Vitreous ethanol concentrations following embalmment were generally consistent with pre-embalmment concentrations, with mean post−/pre-embalming ratios of 0.7 and 1 reported. When rats were injected with succinylcholine, the drug was still detectable in embalmed tissues after 6 months. Carbon monoxide was identified in clots of heart blood from a body after a 2-month embalmment. Measuring iron and carbon monoxide content may be useful in calculating carboxy-heme saturation in embalmed cases.

Table 40.1 Case studies of drugs in embalmed tissues

Case determination	Quantitative results	Time of embalmment
Ethchlorvynol and phenobarbital abuse resulting in an overdose	Ethchlorvynol: 112 mg/L (bile) Phenobarbital: 32.8 mg/L (heart bloody fluid)	52 h
Homicide from acute narcotic intoxication	Morphine (free): 1.5 mg/kg (liver)	3 weeks
Acute heroin fatality	Morphine (total): 2476 ng/mL (bile), 4.3 mg/kg (liver), 4.21 ng/mg (hair) Codeine: 305 ng/mL (bile), 0.23 ng/mg (hair) 6-Monoacetylmorphine: 6.99 ng/mg (hair)	9 days
Fatal asthma attack triggered by mCPP[a]	Laudanosine: 550 ng/mL (blood), 1200 ng/mL (urine) Salbutamol: 30 ng/mL (blood), 120 ng/mL (urine) Atropine: 96 ng/mL (blood), 30 ng/mL (urine) Methylprednisolone: 500 ng/mL (blood), 100 ng/mL (urine) Prednisone: 260 ng/mL (blood), 410 ng/mL (urine) Naproxen: 300 ng/mL (blood), 3100 ng/mL (urine) Hydroxyzine: 60 ng/mL (blood), 40 ng/mL (urine) Benzoylecgonine: 302 ng/mL (urine) Ecgonine methyl ester: 61 ng/mL (urine) Metoclopramide: 5.1 ng/mL (blood), 91.9 ng/mL (urine), 164.7 ng/mL (bile), 2.8 ng/g (liver), 7.5 ng/mL (vitreous) Meta-chlorophenylpiperazine (mCPP): 15.0 ng/mL (urine), 5.1 ng/mL (bile) 0.3 ng/g (liver), 4.7 ng/mL (vitreous)	24 h

[a]Hair results not included

Drugs in Formalin-Fixed Tissues/ Formalin Solutions

Amphetamines

When formalin-fixed liver was stored for 24 h in unbuffered 20% formalin, methamphetamine losses of ≥28% were observed. Methamphetamine concentrations in formalin-fixed rabbit liver decreased by 97% after just 1 day of storage in a 10% formalin solution when compared to pre-formalin treatment; at 4 weeks, only 0.2% of the methamphetamine remained. No methamphetamine was identified in formalin-fixed liver and kidney in 15% formalin solutions (pH 4–5) at 1 month. When methamphetamine was spiked directly into a 15% formalin solution (pH 4–5), methamphetamine was relatively stable for 12 months. Methamphetamine was exposed to 5–20% formalin in water at pH 3.5–9.5. In 20% formalin at pH 9.5, methamphetamine concentrations decreased by ~90% on day 1. Conversion to N-methyl-methamphetamine from methamphetamine and/or amphetamine presumably via the Eschweiler-Clarke reaction was rapidly observed

in high formalin concentrations at neutral and basic pH. In acidic formalin solutions, methamphetamine concentrations showed only small losses by 30 days and little subsequent production of N-methyl-methamphetamine. Although it is important to test for N-methyl-methamphetamine in suspected methamphetamine cases, some caution should be applied to interpretation as N-methyl-methamphetamine is itself an abused drug.

3,4-Methylenedioxymethamphetamine (MDMA) was injected into liver pieces which were stored in 20% unbuffered formalin solution for 24 h. Conversion to N-methyl-MDMA, likely via the Eschweiler-Clarke reaction, was observed after 1 h, and by 24 h, ~10% of the MDMA remained unchanged. As such, N-methyl-MDMA may be a more suitable target for analysis. Similar to methamphetamine, MDMA was not identified in in formalin-fixed liver and kidney stored in 15% formalin solutions (pH 4–5) at 1 month. When evaluated in formalin concentrations of 5–20% at pH 3.5–9.5, maximum stability was achieved in acidic conditions with the greatest decreases observed at high pH. Although losses of up to 95% were observed, MDMA was detected under all conditions at 60 days. When spiked directly into unbuffered 15% formalin, MDMA concentrations rapidly decreased when stored at room temperature, while concentrations were stable for 1 month when stored refrigerated.

Antipsychotics

Although concentrations decreased, chlorpromazine remained detectable in fixed brain, lung, liver, kidney, and skeletal muscle from rabbits stored for 4 weeks in unbuffered formalin, buffered formalin, and buffered paraformaldehyde; highest recovery was achieved in buffered formalin. Chlorpromazine and levomepromazine in formalin-fixed liver and kidney were identified at 13 months in fixed tissue and/or the 15% formalin-fixing solution. Olanzapine spiked into formalin at various concentrations (5–20%) and pH (3–9.5) was determined to be stable for 30 days under all conditions. Although olanzapine has a secondary amine and would be expected to undergo the Eschweiler-Clarke conversion, only 2% of the N-methyl derivative was identified after 30 days. Presumably this is due to the secondary amine group being located in a seven member ring, hindering the reaction.

Barbiturates

Phenobarbital concentrations in liver fixed in 5 and 8% formalin-water solutions (prepared from 10% buffered formalin) decreased by ~40% 1 day after fixation, with losses of >60% at 4 weeks; phenobarbital was present in the formalin-water solutions across the time period. A study evaluating phenobarbital and butalbital in fixed liver and formalin (neutral pH) after 6 months found summed recoveries of 88%, comparable to the extraction efficiency of the method. Formalin solution in which a brain was stored for 15 months was positive for phenobarbital; the tissue itself was negative, although this may have been due to analytical capabilities.

Pentobarbital, phenobarbital, and secobarbital were spiked into formalin (5–20%) at variable pH (3.5–9.5). Higher recovery of pentobarbital was achieved at lower pH, although the drug was detectable at 30 days in all formaldehyde concentrations across the pH range. Secobarbital had recoveries >97% in all experiments. Phenobarbital concentrations were stable at acidic pH and declined by ~20% at pH 7. At pH 9.5, phenobarbital concentrations decreased significantly over 30 days, with the greatest decrease at 20% formaldehyde. 2-Phenylbutyric acid was formed as a decomposition product of phenobarbital in all formaldehyde solutions at pH 9 and may be a viable option for detecting phenobarbital use in these conditions.

Benzodiazepines

Alprazolam, chlordiazepoxide, diazepam, flunitrazepam, flurazepam, lorazepam, midazolam, oxazepam, prazepam, and triazolam were individually spiked into 5–20% formaldehyde solutions at variable pH, with concentrations recorded for up to 30 days. Greater degradation generally occurred under acidic conditions at higher formaldehyde concentrations, although flunitrazepam and lorazepam were more susceptible to decomposition at higher pH. Degradation of oxazepam occurred in all conditions, including control conditions (no formaldehyde). Chlordiazepoxide concentrations decreased at all pH values and to a lesser extent in controls over the 30 days. Similar results were observed for diazepam in 5% formalin-whole blood solutions, with a decrease of >40% observed after 30 days. Diazepam was identified in formalin-fixed tissues from rabbits 4 weeks after fixation; recovery was highest when tissues were stored in 10% non-buffered formalin solution. After 63 days, estazolam concentrations decreased by >97% in fixed tissues from dogs. Bromazepam was identified in fixed liver and kidney tissues and corresponding fixative solutions for up to 6 months. As formaldehyde likely reacts with benzodiazepines through the Eschweiler-Clarke reaction following acid or base hydrolysis, determination of reaction products may be more suitable analytes for the detection of benzodiazepine use.

Carboxyhemoglobin and Cyanide

Carboxyhemoglobin and cyanide in blood solutions were added to formalin; the resulting 5 and 8% formalin-whole blood solutions were evaluated via microdiffusion. A "silver mirror" indicative of the presence of carbon monoxide formed when solutions were initially added to a Conway diffusion cell. Twenty-four hours later, the palladium chloride was darker with a loss of metallic luster, as the formalin diluted the carboxyhemoglobin and interfered with the diffusion process. Microdiffusion was determined not to be a valid technique for cyanide analysis as the formaldehyde reacts with cyanide, interfering with the complexing reagents; other techniques, such as gas chromatography, are recommended. Formalin was added to the blood of individuals who had died from carbon monoxide poisoning. Irregular results were obtained when the formaldehyde concentration was high (9%) and after storage of just 1–2 days.

Cocaine

In buffered formalin (pH 7.4), cocaine concentrations decreased by ~80% after 2 weeks, while benzoylecgonine concentrations simultaneously increased. Hydrolysis to benzoylecgonine was likely due to the pH of the solution and not specifically the presence of formalin. When the pH of the formalin solution was lowered to 3.5, cocaine was relatively stable over the same timeframe, with little conversion to benzoylecgonine. Cocaine and benzoylecgonine behaved similarly in formalin-fixed tissue at pH 7.4 and 3.5. Concentrations initially decreased, with approximately 50% (brain) and 30% (liver) remaining at 2 weeks; concentrations appeared relatively stable for another 2 weeks. Higher concentrations in the brain were attributed to the tissue's greater lipophilicity. Concentrations of cocaine in the fixing solution initially increased, regardless of

pH; however, concentrations leveled off at pH 3.5 while decreasing at pH 7.4. Benzoylecgonine was also present in the fixing solution, with concentrations continuing to rise at day 30.

In a case where cocaine and benzoylecgonine were initially identified at autopsy, cocaine was not detected in formalin-fixed liver 4 weeks postautopsy, while benzoylecgonine concentrations were higher than those initially found. After administration of cocaine to rats, only benzoylecgonine was present in formalin-fixed tissues after 30 days.

Elements and Metals

The essential elements calcium, copper, iron, magnesium, and zinc and metals aluminum, arsenic, cadmium, mercury, manganese, and lead were evaluated in formalin-fixed brain, kidney, liver, heart, muscle, and bone for up to 1 year. Results generally were consistent with original concentrations with the exception of aluminum (concentrations increased over time) and manganese (concentrations decreased over time). Most metals were present at highest concentrations in the liver and kidney. Lead was identified in bone and (non-formalin fixed) hair.

Opiates/Opioids

Morphine was studied in formalin-fixed kidney and liver and in their fixing solutions (10% buffered formalin, pH 7). Morphine was identified in all specimens after 12 weeks and demonstrated good stability as the sums of recoveries between the fixed tissue and formalin solutions were comparable to the extraction efficiency of the method. Concentrations were higher in formalin solutions than in the fixed tissues, with 75% recovery observed in the formalin solution used to fix the liver. Morphine (total) remained detectable at 4 months in formalin-fixed rabbit liver, kidney, lung, and heart, although concentrations were generally considerably lower than those in tissues stored frozen for the same period. Detection was not consistent in the 10%

formalin fixative solutions. As morphine is a tertiary amine, N-methylation of morphine in formalin does not occur, and there was no evidence of O-methylation of morphine to codeine. It has been postulated that normorphine (a secondary amine) is methylated to morphine via Eschweiler-Clarke reaction but at undetectable concentrations.

Concentrations of meperidine in formalin-fixed rabbit tissues were greatly reduced as compared to frozen tissues. Normeperidine was rarely identified in the formalin-fixed rabbit tissues or the formalin solution (10%), likely due to N-methylation of normeperidine to meperidine. Methadone and propoxyphene were detected for 19 and 24 months, respectively, in formalin-fixed tissues (10% formalin); for both drugs, concentrations were variable compared to those quantitated in frozen tissues.

Pesticides

Strychnine concentrations in formalin-fixed tissues decreased but were still detectable after 8 weeks; concentrations were higher in the buffered formalin solutions used for storage. Malathion was identified in fixed tissues 44 days post-autopsy. Paraquat concentrations in formalin-fixed tissue were observed to decrease over time, while concentrations subsequently increased in formalin-fixing solution. Paraquat has been identified in formalin-fixed tissues stored for 6.5 years. At 4 months, tetramine remained detectable at low concentrations in formalin-fixed rabbit liver, but not kidney, lung, or heart; the drug was not reliably detected in the non-buffered 10% formalin fixative solution.

Selective Serotonin Reuptake Inhibitors

Sertraline is converted to N-methylsertraline via the Eschweiler-Clarke reaction with 100% conversion observed at higher formalin concentrations at pH $\geq$ 7. Fluoxetine in rat liver also

indicated conversion to its N-methyl derivative, N-methylfluoxetine, with the reaction occurring more rapidly at higher pH and formalin concentration. The rate of the Eschweiler-Clarke reaction increases with increasing free amine concentration and thus occurs more rapidly in a basic environment. Testing for the N-methyl derivatives of both of these drugs is recommended.

Tricyclic Antidepressants

Nortriptyline and desipramine are N-methylated to amitriptyline and imipramine, respectively, in the presence of formaldehyde via the Eschweiler-Clarke reaction. Recoveries >90% typically were observed for nortriptyline and desipramine after incubation for 60 min in various formaldehyde and paraformaldehyde solutions. There was simultaneous production of small amounts of amitriptyline and imipramine, with increased amounts observed at higher formaldehyde concentrations. Nortriptyline instability increased at higher pH and formaldehyde concentrations. Amitriptyline was detected for up to 12 months in formalin-fixed tissue and the corresponding 10% buffered formalin solution (pH 7), while nortriptyline was not detected at 7 months. Desipramine concentration in fixed liver tissue stored in 5 and 8% formalin for 4 weeks decreased by 72%. Imipramine and desipramine were detected in formalin-fixed tissue and the formalin solution fixative at 14 months; imipramine in formalin-fixed tissue remained quantifiable at 17 months.

Volatiles

Rabbits were administered chloroform, diethyl ether, ethanol, and toluene. Brain, lung, liver, kidney, and muscle were collected and stored in non-buffered 10% formalin for up to 14 days. Although concentrations greatly declined, all analytes were present after 14 days of storage in all specimens. The rate of concentration decrease was ethanol > diethyl ether > chloroform > toluene.

Miscellaneous Drugs

Bupropion was spiked into variable formalin concentrations (5–20%) over a broad pH range and concentrations evaluated at 30 days. More bupropion remained at lower pH and formalin concentration. One hundred percent conversion to N-methyl-bupropion via the Eschweiler-Clarke reaction was observed in 20% formalin at basic pH.

Fenfluramine converts to its N-methyl derivative, N-methyl fenfluramine. When studied over a range of pHs and formalin concentrations for 30 days, no fenfluramine was detected in any formalin solution at pH 9.5 or in 20% formalin at pH 7.0; however, N-methyl fenfluramine was present, making it a more suitable analytical target in these conditions.

Lidocaine concentrations in formalin-fixed brain, liver, kidney, and skeletal muscle were shown to decrease by 67–75% after fixation for 40 days.

Mephedrone and 3-trifluoromethylphenylpiperazine (TFMPP) were spiked into formalin solutions of various concentrations at pH 3.5–9.5. Both drugs were most stable in acidic conditions during the evaluation period (mephedrone 28 days, TFMPP 60 days). At pH 9.5, mephedrone decomposition was rapid, with losses of up to 82% observed after 1 day. TFMPP showed losses of up to 50% over the 60 days at pH 9.5. Although no standards were available for confirmation, putative N-methylated products of the drugs were observed. TFMPP contains a secondary amine in a ring structure versus in an aliphatic chain like mephedrone, likely contributing to its increased stability.

Phenytoin concentrations in formalin-whole blood solutions decreased by more than 33% over 30 days. Concentrations of phenytoin in fixed liver tissue generally were stable over 4 weeks, with some extraction of drug into the formalin-water solution.

Although concentrations decreased greatly, promethazine and milnacipran were identified in formalin-fixed liver and kidney and the 15% unbuffered formalin-fixing solution after 1 year of storage.

Sildenafil was detected in formalin-fixed tissues (brain, heart, kidney, liver, lung, and spleen) and the formalin fixative solution when evaluated at 4 weeks. When compared to concentrations in samples tested at the time of autopsy, the sum of the recoveries in fixed tissue and the formalin solution was $\geq 88\%$ in all matrices.

Conclusions

Analyte concentration in embalmed specimens, formalin-fixed tissues, and formalin solutions generally cannot be considered representative of concentrations present at death. In addition to factors typically affecting postmortem concentrations, formaldehyde concentration, pH, time, and a dilution effect (in embalmed specimens) may all affect drug identification and concentration. Although some drugs appear stable, most experience a decrease in concentration, particularly at higher pH and formalin concentration. The lack of identification of an analyte does not ensure that the drug was not present at death. For some compounds, particularly those with primary or secondary amines, identification of the potential Eschweiler-Clark reaction products may increase chances of identification of drug use. It is recommended that multiple specimens should be analyzed if available as drug affinity between tissues may vary.

Further Reading

Nikolaou P, Papoutsis I, Dona A, Spiliopoulou C, Athanaselis S (2013) Toxicological analysis of formalin fixed or embalmed tissues: a review. Forensic Sci Int 233:312–319

Skopp G (2004) Preanalytic aspects in postmortem toxicology. Forensic Sci Int 142:75–100

Takayasu T (2013) Toxicological analyses of medications and chemicals in formalin-fixed tissues and formalin solutions; a review. J Anal Toxicol 37:615–621

Uekusa K, Hayashida M, Ohno Y (2015) Forensic toxicological analyses of drugs in tissues in formalin solutions and in fixatives. Forensic Sci Int 249:165–172

Correction to: Amphetamines/Sympathomimetic Amines

Michele M. Crosby and Karla A. Moore

Correction to:
Chapter 25 in: B. S. Levine, S. Kerrigan (eds.), *Principles of Forensic Toxicology*,
https://doi.org/10.1007/978-3-030-42917-1_25

The chapter has been inadvertently published with an incorrect figure. It has now been updated with the correct figure in this revised version of the book.

The updated online version of this chapter can be found at
https://doi.org/10.1007/978-3-030-42917-1_25

Cathinone backbone

Substitution Sites	R_1	R_2	R_3	R_4	Compound Name	Acronym	Mol. Wt (g/mol)
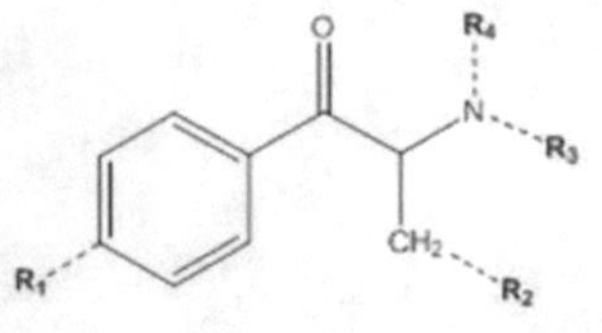	H	H	CH₃	H	Methcathinone	-	163.22
	H	H	CH₃	CH₃	N,N-Dimethylcathinone	-	177.25
	H	H	CH₃CH₂	H	Ethcathinone	-	177.25
	H	H	CH₃CH₂	CH₃CH₂	N,N-Diethylcathinone	-	205.30
	CH₃	H	CH₃	H	Mephedrone	-	177.25
	H	CH₃	CH₃	H	Buphedrone	-	177.25
	H	CH₃CH₂	CH₃	H	Pentedrone	-	191.27
	CH₃	H	CH₃CH₂	H	4-Methyl-ethcathinone	4-MEC	191.27
	F	H	CH₃	H	Flephedrone	-	181.27
	CH₃O	H	CH₃	H	Methedrone	-	193.25
	CH₃	H	C₆H₅CH₂	H	Benzedrone	4-MBC	253.34

Pyrrolidinocathinone backbone

Substitution Sites	R_3	R_4	Compound Name	Acronym	Mol. Wt (g/mol)
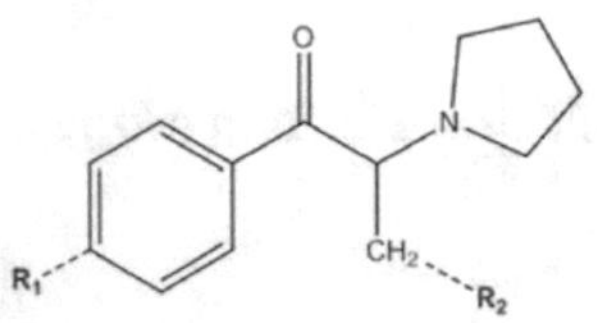	H	H	α-Pyrrolidinopropiophenone	α-PPP	203.28
	H	CH₃	α-Pyrrolidinobutiophenone	α-PBP	217.31
	H	CH₃CH₂	α-Pyrrolidinopentiophenone	α-PVP	231.33
	CH₃		4-Methyl-α-pyrrolidinopropiophenone	MePPP	217.31
	CH₃	CH₃	4-Methyl-α-pyrrolidinobutiophenone	MPBP	231.33
	CH₃	CH₃CH₂	4-Methyl-α-Pyrrolidinopentiophenone	Pyrovalerone	245.36
	CH₃	CH₃CH₂CH₂	4-Methyl-α-Pyrrolidinohexiophenone	MPHP	259.39
	CH₃		4-Methoxy-α-Pyrrolidinopropiophenone	MOPPP	233.31
	CH₃O	CH₃	4-Methoxy-α-Pyrrolidinobutiophenone	MOPBP	247.33
	CH₃O	CH₃CH₂	4-Methoxy-α-Pyrrolidinopentiophenone	MOPVP	261.36
	*Naphthyl	CH₃CH₂	Naphthylpyrovalerone	Naphyrone	281.39

Methylenedioxycathinone backbone

Substitution Sites	R_2	R_3	Compound Name	Acronym	Mol. Wt (g/mol)
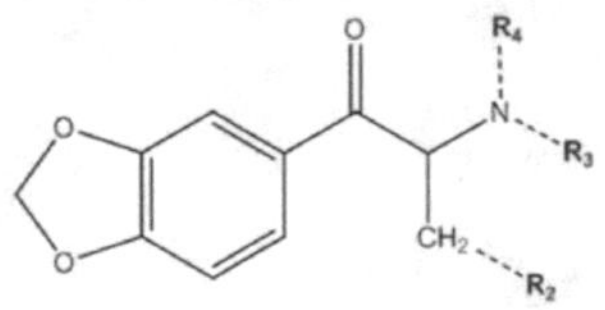	H	CH₃	1-(3,4-Methylenedioxyphenyl)-2-methylamino-1-propanone	Methylone	207.23
	H	CH₃CH₂	1-(3,4-Methylenedioxyphenyl)-2-ethylamino-1-propanone	Ethylone	221.25
	CH₃	CH₃	1-(3,4-Methylenedioxyphenyl)-2-methylamino-1-butanone	Butylone	221.25
	CH₃	CH₃CH₂	1-(3,4-Methylenedioxyphenyl)-2-ethylamino-1-butanone	Eutylone	235.27
	CH₃CH₂	CH₃	1-(3,4-Methylenedioxyphenyl)-2-methylamino-1-pentanone	Pentylone	235.27

Methylenedioxypyrrolidinocathinone backbone

Substitution Sites	R_2	Compound Name	Acronym	Mol. Wt (g/mol)
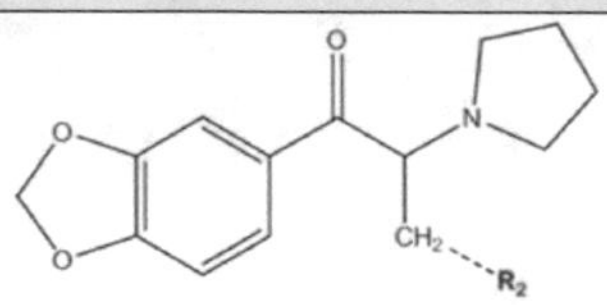	H	3,4-Methylenedioxy-α-pyrrolidinopropiophenone	MDPPP	247.28
	CH₃	3,4-Methylenedioxy-α-Pyrrolidinobutiophenone	MDPBP	261.31
	CH₃CH₂	3,4-Methylenedioxy-α-Pyrrolidinovalerophenone	MDPV	275.34

Fig. 25.2 Structures of synthetic cathinones

Index

Printed in the United States
by Baker & Taylor Publisher Services